Half-Century of Conflict

THE HARPER HISTORICAL SERIES

Under the Editorship of
GUY STANTON FORD

Half-Century of Conflict

By CHESTER V. EASUM

PROFESSOR OF HISTORY, UNIVERSITY OF WISCONSIN

Harper & Brothers – Publishers – New York

To Those Who Served

CONTENTS

Contents

MAPS

EDITOR'S INTRODUCTION

History is in most instances the record of far-off lands, or times, not within the experience of the reader. It is the task of the historian to become a contemporary of the past, to live in it, and to make it live again in his pages. This volume—and many others in these fast-moving years when decades compass changes greater than did past centuries—faces every reader, however young, with the fact that he is a contemporary for a longer or shorter span of the historic period it covers. It is not some other generation's records that he studies. It is, in part at least, his own. It treats of events he knew about in a confused way, perhaps, and of men whose names are current, not legendary. He must share the historian's task of ridding himself of any prejudices that are derived from his sketchy impressions of men and nations. He has the privilege of the second guesser when treaties, battles, national policies, and men's judgments go awry.

But if he is to benefit by history, and especially the history of the last half-century, he must become a contemporary before he becomes a critic. When he has grasped the great and urgent issues and recurring crises, he would do well to ask what he would have done or even perhaps what he did or thought should have been done. I, who lived in mature life through the whole of these fifty years of conflict, am telling you some of the questions I asked myself as I read this record of international conflict. And I asked myself what great forces and portents of change have passed with but casual notice in the preceding half-century and remain to be comprehended and conciliated and controlled by mature nations if the fifty years of conflict are not to become a century.

If you are to get the full benefit of this study, if you are to be a wiser and better citizen of your country, which emerges reluctantly from this past half-century with world responsibilities, you must look forward with a vision clarified by a knowledge of the immediate past.

Many claims may be made for the study of history, and, among others I would recall, is its usefulness for life and action. It may seem only to preserve the past, but to the thoughtful it may equally mark those places where we must break with past traditions.

The catastrophic conflicts through which Easum's *Half-Century of Conflict* guides you have brought most nations to the questioning period about security through unlimited national sovereignty. The volume closes with the proof of their doubts—the establishment of the United Nations and their first concerted steps to restrain the aggression that threatens hopes consecrated by immeasurable sacrifices.

There are many ways of testing what you remember from reading and study. Life alone is the test of what you learned. That test will be applied to you in the next half-century. May you pass it with credit to yourself and the gratitude of the generations that follow you.

GUY STANTON FORD

PREFACE

Neither of the world wars of the first half of the twentieth century was started in or by the United States; yet the United States was eventually involved in both in defense of what its leaders and people thought at the time was its vital long-term interest, seriously threatened. In both cases its basic purpose was the making of a decent peace. In both its people promised themselves, beyond victory, a new and better world. How new, and how much better, would depend upon the character of the peace, upon its general acceptance, and upon the continued coöperation of the peoples and the powers to preserve it.

Twice the optimists were disappointed. Perhaps they underestimated the exhaustion of their allies and the tenacity of totalitarianism. The realization of their hopes depended in each instance upon the readiness of those who had won the war to make and maintain the peace. The study of the wars resolves itself therefore naturally and logically into a study of the problems of tolerance, security, and peace. Such a study of world wars and world peace is here presented in a one-world frame of reference, from an American point of view.

For technical assistance, helpful suggestions, and encouragement the author is indebted and deeply grateful to many of his colleagues: particularly to university cartographer Professor Arthur H. Robinson; Captains Leslie K. Pollard and J. H. Hurff, and Commander Ralph Metcalf, USN; Colonels Willis S. Matthews and W. G. Skelton, USA, and members of their staffs; Professors Robert Lee Wolff, Eugene Boardman, David Fellman, and many others; and above all to Doctor Sidney B. Fay of Harvard, who read the entire manuscript, and to Doctor Guy Stanton Ford, editor of the Harper Historical Series.

CHESTER V. EASUM

Madison, Wisconsin
June, 1951

PART I

The Four Years' War

CHAPTER 1

Origins of the "First World War"

To millions of intelligent and efficient members of the armed forces of the United Nations war was an unnatural phenomenon, even in wartime, something catastrophic but ephemeral and unreal. Reared in the democratic tradition and taught to believe, as their optimistic elders tried to believe, that another world war was as improbable as it seemed unnecessary, they looked upon peaceful exchange and amicable adjustment of differences as the only natural and reasonable bases of international relations. Foreign travel was said or found to be interesting, enlightening, and pleasant. International contests were stimulating. Why should they be dangerous? Suppose some friction did arise. Why should it not be amicably eased?

Young people reasoning thus were the praiseworthy product of their own environment and training. The answer to their question was that the youth of certain other countries, whom they had had to learn to call "the enemy" when some disrespectful nickname did not serve the purpose better, had been differently trained, taught to think that war was wonderful as well as natural, and that peace was prized only by weaklings. They were insufficiently aware of the dynamics of dictatorship in direct conflict with a debilitated or discredited democracy, or of the danger which threatened the world order whenever its natural defenders doubted their ability to defend it or wondered whether it was worth defending. A generation which had learned to dread another economic depression but had dreamed of no greater danger was more amused than alarmed by the strutting of the soldiers and the shouts of the leaders of the malcontent nations of Europe and Asia, and dismissed as incredible the accounts of atrocities and impending aggressions abroad. Mussolini, thought American youth, was quite a

3

showman, but Italy was only a small country. One heard all sorts of things about the Japanese; but where and what was Manchukuo? And Hitler simply "seemed too bad to be true."[1]

The recurrence of war in an at least partially peace-minded world was a result of a resort to the use of armed force by Japan, Italy, and Germany—nations unsatisfied or dissatisfied with the results of the war of 1914-1918. Wars of aggression were contrary to international treaty agreement to which all three nations were parties; but the habit of fighting for territory or other objectives not otherwise easy of attainment was deeply ingrained.

BEFORE SARAJEVO

The German Reich of modern times was a product of power politics. Its nucleus was the state of Prussia, put together and strengthened through the centuries by its kings of the Hohenzollern dynasty, a disciplined army, and an industrious and generally efficient bureaucracy. The principal founder of the empire of 1871-1918, Prince Otto von Bismarck, was in his day the most conspicuous and—superficially at least—the most successful practitioner of what he called *Realpolitik* and others have called power politics.

Bismarck called himself a realist and politics "the science of the possible." He looked upon his world through colored glasses which magnified the vices and weaknesses of mankind but blinded him to most of its virtues. He took this imperfect world as he found it, and made no effort to improve it except when convinced that the improvement proposed would be profitable to Prussia or to the German Empire which he served from 1871 to 1890 as chancellor. Morality, he said, had nothing to do with statecraft, and politics was only organized selfishness; and he did little to raise the tone of either.

The empire, as Bismarck established it and left it nearly twenty years later, was a parliamentary monarchy in form but not in fact. It had, to be sure, a representative national legislative body, the *Reichstag,* freely elected by manhood suffrage; but the Reichstag was unequal either in constitutional powers or in influence to the federal council or *Bundesrat,* composed of representatives of states, chosen by the heads of the states; and most of the states were monarchies. Prussia's Bundesrat delegation, chosen by the king, who was also the German kaiser, and led until 1890 by the Imperial Chancellor Bismarck, was numerically smaller in proportion to population than the

---

[1] Douglas Miller, *Via Diplomatic Pouch* (New York, 1944), preface.

delegations of the other states; but it was large enough to prevent the amendment of the federal constitution. This Prussian state, enabled thus to prevent the democratization or effective parliamentarization of the imperial government, preserved its own undemocratic character until November, 1918, by retaining not only its extraordinarily powerful hereditary monarchy but also a peculiar, indirect, three-class system of voting in state elections. Voters were classified according to the amounts of taxes they paid, in such fashion that property, rather than persons, was represented in the state legislature or *Landtag*.

The making of the state of Prussia had been very largely the work of its Hohenzollern dynasty, a long succession of working kings, most of whom took seriously both their prerogatives and their responsibilities. Characteristic Hohenzollern policies were royal absolutism or the closest practicable approach to it; centralized control of government; expansion by the acquisition of new territories useful to round out or to fill in the gaps between the scattered provinces of which their state—acquired piecemeal—was composed; and militarism—the maintenance of the large armed forces necessary for expansion by conquest or for the defense of crazy-quilt territories without natural frontiers. With few exceptions, the kings of Prussia were faithful to their own code: it was a king's duty to serve, to strengthen, and when possible to enlarge his state; a state must grow and strengthen itself or weaken and die; neither king nor state was subject to any higher political authority or bound by moral obligation to the community of states or peoples.

To these militaristic, materialistic, opportunistic, and rather cynical Prussian traditions the German Empire of 1871-1918 fell heir. The Prussian system of universal military service was applied, with local adaptations of minor importance, to the other German states. The Prussian general staff controlled the whole German army in war, and the king of Prussia became its *Allerhöchste Feldherr* or supreme commander. Demonstrations of the military efficiency of the Prussian army in the wars of German unification, and fear of German aggression after 1871, led to the general militarization of western Europe soon thereafter.

Germany's alliance of 1879 with Austria-Hungary, although ostensibly defensive in character, increased the uneasiness of France and Russia. Bismarck had to be constantly on the alert, and to exert himself to the utmost, to postpone as long as he was chancellor the counteralliance of France and Russia which was formed in 1891, soon after he left office.

Bismarck's foreign policy was based on "balanced tensions." Instead of working for the elimination or permanent easement of tensions between nations, he was willing to perpetuate them and to take advantage of them. Looking upon all other nations as natural or at least potential enemies of Germany, he slyly stimulated their jealousies and fears of one another, so that they would not combine against her. Even his alliances with Austria-Hungary and Italy were built rather upon common enmities than upon a real community of interest.

After 1870 Bismarck started no more wars and called himself a fanatical friend of peace (*Friedensfanatiker*), but his contemporaries were afraid to trust him, especially after the scare of 1875 over his supposed plan to provoke a "preventive" war against France. Intent upon safeguarding Germany, he sought to avoid unnecessary risks, but overlooked few opportunities for improving the empire's position when the gains promised to warrant the risk. Underestimating the fruitful possibilities of good will and coöperation, and discounting all moral considerations in international relations, he contributed little to the development of international law or peaceful procedure, and nothing toward organized international coöperation for peace.

Until he had completed the process of political consolidation at home, and until the necessary surplus capital and industrial capacity were in evidence, Bismarck refused to be hurried into expensive and hazardous colonial enterprises. Meanwhile, so as not to arouse too soon or too seriously the suspicions of the other colonial powers, especially the British, he professed not to be interested in colonies. Eventually he permitted himself to be pushed by a growing "colonial movement," which he had done nothing to discourage, into extending the protection of the imperial government over German traders and adventurers in virtually all the areas ever to be included in the German colonial empire. He always kept colonial policy, however, in what he considered its proper place, subordinate to domestic political considerations and to general foreign policy, refusing to make it an all-important end in itself or his first objective.

The Germans of the Baltic and North Sea ports, such as Danzig, Lübeck, Hamburg, and Bremen, have been sailors and overseas traders since early medieval times; but the modern German navy was the creation of Bismarck's successors. In his naval policy the Iron Chancellor was even more careful than in the colonial field not to challenge too soon or too sharply. He engaged in no navy-building race against Great Britain and probably would have engaged in none.

The Boer War of 1899-1902, however, while revealing anew to Englishmen like Joseph Chamberlain the cost and the risks of overseas empire, and impelling Chamberlain therefore to seek an alliance for Britain, seemed to the restless and impulsive Kaiser William II to be Germany's cue for the building of a war fleet which not even the strongest naval power would dare to challenge. So, with the German Navy League stridently pointing out the imperative and immediate necessity of an ocean navy of which very few of the German people had felt any conscious need, just as the Colonial League had been working for years to make them aware of their alleged need of colonies, the Reichstag was induced to provide the funds for a naval building program which soon seemed to the British to threaten British naval supremacy even in home waters.

By their very ineptitude, as well as by their adherence to the worst rather than the best of his principles, Bismarck's successors were more dangerous to world peace than he had been. Prince Bernhard von Bülow, chancellor from 1900 to 1909, continued his system of "balanced tensions" but was never the master of circumstances that Bismarck had been. Bülow gave the kaiser bad advice on many critical occasions and failed to prevent him from making many tactless and costly blunders. Count Friedrich August von Holstein, unofficial but quasi-permanent and politically irresponsible director of foreign policy from 1890 to 1906, was an able but eccentric misanthrope, governed often by personal dislike and suspicion, controlling others by methods little better than blackmail, willing to advance Germany's interests by trading on her potential nuisance value, and incapable of crediting the spokesman of another nation with more amiable intentions or higher standards of honesty or good faith than his own. Theobald von Bethmann-Hollweg, chancellor from 1909 to 1917, could not control the kaiser, the admirals, the generals, or the Foreign Office.

The character of German leadership and alliances only increased the distrust with which the already established imperial powers looked upon the newest, inevitably aggressive, great naval and colonial power. So for twenty years before the outbreak of war in 1914 the status of the peace was increasingly precarious because of fear and friction between rival armed camps.

Japan's easy victory over China in 1894-1895, followed by her annexation of Formosa and the Pescadores Islands, by her gaining a foothold on the tip of Liaotung peninsula in southern Manchuria, and by China's renunciation of suzerainty over Korea, warned Europeans that a modern Asiatic power had arisen that would demand a voice thereafter in Far Eastern affairs. Admiral Dewey's destruction of the Spanish fleet in Manila Bay, May 1, 1898, and the subsequent annexation of the Philippine Islands and Guam by the United States signalized a new American interest in the Orient. Germany, which had already secured from China, in March, 1898, a ninety-nine-year lease on a port and naval base on Kiaochow Bay and important economic concessions in Shantung province, expedited the liquidation of bankrupt Spain's overseas empire by purchasing for $4,200,000 the Caroline, Palau, and Marianas islands except Guam. Great Britain, seeking reinsurance for her Far Eastern interests, made in 1902 a defensive treaty with Japan as a counterpoise to Russia, and in 1907 an entente with a defeated and weakened Russia which then seemed less dangerous to her, and more amenable to reason, than Germany. This completed the formation of the "Triple Entente," France and Great Britain having formed an entente in 1904 for the amicable adjustment of outstanding differences and alignment of foreign policies.

While rival imperialisms jockeyed for position all around the world, international fears and jealousies came to focus in the Balkans. For the sake of the water passage through the Bosporus and Dardanelles, Russia had for more than two hundred years shown an active interest in the lands along the northern and western coasts of the Black Sea and in the twentieth century was encouraging their peoples to look to her for leadership. Austria-Hungary, with millions of South Slavs already living within her boundaries, and clearly unable to expand in any other direction but southeastward, looked southeastward and found Serbia an obstacle to expansion and a center of subversive agitation among the Serbs of Bosnia and Herzegovina. Germans were building a railway through Turkey and planning a Berlin-to-Bagdad connection at Constantinople—intersecting Russia's coveted water outlet at that point.

These rivalries found expression in a series of international crises. On March 31, 1905, the German kaiser, by landing at Tangier to visit the sultan of Morocco, served notice upon Great Britain and France that Germany had not authorized them to determine the future of Morocco without reference to her. At Germany's insistence an international conference was held at Algeciras, Spain, early in 1906 to reassert the principle that the development of retarded or dependent areas in Africa was a matter of international concern; but the outcome of the conference, owing to British, Russian, and Italian support of France's claims, was more satisfactory to the French than to the Germans. Smarting under the realization of something approaching diplomatic isolation at Algeciras, the German delegation to the second general peace conference at The Hague in 1907 more or less isolated themselves morally also by being among the most outspoken opponents of proposals for the establishment of an international court of arbitration, just as in 1899, at the first Hague conference, they had opposed the limitation of armaments.

German distrust of other peoples became increasingly marked. This was indicated by the acceptance of the opinion that the conference at Algeciras had been unfriendly, that an international court of arbitration would be unfair, and that the limitation of Germany's armed forces would tend to freeze her navy in a status inferior to the British and to keep her army permanently at a disadvantage with reference to the combined strength of the French and Russian armies. After the formation of the British-Russian entente of August 31, 1907, Germany's distrust grew into an actual fear of "encirclement."

"Fear and be slain." The alleged danger of encirclement was useful propaganda material in the hands of militarists, the Navy League, colonial imperialists, and other Pan-Germans, who publicized and exaggerated it for their own purposes, accusing Great Britain in particular of making it (*Einkreisungspolitik*) a cardinal policy.

The tone of German foreign policy became more and more truculent. When Austria-Hungary took advantage of Turkey's temporary embarrassment following the Young Turks' revolt by announcing in 1908 the outright annexation of Bosnia and Herzegovina, Germany supported her in that violation of the general Treaty of Berlin, made in 1878. Serbia objected, but Russia's support of Serbia's protest had to be withdrawn when Germany made it clear that she would declare war in defense of Austria-Hungary if Russia intervened. Russia, weakened by her recent defeat in Manchuria and by political revolution at home, was in no position to make war. Great Britain also protested in vain against the unilateral infraction of the Treaty of Berlin, of which she was one of many signatories. So the accomplished fact of the illegal annexation stood, not unchallenged but unchanged. The German kaiser boasted of the success he had achieved by taking his stand "in shining armor" beside his ally, while Serbians and Russians nourished their resolution never again to be so intimidated.

Again in 1911 the German saber rattled in its scabbard. France had announced that she was about to establish a protectorate over Morocco. A small German cruiser, the *Panther,* was sent to the West African port of Agadir, ostensibly to protect German interests there, actually with so little warning or excuse that the potential victims of

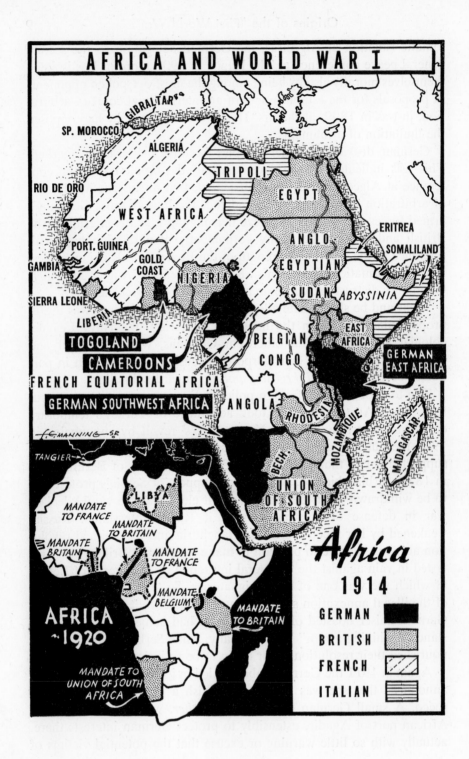

AFRICA AND WORLD WAR I

GIBRALTAR

SP. MOROCCO

ALGERIA

TRIPOLI

EGYPT

RIO DE ORO

WEST AFRICA

ERITREA

SOMALILAND

PORT. GUINEA

ANGLO

GAMBIA

GOLD COAST

NIGERIA

EGYPTIAN

SIERRA LEONE

SUDAN

ABYSSINIA

LIBERIA

TOGOLAND

EAST AFRICA

CAMEROONS

BELGIAN CONGO

GERMAN EAST AFRICA

FRENCH EQUATORIAL AFRICA

GERMAN SOUTHWEST AFRICA

ANGOLA

RHODESIA

MOZAMBIQUE

MADAGASCAR

f. G. MANNING SR

TANGIER

BECH.

UNION OF SOUTH AFRICA

LIBYA

MANDATE TO FRANCE

MANDATE TO BRITAIN

MANDATE BRITAIN

MANDATE TO FRANCE

MANDATE BELGIUM

MANDATE TO BRITAIN

Africa

1914

GERMAN

BRITISH

FRENCH

ITALIAN

AFRICA ~1920

MANDATE TO UNION OF SOUTH AFRICA

alleged injustice were barely able—some of them unable—to get there ahead of the cruiser which was to protect them. The French ambassador Jules Cambon asked bluntly in Berlin what Germany wanted, and was told that the French Congo might well be considered proper "compensation" for what Germany would lose in Morocco if France established a protectorate there. Not knowing just what Germany wanted, and fearing that she might demand a Mediterranean naval base, Sir Edward Grey, British secretary of state for foreign affairs, suggested that Great Britain enter the negotiations as mediator. While Grey was speaking softly, his colleague David Lloyd George shook a big stick by intimating, in a well-publicized address, that Great Britain would not permit herself to be excluded from negotiations in which her vital interests were at stake. This thinly veiled threat of war moved the German government to assure Great Britain confidentially that it did not intend to go to war; but lest the threat should lose its effect, and so as not to lose face, it would not authorize the publication of that assurance or permit France to be informed of it. Germany moderated its demands, however. France was authorized to establish a protectorate over Morocco but had to agree to maintain the "open door" there, and to cede to Germany enough of the French Congo to give German Kamerun access to the Congo River.

Boldness seemed to have paid. Aggressive diplomacy, backed by the threat of force, had gained territory for Germany. By refusing to capitulate in the face of the German demands, France had apparently saved a considerable part of what had been demanded, and secured new recognition for her Moroccan protectorate. And Lloyd George seemed to some observers to have averted war by threatening war.

In 1911 Italy declared war on Turkey and seized the North African provinces of Tripolitania and Cyrenaica, and the west Balkan Turkish province of Albania rose in revolt, demanding autonomous status. Turkey was compelled by the threat of even more serious troubles in 1912 to give way in both instances, ceding Tripolitania and Cyrenaica to Italy, permitting the Italians to continue to occupy the Dodecanese Islands which they had seized, and giving the Albanians control of their own government under Turkish suzerainty.

The inclusion within the newly delineated Albanian boundaries of certain areas coveted by the neighboring Balkan states was one of the causes of the first Balkan war of 1912. Serbia was particularly interested in seaports such as Durazzo on the Adriatic, Greece in Salonika, and Bulgaria in Thrace. All three wanted all they could get of Macedonia, and all were more interested in their own expansion than in the preservation of Albania. A short war against Turkey, fought by Serbia, Greece, and Bulgaria with the aid of Montenegro, resulted in the comparatively easy conquest of nearly all Turkish-controlled territory in Europe except a small area including Constantinople. Serbia and Greece had made most of their gains in Albania and Macedonia, Bulgaria in Thrace.

Then the great powers intervened with the proposal of a conference of ambassadors in London. Austria-Hungary was afraid of the new impetus that might be given the Yugoslav national movement by Serbia's acquisition of a useful outlet to the Adriatic, but both Italy and Russia would have objected if Austria-Hungary had taken Albania for herself. The other great powers, fearing a general involvement and apparently seeing no hope of a "perfect" settlement of the complicated Balkan question, sought instead a "practical" solution for it—one that Europe would accept rather than go to war. Albania was made an independent state; and Greece, Serbia, and Montenegro thus lost part of what their victory over Turkey had put into their hands.

In 1913 the disappointed west Balkan states demanded that Bulgaria forgo in their favor the part of Macedonia which their prewar agreement had contemplated should be hers, and content herself with Thrace and Adrianople. Bulgaria refused, and the second Balkan war followed—Serbia, Montenegro, and Greece against Bulgaria. Turkey availed herself of the opportunity to retake Adrianople and the Aegean coast as far west as the mouth of the Maritsa River, and Rumania took advantage of her neighbor's distress to seize a large part of the Dobruja. Bulgaria lost land on all sides.

The most unfortunate result of the Balkan wars and other crises of the years 1904 to 1914 was the embitterment engendered by the fears and jealousies that marked international relations, particularly between Bulgaria and Serbia and between Serbia and Austria-Hungary. With so many rival imperial interests also involved, it was not surprising that the Balkan peninsula was sometimes called "the tinder box of Europe."

In summary: For the tension which was so generally felt in 1914, for the alliances and other commitments which threatened to involve many nations in a war between almost any two, and for the ultimate failure of the "balance of power" to preserve the peace, no one person or people was entirely to blame. Responsibility for the failure must be shared by many—but not quite equally. Bismarck, master of Germany for twenty formative years and often arbiter of Europe, set his people's feet upon a path from which they found no turning. Fear and ambition alike prompted them to look to their arms and their alliances as he had taught them to do; but they were afraid, and were feared. Germany had no monopoly on militarism or imperialism. She was not the only power prone to use the threat of armed force in world politics or the only one to trade on the fears of others when possible. But her share of responsibility for the precarious state of equilibrium in world politics in 1914 was surely as great as any and greater than most.

JULY, 1914

On June 28, 1914, at Sarajevo in Bosnia, the Archduke Franz Ferdinand, crown prince of Austria-Hungary, was assassinated as he rode with his wife—who was killed with him—in an open car on an official visit. The assassins were Bosnian Serbs seeking the ultimate detachment of Bosnia from Austria-Hungary and its union with Serbia. The imperial government immediately assumed and announced as an established fact that the Serbian government was responsible for the crime. Doubly shocked by the murder of a prince and a personal friend, the German kaiser authorized the sending of a message assuring Franz Josef, emperor of Austria and king of Hungary, that Germany would not presume to say what countermeasures should be taken against Serbia, but would not in any event fail to meet her obligations as an ally, i.e., to help the dual monarchy defend itself if it should be "attacked" by Russia.

It was dangerous for Germany thus to give her ally a blank check; but it was done, perhaps in the hope that, if Germany herself did not intervene in the imminent two-party Balkan dispute, she would be in a better position to insist that no other power—e.g., Russia—should do so.

No one expected Austria-Hungary to let the incident pass unnoticed. The critical questions were whether her demands for satisfaction from Serbia would be exorbitant, whether Russia or any other power would intervene on Serbia's behalf, and whether Germany would then be involved as Austria-Hungary's ally, and France as the ally of Russia. Italy was the third member of the Triple Alliance. But since she would be jealous of any Austro-Hungarian territorial expansion, and had in fact some territorial ambitions of her own concerning the Trentino, Istria, and the Dalmatian coast, which could be realized only at Austria-Hungary's expense, neither side could be sure of help from her. Great Britain, vaguely rather than specifically committed by the general terms of her ententes with France and Russia, was reluctant to encourage them with renewed promises of assistance. Thus she may have missed an opportunity to discourage the Central Powers by warning them that she would not remain neutral if France were invaded. Turkey and Bulgaria were looked upon as probable allies of Germany and Austria-Hungary if a general war should break out—Turkey for fear of Russia, Bulgaria for land in Macedonia and revenge for the part Serbia had played in her defeat in the war of 1913.

An apparently irreconcilable conflict between Serbian national aspirations and Austro-Hungarian imperial interests had long been known to exist. Serbia was politically independent but incomplete in the eyes of South Slav nationalists so long as Bosnia, Herzegovina, Croatia, and Slavonia were subject provinces of the Austro-Hungarian empire. With the dual monarchy in a position to deny her the use of the Danube or the most convenient of the Adriatic ports, Serbia feared the strangulation of her export trade, and her leaders were determined to free her, if possible, from economic dependence upon the grace of her powerful neighbor. Neither the ultimate political union of the Serbs, Croats, and Slovenes nor possession of territories giving Serbia direct access to the Adriatic could be secured except at the expense of the Austro-Hungarian empire. Subversive Yugoslav movements among the Bosnian Serbs were not, therefore, unwelcome to the "greater Serbia" group. Indeed, despite treaty agreements not to support them, the Serbian government had more than once been suspected of protecting and encouraging them. The Austro-Hungarian government, on the other hand, threatened with serious disaffection in provinces in which political unrest was already endemic, thought it saw in Serbia the center of the disturbance and a threat to the territorial integrity of the empire.

Determined upon war with Serbia, and depending upon Germany to prevent Russia from interfering or to protect her if Russia should intervene, Austria-Hungary presented to Serbia on July 23, 1914, an ultimatum so stern in its demands as to seem to have been deliberately made unacceptable. At the end of the forty-eight-hour time limit, Serbia returned a conciliatory answer which, in the words of the German kaiser, removed "every reason for war"; but Austria-Hungary declared the reply unacceptable and ordered mobilization against Serbia July 25. On the same day Serbia also mobilized her troops, and Russia took preliminary steps toward mobilization.

Meanwhile many suggestions were made by Sir Edward Grey and others for an extension of the ultimatum period, for mediation or arbitration, for another conference of ambassadors, or for the resumption of direct conversations between Austria-Hungary and Russia. But Austria-Hungary stubbornly refused to accept any intervention between herself and Serbia, and the German government steadfastly upheld her in that refusal and made only half-hearted and belated efforts to restrain her when it became clear that Russia intended to intervene. Russia, during the same critical days, "rejected in advance" any attempt by France or Britain to exert "a moderating influence in St. Petersburg." "We have adopted at the outset," said Foreign Minister Sazonov, "a point of view which we cannot change." France made, in fact, no attempt to restrain Russia, but reassured her that the terms of their alliance would be faithfully observed, even in the event of war.

On July 29 Austro-Hungarian guns fired on the Serbian capital, Belgrade, and Russian mobilization against Austria-Hungary was ordered; next day the Russian army began general mobilization, against Germany as well. To the military men—with the possible exception of General Conrad von Hötzendorf, chief of the Austrian general staff, who was not quite ready to fight anyone but the Serbs and was therefore willing to continue negotiations while mobilizing— mobilization meant war. Meaning war, it meant also that Germany and France were already involved by their dual alliances with Austria-Hungary and Russia, respectively, unless one or the other should have the hardihood to call its ally the aggressor—which neither showed any disposition to do.

So Germany was clearly, in the minds of her own leaders, on the brink of war when on the afternoon of July 31 she took the first publicized step toward mobilization by declaring the existence of a "threatening war-danger situation" (*drohender Kriegsgefahrzustand*) and sent an ultimatum to Russia demanding that all warlike operations against either Germany or Austria-Hungary should cease within twelve hours. At the same time she demanded that France declare within eighteen hours whether she would remain neutral in the event of a Russo-German war. France replied on August 1 that she would "consult her own interests," and Russia did not reply. So Germany declared war upon Russia at 12:52 and ordered general mobilization at 5:00 P.M. on August 1. France had ordered general mobilization only five minutes before Germany did. On August 3 Germany declared war on France.

On topographical and other purely military grounds the German general staff had planned, long in advance, if at war with France and Russia, to attack France through Belgium—this despite the fact that such a move would violate Belgium's neutrality, which Germany, among the many signatories of a general treaty, had guaranteed. At 7:00 P.M., August 2, the German minister in Brussels demanded free passage through Belgium for German troops, offering indemnity and a guarantee of independence if passage were granted, threatening war if it were refused. It was refused at 7:00 A.M., August 3. German troops invaded Belgium August 4, and Great Britain's course was at last made plain.

Sir Edward Grey, the British secretary of state for foreign affairs, had refused to make any fresh promises to France except to say on August 2 that the British navy would protect the northern coast of France against German naval attack. His government had, on the other hand, sharply refused to promise Germany that it would remain neutral, and had asked both France and Germany for renewed assurances that they would respect the neutrality of Belgium—which assurance France had readily given and Germany had refused to give. Great Britain's long-term interest in seeing France maintain herself as a major continental power, and the traditional British interest in keeping Belgium and the Netherlands out of the hands of any predominant land and naval power, might well have been enough to involve her in the war. When informed that Germany had violated Belgium's neutrality and that Belgium was resisting the invasion, the cabinet had a much stronger case to present to its own Parliament and people, to neutrals, and to Germany. So Britain sent Germany an ultimatum, August 4, which was rejected. "Just for a word, 'neutrality,' . . . just for a scrap of paper," the dismayed and exasperated German Chancellor von Bethmann-Hollweg was reported to have exclaimed to the British ambassador, Great Britain declared war.

Later the chancellor himself, speaking in the Reichstag, characterized the invasion of Belgium as a "breach of international law," a "wrong" which Germany should ultimately make good and could justify only on grounds of "necessity which knows no law." The "imponderables" ultimately thrown into the scales against Germany by her flagrant disregard of moral considerations and of international law were even heavier than he realized. Great Britain, on the other hand, defending herself in Belgium by defending Belgium, could represent herself in good faith as upholding at the same time the rights of small nations and the sanctity of treaties.

Turkey secretly signed a treaty of alliance with Germany on August 2. Japan declared war on Germany on August 23 and seized the German naval base and leasehold on Kiaochow Bay, and German influence and enterprise soon gave way to Japanese in the Shantung peninsula—an indication of the insincerity of Japan's announcement that she intended eventually to return Shantung to China.

Italy remained neutral in 1914, claiming freedom to do so on the ground that the treaties by which she was bound to the other members of the Triple Alliance were defensive in character and that Germany and Austria-Hungary were the aggressors. With some difficulty and when it was already too late, Austria-Hungary was induced to agree to some territorial concessions as "compensation" for any eventual Balkan conquests that she herself might make, and as the price of Italian participation as her ally; but Austria's enemies offered the same territories and more—also prospectively at her expense—and the hope of colonial acquisitions in Africa, Asia Minor, and the Aegean if the German and Turkish colonial empires should be reduced in size or broken up as a result of the war. So on May 23, 1915, Italy declared war on Austria-Hungary. Her alliance with Britain, France, and Russia was attested by secret treaties signed in London April 26 and September 5, 1915.

Bulgaria entered the war as an ally of the Central Powers in 1915; Rumania fought briefly against them in 1916. Greece was neutral in 1914. Switzerland, Sweden, Norway, Denmark, the Netherlands, and Spain remained neutral. Portugal proclaimed her loyalty to her traditional alliance with Great Britain on August 7, 1914, and became a belligerent on November 23, 1914, although Germany did not declare war on her until March 9, 1916. The United States proclaimed its neutrality on August 4, 1914.

SUMMARY

Only the omniscient or the unquestioning partisan will lightly assess responsibility for the outbreak of war in 1914, or hold any one nation or person answerable for it. Serbia had long cherished national aspirations inimical to Austria-Hungary. Austria-Hungary seized upon the murder of her archduke at Sarajevo as a favorable occasion for a punitive and preventive war upon Serbia, and would brook no intervention between herself and her victim.

Without her alliance with Germany, Austria-Hungary might have been more amenable to moderating influences; but Germany, her own peace efforts vitiated by her leaders' fatal conviction that a general war was ultimately inevitable, accepted the hazard of war then while sure of at least one ally rather than risk losing that ally by refusing to support her, and rather than face the possibility of having to confront a coalition, later, alone. It must indeed have seemed a sorry world to German statesmen—afraid to see even Germany, strong and well armed as she was, try to stand alone in it. But so they saw it, forgetting or failing to realize how largely they were themselves responsible for the international tensions which had induced that general state of foreboding and alarm. Pan-German imperialists meanwhile, with their war plans, their glorification of war, and their talk of the greater Germany of the future, had caused their restless but apprehensive fatherland to be widely feared. Although one of the last of the great continental powers to order general mobilization, Germany was the first to complete it, one of the first to make it clear to all that she had decided to resort to the use of armed force and not the mere threat of it, and the first to declare war upon another, thus making that decision irrevocable.

Russian leaders in 1914 also thought an eventual test of strength between Slav and Teuton and their respective allies inevitable. Russia claimed a protector's interest in the Slav peoples of the Balkans, viewed with alarm any diminution of Serbia in size, strength, or influence, at the hands of Austria-Hungary, and preferred a weakened Turkey at the Straits to a strong one or a strongly protected one. So Russia chose to intervene between Austria-Hungary and Serbia, and to convert a bilateral Balkan quarrel into a general European war, rather than renounce those interests. If she had been less sure of the support of France she might have been more amenable to moderating influences; but France encouraged her. Belgium was bound by the general treaty guaranteeing her neutrality to resist invasion. The British Foreign Office tried vainly to avert the catastrophe; but when the war had clearly become a reality Great Britain went into it in defense of interests she considered vital to herself but not exclusively her own.

It would probably not be accurate to say that the advent of war was welcomed by more than a minority of the people of any nation, although there were demonstrations of apparent popular enthusiasm in most metropolitan centers—especially in Berlin and least, at first, in London—when troops marched through the streets to entrain for the front. All were told by their leaders that they were being attacked and must defend themselves; and most of them believed what they were told. During the war, until its final stages, millions on both sides

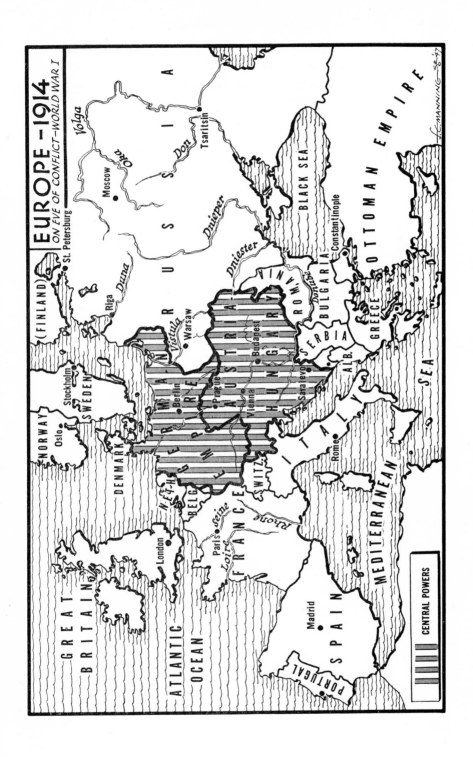

EUROPE - 1914
ON EVE OF CONFLICT - WORLD WAR I

GREAT BRITAIN

ATLANTIC OCEAN

NORWAY

Oslo

SWEDEN
Stockholm

DENMARK

(FINLAND)

St. Petersburg

Riga
Duna

Moscow

R U S S I A

Volga
Oka
Don

Tsaritsin

Dnieper

London

NETH.

BELG.

GERMANY

Berlin

Vistula
Warsaw

Prague
AUSTRIA

Vienna

Dniester

Budapest

HUNGARY

ROMANIA

Danube

Black Sea

Paris
Seine
Loire

FRANCE

Rhone

SWITZ.

ITALY

Rome

Sarajevo

SERBIA

ALB.

BULGARIA

Constantinople

OTTOMAN EMPIRE

GREECE

SPAIN

Madrid

PORTUGAL

MEDITERRANEAN SEA

F.C. MANNING SR '47

CENTRAL POWERS

were heartened by dreams of conquest as well as by hopes of victory. It came, therefore, as a double shock to many of the German people to realize in 1918 that they not only had lost the war, and with it their colonial empire, but would be held responsible for it and for damage done by their armed forces in the course of it.

CHAPTER 2

1914-1916

It was a part of Prussian military tradition to seize the initiative in war and try to paralyze enemy resistance at the outset by effective use of the swift striking power of well-trained and well-equipped armies, boldly led. In August, 1914, the German general staff was ready as usual with a plan which promised a quick and favorable decision. Hoping, as their former chief of staff, von Schlieffen, had done, that the Russian armies would be slow to mobilize and ineffective in any invasion of German territory they might attempt, German strategists assigned a generally defensive role to their relatively small forces on the Russian front, while pouring troops into France in the greatest possible numbers and with all possible speed in an attempt to overwhelm the French armies before a British expeditionary force or reinforcements from North Africa could reach them.

Immediate military expediency was, to the German general staff, a potent argument in favor of an invasion of France through neutral Luxemburg and Belgium. The topography of France is more favorable to an invasion from north to south than to one from east to west, and France was better fortified along her German frontier than along her Belgian border. The Rhine bridges and railway trunk lines were conveniently located for the movement of great armies and their supplies through Belgium, good roads were more numerous, and natural obstacles were fewer and less troublesome. The effect of the outrage on world opinion was adverse; but that was an "imponderable" outweighed at the moment by "practical" considerations.

During the month of August the Germans poured through Belgium, delayed but only delayed by Belgian resistance at Liège and Namur, by a small British expeditionary force that met them at Mons but had to give way before them, and by French troops who met them at Charleroi and in a series of rearguard engagements thereafter. These delays, slight though they were, gave the French commander in chief, Marshal Joffre, time to regroup his forces, many of which had been committed to a defense of the French-German frontier and some to an invasion of Alsace-Lorraine. Others were summoned from French Africa.

The first two weeks of September, 1914, were critical. Paris seemed about to fall. The French government moved to Bordeaux. The apparently irresistible German army, however, almost but not quite equal to its task, revealed under the stress of hard campaigning certain minor imperfections which the most strenuous training maneuvers had not brought to light. Some of its elements had outrun their own services of supply. Internal communications between army groups were inadequate. The chief of the general staff, Helmuth von Moltke, nephew and namesake of one of Prussia's most famous soldiers but less rugged than his uncle, lagged too far behind his front line, lost control as well as contact, and sent six divisions from the western to the eastern front without using them in combat in France. Meanwhile the less brilliant but imperturbable Marshal Joffre was able to keep his forces in hand and strengthen them even while they were being driven back upon themselves, south of the Marne River.

The "first battle of the Marne" was a week of many battles, September 6 to 12, a million men (more or less) on a side, from Paris to Verdun and Belfort, but principally in the valley of the middle Marne, east of Paris. The counterattack of the French armies and what was left of the original British expeditionary force carried them back across the Marne valley, but the Germans dug in along the heights north of the Aisne and, perceiving that the war was about to become one of position rather than of movement, turned their attention to the Channel ports of Belgium and northern France. It was only by the hardest kind of fighting, especially in the first battle of Ypres, and by flooding part of the coastal area that the Allies were able to keep open for the use of the British the ports of Nieuport, Dunkirk, Calais, Boulogne, and an operating area including Arras and Amiens.

The turn to trench warfare indicated, in a sense, a stalemate. The Germans occupied most of Belgium and gained access to the valuable coal and iron resources of the French Briey region and Lorraine—enormous advantages in a long war. But they failed to attain their primary objective, which had been to inflict upon France, in one decisive campaign, a defeat so crushing as to eliminate her from the war. Having failed to win quickly on striking power, and being forced to fall back upon staying power, they had lost a part of their strategic initiative and found themselves compelled to face the prospect of an endurance test in which Russian numbers and distances, British sea power, and the superior economic resources and industrial productive capacity of Britain and France would weigh heavily in the balance against them. So the first battle of the Marne was one of the vital turning points of the war.

RUSSIAN FRONT, 1914

Russia also seized the initiative, and invaded both East Prussia and Galicia in August, 1914. Austria-Hungary was thus distracted from the Serbian campaign for the sake of which she had precipitated the war but, even so, was able to stop the Russian advance only with the aid of the winter snows and the heights of the Carpathians, after most of Galicia had been overrun. She had little help from Germany that year, except indirectly.

Taking advantage of the numerical weakness of the German forces left to face them, while most of the weight of the German army was thrown into France, Russian troops moved rapidly through East Prussia and by mid-August were threatening Königsberg. In that emergency the German general staff recalled from retirement General Paul von Hindenburg, who was thoroughly familiar with the region and was considered an authority on plans for a war against Russia. He was given as chief of staff one of the most capable staff officers the war was to produce, General Erich Ludendorff. Upon arrival on the eastern front the new commanders, with the aid of Major Max Hoffmann (later general, chief of staff on that front, and plenipotentiary at Brest Litovsk), were soon able to divide, entangle, and destroy separately several poorly coördinated and badly led Russian army corps. The culminating engagement of the campaign was at Tannenberg, August 26-29. Russian losses in East Prussia, in casualties and prisoners, were estimated at about 300,000. The invasion failed, and was counterbalanced only by successes in Galicia. A winter stalemate followed there, as in the west. These victories of the German army had served to reduce Russian pressure upon Austria.

1915

The raising and training of enormous national armies and the conversion of industries to war production to supply and equip them were major problems of all the belligerents from the beginning of the war.

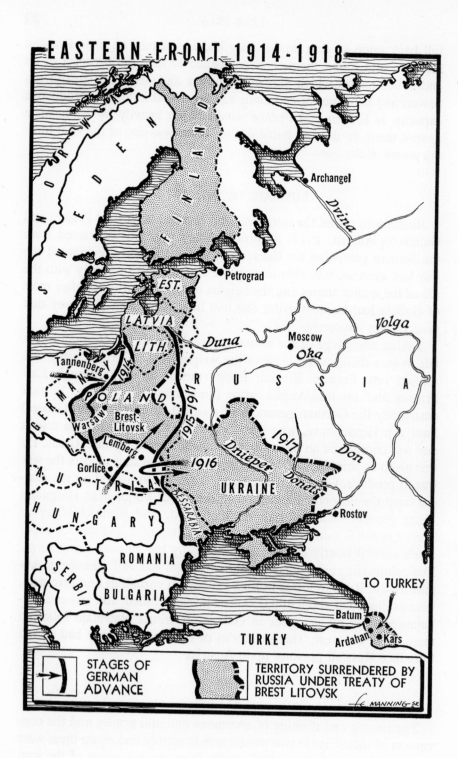

EASTERN FRONT 1914-1918

NORWAY

SWEDEN

FINLAND

Archangel

Dvina

Petrograd

EST.

LATVIA

Volga

Duna

Moscow

Oka

LITH.

Tannenberg

1914

R U S S I A

GERMANY

POLAND

Warsaw

Brest-Litovsk

1915-1917

Lemberg

Gorlice

1916

Dnieper

1917

Don

Donets

A U S T R I A

UKRAINE

HUNGARY

BESSARABIA

Rostov

ROMANIA

SERBIA

BULGARIA

TO TURKEY

Batum

Ardahan   Kars

TURKEY

STAGES OF GERMAN ADVANCE

TERRITORY SURRENDERED BY RUSSIA UNDER TREATY OF BREST LITOVSK

F.C. MANNING SR

In these fields, as in many others, German prewar planning had been more thorough than British or French. By virtue of their system of universal military service, and by mixing veterans and recruits, the Germans were able to put new millions of men into the field in 1915. Also, thanks to the quick conversion of their industry, their munitions supply seemed adequate. The French had fewer reserves of man power, but more than they could then equip or supply. The British, starting with a small standing army, some imperfectly trained "territorial" reserves, and a tremendous war potential in the field of industrial production but with no complete plan ready for its conversion to war work, needed a year in which to extemporize a national army and a munitions industry.

The French and British were therefore unable to undertake any grand-scale offensive on the French front in the spring of 1915, and circumstances would have been favorable for an overwhelming German offensive there. The German commanders on the eastern front, on the other hand, promised a decisive victory over the Russians in Poland if all possible weight were thrown into an offensive there; and the new chief of the general staff, von Falkenhayn, rather reluctantly and half-heartedly adopted their proposal. Von Hindenburg attacked from East Prussia toward Bialystok in February but failed to cross the Narew River. In May German General von Mackensen, with both Austro-Hungarian and German troops and a great concentration of heavy artillery, broke through the Russian line in Galicia. Squeezed between this southern offensive and renewed attacks from the north, and severely handicapped by want of munitions, the Russians were driven out of Poland by the end of August, beyond a line drawn roughly from the southern end of the Gulf of Riga to a point not far west of Dvinsk, thence south through Pinsk and the Pripet marshes.

The inadequacy of Russia's munitions supply was one of many reasons for an attempt of her allies, early in 1915, to open the Dardanelles and establish contact with her by way of the Mediterranean and Black seas. First a naval force, chiefly British, tried to blast its way through with gunfire and (if it had but known it) did not fall far short of success, for the defending Turkish forts were none too well supplied with munitions either; but heavy losses in ships and men caused the attack to be discontinued. Late in April a mixed British colonial force including elements of the Australian and New Zealand Army Corps famous thereafter as the Anzacs made a landing on the Gallipoli Peninsula and tried to open the Straits by land. These men clung valiantly to their beachhead under terrible punishment; but Bulgaria's entry into the war as an ally of Turkey and the Central Powers after the last Allied attacks had failed enabled the Germans to send supplies and staff officers to aid the Turks; and the Russians, trying desperately to defend themselves on their Galician front, failed to make even a diversionary attack on the Bosporus. The Gallipoli campaign was a costly failure, as the action in the Dardanelles had been.

So the Straits remained closed; contact between Turkey and the Central Powers via Bulgaria was maintained; and Turkey was still in a position to threaten Britain's lines of communication with India. The Suez Canal was successfully defended, however, by British and colonial troops, and Egypt was a useful staging area for them throughout the war. A British expeditionary force, moving up through Mesopotamia toward Bagdad, was blocked by the Turks and compelled, on April 29, 1916, to surrender at Kut el Amara.

A third front against Austria-Hungary was opened up on May 23, 1915, with an Italian declaration of war. The Italians tried at once to "redeem" the territories they had coveted as Italia irredenta since unification—the Trentino, Trieste, and Istria. The mountain defenses of the Trentino were easily held by the Austrians, however, despite miracles of military engineering performed by the Italians; and an Italian sweep around the head of the Adriatic was halted a little east of the border, along the line of the Isonzo River. The port of Trieste and an excellent base at Pola on the tip of the Istrian peninsula remained open throughout the war to German submarines, which mines, nets, and patrols in the Strait of Otranto were never able to exclude from the Adriatic.

Austro-Hungarian control of the eastern shore of the Adriatic was no longer threatened after the autumn of 1915. Taking advantage of their interior lines of communication, and assuming that their French, Russian, and Italian fronts could be easily held as they were, the Central Powers turned their attention again in September to Serbia, which had defended itself successfully while they were occupied elsewhere. Bulgaria, smarting for revenge for 1913, was easily induced to join in the attack when offered an opportunity to take Serbian Macedonia immediately, to regain the Dobruja if Rumania should risk the loss of it by attacking her, and Salonika if Greece should live up to the terms of her defensive alliance with Serbia and abandon her rather equivocal position of neutrality.

Austro-Hungarian and German troops commanded by the German von Mackensen moved into Serbia from the north on October 7, and

Bulgarians into Serbian Macedonia from the east November 11. The Serbians and their Montenegrin allies defended their mountainous country as bravely and tenaciously as ever; but their principal cities and railway centers were lost within two months and by the end of February even the Albanian capital, Tirana, and the Albanian seaport of Durazzo were closed to them. Such of the survivors as could escape were picked up off the beaches or off the Greek island of Corfu by Allied naval forces and carried around to a precarious foothold established by the French at Salonika just before the beginning of the October invasion.

The Greek King Constantine, generally considered pro-German, had announced a policy of neutrality after dismissing his pro-Ally premier, Eleutherios Venizelos, who had invited the Allies to send in an expeditionary force to coöperate with Greece in aid of Serbia. Although reinforced in December by veterans of the ill-fated Gallipoli campaign, the conglomerate holding force at Salonika, under the French general Sarrail, was able to do little more than retain its foothold. In July, 1917, having already occupied part of Thessaly and the isthmus of Corinth, it further improved its position by requiring the abdication of the unfriendly King Constantine. The new king, Alexander, recalled Venizelos as premier and brought Greece officially into the war as a belligerent; but the proposed counterattack from Salonika could not be mounted until late in 1918.

To find men and matériel for all these far-flung enterprises was not easy, not even for the Germany of 1915. In France the Germans had to stand generally on the defensive, reluctant though many of them (particularly Chief of Staff von Falkenhayn) were to let pass so golden an opportunity for a decisive offensive. Being committed, however, to the policy of holding that front as economically as possible while trying for a decision in the east, they showed great ingenuity in introducing new offensive-defensive tactics in close-range warfare, elaborate defense systems and underground living quarters for the conservation of their man power, and new weapons to keep the Allies off balance. Among these innovations were the use of poison gas (chlorine released from cylinders and blown along the ground by the wind), the blind bombing of London from zeppelins at night, and the illegal use of the submarine as a commerce destroyer, sinking hundreds of ships, one of which was the British liner *Lusitania*.

French and British offensives that year proved costly and achieved only limited objectives. For the French and British, 1915 in France was the year of the build-up.

1916

In retrospect, as the German high command reviewed it while planning new campaigns to come, 1915 had been for the Central Powers a year of inconclusive victories. Several successful campaigns had overrun vast territories and cost their enemies enormous losses; but none of their principal adversaries had been eliminated. Only Serbia had been totally dispossessed. The Russian army had been pushed far back and seriously weakened, but not destroyed. France and Great Britain, meanwhile, had had access to neutral markets, had got their war industries going, and could be expected to throw strong new armies into an offensive in France.

Both Britain and France had suffered heavy losses already, but neither had been crippled as Russia was thought to have been, and both were potentially dangerous. It seemed imperative that one or the other be eliminated if possible; and Britain, because of her insular position and sea power, was the less vulnerable. She could survive, and strike again elsewhere, even if her troops were driven out of France. The French armies, on the other hand, might never recover their offensive strength if compelled to exhaust themselves in defending some vital point such as Verdun, the anchor of their line and the fortress closest to the German Ruhr and transportation centers.

Supported by the kaiser in his conviction that the western front was not only the most critical at the moment but the one on which, fundamentally, the issue of the war must ultimately be determined, the chief of the general staff, von Falkenhayn, decided to anticipate the Allied offensive by attacking first, at Verdun. On February 21, 1916, after nine hours of the heaviest shelling anyone had then seen, the army group commanded by the Prussian crown prince began pouring infantry into the attack. For more than four months, through June, the attacks continued; frightful losses were incurred by both sides. To both, the battle assumed an ever growing moral significance. To the French, rallying to the battle cry "They shall not pass," holding Verdun meant keeping alive the hope of the survival of France; to the Germans, taking it meant the hope of victory. After July 1 some of the efforts of both were diverted to the Somme River valley by the British offensive there, but intermittent heavy fighting for limited objectives occurred in the Verdun area through the summer of 1917.

The costly failure at Verdun had its repercussions in Germany. Defeatism and silent, almost subconscious, opposition to the war spread widely, underground, as people learned their losses. The crown prince was increasingly unpopular as the rumor spread that, hoping at any price to salvage his prestige as a commander, he had willfully continued the offensive long after his best advisers had realized that it had failed. But most important of all, von Falkenhayn had to give way as chief of the general staff to Field Marshal von Hindenburg, who came from the Russian front, with an aura of success about him and Ludendorff beside him, to assume supreme control over armies, navy, and government in the name of the kaiser. The latter had already surrendered the immediate direction of the armed forces to the generals and admirals and was thereafter little more than a figure-head.

France also felt the effects. Her people had made their supreme effort. Her army had almost been, as her enemy had intended that it should be, "bled white." The military director of her heroic defense, Marshal Pétain, knowing all too well the cost of victory, could never thereafter forget how near he had been to defeat, or how nearly ready to concede it. Defeatists in the Chamber of Deputies, including one Pierre Laval, were convinced that France could never again withstand Germany, and even "the Tiger," Clemenceau, knew that she could not do it alone.

The pressure began to be taken off the French at Verdun in June by offensives mounted by the Allies on other fronts. Lacking the Germans' advantage of a unified command but aiming at coördination of effort, the French, British, Italians, and Russians had agreed in the early spring upon simultaneous offensives, to be begun in July. The German attack at Verdun had been intended not only to forestall at least one of these offensives but to provoke the British into counter-attacking prematurely. The British waited, however, until their new national army, raised by conscription after volunteering had been found unsatisfactory in 1915, was ready and well supplied with munitions.

From July 1 until November 18, when it was slowed down to a halt by the common enemy of all soldiers—cold, rain, mud, and exhaustion—there raged along the valley of the Somme River a battle that surpassed Verdun in the numbers engaged and the expenditure of lives and matériel. It was war at its worst: the war of attrition, wearing the enemy down. The French contributed what they could, but the British weakened themselves on the Somme as the French had been weakened at Verdun, reassuring themselves as best they could with the knowledge that the Germans had been weakened in both battles.

And not only in the west. Austria-Hungary had been tempted in

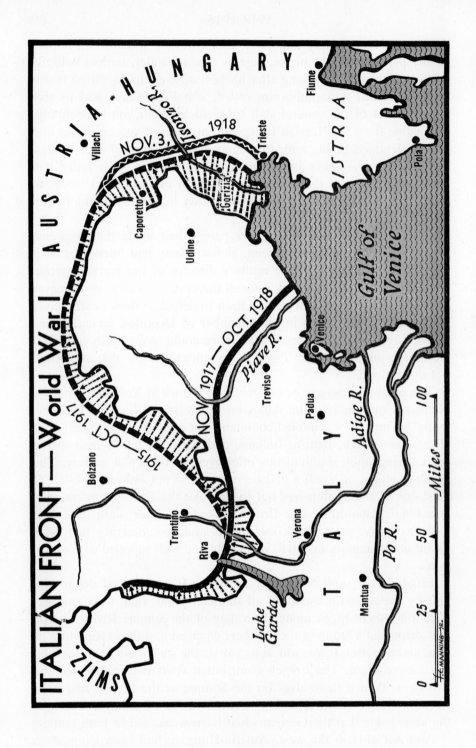

May by what seemed a promising opportunity to attack the Italians from the Trentino salient, hoping to break out into the level country toward Vicenza and Padua, and thus to cut the communications of the Italian armies on the Isonzo. Success in such a movement would have meant the quick collapse of the whole Italian front; but it failed. The Italians held at Vicenza, counterattacked successfully there, and in August improved their position on the Isonzo front by taking Gorizia.

The Austrians had gambled heavily in undertaking the Trentino operation without German support. Troops and guns for it were moved from the Russian front, south of the Pripet marshes. Almost at once, early in June, the Russians under General Brusilov broke through the weakened line and swiftly made great gains in Galicia and Bucovina, surprising even to themselves. German help was required to stop them. With the reinforcements came the generals, von Hindenburg and Ludendorff, to assume command of all Austro-Hungarian and German forces on the Russian front, with headquarters at Brest Litovsk. By the middle of August the Russian advance lost its momentum in the face of stiffening resistance and because of the inadequacy of its supply service.

Before the Russian failure had become apparent Rumania had declared war, on August 27. That Balkan monarchy had been an ally of Germany since 1883 but had remained neutral in 1914. In August, 1916, the Italians at Gorizia and the Russians in Galicia and Bucovina seemed ready to strike the hard-pressed Habsburg empire a fatal blow which Germany, engrossed on the Somme, could not parry; and the Allies promised that Rumania should have Transylvania, Bucovina, and continued possession of the Dobruja, which she had taken from Bulgaria in 1913.

The Rumanian declaration of war was the final incident that brought about the resignation of von Falkenhayn as chief of the German general staff and his replacement by von Hindenburg, who was credited with just having brought the situation on the eastern front again under control. Von Falkenhayn himself assumed command of a strong Austro-Hungarian-German force for the reconquest of the part of Transylvania which the Rumanians had already overrun, and for an invasion of Rumania from the west, while von Mackensen marched in from the south with an army of Bulgarian, German, and Austro-Hungarian troops. The campaign was mercifully short. The Russians could not make good their promise of a diversionary attack in the Carpathians, nor the French from Salonika. By the end of the year all Rumania was held by the Central Powers, and her government, almost-in-exile, had to make peace on such terms as it could get. The terms, which were harsh enough, were held in abeyance pending an ostensible German peace offer; but for the remaining years of the war the Central Powers had access to Rumanian wheat and oil, and control of the railways and the Danube barge lines over which those vital commodities were to be carried.

CHAPTER 3

1917-1918—The United States,
Neutral and Belligerent

THE GERMAN SITUATION AT THE END OF 1916

Such sweeping military successes as there were in 1916 were won, as in 1915, by the Germans and their allies; but victory still eluded them. The German fleet met the British in the battle of Jutland on May 31 and inflicted heavier losses than it suffered; but it was driven back into its havens without breaking the British blockade of Germany or disrupting the heavy sea-borne traffic upon which the life of Britain depended.

Consternation akin to panic seized the kaiser and his confidential advisers when Rumania declared war before it became clear either in Bucharest or in Berlin that the Italian and Russian drives were spent; and it was a personal defeat for the kaiser when he was virtually supplanted by General von Hindenburg, whose fabulous reputation had been sedulously built up for that purpose by Ludendorff. Confidence was quickly restored by the turn of events in southeastern Europe and defensive measures taken by the new military dictators, such as the fortification of the Siegfried or "Hindenburg" line across Belgium and France; but people were hungry as a result of the food blockade and cold for want of fuel in the cities. The physical endurance and morale of civilians and soldiers alike were sorely tested during that third war winter.

As the painful effects of the blockade were ever more acutely felt, the anti-British feeling expressed in the hymn of hate, "God Punish England," helped to prepare public opinion for a strategic decision to revert to unrestricted submarine warfare in hope of compelling Britain to make peace. That decision, when it was eventually taken, was nominally made by the kaiser and his principal military and naval advisers, actually by von Hindenburg, Ludendorff, and Admiral von Holtzendorff, with the kaiser concurring and Chancellor von Bethmann-Hollweg dissenting. But it was not for fear of political opposition that the chancellor dissented. The Reichstag had already assured him by a resolution adopted on October 11, 1916, that it would support a decision "to wage ruthless U-boat war."

The German leaders knew that the resumption of unrestricted submarine warfare would provoke the United States, probably to the point of breaking off diplomatic relations and possibly to a declaration of war. That was a risk which they chose to take. Hindenburg and Ludendorff had realized, on their first general inspection of their western front in August, 1916, that they could neither win the war by any series of attacks on land alone nor afford to stand indefinitely on the defensive. Both Verdun and the Somme had cost them too many casualties. Sea power, the source of Britain's strength and the instrument of the blockade which was crippling Germany, seemed to be the determining factor. If, by use of Germany's most effective naval weapon, the submarine, Britain could herself be blockaded and broken, the war might yet be won before the United States could raise, equip, train, and send an expeditionary force strong enough to determine the issue. The admiralty promised, moreover, to sink such transports as the United States might send into European waters.

THE PROBLEMS OF NEUTRALITY

The effect upon neutral opinion of the ruthless use of the submarine as a blockade weapon, depending for its effectiveness as much upon the terror it inspired as upon the material damage it could do, was another of the "imponderables" which, like their violation of the neutrality of Belgium, the "realists" at German great headquarters never learned to weigh and always underestimated. The interests of the people of the United States were inevitably affected in many ways by the war; but the most serious and direct injury was done them by the submarine.

President Wilson proclaimed the neutrality of the United States on August 4, 1914; but the way of the neutral was neither plain nor smooth. President Eliot of Harvard immediately urged that the United States should send ships to join the navies of the Triple Entente in enforcing a blockade of Austria-Hungary and Germany, on the ground that those powers had shown themselves to be "utterly untrustworthy neighbors and bullies of the worst sort," Germany being (in his opinion) the worse of the two because she had already violated neutral territory. "If they are allowed to succeed in their present enterprises," wrote President Eliot, "the fear of sudden invasion will constantly hang over all the other European peoples; and the increasing burdens of competitive armaments will have to be borne for another forty years. We shall inevitably share in these losses and miseries. . . ."

Ex-President Theodore Roosevelt soon became another of the most outspoken critics of what he called the craven and spineless policy of neutrality; but there were few outright interventionists in 1914. To most Americans, Europe was far away, its troubles imperfectly understood and unreal if not unreasonable and unnecessary. A people fortunate, strong, and self-confident enough to take its own peace for granted did not readily realize how or why the peoples of Europe had lost their grip upon peace and gone desperately to war. Unprepared for war and unfamiliar with fear, Americans were shocked and offended but not seriously alarmed by Germany's flagrant infraction of the treaty guaranteeing the neutrality of Belgium. Contrasting Europe's condition with their own, they were thankful for their supposed security and for peace—a feeling productive, in some, of honest pacifism and, in others, of self-congratulation that Americans were not as other peoples were.

Americans of foreign birth or ancestry were more directly interested. Many of them, so long as the United States was neutral, found their sympathies enlisted on behalf of the lands of their ancestors. Hoping to keep the country out of war and to preserve its unity by discouraging the embittered and partisan discussions in which he feared they might engage, President Wilson at first urged his fellow citizens to be "neutral in fact as well as in name, . . . impartial in thought as well as in action." A public opinion sharply critical of the "hyphenate" soon appeared, wherever the foreign-born or their descendants showed too plainly any "unneutral" partiality.

All the principal belligerents did what they could to influence American opinion through propaganda. In that endeavor, control of the cables gave Great Britain and France an advantage over Germany, enabling them to throw as favorable a light as possible upon their own war reports and upon their own "case" in general. Although German wireless reports got through, and the war communiqués of both sides were printed in the newspapers, the Allies' propagandists were gener-

ally more skillful and understood and anticipated better the psychological reactions of the people whose opinions they sought to influence.
Their comparative success is not, however, to be explained entirely by
saying that they made a better presentation of their case; for other
reasons also, the opinion steadily grew that they had a better case to
present. The Allies interfered often enough with the rights of neutrals,
which the United States was trying to maintain; but Germany's violations of those rights seemed much more outrageous and inhumane.

The United States government recognized at once its obligation,
in its own interest and in the general interest of mankind with which
it identified its own, to maintain the rights of neutrals if it could—
especially the right it had itself traditionally claimed for its citizens:
to trade and to travel outside actual war zones. Only by the maintenance of that right could the war be localized anywhere; only so
could the oceans or much of the earth be kept open to the uninterrupted international exchanges of peacetime. If the world's strongest
neutral nation surrendered that right, others would probably be unable
to maintain it; neutrality would be thereafter a disappearing phenomenon; and the tendency of all wars to involve everyone would be
harder than ever to hold in check.

The right to trade included the right to sell and deliver consumers'
goods, war materials, and munitions to belligerents, unless prevented
by an effective blockade. The United States government was neither
blind nor indifferent to the fact that that trade was profitable to the persons engaged in it. When cash sales to the Allies had led, as eventually
they did, to the flotation of large loans in the United States, some
Americans had thereafter an economic stake in the survival and
solvency of the Allied governments. There were reasons other than
profits, however, for keeping the trade open. By it Great Britain,
France, Italy, and Russia were enabled to make good some of the
deficiencies of their own preparation for war, to compensate to a certain extent for the advantage that Germany's completed war plans
had given her. The German government protested that it was unneutral
to sell, and especially to sell munitions, to belligerents on one side and
not to both; but the American position, fully in accord with previously
established practice, was that it would have been unneutral to refuse
to sell to those belligerents who were able to carry in their own ships
what they purchased, or to whom goods sold could be delivered. To
have refused would have been, furthermore, to put a double premium
on military preparedness and plans for war, such as would in any
circumstances be made beforehand by a deliberate aggressor; any

contemplated attack would be made only when its intended victim was comparatively ill prepared to meet it.

Some sales were made, in fact, directly or indirectly to Germans. A cargo submarine, the *Deutschland,* armed defensively as a merchantman, appeared at Baltimore July 9, 1916, with a cargo of dyes, pharmaceuticals, and mail and was permitted to load and depart with all the zinc, copper, and nickel she could carry.[1] American trade with neutrals having access to Germany, particularly with Norway and Denmark, also increased enormously until Great Britain put it virtually on a quota basis by invoking the convenient doctrine of the "continuous voyage," i.e., that American copper, for example, going into Denmark in vastly greater quantities than in 1913, was clearly on its way to Germany, albeit by way of Denmark, and could therefore legitimately be intercepted under the accepted laws of blockade.

Those "laws of blockade" were only general international understandings of accepted practice, and flexible at best as to details if not in principle. An attempt to codify them had been made by the Declaration of London, 1909, which Great Britain had not ratified and now refused to ratify, as it would have restricted her use of sea power. Instead, she issued at the outset of the war a new contraband list of articles subject to seizure, including many commodities not so listed by the Declaration of London. Many things, she argued, which in previous wars had been classified only as raw materials for the use of civilian population had become essential war materials. One of these, not included until the sinking of the *Lusitania* had so turned American opinion against Germany as to make its inclusion less impolitic than it would have been before, was cotton. Another was food; and, with nation-wide food rationing in effect in Germany, it was no longer possible to differentiate between food imported for civilians' use and food for the German army.

Germany, on the other hand, as the weaker naval power, would have preferred to have the "laws of blockade" more sharply defined and rigidly enforced on those points—but only those—at which strict construction and enforcement would be advantageous to her by restricting Britain's use of sea power and easing the effects of the blockade upon the German people. Germans generally continued,

---

[1] In November, 1916, at New London, Connecticut, the *Deutschland* took on a second cargo consisting chiefly of crude rubber, nickel, chrome, and vanadium. A sister ship, the *Bremen,* disappeared on her outward voyage. Another, the *Bayern,* was converted in 1917 into the armed commerce destroyer U-157. As U-155 the *Deutschland,* also converted and armed, raided shipping in the western Atlantic in 1918.

throughout and after the war, to denounce the food blockade as war upon women and children, the aged and the weak, and as a worse atrocity than any committed by their submarines. Several times during the period of American neutrality the German government sought to embroil the United States more seriously with Great Britain by making concessions contingent upon steps to be taken by the United States to compel Britain to loosen the blockade.

There was friction enough without that. The Department of State was kept busy registering the protests of irate Americans against interference with trade between neutrals, the inclusion of new items in the contraband lists, and the enforcement of the blockade by the establishment of "contraband control points" at which neutral ships were required to put in to be searched—stopping them for search at sea had been found too dangerous in waters infested by hostile submarines. Some Americans were aggrieved also by the publication of British black lists of firms alleged to have "enemy" connections, with which British subjects were forbidden to trade. Censorship of cables and the mails inevitably involved annoying delays and sometimes led to charges that trade secrets were being stolen by the censors and by "listening in" on coded messages sent by wireless, and that unfair advantage was being taken in competitive trade.

The terms of the secret treaties by which the Allies had supplemented their military alliances, distributing among themselves the anticipated territorial fruits of victory, were not widely known in the United States or, though they may have been guessed at, by the president and his advisers; but it was not supposed that any nation was altogether altruistic in its war aims. Nor did many neutrals yet realize that the belligerents were already actually irreconcilable. The propagandists sent over to "explain the war to Americans" had, therefore, enough to do. The task of those working for the Allies was made easier by the offensive blunders of the Germans and Austro-Hungarians; President Wilson was still seeking to end the war by mediation when the German government put an end to any such possibility by announcing the resumption of unrestricted submarine warfare.

German violations of American neutrality were known from 1914 to be serious, and were more serious than they were then known to be. Having failed by argument to prevent the sale of war materials to the Allies, the German government told its ambassador in Washington on January 26, 1915, how to find "persons suitable for carrying on sabotage in the United States and Canada," adding: "In the United States sabotage can be carried out in every kind of factory for supplying munitions of war. . . . Embassy must under no circumstances be compromised."

The German ambassador, Count von Bernstorff, avoided implication; but the Austrian ambassador, Dr. Konstantin Dumba, and the German military and naval attachés, Captains Franz von Papen and Karl Boy-Ed, were handed their passports in 1915 for incitement of strikes and sabotage. When they were gone there were others to carry on their work through the consulates and American offices of German steamship lines. When the United States entered the war the German general staff claimed credit with the Austro-Hungarian for having caused scores of explosions and many millions of dollars' worth of damage in American munitions factories, railway terminals, and warehouses. This boast, the cable of January 26, 1915, authorizing general sabotage, and other evidence belied the subsequent German claim that, although men, money, and materials for sabotage had been sent into the United States in 1916, definite instructions had prohibited any such activity until the United States should actually be at war with Germany.[2]

On February 4, 1915, Germany began a naval and diplomatic offensive against Great Britain by designating the waters around the British Isles and in the eastern Mediterranean as "war zones" in which belligerents' ships would be, and neutral vessels might be, sunk without warning. The impression given out was that this extraordinary step was being taken only in retaliation for illegal acts of Britain. It was implied that greater care might be taken to safeguard the rights of neutrals if the neutrals would assert their own rights more vigorously and compel Great Britain to lift her blockade of Germany as to raw materials and foodstuffs. Great Britain was willing to bargain as to the food blockade but not as to other essential war materials. So the submarine was given a trial as a destroyer of freight and passenger vessels, in open defiance of a plain warning from President Wilson that if an American vessel should be so destroyed or American lives taken on

[2] Two of the most notorious cases of sabotage were explosions that wrecked the Black Tom pier, freight terminal of the Lehigh Valley Railroad near New York, July 29, 1916, and the assembly plant shops of the Canadian Car and Foundry Company at Kingsland, New Jersey, on January 11, 1917. On June 15, 1939, the Mixed Claims Commission (Justice Owen J. Roberts, umpire) found Germany responsible for the Black Tom and Kingsland explosions and guilty of fraud, collusion, and subornation of perjury in its long and stubborn defense. Two previous decisions favorable to Germany (1930 and 1932) were set aside as having been based on false evidence. Damages, including interest, were set at about $55,000,000 in an award made on October 30, 1939. Germany had agreed at Munich in 1936 to pay about $20,000,000, but payment had not been made. See Hall and Peaslee, *Three Wars with Germany* (New York, 1944), 8-10, 134, 166, 184-186.

the high seas "it would be impossible for the Government of the United
States to view the act in any other light than as an indefensible violation of neutral rights . . . [and] the Government of the United States
would be constrained to hold the Imperial German Government to a
strict accountability for such acts."

Trouble was inevitable if Americans maintained their right as
neutrals to trade and travel outside actual war zones and refused to
recognize the German proclamation calling the waters around the
British Isles a war zone. The Americans had both law and precedent
on their side. Neutrals were not bound to recognize any but an effective blockade, one that could stop most of the vessels that might
attempt to go through it; and the submarines could not do that. They
could sink some, and hope that the fear of sinking would deter others
from trying to get through—so frightfulness might add something to
their effectiveness. But they could only interfere with and harass a
traffic which they could not stop and which their government had no
recognized right to prohibit by proclamation. A paper blockade was
neither legal nor binding upon neutrals, and could not be validated by
indiscriminate destruction of lives and property of some of those who
disregarded it.

Nor could the submarine be used effectively against commercial
shipping without violating the established rules. A submarine on the
surface is vulnerable, and innocent-looking merchant ships could be
used as decoys; so it was dangerous for a U-boat to surface and give
warning before attacking, or to stop a ship to search it or establish its
identity. It was usually impossible, because of the more effective
British blockade of Germany, to take a suspected vessel into a German port, even if men could have been spared from a U-boat's crew
(as they usually could not) to serve as prize crews. There was not
room on board a submarine for passengers and crews of vessels sunk;
so provision for their safety was difficult though not always impossible
or always neglected. To all these things a blockading power was obligated; and none of them, the Germans argued, could they be required to do. The submarine, they said, was a new weapon upon
which the old outdated rules of cruiser warfare could not properly be
imposed.

The nub of the matter was that the German government had to
choose between the restricted use of its most potent naval weapon,
which would especially reduce its usefulness as a blockade weapon,
and an open defiance of world opinion, which would surely be shocked
by the inhumanity as well as the illegality of ruthless U-boat war. It

chose to use its weapon. The government of the United States was thus compelled either to abandon its defense of the rights of neutrals and of agreements to mitigate the inhumanity of war, or to reassert them. It chose to reassert them.

Occasion was not long wanting. In 1915 one American went down with the *Falaba,* a British steamer sunk March 28, two with an American tanker, the *Gulflight,* May 1, and 124 (among about 1200 victims) with the *Lusitania,* May 7. The German government, far from disavowing the sinking of the *Lusitania,* defended it, alleging that the ship was in effect an auxiliary cruiser and was carrying soldiers and munitions.

What, then, could "strict accountability" be made to mean? President Wilson was severely criticized at home for the patience with which he argued the American position rather than resort at once to war, although he clearly warned Germany that the United States would look upon another such atrocity as "a deliberately unfriendly act." Great patience was indeed required. It was not until after the sinking of the *Arabic* (August 19), westbound and obviously carrying no contraband but with two Americans on board, that the German ambassador (going beyond his instructions) announced on September 1, 1915, a secret order already given to U-boat commanders not thereafter to sink ocean liners without warning or without provision for the safety of their passengers and crews, unless they resisted or tried to escape. On October 5 von Bernstorff was authorized to "regret and disavow" the sinking of the *Arabic* and to say that his government was prepared to pay an indemnity for the American lives which, "to its deep regret," had been lost.[3]

Before the acrimonious intergovernmental discussion of the sinking of the *Lusitania* had been concluded, the American secretary of state, William J. Bryan, had resigned for fear it would lead to war. Early in 1916 both houses had before them resolutions, introduced by Representative McLemore of Texas and Senator Gore of Oklahoma, which would have warned American citizens against traveling on armed vessels of belligerent nationality and would have directed the State Department to refuse them passports for such travel. President Wilson, in a letter to Chairman Stone of the Senate Foreign Relations Committee, let it be known that he could not "consent to any abridgement of the rights of American citizens in this respect." To him, "the honor and self-respect of the nation" were involved, and "the whole fine

[3] Germany agreed after the war to pay American claims in this and similar cases amounting to between two and three million dollars.

fabric of international law might crumble under our hands piece by piece" if we should "once accept a single abatement of right." The McLemore resolution was defeated in the House of Representatives by a vote of 276 to 142; and an adverse majority of 68 to 14 kept Senator Gore's resolution from coming to a vote.

March 24, 1916, an unarmed channel steamer, the *Sussex,* was sunk without warning. Although no Americans were among the eighty non-combatants killed, some were endangered and were saved only because they were on a part of the vessel that remained afloat. On April 18 the United States served notice that "unless the Imperial Government should now immediately declare and effect an abandonment of its present methods of submarine warfare against passenger and freight-carrying vessels, . . . [it would] have no choice but to sever diplomatic relations with the German Empire altogether."

Grudgingly then, May 4, the German government gave the *"Sussex* pledge" to "do its utmost to confine the operations of the war for the rest of its duration to the fighting forces of the belligerents" by holding its submarine commanders to the instructions already announced by Ambassador von Bernstorff after the sinking of the *Arabic.* It took occasion, however, again to denounce the food blockade and to call the American attitude unneutral: "The German Government cannot but reiterate its regret that the sentiments of humanity which the government of the United States extends with such fervor to the unhappy victims of submarine warfare are not extended with the same warmth of feeling to the many millions of women and children who, according to the avowed intentions of the British Government, shall be starved. . . . The German Government, in agreement with the German people, fails to understand this discrimination."

The German government sought also to make even its *Sussex* pledge contingent upon the United States' holding Great Britain to observance of laws which Germany accused her of violating: "Should the steps taken by the Government of the United States not attain the object it desires, to have the laws of humanity observed by all belligerent nations, the German Government would then be facing a new situation in which it must reserve to itself complete liberty of decision." The United States refused to make its relations with one belligerent contingent upon its relations with another. "Responsibility in such matters is single, not joint," it maintained; "absolute, not relative."

For the rest of 1916 neutrals could sail the seas in comparative safety, the flow of food and war materials to Britain was reduced but never stopped, and the inadequacy of the submarine as a blockade weapon, under the restrictions then imposed upon its use, was demonstrated. The German government, meanwhile, had reserved the right to revoke its *Sussex* pledge, and the United States had so far committed itself as to make almost inevitable the breaking off of diplomatic relations if Germany should at any time revoke or break that pledge.

Both the president and the people of the United States moved a long way in their thinking during 1915 and 1916. In a public address just after the sinking of the *Lusitania,* the president tried to quiet the clamor for war by saying that "there is such a thing as a man being too proud to fight, . . . a nation being so right that it does not need to convince others by force that it is right." The phrase "too proud to fight" was ridiculed at the time by those already angered to the fighting point. It was to be put into circulation again, ironically, by cartoonists and other propagandists during heavy and effective fighting by American troops in 1918. The president certainly did not tell the German government that his nation would not fight, and the asperity of the third *Lusitania* note and of those following the sinking of the *Sussex* should have convinced the Germans that it would if pushed too far. Ambassador von Bernstorff was so convinced, but other German leaders still thought it safe in 1915 to presume upon American patience, which they mistook for pusillanimity.

In 1916 the president spoke more frequently of national honor and lent all his influence to a program of naval and military preparedness intended—belatedly—to put the armed forces into a better position to defend the nation's rights and interests. Early that year Colonel Edward M. House, as the personal representative of the president, suggested to the British foreign minister that the United States might, if a favorable occasion could be found, suggest a conference of belligerents and, if the conference failed, would "probably" itself become a belligerent against the nation responsible for the failure. No such occasion arose, and the policy of the president and Colonel House was not then put to a test. If it had been, American opinion would at that time have been found much more nearly evenly divided than it was a year later.

"He kept us out of war" was a slogan used with telling effect by Democratic speakers in the presidential election campaign of 1916, never flatly disavowed by the president. It attracted much more attention than his own previous public reminder that the time might come when he would find himself unable to preserve both "the honor and the peace of this nation," and that in such a crisis no one must expect him to do "a contradictory and shameful thing." His opponent, Charles

Evans Hughes, while promising to uphold American rights, did not propose to do otherwise than "keep us out of war." The outcome of the election, small though the president's electoral majority was, indicated clearly enough that no more than a small minority of the American people was yet ready to intervene, unless attacked, in what was still generally considered primarily a foreign war.

The president did not forget his mandate or betray his people when, only five months later, he accepted his awful responsibility for leading them into war. Both he and they were influenced by events and decisions made by others. Any peace depending for its maintenance upon the continued keeping of the *Sussex* pledge was plainly precarious at best. The only way, therefore, to keep the country out of war would be somehow to induce the belligerents to make peace by negotiation before the United States became involved, as it probably would be if the war went on—almost inevitably if Germany resumed unrestricted U-boat warfare.

The president needed little urging, therefore, when the German chancellor suggested on November 16 that he should again offer his services as mediator. Only an auspicious occasion was wanted. Ambassador von Bernstorff, informed but not permitted to tell Mr. Wilson that Germany would soon publish a "peace note" of her own if the president did not, advised his government to wait for Wilson. The American idea of a favorable occasion for a peace proposal would have been an announcement, which Ambassador Gerard had urged the Germans to make, that the deportation of Belgian laborers to Germany would be discontinued. The Germans, as became apparent later, were waiting only for the fall of Bucharest. The president was not quite (though nearly) ready to address the other belligerents when on December 12, 1916, the German chancellor handed to Joseph C. Grew, secretary of the American embassy in Berlin, the German "peace note" of that date, saying that he hoped it would be considered evidence of the promised coöperation. It was nothing of the sort.

Confidential correspondence, published after the war, showed that the German leaders, fearful of ultimate defeat, would have been glad to cash in their chips while still ahead of the game. The Austrian foreign minister assumed that the territorial integrity of the dual monarchy would be maintained, and that Germany's colonies would be restored to her with the Belgian Congo added. Bethmann-Hollweg thought it would be "robbery" for Alsace-Lorraine to be taken away from Germany, but that Germany should take Liège from Belgium and the Longwy-Briey iron basin and an indemnity from France.

Hindenburg would have annexed Luxemburg and have demanded a cash indemnity from Great Britain if he evacuated Belgium.[4]

None of these terms was stated in the German "peace proposal" of December 12, but its tone would have belied its purpose equally well if its purpose had been peace. It began with a fanfare of trumpets, then spoke at length of the strength displayed already by Germany and her allies in the purely defensive war which had been forced upon them, and of their ability and indomitable readiness to continue the struggle indefinitely if necessary. Their peace proposals would, they said, "guarantee the existence, freedom, honor, and development of their nations." They would go on to certain victory if the Allies should spurn their offer, but would not then be responsible for the prolongation of the war.

Great Britain, France, and Italy, not yet victorious but hopeful yet of victory, were unlikely to consider an invitation couched in such terms. And by proclaiming on November 5 the establishment of a puppet kingdom of Poland, without returning to it West Prussia, Posen, or Galicia, and so without winning the allegiance of the Poles, the Central Powers had already killed whatever chance they might otherwise have had of making a separate peace with czarist Russia.

In such circumstances President Wilson's general invitation to the belligerents, December 16, to state their war aims and the terms on which they would make peace was most inopportunely timed. It was also ineptly worded in at least one of its phrases, which erred in the direction of complete impartiality by suggesting that, if the statements of their recognized spokesmen could be accepted, all the belligerents seemed to be fighting for essentially similar purposes. It was that phrase to which Colonel House had objected when shown a draft of the note, November 27, fearing the unfavorable effect it might have upon the Allies. The colonel's objection seems only to have delayed the dispatch of the note beyond the last date on which it could con-

[4] When Germany at last transmitted her terms, in confidence, to President Wilson on January 29, 1917, along with notification of her intention to resume unrestricted submarine warfare, they were stated in more general terms, such as: "colonial restitution in the form of an understanding which would secure Germany colonial possessions compatible with the size of her population and the importance of her economic interests.

"Restoration of those parts of France occupied by Germany, on condition that certain strategic and economic adjustments of the frontier be allowed, as also financial compensation.

"Restitution of Belgium under definite guarantees for the safety of Germany, which would have to be determined by means of negotiations with the Belgian government.

"Compensation for German undertakings and private persons who have suffered damage through the war." J. H. v. Bernstorff, *My Three Years in America* (London, 1920), 377.

ceivably have done any good, without eliminating the challenged phrase. The latter had precisely the unfortunate effect Colonel House predicted for it on the susceptibilities of the Allies. People convinced of the righteousness of their cause were deeply hurt and not a little offended by the president's apparent inability to differentiate between them and their enemies.

Government spokesmen indulged in less emotionalism, although to them also the Wilson note seemed to be too much an echo of the German, and to have upon it the curse of something "made in Germany." For a time the Allies showed some disposition to look upon the president as a tool of the Germans, as the Germans had all along called him a tool of the Allies.

The Allies answered the German note first, December 30, in a joint statement challenging its sincerity and bluntly calling it what it was: a war maneuver rather than a peace proposal.[5] To President Wilson they replied through a new British government (David Lloyd George, prime minister; Arthur Balfour, minister for foreign affairs) in general terms elaborating the formula "restitution, reparation, guarantees" and the Allied thesis that Germany was responsible for the war. While moderate and reasonable in tone, the note left little room for doubt that the Allies also had conquests as well as victory in mind. A war which had originally been represented to all the peoples engaged as one of self-defense had become, to leaders on both sides, a war of conquest. None could afford to state its war aims too plainly. None had in mind a peace which its enemy could be expected to accept unless defeated.

Germany, which had ostentatiously suggested a peace conference, refused to state its terms; and Foreign Minister Zimmermann, urged by von Bernstorff to state them, replied that no American participation in peace negotiations was wanted.[6]

[5] The kaiser made propaganda of the Allies' reply by issuing the following proclamation to his armed forces, January 5, 1917:

"In unison with the rulers allied to me, I proposed to our enemies to enter into immediate peace negotiations. The enemies have declined my offer. Their lust for power contemplates the destruction of Germany.

"The war goes on!

"The heavy responsibility before God and men for all the future terrible sacrifices, which my desire wished to spare you, falls upon the enemy governments.

"In righteous indignation over the enemy's insolence and in the desire to defend our most sacred possessions and to secure for the Fatherland a happy future, you must harden into steel.

"Our enemies did not want the conciliation which I offered them. With God's help our weapons shall force them to it." Quoted from the *Norddeutsche Allgemeine Zeitung,* January 6, 1917, by Ralph H. Lutz, *Fall of the German Empire* (Stanford, 1932), I, 400.

[6] See footnote 4, p. 45.

American participation in peace negotiations was by that time "wanted" by President Wilson. More keenly with each passing year of war he had realized that the United States had a vital national interest in the kind of peace to be made at the war's end, in the possibility of a permanently peaceful postwar world. In the first war years he had hoped that he would have most influence as head of a neutral state. By January, 1917, it seemed that belligerents would listen only to a belligerent, that the peace would be made exclusively by those who had won the war.

Hoping that it was not yet too late, the disillusioned president, hurt by the criticism his last attempt at mediation had aroused, compelled to discount the professed idealism of the Allies, and viewing with foreboding the imperialistic war aims of Allies and Central Powers alike, made a last public effort as a neutral to circumscribe and control the character of both war and peace. In a memorable address to the United States Senate January 22, 1917, he called it "inconceivable" that the people of the United States should play no part in the great enterprise of laying "afresh and upon a new plan the foundations of peace among the nations." Renewing his advocacy of a League for Peace, he attempted to formulate the conditions upon which he would feel justified in asking the people of the United States to adhere to such a league.

The present war [he said] must first be ended; but . . . it makes a great deal of difference in what way and upon what terms it is ended. . . . [There must be] a peace that is worth guaranteeing and preserving, . . . a peace made secure by the organized major force of mankind, . . . not a balance of power but a community of power; not organized rivalries but an organized peace . . . a peace without victory, . . . [since] only a peace between equals can last. . . . The right state of mind, the right feeling between nations, is as necessary for a lasting peace as is the just settlement of vexed questions of territory or of racial and national allegiance. . . .

No peace can last, or ought to last, which does not recognize and accept the principle that governments derive all their just powers from the consent of the governed, and that no right anywhere exists to hand peoples about from sovereignty to sovereignty as if they were property. . . .

Peace cannot be made without concession and sacrifice. . . . The statesmen of the world must plan for peace and nations must adjust and accommodate their policy to it. . . .[7]

Unfortunately, the statesmen of the world were too completely engrossed just then in planning for victory first to pay much attention to the president's suggestion that they "adjust and accommodate" their

[7] U.S. 64th Congress, 2nd Session, Senate Document 685.

policies to his principles; and many of them were as deeply shocked
and offended by his advocacy of "peace without victory, . . . between
equals" as they had been by his pointing out the similarity of their
generalized statements of war aims. The Senate address contained or
foreshadowed most of the essential elements of the famous "Fourteen
Points" enunciated almost a year later, January 8, 1918; but the
times were out of joint. What seemed so reasonable to the pacifically
inclined president of a neutral state was denounced by belligerent
peoples as unreasonable, impractical, and based upon an imperfect
understanding of the hard facts of life.

The U-boats were already on their way.

No thought of the possibility of a peace conference seems to have
entered into the calculations of the army and navy leaders who were
making Germany's decisions in 1916 and 1917. Those men were
thinking only of the most effective use of the military and naval
weapons at their disposal; and they estimated during that winter that
it was time for the resumption of unrestricted submarine warfare.
The question had been seriously considered since August, 1916, at
which time, finding the generals on his side in opposition to the proposed change of policy (because they were not ready), the chancellor
had argued (with singular lack of foresight) that, as those ultimately
responsible for the national defense, they should decide. On December
23 they reminded him of his own commitment and informed him
that they had decided in favor of the U-boat. The die was cast at a
crown council at great headquarters in Spa January 9, 1917. The
kaiser favored it, on the basis of Admiral von Holtzendorff's promise
that Great Britain could be isolated and forced to sue for peace within
a few months. The secretary for foreign affairs, von Jagow, had already
resigned in face of the certainty of American intervention, and been
replaced by Zimmermann. Chancellor von Bethmann-Hollweg opposed the decision and was overruled, but did not resign.

The date on which the new sea war was to begin was February 1.
The submarines, with their officers carrying the new instructions,
would put to sea in January so as to reach their assigned areas by that
date. The German ambassador in Washington was not notified until
January 19, and then was not authorized to notify the government of
the United States until January 29.[8] In the interim he cabled his

[8] War zones were again proclaimed, as in 1915, but covered the Atlantic coast of
France as well as waters around Great Britain and Ireland and much of the
Mediterranean, within which the Germans threatened to sink all vessels without
examination or warning. Elaborate provision was offered, regarded rather as an

government repeatedly in a vain effort to change its course or to delay the threatened action, insisting that the American danger was greater than his superiors seemed to think. On February 3, the United States broke off diplomatic relations and sent him home. When he got there he was not questioned by the kaiser or the high command, although he visited them at army headquarters. Their minds were already closed on the subject on which he could best have enlightened them; they were unwilling to try to keep the United States neutral, as President Wilson still hoped against hope they would do. Hindenburg had already said that all necessary steps had been taken to guard against American intervention. The admiralty would have found it inconvenient, and thought it not worth the trouble, to try to safeguard American vessels. Soon afterward, the kaiser, in a marginal note on an admiralty memorandum to that effect, wrote: "Agreed, reject. . . . Now, once and for all, an *end* to negotiations with America. If Wilson wants war, let him make it, and let him then have it."

Wilson did not want war, and was not ready to make it, though he was so soon to have it. The failure, March 4, of a bill to provide for the arming of American merchantmen, although largely due to a filibuster led by what the president called "a little group of wilful men," was timely evidence that there were many others in America who abhorred the thought of war.[9]

There were more, however, than there had been a year or two before who had begun to ask themselves whether the United States could afford to see Germany win the war, and whether Germany might not win it in 1917 unless prevented by the United States. Thinking people startled by the battle of Jutland had had time for some reflection since then. The German fleet had done more damage than had been done to it. Naturally the British had not yet publicly admitted that their commanders in that battle could have lost the war in an afternoon; but suppose the British fleet had been destroyed or driven from the seas? Many Americans not otherwise predisposed to be pro-British had learned long since to look upon the British navy as a stabilizing influence in the world and particularly in the Atlantic, where it could have made the maintenance of the Monroe Doctrine difficult but had made it easy. People who had had to learn by 1917 to

---

insult than as a concession, for the safe passage of one American mail steamer per week to Britain.

At the same time, when it was already too late to alter the situation, the German government submitted a confidential statement of the terms on which it said it was willing to accept American mediation and negotiate for peace. See footnote 4.

[9] Authority to arm the vessels was found in an unrepealed statute of 1797.

think of Germany as a potential enemy of the United States but saw no need to think of Britain as one were seriously disturbed by the thought of Germany's taking Britain's place as the dominant European naval power in the Atlantic. To an increasing number the comparison and the contrast were becoming clear: a victorious Britain would not endanger the safety of the United States, but a victorious Germany might—indeed, seemed likely to—do so.

The traditional friendship of Americans for France had, meanwhile, been strengthened and turned to sympathy. What France had gained, Germany had lost. Stories of German atrocities, especially in Belgium, were not universally believed and might not all have merited belief. But it was known that Germany was waging a lawless, ruthless war, regardless of the rights of other nations. The Germans, therefore, seemed much less likely than the Allies, if victorious, to make a peace which Americans could approve and Europeans would find tolerable.

Political ideologists, accustomed to thinking of the German government as a military dictatorship and of Austria-Hungary as a horrible example of Old World imperialism, found it easier in March, 1917, than previously to associate the cause of the Allies with the defense of world democracy; for on March 11 the authority of Nicholas II, "Autocrat of all the Russias," broke down, and on March 16 the establishment of a provisional government on the model of a parliamentary monarchy was announced.

War clouds gathered ominously while President Wilson waited for the "overt acts" pending which he said he could not believe that Germany would actually do what she had announced that she intended. Public opinion in the United States was even then rather anti-German than pro-Ally. Thunder and lightning answered the publication of the first Zimmermann note to Mexico, and new depredations by German U-boats brought on the storm.

On January 16, 1917, the new foreign minister sent to German Ambassador Eckhardt in Mexico, through the ambassador in Washington, a coded note suggesting an alliance with Mexico and a joint Mexican-Japanese attack upon the United States if Germany's alleged "endeavor to keep America neutral" should fail. In addition to generous financial assistance, Mexico was offered an opportunity to reconquer "lost territory" in Texas, New Mexico, and Arizona. (California was not mentioned. Was it to be used to lure Japan?) Germany's intention to resume unrestricted warfare on February 1 was announced, and Mexico was assured that the U-boats would compel Great Britain to sue for peace within a few months.

A second note, February 8, reiterated that the definite conclusion of an alliance must depend upon an outbreak of war between Germany and the United States, but instructed Eckhardt to broach the matter immediately and to suggest that the president of Mexico sound out Japan. If the president declined for fear of subsequent revenge, he was to be promised a definitive postwar alliance, provided that he had drawn Japan into the alliance against the United States.

The Zimmermann-Eckhardt messages were intercepted by the British naval intelligence service, turned over to the American embassy in London where they were again decoded, and published in the United States March 1. Herr Zimmermann, who six years earlier had expressed surprise that so much fuss had been made over the sending of so small a warship as the *Panther* to Agadir, was officially surprised again at the resentment aroused by the publicizing of the precautions he had thought it proper to take against the possibility of war with the United States.

The U-boats added fuel to the flames. One American vessel was sunk in February. Two American women were among the twelve persons lost with the Cunarder *Laconia* March 5. Five American ships were torpedoed that month. On March 21 President Wilson summoned the new Congress, the old one having expired March 4. On April 2 he appeared before it to advise it to "declare the recent course of the Imperial German Government to be in fact nothing less than war against the government and people of the United States; [and] that it formally accept the status of belligerent which has/[had] thus been thrust upon it."

The president was, that day, in a very real sense the spokesman of his people. He and they had come to the point of belligerency only with the utmost reluctance and when convinced at last that vital principles as well as interests were at stake, which could be safeguarded in no other way.

Property can be paid for [said the president]; the lives of peaceful and innocent people cannot be. The present German submarine warfare against commerce is a warfare against mankind. . . .

We have no quarrel with the German people. . . . It was not upon their impulse that their government acted in entering this war. . . .

We are glad . . . to fight thus for the ultimate peace of the world and for the liberation of its peoples, the German peoples included: for the rights of nations great and small and the privilege of men everywhere to choose their way of life and of obedience. The world must be made safe for democracy. . . .

It is a fearful thing to lead this great peaceful people into war. . . . But the right is more precious than peace, and we shall fight for the things which we have always carried nearest our hearts—for democracy, for the right of those who submit to authority to have a voice in their own Governments, for the rights and liberties of small nations, for a universal dominion of right by such a concert of free peoples as shall bring peace and safety to all nations and make the world itself at last free. . . .

The honest idealism which had so often characterized the American people at its best, and combined with a realistic appraisal of its own interest to motivate its conduct in its greatest crises, has rarely found more eloquent expression. The war of 1917-1919 has more than once, not always inappropriately, been called the First American Crusade, sometimes with implications of hypocrisy or suggestion, on the contrary, that it was a misguided and visionary enterprise—a twentieth-century repetition of the Children's Crusade of 1212.

Subsequent events have thrown a clearer light upon the principles and policies then enunciated by Woodrow Wilson, and shown them better in perspective. If a people is at its best when it most closely identifies its conception of its own interest with the general interest, defending itself when necessary in this world but looking toward a better one, then the president spoke for his people at its best. The world has not yet found any better guarantees of peace than the principles of democracy and collective security and the "universal dominion of right by . . . a concert of free peoples." The most cunning propaganda could then have done no more to raise the hopes of the oppressed or to rouse the fighting spirit of Americans.

Congress declared war on Germany on April 6, 1917.

CRESCENDO, 1918

Beginning February 1, 1917, the German submarine commanders were told to show what they could do. In thirty months of war they had averaged little more than sixty merchant-vessel sinkings per month, but in January, 1917, they had sunk 180. From February to June, inclusive, they averaged nearly ten per day. In April, with total sinkings averaging approximately thirteen per day, about one ship in four that attempted to reach or leave the British Isles went down.

Ships could not be replaced that fast, and some neutrals prudently kept their ships away from the danger zones lest they be sunk. The volume of Britain's imports and exports was materially reduced, and her food stocks, good for only a few weeks or months at best if imports were cut off, diminished daily at a dangerous rate. The promise of the German admiralty to win the war by use of the submarine before the United States could intervene seemed likely to be made good, and might have been if the United States Navy had not intervened first, against the submarine.

The United States Navy had fortunately not been altogether neglected since the war against Spain. It had had its share of the appropriations included in the preparedness legislation of 1916. The Germans knew that, but may have hoped that the natural nervousness of the seaboard communities would cause the government to keep the navy in the western Atlantic for the protection of its own shores or, at most, of its troopships.

There were few troopships for many months. The Allies expressed at first but little interest in the possibility that a large American expeditionary force might eventually be sent to help them. They were not yet ready to admit that such help might be needed. The United States went quickly and vigorously to work, none the less, to raise a large army by selective service, using the small Regular Army as a nucleus and the federalized National Guard as a first reserve. Only a token force under General John J. Pershing arrived in France by way of England in June, 1917, to set up the headquarters and organization of an expeditionary force—a task which took almost as long, and was quite as necessary, as the training of the force itself.

The navy went first. Eighteen American destroyers, vanguard of a force of eighty, appeared at Queenstown (now Cóbh), Ireland, May 4. Rear Admiral William S. Sims was already on his way when war was declared, to establish in London an American naval headquarters to insure the most effective possible coöperation with the British navy in tightening the blockade of Germany and breaking the German blockade of Britain.

American assistance made the difference between success and failure, survival and surrender of all hopes of victory. The United States Navy planted, with mines made in America, about four-fifths of a field of more than seventy thousand mines between the Orkneys and the Norwegian coast; the Norwegians closed the gap at the eastern end of the barrier by mining their own territorial waters at that point, closing them to both belligerents. The English Channel was also extensively mined, and the passage from the North Sea or back into it again was made more hazardous for submarines. Two American inventions, the depth bomb and an underwater direction finder called the hydrophone, were useful counteroffensive weapons in the war of extermination. The Germans had, for the first time, some difficulty in recruiting U-boat crews as more and more of them *kehrten nicht mehr von ihrer Reise zurück, . . . liessen . . . nichts mehr von sich hören*—failed to return, and nothing was heard of them. "Spotting" U-boats from the air, from captive observation balloons or land-based planes, passed through its experimental stages. The convoy system, a joint enterprise of the British and American navies, protected merchant shipping and kept the sea lanes open; and a United States battle fleet based on Britain and added to the British helped to deter the German high-seas forces from another test of strength. Merchant-ship sinkings were cut in the last six months of 1917 to approximately half, and in the first ten months of 1918 to little more than a third, of the April-to-June (1917) rate. The number of submarines destroyed increased by inverse ratio, so that the U-boats failed to make good either of the admiralty's promises: to knock Great Britain out of the war and to keep American troops off European soil.

While waiting for the submarine to do its work, the German armies stood on the defensive in France and Flanders in the spring of 1917. Not so the British. When the British offensive seemed ready to get under way in March, the Germans spoiled its timing by making, "according to plan," a strategic retreat to the previously prepared field fortifications of the *Siegfried Stellung* or "Hindenburg line." Thus the British had the inconvenience of extending their lines of supply and communication across terrain already torn and trampled by heavy fighting and devastated by the Germans as they evacuated it. The British followed up and attacked again early in April, around Arras. They took Vimy Ridge, a part of the vaunted "line" where the front had stood unchanged, inflicted and sustained heavy losses, and captured a considerable number of prisoners; but they did not break through.

During the last half of April the new French commander in chief, General Nivelle, who had led the counterattack at Verdun the year before, tried hard for a breakthrough on the Aisne front east and west of Reims, toward Laon. He also failed. The Germany military intelligence anticipated the attack, and a long artillery preparation would have told them when and where it was coming if they had not got the information through other channels. The weather was unfavorable. The troops making the attack were not imbued with their commander's confident, aggressive spirit. Within two weeks they had lost fifteen thousand killed and suffered sixty thousand other casualties and had not breached the enemy defenses. Their principal achievement was the taking of some prisoners and guns and the attrition of some of the German reserve divisions.

Nivelle's failure led to his replacement by Pétain, a "safer" strategist who was less prodigal in his expenditure of soldiers' lives and less optimistic about winning the war by a knockout that summer. The most aggressive and offensive-minded man left in the French high command was the new chief of staff, Ferdinand Foch. The first task of the new commanders was the restoration of morale. Mutiny and desertion were too common to be punished with the usual severity. The hopeless spirit of defeatism found new expression through the summer in the Chamber of Deputies, played on by peace talk in the German Reichstag. By careful cultivation of the confidence of the army, Pétain succeeded by late summer in so restoring its efficiency that it showed it was itself again in offensives with limited objectives around Verdun and along the Chemin des Dames, east of Reims.

After the discontinuance of their attacks at Arras the British devoted most of their attention in the summer of 1917 to taking the pressure off the French by attacking near the northern end of the line, behind which Ostend and Zeebrugge were serving the Germans only too well as submarine bases. But the bases remained in German hands and had to be neutralized as completely as possible by daring naval action. From June 7 to November 4, in a series of costly attacks around Ypres ending in failure in the deep mud of Passchendaele, the British army exhausted itself, its reserves, and its munitions as it had done a year earlier on the Somme. Prime Minister Lloyd George had authorized the offensive, and Field Marshal Sir Douglas Haig kept stubbornly at it, so as to make impossible any German drive against the French while the French army was being overhauled, and to hold in Flanders German troops that might otherwise have joined in an attack in October upon the Italians. But the British high command was in serious danger of losing the confidence of its troops and people because of the ghastly sacrifices its strategy entailed.

Slavish adherence to a new formula had increased the costliness of the third battle of Ypres, as excessive artillery preparation had defeated its own purpose by making impassable and untenable the ground subjected to it. In the third week of November a new Allied weapon, the heavy tank, broke through the Siegfried line near Cambrai. It was a surprising victory due largely to surprise, which the British were unfortunately not ready to follow up and exploit, and which was nearly turned into defeat by a swift and vigorous German counterattack. The Germans soon developed antitank guns and defenses and used some tanks themselves; but their infantry did not lose during that year or the next its dread and hatred of the "devilish" innovation.

In August, 1917, the Italians under General Cadorna attacked the Austrians on the Isonzo front north of Gorizia. Although that offensive ended after about a month without accomplishing much else, it revealed such demoralization and weakness in the Austro-Hungarian army that the German high command found it necessary to send a reinforcement of six German divisions from the Russian front. These and the Austro-Hungarians counterattacked October 24, taking the war-weary and dispirited Italians by surprise in front of Caporetto and throwing them back, first out of the mountain end of their line (where the Germans struck them), then all along it to the Adriatic. Italian losses were a quarter of a million prisoners, twice as many killed, wounded, ill, or missing, and guns and other equipment in proportion.

By November 9 the elements of the beaten army were re-forming behind the Piave River, and Cadorna had been replaced as their commander by General Armando Diaz. Their recovery from almost complete collapse was creditable, facilitated though it was by the timely arrival of two army corps of reinforcements, one British and one French, along with their own reserves. The Germans and Austrians, furthermore, who had planned originally to advance only to the Tagliamento, had outrun their own supplies and were not able to extemporize an offensive with unlimited objectives with forces adequate only to a more modest enterprise.

Russia caused the Central Powers less trouble in 1917 than Italy. The provisional government established by the Constitutional Democrats ("Cadets") upon the overthrow of the tsar in March was followed, May 15, by a provisional republic with Prince George Lvov as prime minister and the Socialist Revolutionary Alexander Kerensky as minister of war. Although unable to carry on the war effectively, and openly advocating a general peace without annexations or indemnities or intervention in any nation's internal affairs, the Lvov-Kerensky government rashly undertook an offensive in Galicia at the end of June with General Brusilov in command. Where only Austro-Hungarian opposition was encountered the going at first was easy; but a stiff German counterattack in the direction of Tarnopol July 19 stopped Brusilov's offensive and drove him back to Russian ground. Lvov and two other Constitutional Democrats resigned and Kerensky formed a nonpartisan but noncommunist "national" cabinet. The Russian army was then incapable of further offensive action. The Germans captured Riga in September, and in December made a truce with the Lenin-Trotsky Bolshevists who had by that time seized control of government in Russia.

In an autumn campaign in November and December, 1917, the British put an end to the Turkish military threat to Egypt and the Suez Canal by taking Gaza and Jerusalem. The tide turned also in Mesopotamia. Kut-el-Amara, where nine thousand British and Indian troops had had to surrender April 29, 1916, was retaken in February, 1917. With the conquest of Bagdad in March, 1917, the safety of the Anglo-Persian oil concessions between that city and the head of the Persian Gulf was assured; and the British expeditionary force based on Bagdad was in a position to move against Turkey in 1918 while another advanced from Palestine.

A small German force led by the redoubtable Paul von Lettow-Vorbeck kept a much larger British force busy in German East Africa through most of 1917 and was still at large in Portuguese East Africa at the end of the year, but able thereafter to carry on only a guerrilla type of warfare. The other German colonies in Africa had been quickly overrun.

In 1918 such subsidiary campaigns as remained to be completed were more than ever overshadowed by political events and the military climax of the war in Europe.

CLIMAX, 1918

It was a very near thing in 1918. First Russia made a separate peace, then the Germans mounted a *Friedensturm,* or offensive intended to secure them a favorable peace. The war was won and lost in 1918 in the sense that its outcome, only partly or provisionally predetermined by all that had happened in the preceding four years, was only then finally determined.

The separate Russian peace was made at Brest Litovsk on March 3, 1918, as a result of negotiations which had been begun there three months earlier. The German delegation was headed by Foreign Minister Richard von Kühlmann and General Max Hoffmann, Russian nemesis on that front since August, 1914. The threat of further invasion was freely used and once made good, German troops going through Estonia as far as Lake Peipus. The treaty was dictated and imposed by force, not negotiated between equals. The Germans wanted peace; the Bolsheviks had to have it. Lenin and Trotsky, the new leaders of revolutionary Russia, proposed a general peace, which the Germans said they were willing to consider but which the Allies were not ready to make and considered Russia treaty-bound not to make. German spokesmen objecting, after the war, to the "dictated" peace of Versailles were wont to argue (more vociferously than convincingly) that the Treaty of Brest Litovsk was no accurate indication of the kind of peace Germany would have made with her other enemies if she had won the war, because (they said) the Allies' rejection of Russia's general peace proposal had compelled her to make at Brest Litovsk rather a war move than a peace.[10]

The transition from war to peace on the Russian front was anything but rapid; and peace was as costly to Russia as war. The severity of the settlement is indicated by the fact that more than a million German soldiers, sorely needed elsewhere, had to be left in the east to enforce it. For the sake of peace and an opportunity to proceed with the revolution, in which they were more interested just then than in holding or conquering territory or in meeting obligations assumed without their approval or consent by the tsar's government, the Russian revolutionaries had to sign away most of the lands that, since the days of Peter the Great and Catherine II, had made their empire a European power.

Finland was made nominally independent, actually a German satellite state. Estonia, Latvia, Lithuania, Poland, and Ukraine were given up by the Russians and occupied by German troops, who soon established puppet governments to exploit them. Kars, Ardahan, and Batum were ceded to Turkey. Although the Germans had agreed in principle that no indemnities would be levied, they exacted a promise to pay 300,000,000 gold rubles, called "compensation."

Russia's failure in 1917 left the Rumanian government almost in exile at Jassy and nearly destitute, all else but Moldavia having been lost in 1916. Russia's withdrawal from the war, and her quarrel with Rumania early in 1918 over Bessarabia, gave the Central Powers an opportunity to make a profitable peace with Rumania, largely at Russia's expense. As compensation for the Dobruja, lost to Bulgaria, and for concessions to Hungary on the Transylvanian frontier, Rumania was permitted by the Treaty of Bucharest, May 7, 1918, to hold on to Bessarabia. The Central Powers kept control of the Rumanian oil fields and railways and of transportation on the Danube, and continued to exploit for their own benefit all Rumania's resources.

It is not surprising that under the terms of the armistice of Novem-

---

[10] This argument is clearly proved false by German government and army headquarters documents for the year 1918.

ber 11, 1918, the Allies compelled Germany to agree to the nullification of the treaties of Brest Litovsk and Bucharest; but before those armistice terms could be imposed some of the hardest fighting of the war had yet to be done.[11]

In March, 1918, for the first time since 1914, the Germans had more men and war materials available for immediate use in France than all the Allies and the Americans combined.[12] They had also the advantages of unity of command and shorter lines of communication, and were able to concentrate as never before on a single front. Time, to be sure, was not on their side. They knew that behind the two or three American divisions which had seen enough front-line service to be properly classified as combat troops stood an expeditionary force of more than 200,000 men. Behind those were several millions in training in the United States, and behind those was a man-power reservoir of millions more. Only trained soldiers on the front count for much at the front; but the weight of the American reserves oppressed the minds of German generals in the spring as it was to overwhelm their soldiers in the fall.

To make the utmost use of such advantages as they still had, the Germans seized the initiative by launching a very heavy attack, March 21, on the British Third and Fifth armies on a seventy-four-mile front from a little northeast of Arras to La Fère, south and a little east of St. Quentin. The general plan of the attack was to break through the British front, at or near the point where it joined the French, then to swing northwestward and pin the British army back against the sea. The Fifth Army front of forty-two miles, recently taken over from the French, not very strongly fortified, and held by eleven overextended divisions in line with only three in reserve, was the more vulnerable of the two under attack. There rapid progress was made during the week of March 21-28, and some during the week ending April 4, westward from the St. Quentin-La Fère line to one a little east of Amiens, with Cantigny and Montdidier marking the southwestern limits of the salient formed.

New German infiltration tactics were locally and temporarily successful. Ground lost in 1916 and abandoned in 1917, along the Somme, was retaken, with about 90,000 prisoners. The geographical

[11] A new German ministry headed by Prince Max of Baden announced on October 4, 1918, its intention to renounce the treaties of Brest Litovsk and Bucharest. Its request for an armistice had been sent to President Wilson the night before this announcement was published.

[12] The German superiority was later estimated by General Ludendorff at "twenty or twenty-five divisions." See map, between pp. 22-23.

limits of the westward push toward Amiens were set as much by
German problems of supply and concern about the flanks of a salient
nearly forty miles deep as by the strength of the reorganized British
resistance before Amiens. Yet, strategically, the attack failed. The
British Third Army held firm the northern shoulder of the salient
before Arras. Although Pétain, also expecting an attack, in Champagne, was reluctant to send reserves to support the British, twenty
French divisions were finally sent; and the southern flank of the
salient was held along the line of the Oise River and thence westward,
a little south of Noyon and Montdidier, to Cantigny.

Under threat of disaster the Allies agreed at last to the creation
of a supreme command and a strategical reserve, under General
Ferdinand Foch. The Allied strategical reserve was augmented by a
rising flood of American troops, rushed to France on an accelerated
schedule that gave soldiers priority over their supplies although it
compelled them then to use much French and British equipment.
The immediate use of these troops wherever they were most needed,
as soon as they could be readied for action, was made possible by a
self-denying decision on the part of General Pershing, who abandoned
during the emergency his insistence that American troops should be
handled as a separately organized American expeditionary force, not
used as replacements in the Allied armies.

Meanwhile the series of German offensives continued. In April, 9 to
29, another attempt to break the British line was made, on a twenty-
mile front between Béthune and Ypres. The British, Portuguese, and
French were driven back from ten to twelve miles, losing Armentières,
the height called Mount Kemmel, and the hard-won Passchendaele
salient, but managed to hold Béthune, Ypres, and the transportation
center of Hazebrouck. Casualties were very heavy on both sides.

On May 27 another strong attack was launched between Noyon and
Reims, beginning along the hills north of the Aisne River known as
the Chemin des Dames and carrying southward across the Aisne River
and the Aisne-Marne Canal, to reach the Marne River itself within
five days, between Château-Thierry and Dormans. Then again the
offensive was "contained"—stopped by the holding of the eastern
shoulder of the salient at Reims—by the timely arrival and fierce
counterattacks of American troops at Château-Thierry and Belleau
Wood, and by a stiffening of French resistance at the southwestern
point of the bulge, nearest Paris, between Château-Thierry and Vil-
lers-Cotterets.[13]

[13] Several American units distinguished themselves in the Aisne-Marne sector,
particularly the 5th and 6th regiments of United States Marines, forming one

The attackers had been aided in two of their 1918 offensives by fog and mist, which made surprise easier, and in the third by the failure of the French command to give due credit to military intelligence reports that an attack was impending. No one was surprised when on June 9 a fourth drive was launched to pinch off the narrow Allied salient near Compiègne, between the Picardy and Marne bulges created by the March and May offensives. The attempt failed.

The Allies were fully forewarned of the final German push, which began early in the morning of July 15 on a long line hinged on Reims and running roughly eastward across Champagne and southwestward from Reims to the Marne near Dormans. In Champagne, knowing not only where but precisely when the enemy attack was to come, General Gouraud of the French Fourth Army adopted Pétain's device of an elastic defense in depth, virtually evacuating his front-line positions as soon as it was dark on the night of the fourteenth. The Germans, punctually on schedule, wasted on an almost empty area several hours of intense artillery preparation, somewhat weakened by Allied counter-fire, then poured their troops into the attack, only to be stopped by a strengthened second line.

Southwest of Reims the Germans made some progress, and again crossed the Marne both above and below Dormans. For three days they maintained their offensive; but on the second day, July 16, their drive was met by a counterattack along the Marne. On July 18 a strategic reserve force already assembled by Foch and Pétain on the western flank of the Marne salient attacked with tanks, eastward toward Soissons, in a threat to cut off the salient and trap the troops in it. Recognizing their danger, the Germans fought hard to extricate themselves, but lost thirty thousand men as prisoners before they managed, August 5, to form a new line along the Aisne and Vesle rivers. Soissons had been retaken by the Allies, Reims had been held, and the dangerous Marne salient between those two points had been wiped out. In Champagne the Germans had suffered frightful losses and gained nothing worth defending against counterattack.

In that third week of July the war reached its final turning point. On the fifteenth Ludendorff said to the German Foreign Office representative at his headquarters: "If my blow at Reims succeeds now we

---

infantry brigade of the 2nd Division. The "regulars" of the 9th and 23rd Infantry regiments formed the other brigade of that division. The famous 1st Division had already made, on May 28, the first American offensive in the war, reducing a German salient at Cantigny. The 1st, 2nd, 3rd, 4th, 26th, 27th, 28th, 32nd, and 42nd ("Rainbow") divisions and many other American units participated in the Aisne-Marne-Champagne actions in June and July.

have won the war."[14] He soon knew that he could not win. Although he was still meditating another thrust at the British when he was himself attacked by them on August 8, the German commander had lost the initiative and was never able to regain it.

On August 8, called by Ludendorff "the black day of the German army," the British and French punched in the western point of the Amiens salient with a tank-led drive in which, for the first four days, prisoners taken exceeded casualties sustained. The revelation that some of their divisions had not fought well caused the German high command more concern than the loss of territory. The tired German armies were still on French and Belgian soil, but they were being pushed back and were spending the last of their strength and resources, while American reinforcements for the Allies were arriving at the rate of 300,000 men per month.

By August 10 the prosperous state of Allied affairs seemed to General Pershing to warrant the regrouping of American divisions into a homogeneous expeditionary force under American command, which should take over a sector of its own and assume the responsibility for its own offensive operations. A few American divisions and some smaller units continued to serve as parts of British, French, or mixed army groups, and some French divisions operated occasionally under American First Army command; but, in substance, General Pershing's demand was granted. American operations were thereafter coördinated with those of the Allies through the supreme Allied command, but Americans were not used simply as replacements or reinforcements for Allied armies.

While this regrouping was going on, British and French armies were attacking, one after another at intervals of a few days only, all along the line. By September 12 the Germans had been driven back to the old "Hindenburg line" positions from which they had pushed off in March, and the Americans were ready to attack at St.-Mihiel.

The St.-Mihiel position was a naturally strong one, with the heights along the right bank of the Meuse forming its western and southern faces while Mont Sec overlooked the plateau behind them. The Germans had used it since 1914 to strengthen their grip upon the Longwy-Briey iron ore region, and to buttress the defenses of the vital railway center of Metz. The reduction of the salient was, for the Allies, a necessary preliminary to an offensive aimed at one of the German army's principal railway transport channels—to the front from the

---

[14] Others thought later that they remembered having heard Foch say the same thing, the same day. See Harry R. Rudin, *Armistice, 1918* (New Haven, 1944), 15.

Rhine crossings at Mainz and Coblenz, and along the front from Metz to Sedan.

On September 12, 1918, the American First Army attacked at St.-Mihiel with about 500,000 men, supported by French and British air forces and some French infantry and artillery—about 100,000. All of the limited objectives of the attack were taken in two days, and enemy counterattacks were beaten off and the new positions stabilized in two more. The number of prisoners taken (16,000) was more than twice the number of casualties sustained (7500).

The way was open, and American plans were ready, for a move to cut the German railway supply lines through Metz; but the supreme Allied command had already prevailed upon General Pershing to hold that plan in abeyance and to undertake, instead, an offensive west and northwest of Verdun, in closer conjunction with a northward push of the French Fourth Army west of the Argonne Forest.

The Meuse-Argonne offensive undertaken by the American First Army was an enterprise of such difficulty and magnitude that the St.-Mihiel operation seemed subsequently, in comparison with it, only a training exercise. But the training proved useful. The movement of many divisions by night marches, during and immediately after the St.-Mihiel offensive, into position for the Meuse-Argonne attack was a tremendous problem in logistics; but the assault troops were assembled on the new line by September 25. A few divisions had to be used without previous front-line experience, but a good equivalent of what the European armies were then calling "shock troops" was provided by battle-tried veterans in a dozen of the "oldest" divisions.

The defense of the Meuse-Argonne sector was imperative for the Germans. Marshal Foch[15] had planned a sweeping movement across northern France and Belgium, pivoted on Verdun, that would push back against the wooded hills of the Ardennes region all such German forces as could not be funneled out through Aachen and Cologne on the north or through Sedan, the Ardennes gap, and Coblenz or Mainz. Until they had to be used for withdrawal, the railway lines from Metz to and beyond Sedan were indispensable to the Germans as supply lines; and the American offensive was aimed at them at the point where they ran closest to the battle front. Compelled as it was by desperate necessity to hold open those railways, as a supply line or as an escape corridor, the German high command concentrated there sixty-two of its best divisions.

The defense was aided by the terrain. The heights along the Meuse

[15] General Foch was made marshal of France on August 7, 1918.

the ARDENNES in two World Wars

WORLD WAR I

The railroads paralleled the range and were at right angles to the line of advance, leaving the main supply lines to slow-moving wagon and truck trains. The Ardennes then constituted a barrier.

WORLD WAR II

With the advent of mechanized warfare in conjunction with the airplane, swift-moving columns of tanks and trucks advance at will behind a barrage of bombs laid down by the Air Force. The natural barrier of the Ardennes was a less serious obstacle than in 1918.

on the east, and the rugged hills and ravines of the Argonne on the west, heavily wooded and tangled with undergrowth, were serious natural obstacles. The more open ground between was dominated by Montfaucon and other elevations. Four years of continuous occupation had given the Germans ample opportunity to fortify the area and cover it with interlocking fields of fire. Roads were few, and sure to be shelled; so the supply problem was always serious.

The cost was inevitably high in such circumstances, in the face of determined resistance. The number of casualties sustained by more than a million men engaged was 117,000, more than four times the number of prisoners taken. Yet the lines moved forward, intermittently and unevenly at times, but inexorably, from September 26 until the signing of the armistice, November 11. They moved faster, in fact, than those of the French Fourth Army in the more open country just west of the Argonne, until some American divisions were sent to help the French. With the capture of the heights commanding Sedan, November 6-7, and the seizure of the high ground on both sides of the Meuse River around Dun-sur-Meuse, November 7, the German life line was cut. Unable any longer to supply itself, defend itself, or retreat fast enough to save itself, the German Fifth Army was hopelessly beaten and helpless.

Meanwhile, the other German armies north and west of that point had been pushed back to the line Ghent-Mons-Sedan. The Aachen-Cologne escape route could not accommodate them all, and the Sedan-Ardennes gap was closed. If the surrender[16] had not come when it did, pressure on the Belgian front would have been continued while a new (Second) American army moved on Metz. Plans had been made to carry the whole Allied offensive right to the middle Rhine, to cut off the German retreat there, and if possible to destroy the German armies west of the Rhine.

It was not necessary to go so far. Germany's allies had left her to fight alone. Her transportation system could no longer feed or fuel her cities or bring oil enough from Rumania to supply her needs. Her motor transport and air force had neither lubricating oil nor gasoline enough to keep them going. The seamen of her high-seas fleet had mutinied rather than try, by a diversionary foray, to take the pressure off the hard-driven armies in northern Belgium. The Fifth German Army, which had tried so valiantly to defend the most vital sector in the center of the line, was faced with imminent and overwhelming

---

[16] The author's reasons for using the word "surrender" here instead of "armistice" will appear in subsequent paragraphs.

disaster. The armistice terms were ready, and the Germans were ready to sign them. Those terms made impossible the resumption of hostilities by Germany and enormously enhanced the military supremacy of her enemies. So far as further fighting was concerned, the Germans were at the mercy of the Allies and the United States.

ARMISTICE

The decision to ask for an armistice was Germany's public admission of defeat. As early as June 3, 1918, in a memorandum approved by Ludendorff, Foreign Minister von Kühlmann was confidentially informed that the war could not be won by force of arms alone; but he was soon afterward repudiated and dismissed for saying so in the Reichstag.

The failure of the German July offensive and the success of the Allied drives in July and August altered Ludendorff's views of the military situation. Realizing, although still unwilling to admit publicly, that he could not win the war, he wanted peace made quickly lest he lose it. In August, Kühlmann's successor, von Hintze, was instructed by the kaiser and the high command to try at the first favorable moment, when the front was stabilized, to arrange for a peace conference through the mediation of the queen of the Netherlands. That favorable moment never came. An Austro-Hungarian "note" suggesting a general peace conference in a neutral country, sent out despite German protests and published on September 15 along with news of St.-Mihiel and Bulgaria's collapse, caused great consternation in Berlin. Yet the German people did not realize the seriousness of their situation.

On the third day of the Meuse-Argonne offensive, September 28, the German high command decided to ask for an armistice. Bulgaria's defection meant the loss of Rumanian oil, the supply of which was already diminishing because of transportation difficulties. It was estimated that available supplies of gasoline and illuminating oil could be made to last only two months longer, lubricating oil six. Peace must be made quickly; but if an armistice could be made while the German army was still intact, on foreign soil, a promise to evacuate non-German territory on the western front might be advantageously used as a *quid pro quo,* while an army in being might threaten to resume hostilities if things went wrong during the negotiation of terms of peace. So Germany might get better terms. The generals had then no thought of evacuating any territory in the east. They had begun to pose already as protectors of Europe from Bolshevism.

Next day, September 29, the high command informed the kaiser and chancellor, Count von Hertling, that they had lost the war, and that every hour's delay in securing an armistice was dangerous. The kaiser was surprised and reluctant to act precipitately in the matter, but signed that day a decree dismissing Hertling and ordering the formation of a new ministry. The decision to ask for an armistice was made, however, by the generals, and imposed upon the kaiser and the outgoing chancellor.[17]

Assuming that better terms could be secured by a more democratic-looking government, the high command recommended the appointment of the comparatively liberal Prince Max of Baden as chancellor. Prince Max realized that his principal task would be to make peace, but he did not immediately realize that the war policy was already bankrupt when he was called upon to liquidate it. He had to be pushed into sending the armistice note sooner than he thought necessary.

The high command demanded it. A military spokesman for the general staff reported to the Reichstag party leaders on October 2 that twenty-two divisions had had to be broken up to find men to maintain the others at half their normal strength. "The German army is still strong enough to hold off the enemy for months," he said, "to win local successes, and to make the Entente face new sacrifices. But every day brings the enemy nearer his goal and will make him less inclined to conclude with us a tolerable peace. Therefore no time must be lost. Any twenty-four hours can make the situation worse and give the enemy an opportunity to comprehend our momentary weakness."

Finding Prince Max willing to assume the chancellorship but unconvinced of the necessity of an immediate armistice request, the kaiser scolded him: "The supreme command considers it necessary, and you have not been brought here to make difficulties for the supreme command."

Hindenburg was equally insistent: "The Supreme Army Command persists in its demand of Sunday, September 29 of this year, for the immediate sending out to our enemies of the peace proposal. . . . There is, according to all human calculation, no further prospect of imposing peace upon the enemy. . . . In these circumstances it is im-

---

[17] The kaiser, even then, blamed the civilians. "We have lost the war," he reported to admiralty officials. "Army and people have fought brilliantly, the politicians unfortunately have not." See Magnus von Levetzow, *Der letzte Akt*, Süddeutsche Monatshefte, Jahrgang XXI (April, 1924), 58. See also Harry R. Rudin, *op. cit.*, 56-88.

perative to break off the battle in order to spare the German people and their allies useless sacrifices. Every wasted day costs thousands of brave soldiers their lives."[18]

In the evening of October 3, 1918, a new German ministry formed by Prince Max von Baden as chancellor approved and sent off to the president of the United States, via Switzerland, an armistice note already drafted by the army high command and accepted by the outgoing Hertling ministry. The note asked for an immediate general armistice and requested that President Wilson notify all belligerents and invite them to name plenipotentiaries for the negotiation of peace terms. The German government offered to accept, as a basis for negotiation, the program laid down by the president in his message to Congress of January 8, 1918 (the "Fourteen Points"), and his subsequent pronouncements, including one of September 27, 1918, only just then published in Germany.

The Fourteen Points to which the German government thus turned for protection in defeat, although it had scorned them until it knew itself defeated, were broad-minded and generous:

1. Open covenants, openly arrived at; no secret treaties.
2. Freedom of navigation upon the seas, outside territorial waters.
3. Removal of economic barriers to international trade.
4. Reduction of armaments.
5. Adjustment of colonial claims on the basis of the principle of trusteeship.
6. Evacuation of Russian territory and freedom for her to determine her own political development and national policy, with assurance of a sincere welcome into the society of free nations under institutions of her own choosing.
7. Evacuation and restoration of Belgium.
8. Evacuation and restoration of France, including Alsace-Lorraine.
9. Readjustment of the frontiers of Italy along clearly recognizable lines of nationalty.
10. Autonomy for the peoples of Austria-Hungary.
11. Evacuation of Rumania, Serbia, and Montenegro; access to the sea for Serbia.
12. Dissolution of the Ottoman Empire, sovereign status for Turkey, internationalization of the Dardanelles.
13. An independent Poland with access to the sea.
14. A league of nations.

---

[18] It is interesting to compare this statement with one made by Marshal Foch, quoted below. See footnote 25, p. 74.

When the Fourteen Points were published in January, 1918, Chancellor Hertling of Germany professed to agree with only the first five of them, although he said he would be willing to investigate the principle of a league of nations after peace had been made. Belgium, Russia, and Poland, he then said, were not subjects for general discussion. French territorial questions would be settled between France and Germany alone. Alsace-Lorraine would not in any case be given up. Austria must be consulted about points nine, ten, and eleven, and Turkey about point twelve.

As the hope of victory waned, official German interest in the Fourteen Points increased. "Accept Wilson's idea of a league of nations," wrote Major Alfred Niemann of the general staff on July 20, ". . . not for the purpose of realizing this Utopian scheme but in order to open negotiations. The slogan that an end must be made to the massacre of peoples possessing highly valued cultures appeals to most nations. Wilson's cant must become the means of entrapping him."[19]

A considerable body of public opinion in Germany, ignorant of the true military situation and of the army's insistent demand for an armistice—which the chancellor could not publicize without advertising Germany's weakness—was shocked by the armistice request and called it premature. Even Walther Rathenau, coördinator of industrial production for war purposes, who was subsequently murdered by the irreconcilables for his too-conciliatory attitude toward Germany's enemies, called the Fourteen Points "insidious," especially as to Poland and Alsace-Lorraine. He darkly foretold that Danzig might become a Polish harbor, and that an indemnity of fifty billion marks might be demanded. If Germany summoned all her resources and fought on, he thought, she could get better terms than those offered by the Fourteen Points.

Before President Wilson was willing even to notify the Allies of the receipt of the German note, he demanded assurance, October 8, that the German government was accepting the Fourteen Points as a basis for peace terms, not merely as a basis for a discussion of terms. He could not ask the Allies to negotiate, he said, with an enemy whose troops were on their soil; so Germany must agree in advance of negotiations to evacuate France and Belgium at once. Implying unwillingness to deal with a spokesman for the kaiser, he asked pointedly, also,

---

[19] *Ursachen des deutschen Zusammenbruches im Jahre 1918* [Das Werk des Untersuchungsausschusses der deutschen Verfassunggebenden Nationalversammlung und des deutschen Reichstages, 1919-1920. Vierte Reihe, 12 vol. Berlin, 1925-1930.] II, 185. See also Harry R. Rudin, *op. cit.*, 18.

For the full text of the Fourteen Points, see Appendix A.

whether the new chancellor was "speaking merely for the constituted authorities of the Empire" who had so far conducted the war.[20]

Immediately after sending off the armistice request, and before their first meeting with the Reichstag, the majority parties making up the ministry of Prince Max published, October 4, their moderately revolutionary program. When peace was made, they said, they would be ready to join a league of nations to keep the peace, guaranteeing equality and independence to all member nations, freedom of the seas, peaceful settlement of international disputes, and disarmament. Accepting as part of their platform the Reichstag peace resolution of July 19, 1917, they renounced all claims of conquest, including the treaties of Bucharest and Brest Litovsk. They declared themselves ready to evacuate and restore Belgium, but not Alsace-Lorraine. They demanded the reform of the electoral laws of the state of Prussia and the complete subordination of the naval and military to civil authority in the imperial government.

The proposed political reforms were not at once effected. The high command had more to say than the chancellor or the Foreign Office in the drafting of the reply to Wilson. Although unwilling to accept any terms which would make it impossible for them to resume hostilities, the generals wanted to give their troops a respite, and again demanded an immediate armistice. In reply to a direct question, October 9, whether he could hold the front three months longer, Ludendorff replied that he could not. Conservatives and nationalists not in office, such as Count Westarp, Walther Rathenau, and Gustav Stresemann, denounced the president's note as a demand for unconditional surrender. Prince Max thought it an intolerable attempt to interfere in German domestic affairs. The exigencies of the military situation, however, dictated the conciliatory reply sent October 12.

This second note to President Wilson accepted the Fourteen Points outright "as the foundations of a permanent peace of justice," reserving the right to discuss only the practical details of their application but raising (at Hindenburg's suggestion) the question whether the Allies were also accepting them. It promised the immediate evacuation of French and Belgian territory. It assured the president that the im-

---

[20] Ludendorff had, as a matter of fact, warned the chancellor that he was accepting the Fourteen Points only as a basis for discussion, not as a statement of conditions of peace.

Although President Wilson did not transmit the German note to the Allies, the French had intercepted and decoded it. Both French and British offered suggestions as to how it should be answered.

Senator Lodge and others opposed granting an armistice, or any settlement short of unconditional surrender.

perial chancellor was supported in all his actions by the will of the great majority of the Reichstag and was speaking in the name of both government and people.

In the conferences of German officials in which the note of October 12 was formulated, the question of the voluntary abandonment of the use of the submarine against passenger vessels was discussed, but the admiralty officials were unwilling to forgo the use of what they called the most effective offensive weapon then left to them. The day the note was sent, word flashed around the world that a German submarine had sunk an Irish mail and passenger steamer, the *Leinster*. Several hundred lives were lost. Some of the victims were Americans. Many were women and children.

Anger over the sinking of the *Leinster,* and the well-warranted suspicion that the German generals would use an armistice, if they could, only to extricate their armies from a precarious position, were evident in President Wilson's reply, as well as in the unsolicited suggestions which poured in upon him as he prepared it.[21]

The president's reply to the second German armistice note, which he had not transmitted to the Allies, called attention to the continuance of U-boat atrocities and the wanton devastation of the areas then being evacuated, under pressure, by the German army, and declared that the nations associated against Germany could not be expected to agree to a cessation of hostilities while such acts continued. No arrangement would be considered which did not preserve and safeguard the "military supremacy of the armies of the United States and of the Allies in the field." (This the Germans properly interpreted as a demand for virtually unconditional military surrender.) As a further "condition precedent to peace," the "arbitrary power" of the imperial government must be destroyed or reduced to "virtual impotency" by the action of the German people themselves. The governments associated against Germany must know "beyond a peradventure" with whom they were dealing.

Although the president's refusal to deal with an unregenerate autocracy could have been interpreted merely as insistence upon political reform, it was very generally looked upon as incitement to revolution, with the hope of better peace terms as reward.

The chancellor, Prince Max, had hoped to preserve the monarchy by making peace before it collapsed, and to placate President Wilson by completing quickly the political reforms proposed by his ministry on taking office. On October 15, after President Wilson's second note

[21] The British government sent three notes on this subject on October 13.

had been sent but before it was received, the chancellor was declared by imperial decree to be the supreme authority in Germany, and the high command legally subordinate to him; but non-German observers were not convinced of the genuineness or permanence of the change.

German leaders were disappointed and dismayed to learn that President Wilson had not blundered into Ludendorff's trap, and that the only armistice terms to be had would be little less than capitulation. No military resources would be left them with which to bargain or to threaten to resume hostilities. What alternative, then, was open to them? What resources had they with which to continue fighting? And what prospect of ultimate success?

A serious influenza epidemic was raging.[22] The transportation system was breaking down. Berlin had neither meat nor fats, and not enough potatoes. The lighting of homes and factories must be curtailed, and people were beginning to say "better a horrible end than horror without end."

Allied attacks did not cease. On the western front 191 divisions, far below normal strength, were "getting 70,000 too few men a month." They were faced, according to their own staff estimates, by 220 American and Allied divisions, of which the French were reduced to about the same size as the German, the British were larger, and the (forty) American were much larger. A quarter of a million more Americans were arriving in France every month.[23]

"The conditions are intended to put us out of the fight," said Ludendorff in conference. Encouraged by—or taking advantage of—an optimistic and unsupported statement by the minister of war that 600,000 additional recruits could be raised within a short (but unstated) period and 100,000 per month for another six months, by calling up the class of 1901, the general no longer pressed his previous demand for an immediate armistice but proposed, instead, to fight on rather than accept humiliation or terms that would make it impossible for him to resume hostilities after a two or three months' respite. Hearing him declare possible what he had only two weeks earlier declared impossible, the cabinet ministers lost confidence in his judgment and, against his self-contradictory advice, sent a third armistice note to President Wilson.

The third German note denied the wanton destruction of property during the withdrawal in France and Belgium or the deliberate de-

---

[22] The chancellor, Prince Max von Baden, was ill from October 22 to November 5, totally incapacitated November 1-3.

[23] President Wilson announced, before replying to the second German armistice note, that 250,000 men per month would continue to be sent until the actual cessation of hostilities. There would be no slackening or diminution of the pressure.

struction of lifeboats with passengers. The sinking of the *Leinster* could not be denied, but the note announced that orders had been sent to submarine commanders to attack no more passenger vessels. Again it assured the president that the new government was "free from arbitrary and irresponsible influence," "supported by the approval of the overwhelming majority of the German people."

President Wilson replied, October 23, to the effect that he was ready to transmit the whole correspondence to the governments of the Allies, and was taking up with them the question of armistice terms. The military provisions would be drawn up by the military commanders, so as to make impossible any resumption of hostilities by German troops and to insure that the terms agreed to could be enforced.

The political reforms which the Germans said they had made did not satisfy the president: "It is evident that the German people have no means of commanding the acquiescence of the military authorities . . . ; that the power of the King of Prussia to control the policy of the Empire is unimpaired. . . . The nations of the world do not and cannot trust the word of those who have hitherto been the masters of German policy. . . . If it [the United States] must deal with the military masters and the monarchical autocrats of Germany now, or if it is likely to have to deal with them later in regard to the international obligations of the German Empire, it must demand, not peace negotiations, but surrender."

Hoping that the United States would quarrel with the Allies over peace terms and withdraw from the war, or that some other stroke of luck might yet save them if they could force their own government to break off armistice negotiations, Hindenburg and Ludendorff issued on October 24 a proclamation to the troops calling President Wilson's third note "a demand for unconditional surrender, . . . unacceptable to us soldiers." For this act of insubordination Ludendorff was dismissed from his command by the kaiser at the instance of the chancellor. Hindenburg remained. General Groener succeeded Ludendorff as first quartermaster general. The chancellor and cabinet ministers had decided to make the peace which, four weeks earlier, the high command had demanded.

The fourth German armistice note, October 27, was meek in tone, a sign of surrender: ". . . The peace negotiations are being conducted by a government of the people in whose hands rests, both actually and constitutionally, the authority to make decisions. The military powers are also subject to this authority. The German government now awaits the proposals for an armistice. . . ."

The period from October 23 to November 6 was momentous. In the United States vociferous demands for the unconditional surrender of Germany embarrassed the president in his conduct of negotiations for an armistice.[24] Believing, as he was peculiarly prone to believe, that most of the American people wanted what he wanted, and that he could carry them with him in the face of all opposition, he publicly appealed to the voters in the congressional election campaign then in progress to show their approval of, and confidence in, his leadership by returning Democratic majorities to both houses of Congress. The return of a Republican majority to either house would be interpreted in Europe, he said, as a repudiation of his leadership. Republican majorities *were* returned to both houses; and the result of the election *was* interpreted in Europe as a repudiation of his leadership.

In France, in the field, the Allied and American advance continued, at heavy cost. At Marshal Fochs' headquarters at Senlis the military commanders met to draw up armistice terms. Only General Pershing was unwilling to grant an armistice then. Submitting to the Supreme War Council at Versailles the terms recommended by the leaders of the armed forces, and asked to speak only as a soldier, Marshal Foch said in answer to a direct question: "One makes war only for results. If the Germans now sign an armistice under the general conditions we have just determined, those results are in our possession. This being achieved, no man has the right to cause another drop of blood to be shed."[25]

In Britain and France there were lively discussions of the Fourteen Points, and in Paris and Versailles a tense diplomatic struggle over their acceptance by the Allies, in the course of which Colonel House once threatened to recommend to President Wilson that the United States make a separate peace, at once, unless the Fourteen Points were accepted, at least in principle. So the Allies accepted the "principle" of the freedom of the seas without giving up the "principle" of their right to maintain a blockade in time of war. They must, they said, "reserve to themselves complete freedom on this subject" when they entered the peace conference. Another significant reservation gave notice that "compensation will be paid by Germany for all damage done to the civilian population of the Allies and their property by the aggression of Germany by land, by sea, and from the air."

[24] Republican Senator Poindexter introduced into the Senate on October 21 a resolution to make it unlawful for any officer of the United States to negotiate with Germany as to either armistice or peace except after the surrender of the German army.

[25] Compare this statement with one attributed to Field Marshal von Hindenburg, quoted above. See footnote 18, p. 68.

The Allied reservations to the Fourteen Points were transmitted to Germany by President Wilson with his own endorsement on November 5, along with the notification that armistice terms were ready and would be handed by Marshal Foch to the plenipotentiary whom the German government was instructed to send for them. These reservations, and the president's previous warning that the resumption of hostilities by Germany must be made impossible, opened wide the way for Allied demands for the surrender of the German fleet, the virtual disarmament of Germany, the payment of reparations, and the admission of war guilt—or at least of "aggression."

The character of the Fourteen Points was not as materially altered by the Allied reservations, endorsed by President Wilson and clearly stipulated by him to the German government, as it would have been by those which the German leaders had themselves had in mind; but the German people were imperfectly informed about either. It suited the purpose of their leaders better, then and later, to pretend that they had been offered and promised a peace based on the Fourteen Points. They had, as a matter of fact, asked for such a peace only as insurance against a worse one, hoping meanwhile to secure a better one. The German leaders were not deceived on this point by President Wilson, as some of their unreconciled nationalists, especially National Socialists and most notably Hitler, subsequently claimed they had been. As for the German people, they were at first permitted by their own leaders to deceive themselves and to believe what they chose to believe, and were subsequently told what they wanted to hear: namely, that their armies had not been beaten in the field but had been tricked into a premature and unnecessary surrender and that the United States and the Allies had then violated a solemn promise to give them a peace based on the Fourteen Points.[26]

By the time the Germans were notified that the armistice terms were ready for them, they were ready to accept whatever terms they could

[26] The opinions here expressed are different from those hitherto quite commonly held. Professor Harry R. Rudin, for example, says: "The Allies were now no longer free to do as they pleased with Germany; when Germany accepted the agreement and proceeded to conclude the armistice, the Entente nations were bound morally and legally to a pledge that peace with Germany would be made on the basis of the Fourteen Points." *op. cit.*, 283. Count Bernstorff, on the other hand (wartime German ambassador to the United States, who was still a foreign service official at the time of the armistice), wrote after the war: "The charge that Wilson purposely betrayed us over the fourteen points acquired greater prominence from the fact that a legend was fostered in Germany to the effect that we laid down our weapons in reliance on the fourteen points. This legend is a flat falsification of history, as everyone knows who then took any part in the negotiations. We had to lay down our arms because the Supreme Army Command insisted that we should do so, in order to avoid a catastrophe, and then we invoked Wilson's help, with an appeal to the fourteen points." *Memoirs* (New York, 1936), 136.

get. The thought of peace, during the weeks since the armistice negotiations had been opened up, had weakened the people's will to go on
with the war. The military situation had gone from bad to worse, and
many had lost confidence in the high command. A mutiny among the
sailors at Kiel seemed about to take on a revolutionary character.
There was a growing demand for the abdication of the kaiser. Although, in late September, the home front had not yet begun to realize
the danger of defeat when Ludendorff lost his nerve and confessed
himself defeated, the German people were ready by November 6 to
concede defeat rather than face a continuance of the war. Their fighting spirit could not be roused again.

The leader of the delegation sent through the lines to receive the
armistice terms at the hands of Marshal Foch was a civilian, a representative of the Center party in the Reichstag, Matthias Erzberger.
His was an ungrateful task, and ungrateful army leaders subsequently
let him bear alone the odium of having performed it faithfully. Instructed by Hindenburg to get better terms if possible, but in any event
to sign, he signed, November 11.

The German army was to retire at once beyond the Rhine, and all
other non-German territory was to be evacuated. German territory
west of the Rhine was to be occupied by American and Allied troops,
with bridgeheads at Cologne, Coblenz, and Mainz, the maintenance
of the armies of occupation to be charged to the German government.
Enough armament and rolling stock (5000 guns, 25,000 machine
guns, 3000 trench mortars, 1700 airplanes—all Germany then had,
according to Hindenburg—5000 locomotives, 150,000 railway cars,
5000 trucks, etc.) were to be surrendered to make sure that the German army could not fight again. Allied and American prisoners of
war were to be repatriated at once, and interned civilians within a
month, without reciprocity. All submarines were to be surrendered,
and surface ships of the battle fleet interned. "Reparation for damage
done" was to be required, and the treaties of Bucharest and Brest
Litovsk were to be repudiated.

People in Allied countries and in the United States greeted the
cessation of hostilities as the end of the war. Their hope that the peace
would be permanent was strengthened by the abdication of the kaiser,
November 9, and the prospect of the establishment of a moderate
Social-Democratic republic in Germany under the leadership of
Friedrich Ebert. Optimism was not yet tempered either by understanding of the complexity of the problems of peacemaking or by premoni-
tion of the number of Germans still oblivious or defiant of the fact of
Germany's defeat.

CHAPTER 4

Peace Conferences and Treaties

PROBLEMS OF PEACEMAKING, 1919

Peace has to be made, at the end of a war, by people who have just been making war. Its permanence depends to a great extent upon the forbearance and foresight—in short, upon the wisdom—of its makers. It depends also upon the honest acceptance of its terms by the peoples who are parties to it.

When one belligerent or group of belligerents has won an undisputed and overwhelming victory, it is in a position to impose its will upon its late enemy by dictating terms of peace. When no such decision by force of arms has been reached, belligerents may negotiate upon a more nearly equal footing. Such a "peace without victory" is possible only if the differences between belligerents are not irreconcilable.

In contrast with the dynastic wars of the early modern period, fought for limited objectives and directly affecting only a portion of the populations nominally concerned, the world-wide struggle of 1914-1918 was, for each people involved in it, an all-inclusive national enterprise. Almost everyone in Europe lost friends or relatives in the war. Many thousands of maimed men were omnipresent reminders of the price paid for victory. Political responsibility of national leaders to electorates aroused for years to their maximum war effort meant susceptibility of leaders to public demands for vengeance, for indemnification, for territorial gains, or for guarantees against aggression in future. The "peace between equals" which President Wilson had said in January, 1917, was the only peace that would last was psychologically unattainable in 1919. Germany and Russia were not invited to participate in the Paris peace conference.

Treaty makers were pulled and pushed in many directions. Simply to put the clock back and restore all things as they had been before the war was clearly impossible, although nostalgia and extreme conservatism might have led some people to try it. The war effort had occasioned too great a social upheaval. Men of all classes and backgrounds had worked and fought side by side, sharing both rations and dangers. The need for leaders had opened up the officers' corps of all armies to others than aristocrats. Women had taken men's places in war industries and public transportation services, and some had served in uniform as nurses and in organizations such as the British W.A.A.C. (Women's Army Auxiliary Corps), and earned the right to vote in countries in which they had not previously enjoyed that right. Government or community control over travel, raw materials, and foodstuffs, conscription for military service, and (in Germany, at least), compulsory labor service for men not in the armed forces had accustomed people everywhere to many forms of collectivism and social controls.

People had learned everywhere, also, to look to government more than formerly for leadership in social action. Democracy had triumphed over autocracy. Self-determination was everywhere acclaimed if not everywhere attained. But the political liberalism of the nineteenth century, like the individualism of the eighteenth, was on the wane.

The old imperialism seemed dead, at least so far as the Central Powers were concerned. The German kaiser had abdicated and sought sanctuary in the Netherlands. Emperor Karl of Austria-Hungary was also in exile, and his empire had disintegrated. The Turkish Empire clearly could not long survive defeat. Colonial imperialism would be revived or would give way to another form of administration of dependent areas, according to decisions to be reached as to the disposal of the erstwhile colonial possessions of Germany and Turkey.

To peoples like the Poles and Czechs, the day of deliverance from alien bondage seemed at hand. Unity and independence promised happiness to the Poles, freedom and self-government to the Czechs, and to the Serbs their "greater Serbia."

Aged Frenchmen like Premier Clemenceau and President Poincaré, intensely nationalist and emotional in their patriotism, had twice seen their land delivered from invasion and were determined that never again should it be invaded. Frenchmen thought of themselves as looking backward only to the righting of ancient wrongs, forward to security for France; but they were interested in seeing Germany economically and militarily weakened, and her neighbors strengthened as potential allies of France.

Italy looked first to the territorial gains promised her by the Allies, hoped for others, and had tried hard before the armistice to register more reservations when accepting the Fourteen Points. Great Britain was primarily interested in the protection of her naval bases and sea lanes, in the restoration and extension of her overseas economic enterprises, and in supporting the aspirations of the self-governing dominions. Although reluctant to lose Germany permanently as a customer, she would not have been sorry to rid herself of German trade rivalry or of the threat of German colonial imperialism. President Wilson wanted neither a spoilsman's peace nor vengeance but a lasting peace. To him, the task of paramount importance was the establishment of a league of nations which would at first administer and might ultimately revise whatever settlement the conference might formulate.

All said that they sought only justice, but who could judge between conflicting national claims? It was generally agreed that the defeated enemy peoples should be justly treated; but should justice be stiffened by sternness or tempered by mercy? How much in reparations, what cessions or retrocessions of territory, what punishment would be just? Wide differences of opinion, both then and later, between erstwhile allies as between erstwhile enemies, were inevitable.

Versailles

TREATY MAKING

The general settlement embodied in the treaties of Versailles with Germany, June 28, 1919, of St.-Germain with Austria, September 10, 1919, of the Trianon Palace with Hungary, June 4, 1920, and of Sèvres with Turkey, August 20, 1920, was perhaps inevitably the result of uncounted compromises. The spirit of nationalism had been tremendously stimulated by the war, and the numerous "succession states," established generally on the principle of self-determination, competed with the victorious Allies in claiming former enemy territory on whatever grounds best suited their immediate purposes—historical, ethnic, linguistic, strategic, or economic. No one principle was followed quite consistently, or could have been so followed without doing violence to others. No nation was quite satisfied; and in the general dissatisfaction those Germans who could not or would not reconcile themselves to their defeat found sustenance for their hope of ultimately reversing the outcome of the war.

Germany suffered both territorial and material losses by the Treaty of Versailles, but German pride was much worse hurt than Germany was. A delegation headed by Count von Brockdorff-Rantzau was summoned to Versailles in May, 1919, and handed a draft of a treaty of more than two hundred pages, but was given no opportunity to discuss its terms in conference with its authors. Brockdorff-Rantzau's bitter protest won little sympathy, and only a few concessions were made in response to written objections and counterproposals. Under threat of further invasion the new German government had no choice but, even so, was able to bring itself to the point of agreeing to sign only at the very end of the stated period of grace. The treaty was signed on June 28, 1919, on the fifth anniversary of the murders at Sarajevo. The formal ceremony was staged, with the German delegates summoned as malefactors before the bar of justice, in the Hall of Mirrors of the palace of Louis XIV, in Versailles, in which the formation of the German Empire had been so arrogantly proclaimed on January 18, 1871. The *Diktat* (or dictated peace) of Versailles was a catchword of German resurgence, intransigence, and irredentism thereafter.

TERRITORIAL TERMS

Alsace and Lorraine were ceded to France. The reconquest of those provinces had been one of the principal war aims of France. It had been referred to by President Wilson in the eighth of his Fourteen Points as the righting of "the wrong done to France by Prussia in 1871," which he said had "unsettled the peace of the world for nearly fifty years." Most Germans, however, had thought of the cession of 1871 only as the righting of still other, more ancient, wrongs done to the old Germanic empire by France in taking those territories piecemeal, by use or threat of force, when France had been stronger than Germany. Much of Alsace had been under French control for more than three hundred years when Germany took it back in 1871, Strasbourg and most of Lorraine for nearly two hundred; and the French title to the duchy of Lorraine had been recognized by treaty since 1738. Yet Germans were as unready to reconcile themselves to the loss of the provinces in 1919 or thereafter as the French had been between 1871 and 1918. National irredentists referred to the former imperial province as the *Westmark*.[1]

Loss of control of the iron ore deposits of Lorraine left the industrialists of the German Ruhr region uncomfortably dependent upon

[1] Traditionally, a *Mark* was a border province. The same people called Austria the *Ostmark* or East Mark even before its annexation in 1938.

friendly relations with France. This was doubly disappointing to men who during the war had promised themselves that the Longwy-Briey region would be annexed to round out the province, which of course they had expected to retain.

The Saar Basin, valuable especially for its coal, was claimed by France as compensation for damage done to French coal mines during the German occupation. Actual annexation was not permitted; but, "as part payment towards the total reparation due," the French were given the mines for fifteen years, during which time they did what they could by coördination of currency and customs policies to make the prospect of a permanent union with France attractive to the inhabitants of the district. Government of the Saar, meanwhile, was supervised by the League of Nations.[2]

Eupen, Malmédy, and Moresnet were ceded by Germany to Belgium, subject to plebiscites to determine the wishes of the inhabitants. The plebiscite returns favored Belgium.[3]

Northern Schleswig was ceded to Denmark, its southern boundary being determined by plebiscite. The Kiel Canal remained German but was to be open to vessels of all nations on equal terms.

The German-Polish boundary was the subject of much discussion in the conference and a cause of friction afterward. It was generally conceded, and had been stipulated by President Wilson in the thirteenth of his Fourteen Points, that "an independent Polish state should be erected which should include the territories inhabited by indisputably Polish populations, [and] which should be assured a free and secure access to the sea. . . ." Access to the sea obviously meant at least the establishment of a free port at Danzig and opportunity to use it. To Polish nationalists and those, such as the French, who supported them, it meant ownership and control of a continuous strip of territory reaching to the sea, with the possibility of developing on Polish soil (as was subsequently done at Gdynia) a naval base and seaport that would free Polish trade from dependence upon Danzig. This view prevailed, and what the Germans subsequently called the "corridor" was cut through the province of West Prussia, along the west bank of the lower Vistula River. Danzig was again made a free city, as it had been in the days of the Napoleonic grand duchy of Warsaw, and Poland was

[2] In 1935 a plebiscite under strict League of Nations supervision resulted favorably for Germany; so German rule was restored there.

[3] Some German complaints were raised against the administration of the plebiscites. When the provinces were overrun by German troops in 1940, they were at once reincorporated into the Reich.

POLAND

AT ITS GREATEST EXTENT IN 1569

Showing also cessions and partition with territory absorbed by Russia, Prussia, and Austria.

Petrograd

Novgorod

R Moscow

1721

Riga

1772

1667

Dvinsk

Minsk

1793 PRUSSIA

Danzig

1772

1795

1795

1793

1667

Berlin

Warsaw

Luxlin

1793

1795

Kiev

1795

1772 Lwow

TO RUSSIA

TO PRUSSIA   Budapest

TO AUSTRIA

F.C. MANNING SR

DUCHY OF WARSAW
1807–1812
KINGDOM OF POLAND
1815–1863

Riga

Danzig

Berlin

Warsaw

DUCHY OF WARSAW   KINGDOM OF POLAND SET BY CONGRESS OF VIENNA

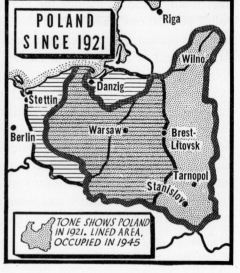

POLAND
SINCE 1921

Riga

Wilno

Stettin

Danzig

Berlin

Warsaw

Brest-Litovsk

Tarnopol

Stanislov

TONE SHOWS POLAND IN 1921. LINED AREA, OCCUPIED IN 1945

again given a free port there. The city was to govern itself, under a League of Nations commissioner.

The population of Danzig was almost entirely German. A Slav settlement there had been taken over during the Middle Ages by German traders, who from 1308 to 1454 were protected by the Order of the Teutonic Knights. After the decline of the Order, Danzig was virtually autonomous as a member of the Hanseatic League but recognized the suzerainty of the king of Poland from 1455 to 1793, when it was annexed by Prussia in the second partition of Poland, along with the fortress town of Thorn (Toruń) and the province of Posen (Poznań). Taken from the Prussians by the French in 1807, it was made a free city and a free port for the grand duchy of Warsaw, in which Posen was included, but both Danzig and Posen were regained by Prussia in 1815 and held thereafter until 1919, when Posen again became a part of Poland.

West Prussia (Pomorze) was seized by Frederick II of Prussia in the first partition of Poland, 1772, and was continuously controlled by Prussia until 1919, when it was ceded to Poland as part of the "corridor."

From the time of the first annexation by Frederick the Great, it had been the policy of the Prussian and German governments not only to develop and modernize their Polish provinces but to Germanize them. Agricultural and industrial development had been more welcome and more successful than Germanization. Poles remained Poles and preferred their own language despite discrimination against its use in public discussion or business; and Polish buyers, by pooling their resources, had purchased more land from year to year than was sold to the government-subsidized German buyers. Polish deputies had been a troublesome bloc in the Reichstag. Germans were still a minority in both provinces in 1919. As such they were legally protected by treaty, but complained often thereafter (not without reason) of harsh treatment, strikingly similar to their former treatment of Poles in the same areas.

Upper Silesia was in 1919 partially inhabited by Poles but had never in the last seven hundred years been politically a part of Poland. In 1740 it was a dependency of the kingdom of Bohemia, one of the hereditary possessions of Maria Theresa of the house of Hapsburg. Its seizure in that year by Frederick II, and the determined efforts of Maria Theresa to regain it, were primary causes of three wars, including the Seven Years' War; but Frederick retained it, and it was German territory, politically, in 1919. Poland, on the other hand, needed its coal, iron, and other minerals and its highly developed industries to supplement and balance her other resources, which were principally agricultural. To have given all Silesia to Poland would have been quite consistent with the French policy of weakening Germany and strengthening her eastern neighbors but inconsistent with the principle of self-determination and difficult to justify historically. So those districts, but only those, which showed local Polish majorities by plebiscite were awarded to Poland.

German spokesmen had argued that Silesia was an indivisible economic unit and that a large majority of its people were German and unwilling to be separated from Germany. This claim as to the attitude of the majority was confirmed for the plebiscite area as a whole, although that area did not cover all Silesia. But in certain small communities in extreme southeastern (or Upper) Silesia local majorities made up largely of Polish immigrant laborers or their descendants sufficed as the basis of the award of those districts to Poland. Though only a small part of Silesia, the lost area included some of the best of its industrial resources.

Unreconciled and irreconcilable nationalists were not the only people in Germany who refused from 1919 to 1939 to concede that the German-Polish frontier had been either justly or permanently established. German public opinion was virtually unanimous as to the "hardship and injustice" imposed upon Germany by the interposition of the "corridor" between Pomerania and East Prussia, by the subjection of the German elements of the population of West Prussia and Posen to Polish control, and by the way the Germans had been "counted out" of Upper Silesia.[4]

Territorial losses to France and Poland might have been made good by the annexation of Austria, with the consent of most of the Austrian people. Both German and Austrian constituent assemblies had provided for the inclusion of republican Austria in the federal union of German states. But the Allies were unwilling to permit it, and explicitly prohibited it in Article 80 of the Treaty of Versailles and Article 88 of the Treaty of St.-Germain.

During the war the German naval base at Kiaochow was quickly seized by the Japanese, and Germany's place in Shantung province was taken by Japan. German-controlled islands in the Pacific south of the equator were taken over by Great Britain, Australia, and New Zea-

---

[4] Boundary lines had been drawn by plebiscite on the basis of local majorities in North Schleswig also, and in Allenstein and Marienwerder in East Prussia; but there the results had been favorable—and acceptable—to Germany. See also pp. 81-82.

land, and those north of the equator by Japan. All were retained in 1919 under mandate by the powers then in possession of them.

In Africa also Germany had lost possession of her colonies and was compelled by the Treaty of Versailles (Article 119) to renounce "in favor of the Principal Allied and Associated Powers all her rights and titles" over them. They were then assigned as mandated territories: one-third of Togoland to Great Britain and two-thirds to France; one-sixth of Kamerun to Great Britain and five-sixths to France; German East Africa to Great Britain, German Southwest Africa to the Union of South Africa, and Ruanda-Urundi (a small area at the northern end of Lake Tanganyika on the northwestern frontier of German East Africa) to the Belgian Congo.

The constantly reiterated Nazi statement that Germany was "poor" between the wars because she had been "robbed" of her colonies was more easily believed by those who wished to believe it than proved to a student of the record. Colonies had been neither profitable to the German taxpayer nor important in German foreign trade. Imports from the colonies had constituted only three-tenths of one percent and exports to the colonies only one-half of one percent of Germany's total prewar foreign commerce, whereas colonial expenditures were 2 percent of total governmental expenditures. Only some of those engaged in colonial business enterprises, employed in the colonial administration, or supplying it as contractors made money out of the colonies. And despite all the Nazi and Pan-German talk about the Germans as a *Volk ohne Raum* with an incontestable claim to *Lebensraum*—i.e., an overcrowded people without room in which to live—they were not using their colonies as an outlet for surplus population when they had them. The entire German population of the German colonies in 1914 was less than 24,000, including soldiers and officials, and was not increasing.

It was politically profitable for recalcitrant German nationalists, however, in the years between the world wars to protest against the loss of the colonies. People associated the loss of empire, in their emotions even more than in their minds, with whatever hardships they encountered. Such emotionalized and irrational thinking was stimulated later by the Nazi government by use of every propagandist device at its command. Schools for prospective "colonials" and colonial officials, and agricultural experiment stations to plan for the development of colonial areas not then under German control, were maintained through the middle thirties, and a flood of publications appeared in praise of Germany's handling of the colonies she once had had.

WAR GUILT AND REPARATION

The loss of Upper Silesia, it was argued by some German spokesmen, would cripple German industry so seriously that payment of reparation would be rendered impossible. But the Allies never saw quite eye to eye as to whether the essential purpose of the exaction of reparation payments should be to cripple Germany (which might reduce the amount she could pay), to collect as much as possible (in which case the economic recovery of Germany must be permitted and encouraged so as to increase her capacity to pay), or merely to require payment for damage actually done to the property of citizens of Allied countries. The pre-armistice correspondence and the terms of the armistice itself had stipulated that Germany should "make compensation for all damage done to the civilian population of the Allied and Associated Powers and to their property" by German "aggression." The Treaty of Versailles (Article 231) affirmed and required Germany to accept "the responsibility of Germany and her allies for causing all the loss and damage to which the Allied and Associated governments and their nationals had been subjected as a consequence of the war imposed upon them by the aggression of Germany and her allies."

No amount could then be stated; but Germany was required by Article 232 of the treaty to repeat the promise made in the armistice agreement to compensate civilians for damage done them and their property. Such "damage" was so defined (by Annex I) as to include pensions and compensation in the nature of pensions to naval and military victims of the war (wounded, invalided, etc.) and to their dependents, the cost of governmental assistance to prisoners of war and their dependents, and allowances paid by Allied and Associated governments to families and dependents of members of the armed forces or others serving with those forces.

The inclusion of pensions and separation allowances as "compensation for damage done civilians" had not been contemplated by most members of the United States delegation and was not readily accepted by them. But certain British delegates argued that the citizen soldier was essentially a civilian, and that personal injury should be paid for as well as the destruction of property. President Wilson, inclined at first to exclude such personal damages, was persuaded to include them. Their inclusion gave the British a larger share of whatever amount might eventually be paid, but the French were not averse to seeing the prospective total so increased.[5]

[5] It was subsequently agreed that France, with nearly thirteen thousand square miles of her territory devastated, should receive 52 percent of whatever amount

The whole question of reparation might have been more satisfactorily solved if the interested parties could have brought themselves to look upon it more as a part of peacemaking and less as a continuation of the war. To the Germans and the French, however, and to a certain extent to the other peoples concerned, the war unfortunately moved on only from one phase into another. The French still sought security by getting all they could for France at Germany's expense; the Germans, resentful of what they called the falsehood and injustice of the "war guilt clause" (Article 231 of the treaty), were determined to "defend themselves" by refusing or evading payment if possible. The Germans expected the French to be insatiable, and the French were equally certain that the Germans would complain in any case and would pay only what they were compelled to pay. Both were right. No amount could have been set during the Paris peace conference, not only because the damage could not be so speedily assessed but also because the French people would have denounced as inadequate any total which anyone might then have had the temerity to suggest, and would have overthrown any government that dared accept the estimate. The Germans, on the other hand, never looked upon reparation as a debt, or upon default or evasion of it as dishonest or dishonorable.

The task of setting the amount which Germany must pay was assigned by the peace conference to a reparation commission. The United States was not represented thereon but would have been if it had ratified the treaty. After a period of negotiation during which Allied claims for more than 200,000,000,000 marks were presented and the "sanction towns" of Duisburg, Düsseldorf, and Ruhrort were occupied to increase the pressure for payment, the reparation commission at a conference in London early in 1921 presented a categorical demand for 132,000,000,000 marks, 1,000,000,000 of which should be paid within three months. The German Reichstag refused to authorize such an agreement, Stresemann and the People's party deputies voting with the majority for refusal, and the Fehrenbach ministry resigned; but on May 11, 1921, the new cabinet of Chancellor Wirth had to promise to pay the amount demanded, equivalent to approximately $33,000,000,000. The first payment, equivalent to about 1,000,000,000 marks, was made on time, in the currencies of a dozen nations; and the supply of cash on hand was virtually exhausted. The foreign exchange problem, much stressed and subsequently overstressed by German spokesmen, was a real one.

Germany paid, Great Britain 22 percent, Italy 10 percent, Belgium 8 percent, all others 8 percent.

The policy of fulfillment, as Chancellor Wirth's compliance with Allied demands was called, was designed to enlist the sympathy and good will of the recipients of reparation payments. Its advocates hoped also, by making an ostensible effort at fulfillment, to convince the Allies that the reparation terms of the Treaty of Versailles were actually *undurchführbar*—incapable of fulfillment—unless Germany were permitted to retain most of her prewar economic assets and German industry to recover quickly from the effects of the war. They hoped thus, against hope, to be permitted to retain Upper Silesia despite the result of the plebiscite held there on March 20, 1921.

No such hopes were realized. The mark lost steadily in purchasing power and exchange value, and the government was suspected of inflating its currency to evade its obligations. The partition of Upper Silesia in October, 1921, brought the total German treaty losses to approximately one-eighth of the territory, one-tenth of the population, three-fourths of the iron ore, two-thirds of the zinc, and one-fourth of the coal production of prewar Germany.

These losses so deranged the national economy as to make reparation payments more difficult. The murders of former Finance Minister Matthias Erzberger in August, 1921, and Foreign Minister Walther Rathenau in June, 1922, indicated increased domestic discontent and the unpopularity of the government's financial and foreign policies.[6]

Rathenau had induced the Allies to agree to some diminution of the cash payments called for in 1922 and to accept some payments in kind, such as deliveries of coal, chemicals, and building materials. But by the end of the year Germany had asked for a partial moratorium on cash payments and had fallen behind schedule in the delivery of telegraph poles.

In January, 1923, France and Belgium, without the coöperation or consent of Great Britain or the official approval of the United States— which was then withdrawing the last of its troops from the old occupation zone on the Rhine—declared Germany in default and sent troops to occupy the Ruhr, a "sanction" which the Allies were authorized by the Treaty of Versailles to apply in case of default. (The right of *some* of the Allies to take such action separately was less clear, and was questioned by Great Britain.) The German government stopped all reparation payments and deliveries to France and Belgium, ordered its officials in the occupied area not to coöperate with the "invaders," and encouraged the population of the Ruhr in a policy of passive resistance. For some months people simply stopped work in the mines and fac-

[6] Hitler subsequently dedicated monuments to the murderers.

tories of the newly occupied area and let the armies of occupation organize their own transportation system.

Great hardship resulted, as many thousands of men out of work had no income. Ten million people were soon on relief, and the shipment of food into the area was disrupted. The rest of Germany also suffered as a result of being cut off economically from one of its principal producing areas. Relief measures for the benefit of the people of the Ruhr accelerated the already swift decline of the mark to worthlessness, so that before the end of 1923 a million million marks had a dollar value equal to that of only one prewar mark—less than twenty-five cents.

With passive resistance costing the government as much per day as the fighting of 1918 had done, it became clear by August, 1923, that that policy must be abandoned. Chancellor Cuno then resigned, and his cabinet was replaced by one headed by Gustav Stresemann, known generally until then as a parliamentary spokesman of "big business." Stresemann had always been, and still was, an ardent German nationalist. During the war he had been an outspoken advocate of world-power imperialism and conquest. Always after the war he was a revisionist, seeking revision of the peace terms to Germany's advantage. But in August, 1923, his conception of tactics, dictated by circumstances, was: (1) to liquidate the bankrupt Ruhr policy of his predecessor; (2) to stabilize the mark; (3) to recognize the fact that while Germany worked toward the position she wanted in a world such as she wanted it to be, she had to live in the world as it was; (4) to cultivate the sympathy and confidence of other nations, for the sake of the earlier resumption of trade and prosperity.

Stresemann's first step was to order the abandonment of passive resistance in the Ruhr and the withholding of government relief from the population there. His decision was ratified first by a conference of the principal ministers of the German states or *Länder*, then by the Reichstag, which conferred on him the dictatorial powers he needed to carry it out along with other necessary measures. The population of the Ruhr went peaceably back to work, and the occupying powers got some coal for their pains. The enterprise had paid poor dividends, except in the negative sense that it had hurt Germany.

The stabilization of the mark was effected by officially recognizing and legally confirming the worthlessness of the old *Reichsmark* and replacing it by the issuance of a new *Rentenmark* secured nominally by the land and industrial resources of the nation, actually by the government's ability to command confidence. The new mark proved stable for the simple reason that everyone insisted that it should. The German people had had more than enough of inflation. Individuals generally credited with stabilization were Chancellor Stresemann, Finance Minister Dr. Hans Luther, and Dr. Hjalmar Schacht, president of the Reichsbank.

The mark could not have been stabilized without a move toward balancing the budget by reducing government expenditures. Spartan measures for that purpose, reducing salaries, pensions, and social insurance payments, and proposing the suspension of the eight-hour-day law met stout opposition from labor unions and from Social Democrats in the Reichstag.

Emergency powers granted by the Reichstag were barely sufficient to enable the government to maintain its authority. A radical government including three Communists was established in Dresden in October, 1923, and suppressed in November only after some violence and loss of life. A reactionary group led by von Kahr and von Lossow in Munich declared Bavaria's connection with the Reich suspended, and threatened to "save" Germany from the Socialists. Also in Munich, on November 8, occurred Hitler's "beer-hall Putsch," which ended in fiasco partly because the National Socialists failed to enlist the support of von Kahr's group. Republican government now had little prestige left, and did not punish the miscreants severely enough to reëstablish its authority.

In the matter of reparation payments, Stresemann asked the Allies for a moratorium, a loan, and an investigation of Germany's capacity to pay—and was denounced by German irreconcilables for such "subservience" to foreigners, international bankers, and Germans interested only in foreign trade. On November 23 he resigned the chancellorship but remained in the new cabinet as minister for foreign affairs. Dr. Luther also remained as finance minister. Wilhelm Marx, a leader of the Center party, became chancellor.

Germany's capacity to pay was studied during the winter of 1923-1924 by an international committee of nonpolitical experts under the chairmanship of Charles G. Dawes of Chicago. The recommendations of that committee were accepted by the reparation commission and the German government as the so-called Dawes plan, effective September 1, 1924. Neither total nor term was set, but annual reparation payments were scaled down to 1,000,000,000 marks in the first year, from which figure they were gradually to increase to 2,500,000,000 within five years. Money to meet these payments was to be found in the proceeds of certain taxes earmarked for them, including a tax on the nationalized German railways, which for this purpose were to be brought under international control. Four-fifths of the first year's payment came from the proceeds of a foreign loan which Germany was then permitted to float. The transfer of funds was to be effected through the office of an agent general in Berlin. The agent general was another American, Seymour Parker Gilbert.

For five years, 1924-1929, under the Dawes plan reparation payments were made punctually and in full, including 100,000,000 marks per year paid to the United States (55,000,000 to repay the costs of the United States army of occupation and a maximum amount of 45,000,-000 on claims approved by the U.S.-German Claims Commission).

The presence of the agent general in Berlin reassured potential moneylenders in Great Britain and the United States and made it easy for German businessmen as well as for their government to borrow freely. The modernization and expansion of industrial plants kept pace with public improvements. It was a period of great optimism and ambitious building. Those were the years, too, of Locarno, of Germany's admittance to the League of Nations, and of her signature of the Kellogg-Briand Pact renouncing war as an instrument of national policy and promising to settle international disputes by none but peaceful means. While appearing to move in the direction of reconciliation and peaceful and mutually profitable coöperation with other peoples, the Germans quickly won the confidence of many others, restored their own self-confidence, and rebuilt their cities, industrial plants, and utilities.[7]

There was cause for concern, however, in the fact that German

[7] Less than half of any year's reparation payment was made out of the regular national budget, and the "controlled revenues" were always enough to have paid the whole annuity. During the years 1924-1929, 168 German stock and bond issues were publicly sold in the United States by firms such as the Krupp Iron Works of Essen, the August Thyssen Iron and Steel Works, the United Steel Works, and the North German Lloyd. Total foreign investments in Germany during the years 1924-1931, inclusive, were estimated by the reparation commission at $4,800,000,000. Reparation paid by Germany during those years was estimated by the commission at $2,500,000,000, and payments made before 1924 at $1,400,000,000.

Neither government nor business was as badly hurt by reparation payments as it said it was. At the end of the reparation period the payments amounted to only 2.2 percent of the national income. In 1929-1930 Germany used for external and internal debt service only 23 percent of her government expenditures, whereas France was devoting to that purpose 31 percent, Great Britain 46 percent, and the United States 31.9 percent in 1928-1929 and 30.3 percent in 1929-1930. In 1928 the Reichsbank's stock of gold was twice what it had been in 1914. From 1924 to 1929, while still borrowing abroad and paying toward reparation less than they borrowed, Germans saved $5,000,000,000 and invested abroad no less than $2,000,000,000. German exports in 1929 exceeded those of 1913 by 34 percent. See article by Alzada Comstock, Current History, August, 1945; also Gustav Stolper, German Economy, 1870-1940 (New York, 1940), 176-181.

economy was not carrying itself. It was being carried, and its foreign
obligations were steadily increasing. If the inward flow of credit
should suddenly stop, and if a strong demand for immediate payment
of short-term financial obligations should be made, a crisis might be
precipitated. The country could not live indefinitely on its debts. The
Dawes plan, moreover, was seen to be only what its authors had said
it was—a temporary expedient under which annual payments starting
at 1,000,000,000 marks in 1925 had increased to 2,500,000,000 by
1930, with neither term nor total amount yet set.

The Young plan, drawn up in 1929 by another international committee under the chairmanship of another American, Owen D. Young,
and signed January 30, 1930, was designed to set a total and a term for
reparation payments. The nominal total was about 37,000,000,000
marks plus interest, the term fifty-eight years. The actual total, over
the entire term, would have been nearly three times the amount of
the original obligation.

Germany's situation was in certain ways more favorable than under
the Dawes plan. The Dawes report had recommended the evacuation
of the Ruhr; the adoption of the Young plan led to the evacuation of
the whole Rhineland zone of Allied occupation by June 30, 1930,
long before the expiration of the fifteen-year period stipulated by the
Versailles Treaty. German economic autonomy was restored by the
removal of the controls administered under the Dawes plan by the
agent general for reparations. Payments were to be made through a
new Bank for International Settlements to be set up in Basel. The
37,000,000,000 marks (approximately $9,250,000,000) to be paid
(with interest) under the new agreement was but a small fraction of
the 132,000,000,000 demanded and promised nine years before and
never meanwhile reduced as to capital, Dawes plan payments having
been treated as interest only. The annual payments were to be smaller.
Starting at 1,700,000,000 marks per year for the first two years, they
were to increase gradually thereafter to 2,500,000,000 marks in 1965-
1966, then to decrease gradually to 898,000,000 in 1988. Germany
was promised the benefit of two-thirds of any reduction which the
United States might make in its war debt claims on the Allies up to
1965, and of the full amount of any reduction made thereafter.[8]

[8] The Young committee proposed that the United States should receive, out of
continued German reparation payments, an average annuity of 66,100,000 marks
for thirty-seven years, and an average of 40,800,000 for fifteen years thereafter. As
the United States did not become a party to the Young agreement, it made its own
arrangement directly with Germany June 23, 1930, to cover the unpaid balance of
the costs of its army of occupation (minus a 10 percent reduction, agreed to also

The German people voted by plebiscite December 22, 1929, to accept the Young plan, and the necessary laws for its implementation were passed by the Reichstag and signed by President von Hindenburg. But formal acceptance did not mean fulfillment. A total and a term had, to be sure, at last been set; but the total, though reduced, still seemed large to people reluctant to pay; and the term seemed long to people who protested against "seeing their grandchildren enslaved." The "Young plan" years, moreover—1930 and 1931—owing to a rapidly spreading world-wide economic depression were years of falling commodity prices, diminishing foreign trade, and restricted credit. By June, 1931, the Kredit Anstalt of Vienna was on the verge of bankruptcy, and on July 13 what had been reputed to be one of Germany's strongest financial institutions, the Darmstädter und National-Bank, had to close its doors.

The reparation payment of 1930 had been made out of the proceeds of an international loan of 1,200,000,000 marks. Interest and amortization payments on both Dawes and Young plan loans were due June 30, 1931. On June 20, President Hoover proposed the postponement for one year from July 1, 1931, of all international debt and reparation payments except obligations of national governments to private parties. On June 25 a final credit of 420,000,000 marks was allowed the Reichsbank by the banks of the United States, Great Britain, and France and the Basel Bank for International Settlements to meet the payments due June 30 on Dawes and Young plan loans.[9]

Under a "stand still agreement" negotiated in August, 1931, and renewed in February, 1932, and annually thereafter, the German government asserted and secured formal recognition of the inability of German banks to repay the short-term credits previously extended to

---

by the Allies as to their occupation costs) and claims approved by the United States-German Mixed Claims Commission.

The total cost to the United States of its army of occupation was fixed at $292,663,435.79. The 10 percent reduction mentioned above, payments already made, and certain other credits allowed Germany had reduced the total claim by September 1, 1929, to $164,670,421.62. This was to be paid in annual payments over a period of thirty-seven years, the average annuity to be 25,300,000 marks or about $6,000,000. During the year 1930 Germany paid on this account 37,850,000 marks or nearly $9,000,000. The United States treasury's estimate of the awards made and to be made by the Mixed Claims Commission up to August 21, 1929, was almost $300,000,000, of which nearly one-third was accumulated interest. Germany had paid by then nearly $32,000,000 and accumulated about $2,000,000 in other credits. Under the agreement of June 23, 1930, Germany paid the United States 61,200,000 marks (about $14,535,000) during the year 1930 and agreed to make two payments of 20,400,000 marks (about $4,850,000) each per year thereafter until March 31, 1981. *United States Treasury Reports*, 1929, pp. 54, 55, and 1930, pp. 64, 65.

[9] This was repaid in 1933. Stolper, *op. cit.*, 190.

them by foreign banks. British bankers were badly hurt by heavy withdrawals of gold from London by other west European bankers who feared that, unable to reclaim short-term credits from Germany, the British banks would find it impossible to meet their obligations. Great Britain was, in fact, forced off the gold standard in September, 1932. Meanwhile the German banks were hurt both by the depression and by their inability to secure further foreign credits.

At a conference of the signatories of the Young plan agreement at Lausanne in June and July, 1932, Germany finally agreed to pay three billion marks in the form of 5 percent bonds, to be deposited with the Bank for International Settlements and negotiated and sold when and if the bank found it possible, in lieu of further payments. This was less than 10 percent of the amount agreed upon two years before.

The Lausanne agreement was tantamount to an admission that the nations interested in reparation payments had given up hope of collecting them without the help of the United States. The agreement was never ratified because the British, French, Belgian, and Italian delegates had concerted beforehand not to ask their governments to ratify it unless the United States should consent to a further downward revision of its war debt claims upon them. This the United States government declined to do. No further reparation payments were made, nor any further debt payments to the United States except by Finland, and except token payments in 1933 by Great Britain, Italy, Czechoslovakia, Rumania, and Latvia.

WAR CRIMES AND CRIMINAL TRIALS

Under the heading "Penalties" (Article 227 of the Treaty of Versailles) the Allied and associated powers publicly arraigned "William II of Hohenzollern, formerly German Emperor, for a supreme offense against international morality and the sanctity of treaties." He was to be tried by a specially constituted tribunal of five judges, one each appointed by the United States of America, Great Britain, France, Italy, and Japan. In its decision the tribunal was to "be guided by the highest motives of international policy, with a view to vindicating the solemn obligations of international undertakings and the validity of international morality."

The former kaiser had found sanctuary in Holland, and the government of the Netherlands declined to extradite him; so the trial was never held. The whole problem of "war guilt" and punishment would not, in fact, have been solved even by the hanging of the kaiser, for he had not been solely responsible for all decisions made in his name by his government. Nor was there any modern precedent for bringing the head of a state to book before an international court which had not existed when the crimes of which he was accused were alleged to have been committed, under international laws not then codified or clearly stated. The statement of the principles and policies involved, however, was later comparable with the attempt made by the prosecution at the war criminal trials at Nuremberg in 1945-1946 to establish that international law and treaty agreements were enforceable, and that the waging of a war of aggression in violation of them was a crime for which those responsible could be brought to trial before an international court and punished.

Article 228 of the Treaty of Versailles required the German government to recognize the right of the Allied and associated powers to bring before military tribunals, and to hand over to them for trial and punishment, "persons accused of having committed acts in violation of the laws and customs of war."

Those so accused included submarine commanders charged not only with the sinking of passenger vessels without warning but with the subsequent gunning of their lifeboats, commanders of prison camps in which prisoners of war had been maltreated, and officers and men believed to have been responsible for or guilty of other atrocities in combat or against the inhabitants of occupied areas. The proposed international tribunal was not set up. When in 1920 a few of the accused persons were brought before the supreme German federal court at Leipzig instead, evidence submitted by the Allies was discounted. Officers accused of atrocities were treated as if they had been either unjustly or sufficiently punished by being so called to account for war deeds done in defense of their fatherland, or they were permitted to plead in self-defense that they had acted only in obedience to orders of higher authority.[10] Although the trials soon turned

[10] In his opening statement to the court at the Nuremburg war criminal trials of 1945-1946, the principal British prosecutor said, in part: "There comes a point at which a man must refuse to answer to his leader if he is also to answer to his own conscience." In Rome on October 12, 1945, German General Anton Dostler was sentenced to death by a United States military court for having ordered the execution of fifteen United States soldiers without trial near La Spezia, Italy, March 26, 1944, and was executed on December 1 despite his argument in self-defense that he had only obeyed explicit orders from Hitler. In May, 1946, Lieutenant General Karl Maris von Behrens, tried by a British military court for the execution of fourteen British commandos who landed in Norway in 1942, and pleading orders from Hitler as his defense, was acquitted.

Colonel General Eberhard von Mackensen, former commander of the German Fourteenth Army in Italy, and German Lieutenant General Kurt Maeltzer, former commander of the garrison of Rome, were sentenced to death before a firing squad by a British military court sitting in Rome, November 30, 1946, for the massacre

into a farce from the point of view of the prosecution, and were therefore soon abandoned, the Weimar republic was always reproached as if responsible for a national disgrace for having permitted them to be held.

DISARMAMENT AND REARMAMENT

"In order to render possible the initiation of a general limitation of the armaments of all nations," Part V of the Treaty of Versailles provided for the military and naval disarmament of Germany. The German army was to be reduced to a volunteer force of 100,000 men, including not more than four thousand officers, and its general staff was to be dissolved and not to be reconstituted in any form. Universal compulsory military service was to be abolished. All fortified works, fortresses, and field works situated in German territory west of a line drawn fifty kilometers east of the Rhine were to be disarmed and dismantled, and no new fortification was to be constructed in that Rhineland zone. Germany was forbidden to import arms, munitions, or war materials of any kind, or to manufacture them for export, and all her munitions and war materials factories were to be rigidly controlled by an inter-Allied control commission.

The German navy, including the coast guard, was to be reduced to a total of fifteen thousand officers and men including not more than fifteen hundred officers and warrant officers. Only six battleships of the *Deutschland* or *Lothringen* type, six light cruisers, twelve destroyers, and twelve torpedo boats or their equivalents were to be kept in commission—no submarines, no dirigibles, no military or naval aircraft of any kind, no poison gas or materials for making it.

As a safeguard against the form of evasion practiced by Prussia when Napoleon limited the size of her army after Jena—large numbers of recruits being given short periods of training and then discharged to make way for others, so that soon the number of trained men greatly exceeded the number in the army—the treaty provided that the period of enlistment must be twelve consecutive years, and that the number of men discharged for any reason before the expiration of their term of enlistment must not in any year exceed 5 percent of the total.

Many ways of evading the disarmament terms were found, none the less. Uniformed police forces and citizens' corps (*Einwohnerwehr*)

---

of 335 Italian political prisoners held as hostages, in reprisal for the killing of some SS men. Field Marshal Albert Kesselring, acknowledging a commanding general's responsibility for the same offense and other "reprisal" killings, was sentenced to death May 7, 1947, but his sentence was later commuted to life imprisonment.

soon outnumbered the legal Reichswehr as the Landwehr had outnumbered the treaty-restricted Prussian army after Jena. The long-term soldiers of the Reichswehr were thoroughly trained as the officers' and noncommissioned officers' corps of a readily expansible and potentially much larger force, and the standards and traditions of the most famous regiments of the old imperial army were entrusted to its smaller units and kept alive by them. The outlawed general staff put on mufti and an air of outraged dignity but did not forsake its ways or lose its coherence or influence. Its former members continued to contemplate the possibility of reversing the results of the last war, and to discount the possibility of doing that except by winning the next one. Its intelligence section was merely transferred from the ministry of war to the Foreign Office, the military railway section to the ministry of transport, and the topographical section to the ministry of the interior.

Aircraft factories moved across the borders into the Netherlands or elsewhere. Army aviators practiced paratrooping as instructors in the Russian air corps, or flew German planes for overmanned and over-equipped German commercial air lines in South America. "Glider clubs" sprang up all over Germany, so that the youth who could not fly could soar. "Air sports" organizations were popular and numerous—easily convertible into an air force whenever circumstances should permit.

Metallurgy, shipbuilding skill, and general ingenuity, applied in combination to the problem of defeating the purpose of a ten-thousand-ton limitation on warships of the cruiser class, led to the development of what was often called the "pocket battleship." Technological improvement in the making of armor plate, the increased use of welding in place of riveting, new and heavier (eleven-inch) guns, greater speed and cruising range, and similar improvements made the new *Deutschland,* the *Admiral Graf Spee,* and others of their type a new terror of the seas, able—it was thought—to outrun anything of equal armor or gun power or to outgun anything of equal speed.[11]

The treaty provision for the destruction of German weapons and munitions and of machines for making them was no less difficult to enforce. The control commission had no omnipresent Gestapo at its disposal, and its work was not made any easier by the fact that persons who gave it information did so at the risk of being murdered for their pains by some of their unreconciled compatriots. The Krupp concerns

---

[11] Off Uruguay, December 13, 1939, the *Graf Spee* was damaged and driven into Montevideo harbor by three British cruisers, *Essex, Ajax,* and *Achilles.* Ordered to leave that port December 17, the ship was scuttled by its own crew off the estuary of the River Plate.

were subsidized by the republic to carry on in secret an extensive program of research and experimentation in the techniques of armament production, while ostensibly engaged only in producing peacetime consumers' goods. Real and rigorous enforcement of the disarmament provisions of the treaty would have required more policing, over a longer period, than the Allies had the unity or the persistence to undertake.

The leaders of the Weimar republic left it to Hitler to denounce the treaty officially and to flout that part of it publicly, but its terms had already been circumvented in many ways before 1933. Examination of documents carried off from the archives of the French Foreign Office by the Germans during the war and subsequently recaptured and returned by the United States Army revealed that the French government's original document of the Treaty of Versailles had been destroyed (reported in *Time,* June 3, 1946). To "tear up" that treaty, piecemeal and without war if possible but by war if necessary, had been one of Germany's principal national aims ever since its signing.

St.-Germain-en-Laye, with Austria, September 10, 1919

The Treaty of St.-Germain recognized and recorded the dissolution of the Austro-Hungarian Empire, which had been an accomplished fact for nearly a year before the treaty was signed. Centrifugal forces such as nationalism had seriously threatened the conglomerate dual monarchy with disruption before the war. These were intensified by the strains of the war itself, encouraged by the weakness and inefficiency of the central government more clearly revealed in war, and stimulated by President Wilson's wartime proposal of self-determination as a basis for deciding the status of the peoples of the old empire.

Even the semblance of parliamentary government that Austria-Hungary had known in 1914 had been suspended when the Reichsrat was prorogued in March of that year. The parliament had not been reconvened when war impended, and ministerial government by imperial decree had broken down with military failure as the war went on. Complete disintegration seemed imminent when the minister-president Count Karl Stürgkh was assassinated, October 21, 1916, and Emperor Franz Josef died one month later, after an inglorious reign of nearly sixty-eight years.

In an attempt to postpone the inevitable, new leaders made conciliatory gestures at once toward enemy nations abroad and toward hostile nationalities at home. Count Ottokar Czernin, who had succeeded Count Stephen Burian as foreign minister in December, 1916, hoped to avert a more complete and final defeat by making an immediate peace. He was not successful. The German announcement of December 12, 1916, that the Central Powers were ready to negotiate for a general peace was useful for domestic political consumption only and in Germany only, and merely served to stiffen the war will of the peoples of the Allied countries. Little sympathy for Austria-Hungary was aroused when, early in 1917, the new Emperor Karl sought, through his wife's brother Prince Sixtus of Parma, to open up secret negotiations for peace. Italy wanted everything that the Allies had promised her in 1915, which was more than the new emperor could yet bring himself to concede. Austro-Hungarian foreign policy had consequently to be more subservient to Germany. For more than a year thereafter the dual monarchy dared not again· reveal its inclination toward peace. Hopes of victory revived somewhat with early German successes in 1918, but died when the tide turned in France in midsummer.

Meanwhile the empire was falling apart. In the Reichsrat which was convoked in May, 1917, the Czechs and South Slavs showed strong separatists tendencies, and the German Austrians and Magyars made little effort to conciliate them. The national organization of the Czechs was officially recognized by the Allies in August, 1918, as a belligerent power, and a Czech government was set up in Paris October 14. The prospect of independence seemed more promising to the other nationalities than membership in the federal state which the emperor finally offered them October 16.

Defeat and dissolution came swiftly and simultaneously. Bulgaria concluded an armistice, September 29, leaving Hungary exposed to invasion by the Allied force advancing from Salonika, and Hungary demanded the return of her troops to defend their home territory. Another new foreign minister, Count Julius Andrassy, apparently hoping to placate President Wilson and by conciliation even yet to hold the peoples of the old monarchy together in some form of voluntary association, announced his government's acceptance of the principle of self-determination. But nothing less than independence was any longer acceptable to the peoples concerned. On October 30 a new Hungarian government was formed in Budapest, which on November 16 declared itself a republic. On November 3 an armistice was concluded, on terms tantamount to complete capitulation, with the Allied powers and the United States. Allied forces had gone over to the offensive in northern and northeastern Italy, quickly regained the ground lost in 1917, and advanced beyond the lines they had held before Caporetto. Further resistance was impossible.

On November 11, almost unnoticed by a world rejoicing over the cessation of hostilities in France and Belgium, Emperor Karl tried to effect a *de facto* abdication without definitively renouncing his right to the crown. Next day, November 12, a national assembly proclaimed the establishment of a democratic German Austrian republic.

The law of March 12, 1919, of the constituent assembly sitting in Vienna stated, as the resolution of November 12, 1918, of the provisional government had done: "German Austria is a constituent part of the German republic."

The constitution of the new German republic, adopted by the constituent assembly at Weimar on July 31 and signed by President Ebert on August 11, 1919, provided in Article 2: "The Reich territory consists of the territory of the German states. Other territories may be absorbed into the Reich by law if their populations, on the basis of self-determination, so desire"; and in Article 61: "German Austria shall receive, after its union with the German Reich, the right of participation in the Reichsrat with a number of votes proportionate to its population. Until then the representatives of German Austria shall have an advisory capacity."

To write into the German constitution a provision for the admission of Austria into the federal union of German states was a violation of Articles 80 and 434 of the Treaty of Versailles, already signed—a conscious and deliberate reëxpression of a hope already specifically denied by that treaty. According to Article 80, "Germany acknowledges and will respect strictly the independence of Austria, within the frontiers which may be fixed in a Treaty between that State and the Principal Allied and Associated Powers; she agrees that this independence shall be inalienable, except with the consent of the Council of the League of Nations." By Article 434 "Germany undertakes to recognize the full force of the Treaties of Peace . . . which may be concluded . . . with the Powers who fought on the side of Germany, . . . and to recognize the new states within their frontiers as there laid down."

Some of the Germans concerned may conceivably have hoped that the consent of the Council of the League might eventually be secured; for to them the voluntary union of the two German peoples appeared to be an obviously reasonable proposal. They seem to have been either naïvely unaware or obtusely oblivious of the fact—obvious enough to everyone else—that Germany's late enemies could not be indifferent to such a strengthening of Germany or to the reduction of the friendly new state of Czechoslovakia so nearly to the status of an enclave within Germany.

Sharply challenged by the Supreme Allied Council in Paris, the German government pointed out that Article 178 of its new constitution had stated that none of the terms of the Treaty of Versailles could be in any way affected by any provision of that constitution. Paragraph 2 of Article 61 of that constitution, it admitted, could therefore "have no validity" until the Council of the League of Nations should agree to a change in the political status of Austria. In the meantime, the German contention (note of September 5, 1919) was that the provision for the admission of Austrian representatives to the German Reichsrat did not infringe upon Austria's sovereignty or impair her independence, since she was still free to decide whether to send them.

The Supreme Allied Council accepted only the German admission that any part of the Weimar constitution which was contrary to any of the terms of the Versailles Treaty was therefore invalid. Baron von Lersner, chief of the German delegation to Versailles, had to sign, and both houses of the German national legislature had to accept, the Protocol of September 22, 1919, which declared the second paragraph of Article 61 of the German constitution of August 11, 1919, "null and void" and specified further that Austrian representatives could not be admitted to the German Reichsrat except as the Council of the League of Nations might consent to a change in the international status of Austria in conformity with Article 80 of the Treaty of Versailles.[12]

Austria was also compelled to renounce her intention to become a constituent part of the German republic. Article 88 of the Treaty of St.-Germain, signed September 10, 1919, stipulated: "The independence of Austria is inalienable otherwise than with the consent of the Council of the League of Nations. Consequently Austria undertakes in the absence of the consent of the said Council to abstain from any act which might directly or indirectly or by any means whatever compromise her independence, particularly, and until her admission to membership of the League of Nations, by participation in the affairs of another power."[13]

Even the word "German" had to be dropped from the name of the

[12] See M. Margaret Ball, *Post-war German-Austrian Relations: The Anschluss Movement, 1918-36* (London, 1937), chap. 2.

[13] See also Geneva Protocol No. 1, October 4, 1922, p. 275.

state, which had been calling itself "German Austria." In compliance
with the Treaty of St.-Germain it renamed itself the Republic of Austria
and repealed (October 21, 1919) that part of the law of March 12
which had called Austria a part of the German republic.

Universal compulsory military service, according to the treaty,
was to be abolished, and the Austrian army was not to exceed
thirty thousand men, including officers and depot troops, and was to
include no military or naval air forces or dirigibles. The manufacture
of arms and munitions was to be carried on in only one factory, which
was to be government owned and strictly supervised, and limited to
the actual needs of the "treaty" army. The importation of arms or munitions, or their manufacture for and exportation to foreign countries,
was forbidden.[14]

Like Germany, Austria also had to accept responsibility "for causing the loss and damage" to which the Allied and associated governments and their nationals had been subjected "as a consequence of the
war imposed upon them by the aggression of Austria-Hungary and
her allies," and to agree to make such reparation payments as it was
thought that she could.

The disarmament and reparation clauses of the treaties of St.-Ger-
main and the Trianon Palace (June 4, 1920, q.v. below) either duplicated or closely paralleled those of the Treaty of Versailles, already
discussed. Spokesmen for Austria had tried to get the republic recognized as a new nation which had never been at war and which could not
be in any way identified with Austria-Hungary or, presumably, be held
responsible for its acts or its obligations; but both Austria and Hungary
were treated as legal successors to the old Austro-Hungarian monarchy, rather than as new states.

To Italy Austria was compelled to cede that part of the Tyrol south
of the Brenner Pass (with a German population of 250,000), Trentino,
and Venetia Julia (Venezia Giulia), including Trieste and the Istrian
peninsula and its hinterland to which Fiume was eventually added.
Czechoslovakia claimed and was given the lands of the old kingdom
of Bohemia and Moravia, with a German population of three to three
and a half millions. Galicia went to Poland, and Czechoslovakia and
Poland quarreled over possession of Teschen. Burgenland, between the
new Austria and the new Hungary, was claimed by Austria on grounds
of nationality; but part of the province adhered to Hungary by
plebiscite. The former imperial provinces of Bosnia, Herzegovina,

---

[14] This prohibition was imperfectly enforced.

Croatia, and Slavonia (Austrian and Hungarian) were included in the new South Slav state of Yugoslavia.

Territorially, the new federal republic of Austria, reduced by the treaty to an area (32,369 square miles) smaller than Indiana with a population (about six and a half million) less than that of Illinois, was but a truncated remnant of the enormous empire of which it had once been the nucleus. It had, in fact, been the nucleus and nerve center of the empire too long to be able to adjust itself readily to the change. With the establishment of new national boundaries in what had once been Austria's vast Danubian trading area, trade barriers were quickly erected against her. Austrian industries were cut off from old markets and from raw materials, or found access to them much more difficult, as the succession states formed new trading ties or strove for economic self-sufficiency.

Vienna had been one of Europe's greatest capitals, the financial, educational, cultural, and administrative center of the empire. The loss of the empire left it crowded with former *rentiers*, officers, civil servants, government officials, teachers, and artists bereft of their occupations, dislodged from their formerly secure positions in life. It still housed a third of the people left to Austria; but its imposing public buildings and imperial palaces were "surplus"—relics and reminders of departed glory, economically unproductive.

Unable even to feed its people, yet forbidden by the peace treaties to seek salvation by reëstablishing its more ancient connection with Germany as a substitute for its centuries-old association with Bohemia and the Danubian states, the new Austria, politically independent in spite of itself, was always more or less dependent economically upon its former enemies. Vienna was fed, after a fashion, during the first postwar winter, by an American Relief Administration headed by Mr. Herbert Hoover. Unemployment, economic paralysis, deficit government financing, and inflation brought the government to the verge of bankruptcy and the value of the currency unit, the crown, almost to the vanishing point (approximately 1/17,000) by August, 1922.

On September 6, 1922, Austrian Chancellor Seipel appeared before the Council of the League of Nations to ask for an international loan. A large loan previously made (February, 1922) by Great Britain, France, Italy, and Czechoslovakia had already been consumed by current expenditures; the lenders, therefore, were unwilling to make another without a League of Nations guarantee and effective League control of Austrian assets and financial administration. So a control committee was set up and a commissioner general (Dr. A. R. Zimmerman) appointed by the Council of the League, to which they were to be responsible, to protect the financial interests of the lenders.

The powers took good care, also, of their political interests as they understood them. By the first of three protocols signed at Geneva on October 4, 1922, they agreed to respect the political independence, territorial integrity, and sovereignty of Austria and to seek no special or exclusive advantages for themselves. Austria, on her part, was required to undertake not only not to alienate her own independence but also to abstain from any negotiation or economic or financial engagement calculated directly or indirectly to compromise it, and not to grant to any state "a special regime or exclusive advantages calculated to threaten" it. On these conditions a new loan was made, which was to run until 1943.

Another League loan was necessary in 1923. Further inflation led to the introduction of a new currency unit, the schilling, in 1924 to replace the krone at the rate of 1 to 10,000. But in 1925 the budget was balanced, and the foreign controls were withdrawn in 1926.[15]

The question of Austria's national independence had twice been answered for her. She was not to be permitted to abandon it and become a constituent part of the German republic. The restoration of the Habsburg monarchy was also clearly impossible; her European neighbors would not permit it. Parliamentary government, however, was beset with political as well as social and economic problems. The strongest of the moderate "middle" parties upon which the republic would have had ultimately to rely for its maintenance on a democratic basis were the anticlerical Social Democrats led by Dr. Karl Renner, Otto Bauer, and Victor Adler, whose stronghold was Vienna, and the Christian Socialists, principally a peasants' agrarian and provincial party led by Monsignor Ignatz Seipel, in which the Catholic clerical influence was very strong.

Vienna, under progressive and enlightened gradualist socialist leadership, became world famous for its low-cost municipally owned apartment houses for workers and their families, municipal loans for building suburban homes, and many other socialized municipal services. Despite large expenditures, including its contribution of more than two-thirds of the national government's income, and despite its heavy taxes—which drove real-estate prices down—the municipal administration of Vienna was solvent while the federal government

---

[15] See further discussion of the Geneva Protocol No. 1 of October 4, 1922, however, in its connection with the German-Austrian *Anschluss* proposal of 1931, below, pp. 274-276.

was going bankrupt. But other sections of the population, and especially the Christian Socialists, were alarmed by the anticlericalism or the radicalism of the Social Democrats. The latter, on the other hand, never trusted the Christian Socialists as genuine friends either of democracy or of republicanism. The two parties never consistently gave the republic the benefit of their united support after the disruption of the coalition led by Dr. Renner (1919-1920).

Austria's strongest governments, therefore, such as Seipel's and (later) those of Dollfuss and Schuschnigg, were more or less authoritarian in character; and the self-confessed failure of political-party-parliamentary government was signalized by the appearance of the paramilitary *Schützbund* of the Social Democrats and the fascist *Heimwehr* of the clericals, which were frequently in conflict.

There were also extremist parties of the left and right—Communists who were never numerous enough seriously to menace the republic, and Pan-Germans whose voting strength in 1920 was only one-fourth that of the Christian Socialists and one-third that of the Social Democrats. After the National Socialists came into power in Germany, the Austrian Nazi party absorbed the Pan-Germans and soon became a real threat not only to the republic but to the independence of the national state.

Treaty of the Trianon Palace, with Hungary, June 4, 1920

The signing of a treaty of peace with Hungary was delayed until June 4, 1920. The Allies then had to deal with the third government Hungary had had since October, 1918. The war had not been unpopular in Hungary until it had clearly been lost; but as defeat became imminent in October, 1918, "peace" parties began to assert themselves, hoping by political revolution to appease the Allies and conciliate the non-Magyar national groups still subject to Hungary but ready to break away.

The only well-organized or cohesive group of politically liberal or democratic revolutionaries was the Social-Democratic party. The most prominent leader of the October revolution, however, was not a Social Democrat but a pacifist Magyar aristocrat, Count Michael Károlyi, who had at one time been interned in France but had been released to do what he could at home to bring the war to an end.

On October 25, 1918, Count Károlyi and his personal following secured the support of the Social Democrats and the politically liberal bourgeois group who called themselves the Radicals, in forming a

National Council. On October 30 the National Council declared itself
the national government, and Count Károlyi was named premier, still
nominally loyal to the Habsburg king. On November 16, after the
abdication of King Charles, a Hungarian People's Republic was proclaimed, with Károlyi still premier. On January 11, 1919, the National Council named him president of the republic.

The new government, deriving its most substantial support from
the Social Democrats, encouraged the rapid growth of trade unions,
even among government employees, and attempted some agrarian reforms looking toward peasant ownership of land, much of which
was still held in large estates by the magnates. But most of the reforms that it proposed, such as universal suffrage and a general election, were still only proposals when it fell. It had not long to live.
The Allies were not placated by the appearance of a democratic
government; Károlyi himself had signed an armistice at Belgrade
November 13 with General Franchet d'Esperey, commander of the
Allied expeditionary force operating from Salonika, yielding great
areas of former Hungarian territory—more than had been given up by
the imperial delegation in the armistice signed on the Italian front
November 3. His pacifist minister of war, having disarmed the soldiers
as fast as they came home, could do nothing to defend the new government against enemies foreign or domestic. The subject nationalities
paid no attention to offers of conciliation, but welcomed separation.
The conservatives were alarmed by the president's reform proposals,
and the proletariat turned to Béla Kun, who promised them more than
the president could.

So Hungary did what the Germans had talked so much about doing: "went communist," alleging the severity of the peace terms as a
reason. On March 21, 1919, Count Károlyi handed over the government, ostensibly to the proletariat, actually to Béla Kun, a Hungarian
Jew recently returned from prison camp in Russia with a forged passport and continuing Russian-communist support, subsidy, and supervision. The establishment of a Soviet republic was at once proclaimed,
with a mason named Alexander Garbai as president and Béla Kun—
appropriately—people's commissar for foreign affairs. The immediate
nationalization of the land and other national resources, of industry,
banks, trading, and property was announced—but not effected for
lack of personnel and planning. Production was soon halted. Peasants
refused to deliver foodstuffs and resented the requisitions levied to feed
the towns. Labor had to be drafted to work the socialized estates.
Rumanian troops moved in from Transylvania.

A reign of terror was instituted by the Communists in a ruthless and sanguinary attempt to liquidate all opposition at home, and an army was quickly raised and sent against the Czechs in Slovakia as well as against the Rumanian invaders. But Budapest was occupied and put under heavy requisition by Rumanian troops on August 3, 1919. Béla Kun had resigned and fled two days before and with most of his fellow commissars returned by a roundabout route to Russia.

Meanwhile, a counterrevolutionary movement had been organized in the French zone of occupation by Admiral Nicholas Horthy de Nágybanya, former commander of the Austro-Hungarian navy. This assumed more and more the character of a national government as it rallied the anticommunist forces and raised an army. When the Rumanian army withdrew, looting as it went, Admiral Horthy re-entered Budapest as commander of the armed forces of the nation, November 16, 1919. March 1, 1920, a new national assembly named him regent of Hungary.

White terror followed Red terror. The revolution was now at an end; yet the clock was not put back quite to 1914 or to 1918. The monarchy was restored, but the monarch was not. Twice in 1921, in April and October, the former king appeared in Hungary to reclaim the throne, but both times the regent refused to turn it over to him. The Allies would not have permitted a Habsburg restoration in any case, and required the Hungarian government, after Charles's second unsuccessful attempt to restore himself, to declare that he and his dynasty had forfeited the throne.

The Horthy regime was strongly nationalist in character but not politically liberal. The fact that Béla Kun and most of the other commissars of the short-lived Communist government were Jews served as pretext if not as reason for a policy of anti-Semitism. Half a million Jews, who had generally before the war supported the Magyar regime and contributed much to the economic and cultural life of the country, with little occasion to think of themselves as a people apart or as a minority, were made into one by being treated as one.[16] Strenuous efforts were made to Magyarize the other minorities—Germans, Rumanians, Slovaks, and South Slavs. Of the four premiers who held office during the twelve-year period following the signing of the peace treaty, three (Count Paul Teleki, July, 1920-April, 1921; Count Stephen Bethlen, 1921-1931; and Count Julius Károlyi, August,

---

[16] The Jews were between 6 and 7 percent of the population but were restricted to 5 percent of the enrollment in universities and technical schools. Their prewar percentage had been higher.

1931-September, 1932) were aristocrats. None pretended to have reconciled himself to the terms of the Treaty of the Trianon.

The terms of that treaty were similar to those that had been imposed upon Austria. Hungary lost more than two-thirds of her prewar territory and more than half of her population.

Disarmament and reparation clauses duplicated or closely paralleled those of the Treaty of St.-Germain. The separation from Austria and the dissolution of the dual monarchy and empire were recognized. Slovakia and Ruthenia had already been awarded by the Paris peace conference to Czechoslovakia, Transylvania to Rumania, and the South Slav provinces (as mentioned above) to Yugoslavia. Although these territorial transfers had been made principally on a national-ethnic basis and in accord with the wishes of non-Magyar majorities in the areas transferred, the mixing of populations characteristic of that region had been such that approximately half a million Magyars found themselves living as an alien minority in Yugoslavia, a million in Slovakia, and a million and a half in Transylvania.

Irredentism, a perennial source of trouble in modern Europe, was always especially notable, in the period between the wars, in Hungary. The idea of recovering "the lost brothers" by regaining possession of the lost provinces was kept alive by propaganda and did not lose its popular appeal. Those who cherished that idea listened the more readily on that account to the other revisionists when the 1918-1920 settlement began to break up twenty years later.

Treaty of Neuilly-sur-Seine, with Bulgaria, November 27, 1919 (Effective August 9, 1920)

Bulgaria had signed an alliance with the Central Powers September 6, 1915, declared war on Serbia October 12, 1915, and ridden with her allies into temporary possession of Macedonia and southern Dobruja when they overran Serbia and Rumania. However, she had contributed little to their common cause after those objectives had been attained (except that her continuance in the alliance had maintained their military contacts with Turkey). In September, 1918, attacked by an Allied expeditionary force based on Salonika, she collapsed and signed an unconditional armistice (September 29).

The Bulgarian government, like those of the other defeated nations, was faced at the moment of surrender with the threat of revolution. Alexander Stambolisky, peasant-born leader of the Agrarian party, who had been imprisoned throughout the war because of his outspoken opposition to it and had been released and sent to the Macedonian front only when its end was obviously at hand, returned to Sofia with a body of insurgent troops and compelled King Ferdinand to abdicate, October 3, in favor of his son, Prince Boris. Stambolisky became a member of the new cabinet in January and premier in October. He went to Paris and signed the Treaty of Neuilly in November, 1919, but was unable to establish himself with a homogeneous Agrarian majority until February, 1920. Ruling in the name of King Boris until 1923, he was overthrown by a military coup of the irredentist "Macedonian" party, hunted down, and shot.

Stambolisky had had enough influence with the Allies to secure the remission of three-fourths of the $438,000,000 reparation payments Bulgaria had promised by the Treaty of Neuilly to make over a period of sixty years. About the territorial terms of that treaty he had been able to do nothing. His government might argue—and did—that only King Ferdinand, whom it had dethroned, had been responsible for Bulgaria's participation in the war, and that its people ought not to be punished for Ferdinand's misdeeds. The Allies remembered how Bulgaria's entry into the war had doomed their Dardanelles-Gallipoli plan to failure, and how avidly and vindictively she had joined in the invasions of Serbia and Rumania. Yugoslavia was given several small but strategically valuable districts along her Bulgarian border in Macedonia. Rumania regained southern Dobruja, which she had seized in 1913 and lost in 1916. And western Thrace, through which Bulgaria had gained access—unsatisfactory, but better than none— to the Aegean Sea, had to be ceded to Greece. Three wars in six years had not got Bulgaria either Macedonia or Thrace, for which she had fought them; but the areas were still there—with some Bulgarians living in them—to tempt her to fight for them again at the first favorable opportunity.

The disarmament provisions of the Treaty of Neuilly were similar to those of the treaties of Versailles, St.-Germain, and the Trianon, Bulgaria's armed forces being limited to 33,000 including army, frontier guards, and gendarmerie. The required acceptance of responsibility for damage done to the Allies and to Allied peoples was exactly the same; and the constitution of the International Labor Organization was written into all four treaties in the same form.[17] In most other respects the Treaty of Neuilly followed fairly closely the pattern already set at St.-Germain and the Trianon.

[17] There were forty articles: Articles 387-427 of the Treaty of Versailles, 332-372 of the Treaty of St.-Germain, 315-355 of the Treaty of the Trianon, 249-289 of the Treaty of Neuilly.

Treaties of Sèvres (August 20, 1920) and Lausanne (July 24, 1923), with Turkey

Turkey continued the war only a month after Bulgaria dropped out. She had mobilized all her man power at the beginning and her national resources had been strained to the utmost, throughout, to keep her large armies on foot. Some stiffening in the form of German guns, munitions, and troops had been necessary all along, and whole Turkish armies had sometimes (as in Mesopotamia in 1916 and Palestine in 1917 and 1918) been commanded by German generals.[18]

Turkey had done the Central Powers valuable service by successfully defending the Dardanelles. Her reward, at Brest Litovsk three years later, had been permission to regain the territory she had lost to Russia and to annex Kars, Ardahan, and Batum. She had seriously threatened Egypt and the Suez Canal in 1914 and 1915 but had been pushed back into Palestine by December, 1917, when the British captured Jerusalem. In Mesopotamia the first British advance had been stopped and a British army compelled to surrender at Kut-el-Amara early in 1916. But a second and more methodical British campaign had retaken Kut and gone on to Bagdad by March 11, 1917.

In the autumn of 1918 the advance of Turkey's enemies was swift and her collapse was sudden. The defection of Bulgaria September 29 exposed Thrace and Constantinople. The British and imperial forces based on Bagdad moved on Mosul October 23-30; and those in Palestine swept northward through Syria, 360 miles to a point north of Aleppo, September 19 to October 31, when at Turkey's request an armistice was concluded.

Secret treaties concluded between the Allies during the war had anticipated that Turkey would lose all her European territory and all other inhabited by non-Turkish populations. It had been generally agreed among the Allies, in treaties made while the United States was still neutral and to which it had not been a party, that Russia was to take Constantinople, some land on both shores of the Bosporus and Dardanelles, the islands in the Sea of Marmora and two (Imbros and Tenedos) in the Aegean, and certain provinces south of the Caucasus including Erzurum and part of Kurdistan. France was to take Syria, Lebanon, and Adana, Italy the Dodecanese and Adalia, Britain Mesopotamia and Palestine.

After Brest Litovsk Russia was no longer one of the Allies and had

---

[18] Field Marshal von der Goltz in Mesopotamia, von Falkenhayn and Liman von Sanders in Palestine.

THE NEAR EAST
AFTER TREATY OF SEVRES — 1920

///// AWARDED TO GREECE
RETAKEN BY TURKEY 1922
•━━ OIL PIPE LINES
■ OIL FIELDS
✈ PRINCIPAL
AIR FIELDS

U. S. S. R.

CASPIAN SEA

ARABIAN SEA

PERSIAN GULF

Karachi

Kabul

AFGHAN.

Meshed

Isfahan

I R A N

Teheran

Tabriz

Kirkuk

Mosul

Baghdad

I R A Q

Basra

Abadan

SAUDI ARABIA

RED SEA

Astrakhan

Makhachkala

Baku

Batum

Rostov

Black Sea

Bucharest

ROMANIA

Belgrade

YUGOSLAVIA

BULGARIA

TO GREECE

GREECE

Smyrna

Istanbul

Ankara

T U R K E Y

MEDITERRANEAN

LEBANON

Tripoli

Haifa

SYRIA

Damascus

TRANS-
JORDAN

PALESTINE

SUEZ

Cairo

Alexandria

Luxor

EGYPT

LIBYA

renounced her claim on Constantinople, the Bosporus, and the Dardanelles. By the terms of the treaty signed at Sèvres August 10, 1920, Turkey retained Constantinople (soon renamed Istanbul) but had to agree to the internationalization and demilitarization of the Straits, and to admit an Allied army of occupation to the zone of the Straits. Nearly all of Thrace was ceded to Greece. Greece was to have also, for five years, the right to administer Smyrna and its hinterland in Asia Minor. Imbros and Tenedos were awarded to Greece (instead of to Russia). The Dodecanese islands and Rhodes were retained by Italy, although Greece also put forward a claim to the Dodecanese. All Turkey's ancient and attenuated claims to suzerainty over Egypt and the Sudan, Libya, Tunis, and Morocco, Mesopotamia, and Palestine were renounced in favor of the principal Allied powers. Turkey had to agree to grant independence to Armenia and autonomy to Kurdistan. Arabia had already, during the war, broken all ties with Turkey.

The Treaty of Sèvres was never ratified. The beaten and demoralized Turkish imperial government with an Allied army of occupation in the zone of the Straits was ready to ratify it, but Turkish nationalists were not. Some personal pressure was put on members of the old parliament to secure ratification, but that body permitted itself to be dissolved without ratifying. Meanwhile, a revolutionary republican government had already been set up at Ankara (Angora) under the leadership of Mustafa Kemal, a general with a well-established military reputation but an "unknown" in international political affairs, who had been elected president of both the national assembly and the new government, April 23, 1920.

The republic at once broke with the past by abolishing the sultanate and recognizing the loss of the former imperial territories of Syria, Palestine, Arabia, and Mesopotamia. It made a bid for the friendship of other Moslem peoples by deposing the sultan also from his old position as caliph or religious head of the Moslem world.

The first foreign power to recognize the new government was Soviet Russia. Turkey had already occupied Kars and Ardahan and now retained possession of them but returned Batum. Turkish troops quickly suppressed all counterrevolutionary movements, reconquered Armenia, expelled Italian troops from Adalia in southern Anatolia, and stopped a French advance into Cilicia. By midsummer of 1921, France and Italy were ready to deal separately with Mustafa Kemal's Turkey, but Britain was not yet willing to abandon the attempt to enforce the Treaty of Sèvres, and Greece was eager to collect her profit by further use of armed force if necessary.

Greek troops were already occupying Thrace and Smyrna. In July, 1921, a Greek army advanced into Anatolia, but with the help of French and Italian war supplies the Turks rallied and in September, 1922, drove the Greeks right out of Asia Minor, by way of Smyrna. In November, 1922, Istanbul (Constantinople) was occupied by Mustafa Kemal's troops, and the phantom government maintained there until then by the deposed sultan, Mohammed VI, was overthrown. Unable and unwilling to fight the victorious Turkish army for possession of the Straits, the Allies were compelled to negotiate a new treaty.

Peace with Turkey was finally made at Lausanne, Switzerland, July 24, 1923. As by the Treaty of Sèvres, Turkey gave up her claim to Syria, Palestine, Arabia, and Mesopotamia; but she regained Adalia, Cilicia, Smyrna, both shores of the Bosporus and Dardanelles, and eastern Thrace as far west as the Maritsa River. The Straits were to be demilitarized and kept open to the vessels of all nations; otherwise, Turkey became mistress in her own house by securing at last the renunciation of the "capitulations" by which foreigners had retained extraterritorial rights within that country and partial control of its tariff policies.[19] Under the supervision of a commission set up by the League of Nations, a rather remarkable exchange of populations between Greece and Turkey took place, Greeks being moved from Anatolia and eastern Thrace to Greece and Turkish nationals from Greece and western Thrace, with such protection of their property rights and such compensation for financial losses as could be afforded them. Italy still retained the Dodecanese islands, alleging that the nonratification of the Treaty of Sèvres had released her from an agreement to cede them to Greece. Britain retained Cyprus.

SUMMARY

The peace settlement of 1919-1920 was the result of the often imperfect reconciliation of divergent opinions and interests, achieving at best only a certain "equilibrium of dissatisfaction." President Wilson's Fourteen Points were neither entirely disregarded nor everywhere consistently applied. They were not in fact everywhere applicable or quite consistent, one with another; nor were the victors bound by any agreement to apply them in all settlements made. In general, the new map of Europe was more consistent with the prin-

---

[19] In 1936 the other signatories of the Treaty of Lausanne agreed to Turkey's refortification of the Straits.

ciples of nationality and self-determination than the old one had been. Irredentism was by no means eliminated from European affairs, but an attempt was made to reduce its incidence by conceding some of the more easily defensible geopolitical claims of at least some of the nations and providing treaty protection for national minorities.

The settlement was certainly more generous, forward-looking, and generally enlightened than the one which Germany and her allies had had in mind to impose if they had won the war. It was also more generous to the defeated nations and less of a spoilsman's peace than it presumably would have been without the moderating influence of the United States.

No effective world government was set up, but a promising step was taken in that direction with the creation of the League of Nations. The essential principle of collective security was at least clearly stated in the Covenant of the League, and some promising provisions were made for its implementation. Paper provision was also made in the Covenant for peaceful change, without which collective security could be maintained only by superior force, and without which the "sanctity of treaties" might become only a cloak to cover the perpetuation of injustice. The mandates system, substituted for the outright annexations contemplated by secret wartime treaties among the Allies, was based on a recognition of the principles of trusteeship and political tutelage, and promised to eliminate the worst abuses of the old imperialism.

The League of Nations, the Covenant of which was incorporated in the Treaty of Versailles but could be ratified by nations becoming League members without being parties to the Versailles Treaty, had a manifold task: (1) to administer that treaty and others of the general peace settlement, (2) to protect the settlement, (3) to promote peace and international coöperation. The first of those tasks it carried out creditably. It seems, now, ultimately to have failed in the second by concentrating too much upon it, especially during the first ten years, at the expense of the third. Dissidents demanded change and drew together for the purpose of compelling change by use of armed force if necessary. Failure to realize the League's potentialities as an instrument for peaceful change made the resort to armed force, or the threat of it, seem better justified than it was—especially to peoples who, aware of the imperfections of the settlement, had lost sight of their vital common interest in its maintenance against aggression.

PART II

Reconstruction

PART II

Reconstruction

CHAPTER 5

The League of Nations

Nothing had so sustained the spirit of the peoples through the years of war as the hope of a new and better world. Imperialists had hoped for conquests. The most single-sighted, narrow-minded, and myopic nationalists had hoped for immediate national advantage. Enlightened nationalists and all genuinely world-minded people had yearned for peace, hoped for freedom from the fear of war. How new would the better world be?[1]

President Wilson had been but one of many spokesmen of those whose hopes had centered upon what he had called "a general association of nations . . . for the purpose of affording mutual guarantees of political independence and territorial integrity to great and small states alike."[2]

How fully could those hopes be realized? How literally could they be translated into the provisions of the covenant which would be the written constitution of the new international organization? Would that organization be or become a federal world state or only an "association" or a league? Would it aim at eventual universality or permanently exclude the defeated nations or others its members considered unfit for membership? Would its original members, once freed from the compulsion of a cruel war against a common enemy, remember the crisis which had brought home to them the necessity of united action? Or would each remember only its own war efforts and immediate aims?

In the worst crises of the war itself, such as the antisubmarine warfare of 1917-1918 and the climactic land campaigns of 1918, the

[1] See Carl Becker, *How New Will the Better World Be?* (New York, 1944).
[2] Point XIV of the Fourteen Points.

armed forces of the Allies and the United States had fought together for self-preservation through mutual aid under a coördinated if not a perfectly unified command. In all nations, the war itself had stimulated an interest in world affairs and accustomed people to the idea of collective action by the nations. At the same time, the national patriotism also so greatly stimulated by the war made continued international coöperation more difficult when it again resolved itself, as it very generally did, into mere nationalism.

The new world, then, was clearly not to be a single, all-inclusive, unitary or federated world state or super-state. The nations were not ready in 1919 to pay the necessary price for it in surrender of sovereignty or assumption of obligations. The establishment of a voluntary league of national states, on the other hand, seemed historically logical, politically feasible, and necessary.

All known devices for the maintenance of peace in western Europe had ultimately failed. Nineteen-fourteen had again shown that. The most promising of those procedures, however, the ones which had most often been used successfully to deal with danger of imminent war, were the international conference and the established formulas for international conciliation. Two of the principal nations active in the making of the League were republics. Britain, Belgium, Norway, Sweden, and the Netherlands were parliamentary monarchies. Italy and Japan also had their parliaments. To all, the making of national law by a national legislative body was familiar. The idea of submission to the authority of a "parliament of man" was not.

The framers of the Covenant of the League deemed it wise to build upon whatever seemed solid of the foundation already laid, to use what seemed most useful of the prewar peace machinery with which they were already more or less familiar, inadequate though it had admittedly proved to be. So the Assembly of the League of Nations was made an annual international congress in which all member states were represented, not a world parliament representing peoples. The five great powers (France, Great Britain, Italy, Japan, and the United States) were to be permanently represented also, along with four others selected for short terms by the Assembly, in the Council of the League—another international conference meeting on call of its chairman whenever necessary. The Council, always organized and ready though not always in session, could and did meet several times a year, sometimes on very short notice. It was expected that most emergency decisions would be made in the council, which could meet quickly in a crisis, whereas the general long-term policies of the League would be determined in the annual meetings of the Assembly.

No league or federal union of states unequal in area, population, or power could be formed without some attempt to reconcile the theoretical equality of sovereign states with their actual inequality in size and strength and with the inequality of their prospective shares of the collective burden to be borne. Would it have been undemocratic to deny to any member of the league a voice exactly equal to that of any other member in the determination of league policy? Or would it be democratic to ask one of the great powers to assume a proportionately heavy share of the financial burden and other responsibilities of the league—including the danger of war to enforce or uphold league policy—but to content itself with one vote, equal in weight to the vote of the smallest, weakest, and possibly most irresponsible member state in the determination of that policy? The provisions of the League Covenant on this point were dictated by the necessity to compromise these conflicting views.

All member states were represented on a basis of theoretical equality in the Assembly of the League; the great powers held a preponderance of power in the Council as it was at first organized. Each state's financial contribution to the League was fixed by a formula based upon population, total wealth, volume of trade, and other factors. The United States would have made the largest contribution if it had joined the League; Great Britain paid more than any other nation that joined. The smallest powers paid least, and none objected that its payment was too small. Should those who paid the piper, then, call the tune? The League never found a really satisfactory answer to this question but seemed at first to have found a reasonably acceptable compromise solution for it, at a time when compromise was necessary because a formula fully acceptable to the great powers was sure to be unacceptable to the smaller ones.[3]

Conciliation

Although incidents which led to war, or which threatened to do so, had in modern times commanded most of the world's attention, in-

[3] The same question was still very much alive at the San Francisco conference of 1945 and the Paris peace conference in the late summer of 1946, and no better answer seemed yet to have been found for it. By the Bretton Woods agreements (July, 1944) for the establishment of an International Monetary Fund and an International Bank for Reconstruction and Development, each member nation was to have 250 votes, plus one for every $100,000 of its quota of the fund or, in the international bank, one for each share of stock it held.

numerable other disputes had gone almost unnoticed because they were settled peaceably by conciliation, with or without the mediation or good offices of governments not involved as principals. The organization of the League of Nations promised in 1919 greatly to facilitate the settlement of international disputes by conciliation, especially in the Council of the League, which could be made available at any time for discussion of a dispute not settled by direct negotiation, and by which a formula for agreement might be suggested. It was declared by Article 11 of the Covenant to be "the friendly right of each Member of the League to bring to the attention of the Assembly or of the Council any circumstance whatever affecting international relations which threatens to disturb international peace or the good understanding between nations on which peace depends." It was hoped that, by declaring "any war or threat of war" a matter of general concern, peace-loving nations could preserve the peace and prevent aggression by measures short of war.

Permanent Court of International Justice

One of the most promising features of the peace movement of the first ten years of the twentieth century had been the establishment of the Permanent Court of Arbitration at The Hague, following the Hague peace conference of 1899. Only the name and secretarial staff and the building, built by Andrew Carnegie, were really permanent. The court itself consisted only of a long panel of distinguished jurists, from which the judges who were to arbitrate had still to be selected by agreement between the parties after a difficulty had arisen. It was still necessary also to determine by negotiation, after a dispute had arisen, the exact scope of the questions to be submitted to the court and the principles on which it would recommend a settlement. The "court" could only recommend. Its arbitral awards were not judicial decisions and did not have the force of law. It had no means of enforcing them, and there was no international executive authority to enforce them. Nations might—and many did—by general arbitration treaties mutually agree beforehand to submit all disputes or all disputes in certain categories to arbitration by the court; but the actual submission of a dispute or the acceptance of an arbitral award was still voluntary. Russia and Japan, Italy and Turkey, and all the Balkan nations were involved in wars between 1900 and 1914 as if the Hague court had never existed. In the crisis of July, 1914, the suggestion that the Serbian-Austrian dispute be submitted to arbitration by the court was assented to by Serbia but brusquely rejected by Austria-Hungary, upon which Germany was unwilling to put pressure.

As subsequently proved to be the case with much of the peace-keeping machinery of the League of Nations, the Permanent Court of Arbitration at The Hague had failed to fulfill its principal mission primarily because the nations failed to use it when it was most needed. Would a stronger court, able to act more quickly, a really permanent one with greater powers and prestige, empowered to hand down actual judicial decisions based upon international law instead of mere recommendations based upon previous agreement in principle, have been appealed to when the court of arbitration had been ignored, and have succeeded where the old Hague court had failed? There seemed in 1919 to be good reason to hope so.

As authorized by Article 14 of the Covenant of the League, the Council of the League of Nations appointed an international committee of twelve jurists who drew up the statute of a Permanent Court of International Justice "competent to hear and determine any dispute of an international character which the parties thereto [might] submit to it," and also to "give an advisory opinion upon any dispute or question referred to it by the Council or by the Assembly." This statute, which was to be the charter of the so-called "World Court," was executed at Geneva on December 16, 1920, as a protocol of signature and came into effect in September, 1921, after its ratification by twenty-eight states. About sixty states, including Germany, eventually "joined the court" by signature and ratification of the protocol of signature of December 16, 1920.

It was the intention of the authors of the statute that the new tribunal should be more truly a permanent court than the old one at The Hague had been. Its eleven judges and four alternates, elected for nine-year terms by the Assembly of the League and eligible for reëlection, should be always available in annual sessions at The Hague or in extraordinary sessions upon call; and none of them could be dismissed unless he had, in the opinion of the others, ceased to fulfill the required conditions. The court's decisions were to be based upon international law and treaties and—in time—presumably upon its own judicial precedents, and were to be final, without appeal; and the court itself was to decide whether it had jurisdiction in a case in which its competence was questioned.

The jurisdiction of the court was to comprise "all cases which the parties refer[red] to it and all matters specially provided for in treaties and conventions in force." Article 36 of the statute provided further

that a member nation might, at its own option, declare its readiness
to "recognize as compulsory *ipso facto* and without special agreement, in relation to any other Member or State accepting the same
obligation, the jurisdiction of the Court in all or any of the classes of
legal disputes concerning: •

    (a) the interpretation of a treaty;

    (b) any question of international law;

    (c) the existence of any fact which, if established, would con-
        stitute a breach of an international obligation;

    (d) the nature or extent of the reparation to be made for the
        breach of an international obligation."

Approximately two-thirds of the states which joined the court by
signature and ratification of the protocol of signature (of December
16, 1920) accepted also the optional clause just quoted, conceding
to the court compulsory jurisdiction in the cases and circumstances
specified.

The new court could act more quickly and efficiently than the old
one and had more power and prestige. Its first ordinary session was
held June 15 to August 12, 1922. In its first six years it held six
regular and six extraordinary sessions and handed down ten decisions
and thirteen advisory opinions, all of which were accepted. It was
still available in the 1930's when the fabric of the peace was torn
apart, without reference to it, by a series of aggressions by the totalitarian powers.

The court could do nothing which the League could not or would
not do. It could not decide a question or a dispute which was not referred to it, and by its own early decision would not accept jurisdiction
in a cause involving a nation not a member of the League unless that
nation voluntarily recognized its competence in the case. The court
could not enforce its own decisions. It depended upon the League or
upon the member states for the mobilization of world opinion or the
maintenance of the principle of legality that would make enforcement
unnecessary. In brief, it rose and fell with the League.

The closeness of the court's connection with the League was a
primary reason for the refusal of the United States to join it. The
United States had always been a leader in the movement toward peace-
able settlement of international disputes, especially by arbitration, and
might logically have been expected to continue that leadership in the
formation and maintenance of the new court. A distinguished American, Elihu Root, was one of the authors of its statute, and there was

always one American judge.[4] The court, however, as a creature and agent of the League seemed to many Americans not to enjoy the independence they had learned to value in their own judiciary. The judges, though chosen for their individual qualities as accredited representatives of the legal systems of their homelands, not as political spokesmen for their national governments, were elected by the Assembly of the League, and their salaries and the expenses of the court were paid by the League.[5]

The giving of advisory opinions to the Council or Assembly of the League, when asked for them, was the function of the court to which most serious objection was raised in the United States. The first chief justice of the United States Supreme Court had declined President Washington's well-meant request for an advisory opinion as to the scope of his presidential powers in order to keep the docket clear for judicial action on cases brought before the court, and to preserve the court's independence from executive or administrative influence; and the separation of powers was a tradition still potent in American thought, however imperfectly observed in practice.

Every president of the United States from Harding to Franklin Roosevelt, inclusive, recommended that the Senate ratify the World Court protocol of signature. At last, in 1926, the necessary Senate majority was mustered for ratification subject to reservations as to United States participation in the election of judges and the financial maintenance of the court—and one stipulating that the court could not, without consent of the United States, entertain a request for an advisory opinion in any case in which the United States had or claimed an interest. To the nations already members of the court, the United States seemed here to be asking for a special privilege which other members did not have and were not then willing to concede. Three years later, through the mediation of Mr. Root, reservations acceptable to the members and not clearly incompatible with the Senate reservations of 1926 were presented to the Senate by President Hoover but were not accepted. Both of the principal party platforms of 1932 contained statements favorable to adherence to the court, but the proposal was not again voted upon until 1935, and then was voted down.[6]

[4] John Bassett Moore, Charles Evans Hughes, Frank B. Kellogg, Manley O. Hudson.
[5] Reasons for not joining the League are discussed below.
[6] See Chapter IV (Articles 92-96) of the Charter of the United Nations, and compare its International Court of Justice with the League's Permanent Court of International Justice. There are striking similarities.

Nonpolitical International Coöperation

The world of 1919 was already familiar with many forms of international organization and coöperation in nonpolitical fields, of which the International Postal Union was an outstanding example. The League of Nations perpetuated many such organizations and added many to their number, including the International Labor Office. Promising beginnings were made in the direction of intellectual and cultural exchanges, public health, and the world-wide promotion of social and economic welfare. In these fields the League did not fail, although here also its ultimate success depended upon the preservation of the peace, in which it did not ultimately succeed.

Parliamentary Procedures and Persuasion

The powers which created the League and gave it its original character were the United States and the comparatively democratic nations of western Europe. Their peoples were already familiar with the give-and-take, the frank discussion, and the reconciliation or compromise of conflicting interests and opposing views that are component parts of parliamentary procedure and the international conference. It was natural, therefore, and historically logical for such peoples to devise for the conduct of their international affairs an organization such as the League, which carried those familiar procedures into the meetings of its Council and Assembly, giving minorities and minor states alike their right to be heard, without quite depriving the major powers of the influence to which they thought their responsibilities entitled them.

Such an atmosphere would be congenial only to the representatives of comparatively democratic states. Good manners might for a time conceal the cynicism of the skeptic, but the boorish unbeliever—such as Dr. Goebbels—would be an obvious misfit from the moment of his appearance. No totalitarian state, maintaining itself by ruthless liquidation of dissent at home and by trading in its international relations upon other nations' known aversion to war, was ever—or could ever have been—at all at home in such an organization. Dictatorship is not a natural partner of democracy, and President Wilson's wartime appeal to his people to "make the world safe for democracy" had been based upon the stated presupposition that democracy was essentially peace-loving and dictatorship inherently aggressive and warlike. It was therefore natural and not surprising that the League did not invite Germany to membership until (rightly or wrongly) convinced of the democratic character and peace-mindedness of the Weimar republic, or that Hitler took the Third Reich out of the League after his henchmen had quickly demonstrated the incongruity of their appearance there. Japan and Italy withdrew from the League, as will be seen in subsequent chapters, only after having been reproved for acts of unprovoked aggression; but they had ceased to be useful members of the organization when they turned away from the paths of democracy and peace.[7]

Sanctions

The formation of the League of Nations was more a work of evolution than one of revolution. Its organization and procedures were based largely upon whatever was then most familiar and seemed to have been most useful of the international organizations and procedures of the recent past. At the very heart of the League, however, was the revolutionary principle of collective security, designed to give new and better expression to the basic concept of the old "concert of Europe" and eventually to take the place of the discredited theory of the "balance of power." The "balance of power" had worked, in fact, usually in negative fashion only, to prevent any European nation or group of nations from becoming powerful enough to dominate the rest. When one seemed to be about to do this, others combined against it. The result was, all too often, a precarious state of balance as in 1914 in which neither side could be, beforehand, either confident of victory or certain of defeat; and all too often one side or the other had risked defeat in hope of victory. Effective implementation of the principle of collective security, on the other hand, would have foredoomed to failure any lawless act of aggression by immediately bringing into play against it the overwhelming force of an organized world.

To function in such fashion, and to avoid the danger of setting up only a new balance of power, the League needed to be universal or as nearly so as possible, including in its membership all or nearly all important nations. To the extent that it failed at any time to do this, it was weakened.

It was presumed that the League could discipline its members and protect them against nonmembers by measures short of war, exerting

[7] See Article 4, Chapter II, of the Charter of the United Nations: "Membership in the United Nations is open to all other peace-loving states which accept the obligations contained in the present charter and which, in the judgment of the organization, are able and willing to carry out these obligations."

pressure by use of sanctions other than armed force. The first of these sanctions would be an informed and mobilized world opinion. President Wilson, who had appealed often and successfully to world opinion and had spoken often, eloquently and effectively, what was in men's hearts and minds, attached great weight in his own thinking to what Thomas Jefferson had called "a decent respect to the opinions of mankind."

World opinion proved in the event to be inadequate as a sanction, because the leaders of the aggressors despised it and took pains to see that their peoples were uninformed or misinformed about it or impervious to it. But appeals to it, especially by President Roosevelt in 1939, were wasted only on the aggressors; and much that was said in debate in the conferences of 1946 and 1947, spoken apparently for effect upon world opinion, revealed a continuing realization of its importance. Wisely directed by the United Nations, it might yet be a potent factor in world affairs.

Article 16 of the Covenant of the League provided a stiffer sanction, along with some of the clearest statements of the principle of collective security: "Should any Member of the League resort to war in disregard of its covenants under Articles 12, 13, or 15, it shall *ipso facto* be deemed to have committed an act of war against all other members of the League, which hereby undertake immediately to subject it to the severance of all trade or financial relations. . . . The Members of the League agree, further, that they will mutually support one another in the financial and economic measures which are taken under this Article . . . and . . . in resisting any special measures aimed at one of their number by the covenant-breaking State."

Here again the League needed to be all-inclusive, or nearly so. It is doubtful that any nation could long have withstood the pressure of a complete economic boycott; but any boycott, to be effective, would have needed to be both quick and complete. None such was ever imposed. When there was occasion for it, as against Japan in 1931, neither the United States nor Russia was a member of the League, and either would have been legally free to choose whether to join the League in imposing sanctions or merely to take over the trade of those who did. At the time of Italy's conquest of Ethiopia economic sanctions were given a half-hearted trial, but none of the nations nominally imposing them had the necessary legislation ready when it agreed to their imposition.[8]

[8] The Japanese-Manchurian incident is discussed below, pp. 452-461, and the Italian-Ethiopian affair on pp. 476-485.

The League's experience with economic sanctions does not seem to have proved them useless, but indicates quite clearly that the necessary legislation should have been ready and the chief executive of each member state empowered in advance, in certain specified circumstances and at the instance of the League, to impose and enforce them. To have been effective, they would have needed to be imposed immediately and simultaneously by all participating states; and all states but the offender should have participated. The members of the League seem to have lacked the necessary unity of purpose and realization of a fundamental community of interest to give economic sanctions a convincing trial.

It is an inherent weakness of the economic boycott as a sanction, however, that it is in fact a warlike act, a form of warfare, dependent for its effectiveness upon the actual or supposed readiness of its users to maintain it by use of armed force if the nation upon which it is imposed uses force to break it. That third and ultimate sanction the League of Nations did not effectively provide. Neither did it preclude it.

In Paragraph 3 of Article 16 of the Covenant, the members of the League agreed to "afford passage through their territory to the forces of any Members of the League who are coöperating to protect the covenants of the League," and in Paragraph 2 that the Council should "recommend to the several governments concerned what effective military, naval, or air force" they should so use. By Article 10 the members undertook "to respect and preserve as against external aggression the territorial integrity and existing political independence of all Members of the League," and that "in case of any aggression or in case of any threat or danger of such aggression" the Council should "advise upon the means" by which that obligation should be fulfilled. There was no international police force, however, and member states stopped short of contractual agreements to go to war or to use their armed forces to enforce a League decision or in defense of other member states.

How, then, was mutual security to be assured, particularly if the nations materially reduced their armaments as most of them wished to do, both for reasons of economy and in hope of easing the tensions they had so often seen aggravated by uncontrolled competition in armament? An answer to that question was proposed by the fourth Assembly of the League, September, 1923, in the form of a mutual assistance pact to be signed by the member states. Each state which signed that pact would, by so doing, have bound itself to come at once to the assistance of any other signatory state which might have been attacked. The Council of the League would have had to designate which of two or more powers at war was the aggressor, and would have had to make its own definition of what constituted aggression and its own tests to determine when or whether an act of aggression had been committed. Most of the nations to which the draft treaty was submitted (including the United States, Great Britain, Germany, and Russia, three of which were not members of the League) were unwilling to undertake such obligations without a treaty definition of aggression.

The fifth Assembly of the League attempted to define aggression in pragmatic fashion as a resort to war in violation of the undertakings contained in the Covenant of the League and in the Geneva Protocol of October 2, 1924, which made that definition. Any state at war was to be "presumed to be an aggressor," unless the League Council had by unanimous decision declared otherwise, if it had refused to submit the dispute to the procedure of pacific settlement provided by Articles 13 and 15 of the Covenant of the League, or to comply with a judicial decision or arbitral award or with a unanimous recommendation or report of the Council.

The Geneva Protocol of 1924 elaborated all the existing means of pacific settlement of disputes, including arbitration, and linked security with disarmament and with an agreement by every signatory state not to go to war against another "except in resistance to acts of aggression or when acting in agreement with the Council or the Assembly of the League of Nations in accordance with the provisions of the Covenant and of the . . . Protocol," and to "abstain from any act which might constitute a threat of aggression against another State."

The nub of the protocol, however, was in its Article 11, which would have bound the signatories to apply sanctions against an aggressor and to "come to the assistance of the State attacked or threatened." That was more than the nations were willing to promise beforehand to do. Here, as later in the application of economic sanctions (already mentioned) the necessary unity and hardihood of purpose were lacking. Nations hoped not again to have to fight a war to stop a war and punish an aggressor, and were not sure enough that a general treaty agreement to do precisely that would actually prevent war by forewarning the potential aggressor that he could not win.

"Only a League"

Ardent advocates of a federal world state have argued that the League of Nations failed and was foredoomed to failure because it was *only* a league of nations, a loose voluntary association of national states still intent upon keeping their sovereignty intact and motivated more by nationalism than by cosmopolitanism or good world citizenship. A federal union of the peoples, in which the individual citizen owed allegiance immediately to the world state, and in which the particularistic influence of nationalism would have been diminished by the strengthening of the "one world" attitude, might logically have been stronger than any league, and successful where the League was not. But something more than logic was involved.

It was somewhat as if Western civilization stood on its forward-most point of solid ground, looking out across the unknown toward the shining white cliffs of the security to be afforded by effective world government. What lay between? Only a chasm? If only a chasm, could it be crossed at one leap? Suppose one took the leap, fell short, and could not jump again? If it was a chasm that lay between, was it too wide to be bridged? Or was it only a morass, over which a causeway or a bridge could in time be built? There was material at hand with which to begin to build a causeway; the distance seemed too great to be bridged by a single span; and the nations were not ready to take the leap.

The crises of the war had brought home to millions of people in all the Allied countries and in the United States the necessity of united action. The war had also, however, stimulated the spirit of nationalism. For a time, one balanced the other; then, as the fear people had felt in wartime faded in their memories, the memory of the differences and irritations of the war and postwar periods was revived by new disputes over the terms and policies of peace. So the nations naturally interested in preserving the peace settlement began to draw apart long before those disposed to disrupt it began to draw together. The nations were only half-ready for international organization, and less than half-ready for a supernational world state.

The United States proved to be unready for either. Great care had been taken in the framing of the Covenant to meet the wishes of the United States, as it was generally considered highly desirable, if not indispensable, that it should be a member of whatever organization might then be formed. President Wilson had returned to Paris from a trip home during the peace conference with something tantamount to instructions to see to it that the Monroe Doctrine was recognized and that member states were assured of the right of withdrawal from the League. Both of those things were done, so that no known obstacles would stand in the way of the entrance of the United States into membership.

The insistence of the United States upon the right of withdrawal, and upon a plain statement of a legal and dignified withdrawal procedure, might well have been taken not only as an indication of a traditionally cautious attitude but as evidence that its people were willing to think of the League only as a league, not as a federal union or world state. The right of withdrawal from the federal union of the United States had been neither stated nor explicitly denied by its original constitution and had subsequently been claimed by "seceding" states and denied in practice only at the cost of civil war. In 1919, however, citizens of the United States were well accustomed to the ideas that their federal union was permanent, that no state had a right to secede, and that the federal government could, if necessary, coerce a state. Majority opinion seems to have been favorable in 1919 to entrance into a league, but not into anything comparable in centralization of authority with the American conception of a federal world state.

The United States and the League

The refusal of the United States to join the League was a serious blow to it. There seemed for fifteen years to be substantial reasons for considering it a going concern, even without the United States, and its eventual failure to keep the peace is not conclusive proof that a league of which the United States was not a member could not have kept the peace. Nor is it possible to answer definitively the hypothetical question whether a league including the United States would certainly have succeeded where one which did not include the United States did not succeed. It seems reasonable to suppose, however, that the prestige and prospects of the League would have been as much enhanced by the full participation of this country in its activities as they were hurt by its abstention.

Nations "joined the League" by ratifying the Treaty of Versailles, of which the Covenant of the League was Part I, or by ratifying the Covenant separately. Ratification was everywhere a vital step in the treaty-making process but was generally taken for granted when treaties were negotiated and signed. The United States was one country, though by no means the only one, in which ratification was not properly to be taken for granted. The treaty-making power is shared by the president and the Senate. The president or his authorized envoy plenipotentiary negotiates and signs treaties; the Treaty of Versailles had been signed by President Wilson; but the Senate was not legally bound to "honor the president's signature."[9]

The president knew that one-third plus one of the members of the United States Senate could prevent ratification by voting against it. He knew that ratification would be opposed by a determined group of senators, most of whom were Republicans, organized and led by Senator Henry Cabot Lodge, chairman of the Senate Committee on Foreign Relations. Knowing these things, he might well have won over or neutralized some of the opposition by taking to Paris with him more of the outstanding American advocates of international organization, such as Elihu Root or William Howard Taft.[10]

Relations between President Wilson and Senator Lodge, however, were already embittered. The sincerity and intellectual honesty of Lodge's opposition to "Wilson's League" have been seriously questioned. There seems to be little room left for doubt that his oppositional attitude was sensibly stiffened by personal animus and political partisanship. One wonders whether—and doubts that—Lodge would have had the grace to go and serve as a loyal or coöperative member of the delegation if Wilson had had the grace to ask him.

The president might also have sent the treaty to the Senate with a published message to the Senate and people of the United States, paraphrasing the letter which George Washington, as president of the Constitutional Convention of 1787, sent to the Congress with the draft of the new federal constitution which he advised the Congress and the states to adopt: Neither the treaty nor the Covenant it contained seemed perfect to any delegate or delegation, or would probably be perfectly satisfactory to any nation; but it was the best that that conference could do at the time; it was doubtful that that conference could do any better

---

[9] Reproachful remarks were made in Europe, often by men who should have known better, and probably sometimes by men who did, implying that the Senate had been guilty of a breach of faith in refusing to "honor the president's signature." Mr. John W. Davis, while United States ambassador to Great Britain, answered such criticism effectively by delivering a well-timed and well-publicized lecture on "The Treaty-Making Power in the United States."

[10] The chairman of the Senate Committee on Foreign Relations and the majority leaders or other outstanding members of Congress would also have been logical members of the peace delegation. Note that Senators Connally and Vandenberg were so sent and went loyally in a nonpartisan spirit as members of a bipartisan delegation to the 1945 San Francisco conference and to the United Nations sessions and Paris peace conference of 1946.

if it adjourned and later tried again, or that another conference could make a better treaty; the document contained provisions for amendment; and a careful weighing of the advantages probably to be derived from its acceptance against the apparent disadvantages of going on without it would reveal substantial reasons for accepting it.

President Wilson unfortunately sent no such persuasive or placatory message. He had been worn down almost to the point of exhaustion, and his nerves frayed to exasperation, by his labors at the conference and by the criticism of Clemenceau and other French nationalists, who had seemed to think, resentfully, that he had gone to Paris only to rob them of the fruits of their victory. Both Clemenceau and Lloyd George had looked upon him at Paris, as a result of the Republican victory in the congressional elections of 1918, as a "lame duck" leader. But he could not bring himself to believe that his people had repudiated him in that election, or that he could not successfully appeal to them to support him against the congressional leaders of the opposition. Neither could he contemplate with any degree of equanimity the further negotiation necessary to get any American reservations accepted by the other signatories, or think without dismay of the possibility that the Senate might so "water down" the Covenant with reservations that nothing real would be left of the League.[11]

With public opinion generally though by no means unanimously favorable to the League, it was good political tactics for the opposition to fight it not by direct attack but by offering reservations innocuous enough in appearance to be inoffensive to the average voter but real enough in substance to be unacceptable to the president. The maneuver was successful. President Wilson, touring the country in an attempt to

[11] In his published appeal to the voters October 24, 1918, President Wilson had said, in part: ". . . If you have approved of my leadership and wish me to continue to be your unembarrassed spokesman in affairs at home and abroad, I earnestly beg that you will express yourselves unmistakably to that effect by returning a Democratic majority to both the Senate and the House of Representatives. . . .

"I have no thought of suggesting that any political party is paramount in matters of patriotism. . . . I mean only that the difficulties and delicacies of our present task are of a sort that makes it imperatively necessary that the nation should give its undivided support to the government under a unified leadership, and that a Republican Congress would divide the leadership. . . .

"The return of a Republican majority to either house of the Congress would, moreover, be interpreted on the other side of the water as a repudiation of my leadership. . . . It is well understood there as well as here that Republican leaders desire not so much to support the President as to control him. . . .

"In ordinary times divided counsels can be endured without permanent hurt to the country. But these are not ordinary times. . . ."

Just before the president sailed for Europe, ex-President Theodore Roosevelt had issued a statement saying: "Our allies and our enemies and Mr. Wilson himself should all understand that Mr. Wilson has no authority whatever to speak for the American people at this time. His leadership has just been emphatically repudiated by them."

enlighten and arouse public opinion to such a point that the Senate minority would not dare defy it, and publicly predicting another world war a generation later if the motion to ratify should fail, suffered a physical collapse which crippled him permanently but increased his irascibility and hardened his determination not to compromise with his political enemies, whom he had come to look upon as spokesmen for the powers of darkness and evil. The two-thirds majority necessary for ratification with reservations was always ready; but, convinced that the reservations proposed would change the character of the League, rob it of its virtue, and make of it but a useless thing, the president instructed the senators who still accepted his leadership to vote against ratification with reservations. The vote, March 19, 1920, was forty-nine for ratification with reservations to thirty-five against. A change of seven votes would have made the difference between passage and failure of the motion.

Thirty-five votes in the Senate on March 19, 1920, prevented the United States from taking a vitally important step which a rather large majority of its people had been ready in 1919 to see it take, and for which probably a majority would still have voted in a plebiscite. But the constitution made no provision for such a national referendum, and no popular vote was ever taken. President Wilson spoke in 1920 of making that year's national election "a solemn referendum" on that question. Too many other issues were involved, however, and the League question was further obfuscated during the campaign by a published statement of more than thirty prominent Republican leaders, including William H. Taft, Charles E. Hughes, Elihu Root, Herbert Hoover, Henry L. Stimson, Butler of Columbia, and Lowell of Harvard —all known as advocates of international organization—that a vote for Harding would be a vote to "bring America into an effective league to preserve peace." Harding himself was very careful as a candidate not to say anything that might cost him the vote of either friend or foe of the League, and the outcome of the election was not an unequivocal expression of the people's will in that matter; but after his inauguration, as if he considered his election a mandate to that effect, he declared the issue dead.[12]

[12] Never having ratified the Treaty of Versailles, the United States made a separate peace with Germany by a congressional resolution signed by President Harding July 2, 1921, and in treaty form in Berlin by plenipotentiaries of the two countries August 5, 1921. The treaty was brief, consisting principally of an enumeration of the parts of the Treaty of Versailles (I, the League; II, Germany's boundaries; III, political clauses for Europe; IV, 2 to 8, China and Shantung) which the United States was not ratifying, and those (all the rest, including the terms concerning disarmament of Germany, reparation, and Germany's loss of her colonies) which it was.

The League was not dead, and the question need not have been considered closed. The United States could still have joined the League at any time; but only an ardent few went on insisting that it should. The will of the majority had been frustrated by a stubborn Senate minority—partly isolationist and partly only anti-Wilson, anti-Democrat, and anti-administration—but that frustration was not universally or long resented. Gradually through the twenties, and especially in the middle twenties, public opinion changed. That was a period of disillusionment about the war—its origins, principles, purposes, and results. An honest revisionist opinion, based upon convincing new evidence, spread among historians to the effect that Germany's share of original responsibility for the war had been less great than it had seemed in wartime to have been. A "debunking" school of pseudo-historical writing also developed, properly discounting the extravagances of wartime writing and public speaking but inculcating also an unhealthful attitude of skepticism as to all the nation's war aims and leaders.

Year after year revealed an increase in the number of those who saw abroad, especially in Europe, only a world full of "foreigners," of wickedness, and of greed, which seemed but little better—if indeed in any way better—than before a war had been fought to make a new one. Had they then only saved an old one? Could young men only win, and only old men keep? Had only an old men's peace, after all, been made possible by the young men's victory? Would it be ever so? If so, thought many, the United States should hold aloof. At almost any time from five to fifteen years after the Senate's rejection of the League Covenant, a consensus of majority American opinion would probably have been that the Senate minority had, as the founding fathers had foreseen and intended that it might, used its veto in the treaty-making process to prevent the taking of an unwise and ultimately costly step.

It has been smartly said of Americans that too few of them have read the minutes of the last meeting. It would perhaps be more pertinent to say that too many have read the minutes of only the last meeting. Their memories are short. It was given to only a steadily diminishing few during the first fifteen years of the twenty years' truce from 1919 to 1939 to remember the vital considerations of interest and of safety that had impelled the United States to go to war in 1917, or the alternative with which it had then been faced in the event of a German victory. Seeing only that they had gained nothing by participation in the war, people reasoned superficially that they had accomplished nothing. Not knowing what they might have lost by nonparticipation, they either did not ask themselves that question or foolishly assumed that they would have lost nothing.

Participation, then, according to such reasoning, must have been a grave mistake. Why had they made it? Quite clearly they must have been misled. President Wilson must have been pro-British all along, and have betrayed them as soon as possible after having been reëlected because he had "kept us out of war." Or the British and French had duped them by their clever use of propaganda and stories of atrocities. Or the munitions makers or the other money men had done it for their own nefarious purposes. Somewhere someone had blundered.

If it had been, then, so egregious an error for them to permit themselves to be involved in such a war, they would be incredibly stupid, surely, ever to repeat the blunder. If it had been unwise to go into a European war, how could it be other than unwise to risk involvement in another by going then into an international organization including so many nations recently at war, not knowing that they would not soon be at war again over some of their many quarrels, which again already seemed to so many Americans to be interminable, confusing—and remote?

On one point, if on one point only, Americans were essentially unanimous. They wanted no more of war. It is significant, and probably unfortunate, that so many of them thought of membership in the League of Nations not as their surest guarantee against another war but as a foreign entanglement which they feared might sometime involve them in another. They wanted only to stay out of trouble, and hoped to do that by staying away from areas where trouble was or seemed likely soon to be. They hoped to avoid involvement by avoiding international commitments and responsibilities.

Ancient and honorable tradition seemed to support the separatist argument. The first president of the United States had experienced serious difficulty in keeping the new nation from being involved, against its will and interest, in a European war as the ally of France, by the alliance which had been so useful, only a few years before, in its war for independence. Naturally, he had warned his countrymen against permanent alliances although not against temporary ones, and cautioned them against intervention in European international quarrels which were none of their concern. Washington was perhaps the most actual and practical statesman of his day. If he had lived in the twentieth century he would unquestionably have judged the policy of that day also according to his conception of contemporary circumstances, not those of a hundred or a hundred and twenty-five years before. But much of the wisdom in his farewell address was generally recognized as perennial and still pertinent; and membership in any league of nations, involving commitments as to policy, seemed too much like a permanent alliance to look good to those Americans who were not yet in any sense world-minded.

The United States had come into a new relationship with other nations more swiftly than many of its people realized. Their conception of its place in the world had not changed as rapidly as its actual position. Their traditional reluctance to permit their government to make commitments or to assume obligations in their name beforehand, to be made good by them in circumstances which could not be foreseen, made them cautious—even timid—about membership in the League.

If the American people had been convinced that the League of Nations was the only agency likely to be capable of keeping the world at peace, that it could and would do so if the United States were a member of it and not otherwise, they would very probably have pushed their government into it if the government had waited to be pushed. Unfortunately, they were not so convinced. Fearing instead that membership might involve them in a war which the League had failed to prevent and in which they might otherwise not have been involved, they sanctioned, after the fact, the senate minority's decision not to join. Having once gone into a war to end a war because they did not dare not to, they refused to go into a league to prevent another because they did not dare.

The United States coöperated in many ways with the League which it had not joined, and was careful not to hamper it in its efforts to keep the peace. In the first ten years it participated in more than forty League conferences, mostly nonpolitical. An American served on the League's commission of 1932, headed by Lord Lytton, to investigate and report upon the Manchurian incidents of 1931, although the United States could not be officially represented as a voting member in the League Council when it met to deal with that act of Japanese aggression. In 1934 the United States joined the League's International Labor Organization. More American coöperation with the League, not less, might have been foreseen if the League had continued to be active. Nothing that the United States could do as a nonmember, however, could ever counterbalance the loss the League sustained when the strongest of the states which made it failed to join it.

Abraham Lincoln's striking statement of the foremost question of his day—how any government not too strong for the liberties of its people could be strong enough to maintain itself—might have been paraphrased to fit the twentieth-century problem of world government. How could any international organization not too strong for the sovereignties of its member states and the national susceptibilities of their peoples be strong enough to maintain itself and effectively to implement the principle of collective security? The League of Nations proved to be at once too strong for the susceptibilities of citizens of the United States and not strong enough to police the recalcitrants and the insatiables. The price of peace would have been but a fraction of the cost of war; but the peoples who preferred peace were not ready to pay enough for it to keep it. They hoped that they could keep it without paying.[13]

[13] In January, 1947, addressing the twenty-first annual institute of the Cleveland (Ohio) Council on World Affairs, General Omar Bradley said: "Science has at last irrevocably stripped the American people of the treacherous notion that we can ever again find safety in the storm-cellars of isolationism. . . . There are no longer any safe hide-outs from the world. Unless we walk this earth in company with other men from other nations, any refuge that we seek alone will become our tomb. . . . Non-involvement in peace means certain involvement in war." (*Time,* January 20, 1947.)

CHAPTER 6

Quest of Security by Treaty Agreement

During the third decade of the century many nations sought security not only in association, as in the League of Nations, but in treaty agreements recognizing and in certain cases guaranteeing one another's boundaries, restricting offensive armaments, and reassuring one another by promising to settle their differences only by peaceful means.

The trend seemed promising. One of the ideological objectives of the war just fought, exaggerated in relative importance by the propagandists but not without weight or substance, had been the preservation of the sanctity of treaties. The history of war was a record of broken treaties, but the history of civilization recorded the acceptance by the nations of the concepts of legality, good faith, and scrupulous keeping of agreements. It did not then seem Utopian to suppose that treaties would be less lightly broken thereafter than theretofore.

War had bred pacifism of many kinds. Its horrors were fresh in men's minds. Those who every day learned something new about the enormity of its cost, which they could not yet compute, looked anxiously for some less costly and less hazardous provision for the security they still found themselves compelled to seek. Some were so horrified by the very thought of war that they convinced themselves emotionally that nothing could be worse. Some saw in it only such wickedness that they could not see how righteousness could be served or any good accomplished by such wrong and sinful means. Life, they thought, could not be saved by killing, or mankind be served by men acting so in anger. In hatred of evil they saw only—and deplored— hatred of the evildoer, a denial of the Christian doctrine of the brotherhood of man. Nothing that had to be fought for was to them worth

138

fighting for, and nothing of value could be preserved by destroying things of value. To those who reasoned thus, war was the antithesis of reason.

Money saving was another important consideration. The total cost of the war could never be computed, but its money cost to the United States had been estimated at between $40,000,000,000 and $45,000,000,000. The national debt had risen in 1919 to an unprecedented peak of approximately $26,500,000,000. In June, 1921, a budget bureau had been set up in the Treasury Department to prepare an annual statement of the federal government's income and expenditures; and although the wartime excess-profits tax and transportation taxes were soon removed and the surtax on incomes was reduced, taxpayers demanded not only the luxury of tax reduction but also the frugal reduction of the national debt. That involved retrenchment, expenditures less than income, and systematic debt retirement; and the advisability of spending less on naval armament, if security could be insured without it, seemed clearly indicated.[1]

Great Britain's budgetary problems were more serious. Of about twelve million adult workers, more than two millions were registered in 1921 as unable to find employment. Annual interest on the national debt, which before the war had been about £22,000,000, had mounted to £360,000,000. Wartime taxes could not be very much reduced, were called confiscatory by those upon whom they bore most heavily, and seemed to be pointing the way to socialization or to the redistribution of wealth by use of the taxing power of government. The United Kingdom, upon which most of the financial burden of the maintenance of the British navy always fell, could not go on interminably competing with the United States in a navy-building race.

Both Britain and the United States were, at the war's end, still engaged in extensive naval building programs too expensive to be continued unless under pressure of the direst danger. The United States Navy had not yet quite arrived at parity with the British but was growing at a rate that promised soon to surpass it. The two had lately fought together effectively as allies and seemed to be in no danger of again having to fight each other. Either country could without serious misgiving concede naval parity to the other. Neither, however, could well afford a naval armament race with Japan, despite the disparity in total resources. The Japanese government, although a parliamentary monarchy in form, was sufficiently totalitarian in character to be able to

---

[1] By June 30, 1931, the national debt had been reduced by a little more than one-third, to $14,185,000,000. Since then it has increased enormously.

allocate to its army and navy whatever portion of the national resources it might decide. To fight Japan on equal terms in the western reaches of the Pacific, any American or European power would have needed a navy several times as strong as hers. Neither the United States nor Britain had then such an overpowering navy, or cared to contemplate the cost of building one in such unequal competition with Japan. It was doubtful that their combined fleets would have been adequate to such a task; and there was no possibility of their combining while Britain was Japan's ally.

In a war between Japan and the United States, involving those two nations only, Great Britain would not have been bound by the terms of that treaty of alliance to aid Japan, but unless she had denounced the treaty she could not consistently have aided the United States. Neither Canada nor Australia was legally bound by Great Britain's Japanese alliance, but neither could be indifferent to it. Australia, closer to Japan, fearful of Japanese infiltration, with restrictions on Japanese immigration and ownership of land, had been protected in a fashion by the alliance and would want to be assured of protection in some other form if that were lost. Canada, adjacent to the United States and conscious of a close community of interest with her friendly southern neighbor, as well as of similar Oriental immigration problems along the Pacific coast, preferred that the United Kingdom and the empire should also be free, in any crisis, to identify their policy with that of the United States. Both commonwealths made their position known to Britain at an imperial conference of premiers not very long before the Washington conference of 1921.

Although there was no imminent threat of actual war, and talk of "the next war" as one between whites and Japanese in the western Pacific area seemed rather irresponsible, the danger was not all imaginary. Tension which had developed between the United States and Japan before the war over federal restriction of Japanese immigration and Pacific state restriction of the immigrant's opportunity to acquire land had been only slightly eased by the Japanese government's agreement to restrict emigration to the United States, or by American explanation of state rights.[2] American apprehension had been aroused in 1915 by Japan's outrageous Twenty-One Demands upon China, and Japan's resentment of American protests had been only partially allayed by the ambiguous Lansing-Ishii agreement of

[2] The federal Supreme Court subsequently sustained the California land laws in question, and the Immigration Act of 1924 ended Japanese immigration.

November 2, 1917, that Japan had "special interests" in China due to territorial propinquity.[3]

The United States had not been happy over the confirmation at the Paris peace conference of Japan's occupation of the Pacific islands formerly German, north of the equator, or content with the substitution of the mandate system for outright annexation. American opinion had not been appeased by the concession of cable rights on Yap, the only island for which the United States had asked. President Wilson had tried but failed at Paris to restore Shantung to China, and the United States had never approved or ratified, even in its separate peace with Germany, the treaty clauses which sanctioned Japan's continued occupation of it. Under guise of what she called a Japanese Monroe Doctrine for eastern Asia Japan had sought persistently to exclude American trade from all areas in which her own influence was strong. The United States was justifiably uneasy over the attitude and conduct of Japan in China and Siberia. In Siberia a Japanese occupation force was still being maintained, although United States troops had been withdrawn from that area in January, 1920.

THE WASHINGTON CONFERENCE, NOVEMBER 12, 1921-FEBRUARY 6, 1922

There was indeed no dearth of matter for the agenda of a conference much broader in its scope than the one on reduction of naval expenditure by mutual agreement which had been suggested by the Borah resolution adopted by the Senate on May 26 and by the House of Representatives on June 29, 1921. Such a conference met in Washington, on invitation by the United States, November 12, 1921—three years and a day after the signing of the European armistice at Compiègne—to discuss the limitation of naval armament and current problems of the western Pacific and eastern Asia.

Five-Power Naval Limitation Treaty, Signed February 6, 1922, Proclaimed August 21, 1923

Realizing that no state with the possible exception of his own would probably be ready to give up any substantial advantage it had gained or agree to any material diminution of its relative naval strength, the American Secretary of State Charles Evans Hughes opened the discussion of naval limitation at Washington in November, 1921, by

[3] The agreement at the same time reaffirmed the "open door" and the independence and territorial integrity of China.

proposing in effect that Great Britain concede to the United States the naval parity which it had already virtually attained; that Japan, which then had a navy a little less than two-thirds as large as that of the United States or Britain, should remain in that relative position for the term of the treaty; that for a period of ten years no further construction of capital ships should be begun; and that certain designated ships already built or under construction be scrapped by all three to bring them down to an agreed maximum of capital ship tonnage. The ratio he proposed was 5:5:3 for Britain, the United States, and Japan, and 1:67 each for France and Italy.

Endless arguments as to length of coastline to be defended, number and distribution of bases and distances between them, tonnages, gun power, cruising ranges, the proper balance between categories, and the direction from which an attack was feared would have followed if anyone at that conference had tried to assign offhand to any nation a navy "adequate" to its needs. Mr. Hughes found it practical, therefore, to proceed as if he had assumed that what each nation then had was adequate, and to propose a "naval holiday" that, if observed in good faith, would not materially affect the existing relative strengths of the navies concerned.

Similar complications would have ensued if anyone had attempted then to measure or to judge the strength of a navy by any elaborate mathematical formula including gun power, cruising ranges, and ships in all categories. It was less accurate or scientific but easier and diplomatically more practical simply to count first-class battleships and accept the number of such ships in a navy as the measure of its strength for purposes of comparison and limitation, as was done.

The size of capital ships was limited to 35,000 tons, aircraft carriers to 27,000, and other war vessels such as cruisers to 10,000 tons. Capital-ship guns were restricted to a caliber of sixteen inches, others eight. Noncombatant ships such as transports were not made subject to limitation; but no preparation was to be made in merchant ships in time of peace for the installation of warlike armaments for the purpose of converting such ships into vessels of war.

The treaty was to remain in force until December 31, 1936, or longer; i.e., for two years after notification of its termination, which any one of the contracting parties might give the others after December 31, 1934.[4]

[4] Japan notified the United States well ahead of time, on September 18, 1934, that she would refuse to be bound by the treaty beyond 1936. The planning of two giant battleships, *Musashi* and *Yamato,* of 63,000 tons each, with 18.1-inch guns, was begun in 1934. Keels were laid down in 1937.

By the same treaty the United States, the British Empire, and Japan agreed to maintain the *status quo* with regard to fortifications and naval bases in the Pacific. More specifically, the United States was to build no new naval bases or fortifications; nor was she to increase the existing naval facilities on her Pacific islands except (1) those adjacent to the coast of the United States, Alaska, and the Panama Canal Zone, not including the Aleutian Islands, and (2) the Hawaiian Islands.

The British Empire was not to fortify or increase the naval facilities of Hong Kong or other British insular possessions in the Pacific, east of the meridian of 110° east longitude, except (1) those adjacent to the coast of Canada, (2) the commonwealth of Australia, and (3) New Zealand. (Singapore is west of the 110th meridian.)

Japan was not to add to the existing fortifications or naval facilities of the Kurile or Bonin Islands, Amami-Oshima (an island in the Ryukyus, northeast of Okinawa), the Loochoo islands, Formosa, the Pescadores, or any insular territories or possessions in the Pacific she might subsequently acquire. (Japan was not legally free to fortify the mandated islands or to build naval bases on them, but never permitted the inspections which might have determined whether she was doing so.)

Pacific Four-Power Treaty, in Force August 17, 1923

Also at the Washington conference of 1921 a treaty of mutual recognition was signed, December 13, by representatives of the United States, the British Empire, France, and Japan. Ratification was completed August 17, 1923. The parties agreed as between themselves for a period of ten years, and after that indefinitely unless one of them should exercise its right to terminate the treaty upon twelve months' notice, to "respect their rights in respect to their insular possessions and insular dominions in the region of the Pacific Ocean."

The four parties agreed further that, if there should develop between any of them a controversy arising out of any Pacific question not satisfactorily settled by diplomacy which seemed likely to disturb friendly relations between them, they should invite the others to a conference, to which the whole subject would be referred "for consideration and adjustment." If the rights of any of them should be threatened by the aggressive action of any other power, the parties were to "communicate with one another fully and frankly in order to arrive at an understanding as to the most efficient measures to be taken, jointly or separately, to meet the exigencies of the particular situation." The United States was careful to stipulate by reservation that its ratification was not to be deemed an assent to the mandates granted in the Pacific under the Treaty of Versailles.

By ratification of the Four-Power Treaty, August 17, 1923, the Anglo-Japanese alliance, last renewed July 13, 1911, was terminated.

Noxious Gas and Submarines

All nations were invited to adhere to certain treaties supplementary to the five-power naval limitation agreement, which prohibited the use of poison gas in warfare and restricted the use of submarines as blockade weapons. Great Britain, which had suffered most from it, proposed that the use of the submarine be simply forbidden. American public opinion at that time would have supported the prohibition; but France, which called the submarine a defensive weapon, refused to consider its abolition, demanded a U-boat tonnage half again as great as that proposed by Secretary Hughes for the United States or Britain, and prevented the imposition of any tonnage limitation in that category. Great Britain then rejected the idea of any limitation of antisubmarine warcraft.[5]

Rules adopted on motion of Elihu Root to govern the use of the submarine as a destroyer of commerce were reminiscent of the position taken by the United States in its arguments with Germany from 1914 to 1917. The legal requirement of visit and search was restated and reaffirmed, and belligerent submarines were denied exemption from them. It was recognized that the submarine could not be fully effective as a blockader without violation of those rules. But the makers of the treaty asked others to join them in declaring that the use of the submarine as a commerce destroyer without visit and search was an act of piracy, and that the prohibition of such use should be accepted by the nations as international law.

Nine-Power Treaty Concerning China, Signed February 6, 1922, Proclaimed August 5, 1925[6]

Nine powers—the United States, Belgium, the British Empire, China, France, Italy, Japan, the Netherlands, and Portugal—signed

[5] France did not ratify the treaty, but on November 6, 1936, both France and Italy deposited in London their instruments of ratification of Part IV of the London naval treaty of 1930, which would have required submarines to conform to the rules of international law to which surface vessels were subject.
[6] France did not ratify until July 20, 1925.

in Washington on February 6, 1922, a treaty essentially embodying four resolutions introduced by Mr. Root, in line with traditional American policy concerning China. The contracting powers, other than China, agreed:

1. To respect the sovereignty, the independence, and the territorial and administrative integrity of China.
2. To provide the fullest and most unembarrassed opportunity to China to develop and maintain for herself an effective and stable government.
3. To use their influence for the purpose of effectually establishing and maintaining the principle of equal opportunity for the commerce and industry of all nations throughout the territory of China.
4. To refrain from taking advantage of conditions in China in order to seek special rights or privileges which would abridge the rights of subjects or citizens of friendly states, and from countenancing action inimical to the security of such states.

The contracting powers other than China further bound themselves not to support any agreement between their respective nationals designed to create spheres of influence or exclusive opportunities in China, and China promised not to discriminate or permit discrimination against the nationals of any of them in the use of the railways.

The powers further agreed that whenever a situation arose which, in the opinion of any one of them, involved the application of the stipulations of the treaty and rendered desirable the discussion of such application, there should at once be "full and frank" communication between them.[7]

Other powers which had governments recognized by the signatory powers and which then had treaty relations with China were to be invited by the United States to adhere to the treaty.[8]

A supplementary nine-power treaty concerning China permitted her some upward revision of her tariff, and a resolution was adopted providing for the creation of a commission to study the question of the continuance or abandonment of extraterritoriality. Such measures promised to give some substance to the general assurance that China was at last to be given an opportunity to assume control of her own affairs as fast as her government could show the necessary stability.

No such assurance could have any real meaning with the Japanese still in Shantung. So, largely through American and British mediation, a separate agreement was made between China and Japan that the

[7] Japan seems to have violated this clause in 1931 and thenceforth, as well as the other terms of the treaty and its whole sense and meaning.
[8] The Soviet Russian government was not then so recognized.

Japanese troops and police should be withdrawn, the former German leasehold returned to China, and Japanese railway and industrial interests bought out by Chinese.

China fared better this time than at Versailles; and internationally minded Americans drew what comfort they could from the thought that abstention from membership in the League of Nations did not necessarily mean self-seclusion from world affairs.

FURTHER LIMITATION OF ARMAMENT
Geneva, 1927

The five-power naval limitation treaty signed in Washington February 6, 1922, effective August 21, 1923, limited only the sizes of capital ships, carriers, heavy cruisers, and guns, and the numbers of capital ships. It also ended new battleship building except for regulated replacement until December 31, 1931. In 1927 President Coolidge invited the signatories of the Washington treaty to meet again in Geneva to discuss limitation of warships in other categories, such as cruisers, destroyers, and submarines. France and Italy, sensitive especially about submarines, declined even to send delegates. Great Britain, which had already conceded to the United States nominal parity in capital ships, was too apprehensive about the special naval problems of its extended overseas empire to be ready yet to agree to parity in global tonnage or in all categories. It was especially difficult to reconcile British and American views as to cruiser strength. After months of discussion the conference adjourned without having reached agreement.

London, 1930

In 1929 President Hoover and Prime Minister MacDonald tried again. A new conference met in London in 1930, attended by all five signatories of the Washington naval limitation treaty. Here the United States and Great Britain agreed to approximate general naval parity as between themselves, with the understanding that each could build more than the other of the type of cruisers it thought it most needed. Japan was authorized to build up to the same total tonnage in destroyers (150,000) and submarines (52,700) as Great Britain and the United States, and her capital-ship quota was slightly increased over the three-to-five ratio agreed upon at Washington. The ten-year capital-ship building "holiday" was extended through 1936.

Nothing effective was done, however, to reduce any one of those navies. The nations merely accepted certain mutual limitations upon new construction and replacement so as not to disturb too seriously the existing state of balance between them. That "state of balance" was believed to be such as would make it impossible for any one of them to attack another successfully by sea but would not reduce the naval strength of any one to such a point that it could not defend itself at sea.

As to the use of submarines, the following were "accepted as established rules of International Law:

"(1) In their action with regard to merchant ships, submarines must conform to the rules of international law to which surface vessels are subject.

"(2) In particular, . . . a warship, whether surface vessel or submarine, may not sink . . . a merchant vessel without having first placed passengers, crew, and ship's papers in a place of safety. For this purpose the ship's boats are not regarded as a place of safety unless the safety of the passengers and crew is assured. . . ."

All other powers were invited to express their consent to the above rules, and that part of the treaty was to "remain in force without limit of time."

Except the tonnage limitation of 27,000 tons for an aircraft carrier imposed by the Washington five-power naval treaty, nothing had been done by international agreement to restrict the development of naval air power. Only a few forward-looking men had accurately estimated its still unrealized possibilities. Others were only sufficiently cognizant of the new weapon to be wary of long-term limitation in a period of revolutionary changes.

For France, with Mussolini's Italy as a neighbor, both the fear of attack and the problem of defense were more serious. Italy, which the Five-Power Treaty had put on the same footing as France as to capital ships, now demanded parity with France as to submarines also. As France saw it, parity would really mean superiority for Italy in the Mediterranean, as France had her Atlantic and Channel coasts also to defend. She would therefore concede what Italy demanded only if Britain would underwrite the *status quo* in the western Mediterranean as she and others had already underwritten the Franco-German frontier at Locarno.[9] That was more than Britain was prepared to do unless the United States would reinsure her by entering into a consultative pact for the implementation of the Pact of Paris;

[9] Discussed below, pp. 151-155.

and the United States was unwilling to do that.[10] So neither France nor Italy accepted or was bound by the naval limitation treaty signed by the other three naval powers at London April 22, 1930.

Even such limitation on new naval construction as was accepted by the parties to the London treaty was not unconditional. By what was called colloquially an "escalator clause" it was agreed that if any of the signatories, finding its security threatened by naval construction by a power which was not a party to the treaty, should consider it necessary to increase its own construction to keep pace, it might do so; but if it did, it should inform the other signatories, which would then be free to make proportionate increases in the category or categories specified.

The failure of the principal naval powers to find security by treaty limitation of new naval construction served by 1930 to light up the fact that such agreements would never be adequate or reassuring unless they covered all offensive armament and included all the stronger military and naval powers. Something much more comprehensive was needed, something that could be enforced against a nation which evaded or violated its agreements.

Advocates of disarmament still thought that it would promote peace by bringing a feeling of security. Others argued that only some previous provision for security would make disarmament psychologically or practically possible. This was the setting for a League of Nations effort from 1932 to 1934 to do in the direction of general disarmament what the naval powers interested in the Pacific had only partially succeeded in doing among themselves.

Geneva, 1932-1934

The idea of the general limitation of armaments was not new. The Treaty of Versailles had, in Part V, prefaced its provisions for the disarmament of Germany with a statement that that requirement was being laid down "in order to render possible the initiation of a general limitation of the armaments of all nations." By Article 8 of the Covenant, the members of the League of Nations had "recognized" that the maintenance of peace required "the reduction of national armaments to the lowest point consistent with national safety and the enforcement by common action of international obligations." The same article had stated further that, "taking account of the geographical situation and circumstances of each State," the Council

[10] The Pact of Paris is also discussed below, pp. 155-156.

should "formulate plans for such reduction for the consideration and action of the several governments," which were not to exceed the limits of armaments therein to be fixed after having once adopted them.

Prompted by the sixth Assembly of the League, 1925, the Council set up a preparatory commission to formulate certain general proposals for reduction or limitation of armaments. After five years of intermittent effort, the preparatory commission had only a rough draft of a treaty ready for submission to the world's first general disarmament conference when it met at Geneva February 2, 1932. The discussions continued through four sessions, alternating with periods of negotiation through the regular diplomatic channels, until June 11, 1934. About sixty states were represented, including the United States, Russia, and Germany.[11]

This conference did not disarm anyone because, although everyone was interested in disarming everyone else, no nation could convince another that it itself was ready to disarm. The Union of Soviet Socialist Republics, for example, was relatively an unarmed state at the time. It took consistently at the conference the apparently unequivocal position which its representative, Mr. Litvinov, had taken in 1927 in the preparatory commission: The way to disarm was to disarm; his government, he said, would give serious consideration to any reasonable proposal for progressive, but eventually general and total, disarmament. But the fear and suspicion which all too often grow into hatred, which in turn so often produces wars, sat upon the neck of every delegate, as at so many futile conferences. Hagridden by their fears, most of the other nations were especially suspicious of Soviet Russia and skeptical of the sincerity of the Litvinov proposals.

Great Britain, with a very small peacetime army, submitted reasonable proposals for the reduction of continental armies, but had just come away from a naval limitation conference which left her naval superiority in European waters unchallenged and authorized an increase in her naval strength if it should be challenged. The United States suggested the abolition of "offensive" weapons such as mobile siege guns and long-range bombing planes. However, with soldiers' and sailors' pay and production and maintenance costs much higher in monetary terms than those of the European nations or Japan, it was unwilling to consent to any overall limitation of expenditures on military

---

[11] Russia did not become a member of the League until September, 1934. Germany did not give notice of withdrawal from it until October 19, 1933.

or naval establishments. Neither the United States nor Britain was willing to furnish a contingent for an international police force to defend a nation which might, with that assurance of security, have disarmed.

The German governments with which the conference had to deal were the ministries of Chancellor Heinrich Brüning until May 29, 1932, Franz von Papen from June to November of that year, Kurt von Schleicher from December, 1932, through January, 1933, and Adolf Hitler thereafter. Konstantin von Neurath was foreign minister for all of the three last named. He was an able veteran in the Foreign Office service and had been ambassador to Italy in 1921 and to Great Britain in 1930, but was not helpful to the conference. The German delegates must have been aware of their country's numerous evasions of the Treaty of Versailles and by some sort of paranoid "projection" have taken it for granted that others would evade in the same fashion, if they could, whatever agreements they might make. Familiar for years with armed police reserves, paramilitary party troops, and *Einwohnerwehr* (militia), they insisted that trained reserves and organized police forces must be taken into consideration and counted when determining the strength of any nation's army.

The Germans stood fast throughout the conference on two points, steadily maintaining (1) that the declaration of an intention to disarm, written into the Treaty of Versailles as a preface to Part V,[12] was a contractual obligation which the signatories were legally and morally bound to honor and (2) that failure of the other signatories to keep their contract had freed Germany from any legal or moral obligation to keep hers. She considered herself free, therefore, to negotiate on equal terms in the matter, and demanded that the others recognize her complete "equality of right" as to armament, including her right to rearm up to their level if they did not disarm. This "right" had been conceded to Germany by the other principal powers before Hitler became chancellor, although he and his party always claimed credit for having regained for Germany the general recognition of her *Ebenbürtigkeit* (status, by birth, equal to the best; inferiority to none) among the nations.

Meanwhile, the steadily increasing truculence of Hitler's public statements and the habitual use of a war vocabulary by other Nazi propagandists had alarmed the French and served only to strengthen their insistence that security must precede disarmament. France had proposed an international armed force, to be available at any time to enforce decisions of the international authority and to stop aggression. With some such protection, the French argued, the nations could

[12] Quoted above, p. 96.

afford to weaken their national defenses. Without it, they dared not.

Rightly or wrongly, however, France also was feared, and her motives were not universally recognized as unselfish or above suspicion. Ever since 1918 she had maintained the largest standing army in Europe, had cultivated the friendship of Czechoslovakia and Poland, and had helped them arm themselves against any revisionist movement that Germany might think of making. Did she have in mind that the principal component of the international police force which she advocated should be French, the whole commanded by a French generalissimo and staff, the other contingents thus involving their peoples automatically as allies of France in any warlike action of the international armed force under French direction? In the perpetual enforcement of the Treaty of Versailles against Germany, for example, for the benefit of France? Would France ever find security except in something which to other Europeans would look more like supremacy in Europe?

The conference adjourned in June, 1933, but was to reconvene October 16. Discussions were continuing between the interested governments when, two days before the delegates were scheduled to reassemble in Geneva, the German foreign minister, Baron von Neurath, notified Mr. Arthur Henderson, the president of the conference, by telegraph that Germany would not attend the session and was withdrawing from the conference. It had become clear, he said, that the conference would not "fulfill what was its sole function, namely, general disarmament," that this failure was due "solely to the unwillingness on the part of the highly armed States to carry out their contractual obligation to disarm," which had rendered impossible "the satisfaction of Germany's recognized claim to equality of rights."

Five days later, October 19, Germany served official notice of her intention to withdraw also from the League of Nations. With a resurgent Germany rapidly rearming under such leadership, talk of disarmament lost whatever point it had ever had. The conference met on October 16, therefore, only to adjourn. Disarmament was dead. Funeral orations were delivered at a final gloomy session, May 29 to June 11, 1934, with Hitler in the saddle, riding high, in Germany, and France and Britain blaming each other for the divergence of their views and the frustration of their uncoördinated policies.

TREATY OF MUTUAL GUARANTEE—LOCARNO, 1925

The four-power treaties signed at Washington in 1921 and 1922, for the maintenance of the *status quo* as to fortifications and naval

bases on Pacific islands, involved the mutual recognition by the signatories of one another's insular possessions, but did not guarantee them.
The parties were bound only to refer disputes to a conference of the
signatories, or to "consult" or to "communicate with one another to
arrive at an understanding as to the . . . steps to be taken" if the rights
of any of them were threatened by the aggressive action of any other
power. No one was bound to go to war to defend another.

At Locarno in 1925 five nations went—on paper—beyond mutual
recognition to mutual guarantee of the German-French and German-
Belgian boundaries. Early in 1925 the German minister for foreign
affairs, Gustav Stresemann, proposed to Premier Edouard Herriot of
France that a treaty of mutual guarantee be drawn to insure the existing Franco-German frontier against attack from either side. Such a
guarantee promised to do much to clear away the fog of fear and suspicion that still lay heavily on the Rhineland, which the gradual evacuation of the Ruhr and the adoption of the Dawes plan had only
partially dispelled.

M. Herriot's ministry fell for other reasons, and he had to resign
his premiership before he found an answer to Stresemann's proposal.
British Foreign Minister Austen Chamberlain's first reaction was unfavorable. The move would be, he thought, unwise and premature.
Only a few months later, however, Mr. Chamberlain was ready to
join Foreign Minister Aristide Briand of France in pushing the proposal, to which Stresemann naturally assented. So followed the conference and treaties of Locarno.[13]

The principal Locarno Pact was made by Germany, France, Belgium, Great Britain, and Italy. By it they collectively and severally
guaranteed the territorial *status quo* as established by the Treaty of
Versailles between Germany and France and between Germany and
Belgium, and the inviolability of those frontiers. Germany and France
and Germany and Belgium mutually undertook in no case to attack
or invade each other or resort to war against each other, *except* (1) in
legitimate resistance to an unprovoked act of aggression committed
in violation of the Treaty of Versailles or the Locarno Treaty itself,
or by reason of the presence of armed troops in the demilitarized zone,
or (2) in pursuance of Article 16 of the Covenant of the League of
Nations, or (3) as an agent of the League.

By the same treaty the principal parties—Germany and Belgium,
Germany and France—undertook "to settle by peaceful means . . .

[13] As a reward for this distinguished service, the king conferred upon Mr.
Chamberlain—thereafter Sir Austen Chamberlain—the Order of the Garter.

[diplomacy, judicial decision, or conciliation] all questions of every kind" which might arise between them. If at any time one of the parties should allege that another had violated or was violating its pledge not to invade or to resort to war against another, it was to bring the matter before the Council of the League, and all—including Great Britain and Italy as guarantors—were bound to come immediately to the assistance of the one so injured if the Council sustained the charge. Either the crossing of the frontier or the assembly of armed forces in the demilitarized zone was defined as an act of unprovoked aggression and a "flagrant violation" of the treaty.

Great pains were taken to make it clear that the Locarno Treaty was in conformity with the Covenant of the League of Nations, would work no diminution of the League's authority, and was dependent for its administration upon League agencies. Although initialed October 16, 1925, the principal treaty went into effect only when Germany became a member of the League, September 14, 1926, and—according to its terms—should not have ceased to have effect until one year after a decision by a two-thirds majority of the Council that the League of Nations no longer insured sufficient protection to its parties. Before being asked to make such a decision, the Council should have had three months' advance notice.[14]

In addition to the treaty of mutual guarantee of her French and Belgian boundaries, Germany entered at Locarno into arbitration agreements with France, Belgium, Czechoslovakia, and Poland but refused to discuss an "eastern Locarno" accepting her eastern boundaries as permanent. No German government, Stresemann said at home two months later, would ever recognize this frontier. France, however, at the same conference made treaties of mutual guarantee with both Czechoslovakia and Poland.

Because the Rhineland had been recognized as one of the storm centers of Europe for more than a thousand years, the Locarno pacts were hailed by the world as having gone straight to the heart of the problem of peace. Briand, Sir Austen Chamberlain, and Stresemann were all awarded Nobel peace prizes. Stresemann, with whom foreigners found it much easier to deal than with his predecessors or his successors, was almost universally acclaimed as an internationalist. He was in fact the same ardent nationalist he had always been. He had done his country invaluable service by regaining for it, to a very

[14] All these stipulated procedures and legal formalities were disregarded by Hitler when on March 7, 1936, he notified the British, French, and Belgian governments that Germany no longer considered herself bound by the Locarno Treaty and, on the same day, marched his troops into the Rhineland.

considerable degree, the unearned confidence of the world. He had sat with the delegates from other nations at Locarno as an equal among equals—*ebenbürtig* at last—and had got his country invited into the League of Nations without having again to assent to the Treaty of Versailles. Germany would have been wise to continue on the path of conciliation which she seemed then to have taken under his leadership.

The world's generous optimism might have been tempered, however, if it had heard or read Stresemann's address reporting on Locarno and giving an account of his stewardship. The treaty did not guarantee the *status quo* in the west, he said, but only the maintenance of peace. "Our resistance was the fundamental idea of the whole transaction." Germany had not recognized even her western frontiers as permanent but had promised only not to try just then to change them by use of force. "There was no moral renunciation but merely a recognition of the fact . . . that it would today be madness to play with the idea of a war with France." He had refused even to discuss a nonaggression pact with Czechoslovakia or Poland, or the renunciation of war except as to the western boundary. "Membership of the League does not exclude the possibility of war."

As to other boundaries: "What stands in the way of a strengthening of Germany? What stands in the way of a recovery of German soil, or a junction with Austria?[15] What stands in our way is the eternal anxiety that if this sixty-million nation becomes a seventy-million nation we are threatened by France, and we cannot so far endanger our vital political interests. The moment the incessant threat of war on our western frontier ceases to exist, the argument is no longer valid. As a consequence our prospects in this connection are entirely favorable."

As to the League: "The League was in its origin directed against us. Its proceedings were hostile to us. . . . But in the present state of affairs I do not ask whether people are sympathetic to me or not, I ask whether a thing is to my advantage."[16]

It was to Germany's advantage in 1925 to sign the Locarno pacts and in 1926 to join the League. She was weak, and needed to be conciliatory. Lulled then into a false sense of security, her neighbors were

[15] It is interesting to note that Stresemann did not at that time call Austria German soil as Hitler subsequently did.

[16] Address to the Central Association of Provincial Associations, December 14, 1925. See E. Sutton, *Gustav Stresemann: His Diaries, Letters, and Papers*, 2 vols. (New York, 1935-1937), II, 215-229; or W. C. Langsam, *Documents and Readings in the History of Europe Since 1918* (New York, 1939), 662.

taken by surprise and struck with consternation when Hitler challenged them. Hitler, although unlikely to acknowledge it, was one of Stresemann's beneficiaries.

It was indicative of trouble to come a generation later that Russian leaders and press professed to see in the Locarno pacts a sinister combination of western European capitalist states against socialist Russia and a menace to Russian national security, and bestirred themselves at once to win friends and influence neighbors in eastern Europe.

RENUNCIATION OF WAR: PACT OF PARIS, 1928

The years 1926 to 1929 were a period of general optimism. The Dawes plan was in effect. German reparation and inter-Allied debt payments were being made on schedule. German foreign credit was good, and Germany as well as most of Europe seemed to be on the way to recovery from the economic consequences of the war. The fear of war diminished in the light of Locarno and of Germany's admission to the League of Nations.

The movement to seek security by treaty agreement gained momentum. Proceeding from the particular to the general, from the agreement of two nations at Locarno not to go to war over their common boundary to a general declaration of intention not to go to war, Foreign Minister Briand of France proposed early in 1927 the negotiation of a bilateral treaty agreement between the United States and France that neither would go to war against the other. Out of the ensuing correspondence between M. Briand and Mr. Frank B. Kellogg, the United States secretary of state, there grew an international conference at Paris in 1928 where on August 27 the general pact for the renunciation of war, generally known as the Pact of Paris or the Kellogg-Briand Pact, was signed by representatives of fifteen nations. By the time of its formal proclamation by President Hoover in Washington on July 24, 1929, it had been ratified by forty-five nations. Eventually the number grew to sixty-two, including—as events were to prove—the aggressors of 1939-1941.[17]

The text of the Paris Pact was short: the parties solemnly declared that they condemned recourse to war for the solution of international controversies and renounced it as an instrument of national policy in their relations with one another, and agreed that the settlement or

---

[17] The parties named in the text of the treaty as its makers were Germany, the United States, Belgium, France, Great Britain, Italy, Japan, Poland, and Czechoslovakia.

solution of all disputes or conflicts of whatever nature or of whatever origin which might arise among them should never be sought except by pacific means.

Whether the treaty could be said to have outlawed war was a matter of interpretation. No sanctions were provided, no means of enforcement, no penalty for violation—but what a gesture! To the cynics it was only a gesture, camouflage behind which to conceal war plans, or a pious front to enable self-righteous hypocrites to look respectable to themselves in the mirror if they held it carefully. To practical idealists it seemed a step upward and forward to put all nations on record in a public and mutual renunciation of offensive war, so that none could attack another without violating its own public pledge. Believers in moral force still hoped that "a decent respect to the opinions of mankind" might have sufficient weight.

The first ten years of the life of the treaty were disappointing, giving new prevalence to the ugly phenomenon of undeclared war. Nations did not refrain from making war but merely from declaring war, calling war only an "incident," as Japan did her unprovoked aggression in Manchuria, or "self-defense," as Japan did her invasion of North China, or the abatement of a nuisance in Ethiopia, or "protection" of German nationals and a German-speaking minority in Czechoslovakia. Neutrals unable to choose between death and the doctor could also, conveniently, see no evil by acting as if undeclared war were not war. Hypocrisy and self-deception seemed to have spread.

At Nuremberg in the war criminal trials of 1945-1946, however, new steps were taken to carry on from where the Kellogg-Briand Pact left off. Punitive action was based on the ground that the signing of that pact and others like it had been something more than a gesture and that the waging of aggressive war in violation of such a pact was a punishable breach of law. Perhaps world opinion supported by an organized world force could do what decency alone, not so supported, had not done. If that point were once established, perhaps another stone had been well laid in the structure of world peace.

Litvinov Protocol, 1929

The strongest power not represented at the Paris congress of 1928 and not included among the original signers of the Kellogg Pact was Russia, with which neither Great Britain nor the United States was then maintaining normal diplomatic relations.[18] Through the good

---

[18] Great Britain had recognized the Soviet Russian government in 1924 but had severed diplomatic relations in 1927. The United States did not recognize the Soviets until 1933.

offices of France, however, the Russian signature was obtained only two days later, August 29. Soon afterward Maxim Litvinov, successor to Georgi Chicherin as Russian foreign commissar, negotiated an eastern European nonaggression pact, the Litvinov Protocol, signed at Moscow February 9, 1929, by Russia, Poland, Latvia, Estonia, and Rumania. Lithuania, Turkey, Danzig, and Persia (Iran) also signed soon afterward.

NONAGGRESSION AND CONCILIATION: PAN-AMERICAN TREATY, 1933

Refusal to recognize changes brought about through use of force was a natural concomitant of a policy of mutual assurance and non-aggression. After Japan's attack on China in Manchuria and in accord with United States policy, publicly stated in that connection, not to recognize territorial changes so made, and just when the general disarmament conference at Geneva was about to be broken up by Germany's withdrawal from it, six South and Central American states met in Rio de Janeiro. As if to serve notice on the world that the Americas still considered it possible to keep peace among themselves no matter what happened in Europe or in Asia, they made a treaty of nonaggression and conciliation containing this interesting new provision of nonrecognition.

The treaty was signed on October 10, 1933. Its makers were Argentina, Brazil, Chile, Mexico, Paraguay, and Uruguay; but it was open to the adherence of all states, and many others including the United States (March 11, 1936) accepted the invitation to adhere to it. It was concluded for an indefinite time but could be denounced on one year's notice by any state, in which case it should cease at the end of that one-year period to bind that state but should continue in effect for all others that had signed or adhered to it.

By the first four articles of the treaty the contracting parties declared as follows:

1. They condemned wars of aggression in their mutual relations or in those with other states. The settlement of disputes or controversies of any kind that might arise between them should be effected only by pacific means which had the sanction of international law.

2. As between themselves territorial questions must not be settled by violence, and they would not recognize any territorial arrangement which was not obtained by pacific means, or the validity of any occupation or acquisition of territory that might be brought about by force of arms.

3. In case of noncompliance with the obligations contained in the foregoing articles the other signatories were to make every effort to maintain the peace, to adopt in their character as neutrals a common and solidary attitude, to exercise the political, juridical, or economic means authorized by international law, and to bring public opinion to bear, but in no case to intervene. These requirements were subject to the attitude that might be incumbent upon them by virtue of other collective treaties of which they were signatories.

4. The signers obligated themselves to submit to the conciliation procedure established by the treaty any disputes not settled by diplomacy within a reasonable period.

The comparative cordiality of inter-American relations should have had no deleterious effect on friendships between European nations or between Americans and Europeans. The activity and comparative success of the Pan-American Union and other inter-American associations did not in fact interfere or compete with the League of Nations. But numerous comparisons were made, not always appropriate, and often unfavorable to the League. Approval of the Pan-American Union was—whether consistently or inconsistently—about as common in the United States as was skepticism concerning the League.

MUTUAL ASSISTANCE

The Stresa Resolution, 1935

In typical Nazi manner, on March 16, 1935, using the Reichstag as a sounding board, Adolf Hitler announced to a startled world that Germany no longer considered herself bound by the disarmament provisions of the Treaty of Versailles. The Reichstag, with its usual alacrity and manifestations of enthusiasm, passed at once what it called a "law for the building up of a defense force" on the basis of universal military service, which had been forbidden by the treaty. The new peacetime army, including the police forces to be incorporated in it, was to consist of twelve corps commands of thirty-six divisions. That was only the announcement of a beginning already made. Germany was already on her way back to military might.

Nations which had been represented in the general disarmament conference at Geneva, which before Germany's withdrawal from it in October, 1933, had recognized her theoretical right to equality in armament, were more disturbed by the manner in which this new step toward rearmament was taken than by any immediate military threat apparent in it. Meeting at Stresa,[19] April 11 to 14, 1935, representatives of Italy, France, and Great Britain "regretfully recognized that the method of unilateral repudiation adopted by the German Government, at a moment when steps were being taken to promote a freely negotiated settlement of the question of armaments, had undermined public confidence in the security of a peaceful order."

By way of definition of their conception of a proper basis for a peaceful order in Europe, the three participating powers confirmed their previous declarations that "the necessity of maintaining the independence and integrity of Austria would continue to inspire their common policy."

Although Italy and Great Britain had participated in the Treaty of Locarno only as guarantors, at Stresa they formally reaffirmed all their obligations under that treaty and declared their intention, should need arise, faithfully to fulfill them.

Finally, the three powers declared that they were in complete agreement in opposing, by all practicable means, any unilateral repudiation of treaties which might endanger the peace of Europe, and would act in close and cordial collaboration for that purpose.

The so-called "Stresa front" did not stand long unbroken. When Hitler on March 7, 1936, denounced the Treaty of Locarno and marched his troops into the Rhineland in violation of its terms, Italy was actively engaged in the conquest of Ethiopia, then virtually completed.[20] Fear of Germany had—among other considerations—made France afraid to offend Italy by trying to restrain her. Fear of a war with Italy was all the greater, in Britain as well as in France, because of the reawakened fear of Germany. The treaty formalizing the "Rome-Berlin Axis" was not signed until October 25, 1936; but the aggressions of one dictator were already contributing materially to the success of steps taken by the other in preparation for aggression.[21]

Franco-Russian Treaty, 1935

In its memorandum of March 7, 1936, repudiating the Treaty of Locarno and announcing to the Belgian, British, and French governments that it had that day "restored the full and unrestricted sovereignty of Germany in the demilitarized zone of the Rhineland," the

---

[19] Stresa, like Locarno, is on beautiful Lake Maggiore. Locarno is at the northern end of the lake, in Switzerland, Stresa on its western shore in Italian Piedmont.

[20] See pp. 476-485.
[21] See p. 469.

German government pointed accusingly, as the ostensible reason for its action, at the Franco-Russian pact of May 2. This, it angrily alleged, was directed exclusively against Germany, as if neither the Locarno Pact nor the Covenant of the League of Nations were valid or existed. The German argument was that the obligations France had undertaken in her pact with Russia were incompatible with those she had assumed at Locarno and that France, by thus violating the Treaty of Locarno, had so effectively invalidated it that Germany was no longer bound by it.

The Franco-Russian pact in which Germany professed to see such sinister designs upon her safety had not been ratified when she made it a pretext for the remilitarization of the Rhineland; but it was ratified less than three weeks later, March 27, 1936. Russia was by then a member of the League of Nations. The treaty was defensive in its stated terms, kept carefully within the framework of the League of Nations Covenant.

If either party should be "threatened with, or in danger of, attack" by a European state, they were to consult on measures to be taken for the observance of the provisions of Article 10 of the Covenant of the League. If either were the object of an unprovoked attack by a European state in a dispute in which the League Council had been unable to make a report by unanimous vote of its members, not including parties to the dispute, the other should immediately give "aid and assistance." The pact was tied in by its own terms, also, to Articles 16 and 17 of the Covenant.

The Franco-Russian mutual assistance pact seems to have been defensive in purpose as in form, and Germany's violent protest rather a piece of political propaganda than a warranted expression of well-founded fear. As an instrument of security, however, the pact had little value.

SUMMARY

The quest of security by agreement had circled back upon itself. Negotiations for the limitation of naval armament had been hindered by much jockeying for competitive advantage, and the Washington naval limitation treaty was to expire at the end of 1936. Mutual acceptance and guarantee of boundaries, the universal renunciation of war as an instrument of national policy, the universal declaration of intention to settle disputes only by pacific means, and general non-aggression pacts had all failed to free the peoples from the fear of attack and consequent necessity of self-defense. Finally, mutual assistance pacts among three nations for the preservation of the *status quo* in an area, or between two for defense against one situated between them, were sadly reminiscent of the Entente of 1907-1914 or of the old dual alliances of the nineties.

Enough peace-keeping treaties had been made to have insured peace forever if the treaties had been made in good faith and faithfully kept. Some hypocrisy and deceit were probably concealed beneath the verbiage of the diplomatic discussions and the treaties, but the failure of the peace movement seems to have been due rather to weakness or lack of faith than to bad faith. Fifteen years after having established the League of Nations at Geneva, the nations turned to it in vain, or turned to other agencies as if it were not there. They had not sufficient faith in it to make it justify their faith.

CHAPTER 7

The Succession States

CZECHOSLOVAKIA

Independence and Union

The end of the multinational Habsburg monarchy of Austria-Hungary was the beginning of a new era for its subject peoples. For the most numerous and homogeneous of them the right of self-determination promised by President Wilson in one of his Fourteen Points meant a long-sought opportunity to win or to regain their independence. The national minorities problem was not solved thereby, for there were minorities within minorities; but it was brought somewhat nearer to a solution on an ethnic basis. This was especially true of Czechoslovakia.

New republican leaders in the one-time independent kingdom of Bohemia freed it in 1918 from its centuries-old Habsburg connection and reëstablished it as a nation, enlarging it with the consent of the peoples concerned to include the mixed but predominantly Slav populations of Moravia, Slovakia, and sub-Carpathian Russia or Ruthenia. Moravia had been for practical purposes, since the sixteenth century, connected with Bohemia. Slovakia and Ruthenia had been the northernmost provinces of Hungary. The new state was bounded, therefore, on the west and north by Germany, on the north and northeast by Poland, and on the south by Austria and Hungary.

The father of the new country, if any one earned that title, was Professor Thomas G. Masaryk of the Charles University at Prague. Both as a teacher and as a member of the imperial parliament and delegations, he had long been known before 1914 as a democrat and as a leader of the Czech nationalist group called the Realists. At the outbreak of the war he realized at once that the Central Powers, with all their initial advantages, might not win the war, and that the Czechs and Slovaks, although many thousands of them were compelled to take their places in the ranks of the Austro-Hungarian army, had better reason to hope that the empire would be defeated than to fight for its preservation.

While in neutral Switzerland in December, 1914, on his way home from a trip to Italy, which was also then still neutral, Thomas Masaryk was informed that the imperial authorities had planned to arrest him on his return. So he did not go home. For nearly four years thereafter, Czechoslovakia was where Masaryk was—in Paris, London, Moscow, Washington, or Pittsburgh. Closely associated with him were his Charles University colleague Eduard Beneš, the Slovak scientist Milan Štefánik, and a former Czech deputy, Josef Durich.

In July, 1915, in a John Hus anniversary address at Geneva, Professor Masaryk took his stand publicly in favor of the Allies and of Czechoslovak independence. On November 14, 1915, a similar manifesto was issued by Masaryk and Durich on behalf of the nationalist underground at home and revolutionary committees in Allied countries and the United States. In January, 1916, the self-constituted foreign committee became a Czechoslovak National Council: president, T. G. Masaryk; vice-president, Josef Durich; general secretary, Dr. Eduard Beneš; Slovak representative, General Milan Štefánik. This council kept in touch with the nationalist movement at home, and sought recognition and help for it abroad.

Recognition came step by step. In January, 1917, the Allies, replying to President Wilson's request for a statement of their war aims, included among them the liberation of the Czechoslovaks. In Russia in 1917 Kerensky renewed a promise previously made by the tsar to permit the recruitment of a Czechoslovak legion from among the prisoners of war then in Russian hands. Later some of these were transported across Siberia and home around the world, too late to affect the outcome of the war materially but soon enough to contribute something to the achievement of an important political purpose.[1]

After having spent some time in Russia in 1917 arranging for the

---

[1] The presence of the Czechoslovak legion in Siberia may have done something to keep both revolutionary Russia and the Germans in the Ukraine cut off for a time from the resources and the prisoner-of-war camps of eastern Siberia, and so have helped to make the German Ukrainian enterprise more costly and less profitable. The Lenin-Trotsky government insisted upon disarming the Czechoslovaks before it would permit their transport, and they resisted rather than be disarmed, holding out for months in the valley of the Volga and along many miles of the Trans-Siberian Railroad.

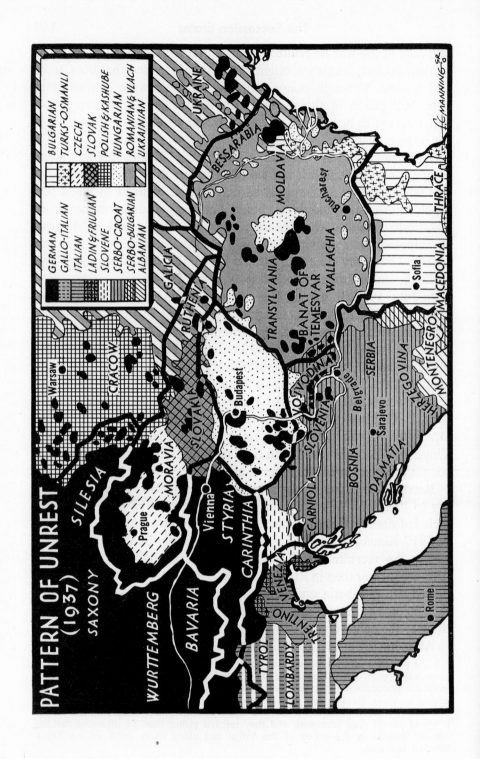

PATTERN OF UNREST (1937)

Legend:
- BULGARIAN
- TURKS-OSMANLI
- CZECH
- SLOVAK
- POLISH & KASHUBE
- HUNGARIAN
- ROMANIAN & VLACH
- UKRAINIAN
- GERMAN
- GALLO-ITALIAN
- ITALIAN
- LADIN & FRIULIAN
- SLOVENE
- SERBO-CROAT
- SERBO-BULGARIAN
- ALBANIAN

SAXONY, SILESIA, Warsaw, CRACOW, GALICIA, RUTHENIA, UKRAINE, BESSARABIA, MOLDAVIA, THRACE, Sofia, MACEDONIA, WALLACHIA, Bucharest, TRANSYLVANIA, BANAT OF TEMESVAR, VOJVODINA, SERBIA, Belgrade, MONTENEGRO, HERZEGOVINA, DALMATIA, Sarajevo, BOSNIA, SLOVENIA, CARNIOLA, CARINTHIA, STYRIA, Vienna, Budapest, SLOVAKIA, MORAVIA, Prague, WURTTEMBERG, BAVARIA, VENEZIA, TRENTINO, TYROL, LOMBARDY, Rome

A.G. MANNING SR.

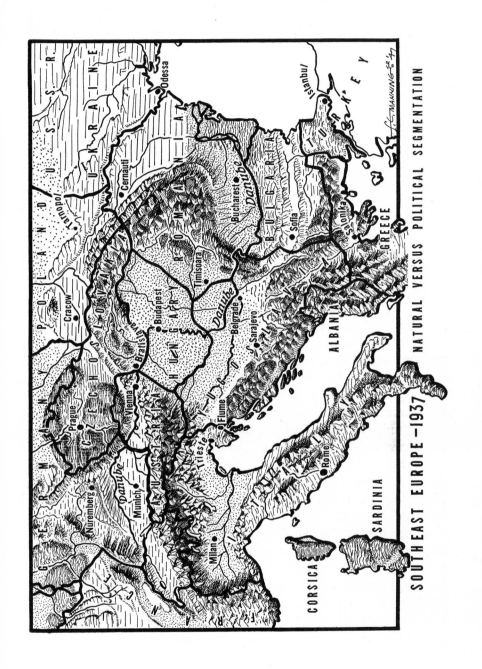

SOUTHEAST EUROPE — 1937   NATURAL VERSUS POLITICAL SEGMENTATION

formation of the Czechoslovak legion there, Professor Masaryk made his way in 1918 to the United States, where he secured from Secretary Lansing, May 29, a public declaration of sympathy for the cause of Czechoslovak and Yugoslav independence. Just a week before, Lord Robert Cecil had put Great Britain publicly on record in favor of independence for Czechoslovakia. On June 3, 1918, the Allied War Council at Versailles announced its support of the Lansing declaration. On June 29 the French government recognized the Czechoslovak National Council as the responsible controlling body of an organized national movement, and President Poincaré participated on June 30 in the ceremonies marking the formation of a Czechoslovak regiment. Italy also agreed to the recruiting of Czechoslovak troops in Italy. On September 3 Great Britain and the United States recognized the National Council as on the same footing as the Belgian and Serbian governments in exile, and Japan granted it similar recognition September 9.

Having been so recognized, the National Council began on October 14 to call itself an interim Czechoslovak government, with Masaryk provisional president and Beneš minister for foreign affairs. On October 18 it declared the Czechoslovak nation independent.

Fortunately no serious friction then developed between nationalists at home and nationalists abroad. Immediately upon the capitulation of Austria-Hungary a Czech National Committee in Prague proclaimed, on October 28, the independence of the Czechoslovak state and assumed control of its administration. The principle of Czechoslovak unity was sustained two days later by a manifesto adopted by the Slovak National Council. The National Committee at Prague quickly agreed with the Masaryk-Beneš government in exile that the new government should be a democracy and a republic; and on November 13, 1918, the National Committee announced an interim constitution for it.

Under the interim constitution a national assembly met November 14, constituted on the basis of proportional representation, with the exception that the German national minority refused to participate in it. The assembly unanimously elected Masaryk president of the republic, although he did not return to Prague until December 21. Beneš was foreign minister.[2] The new prime minister was Kramář, and General Štefánik became minister for war. The first goals of the Czechoslovak nationalists were achieved: independence and a national government.

[2] Dr. Beneš was foreign minister for seventeen years (1918-1935) and president for three (1935-1938).

Government and Politics

As organized under its national constitution of February 29, 1920, Czechoslovakia was a centralized rather than a federal state. This disappointed the more extreme Slovak and Ruthenian nationalists, who were willing to enter a federation but had hoped for more complete autonomy than the constitution gave them.

The president of the republic was to be elected for a term of seven years and might be reëlected, but only T. G. Masaryk could be reëlected more than once.[3] Political power was concentrated in a bicameral legislature, to which deputies were elected for six years and senators for eight by universal, equal suffrage. The ballot was secret, and voting was compulsory. The premier and cabinet, appointed by the president, were politically responsible to the parliament. The judiciary was independent.

Elections were on the basis of proportional representation, which showed there the same merits and the same disadvantages as in Weimar Germany and elsewhere. The parliament reflected well the political complexion of the country, and minorities were faithfully represented. But more than twenty parties developed, none could gain power and accept responsibility for the determination of government policy except merely as the strongest of several in a coalition, and the voter could cast his ballot only for the "bound list" of candidates of one party or another, not for an individual candidate.

The Agrarian party was the one most often and longest in power, not as an actual majority party but as the strongest in one coalition after another. It was originally the party of land reform, setting 150 hectares (about 375 acres) as the legal maximum holding of arable land and parceling out estates larger than that, with compensation to previous owners at the 1913-1915 average price. Land was thus sold to 235,000 peasants who had previously owned none, and 415,000 who owned less than ten hectares (about twenty-five acres) each were permitted to buy more. These beneficiaries of the landownership reform were the backbone of the Agrarian party, but it gained many middle-class members also in the towns, not only by its moderate democratic republicanism but simply by its long-continued tenure of power. Four of the republic's seven premiers before the German occupation were Agrarians. The last of them was Milan Hodža, November 5, 1935, to September, 1936.

[3] Masaryk was reëlected in May, 1920, 1927, and 1934, and resigned at the age of eighty-five in December, 1935. His successor was Beneš.

Although Dr. Hodža and many other national government officials were Slovaks, there was always an autonomist party in Slovakia, pressing for the fulfillment of a promise made or implied before independence had been achieved. Roman Catholicism was stronger in Slovakia than in old Bohemia, the homeland of Hus, and was offended by what it called the anticlericalism of the Czechoslovak government. The Slovaks always objected also to the influx of Czech officials, although the level of literacy, general education, and administrative efficiency was higher among the Czechs than among the Slovaks, and more people properly qualified and trained for government service were available there. A leader of the Slovak autonomist movement was a Roman Catholic priest, Father Andrej Hlinka. After Hlinka's death in August, 1938, another priest named Tiso took over the leadership of a nominally autonomist but in effect pro-German party.

Ruthenians were also disappointed by their failure to attain autonomy, and resentful of the presence of numerous Czech officials; but Ruthenia was in all ways the most "backward" part of the country, its people the farthest from being ready for self-government.

In general the national administration, although top-heavy with Czechs, was honest, intelligent, efficient, and beneficent. New universities were established in Brno (Brünn) in Moravia and Bratislava (Pressburg) in Slovakia. There was an excellent social insurance system; the currency was sound; and stability was achieved with tolerance.

Economic Resources and Problems

Czechoslovakia was the most richly endowed of the succession states, in natural resources, industry already developed, and industrially skilled people. In all, approximately three-fourths of the industrial plant of the old Austro-Hungarian empire was located there—nearly all of the porcelain making, 92 percent of the sugar refining, 87 percent of the barley, 75 percent of the cotton goods, and nearly half of the alcohol production. It had three-fourths of the coal, two-thirds of the graphite beds, nearly all of the silver, and most of the gold of the whole area that had been Austria-Hungary. Its resources and its industries were sorely missed by what was left of Austria and Hungary.

Conversely, Czechoslovakia missed its old markets in what had been the great free-trading area of the empire. It was helped somewhat by the internationalization of the Danube and by valuable shipping privileges on the Elbe and a free port at Hamburg, and managed much of the time to build up an excess of exports over imports. Its most valuable exports were those requiring personal artistry and skill as well as mechanical efficiency in their production: porcelains, glass, laces, shoes, musical instruments, textiles, light arms, machinery, locomotives, railway equipment, etc.[4]

The prosperity resulting from industrial and agrarian production was shared by many elements of the population, especially in Bohemia and Moravia, but was not evenly distributed to or among the Slovaks and Ruthenians. In the eastern provinces increasing economic hardship was the rule and contributed to the political dissatisfaction already mentioned. The iron and textile mills of Slovakia, cut off from their old Hungarian markets, could not compete with the metallurgical and textile industries of the Czechs; so many of them closed down or were taken over by their stronger competitors or by Czech banks. The Slovak forests, also cut off by new political barriers from Hungarian markets they had once supplied, became less profitable. Slovaks, who produced less of their own food than the Czechs did, profited less than the Czechs from national legislation in support of agricultural prices. Less fortunate than the Czechs in natural resources, the Slovaks thought themselves less favored by national economic policy.

Ruthenia was poorer than Slovakia. It also had formerly exported timber to Hungary. That market had been lost temporarily and was only partially restored. Some of its land was held in large estates, and Czech colonists seemed to the Ruthenians to have been favored in such redistribution as had been effected by the new land laws. Most peasant holdings were too small to support any but the barest existence. Overpopulation, unemployment, and poverty were constant serious problems. The national government was not unaware of or indifferent to these, but twenty years did not give it time to solve them.

National Minorities

Government's failure to equalize economic conditions in areas which had never been economically alike, or to spread prosperity evenly throughout a population which had been quite uneven as to education and economic status when the government was formed, contributed as has been shown to continued discontent. The attitudes of national minorities contributed more.

[4] J. S. Roucek, *Central-Eastern Europe* (New York, 1946), 350. See also Hugh Seton-Watson, *Eastern Europe Between the Wars, 1918-1941* (Cambridge, England, 1945), chap. 6, sec. 2; and, for Ruthenia, Elizabeth Wiskemann, *Prologue to War* (New York, 1940), 211-217.

Grouped together as Czechoslovaks, the Czechs and Slovaks were about two-thirds of the entire population of 13,374,364 in 1921, 14,729,536 in 1930. Czechs alone numbered perhaps a little less than 7,000,000 in 1921 and more than 7,000,000 in 1930, Slovaks from 2,000,000 to 2,500,000. The other third of the population was made up of Germans (23.4 percent of the total in 1921, 22.3 percent in 1930), Magyars (5.6 and 4.7 percent), Ruthenes (3.5 and 5.7 percent), Poles (0.5 percent), Jews (1.3 percent), Rumanians (0.1 percent), and (in 1930) 52,209 gypsies (0.2 percent).[5]

The Hungarian element in Ruthenia was only 15.4 percent in 1930, but before 1918 Hungarians had been the favored people there and had owned many of the large estates which the Czechoslovak land-ownership reforms had redistributed—not without remuneration, but without the dispossessed owners' ever reconciling themselves to the change. The Hungarians who were left there or who could return in 1939 welcomed, then, the annexation of Ruthenia by Hungary on March 15 after one day of nominal independence.

There were Hungarians also in Slovakia. Béla Kun's attempt to "rescue" them by reconquest of the region has already been mentioned.[6] They were not abused. The University of Bratislava (Pressburg) was rather thoroughly de-Magyarized by the exclusion of Hungarian studies from its curriculum and the disuse of the Hungarian language in instruction; but schools still offered elementary instruction in the vernacular in predominantly Hungarian communities, and Magyar deputies to the Czechoslovak parliament were free to speak there in their own tongue. If any comfort could be found in comparisons, Hungarians in Slovakia could have congratulated themselves that they were better treated than their similarly situated compatriots in Yugoslavia or Rumania. Some of them, indeed, preferred Czechoslovakia as it was to Hungary as they had known it and still saw it; but more of them cherished a preference for Hungary, and some, at least, were found in 1939 to welcome the Vienna "award" of part of Slovakia to Hungary.

The Slovaks are not mentioned here as a national minority; nor are the Moravians. The Slovaks were both racially and linguistically quite closely related to the Czechs. The principal differences between them were economic and cultural, as a result of Bohemia's centuries of close connection with Austria while Slovakia had been controlled by Hungary. There was a self-conscious separate Slovak nationalism,

[5] *Czechoslovak Statistics*, IX, 65-66, quoted by Hugh Seton-Watson, *op. cit.*, 431.
[6] See p. 107.

language, and literature; but the Czechs and Slovaks were fundamentally kindred peoples. Moravia was a province of Bohemia. Both Moravians and Bohemians were Czechs.

The most numerous, most prosperous, and most vociferously malcontent of the national minorities was the German. There were between three and three and a half millions of these people, living principally in the industrialized mountain regions of the west, northwest, and north, nearest Germany, and in northern and southern Moravia, which had for centuries been a sort of connecting link between German Silesia and German Austria. From the Sudeten mountains of the Bohemian-Silesian border, where many of them lived, they all came in the 1930's to be called, rather indiscriminately, the Sudeten Germans.

These were not subject people inhabiting land newly seized by conquest or acquired by negotiation. Only one tiny border district, Hlučín, was transferred by the treaty makers from German to Czechoslovak sovereignty. When the new state was established, the centuries-old Bohemian-German border was kept otherwise unchanged for valid economic, military, and historical reasons. The Sudeten Germans were not "taken into" Czechoslovakia in 1919. They were already there. Most of them had been there all their lives, as their ancestors had been for generations. They were citizens of Czechoslovakia and members of that nation just in so far as they wished to be. As such, they were as fully protected in the exercise of their rights as other national minorities were, either there or elsewhere in central eastern Europe, and were not seriously abused; but they considered themselves abused.

Germans in old Bohemia had been a privileged minority, favorites of the Habsburgs, for three hundred years. Some had gone there as refugees from states turned Protestant during the troubled times of the Thirty Years' War. Others had been given, or permitted to buy cheaply, the confiscated lands of defeated Czech rebels. Others had gone in as government officials, trusted by the imperial authority and permitted to pay themselves well for their maintenance of it. There as elsewhere German industry and thrift were generally in evidence. There were Germans of all classes, in all parts of the country, and in all trades and professions; but whether favored, fortunate, or worthy of their hire they had, as a group, up to 1918 done rather well by themselves. In the nineteenth century the villages and the language of the villagers were still Czech, but the towns and the principal university at Prague seemed rather German than Czech. The German language was preferred by imperial officialdom, and Germans considered themselves a ruling class or, at least, superior citizens.

Knowing that they would lose their privileged status, and fearing that they would be treated as second-class minority citizens—at best—by any government controlled by the Czechoslovak majority, the Germans in Czechoslovakia hoped and worked during the war for maintenance of the monarchy and victory for the Central Powers. They took no part in the independence movement and were unsympathetic toward it, sent no delegates to the constituent assembly, and demonstrated on March 4, 1919, against the new government. Fifty people were killed in disorders, which were quickly suppressed. Yet the Czechs and Slovaks took no revenge. Later the German minority complained because the imperial war bonds for which they had subscribed quite heavily were honored for "only" two-thirds of their face value.

In the middle and later twenties the Germans seemed for a time to have chosen the path of coöperation in the national government. This was the period following Locarno when the peace movement seemed strongest and conciliation was the catchword of the chanceries. First the German Agrarians and the German Clericals participated in a government coalition in 1925, then in 1929 the German Social Democrats also joined one.

The opportunist policy of coöperation was only temporary. Before they were affected by the world depression German industries in Czechoslovakia, like all others there, had lost some foreign markets as a result of the separation from Austria-Hungary; and the Germans thought that their Czechoslovak competitors had had more government help than they in finding new ones. During the twenties they had complained that government encouragement and help, contracts and subsidies, were going to Czechoslovak firms in preference to German. Although Germans could be officials, they complained of unfair discrimination, as Czechoslovaks seemed generally to be preferred as more "reliable."

The Germans had their schools and used their own language freely and with safety, but were aggressively uncomfortable in their enjoyment of those rights. The tolerance of the Czechoslovaks was a poor substitute for the privileges they had once enjoyed.

In the depression they experienced real hardships. Their sense of injury fed upon the fact that government relief measures seemed to benefit first the "loyal" Czechoslovak, and the German malcontent of doubtful or divided loyalty only later if at all. So they listened to the

Nazi voice which promised to make Germany again the homeland of all Germans everywhere, benevolently interested in their welfare wherever they might be.

The advent of Hitler and the success of Axis intervention in the Spanish civil war meant the end of coöperation between the Bohemian Germans and the democratic Czechoslovak republicans. So-called physical-culture or other nominally cultural societies served as fronts for subversive political organizations. The leader of one of those, Konrad Henlein, began in 1933 to call his group the *Sudetendeutsche Heimatfront,* after the Nationalist and National Socialist parties had been legally dissolved. In 1935 the *Heimatfront* became the *Sudetendeutsche Partei,* a Nazi organization in all but name, with German Nazi affiliations, guidance, and support.

This soon became the strongest German party in the nation, winning in 1935 forty-four of the seventy-two German-held seats in the Parliament. Its parliamentary representation was already second in numerical strength only to the Agrarian. There were at that time three other German parties, the German Agrarians, the Clerical Christian Social party, and the German Social Democrats, all of which were willing in 1935 to coöperate with the Agrarians in a coalition government. The principal opposition parties then were the Sudeten, the Communist, and Father Andreus Hlinka's Slovak People's party, a reactionary group not noticeably unfriendly to fascism, ostensibly advocating autonomy for Slovakia.

The Sudeten German party protested at first its undivided loyalty to Czechoslovakia, as the Sudeten Germans had done since the failure of their secession movements in the early years of the republic. They claimed at first only autonomy for the German districts and the reorientation of the national foreign policy so as to align it with that of Germany. Instead of turning to Germany in foreign policy as the Sudeten party demanded, Dr. Beneš tightened the existing alliances with France and with the Little Entente, and made a new defensive mutual assistance pact with Russia, May 16, 1935.[7]

In its domestic policies the Hodža coalition government did what it could to appease the Sudeten Germans by promising that there would be no discrimination against Germans in favor of Czechs in

---

[7] President Thomas Masaryk resigned in December, 1935, and Dr. Eduard Beneš, who until then had been the republic's only minister for foreign affairs as Masaryk had been its only president, succeeded him. On March 1, 1936, the historian Dr. Kamil Krofta followed Beneš as foreign minister. Czechoslovakia's last freely chosen premier before the Munich conference was a Slovak Agrarian leader of peasant origin, Milan Hodža. Masaryk died September 14, 1937.

the public use of language, the choice of civil servants, or the allocation of government funds, contracts, or economic enterprises. Such
promises were hard to keep, however, in 1937 and 1938, as the public
demonstrations of Henlein and his followers were more and more
openly pro-German and provocative. Police measures for the preservation of order and the protection of life and property were denounced
by Henlein and the Nazi press—in Germany as well as in Czechoslovakia—as persecution.

Sudeten-Nazi intimidation was bolder and more successful after
the German occupation of Austria in March, 1938. Henlein publicly
called upon all Germans in Czechoslovakia to join the party political
front at once, implying that those who did not do so would not be
recognized as Germans in the day of reckoning which was to come.
Before the month of March was out, the German Agrarians, German
Clericals, and German Social Democrats had withdrawn from Dr.
Hodža's government coalition, and the Agrarians and Clericals had
joined the Sudeten party. Before Munich, fifty-five of the German
members of the Czechoslovak parliament were followers of Henlein.
The German deputies not so regimented were eleven Social Democrats
and five Communists. The avowed domestic enemies of the independence of the state were already legally—whether properly or not—
in virtual possession of the citadel.

Foreign Affairs

Bohemia-Moravia is a natural fortress centrally located in Europe,
with the mountainous Böhmer Wald, the Erz Gebirge, and the Sudetes
forming its western, northwestern, and northeastern ramparts. It is
open only on the east toward Slovakia and Ruthenia, eastern provinces
of the Czechoslovak state, and on the south toward Austria, with
which its ancient connection was severed only in 1918. Bohemia-
Moravia is also a natural trading center, with the Elbe and Morava-
Oder river systems to carry exports to Hamburg and Stettin, and the
Danube (internationalized in 1919) to give it access to a great trading
area in southeastern Europe and to the Black Sea. Friendly relations
with Austria, Yugoslavia, and Italy meant commercial access to the
Adriatic.

The most immediate menace to the peace and security of Czechoslovakia in 1920 was revisionist Hungary, unreconciled to the terms
of the Treaty of Trianon, determined to regain the territories it had
lost—Slovakia and Ruthenia for example—and in position to close

the Danube if it dared. Austria was then too weak to be either very useful as a friend, if indeed her friendship could be won again, or dangerous as an enemy unless in German hands. The danger from a resurgent Germany could never be forgotten but seemed in 1920 to be comparatively remote. Czechoslovak foreign policy had, therefore, (1) to concern itself with the closest possible collaboration with the other principal beneficiaries of the Treaty of Trianon, Yugoslavia and Rumania, (2) to fit itself into France's system of alliances with other beneficiaries of the Treaty of Versailles—notably Poland—for security against eventual revisionist attempts by Germany, and (3) to support the League of Nations in all its measures to keep the peace by preventing the revisionists from using force. This was the geopolitical basis of the foreign policy of Dr. Eduard Beneš, which was the policy of Czechoslovakia for twenty years.

This step-by-step progression from nationalism through regionalism and continentalism to universalism did not seem, as Dr. Beneš conceived it, either inconsistent or impractical.

The attempt to secure for Czechoslovakia the closest possible coöperation of Yugoslavia and Rumania for the service of their common political and economic interests took the form of what has been called the Little Entente. The entente grew out of bilateral pacts negotiated by Dr. Beneš on a trip to Belgrade and Bucharest in August, 1920. By the treaty of August 12, 1920, Czechoslovakia and Yugoslavia agreed each to aid the other if Hungary should make an unprovoked attack upon either, and to make no other alliance without the consent of the other. Rumania made similar treaties with Czechoslovakia April 23 and with Yugoslavia June 7, 1921.

In 1922 the treaty basis of the Little Entente was broadened as each party gained from the other two recognition of its treaties of friendship with nations not in the entente: Czechoslovakia with Rumania, Austria, and Poland, Yugoslavia with Rumania and Italy. The three further undertook to support one another in their international political, and diplomatic relations, and to take common measures if their common interests should be threatened.

On May 21, 1929, the Little Entente was indefinitely continued by a trilateral agreement that the treaties of alliance of 1920 and 1921 upon which it was based should thereafter be automatically renewed at the expiration of every five-year period. The parties also bound themselves to settle all differences among themselves peaceably, by arbitration or conciliation as suggested by the League of Nations in its model treaty of 1928.

Hitler's seizure of power in Germany foreshadowed his seizure of Austria and Czechoslovakia. Beneš knew that.[8] He also knew that, to have any hope of survival, his country would need all the help he could find for it. He therefore proceeded immediately with Titulescu of Rumania and Jevtić of Yugoslavia to set up a permanent council of foreign ministers of their three powers, and to tighten the entente in other ways. The new pact of organization, signed February 16, 1933, bound each of its parties to make no new political or trade treaty materially affecting its relations with any fourth power without the knowledge and consent of the others. An economic council was established to coördinate the business interests of the three, and a permanent secretariat was set up at Geneva. Conscious alignment with the League of Nations was indicated also by Article 10 of the new pact, which stipulated that nothing in it could be contrary to the principles and dispositions of the Covenant of the League.

Thus strengthened as spokesmen for the Little Entente as well as for their own governments, Beneš and Titulescu continued their vigorous protests in the Assembly of the League against Japan's aggression in Manchuria and urged the use of sanctions to stop her there.

In January, 1934, a bilateral agreement between Marshal Pilsudski and Hitler indicated that Poland had abandoned the principle of collective security to make her own deal, separately, with the power then threatening the peace. The murders of the Austrian chancellor, Dollfuss, July 25, and of King Alexander of Yugoslavia, plus the incidental shooting of Foreign Minister Barthou of France, October 9, 1934, were warning signals which no one could disregard. Czechoslovakia, however, still preferred the protection of its friends to the appeasement of its enemy. Foremost among those friends, ever since Versailles, was France. Since January 25, 1924, France and Czechoslovakia had maintained a bilateral defensive alliance, the treaty terms of which had stressed its complete compatibility with the Covenant of the League of Nations.

Both directly and through Czechoslovakia, by trade agreements and by loans, France had worked through the years to strengthen her relations with the Little Entente. The killing of her foreign minister, Jean Louis Barthou, in the company of King Alexander of Yugoslavia in Marseilles, October 9, 1934, by a Macedonian terrorist in the pay of

---

[8] Beneš predicted in May, 1933, that Hitler would try to absorb Austria and Czechoslovakia, to create an independent Ukraine as a counterpoise to Russia and Poland, to suppress the Danzig corridor, and to reduce Poland to subservience. Lord Robert Cecil, *A Great Experiment* (London, 1941), 247; R. W. Seton-Watson, *A History of the Czechs and Slovaks* (London, 1943), 345.

the Croatian terrorist Ante Pavelić and his Italian and Hungarian accomplices, was correctly interpreted as a warning that French influence in southeastern Europe would soon be seriously challenged.[9] Hungary and Bulgaria might be held in check by the Balkan Entente formed February 4, 1934, by Yugoslavia, Rumania, Greece, and Turkey, mutually guaranteeing one another's boundaries against aggression except by a great power; but Italy was—or was still thought to be —a great power, and Mussolini more self-assertive every day. If Duce and Führer should form a working partnership to lead their peoples into the sunlit living spaces about which both were already talking, the peace of Europe, the safety of France, and the existence of Czechoslovakia would be threatened.

For both France and Czechoslovakia a reorientation of foreign policy to enlist the aid of Russia seemed wise and necessary. This reorientation was made easier by the fact that by the end of 1924 Soviet Russia had been diplomatically recognized by most of the nations of Europe, including all the great powers, in 1933 by the United States, and in 1934 by Rumania, and had become a member of the League of Nations in September, 1934. The Franco-Russian pact was signed first (May 2, 1935) but not ratified until March 27, 1936. If either party should be threatened with, or in danger of, attack by a European state, the other was to consult with it immediately as to measures to be taken in fulfillment of obligations assumed under Article 10 of the Covenant of the League of Nations, guaranteeing the territorial integrity of members of the League as against external aggression. If either should be the object of an unprovoked attack as a result of a failure of the League Council to effect a settlement of a dispute, as provided for in Article 15 of the Covenant, the other should give it immediate "aid and assistance." The mutual obligation to wage defensive war was meshed also into Articles 16 and 17 of the League Covenant.

In Section IV of this mutual assistance pact France and Russia declared that the negotiations which had resulted in its signature had originally been begun with a view to drawing up a security agreement covering the USSR, Germany, Czechoslovakia, Poland, and the Baltic states, neighbors of the USSR, and that a treaty of assistance was to have been concluded between the USSR, France, and Germany under which each of those three states would have been pledged to "come to the assistance of that one among them which had been the object of an attack by one of those three states." They further declared that they

[9] Pavelić was the Croatian Quisling of 1941-1945.

continued to regard as desirable the conclusion of such a treaty with Germany.

If the Germans really feared encirclement, as some of Hitler's subsequent statements indicated that they did, such a general guarantee, if made in good faith and made effective, would seem to have offered them adequate protection. But the Nazi never supposed that others acted in good faith. Having themselves no confidence in international agreements, written or unwritten, they probably assumed that the pointed phrase "an attack by one of those three states" had been pointed at them. Whatever their reasons, they did not participate. Instead, they used the Franco-Russian pact as a pretext for their own repudiation of the Treaty of Locarno.[10]

Following the lead of France, Czechoslovakia on May 16, 1935, made a defensive treaty of mutual assistance with the USSR, to be implemented only if and when France had already come to the aid of either party, under attack, under the terms of her treaty with it. In other words, neither was bound by this treaty to aid the other unless France did.

Meanwhile, Dr. Beneš had always been active in the League of Nations, having gone as Czechoslovakia's delegate to its first Assembly and been elected to the Council in 1923 and reëlected in 1925. He had helped twice to prevent the return of the Habsburgs to Hungary in 1921, and had been coauthor and enthusiastic and persistent advocate of the Geneva Protocol of 1924. While working with the great powers he had worked unceasingly for the small ones, and always but not exclusively for his own. He had attended the Locarno conferences, initialed the agreements negotiated there, and later signed the Locarno treaties for Czechoslovakia in London. He had urged decisive action against Japan. He would have preferred the Geneva Protocol and the Locarno system to the Little Entente and dual alliances with France and Russia upon which he had to fall back ten years later; but he had to take what he could get. He knew that the new position was the result of a retreat, and that his country's situation, like that of Europe, had deteriorated; but he was not ready to surrender.

In January, 1934, Hitler made a nonaggression pact with Poland and the disciplined Nazi press dropped for several years all discussion of Danzig, the Danzig corridor, and Silesia, although virtually no German ever gave up the idea of eventually recovering those territories. The press turned its attention then to daily denunciations of Soviet Russia (one word in German), and to sentimentalizing over the syn-

[10] See footnote 14, p. 153, and pp. 471-472.

thetic sufferings of the Germans "exiled from home" in Austria or broken in bondage to the "bolshevist" Czechs and Slovaks.

After Czechoslovakia had made with Russia in 1935 a treaty not altogether unlike the one that Germany had chosen not to make, the Nazi press pictured that country as one vast airfield and army base covered with Russian planes and tanks ready to fan out over and into defenseless Germany. The sufferings of the German hostages in that hostile camp, the Nazi papers said, were beyond belief.[11]

After the German occupation of Austria in March, 1938, the tone and tempo of denunciations of the Czechoslovaks and of Beneš personally were stepped up to a pitch attainable and sustainable only by experts. Trading upon the patent fact that no one in France or Britain wanted war, although none but a fanatical few of his own people wanted one either, Hitler rightly judged it safe to threaten. Czechoslovakia could not fight Germany alone. Neither Britain nor Russia was treaty-bound (by bilateral defensive treaty, without raising the question of general obligation as a member of the League of Nations) to go to war in her defense unless France did. And France would fight only in self-defense.[12]

Emboldened by the occupation of Austria and presumably acting on instructions from Berlin, Konrad Henlein publicly proclaimed at Carlsbad, April 24, 1938, an eight-point "program" which challenged the sovereignty of the Czechoslovak government. He demanded for the Sudeten Germans not only "full equality" with the Czechs, which the government was not disposed to deny to any whom it could trust, but many special privileges, such as recognition as a separate folk group with an autonomous government and only German state employees within defined areas and special "protection" of those living outside those areas. He would have reopened old records and revived old quarrels by claiming reparation for all injustices done to Sudeten Germans since 1918. For the people of this alien state within a state Henlein claimed full liberty to demonstrate their Germanism and acceptance of Nazi ideology. In the same address he denounced the foreign policy of the Czechoslovak government, saying that it should cease to make itself an obstacle in the way of Germany's eastward movement, and for the sake of more friendly relations with Germany should abandon its alliances with France and Russia.

In May, with municipal elections in the offing, already twice post-

---

[11] The Nazi descriptions of them were incredible.
[12] For further discussion of the behavior of France and Britain in the Czechoslovak crisis see pp. 417-421 and 508-523.

poned, the government lifted its ban on public meetings and political demonstrations, and Henlein came promptly into the open with a storm troopers' organization on the German Nazi model. German troops massed for maneuvers on the Czechoslovak borders and were countered by a partial Czechoslovak mobilization, carried out with convincing quickness and precision; but during the summer a million Germans were called up for military service, while many thousands more were fortifying their French frontier.

In August the British government sent Lord Runciman to Czechoslovakia, ostensibly to investigate and if possible to mediate the dispute. Mediation proved to be impossible. The government was conciliatory; the Henleinists were not. Lord Runciman seemed to have listened more sympathetically to the dissidents than to spokesmen for the government. He confessed in his report "much sympathy with the Sudeten case." "It is a hard thing," he said, "to be governed by an alien race"—as if he considered Czechoslovaks intruders in predominantly German-populated Czechoslovak territory, and found the German nationalism which would disrupt the state preferable to the Czechoslovak nationalism which would maintain it. The Czechoslovak Germans, he thought, were moving inevitably toward revolt; there would be endless disturbance until they got what they wanted; so the way to quiet them was to give them what they wanted. It would be better to cede the disputed territories than to go on disputing their inevitable cession; and Czechoslovakia should abandon her defensive alliances (as Henlein had said) so as to cease to threaten Germany with attack. Then an international guarantee might be given what Neville Chamberlain had already called "a smaller and sounder" Czechoslovakia, and Germany might make a favorable trade agreement with it. Henlein had already gone off to the Nuremberg party congress, where Hitler denounced Czechoslovakia and vilified President Beneš in outrageous and unprecedented fashion, swearing vengeance on the torturers and oppressors of "his" German people.

The story of the fatal series of September conferences with Hitler is told elsewhere.[13] Chamberlain flew off to Berchtesgaden without waiting to talk to Runciman. As Henlein had been, Hitler was found to be insatiable. Back-pedaling before him, meeting his demands and hearing him brazenly double them in the middle of a report that they had been met, the British first minister Neville Chamberlain probably realized at Godesberg that he could not do business with Hitler. But he seems to have seen no better way out of a losing venture than to

[13] Pp. 513-523.

take his losses—letting Czechoslovakia pay the first installment on them—and leave the game. France was equally unready to fight to hold the ramparts of Czechoslovakia. Neither France nor Britain could afford to see that bastion surrendered, but neither thought that it could afford then to defend it. France notified Czechoslovakia that if Czechoslovakia did not immediately accept the Franco-British proposals, and war resulted, she would hold it responsible for having caused Germany to resort to force and would not associate herself with it.

At Munich, September 30, 1938, Czechoslovak delegates who had been peremptorily summoned for the purpose but not consulted were informed by friend and foe together that five zones were to be ceded to Germany, the transfer to be made under international supervision. Germany took six zones immediately without supervision. Zones five and six were largely Czechoslovak in population. In northern Moravia, for example, zone five included 254 Czech communes with a population of 221,000 Czechs to 145,000 Germans, and in southern Moravia 38 communes with 54,000 Czechs to 16,500 Germans; in all, 719,000 Czechs in five zones. Then a sixth zone not mentioned at Munich was occupied, with 60,000 more Czechs in seventy villages.[14] The Czechs in the areas so seized had no effective guarantees of national minority rights. Nazi rulers conceded dissidents no rights.

After Munich it was not long until Czechoslovakia was submerged. Beneš and Premier Syrový resigned October 5. Beneš flew to London October 22. No national election of a president was held; but on November 30 what was left of the parliament, with Germans and Communists not voting, elected Dr. Emil Hácha, former president of the supreme administrative court. A ministry headed by Rudolf Beran of the Party of National Unity replaced the interim government which General Syrový had meanwhile held together.

Poland had already taken Teschen. On the very day of the Munich conference, September 30, 1938, the Polish minister for foreign affairs, Colonel Beck, had sent a note demanding the immediate cession of the area disputed between the two countries in 1919. By October 10 Polish troops had taken the formerly disputed area, and in November they went on into Czechoslovak Silesia and Slovakia, taking the railway town of Bohumin (Oderberg) and many of the coal mines and industries around Ostrava and Karvinná. Wherever they went, Czech schools were closed at once.

The total population of Czechoslovak territories annexed by Poland

[14] R. W. Seton-Watson, *op. cit.,* 369.

was more than a quarter of a million persons, of whom less than one-third were Poles, and Czechs outnumbered Poles almost two to one. A German minority of 17,351 was involved there also.

Slovakia soon followed suit. The autonomist party already there had fallen under the new and more aggressively separatist leadership of Father Josef Tiso after the death of Father Andreus Hlinka in August, 1938. On October 7 Slovakia "seceded," but within a month (November 2) the first Vienna award, the work of Ribbentrop of Germany and Count Ciano of Italy, gave southern Slovakia to Hungary. Nearly a million people lived in the ceded area. A bare majority were Hungarian. Nearly 19,000 Czechs and 270,000 Slovaks were handed over to Hungarian rule. Father Tiso sadly pointed out that the change gave Hungary a Slovak minority of 20 percent and left Slovakia with a Magyar minority of only 6 percent. What was left of "independent" Slovakia contained only 17 percent of the industry, and produced only 10 percent of the income, of the second Czecho-Slovakian republic to which it returned, November 30, 1938.[15]

The reconstituted national state was federal in form, with federal departments of national defense, foreign affairs, and finance; but Slovakia had autonomy at last. Father Tiso put his own government on a one-party basis. Mindful of the way the Sudetenland had gone, the federal government attempted on March 12, 1939, to overthrow the neo-Nazi Slovakian regime and put Karel Sidor in Father Tiso's place. Next day Tiso was summoned to Berlin and ordered to declare Slovakia independent. He seemed willing, but the diet at Bratislava adopted the declaration, March 14, only under pressure of German threats of gunfire.

Cut off from Bohemia-Moravia (or "Czechia") by the intervening territory of an independent Slovakia, Ruthenia, which had followed Slovakia's example by demanding autonomy on October 11, 1938, followed it again in March, 1939, by declaring itself independent. Within twenty-four hours it had been taken by Hungary. In its easy annexation Hungary had the support of Poland, no help from Germany.

The day after Father Tiso had been ordered to Berlin and sent right back to Bratislava to declare Slovakia independent—of Czecho-Slovakia—President Hácha was summoned. Received by Hitler, Ribbentrop, and Göring with the news that Moravská Ostrava (Mährisch Ostrau) was already occupied by German troops, and bullied to the point of physical collapse, "in order to secure final pacification" he signed at last a statement that he was placing the destiny of the Czech

[15] Czechoslovakia became for a time Czecho-Slovakia.

people and country "with confidence" in the hands of the Führer of the German Reich.

That day Hitler went to Prague. Next day, from the historic Habsburg castle there, which had lately housed Presidents Masaryk and Beneš, he proclaimed the Protectorate of Bohemia and Moravia. Two days later, March 16, he announced from Vienna that Slovakia also would be "protected." The protector of Bohemia-Moravia was to be Konstantin von Neurath, not an original Nazi party member but always useful to the party in the Foreign Office. (See pp. 799-805, on the war criminal trials, Nuremberg, 1945-1946.)

POLAND

Resurrection

After the third partition, 1795—except from 1918 to 1939—a free and united Poland existed only in the minds and hearts of those people whose belief in it, nourished on historical memories of a past long gone, was strong enough to keep alive their faith in the possibility of its resurrection. The Polish nationalist of the nineteenth century could not be too realistic. There was little actual similarity between the ideal Poland of the past which his nostalgic imagination conjured up and the Poland, paralyzed by internal strife and political ineptitude, which was taken apart by its neighbors in the late eighteenth century. The Poland of the patriot's dream was not on the map or in this world at the dawning of the twentieth century. Unless three powerful empires —the German, Austro-Hungarian, and Russian—should be simultaneously destroyed, it could never again be put on the map; and the odds against such an occurrence would have seemed prohibitive to almost anyone else. The Polish nationalist could not, then, afford to count the odds. In his indomitable belief in something which others could not see he often seemed impractical, unreasoning, uncompromising, quite "out of this world."

The hopes of the Polish nationalists of the early nineteenth century had twice been disappointed. Napoleon, setting up the grand duchy of Warsaw and giving it access to the sea by establishing a free port for it in Danzig, which he made for a while a free city, had promised them a new national existence if they would show themselves worthy of it by fighting for it. They fought for it in his armies but did not gain it. When Napoleon was gone and the Russians were again in Warsaw, the Congress of Vienna set up "Congress Poland" as a constitutional

kingdom of which Tsar Alexander would be king. But the new kingdom of Poland did not include Pomorze (West Prussia), Poznań
(Posen), or Galicia; and it soon ceased to be a kingdom, becoming
only a Russian province misgoverned by officials unfit to govern elsewhere in tsarist Russia.

In 1914 Poles living in Posen and West Prussia were summoned to
fight for Germany, those in Russian Poland to fight for Russia. Those
from Galicia were called up by Austria-Hungary but used at first on
other fronts than in Galicia. Seven hundred thousand of them served
on either side. The Central Powers proposed to free the Russian Poles
and create an independent Poland, without saying clearly that the new
Poland would include all the Poles. Russia promised to free the Polish
subjects of the Central Powers and give them place in an autonomous
Poland within the Russian Empire.

While both sides tried to use the Poles, the Poles tried to use each
against the other. The Russian proposal was accepted by an all-
Polish National Democratic committee in Warsaw, led by Roman
Dmowski, leader also of the Polish delegation in the Russian Duma.
Dmowski thought in 1914 that the Poles could best promote the cause
of Polish nationalism by supporting Russia.

Not so Joseph Pilsudski. Pilsudski, though born in Lithuania, had
always been an enemy of Russia and had won his service badge as a
Polish patriot by having been expelled from medical school for
revolutionary activity, by having once been banished to Siberia for
complicity in a plot to kill the tsar, and by having edited for seven
years, underground, a revolutionary paper. Convinced that nothing
good for Poland could come out of collaboration with Russia, Pilsudski
went to Galicia in 1914 and raised there a small volunteer force, later
swelled in numbers and importance to the point of being called a
"legion," to fight the Russians.

After pushing the Russians out of Poland, the Germans set up a
provisional government in Warsaw and the Austro-Hungarians one in
Lublin. Hungary was unwilling to grant the Poles equality of status
with Hungarians in what at that time was still a dual monarchy. Austria
was unwilling either to permit Germany to annex Congress Poland or
to see an independent Poland set up as a buffer state between Germany
and Russia.

Pilsudski and his legion had been fighting not for Germany or for
Austria-Hungary but for Poland. When he thought he saw himself
and Poland being cheated by the indefinite postponement of the
recognition of a Polish state, he said so. He continued in 1917 to make

plans for the raising of a Polish army without, however, raising one for Germany to use. When Poland was not made independent by the Treaty of Brest Litovsk and land that she considered Polish was allocated elsewhere, he protested so vigorously that the Germans imprisoned him at Magdeburg. Released when the war ended, he hurried back to Warsaw and took command of the confused situation there when the German-controlled provisional government collapsed. The Allies had made the establishment of an independent Poland one of their war aims and General Haller had raised a Polish army in France. Meanwhile, after the communist revolution, Roman Dmowski had gone to Paris and established there a Polish National Committee which the Allies had recognized as representative of the new state, as the Masaryk-Beneš committee represented Czechoslovakia. Dmowski was a conservative and was supported by the more conservative elements of the Polish population. Pilsudski was not a party man but a nationalist and was supported as a nonpartisan by the army. But being a former Socialist and still something of a leftist, he was supported in 1919 by the Socialists and distrusted as a former revolutionary by the conservatives.

Here the world-famous Polish pianist Ignace Paderewski did his country another invaluable service. He had devoted himself all through the war to winning sympathy for Poland in the capitals of the world, where he was already known and universally admired. He had done much to secure Allied recognition of Polish independence and of Dmowski's National Committee. Now, recognizing the danger of dissension between the National Committee in Paris and the regency council in Warsaw, Paderewski went to Warsaw and reconciled them. Pilsudski became "chief of state" of the provisional government and remained in control at home. He was the one man Poland then had who could do what had to be done. Paderewski became premier and returned to Paris, where he and Dmowski represented Poland at the peace conference. Having just seen his country achieve the impossible in winning its independence, no ardent nationalist like Paderewski or Pilsudski would suddenly become too modest to assert her claims with boldness. Neither did. Both were bold enough. They claimed for the new Poland nothing less than the boundaries of 1772, before the first partition.

Poland's boundaries had never been dictated by geography. She had no natural frontiers unless the Carpathians, the natural southern boundary of Galicia, were so considered. East and west, the country was wide open. Historically, when Poland had been strong and Germany and Russia weak, Poland had pushed her boundaries outward, usually eastward. When Poland had been weak and her neighbors strong, the latter had pushed her boundaries in upon her and eventually obliterated them. In 1919 Austria-Hungary was gone, Germany and Russia were weakened by defeat and revolution, and Poland had powerful friends interested in strengthening her as a buffer state between Germany and Russia.

The Allies' statements about the boundaries of the new Poland had been as vague as their ideas on the subject, which were very vague indeed. In general, however, France wished her to be strong enough to replace Russia as an ally against Germany, and Britain, less pessimistic than France about the possibility of eventual reconciliation with Germany, was more cautious about giving Germany a grievance that might lead to a new irredentism between her and Poland.

Point XIII of President Wilson's Fourteen Points had said only: "An independent Polish state should be erected which should include the territories inhabited by indisputably Polish populations, which should be assured a free and secure access to the sea, and whose political and economic independence and territorial integrity should be guaranteed by international covenant."

The Versailles award to Poland of the Danzig corridor through West Prussia and of the provinces of Pomorze (West Prussia) and Poznań (Posen), and the outcome of the plebiscite in Upper Silesia have already been discussed.[16] The dispute with Czechoslovakia over the Teschen area has also been mentioned.[17]

Although Poland had once perished by the sword, she had been restored by it and seemed ready to live by it if necessary to get back to her boundaries of 1772. The Supreme Council of Allied and Associated Powers assembled for the Paris peace conference asked Lord Curzon of Great Britain as chairman of a committee to make a quick study of the question of Poland's eastern boundary and recommend a solution for it on an ethnic basis. The "Curzon line" accepted by the council was the only one ever drawn on that basis. So far as the Curzon committee could determine, most of the people then living west of that line were Polish; east of that line the population was predominantly Lithuanian, White Russian, or Ukrainian, and only a minority was Polish. The line ran close to what had been Russia's western boundary after the third partition of Poland in 1795, roughly

[16] See pp. 81-84.
[17] See pp. 181-182.

south from Grodno. Bialystok and Lublin were west of it, Wilno (Vilna) and Lwów (Lemberg) were east of it.

The towns of Wilno and Lwów had larger Polish populations, in proportion to their totals, than the provinces of the same names had. Poland claimed both. Her troops were already far east of the Curzon line when the peace conference accepted Lord Curzon's recommendation, and she rejected it.

In western Galicia the people were Polish and the idea of a Polish national union was readily accepted. In eastern Galicia the Ukrainian majority would have preferred independence or union with the new Ukrainian People's Republic, or at least autonomy within Poland. Poland claimed the whole area and in November, 1918, Polish troops occupied Lwów. In 1919 they conquered the three provinces, Lwów, Stanislawów, and Tarnopol, which were at once incorporated into Poland. The Paris peace conference and the Allied Conference of Ambassadors continued until 1923 to advocate self-determination and self-government for the people of eastern Galicia, and then in the face of Polish obduracy recognized what Poland had done.

Meanwhile Poland was at war with Russia, and on May 8, 1920, her troops entered Kiev. By that time, however, the Soviet army had disposed of some of its internal enemies, Kolchak and Denikin, and was better able to concentrate on the Poles. By July the Polish army was in so serious a position that it had to ask the Allies to mediate. The Allies suggested that it fall back to the Curzon line and that a conference then be called. While winning, the Russians refused mediation, and by August had driven the Poles back almost to Warsaw. Then in mid-August an Allied commission under General Weygand arrived and, with the aid of supplies from France, helped Pilsudski drive the Russians back.[18]

The new boundary established by the Treaty of Riga, March 18, 1921, was east, but not far east, of that of 1793. In other words, Poland took from Russia the territory east of the Curzon line which had been taken from her by Russia in the third partition in 1795, with a very small part of what had been taken in the second partition. Russia still held all that she had taken in the first partition and most of what she had taken in the second. Poland did not get back to the boundary of 1772, and was not satisfied. Russia was no better pleased than Poland.

Wilno, town and district, also east of the Curzon line and allocated

[18] Germans in Danzig handled munitions for Poland as slowly as they dared, and seriously impeded their shipments.

by the Paris peace conference to Lithuania, was also seized by Poland in 1920 by use of armed force. Russia, at war with Poland, had recognized Lithuania's claim to the town and area. Polish troops, driving the Russians back in October, 1920, came into conflict with the Lithuanians, made an armistice with them and agreed upon a line of demarcation, then broke the armistice on October 9 and seized the town and district. Their government disavowed the seizure but continued the occupation; and nearly two and a half years later (March 14, 1923) the Allied Conference of Ambassadors recognized it. Lithuania did not concede the territory until seven years after its seizure.

Plebiscites in the East Prussian districts of Marienwerder and Allenstein, held in the summer of 1920 when Poland's war with Russia was going very badly for her, resulted in the retention of the plebiscite areas by Germany. So were rounded out, by war and plebiscite over a period of something more than two years, the boundaries of resurrected Poland.

Government and Politics

The new government was confronted by peculiar political difficulties of historical origin. There was great disparity between the three principal parts of the country. The Poles in Galicia, although subject to Austria-Hungary, had been permitted to handle most of their own affairs through elected assemblies, and politically experienced Poles had been active in the Austrian diet or Reichsrat. They were quite ready to participate in Polish national life. Poles in the areas previously held by Germany had been less favored and had had less political experience. The Germans in those areas were usually prosperous, literate, and self-confident; but they were neither wanted in Polish politics nor ready to act whole-heartedly as citizens of Poland. Most inhabitants of the areas previously controlled by Russia were poor, uneducated, without political experience, and unready for self-government.

Each of the three sections, when freed from alien control, had as its inheritance from the power that had controlled it a different currency, law code, minor officialdom, and administrative organization and procedure. It took ten years to unify and coördinate the administration of the various areas and give the country a code of judicial procedure. People who had lived under dissimilar regimes had naturally developed different attitudes toward government and different thought and behavior patterns. As subject people, many of them had always been instinctively distrustful of government, habitually unfriendly and uncoöperative in their attitude toward it; and they were slow to change in that respect. Poles were alike and unanimous only in their determination to maintain their national independence and to make life miserable for anyone living in Poland whom they suspected of endangering the nation by disloyalty to it or by cherishing the memory of another allegiance.

With proportional representation, eighty political parties arose. Fifteen were represented in the first national diet.

There were three national constitutions, of which the last was the least democratic. The first was only a provisional "little" constitution adopted February 10, 1919, by a democratically elected diet. Paderewski was then premier and Pilsudski chief of state. The second was adopted March 17, 1921, by a constituent assembly elected by universal adult suffrage with proportional representation. Many of its provisions resembled those of the constitution of the Third French Republic. The titular head of the state was to be a president elected for a term of seven years by a national assembly consisting of the two houses of the national legislature sitting in joint session for that purpose. The president's powers were limited and were to be exercised only through cabinet ministers, whom he appointed but who were to be responsible to the lower house of parliament, the Diet or Sejm. Real political power was concentrated in the hands of a bicameral parliament consisting of a Diet and a Senate.

The constitutent assembly had done its work in troubled times, during the war with Russia, with Pilsudski serving as chief of state and commander of the army and the Galician peasant leader Witos as premier. In the first parliamentary elections, in November, 1922, the largest number of seats (163) was won by the National Democratic party. The National Democrats were nationalistic but not democratic. Before 1914 and until the Russian revolution they had advocated coöperation with czarist Russia. In the new Poland the party was anti-Semitic. Peasant parties, not effectively combined, elected 150 members. The numerous minority groups, with proportional representation, elected eighty-three deputies who soon increased their legislative influence by forming a minorities bloc. The Socialists had only forty-one seats, and there were never more than a few Communists; but the parties of the left could, by combining with the Peasant parties, outweigh the right for as long as they could hold their coalition together.

It was such a coalition that elected the first president under the new constitution, a friend of Pilsudski, G. Narutowicz. President Narutowicz was almost immediately assassinated, and Stanislaw Wojcie-chowski was elected to succeed him. General Wladislaw Sikorski became premier. Marshal Pilsudski retired for a while from public office.

The period of parliamentary government, 1922 to 1926, was one of personalities and political instability. Within four years there were fourteen cabinet changes. Neither people nor leaders had had much political experience. Parties represented special interest groups only, and most members of the diet seemed as devoid of national vision and as irresponsible as those of the prepartition diets of the eighteenth century. The Socialists wanted to reduce appropriations for the army, but were unwilling to reduce the numbers or the salaries of other government employees, and advocated increased appropriations for public works as a cure for unemployment. The conservatives, on the other hand, would have increased military and decreased civilian expenditures. With power concentrated in the hands of a legislature so divided and with no constitutional provision for breaking deadlocks, efficient government seemed impossible.

A crisis developed in May, 1926, over a proposal to reinstate Pilsudski, who had resigned, as chief of staff. The army was still loyal to him. With little disorder, because he met little resistance, he used the army to compel the resignation of Premier Witos and President Wojciechowski. In lieu of a vote of confidence, he let the national assembly elect him president, then declined the honor and had it given to Professor Ignace Moscicki.

By constitutional amendment the president was empowered to dismiss parliament with consent of the cabinet and, within certain limits, to govern by decree which should have the force of law. The president could constitutionally control appointments, including military ones; but Pilsudski proved in practice to be able always to control the president. He thus made Casimir Bartel premier and himself inspector general of the army.

Subsequently, until he died on May 12, 1935, Pilsudski was now and then premier or minister for foreign affairs, usually only leader of the army; but no matter where he sat he was always Pilsudski, always head of the table and leader of the nation. His strong-man government has been rather sympathetically described as a quasi-dictatorship. He postponed a national election until 1928 when he was sure he could control it, and would brook no interference with policies he considered vital to the nation; but although thinking of himself only as one who had risen above political partisanship, he did not establish a one-party system or consciously give his love of power priority over his love of country. Like Cromwell in that respect, he may sometimes have mistaken the former for the latter.

Political attitudes were very personal. People were for Pilsudski or against him. Pilsudski trusted persons or distrusted them, as he considered them good Poles or bad. Those whom he trusted most he used most, especially his "colonels"—the men who had joined his "legion" in 1914 and 1915 to fight the Russians and had kept his confidence. The parties of the left, which had supported him until his coup d'état of 1926, withdrew their support soon thereafter, and he then had to depend more heavily than ever upon his "colonels" and upon the landowners and aristocrats. Old family names such as Radziwill, Poniatowski, and Potocki began to appear again more prominently than at any other time since 1914. Elections were never free from intimidation or fraud; yet the government found them difficult to control.

In 1935 the government proposed again to amend the constitution. It had not the two-thirds majority in the national assembly which the constitution required for its amendment, but by taking advantage of the temporary absence of the opposition members (following a parliamentary quarrel which it was later accused of having provoked for that purpose) it rushed the measure through three readings at one sitting and declared it ready for the president's signature. The president signed it, and there was no court with power to review it.

The new constitution strengthened the executive at the expense of parliament, to which neither the president nor any of his ministers was any longer responsible. The president would no longer be chosen by the national assembly but would be elected by universal suffrage. Voters, however, would have only to choose between two candidates, one of whom would be nominated by the retiring president and the other by an electoral college, two-thirds of whose members would be chosen by the Diet and one-third by the Senate.[19] As chief of the executive, the president would make executive appointments and appoint one-third of the members of the Senate. He could summon, adjourn, or dissolve the parliament, and govern by decree when he and his ministers deemed it necessary.

Who would really exercise the almost unlimited authority of the president would depend upon his personal strength and relations with his ministers. While Pilsudski lived, he ruled. When he died, May 12,

[19] No election was held under the new constitution. President Moscicki had been reëlected in 1933 for a second seven-year term and was still in office when the Germans invaded.

1935, his "colonels" took over. One of them, Edward Smigly-Rydz, took Pilsudski's place as inspector general of the army and virtual dictator, but could never measure up to his stature as a leader.

Among the more influential of the new governing group were the minister for foreign affairs, Colonel Joseph Beck, who had held the same position under Pilsudski since 1932, and Slawek and Koc, both reactionaries and totalitarians. One of their first acts was to restrict the franchise so as to permit only persons twenty-four years old or older to vote in elections to the Diet, thirty or older in elections to the Senate (of which only two-thirds of the members were elected). Even the nomination of candidates for election to the Diet was controlled by government commissions.

The government of the colonels was less popular than Pilsudski's had been, but the people's dissatisfaction found few political outlets. A peasants' strike in 1937 which, until it was suppressed by force, made Poland seem to be on the brink of civil war was a protest against the character of the government as well as against the economic status of the peasants. Municipal elections of 1938 were swept by the Peasant and Socialist parties, which boycotted the parliamentary election of that year in continued protest against the restrictions under which it was held. The government was not in sound political condition to stand the test of war.

Economic Resources and Conditions

Two-thirds of Poland's people in the period between the wars were peasant farmers. Poland was one of Europe's foremost producers of rye, wheat, oats, potatoes, sugar beets, and livestock. Seven years of war and military occupation had, by 1921, devastated much of her farm land. Buildings had been destroyed, livestock killed or driven off, fields left untended or unfertilized. The building of two enormous plants for the production of commercial fertilizers by a chemical process invented by President Moscicki, and government loans to farmers at low interest rates for their purchase, were two of the government's best answers to the problem of restoring the fertility of the soil. Eventually, also, the land was restocked with animals.

Some progress was made toward a solution of the landownership problem, though never enough to satisfy the peasants or to encourage efficient mechanized farming, to which much of the level land of the country was well adapted. In 1921 nearly half of the land was in estates of more than one hundred hectares (250 acres) each, so large that their number was only 0.6 percent of the total number. About 5 percent of the total area was owned by the national government and included many square miles of forest, swamp, and barren land; but the percentage of arable land held in large privately owned estates was still high. Among the obstacles to redistribution of the land was the minorities treaty which protected the larger-than-average holdings of some of the Germans in Poznań and Pomorze.

Some redistribution was made, with compensation to the owners paid partly in cash and partly in government bonds; but when the war came nearly two-thirds of the total arable land was still in small holdings of less than twenty hectares (fifty acres) each, and nearly two-thirds of those holdings were of five hectares (about twelve acres) or less each.[20] Such small farms would not support the families of their owners, who had to supplement their incomes by working for someone else for wages. Yet the rural population was relatively large. Industry was drawing some landless laborers off the land, but not many. As there was always an abundant supply of farm labor available at low wages, mechanization was slow and the peasant standard of living remained low. All levels of production and peasant living standards were lower in the predominantly Lithuanian, White Russian, and Ukrainian provinces along the eastern frontier than in western Poland. Many peasants there may well have welcomed collectivization, with its large-field farming, mechanization, introduction of scientific agronomy and animal husbandry, and increased production.

Poland had enough oil in her southern regions, near the Carpathians, to make her one of Europe's principal oil producers and to enable her to export 40 percent of the output of her wells. But some of the profit must also have been exported, as 87 percent of the capital invested in the oil industry was owned by foreigners.

Poland ranked seventh among the nations of the world in coal production in 1936, fifth among those in Europe, third in Europe (after only Great Britain and Germany) in coal export. Nearly a third of the coal she produced was exported, much of it going by water from Gdynia across the Baltic to Sweden. Three-fourths of what she produced came from Upper Silesia, most of the rest from around Dabrowa and Cracow. Sixty percent of the capital invested in coal production was foreign. In Upper Silesia most of it was German.

Germany's loss in Upper Silesia was Poland's gain in many ways.

[20] George Kagan, "Agrarian Regime of Pre-war Poland," *Journal of Central European Affairs,* III (October, 1943), 241-269; Wladislaw Malinowski, "Note on the Agrarian Regime of Pre-war Poland," *ibid.,* IV (April, 1944), 71-75; Wiktor J. Ehrenpreis in J. S. Roucek, *op. cit.,* 378.

Ninety percent of the zinc production which made Poland the fifth ranking zinc-producing nation in the world, third in Europe, was Silesian. (Yet Germany was still one of the two nations whose zinc production exceeded Poland's. The other was Belgium.) Upper Silesia contributed heavily also to Polish lead, iron, and steel production.[21]

The Polish government did all it could do to capitalize on its access to the sea. As soon as it could make good the wastage of the war in ruined railway stations and disrupted signal systems, worn-out rolling stock, blasted bridges, and broken railway lines, it turned its attention to improving its river and rail connections with the Baltic, building at great expense through difficult terrain a new railway to carry coal down the corridor from Silesia to the new port of Gdynia, rather than use the parallel Danzig-to-Poland railway, only a few miles away, or cross German or Danzig territory.

Gdynia was literally new. The peace settlement of 1919 gave Poland a free port at Danzig, but Polish trade through that port was often subject to inconvenience. There were delays in docking or unloading ships. German harbor masters and warehousemen were suspected of discrimination, German longshoremen of slowing down. Polish shippers questioned whether Danzig could handle the increased volume of the new Poland's trade, and doubted that it would try very hard to do so; and they hated the thought of dependence upon German Danzig, no matter whether it was able or unable, willing or unwilling, to handle their cargoes. So they built Gdynia, on Polish soil, just west of Danzig.

Gdynia had been only a fishermen's village of three hundred people. By 1929 it had a population of fifteen thousand, by 1939 nearly ten times as many. In the last years before the German invasion it was the busiest seaport on the Baltic, handling four-fifths of Poland's overseas trade, which was increasing in volume as Germany, Austria, and Czechoslovakia took fewer of her exports and Britain and the Scandinavian countries took more. By that time it had many miles of breakwaters, piers, and railway spurs of its own, and more than fifty shipping lines to all parts of the world—half of them, however, to Baltic and North Sea ports. It was also by then a naval base, and Poland was building a navy.

Danzig had not been put out of business and still had trade to handle, but she felt the competition and for a time was more accommodating. Some agreements were negotiated for the allocation of

[21] See pp. 83-84.

traffic to the two ports; but when the Nazi got control of Danzig negotiation was made more difficult, and Poland put her trust in Gdynia.[22]

Poland started with a heavy handicap as to motor roads. She contrived after 1920 to increase her modern road mileage by 50 percent and to replace some of her wooden bridges with newer ones of steel and concrete, but most of her highways were still dirt roads in 1939. Poland's well-wishers hoped the autumn rains would turn them to mud that would mire the German army down, but the German army churned them to choking dust in weeks of rainless weather.

National Minorities

Nearly a third of the people living in Poland in the period between the wars were not Polish: more than 8,000,000 in a population only slightly in excess of 27,000,000 in 1921, nearly 10,000,000 in a population of nearly 32,000,000 in 1931. The percentage of Poles in the total population had decreased in the ten-year period from 69.2 percent to 68.9 percent, although the government had tried hard to increase it by offering material inducements to Polish families to maintain a higher birth rate. By 1939 the total population had grown to approximately 35,000,000, with minorities estimated at ten to eleven millions.[23]

Recognizing that some violence was being done in the name of Polish nationalism to the national feeling of the minorities and to the principle of self-determination which it had itself acclaimed and followed when convenient, the Paris peace conference required Poland to subscribe to a treaty defining and guaranteeing minority rights.

The Polish minorities treaty was signed at Versailles on the same day as the Treaty of Versailles, June 28, 1919, and guaranteed by the League of Nations. It provided that in addition to all rights and privileges of Polish nationality and citizenship the minorities should enjoy without interference or discrimination the special privilege of using their own languages and receiving elementary instruction in them, of maintaining their own institutions, and of benefiting in proportion to their numbers from the expenditure of public funds. Jews were specifically recognized as a minority and protected in their religious observances, including the keeping of their Sabbath, and in the use of the Yiddish language.

[22] See p. 528.
[23] Polish censuses of 1921 and 1931. Hugh Seton-Watson, *Eastern Europe Between the Wars, 1918-1941*, Appendix A.

The Jews, though not quite a tenth of the whole people, had so congregated in the towns, and particularly in the eastern ones, as to constitute about a third of the population of cities of more than 100,000 inhabitants. There they were active in business, controlling nearly three-fourths of the mercantile establishments. Half of the employers of labor and nearly half of the skilled artisans were Jews. Jews were prominent in the legal, medical, and other professions, and in banking.

Being present in larger numbers and more closely grouped together than in most other countries, the Jews showed more of a tendency in Poland than elsewhere to form separate communities and live apart. Yet 400,000 of them listed themselves in the last census as Poles rather than as Jews, Jewish only in religion. In Poland as in other countries the nationalists least willing to see them assimilated were the first to condemn them as clannish for holding themselves aloof.

Jewish preëminence in certain lucrative professions and the apparent prosperity of certain Jews aroused the envy and cupidity of some of their non-Jewish neighbors. Although communism was never strong enough to be seriously thought a menace, Polish fascists of the Nazi type found it useful as a whipping boy; and there were enough Communists among the Jews to serve the Jew-baiters as a pretext. Nothing was ever so bad that a Nazi occupation could not make it worse; but there was ugly and violent anti-Semitism in Poland before the Nazi aggravated it.

The unhappy situation of the Lithuanian, White Russian, and Ukrainian populations of the eastern districts has already been mentioned.[24] Some amelioration of their condition was afforded after 1922 by the grant of some self-government in purely local affairs. In 1920 a new law promised them the use of their own languages in administrative offices, courts, and schools; but the Polish administration of the eastern areas was never enlightened or liberal enough to win their allegiance or to enable them to prosper under it. There was great confusion in those areas, much ignorance, and little unanimity of political opinion. Many of the people seem to have seen no reason why they should endanger or exert themselves to maintain a connection which they had never chosen to make, found advantageous, or learned to contemplate with any satisfaction.

The German minority was not Poland's largest, but it was her most troublesome. The combination of the German minority and the Versailles minority treaty was awkward for her, as the treaty was not

24 See pp. 186-189.

reciprocal. It gave the Germans living in Poland the right to appeal to the League of Nations and the World Court if they considered themselves mistreated. They availed themselves of that privilege several times, and were sustained in their complaints.[25] Poles living in Germany might be similarly ill used, and were, but had no such statutory protection. Finding them inadequately protected by a fifteen-year bilateral treaty she had made with Germany in 1922, Poland did not renew that treaty. Germans living in Poland who did not choose to become Polish citizens she ordered to leave the country by July 31, 1925. Finding her own landownership reform legislation blocked where German landowners were concerned by provisions of the minorities treaty of Versailles, she announced in the League of Nations Assembly of 1934 that she would no longer recognize the obligations which that treaty imposed upon her. After the adoption of the new electoral law of 1935 no more Germans were elected to the parliament.

There was provocation and terrorism on both sides in western Poland as relations between Germany and Poland deteriorated. While Hitler was busy elsewhere with his "redemption" of the Austrian and Sudeten Germans, those in Poland were reasonably circumspect, well watched by Polish police and discreetly encouraged by the German Gestapo. As soon as he was free to turn his attention farther eastward, Hitler found much to say about Poland's persecution of her German nationals. When the invasion came, the Germans already in Poland thought their day had dawned. It had; and they served their other country well as informers, spies, and saboteurs. While the occupation lasted, they enjoyed their day of power and of profit. When the Russians expelled the German armies, those who were not overtaken by a swifter vengeance fled or were thrown across a new border line, far west of any they had known, into the fragment that was left of Germany.

Foreign Policy

During Poland's first few years as a restored national state she put her trust, necessarily, in the Allies and League of Nations which had restored her, in the anti-German alliance policy of France, and in her own new-found military strength. By use of armed force she took disputed territory from Czechoslovakia, Russia, and Lithuania, thus making temporary enemies of all three. Teschen always stood in the way of good relations with Czechoslovakia, and because of Wilno

[25] See p. 83.

Lithuania refused to reëstablish diplomatic relations until 1938. Reconciliation with Russia was a little easier. With Litvinov in the ascendant, the two nations signed first the multilateral Litvinov Protocol of 1929, then a bilateral nonaggression pact in 1932, which was extended in 1935 for a period of ten more years.

France sponsored Poland and helped her in many ways. She was Poland's strongest friend at court, at the Paris peace conference and in the Allied Conference of Ambassadors. French money, munitions, and a military mission aided her in her post-Versailles war against Russia. Before that war was ended a treaty of alliance against Germany had been signed by France and Poland, February 19, 1921, supplemented by a military convention in September, 1922. Either was pledged to help the other if the other should be attacked by Germany. That treaty was still legally in effect in September, 1939. French capital played an important part in the improvement of Poland's railways and in the building of the port and naval base of Gdynia.

At Locarno in 1925 Germany and Poland made an arbitration treaty, but Stresemann rejected the idea of an "eastern Locarno" to guarantee the German-Polish boundary against change by use of force. When France renewed the suggestion in 1935 Poland was also unenthusiastic about it, as Pilsudski and Colonel Beck suspected her of hoping to evade some of her treaty obligations as an ally by sharing them with Russia.

Poland was a member of the League of Nations, a signer of the Kellogg-Briand Pact, and a participant in the general disarmament conference at Geneva in 1932; but Pilsudski, always the vigilant old soldier, watched constantly the current strength of all his neighbors' battalions. Seeing France and Britain permit their armed strength to decline, and at the same time fail to replace it with anything he could recognize as convincing guarantees of security on an international basis, he was all the more impressed by the self-confident and aggressive spirit of Nazi Germany. A bilateral pact with a neighbor conscious of its strength—his nearest western neighbor, too—seemed to him more real and practical than continued dependence upon a friendly nation far away and clearly conscious of its weakness.

So in January, 1934, Hitler and Pilsudski made a bilateral ten-year nonaggression pact which probably did as much as any other treaty of that year to weaken Europe's confidence in the League-and-general-treaty system of security. The bilateral agreement was one of Hitler's favorite weapons. It advertised to all who might be interested that the other party to it was making his own deal separately with the only central European nation that had refused to deal any further through the League of Nations, had voluntarily withdrawn from it, and was daily denouncing it and all its works—especially the Versailles territorial settlement which it had in general maintained.

Poland was here reacting differently from Russia. As Russia saw herself threatened by Germany's renascent military strength and the constantly growing prestige of a blatantly anticommunist German government, she turned toward collective security rather than away from it, joined the League of Nations, publicly advocated universal disarmament, and let Litvinov say repeatedly for the record: "Peace is indivisible." Poland's leaders, however, feared and distrusted Russia more than they did Germany, and turned to Germany for protection.

How far Colonel Beck had gone in giving Poland's foreign policy a German-Italian orientation was indicated by the haste with which he recognized Italy's conquest of Ethiopia. Poland served the Axis, not the League, on that occasion. When Czechoslovakia was threatened by Germany and Litvinov argued publicly that it was not yet too late for the powers to act in concert to stop the brazen aggression, Poland made it known that she would not permit the passage of Russian troops across her territory. Her attitude was one of many reasons why Czechoslovakia was not defended. Instead, Poland seized Teschen on the very day of the debacle, so punctually as to indicate that she must have known beforehand just what was to be done that day in Munich.

With Czechoslovakia gone, Poland was clearly indicated as Hitler's next objective, and the British ministry realized at last the falsehood of the Führer's oft-repeated statement that he had no more territorial demands to make. Yet Hitler kept the initiative. In his anniversary address of January 29, 1939, he lauded the German-Polish nonaggression pact as a pillar of the peace. Less than two months later he demanded Danzig. Poland refused, and accepted (on a mutual basis) a British guarantee of her independence and territorial integrity. Hitler made that acceptance of the British guarantee his pretext, in a speech on April 28, for orally denouncing his nonaggression pact with Poland.[26]

Then, if ever, was the time for Poland to have made a general defensive treaty to supplement and strengthen her old dual alliance with France. Still mortally afraid of Russia, however, she would have

[26] Only four months and two days were to elapse between this informal and illegal denunciation of the treaty and the aggression against which Poland's leaders had vainly hoped it would afford protection.

nothing to do with defense plans or alliances which contemplated the use of Russian troops on Polish soil. France had, by then, a dual defensive treaty of alliance with Russia. Britain had none. Distrust of Russia, both in Britain and in Poland, stood in the way of a four-power military alliance.

Geography stood in the way of direct British aid to Poland. A glance at the map showed clearly that, if Germany attacked Poland, France and Britain could help her only by attacking Germany from the west or from the air. There was known to be a German west wall of unknown strength which would slow down a land attack if it did not stop it, and a German air force and anti-aircraft defense which could have made an air attack extremely costly if the Allies had had the equipment and the hardihood to start that sort of thing. It was not difficult, therefore, for a Russian realist to predict that Germany would (as she did) win her war in Poland in a few weeks, confront the French and British with an accomplished fact, and let them then decide what they would do in the face of the new situation. Russia would in that event, as their ally, have found herself at war with a mobile, mechanized, victory-stimulated German army and an overshadowing German air force on her western frontier or in wide-open eastern Poland; and she was not ready to face it.

As an alternative, on August 23, 1939, Russia made a nonaggression pact with Germany. On August 25 Great Britain and Poland signed a treaty of alliance. On September 1 the German air force swarmed over Poland and German troops swarmed into it. Great Britain and France declared war on Germany September 3.[27]

RUMANIA

Territorial Gains, 1918-1919

Rumania lost and won in light-opera fashion in 1916 and 1918, and has experienced frequent violent changes since that time. By participation in the second Balkan war she had taken the southern Dobruja from Bulgaria in 1913. In August, 1914, she had a defensive treaty of alliance with Germany and Austria-Hungary, and a German-born Hohenzollern of the south German branch of the family as king, Carol (Karl, or Charles) I. A strong pro-German faction hoped with the aid of the Central Powers to take Bessarabia from Russia, which had held it for a hundred years.

[27] See p. 540 and maps, pp. 164-165.

King Carol died, however, on October 10, 1914. His successor, his nephew Ferdinand I, was also a Hohenzollern and German-born, but not actively pro-German. The new queen, Marie, a member of the British royal family with a wide acquaintance among the others and a lively interest in international affairs, thought that the Allies might win the war. This seemed not improbable as Russia drove the Austro-Hungarian armies out of nearly all Galicia in the 1914 campaign. Both liberals led by Ion Bratianu and conservatives led by Take Ionescu favored intervention on the side of the Allies with a view to the conquest of Transylvania, which had never been part of the king-dom of Rumania but in which a majority of the population was Rumanian.

Enthusiasm for the Allied cause waned noticeably in 1915, a year of sweeping victories for the Central Powers. The failure at Gallipoli, the conquest of Serbia, and Russian reverses in Poland were warning signs to Rumania that to associate herself with the Allies might be to court disaster. Help comes most readily in war to those who need it least. By midsummer, 1916, however, the great German offensive at Verdun had failed, the Allied offensive on the Somme had not yet bogged down, an Austrian offensive in the Trentino had failed, and the Italians had gained some ground at Gorizia; and the Russians were again on the offensive in Galicia.

The Allies were generous with offers of other peoples' territory. Russia had already suggested that Rumania take Transylvania, and offered to guarantee her possession of the Dobruja. Now, by treaty, August 17, Bucovina and the Banat of Temesvár as far west as the Theiss (Tisza) River were also offered, and Rumania declared war on Austria-Hungary on August 27, 1916. Transylvania was her first ob-jective, and her troops poured into it. They went in unready, inade-quately supplied and insufficiently equipped, depending upon Russian promises of munitions and assistance of Russian troops already in Bucovina and the help of Allied troops then at Salonika, which might have been expected to divert the attention of the Bulgarians.

Very little of the promised help was forthcoming. General Sarrail sat tight at Salonika while the Bulgarians reëntered the Dobruja, and the Russians could not hold their own in Galicia or Bucovina. The Central Powers, on the other hand, sent strong and well-supplied forces not only into Transylvania but on into Rumania, occupying Bucharest December 6. The Rumanian government fled but went on with the war until August, 1917, then signed a truce December 6. At Bucharest, May 7, 1918, a Germanophile ministry signed a treaty of

peace recognizing a situation which had existed in fact for more than
a year already. The Dobruja south of the Danube, which Bulgarian
troops had taken in 1916, was ceded back to Bulgaria. Hungary kept
what had been hers and improved her border lines in the Carpathians.
Rumanian grain, oil, and other war materials were all available to the
Central Powers, and Rumanian economic interests were in all ways
subordinated to those of her conquerors.

One temporary advantage only was gained from the new situation.
In May, 1917, Rumanian elements in Bessarabia had formed a "National Moldavian Committee." In December, 1917, that group invited
Rumanian troops into Bessarabia to defend the independence of the
new Moldavian republic which it then proclaimed. The troops were
sent, and from January to March, 1918, a state of war existed between Rumania and revolutionary Russia. In April the Rumanian
elements in the Bessarabian supreme council, with the Ukrainian delegates abstaining, voted for union with Rumania, reserving the right of
autonomy for Bessarabia. In May, by the Treaty of Bucharest, the
Central Powers recognized the transfer, to weaken Russia and compensate Rumania for what she was losing to them and to Bulgaria.
Russia was not reconciled to the loss of Bessarabia and did not then
recognize Rumania's title to it, but was not able then to take it back.

In November, 1918, Germany and her allies lost their grip. Armistice agreements were signed by Bulgaria September 29, Turkey October 31, and Austria-Hungary November 3. Anticipating Germany's
surrender by only three days, on November 8 Rumania denounced
the Treaty of Bucharest by which she had made a separate peace, repealed all acts of the pro-German government, and again called
herself a belligerent and one of the Allies. Ion Bratianu, who had
brought her into the war in 1916, again became premier, December
14, 1918, represented his country at the Paris peace conference, and
collected on almost all its territorial claims based on the treaty of
alliance of August 17, 1916, as if it had never made a separate peace.

By the general Versailles-Trianon-Neuilly territorial settlement,
Rumania had to share the Banat of Temesvár with Yugoslavia, getting
only the eastern portion of it; but the union with Transylvania, already
proclaimed by Juliu (Julius) Maniu and the Transylvanian-Ruma-
nian nationalists, was confirmed. Rumania then regained also the
Dobruja south of the Danube, gained Bucovina, which had been part
of the crown lands of Austria, and retained Bessarabia, which she
had taken from Russia early in 1918. Having made sure of her possession of Bessarabia, she forgot about autonomy and, working

through the Rumanian members of the Bessarabian supreme council, incorporated the territory as a Rumanian province. The supreme council voted for incorporation, then for its own dissolution. The principal Allied powers did not recognize the annexation until October 28, 1920, and Russia not until 1934.

Having been on the winning side in the war, although herself defeated, overrun, and economically exploited by the enemy, Rumania had more than doubled both her area and her population. Her area from 1918 to 1940 was 122,282 square miles. Her population in 1936 was 19,319,300. Even so, Ion Bratianu refused to sign the treaties because of his objection to the clauses for the protection of national minorities and because he had not got all the land he asked for in central Hungary. Rumania's attempt to make further gains at Hungary's expense during the Béla Kun period has already been mentioned.[28]

Government and Politics

As it had been before the war, the government was a parliamentary monarchy in form only. An expropriation law of July, 1917, had promised a radical redistribution of the land. The right of suffrage by secret ballot had been decreed for all men over twenty-one when the royal government redeclared war November 8, 1918. But political parties really represented classes, economic-interest groups, or areas; and control of the national government was only the rich prize for which those groups or ambitious individuals contended, the winners using it for their own advantage.

Ion Bratianu's following called itself the Liberal party but was none too liberal politically. The party of business, banks, and light industry, it consisted principally of the wealthier bourgeoisie, rather nationalistic and unfriendly to foreigners than patriotic, willing to use the land reform to reduce the economic strength and political influence of the old landed aristocracy, and willing to permit all men to vote who would vote consistently to keep the Liberals in office. It advocated the centralization of administrative authority and, wherever possible, strengthened bureaucratic controls. It sought also to further the industrialization of the country and to promote its foreign trade. It was in office in 1918-1919, returned in 1922, and held office until 1926.

The People's party, organized and led by the war hero Marshal

[28] See pp. 106-107.

Averescu, shared his aversion to Bolshevism or anything called "communism" and was even more conservative than the Liberals. It was most interested in what it called the reëstablishment of order. Averescu was in office with the support of Take Ionescu and the Conservative Democrats in 1920-1922, pushing land reform in Bessarabia so as to eliminate Russian influence there, and again in 1926-1927 with Liberal support, vainly opposing the return of Crown Prince Carol.

Late in 1925 Crown Prince Carol, who had been estranged from his wife the Princess Helen, left Rumania with a Madame Magda Lupescu. From Venice, en route to Paris, he issued a statement renouncing his right to the succession to the throne and to the tutelage of his little son Prince Michael, who by his renunciation became heir apparent to the throne. Carol announced that it was his intention completely and permanently to sever his connection with his homeland. A provisional regency council was appointed in January, 1926, consisting of the patriarch of the Orthodox Church, the president of the Supreme Court, and Carol's younger brother Prince Nicholas.

The reasons for the crown prince's abdication were more political than personal. His personal immorality, though scandalous, had not so scandalized his countrymen as to have compelled him either to renounce his right to the succession or to leave the country. He was known to be an admirer of Mussolini and to cherish an ambition to make the monarchy into a royal dictatorship. The Liberals, led by the Bratianus, had been able to do business with King Ferdinand to the mutual advantage of monarchy and party but knew that they would be thrust aside by Carol. So in the last days of their political preeminence they quietly banished him.

King Ferdinand died on July 20 and Ion Bratianu November 24, 1927. The new premier, under the regency, was Vintila Bratianu. Policy was not greatly changed and continued to exclude Carol, but Vintila Bratianu was less forceful than his brother had been, and less successful in preventing the growth of a new movement combining a narrow nationalism with a demand for Carol's return. The new movement was fostered and utilized by the National Peasant party formed in 1926 by the fusion of the older National and Peasant parties.

The Liberals and the People's party had kept themselves in power by controlling the elections, either separately or jointly. The last election before King Ferdinand's death had been so managed by Ion Bratianu that the Liberals won 70 percent of the votes and the National Peasant party only 20 percent, although a reversal of those percentages would have reflected more accurately the actual popularity of the two parties at the time. But in November, 1928, Premier Vintila Bratianu resigned and, in what was generally conceded to have been the freest and fairest election held in Rumania between the wars, the National Peasant party won three-fourths of the votes cast. Dr. Maniu, who had served his political apprenticeship in the prewar Hungarian parliament as spokesman for the Rumanian element in Transylvania, was the new premier.

Rumania's only peasant government was popular at first, but not with the most influential people. Dr. Maniu's personal integrity was above challenge in a country where venality, favoritism, and personal profit-taking by officeholders were only too common. Some of Maniu's associates were little better in that respect than the politicians they replaced. Although decentralization of administration had been promised, little was done in that direction, and Rumanian administration was still compared unfavorably with what the people remembered of the Russian or Hungarian in Bessarabia, Bucovina, or Transylvania.

The peasants who had helped elect the National Peasant government expected it to do something for them. Export duties were repealed. Some coöperatives were encouraged, and some instruction was offered in better methods of cultivation. But the most significant land reform attempted was disappointing. The landownership reforms effected by previous postwar governments had expropriated the owners of very large estates with little compensation but had greatly increased the number of dwarf-size holdings. In 1929 the Maniu government made it legal to sell such holdings, hoping so to facilitate the formation of farms of medium size. Some very small holdings were sold, but the sellers only dropped so much the deeper into the rural proletariat of landless laborers or dwarf holders, already too numerous, for whom little more was done.

At the other end of the financial scale the government opened up the country to the influx of foreign capital, which aroused the bitterest resentment among the bourgeois Liberals. The latter had been inhospitable to money from abroad and clung to their monopoly of opportunity to exploit the country's forest and oil reserves for their own benefit. New taxes were found necessary but were universally resented.

Bedeviled on both sides by the discontented, finding their program sabotaged by bureaucrats appointed by previous governments, and realizing that their government had already lost much of the popularity it had enjoyed during its first months in office, the party leaders thought again of the exiled Carol, whom they hoped they could use.

Young King Michael was still a boy, and the regency was but a feeble substitute for a king. On the theory that the country needed a king, that Carol was the king it needed, and that he would be decently grateful to the party that brought him back—assumptions all of questionable validity—they permitted Carol to return in June, 1930. The regency and the boy king Michael acquiesced and, after going through the formality of resigning, Dr. Maniu stayed in office as premier.

Carol II seemed for a while to be what the country wanted, but he was not the king it needed. In a reign of only ten years he did it incalculable harm. Lacking at first the strength to rule by force and intimidation as Mussolini did, he strengthened himself by bribery and personal intrigue.

Maniu was not the king's kind of man. Carol had promised before his return not to bring his mistress Magda Lupescu back with him; but she came, and was soon powerful in palace politics, which dominated national politics and directed national policy. As Madame de Pompadour had done, she ticketed men for favors, for advancement, or for oblivion. Something of a Puritan personality, and objecting to Madame Lupescu on grounds of personal morality as well as to her abuse of influence, Maniu protested in vain—and resigned. Two years later he was again premier for a few weeks, vainly tried again to rid the government of the Lupescu, and again resigned.[29]

Lesser men than Maniu, such as Vaida, were drawn away from the National Peasant party and into the king's personal following. The king secretly encouraged the Nazi-like Iron Guard, and used it to eliminate officials who embarrassed him by taking their offices too seriously. Premier Duca, for example, outlawed the Iron Guard on the eve of the elections of 1933 and was soon thereafter murdered by it. Duca's successor, Tatarescu, was more obliging and did the king's will when he could.

The Iron Guard was a fanatically nationalistic and hysterically anti-Semitic organization with Nazi-Ku-Klux trappings—green shirts, white horses, fiery crosses, clubs, knives, and firearms. Its founder, Corneliu Zelea Codreanu, a young man of mixed Polish and Hungarian ancestry and so an outsider in Rumania in much the same

---

[29] In August, 1944, Dr. Maniu participated with King Michael in the overthrow of the pro-Nazi government of Ion Antonescu and in the consequent rapprochement with Russia; but in 1945 he was excluded from the communist-led government of Dr. Petru Groza. On July 18, 1947, he was arrested on a charge of treasonable communication with the United States and Great Britain and of having aided four Rumanian Peasant party leaders to escape secretly from Rumania. In November, 1947, he was sentenced to imprisonment for life.

sense as Hitler was in Germany, was notorious as the reputed murderer of a prefect of Jassy who had tried in 1929 to suppress disorder started by the students there. As Codreanu and his fellow hooligans had been the agents of the police more often than they had been its enemies, he was acquitted and continued in the name of patriotism to wage war by violence on "Jews," "communists," and others labeled for convenience as enemies of the people. Kindred organizations with duplicate aims and methods and interchangeable membership were the Legion of the Archangel Michael and the All for the Fatherland party.

As the Nazi were then doing in Germany, the ardent and eloquent young men of the Iron Guard promised to free the poor from poverty by giving the peasant more land and the industrial worker better wages, to free the country from misgovernment by dishonest politicians, to free everyone from exploitation by Jewish merchants and moneylenders, to free the professions from unfair Jewish competition in them, to free property and capitalist enterprise from Jewish and other alien control and from the ever present threat of communism. People who did not know what freedom was but thought they wanted to be free listened to them, and lost the little freedom they then had.

Having used the Iron Guard without acknowledgment to intimidate or to eliminate the Liberals and Democrats, Carol himself began in 1937 to be afraid of the thing he had let loose. If he depended too much upon it or let it get too strong, it might turn upon him and destroy or dominate him. In the elections of that year the government party, which by an undemocratic law adopted by the Liberals in 1926 needed only 40 percent of the votes cast to give it a majority of the seats in parliament, got only 38 percent. The National Peasant party had polled only 22 percent of the votes cast, the Iron Guard 16 percent, and the equally anti-Semitic National Christian party 9 percent. The king's choice as premier was Octavian Goga of the National Christian party.[30]

The Goga ministry lasted only a few weeks. Then the king openly declared a dictatorship, and a well-controlled plebiscite overwhelmingly endorsed an appropriate constitution. A typical fascist one-party system was announced in December, 1938, to unite all parties in a "Front of National Renaissance," and the wastrel king corruptionist declared war on waste and on corruption. The voting age was raised to thirty, and thousands of the younger members of the Iron Guard were so disfranchised. The patriarch Miron Cristea of the Orthodox

[30] Hugh Seton-Watson, *Eastern Europe Between the Wars, 1918-1941*, 209.

Church was called premier. Corneliu Codreanu of the Iron Guard was arrested and sentenced to ten years' imprisonment; but late in November, 1938, he and thirteen fellow prisoners, all Iron Guardists, were machine-gunned by the police, who said they had attempted to escape while being transferred to a safer prison.

Government gunmen and Iron Guard terrorists were equally jittery, ruthless, and quick on the trigger. The summer of 1939 was a period of numerous arrests and outrages. In September Armand Călinescu, a strong man who had held the key position of minister of the interior in the short-lived Goga ministry and had become premier upon the death of Miron Cristea, was assassinated. At once in retaliation for his murder the government publicly executed nine members of the Iron Guard. Many others were liquidated later. Thousands were arrested.

The regime solved nothing. The king had destroyed all legitimately organized and law-abiding political opposition and made himself master of a police state. People were at the mercy of lawless law-enforcement agencies which only the king or the king's friends could control. Carol was popular only among those who hoped to profit from his favor, including the army, upon which he lavished all the money he could spare from his own indulgences and the extravagance of his personal favorites. Taxes were heavy and government officials were rapacious and irresponsible.

The Iron Guard had the support of Nazi Germany. While Poland stood and Germany and Soviet Russia seemed unlikely to combine, Carol dared to fight the Guard for control of the Rumanian government. When Germany and Russia collaborated in the fourth partition of Poland, Rumania's tenure of Bessarabia was at once made more precarious. When France proved unable to withstand invasion, "the wave of the future" appeared to be a Nazi wave, and the British-French guarantee of Rumanian independence, previously given and accepted, seemed to lose some of its value.

Hoping in desperation that the patriotism of the Iron Guard would be stronger than its affinity with the Nazi, and that with its support he might yet maintain Rumania's independence without loss of territory, the king changed horses in midstream. On June 21, 1940, he proclaimed the conversion of the Party of National Renaissance into a new Party of the Nation, of which the Iron Guard would be the nucleus. With that end in view, he staged a public reconciliation with Horia Sima, the leader of the Guard, and appointed a pro-German foreign minister, Ion Gigurtu.

It was a last-minute recognition of the way the world was going. Two days later, June 23, France signed an armistice with Germany, June 24 with Italy. On June 27 the Russians moved into Bessarabia, which had once been theirs, and Bucovina, which until 1918 had been part of Hungary. The Axis did nothing to stop them. Great Britain did not withdraw her guarantee of Rumanian independence but was subsequently said by the Rumanian foreign minister Gafencu to have given warning in December, 1939, that that guarantee would not hold against an attack by Russia unless Turkey should promise Rumania immediate assistance and Italy should promise neutrality; so Rumania renounced it. British oil interests were expropriated, and German troops took over the defense of the oil fields.

Helpless in German hands, the king made Gigurtu prime minister and Horia Sima minister of culture; but when he was compelled at the end of August to cede northern Transylvania to Hungary, with a population of 1,400,000 Rumanians to 900,000 Hungarians, the nationalism of the Iron Guardists was aroused to the point of protest.

That was all. The king was made to take the brunt of the nationwide resentment, and to abdicate. Going a second time into well-earned retirement, this time overseas, he carried with him to Mexico and later to South America his precious Magda Lupescu and the valuables they would need for a long sojourn abroad.

Nineteen-year-old Crown Prince Michael became king again in name, and General Ion Antonescu tried to take control of the government. He could no more resist the Germans or refuse to obey their orders than Carol had found that he could. On September 6, the day of the abdication, he had to give back to Bulgaria the territory of the Dobruja south of the Danube, which Rumania had taken in 1913, lost in 1916, and retaken in 1918.

Losses of population from June to September, 1940, were approximately as follows: to Russia in Bessarabia and Bucovina 4,000,000; to Hungary in Transylvania 2,400,000; to Bulgaria in the Dobruja 350,000.

Appealing publicly for unity on the nationalist principles of the League of the Archangel Michael, General Antonescu tried, as Carol had tried, to use the Iron Guard without permitting it to use him; but, accusing him of having sold out the country to the Germans, it turned against him, still led by Horia Sima, whom he had made vice premier. The new war between government and Guard was worse than anything the unhappy country had yet seen. The bodies of Corneliu Codreanu and his "fellow martyrs" were exhumed and honored with an elaborate funeral. The common grave from which their bodies had been taken was left open by the Iron Guard until it had sixty-four "enemies of the people," supporters of the government—four for one —lined up before it, to be machine-gunned as they had been. Jews were, as usual, special objects of the attentions of the Iron Guard. Thousands were killed.

Yet the government forces won. The Germans, who had used the Guard as Carol had used it to cripple government in Rumania, betrayed it as he had done, but for a different reason. It was too Rumanian, too nationalistic, for them. But when its power to oppose them had been broken they sheltered its refugees, to have them in hand for future use as needed.

General Antonescu formed another government in January, 1941, this one almost entirely military, without the Iron Guard. It was totalitarian, openly pro-German and controlled by Germany. The general had signed the Axis pact November 23, 1940. The country was occupied by German troops, their concentrations facing toward Bulgaria and Bessarabia. Great Britain severed diplomatic relations with Rumania February 10. In June, for the sake of Bessarabia and whatever else she might hope to get as compensation for territories she had had to cede to her fellow satellites, Rumania went with Germany into her war against Russia.[31]

Economic Conditions and Problems

Rumania possessed great natural wealth, of forest, field, and subsoil, never fully utilized or equitably distributed. That there was always a close connection between economics, domestic politics, and foreign relations will have been apparent in the discussion (above) of government and politics.

Crude oil and gasoline have drawn the attention of investors and invaders to the Ploeşti oil fields; but cereals bulked larger in the country's export trade before 1914 and were second only to petroleum products in the later part of the period between the wars. There is rich black soil in the old kingdom of Rumania, and good grain-producing land in Transylvania and Bessarabia. The soil of the Dobruja needs only to be better watered to be extremely fertile. Nearly 83 percent of the population of 1919 were engaged in agriculture, forestry, or kin-

[31] The peace treaties of February, 1947, provided that Hungary should return northern Transylvania to Rumania and that Rumania should return Bessarabia and cede northern Bucovina to Russia (Ukraine), and return the southern Dobruja to Bulgaria.

dred pursuits. Wood products and livestock ranked next to cereals and oil among exports.

Until 1914 much of the land was owned by a few in large estates, many of which were devoted to wheat production. Rumanian wheat was of excellent quality and found a ready market in Germany, Belgium, and Britain, where the exchange it earned was used to purchase textiles and other imports. Prosperity for wheat-land owners depended upon the purchasing power of wheat. This landlords' country, however, was populated by a peasant people, few of whom owned the land they tilled. One of the first reforms announced by the Liberal party in the early twenties, therefore, was agrarian. The Liberals were a bourgeois, not a peasant, party. Their land reform expropriated owners of the largest estates, foreigners and other absentees who owned land, and large estates held in mortmain. Some indemnity was offered, but when paid at prewar prices in inflated postwar money it was poor consolation for the landlords' loss of economic and political importance.

The peasants profited little. Landownership had been made possible for them, but land use involved machinery and seed which they had to buy with money borrowed at exorbitant interest rates. The per capita debt of the agricultural population increased enormously. Many holdings, moreover, were too small for efficient grain farming. Legislation in 1929 permitting the sale of such small holdings, to encourage the formation of farms of medium size, achieved only a partial solution of that problem and incidentally complicated another. Those who sold their holdings stayed on the land as laborers for low wages, and the land already had more such laborers than it could well support.

The Liberals had nationalized the forest and mineral resources of the nation and restricted the influx of foreign capital. Sixty percent of the capital invested, two-thirds of the members of the board of directors of any company operating there, and most of the employees had to be Rumanian. That did not mean socialization, however, or any general distribution of the profits from the forests, mines, or natural gas or oil fields. Those were bourgeois monopolies of the Liberals or their friends. Maniu and the National Peasant party, during their brief tenure of office, greatly liberalized the laws governing foreign-owned enterprise; but exports of petroleum products were always heavily taxed.

The oil industry of the country did not keep pace with world production. In 1913 Rumania ranked fourth in total gasoline production. In 1939 it produced far more petroleum than in 1913 but only 2 percent of the world total. Yet petroleum exports had by that time exceeded cereal exports in value. Cereals were declining then in relative importance, petroleum products were gaining.[32] The location of the Ploeşti oil field, and the nonexistence of any other comparable with it in southeastern Europe, made it indispensable to the Germans in both wars. One of the world's most valuable deposits of methane gas was in Transylvania. There was also coal and lignite. Salt and tobacco were state monopolies.

National Minorities

On October 15, 1922, Ferdinand of Rumania was recrowned as king of all the Rumanians. Nearly a fourth (4,500,000) of the 18,000,000 to 20,000,000 inhabitants of the greatly enlarged kingdom to which his new title referred were minorities not of Rumanian nationality. Of these the most numerous were the 1,500,000 Hungarians, most of whom lived in Transylvania and the eastern section of the Banat of Temesvár, some in Bucovina. Next in number if classified by religion were 1,500,000 Jews; but more than half of these were included in the census reports as of Rumanian nationality, less than half as Jews. Although Jews were scattered throughout the country, they were more numerous in Transylvania and Bucovina than elsewhere. There were nearly 800,000 Germans, most of them in Transylvania and the Rumanian Banat of Temesvár. In the Dobruja were nearly 200,000 Turks and twice as many Bulgars. In Bucovina were 37,000 Poles, and in Bessarabia and Bucovina perhaps a million Ukrainians and other Russians.

Among these people of many nationalities were many religious denominations, all enjoying constitutional freedom of religion; yet the country was overwhelmingly Greek Orthodox, with 13,200,000 of its people in the national church. Second in numerical strength was the Jewish faith with 1,500,000. The Uniat Church had nearly a million and a half, the Roman Catholic nearly a million and a quarter. There were 260,000 Moslems, and many of other religions.

Anti-Semitism was peculiarly bitter and violent in Rumania. The Iron Guard was not the only group guilty of it. But anti-Semitism was not a matter of religion. Jews were more numerous there than in most of Europe. They were active in trade and banking, and in law, medi-

[32] Cereals were 32.3 percent of the exports of 1937, 23.9 percent of those of 1938; petroleum and petroleum products were 40.4 percent in 1937, 43.2 percent in 1938.

cine, journalism, and the other professions open to them. Some were teachers, but not many. Rumanian universities were centers of anti-Semitism. The army officers' corps and civil service were not open to Jews. They were the governed, not the governors, with privileges rather than inalienable rights—privileges which they often had to buy and buy again.

The national minorities (German, Hungarian, Bulgar, and Russian or Ukrainian, but especially the Hungarians) often complained of unfair and official discrimination. It was the government's policy to assimilate them, by use of whatever pressure proved necessary, not to go on governing a polyglot people without unity or homogeneity. Jealousy and friction between the old kingdom and the areas acquired in 1918 were perhaps inevitable and always serious, the newer portions of the state complaining that they were being governed and exploited by the old. The complaint was not without justification, but there seems to have been less deliberate abuse of minorities as such (except the Jews) than the widespread discontent would have implied. Rumanians were themselves in the minority in the towns of all the new provinces, despised as inferior people by the non-Rumanian owners of the better houses, the more prosperous businesses, and the more popular vernacular newspapers. Hatred of foreigners was common among Rumanians, but they were themselves hated as foreigners in the new provinces.

No part of Rumania was well governed between the wars. Some parts were governed worse than others. The worst misused of all seems to have been Bessarabia, called by Hugh Seton-Watson "perhaps the most mis-governed province in Europe." There grape growing, which had flourished, was discouraged because Rumania also grew grapes and its growers did not want to meet the competition of Bessarabian wine. Bessarabia had once been, but ceased to be, a richly productive province. Its peasantry was kept primitive and ill equipped. The Rumanians refused or failed even to build good roads there, apparently for fear the Russians would use them for invasion. If any province was justified in complaining that it was being treated only as a colony and exploited, that province would certainly have been Bessarabia. People there would have welcomed reannexation to Russia or the Ukraine long before it came.[33]

Germans, Hungarians, and Bulgars were found in great numbers to welcome the change when Transylvania and the Dobruja were taken from Rumania in 1940. Germans had worked with the Iron

[33] Hugh Seton-Watson, *Eastern Europe Between the Wars, 1918-1941,* 336-337.

Guard for years to "Romanize" Jewish-owned businesses and proper-
ties, i.e., to take them from their Jewish owners. There had been a
strong Nazi movement among the Germans in Rumania since 1931,
outlawed in 1934 but only gone underground, openly Nazi again since
1939. But the disloyal attitudes of the other minorities had been induced perhaps as much by stupidity and weakness of the national
government as by deliberate discrimination against them. They had
generally been better treated than Rumanians had been in the same
provinces before 1918.

Foreign Policy

It would have been natural to suppose that, as one of the principal
beneficiaries of the territorial settlement of 1919-1920, Rumania
would align herself in foreign policy with the other nations interested
for the same reasons in the preservation of that settlement. After the
failure of her attempt in 1919 to push her western boundary farther
into Hungary, her policy was in general just to hold what she had. Her
alliances with Czechoslovakia and Yugoslavia, forming the Little
Entente from 1920 to 1939, have already been discussed.[34] The
Little Entente was intended to serve as a safeguard primarily against
Hungary, but also to discourage revisionist attempts against Rumania
or Yugoslavia by Bulgaria or against Yugoslavia by Italy. The Balkan
Entente of 1934 was formed to provide its members some insurance
against attack by Bulgaria, and to make Rumania's possession of the
Dobruja more secure.[35]

Beyond southeastern Europe, in the broader field of general European politics, Rumania looked usually to France for political loans
and leadership, and hoped for the preservation of an independent
Poland. Rumania and Poland were the buffer states of east central
Europe, confronting Russia. Both held land taken from her after her
revolution, were aware of the danger in which they would find themselves if the USSR should at any time try to recover the lost territory or should revert to the expansionist policy of tsarist Russia, and
were equally fearful of the more immediate threat of communist infiltration. This community of interest in a common danger was recognized in a treaty of alliance made by Poland and Rumania in 1921 by
which each promised to aid the other if the other were attacked on its
eastern frontier. The eastern boundary lines so guaranteed were, for

[34] See p. 175.
[35] See p. 109.

Rumania, the Dniester, so as to include Bessarabia, and, for Poland, the line already established (March, 1921) by the Polish-Russian Treaty of Riga. After Pilsudski of Poland had made a nonaggression pact with Hitler in January, 1934, Rumania turned to Russia and made with her in June of that year a nonaggression pact by which she and Russia mutually guaranteed their common boundary as it then stood.[36] To themselves the Russians seem to have interpreted that treaty as Stresemann interpreted Locarno to his German friends.

For the first ten years of the period between the wars France took the lead on the continent of Europe in organizing the defenders of stability—those who for their own reasons chose to consider Europe's boundary questions closed. Rumania followed that lead, not blindly but always alert to her own interest, and got help from France and Czechoslovakia in her new armament program of 1937.

Fascism of the Nazi type appealed as strongly to many of the Rumanians as dictatorship to their king. Democratic safeguards and political procedures had disappeared before what may be called the western European orientation of foreign policy was abandoned. From the time when National Socialists took control of government in Germany, France's influence waned with her strength and her waning confidence in herself, and German economic and political influence grew in proportion throughout southeastern Europe.

Before the invaders went into Rumania in uniform in 1940 the way had been well prepared for them. The country was already at war with itself and had learned by bitterest experience to have little confidence in its own leaders, hereditary, appointed, or elected. Numerous elements of the population welcomed the impending changes. Czechoslovakia, Poland, and France had already gone the way of all those who opposed the Germans with insufficient means. A timely compliance with the will of the Axis powers promised to be profitable. The immediate consequences of resistance then would certainly have been painful. Rumania complied.

YUGOSLAVIA

Independence and Union

The first shots of the war of 1914 were from Austrian guns firing on Belgrade July 29. One of its immediate causes was Austro-Hungarian hostility to Serbia, due in part to Serbia's ambition to free

[36] See p. 203.

Croatia, Slovenia, Bosnia, Herzegovina, Dalmatia, the Banat of Temesvár, and the Vojvodina from Austro-Hungarian control and to include them and Montenegro in a new and greater Serbia. One of its first results was the realization of that ambition.[37]

Serbia was overrun by armies of the Central Powers and Bulgaria in the autumn of 1915 and occupied thereafter until 1918; but a government maintained itself in exile, and some troops which, after fierce resistance and an arduous retreat, had found refuge on Corfu and been reorganized at Salonika joined in the final campaign against Bulgaria in September, 1918. On November 1 Serbian troops reoccupied their capital, Belgrade. When the Habsburg grip loosened, Serbia was ready to take hold.

There was no long interregnum, but there was uncertainty about boundaries and form of government. As in 1912, Yugoslavia and Greece might have partitioned Albania between them but were prevented by Italy's interest in Albania and President Wilson's opposition to such ruthlessness. So Albania was again called independent, with approximately the boundaries of 1913. The Serbian-Greek boundary of 1913 also stood unchanged.

On the southeast a few strategic changes favorable to Yugoslavia were made in her Bulgarian boundary, with which neither side was satisfied. Macedonia, through which the southern reaches of that boundary ran, is a region of mixed population among which opposition to the authorities and intimidation of one group by another are endemic. With Rumania there was rivalry over the Banat, formerly Hungarian, which was eventually divided between the two countries. Austria was too weak in every way to contest her new boundaries very seriously. There was no further question about the cession of the Serb-Croat-Slovene provinces, but a plebiscite in a disputed border zone, supervised by an inter-Allied commission at Klagenfurt, resulted in the award of the plebiscite area to Austria.

Boundary disputes with Italy were more serious. The first of these centered around Fiume, a town with a considerable Italian population and Slav hinterland, wanted by Italy as a useful Adriatic port and

[37] Banat means frontier province, Vojvodina a duchy. The Vojvodina and the Banat were in 1914 the central southern provinces of Hungary, adjoining Serbia on the north. The southern part of the Vojvodina is east of Slovenia, between the lower Sava River and the Danube; its northern section is north of the Danube, between that river and the Theiss (Tisza). The Banat is east of the Theiss River and north of the Danube, extending eastward to the Transylvanian Alps and northward to the Maros River. The Maros flows westward into the Theiss, the Theiss southward parallel with the Danube, then into it below the point where it has swung eastward toward the Black Sea. See maps, pp. 164-165.

needed by Yugoslavia as an outlet. Yugoslavia indicated its readiness to submit the question either to arbitration by President Wilson or to a plebiscite; but Sonnino, for Italy, insisting that the area had been promised to Italy as part of her price for entering the war in 1915, refused to compromise the issue.

On September 12, 1919, the Italian prefascist poet-aviator-adventurer Gabriele d'Annunzio, with his Arditi dressed in black shirts reminiscent of the red ones worn by Garibaldi's men and reviving the salutes and symbolism of early Rome, seized the town. By the Treaty of Rapallo, directly negotiated between Italy and Yugoslavia and signed November 12, 1920, the Dalmatian coast town of Zara was made a free city under Italian sovereignty. It was stipulated by the treaty that Fiume should become a free city under League of Nations supervision and Yugoslavia should be free to use it as a port. But Italy kept control of it in violation of the treaty until January 27, 1924, when Premier Pašić signed it away to Mussolini, recognizing Italy's possession of it, receiving in return only the right of access to a free commercial zone in it. By the same treaty, Yugoslavia retained her sovereignty over the adjoining Croat village of Sušak and the left bank of the Baroš River mouth.

As had been contemplated by Italy's wartime treaties with her allies, the Istrian peninsula and its hinterland (Venezia Giulia), north of Fiume and north and east of Trieste, went to Italy. That boundary was not drawn on strictly ethnic grounds, and included on its Italian side nearly half a million Croats and Slovenes.[38]

Government and Politics

Until the boundaries of the new state had been defined, Prince Regent Alexander (later king), of the Serbian Karageorgevich dynasty, postponed the election of a constituent assembly to determine the form of government. A manifesto issued from Corfu in 1917 by the Serbian premier Nikola Pašić and the Dalmatian Croat Dr. Trumbić had announced that the Serbs, Croats, and Slovenes were all one nation and would be united under the ruling house of Serbia in a democratic parliamentary monarchy to be called the Kingdom of the Serbs,

[38] After the defeat of Yugoslavia in 1941 Italy organized Croatia and part of Slovenia as Italian puppet states, and the Italian Duke of Aosta was made king of Croatia. Upon the defeat of Italy, Italian establishments were taken over by Germans. The area was reoccupied, along with the Istrian peninsula and province, by Yugoslav troops in 1945. In 1946 a dispute like that for Fiume developed over Trieste and the new boundary to be established between Italy and Yugoslavia, running roughly northward from Trieste. See p. 816.

Croats, and Slovenes. The manifesto had further declared that the three peoples and their three states were to "rank equally," and to have the right to display their state flags as freely as the national emblem. Both of the alphabets, Roman and Cyrillic, then in use among them were to be official, and all religions equally free. Elected officials would be chosen by direct election by universal and equal suffrage and secret ballot.

In the election of a constituent assembly, November 28, 1920, the issue between centralists and federalists was clearly drawn. The Corfu manifesto had not been explicit on that point, but had seemed to promise a federal state with political autonomy and complete cultural freedom for the peoples of the component states. The exigencies of the national situation, on the other hand, argued the centralists—led by the prince regent, the 1914 premier, Nikola Pašić of Serbia, and the Serbian Radical party—required a strong and highly centralized national government. The Radicals would virtually have made the whole into a greater Serbia under Serbian control. The Democrats, however, the Croatian Peasant party led by Stjepan Radić, and the Slovenian Peasant party advocated decentralization and what Americans would have called state rights in a fairly loose federal union.

The greater Serbia party won the election. Only fifty-five deputies were elected by the Croatian Peasant party. Knowing that they would be outnumbered in the constituent assembly, their leader Radić ordered them to stay away. Although the Communist party was the fourth largest in Yugoslavia, Communists were soon excluded from the government. The murder of the minister of the interior, Drašković, by a young Communist moved the delegates from the other parties— or gave them their cue—by majority vote to unseat the fifty-four Communist delegates and annul their mandates, and to outlaw the party and its press. The extreme left was thus permanently disfranchised and driven underground, where it did not die. A large part of the nation had excluded itself or been excluded from legitimate participation in national political affairs. Only obstructionism or illegal opposition remained open to unfavored groups.

Pašić and his Serbian Radical party were therefore able with the help of their political allies to create on paper a rightist national government of a unitary type making little allowance for state rights or localism of any sort. This "Vidovdan (St. Vitus's Day) constitution" was adopted by the assembly on the seventh anniversary of Sarajevo, June 28, 1921.

The election of the first parliament was postponed until March,

1923, when the cleavage between autonomists and centralists was shown to be deeper than before. For another year Radić and the other Croatian Peasant deputies boycotted the parliament, as they had done the constituent assembly, by refusing to take the seats to which they had been elected. Pašić died in December, 1926. In 1928, after four years of persistent advocacy of the special interests of the Croats and Slovenes, which the government called obstructionism, Stjepan Radić was shot and mortally wounded by a Montenegrin deputy, during a session of parliament, for opposing ratification of a commercial agreement (Nettuno) with Italy which he considered prejudicial to the Croats. Two of his followers, one of them his nephew, were killed, and several others wounded.

The other Croatian deputies then withdrew from Belgrade and set up a separate parliament, inviting other dissidents to join them in a boycott of Serbia and nonrecognition of the Belgrade government. King Alexander's statement that parliamentary government had broken down and resulted in disunion rather than in unity was not an inaccurate description of current political conditions, although a firmer believer in parliamentary democracy might well have raised the question whether it had really been responsible for the failure or had not been tried.

The king turned to authoritarianism. On January 5, 1929, he dissolved the "rump" that was left of the parliament, abrogated the constitution of 1921 and announced that a new one would be promulgated —and meanwhile set up a royal dictatorship.

On September 3, 1931, the king announced that the dictatorship had served its purpose and the country would return to a constitutional regime; but the new constitution also was king-made. The parliament was to be bicameral, with the king appointing half of the members of the Senate. The members of the House of Deputies were to be directly elected by equal suffrage of men and women, but by open ballot under qualifying conditions which only members of the officially sponsored National party could hope to meet. Again the opposition boycotted the elections, and again the king got a docile government to handle an angry people.

After General Živković retired from the premiership on April 4, 1932, his position was held by civilians in rapid succession; but cabinet changes, however numerous, brought no fundamental change of system. The liberties promised by the Corfu manifesto were generally denied as the government sought to impress upon all a uniform national stamp without regard for regional, religious, or political differences.

In an attempt to obliterate traditional territorial lines the government gave its nine provinces new names, each for its principal river. The very name of the state was changed by royal proclamation in October, 1929, from the Kingdom of the Serbs, Croats, and Slovenes to the Kingdom of Yugoslavia; but Serbian and Croatian chauvinism left no room for the conception of a Yugoslav national patriotism.

Older leaders had lost touch with people. A middle generation interested in officeholding only for self-enrichment cared nothing for the welfare or wishes of the people. Young men were extremists, right or left. Young intellectuals were usually radicals, considered dangerous. The university at Belgrade was a center of radicalism.

Fortunes were made in politics, in Zagreb as in Belgrade, while the people lost confidence in politicians. Although social discontent was ruthlessly repressed its causes were not removed, and its bitterness increased in underground activity. About all that the dictatorship could achieve was "order" and some increase of industry and trade. Croats still complained that Croatia was treated as a colony and exploited for the benefit of Serbia, that money raised there by taxation was spent by Serbs in Serbia.

In October, 1934, the unpopular monarch left the protection of his own police to visit France. He had scarcely left Yugoslav soil, technically, by debarking from his destroyer *Dubrovnik* in Marseilles when he and French Foreign Minister Barthou, who had gone to the port to meet him, were murdered by a Macedonian terrorist. The guards were quick enough to kill the assassin immediately; but Mussolini refused to extradite Ante Pavelić, head of the Croatian Ustashi, the organization of the extreme right-wing Croatian nationalists which had planned the crime and furnished the murderer his forged Hungarian passport. Italy and Hungary were as unwilling to see the Yugoslav government strengthen itself abroad as the Croatian irreconcilables were to see it strengthen itself at home.

Alexander's son and legal heir, Peter II, was then a boy in school in England. So a regency was formed by the late king's cousin, Prince Paul. The most influential minister from 1936 to February 4, 1939, was profascist Dr. Milan Stojadinović. Two Croats, Dr. Stanković and Dr. Perović, at first shared the regency with Prince Paul. Monsignor Anton Korošec, leader of the Slovene clerical party, was in a position as minister of the interior and later as minister of education to favor Slovenes as government officials, and was accused of doing so although the favored ones may well have earned promotion. Slovenia was one of the more enlightened and prosperous regions of that kaleidoscopic country. Korošec shared Stojadinović's aversion to "bolshevism" and all forms of leftist radicalism, which was usually anticlerical. Closely associated with those two conservatives was Dr. Spaho, leader of the Bosnian Moslems and notably successful in securing advantages for them.

As a Roman Catholic and a Slovene, Monsignor Korošec would have been happy to make a new concordat with the Roman Catholic Church, giving it greater privileges in Croatia and Slovenia, to give the Slovenes their autonomy, and to effect a more cordial *modus operandi* between Croatia and the national state. Radić's moderate successor as leader of the Croatian Peasant party, Dr. Vladko Maček, was willing to negotiate when released from prison, and was given an ovation when he visited Belgrade in August, 1938.

After more than a year of negotiation with the new government formed by Dragisha Cvetković when Stojadinović resigned (February 4, 1939), arrangements were tardily completed in August, 1939, for an autonomous *banovina* (province) of Croatia with its capital and separate legislature at Zagreb. Matters such as foreign policy and trade, defense, public security, and religion were to be reserved to the national government. The *ban* or governor was to be a Croatian, Dr. Ivan Subašić, a man well known for his Yugoslav sentiments, but nine of his eleven governmental department heads were Croat nationalists. Maček was satisfied with the progress being made and became vice-premier in the new Yugoslav government, in which five other Croats also participated. There Dr. Maček continued to work for a democratic federation of all the South Slavs; but the concessions so reluctantly made by the national government had only whetted the appetites of Ustashi like Pavelić, who were soon to serve the Italians as Henlein served the Germans.

Economic Resources and Problems

Agriculture was the occupation of four-fifths of the people of Yugoslavia but brought them only half of the national income; so the peasant standard of living was rather low. Industry earned almost a third of the national income although it occupied only 11 percent of the population. The 3 percent engaged in banking and commerce enjoyed 11 percent of the national income.[39]

Exports in 1938-1939 were chiefly timber, agricultural surpluses, and industrial ores and raw materials. Timber led the list in value, with Italy a leading buyer of it. Prosperity depended literally also, as in 1914, on sending the pigs to market. Swine exports were second in

[39] J. S. Roucek, *op. cit.*, 506.

value only to timber in 1939, fourth in 1938. Fresh meat was fifth. Great numbers of horses, cattle, sheep, and goats, as well as hogs, were raised.

Copper ore was third in value among exports in 1938 and 1939. The largest copper mine was financed by French capital. Iron, lead-zinc ore, and chrome ore were also produced in considerable quantities, the lead and zinc largely by British enterprises; and bauxite was sent to aluminum plants of Germany, on a barter basis always advantageous to Germany.

Imports of greatest value and volume were textiles and machinery. More of these imports came from Germany than from any other nation.

Germany took more of Yugoslavia's exports in 1938 than the combined purchases of the next five nations on the list—Great Britain, Czechoslovakia, Belgium, Italy, and the United States. In 1939, thanks to new economic agreements with the Little Entente and Italy, exports to Czechoslovakia nearly doubled and exports to Italy increased considerably. But Germany still took as many of the country's exports as the next three nations on the list of buyers—Great Britain, Czechoslovakia, and Italy. In 1939 exports to Great Britain, Belgium, and the United States were less than in 1938, but total exports exceeded imports in value by what would have been a substantial margin if Germany had paid for what she bought. The unctuous but elusive Dr. Hjalmar Schacht, however, usually saw to it that Germany lagged far behind in its deliveries, so as to be in a good position to threaten at any time to break off without completing an exchange or negotiating for a new one.

Doing business with Nazi Germany was always a speculative venture and eventually unprofitable; but it often promised initially to pay dividends. Germany was, because of her location and advanced industrialization, a natural user of the agricultural and raw-material exports of Yugoslavia, and a natural supplier of the machinery and finished goods which that country had to import. A sense of the importance of the trade with Italy and Germany, as well as the fascist inclination of many of the national leaders, may well have influenced the direction of Yugoslav foreign policy in those last years before the new outbreak of the war in Europe.

National Minorities

Yugoslavia had nearly twelve million people in 1921, nearly fourteen million in 1931. Of those, about 85 percent were Yugoslavs, i.e.,

Serbs, Croats, or Slovenes. The other 15 percent were Germans, Magyars, Albanians, Italians, Macedonians, and others.

The differences between Serbs, Croats, and Slovenes were linguistic and religious rather than racial, resulting from propinquity to other peoples and from different historical backgrounds and experiences. The Serbs and Croats used a common language with certain variants; but the Croats, who had lived in Austria-Hungary, used the Roman alphabet and the Serbs the Cyrillic. The Slovenes were Roman Catholics, with a language of their own, using the Roman alphabet. Most of the Croats and Slovenes were Roman Catholic in religion, Serbs in Serbia generally Orthodox. There were 729,000 Bosnian (Serb) Moslems, and more than 800,000 others. The census of 1931 showed also a quarter of a million Protestant Christians (most of them found among half a million Germans), and 68,405 Jews.

The populations were mixed in almost all parts of the country; but nearly 6,000,000 Serbs lived in Serbia, Bosnia, Herzegovina, and Montenegro, and 3,221,000 Croatians in Croatia and Dalmatia. The home of the 1,134,000 Slovenes was in the northernmost part of the country, adjoining Austria, Hungary, and Italy. The capital of Slovenia was Ljubljana (German Laibach) in the old province of Carniola. A quarter of a million Slovenes and 92,800 Croats lived beyond the line in Italy. Italians in Yugoslavia were only 12,533 in 1921—one-tenth of one percent of the total population.

In the Danube Valley north of Belgrade, in the Vojvodina, lived between 325,000 and 350,000 Germans and nearly as many Hungarians. This territory was taken from Hungary only in 1918. Its Magyar inhabitants had been citizens first class in Hungary, and the Germans had enjoyed autonomy under the Habsburg monarchy. Both were and had been more prosperous than the Serbian average, and the maize and wheat fields of those districts were the most productive in the nation. German, Czechoslovak, and Magyar minorities there, although thrifty and productive, complained bitterly and had some reason to complain against tactless and often brutal treatment by Yugoslav officials. This was especially true of the once-dominant Magyars, more especially after the royal dictatorship was established in 1929.

About 123,000 Germans lived in Croatia, 40,000 in Slovenia, and 15,000 in Bosnia. Many of them had gone there as civil servants of the old imperial authority but had chosen to live there rather than go back to Austria. They were not popular, but they were not persecuted. After 1933, however, Nazi ideas spread among the Germans throughout Yugoslavia, and their *Kulturbund* became a Nazi organization and a menace to any advocate of any but a Nazi and pro-German policy. It supported Premier Stojadinović in 1938, and in return he legalized the sale of land in frontier areas to Germans, who took advantage of the opportunity for the benefit of Germany. Germans in Yugoslavia seem to have been as disloyal to the land in which they lived in 1941, and as useful to Germany, as the Germans living in Czechoslovakia had been in 1938 and 1939.

There were more than 400,000 Albanians in Yugoslavia, most of them living in the southwest, near Albania. The national government attempted their assimilation without much success. They considered themselves harshly treated, and were considered undependable as Yugoslavs.

In the southeast the Macedonians were a problem, not because they were so numerous but because of the terrorist activities of their Internal Macedonian Revolutionary Organization (IMRO). From its headquarters in southwestern Bulgaria the IMRO organized raiding expeditions into Yugoslavia, hoping to embroil the two governments and making itself troublesome to both.

Macedonia was only a regional term. Part of the region was in Serbia, part in Bulgaria, part in Greece. Greek Macedonia was populated principally by Greeks, the percentage of Greeks among the population having been increased in 1923 when exchanges of populations with Bulgaria and Turkey had moved out a considerable number of Slavs and brought in Greek émigrés and refugees from Bulgaria and Turkish Asia Minor. Most of the Macedonians in Serbia and Bulgaria were Slavs. They were, strictly speaking, neither Serbs nor Bulgarians; and what they called themselves at any moment depended upon the circumstances and tactics of the moment. Usually someone controlled a village or a community and could tell its people how to answer when asked whether they were Yugoslavs, Bulgars, or Greeks, and they answered as he had told them—unless the questioner seemed stronger than he, or temporarily to have taken his place and gained control. Then also their answers were dictated by their circumstances.

In 1924 the IMRO joined Bulgarian Communists in advocating an autonomous Macedonia in a Balkan federation. At other times, as after 1928, it opposed the Communists. The program of the Yugoslav Communists for Macedonia was said to be autonomy within Yugoslavia. Communism was stronger in Macedonia than elsewhere in Yugoslavia. Peasants who hated their national government because they thought it heavy-handed, unjust, and oppressive hoped that communism would weaken that government and free them from it. Many of them fell, in Macedonia as elsewhere in Yugoslavia, into the rather strange psychological habit of associating communism in their minds with dreams of civil liberties.

As has just been indicated, some of the Yugoslav government's trouble in its Macedonian quarter was communist trouble; but some was Bulgarian. Especially along the left bank of the Vardar River there were people who thought of themselves and acted rather as Slavs and Turks than as Yugoslavs, did valuable fifth-column work in 1941, and welcomed annexation to Bulgaria. Others accepted Yugoslavia, and welcomed restoration in 1945. Still others might have preferred an autonomous or an independent state of Macedonia, however impractical such a proposal might have seemed to anyone else.

In summary, political confusion in Yugoslav Macedonia was such that it would have been difficult to discover what the people living there were thinking—and certainly they were not all thinking alike. Except in the last weeks before it was attacked, when it was trying in desperation to placate its enemies and to find friends where it could, the Yugoslav government does not seem to have concerned itself at all seriously over what its Macedonian subjects thought. Instead, according to one qualified observer, "administrative brutality, Serbian chauvinism, political corruption and economic exploitation were more flagrant in Macedonia than in any other part of Yugoslavia."[40] Yugoslavia was vulnerable in Macedonia in 1941.

Foreign Policy

The goals of Yugoslav foreign policy from 1918 to 1941 were, naturally and necessarily, prosperity and security. To those a third might have been added if the state had been strong enough to hope to realize it: the inclusion of Trieste, Istria, and more of Macedonia; but after the international discussions of the first few years after 1918 the national boundaries had been established and those territorial ambitions had to be held in abeyance.

Security seemed to depend primarily upon Hungary's continued acceptance of the territorial terms of the Treaty of Neuilly. No Hungarian national leader since Count Karolyi had pretended to be reconciled to the cession of Slovakia and Ruthenia to Czechoslovakia, Transylvania and part of the Banat of Temesvár to Rumania, or the rest of the Banat and Vojvodina to Yugoslavia. A common interest in

[40] Hugh Seton-Watson, *Eastern Europe Between the Wars, 1918-1941*, 316.

holding what they had gained at Hungary's expense helped, therefore, to bring Yugoslavia, Rumania, and Czechoslovakia together in the Little Entente, and to induce the Little Entente to respond favorably to France's efforts to build up a system of commercial agreements and alliances to maintain the general peace settlement of Versailles, the Trianon, Neuilly, and Lausanne.

Relations with Hungary were naturally not cordial, although some effort was made to improve them. This effort promised to be successful only in November, 1940, when a treaty of perpetual friendship was negotiated in Belgrade and later signed in Budapest, February 26, 1941.[41]

Relations with Bulgaria were never cordial. Serbia had been one of the allies which in 1913 in the second Balkan war had taken from Bulgaria some of the territory she had won in 1912 in the first Balkan war, in Macedonia and Thrace. Bulgaria had joined the Central Powers in the invasion of Serbia in 1915 but eventually lost ground in both Macedonia and Thrace as a result of the defeat of 1918. It was only realistic to assume after the rise of Hitler and Mussolini that she would join them also, or either of them, in a new invasion if a favorable opportunity were found. Those of Bulgaria's neighbors who in 1913 and in 1918 had taken territory from her, or territory she had coveted, therefore made a pact in 1934 to hold their ground and, if possible, to discourage her from trying for revision by warning her that such a move would meet resistance. The pact, signed February 4 by Yugoslavia, Rumania, Greece, and Turkey, committed them all to a mutual guarantee of their Balkan boundaries against attack by any but a great power. Bulgaria, surrounded on three sides by the territories of the four parties to the pact and bounded on the fourth side by the Black Sea, seemed clearly indicated as the power—if any—against which the others were combining.

The Balkan pact, however, offered Yugoslavia no protection against Italy. After Italy's conquest of Ethiopia, the formation of the Rome-Berlin Axis and its successful intervention in the civil war in Spain, the occupation of Albania by Italy in April, 1939, and possible further Italian expansion eastward from the Adriatic were ever more imminent threats which Yugoslavia could not ignore. The fate of Austria and Czechoslovakia was not encouraging.

Germany, on the other hand, took in 1938 more than four times as

[41] The treaty was soon broken when Hungary joined Germany, Italy, and Bulgaria in their attack upon Yugoslavia, seizing first the Banat and Vojvodina. Count Teleki, the Hungarian premier who had made the treaty, committed suicide when Horthy broke it.

much (by value) of Yugoslavia's export trade as Great Britain did, nearly five times as much as Britain in 1939, more than four times as much as Czechoslovakia in 1938 and more than twice as much as Czechoslovakia in 1939. Exports to Italy increased 80 percent in 1939 over 1938. In April, 1939, Mussolini seized Albania.

The Axis side of the bread seemed to Prince Paul and his premiers Stojadinović and Cvetković to be better buttered; the course of appeasement seemed safer; and they found fascism more congenial than democracy. So did Father Anton Korošec, minister of education, whose sympathies were with fascist Italy, although his talk was of neutrality.[42] Vice-premier Maček and several other Croatian ministers believed that the Allies might win the war, but were more anxious to avoid having to help the Axis than to go to war to help the Allies.

The German occupation of Rumania, late in 1940, put an end to the Little Entente. Late in February, 1941, German troops poured into Bulgaria from Rumania. As Hungary, Rumania, and Bulgaria had all adhered to the Axis pact and the attitude of the Axis powers was every day more menacing, Premier Cvetković and Foreign Minister Marković went finally to Vienna and on March 25 signed the Three-Power Pact.

Protesting that their government had gone over to the enemy, the ministers of justice, social welfare, and agriculture resigned. Two days later, March 27, a military coup d'état overthrew the ministry, banished Prince Paul, and made young Peter (II) king and General Dusan Simović premier. The Croatian leader, Dr. Maček, carried over as vice-premier; but Ante Pavelić's Ustashi seized power in Croatia and declared it an independent state. On April 10, German planes were over Belgrade, and Yugoslavia's boundaries were simultaneously overrun from all directions but the south, where Italy was already occupied with the Greeks.

GREECE

The ancient Greeks were a seafaring people and great colonizers. Many of the modern Greeks have also gone down to the sea in ships as merchant seamen and enterprising tradesmen. The Aegean Sea, its islands and all its coasts, and the eastern Mediterranean have always been inviting fields for Greek expansion, economic and political.

One of the most aggressive and ambitious of the modern Greeks was Eleutherios Venizelos, born in Crete in 1864. Venizelos was at

[42] Korošec died in December, 1940.

once a liberal in domestic politics and an expansionist. He was one of the prime movers in the formation of the Balkan League, and in the Balkan wars of 1912 and 1913, which resulted in the union of Crete with Greece and in the acquisition of additional territory in the north-west (Epirus) and the northeast (Macedonia, Salonika, and western Thrace). He was ready in 1914 to keep right on going, honor his country's treaty of alliance with Serbia by joining in her defense, and depend upon the generosity and justice of the Allies—and his own bargaining skill—to see to it that the righteous were rewarded.

The Greek King Constantine was pro-German. Venizelos was strong in parliament. The deadlock resulted in a policy of neutrality. When the Dardanelles campaign of 1915 was in prospect and the Allies wanted help, Venizelos would have helped them but the king prevented him. When Bulgaria mobilized for war, Venizelos managed, despite the king, to see to it that Greece also mobilized. When Bulgaria joined in the attack on Serbia he would have joined in her defense, hoping that the Allies would eventually force Turkey to cede to Greece some territory in western Asia Minor; but the king was in the way. Even after the Allies established a beachhead at Salonika in October, 1915, the pro-German king dismissed Venizelos and kept the Allied forces there immobilized for nearly two years.

Meanwhile, from Crete, Venizelos urged the Greeks to join the Allies. On October 1, 1916, he formed a provisional government at Salonika to aid the Allies. In June, 1917, King Constantine was at last compelled to abdicate in favor of his second son, Alexander, renouncing also Crown Prince George's right to the succession.[43] Venizelos again became premier and, with the consent of the new king, Alexander, brought Greece officially into the war. A year later, in 1918, Greek troops took part in the invasion of Bulgaria from Salonika which brought the war there to an end.

Being on the winning side in three wars in only a little more than six years brought Greece the promise of territorial gains beyond the expectations of any but the boldest—like Venizelos. For two more years that promise seemed to be about to be fulfilled, as Venizelos represented his country at peace conference after conference and sat among the plenipotentiaries of the great powers. Greece lost no territory to Albania or Yugoslavia, was promised much of Thrace at the expense of Bulgaria and Turkey by the Treaty of Sèvres (q.v.), and gained at Smyrna a good foothold in Turkey.

Then a pet monkey bit the king. Alexander died October 25. His

[43] See p. 819.

younger brother Paul declined the government's suggestion that he take the throne; so the restoration of the deposed and exiled ex-King Constantine became an issue in a general election, November 14, 1920. The Allies were already at cross-purposes as to the Dardanelles and their relations with the revolutionary Turkish government of Mustafa Kemal, and as to the future of the Greeks in Asia Minor. They did not welcome the return of Constantine to Greece; but he returned, December 19, 1920, following a plebiscite in which Venizelos suffered a severe defeat.

It was part of the pattern of Greek politics that elections were often won and lost by large majorities. Those who were politically wise could usually predict the outcome of an election, and those who knew they could not win sometimes refused to vote. It was not unusual for the leader of the losers to go abroad for a time, immediately after an election, and to reconnoiter cautiously before returning.

Thus Venizelos left the country when the election of November, 1920, went against him, as he had done when dismissed by the same monarch in 1915. He stayed abroad without political responsibility while King Constantine and the king's friends went on to disaster in the war against the Turks. France and Italy were already something less than lukewarm in their support of Greek claims on Turkey, and the British had not forgotten that Constantine had been more friendly to their enemy in wartime than to them. The Allies refused to recognize him and gave Greece no further help while he was king.

Yet, not content with what they had, the Greeks attacked the Turks again in Anatolia. They made some gains at first but in September, 1922, were driven out of Asia Minor into the sea at Smyrna. All but the Turkish quarter of the city of Smyrna was destroyed.

The king ordered demobilization. He may have hoped so to forestall a revolt of the beaten army; but, if so, he failed also in that. The returning troops revolted, and the king fled, September 27. Before he died in his second exile in January, 1923, eight of his principal ministers had been indicted, tried and condemned by court-martial, and shot. His eldest son, George II, whose right to the succession he had forfeited with his own in 1915, succeeded him.

Venizelos returned to represent his country at the Lausanne conference of 1923 and save what he could from the wreckage. It was not much, but something.[44]

Although Venizelos cut its losses at Lausanne with his customary skill, the monarchy was still unpopular because it had lost the last war.

[44] See p. 113.

Venizelos would have maintained it on a constitutional basis but could not, so again absented himself. In his absence a plebiscite was held, April 13, 1924, which abolished the monarchy and established a republic. King George abdicated for himself this time, and went for the second time into exile. Venizelos remained in retirement for four years (1924-1928).

Those were troubled years, notable chiefly for frequent cabinet changes, during which more was done to discredit republican forms of government in Greece than to vindicate them. Then Venizelos came back, became premier as leader of the Liberal party in July, 1928, after an overwhelming victory at the polls, and for four years gave the government the stability it had lacked.

Those years saw the completion of the exchange of populations which had been agreed upon in the treaty of Lausanne and in a Greek-Bulgarian convention of 1919. Nearly 1,500,000 people of Greek origin or ancestry came from Asia Minor, European Turkey, and Bulgaria, replacing Turks and Bulgarians who were moved out. It was a complicated, costly, and time-consuming exchange, accomplished only with the aid of the League of Nations and generous foreign loans. The supervisory agencies set an example worthy of emulation (which the Nazi, later, did not emulate in their wholesale removals) by doing what they could to safeguard the economic interests and, as much as possible, to consider the wishes of the people being moved.

In the long run, the operation paid Greece good dividends. When it was completed, she had a fairly homogeneous population and none of the serious national minorities problems by which the other Balkan states were plagued. Macedonia and Thrace were more productive and more prosperous after the influx of Greek repatriates than before.

The general level of prosperity was rising under the comparatively stable government of Venizelos and the Liberal party until the world depression checked its rise. There as elsewhere, government was blamed. Venizelos gave way in November, 1932, to Panagis Tsaldaris of the royalist People's party, returned to office two months later, and was again overthrown and replaced by Tsaldaris in March, 1933. The parliamentary elections of March 5, 1933, gave the People's party 135 seats and the Venizelist Liberals 111. Venizelos retired to Crete.

Two years later, in March, 1935, alleging that the royalist premier Tsaldaris was about to restore the monarchy, part of the army and navy revolted against him in the name of the republic. The finger of suspicion, pointing already in the direction of Venizelos, was put directly on him when some of the rebels turned their ships toward

Crete, where he was living. He fled to Paris, where he died a year later. Meanwhile Marshal Kondyles, an officer of the fascist type, suppressed the rebellion, ousted Tsaldaris and took his place as premier, abolished the republic, won another plebiscite by a rather unconvincing vote of 98 percent, and restored the monarchy.

George II returned to Greece as king for the second time November 25, 1935. He pardoned Venizelos, whom Tsaldaris had exiled, released political prisoners, and behaved at first in a generally ingratiating manner, permitting a fairly free election on January 26, 1936.

Kondyles, who had restored the king but disapproved of his conciliatory attitude toward those who had opposed him, resigned within a week of the restoration and died only a few weeks after his resignation. With Kondyles and Venizelos gone, a new strong man was chosen by the king to be premier. He was General John Metaxas, whose personal party had filled nine seats in parliament in the January election in which the Venizelist (Liberal) party had filled 135 and the royalist People's party 125. Metaxas dissolved the parliament on August 4, 1936, and established a dictatorship in the king's name, proclaiming a Third Hellenic Civilization in imitation of the Nazi Third Reich but professing that it was all in the best tradition of ancient Sparta. Such was the constitutional monarchy of Greece under George II in the last years before the war which made him again an exile.

It was the government of George II and Metaxas which accepted the offer made it by Great Britain and France on April 13, 1939, of a guarantee of its independence and territorial integrity, and which subsequently defended itself as long as possible with insufficient help from them. (Rumania accepted a similar guarantee on the same day, and renounced it before she was attacked.) It was the government of George II with which Great Britain later made a treaty of alliance. Britain's continued interest in Greek affairs after the withdrawal of the Germans and Italians in 1945 was a natural consequence of that alliance and of more than a century of close, friendly, and mutually advantageous relations between the two countries.

CHAPTER 8

Weimar Germany

ESTABLISHMENT AND IMMEDIATE PROBLEMS

Extent of the Revolution

Rebellion against the regularly constituted political authority has been a rare phenomenon in German history. The "Weimar" republic of the period 1918 to 1933 was established rather by default than by design, and was the only government Germany has had in modern times which was seriously embarrassed by its own people's active opposition to it.

There was always, to be sure, some parliamentary criticism of the Hohenzollern empire. An outspoken few, Social Democrats or left-wing liberals of the Catholic Center or National Liberal party, would have welcomed some diminution of the discretionary powers of the executive and the conversion of the imperial government into a genuinely constitutional monarchy of the parliamentary type. Some such revisions might eventually have been made if the war of 1914-1918 had not occurred, or if Germany had won that war; but it was the loss of the war that caused the collapse of the monarchy in November, 1918. The change in the form of government was not the cause but the consequence of defeat. The republic took the place of an imperial government which it had not overthrown but which had been destroyed largely by pressure from outside. It was fear of civil war, rather than the will to wage one, that prompted those who demanded the kaiser's abdication, and the hope of securing better peace terms without than with him that guided those who advised him at last to abdicate.[1]

[1] See pp. 73-76.

The demand for the parliamentarization of the monarchy had reached a peak in 1908, when Chancellor Bernhard von Bülow had failed to warn the kaiser against permitting publication of some tactless and inaccurate remarks he had made for publication in the London *Daily Telegraph,* and then left him undefended to bear the brunt of the public criticism aroused by his indiscretion. The opportunity was lost, however, when the political parties failed to coöperate for that purpose. The government suffered another serious loss of popularity in 1913-1914, when public anger was aroused by the leniency shown certain army officers who seemed with comparative impunity to have set themselves above the civil law in their treatment of civilians in the Zabern incident.

Then the fear of war put an end to the Reichstag's efforts to tie the hands of government. When the kaiser, in uniform, announced the outbreak of the war in August, 1914, and asked for a *Burgfrieden* or civil peace, a cessation of all partisan activity, saying that in such a crisis he knew no parties, "only Germans," the members of the Reichstag responded as Germans, not as party members, and granted him his wish. Even the Social Democrats, explaining that they considered the war a defensive one, declared themselves ready to support it. Only the radical Karl Liebknecht opposed the voting of the necessary war credits.

The *Burgfrieden* was threatened by the formation in 1915 of the Spartacus Union, forerunner of the Communist party, by Liebknecht, Rosa Luxemburg, Franz Mehring, and Clara Zetkin. Liebknecht and Rosa Luxemburg were soon imprisoned for their open opposition to the war. They had few followers, however.

No very serious breach of the civil truce occurred until the summer of 1917. Then the Social Democrats demanded that the government state its war aims, renouncing annexations and indemnities. After their delegates had returned in June from an international conference in Stockholm, the more radical socialists began to demand that the government state its policy on domestic as well as international affairs. On July 19, 1917, defying both the chancellor and the military high command by a vote of 214 to 116, a combination of Social Democrats, Progressives, and the Catholic Center party passed a resolution calling for a peace without annexations or indemnities, "a peace of understanding and of lasting reconciliation."

One of the principal advocates of the peace resolution of July 19, 1917, was the leader of the Center party, Matthias Erzberger, who was subsequently to head the delegation to sign the armistice agreement of November 11, 1918. Spokesman for the Catholic labor group was Konstantin Fehrenbach, later chancellor of the republic. Philipp Scheidemann spoke for the Social Democrats, who supported the motion, but less actively than the Centrists.

Erzberger and his Catholic colleagues were eager to push through the peace resolution as part of the preliminary groundwork for a papal peace note which had been in preparation since June, and which the pope sent to all the belligerents in August, 1917. The note did less toward shortening the war than its sponsors had hoped it would. It was resented and discounted in anticlerical French circles on the ground that it was issued only when it became clear that Austria could not win the war. The British government replied with a statement of general war aims, including evacuation, restitution, and guarantees, much like those of 1918, to which the Central Powers would never assent until ready to confess themselves completely beaten. President Wilson's reply, that the American people had no quarrel with the German people but were at war only with the imperial government, elicited an editorial reply from the Social-Democratic newspaper *Vorwärts* that Social Democrats were still willing to defend Germany but not to go on fighting merely for the monarchy. The German government was not yet willing to promise unconditionally to evacuate and restore Belgium as the pope had hoped it would. It still hoped to hang on to Liège as a pawn until satisfied with Belgium's compliance with the peace terms. So the papacy's effort at peace-making, though it may have done something to clarify the issues, was a comparatively useless gesture.

As a move toward peace, the Reichstag resolution of July 19, 1917, was equally useless. There were "peace" parties in France and England, more vocal in the French Chamber of Deputies than in the British House of Commons, but they drew no more encouragement from the Reichstag's action than the war parties did. The resolution in favor of a peace without annexation or reparation charges, coming as it did only after nearly three years of war, after the United States had become a belligerent, and after the Germans had had to begin to ask themselves whether they or their enemies would be in the better position to make annexations or collect reparation payments, could easily be interpreted rather as a confession of weakness than as a generous offer of peace. It therefore encouraged the "victory" parties in all enemy countries at least as much as it did the peace parties; and those demanding nothing less than victory were more numerous in 1917, and politically more influential among the peoples then at war with Germany, than those seeking reconciliation.

Another opportunity for the parliamentarization of the German government was offered by the passage of the peace resolution, but was lost. The Reichstag majority adopted a resolution to which the kaiser, cabinet, and army and navy high command were known to be strongly opposed. It did not follow up this self-willed action, however, with any determined assertion of a will to power. It did not try to take control of government. Its leaders let it be known that they wanted a new chancellor, and they were given one; but they were not consulted as to who he should be, and the change was no improvement from a parliamentary point of view. Dr. Georg Michaelis, the new chancellor, was less likely to defend the powers of the Reichstag against the high command than his predecessor Bethmann-Hollweg had been, and accepted the peace resolution only "as he interpreted it." Soon afterward the Fatherland party was founded by some of the less democratic but more strongly nationalist elements of the old parties to try to rouse the people again to an unquestioning and unflagging continuance of the war effort.

In October, 1917, the moderate "middle" parties again asserted themselves in the Reichstag by demanding a change of ministers. Chancellor Michaelis had distinguished himself chiefly by obsequious conformity to the wishes of the high command and by his readiness to accuse the radical Reichstag leaders of treasonable responsibility—which, generally speaking, he could not prove—for a minor mutiny in the high-seas fleet.[2]

The high command did little to defend Chancellor Michaelis when he came under fire from the Social Democrats, Centrists, Progressives, and National Liberals, after only three and a half months in office, but permitted him to resign under Reichstag pressure, October 26, 1917. His place was taken by the premier of Bavaria, Count Georg von

[2] Superficially, the mutiny of July, 1917, was a protest against the quality of the food, the privileges of the officers, especially as to food, and the rigorous discipline. Fundamentally, it was an expression of the restlessness and discontent of men long confined in close quarters in comparative idleness, without the emotional compensation of action or achievement to relieve their boredom or alleviate the irksomeness of the restraints thought necessary to keep them in order and constant readiness for action. Submarine crews and front-line troops, in constant danger, endured much greater hardships without thought of refusal. Order and discipline were quickly restored, but not morale. Punitive action taken by the navy was not extraordinarily severe. Two of the leading mutineers were shot. Death sentences imposed on three others were commuted to fifteen years' penal servitude. Great discontent persisted among the crews of the idle battleships, a fertile field for the propagation of communism and other radical ideas, to flare up anew in the revolt of early November, 1918.

Hertling, a conservative right-wing member of the Center party, who had been offered the position on the resignation of Bethmann-Hollweg in July but had then declined to take it. Although the dismissal of Michaelis may have been considered a victory for the Reichstag majority, the appointment of Hertling could not be so considered. Hertling was no advocate of constitutional reform, and thought it his patriotic duty to support the kaiser and the high command, not to try to bring them under Reichstag control.

The victor's peace of Brest Litovsk, the way in which it was dictated to the defeated Russians, and the incidental betrayal of the nationalist aspirations of the people of Poland were criticized in the Reichstag by Philipp Scheidemann of the Social Democrats; but his criticism, like so much that was said in Reichstag debates, was empty words. Because the treaty had actually brought the war in the east to an end, said Scheidemann, the men of his party would not reject it. They would refrain from voting. Only the Independent Socialists voted no. Stresemann's National Liberals, as nationalistic as anyone, favored ratification; and Erzberger told the Reichstag—could he have told himself?—that the treaty's terms were quite consistent with the principles of his peace resolution of July, 1917. So the Reichstag exercised neither positive nor negative control over national policy as to the making of peace in the east.

The war itself was denounced in the Reichstag on July 13, 1918, by Independent Socialist Deputy Geyer as an imperialist enterprise which he said had been wrong in Belgium, reactionary and brutal in the east, and never an honest war of self-defense; but the initiative for broadening the parliamentary base of government had to come from outside the Reichstag. A memorandum sent from the Foreign Office in Berlin to Ludendorff at military headquarters September 28 suggested the resignation of Chancellor Hertling and a broadening of the powers of the Reichstag as a concession to President Wilson's well-publicized condemnation of the "military dictators" of the old regime, to be followed by a request for an armistice and a peace based on the Fourteen Points.

Next day Ludendorff had a conference with the kaiser and Foreign Minister von Hintze. Confessing himself defeated and eager to end the fighting because every hour's delay was dangerous, he recommended such a revolution from above, on the ground that a dictatorship could not get a hearing and a more democratic-looking parliamentary government might be given better terms. An imperial decree announcing the resignation of Count Hertling (who resigned unwillingly) was signed that night reluctantly by the kaiser and published in Berlin the next morning. Prince Max of Baden accepted the chancellorship dutifully but with great misgiving, and soon found himself embarrassed both by the supreme authority nominally thrust upon him and by the kaiser's continued practice of ordering him to exercise it as directed by the high command.

Prince Max found it difficult to persuade the reluctant Reichstag to share responsibility with him. Why, asked Scheidemann in a conference of Social-Democratic party leaders, should they at that late date participate in a bankrupt enterprise? Because it was their duty as Germans, not as party members, replied Friedrich Ebert, to get tolerable peace terms while they could be had, and to save the country from the consequences of a worse defeat than it had already suffered—and from a communist revolution. So under Ebert's leadership the Socialists consented to enter a coalition cabinet to make as soon as practicable the peace which the high command, to their great surprise and consternation, so urgently demanded.

Both Prince Max and Ebert would have preserved the monarchy by putting it on a constitutional basis, rather than establish a republic, if they had been free to choose. The prince was advised by a colleague in the middle of October that President Wilson was willing to make a reasonably generous peace but Marshal Foch wanted a sterner one; so Germany must get on at once with the democratization of her own government so as to strengthen Wilson against Foch. The chancellor doubted that a republic, established then in Germany, would be either real or permanent. "A relapse is to be feared," he wrote in a draft of a third armistice note which was never sent, "only if Germany, to please other countries, permits the hasty and insincere imposition upon her of a constitutional form irreconcilable with her peculiar character and history." His words were prophetic.[3]

On October 20 a Socialist *Vorwärts* editorial expressed the hope that Germany would strike its war flag forever, without having brought it home for the last time victorious. This readiness to accept peace without victory was based on the realization of the futility of fighting on stubbornly and blindly for a victory that was clearly unattainable, and also on the theory that victory would strengthen only the most reactionary elements and retard the revolution. This stand was taken, how-

[3] Max von Baden, *Erinnerungen* (Stuttgart, 1928), 456-458; Rudin, *Armistice, 1918* (New Haven, 1944), 159. Compare this statement with the opinion of Montesquieu (expressed in his *L'Esprit des Lois*) that there is no form of government perfectly suitable for all peoples, but that for any people the best is the one best adapted to its situation and the habits and thought patterns growing out of its experience.

ever, by only a few of the more radical Socialists. Most of the German people were at that time more afraid of civil war and revolution than of the other foreseen consequences of defeat.

The least volatile and most influential of the Social-Democratic leaders, Friedrich Ebert, was more patriot than party man and on principle more revisionist than revolutionary. Although a sturdy political controversialist, he was essentially a man of peace, primarily concerned in October, 1918, with sparing his distressed fatherland further destruction. He wanted no more of war, offensive or defensive, foreign or fratricidal. He wanted no revolution on the Russian model, only evolution. On October 22 he proposed in the Reichstag certain constitutional changes to put an end to arbitrary government. The chancellor, he said, should thereafter be nominated by the Reichstag, removable by Reichstag vote, and responsible before civil courts of law. The military should cease to be a state within a state and should be brought under the control of civil authority. Woman suffrage should be granted.

Ebert did not then demand either the abdication of the kaiser or the abolition of the monarchy. Many others, however, while considering the constitutional changes proposed by Ludendorff and Ebert, were soon ready to demand at least the abdication of the kaiser, not because of any very general change of attitude toward him or his position but for the sake of easier peace terms. Reports poured in from German diplomats in neutral European capitals to the effect that the United States and the Allies would make no peace with the kaiser or the crown prince. Friends of the imperial monarchy in Bavaria and Baden besought the chancellor, himself a prince, to save the system by inducing the kaiser to lay aside his crown. Gustav Noske, a Social Democrat, said bluntly that if the kaiser got out Germany could get a good peace. Colonel Hans von Haeften of the general staff stated with equal frankness that, if the kaiser refused to abdicate, the negotiations with President Wilson must be broken off and Germany's situation would be hopeless.[4]

New constitutional laws were passed October 26, 1918, and proclaimed in a decree signed by the kaiser two days later, giving the Reichstag concurrent power with the Bundesrat in making treaties and declaring war, making the chancellor responsible to the Reichstag for political acts of the kaiser, and giving the chancellor greater power over the appointment, promotion, or retirement of army, navy, or

[4] Prince Max of Baden, *op. cit.*, 497-498; Rudin, *op. cit.*, 205.

other officials—a power which he soon used in forcing the retirement of Ludendorff.

Many students of the question have been convinced that these reforms were spontaneous and genuine; others that they were insincere and fraudulent. A spokesman for the chancellor got word confidentially to the United States embassy in Copenhagen that the reforms were genuine and sincerely made, but that the establishment of a republic at that time, merely to make a favorable impression on the entente, would be insincere and not an actual expression of the people's will.

When or whether the German people would on their own initiative have set up a system of democratic control of government was still an open question. It was clearly indicated, however, that they would not have demanded the kaiser's abdication when they did if they had not hoped for more favorable peace terms without than with him, or have changed of their own volition then—if ever—from monarchy to republic.

Prince Max, the last imperial chancellor, offered his resignation November 7, the day after the decision to capitulate; but it was not accepted. So it was he who announced the abdication at noon on November 9, before the kaiser had finally agreed to it. The new chancellor, Ebert, who took over on November 10, had by that time come to look upon the kaiser's abdication as essential not only to the making of a tolerable peace but also to the maintenance of internal order and the prevention of a social and economic revolution—which he said he hated "like sin." He would have preferred to leave the question of the eventual form of government to be settled by a constituent assembly. He was more than a little disturbed when his impulsive colleague Scheidemann, having been told on November 9 that the kaiser's abdication had been announced, people were rioting in the streets, and Karl Liebknecht was about to proclaim a soviet republic, tried to anticipate the Spartacists by himself announcing the establishment of a socialist republic. Next day a Berlin mass meeting of Social Democrats, Independents, and Spartacists endorsed a provisional government by a Council of People's Commissars composed equally of Social Democrats and Independent Socialists, headed nominally by Hugo Haase and Ebert, actually by Ebert.

Making it his mission to preserve as much as possible of the social and economic structure of the Germany he knew and loved, Ebert did what he could to control the pace and restrict the scope of the revolution, confining its changes to the political field. The Spartacists, on the other hand, who had been receiving arms, money, propaganda materials, and revolutionary guidance and encouragement from Russia since Brest Litovsk and were communists already in everything but name, were driving hard for a total political, social, and economic revolution on the Russian model.[5]

To dissociate himself and the other moderate Socialists from the revolutionary radicals and retain or win the confidence of the millions of the middle and upper classes who, like himself, were ready to accept the republic and welcome some political reforms but abhorred the thought of total revolution, Ebert tried to convince everyone but the communists that his government was liberal but safe. As evidence of its liberalism he issued a proclamation on November 10 lifting the "state of siege," restoring freedom of association, assembly, and utterance, and granting amnesty to political prisoners under punishment for offenses against the kaiser's government. Recognizing that his was only a provisional emergency government, he proposed the election, as soon as should be found practicable, of a national constituent assembly, by proportional representation, by equal, direct, universal suffrage of persons twenty years old or older. To make it "safe," he called upon all officialdom, the enormous and efficient civil service, and the police to keep the country's communications system and national, state, and municipal public services in uninterrupted operation and to protect life and property—which, generally speaking, they did, although most of them were still loyal to the monarchy and would have been happier in its service than in that of the republic.

As further insurance against Bolshevism and civil disorder Ebert enlisted the aid of the army through the coöperation of General Groener, Ludendorff's successor as chief of the general staff. It was agreed that the government would concentrate on the preservation of law and order, housing, and the reconversion of industry from war to peacetime production. The army would recognize the republic and, for the sake of order and the preservation of property and of the social structure as it was, would help it hold down the "bolshevists." This agreement prevented the immediate dissolution of the army, kept its officer caste intact despite demobilization, and put the republic in an unfortunate position of dependence, from the start, upon one of the least democratic and essentially antirepublican elements of the population. Later the Reichswehr, in which the best and worst traditions of

[5] The Russian embassy had been closed only on November 6 and Ambassador Adolf Joffe had been sent home for abuse of his diplomatic privileges and immunities.

the professional officers' corps were perpetuated, never hesitated to take advantage of its indispensability or to assert its independence of political—which meant civilian government—control. So Ebert, moderate Socialist and devoted patriot, intent upon safeguarding life and property, saving his country from danger of civil war, and making the new government seem "safe" to those who had most to lose by revolution, has been said to have succeeded only in making republican Germany safe for militarism.

Still trying to control and confine the revolution, the Majority Socialists (Social Democrats) and left-wing Independent Socialists participated in a national congress of workmen's and soldiers' delegates of the soviet type, December 16 to 20, which refused to seat the communists Rosa Luxemburg and Karl Liebknecht. Much bitterness of feeling between moderates and radicals revealed the continuance of the old cleavage between revisionists and revolutionaries. Ebert's provisional government group was called "bourgeois" and reactionary by the Spartacists and Independent Socialists.

The national congress of workmen's and soldiers' councils attacked with special bitterness the government's alliance with the army and adopted resolutions ordering the transfer of all powers of the supreme command to the cabinet and the executive committee of the congress. The resolutions ordered also that army officers should thereafter be elected and that the wearing of insignia of rank should be forbidden; but Ebert, true to his understanding with General Groener, made no attempt to implement any of these resolutions.

More decisive actions taken by the December congress of workmen's and soldiers' councils were the rejection by a vote of 344 to 98 of an Independent Socialist motion to make the soviet system basic for the new Germany, and provision for the election by universal suffrage, on January 19, 1919, of a national constituent assembly.

Disgruntled by their failure to set up a dictatorship of the proletariat, the left-wing minority group of Independent Socialists (Haase, Dittmann, and Barth) withdrew from the six-man Council of People's Commissars. Three Social Democrats took their places. One of these was Gustav Noske, the heavy-handed authoritarian who had restored order in Kiel after the sailors' and communists' rebellion there. He was ready to use such force as was found necessary to suppress disorder elsewhere.

There was much for Noske to do. Demobilization had progressed so far that the authorities had called for volunteer enlistments; but many demobilized war veterans had shunned the army and joined, instead, the irregular organizations later called the Free Corps. Some of these saw something like real service against the Soviets in the Baltic states; but they were generally ill disciplined, unreliable, and antirepublican in all their attitudes. With such dependables as he could find, Noske had to quell the undependables.

The last week of December, 1918, and the first half of January, 1919, were periods of violence in the Berlin area. On December 30 the Spartacists repudiated their uneasy alliance with the Independent Socialists, openly took the name of Communists, and (against the advice of their leaders Karl Liebknecht and Rosa Luxemburg) ordered their people to boycott the approaching national election. On January 6, acting again against the advice of Rosa Luxemburg but with Liebknecht concurring, Communists and Independent Socialists filled the Berlin streets with rioters, to discredit the provisional government on the eve of the elections. Noske struck back ruthlessly on January 11, with Regular Army troops and volunteers. There were a thousand casualties. "Spartacus week" ended with order restored and the government, which had been forced to act as a police state, in control. Liebknecht and Rosa Luxemburg were taken prisoner and killed by their captors without trial on January 15, after the rioting had ceased.

The Weimar Assembly

The election was held as scheduled, January 19, and resulted in an overwhelming victory for the parties most friendly to the republic. The Communists boycotted the election as they had said they would. The right-wing nationalists, militarists, and imperialists who subsequently ruined the republic kept discreetly quiet and stood haughtily aside. They let the Social Democrats, the Center party, and the Democrats shoulder the responsibility for creating a new government, concluding peace on terms not yet revealed, and attempting reconstruction after a long and losing war. No one then knew how difficult those thankless tasks would be; but it was already evident that none of them would be easy.

One of the immediate tasks of government during the interim between war and peace was to free the country from the food blockade. Article 26 of the armistice agreement read: "The existing blockade conditions set up by the Allied and Associated Powers are to remain unchanged, and all German merchant ships found at sea are to remain liable to capture." Erzberger tried hard before signing to induce Marshal Foch to strike out or soften that provision; but the only concession he could get was the addition of a statement that:

"The Allies and the United States contemplate the provisioning of Germany during the Armistice as shall be found necessary." No immediate steps toward the general provisioning of Germany were recognized by the Allies in 1918 as necessary. Germans of all classes and parties protested at every opportunity that the continuance of the food blockade after the cessation of hostilities was an atrocity far worse than any ever committed by the commander of a German submarine—and a breach of faith.

In January, 1919, the Allies offered food if German ships would carry it from England. There were some ships available, but their owners refused at first to send them for fear they would be seized for reparation. It was not until March, 1919, that these German owners were sufficiently reassured as to the safety of their ships to be willing to permit them to carry food to their own hungry people. Meanwhile the Allies and the provisional government which could not dictate to them—and failed to dictate to the shipowners as it might have done—were blamed for the continuance of the "hunger blockade."

The national assembly elected January 19 met at Weimar February 6, 1919, and assumed the difficult double role of provisional government and constitutional convention. The central council of workmen's and soldiers' soviets had formally surrendered its powers to the assembly on February 3. The assembly elected Friedrich Ebert president of the Reich on February 11, and a new cabinet was then formed with Scheidemann chancellor, Noske minister of defense, and Erzberger minister without portfolio. Rather optimistically, they named a minister for the colonies. The minister for foreign affairs was an experienced official of the foreign service, Count Ulrich von Brockdorff-Rantzau. He was not affiliated with any political party. Professor Hugo Preuss, a nationally recognized authority on the science of government, who was to earn the honorable title of principal author of the constitution, was minister of the interior.

While working at the making of a constitution, the national assembly was seriously distracted by the current problems of demobilization, reconversion, and adjustment to new conditions, which included the occupation of the left bank of the Rhine and several bridgeheads on the right bank by United States and Allied troops. In June all other work was interrupted by discussion of the dilemma: to sign or not to sign the Treaty of Versailles. On that issue the Democrats—the politically liberal middle-class party of Theodor Wolff of the *Berliner Tageblatt,* historian of religion Ernst Troeltsch, sociologists Max and Adolf Weber, publicist of social reform Friedrich Naumann, capitalist and industrialist Carl von Siemens, economic and foreign affairs expert Walther Rathenau, former colonial minister Dr. Dernburg, former Ambassador von Bernstorff, and financial manipulator Hjalmar Schacht—withdrew from the cabinet coalition and refused even to permit members of their party to accept positions in the new cabinet as individuals without party sponsorship. Chancellor Scheidemann resigned and another Social Democrat, Gustav Bauer, formed a new cabinet of representatives of two parties only, in which Social Democrat Hermann Mueller became minister for foreign affairs and Centrist Erzberger finance minister.

Count von Brockdorff-Rantzau fought hard against acceptance of the treaty about which he had spoken with such bitterness when it was handed to him in Paris. Two hours before the expiration of the Allies' ultimatum on June 23, 1919, still strenuously objecting to what it called the unparalleled injustice of the treaty and registering the strongest mental and moral reservations as to its "honor clauses"—on which the Allies would accept no written reservations—the Bauer government agreed to sign rather than face the consequences of refusal.

The application to Germany of the territorial, war guilt and reparation, war criminals and trials, and disarmament provisions of the Treaty of Versailles, and the German people's reaction to them, have already been discussed.[6] It was unfortunate for the republic and for the political parties then most friendly to it that it and they were generally blamed by their own people for the real and alleged—always exaggerated—severities of a treaty imposed upon a country physically unable to reject it, as a result of a war begun, fought, and lost (so far as Germany was concerned) by the kaiser's government, not by the republic. The sober citizens who accepted the responsibility of office in those trying days were better patriots than the patrioteers who avoided office and undermined their government with irresponsible talk of patriotism. No people can or should expect, either by revolution or by disclaimer of responsibility, to escape the consequences of things that it has done or that have been done in its name by agents of its government; but paying for the sins and failures of the empire was made a crippling handicap for the Weimar republic when its domestic enemies saddled it unjustly with blame as well as burden.

The Weimar Constitution

A constitution was adopted by the Weimar assembly July 31, 1919, by a vote of 262 to 75. Opposition was offered inside the assembly by

[6] See pp. 80-98.

representatives of the Nationalist, Independent, and People's (formerly National Liberal) parties and, outside the assembly, by unreconciled reactionary imperialists and the radical revolutionaries, mostly communist. The assembly then moved to Berlin and continued to function as an emergency national legislature until May 21, 1920. President Ebert and the Bauer cabinet continued in office and promulgated the new constitution August 11, 1919. The first national Reichstag election was on June 6, 1920.

Although it seems improbable that the republic would have been established when it was if defeat had not destroyed the monarchy, its establishment constituted a very real advance for Germany in the direction of democracy. It gave the Germans their first national bill of rights. It is true that some civil liberties were only conditionally guaranteed, and that duties as well as rights were detailed; but it was written that "sovereignty emanates from the people" and that the citizen had rights inalienable by the state, as well as obligations to the state. Among such rights were equality before the law, freedom of religion, the secret ballot, and the right of petition.

Centralization

The new national government was less highly centralized than Dr. Preuss would have liked to make it but more so than the empire had been. It was a federal union, of which Prussia was the largest member state or *Land,* larger than all the others combined. Each state had its own government, ministry, and minister-president or premier, of which Prussia's rivaled the national government and officials in power and prestige. Particularism comparable to regionalism or states' rights in the United States was still very much alive, particularly in Bavaria and the southwestern states or *Länder.* Bavaria, for example, had maintained a foreign office and sent ambassadors abroad. Yet, constitutionally, the national republic had more power over the *Länder* (which had also been made republics) than the imperial government had had when most of them were monarchies with dynasties of their own to sustain them in their particularism. The state-owned railways were soon well on the way toward nationalization. The constitution gave national law precedence over state law where both were applicable, and made it a duty of state courts, administrators, and police to administer and enforce national law. All Germans enjoyed equal rights of citizenship everywhere in Germany.

The national government was given powers of direct taxation which the empire had not had. Thus it was freed from dependence upon the proceeds of indirect taxation or upon matricular contributions from the states. The first section of Article 48 expressly authorized the federal government, when necessary, to coerce a state.

Constitutionally, the powers of the national government were concentrated in the democratically elected Reichstag. There was again a federal council (Reichsrat) replacing the old Bundesrat, made up of members of the cabinets of state governments, and therefore representing the state governments which paid their salaries, as the Bundesrat had represented the heads of states by whom its members had been appointed. Representation in the Reichsrat was apportioned among the states at the rate of one member for every 700,000 people, with the exception that no state could have more than two-fifths of the total (Prussia's population would have entitled her to two-thirds) and no state should have less than one delegate. Some of the smallest *Länder* of central Germany were combined to form Thuringia. In 1921 Prussia had twenty-six seats, Bavaria ten, Saxony seven, Württemberg four, Baden three; Thuringia, Hesse, and Hamburg two each; others one each. Representation was to be reapportioned by the Reichsrat itself after each census. The Reichsrat could initiate legislation to be submitted by the cabinet to the Reichstag and, by withholding its consent, could delay the enactment of Reichstag legislation; but a law could be passed over its suspensory veto by a two-thirds Reichstag vote. In general, it was much less powerful than the Bundesrat had been.

Reichstag, Supreme Court, and Ministry

Theoretically, the Reichstag was more powerful than the Reichsrat and more powerful than the imperial Reichstag had been. A national Supreme Court, to sit at Leipzig, was empowered to handle cases in dispute between states or between the national government and a state, but was not specifically authorized to judge the constitutionality of an act of the Reichstag and Reichsrat.

The people's will which was to rule the state was expected by the constitution makers to find its usual and most direct expression through this national legislature, elected by universal suffrage and proportional representation, rather than through the *Länder* or the Reichsrat. Though federal in form, the national government was thus apparently intended by its founders to become in fact progressively unitary. The national administration was entrusted to a cabinet or ministry selected and headed by a chancellor.

The chancellor was appointed by the president but was responsible to the Reichstag. The position of the Reichstag in the national government was thus made comparable with that of the French Chamber of Deputies or of the British House of Commons. Election was for four years; but a Reichstag dissolution, which could occur at any time, would call for a new election.

The Presidency

The *Reichspräsident* was to be something more than a figurehead but normally less powerful than the president of the United States. His stated prerogatives as chief of the executive and director of defense and foreign policy were very great, but the requirement of his ministers' countersignatures on all his official acts was expected to make his powers more nominal than real. Instead of a veto, he was given power to require the submission of an act of the national legislature to the voters in a referendum. A referendum could also be used instead of an impeachment trial, following an impeachment of the president; but if vindicated in such a referendum the president was to be declared reëlected for seven years from that date, and the Reichstag which had impeached him would be dissolved. The president could act only through his ministers, and they were responsible to the Reichstag except in an emergency.

Article 48 of the constitution made extraordinary provision for presidential action in an emergency. As head of the national government the president could coerce a state. If public safety and order were seriously disturbed or threatened he could take the necessary measures to restore them. In such an emergency he was empowered to use the armed forces, temporarily to suspend civil liberties, and to adjourn the Reichstag and govern by decree, subject to subsequent Reichstag approval or rejection of his decrees.

Article 48 was one of the most fateful articles in the constitution and has been the subject of much discussion. Was it a "joker" put into the constitution by some enemy of democracy to cripple the republic? Or did its authors only recognize that the republic was being set up in troubled times and that some crisis might arise in which the president would need extraordinary authority to save it? Did its inclusion indicate that even the authors of the constitution lacked confidence in democracy and would turn instinctively in a crisis, in time-honored

German fashion, to a man rather than to men? Would the people in some emergency—hungry, endangered, or perplexed—turn less readily away from self-reliance to self-surrender? The record seems to indicate that that article was put into the constitution for the preservation of the republic but that the result of its eventual use was the destruction of the republic.

A similar lack of confidence in the electorate and uncertainty as to whether a popularly elected president could be depended upon to use his emergency powers for the preservation of the republic were revealed by the reluctance of the republican parties to arrange for the election of a president. Friedrich Ebert had been chosen only by the Weimar national assembly. Cynical as to the wisdom of the voters and confident in their own ability to influence the unwise, the monarchists and other reactionaries repeatedly demanded an election "by the whole people," which the republican coalition of the Social Democrats, Democrats, and Center party, constituting a majority in the Reichstag, repeatedly deferred. In February, 1922, President Ebert asked the Reichstag to arrange for an election; but on October 24, 1922, by a vote of 314 to 76, it prolonged his term through June, 1925.

Ebert died in office February 28, 1925, without ever having been directly elected president by the people. The Reichstag then had to make provision for an election, and did so by revising its own earlier legislation on that subject. A law of May 4, 1920, had provided that a majority of the popular vote was necessary for election. If no candidate had a majority in the first balloting, there should be a *Stichwahl* or run-off election between the two leading candidates. In March, 1925, that law was changed. A majority of all votes cast was still required for election on the first ballot. If no candidate had such a majority a second vote would be taken. All candidates might run again, new ones might be nominated, or parties might combine in support of certain ones. There might then again be several candidates, of whom none might win by a majority; but, so as not to prolong the process indefinitely, it was provided that the candidate who received the largest number of votes in the second balloting should be elected.

In the election necessitated by the death of President Ebert, the voters first went to the polls March 29, 1925. Karl Jarres, mayor of Duisburg, candidate of a conservative coalition of Nationalist, People's, and Economic parties, won more than 10,500,000 votes, a large plurality but not a majority. Social Democrat Otto Braun won the largest single-party vote, nearly 8,000,000. The Center party candidate, former Chancellor Wilhelm Marx, had about half as many as

Braun, and Communist Ernst Thälmann half as many as Marx. There were three others. Former General Erich Ludendorff ran last, with less than a quarter of a million votes. Hindenburg was not a candidate.

The second balloting took place on April 26. Meanwhile the Social Democrats and Center party had formed a liberal republican coalition in support of the Centrist Wilhelm Marx, Otto Braun withdrawing. The conservative coalition held together, but chose a new candidate, Field Marshal Paul von Hindenburg.

As a candidate, the old soldier and self-confessed monarchist, coming for the second time out of retirement, professed only to be responding again as he had done in 1914 to the call of duty. Ebert had not ceased to be a Socialist while president, said he; neither would he change or conceal his personal political views. While Germany had been a monarchy, he had been a monarchist. He had served the fatherland in war; he would serve it also in peace. He had never been a politician or a party man. He would put the presidency above politics and parties and extend a cordial hand to everyone "conscious of himself as a German."

In the light of subsequent events it seems significant that von Hindenburg's strongest appeal to the voters, first and last, was made as a national military hero on a personal, nonpolitical, patriotic or patrioteering basis. The response indicated that people had more confidence in the old monarchist as an individual than in the new republic as an institution. The inferior status of the party politician in popular esteem was indicated by the ease with which von Hindenburg made political capital out of being "no politician"—and later Hitler out of not being an ordinary one.

In the balloting of April 26, 1925, 2,500,000 more votes were cast than in the first. The conservative coalition, with von Hindenburg as candidate, drew four million more votes than in March, about a million of the increase apparently being accounted for by the Bavarian (Catholic) People's party, which had had a candidate of its own in the first balloting and in the second had joined the conservative coalition (Nationalists and People's party) rather than the liberal one (Democrat, Social Democrat, and Catholic Center). Another bloc of nearly two million votes was withheld from the liberal coalition candidate by the Communists, who voted for Ernst Thälmann as before. One million more, from whatever source, would have given the liberal coalition candidate, a friend of the republic, the plurality necessary for election. Two millions would have given him a majority. By actual count von Hindenburg, candidate of the coalition less friendly to the republic, was elected president by a plurality of about 900,000 votes, his total being half a million less than half of all votes cast.

In office, although he owed his election to the support of the conservatives, von Hindenburg disappointed his more reactionary supporters by not moving immediately toward the restoration of the monarchy. After reëlection as the bulwark and defender of democracy, seven years later, he disappointed his more liberal supporters by lending the prestige of his position to movements inimical to the republic.

A turning away from parliamentary democracy was already noticeable when the newly elected President von Hindenburg made his triumphal entry into Berlin on May 11, 1925. It was perhaps natural, but it was none the less significant that the black-white-red of the monarchy predominated over the black-red-gold of the republic among the flags with which the city was bedecked, and that the *Stahlhelm,* supposed to be composed of veterans of the wartime army, was prominent among the many guards of honor. Other right-wing paramilitary organizations were out in force, in uniform and formation, but not the republican *Reichsbanner.*

The Political Party System

The very existence, within a few years of the establishment of the republic, of street-fighting organizations such as the nationalist *Stahlhelm*, the Nazi storm troops (*Sturmabteilungen,* or SA), or the republican *Reichsbanner* was an indication that the political party system was already in a bad way. Political life was a struggle for existence and control in which the law of natural selection did not insure the survival of the fittest unless the fittest was merely the readiest to fight. Each party strong enough to raise an army had one, organized in military fashion for parades and demonstrations, fighting in the streets, breaking up others' meetings or preventing its own from being broken up, intimidating the unsympathetic or protecting its own sympathizers from intimidation. In addition to those already named, there was the hand-picked Nazi *Schutzstaffel* or SS (euphemistically called a defense corps), the Communist *Red Front,* and others. The *Reichsbanner,* somewhat less aggressive and more honestly defensive in character than the others here named, was a Social-Democratic organization drawing some support from other groups of moderate republican views.

The press was equally partisan and belligerent. One of the more conservative Center party organs was the Catholic *Germania,* owned in the later years by Colonel Franz von Papen. The *Frankfurter Zeitung* and *Berliner Tageblatt* were liberal and democratic. The *Hamburger Nachrichten* was politically reactionary and critical of the republic. *Vorwärts* was, as before the war, Social Democratic. The Communists had their *Rote Fahne* or *Red Flag,* the Nationalists their *Stahlhelm,* and Hitler his *Völkischer Beobachter.* Many newspapers and periodicals were special-purpose publications, dedicated to the peculiar political or economic interests of their publishers or the industries or groups by which they were maintained. The *Essener Zeitung,* for example, was an organ of the Rhenish-Westphalian heavy industry. A genuinely independent paper, free from partisanship, prejudice, and propaganda, was a rare phenomenon.

Political irresponsibility seems to have been one of the unfortunate by-products of the system of proportional representation as it worked out in practice in Weimar Germany. Any party that could muster sixty thousand votes could send a deputy to the Reichstag, and a larger one could send a deputy for every sixty thousand votes cast for its list of candidates. With each party standing definitely for a known principle, an idea, an interest, or a policy, the Reichstag ought to have mirrored faithfully the political complexion of the country and the views and preferences of its people. In a sense it did; but different views, conflicting interests, and irreconcilable conceptions of national policy found expression so easily that enmity and great bitterness took the place of rivalry between parties.

Parties multiplied by fission. The multiplicity of parties compounded the confusion in the Reichstag. Every government had to be a coalition government serving several masters; every cabinet contained representatives of several parties, always mindful of their party ties, not always equally concerned about cabinet cohesion. Every chancellor knew that his ministry could be overthrown at any time by the defection of one of the parties composing his coalition, and often found his hands tied by one or another of them. He was thus constantly weakened by a feeling of insecurity, and frequent cabinet changes gave the government an appearance of instability and undermined people's confidence in it.

Party control of government was often negative. Instead of insisting upon its own inclusion in a government coalition, a party not infrequently refused to participate in one if a certain other party did, or unless certain policies or proposals were abandoned. A time when unpopular decisions were clearly soon to be forced upon a government was recognized as a bad time to be in office, and parties sometimes held aloof for that reason, hoping to utilize to their own advantage the consequent popular dissatisfaction. For the sake of certain policies which it approved, a party sometimes agreed temporarily to "tolerate," i.e., not to move to overthrow, a government in which it refused for some other reason to participate. The Social Democrats, for example, withdrew from a Stresemann cabinet in 1923 because the chancellor proposed to abandon the eight-hour day and reduce pensions and unemployment insurance benefits. However, they "tolerated" another Stresemann government that year and others led by Chancellors Wilhelm Marx and Hans Luther in 1924 and 1925 for the sake of the advantages they hoped were to be won by the abandonment of resistance in the Ruhr and the adoption of the Dawes plan. The businessmen of Stresemann's People's party, at the same time, while accepting his foreign policy for the sake of better business, would have refused to participate in a government which kept the eight-hour day and the high insurance benefits which the Social Democrats demanded; and the Nationalists withdrew their support because they did not like the Dawes plan.

Parliamentary responsibility implies ability to formulate, carry through parliament, and execute a consistent policy or program. It implies at least a minimum of cohesion in the cabinet and the existence of a reasonably dependable and friendly parliamentary majority. Without these, the chancellor, prime minister, or other official leader soon finds himself frustrated, and is not unlikely to believe that someone other than himself is responsible for his frustration; yet no one else will assume responsibility for his failure. The irresponsibility of parties intent upon evasion of responsibility rather than acceptance of it often brought the German chancellor to precisely this position.

Another type of political irresponsibility developed inside the parties. Party membership involved the inscription of a member's name upon the party roll, and payment of dues. Funds thus raised were handled by a full-time, salaried, professional secretariat. Policy was made by party leaders and officials and confirmed, not made, at an annual convention or *Parteitag*. The ordinary party member paid his dues and dutifully helped make a crowd when summoned to a meeting, street demonstration, or *Parteitag*; but he had little voice in the formulation of party policy, and none in the choice of candidates. In an election, he cast his ballot for a party list, not for a candidate of his own choosing. If only half of those nominated could hope to be elected, the position of a candidate's name on the list was all-important, and top position was tantamount to election. That also was handled by the party leaders and the secretariat. They were the "politicians." The little man (who could not see later why he should be punished for what "they" had done) might be a party member, but he played no leading part in politics. He only acquiesced. There came a time, however, when, accustomed as he was to accepting policies and choices made for him by his leaders, he chose to transfer his allegiance to new leaders who said they would do more for him than his old ones had done.

However irresponsible and particularistic the parties were in their attitude toward the national government, their internal discipline was effective. The constitution provided that a Reichstag deputy should vote on every question as an individual according to his own judgment, not as a member of a bloc instructed by a party caucus; but that clause of the constitution was consistently disregarded. Party delegations still met in caucus and decided how the deputies should vote. With the vote on any question thus predetermined, parliamentary discussion lost all but propaganda value, and the Reichstag could not be a deliberative body.

Political party particularism, irresponsibility, and obstructionism, which by 1930 induced a state of parliamentary paralysis, had already seriously discredited the Reichstag by 1925 and partially accounted for the favorable response to Field Marshal von Hindenburg's persistent presentation of himself as not a party man, in fact "no politician." It was already good politics in 1925 to sneer at politicians.

Insurrection and Militarism

During the first six stormy years of the life of the republic, acts of violence and disorder serious enough to threaten its existence were committed by extremists of both right and left. While the constituent assembly was in session at Weimar, Communist outbreaks against the provisional government occurred at Eisenach, Magdeburg, Dresden, and Berlin, and in the Ruhr. These were suppressed with great severity, indicated by Noske's order of March 9, 1919, that government troops should shoot down anyone encountered with a weapon in his hand opposing them. During the same period the provisional republic set up by Kurt Eisner in Bavaria in November, 1918, was overthrown by a moderately conservative bourgeois group. Eisner was assassinated. The Spartacist-Communists revolted. Munich was besieged and eventually retaken by government troops and volunteers. It became a center of reaction. In 1922 and 1923 Bavaria alternated threats of secession with talk of "saving the Reich" by seizing the national government for the radicals of the extreme right.

In March, 1920, the government buildings in Berlin were seized and held for a few days by a band of nationalist reactionaries nominally led by Wolfgang Kapp. Kapp was the American-born son of a liberal émigré but had spent most of his life as a comparatively obscure provincial German bureaucrat. What he lacked in character and ability he made up for in chauvinism. During the last years of the war he had collaborated with Admiral von Tirpitz in forming the Fatherland party, so called, for unfaltering continuance of the war.

Kapp was supported by Traugott von Jagow, who had been chief of the Prussian police from 1909 to 1918, by General Baron Walther von Lüttwitz, commander of Reichswehr troops in the Berlin area, by a veteran cavalry officer, Major Waldemar Pabst, by Ludendorff's former adjutant, Colonel Max Bauer, and others. Ludendorff was in sympathy with the insurgents. The spearhead of the insurrection was the so-called Marine Brigade, one of the most efficient units of the volunteer defense corps, which had already helped suppress the Bavarian soviet republic and was then quartered in Döberitz, near Berlin. The Marine Brigade commander was naval Captain Herman Ehrhardt, a hard-bitten, unreconciled enemy of democracy and of the republic.

Kapp's attempted coup d'état or *Putsch* came at a bad time for the republic. It had been compelled by pressure of the Allied powers during the months just past (1) to sign at Versailles a protocol (September 22, 1919) declaring null and void the second paragraph of Article 61 of the Weimar constitution, which had made provision for the inclusion of Austria as a member state of the German federal union on a voluntary basis and on equal footing with the other states; (2) to agree to try in the German court at Leipzig some of the men listed by the Allies as war criminals; (3) to disarm Germany at once, down to the limits set by the Versailles Treaty; and (4) to recognize anew a heavy but undefined liability in reparation payments.[7] This compulsory submission to the will of victorious enemy powers was only sensible and could well have been defended as at once intelligent and patriotic, but it could not well be pointed to with pride before an arrogant and sensitive people only then beginning to be aware of what it had cost them to fight a war and lose it.

The Kapp *Putsch* was precipitated by government plans to abolish the volunteer defense corps and reduce the Reichswehr in compliance with treaty agreement. Captain Ehrhardt declared that his Marine

[7] See pp. 100-102, and 88-98.

Brigade would refuse to disband, and von Lüttwitz that the officers and soldiers of the Reichswehr would not permit the dissolution of the Marine Brigade or accept their own dismissal from the service.

Anticipating and attempting to forestall rebellion, Defense Minister Noske ordered the removal of Lüttwitz from his command and the arrest of Kapp, Colonel Max Bauer, and Pabst. The rebels escaped arrest, however, and the Marine Brigade marched into Berlin. Noske and General Walther Reinhardt, chief of the army command, might have had the courage if they had had the power to use the regular troops of the Reichswehr to stop the irregulars; but General Hans von Seeckt, head of the *Truppen Amt* or troops office which had been set up in place of the outlawed general staff, piously protested that German soldiers must not be made to fire upon one another. This meant that, so long as they obeyed their officers, which none of them had refused since 1918 to do, German soldiers, always available for use against rebels of the left, could not be depended upon for use against rebels of the right.

The Reichswehr offered no real resistance to the armed insurrectionists invading the national capital. Ebert and Noske, uncertain whether the forces loyal to them, including the police, would be able to quell the rebellion quickly, and unwilling to be responsible for bloodshed that might be preventable, withdrew with the government to Dresden, then to Stuttgart, where Konstantin Fehrenbach, president of the national assembly, summoned the assembly to meet at once.

Kapp and his associates moved into the government buildings in Berlin and began calling themselves a government. Kapp was to be chancellor, von Lüttwitz defense minister. Both would have been puppets of the parties of the right, which had already been defeated in the assembly on the platform proclaimed by Kapp: direct election of a president, no further reduction of the armed forces, government by experts—on the old Prussian civil service model. Ungrateful and disloyal to their own servants, those parties did little to identify themselves with the rebel government and nothing to defend it. They were waiting, as their custom was, to see whether it could maintain itself.

The trade unions, on the other hand, responded to the legal government's call for a general strike. The strike was immediate, general, and real. Everything stopped. Kapp could do nothing. He lost his nerve and fled, and the Ebert-Noske-Gustav Bauer government returned to Berlin.

Few were punished, and none severely, for rebellion in the name of nationalism. Kapp himself subsequently surrendered, and died awaiting trial, June 12, 1922. Colonel Max Bauer left the country. General von Lüttwitz was deprived of his command and went into retirement at Schweidnitz. Jagow was sentenced to imprisonment for five years but was soon granted an amnesty. Ehrhardt, far from abandoning his evil ways, merely moved down to Munich and founded there a secret murder society called Organization C or *Consul,* dedicated to the destruction of the Weimar constitution and the liquidation of those conspicuous for their support of the republic and acceptance of the terms of peace. These its *Vehm* courts "condemned" as traitors, and its murder squads "executed." Matthias Erzberger was one of the most prominent of its many victims. In signing the armistice agreement of 1918 at Compiègne he had signed his own death warrant. By advocating the acceptance of the Treaty of Versailles he had confirmed the sentence. His execution waited only for an opportunity, and the opportunity was found on August 26, 1921. Walther Rathenau, shot June 24, 1922, was another victim. He was a Jew; he had supported the policy of fulfillment; and he had accepted appointment as foreign minister only three months after Upper Silesia was lost to Poland.

More aroused by the easy first success of the Kapp *Putsch* than reassured by its collapse, the Allies insistently demanded the immediate abolition of the *Freicorps* or volunteer force in excess of the authorized strength of the Reichswehr. So the *Freicorps* was legally abolished and went underground. Bavaria was especially hospitable to it. There Ehrhardt and members of his old brigade were active in it. Although legally nonexistent, it never lacked arms, ammunition, or encouragement.

As a result of Noske's failure to control the generals or to use the Reichswehr to restrain the Kappist rebels, President Ebert had to ask for his resignation; but having himself always depended upon the generals as his allies instead of trying to control them as servants of the state, he was in poor position to reproach Noske for the same offense. Democrat Otto Gessler, the new minister of defense, was no less complaisant. He also permitted the generals, under their usual pretense of keeping the army free from politics, to free themselves from political control and dictate the military policy of the government.

The army might well have been thoroughly discredited as a result of the Kapp *Putsch,* and properly subordinated to civil authority and the law, but was not. Nor could the Allies depend upon the German government to enforce the disarmament provisions of the Treaty of Versailles. That was a task for which it had neither strength nor inclination. It reduced the Reichswehr legally on December 30, 1920, to treaty strength of 100,000, with officers sworn in for twenty-five years and men for twelve. But it maintained at the same time a constabulary (*Schutzpolizei*) of 150,000 men, and usually ignored the existence of other illegal forces such as the Bavarian *Einwohnerwehr*. Public opinion did not demand complete disarmament and would have been alienated by it.[8]

Communists contributed indirectly to the continued popular tolerance of government's dependence upon the army by repeatedly attempting revolution in times of great distress. Under the guidance of the Third International they took up temporarily, during the occupation of the Ruhr in 1923, a fiercely nationalistic propaganda line designed to discredit the national government for having failed to prevent the occupation. Meanwhile they formed fighting organizations of their own, called Hundreds. The Prussian minister of the interior banned the Hundreds, but in Saxony and Thuringia, early in October, 1923, a proletarian combination of Social Democrats and Communists led by a Social Democrat seized control of both state governments.

The Reichstag had just granted the national government extraordinary emergency powers. The defense minister at once delegated full authority to the commander of the Reichswehr in Saxony. The Communists talked of fighting, and were ousted from the Saxon cabinet. Lives were lost and people wounded at Pirna and at Freiberg, but the Social Democrats would not fight the Reichswehr, so remained in office. A People's party colleague of Chancellor Stresemann, federal Minister of Justice Dr. Rudolf Heinze, was made Reich commissioner for Saxony with plenary powers. Communists were forced out of the Thuringian cabinet in similarly cavalier fashion. In Hamburg in the last week of October a Communist revolt was suppressed by the police.

Militarism was strengthened and republicanism weakened whenever a republican government found it necessary, as the monarchy had almost never done, to use German troops for internal police purposes. Stresemann's government was hurt by its use of force in Saxony and Thuringia in 1923 to the extent that the Social-Democratic members of his cabinet resigned, November 2, in protest against what they called abuse of power. Bourgeois middle groups were somewhat reassured, but the radicals of the right were as recalcitrant as ever. In Munich a loosely knit combination of discontented reactionary and

---

[8] The Treaty of Versailles had stipulated that the number of customs officers, foresters, and coast guards should not exceed the number employed in 1913, and that constabulary and police forces might be increased only in proportion to any increase in population.

separatist elements was in control of the Bavarian government and needed only organization and unity of purpose to make it a real danger to the Reich; and Hitler and his followers threatened to get control of it, give it strength and unity, and use it to overthrow the government.

In Munich on November 8 and 9, 1923, the National Socialists made their first serious attempt at insurrection. On the evening of November 8 a political meeting was being held at which General von Lossow, commander of the local division of the Reichswehr, and Colonel Hans Seisser, commander of the Bavarian police, were to be present and the Reich commissioner for Bavaria, Gustav von Kahr, was to speak. With only a handful of followers but with his own security measures well prepared, Adolf Hitler invaded that meeting. Wildly brandishing a pistol, and supported by General Ludendorff who soon also appeared, Hitler compelled Kahr, Lossow, and Seisser to agree to join the National Socialists next morning in a march on Berlin, to set up a new national government under General Ludendorff with Hitler as chancellor.

Kahr and Lossow had previously made known that they regarded Lossow's 5th Reichswehr Division as in the service of Bavaria, not the Reich; but they broke their forced promise to Hitler as soon as they could get away from him and his pistol. During the night, also, President Ebert issued a proclamation declaring guilty of high treason anyone who supported the movement which he called "this mad attempt at Munich," and General Hans von Seeckt announced that the Reichswehr would deal sternly with any breach of public order.

By the morning of November 9 all but National Socialist support for Hitler's proposed *Putsch* had evaporated, and the Nazi force itself seemed about to melt away. So the leaders ordered a march through Munich streets rather than slink away without making some sort of demonstration. The marchers soon came under fire from a road block set up by Reichswehr and police. General Ludendorff, at the head of the marching column, stalked straight ahead; the soldiers were careful not to hurt him. They had to arrest him but did not want to hold him. The parade disintegrated.

Hitler, who had a car ready for the purpose, ran away and was sheltered in a suburb of Munich in the home of his friend Ernst (Putzi) Hanfstängel. Göring was wounded but got away to Austria, then Italy, then Sweden. He became an active leader in the movement again only in 1927. Rudolf Hess escaped to Austria but returned later and was sentenced to eighteen months' fortress imprisonment at Landsberg, where he went on serving Hitler. Captain Hans Roehm and Wilhelm Frick were taken into custody and found guilty of the offenses charged against them but were soon released.

Hitler and Ludendorff were brought to trial on charges of treason on February 26, 1924. Judges who had been trained and reached maturity under the old regime treated the old general with all the deference to which his rank and war service had once entitled him, and disregarded his disloyalty to the republic by acquitting him of the charge of treason.

Hitler was permitted to use the occasion of his trial for several characteristic diatribes against the republic and the "November criminals" who betrayed the monarchy. The old flags, he warned, would wave again. He defied the court, which he knew must find him guilty of high treason, and publicly appealed to "the eternal court of history," which he said would recognize that he and the other officers and soldiers of "the Quartermaster General of the old army" had, as Germans, wanted and desired only the good of their people and fatherland, only to fight and die. History, he said, would therefore acquit them. The general behind whose name he tried to hide was found not guilty, but Hitler was found guilty of high treason and given the minimum sentence the law allowed: imprisonment for five years, of which he served less than eighteen months.[9]

The double standard of justice, as applied by the republic to its rebels of the left and right, infuriated the parties of the extreme left, cost it the confidence of the moderate liberals, and encouraged the rebels of the right in their defiance of it. Before the death of Ebert in 1925, whatever popularity the republic had had was already on the wane.

The government of the republic was not, in its first six years, unrepresentative of the German people or unresponsive to their will. It surrendered neither rights nor territory except under pressure which it could not resist, and paid or agreed to pay reparation only under the most vigorous protest. It was always as nationalistic as it dared to be, and evaded the disarmament provisions of the peace treaty in many ways. Yet the militarists and other right-wing reactionaries brazenly blamed it for the consequences of defeat in a war which they, not it, had lost, as well as for the defeat itself. Among the consequences of defeat were poverty—falsely attributed to the loss of colonies—the

[9] Halperin, *Germany Tried Democracy* (New York, 1946), 275-279, 285. The story of the rise of National Socialism will be told later. It was just four days before Hitler's trial started that the Social Democrat street-fighting organization, the *Reichsbanner*, was formed. Kahr and Lossow hung on to their posts in Bavaria for more than three months after Hitler's *Putsch*.

cession of valuable territories and industrial resources, the French and Belgian occupation of the Ruhr, the fantastic inflation of the currency which meant financial ruin to millions and wealth to clever operators only, and agreements to disarm, to try alleged war criminals, and to pay reparation.

By 1925 the facts of 1918 had been forgotten, or had become unrecognizable as misrepresented by protest propaganda, with the result that a considerable number of the people turned away from the liberal republican parties of the "Weimar coalition" which had had the hardihood to accept the responsibilities of office in the darkest days of that dark period. Gustav Stresemann, who was chancellor from August to November, 1923, and foreign minister for six years thereafter, freed the Ruhr from foreign occupation and greatly improved his country's international standing; but he did not strengthen the republic. His successes in the international field, on the contrary, restored the strength and confidence of conservative and bourgeois groups who preferred authoritarianism to trade unionism, state socialism, or republicanism. The election of von Hindenburg to the presidency was the work of such groups, not of convinced believers in socialism or democracy.

The republic had not yet lived out half of its span when von Hindenburg was elected president, and some years of stability and apparent prosperity were just ahead; yet, in a sense, its best years were already past. The militarists and money men merely tolerated it and used it in good times, then turned against it when hard times again threw millions into consternation, thus readying them for totalitarianism.

GEOPOLITIK: OR ECONOMICS, POLITICS, AND FOREIGN POLICY

Policy of Fulfillment

German national policies, before as well as after the advent of the Nazi, were necessarily cut according to the cloth. The country was weakened economically, and worse hurt psychologically, by the wastage of the war, the loss of Alsace and Lorraine, Upper Silesia, Danzig, and the corridor, and the temporary losses of the Saar and Ruhr. Its pride was hurt, and its publicists said it was crippled, by the loss of its colonies. Germany's helpless condition dictated a policy of conciliation. Armed defiance of its victors was impractical. The Wirth-Rathenau policy of fulfillment—i.e., compliance with the peace terms and recognition of a reparation obligation—was inexorably dictated by circumstances in 1921 and 1922. He served his country best who faced these facts most fearlessly; and in that respect Ebert, Wirth, and Rathenau served it well.

Rapallo

Rathenau, as minister for reconstruction in Wirth's first cabinet (May 10 to October 20, 1921) and as foreign minister in his second, immediately following the first, was especially active and ingenious in attempts to improve Germany's condition and international status. Taking his opportunities and his personal allies where he found them, he turned toward Russia in 1922 in the otherwise uncongenial company (so to speak) of General von Seeckt, principal organizer of the Reichswehr.

Von Seeckt, to whom ideology was always subordinate to military considerations, considered it his duty to estimate as accurately as he could all dangers by which Germany might conceivably be threatened, and the resources at her command with which to meet those dangers. He was aware of the enmity of France, and assumed that Poland and Czechoslovakia, as beneficiaries of the Versailles Treaty, would always be natural enemies of a Germany unreconciled to acceptance of that treaty, and natural allies of France. Britain might not be willing to make a military alliance with France to defend the Versailles settlement but would surely not make one with Germany to break it. At least a temporary community of interest might be found, however, with Soviet Russia—and used to Germany's advantage.

Russia might, in the opinion of the geopolitically-minded officers of the revamped German general staff (*Truppen Amt*), be found to have a common interest with Germany in the destruction and territorial absorption of Poland. Allied or coöperating effectively with Russia, Germany would be better able to withstand another wartime blockade. Behind the iron curtain, not yet so named but already drawn around Russia, the Reichswehr hoped to carry on in secret the experiments with new armament and tactics which the peace treaty had made illegal and surveillance of Allied military commissions would have made more difficult at home. As a *quid pro quo*, German officers could continue the practice of their profession by helping to train the new Red Army.

Rathenau was interested primarily in the business aspects of a German-Russian rapprochement. Industrialization, modernization of existing industry, expansion of transport and communication facilities, and mechanization of the great farms to be formed by collectivization were clearly indicated as the imperative first tasks of any Soviet government. Why should not German heavy industry supply the machines the Russians must have to make machines, the electrical, mining, and oil-drilling equipment, and the engineers and technicians needed to set up and operate these machines and the pilot plants? Money might not be asked to immigrate, but capital investments in Russia, in the form of industrial machines, materials, and skills, might well be made with an alluring prospect of profit. Rathenau seems to have thought also that Germany might be in a better position to bargain with the nations of western Europe if she could make herself appear to be on better terms with eastern Europe than they were.

In April, 1922, an international conference was being held at Genoa to discuss the possibility of general diplomatic recognition of Russia's Soviet government if it would recognize the international debts of the government of the tsars and obligate itself to pay at least a portion of them. On April 16 Rathenau made with Russia the separate Treaty of Rapallo, which when reported at Genoa created something of a sensation there. Germany, it was revealed, had not waited for the others but had already recognized the new government in Russia, *de jure* and *de facto*. Although the others had recognized it only *de facto* by agreeing to discuss the question of its recognition as a legally and properly established government, Germany had declared herself ready to resume regular diplomatic and consular relations with it at once. While others were bickering over debts incurred by Romanov Russia, Germany waived indemnification for losses incurred by German citizens through the abolition of private property in Russia, and Russia and Germany mutually waived reparation claims. Trade between the two countries was to be resumed and facilitated.

Representatives of other nations at Genoa were surprised and angry. Their demands and Russia's offers had been far apart, and little was done to bring them together. Germanophobe parties everywhere, especially in France and Belgium, already advocating greater sternness in the collection of reparation from Germany, were strengthened.

The immediate diplomatic consequences of the making of the Treaty of Rapallo were therefore not altogether fortunate. If the secret terms of that treaty had then been revealed, they might have caused a more serious explosion. The Reichswehr had got what it wanted. In return for the annual payment of a stipulated sum, Germany was permitted to establish in Russia the aviation schools which the Versailles Treaty had forbidden her to maintain at home. German tank and artillery units trained in Russia as if parts of the Russian army but under German command. German armament and munitions—guns, planes, tanks, shells, and gas—were produced by Germans in Russian factories; and war research and experimentation went on beyond the ken of the Allied control commission.

Yet nationalist anarchists of the Ehrhardt type called Rathenau a Jewish internationalist, a pacifist, and a traitor. On June 24, 1922, a wave of protest swept over Germany in response to a government announcement of the costs of the Allied occupation of the Rhineland, and to the realization that Upper Silesia had really been lost to Poland. In the midst of the outcry, Foreign Minister Rathenau was murdered in gangster fashion on a public highway a few miles from the center of Berlin.

Chancellor Wirth struck back at Rathenau's assassins. One, naval Lieutenant Erwin Kern, was killed by the police while resisting arrest. Engineer Hermann Fischer, cornered with Kern, killed himself. Ernst Werner Techow, nephew of an industrialist, was captured and sentenced to prison for fifteen years but was granted an amnesty seven years later. Ten others were given terms of two to eight years, the longer sentences subsequently shortened. Three accused persons were acquitted.

Murderers of persons less prominent than a government minister were usually not apprehended or were only perfunctorily punished if their victims could be accused of collusion with the occupying forces; and any voluntary compliance with the peace terms or conciliatory gesture toward the former foreign enemy was likely to be called collusion. What Rathenau had done for Germany with respect to Russia was not generally known. What had been done to Germany by the western powers and Poland was known only too well; and Rathenau was made the scapegoat. Such lawless acts of violence were outlawed again, and often again committed. The wrathful were readier to defy their government than were the authorities or timid citizens to defy the men of wrath.

Recognition and Recovery

Ebert, Wirth, Rathenau, Cuno, and Stresemann were all realists and all revisionists. They recognized their country's weakness in the first five years after the war and the necessity of at least formal and partial reconciliation with its former enemies for the sake of the resumption of trade, upon which economic recovery depended. When it had regained its strength it could be bolder in demands for revision of its treaty status; but until capable of controlling its circumstances it must adapt itself to them. Stresemann, especially, was driven to this conclusion by the French and Belgian occupation of the Ruhr in 1923.

The Hamburg shipowner Wilhelm Cuno became chancellor November 16, 1922. He was a Roman Catholic but had formerly been a member of the People's party rather than the Center. The Social Democrats, apprehensive about the eight-hour day and social insurance, refused to participate in his "bourgeois" government but tolerated it. On December 2 the Cuno government notified the reparation commission that it would be late with certain deliveries of timber and asked that they be deferred until April 1, 1923. On December 27, with the British representative dissenting, Premier Poincaré of France induced the commission to declare Germany in default on the delivery of 140,000 telegraph poles. By a vote of three to one, Great Britain again dissenting, the commission on January 9, 1923, found Germany in default also on coal deliveries; and next day the occupation of the Ruhr by French and Belgian troops began. The British army did not participate, and United States troops were soon withdrawn from the Coblenz occupation zone.[10]

The Cuno ministry resigned August 13, 1923, as a result of the cost and ineffectiveness of its policy of passive resistance in the Ruhr and the bankruptcy of the government and great sections of the population through inflation of the currency. More realistic than Cuno, Cuno's successor Gustav Stresemann ordered the people of the Ruhr to go back to work and resume deliveries of reparation materials. With the help of Hans Luther, Hjalmar Schacht, and others, he established a new currency.

Such steps were necessary but not popular. Emergency powers were granted and had to be used, as has been told above, to suppress Communist disturbances in Saxony, Thuringia, and Hamburg, and Nationalist and National Socialist opposition in Bavaria.[11] The number of the unemployed increased from 180,000 in July to 1,500,000 in December. Yet as a measure of economy the government abandoned the eight-hour day. Recovery seemed likely to be retarded as long as the nation's status with reference to reparation remained undetermined.

Nationalist and Socialist opposition, right and left, defeated Stresemann on a motion for a vote of confidence November 23, 1923, two

[10] See p. 76.
[11] See pp. 257-259.

weeks after Hitler's Munich *Putsch*; but he continued as foreign minister in the cabinets of the Centrist Wilhelm Marx and succeeding chancellors until October, 1929.

If Stresemann had had a saber he might have rattled it. Having none, he refused, as he said, to "rattle an empty scabbard." It was more prudent and more profitable to accept the Dawes plan, as he did, and to solicit foreign loans with which to meet the first reparation payments under it and finance industrial reconstruction and public building.

The period 1924-1929 was one of great activity and apparent but in many ways illusory prosperity for Germany.[12] The rationalization and cartelization of industry begun under the guidance of Rathenau continued, increasing volume and lowering costs of production by eliminating waste and allocating markets so as to control competition. National government, *Länder*, municipalities, and businesses found borrowing easy and spent prodigally what they borrowed. While manufacturers quickly converted much of their easy money into modernized and enlarged industrial plants, increasing their capacity to produce, many of the municipalities spent theirs on parks and public buildings—commodious, imposing, and not without social value but not self-liquidating or productive of material goods or revenue. Repeatedly but vainly Stresemann and Seymour Parker Gilbert, American agent general for reparation money transfers, warned them all that a day of reckoning would come when repayment would be demanded or the sources of credit would dry up; but until that day came Germany seemed to prosper.

Prosperity and the promise of stability seemed at first to hurt the political prospects of the extremist parties. In the first Reichstag elections (December 7) after the implementation of the Dawes plan by Reichstag legislation, August 29, and the granting of the first Dawes plan loan in October, 1924, the Communists lost seventeen (more than a fourth) of their seats, and the Nazi eighteen (more than half). The Communist popular vote was 1,200,000 less than in the last previous election, and the Nazi 1,100,000 less. The greatest numerical gain (thirty-one seats) was made by the Social-Democratic party, which was still numerically the strongest in the Reichstag with 131 seats.

Yet there were neither Democrats nor Social Democrats in the new cabinet formed by Dr. Hans Luther on January 9, 1925. His was a conservative nationalists' and businessmen's government, supported by the second and third strongest parties, the German Nationalists and Center, more concerned about quick economic recovery at the top

[12] See pp. 90-94.

than about restoring the eight-hour day, lowering tariffs or prices, or perpetuating the republic unless they could continue to control it. The election of von Hindenburg to the presidency was, as has been shown, a victory for economic conserratism and political reaction. The republic was restoring public confidence and bringing at least a promise of prosperity; but with restored confidence many of those turned against it who in 1918 had accepted it reluctantly, in form but not in spirit, and had tolerated it only while they dared not do otherwise.[13]

The success of the counterrevolution in the election of von Hindenburg in 1925 caused some consternation outside Germany, where it was feared that he might try to restore the monarchy. That such fears were so soon forgotten was due to the appearance of good faith with which the new president seemed to accept his position and to the continuance of Stresemann's policy of conciliation, which was in those days the German nationalists' greatest asset.

When President Ebert died, February 28, 1925, Stresemann was already deeply engaged in the negotiations leading to the Locarno agreements along a line suggested by Chancellor Cuno as early as December, 1922, before the French had gone into the Ruhr. He went right on with them under President von Hindenburg. The principal obstacle in his way in 1925 was French insistence upon linking a western with an eastern pact, setting up international guarantees of Germany's Czechoslovak and Polish boundaries as well as the French and Belgian. Stresemann was unwilling even to discuss a proposal that Germany should repeat her recognition of her eastern boundaries or sanction any international guarantee of their permanence.

Stresemann had simply chosen conciliation as the best tactical maneuver for improving Germany's relations with her western neighbors and promoting her other interests. His nationalist strategy remained unchanged. In September, 1925, just before accepting the Allies' invitation to a conference at Locarno, he explained in letters and newspaper articles for home consumption that he was not giving up anything not already lost, or surrendering anything forever. His long-term policy was as always, he said, to revise the eastern frontier so as to recover Danzig, the corridor, Upper Silesia, and Memel; to claim "the right of self-determination" for Austria so that it might join Germany; to recover the lost colonies; and to protect all Germans living under foreign yokes abroad.[14]

[13] See pp. 236-242.
[14] See pp. 151-155. Adolf Hitler, whose subsequent policy statements so closely resembled these, was released from prison and granted an amnesty as a person of no consequence in December, 1924, and his party dwindled into apparent insignificance.

By the treaties initialed at Locarno October 16 and signed at London December 1, 1925 (terms of which are given in Chapters 6 and 7), an atmosphere of greater confidence was created in Germany's relations with western Europe. The international guarantee of her western frontier, however, was not to take effect until she became a member of the League of Nations; and Germany raised as many questions before applying for League membership as other members raised before admitting her. She had to be assured that she would not be required to renew her ratification of the Treaty of Versailles or make again that hateful forced confession that she had been guilty of aggression in 1914. Negotiations for her admittance were complicated by demands of other nations that they also be given permanent Council seats if she was given one.[15]

While agreeing at Locarno that Germany should join the League of Nations, Stresemann was careful to commit the other signatories to an understanding that no member was to be obligated to coöperate against an aggressor except to an extent compatible with its military and geographical situation. What he then had in mind was made plainer in the course of the negotiations for Germany's admittance to the League. To establish a basis for any future demand he might be in a position to make that Germany be permitted to rearm, Stresemann pointed out that, disarmed, she could assume no military obligations under Article 16 of the League Covenant.

More plainly put, these two contentions meant that Germany would take no action in defense of Poland, even as a member of the League acting in conjunction with other members. It was not generally known, although Stresemann may be presumed to have known, that the geopoliticians of the Reichswehr would have been more inclined, if Russia attacked Poland, to join her in a fourth partition of that country than to try to stop her.

Russia wanted reassurance. Russian Foreign Commissar Chicherin expressed alarm at what he called the Locarno reversal of the Rapallo policy. He professed to see a threat to Russia in Germany's inclusion in the League, a step toward the isolation of Russia by the League. As Rathenau had done at Rapallo before going to Genoa in 1922, so on April 24, 1926, before going to Geneva in September, Stresemann made a new treaty with Russia.

The German-Russian reinsurance treaty of 1926 was no more likely

[15] Germany was given a permanent place on the Council. Three new nonpermanent seats were added. Poland accepted one. Brazil was offered one, but withdrew from the League. Spain refused one, then accepted it.

to ingratiate Germany with the other members of the League than the Treaty of Rapallo had been to make friends for her at Genoa. It envisaged close and friendly relations. If either party should be attacked, the other was to remain neutral. With the treaty Stresemann sent a letter assuring Russia that, as a member of the League, Germany would oppose any anti-Russian move the League might make. It was almost an alliance; yet the Reichstag approved the treaty on June 30 with only three dissenting votes.

Germany was made a member of the League at the 1926 session of the Assembly, and Stresemann took her seat on the Council September 10.

The Luther-Stresemann government had told its own people in February when applying for membership that, far from recognizing the Treaty of Versailles again, Germany would be in a better position as a member of the League to work for its revision. But the League did not develop into a revising agency. The Cologne occupation zone had been evacuated according to plan at the end of January, 1926, and the Allied military control commission was withdrawn at Stresemann's insistence January 31, 1927. These moves, however, did not constitute treaty revisions, and Europe was disturbed but not moved to compliance by occasional German references in 1927 and 1928 to the revision of Germany's eastern boundaries.

There were other indications that success had not strengthened the republic and that the admittance of Germany to membership had not greatly strengthened the League of Nations. The national unemployment insurance program adopted July 7, 1927, by the bourgeois coalition cabinet of Centrist Wilhelm Marx provided assistance to the unemployed for a period of twenty-six weeks. This was not generous enough to placate the Social Democrats, who were still willing only to tolerate the government and were not participating in it. In August, 1927, the first Nazi *Parteitag* at Nuremberg was attended by twenty thousand persons. Hitler and Alfred Rosenberg were the orators. At the dedication of a Tannenberg monument that autumn old Field Marshal von Hindenburg, in an address written for him in part by Stresemann, categorically denied for Germany the old treaty-confirmed charge of war guilt, from which she had not been freed by treaty revision. That autumn the Junker landowners made Hindenburg more fully one of themselves by causing him to be given an imposing but impoverished estate at Neudeck, with provision made for evasion of the inheritance tax but not for payment of taxes already in arrears. He valued the estate; but its bad financial status made it his Achilles heel and predisposed him to consider sympathetically the tax delinquencies and subsidy requests of the other landlords.

On August 27, 1928, Stresemann signed for Germany the Kellogg-Briand Pact of Paris, renouncing war as an instrument of national policy. As interpreted and enforced at Nuremberg in 1945-1946, the pact made the planning and initiation of a national war of aggression a capital offense. In November he explained apologetically to the Reichstag that his conciliatory foreign policy had been dictated by military weakness. Meanwhile, in September, the rabidly nationalist *Stahlhelm* had proclaimed its hatred of the regime, which it accused of having made impossible the liberation of the enslaved fatherland, the destruction of the war guilt lie, or the winning of needed *Lebensraum* in the east.[16]

By setting a term and a total of reparation payments, thus ending some uncertainties left by the Dawes plan, the Young plan might have strengthened the republic in 1929 but did not have that effect. The certainties it established were too unpleasant and left open to the domestic enemies of the republic too many avenues of attack.[17]

Depression, Discontent, Disunity

While the Young plan negotiations were in progress, the government tried to identify itself in spirit with the whole people by proclaiming June 28, 1929, a day of sorrow, but added nothing thereby to its own popularity. Its proclamation only reopened old wounds by adverting to the tenth anniversary of the signing of a treaty which it called "a bitter disappointment to all friends of justice and true peace." No one was convinced by the reiteration that Germany had signed that treaty without thereby acknowledging that the German nation had started the war. Because neither leaders nor people would forget it, there was some truth in their contention that that accusation made it impossible for them to regain their tranquillity and undermined the feeling of trust between the nations.[18]

Also while the Young plan was still being negotiated, German nationalist opposition to it was organized. The Nationalist leaders Alfred Hugenberg and Franz Seldte, founder of the *Stahlhelm*, joined Adolf Hitler and other Nazi in promoting a petition, by exercise of the

[16] Halperin, *op. cit.*, 366. The *Stahlhelm* was not a Nazi organization, although many of its members subsequently joined the Nazi, taking their slogans and ideologies with them or finding themselves at home among kindred ones.
[17] See pp. 92-94.
[18] Quoted by Halperin, *op. cit.*, 391-392.

popular initiative in legislation, to bring before the Reichstag a bill which with characteristic overstatement they called "A Law Against the Enslavement of the German People." It was the declared purpose of this bill, colloquially called the "freedom law," to reject the Young plan in advance, to attaint with treason the chancellor, cabinet, and plenipotentiaries responsible for it, and to repudiate all further obligation in respect of reparation. (Hjalmar Schacht was head of the German delegation which negotiated the Young plan, and signed it; but he later took advantage of some slight further concessions made by Stresemann to join the Nationalists, Nazi, and Pan-Germans in denouncing the agreement he had made. Some months later, as a further gesture of protest, he resigned the presidency of the Reichsbank.) The recalcitrants secured barely enough signatures to bring their "freedom law" before the Reichstag, where on November 29 the government forces, led by the Social Democrats and a new foreign minister from the People's party, Dr. Julius Curtius, defeated it.[19]

The Young plan was accepted by the voters in a referendum December 22, 1929. Less than six million votes were cast against it. Its acceptance was due in part to the publication of the last concession Stresemann had induced the Allies to make, at a reparation conference at The Hague, August 28; the military evacuation of the Rhineland began September 15 and was to be (and was) completed by June 30, 1930, five years before the time prescribed by the Treaty of Versailles.

The legislation necessary to implement the Young plan was passed by the Reichstag March 12 and signed by the president March 13, 1930. Five days later a sharper law was passed for the protection of the republic and the suppression of disorder, which had become so serious that the minister of the interior, Carl Severing, reported that three hundred policemen had been wounded and fourteen killed in Prussia in the year just past. The new law was not enforced, however; and within two more weeks the political coalition which had been responsible for the acceptance of the Young plan had fallen apart.

The Cabinet headed by the Social Democrat Hermann Mueller, which had been in office since June 28, 1928, and had been responsible, with Stresemann, for the Young plan policy, proposed in the interest of economy to increase the premium on government unemployment insurance, stipulating at the same time in the interest of the unemployed that the insurance benefits could not be decreased without appropriate legislative action. Spokesmen for the People's party, bent on tax reduction and freed from the moderating patriotic influence

[19] Stresemann died October 3, 1929.

of Stresemann, objected to the new measure because it did not reduce expenditures as they wished. The trade unions and more radical Social Democrats objected because it would have increased the cost of the insurance to the insured. Upon the resignation of Hermann Mueller, the chancellorship was assumed by a leader of the Center party, Heinrich Brüning, with the Social Democrats again only tolerating a government in which they would not participate.

Brüning's was always a minority government with little dependable parliamentary support or cabinet cohesion. With little prospect of winning a Reichstag vote of confidence, he was hard put to it to fight off persistent Communist, Nazi, and Nationalist resolutions of "no confidence." Although the Social Democrats had no quarrel with his foreign policies, they assumed that whatever government was in power during the depression would come to grief, and hoped to gain popularity as champions of social insurance for the workers and the poor by opposing the government's efforts to economize on civil service salaries and pensions and on its contribution to the unemployment insurance fund.[20]

The German civil service was traditionally nonpartisan and nonpolitical, but its members constituted a large, fairly homogeneous, cohesive, and very influential group. It hurt the republic politically when Brüning's proposals to reduce expenditures by reducing the number of civil service employees as well as their salaries and pensions cost him the support of that group. The *Beamtentum*, officialdom of the civil service, would not overthrow the republic but would do nothing to defend it at the risk of salary or position. Better change the buttons again than give up the uniform.[21]

With so many groups against him, Brüning was forced to purchase support or tolerance from day to day, or to fall back upon presidential authority under Article 48 of the constitution and govern by decree. He depended principally upon the middle parties (Center, People's, and others) and, outside the Reichstag, upon the manufacturers and landowners. He tried not to burden business with taxes, and he tried

---

[20] There were more than three million unemployed in the autumn of 1930, two-thirds of whom were receiving unemployment insurance benefits. Although it met for the unemployed only a fraction of the minimum cost of subsistence, the insurance program did not pay its way. Its fund showed a deficit of 450,000,000 reichsmarks in June, 1930, and the poor-relief fund a deficit of 150,000,000; and revenues earmarked for these purposes were insufficient. Halperin, *op. cit.*, 422.

[21] Some of the older and bolder of these men were reported to have said during the Nazi period that they had changed their buttons twice already, from monarchy to republic and from republic to Third Reich, and would be glad to make a third change at any time.

to subsidize industries that promised to put more men on their pay rolls. Another subsidy policy, dictated to him by the Nationalists, was aid to owners of large estates, most numerous in northeastern Germany. This was the infamous *Osthilfe*.

The landowning aristocracy of old Prussia, commonly called the *Junker*, was probably the most homogeneous, compact, and influential special-interest group in Germany. Men of a few thousand families had always held positions of trust and profit in the army and diplomatic corps and in the higher echelons of the civil service. For many generations men of their class had served the state and had generally been found worthy of their hire. They still considered themselves the backbone of society, essential to the state, and entitled to whatever subsidy or bonus they said they needed. Being in a position to dictate to Brüning with the sympathy of von Hindenburg, they joined the industrialists in insisting upon the downward revision of social insurance payments and, for themselves, demanded a high protective tariff on agricultural products and cash subsidies for impoverished estates.

Many of the estates which were represented as impoverished were large. Some 11,000 landowners held more than 16,000 estates. Of these, 113 owned from 12,000 to 25,000 acres each, 46 more than 25,000 each. Richest of all were the holdings of the Hohenzollern family, 415,000 acres.[22] Yet the Hohenzollern took whatever *Osthilfe* money they could get. As master of Neudeck, President von Hindenburg accepted instead a "contributed gift." It would indeed have been a bold underling official who dared challenge the claim of the local magnate, arrogant scion—perhaps—of a proud old family. One such landed aristocrat was reported to have drawn subsidies for the relief of three impoverished estates and used them for the purchase of a fourth. Others induced the government to buy what they had to sell— potato spirits, for example—at prices fixed well above the market, and store what it could not sell or use. More money was drained out of the

---

[22] In a referendum on June 20, 1926, nearly fourteen and a half million votes were cast for a proposal to dispossess the Hohenzollern without compensation. This could have been done constitutionally only by a majority of the qualified voters. The initiative had been taken by the Communists. The Social Democrats would have preferred expropriation with nominal compensation but, like most of the voters, had too much respect for property rights to be willing, at the risk of being called "Reds," to vote for the proposal as it was presented to them.

Public or semipublic buildings such as the royal palaces in Berlin and Potsdam and the Hohenzollern family archives of the house of Brandenburg-Prussia in Berlin-Charlottenburg were taken over by the castles and parks administration and handled as joint state and family property. Twice a year an official went to Holland to present to the exiled kaiser a report on the handling of that property, and let him pay his family's half of the operating deficit.

treasury through this private pipe line of the Junker than could ever have been saved by the Brüning policy of plugging little leaks in the salary, pension, and unemployment insurance budgets to the discomfiture of millions of little people.

Government by Decree

In mid-July, 1930, a budget which the Reichstag had just refused to approve was proclaimed as in effect in defiance of the Reichstag by presidential decree under Article 48—the first open and official violation of the principle of ministerial responsibility. With the Social Democrats spearheading the offensive, the Reichstag adopted a resolution abrogating the decrees. The chancellor retaliated by dissolving the Reichstag and carrying his case to the people in a manifesto saying that the majority parties had shown themselves incapable of assuming the responsibilities of government yet had denied him the means of governing.

It was in just such periods of economic disorder and distress and parliamentary paralysis that the antiparliamentarians found their finest opportunities. Speaking to his party leaders at Munich on July 27, in the interim before a new Reichstag election, Adolf Hitler said, in part: "It is not parliamentary majorities that decide the fate of nations. They can destroy nations. But we know that in these elections democracy must be destroyed with the weapons of democracy."[23]

On the eve of an earlier election, May 19, 1928, he had told his followers that they must grow into "a mighty army of termites" before their hour could come. In 1930 the termites were still at work, and their leader was growing bolder as the timbers of the republic seemed almost ready to give way.

More than half of the 35,000,000 votes cast in the Reichstag election of September 14, 1930, were cast for the less democratic parties least friendly to the republic. The Nazi, who two years earlier had commanded less than a million votes and only twelve Reichstag seats, had become the second strongest party in the nation, with more than 6,400,000 votes and 107 seats. The Communists, third strongest, had increased 40 percent in popular strength since 1928, to a total of 4,587,000 votes and seventy-seven Reichstag seats instead of fifty-four. The Social Democrats were still the largest party numerically but had lost something in numbers and more in unity and strength.

Between the election and the first session of that Reichstag, three

[23] Quoted by Konrad Heiden in *Der Führer*, 348.

Reichswehr officers were brought to trial before the Supreme Court at
Leipzig and sentenced to eighteen months' fortress imprisonment for
treasonable activity on behalf of the Nazi party. Hitler testified at their
trial. Reminded by the judge of a threat already attributed to him, he
repeated it: "If our movement succeeds we shall (set up) a people's
tribunal before which the November criminals of 1918 shall expiate
their crimes and I frankly predict you shall then see their heads rolling
in the sand."[24]

When the new Reichstag assembled October 13, 1930, the uniformed Nazi delegates marched in in military formation, creating a
great commotion, rivaled in rowdyism only by the Communists.

Although it could never command a dependable Reichstag majority
at home, the Brüning government was not at first quite without credit
abroad; and it sought diligently to improve domestic conditions by a
vigorous foreign policy. On June 23, 1930, to match a concession
already made by the Allies as part of the Young plan, the United
States government agreed to reduce by 10 per cent its claim for reim-
bursement for the expenses of its army of occupation.[25] The principal
amount of the bonds payable on this account in 1930 was paid when
due, as were also the amounts payable under an agreement with the
United States covering claims for war damage.

Also in June, 1930, under the Young plan, Germany received a
loan of 1,200,000,000 reichsmarks. A year later a credit of 420,000,-
000 marks was extended to the Reichsbank by the central banks of
the United States, Britain, and France and the Basel Bank for International Settlements, to cover payments due June 30 on reparation loan
service.[26] There the borrowing stopped, but repayment was suspended
after July 1, 1931, by the Hoover moratorium and the August, 1931,
standstill agreement on short-term loans, made originally for six
months only but repeatedly renewed.

The most ambitious of Brüning's international economic projects
was the announcement March 19, 1931, of a proposed economic
union or *Anschluss* with Austria. It was sponsored by Dr. Schober of
Austria, as well as by Foreign Minister Curtius of Germany, and might
have been advantageous to both countries. But it was not permitted

---

[24] Guido Enderis, special cable to the New York *Times*, Leipzig September 25,
New York *Times* September 26, 1930. Too many readers of these words simply
dismissed them with the thought that the man was mad.

[25] The original amount of the claim was $292,663,435.79. Nearly $100,000,000 had
been paid. The balance was to be paid through a period of thirty-seven years. *U.S.
Treasury Reports*, 1930, p. 64.

[26] This last item was repaid in 1933.

because too many of Germany's nervous neighbors thought that they saw in it a step toward a political union, which had been prohibited by the peace treaties and subsequent loan agreements.[27]

The opposition to the German-Austrian *Anschluss* was led by France and Czechoslovakia, which feared that it might endanger them by strengthening Germany. They induced the Council of the League of Nations at its sixty-third session May 18-19, 1931, to ask the Permanent Court of International Justice for an advisory opinion as to whether such an assimilation of the tariff and economic policies of Germany and Austria would be compatible with Article 88 of the Treaty of St.-Germain (which had declared the independence of Austria inalienable otherwise than with the consent of the Council of the League of Nations) and with Protocol Number One signed at Geneva on October 4, 1922 (by which Austria had undertaken not to alienate her own independence, or to make any economic or financial engagement calculated directly or indirectly to compromise it, or to grant to any state a special regime or exclusive advantages calculated to threaten it).

The court's opinion was that the proposed economic union endangered Austria's independence and might result in the granting of special and exclusive advantages to Germany (although it had been publicly announced that other states would be invited to join the *Anschluss* on equal terms with the original parties), and was therefore incompatible with the Geneva Protocol in question.

That opinion had been reached by an almost evenly divided court. Six judges—from France, Poland, Spain, Rumania, Salvador, and Colombia—concurred in the opinion written by Bustamente of Cuba, and would in fact have gone farther and declared the *Anschluss* incompatible with either Article 88 of the Treaty of St.-Germain or the Geneva Protocol. Seven—from Great Britain, the United States, the Netherlands, Belgium, Germany, Japan, and China—held in a dissenting opinion that such an economic agreement as was proposed, on a basis of equality, need not rob Austria of the right to exercise her own judgment in making the decisions it involved or endanger her independence if the treaty and protocol appealed to had not already restricted it. Other customs unions, the minority opinion pointed out, had not generally been considered incompatible with independence.

The fifteenth vote determined the issue. It was cast by the Italian, Anzilotti, in a separate opinion. It was not customs unions in general,

[27] See pp. 103, 104; also M. M. Ball, *Post-War German-Austrian Relations* (London, 1937), chap. 2 and Appendix 1.

he said, about which the court had been asked to give its opinion, but one between Germany and Austria. Austria might have entered some other customs union without compromising her independence; but one with Germany might endanger it and would therefore be incompatible with the treaties cited.

The fact that Germany was involved and might be strengthened made all the difference to those who feared her most. The judges were not negotiators acting on instructions from their foreign offices to reach a political decision. Each may be presumed to have formed his own opinion. Bustamente of Cuba and Kellogg of the United States decided differently; so did the French and Belgian members of the court. Yet the judges' individual opinions were generally quite similar to the political positions already taken by the governments of the countries from which they came, and each reflected fairly faithfully the current trend of public opinion at home. The court's opinion in this case has sometimes been called in the United States its Dred Scott decision.

Two days before the adverse advisory opinion was announced, Germany and Austria made public their decision to abandon the *Anschluss* plan. They were in desperate financial straits, and France seemed to be better able than any other nation to help them; so the good will of France, without *Anschluss*, seemed to be worth more to them than *Anschluss* with the ill will of France and other nations. At a meeting of a Commission of Inquiry for European Union, Schober for Austria and Julius Curtius for Germany explained that they had hoped *Anschluss* would open the way for a wider union of peoples. Since it seemed, instead, to be looked upon by others as an obstacle to such a union, they said, they would withdraw their proposal. Their renunciation was denounced by nationalists in both their countries as a capitulation. Curtius was forced by adverse German opinion to resign. Brüning had to take over from him the Foreign Office portfolio and form a new cabinet without him. Former chancellor Joseph Wirth, who had been minister of the interior, was also dropped from the cabinet, and his post was taken over by General Groener, who continued as minister of defense. A cabinet of personalities became one of fewer personalities.

Other ambitious proposals advanced by Brüning for the rehabilitation of Germany by increased coöperation with the rest of Europe fared no better than his attempt at *Anschluss* with Austria. He had in mind the improvement of international inland waterways, such as Danube-Rhine canal connections, and some vast international electrification projects for central Europe. He would have been willing to offer France some cash compensation for the immediate return of the

Saar to Germany without waiting for the contemplated plebiscite at the end of a fifteen-year occupation period. To get Danzig and West Prussia back, he would have been willing to guarantee Poland a free port on the Baltic and free access to it. At the Geneva disarmament conference he had almost succeeded in securing the concession, in principle, of Germany's equal right to armament when he was undermined there by General Kurt von Schleicher, who told the French ambassador that he would soon be forced out of office and that France would be wise to wait and deal with his successor—which she did.

Schleicher was an inveterate intriguer in the ministry of defense, with high connections in the Reichswehr, and a member of the "palace camarilla" surrounding and influencing the aged president. By 1932 he had almost realized his ambition to combine a maximum of power and influence with a minimum of political responsibility, to control both Reichswehr and government from behind the scenes as confidential adviser to von Hindenburg. His fellow favorites in the camarilla in 1932 were the president's son Oskar and Secretary Otto Meissner.

It was Schleicher who had suggested the appointment of Brüning to the chancellorship in March, 1930. It was Brüning, more than anyone else, who was responsible for the reëlection of von Hindenburg in April, 1932. In the first balloting, March 13, the middle parties gave the old president a plurality of more than 7,300,000 votes over Hitler. Nearly 5,000,000 votes were cast for the Communist candidate Ernst Thälmann and more than 2,500,000 for the Nationalist Colonel Theodor Düsterberg. In the second balloting, April 10, the Nationalists, who had withdrawn their own candidate, threw about two million of their votes to Hitler, but Hindenburg got the rest—about half a million. More than a million Communists who had voted in March seem to have stayed away from the polls in April. Thanks to Brüning and the parties still friendly to the republic, Hindenburg had in the second balloting a majority of about two million votes over Hitler and Thälmann combined. A plurality would have been enough for election.

Brüning was believed to have wished to reëlect von Hindenburg so as to use him, as his original supporters for that office had hoped seven years earlier to do, to restore the Hohenzollern dynasty. Brüning would presumably have preferred a constitutional monarchy on the British model. No effective steps were taken in that direction.[28] There was not time.

In May the president for whose reëlection Brüning had been

[28] Halperin, *op. cit.,* 475, 476.

responsible in April turned against him. Schleicher had promised Hitler to induce the president to force Brüning to resign. The ban which he had imposed upon the SA and SS by presidential decree of December 8, 1931, would then be lifted and the Reichstag dissolved. The Nazi always thought that they could win more seats in the next election. Meanwhile they promised to "tolerate" Brüning's successor, Franz von Papen. At the same time Schleicher was promising the president that he would either control the Nazi or destroy them.

Brüning incurred the enmity of the Junker group, and lost the confidence of the president, by proposing to partition some bankrupt estates for the relief of some of the unemployed. Neudeck was not threatened; but its proud owner listened readily to the cry of "agrarian Bolshevism" raised by his Junker neighbors, the group he had known best and longest—and sometimes seen at its best—in the army and in which he most implicitly put his trust. He agreed to dismiss Brüning, whom he disliked, and make his personal favorite Franz von Papen chancellor.[29]

As military attaché to the imperial German embassy in Washington in 1914, Captain Franz von Papen had abused his diplomatic privileges and immunity to incite strikes and organize sabotage in the United States. In 1915 one of his blunders led to his being handed his passport and sent home. In 1932, still a saboteur, he helped wreck the Weimar republic. Then the president put him in charge of a prize crew from the *Herrenklub* to bring what was left of it into port. Less than half the members of his "presidial" cabinet were members of the Reichstag, and parliamentary government was only a memory to be mocked at. Presidential absolutism, through a chancellor dependent upon presidential favor for his tenure of the office, had become the basic feature of German political life.

Then followed, as in any despotism under an aging despot, a period of rivalry between palace favorites. Having made and broken Brüning, General von Schleicher credited himself also with having made Papen chancellor, and expected to control him. Able General Groener had had to resign, May 12, as minister of war; and Schleicher took Groener's place in Papen's "Almanach de Gotha" cabinet of monocles May 31. This opened the way for the lifting, June 15, of the ban of outlawry from the SA and SS, for which the Nazi had had

---

[29] Hindenburg was a Lutheran; but his belief in the old army and the soldier caste that had furnished it so many of its officers transcended his religious faith. Brüning was Catholic, had been a wartime army officer but not a professional soldier, and was suspected of some sympathy for socialist ideas. Papen was also Catholic, but his family was wealthy and aristocratic, and he had once been a professional soldier.

reason to blame Groener quite as much as Brüning or von Hindenburg. Schleicher and Papen both thought that they could control the Nazi. Apparently each thought he could use them if necessary against the other. In underground intrigues they competed for the support of the Nazi whom they despised.

Faithless to their previous agreement with Schleicher to tolerate the Papen-Schleicher government, the Nazi announced in June, in the interim between dissolution of the Reichstag and the next Reichstag election, that they had not created the new government and were not disposed to tolerate it.[30] Even the Lausanne agreement to put an end to reparation with a final token payment (which was never made) they denounced as "a new tribute pact."

The preëlection campaign was marked by widespread violence. On July 20 Chancellor von Papen, taking advantage of a Nazi-provoked Nazi-Communist riot which had occurred in Altona, a suburb of Hamburg, three days before and had been quickly quelled, accused the Prussian government of failure to maintain law and order. He made his accusation a pretext for the seizure of the government of Prussia.

Premier Otto Braun and Minister of the Interior Carl Severing of Prussia had at their disposal in that last stronghold of Social Democracy and republicanism[31] the *Reichsbanner* and a strong and well-disciplined state police force, and so might have made a fight of it. But they were not fighters. They abhorred the thought of civil war, blinding themselves or somehow blinded to the fact that a civil war was already being fought against the German state and people.

Precisely as the spokesmen of the old Prussian Landtag of 1848 had done when ordered by General Wrangel to discontinue their discussion of a constitution and disperse, Severing declared in high dudgeon for himself and his associates that they would not give up their offices unless compelled by force. As Wrangel had done in 1848, so General Gerd von Rundstedt in 1932, commanding the Berlin division of the Reichswehr, assured the heads of the civilian government of Prussia that he had at his disposal and would use whatever force was necessary to carry out the chancellor's orders. An officer and ten men arrested Albert Grzesinski, chief of a police force of sixty thousand. Severing was obdurate until told by the new police chief, Grzesinski's successor, that force would be used if he did not

[30] Schleicher had made good on his promises to Hitler, to tolerate the SA and SS and dissolve the Reichstag.

[31] The Nazi were rapidly gaining strength in the smaller southern states.

yield; then, knowing that the Prussian police could at any time be taken over by the president under Article 48 as Ebert had done more than once, he yielded.[32]

Hoping to foil von Papen as Kapp had been foiled in 1920, the Communists called for a general strike; but the unity which had frustrated the Kappist group was lacking in 1932. So as to shun provocation and give the chancellor no excuse for further usurpations, the Social Democrats emphasized what they called the maintenance of discipline—which meant submission without even such passive resistance as a general strike would have involved. Papen was in power; so obedience was prudent and was preached in the name of discipline. Then the Communists talked revolt; but the police broke up their meetings and stopped the publication of the *Red Flag* for five days; and there was no revolt.

In the last weeks of the preëlection campaign Papen made good use of a slogan which was later to be further popularized by National Socialists: *Gemeinnutz vor Eigennutz*—the general interest of the community comes first, taking precedence over the interest of the individual. Hitler made a whirlwind campaign, traveling by plane and speaking several times a day, shouting nationalism, while Gregor Strasser, one of the most active and persuasive of the other Nazi orators, stressed socialism.

In the election, July 31, the government parties lost ground. The Reichstag representation of the Nationalists and the People's party—the only parties on which Papen could depend for support—declined to thirty-seven and seven, respectively. The Communists gained, largely at the expense of the Social Democrats, who thus paid a penalty for their futility in the face of the seizure of the government of Prussia. With fourteen million votes and 230 deputies, the Nazi had become the strongest group. Their 38 percent of the Reichstag could have combined with the 6 percent of the Nationalists to form a reasonably solid minority government bloc but was more often combined with the Communist 15 percent to form a majority in opposition. They did not coöperate with the Communists in much else but in making parliamentary government impossible; but that, for

[32] It would be easy to exaggerate the significance of these incidents; yet if they are typical they are significant. Compare them with Sir John Eliot's defiance of King Charles I in the second session of his third Parliament in 1629, the Long Parliament's refusal to be dissolved without its own consent, and Mirabeau's defiance of the king's troops after the taking of the Tennis Court Oath in 1789—and compare the subsequent constitutional histories of England, France, and Germany.

different reasons, suited them both and was enough for their immediate purposes.

The newly elected Reichstag met August 30, 1932, only to elect Hermann Göring speaker and adjourn for six weeks. When it met again September 5 Papen was ready with an order for its dissolution, signed for him beforehand by the president as the first of the kaisers had on occasion signed one for Bismarck, but he fumbled momentarily and Göring forestalled him by calling for immediate action on a Communist motion of "no confidence." Papen tried to interrupt with his presidential order of dissolution, but Göring ruled him out of order on the ground that no new business could be introduced while a vote was being taken. The chancellor laid the dissolution order on the speaker's desk and left the room. The voting proceeded and the motion of "no confidence" was passed. Göring then declared that the chancellor's government had fallen as a result of the motion, and Papen said the vote was invalid, having been completed after the legal dissolution of the Reichstag. The law and the privileges of parliament had indeed fallen into the hands of strange defenders.

Another election was held November 6. This time it was the Nazi who lost ground. Foreign opinion was known to be generally apprehensive of them, and some fear was felt that a Nazi victory would have an unfavorable effect upon Germany's international position. Foreign Minister Baron Konstantin von Neurath had gone further than the public knew, to warn the chancellor that the Foreign Office would not be responsible for the consequences if Hitler became chancellor. Less cash than usual was available for the campaign, as Papen had induced his wealthy friends to withhold the contributions he had, years before, first persuaded them to make to Hitler's funds. More moderate and bourgeois support was lost by public Nazi association with a Communist-instigated strike of Berlin transport workers, by which the party tacticians had hoped to embarrass the government and win some radical labor members away from the Communists with whom they were temporarily joining hands. They drew two million fewer votes than in July, and lost more to the Communists than they won from them. The Nazi Reichstag delegation dropped from 230 to 196, from 38 percent to 33 percent. The party seemed to have passed its peak. But the gains registered by the Nationalists and Communists were no promise of a return to parliamentary government. The Communists, with a hundred deputies in the Reichstag, had gained more than the Nationalists and seemed to be on the march.

The fear of Bolshevism led the capitalists to wonder whether the socialite von Papen, clever only at intrigue and always a bungler in performance, would ever be strong enough to save them and whether they had erred in judgment when they permitted him to persuade them to discontinue their subsidies to Hitler. Schleicher also, as minister of defense, turned against the chancellor, whose appointment he had himself recommended, and carried a majority of cabinet members with him. He said he favored a working partnership with Hitler.

Forced to resign November 17, but flattering himself that he would soon again be found indispensable, and confident that Hitler would be discredited by trying and failing if asked to form a government, Papen advised the president to offer the chancellorship to Hitler. Hindenburg and Hitler agreed that Schleicher might remain as minister of defense and von Neurath in the Foreign Office; but Hitler demanded full use of the emergency powers of the president, and that was more than the president was ready then to give him. Such powers in the hands of a party leader, he said, would lead only to a party dictatorship.[33]

The president would have preferred to bring back Papen; but the ministers, led by Schleicher, refused to serve under him. Schleicher would have preferred to have Hjalmar Schacht made chancellor, and hide behind him as he had hidden behind Brüning and Papen; but after an interim of more than two weeks of confusion Hindenburg told him gruffly that he would have to undertake the task himself.[34]

Schleicher's government lasted less than two months. No one trusted him, not even the president. He had no party or personal following. He sought to win the support of the Nazi, or to split the party and keep part of it, by negotiating with Gregor Strasser; but, after several arguments with Hitler, Strasser went away. The disgruntled but still dangerous ex-Chancellor Papen was ready to betray his own betrayer, Schleicher, by bargaining with Hitler to oust him.

The chancellor and the Reichstag which met December 6 to 9, 1932, agreed upon a few palliative measures on a bargaining basis. A law permitting employers who took on additional workers to reduce wages at the same time was repealed. An amnesty to political prisoners

[33] Nazi propagandists then generally pretended to agree with Hindenburg that the national government should be nonpartisan in character, above all parties; but National Socialism, they said, was a great national movement, nonpartisan and above all parties, as nationalism should be.

[34] There is nothing to indicate clearly that Schacht would have accepted the position. He was a canny individual, far more clever than Schleicher, and equally unscrupulous. It was characteristic of him to use others, not to be used by others without his knowledge or against his will. He would not stay with a sinking ship, and it would not have been in character for him to accept command of one.

was supported by the unusual combination of National Socialists, Social Democrats, and Communists—all of whom hoped to welcome at the prison gates some valued members of their parties. At adjournment it was left to Göring and the standing Reichstag committee on procedure to set the date for the next meeting.

One small diplomatic success—if it be called that—came Schleicher's way. As minister of defense under Brüning and Papen he had insistently demanded for Germany the right, "in principle," to equality with other powers with respect to armament. From Geneva on December 11 came a five-power declaration conceding that equality. There was still a general implication that the others might come down to Germany's level. She was not specifically authorized to build up at once to theirs.[35]

It was not enough. Because of his "pampering of labor," heavy industry and big business called him a socialist and agreed with the wily Papen that Hitler was safer. The Social Democrats and landowners, on the other hand, accused him of having sold out to "big business." When he proposed to discontinue Papen's quota system for restricting agricultural imports, instead of increasing the tariff as its members wished, the Junker Land League was ready to be rid of him. It demanded his dismissal when it learned that he was contemplating, as Brüning had, the expropriation of some 1,300,000 acres of the sort that had run the last three governments into bankruptcy by way of the *Osthilfe*. He would use this land, he said, for the resettlement of some of the unemployed. The only political leaders of any consequence still loyal to him were Alfred Hugenberg of the German Nationalists and Gregor Strasser, who had recently returned to Berlin but whose influence in the Nazi party could not just then be accurately estimated.

Meanwhile Joachim Ribbentrop brought his friends Papen and Hitler together January 4 at the home of Baron Kurt von Schröder, a Cologne banker. There a Rhenish-Westphalian industrialists' group headed by Fritz Thyssen, head of steel and other corporations, and including Schröder and the Krupps undertook to pay a large part of the Nazi party debt, which amounted at that time to about twelve million marks.[36] Papen wanted to be chancellor again, and Hitler permitted him to think he might be, provided only that a suitable person was made minister of defense. A week later, encouraged by some

[35] See discussion of the Geneva disarmament conference in Chapter 6, pp. 148-151.

[36] Thyssen's purported autobiographical confession, *I Paid Hitler*, is an interesting though not altogether convincing document. It makes him appear so simple minded that one wonders how he headed a complex industrial empire.

Nazi success in a local election in Lippe, Hitler was again emboldened to demand the chancellorship.

Rightly anticipating difficulty with the Reichstag which was soon to meet, Schleicher asked the president to provide him, as he had provided Papen, with an undated order for its dissolution. He said he must have such an order in his hand to prevent public discussion of some scandals recently uncovered by the Reichstag budget committee in the administration of the *Osthilfe*; but on that sensitive point the president would not be blackmailed. He refused the request. Schleicher resigned January 28.

Because he hated Papen, Schleicher on resigning recommended Hitler, just as Papen had done for jealousy of Schleicher when he resigned. Presidential secretary Otto Meissner seconded the nomination. Grudgingly, on January 30, the old field marshal appointed "the Bohemian corporal," for whom he had only recently said that the position of a postmaster would be more appropriate.

Papen agreed to the appointment and accepted the subordinate position of vice-chancellor but tried to save face and protect himself by stating terms: the authority of the president should always be supreme; as vice-chancellor he, von Papen, should be present at all interviews between president and chancellor; the chancellor should govern in strictly parliamentary fashion; Neurath should stay at the Foreign Office; Nationalist manufacturer Franz Seldte of the *Stahlhelm* should become minister of labor; and Nationalist leader Hugenberg minister of economics and agriculture.

There were only two Nazi other than Hitler in that first Hitler cabinet, but they held key positions. Wilhelm Frick was minister of the interior. Hermann Göring was aviation minister, minister without portfolio, and deputy commissioner for Prussia. A Nazi sympathizer, General Werner von Blomberg, was minister of war.[37]

Papen and his friends flattered themselves that they could handle Hitler. Industrialists, imperialists, and generals thought they could use him but keep him always dependent, under their control. Millions of moderate-minded and mild-mannered people hoped he would give them stable government, bring them prosperity, and forget the wild talk in which like other revolutionaries he had sometimes indulged. With the malevolence, cupidity, and power lust of little men long frustrated, then shown at last the promised land, his followers looked to him to make them rich and powerful, to help them avenge themselves upon those who had been successful where they till then had

[37] Halperin, *op. cit.*, chap. 39.

failed and who had made them wait so long. Only the last group knew their man, and they did not know him well.

NIHILISM IN THE NAME OF NATIONALISM

How could such a party as the National Socialists, such a man as Hitler, have gained by legal means almost complete control of the German Reich? The answer is twofold, and only half of it has been given. Democracy had not really been tried and found wanting. It had been tried but briefly and in faint-hearted, bungling fashion. Its defenders were too few. Too many Germans wanted something else. The republic had been permitted, before Hitler, to fall into other enemy hands than his. He did not have to overthrow it; he only took it over.[38] The last three chancellors had been politically responsible only to the president and had governed by decree by virtue of his extraordinary authority. The extraordinary had become the ordinary. People already familiar with government by authority wanted a stronger, more efficient government more urgently than they wanted a restoration of parliamentary control of government.

The other half of the explanation is that, fraudulently but plausibly, the Nazi offered the German people much that many of them wanted. The Nazi voice, strident and challenging, alien and offensive to the better ones, was yet in some ways theirs, demanding what they wanted but had not dared demand, shouting defiance as if strong where, being weak, they had had courage only for denunciation. Based on hatred and cupidity, the movement spread most rapidly in hard times, as during the enemy occupation of the Ruhr, the inflation, and the depression of 1929-1932. By promising effective use of returning strength and fostering the spirit of national self-confidence, it gained adherents also in periods of recovery. It showed serious signs of disintegration only in the year of anticlimax, 1932, after having sent the most numerous delegation into the Reichstag and before gaining control of the government. The republic had, as has been shown, revealed some serious structural weaknesses before it fell, and its foundations had been undermined at many points. One of the largest and most voracious, but only one, of the several "armies of termites" which had eaten away its timbers and weakened it to the point of imminent collapse was the Nazi, which in 1933 destroyed it.

---

[38] The German word for what had happened was *Machtübernahme* (the taking over of power), more frequently and more accurately used than *Machtergreifung* (the seizure of power).

The Nazi Appeal

National Socialism appealed to many people in many ways. Its turgid philosophy was unscientific, inconsequential, and infinitely repetitious; but an uncritical person willing to accept its premises without examination and to follow its maunderings without serious question could easily be made to think that he was being introduced to a new interpretation of the universe. He was, but it was not what he thought it was. With undeniable cleverness, uninhibited by intellectual honesty, reverence, or scruples of any sort, its propagandists knew how to appeal to the more generous instincts and best qualities of a decent people for indecent purposes, to appeal to their basest instincts and most selfish motives in the name of unselfishness and service.

It aroused their patriotism, referring constantly to love of father-land as if that generous emotion had been a virtue peculiar to National Socialists, as if in that respect "German" and "National Socialist" were synonymous. Loyalty to comrades, compatriots, and country was honored publicly in word, dishonored secretly in deed. Jews, pacifists, Bolshevists, democrats, or internationalists were called traitors and made scapegoats for all defeats and national disasters, as if the Nazi would have won the war and prevented the occupation, the loss of territory, the inflation, and the depression. Any patriotic German grieving over the condition of his fatherland, concerned about its future, and eager to put it on a pinnacle above other nations was re-minded of departed glories—exaggerated for the purpose—and offered an opportunity to share in their restoration. If he was humiliated by its weakness and called its weakness shame, he was challenged to offer it any strength he might have in him.

The mutual obligation of the subject and the state had always been emphasized in Germany, especially in Prussia, and had been restated in the Weimar constitution. National Socialist propaganda reëmpha-sized the paramount interest of the community, the obligation of the individual to serve. To serve the state was, it said, to serve the people. To serve the people was to serve God, to fulfill man's highest function. In practice, the slogan the Nazi had taken over from the Nationalists, "The general interest takes precedence over self-interest," meant that the individual should forget his personal freedom and surrender him-self and his country to the National Socialists for the sake of the national freedom of which they said Germany had been deprived and which they promised to restore. The Nazi would supply the leadership. Citizens should conform and follow.

National Socialist propaganda appealed to the German's pride. The most insignificant person could be told, and was, that he could enhance his own importance by identifying himself with a dynamic organization which soon would move the nation and shake the world. If his ego could be inflated by the wearing of a uniform, the Nazi had a uniform for him and probably some sort of pseudomilitary title, could clothe him with authority to censor or control his neighbors, and offered him opportunity to march often in parades and listen to addresses which assured him that he and his comrades in the party uniform were the last best hope of Germany and of the world.

The young German was taught to value physical hardihood and be proud of a fine physique. A strenuous, continued, and generally successful effort was made to overcome whatever harmful effects the malnutrition of the leanest years of the food blockade and depression period had had. All that was best in eugenics, prenatal care, pediatrics, child welfare, nutrition studies, physical education, and scientific public health measures was brought to bear to give Germany a generation of sturdy youngsters, conscious and proud of their health and strength. A good physical inheritance was talked of as a legacy which the individual was not free to dissipate by neglect or self-indulgence, or by marriage with one not so qualified.

In time, most of the good in the Nazi emphasis on eugenics, physical education, and public health was overshadowed by the bad. Physical hardihood and a high birth rate were valued as military assets by men contemplating aggression, not defense. A generation of deliberately hardened pagan youth, abstemious as to alcohol and tobacco, masters of their appetites in eating, and rather contemptuous of the self-indulgent gluttony and heaviness of their elders, had been taught to admire only hardness and strength, to indulge in wild excesses of only the Nazi type, such as emotional orgies of fanatical devotion to their so-called ideals or frantic hatreds of those pointed out to them as foes. Great sexual license was allowed them in the interest of the birth rate among the self-styled Aryans, but union with a Jew was called race pollution. So whatever was legitimate of pride in family, good blood, and physical inheritance was turned into an arrogant belief in racial superiority and the ugliest intolerance. The sterilization of those physically or mentally unfit to have sound and healthy children was advocated with the same cynical disregard for religious or moral scruples as subsequently characterized the use of euthanasia to dispose of the incurably ill and the insane.[39]

[39] In the first war-crimes trial of Germans by a German court, at Frankfort at the end of December, 1946, a former SS lieutenant colonel, Dr. Friedrich Mennecke, was sentenced to death and three of his subordinates to prison terms for the murder by euthanasia of inmates of the Eichberg insane asylum.

The uglier aspects of these propaganda programs, however, had not yet made themselves obvious in 1933 to any but a close and critical observer. What was apparent was a commendable community interest in public health, especially in the physical well-being of the young, and in the improvement of the breed.

National Socialism glorified work and stimulated the workman's pride in it. A certain inconsistency was apparent in the fact that the party propagandists were personally doing none of the work they sought to glorify, and that full-time party workers were not working at all in the ordinary sense; but it was none the less a useful propaganda line. Germans were no exception to the rule that the skilled artisan is usually proud of his skill and of the quality of his product. Luther's teachings had always done something to dignify the laborer and strengthen his self-respect. Expert photography, making the most of scenic beauty and fine old buildings or bright-shining new ones, and playing up the artistry of skilled craftsmanship, turned out attractive propaganda films under the heading *Schönheit der Arbeit,* "the beauty of work." After the Nazi took control of government and command of its resources, a movement calling itself *Kraft durch Freude,* "Strength through Joy," did something to bring within the worker's reach cultural advantages, recreational opportunities, and organized vacation tours. He was constantly assured of the importance of his craft and encouraged to believe that National Socialism offered him a richer life and a future full of happiness in fruitful work.

Skillfully National Socialism appealed to the imagination. No one knew the strength a united people could discover or the pressure it could bring to bear upon an object if genuinely united, everyone pushing at once with all his might in one direction. The German people were not doing that, but were told that if they would only do it they would find themselves irresistible. No obstacle would be immovable or insurmountable. It heartened them and quickened their imagination to be told that they did not know their strength and that unity would make each man's strength as the strength of ten. A calculating person gifted with some imagination might recognize, as Paul Joseph Goebbels did, that the party was likely to go far, and decide to go along with it for his own advancement. An imaginative, uncalculating one might be so impressed by the apparent dynamism of the movement as to wish to surrender himself to it and be an infinitesimal part of something transcending the imagination. The old political parties had too often seemed to speak for factions, fractions, or special interests only. The Nazi party prospered by representing itself as the only party of a truly national character, and the one-party system as the only one capable of achieving national unity.

Behind a façade of patriotic phrases the Nazi gave free rein to cupidity and malice in all their ugliest forms. Most of the earlier members of the party were misfits and failures, maladjusted and malcontent. Many were lawless freebooters out of the old "Free Corps," conscious of no kinship with peace-loving Germans, knowing no comradeship save with others of their kind who marched beside them in the ranks, failing often in loyalty even to them.[40] Some had been members of the *Stahlhelm,* others Communists. Few had been successful, happy, or contented. Many had been irregularly employed. Others, completing their training during periods of depression when unemployment was at its worst, faced a dismal future as merchants or professional men unless openings which they could not find were found for them.

Such men easily convinced themselves that they had been cheated, and that those then in control of business and the professions had cheated them. Any competition in which Jews had been successful and non-Jews unsuccessful must, they told themselves or were told, have been unfair. They coveted the banks, merchandising marts, newspapers, publishing houses, and theaters owned and staffed by Jews. Successful Jews were commonly accused of favoring Jews as against non-Jews in businesses and professions which they controlled or in which their influence counted.

Until the Nazi came into power in 1933 their anti-Semitism was generally glossed over as Germanism, as an attempt only to break the alleged strangle hold of an alien and alien-connected element of the population on business and the professions. After 1933 the rank and file called it more frankly "frying the fat out of them," plundering them of their property, taking their positions, and terrorizing them by sending or threatening to send them to the concentration camps. The most atrocious persecutions occurred only after the rest of the population had been too thoroughly intimidated or poisoned by the deadly drug of racialism to prevent them or protest too much against them. Talk of the extermination of the Jews sounded, in prewar Nazi Germany, like the raving of a lunatic. The Jews were not abused because all the other Germans hated them, as Jew-baiters Julius Streicher, Hitler, and others would have had the world believe; they were plundered first, then otherwise persecuted, then hated in an

---

[40] The sentimental wartime ballad "I Had a Comrade" was revived in an attempt to recapture the fine spirit of camaraderie the best of the troops had known in wartime.

attempt at self-justification by those who had abused them. A German who had wronged a Jew and had on that account a queasy conscience, or who had a personal grudge against one or against Jews in general, or who hated the Jew as an alien and an enemy of the people, could find congenial company in the Nazi party.

Nazi Propaganda Methods

The Nazi propagandists were masters of pageantry, clever in their control of the psychology of crowds, uncomplimentary but not usually inaccurate in their estimate of the intelligence of the people who composed their crowds. Hitler had told them in *Mein Kampf* to shoot at the bottom of the pyramid, to aim their arguments at those of the lowest level of intelligence; and he and Goebbels showed them how to do it. Goebbels could compliment the SA and SS on being primitive in their thinking. He could make them glory in their atavism by calling them "ripe for action," in contrast with the aristocrats, the bourgeois, the pious, the politicians, and the intellectuals, whom he encouraged them to deride and to despise. The fantastic exaggeration and endless repetition which most foreigners and many Germans found first boring, then repulsive, did not offend the crudest listener, but had upon him eventually the desired effect, as Hitler had said in *Mein Kampf* that it would have. Falsehood could be made as convincing as any truth, and was as freely used.

The party made effective use of slogans, such as "Germany, awaken!" or "One folk, one Reich, one leader!" or "Make possible the impossible." By use of excellent sound equipment they carried the spoken word constantly to every nook and corner of the country, dinning into people's ears their talk of unity, of patriotism, of the rescue of the fatherland from great danger, of confounding its many enemies.

They were great dragon slayers, the Nazi. It was often necessary for them first to create some dragons, then to slay them; but they were equal to both tasks. People were told of needs of which they had not been conscious, which the Nazi would supply; of dangers of which they had not been aware, against which the Nazi would defend them; of wicked neighbors just across the hall of an apartment house or beyond a national boundary whom they had not suspected of ill will or wrongdoing, but against whom the watchful Nazi warned them just in time. Here at last, as self-described, was an ever vigilant and devoted band of knights, led by a strong-willed fearless Siegfried who would kill any Fafnir and confound all the malicious Mimes by whom Germany was troubled. Politically intelligent people were not deceived; but many were not intelligent enough, politically, not to be deceived.

The youth program of the party was ambitious and, at first, superficially attractive. The Germans had always taken seriously the training of their children. Organizations for the direction of youth activities had multiplied in the republic. These the Nazi proposed to coördinate; and when they were in power their youth movement absorbed or destroyed all others. To the casual and uncritical observer, the Hitler youth (*Jugend*) and German girls (*Mädel*) looked surprisingly like Boy and Girl Scouts, except that they marched better and seemed to take their drum-and-bugle business more seriously, and that more of their young leaders gave one the impression of being zealots. Those leaders knew how to make their outings pleasant by mixing nature study, folklore, and group singing around bonfires at night with strenuous physical training and premilitary marches and maneuvers, all calculated to stimulate a small boy's natural urge to grow quickly into a bigger one, and a big boy's ambition to become a man. Health, hardihood, and racialism were glamorized for boys and girls alike. They were told early, suggestively, and plainly that they must serve their state and people, and that part of their service must be to give Germany more children—many more, and that right soon.

Agreements called concordats were made in 1933 with both the Lutheran and the Roman Catholic Church that the religious training of the youth would be left to the churches and that the secular youth movement would not obstruct or try to counteract it. After 1933 the Nazi habitually violated those concordats. Outings on Sunday mornings took the young people from their homes and kept them from the churches at the hours that had usually been given to religious instruction. The whole trend of the Nazi youth movement was amoral and immoral, unchristian and antichristian, and meant to nullify all nonconformist influence of parents, family, tradition, or religious teaching. The youth leader, Baldur von Schirach, was known to be a man of questionable character but was not yet generally recognized in 1933 as the Pied Piper he eventually proved to be.

One of the most successful of the Nazi propaganda programs, advocated before 1933 and implemented after, was the labor service (*Arbeitsdienst*). Everyone, it was argued, should earn his right to membership in the community by doing it some service. Everyone should know from experience what manual labor was, should learn to live with others of all classes and from all backgrounds on entirely equal terms, should become familiar with the land in which he lived by living for a while on the land and working there for its improvement. Roads were built, forests were cut or cleared, cut-over areas were reforested, drainage and erosion control were improved, new acres were made available to farmers.

The labor service offered an immediate though only partial solution of the unemployment problem and at the same time paid some dividends in the public value of the work done. The Nazi used it also, effectively, as premilitary training. Within a few years the uniformed labor corps, carrying painted spades on their shoulders as parading infantry carried rifles, could march past a reviewer in creditable military style; but few Germans and not many foreigners seemed to be offended or seriously alarmed by the military features of the program. That it gave the Nazi another excellent opportunity for indoctrination, and that they were assiduously so using it, was obvious.[41]

Nazi Promises

Until they were in power, the Nazi were all things to all men and, with a light-heartedness attainable only by those who know not or care not what they say, promised to perform miracles. Their promises were often contradictory or went beyond the possibility of fulfillment, but millions listened gladly to the Nazi voices promising them what they wanted, no matter what, and telling them what they wanted most to hear.

There would be an end of interest slavery; debtors welcomed the suggestion of lower interest rates. Payments on debts owed to foreigners were soon defaulted by the Nazi government, not the private debtors, when Schacht as president of the Reichsbank diverted them into a "conversion fund." Claiming he could not convert them into foreign currencies, he dishonestly withheld from foreign creditors the funds he continued to collect from German debtors. Interest rates on land purchases by peasants were lowered; but the new peasant owner (*Bauer*) had little freedom in his use of the land, might lose it if he did not use it as ordered, and had only a restricted right to sell it. Soon prices also were controlled.

Employers were assured that soon trade unions would be merged

[41] This is well illustrated by the labor service sequences of the sound-film record of the sixth annual party congress at Nuremberg, 1934. The film was called *The Triumph of the Will*.

in one great "Labor Front" and so disciplined that strikes and other labor troubles would no more retard production, reduce profits, or disturb industrial relations. Labor was told at the same time that one great "Labor Front" would soon secure for them higher wages, better working conditions, and insurance against unemployment due to shutdowns or to lockouts. Employer and employee both paid high, eventually, for everything the Nazi did for either; both hoped in 1933 to gain much while paying little.

Those who had anything to lose, either property or position, were offered protection for it. Those who had nothing were permitted to hope for much—in new employment, new prosperity, or pensions. To the aged, rich or poor, the prospect of security was alluring. To the young, the insecurity inherent in adventure was no deterrent, while excitement and wild dreams of power lured them on. No one ever worked both sides of the street more unscrupulously or more successfully than the National Socialists before 1933.

The differences between Nazi leaders, active party members, Nazi sympathizers, and those who for reasons of self-interest or self-preservation more or less willingly "went along" with the movement will always baffle students as for years after 1945 they perplexed denazification boards and military governments. Estimates can be only estimates, but need not for that reason be uninteresting or altogether valueless. The number of active National Socialists in Germany in 1933 was variously estimated at from 10 to 25 percent of the population. They were only a militant minority. They were probably considerably outnumbered by their active and determined enemies; but their enemies, distributed among many uncongenial and often mutually antagonistic groups, had no common organization and no common aim, and so were generally ineffective.

Weight was always given to the movement by one of the two largest groups—those who "went along" with it for their own advancement or convenience, giving it their uncritical approval as long as it gave them prosperity and what might pass for law and order if they could overlook or pretend not to see the essential lawlessness of all Nazi law or law enforcement. Passive opposition, unwilling but unresisting compliance, was the unspoken policy of the other of the two largest groups. These people were non-Nazi. They could not bring themselves to believe before 1933 that Germany would ever have a Nazi government. They were never proud of it, but prudently accepted it, however reluctantly, for want of anything better, for fear of communism or of anarchy, or for want of civic courage and of leaders bold enough to fight it. A sizable majority of the German people seem to have been about equally divided between these two groups of fellow travelers (*Mitläufer*)—the willing and the unwilling. The proportion seems to have varied with the party's prospects of success, not to have been much affected by its excesses. Many thousands, perhaps millions, of Germans stayed alive and hung on to their positions, property, or employment in Nazi Germany by occasional conformity; but no one will ever know how many. Few would confess, when the Nazi government was gone, that they had served it willingly, conformed more often than occasionally, or been honest when they prudently conformed. The Nazi always had some help from the willing conformists and were never seriously embarrassed by the reluctance of the unwilling. No effective opposition or overt criticism was offered even by the most reluctant of the "occasional conformists."

Nazi Performance

The Nazi soon made good, after a fashion, on some of the most attractive of their promises. In January, 1933, Germany had six million unemployed. Within eighteen months that number had been cut in half. By 1936, virtually all who were employable were employed, although not all in economically productive work. Remilitarization had taken millions either into the armed services or into industries making equipment or munitions for them. The numbers of party functionaries, in offices often duplicating government departments already existing and still at work under constant party-man surveillance, continued to increase. The SA, SS, and secret police (*Geheime Staatspolizei* or *Gestapo*) enrolled, all together, several hundred thousand men. More and more officials were employed as more fields of activity and aspects of daily life were regulated. But people were busy, and those not barred on racial grounds or as political nonconformists had steady incomes.

National Socialism was economically parasitical. It exploited but did not create, plundered but did not produce. Yet in its first years it was credited with an enormous increase in business activity and industrial production. By a number of ingenious international trade agreements, exchanging German goods for materials on a barter basis, Dr. Schacht managed in the middle 1930's to keep open some foreign markets for German manufactures and to go on drawing for Germany's benefit upon the raw-material resources of other countries for years after foreign sources of financial credit had dried up. Called a wizard for his ability to carry on foreign trade without money, he soon revealed himself to be a genius at buying without paying. Many of the materials used in rearmament and much of the huge stock pile of food and other war material with which Germany entered the war in 1939 had been imported under Schacht's insatiable barter agreements and only partially paid for by lagging German exports.

There had been disorder in the last years of the republic, ranging upward from petty thievery in the streets through housebreaking and highway robbery, all traditionally rare in Germany, to open defiance of the national government—in which respect the Nazi had been the worst offenders. Once in power, they quickly put an end to all lawlessness and violence but their own, and legalized their violations of the law by making new law to suit their own purposes. Life and property were again made safe from gangsters operating independently. Neither was ever safe from the SA or the Gestapo. Both might be forfeited by anyone who fought the party that controlled the state.

Nazi propaganda always stressed what it called the dynamic and creative character of National Socialism and boasted about a "wonderful new Germany." The movement was dynamic in the sense that its leaders were energetic and ambitious. Their appetite for power grew with eating, and was never sated. National Socialism, however, was not creative, but rather what one of its own renegades called it, a "revolution of Nihilism," all destructive.[42]

Hitler talked a great deal about legality before 1933, and became chancellor legally. The lawless character of his government was immediately revealed; yet it was endorsed by plebiscite, and constitutional consent to its continuance was given after the revelation. The world wondered why. One reason seemed to have been the fatuous hope cherished by millions of Germans, Nazi and non-Nazi, that Hitler would somehow, without war, reverse the results of the war they had lost. His foreign policy, which promised recognition, prosperity, and peace, and led to war, some years of victory, and eventual defeat, will be discussed later.[43]

The excuse was later offered in extenuation that no one realized in 1933 the true character of the man or of his associates. There was some truth in such a statement; yet it was not more than half true, and was quite misleading. One did not need to know how bad Hitler was to know that he was bad—"a flame kindled from foul gases."[44]

---

[42] Hermann Rauschning, *The Revolution of Nihilism* (New York, 1939).
[43] See pp. 462-476.
[44] Heiden, *op. cit.,* 764.

It was true that everyone had then much yet to learn about the Nazi. They grew in office—grew stronger, more arrogant, more ruthless, more ambitious, revealing enormities of wickedness surpassing anything anyone could have imagined in 1933. Yet it could not be said of them in charity that they knew not what they did, or of those who voted for them in the plebiscite of 1933 that they did not know for what manner of men they were voting. They had not yet seen everything that they were soon to see; but surely they had seen enough.

Industrialists who had heard Hitler speak under Thyssen's sponsorship in Düsseldorf January 27, 1932, or to whom his speech of that day had been relayed, had supported him thereafter because they thought he would give Germany the strong government that they wanted, and big business the protection they demanded, against "bolshevism." They knew that he had then, as always, repudiated internationalism and democracy in favor of a narrow nationalism, "the authority of personality," and the "principle of inequality." Hoping to make the state the servant of business, they were ready to attribute the failures of business to the weakness of the state, and were willing to see him try to make good, if he would, on his statement that economic crises, having arisen only through the folly and weakness of the state, could be solved by a stronger state by the exercise of political power. The reconquest of power, he had said, must precede economic recovery; then, and only then, could the power state create for the business world the conditions necessary for its prosperity. The nationalism and authoritarianism of the Hitler program appealed to the industrialists, and he had assured them that they need not worry about its so-called socialism.

Everyone knew that, however much he might talk of peace and freedom, Hitler was not a man of peace, and wanted freedom only for the Germans. Not everyone had read the *Völkischer Beobachter* of January 29, 1930, or remembered three years later just what it quoted Hitler as having said about the naval limitation conference then in session in London, with the Young plan just reaching the point of final agreement:

We Germans have no desire even in the slightest that events of any kind whatsoever will preserve a "world peace" whose sole result, as recent events show, is to make possible, to encourage in fact the most horrible plundering and exploitation of our people. . . . Germany can harbor only the single ardent desire that over every conference the spirit of misfortune should reign, that discord should arise from it, and that finally in blood and fire there should be an end to a world peace which otherwise will be the end of our people. . . . As long as peace prevails, Germany has nothing at all to hope for, and only when this world is again thrown into disorder can it be possible for a gifted German government to recognize German interests and, where possible, secure advantage for the German people in these conflicts.[45]

Millions of Germans who wanted peace also wanted the changes of which Hitler talked. With returning national confidence, more of them than formerly were willing to risk their peace for the sake of change, though still wanting the fruits of victory without a war if they could get them so. Others, more honest with themselves, knowing that they could not get what they wanted without fighting for it, wanted war—and supported Hitler as the man most likely to be able to bring the German people to it.

If anyone had been ignorant of the brutal methods of the Nazi strong-arm squads, or had supposed that those methods were not sanctioned by the highest party leaders, he might have been enlightened as late as August, 1932, by the Potempa murder case. A gang of Nazi terrorists were brought to trial in Beuthen for having invaded the home of a Communist in the Upper Silesian village of Potempa and kicked and beaten him to death. High and low, in court and in the press, the Nazi identified themselves with the murderers. Goebbels warned the government of dire consequences to follow if it dared condemn any of them to death. When five of them were none the less sentenced to death and two to life imprisonment, Captain Roehm visited them in prison and assured them that the party would never permit the government to execute them. Hitler called the court's action "legal assassination" and wired the condemned men: "In the face of this most monstrous and bloody sentence I feel myself bound to you in infinite loyalty. From this moment, your liberation is a question of our honor. To fight against a government which could allow this is our duty."[46] The sentence was not carried out, but furnished Hitler occasion to attack Chancellor Papen and President Hindenburg repeatedly, publicly, and with unparalleled ferocity. A leopard could have changed his spots as readily as Hitler or his associates could have developed an honest respect for law within less than half a year after having so identified themselves with the Potempa murderers.

The character of the new regime was not long in doubt after Hitler's appointment to the chancellorship—if it had ever been in doubt. One of his first official acts was to dissolve the Reichstag and the Prussian diet. So as to control the election of a new Reichstag, the Nazi bullied

---

[45] See also *ibid.*, 325-326.
[46] Halperin, *op. cit.*, 503.

their opponents in every conceivable way. They broke up or "policed" all party meetings but their own and the Nationalists', monopolized the radio, banned the Communist paper, *Red Flag,* compelled the Socialist *Vorwärts* to suspend publication for several short periods, and finally "outlawed" the Communists altogether, accusing them of having set fire to the Reichstag building as the first step in an attempt at revolution.

Someone set fire to the Reichstag building in the night of February 27, 1933. It was quite generally suspected at the time, and was later revealed, that the Nazi did it themselves, or caused it to be done by duped incendiaries whom they smuggled into the building through a tunnel from the basement of the house occupied by Göring as president of the Reichstag, just across the street. "A sign from heaven," Hitler called it, invoking curses from heaven upon the Communists whom he accused. "A gift from heaven," less partisan observers called it, referring to the political use he made of the incident and the accusation. A wave of anticommunist hysteria swept the country—or was made by Nazi propaganda to seem to do so. Hitler at once induced the president to issue an emergency decree suspending all guarantees of personal liberty, freedom of utterance and assembly, and even freedom from censorship of personal letters and private telephones.

Despite the severity and the pseudo-official character of the measures taken against them, the Communists cast 4,800,000 ballots which had to be counted in the Reichstag election of March 5, 1933; but their eighty-one deputies were not permitted to take the seats to which they had been elected. The Nazi, with whom they had so often coöperated to hamstring parliamentary government, would run no risk of being hamstrung by them.

The Social Democrats polled 7,000,000 votes, a million less than on July 31, 1932, the Center 5,500,000, a million more than then.

The Nationalists had gained a million, polling 3,000,000. The Nazi had gained three millions, polling 17,000,000 or about 43.6 percent of the 39,000,000 ballots cast. With a fraction over 51 percent of the popular vote, the Nazi-Nationalist combination had a majority also in the Reichstag, with 288 Nazi and 53 Nationalist deputies in a house of 648. Hitler was still a minority chancellor, and dependent upon the Nationalists for a parliamentary majority; but the popular vote cast for his party alone had exceeded by 4,500,000 the combined totals of those cast for the Center and the Social Democrats. These two were the only parties that would still have restored parliamentary government, and he had no thought of restoring it.

The first meeting of the new Reichstag was staged with due attention to history and tradition, to give it the appearance of a national occasion. On March 21, the anniversary of the opening of the first imperial Reichstag in 1871, the deputies assembled in the garrison church in Potsdam, filled with the battle flags captured in the Seven Years' War, where President von Hindenburg laid a wreath on the tomb of Frederick the Great. Hitler appeared, as usual, in party uniform.[47]

Two days later, by a vote of 441 to 94, with Communists excluded, some members absent or not voting, and only the Social Democrats persisting in their hopeless opposition, the Reichstag surrendered its powers to the chancellor for four years. If he failed the nation in that period, Hitler said, the people might hang him if they would.

The people did not hang Hitler. He gave too many of them what they wanted and made revolt too dangerous. Much as Mussolini had done in Italy, he steadily strengthened his grip upon them and gradually extended his controls until any attempt at rebellion seemed hopeless. His government soon earned the unenviable distinction of having given the world its most convincing demonstration of the uses of intimidation. By calculated cruelty, the Nazi broke the bodies of their immediate victims and the spirits of their victims' relatives and friends. The extent to which they managed within half a dozen years to undermine the character and break down the moral fiber of the whole people surpassed anything that most of the world would have believed possible.

For that general deterioration of a decent people, the Nazi were principally but not primarily or exclusively responsible. Something that Hitler said in an address to representatives of the Labor Front in Berlin on May 10, 1933—the day of the ceremonial burning of the books of 160 writers, participated in by Nazi students in university towns throughout the land—merited thoughtful consideration:

Important changes cannot take place in the life of a nation unless there is the most urgent necessity for them. No one can bring about a really decisive revolution unless the people themselves in their inmost souls are crying out for one, unless the state of affairs makes such a revolution inevitable. It is easy to alter the form of government of a state, but a nation can be remolded from within only when a certain process of development has already more or less taken place of itself, when that nation has discovered—perhaps

---

[47] Subsequent meetings of the Reichstag, throughout the life of the Third Reich, were held in the Kroll opera house in Berlin. The Reichstag building was deliberately left unrepaired, and shown to sightseers as a symbol of the wickedness of Communists and the futility of democracy.

not quite clearly and only subconsciously—that it has been following the wrong path, and would like to leave that path, and is only prevented from doing so by the sheer inertia of the masses until, from somewhere or other, the impulse comes, or until a new movement which has seen the new way one day leads the nation into it.[48]

The real twentieth-century German revolution occurred not in 1918 but in 1933. It occurred then not only because new leaders popularized a new path and coerced those who did not choose to take it but because a very considerable number of people were ready to leave the old path or to try to find their way back to an older one. As a form of government for Germany, the Weimar republic had far more foreign friends than foreign enemies. Its failure was not inevitable, or due to weaknesses in its ingenious and democratic constitution. It failed for want of friends at home. What happened afterward to the people who permitted it to fail was a heavy but not altogether unmerited punishment for their failure. The tradition of the *Machtstaat* or power state from Frederick the Great to Bismarck tended to strengthen the *Führerprinzip* or leadership principle. In Germany there was no long tradition of personal liberty and self-government, broadening down through the centuries from precedent to precedent, which might have laid firm the foundations for a republic or have erected a fortress no Hitler could storm.

[48] *Collected Speeches* (Berlin, 1933).

CHAPTER 9

Great Britain, Commonwealth, British Empire

GREAT BRITAIN

New Position and General Problems

Great Britain found herself in 1919 in a prominent but uncomfortable position. Her existence, which had been threatened, had again been made secure against danger of invasion from across the Channel, and the vital food ships could again ply the sea lanes to her ports without fear of lurking submarines. Her political institutions had stood the strain of war, and she was faced with no threat of revolution. While elsewhere thrones had fallen or were falling, her constitutional monarchy had been strengthened. Russian, German, and Turkish imperialism seemed dead and, if mandates were to be considered new imperial acquisitions, Britain and the British dominions seemed to have gained much of what Turkey and Germany had lost, and to have been rid by the Russian revolution of a potentially dangerous rival. The United States, as a new counterpoise from the Western Hemisphere, had completely upset the prewar power balance of Europe but was already showing a disposition to withdraw from Europe and leave it to France and Britain to bring things back into equilibrium there. France, showing the petulance of one badly hurt but not yet realizing or revealing quite how badly hurt she was, would have her own ideas about how the peace they were making should be kept; but perhaps Britain also could withdraw into some sort of semi-isolation, concentrate on home and empire problems, and let continental France assume the responsibility she could not escape for conditions on the continent. Neither the cost of victory nor the continuing day-to-day price of peace was yet fully realized.

Only the brighter aspects of the situation were presented to the people by David Lloyd George's ministry in the election of December 14, 1918, called soon after the armistice so that the momentum of the war effort and patriotic wartime unity of spirit would return to office the coalition ministry that had "won the war" and promised also to "win the peace." In this second "khaki election"—the first had been held during the Boer War—the ministry profited politically by arousing anew the unthinking spirit of belligerence. The government speakers talked freely and irresponsibly of "hanging the kaiser" as a war criminal, making Germany pay for the war "to the last penny," and making Britain (as the prime minister had promised during the war) "a land fit for heroes."

The electorate to whom this incendiary oratory was addressed included many thousands of naval and military "heroes" who had reached voting age since 1910, so were voting in their first parliamentary election. (A civil truce had been declared in Britain as in Germany, and the election of a new Parliament, which must otherwise have taken place in 1915 if not sooner, had been postponed.) These young men had been taught during the war to hate and deride the kaiser and to hold him responsible for the war—which most of them had hated. They wanted to punish someone, to make someone pay, and to enjoy some tangible fruits of victory. Other new voters were the women over thirty who had just then been enfranchised by the Fourth Reform Bill, a majority of whom were expected, out of gratitude, to vote for the government which had given them the right.[1]

As a tactical maneuver in domestic politics, the "khaki election" of December, 1918, was a complete success. The government coalition won 467 seats. Former Prime Minister Herbert Asquith, who had been a leader of the Liberal party in the House of Commons for thirty years, lost his seat. Seventeen of his former colleagues who, with him, had repudiated the leadership of Lloyd George were also defeated. Some of the more prominent leaders of the Labour party—Arthur Henderson, Philip Snowden, and pacifist Ramsay MacDonald—were not reëlected. There were only twenty-eight Independent (Asquith) Liberals and sixty-three Labour members in the new House of Commons. Seventy-three Sinn Feiners were elected from Irish boroughs but refused to come to Westminster to take their seats.[2]

[1] There had been some unsuccessful agitation for woman suffrage in Britain before the war. During the war it was generally conceded that the women had earned the right to vote by their indispensable contribution to the war effort. To have permitted them to vote at age twenty-one, however, with women outnumbering men in the United Kingdom as they did in December, 1918, would have meant that more than a majority of the electorate would have consisted of inexperienced voters.

[2] See p. 323.

In the long view, the political victory of December, 1918, looked less imposing. It meant that the prime minister went to the Paris peace conference rather as the leader of a war party than as negotiator of a peace treaty. Changing his positions in the direction of moderation or conciliation while there, as he did in some instances under President Wilson's influence, involved some inconsistency. It also involved some disappointment among those of his constituents who had not thought enough about the peace to see the unwisdom or impossibility of doing what he had said or implied that he would do.

The self-made Welsh labor leader had been an inspired standard bearer in the Liberals' war on poverty before the war, an energetic administrator as chancellor of the exchequer and minister of munitions, and a courageous and inspiring national leader in the war, truly one of the fabricators of the victory. But his was not the genius for making a world peace. Immediate expediency meant too much to him. The future was too far away for him to see it. He could serve, and did, as mediator between Clemenceau and President Wilson, and some of his criticisms of them were clever; but he had not the judicial temperament to serve as arbiter between them. He could arouse enthusiasm or anger as few others could, but could not inspire complete confidence.

He soon lost the confidence of his Conservative supporters in the British Parliament. After a quick revival in the first two years of peace, filling deferred orders and catching up on consumer-goods demand, British export trade declined and unemployment rapidly increased. Thousands of demobilized war veterans, many of whom had gone directly into the armed forces from school or university, leaving their technical or professional training uncompleted, and were therefore untrained and inexperienced in peacetime industry or business, had never found employment and were living unhappily on insufficient unemployment allowances commonly called "the dole." Others, previously employed, were eligible for unemployment insurance benefits; and the government had to support the insurance fund, which would otherwise soon have been exhausted. To stimulate trade and revive employment, the government negotiated a trade agreement with Soviet Russia without recognizing the government of that country *de jure*—which was not quite satisfactory to Labour but disturbed the British Conservatives, as did the "dole" and concessions made to Ireland in the establishment of the Free State in 1921.[3]

At last, to safeguard and retain conservative political support, Lloyd George imposed a protective tariff of 33⅓ percent on imports

[3] See pp. 324-326.

that competed with the output of certain "key" industries considered vital to the national welfare or defense, or that came from countries with depreciated currencies. These concessions were not enough, however.

In October, 1922, the Conservative party decided to dispense with Lloyd George's services as coalition leader and to set up a ministry of their own if successful at the polls. They won the election in November, and Bonar Law became prime minister with the first one-party government since 1915.

International Debts and Reparation

One of the first and most important acts of the Bonar Law ministry was to send Stanley Baldwin, chancellor of the exchequer, to arrange for the refunding of the British debt to the United States. During the war the United States government had granted credit freely to the Allies, to the extent of something more than ten billion dollars, which with postarmistice credits and accumulated interest had increased to nearly twelve billion dollars. The credit had been granted by the United States government in the form of demand loans at 5 percent. It had been used largely for the purchase of war supplies in the United States at high wartime prices and postarmistice purchases of surplus war equipment and supplies in Europe at liquidation prices, while the United States government was paying only 4¼ percent interest on its own war bonds (called Liberty and Victory bonds). Meanwhile, for supplies, weapons, munitions, and services such as transportation, housing, and warehousing, the American Expeditionary Force had paid in cash, in European currencies at exchange rates sustained by American loans, about ten billion dollars—an amount approximately equal to the total prearmistice credit granted the Allies. There had been no lend-lease arrangement and no return lend-lease. If there had been, the books would not have been far out of balance.

In 1922 the United States government invited the debtor nations to make arrangements for the funding of the debts. Britain had borrowed in the United States something more than four and less than five billion dollars. She had lent to her allies more than twice as much. She would therefore have been canceling for others more than she was asking the United States to cancel for her benefit, if the latter had accepted the suggestion made on her behalf by Arthur Balfour that all international war debts and reparation claims be canceled in the interest of reconstruction and general recovery.

Balfour knew that Britain would be unable to collect more than a small fraction, if any, of what it had lent unless the money came out of Germany in reparation payments. France had borrowed from Britain and the United States about seven billion dollars and had lent half that much to Belgium, Italy, and others. Italy had borrowed more than ten times as much as she had lent, and more than she could hope to get as her share of German reparation.

The United States, on the other hand, expected to recover very little in reparation from Germany and had paid its way in cash in its relations with the Allies. General cancellation would have been for it a one-way transaction, offering no compensating advantage except intangibles such as good will or imponderables such as the incalculable benefits to be derived from an earlier revival of general prosperity and international trade. The United States did not agree to the Balfour proposal.

Balfour then announced that Great Britain must reluctantly ask the others to pay enough on their debts to her to cover, with her share of German reparation, the payments she must make on her debt to the United States. If her debt to the United States should be reduced, she would give her debtors the benefit of an equivalent reduction. The United States was thus left isolated as the object of whatever resentment anyone might feel against the uncomfortable necessity of paying anything on account of international war debts, even to France or Britain.

There was a rather general feeling among the Allies that the war debts should be canceled or materially reduced. It was remembered that much of the money had been spent in the United States, that people there had profited from the sale of war materials to belligerents, and that the government had retrieved some of the money by taxing extraordinary incomes. Uncle Sam was called Uncle Shylock because of the apparent margin of three-fourths of one percent between the interest rate he had charged (on paper, without yet collecting any of it) on war loans to other nations and what he had at the same time been paying to the holders of his own war bonds.

Soon the fact that the United States was richer than the debtor nations began to appear to some of the people of those nations to be an argument against repayment. It could spare the money more easily, they said, than they could find it. Eventually the objectors, especially in France, convinced themselves that they had fought for years in the general interest, in defense of civilization and for the common good of humanity, before the United States had recognized its vital interest in the outcome of the war, and even then had had to hold off the common enemy for more than another year before the A.E.F. had begun really to make itself felt on the fighting front. If the United States were never to be repaid, it would be less badly hurt by loss of the money involved than the Allies had been by loss of men killed and wounded in that period. Such opinions were presumably not quite universally held. Edouard Herriot of France was one of those who recognized the obligation and insisted that France meet it. There were many, however, in France and other debtor countries who did not think of international war debts as immutable contractual obligations, or of their revision or nonpayment as a default or breach of faith.

Faced with the alternatives of cancellation, revision, or a probably unsuccessful attempt to collect the war debts in full, the United States government chose revision downward by reduction of the interest rate and extension of the period of payment, adjusting the interest rate according to the debtor's own statement of ability to pay. By accepting the agreement negotiated by Stanley Baldwin in 1923, Great Britain was the first great power to arrange for the funding of her debt. The interest rate was reduced from 5 to $3\frac{3}{10}$ percent. The period of payment was extended to sixty-two years.

The British funding agreement was made the model for several other nations. Those that said they could not pay so high an interest rate were permitted to settle at a lower one. Belgium was to pay 1.8 percent, France 1.6 percent, and Italy—which at the same time was maintaining the largest standing army in Europe in proportion to population—0.4 percent. Figured on the basis of the original demand notes at 5 percent, although principal and interest over the whole period would have totaled $22,000,000,000, these funding agreements represented a reduction to about half of the original amount; but Britain's reduction was less than half, and France, Belgium, and Italy were given a much lower interest rate than she. The time was soon to come when British taxpayers would begin to tell themselves that they had been penalized for their government's promptness and expressed readiness to pay.

Britain, in turn, made funding agreements with the nations owing war debts to her, on such terms that if all promised payments had been made, and if German Dawes and Young plan payments had been continued, receipts on one account would approximately have balanced payments on the other. Up to the time of the Hoover moratorium (July 1, 1931, to July 1, 1932), however, receipts had not equaled payments, and provision for the difference had had to be made in the budget.[4]

Semiannual payments were made by Great Britain until the moratorium, another was made on December 15, 1932, but only a token payment June 15, 1933. France defaulted on both dates and regularly thereafter, on the ground that she should not be expected to pay unless Germany kept up her reparation payments. Italy, Czechoslovakia, and Latvia did as Britain did on both due dates here mentioned. Lithuania paid in December, defaulted in June. Only Finland paid in full, and continued year after year to do so. In December, 1933, Britain and four others made token payments. After that, none were made. In April, 1934, the Johnson Act made it illegal for nationals of the United States to grant loans to nations in default on debts to the United States. Thereafter only Finland continued to qualify.

Unemployment, "Protection," Socialization, Managed Economy

Within four years after the end of the war in 1918, the changes the war had made in Great Britain's world position had become uncomfortably apparent. She was no longer undisputed mistress of the seas, but at Washington in 1921 had had to concede to the United States naval parity and to Japan a comparative status that meant naval supremacy in the northwestern Pacific.[5] She was no longer the world's principal creditor nation but was heavily indebted to the United States. Interest charges on the national debt were nearly sixteen times what they had been before the war. Although the self-disciplined British citizenry was still taxing itself more heavily than Americans, Frenchmen, or Germans were then being taxed, it did not pretend not to find the tax load burdensome. Owners of large estates, forced by taxation to break them up and sell them, grumbled at what they called confiscation. Serious budgetary problems were faced by government, trade and industry, and the individual.

Agriculture was the largest single industry, affording employment to about 1,300,000 people. By intensive methods of cultivation and scientific animal husbandry, good yields of cereal grains per acre and great numbers of beef cattle, sheep, and hogs were produced. As had been done during the Napoleonic period, and as was to be done

[4] While the Dawes plan was in operation and international war debt payments were being made as scheduled, France was receiving in reparation and war-debt payments something more than enough to meet her debt payments to Great Britain and the United States and service her special reconstruction bonds. See pp. 90-94.

[5] See the Washington conference of 1921, in Chapter 6, pp. 141-146.

again from 1939 to 1945, every effort had been made during the war to increase production of foodstuffs. Much marginal land had been plowed for crops or converted into vegetable gardens. Landowners of the twentieth century were less successful in securing tariff protection than the beneficiaries of the nineteenth-century "corn laws" had been, but prices of all foodstuffs and the minimum general cost of living were higher than before the war. Sixty percent of the population lived in urban areas, highly industrialized, closely packed together. Although there were many square miles of open country in the north and southwest, the average density of population for the whole island was comparatively high. Although no single industry equaled agriculture, the many manufacturing industries, together, dwarfed it in volume and value of output and in number of persons employed. Four-fifths of the breadstuffs and fruit, half of the eggs, meat, and dairy products, and a third of the vegetables and fish consumed in Britain had to be imported.

Any country so highly industrialized, importing such portions of its food as well as vital raw materials for its industries, is dependent upon markets for its exports. Britain had always known that but had lost many of her markets. In that field the United States had become a more formidable competitor than formerly.

Cotton cloth, cheaply produced in great quantity, had for many years been a staple of Britain's export trade. Much of it had gone to India, but when the war ended the Indians were making more of their own cloth than formerly. In China and Africa, and soon almost everywhere, British cloth and other manufactured goods had to compete with Japanese products, more cheaply made and marketed. Lancashire, the old center of the cotton spinning and weaving industry, became one of the depressed areas.

The revival of the German iron and steel industries and the inflation of the mark made world-market competition difficult for British machines and cutlery, produced without benefit of subsidy by companies paying comparatively high wages and taxes in a relatively stable currency.

Shipbuilding normally gave the British an opportunity to export at once the skilled services of their artificers and seamen and finely finished materials by building ships for foreigners or for their own manifold maritime enterprises. Construction had been artificially stimulated during the war, as British and American yards worked feverishly to launch ships faster than enemy submarines could destroy them, and fast enough to carry armies and the mountains of supplies that had to follow them. When sinkings stopped, building slackened. When the expeditionary forces had been carried home, remote estuaries and backwater bays in the United States began to fill up with surplus ships tied together, rusting at anchor. While the great ship-yards of the United States and Britain stood virtually idle and British and American lines used aging German vessels seized in war and retained as reparation, German yards were busy building better ships with which to make a new bid for the ocean carrying trade. It was not until after years of deep depression that the Cunard and White Star lines were combined for the sake of efficiency, and government loans at low interest rates encouraged new shipbuilding. The French lines' *Normandie* and the North German Lloyd's *Bremen* and *Europa* had headed the parade of transatlantic liners for ten years before the "Queens" *Mary* and *Elizabeth* were ready. Some fine new ships, however, appeared after a time on the Canadian and South African routes.

Britain's principal raw material export was coal, which before the war had gone in great quantity to the Scandinavian countries, Italy, and France. Smaller quantities had been carried surprisingly great distances, to coalless countries or to steamship coaling stations.

Many circumstances and conditions combined in the first five years of peace to depress the British coal industry. German deliveries to France and Italy on reparation account reduced the demand for British coal in those countries. Soon France increased her output by bringing her own war-damaged fields back into production to supplement the Saar, and was thereafter less dependent upon imported coal. Germany, having lost Lorraine, was importing iron ore from Sweden and would have preferred to pay for it with coal if Poland had not come into the market with Silesian coal, formerly German. Electrification sometimes meant the substitution of water power for coal. Naval vessels and ocean liners were being converted so as to burn fuel oil instead of coal, and new ships were powered by oil-driven motors. When Britain's own iron and steel industries were forced to cut production, less coke and smelting coal were used; so the coal industry also suffered.

Britain still had abundant coal reserves, and her mines were by no means worked out; but many of the seams which were easiest of access had been worked to the point where, with obsolescent equipment and old but inefficient methods still in use, their further exploitation was uneconomical. When in 1925 lessening demand and price reductions made coal production financially unprofitable, mine owners proposed to reduce wages and lengthen the working day from seven hours to eight. The miners refused to accept the change. For almost a year, to avoid a strike, the government supervised and subsidized the mines so as to maintain the existing wage scale; but during that period three-fourths of the coal that came up had been mined at a loss. A government commission then recommended a wage cut, to go into effect May 1, 1926. The miners refused to accept the reduction and stopped work.

The coal strike which began May 3, 1926, threatened to grow at any moment into a general strike as some millions of trade-union members were called out in other industries in sympathy. It was one of the most serious labor crises in British history. With characteristic moderation, however, the trade-union leaders made no attempt to stop services essential to public health. Food, gas, electricity, water, sanitation, and hospital services were still available, and volunteers provided the most essential transportation. Even so, the strike was generally regarded as inimical to the public interest and as an attempt to coerce the nation, and was generally resented.

After nine days the general strike was called off by the Trades Union Congress, but the coal strike continued until November 19. When at last, then, the miners went back to work, the eight-hour day had been legalized by Parliament and wages had been reduced. Labor paid for the strike failure in many ways. Other legislation of 1927 increased the financial responsibility of the miners' unions by making them liable for damage due to strikes (as they had been after the Taff Vale decision of 1901 until exempted by the Trades Disputes Act of 1906). New legislation also made union funds subject to injunction or attachment, prohibited picketing (which had been legalized in 1906), and restricted the unions' disciplinary control over their members in matters such as strike participation and payment of political levies. Ramsay MacDonald's second Labour government, which took office June 5, 1929, tried to revise this restrictive legislation but, as a minority government dependent upon Liberals or liberal Conservatives for support, could not muster the necessary votes in Parliament.

The depression in the coal industry seemed permanent. Some of the most seriously affected of the depressed areas were in south Wales and northeastern England. Compulsory price fixing, controlled marketing, and the closing of unprofitable pits—all under government supervision—were considered necessary. Coal royalties were already nationalized, and the nationalization of the mines (effected in 1946 but closely approached years earlier) was foreshadowed.[6]

MacDonald followed Baldwin and Baldwin followed MacDonald as prime minister. Labour and Conservative parties wrestled alternately with the problems of unequal distribution of wealth, insufficient overseas trade, and unemployment. However different their points of view may have been, their handling of similar domestic problems was not totally dissimilar. MacDonald (though a socialist) was not a violent revolutionary, or Baldwin a very extreme reactionary, though conservative enough. Each, in his first ministry, had to depend upon Liberal support for his parliamentary majority. MacDonald did not propose, as prime minister, the capital levy of which his party had freely talked, and Baldwin had to continue government aid to the unemployed and the depressed areas. Both were plagued by strikes and tried hard to prevent them. The Conservative government, in 1927 for example, enacted more restrictive labor legislation. Laws increasing the pensions paid to widows, orphans, and aged persons and giving women the same voting privilege as men were passed by the Conservative government in 1928.

The Labour-Liberal government of January to November, 1924, adhered in general to the traditional policy of free trade. Mr. Baldwin and the Conservatives, 1923-1924 and 1924-1929, turned rather to tariff protection of key industries, as the last Lloyd George coalition had done, and to imperial preference, advocated by Joseph Chamberlain nearly thirty years before, giving preferential tariff treatment to imports from the colonies and dominions under a general protective tariff system.

Conservatives favored key industries also by reducing their taxes. Socialists in the Labour party welcomed the wider distribution of the ownership of land when their tax policy forced the sale of some large hereditary estates, and would have welcomed some further redistribution of wealth.

Improvement in diplomatic and trade relations with Russia, and a generally conciliatory and coöperative foreign policy (to be discussed later), were not enough to carry Britain through the years of the world depression unscathed. Foreign trade declined, successively, in 1929, 1930, and 1931. Iron and steel production and cotton cloth

[6] In February, 1947, Britain suffered a serious coal shortage, to which extraordinarily severe winter weather traffic stoppages on snowbound roads and railways, and the war's depletion of man power in the mines were contributing factors. Opponents of the recently effected nationalization accused the government of mismanagement.

manufacturing, always heavily dependent upon export trade, were especially hard hit. Unemployment and government budget deficits due to shrinking tax receipts and mounting costs of maintenance of the unemployed reached new and alarming totals. Short-term credits such as those then outstanding in Germany could not be recalled after the general agreement to the Hoover moratorium and subsequent stand-still agreements, but the money would probably not have been forthcoming out of Germany if there had been no moratorium, or have gone far toward solving Britain's economic problems.[7]

Drastic economies were recommended by a government (May) committee of experts, including the reduction of government salaries, pensions, other social insurance benefits and social services, and appropriations for the national defense. Opinion in the Labour party was sharply divided. Many of the members objected to the economies proposed and would have tried to balance the budget by increased taxation. Prime Minister MacDonald and Chancellor of the Exchequer Philip Snowden, on the other hand, would have done as the May committee had advised.

The division of the party and the national economic crisis combined to bring about the resignation of the Labour government on August 24, 1931. MacDonald again became prime minister and Philip Snowden chancellor of the exchequer in a national coalition cabinet of Laborites, Liberals, and Conservatives; but both were read out of the Labour party. On September 21, 1931, Britain abandoned the gold standard, to the dismay of people everywhere to whom the Bank of England and the gold standard had been synonymous with financial soundness and integrity.

In the national election of October, 1931, both Labour and Liberal parties were divided. Lloyd George opposed the coalition. Sir Herbert Samuel and Sir John Simon, former Liberals, supported it. The national coalition won the election by a large majority, and Mr. MacDonald formed his fourth ministry in November with strong parliamentary support, more than half of it Conservative.

The budget was balanced in 1932 and for five years thereafter, rather by reduction of expenditures, as had been proposed in 1931 by Snowden and the May committee, than by increased taxation. Renewed industrial activity reduced the amount required for maintenance of the unemployed. But rearmament, made imperative after 1936 by Italy's aggressiveness and the arming of Nazi Germany, compelled the government again to borrow money and increase the national debt, to meet its annual budget deficits.

[7] For the Hoover moratorium, see p. 93.

Insufficient export trade and an excess of imports over exports were still serious problems. The year 1932 saw Britain take the remaining steps (March 1) to the adoption of a protective tariff policy and, at an imperial conference at Ottawa, Canada, toward imperial economic preference. Equally strenuous efforts were made to stimulate production and spread employment at home, and ambitious road-improvement, traffic-control, slum-clearance, and new housing projects were planned and partially carried through. Unemployment, which had reached a peak with nearly three millions unemployed in the worst period of the depression in 1932, had been reduced to half that number within five years. Then it increased again until abruptly ended by the war.

Ramsay MacDonald resigned as prime minister on grounds of ill health June 7, 1935, but was able to accept a position in the cabinet of Stanley Baldwin, who succeeded him. The Baldwin government was confirmed by the outcome of a general election November 14, 1935. Most of the ministers of the national coalition cabinet were carried over. The new government was largely Conservative but included some National Liberals and National Labour members like Ramsay and Malcolm MacDonald. A similar coalition cabinet, largely Conservative, was formed by Neville Chamberlain, son of Joseph Chamberlain and younger half-brother of Sir Austen Chamberlain, who succeeded Baldwin May 28, 1936.

The domestic problems of the Neville Chamberlain government were largely economic, like those of the previous national governments. Declining foreign trade reduced the national earning power, while increasing expenditures for armament, undertaken in a belated attempt to prepare for impending war, increased the public debt to a new all-time high of eight billion pounds. The government's eventually ineffectual attempts to avert or to postpone the war will be discussed later, under the heading of foreign policy and in a chapter on the general diplomatic background of the war.[8]

The Dynasty

The years 1935 and 1936 witnessed two striking though strikingly different demonstrations of the continuing importance of the position of the king. In 1935 the whole empire and commonwealth except Ireland joined enthusiastically in the celebration of the twenty-fifth anniversary of the accession of King-Emperor George V. The observance of the silver jubilee, however official in character, brought out

[8] See pp. 372-377, 422-523.

innumerable expressions of genuine affection for the monarch who had
so loyally accepted both the constitutional limitations of his authority
and the many remaining responsibilities of his exalted office, and who
had gone through war and hardship with his people, doing his duty
as one of them and identifying himself with them. Occasionally a
radical socialist had voiced some criticism of the cost of maintaining
the royal establishment, or of the generous allowances paid the king's
four "idle" sons; but such rude criticisms attracted neither sympathy
nor much attention. Although scoffers sometimes called the royal
couple "stuffy," or ridiculed the queen's conservatism in the choice of
parasols or hats, fundamentally people respected the conscientious
king and queen because they took themselves and their position seriously—and were personally respectable, above reproach. The prestige
of the crown, at home and in the dominions overseas, was enhanced
by the eventful reign of George V.

On the death of George V, January 20, 1936, his eldest son was
proclaimed king as Edward VIII; but he was never ceremonially
crowned. As Prince of Wales, Edward had been immensely popular.
Aged twenty at the outbreak of the war in 1914, and a student at
Magdalen College, Oxford, where he had been a private in the university officers' cadet battalion, he had gone at once into the army as
a staff officer and in France, Italy, and Egypt had served as actively
as his military seniors would permit. After the war he had shown a
natural and commendable interest in the care of disabled war veterans
and their families. Within ten years, as the peripatetic representative
of the royal family and of Britain, he had traveled extensively in all
the self-governing dominions overseas, India, and Burma, and had
visited many of the smaller colonies and British bases in Africa and
the Near East. He had gone once to Japan, twice each to Argentina
and the United States, and once or more than once to nearly every
national capital of central, southeastern, and western Europe. He was
a good traveler and a fair linguist, useful as a promoter of international good will and of British international trade. He had served a
long and arduous apprenticeship and seemed in most respects well
trained and qualified for the position indicated for him by the law
of primogeniture.

At forty-one, however, when his father died, Edward was still a
dilettante. The war had overtaken him before his academic education
was completed, and he had never continued it except in desultory
fashion. His mind was keen and quick; but he had not the patience,
when he had the time, to study any problem exhaustively enough to

master its fundamentals. In music he showed a preference for dance bands and in personal amusement for the atmosphere of the night clubs. People remembered the gaiety, good nature, and general good sense and popularity of his grandfather Edward VII, which had been welcomed as a change from the unnatural solemnity of the later years of Queen Victoria. They compared him with his grandfather, were tolerant of his escapades, and loved him for his friendliness and informality; but they wondered sometimes when the boyish-looking prince would give them evidence of greater mental and emotional maturity, or indicate a deeper realization of the restraints which his position inevitably put upon him. As king in 1936 he occasionally embarrassed his ministers by making generous but impulsive public statements about problems, such as those of the miners in south Wales, of which they had not been unaware but which they had been unable yet to solve.

Life had rushed Edward, and had given him little opportunity to learn to live quietly at a tempo comparable with that set by his parents. He was a restless, sometimes almost a rebellious, person. Always in the spotlight, denied the luxury of a private life free from prying and publicity, he found it especially difficult to reconcile himself to the fact that birth and position had restricted him more narrowly than others in the exercise of some of the fundamental rights of the common man, such as the choice of companions and the selection of a wife. When a king of England marries, he chooses not only a wife for himself but a queen for all Britain, a first lady for many British lands.

Churchmen and moralists, and many others not primarily concerned with religion or with personal morality but seriously interested in the character of the king's example, were deeply disturbed during the short reign of Edward VIII by his apparent indifference to public religious observance, and by his more than merely friendly interest in Mrs. Wallis Warfield Simpson. Mrs. Simpson had been twice married and already once divorced. In October, 1936, her second marriage also was terminated by divorce (nisi, to become final in 1937). She was an American by birth and so, to British genealogists, a "commoner." Neither of these handicaps, however, weighed so heavily against her as the fact that she had two ex-husbands still living when the king let it become known publicly that he wished to marry her.

The king is, ex officio, secular head of the Church of England and protector of the Presbyterian Church in Scotland. The former looks with some disfavor upon the remarriage of divorced persons, and both frown upon frivolity in high places. To both, the proposed marriage seemed improper. It would have set a conspicuous example of which they could not have approved. Prime Minister Stanley Baldwin finally let Edward know that ministry and parliament considered the king's choice of a wife a question of national and imperial, not purely personal, concern. The dominions, when consulted, indicated that they also disapproved. After once tentatively suggesting that Parliament legalize a morganatic marriage, with the right of succession to be settled upon the heir presumptive (the Duke of York) and his children, the king notified the prime minister that he would rather abdicate than forgo the privilege of living as he chose.

Parliament passed the act of abdication December 11, 1936. Edward's brother, the Duke of York, immediately became King George VI and was crowned in Westminister Abbey on May 12, 1937. His conduct as king in trying times during the first ten years of his reign indicated that he was a true son of his father in his acceptance of the conditions of the kingship and in his realization of its responsibilities. One of his first official acts was to confer upon the ex-king, his brother, the title of the Duke of Windsor.

The powers of the crown are limited by the British constitution; yet its usefulness is great. Its importance in the minds of the peoples of the kingdom, commonwealth, and empire is such that he who wears it is compelled to qualify; and Parliament can define the terms on which it shall be worn.

COMMONWEALTH

"When Britain is at war Canada is at war." Without waiting for any other interpretation of their obligations, the self-governing dominions joined the mother country and the empire in the Four Years' War in 1914, as Canada and Australia had done in the Boer War. Some reluctance was apparent among the French Canadians and among the Boer element in South Africa, but loyalty, not disaffection, was the general rule. Canada adopted conscription for overseas service; Australia did not, but raised a proportionately large expeditionary force of volunteers. New Zealand, most British of all the self-governing dominions though geographically remote, adopted conscription and sent a higher percentage of her man power to the war than any other. The Germans tried with slight success to incite a Boer rebellion in South Africa. Many of the Boers, such as the great leaders Smuts and Botha who had once fought against the British, participated in the conquest of the German colonies in southwestern and middle eastern Africa; and the South African uniform was seen in Britain and in France. About a million men from India and two million others from overseas, largely from the self-governing dominions, fought for Britain in the war.

The services of the overseas contingents were not accepted without acknowledgment. Properly grateful for them, happily reassured by such a demonstration of loyalty and community of interest, and not averse to using it in propaganda to convince the world of the beneficence of the British system, the public information services played up the performance of the men from overseas more often than they played it down. Some jealousies were thereby aroused. The Anzacs (Australian and New Zealand Army Corps), for example, did not fight alone at Gallipoli; but their losses were so heavy that their people back home asked themselves whether they had been "sacrificed" by British blundering, while the families of men of less-publicized British regiments which also fought there protested: "Our boys died as dead as they." Britain's enemies, meanwhile, could point to the British press for proof of their propaganda statements that her battles were being fought for her not by her own sons but by her misguided minions. Men from the dominions who asked themselves, not unnaturally, why and for what they had come so far to fight were usually quick to answer that they had done it in the interest of their own home-lands, not "the homeland," not the empire.

Equality of Status, 1926

The war years witnessed some growth and strengthening, in the dominions, of the opinion that their involvement in any subsequent war in which Britain might be engaged ought not to be immediate or automatic—that each of them should be free to decide for itself how far it should be bound by any of Britain's commitments, or whether it must in all cases or in any case accept British foreign policy as its own. That idea was expressed as early as 1917, at an imperial conference called for the coördination of the common war effort. It was thus made clear that the self-governing dominions were thinking of themselves as autonomous nations, although still willing in that war, in the interest of efficiency, to combine their armed forces with those of Great Britain under the supreme command of the British admiralty and army staffs. General Jan Smuts of South Africa was a member of the emergency war cabinet.

At the Paris peace conference of 1919 Canada, Australia, New

Zealand, and the Union of South Africa were represented by their own delegations. All of them but Canada were given mandates over some of Germany's former colonial possessions, and all became members of the League of Nations.

Irish nationalists claimed equal privileges for Ireland, and their claims were disputed by Great Britain only until the establishment of the Free State (to be discussed later) in 1922.[9]

In 1919 Canada was permitted to name her own minister to the United States. In 1921 the dominions were represented at the Washington conference as at Paris two years before. In 1923 Canada negotiated directly with the United States (rather than through the British Colonial or Foreign Office) a treaty for the regulation of the halibut fisheries in which both were interested. This innovation was accepted as a precedent by the other British nations, with the understanding that all should always be informed of such agreements and included in their negotiation if immediately affected. The others were equally free to open ministries in Washington, and some of them subsequently did so. None need ratify a treaty entered into by Great Britain, and none was bound by such a treaty which it had not ratified. There were "republican" independence movements afoot, however, in the early twenties in Ireland and the Union of South Africa, among those to whom autonomy seemed not to be enough.

Equality of status was accepted by an imperial conference in 1926 as "the root principle governing . . . Inter-Imperial relations" so far as Britain and the dominions were concerned, and as the basis for continued voluntary association in a commonwealth of nations. As defined in a committee report to that conference, worded by Lord Balfour, equality of status meant that the members of the commonwealth were to be "autonomous communities within the British Empire, equal in status, in no way subordinate one to another in any aspect of their domestic or external affairs, though united in a common allegiance to the crown, and freely associated as the British Commonwealth of Nations."[10]

[9] The representatives of the other British nations did not always follow Britain's lead in the Assembly of the League; but their presence there was made the basis of the charge that Great Britain was being given five or six votes in the Assembly instead of one. This was one of the arguments adduced in the United States against ratification of the League Covenant and subsequently as a pretext for the USSR's insistence upon similar representation of the Ukrainian and White Russian soviet republics in the Assembly of the United Nations.

[10] "Imperial Conference, 1926. Summary of Proceedings," in *British Parliamentary Papers*, 1926, Vol. XI, Cd. 2768, p. 18. See also Paul Knaplund, *The British Empire, 1815-1939* (New York 1941), 603.

The republican movement in the Union of South Africa, of which Premier Hertzog had been a leader, was weakened by the assurance of complete autonomy with equality of status offered by the Balfour report to the imperial conference of 1926, with which Dr. Hertzog, head of the South African delegation to that conference, was satisfied. A stronger Irish republican movement persisted.

Statute of Westminster, 1931

After years of planning in committee, the legislation necessary to implement the declaration of 1926 was ready for presentation to the national legislatures. The Statute of Westminster, passed by the British Parliament in December, 1931, defines the relations of the member states of the commonwealth and serves in effect as its written constitution. As so defined, Britain's primacy is only that of a "first among equals." Acts of the British Parliament are not law in any of the other member states unless specifically reënacted or accepted as its own by the Parliament of that state. Legislation enacted by the Parliament of a member state cannot be annulled, nor can the assent of the crown be withheld from it, on the ground that it is contrary to an act of the British Parliament. The assent of the crown to dominion legislation is given in each case through a governor general nominally appointed by the crown but chosen in fact by the dominion, to which he must be acceptable. The sole legal bond remaining to hold the member states together is their common allegiance to the crown; but the significance of that bond is indicated by the provision of the Statute of Westminster that no change in the laws governing the succession to the crown can be made without the consent of the Parliaments of the member states.

Allegiance to a common crown is effective as a bond of unity within the commonwealth because it is a familiar and time-honored symbol of a common heritage and a certain community of interest. It symbolizes an association which has endured because it balances so nicely the centripetal forces of common membership in an old and powerful league of peoples against the centrifugal forces—such as location, peculiar population or defense problems, special interests, or relations with neighboring nonmember states—which tend at times to draw a member state away in the direction of independence or of other international alignments. Members of the commonwealth have remained members for the sake of sentiment, kinship, safety, and mutual advantage. The loosening of the bonds seemed in 1939 to have strengthened the bond. All member states but Ireland, which had already claimed a different status, joined Great Britain in the war against Nazi Germany in 1939 as they had joined her in the war against imperial Germany in 1914.

IRELAND

Home Rule Question, 1914-1920

The outbreak of war in 1914 found Ireland in turmoil over the question of "home rule." A new Government of Ireland Act, the "Third Home Rule Bill," had been passed by the British House of Commons and rejected by the House of Lords in 1912 and 1913. Under the provisions of the Parliament Act of 1911, the new Government of Ireland Act could become law without the consent of the House of Lords if passed a third time by the House of Commons. It was so passed in May, 1914, but amended by the House of Lords so as not to include Ulster; so the king's assent was withheld while an unsuccessful attempt was made to reconcile conflicting views. In September, 1914, it was again passed by the Commons, without the amendment excepting Ulster, and became law; but it was held in abeyance by a companion act suspending it until after the war and pledging the government to bring in then a new bill on the Ulster question. When that time came, other legislation was ready, but Ireland was not ready to accept either the law of 1914 or the proffered substitute.

The question was an old one, complicated by geographical, historical, religious, economic, and political considerations. Fundamentally, it was made difficult of solution by Irish resentment of the fact that, as the Irish saw them, the British were intruders in Ireland, with a long record of exploitation and oppression, and by British reluctance to "quit Ireland" for fear that that island might, in wartime, be seized and used as a base by some enemy of Britain. By the Government of Ireland Act of 1914, therefore, although Ireland was offered autonomy at home, the control of foreign policy and defense were reserved for the British Parliament, in which Ireland was still to be represented by forty-two members empowered to vote on such imperial questions only.

The Irish were divided, first, among Ulstermen and others. Of the nine counties of northern Ireland or "Ulster," four were predominantly Protestant, three strongly Catholic, and two fairly evenly divided but with Catholics slightly in the majority. The four predominantly Protestant counties were the most populous and most highly industrialized. They accounted for about 80 percent of the population and much of the wealth of the nine. If Tyrone and Fermanagh, the counties with the largest Protestant minorities, were included in a census with the four with the largest Protestant majorities, a strong Protestant majority would be found in the six—often called the "Six Counties."

Irish nationalists naturally wanted the new national government to encompass all Ireland. The island seemed to them too small to be divided. To separate Ulster from the rest would have been, as they saw it, a truncation of the country. Even the Protestants of the Six Counties, they thought, ought not to be—and in fact were not—insensible to the spirit of Irish nationalism. (Sir Roger Casement, one of the most ardent nationalists, was an Ulsterman and a Protestant.) Most of the Protestants of the Six Counties feared domination by the Catholic majority in a united Ireland; but their apprehensions were not based entirely upon religious differences. They feared also that, as the most highly industrialized section of the country, with more accumulated wealth than the general Irish average but with only a minority voice as to the levying of taxes or the expenditure of public funds, North Ireland would find itself paying disproportionately heavy taxes for the benefit of the rest, which had been less favored and had prospered less during the period of union with Great Britain.

The Unionists of Ulster preferred separation from the rest of Ireland to separation from Great Britain, and threatened rebellion against "home rule" if it meant, for them, submission to an Irish parliament in which they would be represented only as a minority group and which they feared might discriminate against them. They found an eloquent and effective leader in Sir Edward Henry Carson, born in Dublin, educated at Trinity College, Dublin, and in 1914 a member of (the British) Parliament for the University of Dublin. The arming of the Unionists in the summer of 1914, in protest against the Government of Ireland Act of that year, and the coming of the war were the principal reasons for the British government's decision to delay the implementation of that act for the duration of the war.

The people of Ireland were further divided in 1914, and more seriously later, between the moderate nationalists who would have been at least temporarily content with free dominion status within the empire and more radical separatists who wanted nothing less, even then, than complete severance of all legal ties with Great Britain and the establishment of an independent Irish republic.

Officially, as a part of the United Kingdom, Ireland was at war when Britain was at war; yet Ireland was in many ways a special case. A great part of her population was loyal to the United Kingdom, and many thousands of her young men served in the British armies as volunteers. Yet there was some discrimination. Those from the south of Ireland were not encouraged to recruit their own divisions as those from Ulster were doing. When conscription was adopted by the British in 1915, it was not made applicable to the Irish, who would have resented any attempt to impose it by use of force. In 1918, when an attempt was made to impose a new and more comprehensive conscription law upon the whole United Kingdom, the government thought it prudent to compromise with the Irish opposition to the act by offering to suspend its provisions so far as Ireland was concerned if enough new volunteers came forward. Few volunteered, and the question of conscription in Ireland was still unsolved when the war ended.

Yet Ireland was more help than hindrance to Britain in the war. Such surpluses of food and other war materials as Ireland could produce were needed, and were correspondingly useful in Britain; and naval bases such as that at Queenstown (Cóbh) were of incalculable value in the war against the submarine and in keeping the sea lanes open.

The only serious insurrection was on Easter Monday, 1916, when certain members of the ardently nationalist Irish Republican group, closely associated with the Fenian Society, an organization otherwise known as Sinn Fein ("We ourselves")—not to be confused with the more moderate Irish Nationalists led by Sir John Redmond, who were willing to accept home rule and dominion status and who had announced that they would support Britain in the war—seized some of the public buildings in Dublin and issued a proclamation in the name of the "Provisional Government of the Irish Republic."

The British were frightened and angry. What they had always feared most was Irish coöperation with an enemy of Britain in time of war; and such coöperation had been planned, although the plan failed. Sir Roger Casement, who had gone to Berlin to plan the rebellion, was brought back to Ireland by a German submarine but was soon captured. A German surface vessel carrying arms for the insurgents was seized off the Irish coast. No further help came from Germany, and the little that had come served only to brand the Irish, in British eyes, as traitors in league with the national enemy. The rebellion was quickly and rather ruthlessly suppressed, and the country was put for a time under martial law. Sir Roger Casement was hanged August 3. A few of the other leaders were shot. Many of the insurgents, or of those suspected of participation in the rebellion, were imprisoned. Feeling on both sides was embittered.

One of the leaders of the Easter rebellion of 1916 was Eamon de Valera. He was captured and condemned to death, but his sentence was commuted to life imprisonement. In 1917 he was one of the beneficiaries of a general amnesty. In 1918 he was again imprisoned but escaped to the United States, where he was sympathetically received by those most friendly to the Irish republican cause, and whence he returned to Ireland after the war as the leader of the Sinn Fein separatist movement.

In the general British parliamentary election of 1918, the Unionists won twenty-six seats, the Nationalists (favoring home rule but not insisting upon immediate independence) six, and de Valera's Sinn Fein seventy-three. Refusing to attend the Parliament in Westminster, the Sinn Fein deputies preferred to consider their election a mandate to establish an independent Irish republic—which they did, at least in name, in January, 1919, at Dublin despite determined British opposition. Some of the members of the new Dail Eireann, so self-constituted, were imprisoned. Others went into hiding. None went to the Parliament in Westminster to which all had been elected. The new Dail chose a ministry, elected de Valera president and Arthur Griffith vice-president, and sent delegates to Paris in an unsuccessful attempt to secure an invitation to the peace conference then in session there and international recognition for Ireland as a sovereign state.

The years 1919 and 1920 were a period of disorder and violence in Ireland, of raids and ambuscades, between the "Irish Republican Army" led by Michael Collins and the constabulary reinforced by special auxiliaries recruited largely from among the unemployed in Britain—youngsters who had missed the war or veterans who had been unable as civilians to adapt themselves to postwar conditions. The use of these so-called "Black and Tans"—clothed in surplus army uniforms with black armbands and black bands on their caps— was especially resented by the Irish and did not justify itself by its results.

Fourth Home Rule Bill

In December, 1920, the Lloyd George government secured the passage by the British Parliament of yet another Government of Ireland Act. This offered southern Ireland more nearly complete autonomy than ever, but the new Irish parliament was not to legislate for Ulster. Northeastern Ireland was to have a separate parliament for the handling of its local affairs and to continue to enjoy its old right to representation in the British Parliament at Westminster. This offer was accepted by the Unionists of the northeastern counties, and the new parliament of northern Ireland was formally opened in Belfast by King George on June 22, 1921. Northern Ireland was to be further represented by thirteen members in the House of Commons at Westminster. As defined by the Parliament Act of 1920, northern Ireland included the Six Counties—Antrim, Armagh, Down, Fermanagh, Londonderry, and Tyrone—and Belfast and Londonderry county boroughs. In the whole area included, Protestants outnumbered Roman Catholics nearly two to one (in 1937, 851,455 to 428,291). In Tyrone and Fermanagh Roman Catholics slightly outnumbered Protestants. Religious toleration was assured.

The Irish Republicans objected to anything less than independence from Great Britain, and to the establishment of any new regime for anything less than all of Ireland. The Sinn Feiners again stood for parliament, captured all but four of the parliamentary seats except those for northern Ireland, then boycotted the proposed Irish parliament to which they had been elected, as they had previously boycotted the old British Parliament itself. A personal conference with de Valera having failed to produce an acceptable solution of the problem of the relations of the two countries, Lloyd George turned at last, early in December, 1921, to a more accommodating Irish Nationalist, the founder and former leader of the Fenian Society and vice-president of the unrecognized Irish "republic," Arthur Griffith. Michael Collins was a member of Griffith's delegation.

Free State Agreement, 1921

By signing a treaty agreement with the Irish delegates (December 6, 1921), as with the plenipotentiaries of a sovereign state, the British prime minister took a long step toward *de facto* recognition of the right of the Irish, as one people, to sever the political bonds which had united them with another and to assume a separate and equal station among the nations of the world. Yet geographical propinquity and many years of close though not always pleasant association had bound Ireland and Britain too closely together, with bonds by no means all political, for any sudden and total severance to be quite practicable. The treaty gave Ireland, therefore, in lieu of independence, the same constitutional status as was then enjoyed by the self-governing dominions—Canada, Australia, New Zealand, and South Africa.

Ireland was to become the Irish Free State. Its people still owed allegiance to the British crown, which was to be represented in Ireland as in Canada by a governor general. His authority in Ireland was to be analogous to that of the king in Britain. Its officials were to take an oath of allegiance to the king. The Free State was to have its own army, coast guard, and revenue cutters, subject only to certain limitations upon the relative size of its armed forces in comparison with the British and to the reservation on behalf of the British navy of the right to defend the coasts of Ireland and to use harbors, bases, and radio stations for that purpose. Ireland agreed to assume an unspecified share of the British national debt and to continue the annual payments still due under the land purchase acts.[11]

North Ireland was to choose by vote of its people whether it should be included in the Free State of Ireland or maintain its connection with the United Kingdom, with the autonomy granted it under the act of 1920. It chose to continue as it was. A commission was set up in 1925 to fix the boundaries between it and the Free State. Insisting upon retaining all of the Six Counties, North Ireland refused to send a delegate. So, by agreement with the Free State, the British government appointed a delegate for Britain and one for North Ireland; but the Free State delegate withdrew when his claim on counties Tyrone and Fermanagh was not confirmed. By direct negotiation between the British and Free State governments late in 1925, it was agreed that the boundary established in 1920 (with Tyrone and Fermanagh included in North Ireland) should stand unchanged, but that the Free State should be relieved, as of 1921, of the share of the British national debt which it had agreed in 1921 to assume. The more moderate Irish Nationalists reconciled themselves, at least as a matter of immediate and practical politics, to the division. To de Valera and the Republi-

[11] The Land Purchase Act of 1885, with subsequent revisions, had facilitated the purchase of land by those who lived on it and worked it. If an owner was willing, for example, to sell at "eighteen years' purchase" (i.e., a sum equal to eighteen times the annual rental), the government would guarantee him that amount. The tenant could then become the owner of the land, subject to forty-nine annual payments of 4 percent each of the purchase price, with the government guaranteeing payment. By 1921 nearly two-thirds of the land in Ireland had been sold by landlords to tenants by voluntary transactions of this sort, but many of the amortization payments were yet to be made, and the British government and its bondholders were deeply involved. Under the Land Act of 1923 the purchase price was more commonly fifteen years' purchase, and the annuity rate 4¾ percent.

cans the separation of Ulster from the rest of Ireland was still anathema.

The same division between Nationalists and Republicans was revealed in the discussion over the acceptance of the Free State agreement. De Valera resigned the presidency when the Dail, by a close vote, ratified the treaty, and Griffith and Collins assumed the responsibility of forming the government for which the pact provided, meanwhile going on, respectively, as elected president of the Irish republic and appointed chairman of a provisional government. Their task was made difficult by the active opposition of de Valera and the other irreconcilables, which was carried to the point of civil war as the British constabulary was withdrawn. Both Griffith and Collins were reluctant to act ruthlessly against their former Sinn Fein comrades in the cause of Irish nationalism.

On August 12, 1922, exhausted by nerve strain and hard work, Arthur Griffith fell dead on his way to his office in Dublin. Ten days later, Michael Collins was killed in an ambuscade, attributed to "Irish Republicans." Leadership of the Free State forces devolved upon William Cosgrave, who was elected president, and Kevin O'Higgins, minister of justice. After half a year of further fighting, marked by serious loss of life, destruction of property, and numerous imprisonments, de Valera recognized the superior strength of the government forces to the extent of ordering his Republican followers to refrain from further violence.

Meanwhile the provisional government of 1922 completed a constitution, republican in form, which the British Parliament accepted. The establishment of the Free State was proclaimed by the king December 6, 1922.

The uneasy truce between Free State and Republican parties lasted four years, during which Republican candidates continued to stand for office but boycotted the Free State parliament by refusing to take the oath of allegiance to the king when elected to it. In 1927 O'Higgins, then vice-president of the executive council, who as minister of justice had most boldly asserted the authority of the government and its right to maintain itself by suppressing illegal opposition, was assassinated. Although de Valera was not charged with the murder and disclaimed complicity in it, the subversive tactics and recalcitrant attitudes of his followers were held by government and a considerable segment of public opinion to have been at least indirectly responsible for it, and the Irish Republicans lost face with their foreign and domestic supporters, to a certain extent, as a result of it. A new public safety act gave the government extraordinary police powers and a new electoral law required all candidates for parliament to certify their intention to take their seats and serve in parliament if elected—which they could not do if they continued to refuse to qualify by taking the oath of allegiance. De Valera then changed his tactics. He instructed his followers, if elected, to take the oath and take their seats. He himself took the necessary steps to qualify, and in 1927 became the leader of the opposition in the Irish parliament or Dail Eireann. His party was then the second largest in the Dail, with 57 of the 153 seats.

The ten-year Cosgrave administration made great strides in the direction of Irish nationalism without attempting to withdraw from the empire or commonwealth of British nations. With dominion status it secured the right, which it promptly exercised, to send its own diplomatic representatives to other nations. In 1923 Ireland was made a member of the League of Nations. With the other self-governing dominions it was represented at the imperial conferences of the middle twenties, participated in the definition of equality of status at the conference of 1926, and became a member of the commonwealth under the Statute of Westminister in 1931. The spirit of nationalism was emphasized by use of an Irish flag and Irish coins and postage stamps, and by encouragement of the use of the Gaelic language in literature, law courts, family and place names, and addresses to the Assembly of the League of Nations. Public education was improved, further land purchases by tenant farmers were subsidized, and hydroelectric power installations were developed on the rivers—especially the Shannon.

Yet the Cosgrave government, advocating the maintenance of membership in the commonwealth of British nations, could not survive the wave of discontent and economic nationalism which accompanied the world-wide depression of the early thirties. Forced to economize on salaries and pensions, and unwilling to adopt the high tariff demanded by Irish manufacturers, the government in power found itself increasingly unpopular. The de Valera party, free to criticize while not in power, won the election of March, 1932, by a narrow margin on a promise of national economic self-sufficiency.

In office as Cosgrave's successor as president of the executive council, de Valera moved steadily in the direction of the goal he and his party had always set for themselves: independence for an Ireland which would include the whole island, and in which northern Ireland would be incorporated as an integral part.

Independence and self-sufficiency should come first. Members of the Irish parliament were no longer required to take the oath of allegiance to the British king. Land-purchase annuities in the amount of about five million pounds per year, still made to the government by the purchasers, were withheld by it from the British creditors to whom they were due under the terms of the Free State agreement as amended.

The British government refused to countenance the unilateral repudiation either of the oath of allegiance or of the land-purchase payments and authorized the imposition of duties on imports from Ireland high enough to compensate for the annuities withheld. The duties proved to be so nearly prohibitive as almost to kill the trade, without raising half enough to balance the annuities. Ireland retaliated with a tariff on imports from Britain, and both countries suffered economically from the diminution of their trade. This unfortunate economic situation was partially corrected by new trade agreements in 1936 and 1938.

One by one, the remaining symbols of recognition of allegiance to the British crown were liquidated. In 1933 the Dail ceased to regard the assent of the crown as essential to legislation, and terminated the right of appeal from Irish courts to the British privy council. Irish citizenship was redefined as something distinct from British citizenship. In 1934 the prerogatives of the governor general as personal representative of the crown were further diminished when foreign diplomats were instructed to present their credentials to the president of the executive council rather than to him. The Free State government sent no official representative to the silver jubilee of King George V in 1935, or to his funeral in 1936 or the coronation of his second son George VI in 1937. It did not proclaim the accession of either Edward VIII or George VI. It assented, however, to the abdication of Edward in December, 1936.

Republic of Eire, 1937

A new constitution published in April, adopted by plebiscite July 1, and effective December 29, 1937, was in effect a new declaration of independence and a reassertion of Irish nationalism. The British Parliament was not asked to accept it. The Irish had made it "for themselves." It did not mention king, crown, or commonwealth of British nations, or acknowledge any further political connection with them. The new Irish republic gave itself the old Gaelic name of Eire.

In the name of territorial integrity the constitution claimed the whole island and its territorial waters as the rightful and ultimate national territory, but provided as a practical matter that, until the "unity of the country" should be "restored," the government would not attempt to exercise authority over northern Ireland.

The new constitution provided for a popularly elected president, chosen for a seven-year term and eligible for reëlection, but with only nominal authority. In the first presidential election, April 22, 1938, de Valera and Cosgrave agreed upon the nomination of an elderly Protestant nationalist, Douglas Hyde, a man widely known and respected for his character and scholarship, not famous "for the enemies he had made" in politics. There being no other nominations, Hyde was declared elected without the formality of an election.[12]

The basic law further provided for a bicameral legislature consisting of a Senate and a directly elected House of Deputies, and for a cabinet responsible to the House of Deputies. The cabinet was to be headed by a prime minister in whom all executive authority and responsibility were to be centered. As leader of the strongest party, although its deputies constituted only half the membership in the new house elected July 1, de Valera became prime minister.

Having gone so far toward achievement of his major objectives, and dealing (from May, 1937) with a placatory British prime minister, Neville Chamberlain, the Irish leader could afford to be less implacable than formerly on matters of secondary importance. By agreements signed April 25, 1938, the tariff war was terminated. In lieu of the suspended land payments, Ireland agreed to pay a lump sum of £10,000,000 and, as indemnity for damage done to British property in Ireland during the civil wars of the early twenties, annual installments of £250,000 for a period of forty-nine years.

By another agreement signed April 25, 1938, Great Britain appeased Eire in the matter of her territorial integrity by consenting to turn over to her before the end of that year the naval bases and harbor facilities which Britain had retained at Cóbh (Queenstown), Bere Haven, and Lough Swilly under Articles 6 and 7 of the Free State agreement of 1921. Winston Churchill sounded a warning that those bases would be needed if Britain should again become involved in a general European war such as even then seemed possibly to be im-

---

[12] In 1945 Dr. Hyde retired after seven years in office, and Seán T. O'Kelley, deputy prime minister and minister for finance, was elected from a field of three candidates to succeed him.

pending; but Chamberlain hoped for peace and gambled, in the event of war, upon the good will of Eire.[13]

When the war came, in 1939, Eire at once proclaimed its neutrality and stubbornly maintained it, being particularly solicitous, it sometimes seemed to the British and United States governments, not to offend Nazi Germany in any way. The British air and naval forces were unable to use the bases in question, although they were desperately in need of them. But Britain's worst fears—that Eire would be used as a German base for an air-borne invasion—were never realized. De Valera had stated in the Dail as early as May 29, 1935, that the Irish would never permit their territory to be used as a base for attack upon Britain. During the war he announced repeatedly that Eire would resist invasion from any quarter at any time. Some bombs fell on Dublin, but the country was spared the more extensive devastation which would presumably have been visited upon it if it had participated in the war either as an active belligerent or to the extent of permitting the armed forces of a belligerent to use its bases.

In November, 1939, de Valera protested against the application of the United States neutrality laws to Irish waters as to a war zone. When the United States had become a belligerent and established bases and staging and training areas in northern Ireland, he professed uneasiness about the presence of the troops there but was assured by President Roosevelt (February 26, 1942) that there was not and had not been "the slightest thought or intention of invading the territory of Ireland or of threatening the security of the Irish." To de Valera, northern Ireland was always an integral part of "the territory of Ireland." In a subsequent note to the United States government in March, 1944, rejecting its request that he exclude diplomatic and consular agents of the Axis powers from Eire on the ground that their presence there was endangering the lives of United States troops and the secrecy essential to the success of Allied operations, he referred to Irish neutrality as "the logical consequence of Irish history and of the forced partition of national territory."

North Ireland supported Britain in the war, and thousands of other Irish volunteers served in the British armed forces. The people of Eire were assured an insatiable market for such foodstuffs and other war materials as they could produce, but suffered some real hardships resulting from shortages of coal and other essential raw materials.

[13] Cóbh and Bere Haven are on the southern coast of Eire, the latter near the southwestern extremity of County Cork. Lough Swilly is on the far northwestern coast, west of Londonderry, beyond the boundary of Ulster or "North Ireland." All are well situated for protection of the Atlantic sea routes around Ireland to Britain.

More than fifty thousand Irish workers, many of them unemployed at home because of factory shutdowns due to shortages, found employment and made their contribution to an Allied victory as industrial workers in British war industries.

EMPIRE

Newfoundland

The general twentieth-century trend among the many peoples of the British Empire was toward nationhood and control by each of its own affairs. Newfoundland was an exception.

Newfoundland was one of the older British colonies in the Western Hemisphere, France having ceded her claims to it, as to the Hudson Bay region and Nova Scotia, by the Treaty of Utrecht in 1713. It was less easily tied in with the mainland provinces than Nova Scotia, however, after the completion of the conquest of Canada in 1763, and continued as a separate colonial community. As early as 1832 it had its own elected legislature. When the Dominion of Canada was formed in 1867, Newfoundland chose not to be included. In 1914 it still stood alone, and sent its own contingent to fight as part of the British Expeditionary Forces on the battlefields of France.

Politically, in the Versailles period, Newfoundland enjoyed dominion status much like that of Canada. The first years of peace were a time of great expectations in which it was optimistically assumed that the high prices and extraordinary prosperity of the war years would continue. Newfoundland's claim to Labrador was judicially confirmed in 1927, and the timber and mineral resources of Labrador were valuable assets. Roads, railways, and other public works were expanded at extravagant expense in anticipation of great waves of immigration and of tourist trade which never came and of a continuing business boom which did not materialize.

Instead, the annual export of salt cod, which had amounted to nearly $26,000,000 in 1918-1919, had dropped by 1931-1932 to little more than $5,000,000. A comparable decline in the export of pickled herring occurred, and the bulk herring trade shrank by 1931-1932 to little more than a fifteenth of its 1915-1916 volume. Falling prices caused the value of the island's exports to decline faster than their volume. The iron mines had to reduce production far below capacity. Only the paper mills held up. The government's budget could not be balanced. The annual deficit averaged $2,000,000, and the national debt increased from $43,000,000 in 1920, to $100,000,-000 in 1933.

Savings amounting to $5,000,000 were effected in 1932 by drastic reductions in salaries and pensions, public services, and the number of public service employees, by discontinuing the operation of branch railway lines which were not paying the cost of operation, and by cutting in half the government's contribution to the support of education; but government income had also declined, and unemployment led to new demands for government relief. The budget was not balanced, and Canada and Great Britain had to advance the $3,100,000 needed to meet obligations payable July 1, 1933.

As a last resort, Newfoundland asked Great Britain for advice and further help, and on February 16, 1934, by action of its own legislature, subsequently approved by the British Parliament, gave up its dominion status and went into a sort of receivership. The operation of the existing dominion government was suspended in favor of a commission consisting of a governor and six commissioners, three each from Newfoundland and Great Britain, appointed by and responsible to the imperial government. Some further economy was effected by refunding the public debt under imperial guarantee; but after thirteen years of government by commission Newfoundland was not yet in a position to restore self-government by elected legislature and executive council.[14]

India

India contributed materially, in fighting men, money, and services, to the British effort in the Four Years' War. In India, as elsewhere, the spirit of nationalism was stimulated by the war. The idea of self-determination appealed to Indian nationalists as to others, and high hopes were raised that dominion status would be attained as soon as the war was over, and membership in the proposed new league of nations as soon as such an organization should be formed. These hopes were encouraged by the inclusion of some Indians in imperial councils during the war.

To the most thoroughgoing Indian nationalist the simple proposition that the British should "quit India" at once was self-evident. The only questions he recognized as debatable were as to the mechanics of withdrawal and the establishment of a new national government, which he knew would not be easy but was sure would not be

[14] Paul Knaplund, *op. cit.*, 643-647.

found too difficult if Indians who wanted it were free to undertake it without further British tutelage or interference. To an equally convinced and uncompromising imperialist, India was an asset vital to the empire, an outpost which could not be abandoned, a responsibility which could not be abdicated. Mohandas Gandhi was an Indian nationalist, Winston Churchill an imperialist.

To no one but a protagonist of one side or the other, or a hasty or uninformed observer predisposed to be easily convinced one way or the other, was the "Indian problem" simple. The teeming populace of that vast subcontinent did not constitute a nation. It was not homogeneous. India was a land of many peoples, of the greatest inequalities and glaring contrasts. Peoples of what had once been different nationalities still differed widely in their folkways and languages or dialects. No other language was so generally understood as English.

The Hindu majority was divided horizontally by the caste system, the Brahmans being the highest of many castes and the so-called "untouchables" unclassified, lower than the lowest caste. There were about forty million unprivileged people in these "depressed classes" at the bottom of the social scale, sharing their poverty with other millions not so handicapped by the caste system but unfortunate in other ways. Legal and educational reforms were doing something toward providing equality of opportunity for the people of the depressed classes, and certain able, persistent, and lucky persons were demonstrating that it was possible for individuals to forge ahead against the odds; but many millions of Indians were still exploited by other Indians in many ways.

The peoples of India were divided also along religious lines, the most numerous and self-assertive religious minority being the Moslems or Mohammedans.[15] When especially offended by British policies elsewhere—as they were in the early twenties by Britain's support of Greece against Turkey in Thrace and Asia Minor, by the deposition of the Turkish caliph, the religious head of Islam, and by Lord Balfour's declaration in favor of Zionist aspirations for a Jewish national home in Palestine, which the Moslem Arabs would not welcome —they occasionally lent the support of their political organization, the Moslem League, to the Hindu National Congress party in opposition to British rule. When confronted with any real prospect—im-

[15] The principal Indian religions and the numbers of their followers according to the census of 1931 were: Hindu, 239,195,140; Mohammedan, 77,677,545; Buddhist, 12,786,806; Sikh, 4,335,771; Jain, 1,252,105; Christian, 6,296,763; Parsee, 109,-752; and Animist 8,280,347.

mediate or remote—of finding themselves governed no longer in common with but by a dominant Hindu majority, they expressed more apprehension about their own minority rights than enthusiasm for all-Indian nationalism. Similarly, many of the people of the depressed classes were not sure that the British—if they stayed—would not be more likely to grant them equality of political opportunity, or the right to form political organizations of their own to secure equality of opportunity, than a dominant higher-caste Hindu majority would be.

Liberal opinion in Britain was friendly to the idea of self-determination for the peoples of India, and unwilling to see them held within the empire against their will. The habit of holding what one has, however, is not easily broken. For nearly two centuries "India" had been one of Britain's greatest national-imperial enterprises. Investment, as well as profits, had been considerable. Millions of pounds and the lives of thousands of devoted missionaries, civil servants, and conscientious administrators had been invested there.

The license and uncontrolled exploitation of the early days of the East India Company were long gone; but the Indians were less ready than the British to forget them. British trade with India was being carried on by 1920 upon a fairly equal and mutually advantageous basis, but advocates of Indian self-sufficiency called that trade exploitation of India by Britain. Payment of interest on British capital invested in India was described as draining away the lifeblood of the Indian people.

However reluctantly, Britons had to recognize that the old colonial enterprise in India was either bankrupt or in serious danger of bankruptcy; but they would liquidate it gradually and by orderly process if possible. If the old imperialism was dead in India, they would prefer to see all its heirs come into their inheritance, each into his own, without violence or bloodshed, without the awakening of new hatreds or the reawakening of old ones. The consciousness of an obligation to those elements of the Indian population which had worked with them most cordially, or had learned to depend most heavily upon them, also contributed something to the British feeling of reluctance to abandon those "loyal" groups to the tender mercies of Indian nationalists who might treat them as traitors to their own people, or who might at best discriminate against those suspected of having sympathized with the outsiders.

British opinion was not altogether unfriendly to the national aspirations of the peoples of India, nor were the British very much surprised to find India following the trend toward nationhood which was already so evident in the dominions. Indeed, even Indian resentment of continued political tutelage could be viewed with a certain equanimity as a natural consequence of British teaching and example. From whom but the British had the Indians got these ideas about nationalism and self-government, and the political training and experience which made them so confident that they were ready to handle their own affairs?

The question was not whether India should move toward a greater degree of self-government, dominion status, or independence, but only when, how, and how fast. To the more impatient Indian nationalists it was axiomatic that Britain would make concessions grudgingly, as slowly as possible, and only when compelled to do so—a charge which was probably not altogether unfounded, in a situation not without precedent. To the British it was a matter of constitutional safeguards of the rights and liberties of the Moslem minority, the depressed classes, British investments and business interests —and the native princes who had coöperated with the British. All these considerations tended to complicate still further the already difficult task of making the constitutional changes required for any move toward dominion status.

Dominion status presupposed the formation of some sort of national government, unitary or federal. More than two-fifths of the area and nearly one-fourth of the population of India—more than eighty millions—were not included in British India but were in hundreds of "native states," ruled by native princes. The exact relationship of these princes to the imperial government varied greatly, as did the size, character, and general importance of their states. Generally speaking, they had to recognize the imperial government as the paramount power in India. They might not make alliances or war, either with one another or with foreign powers. Otherwise, they were free to manage their own affairs as allies of British India. As the paramount power, the imperial government reserved the right to intervene in the internal administration of a native state notoriously guilty of misgovernment, but only in such circumstances. The right was rarely exercised. Although some of the native governments were arbitrary and unenlightened, others were comparatively enlightened despotisms. Some of the largest and best governed were Baroda, Mysore, Hyderabad, and Travancore. The native states varied as greatly in size and importance as in character. Some were insignificant. The rulers of the richer states were, in several instances, among the world's wealthiest men; and their conspicuously wasteful spending appeared in ugly contrast against the drab background of the poverty of most of their people.

No all-inclusive national Indian government could be formed without the native states. Should they be absorbed and lose their identity entirely? Could their rulers be expected to surrender voluntarily such wealth and power? If not, how should they be liquidated and their lands nationalized? Or as an alternative, could they be somehow left intact and federated with British India? Those questions went unanswered in 1919 because the princes of the native states resisted change, the imperial government, which had dealt with them as they were for many years, could not well coerce them, and the other Indians could not effectively combine against them. The relation of the native states to the new Indian government or governments which would take the place of the British administration upon its withdrawal was still an unsolved problem in 1947 when the British government reiterated its intention to withdraw.

The extremely unequal distribution of wealth, glaringly exemplified in the contrasts between opulence and penury in many of the native states, was a problem common to all India—to the growing industrial areas in the great cities, to the trading centers and the seaports, but especially to the agricultural areas. A very high percentage of the people were tillers of the soil, or were directly dependent upon those who labored on the land. Millions of small farmers worked land which they did not own, or of which they were only nominal owners, burdened with debt which they could not pay, at rentals or at interest rates which kept them perpetually obligated to the moneylenders. Poverty prohibited the purchase of better agricultural machinery, while ignorance and poverty retarded the application of commercial fertilizers or the adoption of more scientific agricultural methods.

Irrigation and flood control were equally essential, and the need for them was realized; but existing governments had not had the authority or the means to do more than a small fraction of what needed to be done. The population directly dependent upon the land had increased greatly and was increasing, while the fertility of the soil had not been maintained or its productivity stepped up to keep pace with the demand upon it for food, for mere subsistence. The danger of famine was ever present, and famine often stalked the land. Millions of people were always underfed and ill nourished. The whole land economy of India needed to be revolutionized, as its agriculture needed to be modernized. Between 1919 and 1939 some progress was made in both directions—but very little, measured by the need of it.

Much of the appeal of nationalism in the 1920's and the 1940's was in its demand for a government capable of giving India a new land-ownership and land-use economy and a modern agricultural and industrial system which could feed its people.

The reforms made or conceded by the British administration in the period between the wars were largely political in character, and most of them affected British India only. Communal strife (between Moslem and Hindu "communities" or groups of people in any area, not usually strife between areas) and understandable concern for the interests of the princes who had been Britain's friendly allies in India, and of the depressed classes who were in certain ways her protégés, were ever present obstacles to the immediate recall of the referee. (Or, as Indian nationalists put it, ever ready excuses for refusal to recall him.)

Outbreaks of violence such as, twenty-five years later, may have hurried the British in their decision to "quit India" had the effect in 1918 or 1919 only of convincing them that then was no proper time to quit. In 1917 and 1918 a new secretary of state for India, Mr. Edwin Montagu, and a new viceroy, Lord Chelmsford, conducted a long series of inquiries with a view to the revision of the status of India. Mr. Montagu went into that investigation with an opinion already formed and publicly stated in Parliament that Indians ought to be included in all branches of the Indian government, but that the change must be made gradually and that the British government must continue to be the judge as to the pace at which it was expedient to make it. The Montagu-Chelmsford *Joint Report on Indian Constitutional Reforms*, 1918, was made the basis of the new Government of India Act of 1919.

The act of 1919 provided for greater Indian participation in government on the principles of decentralization and diarchy. The powers of the provincial legislative councils were increased. Not less than 70 percent of their members were to be chosen by a limited electorate, with safeguards guaranteeing communal representation for each religious community numerous enough in the province to warrant it. Toward decentralization, more of the functions of government than formerly were to be performed by the provincial governments.

Diarchy was the division of powers, within the provincial government, into two categories, those transferred to native provincial control and those reserved for the representative of the imperial authority. Public health, education, agriculture, and public works administration were transferred. In handling them the governor was advised by a ministry responsible to the legislative council. Irrigation, the collection of land revenue, police power, and the administration of justice were reserved. In those fields the governor's advisers were not politically responsible to the legislative council, although half of them were to be Indians. By declaring a state of emergency, the governor could assume extraordinary authority as representative of the crown, and could intervene in almost any matter—a power which in practice was very rarely exercised but which aroused resentment when it was used. In several instances, the Indians in the provincial governments were reluctant to put diarchy into effect, even on a temporary or experimental basis, unless the British governors would first agree never to use their emergency powers, a promise which the governors were not free to give.

Indians were offered a smaller share in the central imperial government. Real authority was vested as before in the British Parliament, to which the governor general and his executive council were responsible. The powers of the governor general were not diminished by the act of 1919, and the Indian Legislative Assembly and Council of State, elected by a closely restricted electorate, could not, in any real test of strength, control him. The Legislative Assembly opened at Delhi on February 9, 1921, was therefore not a real parliament analogous to the "mother of parliaments" at Westminster, and its members were aware and (many of them) resentful of that fact.

The establishment of the new regime in India under the act of 1919 was not inaccurately described by King George V as a promising beginning, opening the way for India to the same freedom and the same degree of self-government as were already enjoyed by the dominions; but it was only a beginning. India wanted more, and Indian nationalist leaders of the Congress party did not want to wait.

Some approach to equality of status with the dominions seemed to have been conceded, as India continued to be represented as an equal at imperial conferences and was made a member of the League of Nations as if she were a sovereign state. She was unsuccessful at the imperial conferences, however, in her attempts to secure the repeal of legislation by Canada and the Union of South Africa discriminating against immigrants from India and residents of Indian origin.

The most influential Indian leader of the period, already identified both with the nationalist cause and with the struggle for equal rights for Indians in South Africa, was Mohandas Gandhi. Gandhi had always been politically-minded, conscious of his kinship with his own people, and determined to do what he could toward the improvement of their condition. He had been educated first in India, then in the English law in London. During twenty years' residence in South Africa he had distinguished himself as an attorney for the Indians there, attempting to free them from the legal restrictions imposed upon them. As the Boer states were less generous in their treatment of the Indians than the British, Gandhi sided with the British in the Boer War. He supported Britain again in the Four Years' War against Germany. After that, disappointed, disillusioned, and dissatisfied with the meager concessions made by the government act of 1919, he fought the British—in his peculiar but effective fashion.

Gandhi knew his followers and he knew his opposition. So he soon made of himself precisely the type of opposition leader by whom the British would be most likely to be baffled. His watchword was non-coöperation. There had never been more than a handful of the British in India. They performed no manual labor. Let the Indians then cease to labor for them and they would soon leave—or starve. While Englishmen in India had been permitted to depend upon Indians for personal services, Indians had permitted themselves to become dependent upon British goods, gadgets, and professional services. Let Indians spin their own cotton, by hand if necessary, become self-sufficient and self-reliant, and they would find that they could manage better without the British than the British could manage without them. If the Indians would simply refuse—all of them—to go on running India for the British or under British tutelage, they would soon be in a position to run it for themselves.

It was a very plausible platform. Gandhi was personally a pacifist, preaching only passive resistance. His voice was always and only the voice of a dove, but to the exasperated authorities his tongue was often that of a serpent; for violence, which he invariably disowned and decried, seemed to them often to have been the inevitable consequence of his teachings. Yet how could they appropriately discipline so harmless an individual? He was almost a saint. Several terms in prison made a martyr of him. He could go on a hunger strike in prison—or at liberty—and let them be censured by the world for starving him or for driving him to self-starvation. By fasting, prayer, and asceticism —all cleverly publicized by his devoted followers, a remarkably efficient bureau of public relations—he seemed to have become something of a mystic, to have lifted himself or to have been lifted above the mundane things of this world, beyond the reach of temporal punishment. He captured the imaginations of millions of the Indian people and, combining boldness of concept and of speech with meekness of behavior, kept alive in them the hope that, if they were sufficiently consistent and persistent, the meek might yet somehow inherit the earth.

India had millions of the lowly, but they were not always meek. Strikes and disorders in 1918, while the Montagu-Chelmsford report was being studied and the government act of 1919 was being prepared in Parliament, were the subject of the Rowlatt committee report on sedition in India and led to a series of repressive acts of 1919 (pending the passage and application of the government act) suspending jury trial, curtailing the right of appeal, and restricting freedom of assembly and of utterance. Outbreaks in violation of the Rowlatt acts were numerous, and some outrages were committed in the name of their enforcement.

At Amritsar in the Punjab on April 10, 1919, four Europeans were killed by a mob, and a lady missionary, Miss Sherwood, was brutally beaten. Three days later, an illegal mass meeting was broken up by Indian troops under British command. For ten minutes they fired into a close-packed crowd. Nearly four hundred people were killed and about twelve hundred wounded. For a week, April 19 to 26, Indians passing the place where Miss Sherwood had been hurt were made to crawl through the street. The ferocity displayed on both sides, and the quick resort to terrorism, indicated both fear and hatred. General Dyer, the military commander responsible for the conduct of the troops at Amritsar, had been responsible also for the protection of Europeans and the suppression of disorder. He was recalled to England and disciplined for abuse of his authority and excessive (therefore unnecessary and unjustified) use of force; but the policy of ruthless intimidation found defenders among his military and political superiors. Indians thought him inadequately punished, resenting his humiliating police regulations perhaps even more than his use of gunfire. The incident further poisoned the already unpleasant atmosphere in which the reforms proposed by the government act of 1919 had to be attempted.

In 1919 also, while Parliament was still at work on the government act passed later in that year, the government in India was embarrassed by a spreading boycott of British goods and by a campaign of civil disobedience, both incited by Gandhi. Fierce fighting featured a new outbreak of communal strife in August, 1921. The rebellion was suppressed, but the military authorities did not behave much better than at Amritsar. Serious strikes and riots for the special edification of the Prince of Wales when he visited India in 1921 culminated in the murder of twenty-one police officers in 1922 and the imprisonment of Gandhi, who had publicly deplored the murders but was thought to have been at least indirectly responsible for them.

In prison or at large, Gandhi was always the *mahatma*, the great one, to his followers; but during his incarceration the leadership of the National Congress (which was not a national legislative body but the principal political organization of the *Swaraj* or home-rule party) was assumed by Pandits Motilal and Jawaharlal Nehru and C. R. Das. These leaders, less pacifistic and less patient than Gandhi, began by 1927 more and more urgently to demand immediate independence for India, while the mahatma would have been temporarily content with dominion status, as a first step involving less danger of civil war and retaining the advantages of continued association with the British Empire and with the commonwealth then in process of formation.

In 1927 and 1928 a commission headed by Sir John Simon was at work in India, making the new study of conditions there which the government act of 1919 had stipulated should be made within ten years. As usual, it was soon demonstrated to the investigators that not all was well in India. Indians were invited to work with the statutory commission but resented the fact that they had not been made members of it, and generally boycotted it. The vehemence with which the British were being told to "quit India" at once, and the disorders which had died down somewhat during the five years just past but at once broke out again, brought the conscientious and conciliatory Lord Irwin (later Lord Halifax, viceroy since 1926) to the point of returning to London for conference and publishing there an official statement that "the natural issue of India's constitutional progress" was the attainment of dominion status. Others in Britain, however, such as Lord Birkenhead, a former secretary of state for India, unequal to Lord Irwin in forbearance, demanded editorially that the Indians should first make an acceptable and workable constitution for themselves and demonstrate some capacity for orderly self-government before demanding that the British leave. In 1929 an All-Indian National Congress, in which Moslems as well as Hindus were represented, but not the native states, demanded dominion status and drafted a constitution; but it was never given a practical test in operation. The two-volume report of the Simon commission, completed in 1929 and published in 1930, revealed the obstacles in the way of the immediate grant of dominion status as well as the arguments in its favor, and did not recommend it. Instead, it recommended the strengthening of the authority of the viceroy and the gov-

ernors of the provinces and referred to the provincial governments as
training schools in which Indian political leaders might gain some
useful experience. Such condescension was offensive to the proud—
in some cases caste-proud—intellectuals in the forefront of the Indian
nationalist movement.

Unsatisfied by the viceroy's recommendation that dominion status
be recognized as a goal soon to be attained, Gandhi demanded in
something like an ultimatum in March, 1930, that it be attained immediately. When his demand was rejected, he renewed his civil disobedience campaign in characteristically spectacular fashion by making a public and well-publicized pilgrimage to the seashore at Dandi
to make some salt from sea water in token violation of the government salt monopoly and excise law. The authorities prudently refrained at first from again arresting the mahatma, but the disaffection
spread rapidly and widely and led to further violence, so he was interned at Poona from May, 1930, to January, 1931.

Meanwhile, at the suggestion of the viceroy, the first of three
sessions of a round-table conference was held in London. All of the
principal Indian parties and group interests were invited to send
spokesmen, but the Congress party refused to send delegates to either
the first session or the third. None too conciliatory but less intransigent
than some of his fellow nationalists, Gandhi, by agreement with the
viceroy Lord Irwin, in March, 1931, called a truce in the civil disobedience campaign and in the autumn of that year attended the
second session of the conference, which met in London September 7
to December 1. During the next year, however, disorders in India
again led to repressive measures, and Gandhi resumed his advocacy
of civil disobedience and was again imprisoned. The third session of
the round-table conference met in November and December, 1932.
Having found no way out of its Indian dilemma by asking the mutually
antagonistic Indian groups for a solution, it reluctantly reverted to
the older policy of trying to find a solution of its own.

The conference therefore summed up its findings and those of its
investigating committees in a white paper published in March, 1933.
Its recommendations were embodied in the new Government of India
Act of 1935. This act provided for a federal union of the provinces of
British India and the native states, provided that the princes of the
latter would join it voluntarily. The eleven largely self-governing
provinces of British India, called governors' provinces, and six chief
commissioners' provinces to be administered by representatives of the
governor general, were less free to choose. They had either to co-

operate or to refuse and let goverment go on as best it could in the face of their opposition. In the first elections, in 1937, Congress party candidates were in the majority in six of the eleven new provincial legislatures. Although not satisfied with the new government or happy in their relations with it, they decided for the moment not to boycott it. The princes of the native states held aloof, so no real all-Indian federation was effected; but such provisions of the act of 1935 as were recognized as applicable to British India only were declared effective April 1, 1937.

The act of 1935, effective 1937, required no changes in the internal administrations of the native states. It provided for the separation from India of Aden and Burma—which was displeasing to imperial-minded Indian natiqnalists.

Provincial government was to be made more democratic by the extension of the franchise, which, however, was still limited by a comparatively high property qualification. Most of the members of the provincial legislative assemblies were to be elected, and provincial ministries were to be responsible to the legislatures. At the federal level diarchy was proposed. There was to be a bicameral parliament without full parliamentary powers, consisting of a Legislative Assembly and a Council of State. So far as British India was concerned, members of the Assembly were to be indirectly elected on the basis of communal representation, through the provincial legislatures. Most members of the Council were to be elected; a few were to be appointed by the governor general. If the princes had brought the native states into the federation, they would have been represented to the extent of approximately two-fifths of the membership of the Council and one-third of the Assembly, by deputies selected as they saw fit. The powers of the two houses were approximately equal, except that money bills were to originate in the Assembly.

Such reforms, though real, were not what Indian nationalists had wanted and, especially after the round-table conference, expected. This was not dominion status, and neither dominion status nor independence was mentioned in the act of 1935.

Disappointment and protests centered around the reserved powers of the federal government, the position of the governor general, and the emergency powers of the governors of the provinces. The offices of the governor general and viceroy could have been held separately, but both were held by the three successive viceroys, Lord Linlithgow (1935-1943), Field Marshal Viscount Wavell (1943-1947), and the king's second cousin, Rear Admiral Viscount Louis Mountbatten (from March 24, 1947).[16] As head of the federal government, the governor general was powerful as a prime minister is powerful, without a prime minister's usual political responsibility. The viceroy was the personal representative of the crown. Whether held by one man or by two, the offices of viceroy and governor general were supremely important, and their powers were not diminished by the act of 1935-1937. The federal government retained control of foreign policy and defense; and governor general and provincial governors alike retained emergency powers which, if successfully invoked, would have enabled them to override their respective legislatures in matters of religion, communal strife, minorities, treatment of foreigners, or "emergency" use of funds. Their power to define "emergencies" was not as strictly circumscribed as the Indian nationalists would have liked to have it.

Congress party leaders tried but failed to make their coöperation with the government in the provinces of British India dependent upon pledges by the governors not to use their overriding powers. The viceroy pointed out that no such pledge could constitutionally be given, but authorized an agreement that the emergency powers would not be used unnecessarily or without consultation. They were subsequently used in several provinces to prevent the unconditional release of political prisoners.

During the period of two and one-half years just preceding the outbreak of the Six Years' War in 1939, more Indians were constitutionally governed by Indians than ever before. New schools and universities at home made Indians less dependent upon foreign—which before 1914 had usually meant British—universities for their higher training. With a larger pool of trained native personnel to draw upon, the factories, trading enterprises, press, hospitals, and government services used more native artisans, specialists, and professional men and fewer Europeans or foreign-trained Indians. Army officers were being trained in Indian cadet schools, and Indian officers outnumbered European officers in the army two to one. Gandhi was speaking out against "untouchability" and advocating better opportunities for all of the depressed classes, although he opposed the formation of a separate communal electorate or political organization for them.

With natives participating in it to a greater extent than formerly, government showed an active interest in the improvement of living conditions throughout the country. Great irrigation projects were pushed forward—one of the world's largest in the Punjab—and

[16] Lord Linlithgow had been chairman of the committee which drafted the act of 1935.

agricultural production was increased, although not fast enough to keep pace with the increase in population.[17]

Industrialization and urbanization were drawing some workers into the cities, often into terribly congested, squalid slums; but more than 80 percent of the people still lived off the land. Birth rate and death rate, especially the mortality among infants and young mothers, were very high. Modern science had added several years to statistical life expectancy, which had been only twenty-three years in 1920 and in 1930 only twenty-six and one-half. In public sanitation and public health measures, popular education, general standard of living, and modernization of its agriculture and its ways of living, most of India was many years behind the United States, Great Britain, and much of western Europe. These unfavorable comparisons could easily be made, and were made and keenly felt, by well-informed Indian intellectuals, to whom patience and humility soon ceased to seem like virtues when they found themselves retarded in their efforts to modernize their country.

The four oldest and most stubborn obstacles to unity and national status still stood in the way: (1) the ignorance, illiteracy, poverty, and alternating docility and discontent of the long-suffering peasantry and the urban proletariat, turning occasionally to xenophobia and violence;[18] (2) communal strife and caste prejudices; (3) the particularism of the princes and the undemocratic political and economic structure of the native states; (4) British reluctance to risk the conquest of India by another power by permitting the paralysis and division or civil war which her leaders feared would follow her withdrawal if she withdrew before national unity was achieved.

Britain had erected none of these barriers except possibly the last, which need not have continued to be a barrier if the others had been removed. Had the British deliberately maintained and perpetuated the first three, making themselves seem essential, as a pretext for staying there? Many an ardent young Indian convinced himself or was convinced, and tried to convince others, that they had. Most American observers naturally and generously sympathized with the Indian peoples in their struggle toward a better life, and in their assumption that national unity and independence were logical and necessary steps in

[17] The population of India in 1947 was estimated by the New York *Times*, June 8, 1947, at 414,000,000: 260,000,000 Hindus, 90,000,000 Moslems, and 64,000,-000 others.

[18] In 1944 it was estimated that only 15 percent of the people could read or write, and that the average per capita annual income was equivalent to less than twenty dollars.

that direction. Enemies of Great Britain, on the other hand, with less good will or sincerity, made plausible but unprincipled propaganda out of implications, and sometimes out of charges, that Britain had always been responsible for all that was wrong in India, had not merely failed to correct unfavorable conditions there but created them and maliciously prevented their correction. Such innuendoes and such charges were more easily made than proved, but often more easily believed than proved false. So many of them went unchallenged, survived by repetition, and gained wide circulation.

More people lived in India, and many of them lived better, in the twentieth century than in the nineteenth or the eighteenth. Would such progress have been made, or greater progress, if the British had not been there? Had the British, as some trained observers said, carried more liberty to India than they had taken from it, and developed more wealth there than they had drawn away? Had such social, economic, and political progress as had been made been due in any part to British influence, or had it been made despite the presence of the British? The answers an inquiring reporter in British India might have received to questions such as these in 1939 would probably have varied with the age, nationality, and personal circumstances of the persons questioned. Quite apart from contradictory interpretations of the history of British-Indian relations, however, there seems to have been a steadily growing body of opinion in India that India owed Britain nothing and that Britain owed India her independence.

British spokesmen said repeatedly that Britain was ready to withdraw whenever she was certain that obstacles (1) to (3) (above), inclusive, had been removed, and when she knew that she had no further need to be uneasy on point (4) (above). Would those obstacles ever be removed unless the British first withdrew? Must Indians themselves determine, by civil war if necessary, the character of their own national government, or find out at the cost of failure and great sacrifice of life that they could not make a nation of themselves? Many an enthusiastic or embittered young Indian would have said that, at whatever cost, Indians must assume full control of their own affairs and make their own successes or pay the price of their own failures. No one knew what the price would be, but everyone knew that it might prove to be appalling and that the poor would have to pay it. Was life so cheap and liberty so dear—such liberty as India did not already have? If liberty could be won only at the price of national disunity and possible fragmentation, could it bring prosperity and peace?

India was one of the United Nations in the war against the Axis powers, 1939-1945; but it was a decree of the imperial government, no surge of popular feeling or spontaneous resolution of a national legislature, which made her one. It was soon apparent that, as Gandhi said, nothing like general Indian support of the war effort would be forthcoming without a clear and unequivocal statement of British intentions with respect to India. Ultimate independence or dominion status had already been repeatedly announced as Britain's clear intention; so it was immediate independence which was thus peremptorily demanded. To those responsible for the defense of the whole empire, the granting of immediate independence seemed tantamount to abandoning the defense of India—less seriously threatened in 1939 than three years later, but never to be prudently neglected—and to depriving the imperial forces of whatever support a loyal and well-ordered India might have given them. So the imperial authorities tried to postpone all major constitutional changes for the duration of the war, and meanwhile to retain control of the defense of India. The Indian Congress governments in those provinces in which the Congress party was in the majority in the legislative assemblies thereupon resigned, and government had to be carried on by executive authority by the governor general and provincial governors. There was some volunteering for the Indian regiments, some war production, and some voluntary support of the war effort; but relatively few of the Indian people had their hearts in it or thought of it as their war.

Pearl Harbor and the attack on Hong Kong made it India's war in the sense that Indian regiments shared with other British troops the humiliating experience of defeat and surrender at Hong Kong, in Malaya, and at Singapore, and the horrendous retreat from Burma to northeastern India. Burma was lost in March, 1942. For months thereafter refugees, including the American General Stilwell and the remnants of the Chinese force he commanded, straggled across the Burma-India frontier. British naval facilities on Ceylon were bombed, Madagascar seemed in danger of being used by the Japanese as a submarine base to cut the long British-American supply line around Africa, and naval and air supremacy in the Indian Ocean hung in the balance. It was not then apparent that Japan had already overreached herself, or clear that she would not soon invade India.

Enemy agents had long been busy in India promulgating the nebulous idea of "Asia for the Asiatics." Calling India, Malaya, and the Netherlands Indies capitalist-imperialist countries, and representing communism as the antithesis of capitalist imperialism, the Japanese encouraged communism in those areas to weaken the existing governments and economic structures while offering the inhabitants a share in a new "co-prosperity sphere" under Japanese leadership and protection. Experience would soon show Japanese occupation to be something less idyllic than what had been pictured by propaganda. India was fortunately spared that experience; but, never having had it, some of her more radical leaders saw in Japan only an available force to be used at their convenience to free India from Britain, and in the current crisis only an opportunity to win India's independence. They did not necessarily love Japan more; they only loved Britain less.[19]

With the enemy at her gates, India was divided and made no self-coördinated effort to defend herself. Too many of her people, knowing little or nothing of world affairs or the grand strategy of the war and conscious chiefly of their own wretchedness, for which the agitators told them Britain was to blame, gave more thought to the European alien within than to the alien Asiatic then threatening the country from without.

In an attempt to secure more active Indian coöperation in the war effort, the British government sent Sir Stafford Cripps to India in 1942 with new proposals. These were that after the war a new constitution should be made by an elected constituent assembly, and that in the meantime a provisional interim government should be formed in which internal order, police, war finance, railways, procurement of supplies (including munitions) for the armed forces, labor, and propaganda should be subject entirely to Indian control. More Indians, including an Indian minister of defense, would have been taken into the governor general's cabinet. Virtually the whole internal administration of the country would have been Indian. But it was not independence. The supreme commander of all the armed forces was still to be the British commander in chief, who in his conduct of the

[19] Notably Subdar Chandra Bose, who had been president of the Congress party in 1938-1939 but had lost the presidency because of his communist views, his opposition to the war, and his intransigence on the matter of immediate independence. During the war Bose was reported to be working for the Germans in Berlin, then with the Japanese in Malaya and Burma, where they called him head of a "Free India" movement under Japanese sponsorship. He was reported by the Japanese to have been killed in an airplane crash on Formosa August 19, 1944.

On May 26, 1942, Great Britain made a twenty-year military alliance with Soviet Russia. On July 22 the Indian government lifted its legal ban on communism.

defense of India was to be subject to no political control but by the viceroy.[20]

The Cripps proposals were rejected by both Hindus and Moslems. A. K. M. Azad, a Mohammedan theologian then president of the All-Indian National Congress, the political organization of the Hindu majority nationalists, called the offer inadequate. He wanted independence. Soldier and civilian, he said, must feel that they were fighting for their country's freedom under national leadership. To the Moslems represented by the Moslem League, on the other hand, home rule for India meant Hindu majority rule; so too many concessions seemed to have been made by the British to the Congress party. India, said Jinnah, was not one nation but two, and the price of Moslem coöperation must be the establishment of a separate Moslem state or states in predominantly Moslem areas.

To the British authorities, the Cripps proposals seemed certainly to have gone quite far enough for wartime, if not in fact too far. Gandhi was still one of the most influential men in India. He was an uncompromising pacifist. Although the working committee of the Congress party stated on August 5 that India, if independent, would be one of the United Nations, no one had forgotten that on May 2 the same body had adopted a resolution in favor of nonviolent non-coöperation as a form of passive resistance to a Japanese invasion. So it seemed probable that Gandhi's influence would be sufficient in the event of an invasion to deliver India helpless into the hands of the Japanese either by trying his favorite tactic of passive resistance to the invader or by civil disobedience to a government which tried to fight. His statement that he would rather be shot than submit to or coöperate with Japan or any other power was not sufficiently reassuring to the military authorities, already familiar as they were with civil disobedience as a means of embarrassing a government but skeptical of the efficacy of passive resistance as a device for stopping an invader. The Japanese would probably have asked for nothing better than to be met with only passive resistance, and would have found effective ways of dealing with civil disobedience. The British commander in chief retained command of the armed forces for India, and Sir Stafford Cripps returned to England, his mission generally judged a failure.

By a vote of 250 to 13 the working committee of the Congress

[20] The commander in chief from July 1, 1941, to June 18, 1943, was Field Marshal Sir Archibald Wavell. When Wavell became viceroy and governor general in June, 1943, General Sir Claude Auchinlech returned as commander in chief. Both officers had seen many years' service in India. General Auchinlech had been commander in chief from December, 1940, to July 1, 1941.

party on August 8, 1942, authorized Gandhi to lead a campaign of passive resistance and civil disobedience against the existing government. Gandhi, Nehru, and other Congress party leaders were at once imprisoned. Hundreds of persons were killed and thousands wounded in the rioting which followed. Order was restored by use of force, but strikes, sabotage, political opposition, and occasional outbursts of violence interfered with the war effort throughout the war.

The war years brought prosperity to certain parts of India, especially to her industries, and reversed her debtor-creditor relation with Great Britain so that when the war ended she was financially the creditor. The same years, however, brought natural catastrophes and famine. In October, 1942, part of the rice-growing district of southwestern Bengal was swept by a hurricane and tidal wave which killed eleven thousand people and three-fourths of the cattle of the district of Midnapur. Standing crops and stored grain were destroyed, and fields were salted with sea water. Rice production in eastern Bengal was reduced in 1942 and 1943 by an outbreak of rice disease. Both of these disasters occurred at a time when grain reserves had already been depleted by the export of food for Indian troops on active service and when it had become impossible because of the war to import rice from Burma.

The last half of the year 1943 was a period of famine in Bengal. In the late summer and early autumn it was estimated that more than a thousand persons per day died of starvation in Calcutta alone, many of them refugees who had crowded into the capital from stricken country districts. A stronger provincial government or an authoritarian national government with unlimited powers might have done more, or have done more quickly whatever could be done, to prevent hoarding, to commandeer food in other areas which had more, and to distribute equitably whatever was available. The military authorities, led by General Auchinlech and the new viceroy and governor general, Lord Wavell, did what they could. It was difficult to reach remote rural districts because bridges had been destroyed to impede the Japanese when an invasion had seemed imminent, and had not yet been replaced; but more than five thousand free kitchens were set up and, at the peak, two million persons were fed daily by public relief agencies.

Both northwestern and northeastern India saw something of the United States expeditionary forces, as great air bases were established at Karachi (in Sind), and in Bengal and Assam.[21] India was both

[21] See discussion on the China-Burma-India theater, pp. 772- 774.

recipient and contributor of lend-lease aid. More on British or Chinese account than Indian, lend-lease goods to the amount of $2,123,609,-000 were shipped from the United States to India and Ceylon before the end of 1945. Reverse lend-lease from India to the United States, principally in the form of facilities, supplies, and services rendered, amounted by September 2, 1945, to $608,500,000.[22]

In 1942 and 1943, while British and Indian troops held the India-Burma border and the United States Tenth Air Force built up bases from which to bomb Japanese installations in Burma and fly supplies over the "hump" of the Himalayas to China, American General Stilwell labored at the dual task of training and equipping a new army consisting largely of Chinese soldiers, and of opening up the Ledo (Stilwell) Road to by-pass southern Burma and reopen the old Burma Road to China. Also in 1943, British Major Charles Wingate and his "Chindits" pioneered a new kind of warfare, raiding enemy depots and communications deep into Burma in "impenetrable" jungle country, maintaining their own contacts meanwhile by radio and plane, and subsisting on supplies dropped to them from the air.

In February and March, 1944, the Japanese invaded India, aiming first at Chittagong on the coast, Imphal, capital of Manipur, and Dimapur on the Bengal-Assam (Calcutta to Ledo) railway. The Japanese radio announced the beginning of a march on New Delhi. The move may have been seriously intended only as a tactical offensive to parry the anticipated Allied thrust into Burma; but if it had attained its first objectives General Stilwell would have been cut off and the Brahmaputra River valley would have offered it an invasion route down into Bengal above Calcutta. Fortunately for India, it did not attain those objectives. The British Fourteenth Army checked it, then by mid-August drove the last invader out of India. In this fighting on the frontier at least four Indian divisions (the 5th, 7th, 17th, and 23rd) figured prominently and creditably, as they and others did in the 1945 campaign in Burma, in which more than half of the million troops engaged were Indians.[23]

In 1944 and 1945 the war rolled away from India across Burma. By 1945 the total strength of the Indian armed forces had increased with-

---

[22] *Twenty-Second Report of the President of the United States to Congress on Lend-Lease Operations* (Washington, June, 1946), 29, 20. The Indian estimate of this item was $516,713,000. (Government of India Information Services release No. 4/188, May 2, 1946.)

[23] On December 12, 1944, Leopold S. Amery, secretary of state for India and Burma, announced in the House of Commons that it was the intention of the British government to help Burma to dominion status as soon as possible after the war.

out national conscription to between two and two and a half million
men, of whom approximately 375,000 had been furnished by the
native princes' states. The 4th, 8th, and 10th Indian divisions
fought bravely and well in North Africa and Italy, the 5th in Ethiopia
and Burma. Three others guarded the oil supply in Iraq and the
supply routes to Russia, from Karachi and through Iran. A million
men of the Indian armed forces were on active service in southeastern
Asia or overseas when the war ended. These were all subject to the
supreme British and Allied command, and the cost of their maintenance and operations was borne by the British government. Half
of the cost of expansion of war industry plants in India was borne by
Britain with no expectation of repayment or transfer of ownership. The
whole cost of mechanization of the Indian army was borne by Britain,
three-fourths as a gift, one-fourth as a long-term loan. With Britain
always paying more than half of all war costs incurred, the whole
cost of the war in India paid by India was estimated at more than
four and less than five billion dollars. Indian casualties were estimated at 179,935: 24,338 killed, 64,354 wounded, 11,754 missing,
and 79,489 made prisoners of war.[24]

Politically the Indian situation did not improve. Beginning February 10, 1943, Gandhi was permitted to undergo a self-imposed
fast of twenty-one days in protest against his internment (since August
9, 1942) in the palace of the Aga Khan at Poona. He finished
the fast without suffering any apparently serious physical ill effects and
without accomplishing anything politically, but on May 5 a year later
(1944) was discharged on grounds of health. When India had been
cleared of Japanese troops he offered to support the war if India were
given immediate independence. The viceroy rejected his request for an
interview.

Wavell would not see Gandhi to discuss Indian independence in
August, 1944, he said, because there was yet no genuine agreement
among Indian communities. One of the right-wing moderate leaders
of the Congress party, its former president Chakravarti Rajagopa-
lacharia, had all along advocated acceptance of the Cripps proposals
and had tried repeatedly to bring Congress party and Moslem League
leaders together to form a national government to win the war first,
leaving the question of Pakistan (the proposed separate Moslem state
or states, to the establishment of which he was personally opposed)
to be answered later. But Jinnah would permit his Moslem League

[24] Government of India Information Services, releases 281, 3085, 3128, and letter
to author June 23, 1947.

followers to participate in an interim government only if he were assured beyond all peradventure, in advance, that Pakistan would be established immediately after the war.

At a series of conferences with party leaders at Simla, June 25 to July 14, 1945, the viceroy proposed on behalf of the imperial government that he form an interim national government in which all communities should be represented by choosing his ministers from a list to be submitted to him by the Indian parties, and that that government hold an election of a constituent assembly to make a constitution for an independent or autonomous India. But Jinnah, demanding equal representation for Moslems although they were outnumbered by Hindus almost three to one and by non-Moslems four to one, would not agree with the Congress party leaders on a common list of acceptable ministers. He insisted upon the exclusive right to nominate all Moslem ministers although not all of India's Moslems were members of his league. On that point the viceroy would not give up his prerogative. His Simla proposals were accepted by the Congress party leaders, including Nehru and Gandhi, rejected by Jinnah.

On September 19, 1945, Prime Minister Attlee and the viceroy simultaneously proposed by radio that an executive council representative of all Indian parties be set up and a constituent assembly elected. In January, 1946, the viceroy announced that he was determined to carry through that program. In February Jinnah threatened revolt by Moslems if a single constituent assembly for all India were set up, and within two days after the publication of his threat thirty-six persons had been killed and nearly four hundred injured in Moslem *vs.* Hindu rioting.

In March, 1946, a new British cabinet mission headed by the new secretary of state for India, Lord Pethwick-Lawrence, and including Sir Stafford Cripps and A. V. Alexander, first lord of the admiralty, arrived in New Delhi "to help India work out her own solution." The problem was no longer independence or dominion status but Pakistan —the splitting or "vivisection" of India. To this the Congress party leaders would not agree, and Jinnah would agree to nothing else. So another series of round-table conferences (April 27 and 28, May 5, 6, and 12) ended in failure.

In a white paper read to the House of Commons May 16, 1946, the prime minister rejected Pakistan "for the present." He announced the government's intention to form a new executive council by selection from nomination lists submitted by the Indian parties, and to hold an election of a constituent assembly. The Congress party accepted the proposal and in the elections of July 25 won 201 of the 210 seats allocated to general constituencies. The Moslem League, although it had won 73 of the 78 seats allocated to Moslem constituencies, soon denied the authority of the assembly to make a constitution for Moslem India, threatened revolt, and proclaimed a "direct action day." Ninety persons were reported killed and nine hundred injured in Calcutta on August 16. The death toll in that city during August was estimated at more than 3500, and property damage at more than a million pounds. By November 4 the estimates for India had risen beyond five thousand killed and thirteen thousand casualties.

In recognition of their special position and despite their disparity in numbers, the Moslems were offered five of the fourteen places on the new executive council named August 24; but those places had to be filled by Mohammedans who were not members of the Moslem League, because the league refused to name the men to fill them. Seven of the fourteen council members were members of the Congress party chosen from its list of nominees. Nehru became vice-president of the council, and three weeks later resigned the presidency of his party. On October 25 the Moslem League entered the interim government after all, being given the five places on the executive council which had originally been offered it. One of its first five representatives there was an "untouchable."

The constituent assembly met December 9, 1946, to adopt rules of procedure. The princes of the native states were not represented, but their spokesmen indicated that they would coöperate with the new government. The Moslem League refused to send delegates. Communal rioting broke out in Bombay. The All-India Scheduled Castes Federation was reported to have decided to seek United Nations intervention in behalf of the eighty million "untouchables" whom it claimed it represented. In January, 1947, the constituent assembly unanimously adopted Nehru's statement of its purpose: the creation of an independent sovereign republic. On February 20 Prime Minister Attlee announced that it was the intention of His Majesty's government to turn over all political power in India to Indians by June, 1948. At the same time the appointment of Lord Louis Mountbatten to succeed Viscount Wavell as viceroy was announced. He took office March 24.

The new viceroy was not unfamiliar with India. He had commanded the armed forces in the Burma theater in 1944 and 1945. He made no secret of his opinion that the breaking up of India was to be deplored; but a quick study of the situation and a series of conferences with Indian leaders apparently convinced him that partition was preferable to coercion, and that federal union without coercion was unattainable. On June 3 he and the British prime minister announced simultaneously over the New Delhi radio and in the House of Commons that Britain was ready to offer India dominion status in 1947 and let the peoples of India decide then for themselves between union and partition, and in 1948 between independence and continued association with Great Britain. If an independent Pakistan should be established, its constitution would be written by its own constituent assembly. Within twelve days the offer had been accepted, first by the Moslem League and then by the All-Indian Congress party.

It was generally assumed at the time that Pakistan, if established, would consist of two widely separated states, in northwestern and northeastern India, separated by many miles of Hindu-controlled territory. Jinnah's earlier suggestion of a corridor across northern India to connect them was generally dismissed as impractical. Western Pakistan, it was assumed, would include Sind and most of Punjab; but Punjab would probably have to be divided. The eastern segment of Pakistan would be the eastern part of Bengal and possibly part of Assam. Hindu-majority districts of northeastern Punjab and southwestern Bengal, including Calcutta, would presumably go to what might be called Hindustan. As a way of determining the division of Punjab and Bengal provinces, the British suggestion of June 3 was that the Indian members of the legislative assembly of each of those provinces should meet in two bodies, composed respectively of representatives of predominantly Moslem and predominantly Hindu districts. If a majority of either group voted for partition, partition should take place, the boundary line between sections to be determined by a boundary commission appointed by the governor general in consultation with party leaders.[25] It was thought that some of the northwest frontier provinces and possibly part of Baluchistan might also join Pakistan, giving it an area of approximately 300,000 square miles and 70,000,000 people. It would be well supplied with wheat in Punjab and rice and jute (but not jute mills) in Bengal, but would have at first comparatively few industries and only Karachi as its major seaport. Whether eastern Pakistan could still use Calcutta as a seaport as freely as eastern Bengal had done was one of the many problems to be solved.

The predominantly Hindu Dominion of India would include seven complete provinces and the Hindu portions of Punjab, Bengal, and Assam—about 575,000 square miles and 230,000,000 people. It

[25] On June 23 the Punjab legislature voted for division.

would have most of the industries and great cities such as Bombay, Madras, Calcutta, and New Delhi.

The communal minorities problem had not been solved. There would still be a Hindu minority in every Moslem state, a Moslem minority in every Hindu state, and other minorities in all states. Hindu-Moslem rioting continued in the provinces most likely to be divided. If the armed forces were divided on communal lines, a proportionately large portion of them would go to Pakistan, as proportionately more Moslems than Hindus had previously gone into military service; but whether Pakistan could defend the northwest frontier better as an independent state than as a part of greater India had not yet been demonstrated. Thoughtful observers feared that the dissevered parts of India would be only too well armed against one another and not well enough against any strong invader.

There remained also 562 native princes' states, scattered in all parts of India. Their total area was about 712,000 square miles, and their combined populations amounted to about 100,000,000 people. Some of their rulers indicated that they would join Pakistan if Pakistan were made independent. Others would join Hindu India. Others, including Hyderabad and Travancore, proposed to remain independent—as the Congress party officially declared that they had no right to do. Nehru went so far in mid-June as to say for his party that it would not recognize the independence of any state in India, and would regard as an unfriendly act any recognition of the independence of any such state by any foreign power. How the Congress party's declaration of Nehru's statement could affect existing relations between Britain and the Indian princes was less clear than the Congress party's stand on the matter. The viceroy and the prime minister indicated that Britain would give provisional dominion status to either Pakistan or Hindu India if partition should be decided upon, but then made no such offer to any of the princes' states. Britain would continue to be the paramount power among them until her withdrawal. Then responsibility for India would at last be put—perhaps thrust—into the hands of the Indians. Britain officially refused, as of June 3, 1947, to try any longer either to hold India in the commonwealth or to push her out of it—or to hold herself responsible for conditions there. On July 4, 1947, Prime Minister Attlee introduced for its first reading in the British House of Commons a bill which became law with the royal assent July 18, to set up dominion governments in Hindu India and in Pakistan by August 15, 1947. Each dominion so created would make its own laws. No act of the British Parliament would be law in either unless accepted by it. The crown would be represented in each by a governor general, who might or might not serve at the same time as governor general of the other.

Meanwhile, under interim government, an India not yet partitioned acted as a sovereign nation in international affairs. It had already announced that it would pay the first installment on its shares of the capital stock of the International Bank for Reconstruction and Development, ratified the convention on international civil aviation signed at Chicago December 7, 1944, and in December, 1946, sent Asaf Ali, a Moslem member of the Congress party, as its first ambassador to the United States.

On August 14 and 15 respectively, 1947, two new dominion governments were established. Lord Louis Mountbatten, ceasing to be viceroy, remained as governor general of the Dominion of India and was made an earl. Jawaharlal Nehru was the first premier of that dominion. Mohammed Ali Jinnah, already functioning as president of the constituent assembly of Pakistan, was appointed governor general of the dominion he had so long striven to set up and to separate from the rest of India. The secretary of the Moslem League, Liaquat Ali Khan, was Pakistan's first premier. Sir Claude Auchinlech, commander in chief of the armed forces, continued to serve both dominions in that capacity until he could divide the forces between them. Boundaries between the dominions were drawn by the British chairman of the boundary commissions when Hindu and Moslem members of the commissions failed to come to an agreement. Sir Patrick Spens was named arbiter of the constitutional questions which it was foreseen would almost inevitably arise in the process of separation. Both governments proclaimed freedom of religious belief, association, and worship, and complete equality in rights and privileges; but Gandhi announced that, although he accepted the new settlement, he could not join in the rejoicing over the winning of independence because he was grieving over the division of his beloved India and over the violence then still raging between Moslem, Sikh, and Hindu. On January 30, 1948, Gandhi was shot by a Brahman fanatic. The horror occasioned by his murder shocked leaders and people into a renewed and more earnest effort at peaceful separation and reconciliation.

At the end of 1948 both Pakistan and the new India were self-governing members of the British Commonwealth of Nations, otherwise independent of each other and members of the United Nations. Each had absorbed the territories of the native princes' states within its area—not without difficulty. A quarrel between the two over Kashmir had to be referred to the Security Council of the United Nations, and India used troops to coerce Hyderabad. The princes were permitted to retain their titles, dignities, and personal estates but were required to surrender to the union control of defense, external affairs, and communications, and to establish politically responsible government. Untouchability was abolished by the new constitution. The last British governor general of India, Lord Louis Mountbatten, relinquished his office in June, 1948. Prime Minister Nehru was Gandhi's successor as India's most outstanding leader. Until his death, September 11, 1948, Jinnah was governor general of Pakistan. His successor was Khwaja Nazimuddin, formerly premier of eastern Pakistan.

Egypt

It was by no mere coincidence that Napoleon said he would strike at Britain in Egypt, or that his fleet was destroyed by Admiral Nelson at Alexandria. Britain was much preoccupied, then and thereafter, with the maintenance of all possible routes to India. Her interest in the Red Sea route, to which Napoleon had referred, was intensified by the construction of the Suez Canal, which reduced the length of the unbroken sea voyage from England to India from more than eleven thousand miles (around Africa) to not much more than six thousand, and which was obviously destined to become the principal highway for British-Indian trade. In 1875 Disraeli, then prime minister, bought for the British government from the bankrupt khedive of Egypt the khedive's shares (about 45 percent) of the stock of the company operating the canal. In 1882, to protect that investment, the route to India, and other imperial interests, the British set up in Egypt what soon grew into something closely resembling a protectorate. But so as to avoid complications with Turkey, which had not abandoned its claim to suzerainty over Egypt although unable since 1811 to enforce it, the ever practical British government did not publicly call its protectorate a protectorate until December, 1914, when it was already at war with Turkey and no further diplomatic damage, therefore, was to be done. Then it deposed the khedive and called his successor (Prince Hussein Kamel) sultan of Egypt, thus advertising the extinction of Turkey's claim.

Egypt was valuable to the British Empire in the Four Years' War because of its location. Armed camps along both banks of the Suez

Canal kept that great channel open throughout the war, although it was once threatened by the Turks. Troops from Australia, New Zealand, and India used Egypt as a staging area on their way to Gallipoli, Salonika, and other fronts, and Allenby's campaign for Palestine was based on Egypt. The fleet made good use of its base at Alexandria. Conscripted Egyptian labor and supplies procured by requisition were direct contributions, made with little evidence of enthusiasm. An anti-British nationalist movement gained strength during the war, and when the war ended, the nationalists demanded that Egypt be recognized by the peace conference as an independent national state and made a member of the League of Nations. These demands met determined British opposition and were rejected. The nationalist leader, Saad Zaghlul Pasha, was arrested and sent to Malta.

The Egyptian nationalists were still uncoöperative when in 1920 a British commission headed by Lord Milner visited the country to investigate and report. Troops were needed to keep order while the investigation was being made. The commission recommended the termination of the protectorate and the granting of independence, subject to certain reservations as to the protection of Egypt and of the Suez Canal, and as to the Sudan, where the Egyptian nationalists were eager to substitute Egyptian supremacy for the old system of joint control. Egypt would be expected, also, to make a treaty of alliance with Britain. This would set up what one British spokesman called a sort of "British Monroe Doctrine" for Egypt.

The Milner proposal was accepted by the British government in 1922 but was rejected by the Egyptian nationalists. A new constitution for Egypt embodying the fundamentals of Milner's recommendations was thereupon promulgated by unilateral act of the British government. Egypt was called independent, and its sultan (Ahmed Fuad, who had succeeded Hussein Kamel in 1917) was called King Fuad I.

Martial law was discontinued, but the nationalists resented the presence of British troops for the defense of Egypt and the canal. Feeling ran high in 1924 when Sir Lee Stack, the British commander of the defense forces and governor general of the Sudan, was murdered in Cairo. The British government took sharp punitive measures, and Zaghlul Pasha, the nationalist leader who had returned from political exile and had become premier under the new constitution, with which he was still dissatisfied, had to resign. Before resigning, Zaghlul paid the $2,500,000 indemnity which the British government demanded. His successor agreed also to British control of the protection of foreigners and foreign interests in Egypt, and to the withdrawal of more water from the Nile for irrigation purposes in the Sudan, to the disadvantage of competing cotton interests in Egypt.

Any government acceptable to the British was unpopular. A new constitution was promulgated in 1930 and abrogated in 1934 by King Fuad's rather autocratic government, and the old one of 1923 was restored only under popular pressure, December 12, 1935. Fuad died in April, 1936, and was succeeded by his son Farouk.

The treaty of alliance which the British had sought did not materialize until August 26, 1936, when the Italian conquest of Ethiopia had given both Britain and Egypt new reason to reconcile their differences and look to their defenses. By the terms of the treaty, Britain was to have the right to maintain a naval base at Alexandria, to use Egyptian air bases, and to garrison the canal zone but not the rest of Egypt. The defense of Egypt was to be the joint responsibility of the armed forces of both countries, and the Sudan was to be jointly administered, with troops of both nations participating. On these conditions Britain agreed to use her influence to secure the abolition of the capitulations under which foreigners had been granted extraterritorial privileges in Egypt, and to recommend Egypt's admission to the League of Nations.

Through the good offices of Britain, as promised, a convention was signed at Montreux May 8, 1937, by Egypt and the capitulatory powers, which recognized the authority of the Egyptian government over foreigners and foreign-owned property in Egypt. The convention was to go into effect October 15, 1937, but to be gradually applied over a period of twelve years as consular courts were abolished and their functions taken over by mixed or purely Egyptian courts. On British initiative a special meeting of the Assembly of the League of Nations was summoned May 26, 1937, at which Egypt was unanimously elected a member of the League.

During the Six Years' War beginning in 1939 the Egyptian government declared itself neutral. King Farouk was believed by the British to be profascist in his sympathies; so Britain supported the nationalists in opposition to him. Egypt took no active part in her own defense; but her territory, which had been valuable to the British as a base and staging area in 1914-1918, was invaluable from 1939 to 1945. The Suez Canal was kept open to traffic to and from India whenever the Mediterranean was open. From Egypt the British and imperial forces moved westward to the conquest of Libya and Cyrenaica. In Egypt when driven back they re-formed and were reëquipped, again to push westward across Italian North Africa, eventually to join hands with the Americans and Free French in Tunisia. In Egypt the airfields, bases, and depots were established which protected Palestine, facilitated the delivery of lend-lease war materials, and denied the Axis powers access to the oil of Iraq or more than temporary use of Syrian airfields.

After the war Britain indicated an intention to withdraw. The ultimate economic effects of the political withdrawal from India were yet to be revealed, but there seemed to have been a certain shifting of interest from the Suez Canal to the pipelines from the Iraq oil fields across Palestine to the Mediterranean at Haifa and Acre, and from the sea route through the Mediterranean and the Red Sea to the air routes across Syria, Palestine, and Arabia. Anti-British political leaders with visions of a league of Near Eastern Moslem states would in any event have insisted upon the removal of all remnants and reminders of the old protectorate.

British troops began the evacuation of the Cairo citadel May 20, 1946, and on July 4 turned it over to Egyptian troops who on August 9 hoisted the Egyptian flag over it to mark the end of the occupation. By November 27, 1946, the British evacuation of the naval base at Alexandria was completed. The liquidation of the condominium over the Sudan was more difficult and would take longer.

On March 22, 1945, upon initiative of Egypt and of the Mufti Haj Amin el Husseini, who was then in Cairo as a political refugee from Palestine, the League of Arab States for which the mufti had so long used all his influence was formed. Its founding members were Egypt, Iraq, Syria, Lebanon, Saudi Arabia, Yemen, and Trans-Jordan, all signatories of the Alexandria protocol of October 7, 1944, which had proposed it. As stated in the pact, the aim of the league was "to strengthen the close relations and numerous ties which link the Arab states" and "to support and stabilize these ties upon a basis of respect for the independence and sovereignty of these states and to direct their efforts toward the common good of all the Arab countries."[26]

Palestine

Syria, Lebanon, Mesopotamia, Arabia, and Palestine were in 1914 parts of the Turkish Empire. Point XII of President Wilson's Four-

[26] The founders of the league did not conceal the fact that they were thinking of Palestine as an Arab country. The door was pointedly left open for other Arab states to join as they attained their independence, Palestine being specifically indicated in an appendix to the pact. See section on Palestine.

teen Points gave it as his opinion that, although the Turkish portions
of that empire should not be subjected to any alien sovereignty, the
other nationalities then under Turkish rule should be assured "an
undoubted security of life and an absolutely unmolested opportunity
of autonomous development." The Allies were in entire agreement as
to their intention to deprive Turkey of the non-Turkish portions of her
empire, but had planned to retain control of the areas they liberated
from her. The mandates system was the result of a necessary compromise.[27]

In a letter to Lord Rothschild November 2, 1917, while General
Allenby's British and imperial forces were moving up on Jerusalem,
the British secretary of state for foreign affairs, Arthur James Balfour,
made the somewhat self-contradictory statement of policy concerning
Palestine which came subsequently to be known as the Balfour Declaration.[28]

His Majesty's government, said Mr. Balfour, viewed with favor
the establishment in Palestine of a national home for the Jewish people
and would use their best endeavors to facilitate the achievement of
that object. It was to be understood that nothing should be done which
might prejudice the civil and religious rights of existing non-Jewish
communities in Palestine, or the rights and political status enjoyed by
the Jews in any other country.

In 1922 the League of Nations assigned Palestine to Great Britain
as a Class A mandate, accepting and confirming the Balfour Declaration. Recognizing the ambiguity of Britain's position as mandatory
power, and anticipating the difficulty of reconciling Jewish and Arab
nationalisms in Palestine, Mr. Winston Churchill, then secretary of
state for the colonies, attempted in June, 1922, to clarify the situation
by interpretation of the Balfour Declaration. That statement of policy,
he said, had never contemplated, and the British government did not
contemplate, the conversion of all Palestine into a Jewish national
home, or the disappearance or subordination of the Arabs, their language, or their culture, but only the establishment of a Jewish national
home in Palestine by the further development of the existing Jewish

[27] Syria and Lebanon were mandated to France and did not gain their independence until after the Six Years' War. The Arabian states had revolted during the
Four Years' War and fought the Turks as allies of the British, so made good their
independence at the end of that war. For Mesopotamia see Iraq, below.

[28] Arthur James Balfour succeeded Lord Grey as secretary of state for foreign
affairs in December, 1916, and held that office until the dissolution of the wartime
coalition of British political parties in 1922. It was he who headed the British Foreign
Office delegation at the Paris peace conference and at the Washington conference on
naval limitation in 1921. He was made an earl in May, 1922.

community there. Mr. Churchill did not emphasize in that statement, but would not be one to forget, that Britain's imperial interest in the land bridge from the Mediterranean to the Persian Gulf, and in the airfields and pipe-line terminals of Palestine, was a continuing third-party interest there which could not be forgotten or neglected while Britain was a world power. Nor could government be indifferent to the interests or sentiments of the Christians there, to whom (as to both Jews and Moslems) Jerusalem was a holy place.[29]

Classification as a Class A mandate implied that the country should be largely self-governing from the beginning, should be expected soon to be ready for independence, and should be granted independence when ready. Self-government, however, because it presupposed coöperation of mutually hostile Arab and Jewish populations, proved impractical from the beginning. Upon recommendation of the first British high commissioner, Sir Herbert Samuel, a constitution was promulgated September 1, 1922, providing for government by the high commissioner, an appointed executive council, and a legislative council of twenty-two members, ten of whose members were to be appointed by the high commissioner and twelve (eight Moslems, two Jews, and two Christians) to be elected. But the Arabs, resenting what they considered the intrusion of the Jews, refused to participate in elections or in government if Jews were permitted also to participate.

Meanwhile Jewish immigrants poured in. It has been estimated that there were less than 60,000 Jews in Palestine in 1919, 83,000 in 1922, 160,000 in 1929, more than 200,000 in 1933, 400,000 by 1937, 463,535 (roughly one-third of the total population) in 1940. Four-fifths of the increase was due to immigration, which reached peaks of 33,801 persons in 1925 and 61,458 (net, excess of immigrants over 396 emigrants) in 1935, besides whatever illegal entries were effected. Tel-Aviv, a new Jewish seaport near Jaffa, claimed 46,000 inhabitants in 1931, 60,000 in 1933, 125,000 in 1937, 140,000 in 1940. By virtue of a high birth rate, the Arab population also increased during the same period, but less rapidly than the Jewish.

Many of the Jewish immigrants of the 1920's were refugees from Poland and Rumania, where their people had been persecuted. They carried little money with them but were aided financially by the World Zionist Organization and the Jewish Agency for Palestine, and a Jewish Foundation Fund. Unwelcome as they were in Palestine, they held

[29] In 1922 the number of Christian Arabs was estimated at 73,000. The census of 1940 gave the whole number of Christians as 120,587.

together in tight little communities on a mutual-help, more or less com-
munistic basis. Their Jewish Foundation Fund forbade the employment of Arab labor on land it leased to colonists, and their General
Federation of Jewish Labor preferred the importation of more Jewish
laborers to the employment of landless Arabs. An urban industrial and
commercial civilization new and foreign to agrarian Palestine was
developing in the bustling Jewish towns; but what alarmed the Arabs
most was the rate at which the Jews, subsidized by Jews of other countries, were buying land. With great energy, the unquenchable optimism
of a long-suffering, all-enduring people, and the incessant industry of
those who work to live, the Jews held on tenaciously wherever they
took hold. In competition with the Arabs on the land, they had the
advantages of capital, science in agriculture, and community cohesion.
They were more aggressive, more industrious, and more successful.
By 1930 the Arabs were complaining bitterly that, of the limited
acreage of arable land in Palestine, 250,000 acres had been bought
up by the Jews, while the number of landless Arabs had increased.

In October, 1930, a British commission of investigation, Sir John
Hope Simpson chairman, reported that the Arabs in Palestine were
hostile to the Jews because they were apprehensive about their own
economic and political future. Upon recommendation of the Simpson
commission, the British government temporarily suspended immigration, a step bitterly resented by the Jews.

Somewhat conciliated and reassured by the Simpson report, the
Arabs were more willing than previously to coöperate in the election
of a legislative council. No election was then held, however, because
the Jews, although they were then outnumbered by the Arabs roughly
four to one, demanded that any council to be elected should include
as many Jews as Arabs.

The 1930 ban on immigration was only temporary, and after 1933
the stream of refugees was swollen by fugitives from European countries in which Nazi-fascist governments were established and anti-
Semitism was unleashed or aroused. The conditions which had caused
the anti-Jewish Arab outbreak of 1929 were aggravated. In November, 1935, the Arabs demanded that democratic government be
established (in which they would have constituted an overwhelming
majority), that no more Jewish immigrants be admitted until someone
determined how many the country could absorb, and that no more
land transfers from Arab to Jewish owners be permitted. To push these
demands an Arab "Higher Committee" of ten members was formed
under the presidency of Haj Amin el Husseini, the mufti of Jerusalem,

religious leader of the Moslems, largest landowner in Palestine and the country's leading politician. Two members of the committee were Christians. Nationalism and land hunger were more provocative of discord than religious differences.[30]

A royal British commission of which Lord William Robert W. Peel was chairman was sent to Palestine in November, 1936, to investigate and report on conditions there. Its report was published July 7, 1937. Its findings were that the claims of Jews and Arabs concerning Palestine were irreconcilable and the existing British mandate unworkable. With cabinet approval, it recommended, therefore, the partitioning of Palestine into a Jewish maritime state and an Arab state inland, both to become independent upon the termination of the mandate in so far as it had applied to them, and a diminished mandated area in the zone of special interest to the Christians, to include Jerusalem, Bethlehem, and a corridor to the sea at Jaffa. Britain would also have continued to accept some responsibility for the Christian shrines in Nazareth and for coastal towns with mixed populations, such as Haifa and Acre.

Neither Arabs nor Jews would accept the Peel proposals, but the more violent opposition was voiced by the Arabs. The Jews wanted a larger portion of the land. The Arabs opposed partition on any terms. Some of the Arab leaders of the opposition were arrested. Mufti Haj Amin el Husseini, president of the Arab Higher Committee, fled to Lebanon but continued his opposition from there, advocating an unpartitioned Arab-dominated Palestine and an alliance with Moslem neighbor states. Hundreds of persons were killed and thousands wounded in disorders, largely of Arab origin, in 1938.

During 1938 a British commission was at work in Palestine, trying to determine boundaries for partition along the lines suggested by the Peel commission. It could find no boundaries which the parties would accept. Meanwhile neighboring Moslem states supported the Moslem Arabs of Palestine in their demand that the Balfour Declaration be abrogated and further Jewish immigration into Palestine prohibited.

[30] American reclamation experts have estimated that full development and utilization of natural resources such as the potentialities of the Jordan River and river valley would furnish enough water power for industrial purposes and the manufacture of fertilizers, and enough water for irrigation, to enable Palestine and Trans-Jordan to support four million more people than were living there in 1944. A $150,000,000 irrigation and hydroelectric development to be known as the Jordan Valley Authority was sponsored by the Zionists from May 20, 1944; but that economic development would have been the work of years, and might have aggravated the clash of nationalities instead of alleviating it. See Walter Clay Lowdermilk, *Palestine, Land of Promise* (New York, 1944), pp. 169, 227.

The Arab spokesmen were ready to promise the Jews in Palestine, in the area they then occupied, the enjoyment of full minority rights and complete cultural autonomy. The Jews rejected the proposal because it precluded the establishment of an independent Jewish state. Temporarily abandoning its partition plan, in a final futile effort to reconcile the claims of Jews and Arabs, the British government in 1939 proposed that for the next five years an average number of fifteen thousand Jewish immigrants per year be admitted, and that before the end of a ten-year period a new government be established in an independent Palestine, in which both Jews and Arabs should participate and under which the rights and interests of both, including Arab ownership of land in certain parts of Palestine, should be protected. Neither Jews nor Arabs accepted the proposal, but the restriction of Jewish immigration was announced as a policy without popular acceptance.

The outbreak of war in Europe in 1939 found Palestine torn with strife, neither self-governing nor capable of self-government on a democratic basis equitable at once to its majority and to its minorities. During the war there was less disorder, and some Jewish battalions were recruited to help the British fight the German and Italian tormentors of the European Jews; but some terrorism, usually disavowed by the Zionist organization and Jewish Agency for Palestine, was perpetrated from time to time by Jewish nationalist extremists. It was announced by the Cairo police November 8, 1944, for example, that two Jews had confessed that they had assassinated Lord Moyne, British minister of state resident in the Middle East, on orders from the "Stern gang."

Some Arabs also fought on the side of the British, but Mufti Haj Amin el Husseini was constantly active wherever anti-British sentiment could be aroused, in the interest of an independent Arab state of Palestine. In 1939 he was in Iraq, where with the financial and other assistance of Franz von Papen, German ambassador to Turkey, he helped engineer the Rashid Ali revolt of 1941. When that revolt failed he fled to Teheran, where he took refuge in the Japanese legation. Later he launched from Rome and Berlin an extensive program of anti-British propaganda and espionage. After the Nazi collapse he sought sanctuary in Switzerland, where he was denied it as a war criminal. Then he found refuge in France, whence he was permitted to escape by plane to Egypt, where he was protected by King Farouk. His return to the Middle East was bad news to British and Zionists alike, his simple slogan "Palestine for the Arabs" a constant and insuperable obstacle to any but an Arab solution of the problems of Palestine.

The end of the war of nations in Europe meant only an intensification of the war of nationalities in Palestine. Of the million or more Jews in Europe, between the western boundary of Russia and the Rhine, it was estimated that nearly a fifth were refugees, unwilling to return to homes from which they had been driven, or longing for an opportunity to escape from renewed persecution. Desperately they fought for admission as immigrants to Palestine, despite attempts by the British to limit immigration. Although dependent upon the British for protection against the Arab majority, they assailed them bitterly for restricting immigration in an attempt to placate the Arabs. As the mandatory power, Britain was at the same time being assailed with equal bitterness by the Arabs of Palestine, the latter vociferously supported by those of all neighboring Arab states, for its failure to stop all immigration immediately. The Arabs threatened war if an attempt were made to set up in Palestine an independent Jewish state. The claims of the contesting nationalities were as completely irreconcilable as ever, and the mandatory power was caught between them, unable to keep the peace. Both Jews and Arabs resorted to terrorism—against the occupying British troops, against one another, and each nationality against any of its own people accused of dealing with the other. The Arab League announced in December, 1945, that its seven member states would boycott, from January 1, 1947, all goods produced by Jews in Palestine.

After months of study of the problems of European Jews and of Palestine, a joint British and American committee published a report March 29, 1946. It recommended the immediate issuance of 100,000 immigration certificates to victims of Nazi and fascist persecution, those certificates to be used as far as possible in 1946. It suggested also the rescinding of existing restrictions on sale or lease of land to Jews and on use of land by them. As any attempt to establish at that time an independent state or states in Palestine seemed to the committee sure to lead to civil strife which might endanger the peace of the world, it recommended that the mandate be continued, with a strong federal government, pending the setting up of a trusteeship under the United Nations.

The recommendations of the Anglo-American committee were never put into practice. Jamal el Husseini, chairman of the Palestine Arab Higher Committee, threatened that the Arabs would resist them "to the last man." King Farouk of Egypt and King ibn-Saud of Saudi Arabia seemed to have been speaking for the whole Middle Eastern Arab world when they had said in January, 1946: "Palestine is an Arab country." The Zionists had proposed to the joint committee that a million more Jews be brought in within ten years to make it a Jewish country. The Jewish Agency subsequently countered with a proposal for the creation of "a viable Jewish state in control of its own immigration and economic policies in an adequate area of Palestine instead of the whole of Palestine." President Truman ventured the opinion that 100,000 immigrants ought to be admitted in 1946 but was in no position to offer to share responsibility for the consequences. Illegal immigration increased to flood proportions by midsummer (3800 in July, 1946), and on July 22 the military organization of the anti-British Jewish underground, *Irgun Zvai Leumi*, in retaliation against continued British efforts to restrict immigration, blew up the portion of the King David Hotel in Jerusalem which housed the British military headquarters and civil secretariat. Ninety-one persons were killed and forty-five injured. This was but one of many such outrages, more than a few of which were acknowledged, with threats of more to follow, by the clandestine *Irgun Zvai Leumi* radio. In the face of a refusal of consent by the Palestine Arab Higher Committee, a temporary immigration quota of 1500 Jews per month was set up (1600 permits to be issued, 1500 of them reserved for Jews). Illegal immigrants intercepted by the British navy were sent to concentration camps in Cyprus to wait their turn under that quota. They invariably resented being sent there and usually resisted.

September 9, 1946, a new conference on Palestine was opened in London, but both the Jewish Agency and the Arab Higher Committee of Palestine boycotted it. In December the twenty-second World Zionist Congress, meeting in Basel, disavowed the acts of violence still being perpetrated and belligerently acknowledged by the *Irgun Zavi Leumi* in Palestine, but reëmphasized its demand for the creation of a Jewish state. In January, 1947, the National Council of Palestine Jews adopted resolutions denouncing terrorism but refused to help the British enforce the law against the terrorists.

With the situation steadily deteriorating, Great Britain on April 2, 1947, formally requested that the General Assembly of the United Nations be convened in special session to consider Palestine. The Assembly met April 28. It was soon revealed that the five Arab states represented, with Egypt and Saudi Arabia in the forefront and Haj Amin el Husseini always in the background, were unanimously supporting the demands of the Palestinian Arabs for (1) the immediate establishment of an independent "democratic" (i.e., majority-ruled) Palestine while Arabs were still in the majority there by approximately 1,000,000 to 600,000 and (2) no more immigration, so that the ratio of Jews to Arabs in the population would not continue to increase by immigration. What the Jews wanted was protection against the Arab majority in Palestine, the removal of restrictions on land use, lease, and purchase by Jews, and unlimited immigration until Jews were in the majority there—then, but not until then, independence. At the instance of Great Britain and the United States, a new commission composed of men from several of the smaller noncolonial powers was sent out to study the problem of Palestine once more, in the name of the United Nations. As mandatory power, until May 15, 1948, Great Britain went on maintaining a police state there and trying to keep the peace. It was a burdensome and thankless task. On November 24, 1947, the United Nations recommended the partition of Palestine and the internationalization of Jerusalem.

Immediately upon termination of the British mandate, the Jewish National Council in Palestine proclaimed the establishment of the new state of Israel, which was recognized at once by the United States as the *de facto* government of Jewish Palestine, and on May 17 by Russia. David Ben-Gurion was made prime minister and minister of security, Moshe Shertok minister of foreign affairs, and the veteran Zionist leader Chaim Weizmann president. By the end of the year the new state had a functioning government, currency, and postal system, and had established diplomatic relations with other nations. Its relations with its immediate Arab neighbors, however, were still bad. The year 1948 was one of intermittent Arab-Jewish warfare, largely over boundaries. The League of Nations mediator, Count Folke Bernadotte, was shot by Jewish dissidents September 17, 1948. Count Bernadotte was replaced December 11 by a conciliation commission of three members with the American Ralph Bunche as chairman. Action on Israel's application for admission to the United Nations was postponed pending the establishment of peace and of recognized frontiers. By a vote of 37 to 12 on May 11, 1949, with the United States, Britain, and Russia voting for the motion and India, Pakistan, and the six Arab states against it, Israel became the fifty-ninth member of the United Nations.

Iraq

Iraq is a predominantly Arab state, with some Kurdish and other minorities. British troops, many but not all of them from India, campaigning throughout the Four Years' War in what was then known as

Mesopotamia, had wrested that region from the Turkish Empire by October, 1918, and at the war's end remained in military possession of it. The very considerable oil reserves of the Mosul and Persian Gulf areas enhanced its value. Britain was especially interested in it also because of its location athwart the overland route to India or to the Indian Ocean. In May, 1920, Great Britain announced its acceptance of a Class A mandate over the territory, subject to the authority of the League of Nations.

Iraq would have preferred immediate independence, and chose whenever possible to act toward Britain, as toward other countries, as if already independent. On July 11, 1921, its council of ministers named Feisal, a son of King Husein of Hejaz, king of Iraq. Feisal was crowned August 23, 1921. To define the relation of mandated territory to mandatory, in a fashion not altogether incompatible with the national pride of the people of the former, a twenty-year treaty of alliance was drawn up in 1922, to lapse when Iraq should become a member of the League of Nations; but before it was ratified in 1924 its term had been shortened to a period of four years after the ratification of peace with Turkey, which took place August 6, 1924. So, unless renewed, the alliance would have expired in 1928. The treaty of 1924 was accepted by the League of Nations in September, 1924, as a definition of the status of the mandate.

Also on August 6, 1924, Great Britain presented to the Council of the League, for settlement, Iraq's claims in a boundary dispute with Turkey over the Mosul oil region. Under the terms of the Treaty of Lausanne, 1923, that boundary was to have been drawn if possible by direct negotiation between Turkey and Great Britain. Failing that, it was to be referred to the Council of the League; and direct British-Turkish negotiations had failed. The Council accepted jurisdiction and invited Turkey to send a representative to participate in its discussion of the question.

The Turkish claim was based on previous possession and on the charge that two-thirds of the district or vilayet had been illegally occupied by British troops after the signing of the armistice of October, 1918. But Turkey hurt her case by perpetrating military raids in the disputed area while the League's investigation was in progress.

The League commission of investigation reported that, if Britain intended to withdraw in 1928 as her revised treaty with Iraq implied, the area might as well be awarded to Turkey. However, if Britain would accept responsibility as mandatory power for twenty-five years or until Iraq should become a member of the League of Nations, and would guarantee the rights of the Kurdish element of the population to hold office and to use its own language, the disputed area should be awarded to Iraq without plebiscite, so as to give the new state a more easily defensible frontier. Supported by an advisory opinion of the Permanent Court of International Justice, to the effect that it was empowered by the Treaty of Lausanne not merely to make a recommendation but to settle the dispute, the council awarded to Iraq approximately the area which had been occupied by British troops since 1918.

Neither disputant participated in the final Council vote. Turkey had, in fact, recalled her representative because he had no veto power, and had further prejudiced her case by renewed raiding in the disputed area. She eventually accepted the settlement, however, with some slight boundary line adjustments in her favor, in a three-power treaty with Britain and Iraq June 5, 1926, receiving in return the promise of 10 percent of the Iraq government's royalties on Mosul oil for a period of twenty-five years.

In January, 1926, Great Britain and Iraq redefined their mutual relations by negotiating a new treaty for a twenty-five-year term, or until Iraq should become a member of the League of Nations. In 1927, in a third bilateral agreement on the subject, Britain agreed that five years later, in 1932, she would support Iraq's application for membership in the League. Britain was to continue meanwhile to control and use military air bases in Iraq, to control the defense of the country, and to train and equip the new Iraq army; and her special diplomatic position was to be signalized by the precedence her ambassador should enjoy over all others.

In 1932 Iraq entered the League of Nations as an independent member state. In return for certain guarantees required by the mandates commission—of freedom for minorities and protection of the rights of foreigners—she was freed from the humiliating capitulations under which foreign powers had reserved the right to protect their own nationals there. Her military alliance with Britain was not abrogated.

The outbreak of the Six Years' War found Iraq being governed by a rather weak pro-British regency in the name of a boy king, Feisal II. With the fall of France, Nazi activity and influence in Syria increased, and doubts as to the British Empire's ability to defend itself emboldened certain pro-Axis elements in Iraq also. In 1941 revolt broke out, fomented by Haj Amin el Husseini (mufti of Jerusalem) and other

Palestinian Arab exiles, led by Rashid Ali el Gailani, and eventually supported by the formerly pro-British premier, Sharif Sharaf. The rebel government was recognized by the Axis powers and Russia (not yet one of the Allies), and the Vichy French administration in Syria did not prevent German planes from refueling there en route to Iraq. But British troops occupied Basra and Bagdad and successfully defended the air base of Habbaniya. A new government was set up under Jamil Midfai, which broke off relations with Germany, Italy, and Japan; so the Axis powers were denied the use of Iraq's oil and airfields, and access to the Persian Gulf. Rashid Ali, like Husseini, escaped to Iran and subsequently to Germany.

The new administration based its policy upon the hope of a United Nations victory, and served both the economic interest of Iraq and the strategic purposes of the United Nations by permitting the shipment of lend-lease supplies through Iraq to Russia. Iraq also received lend-lease supplies, and on January 16, 1943, declared war on the Axis powers. As a member of the League of Arab States, Iraq was always in the postwar years an active supporter of the Palestinian Arabs against the Zionists and in opposition to further Jewish immigration into Palestine.

FOREIGN POLICY

British foreign policy during the twenty-year truce from 1919 to 1939 had more than ever to be cut according to the cloth, being determined by events and circumstances more often than it could determine them. Britain was properly classified during that period as a "peace-loving" nation, not only because the British people sincerely preferred peace to war and desired tranquillity for its own sake, but because they needed quiet for recuperation. A satiated power in the sense that it did not then contemplate any further territorial conquests or annexations, Great Britain had much to lose and nothing to gain by any war of aggression or by involvement in a general war of whatever origin. She knew that, in a lawless world, the possession of either property or position coveted by another power is dangerous, and that the expense of maintaining armaments sufficient to insure her property and position by armed strength alone in such a world would be prohibitive. Only in an orderly world might equal safety be found for small nations and great empires. Enlightened self-interest and practical idealism alike indicated the desirability of identifying British world interests with the interests of other pacifically inclined peoples in support of the principle of collective security. Great Britain was therefore one of the founders and always one of the leading members of the League of Nations, bearing the largest nation's share (since the United States did not join it) of the cost of the League's maintenance and a full share of its other responsibilities.

As far as proved practicable, Britain would have preferred to substitute its general obligations as a member of the League for more specific bilateral commitments to continental European powers, such as her wartime treaty of alliance with France. The tripartite treaty negotiated at the Paris peace conference of 1919, for example, by which Britain and the United States would have been bound to defend France against an unprovoked invasion by the Germans, was never ratified. Reluctance of the self-governing dominions to assume obligations such as those proposed by the Geneva Protocol of 1924, for fear of being involved by them in a European war, made the British government itself doubly reluctant to assume them. The five-power Rhineland Security Pact (Locarno, 1925) was more to her liking. She lent but little support at that time, however, to France's proposal of an "eastern Locarno" to guarantee the western boundaries of Poland as they were then drawn. In 1935 a poll of public opinion revealed an overwhelming majority in favor of the principle of co-operation with other nations through the League of Nations in the name of collective security, as an alternative to alliances or unilateral action even for the preservation of the peace upon which Britain's own security was well known to depend.

Throughout the period here under discussion, a cardinal point of British foreign policy was the maintenance of cordially friendly relations with the United States. That friendship was slightly strained but never broken by the decision of the United States not to ratify the Treaty of Versailles or join the League of Nations. The war debt question[31] was the subject of occasional reproaches by individuals on both sides of the Atlantic but led to no serious quarrel between governments. Discussion of proposals for limitation of naval disarmament sometimes emphasized divergent views of national interest rather than community of interests, but generally revealed that neither nation was very seriously thinking of the other as a potential or even a hypothetical enemy.[32] Neither was disposed at first to forget about self-determination and its own tradition of aloofness and to intervene

[31] See pp. 304-307.
[32] See pp. 138-148.

between government and people in Italy, Germany, or Spain. Both tried too long to do business with the dictators. They failed to co-operate effectively, in time, to stop aggression by measures short of war.[33]

With France British relations were always friendly, but the international policies of the two countries diverged more widely than during the prewar years of the *entente cordiale*. There was some friction at first over the distribution of German reparation payments, and over France's insistence upon occupying the Ruhr. In general, Britain was naturally less uneasy than France was over the threat of the military and industrial recovery of Germany, more interested in Germany's ability to pay reparation and in her potentialities as a peacetime customer, less inclined to use reparation claims to keep her crippled, more optimistic about the possibility of ultimate and permanent reconciliation.

Relations with Russia varied at first with the government in power. Hoping to accelerate the resumption of industrial production for purposes other than war, and to quicken the revival of foreign trade, the Lloyd George coalition government made a trade agreement with Russia, March 16, 1921, which could serve as a *de facto* basis for a resumption of commercial intercourse without constituting recognition of the revolutionary Union of Soviet Socialist Republics as the legal or rightful government of that country. Such *de jure* recognition would have to await the conclusion of a formal treaty and might depend upon the Soviets' readiness to recognize the international obligations of the old imperial Russian government.

One of the first acts of Ramsay MacDonald's first Labour government was the *de jure* recognition of the Soviet government, February 1, 1924, nearly two years after Germany had recognized it but ten years before the United States was ready to do so. Negotiations were at once begun to broaden the Lloyd George trade agreement of 1921 so as to give British trade "most favored nation" treatment in Russia. With a view to securing a new loan, the Soviet government agreed to consider also the recognition and partial payment of prerevolutionary Russian debts; but Stanley Baldwin, succeeding MacDonald as prime minister in November, 1924, refused to submit the new treaties to Parliament, so permitted trade relations to continue only on the limited basis of the 1921 agreement.

The recognition of Soviet Russia in 1924 was called dangerous by conservatives. Their fears seemed to be confirmed, and the Labour party's popular vote in the November election of that year was ma-

[33] See pp. 513-517.

terially reduced, by the publication of a letter attributed to Gregory Zinoviev, head of the Third International in Moscow, summoning Communists in Britain to work for a proletarian revolution there. The authorship and authenticity of the letter were denied, but the denials were not generally found convincing. Russian Communist agitators were blamed for the general strike of 1926, the extent of their influence possibly being exaggerated by their accusers. A new and stronger unfavorable reaction followed a government police raid on the London offices of the Russian trading agency, Arcos, Ltd., May 12, 1927. Secret documents found missing from the War Office files, which were the primary object of the search, were not discovered; but the government announced that it had found documentary evidence of widespread espionage and Communist incitement to revolution. As a result, diplomatic relations were broken off.

MacDonald became prime minister for the second time, again with a Labour party plurality but less than a majority in Parliament, on June 5, 1929. His government resumed diplomatic relations with Soviet Russia in December, 1929, and in April, 1930, made a new treaty putting British trade with Russia again on the "most favored nation" basis. Mindful of the Arcos affair, the Soviet Union stipulated that its trading corporation should enjoy full diplomatic immunity. Not unmindful of the gravity of British charges against Arcos but with determined optimism, the MacDonald government exacted only an assurance that Soviet agents would not engage in subversive activity in Britain or the empire. On those terms it was willing to grant a substantial credit to prime the pump and start a new flow of export trade to Russia.

Britain welcomed Russia as a participant in the League of Nations economic conference of 1927 and the conferences for limitation of armament in 1928, 1929, and 1932, and as a member of the League of Nations from 1934 to 1939, but was always a little—and sometimes more than a little—distrustful of her. Conservative leaders of the later 1930's were generally less optimistic about the possibility of cordial coöperation with her than Labour leader Ramsay MacDonald had been; and their suspicious fear contributed to their failure to form an alliance with her for restaint of Nazi Germany in 1939.

SUMMARY

Great Britain was much preoccupied from 1919 to 1939 with problems of domestic, imperial, and foreign policy. In men, materials, and money the war costs had been heavy, and her people had been

badly hurt. The national debt was enormous, taxation approached
the confiscation level, and trade balances were unfavorable. Only
by Spartan efforts could living standards be maintained above the
Spartan level. Whether gladly or reluctantly, government was compelled to concern itself with the welfare of individuals and of whole
industries, and to try to control the conditions of their existence by
socializing some of their risks. It did this, however, by measures short
of outright socialization.

Relations with the self-governing dominions were eased and the
bonds which bound them together and all of them to Britain were at
the same time loosened and strengthened by conceding them equality
of status, none to be in any way subject to another but all to remain
united in common allegiance to the crown and in voluntarily continued association within the commonwealth. Only Ireland, established
as a free state and a member of the League of Nations in 1921 and as
a member of the commonwealth under the Statute of Westminster
in 1931, was dissatisfied with her status and the noninclusion of
northern Ireland in her national territory. She declared herself an
independent republic in 1937 and a neutral in 1939.

Imperial and foreign policy, especially in the Mediterranean and
Near East, revolved around the maintenance of friendly relations with
the Moslem Arab world, and around the routes to India; but the
British position in India could not be maintained. British concern
for the defense of India seemed during the Six Years' War to have
been only too well founded, when Japanese troops stood at the gates
of a country at odds with Britain and divided against itself. Unable
to reconcile Moslem and Hindu communities or to secure adequate
constitutional protection for Moslems or the depressed classes in a
united India, the imperial government in 1947 offered dominion
status to each of two Indian states, one predominantly Moslem and
the other predominantly Hindu. In Palestine the mandate to establish
there a national home for the Jews without prejudice to the rights
or interests of the Arab population proved unworkable. Arabs and
Jews were more and more embittered against one another. The
Palestinian Arabs were supported by a League of Arab States in
their violent objection to further Jewish immigration, and further
Jewish immigration was financed and encouraged by Zionist organizations and by individuals moved by sympathy for European Jews
as persons in distress. Caught in a cross fire and compelled to turn
Palestine into a police state to maintain even a semblance of law and
order, Britain asked the United Nations in 1947 to make a new study

of the problem the League of Nations had once assigned to it as mandatory power.

The British people preferred peace to war, and collective security to unilateral defense measures or bilateral treaty agreements; but preoccupation with immediate affairs, and disinclination as well as material unpreparedness to face the prospect of a threat of war, made them unready until September, 1939, for the risks of a bold League of Nations policy in restraint of the aggressors. So they ran eventually into the greater risks of a war with few allies, against a strong enemy coalition consisting of former misfit members of the League.

CHAPTER 10

Russia: USSR

BACKGROUND OF ESTRANGEMENT

The failure of Great Britain, France, and Russia to combine effectively and to carry the other members of the League of Nations with them in determined collective resistance to the acts of unprovoked aggression by which the Axis powers disturbed the world's peace and equilibrium, both before and after their withdrawal from the League and formation of the Axis, is only partially explicable on the grounds that each was preoccupied with its own most immediate affairs and none had sufficient confidence in the procedures prescribed by the Covenant of the League. They also distrusted one another. Soviet Russian leaders of 1939, established beyond further challenge as the governing group at the peak of an authoritarian pyramid, were old revolutionaries who had not forgotten, perhaps could not forget, that they had had to fight their way up to that position against foreign as well as Russian opposition. Noncommunist peoples, on the other hand, had seen and heard too much of the Third International's encouragement of Communist revolutionaries in their own "capitalist" countries, and too many tales of the liquidation of all opposition to the Communist government of the Union of Soviet Socialist Republics, to be able to forget all that at will and wholeheartedly welcome the prospect of a partnership.

Both Russians and non-Russians, Communists and noncommunists, remembered perhaps too much that would better have been forgotten, and forgot much that should have been remembered. British and French remembered with some resentment that revolutionary Russia had committed a breach of treaty agreement by making a separate

378

peace in 1918 and had repudiated the debts and other obligations of the imperial government which the revolution had just overthrown. Russians remembered that their former allies had blockaded Russia's Baltic coast in 1919 and had encouraged and aided Poland and the Russian counterrevolutionaries with money, weapons, war materials, and the services of some staff officers. The Allies forgot the frightful casualties suffered by the Russian armies in the first three years of war, and remembered their defection in the last. Russians remembered the 1920's as a period of hardship in an unfriendly world, and forgot (those of them who knew) that their government's active promulgation of a world-revolutionary doctrine had alienated many peoples who would otherwise have been more friendly. Western Europeans did not know in the middle 1930's whether the USSR had permanently abandoned or was only waiting for an opportunity to revive the territorial expansionism of the tsars, whether it was ready to curb the subversive international activity of the Comintern (Communist International) and be content with "socialism in one state," or whether its outspoken advocacy of an aggressive League of Nations collective security policy was only a tactical maneuver, to be followed shortly by a return to the world-revolutionary policy of the early Bolsheviks.

REVOLUTION, 1917, 1918

The early Bolsheviks—Lenin, Trotsky, Kamenev, Zinoviev, Chicherin, Stalin, Kuibyshev, Kalinin, Voroshilov, Dzerzhinski, and their associates—were tall men who cast long shadows. The very name "bolshevik" had come in the early twenties to be widely though loosely used as a common noun to designate a destructive person, a lawless rough-and-tumble fighter, or a malicious troublemaker. As thoroughgoing revolutionaries, in 1917, the Lenin-Trotsky group cut the ground from under the Liberals such as Prince George Lvov, the moderate Constitutional Democrats led by Professor Paul Miliukov, and the Socialist Revolutionary leader Alexander Kerensky, and paralyzed Kerensky's war effort in the face of the German enemy, by offering a more sweeping and faster moving program than those men had offered. People were sick of the ghastly losses of a mismanaged and unsuccessful "imperialist" war. The Bolsheviks offered the alluring prospect of an immediate general peace. The land, they said, should be confiscated without compensation and immediately possessed by the peasants, who had earned a right to it by living and working on it. The men who worked in the factories should dictate their policies and control their operation. A government composed of soviets or councils of proletarian workmen, peasants, and soldiers should control production and distribution. Possessors of property and former government officials, as natural enemies of the revolution which would dispossess them, were to be deprived of political rights lest they impede its progess. The Marxian dictatorship of the proletariat would be established. Armies fell apart. Their fragments melted away as soldiers shot their officers if the officers tried too hard to stop them, and hurried homeward hoping to be there at the dawning of the new day, to get their share of the plunder which was to be taken from the "capitalist plunderers" and redistributed.

The new day dawned for the Communist party leaders with the Bolshevik revolution or coup d'état of November 7 (October 25, old-style reckoning), 1917. On the eve of the meeting of an All-Russian Congress of Soviets which acted as a constituent assembly, the Bolsheviks of the Petrograd soviet seized public buildings, power plants, and transportation and communication centers in the national capital, and arrested and imprisoned most of the principal officials of the Kerensky government. Kerensky himself escaped to Finland and, like many other Russian refugees from the revolution, eventually found asylum in Paris. The All-Russian Congress at once acknowledged the accomplished fact and approved the establishment of a new provisional government by a "soviet of the People's Commissars," of which Lenin was to be chairman and Trotsky commissar for foreign affairs.[1] To emphasize the national Russian (rather than imperial) character of the new government, the national capital was transferred from Peter the Great's Petrograd to Moscow, capital of old Great Russia.[2]

REVOLUTIONARY COMMUNISM

Government

The new provisional government was a dictatorship, not of the proletariat but of an oligarchy of politically self-made leaders of a well-organized and thoroughly disciplined minority party, acting in

[1] In public life the party leaders used party names. Nikolai Lenin's family name was Vladimir Ilich Ulyanov. Leon Trotsky's was Lev Davidovich Bronstein. Joseph Stalin's was Josif Vissarionovich Dzugashvili. Molotov's was Viacheslav Mikhailovich Skriabin.

[2] During the "great patriotic people's war" against Nazi Germany, twenty-five years later, the tradition of Peter I was revitalized to strengthen the national defense.

the name of the workers. The party hierarchy, which constituted the one-party government, was dominated by Lenin and, after Lenin's death on January 21, 1924, by the general secretary of the Central Party Committee of the Communist party, Joseph Stalin. Trotsky seconded Lenin and served him at first as commissar for foreign affairs and later as commissar for war. After Lenin's death, Trotsky and Stalin quarreled, ostensibly over whether world revolution should be actively encouraged through the Comintern but also as rivals for the succession to Lenin as leader. Stalin was the stronger. Trotsky fled from Russia and, from various temporary refuges in exile, until assassinated in Mexico in 1940, denounced Stalin as a betrayer of Lenin and of the revolution. Stalin meanwhile steadily strengthened his position and, in the war against Nazi Germany, acted with unchallenged authority not only as boss of the party but as head of the government and leader of the people.

A series of constitutions in 1918, 1923, and 1936 offered some apparent opportunity for popular participation in government; but the opportunity was open at first only to a strictly limited electorate, and the right to participate meant little in most matters but the right to signify approval. Government was always, in theory, an integrated pyramidal affair resting upon a broad base of local soviets and reaching its peak in the All-Russian Congress of Soviets (1918), All Union Congress (1923), or Supreme Council (1936); but the voter in a rural soviet was six steps removed from the Supreme Council, and in an urban soviet four steps removed. Inside that pyramid, moreover, at every level, was the corresponding organization of the Communist party, culminating in the party Political Bureau (Politburo). Nominations of candidates could be discussed beforehand in the soviets; but the party made the nominations, and only the official list of candidates was presented in elections, to be voted on (until 1936) by show of hands. Government policies were presented to the soviets at various levels for discussion and approval, most commonly at the local government level; but the party leaders and government officials (often the same persons, in interlocking positions) made the decisions, and dissent was always dangerous.

In the earliest years of the revolution its leaders did not dare temporize with dissent. Those (1918-1920) were the years which saw French troops seize Odessa, liberated Czechoslovak prisoners of war (not yet repatriated) forming a counterrevolutionary legion in southern Russia, British troops closing up on the Caucasus from the south, Allied expeditionary forces guarding piled-up military supplies at Murmansk, Archangel, and Vladivostok, Polish troops operating east of the Curzon line and advancing on Kiev, and counterrevolutionary "White" leaders such as Generals Wrangel, Yudenitch, and Denikin and Admiral Kolchak collaborating with the "invaders" for the overthrow of the new regime. The so-called "Red" revolutionaries were at that time only the nucleus of what they had begun in 1918 to call the Russian Communist party, never numerically more than 3 or 4 percent of the population and at that time probably less than 1 percent. They rode out those early storms only by making free use of the secret police (Cheka) to discover and liquidate all dissidents, and by imposing upon themselves a rigorous discipline, achieving thus a unity of purpose and action which their enemies could not match. The aid their enemies got from foreigners enabled the Reds to win some national support also as defenders of the soil of Russia against alien invaders. In that sense, however, as nationalist defenders of Russian territory, they took heavy losses by the treaties of Brest Litovsk and Riga, signing away enormous areas formerly included in the Russian Empire (Finland, Estonia, Latvia, Lithuania, western White Russia and Ukraine, and Bessarabia).[3]

Radical Economic Policy

Those first years of struggle for control of Russia were years of radical revolutionary activity in the areas controlled. To clear the way for the ushering in of a new world, a clean sweep was to be made of the old. The monarchy had already been abolished; the Orthodox Church which had supported it by preaching obedience to it and offering the "opiate of religion" to the victims of its injustice and oppression must also be destroyed. With it should go the "bourgeois" institutions and moral standards it had fostered, such as the family, marriage as a sacrament, and Christian religious beliefs. Marriage was made a civil contract only, divorce made easy. Government was not only anticlerical but actively antichristian. Church buildings were destroyed, left empty, or put to secular uses. Monastic orders were dissolved. Private trading, the ownership of private property, and the employment of labor for the employer's private profit were to be prohibited. Living on inherited wealth or the interest earnings of other capital was to. be made impossible. Everyone must work, not for himself but for the common good. He would be paid not according

[3] See pp. 57-59 and 187.

to the work he did but according to his need, not in cash but in coupons for rent, food, clothing, entertainment, and other necessities. All the principal means of industrial production, transportation, and communication and the sources of power would be owned and operated by the state.

No such changes could be made without confusion. Great indeed was the confusion. Throughout industry, experienced management identified with the old regime was eliminated, and inexperienced management had much to learn. Production, transportation, and finally the provisioning and fueling of the cities generally broke down. Requisitioning aroused resistance. Famine and typhus swept large areas in 1921-1922, causing the deaths of several million people, although the lives of many others were saved by charitable donations from peoples of allegedly "unfriendly capitalist" countries through international relief agencies. Revolutionary zeal was not generally enough to keep people working their hardest, indefinitely, without other incentive or compulsion. Coercion was impossible without an all-pervading police power and an enormous new bureaucracy, which had to be extemporized, indoctrinated, and trained in service. All this took time, and would have taken more if fear of the government in power—no new thing in Russia—had not been kept alive by ruthless use of the "Red terror" for the purpose of intimidation, and of a lawless police power to crush all opposition. Many thousands of the dispossessed, from whom only opposition was expected, and of others who for any reason raised objection to the changes being made or the methods being used, were imprisoned. Many of those imprisoned as "enemies of the people" were executed.

Much that was attempted in the name—and for the benefit—of some of the people (called the workers) was clearly to be done, as the outside "capitalist" world saw it, only at the expense of others, the owners of the property and holders of positions, the former favored ones, the fortunate ones, the *beati possidentes*. This startled the "capitalist" world, not yet accustomed to the atrocities of totalitarianism. The world was further horrified by what it heard about the summary execution of opponents, critics, skeptics, and victims of the new regime. Many people in other countries found it impossible, twenty or twenty-five years later, to forget this demonstration that the class warfare which Marx once called inevitable could mean the extermination of the numerically weaker class by the numerically stronger, boldly led.

USSR: UNION OF SOVIET SOCIALIST REPUBLICS

Government

By 1923, within the new national frontiers, the revolutionary government had passed the danger zone and had little more to fear from counterrevolution or from foreign intervention. A favorable moment had come for the consolidation of political gains already made. A new treaty of union signed at Moscow, effective July 3 upon ratification by the constituent states, reconstituted the national government as the Union of Soviet Socialist Republics (USSR).

The largest state of the new union was the Russian Soviet Federated Socialist Republic (RSFSR), old Great Russia, which with its population of more than 100,000,000 people had been the nucleus of the old. Its language was the lingua franca of the union, although the use of other languages was legalized. Other member states included White Russia and Ukraine, freed from German control by Germany's defeat and compulsory renunciation of the treaty of Brest Litovsk in 1918, and a new Transcaucasian republic formed by consolidation of Georgia, Armenia, and Azerbaijan, which had declared their independence at the time of the revolution.[4]

The union formed in 1923 was so highly centralized as to seem more nearly unitary than federal in character. Member states might legislate freely on comparatively minor matters of local significance only. It was not until February 1, 1944, that it was announced that several of them were sovereign states, free to make their own separate foreign policies and treaties and entitled to separate membership in an international organization such as the United Nations, then being proposed.

Under the Union constitution of 1923 a Union Congress of Soviets of some fifteen hundred members was chosen by the city soviets and the provincial congresses in which village soviets were indirectly represented (two steps removed). The Union Congress met briefly, biennially, to approve general policies and to choose the members of a Union Central Executive Committee. The latter was bicameral, in some ways similar to a legislature. In its Soviet of Nationalities the numerous nationalities were represented on a basis of approximate

---

[4] Georgia, Armenia, and Azerbaijan were subsequently again made separate republics. The Far Eastern Republic, which had called itself independent in 1920, was reabsorbed by Great Russia (the RSFSR) as soon as the Japanese troops were withdrawn in 1922. Estonia, Latvia, and Lithuania were taken into the USSR in 1940, raising the total number of member states to sixteen.

equality. In the Soviet of the Union the peoples of the constituent republics were represented in approximate proportion to population, except that the urban proletariat had three times as many representatives per 100,000 people as the rural population had. At the head of the government was a Union Council of Commissars, analogous in position to the national ministries of other countries. Although not politically responsive in the same sense as the British cabinet to Parliament, the members of the Union Council of Commissars were chosen by and in general responsible to the Central Executive Committee.

Only a tried and proved member of the Communist party could hope to be a member of the Union Council of Commissars. Position in the hierarchy of the party was more important than position in the council. After Trotsky's disappearance from the Russian scene it did not matter what official title Stalin held or whether he held any office in the government. Wherever Stalin sat, there was the head of the table.[5]

New Economic Policy (NEP) and Five-Year Plans

The political stability achieved by 1923 could be partially attributed to the New Economic Policy adopted in 1921. In that critical year the demoralization of urban industry and transportation and the reluctance of the peasants to produce more foodstuffs than they needed for themselves, under a system which ordered them to surrender their surplus to feed the cities, combined with an unusual drought to cause such a famine that thirty million people needed relief. In such circumstances Lenin deemed it wiser for the Communist party to retain political control of the country by compromising where necessary in the application of its economic theories than to wreck itself politically by refusing to distinguish between what seemed practical and what seemed impractical, economically, in the world as it then was. Trotsky was less easily convinced of the necessity of compromise. Stalin, when he succeeded Lenin, maintained the New Economic Policy and tried to schedule its operation through a series of five-year plans, the first of which was announced in 1928.

The new policy adopted in 1921 was less radical, economically, than the original one had been. Factories and shops employing

[5] During the war against Germany, Stalin assumed the titles of field marshal and premier, or chairman of the Council of People's Commissars (1941). After the war he resigned the latter.

fewer than twenty workers were considered small enough to be denationalized; so private ownership and management of such industries were restored, along with private ownership of small homes. Wages were again paid in money, and private trading on a small scale on a money basis was resumed. Peasants were permitted to use the land they held and sell their surpluses, and some of them (the Kulaks) prospered by enlarging their holdings and working them with hired labor drawn from a growing reservoir of impoverished, usually landless, peasants. Growing inequalities in the distribution of wealth among the peasant population were only partially corrected by discriminatory taxation which had supplanted the old requisition system.

Government focused its attention on the first essentials: heavy industry, the restoration and improvement of the transportation system, and foreign trade. The latter was necessary to secure the industrial equipment Russia needed and did not have, the services of the engineers and other experts needed to install that equipment and teach Russians how to use it and to make more of it, and the money to pay for this equipment and these services.

Government agencies retained control of the principal means of industrial production, transportation, and communication, and of foreign trade. The natural resources of the country were known to be almost incalculable but largely undeveloped and unused. The new policy was not to adhere too stubbornly to an economic program which had in effect isolated Russia, but to attract foreign capital or at least to get and use the industrial equipment, techniques, and technicians of the more highly industrialized nations until Russia could supply them for herself and utilize them in the modernization of her heavy industries and the exploitation of her natural wealth.

The most immediate need was in heavy industry, for machines to make machines to be used in the making of steel, steel rails, and roads and in the manufacture of locomotives, railway rolling stock, motor trucks and tractors, dams and dynamos, mining machinery, and the drills, pipe lines, refineries, tank cars, and tankers of a petroleum industry. These, under the NEP, Russia proposed to import, since she could not make them fast enough or (at first) well enough to satisfy her needs.

Such imports had to be paid for, as did the imported skills of the engineers and other experts brought in with them. So exports were called for. Russia had to sell what she could, for what she could get for it, to get what she had to have. To Great Britain she sold timber products, furs, wheat, butter, flax, hemp, and petroleum products, buying in Britain principally cotton, wool, and yarn for her textile industries, machinery, and rubber. In the United States she sold principally furs, manganese, and flax, and bought producers' goods such as cotton, factory equipment, agricultural machinery, tractors, and motor trucks. In the two-year period 1923-1925 her purchases in the United States amounted in dollars to almost eight times as much as her sales, in the five-year period 1923-1928 to only a little less than three and three-fourths times as much. Exports included wheat which the people might have eaten without being overfed. Imports could not include consumers' goods, which in such circumstances could not have been considered otherwise than as luxuries. Austerity was clearly indicated, and government economic planners made a hard but realistic choice. Comforts and luxuries must wait while priority was given to the modernization and expansion of industrial plants which would presumably soon enable the Russian people to produce more for themselves.

Under the five-year plan announced in 1928 long strides were taken in the direction of the collectivization and mechanization of agriculture. In the early stages of the revolution, ten years before, much of the land had gone into the hands of peasants in small holdings. The new economic plan had not at first prevented the accumulation of some larger holdings in the hands of the more successful peasant holders, the kulaks; but farming was still done generally on a traditional haphazard, small-scale, unscientific basis without benefit of modern mechanization. A certain amount of customary control was exercised by the agricultural village community or *mir*, and some of the work was done coöperatively by those who shared in it. Great open expanses of rich level land seemed in the twentieth century, however, to offer a clear and constant invitation to tractors and tractor-drawn plows, seeders, and combines to tend and harvest them. Scientific husbandry and the use of modern agricultural machinery promised to increase enormously the productivity of the naturally fertile soil and at the same time, by the more efficient utilization of man power on the land, to release for service in the mines, factories, and transport services some of the laborers they needed.

Large-scale power farming is big business. Land, buildings, livestock, and machinery on a big farm in a capitalist country represent a considerable investment, always somewhat speculative in character, subject to hazards of wind and weather, plant pests, livestock diseases, taxes, and price fluctuations. Such farming had been a gradual development in the United States, involving often the inheritance of land

and almost always and everywhere the use of credit and of risk capital. The sudden change-over which the Russian agricultural economic planners contemplated, from the peasant farming Russia knew to the power farming for which much of her terrain was naturally so suitable, could be made only by bold and vigorous state action. The state might reduce the risk by controlling prices but would have to provide the backing which had been a function of risk capital in capitalist countries.

The state acted boldly, vigorously, and with determination. Large farms were formed by consolidation of peasant holdings. On some state-owned farms (too few in number to be called typical) government owned everything, managed everything, and took everything. The work was done by men hired for the purpose, supervised by government officials.

The government-supervised collective or coöperative farm was more nearly typical of the system than the state farm was. Such a collective or coöperative farm became the characteristic unit of agricultural production, much as the manor had been the characteristic rural community and the unit of economic land exploitation of medieval France or England. The agricultural village and the land around it became one farm instead of many. Government provided expert management, or supervision by such experts as it could find or could train quickly. Progressively, as fast as industrial production and importation made it possible, government tractor stations furnished tractors and tractor-drawn power-driven equipment to the collectives in their vicinities, which might also have some such equipment of their own. Government controlled the sale, at fixed prices, of whatever surplus the collective farm produced. Then, after deductions for taxes, the use of government-owned equipment, local public improvements, and other charges the collective earnings of the coöperative were divided annually among the members, according to the number and character of the work hours each of them had done. In addition to its share of the collective earnings of the coöperative, each farm-village family usually enjoyed the exclusive use of a small bit of land, with the privilege of keeping privately such poultry or animals as its land plot would support, and of selling independently any surplus it might produce.[6]

A constant effort was always made to make the village community of the collective farm the center of the political and social as well as

[6] In 1946 and 1947 there were reports of some restriction of this privilege, as a result of alleged abuses of it.

the economic life of the people of the rural community. A revolutionary improvement in the village schools, a noticeable awakening and quickening of the minds and spirits of the villagers, and the growth of a new optimism among them seemed to have been among the results achieved, as attested by the accounts of friendly visitors, by the tenacity with which these people defended their land against invasion from 1941 to 1945, and by the courage with which they set to work in 1945 to restore to fruitfulness its devastated areas.

Such sweeping changes, made at revolutionary tempo at government command, aroused determined opposition, especially among the kulaks, who as the most successful and prosperous of the individual peasant enterprisers resisted collectivization. With the impatient zeal of reformers in too great a hurry to temporize with opposition, the executors of the new land policy used the police power of the state to liquidate the nonconformists. Many of the objectors were killed by police or troops brought in to enforce the change. Thousands of others were sent off as political prisoners to work in labor camps while the land they had held was incorporated into state farms or collectives.

The optimism, vigor, and ruthlessness which marked the collectivization of agriculture were shown in other industries throughout the series of five-year plans. An attempt was made to schedule every hydroelectric development at the maximum speed attainable, to assign to every factory the highest quota it could hope to meet, to demand from every mine the maximum output—then to revise all estimates upward if the impossible, which had been demanded, was found after all to have been possible. The essence of the five-year plans was large-scale long-term total planning, and the assigning of priorities to those phases of modernization and industrialization which needed to come first.

By the time the imminence of war necessarily determined the character of the third five-year plan, a system more like state capitalism than the radical anticapitalist communism of the early days of the revolution had developed. Russian plants were turning out a hundred times as many tractors as in 1928, and agricultural machinery in proportion. The production of electric power was twenty times what it had been, with one of the world's greatest hydroelectric developments at Dniepropetrovsk on the lower Dnieper. Russian steel mills were almost equaling the German in their total output, and chemical production was fifteen times what it had been ten years before. Transportation facilities of all kinds were enormously extended and improved. Urban population had increased and was increasing rapidly, while rural population had decreased slightly.

Incentive Pay and Benefits

As an inducement to keep every worker as well as every mine or factory producing at top speed, a system of incentive pay was introduced, so that the workers' earnings varied widely according to the kind and quantity of the work done. The old equalitarianism of the early days of the revolution was forgotten and a new industrial aristocracy arose, made up of the planners and the managers, the most skillful of the artisans, the most productive of the workers.

Some real social and economic gains were made and kept by the industrial proletariat under the Communist regime. The status of women in industry was in many ways equalized with that of men. Elementary education was offered to millions of children who might conceivably by that time have been offered it by the imperial government but to whom it had not in fact been offered by the old regime. Confiscated Crimean palaces and playgrounds of the prewar nobility and the prerevolutionary rich were opened as recreation centers at low rates to workers on vacation; and the socialist idea that a laborer was entitled to a vacation was at least theoretically sanctioned. Some factories provided educational and recreational facilities for their employees, in an attempt to make themselves the social centers of the lives of those who worked there.

Russia had not become a workers' paradise. Many of the great gains hoped for had not been made. Workers were not free to strike, or to leave one employment for another without permission. In industrial production, as had been true of imports under the new economic plan from ten to fifteen years earlier, the emphasis was on producers' goods, and consumers' goods were scarce and high in price. A good pair of shoes or a shoddy suit of clothes, if he could get them, cost the average worker a month's earnings in 1937. Housing shortages were acute in all the rapidly expanding cities, and life in the new mining towns beyond the Urals was extremely raw and crude.

The New Aristocracy

Although elementary education was theoretically free to all, the technical training and higher education that enabled a young person to work his or her way up into the industrial aristocracy of the well paid was on a fee basis, beyond the means of the average laborer, open in practice only to the sons and daughters of those already privileged—party men and bureaucrats, engineers, technicians, and plant managers. So the new aristocracy of the bureaucrats and the technicians seemed already to have become to a considerable degree exclusive and self-perpetuating. To these were soon to be added a third privileged group—the army officers.

Militarization and Production of War Materials

Whether, but for the threat of war with Germany, industry might at some time during the period of the third or fourth five-year plan have been turned more largely to production of consumers' goods and the raising of the general standard of living, or whether militarization would have been adopted as a policy without threat of invasion, remained an unanswered question. How much farther the revolution might within a few more years have gone along the road Marx had imagined for it—toward a free and democratic world in which all who worked would be adequately rewarded and none need be poor or be denied the benefits of an abundant life—was a question which had not yet emerged from the realm of speculation. The hard facts were that Adolf Hitler openly coveted Russian territory and resources and was not repudiated by his people or effectively rebuked in Germany for saying so. Whether willingly or unwillingly, for offense or for defense, for war or only for fear of war, Russian economic planners turned their country's industrial production more and more to war production, to the equipment of a large army and the development of the war industries indispensable to its maintenance. One-fourth of the government appropriations of 1939 was for preparedness for war. Again comforts and luxuries had to wait; and the total controls needed to hold a whole people indefinitely to such a program of unremitting toil and self-denial, with only a beckoning but receding vision of brighter and better times somewhere on ahead, were (perhaps necessarily) continued.[7]

[7] The non-Russian world wondered in 1946 and 1947 why similar controls seemed still to be maintained, whether war production still held its precedence over reconstruction and the peacetime production of consumers' goods, and—if so—why. What new war threatened Russia then?

RUSSIA AND WESTERN EUROPE

How Radical Was Russia?

It was not clearly apparent from outside in 1938 or 1939 whether the Marxian revolution had been purposely arrested by Stalin and his associates or had been retarded only by the Nazi threat of war, whether the moderate trend then manifesting itself was real and permanent or only a temporary manifestation of patience and of prudence.

If accepted at face value, the publication of a new constitution in 1936 would have indicated that the revolution was calming or slowing down, as others had done before it, to a new level of moderation. Civil and religious liberty were guaranteed by the constitution, and the Soviet Union was generally believed to be genuinely tolerant of cultural, racial, and national differences among its many peoples, encouraging diversity and permitting local cultural autonomy, insisting upon complete conformity only in the political and economic fields. The constitution recognized the right of inheritance and of private ownership of property in the form of personal possessions. It was only income-producing property that the individual might not own. He could accumulate some savings but could put them only into government bonds or savings banks at moderate fixed interest rates. Rents and royalties were taboo.

The new constitution published in 1936 did not mention, as earlier ones had done with emphasis, the inevitability of an eventual conflict between communist and capitalist worlds. Was such a conflict inevitable? Were the two systems antithetical? Or were they incompatible only within one country, and was international coöperation of communist and noncommunist national governments still possible? The old world-revolutionary Chicherin had been replaced as commissar for foreign affairs by the more conciliatory Maxim Litvinov, who had hastened to sign the Kellogg-Briand Pact of Paris and who since 1929 had conducted Russian foreign policy along the line of international conciliation and coöperation.

In 1934, after Hitler had taken Germany out of the League of Nations, Stalin and Litvinov had taken Russia into it, although her earlier spokesmen had professed to see in the League only a threatening combination of her enemies. Was her apparent conversion genuine, or only sickbed repentance induced by fear of death or dire distress at the hands of Nazi Germany? National leaders who did not know the answers to these questions were afraid to gamble on the sincerity and permanence of her conversion, so were handicapped by their doubts in the test of nerves and wills in which they confronted Adolf Hitler, and gave him ground, in 1938 and 1939. Differences in political concepts and practice were more serious obstacles to coöperation than differences in economic theory or practice.

How Dependable Was Russia?

Doubt of the dependability of Russia in international affairs may have been based, to a larger degree than actual conditions warranted, upon doubt of the stability of the Stalin regime. In 1937 and 1938 a series of sensational public trials resulted in the execution of a number of old Bolsheviks including Zinoviev and Kamenev, high-ranking army officers including Marshal Tukhachevsky, and other Communist government officials on charges of treasonable commerce with agents of foreign powers. The trials were marked by confessions by the accused, so abject and hysterical in tone as to give rise to the suspicion that they had been dictated by the prosecutors. Foreign observers did not know whether to interpret the necessity of the purge as an indication of a fatal weakness in the foundation of the Stalin government or to see in the purge itself a convincing demonstration of the Stalin party's strength. Subsequent events indicated that it was the last step necessary to establish Stalin's dictatorship. Instead of weakening Russia militarily as it was at first thought outside Russia to have done, the purge soon seemed rather to have strengthened her. It soon became apparent that a similar though less widely publicized purge had at the same time been made the order of the day in all departments of the government for the elimination of the inefficient as well as of the unfaithful and the unenthusiastic, and that the administration had been strengthened by it.

To most people, including many of those responsible for the foreign policies of the United States and the western European nations, Russia in 1938 was an enigma. Her foreign commissar, Maxim Litvinov, was the most eloquent advocate of collective security in the League of Nations. But did they dare believe and trust him? Did he really speak for his party or for Russia? Communist parties in France and elsewhere, after the formation of the Axis and the signing of the anti-Comintern (anti-Communist International) pact by Germany, Japan, and Italy, had abandoned their former policy of implacable opposition to other parties and to governments of any type but communist, and had signified their willingness to join "popular front" coalitions with other nonfascist parties, such as the Léon Blum government of 1936 in France. But had they adopted this new policy of coöperation on national patriotic grounds or been ordered by the Comintern to adopt it not as patriots but as Communists, as a tactical maneuver, to get some non-Communist help in an impending world-wide struggle between international communism and international fascism? The government of the USSR had bound itself repeatedly by treaty agreements with western powers not to sponsor or to countenance subversive propaganda, espionage, or treasonable activities among their peoples. But the Comintern still maintained headquarters in Moscow, the Russian government was commonly credited with knowing what it was doing, and Communists and Communist sympathizers in other countries continued to dance to whatever tune they thought they heard played in Moscow.

How Democratic Was Russia?

The Russian government called itself democratic and progressive, and its people free, freedom-loving friends of peace. Those words seemed to have different meanings in communist and noncommunist vocabularies. If political democracy is government of a country by its people the USSR was not in 1938 politically democratic. It had exalted the names of economic and social democracy; but it was not governed by its people, or by a majority of them, or even by an ordinary minority. It was governed by one man, advised by a closely knit self-perpetuating oligarchy in the political bureau of a small minority party, effectively responsible primarily to him. The party line, a daily guide to conduct and a comprehensive statement of authorized beliefs and orthodox attitudes on all current questions, was carried to the people by the members of the party—less than one in thirty of Russia's many millions—and by a controlled press free to print only what government-party censors wanted printed.

If democracy is tolerant of minorities and dissidents the USSR was not in that sense democratic. It was tolerant of racial, national, religious, and cultural diversity but intolerant of criticism and of economic or political nonconformity.

If democracy is interested in the integrity and dignity of the individual the USSR was not in that sense democratic; it concerned itself with masses, but with the individual only as a molecule in a mass.

As a police state, and as a user of the labor of political prisoners held indefinitely in involuntary servitude it was as ruthless as the tsars' secret police had ever been. Its people were naturally freedom-loving as other peoples are, and by nature no less friends of peace. Russia was free from foreign domination or interference, and her people were free from foreign influence; but within Russia they were not free.

How Friendly Was Russia?

Were communism and democracy antithetical? Within one country, as anyone not a Communist used those terms, perhaps they were, as Marx had said communism and capitalism were. Was the Marxist idea of the inevitable ultimate self-destruction of capitalism and its replacement by communism an insuperable psychological obstacle in the way of coöperation between communist and noncommunist states? One hoped not but was not sure. Would any dictatorship ever find the atmosphere of an international organization such as the League of Nations more congenial than the fascist-military dictatorships of the anti-Comintern group had found it, or prove to be a congenial partner of the political democracies in such an enterprise?

The leaders of the western European powers were confronted by a common danger, totalitarian fascism; but they thought they saw also a second danger, totalitarian communism. The political character and practices of the government in question were in either case a more serious obstacle to coöperation than its economic theories. They would have preferred to set one against the other and avoid involvement; but when eventually they found themselves about to be involved in war with one they failed to make an ally of the other until it also was attacked. That failure cost them more than could be calculated. Russia was not as well prepared for war in 1939 as Germany was, or as she herself was two years later; but her immediate entrance into the war as a belligerent on the side of the Allies in 1939 would have insured its outcome at the outset, and have shortened it. Instead, she participated in a fourth partition of Poland, reoccupied the Baltic states and Bessarabia, attacked Finland, delivered great quantities of essential war materials to Germany until her own territory was invaded, did not declare war on Japan until three months after Germany had surrendered, and then had to hurry to get into the war in eastern Asia before it ended with the surrender of Japan.

PART III

Disintegration

CHAPTER 11

Decline of the Third French Republic

One broadly generalized but generally valid explanation of the course of events which culminated in the Fourteen Years' World War (begun by Japan's attack on China in Manchuria in 1931, extended into Ethiopia by Italy in 1935, brought back to Europe by armed intervention in Spain in 1936 and 1937, merged into the Six Years' European War by the German invasion of Poland in 1939, and ended by the surrender of Germany and Japan in 1945) was that, while the revisionist powers stiffened themselves militarily, whipped up a war spirit among the best organized elements of their populations, and drew together in a military alliance directed ostensibly only against the Comintern but effective in the event as an instrument of aggression in any direction, the more nearly satiated powers legitimately interested in the maintenance of peace and of the *status quo* were losing much of their cohesion, self-confidence, and confidence in one another. Great Britain (as has been pointed out in Chapter 9) was preoccupied with domestic economic difficulties, problems of empire and of mandates. Maintenance of her position, which would be safest in a well-ordered world, put on her a heavy share of the burden of the ordering of the world. Russia (see Chapter 10) was developing a strong new national state. It might have exerted a determining influence for stability and peace if the Axis powers, those whom the Axis threatened, and those disposed to defend the threatened ones had been quite sure beforehand that Russia would at once use all her resources to stop the Axis if the Axis started a war. No effective collective action to stop aggression by the Axis powers anywhere in Europe was likely to be taken, however, without France. Much of continental Europe looked to her for leadership. All of it not already dominated by the Axis looked to her for help. And France, unfortunately, was unable to give it either help or leadership. She had survived the Four Years' War but had been exhausted by it and had not recovered from her exhaustion. Her people had lost, at least temporarily, the remarkable cohesion and self-confidence which had made her First and Third Republics indomitable and well-nigh invincible. The France of 1939 was not the France of Valmy or Verdun. Her leaders were not comparable with Danton or Carnot, Clemenceau or Foch.

WAR COSTS AND RECONSTRUCTION

Most of the heaviest fighting on the western front from 1914 to 1918 took place in France. Thousands of square miles of land and hundreds of towns and villages, in which before the war one-eighth of the French people had lived and earned their living, were devastated with a thoroughness matched only here and there in the more mobile war of 1939-1945. Eventually France was to receive a little more than half of whatever Germany paid in reparation. No Frenchman could imagine in 1919 a postwar world in which France, which had contributed so much to the winning of the victory, could fail to collect enough in reparation to pay for repairing the damage done; but the repair work could not wait for reparation payments. People's homes, shops, and factories had to be rebuilt at once, trenches and field fortifications filled in and leveled off, fields cleared of wire entanglements, mines, shell fragments, and unexploded shells, farms restocked and reëquipped. Some of the livestock was replaced out of deliveries in kind which the Germans were required to make. Some of the timber and other structural materials were also received from Germany in reparation, along with considerable deliveries of Ruhr region coal in addition to what was brought in from the Saar. The immediate cash cost of reconstruction, however, had to be paid by the national government, which then had to recover its expenditures out of reparation if it could.

Government raised the money for immediate reconstruction by a series of special loans and at first carried that account in a separate budget of recoverable expenditures, this indebtedness to be retired as funds became available out of German reparation payments. While the Dawes plan was in operation and the payments for which it provided were being regularly made, France's share of those receipts would have been sufficient to meet her scheduled debt payments to

Great Britain and the United States and to keep up to schedule in the retirement of her special reconstruction bonds. But a prolonged financial crisis in the middle 1920's led in 1927 to the absorption of the special budget of recoverable expenditures into the regular national budget, before the Dawes plan reparation payments had lifted much of the debt burden.

The national budget was a perennially serious problem. The domestic debt had been very greatly increased by several war loans, and continued to increase at an average annual rate of thirty billion francs for the first five years after the war. Domestic debt service charges were more than five times as heavy after the war as they had been before. In the face of recurrent deficits and occasional suggestions that government should reduce its expenses by lowering the interest rate on the national debt, investors were afraid to buy more bonds. With tax rates already heavier than contemporary German rates, though lighter than the British, ministries hesitated to impose heavier taxes. These might have yielded the increased revenue without which, unless they reduced expenditures, they could not balance the budget. Proposals to reduce the interest rate on the national debt would always arouse the opposition of the influential moneyed people whose interests were well guarded by the Bank of France. To have tried to achieve the same result by cutting government salaries and pensions would have been equally certain to evoke vigorous protests from government employees in essential services.

Unable to bring income and outgo into balance, successive governments printed more money. By 1924 the value of the franc had declined to less than five cents, and in May, 1926, to only a little more than two cents, not much more than 10 percent of normal value. At the end of 1926 an emergency ministry of national union led by former President and Premier Raymond Poincaré managed to restore the gold standard and stabilize the franc at a value of approximately four cents.

The period of reviving optimism and renewed confidence in government which followed the stabilization of the franc (1927-1928) was contemporaneous with similar trends elsewhere. This was the Dawes plan period, following Locarno and Germany's admission to the League of Nations, when Briand and Stresemann were talking peace and conciliation, Germany was being revitalized and rebuilt, largely with foreign capital, and the Kellogg-Briand Pact of Paris was being prepared for signature. France was not dependent during that period upon reparation payments from Germany, but she was receiving those payments regularly and finding them useful. When they were discontinued as of July 1, 1931, under the provisions of the Hoover moratorium, although her own international debt payments were also suspended, the times were again financially out of joint and another period of political instability ensued for France.

REPARATION AND WAR DEBT POLICIES

The policies of France as to reparation, the occupation of the Ruhr, and the payment of inter-Allied war debts have already been discussed in other contexts.[1] Considered from the French point of view, they will be seen to have been inseparable from her concept of the problem of her own security. There were thirty million more Germans left in Germany than Frenchmen then in France—thirty millions too many. France was afraid to see Germany recover economically and nationalize and modernize her industries to such an extent as to increase the existing disparity between her war potential and that of France. If reparation claims could be used to retard Germany's economic recovery, it was logical for France to use them for that purpose so long as she thought of strength as something relative and of herself as relatively weak in comparison with Germany. Her more unregenerate nationalists were keenly interested rather in detaching the Rhineland from Germany than in getting coal out of the Ruhr, and rather in ruining Germany financially than in the money to be got out of her in the process.

As for her war debts to Great Britain and the United States, those had not been economically productive self-liquidating commercial or industrial loans increasing the earnings of the borrower or enabling him to repay them out of the profits they made for him. Most of the money had been spent for expendables such as war supplies and food for a people temporarily unable because of the war to feed itself or pay for food. The war effort had consumed the proceeds of the loans, and along with them many thousands of the men of France. It had been an effort made in common with the nations which had made the loans. Had not France's human and material contribution to the common cause balanced the financial contribution of her allies and associates? Were not her creditors ungenerous in their insistence upon repayment? If she must pay, then those other nations to whom she had granted credits also must pay; and obviously Germany must pay. The Treaty of Versailles had made German reparation a legal obligation.

[1] See pp. 86-94, 264, and 304-307.

France needed the money to meet her own obligations and to provide a large army for her own defense, which in the minds of most of her people was synonymous with the maintenance of the peace of Europe and the world.

ALSACE-LORRAINE, COLONIAL EMPIRE, MANDATES

Alsace-Lorraine

To France, and particularly to her elder statesmen such as Clemenceau and Poincaré, the reacquisition of Alsace-Lorraine in 1918 was a simple act of justice long deferred, the righting of an ancient wrong. Metz had been under French control for more than three hundred years when the Germans recaptured it in 1870, took title to it by the terms of the Treaty of Frankfort in 1871, and made of it a defensive bastion and a spearhead pointed at the heart of France. Much of Alsace had been French territory for more than two (some of it for more than three) centuries when Germany recovered it, Lorraine for more than one.

Under the old Bourbon monarchy of prerevolutionary France these provinces had retained many of their local laws and customs. One of the stated reasons for the Habsburg emperor Leopold II's intervention against the French revolution in 1791 was its anticlerical legislation and nationalization of the property of nobles and the church, acts which he claimed violated certain rights of German landholders and ecclesiastical foundations guaranteed by the Treaty of Westphalia in 1648. As emperor of the Holy Roman Empire of the German People, he represented himself as the defender of those rights. Yet the Congress of Vienna did not deprive France of the provinces. There was no national German government ready to make them into an imperial province and administer their government. No German state was willing to see another take them. And the Duke of Wellington warned the congress that no permanent peace could be made with France if she were required to give them up. The governments of post-Napoleonic France (to 1871) were not usually strong enough or so strongly anticlerical as to deprive Alsatians and Lorrainers of their right to be a little different from other Frenchmen. So although French enough in political loyalty they were always rather different in other ways.

The imperial German government of 1871 made the newly recovered territory into an imperial province or *Reichsland*. German officials swarmed in and showed themselves heavy-handed, high-handed, and tactless, needlessly and inexcusably disagreeable in their insistence upon acceptance of the new German order. They were, however, generally honest and efficient, so that Alsace-Lorraine prospered when the rest of Germany was prosperous. The traditional Prussian-German policy of religious toleration was followed there as elsewhere; so there was no interference with the churches, ecclesiastical foundations, church schools, or elementary education in parochial schools in that predominantly Roman Catholic province. The province was given representation in the national Reichstag and eventually in the federal council or Bundesrat. The German language was made official and given preference over the French which the people of the province, after generations of living as Frenchmen, naturally found easier, preferred, remembered, and romanticized as one of the advantages of "the good old days" in France.

French or pro-French agitators could always find some example of egregious tactlessness or stupid abuse of authority by German government officials or army officers, and could raise a chorus of objectors in or about "the lost provinces" to the effect that the inhabitants were being shamefully persecuted and abused; and the Alsatians and Lorrainers were never perfectly reconciled to their German status. They would have preferred complete autonomy, which they did not have; but their principal objection to Germany was that it was Germany that ruled them.

From 1919 onward it was Germany that gained and France that lost popularity from the sentimental attitude that "it was better before." Since the detachment of Alsace and Lorraine in 1871 the Third French Republic had adopted anticlerical legislation secularizing all public education. This meant depriving the Catholic Church of the control of elementary schools of these provinces, which the German government had permitted it to retain. French replaced German as the official language and the medium of compulsory instruction. School strikes led by priests indicated objection to the change until the policy was revised so as to permit religious instruction in separate schools while still requiring secular instruction in public schools.

Freedom of religion was conceded by the French as it had been by the Germans. But national French laws disestablishing the church and governing the salaries of the clergy and the use of church buildings, to which the rest of France had become accustomed long before, aroused opposition in Alsace-Lorraine, which had not until then been affected by them. In general, the extension to Alsace-Lorraine of the principle of nation-wide uniformity of national legislation and administration, characteristic of the highly centralized, fairly unitary government of the Third Republic, was irksome to these provinces. Under it French law denied them some of the special privileges and the separate provincial parliament which the German Empire had since 1911 permitted them to enjoy. They were especially displeased by the abolition of the historical geographical designation of Alsace and Lorraine, and the redivision of the area into three new French departments of the Upper and Lower Rhine and the Moselle. They longed again for autonomy.

By the Treaty of Locarno German Foreign Minister Stresemann renounced all German claims to Alsace-Lorraine, meanwhile offering his fellow Germans, presumably for home consumption only, an explanation full of casuistry to the effect that he had not really given away anything or renounced anything permanently but, seeing Germany temporarily too weak to start a war of reconquest with any prospect of success, had merely made a temporary agreement not to start one. In public statements intended for foreign publication, as in March, 1935, Hitler, despite his constant denunciation of the Treaty of Versailles and of the temporary loss of control of the Saar, repeatedly confirmed the Treaty of Locarno's renunciation of Alsace-Lorraine and denied any intention of making a war for its recovery. Nazi party propaganda meanwhile belied Hitler by referring to the region as the German *Westmark* or western border province. When it was reoccupied in 1940 it was at once reincorporated into the Reich, which would have retained it if Germany had won the war. Troops of the United States Third and Seventh armies and the First French Army using American equipment and supplies fought their way into it in 1944. When Germany surrendered in May, 1945, French troops were in possession of both Alsace and Lorraine, and it was a foregone conclusion that the area would again become a part of France.

Colonies

The French colonial empire was a reservoir of military man power from 1914 to 1918, supplying Moroccan and Senegalese troops in considerable numbers, and some labor battalions from Indo-China. (Algerians also fought for France and were commonly thought of as "colonials" although Algeria was technically not a colony but a part of metropolitan France and as such its three departments were represented in the French parliament.) After the war there was some discontent and disorder in Morocco but, generally speaking, northwest

Africa continued to supplement the natural resources of continental France.

France included her colonies in her tariff system, took more than three-fourths of their exports, and sent them about the same portion of their imports. Natives were trained to participate in the colonial administration, and those who did so were paid on the same scale as Frenchmen doing comparable work. Some self-government was granted, but generally less than in the British colonies. The French colonies were never comparable with the self-governing British dominions because French people did not migrate to them. The comparatively small French element in the colonies consisted principally of tradesmen, professional soldiers, colonial administrators, and civil servants who went there on a career basis. The defense of the colonies depended heavily upon the French navy based at Dakar, Casablanca, Oran, and Bizerte, and upon colonial troops.

The general peace settlement of 1919 gave France some new colonial responsibilities in the form of mandates over the former German west equatorial African colonies Togoland and Kamerun, and over Syria and Lebanon, formerly parts of the Turkish Empire. There was some objection to France as the mandatory power in Syria and Lebanon, which wanted independence and, if denied that, would have preferred to be mandated to the United States or Great Britain. On more than one occasion the unpopular character of the French administration there was brought to the attention of the League of Nations mandates commission, which recommended its liberalization.

The outbreak of war in 1939 found most of the French colonial empire loyal to France. Colonial troops from north and west Africa were again used in France as in 1914. When northern France was overrun by German armies in 1940 there was some thought of moving the government to north Africa and continuing the war from there. That was not done, but the Germans never gained quite such complete control of that area as of France itself, and the Allied expeditionary force which landed there in November, 1942, was eventually given some assistance by colonial and Free French troops. French Indo-China, on the other hand, showing little loyalty to France, was easily overrun by the Japanese in 1940. Syria had to be taken from its Vichy French administration by Free French and British troops in 1941 to prevent the use of its landing fields by German planes en route to Iraq.[2]

[2] See pp. 371-372, and 591-593.

THE PROBLEM OF SECURITY: REVIEW OF FOREIGN POLICY

As has already been indicated in the matter of reparation policy, security was an obsession with the leaders of France in the twentieth-century period between world wars. Only in their purpose, however—which was to provide for the safety of France and if possible for the maintenance of her position as a great power—were her leaders unanimous or consistent. In their methods they seemed unable to choose between the old and the new, tried to use both, and ended by using neither effectively enough.

The first phase of the old method was to strengthen France comparatively by crippling the defeated enemy. France's efforts to use reparation payments and the cession of German territory and industrial assets to Poland for that purpose, and to detach the Rhineland, have already been discussed.[3] The second phase was to strengthen France potentially by making defensive alliances for her protection against attack by Germany. One such alliance, with the United States and Great Britain, was drafted at the Paris peace conference of 1919 but never ratified. (British ratification was conditional, depending upon ratification by the United States. The United States did not ratify.) Others were with Belgium (1920), Poland (1921), and Czechoslovakia (1924). In 1926 and 1927, respectively, France signed treaties of friendship and consultation with Rumania and Yugoslavia, providing for consultation as to joint action to be taken "within the framework of the covenant of the League of Nations if any neighbor nation should attempt or threaten to disturb the status quo." In May, 1935, a defensive treaty of mutual assistance was signed with Soviet Russia. France had friends enough on paper, but never enough in fact to give her the desired feeling of security.

A third old-style method of providing for security was the maintenance of large armed forces. The French army was not modernized or mechanized as rapidly as the German, nor was its efficiency as well maintained. It was found deficient in 1940 in airplanes, tanks, mobile weapons, and motorized infantry. But it was always large, and solicitude about it made it difficult for the French government to enter without crippling reservations into any international negotiations for disarmament or limitation of armament. Similarly, French objection to restriction of the use of submarines was at once an indication of the jealous watch France was keeping on the British and Italian navies and a stumbling block at every conference for the limitation of

[3] See pp. 80-84, 88-89, and 264.

naval armament. Until after Hitler came to power France seemed to
be seeking supremacy in Europe rather than security. After 1933
she would have settled for security. From 1930 onward, she constructed an elaborate and very expensive system of steel and concrete
fortifications, largely underground, along the whole Franco-German
frontier. This was known as the Maginot line. Outside France, the
purely negative self-defensive attitude which it advertised was sometimes called the "Maginot mentality."

A new security system was offered by the League of Nations, of
which France was a founding member. The League aimed at the
eventual reconciliation of the late enemy nations, and at their inclusion in a universal international organization. It aimed to substitute
an overwhelming weight of world opinion and general economic
pressure for the old "balance of power" idea sustained only by
alliances and armaments. Article 16 of the League Covenant clearly
stated that a resort to war by any member in disregard of its covenants
should be deemed an act of war against all members.

France never openly or officially disavowed the League. As a member she consistently took pains to write into her treaties specific statements that their making was consistent with its spirit and that the
parties were assuming no obligation inconsistent with their duties or
commitments as League members. Yet her continued and constant
manifestation of concern about her own security was an open admission of her lack of confidence in the League. Her skepticism about it
may have caused others to have less confidence in it than they might
otherwise have had.

The French leader most notable as a "good European" for his
conciliatory attitude toward Germany, his enthusiasm for the League
of Nations, and his predilection for the League's procedures for peaceful change and amicable adjustment of international differences was
Aristide Briand, one of the men of Locarno and co-sponsor of the
Kellogg-Briand Pact. Others who showed a similar disposition were
Radical Socialist Edouard Herriot and Socialist Léon Blum.

France seemed to be trying to play both the black and the red at
once, hoping that by so doing she could not lose. It was questionable
whether, playing against herself in such fashion, she could ever in
the long run have won. Not inconceivably, by a more consistent and
far-sighted policy identifying the security and other interests of
France more closely with those of all other peace-minded nations,
strengthening the League of Nations by using the procedures it provided for the maintenance of peace instead of undermining its prestige

by acting in the fundamental sphere of national security as if it did not exist, France might have come nearer to finding the security she sought. She might have been safer if she had not hedged so much. By 1935 it had become apparent that, without help, she would do nothing to check international aggression unless attacked. And she would need help if attacked.

INSTABILITY OF PARLIAMENTARY GOVERNMENT

To those who believed that democracy was the most beneficent principle of government and that the parliamentary form of it was the one best devised to give practical expression to the sovereign will of the people and to translate it into law by which government itself should be governed, one of the most disheartening phenomena of the twenty years' truce was the decline of parliamentary government in Europe. Britain, first to develop it, preserved it; Czechoslovakia adopted and maintained it, but with difficulty; Poland gave it only a perfunctory trial; Weimar Germany permitted it to fail; Italy, Spain, and Austria abandoned it; tsarist Russia had never known it, and the USSR did not introduce it; even the French seemed to lose confidence in it.

Many factors contributed to the political instability of the Third French Republic during that critical period. Whatever its form or character, the government in power would have found the first years of reconstruction expensive and the balancing of the national budget difficult. Taxpayers of a victorious but exhausted nation would have blamed whoever was in office for failure to compel the defeated but rapidly recovering Germans to pay enough in reparation to make "the fruits of victory" something that a Frenchman could relish and find nourishing. A people conscious of comparative weakness and apprehensive about its security might turn in exasperation upon a government that missed an opportunity such as the Paris peace conference of 1919 to strengthen and secure it, at least comparatively, by weakening its most dreaded enemy. Out of dissatisfaction with the Treaty of Versailles the voters turned in fact upon Clemenceau and denied him the presidency of France, a crowning honor which he thought he had earned by a long life spent in the service of his country. The general economic depression of the early 1930's affected France a little later and less seriously than countries with less well-balanced national economies; but she felt it also; and in France as elsewhere political instability was one of its effects.

Two other factors contributing to instability were the multiplicity of political parties and the constitutional inability of the premier to dissolve the Chamber of Deputies and force a new general election when defeated on a government measure in the Chamber or on a vote of confidence.

As in Weimar Germany, the plethora of parties meant in practice that no one party could command a majority in the Chamber or form a ministry. Every ministry represented a coalition and was compelled to serve several masters. It could rarely satisfy all of them long. Whenever one or two withdrew their support the parliamentary majority might be lost and the ministry have no choice but to resign, although several of the same ministers might immediately resume office under the same premier if he was able at once to form a new coalition. In little more than a year, for example, 1931-1932, Premier Pierre Laval reorganized his cabinet three times.

Or the new premier might have been a member of the last ministry, his being made head of the new one indicating some shifting of emphasis in government policy or some slight change in parliamentary opinion or alignments rather than a major reversal of policy. A change of ministry did not, therefore, always mean a complete political overturn or a reversal or abrupt change of direction. The swift succession of six leftist ministries in fifteen months, the last three of them in three months (Edouard Herriot, Joseph Paul-Boncour, Edouard Daladier, Albert Sarraut, Camille Chautemps, and Daladier again—December, 1932, to February, 1934, inclusive) was less kaleidoscopic than it would have been if the five premiers had not been of approximately the same political color, all Radical Socialists.[4]

The resignation of Daladier in February, 1934, was occasioned by serious rioting, a symptom of angry distrust of politicians in general and of the Chamber of Deputies in particular. Several serious railway accidents had given rise to some suspicion that government had been lax in its enforcement of the public safety regulations. Failure to prevent some scandalous financial frauds or to punish those responsible for them was attributed to the connivance of dishonest politicians.

The most conspicuous of these scandals was the case of Alexander Stavisky, a Polish Jewish immigrant equally notorious as a swindler and for his remarkable ability to go on purchasing immunity after numerous accusations. Stavisky managed somehow to become direc-

---

[4] The Herriot ministry resigned in December, 1932, when defeated on a motion to make a payment of about $19,000,000 on the war debt to the United States, due December 15.

The Radical Socialists were a moderate liberal republican party, less radical than the Socialists and much less than the Communists.

tor of the municipal loan office of Bayonne and to defraud it of nearly 200,000,000 francs. Caught in this crowning act of chicanery, and released on bail, he secured numerous unexplained postponements of trial. Prominent politicians were believed to be protecting him, and at least one cabinet minister was thought to have recommended purchase of the forged loan-office bonds. When in January, 1934, it was announced that Stavisky had committed suicide when the police attempted to arrest him, there was an immediate outcry from the antirepublican elements of the right, some of which were strongly anti-Semitic, to the effect that Stavisky had been murdered by the police to prevent him from betraying his political connections. Such stories readily found credence among people who had lost confidence in most of their professional politicians and were already psychologically prepared to believe unfavorable reports about them.

The extremists of the right—royalists, clericals, and fascists in various paramilitary organizations such as Colonel François de la Rocque's fascist war-veteran *Croix de Feu*, the *Action Française* and the blue-shirted *Solidarité Française*, the royalist *Camelots du Roi* and *Cagoulards*, and the Patriotic Youth, all enemies of the republic pretending to be acting on national-patriotic principles—were so quick to denounce the Daladier government and so violent in their demonstrations against it that the premier considered it necessary to station troops and gendarmes around the Palais Bourbon for the protection of the Chamber of Deputies which was meeting there. In the evening of February 6, 1934, nervous soldiers and armed police fired into a contingent of demonstrators approaching the Palais Bourbon through the Place de la Concorde. In a series of disorders lasting several days and nights and participated in by Communists as well as the street-fighting organizations and demonstrators of the extreme right, a score of people were killed and hundreds wounded. Daladier resigned, and President Lebrun asked former President Gaston Doumergue to form an emergency government of national union.

RADICALISM OF RIGHT AND LEFT

The Middle Group

The change from Daladier to Doumergue was a swing from slightly to the left of center to slightly to the right of center. Doumergue was a conservative. His cabinet included five former premiers (among whom were Herriot, Laval, and Tardieu) and the authoritarian old soldier Marshal Pétain.

The parties participating were liberal or moderately conservative, the Radical Socialists forming the left wing of the coalition. The Doumergue cabinet enjoyed the confidence of these moderate "middle" groups sufficiently to be authorized, as an emergency measure, to introduce economies by decree. It reduced expenditures by dismissing tens of thousands of its civil service employees and lowering the salaries of those whom it retained.

Doumergue's economy measures were unpopular with the Socialists; so the ministry was soon under constant fire from both right and left. Doumergue had to resign when in November, 1934, he asked for and was refused the constitutional amendments necessary to empower the cabinet and only the cabinet to initiate money bills, and the premier to dissolve the Chamber of Deputies without consent of the Senate. It was argued that the Chamber would be less likely to overthrow a ministry on insubstantial grounds if it knew that it would immediately then have to face a new election; but the amendments reducing the powers of the parliament and increasing those of the premier over it would have had to be adopted by a national assembly consisting of the two houses of the parliament, sitting in joint session for that purpose, and they were not ready for any such self-denying ordinance. Public opinion, moreover, was skeptical of such a move in what seemed to be a fascist direction. People had little enough confidence in the petty politicians in the parliament, but not much more in their national leaders. Their attitude toward government and government officials was largely negative.

Political opinion was less friendly to the idea of giving the premier greater political power than to that of entrusting him temporarily with extraordinary authority in the field of government finance. This was especially true of the more conservative groups. Pierre-Etienne Flandin, who followed Doumergue as premier with a very similar program and a similar coalition cabinet (from which the most conservative members, Tardieu and Pétain, had been dropped), was overthrown by a vote of no confidence (June, 1935) when he asked for unlimited authority to balance the budget. His immediate successor, however, Pierre Laval, whom the rightists considered safer, was immediately given the control of financial policy which Flandin had just been denied.

Right

Pierre Laval was a man of peasant origin who seemed never to be able to forget that he had once been poor, and to have resolved never to be poor again. He would gladly have forgotten the obscurity of his background by enjoying power and the company of the prominent and powerful; but he failed in his lifelong effort to induce others to forget it. He reduced government salaries and pensions and the interest rate on government bonds, as Doumergue had, but resisted the pressure put on him for the devaluation of the franc. He dissolved some of the smaller antiparliamentary organizations but would take no action against the strongest of them all, the *Croix de Feu*, whose fascist-minded members he called "the true French patriots."

It was Laval who, as Flandin's foreign minister from November, 1934, to June, 1935, and as premier from June, 1935, to January, 1936, negotiated a defensive treaty of alliance with Russia but soon seemed to lose interest in its ratification. It was he who shared with Sir Samuel Hoare the dubious distinction of responsibility for the policy of appeasement of Mussolini in the Ethiopian crisis (to be discussed later). He was deeply impressed by what he knew of Nazi Germany's war potential and never optimistic about France's ability, unaided, to withstand it. So far as Germany was concerned, he had been defeated and a defeatist since the battle of Verdun in 1916. He had faith only in "strong men." If he could not use Mussolini to hold Hitler in check, he saw no way to stop Hitler. If Hitler and Mussolini marched together, he did not know who would stop them. Stalin's strength had not been fully demonstrated, and Laval underestimated it. If choosing between communism and fascism, he would instinctively have chosen fascism.

It is a striking example of the chronological interrelation of events in Europe that the period of greatest ministerial instability in France, 1932-1934, saw the end of the Weimar republic, the firm establishment of Hitler as the Nazi Führer, and the withdrawal of Japan and Germany from the League of Nations. While the defeatist appeaser of the totalitarians, Pierre Laval, was directing French foreign policy in 1935 Mussolini took Ethiopia; and the signing of the German-Italian Axis agreement and of the German-Japanese-Italian anti-Comintern pact followed within a year. France's moments of indecision were always likely to be Hitler's moments of decision; he was on the alert for them and usually took advantage of them.

Left: The Popular Front

Emboldened by the success of National Socialism in Germany and fascism in Italy, some members of the royalist *Action Française* made in February, 1936, a public and viciously brutal attack upon the scholarly Jewish Socialist leader Léon Blum, beating him nearly to death. Startled by the atrocity, President Lebrun decreed the dissolution of the *Action Française* and the *Camelots du Roi*; but the *Croix de Feu* was left undisturbed. Equally startled, and frightened into an attempt at coöperation despite their party differences, the parties of the left—of which the largest were the Radial Socialist, Socialist, and Communist—united in an antifascist bloc called the *Front Populaire* or Popular Front. Also startled, the voters in the April-May elections for the first time in French history elected more Socialist deputies than men of any other party, and gave the Popular Front a comfortable majority (nearly two-thirds) in the Chamber of Deputies.

Léon Blum, leader of the Socialist party since 1924, his national reputation and popularity enhanced by the attack the royalists had made on him, became premier June 6. The Communist party, led locally by Maurice Thorez, had followed the new Moscow line to the extent of coöperating with the other antifascist parties in the election and promising to support the Blum ministry in the Chamber of Deputies, but refused to share its responsibility by accepting any cabinet positions.[5]

So M. Blum, dependent upon Communist support in the Chamber of Deputies, as Radical Socialist premiers had often been dependent upon him and his Socialists, had to concede to the Communists the same tactical advantage he had himself so many times enjoyed. They could control his policy without sharing his ministerial responsibility, as he had often controlled Radical Socialist policy without holding cabinet office. Patriots who had at heart the welfare of the whole French nation could find some encouragement in the national aspects of the Popular Front; but party particularism, evasion of political responsibility, and irresponsible obstructionism both parliamentary and extraparliamentary were generally prevalent even in periods of national emergency. The Third French Republic was traveling a downward path distressingly similar in that respect, and similar for kindred reasons, to the road already traveled by the Weimar republic —to its ruin.

The Popular Front government took office (June, 1936) at a time when France was still beset by the general depression and plagued by sit-down strikes in which the strikers took possession of the establishments in which they worked, left their machines but refused to leave the plants, and thus made it impossible for their employers to replace

[5] See pp. 393-395.

them or go on without them. The Blum government managed some improvement of the strike situation by negotiating new labor contracts involving higher wages and giving clearer recognition to the right of collective bargaining. New national legislation was enacted establishing the forty-hour week and holidays with pay which the Socialists had long advocated. Government was authorized at its discretion to require mediation or arbitration of industrial labor disputes. The charter of the Bank of France was so revised as to spread control of its financial policies more widely among the owners of its stock and loosen the grip which a relatively small number of the largest shareholders had had on it. An attempt to protect the vital interests of both producer and consumer of a basic commodity was made by the creation of a new government agency to control the price of wheat. The railways administration was reorganized and brought under unified government supervision.

Against all these reforms the antirepublican elements of the extreme right protested violently, declaring that the radicals were ruining the country. In retaliation, in June, 1936, charging the organized hoodlums of the right with lawlessness and responsibility for the prevalent disorder, Premier Blum decreed the dissolution of several of their organizations, which then went underground or reappeared wearing new disguises. The *Croix de Feu*, for example, was dissolved by the decree but was at once reorganized as the *Parti Social Français*.

Blum's Communist supporters demanded the nationalization of defense industries, a demand which was at that time being made also in the United States by pacifists and defense saboteurs pretending to be pacifists, under the slogan: "Take the profit out of war." Much publicity had been given in Europe and America to revelations of the international ramifications of the munitions industry and the "profit motive" which was alleged to have inspired the armament makers to sabotage international peace movements and all honest proposals of disarmament.

In the United States in 1934 *Fortune* magazine had devoted a whole issue to the evil machinations of the munitions makers. H. C. Engelbrecht and F. C. Hanighen's *Merchants of Death* had been widely read. In 1936 Senator Gerald P. Nye of North Dakota was cleverly publicizing his own stanchly isolationist views, spiced with some of the revelations of the senatorial committee of which he had been chairman. The committee, investigating the munitions industry from 1934 to 1936, had found that the bankers and munitions makers had made money in the war and used some of their profits to promote

their business by subsidizing unneutral propaganda before 1917 with
the intention of involving the United States in the war for their gain,
against its interest. The implication of Senator Nye's polemics was
that the greed of the munitions makers and the other money men had
been a primary cause of the war, and that the way to peace could be
cleared only by preventing anyone from making profit out of war.
One way to do that, according to the "merchants of death" thesis, was
to nationalize war industries.[6]

M. Blum's Popular Front government took the decisive step toward
nationalization of the French armament industry by securing the
passage of a law authorizing the executive to expropriate, with the
compensation to be fixed by arbitration, any privately owned industry engaged in the manufacture or sale of armament. Some munitions
works and military airplane factories were so expropriated and
operated by the government. Although the Popular Front was politically committeed to the strengthening of France's military defenses
against fascism, and although the Socialist program of concessions to
labor in such matters as hours, wages, vacations, working conditions,
and social insurance plans was carried out in the nationalized industries, those industries slowed down. The rearmament of France lagged
far behind that of Germany, where the Nazi Labor Front had people
working at forced speed, purposefully, not forty hours per week but
nearer sixty. Only when it was already too late was it realized that
France no longer had the best or best-equipped army in Europe, and

[6] Someone might have pointed out in rebuttal the possibility that the nationalization of war industries would merely spread over into new fields the mutual fears and
rivalries already rampant in the military and naval building fields, in which numerous
attempts to limit competitive building by treaty agreement had failed. What nations
would have submitted to the international inspection necessary to insure enforcement
of a treaty restricting munitions making? Or have agreed upon a definition of the
war materials in the manufacture of which they had accepted "in principle" any
form of treaty limitation and regulation? Would not the nationalization of the
munitions and war materials industries have put a higher premium than ever upon
total and constant industrial, military, and psychological preparedness for war, thus
increasing the advantage already enjoyed by the more aggressive-minded nation with
the greater industrial war potential? Would not the weaker and possibly more
pacifically inclined nations have been compelled then either to go into the armament
business in self-defense or each to standardize its military equipment with that of
like-minded neighboring nations in a defensive alliance? Or would each nation
strong in war potential have to equip all its weaker neighbors with armament like
its own? If it did, what of their sovereign independence? And in what respect would
such a grouping be different from one of the rival prewar military alliances so widely
believed to have been a primary cause of war? Would the total amount of armament
making, and the tensions occasioned by it, have been decreased or increased? Would
there be less selling to belligerents if the trade were in the hands of the other governments? Would an international agreement not to sell to a belligerent deter an
aggressor or only dishearten the nation threatened with aggression? Would any peace
but by propitiation and appeasement be promoted by such a prohibition?

that her air force, which had once led its field, was far back out of the running, with only a somnolent and obsolescent military aircraft industry behind it, unable to recover the ground it had lost.

By September, 1936, dissatisfaction with the Blum government was bitter and outspoken. Huge billboards beside Paris streets reminded their readers, who could read easily as they ran, that the Popular Front had promised them work, bread, peace, and security. What had it given them, asked the posters rhetorically, citing an appalling number of unemployed, quoting current high prices of all foodstuffs, even bread. Where was the peace, with Spain aflame? (The Communists and Socialists sympathized with the Loyalists and would have sold them equipment and munitions. The French fascists favored Franco. The government officially supported the British policy of nonintervention.) Where was the security, with fascist governments strengthening themselves on every hand?

In September, with Great Britain and the United States already off the gold standard, France again devalued the franc, reducing its value by another 33 percent. Still industrial production and export trade declined, refugee capital which had fled the country at the inception of the Popular Front government did not return, and government was faced with another heavy deficit in 1937. When Premier Blum asked in June, 1937, for the same extraordinary authority as had been given Pierre Laval two years earlier to enable him to balance the national budget, the Chamber of Deputies refused. Blum resigned, and the Chamber then voted Radical Socialist Camille Chautemps and a second (very similar) Popular Front government for two months the authority it had just refused to give to M. Blum.

Chautemps needed more than a free hand, however, to deal successfully with a 1937 deficit of eight billion francs. Prices continued to rise, out of control. The franc fell to a value of less than four cents. A monarchist plot by *Les Cagoulards* (The Hooded Ones) to overthrow the republic was frustrated; but the Chautemps ministry resigned January 14, 1938.

The Popular Front had broken up. Chautemps immediately formed a new Radical Socialist ministry with Delbos continuing as minister for foreign affairs and Daladier as minister for war. But the Socialists and Communists would not support it, so it had to resign March 10. Léon Blum tried to form a government of national union comparable with Poincaré's of 1926 or Doumergue's of 1934, but failed. Then he formed a new Popular Front government; but the Senate refused it the plenary powers for which it asked, and it lasted only twenty-eight days. On April 10 "strong man" Edouard Daladier formed a largely Radical Socialist cabinet in which he himself was again minister of war, Paul Reynaud was finance minister, and Georges Bonnet was minister for foreign affairs.

PRE-DEFEATISM

The Daladier ministry was one of the strongest France had had in recent years. It lasted until Reynaud succeeded Daladier as premier March 21, 1940, Daladier having meanwhile taken over the Foreign Office portfolio from Bonnet while continuing as minister for war. The imminent threat of bankruptcy of the national government and the new Nazi aggression against Austria had forced the French to try again to recover their national solidarity, but not until after irreparable damage had been done.

Again a period of political paralysis and uncertainty in France had given Hitler a favorable opportunity for action, for which he was prepared and poised. On February 12, while the Chautemps government was breaking up, the German chancellor had summoned Chancellor Schuschnigg of Austria to Berchtesgaden and bullied him into agreeing to take some German-designed Austrian Nazi into his cabinet as ministers of the interior, justice, and foreign affairs. On March 12, while Blum was vainly trying to form a stable new government in France, German troops occupied Austria and Hitler proclaimed its return to the Reich. France, which had played a leading part in preventing the German-Austrian customs union proposed in 1931, was unable to do anything in 1938 in the face of a much uglier accomplished fact—the *fait accompli* of the Nazi occupation, against which Italy refused to join in any protest.

Warned by the fall of Austria, the French Senate agreed to the granting of plenary financial powers to Daladier, whose cabinet contained no Socialists or Communists. The new government devoted itself assiduously, too late, to the military strengthening of France. The army was enlarged and the Maginot line supposedly perfected. Employers were authorized to extend the work week from forty hours to fifty, with hours worked in excess of forty per week rated as overtime and paid for at a slightly higher rate than the normal forty. The employer, however, was to be subject to a 10 percent tax on the profits earned in the overtime periods. War veterans' pension payments were reduced.

Communists, Socialists, trade unions, and the veterans' association objected to these "rightist and centrist" economies. A one-day general strike, November 30, 1938, called rather as a demonstration than as a serious strike, revealed the readiness of the national government to mobilize the workers, order them to work under military discipline, and summarily punish those who might refuse.

The strike crisis of November came between crises concerning Czechoslovakia and precipitated one in relations with Italy. After the annexation of Austria the Nazi centered their attention upon Czechoslovakia, pretending righteous indignation over the alleged abuse of the Sudeten Germans by the Czechoslovak government.[7]

Convinced that Hitler was not bluffing, and knowing that they would be only bluffing if they threatened to oppose him by use of armed force which they did not have and would not then have dared to use, Premier Daladier and Foreign Minister Bonnet decided that appeasement was the only practicable policy. France still had, to be sure, defensive treaties of alliance with Czechoslovakia and with Russia and early in 1938 had made a new one with Great Britain; but Belgium had repudiated hers; and Bonnet, who had always been lukewarm about the one with Russia, had lost all confidence in it after the Soviet purges of 1936-1938. Neither Poland nor Rumania would have been willing to permit the passage of Russian troops to Czechoslovakia to check a German invasion of that country. So France advised Czechoslovakia to accede to Hitler's Godesberg demands, and warned her that if she refused them she would be held responsible for causing him to use force, so must face the consequences without help from France. The beleaguered Czechs despairingly faced the facts of their unhappy situation by signing the Munich pact September 29, 1938.

Daladier was well received, on his return from Munich, by a people glad to be relieved, even momentarily, from the threat of war. (At the same time Hitler and Ribbentrop were being welcomed in Berlin for similar reasons, as reported by well-informed American observers.) The relief, however, was only temporary. The strike of November 30, announced beforehand, was made the occasion of fascist demands, boldly spoken in the Italian Chamber of Deputies, for French Tunisia and the "return" of Corsica and Nice. On December 2 Bonnet and Ribbentrop signed in Paris a nonaggression pact declaring that it was the intention of the French and German governments to settle only by diplomatic means whatever disputes might arise between them. But fifteen days later Mussolini repudiated the

[7] See pp. 171-174, and 508-523.

Franco-Italian pact of January 7, 1935, which had assured France of Italian support against Germany.

Bonnet was only buying time, at a high price. He said afterward that he knew it but knew he had to do it. Neither France nor Britain was then ready to fight Germany. Germany was not fully ready for war either, but was more nearly so than they; and they dared not depend upon Russia, which had not been invited to the conference at Munich.

Immediately after the German annexation and military occupation of the broken remnants of Czechoslovakia in March, 1939, France was put virtually on a war footing. The emergency powers of the Daladier government were made all-inclusive. The national legislature authorized the premier to govern by decree for a period of eight months, then extended its own term by postponing the 1940 election to 1942, so that whatever national solidarity he could achieve would not be disturbed by an impending general election. Daladier used his plenary powers to extend the work week generally to fifty hours (reserving the right to make it sixty if necessary), to enlarge the army, to push industrial production and war preparedness, and to control the press. When the Communists, after the signing of the Nazi-Soviet pact late in August, objected to his defensive measures as provocative of war and inimical to Russia, he outlawed the Communist party and banned its propaganda.

Thanks to Daladier's energy and determination, some use was made of the time he had bought at Munich. France was better prepared for war, both materially and psychologically, in 1939 than in 1937 or in 1938. So was Great Britain.

Neither in 1939 nor in 1940, however, was France really ready. She kept her agreement with Great Britain and declared war on Germany when Britain did, upon the invasion of Poland. But she went to war without confidence or enthusiasm—fatalistically, as if without hope. She fought half-heartedly, defensively, in 1939 because she had no more than half a heart for the war. She collapsed in 1940 because she was hard hit, by an army of such striking power as the world had never seen till then, but also because of her own internal weakness. She had never recovered her resilience since the ordeal of Verdun, 1916. She capitulated because her leaders could not see how she could survive by continuing to struggle, and some of them (Pétain and Laval) thought that she might keep herself alive by floating with the Nazi flood.

The old French confidence in France was gone. France had sought security diligently and at last desperately, in the period between wars, but had not found it, perhaps because she had been inconsistent and short-sighted in her search, seeking it in several directions simultaneously, finally frustrating herself by asking fate for security only, from day to day, and for herself only.

CHAPTER 12

Depression, Aggression, and Appeasement, 1931-1939

DEPRESSION AND DISINTEGRATION

It would be impossible to estimate exactly, but difficult to exaggerate, the political consequences of the world-wide economic depression of the early 1930's. In Germany the Brüning ministry could not survive the rejection of its plans for the revival of central European trade and for the formation of a customs union with Austria.[1] Engelbert Dollfuss, enemy of both Socialists and National Socialists, became chancellor of Austria in May, 1932, was vested with emergency powers during a parliamentary deadlock March 4, 1933, used troops and cannon fire to crush the Socialists in February, 1934, and proclaimed a new authoritarian constitution on May 1, 1934. France's economy was better balanced than that of some of her neighbors, and so at first was less seriously disturbed by the depression. But financial difficulties contributed materially to the political instability of her government, especially in 1932 and 1933, while her inability to offer a market for the exports of southeastern Europe contributed to her loss of influence there and to a corresponding increase of German and Italian influence in that area. In Britain in November, 1931, a national coalition government was formed, less consistent in its support of the principle of collective security than the MacDonald Labour governments had been. In Japan the militarists got control of policy, and Premier Hamaguchi, who was not aggressive enough to satisfy them, was assassinated by a fanatical nationalist November 14, 1930.

[1] See pp. 274-276.

In Spain the monarchy was abolished in 1931, but the republic which was then established was eventually unable either to cure the economic ills with which the country was afflicted or to maintain itself against the combined forces of reactionary rebels and Nazi-fascist interventionists.

International tensions and disintegration meanwhile reflected the deterioration of international economic relations. On March 1, 1932, Great Britain, which had already gone off the gold standard, finally abandoned her traditional policy of free trade and adopted a protective tariff, soon to be slightly modified by a policy of imperial preference and tariff-bargaining for markets. The United States cut the ground from under an international monetary conference in London in 1933 by suddenly reversing itself on the policy of adherence to the gold standard and indicating its intention to devalue the dollar.

The general optimism, amiability, and coöperative spirit characteristic of the later twenties, indicative of a realization of a general community of economic interest, had disappeared with the (partly false) prosperity of that period. Economic nationalism appeared in place of internationalism, each nation striving to save its own currency, price scales, standard of living, markets, and prosperity by becoming economically self-sufficient, no matter what might happen to any of the others. In that mad scramble, after 1933, Germany, by systematic and scientific cheating on bilateral bartering agreements, fared better than her neighbors or the people with whom she bartered.

The economic balkanization of Europe threatened to balkanize it politically also. In an attempt to re-cement relations on a regional basis within the League of Nations, the representatives of several European nations at the 1929 meeting of the League Assembly had proposed a conference to consider the formation of something like the United States of Europe which Aristide Briand of France had long eloquently advocated. At its first meeting, on invitation of the government of France in January, 1931, the Commission on European Union found that it must consider economic questions as well as problems of continental security. The depression and the political disturbance caused by the German-Austrian proposal of a customs union (although Germany and Austria invited the other European nations to join their union on equal terms as a step toward a mutually profitable economic union without loss of sovereignty) showed European opinion not yet ready for European union.

Briand then proposed another scheme for economic coöperation, including loans to the agrarian countries of southeastern Europe and a preferential tariff system among the Danubian states; but what those states wanted most was markets. Briand's program did not appeal to them as the Nazi *Grossraumwirtschaft* (large-scale regional economy) did soon afterward, and France could not absorb their exports as Nazi Germany later did. Conferences on this subject in April and September, 1932, accomplished nothing. As harder times followed hard times in southeastern Europe, French influence waned there. The area was left open for Nazi economic and ideological penetration.

With the one-year Hoover moratorium beginning July 1, 1931, international war debt and German reparation payments ceased, and the Young plan, although adopted, did not effect their general resumption or continuance. National budgets based upon the assumption that those payments would be continued had to be revised or stand new strains. International confidence in the good faith, good will, and financial integrity of the governments concerned was also subjected to new strains.

Everywhere the depression helped to bring about an emergency situation, not altogether unlike the crisis faced by the Soviet Russian government ten years before, when it adopted its New Economic Policy. Emergency planning was required, testing the ingenuity, resilience, and strength of governments. New forms of control of economic enterprise, of production, distribution, hours and wages, had to be devised to meet the new problems of unemployment, undernourishment, and inadequate social insurance programs.

Democracy was not everywhere immediately triumphant in its struggles with such problems. The more unwilling people were to carry one another out of the depression by voluntary submission to government control of phases of economic life not ordinarily so controlled, or to pay the necessary taxes to finance public works programs as palliatives for unemployment or to care decently for the indigent unemployed, the more reluctant their governments were to impose controls or taxes on them. The authoritarian states seemed to have there an advantage.

Democracy, argued the totalitarians, advocates of the "principle of leadership," was outmoded. It could not act quickly, decisively, or authoritatively enough to meet the emergencies of the modern world. Truly responsible government, they said, was responsible for its people and recognized its responsibility but was not necessarily immediately answerable to them in a parliamentary or political sense. Rugged individualism produced too many ragged individuals. By quickly ending unemployment, Nazi Germany seemed superficially to have proved the totalitarian case (until the observer noted how much of the activity in which the German millions were so busily engaged was economically unproductive).

The long-continued emergency of the depression severely tested the internal social and political structures of all the nations affected by it. Only the strongest of the democracies stood the test without substantial change of character. While many governments nominally democratic were being weakened and confessing their weakness by turning to "strong men" and conferring extraordinary emergency powers upon them, then asking them to lead the way out of the wilderness, totalitarian governments seemed to be going daily from strength to strength. Contrary conditions were concealed by censorship.

As self-confidence declined among the nonfascist, non-Nazi, and noncommunist peoples of Europe, so did their confidence in one another. The pessimism with which many of them faced the future was a poor foundation upon which to build a solid wall of international resistance to any violence which the restless revisionist powers might attempt.

DISRUPTION OF SECURITY SYSTEM BY TREATY VIOLATION

During the 1920's (see especially Chapter 6) a persistent and not altogether inconsistent effort was made by men of many nations to achieve world stability and insure national security by treaty agreement. By the Washington conference treaties of 1921-1922 the four principal powers of the Pacific area recognized one another's possessions there and agreed to respect and not to attack them. If the treaties had held, they would have been an adequate guarantee of peace in that area. The five strongest naval powers accepted the principle of naval limitation by agreement. That should have eased the tensions arising out of competitive navy building by leaving each interested party in a good defensive position, unable to attack another with any prospect of success. Nine powers interested in the southwestern Pacific and eastern Asia trading area put themselves on record as recognizing the sovereignty and territorial integrity of China. Japan was a party to that treaty. At Locarno in 1925 Germany confirmed the cession of Alsace-Lorraine and the demilitarization of the Rhineland, and Italy and Britain guaranteed the German-Belgian and German-French boundaries against any attempt to change them by use of armed force. By the Kellogg-Briand Pact of Paris (signed at Paris

August 29, 1928, officially promulgated at Washington July 24, 1929) the signatories, including eventually all the nations, renounced war as an instrument of national policy, reserving the right to fight only in a war of self-defense, which could not occur unless one or more of them broke the treaty by waging offensive war.

In the 1930's the seamless but rather flimsy fabric of international organization to provide security and peace by mutual agreement was torn to shreds by cynics who had used it only while they found it prudent to cover their designs for its destruction. Japan was in good geographical position to compete with other manufacturing and trading nations for Chinese raw materials and markets. She was unwilling, however, merely to compete. Her bolder leaders thought the time had come when she could exclude others from that area and exploit it for herself.

Mussolini was by that time well out into the open with his pretensions as successor to the Caesars and his promises to revive the glories of ancient Rome and restore the Roman Empire. At the same time a resurgent Germany, under bold and recalcitrant Nazi leadership, denounced the disarmament clauses of the Treaty of Versailles, claimed the right to rearm as an essential attribute of sovereignty and equality with other nations, and talked alarmingly about the reacquisition of lost colonies and the conquest of new *Lebensraum*—space in which to live.

All three—Germany, Italy, and Japan—called themselves crowded countries. All three claimed *Lebensraum* for excess population as a natural right, in the name of humanity. All three told their own people at the same time, incessantly, that the world and the future properly belonged only to those youthful and vigorous peoples whose vitality was evidenced by a high birth rate, that the decadence of the old imperial powers was indicated by their static populations and declining birth rates. At home, all offered tax exemptions, public honors, and state aid to parents of large families, to increase the pressure of surplus population about which they were complaining so vociferously abroad.

There was much talk in that decade about the "satiated" and the "unsatiated" powers, the "haves" and the "have nots." Most of that talk emanated, naturally, from the "have nots" eager to dispossess the "haves." The satiated powers, as the term was used in those days, were those which did not then intend to wage aggressive war for the acquisition of more territory, but which naturally associated the maintenance of the territorial *status quo* with the maintenance of peace. Such renunciation, said Mussolini, was a symptom of decadence, characteristic only of a dying people. Fascism saw, on the other hand, he said, in the natural aspiration of a people to rise, to revive, or to expand, a manifestation of vitality. He evidently intended that Italy should not go on much longer as a "have not" nation but should become one of the "haves" by taking what she wanted, wherever she could find it inadequately defended.[2]

Why, asked Hermann Göring rhetorically in 1936, should 40,000,-000 Englishmen own the world-wide British Empire (in which he included the dominions, India, and the mandated territories) and fatten themselves on it while 67,000,000 Germans were squeezed into the narrow confines of "Versailles" Germany to starve? God, answered Hitler, had not created the universe for the sole benefit of the British. Both speeches were published in Germany and widely quoted elsewhere, but few people knew how seriously to take them.

Was it only the return of the lost German colonies that Hitler had in mind? Did he think that those colonies would ever be returned? Nazi Germany was then maintaining a colonial office, schools for colonial officials and prospective settlers, and agricultural experiment stations planning the development of the natural resources of colonies which she did not then possess. Or was the talk about colonies, and the propaganda "proving" how well Germany had handled them when she had had them, intended only to popularize the regime which so encouraged it, to restore German pride and confidence in Germany as a colonial power, and to remind the Germans daily of the "injustice" done them when they were "robbed of their colonies," lest they some day forget it? Or was the propaganda campaign for the regaining of the colonies intended only to disturb the British (who had got some of them under mandate) just enough to make a policy of appeasement seem to timid British leadership to offer an inviting way out of its predicament if German expansion should some day take a different direction? Hitler did not say, and may not then have known. He said only, when he found it expedient to propitiate the British, that he would not fight a war for colonies. They were not worth it. He also told the world, which wanted to believe him, that he would not fight any war unless attacked.[3]

[2] Benito Mussolini, *The Doctrine of Fascism* (Florence, 1936), 45.

[3] On May 23, 1939, at a briefing conference in preparation for the war on Poland, Hitler told his generals: "Living space in proportion to the magnitude of the state is the basis of all power. . . . It is a question of extending our living space to the east, of gaining food supplies. . . . Colonies are no solution. . . . They are too easily

It would not have been impossible for the revisionist powers to bring about some changes by direct negotiation or by conference. The League of Nations Covenant had provided some promising procedures for peaceful change; and at Montreux in 1936 a conference of the signatories of the 1923 Treaty of Lausanne, requested by Turkey to permit her to refortify the zone of the Straits, agreed to authorize that very significant departure from the terms of the Treaty of Lausanne.[4]

Changes as great as the Japanese, Italian, and Nazi leaders apparently already had in mind, however, could hardly have been made with genuine consent. Continued bullying, accompanied by the constant threat of force, must some day reach its limit; and the peaceful-change potentialities of the League of Nations had never been fully realized or utilized.

Eventually, if the revisionist powers meant to take, and then to go on taking, territory owned and occupied by others, they would have had to fight for it. Space, said Hitler to his generals in 1937, was never found without an owner. "The attacker always comes up against the proprietor. The question for Germany is where the greatest possible conquest could be made at the lowest cost."[5] Considerations of right or wrong, or treaties, did not enter into the matter.[6] Japan, embarking upon a career of conquest in Manchuria and China in flagrant violation of the Washington Nine-Power Treaty concerning China and the Kellogg-Briand Pact of Paris, both of which she had signed, blandly pretended to be defending herself in China, acting only in the interest of world peace. She refused to call the China "incident" a war or a treaty violation.

Against marauders such as these, treaty protection was paper protection only, transparently paper-thin. Good will among the nations would have strengthened it, and have diminished the apparent need for it. Good faith was an essential if the peace fabric was to hold; but the totalitarian leaders scoffed at the old nineteenth-century notion that good faith between the nations had aught to do with statecraft. Without security by agreement there was no confidence. Without confidence there could be no security by agreement.

blockaded." See Peter de Mendelssohn, *Design for Aggression* (New York, 1946), 87, 88; International Military Tribunal, *Nazi Conspiracy and Aggression* (Washington, 1946), VII, 848-849.

[4] See pp. 113 and 161.

[5] Hossbach minutes of conference in chancellery, Berlin, November 5, 1937. *Nazi Conspiracy and Aggression*, III, 295-305.

[6] Hitler to his commanding generals at a briefing conference May 23, 1939. *Ibid.*, VII, 847-854.

BEGINNING OF THE WAR IN ASIA—1931

Economic Imperialism in China

The second world war of the twentieth century began in Manchuria in 1931 as a clash between Chinese nationalism and Japanese imperialism. It was occasioned by Japan's decision to seize and assume complete control of the area before the Chinese national government could strengthen itself sufficiently to prevent the conquest. It came at a moment when, because of the general depression and the consequent decline of international confidence and coöperation, effective interference in defense of China by any other power or powers was improbable.

Manchuria was the great northern gateway to China. Through it had swept some of the Mongol hordes of Genghis and Kublai Khan which overran China. From it had come the Manchu dynasty, the armies which conquered China for it, and men for the garrisons which maintained it. Manchuria was not only the land bridge into China from the northeast; Dairen, in Kwantung province at the southern end of the Liaotung peninsula, was a natural ice-free seaport for a hinterland extending beyond Manchuria into Mongolia and Siberia.

The long history of Japan's expansion at the expense of China, therefore, centered for geographical reasons around Korea and Manchuria. But although the Japanese clearly intended in 1931 to be the last outsiders to push into China, they had not been the first. Trade with China had attracted Europeans ever since Marco Polo had publicized the wealth of Kublai Khan. Imperial China had not at first welcomed the traders. The Manchus had treated all foreigners as inferiors, or as subjects bearing tribute to a suzerain as the Koreans did.

In the late eighteenth and early nineteenth centuries—the clipper ship era—American traders shared with Europeans the inconveniences, hazards, and speculative profits of a trade at once officially forbidden and unofficially tolerated as a privilege, not a right. The trade was carried on through intermediaries, the hong merchants at Canton, who monopolized it, upon whom the traders were kept dependent for protection, and for whose indispensable services as interpreters and agents they paid at every step of every transaction an unregulated "squeeze" which they were likely to think extortionate. Friction frequently developed out of fundamental differences between Occidental and Oriental concepts of contractual obligations, the Chinese having been long accustomed to the practice of renegotiating and revising a contract when either party found it working a serious and unforeseen hardship on him and asked therefore for its revision. How then, asked a European, could he hold a Chinaman to a contract? Misunderstanding easily arose also out of the Chinese theory of responsibility—that someone, ever so remotely connected but not necessarily the responsible or guilty one, could be held responsible for every obligation or offense.

Personal hazards of the China trade included the danger that a foreigner might run afoul of the police, be thrown without a warrant or benefit of habeas corpus writ into a prison purposely made uncomfortable and unpleasant, possibly be tortured or abused to extort a "confession" from him, and (if brought to trial) be prosecuted in a Chinese court in a language he could not understand, under a legal system equally incomprehensible to him, on charges which he might or might not understand if they were translated. He was likely to think himself abused and was not always mistaken. The traders were intruders and could not count on being hospitably received.

In the face of such strange hazards and man-made difficulties the uninvited visitors might prudently have stayed away, but the profits of the trade attracted them despite its inconveniences and incidental costs. Their willingness to submit to the conditions and pay the charges imposed on it merely convinced the Chinese officials that, while China could quite well do without the ginseng, furs, sandalwood, cotton cloth, and other goods brought in by foreigners, the traders' peoples must have found that they could not live without China's tea, silks, nankeen cloth, lacquered wares, and objects of art; else they would not have sought those things so eagerly. So, like the goose that laid golden eggs, the trade should be kept alive, and the agents who handled it and officials who permitted it should share the profits of the uncouth foreigners engaged in it. (In 1820 the China trade took 11.8 percent of the exports and furnished 10.9 percent of the imports of the United States.)

The traders' governments would have preferred to legalize the trade by making commercial treaties with China giving their nationals access at least to warehouses and to the courts, for the protection of their property, contracts, and personnel. Thus the China trade would have been raised from the demimondaine level of a clandestine traffic carried on by favor of corrupt and irresponsible Chinese officials and the hong monopolists to the dignity of an established trade authorized by treaty.

Until about 1830 the balance of the trade was "favorable" to China.

The foreigners bought more than they sold, and paid the balance in specie or in bullion, principally in silver dollars. Then a steady increase in the opium trade seemed at first, superficially, to have solved the traders' adverse cash-balance problems. As the use of opium as a narcotic became more general in China and the demand increased, the opiate commanded high cash prices. By 1830 the flow of specie had been reversed, the opium then being imported exceeding in cash value all commodities exported. Specie was thus being drained out of the country, much of it to India, which supplied the opium and used the cash it brought to meet its own adverse trade balance on its trade with Britain. Responsible Chinese officials were justifiably concerned about the ultimate economic consequences of the adverse trade balance and the loss of specie, as well as about the deleterious effect of the opium habit upon the health and morals of the people. Some of the more far-sighted traders also realized that the opium trade might kill itself as the stuff might eventually be produced in China, that Chinese land producing opium poppies would not be producing food, and that a China impoverished and demoralized by such a habit would cease to be a profitable trading area for any other trade.

From 1800 onward the importation of opium was prohibited by Chinese law. The Chinese Co-hong and the British East India Company ceased to engage in it. But there were customers enough, and purveyors of the forbidden opiate found its importation easy with the connivance of Chinese officials for whom the illicit trade provided a richer source of revenue in the extortionate form of the "squeeze" they could put on it than if the government had legalized and taxed it.

In 1834 the British government abolished the British East India Company's monopoly of the British China trade. Thereafter a new need arose for the establishment of a substitute authority or single agent with whom Chinese officialdom would deal and through whom they would if possible control the other traders. Lord Napier was sent to try to negotiate directly with the Chinese imperial government but was rebuffed. In 1838 a new policy of rigorous enforcement of the prohibition of the opium trade was rather suddenly adopted. Opium stocks of all foreigners were confiscated. Some other cargoes belonging to British nationals were seized, trading posts ("factories") were blockaded, and all trade was stopped. The foreigners withdrew from Canton to Macao, then to Hong Kong where British warships protected them. Hostilities ensued. So opium was the occasion, but only one of many causes, of the "Opium War" of 1840-1842.

By the Treaty of Nanking, 1842, China had to open Canton, Shanghai, and three other ports (Amoy, Foochow, and Ningpo) to British trade, and cede Hong Kong outright to Great Britain.[7] China had also to agree to pay a cash indemnity of $21,000,000 to cover the cost of the expedition, the value of the opium destroyed, and accounts payable to British merchants. In 1843 a new treaty gave British subjects extraterritorial rights in China as guarantees of protection for their property rights, contracts, privileges, and persons. In 1844 the same privileges were granted to nationals of other nations. China was "open," and the monopoly of the hong merchants was broken.[8]

From 1857 to 1860 another series of incidents occurred, sometimes called a second "Opium War," with the British again spearheading the advance of the aliens and aided this time by France, which was demanding reparation for the execution, by order of a Chinese magistrate, of a French missionary, the Abbé Chapdelaine. Eight European bishops and fifteen missionaries had been put to death in Indo-China since 1833. By successive treaties signed at Tientsin in June, 1858, and at Peking October 24, 1860, after the destruction of the emperor's summer palace at Peking, eleven more "treaty ports," including several on the Yangtse River, were opened up to foreign trade, and all China soon thereafter to Christian missionary enterprise. At Shanghai, where relations between local officials and the foreigners were fairly amicable from the beginning, land was set aside for a foreign settlement. Similar concessions were soon made at other treaty ports. By the "most favored nation" convention, concessions made to the nationals of one power were enjoyed by all.

The United States minister to China followed the British-French forces to Tientsin, under instructions to coöperate in peaceful measures

[7] Hong Kong had been legally a British possession for approximately a hundred years when it was seized by the Japanese December 25, 1941; so British spokesmen never, during or after the war, indicated that they thought of its recovery as an open question. If there should be any discussion of the status of Hong Kong, they contended, only Britain and China should be parties to it.

[8] Article XXI of the treaty negotiated by Caleb Cushing as the first United States minister to China in 1844 stated the principle of extraterritoriality as follows: "Subjects of China who may be guilty of any criminal act towards citizens of the United States shall be arrested and punished by the Chinese authorities according to the laws of China, and citizens of the United States who shall commit any crime in China shall be subject to be tried and punished only by the Consul or other public functionary of the United States thereto authorized according to the laws of the United States; and in order to secure the prevention of all controversy and disaffection, justice shall be equitably and impartially administered on both sides." See Harold M. Vinacke, *A History of the Far East in Modern Times* (New York, 4th ed., 1942), 46.

to improve the treaty status of Americans in China but to take no part in any hostile demonstration. His government had no territorial designs on China. He took no part in the actual coercion of the Chinese government, and took less advantage of it than some others did, yet utilized the opportunity it offered. At his request the opium trade was legalized and regulated, and an import tax imposed on it. It was the United States treaty which first secured legal recognition and toleration for Christian missionaries and converts without restriction to prescribed areas. The French pushed the protection of missionaries further by compelling the Chinese government to acknowledge publicly an obligation to protect them.

Taking advantage of China's continued political and military weakness, in 1862, France seized the three southeastern provinces of Cochin-China. Russia, whose minister to China had kept on good terms with the United States minister during the British-French advance on Tientsin in 1858 and had posed as a friend of China throughout the incident, arranged for the territorial expansion of Russia to the Pacific by the annexation of the maritime province north and east of Manchuria. Thus she secured the site for a seaport at Vladivostok looking out upon the Sea of Japan, and came into contact with Korea there as well as with China in Manchuria.

For half a century after the signing of the treaties of Tientsin and Peking, the process of opening up China to European and American trade and both missionary and commercial enterprise went forward rapidly. If the development and exploitation of mineral resources, the provision or improvement of transportation facilities and means of communication, and the eventual introduction of railways and power-driven machinery meant progress, then China was helped by foreigners and foreign capital to make such progress more rapidly. The people who did most for the Chinese and asked least of them in return were the Christian missionaries, especially the teachers, doctors, and nurses with their missionary schools and hospitals. Sometimes even they aroused resentful opposition by their interference with old folkways and customs and with vested interests. Another comparatively disinterested group were the customs officials—mostly British, many of them Scotsmen—employed by the Chinese government because it found them honest and efficient. Others also found them easier to do business with than Chinese imperial officials generally were.

Few of the foreigners, however, had gone to China for purely altruistic reasons. When a foreign-owned company opened up an oil well or a mine, the investors expected the enterprise to be profitable to them—to pay a good return and to cover losses on their unsuccessful speculative ventures. When government borrowed money, it had to give its creditors, as security, a lien on some of its revenues; so it lost control of its tariff policy. When a public utility was built with alien capital, the service of its indebtedness had to be given a preferred claim upon a portion of its earnings. The price paid by the Chinese for the benefit of such modernization of their country as they enjoyed depended upon the moderation of the concessionaires. It cost them less where concessions were competitive, more wherever national spheres of preponderant economic interest meant paramount political influence also, and so approached economic exclusiveness and monopoly.

Its energies largely employed at home in its own industrialization and the absorption of its own frontier, the United States made no attempt to block out spheres of interest for itself in China and sought no exclusive privileges for its nationals. It insisted upon "most favored nation" treatment, which meant that its nationals must be as well treated as any others, even those of the nation anywhere most favored. It was willing that they should compete on equal terms but wanted the competition kept open. China, then, should be accessible to the trade and enterprise of all nations with which she had treaty relations; so China should be enabled to maintain itself as a sovereign state and kept territorially intact.

Such was the consistent background of the policy of the open door promulgated by Secretary of State John Hay, beginning in 1899. American nationals and trade should not be discriminated against, even in such matters as customs or railway rates, in existing spheres of interest. This recognized the existence of such spheres, yet would militate against their extension or the establishment of new ones, since the concepts of the open door and of spheres of exclusive interest and privilege were fundamentally incompatible. So a policy of enlightened self-interest, that sought in the first instance to prevent the exclusion of American economic enterprise from an extensive and inviting trading area in which other commercial powers had staked out spheres of interest and influence while the United States had none, was beneficial also to China, and marked the United States as friendly in principle to the sovereignty and territorial integrity of China.

Emergence of Japan as an Imperial Power

The United States took the initiative and the leading part in inducing Japan to reopen her ports to foreign intercourse and her territory to alien residents by treaties made with Commodore Perry in 1854 and Townsend Harris in 1858. Thus ended for Japan a period of approximately 250 years of self-imposed seclusion complete except for some strictly limited contacts with and through a few Dutch and Chinese traders tolerated at Nagasaki. Not content with excluding foreigners, the government forbade its own people to go abroad or to build ships large enough for any but coastal and interisland voyages.

The isolation of Japan was the work of a long line of regents, called shoguns, of the Tokugawa clan who during that period ruled the nation from their capital at Yeddo (Tokyo), in the name of the emperor or mikado. The emperor was kept in retirement at Kyoto, wrapped in mystery and exalted by the Shinto religion as the Son of Heaven, but was permitted no personal exercise of his theoretically supreme authority. The long period of national seclusion was a time of peace, during which the other powerful clans, rivals of the Tokugawa clan, became jealous of it and restive under its control, and during which the restless energies of the warlike samurai were turned to the development of a culture and an ideology ever more intensely nationalistic, imperialistic, and expansionist in character. It suited this ideology to reëmphasize the supposed heavenly origin of the emperor, to refurbish his time-tarnished authority, and to use him and the prestige of his position as a symbol of a new and aggressive nationalism. The Tokugawa shogunate could not survive the loss of face it suffered when compelled to yield to pressure from outside; but in a period of economic and social change it was already subject by 1853 to increasing pressure by the other clans and might soon have lost its grip without the American intrusion.

The Perry expedition of 1853 was the culmination of a long series of attempts to secure at least the right of refuge in Japan for mariners engaged in whale hunting, sealing, and fishing in the northwest Pacific. These men were sometimes tossed by typhoons upon inhospitable Japanese shores or forced by storm damage to their ships to put in there for necessary repairs. It would have been convenient for them to secure fresh water and provisions there. With the introduction of steam-driven ships in the north China trade arose a new need for a conveniently located coaling station. Formosa had been considered, but Japan seemed likely to be much more useful. Russia had sent expeditions in 1792 and 1804 to open negotiations for purposes such as these but had been twice rebuffed. Both Britain and the United States had tried repeatedly, without success. Japan's harbors continued closed not only to foreign seafarers in distress but even to those repatriating Japanese refugees who had been blown out to sea or shipwrecked and whom they had rescued. Government officials may have suspected in such cases that Japanese returning in the company of aliens in alien ships had gone abroad illegally or been captured, not rescued, and used by the intruders as credentials to effect an admission otherwise prohibited.

The Perry naval expedition which sailed from Norfolk November 24, 1852, had been long in preparation. The United States had notified other governments in 1849 of its intention. Perry entered Yokohama Bay without Japanese permission July 3, 1853, and anchored off Uraga July 8, with a message from the president to the emperor which he would present only to an official of the highest rank. He refused to go to Nagasaki to receive his answer through mediaries—who would have been the Dutch or Chinese there established. He demanded succor and protection for seamen in distress, the opening of ports for the coaling, provisioning, and refueling and refitting of American vessels, and most favored nation treatment for all citizens of the United States. Then he withdrew to the China coast and returned in February, 1854, for his answer.

Meanwhile a Russian fleet visited Nagasaki soon after Perry's first visit to Yokohama, and a French fleet was known to be available for service in Japanese waters. The shogun had little choice but to yield to the show of force and grant what Perry had demanded. He used the emperor's sanction to make the bitter pill (Treaty of Kanagawa, March 31, 1854) more palatable to his people but lost more prestige than the emperor did by being so controlled by circumstances.

Britain, Russia, and the Netherlands quickly took advantage of the opening made by Perry. That opening was enlarged and the Treaty of Kanagawa was confirmed and amplified by treaty in 1858 by the first United States consul, Townsend Harris. The later treaty established diplomatic and consular relations between the United States and Japan, and opened six ports to trade as well as to vessels in need of refitting or supplies. Other nations soon secured similar privileges, the more easily since China was just then being induced to sign the treaties of Tientsin and, soon thereafter, Peking. Import and export taxes were regulated by agreement, which meant that Japan soon lost control of her tariff policy as China had already done; but she was able (as China had not been) to exclude the opium trade. Extraterritorial rights were asked and granted, although the Japanese found them humiliating. Christian missionaries were protected by the treaties and permitted to try to win converts, although Commodore Perry had been instructed to reassure the Japanese on that point by telling them that the United States would not try to impose Christianity upon Japan.

During the half-century following Commodore Perry's visits Japan was outwardly modernized in many ways. Under tutelage of British engineers and naval officers, harbor facilities for ocean-going vessels were developed, shipyard workers learned to build such ships, and the nucleus of a modern navy was constructed. German officers supervised the training of a conscript army, which diminished the importance of the traditional warrior caste, the samurai. American engineers directed the construction of bridges, dams, railways, telegraph lines, and new metropolitan buildings. The modern industrialization of the country was begun.

Rival clans used the restored powers and prestige of the emperor to end the shogunate of the Tokugawa, and the new emperor Mutsu-hito (1867-1912) earned his reign-title of Meiji Tenno or Enlightened Ruler by reorienting his people in their relations with foreign powers. The emperor's restored position was symbolized by his moving his capital from Kyoto to Yeddo, the seat of the shoguns, and renaming the latter city Tokyo (meaning "eastern capital").

Feudalism was formally abolished by imperial rescript in 1871, and the former feudal lords (daimyo) were retained as regional governors with liberal emoluments.

The national government was eventually made pseudo-parliamentary in appearance. Certain constitutional forms were established, such as a judicial code patterned after the Code Napoléon, although government was always essentially undemocratic in character. The constitution, drawn up by an imperial commission headed by Count (later Prince) Ito, who had traveled for a year and a half in the United States, Great Britain, France, and Germany, resembled the Prussian more than the British, leaving the army and navy ministers responsible only to the emperor, not the diet. Real power was concentrated in the hands of the emperor, the army and navy leaders, big business, and the genro or elder statesmen who advised the emperor.

As soon as it was strong enough, the imperial government took steps to rid itself of the hateful extraterritoriality clauses of its treaties with other powers, conceding special treaty rights to their nationals in Japan. Great Britain and the United States gave up extraterritoriality in 1894, and by 1901 the last of those clauses, so obnoxious because of their implication of inferiority, had been eliminated from the treaties. Whether she had really put her house in order or had only seemed to do so, she had again become its undisputed mistress.

The new Japan was energetic, eager to expand, and quick to treat its neighbors at least as cavalierly as the old Japan had recently been treated. It took naturally to the sea, and in 1874 embarked upon its modern career of conquest overseas by sending a punitive expedition to Formosa to avenge the murder of some shipwrecked natives of the Liu-Ch'iu (Loochoo, Ryukyu) islands, who it said were under its protection. China at that time claimed suzerainty over both the Liu-Ch'ius and Formosa but could neither defend nor govern them. Japan, however, kept its hold on the Liu-Ch'ius after 1875, and in 1881 China conceded both title and possession. In 1876 the island empire annexed the Bonin Islands, and in 1878 it secured Russian recognition of its possession of the Kuriles in return for the abandonment to Russia of its claim on the southern half of Sakhalin.

In the same years an ancient claim of sovereignty over Korea (then a virtually independent "hermit kingdom," paying only occasional tribute to China as an acknowledgment of a shadow suzerainty) was revived, and Korea was invited to return to her "old allegiance" to Japan. The invitation was declined. In 1875 a Japanese warship making surveys in Korean waters was fired upon from the shore. A mission supported by a show of force was soon sent to demand reparation, and Korea was compelled in 1876 to sign a treaty of amity and commerce, granting to Japanese nationals extraterritorial rights similar to those which Japan had so resented having had to grant to foreigners in her own country. By pointedly referring in the treaty to the freedom and independence of Korea, Japan denied by inference that China had any sovereign rights there. For the next twenty years there was disorder in Korea, fomented by both Chinese and Japanese intrigue, each trying to exclude the other while Russia waited—not always passively—for them both to be excluded.

Korea was potentially useful to Japan as a source of foodstuffs and industrial raw materials, and as a market. She valued it more highly, however, as a foothold on the continent of Asia, from which to go on into Manchuria. Manchuria was richer in unexploited minerals and timber. From Manchuria she could threaten or move into northern China. Its Liaotung peninsula, projecting southward toward Shantung, partly enclosed the Gulf of Chihli; and a naval base at Port Arthur could dominate the sea approaches to Tientsin and Peking (renamed Peiping by Chinese nationalists in 1928). Manchuria was a province of China, the place of origin of its Manchu dynasty, but Japan had more reason to fear Russian interference than Chinese, both there and in Korea.

How little she feared China was demonstrated to a startled world when in 1894 she suddenly attacked her flabby giant neighbor. Her new navy first swept the sea in the war area by defeating an antiquated Chinese fleet off the mouth of the Yalu River and driving the rest of the northern Chinese naval forces to seek shelter at Weihaiwei, where they also were subsequently destroyed. Thus assured of the safety of its sea-borne service of supply, the Japanese army, also modernized, comparatively well equipped, and boldly led, poured troops into Korea. Gaining control of that peninsula, it then invaded southern Manchuria where it captured the fortress city and naval base of Port Arthur. From there it could probably have gone on beyond the Great Wall toward Tientsin and Peking if China had not sued for peace. Only the northeastern Chinese forces had taken part in the war. China south of the Yangtze seemed scarcely to have felt the blow, or to feel the amputations that followed.

By the Treaty of Shimonoseki, 1895, China had to recognize the independence of Korea, which meant that she was no longer able to prevent anyone from ocupying that strategically located country, and that so far as she was concerned Japan and Russia might fight out between themselves the question which of them should have it. She ceded outright to Japan: Formosa, of which Japan had already made an easy conquest, the Pescadores, and the Liaotung peninsula. She agreed also to pay an indemnity of $150,000,000, and to permit the Japanese to occupy Weihaiwei until the indemnity was paid and a satisfactory commercial treaty signed and ratified. The commercial treaty, 1896, gave Japanese the right to trade in China on equal footing with Americans and Europeans, opened up more Chinese ports to trade, and authorized the Japanese to engage in industry in the treaty ports.

Rival Imperialisms in Korea and Northeastern China

Japan was not long permitted to remain in undisturbed possession of the gains she made by the Treaty of Shimonoseki. Supported diplomatically by her alliance partner France and also just then by Germany, Russia soon demanded that she return the Liaotung peninsula to China.[9]

[9] The kaiser was at that time cultivating the friendship of the tsar in hope of winning Russia away from France, to Germany's advantage. He was willing to encourage Russian adventures in the Far East if that would distract Russia from the Black Sea and the Straits and leave Turkey free to coöperate with Germany and Austria-Hungary. He was beginning then, also, to publicize his fears of a "yellow peril" which he said would threaten the world's peace if Japan should get control of

Japan had to give up her Manchurian gains and accept as compensation for them an additional cash indemnity. Soon Russia, who had professed that she had had to block Japan to preserve the territorial integrity of China, was taking steps to make Manchuria a sphere of Russian interest. Her geopolitical reasons for such a policy were selfish, to be sure, but sound. To reach Vladivostok from Chita (east of Lake Baikal) without crossing Manchuria, an all-Russian trans-Siberian railway would have to make a long detour to the north. The most direct and practical line would go across Manchuria, via Harbin. On September 8, 1896, less than five months after the signing of the Treaty of Shimonoseki and four months after the revision of its terms concerning southern Manchuria, a Russian-Chinese railway convention was signed providing for the building and operation, by a syndicate to be formed by the Russo-Chinese bank, of the Chinese Eastern railway across Manchuria.

The port of Vladivostok, however, was not entirely satisfactory, being closed by ice in winter. The logical next step, therefore, the building of the South Manchurian railway from Harbin via Mukden to Port Arthur and Dairen (Dalny, Talien-wan), was taken two years later to secure an ice-free year-round terminus for the eastern Russian railways and an open warm-water seaport for Siberia. Economic and strategic considerations combined to interest Russia in Manchuria, with or without conscious or subconscious mental reservations about eventual further imperialist expansion southward into eastern Asia.

Neither Russia nor Japan respected the independence of Korea. For years the two were rivals for economic concessions and political influence there, although by an agreement in April, 1898, Russia conceded that the Japanese interest was paramount.

By 1898 the "battle of the concessions" in China was approaching a stage requiring regulation. Regulation would have to be by general consent. The one rule commonly recognized was that one commercial power, having established a sphere of interest in which it claimed for its nationals priority of privilege, if not outright monopoly of railway and mining rights and other economic concessions, would not compete for such concessions in the recognized sphere of interest of another. China had usually to agree, with the nation claiming such a sphere of interest, not to grant material concessions within that sphere to na-

the resources of eastern Asia and use them in war against the West. Japanese leaders were more surprised by Germany's intervention than by Russia's, and resented it more keenly. Britain, conversely, gained favor with the Japanese by not intervening. The United States made no move toward intervention but warned the Japanese that other states might intervene to Japan's disadvantage.

tionals of another, or to alienate to another any territory within the area affected.

This practice of staking out, with China's forced consent, claims of spheres of interest covering great areas had been initiated by France in southern China in 1895. It reached its peak in the northeast in 1898. In that year Germany, after casting an appraising and approving eye upon Port Arthur but finding that Russia was already on the point of preëmpting that valuable base, seized upon the murder of two German missionaries in Shantung province as a pretext to demand and get a ninety-nine-year lease on Tsingtao and the land around Kiaochow Bay. By the same general agreement Germany secured railway and mining concessions in Shantung and the privilege of being the first nation to be called on for capital and materials for the industrial development of the province.

Russia then at once demanded a lease on the Kwantung area at the southern end of the Liaotung peninsula, with Port Arthur and Dairen, and the privilege of building the South Manchurian railway to connect Port Arthur and Dairen with the Chinese Eastern at Harbin. The Cassini convention gave Russia, secretly, a sphere of influence in southern Manchuria. Britain, to keep things in balance from her point of view, asked for and got a lease on Weihaiwei, near the northeastern tip of the Shantung peninsula, opposite Port Arthur and between that strong point and Tsingtao. Her lease was to run as long as the Russians held Port Arthur.[10]

With interimperial rivalries thus in precarious equilibrium, the rival powers tacitly or explicitly recognized Manchuria as a Russian sphere of interest, Korea as a Japanese sphere, and the Yangtze Valley as a British one. Such spheres of interest had a natural tendency to develop into spheres of influence, then into protectorates, then to be annexed by the protecting powers. China, handicapped by her own size and the inefficiency of her provincial organization, by the paralysis of her governmental nerve centers or ganglia, and by the venality of many of her provincial and national officials, could not defend herself. The ease and expedition with which the antiforeign Boxer uprising of 1900 was snuffed out by an international task force was convincing proof of her utter helplessness. What remained of her national sovereignty and territorial integrity would be preserved only if the carving-up process should be arrested by the outsiders' mutual fears and jealousies of one another, or if some *deus ex machina* should somehow convince the

[10] At the Washington conference of 1921-1922, Britain promised to restore Weihaiwei to China.

imperial powers that the practice of forbearance would be wiser, and that it would be better for them all if China were strong, free, and united. Some influence favorable to the establishment of a free, strong, and united China was exerted by the United States policy of the open door. The essence of this policy was equality of opportunity in all parts of China for the trade and industry of all nations with which China had trade treaty relations. Its ultimate effect was to discourage the establishment of exclusive spheres of interest. The United States had no such sphere in China but was indicating by its actions that it was in the Philippines to stay. The same impulses which had brought it there, and which had long interested its nationals in the China trade, seemed likely to be stronger in the twentieth century than they had been in the clipper ship era; and the open door policy was designed to safeguard the most-favored-nation privileges which Americans had long enjoyed in China.

In July, 1900, while the Boxer uprising was occupying the attention of the other powers, Russian troops invaded Manchuria to "restore order and protect the railways." Japan was as quick to express alarm over the presence of Russian troops in Manchuria, and to denounce it as a threat to China, as Russia had been in 1895 to protest against the presence of Japanese troops there. Japan, therefore, vociferously joined Britain and the United States in support of China's refusal of assent to the occupation. But it was not until after the formation of the British-Japanese alliance (1902) that Russia could be induced to make a statement of intention to withdraw her troops; and she did not withdraw them until the Japanese defeated them in the war of 1904-1905.

The alliance with Great Britain signalized the world's recognition of Japan as a new member of the company of great powers and gave her new assurance. Intended as reinsurance for Great Britain, not only against further expansion of Russia into China but against attack upon any of her own eastern Asiatic interests by Japan if involvement in a European war should at any time so engross her that she could not herself defend them, it also insured Japan against the danger of intervention by a third power in a war between her and Russia.

The stated purpose of the alliance was the maintenance of peace in eastern Asia through the preservation of the independence and territorial integrity of China and Korea, i.e., though not so stated, to stop Russia in both areas. If either signatory should find itself at war against a single enemy power in defense of its recognized interests in those areas, the other was to remain neutral but to exert itself if necessary to insure the neutrality of other powers. If either were so involved in war against two major powers the other should come at once to its assistance, the two should wage war jointly, and neither should make a separate peace.[11]

By 1903 Japan had made notable progress in developing her industrial and commercial interests in Korea, had settled a number of her people there, and, while still pretending to preserve the independence of the kingdom, had greatly extended her influence in and over it. Russia was sufficiently alarmed to suggest the demarcation of the portion of Korea north of the thirty-ninth parallel as a neutral zone. Negotiations failed to reconcile either nation to the other's ambitions in either Manchuria or Korea, or to induce either to abandon plans for continued exploitation which it was well aware that the other would never voluntarily permit. Even so, the tsar and his advisers had probably never quite convinced themselves that Japan would have the temerity to attack so great a power. The Russian forces in Manchuria were surprised in February, 1904, by the suddenness, swiftness, and efficiency of the Japanese attack.

Preparedness paid dividends. Much of the cash indemnity extorted from China since 1896 had been used for the enlargement and further modernization of the navy, but the army had not been neglected. Both were ready. Again, as in the war against China, Japan made certain of the safety of her water-borne service of supply by attacking without warning, sweeping the seas between her island base and her continental objectives, crippling the Russian naval forces at Port Arthur by surprise attack, occupying Korea, then using Korea as a staging area for a land-based invasion of Manchuria. To the amazement of a world which had not realized her new war potential, she successfully deployed, used effectively in combat, and maintained armies of several hundred thousand men. Although victory was not so easily or cheaply won as it had been against China, Port Arthur was besieged and captured, and the Russian armies were pushed back up the line of the South Manchurian railway toward Mukden and decisively defeated in the field.

Virtually exhausted by her exertions in a year and a half of war, but before she had quite played out her string of victories or given her enemy any indication of the depletion of her resources, Japan listened gladly to President Theodore Roosevelt's offer of the "good offices" of the United States to bring the belligerents together for the purpose of

[11] The term of the alliance was five years. Renewals kept it continuously in effect until it was supplanted by the Washington treaties of 1922. (See pp. 140, 144.)

making peace. Russia's total resources had been scarcely tapped; but despite the extreme disparity of the reserve strength of the adversaries, Japan had shown herself able—as she was again to show herself able in the Philippines in 1941—effectively to dispose of such forces as her much stronger antagonist had then at his disposal in the combat area. In 1905 that was enough. Russia was crippled not so much by her heavy losses in Manchuria, which she had abundant man power and material resources to replace, as by revolutionary disturbances in European Russia, induced partially by revelations of inefficiency, dishonesty, and treason in the conduct of the war. The imperial Russian government was therefore compelled by its own domestic weaknesses reluctantly to make peace.

Thanks to the good offices of President Roosevelt, the treaty was signed at Portsmouth, New Hampshire, September 5, 1905. Russia had to recognize Japan's paramount political, military, and economic interest in Korea (which was more than the economic interest Japan had previously claimed there) and to transfer to Japan her (i.e., Russia's) title to the southern Manchurian railway and all her other treaty rights and concessions in the Liaotung peninsula—which Japan had pretended to consider dangerous to China when Russia held them. It was agreed that the Manchurian railways, except those in the Liaotung peninsula, should be exploited for only commercial and industrial, not for military or strategic, purposes. In lieu of cash indemnity, that portion of the island of Sakhalin south of the fiftieth parallel of latitude—about half—was ceded by Russia to Japan.

The use that the island empire would make of its victory was soon indicated by a series of treaties with Korea. A virtual protectorate, in the form of an alliance, had been established by protocol February 23, 1904. Two months after the war's end, November 17, 1905, by a new treaty imposed upon Korea, Japan made the protectorate official and assumed control of Korea's foreign policy. In July, 1910, again by treaty, Korea was annexed and became a Japanese province, called Chosen. Its people and its other resources became Japanese assets and were exploited as such thereafter until 1945.

In Manchuria, from 1905, Japan took advantage of her treaty rights, extending the area of her nationals' activity in trade and industry, invoking the policy of the open door whenever Germany behaved in similar fashion in Shantung, but keeping the door to opportunity in southern Manchuria open only to Japanese. China's treaty agreement not to authorize the building of a competing railway parallel with the South Manchurian was so interpreted as to block the construction of any other railways in the area. By 1910 Japan's ally

Great Britain had tacitly recognized her position there by making no further serious protest against her disregard of the policy of the open door. In that year Russia made an agreement with her by which each recognized the other's exclusive and preferential interest in its own sphere, Russia along the Chinese Eastern railway and in northern Manchuria, Japan along the South Manchurian railway and in southern Manchuria. The door to Manchuria was no longer open, and China's sovereignty there was disregarded.

The British-Japanese alliance was in effect when war began in 1914 but was not the reason for Japan's participation in the war. Germany's involvement gave her an opportunity to seize the German naval base at Tsingtao and to take over Germany's economic concessions in Shantung. Meanwhile the Allies, also involved in Europe, with their Pacific possessions and sea lanes open in the first months of the war to German raiders sailing out of Tsingtao, welcomed the assistance of a Pacific naval power.

Yüan Shih-kai, the president of China, offered to retake Tsingtao; but Japan vetoed the suggestion, and the Allies permitted her to chart her own course. Great Britain, in particular, showed no enthusiasm for independent Japanese action in that theater, and did not call upon her Far Eastern ally for help when, on August 10, 1914, Japan suggested that she might do so. So Japan was acting on her own initiative when on August 15 she sent an ultimatum to Germany demanding the surrender of the leasehold in Shantung by September 15, "with a view to the eventual restoration of the same to China." Her naval forces had then been hovering off Tsingtao for a week, but Great Britain was not notified of her intention until after the ultimatum had been sent.

Tsingtao fell November 7, 1914. Although the Japanese ultimatum had indicated that the territory would eventually be returned to China, and although Premier Okuma had declared in a cable message intended for publication in the United States that his government had no territorial ambition in the region and was acting only to preserve the peace, Japan quickly took over all German interests in Shantung, outside as well as inside the leasehold area. In fact, she went on beyond them, as in the policing and administration of the Tsinanfu-Tsingtao railway and control of the railway area. There was no indication of an intention to restore the area to China. Realistically, the president of China remarked to the American ambassador: "Japan is going to take advantage of this war to get control of China."[12]

In an attempt to circumscribe Japan's activities in Shantung, Presi-

[12] January 15, 1915. Paul S. Reinsch, *An American Diplomat in China*, (Garden City, 1922), 129; Harold M. Vinacke, *op. cit.*, 367.

dent Yüan Shi-kai on January 7, 1915, issued a new proclamation of
neutrality. He declared that China's neutrality would again cover all
of Shantung province outside the leasehold area, hostilities there having ceased. Japan used his proclamation as a pretext for twenty-one
demands which, if granted, would have accomplished the purpose
which Yüan had already all too clearly realized that she had in mind.
These demands were presented to the president personally, by-passing
the Chinese Foreign Office, with a warning that he must keep them
secret until negotiations were completed; but news of their character
leaked out. It was implied that unless Yüan proved properly coöperative Japan would aid the political opposition then seeking his overthrow. By inference, at least, it was indicated that if he were compliant
enough she might support him against his personal enemies. But he
mistook the popular nationalist resentment against the Twenty-One
Demands for evidence of personal popularity and was tempted thereby
to attempt to overthrow the republic and make himself emperor. The
attempt was unsuccessful. Yüan died June 6, 1916, and the republic
was strengthened by the nationalist opposition to Japan, but not until
after many of the Japanese demands had been granted by treaty May
25, 1915.

Most of the concessions made in 1915 were economic rather than
territorial in character. Japan was expanding her industries rapidly
during the war and was reaching out for raw materials and markets,
hoping to compete more successfully with the United States and Britain
in the world market and to be less heavily dependent upon the United
States and India for raw materials. Manchuria was to become an area
reserved for Japanese colonization and capital. Fukien province and
Inner Mongolia were to be economically assimilated to it. German
treaty rights in Shantung were to be taken over and extended into
Honan and Shansi provinces. Railway and mining rights of enormous
value, in central and eastern China, were to be granted. Everywhere,
Japan seized and exploited the opportunity offered her by the preoccupation of the Western powers—Europe with the war and the United
States with the problems of neutrality—and by the military weakness
of China.

Group V of the Twenty-One Demands, which were not acceded to
by China in 1915 but were held over her thereafter as a threat, would
have completed the process of depriving her of her independence. She
would have had to take dictation from Japanese advisers in political,
financial, and military matters. Japanese-dominated joint police forces
would have controlled her vital areas, her arsenals would have been

"jointly" operated—which would have meant Japanese-controlled—and more than half of her munitions would have had to be purchased from Japan.[13]

During 1916 and 1917 Japan continued to entrench herself economically in China, to exploit the areas she dominated, and to improve her international position as she found opportunity. In the summer of 1916 Russia, disastrously defeated on her western front, had to make an alliance with Japan, recognizing the changes already made in China and Manchuria. Japan recognized, in return, a Russian interest in Outer Mongolia. And the two imperial powers agreed upon a delineation of their spheres of interest in northern Manchuria. The stated purpose of the alliance was "to keep peace in the Far East."

Also in 1916, while continuing German military successes suggested the probability of an eventual German victory and accentuated the Allies' need of naval reinforcement, Japanese diplomats talked openly—possibly for effect—of the advisability of terminating the British alliance and making one with Germany. As a *quid pro quo*, to hold her, Britain had to promise to support her claim, after the war, to the former German-owned islands in the Pacific north of the equator. Japan would support the claims of the British Empire and dominions to the German islands south of the equator. With Germany's resumption of unrestricted submarine warfare on February 1, 1917, the need for light naval vessels for antisubmarine warfare and convoy work was more desperate than before. Both Italy and France had secretly endorsed the secret British-Japanese agreement concerning the Pacific islands before the United States declared war in 1917. The United States government was not a party to it and was not then informed of it.

By the Lansing-Ishii agreement of November 2, 1917, Japan secured from the United States a written recognition of the obvious fact that because of her location she had special interests in China. This diplomatic recognizance of the natural consequences of geographical propinquity was partially counterbalanced by a repetition of the familiar formulas upholding the principles of the open door and the integrity of China, and by a mutual declaration that both parties were opposed to the acquisition by any power of special rights or privileges in China which would abridge the rights of citizens or subjects of other friendly states.[14] Events and circumstances would determine how

[13] Reinsch, *op. cit.*, 134.
[14] U. S. Department of State, *Foreign Relations of the United States*, 1917, 264-265; *ibid., 1922*, II, 595; A. W. Griswold, *The Far Eastern Policy of the United States* (New York, 1938), 215-216; Vinacke, *op. cit.*, 373.

effective this counterbalancing would be. Japan presumably expected to be able to enforce her own interpretation, and might well have been expected to demand—as she did—greater concessions than Mr. Lansing would concede that he had meant to make.[15]

Meanwhile, in August, 1917, China declared war on Germany. Her resources and man-power reserves were thus made more readily available to the Allies, and Chinese labor battalions did useful service in the seaports and in France, thus releasing replacements for the combat forces. China sought no new territory in the war, wanted only to regain control of her own. She was well represented at the Paris peace conference in 1919, and her claim for the recovery of Shantung was warmly supported there by President Wilson. But Japan, holding her allies to their bond of 1916-1917, retained the economic rights and privileges there which she had taken from the Germans and materially extended since taking them, and promised only orally that she would restore political control of the province to China. The shadow so promised was a shabby substitute for the substance lost. China refused for that reason to sign the Treaty of Versailles. The treaty's failure to restore Shantung to China was one of many criticisms expressed in the United States as arguments against ratifying it. The United States did not change its position on the Shantung question; and Japanese resentment of that fact accumulated through the next twenty years.

The Shantung question was only one manifestation of several fundamental and potentially dangerous differences of policy between the United States and Japan. The navy-building race referred to by the resolution initiated in the United States Senate by Senator Borah of Idaho in 1921 was another. The Borah resolution invited the president to explore the possibility of reducing naval expenditure by mutual agreement.[16] Far Eastern observers, however, saw primary sources of discord and danger in the condition of China and in continued manifestations of the aggressive character of Japanese policy there and in Siberia. The promise to restore political control of Shantung to China had not been kept. The United States had withdrawn its troops from Siberia; Japan had not, although she had repeatedly declared that she intended soon to do so. Three successful wars had enabled Japan to replace China in Korea and Formosa, Russia in southern Sakhalin and Manchuria, and Germany in Shantung and many of the Pacific islands. She showed by her behavior that she was

[15] The agreement was superseded by the Washington Nine-Power Treaty of 1922 concerning China. At the request of the United States it was canceled in April, 1923.

[16] Adopted by the Senate in May and by the House of Representatives June 29, 1921.

aware of the strength of her position. Strategically she was impregnable and in fact unapproachable from the westward and could not be seriously threatened from the eastward, across the broad Pacific, by a navy less than two or three times as strong as hers—which the United States did not then possess and thought it could not afford to build if the desired assurance of security and peace could be otherwise provided.

It would have been reassuring to be able to depend upon the support of the British fleet in a war in the Pacific. Many Americans were disposed by then to take British friendship for granted and to reject the thought of a war between the United States and Great Britain as something quite unthinkable. But those responsible for the national defense against all conceivable contingencies could not well afford to dismiss the uncomfortable or even the improbable as inconceivable; and there remained the awkward fact of the British-Japanese alliance. As renewed in 1911 that treaty of alliance had in it an escape clause to the effect that it would not be applicable against a nation with which Great Britain had a general arbitration treaty—such as she had just then negotiated with the United States. But the Senate had not ratified that arbitration treaty, so Britain could not be sure of her escape clause unless the subsequent Bryan peace commission treaty, which had been ratified, should serve the purpose—to which proposition it was improbable that Japan in case of conflict would agree. Dominion pressure, especially Canadian, made abrogation of the embarrassing alliance a major item of the agenda of the impending conference.

The scope of the Washington conference, originally suggested by Senator Borah as a way of reducing naval building expenditures, was thus considerably broadened before the conference convened. If the treaties there negotiated had been made and observed in good faith by all parties to them, both the United States and Japan would have found security in them and other advantages as well.[17] If the treaties held, each was insured against attack by the other, as neither had a navy strong enough to cross the Pacific and attack the other with any prospect of success; and the treaty established a 5:3 ratio as to capital ships and aircraft carrier tonnage, declared a ten-year building holiday, and prohibited for fifteen years the building of any battleships of more than 35,000 tons.[18] The agreement to main-

[17] For terms of the Washington treaties see pp. 141-146.

[18] Detailed planning of the giant Japanese battleships *Musashi* and *Yamato*, 75,500 tons (full-load displacement) each, built for conquest, with 18.1-inch guns, was begun in 1934, more than two years before the expiration of the treaty term. Building began in 1937, *Musashi* at Nagasaki, *Yamato* at Kure. *Yamato* was com-

tain the *status quo* as to fortification of Pacific islands outside territorial waters should have given all parties an assurance of safety, each within its own area.

Equally important to the United States was the conference's redefinition of the policy of the open door, and the incorporation of that traditional American policy into the Nine-Power Pact with reference to China. The parties to that treaty, including Japan, formally agreed to respect the sovereignty, independence, and territorial and administrative independence of China, to maintain and advance the principle of equality of commercial opportunity, and neither to take nor to support any action designed to result in the enjoyment of exclusive opportunities there. China herself was bound to maintain the principle of the open door, to alienate or lease no territory, and to maintain her own integrity and independence.

From 1927 to 1931 the Chinese national people's party Kuomintang struggled with some apparent prospect of success against Communist opposition and the quasi-independent war lords of the great provinces to establish an effective national government. In 1928 Japan interfered with the nationalist program of reconquest and unification by pushing troops westward along the Tsingtao-Tsinan railway in western Shantung province, thus impeding the movement of nationalist troops from Nanking toward Peking, which was then held by the rebel war lord of Manchuria, Chang Tso-lin. The nationalist leader Chiang Kai-shek succeeded finally, despite Japanese interference, in driving Chang Tso-lin out of Peking and back beyond the Great Wall into Manchuria, where he was protected by the possibility of Japanese intervention. Chang Tso-lin, however, was killed by a bomb explosion, and his son and successor Chang Hsueh-liang accepted the authority of Chiang Kai-shek, who was then able to move the nationalist capital from Nanking to Peking.[19]

By 1929 the Chinese national movement made some headway toward achieving the actual as well as the nominal independence of China. Tariff autonomy was regained under a treaty with the United States signed July 25, 1928, effective February 1, 1929, and by similar treaties with other powers. Japan agreed in advance to respect the new national tariff laws which China was thus free to

---

pleted December 16, 1941, *Musashi* early in 1942. Both were sunk in battle action by carrier-based United States naval aircraft, *Musashi* in the Sibuyan Sea in the battle for Leyte Gulf October 24, 1944, and *Yamato* southwest of Kyushu, north of Okinawa, April 7, 1945.

[19] The city was then (1928) renamed Peiping (Northern Peace). The Japanese who occupied it from 1937 to 1945 continued to call it Peking.

pass. Foreign powers which had previously claimed extraterritorial rights for their nationals gave them up, lost them, or agreed to their gradual termination. Whether continued successes or new reverses were in prospect for Chinese nationalism would depend upon whether Japan's policy toward China should be one of friendship and moderation, as had seemed to be promised by her rather liberal ministries of the middle twenties, or one of aggression, as seemed to be indicated by the "positive position" taken by the government of Premier Tanaka in Shantung in 1928 and in Manchuria from 1927 to 1929.

One of Baron Tanaka's more moderate predecessors in the office of Japanese foreign minister, Baron Shidehara, had said: "It is . . . of the utmost importance for us to concentrate our attention and energy on the promotion of foreign trade, without unjust infringement upon the interests of any nation. It is not territory but markets that we have in view. It is not alliances but economic solidarity that we seek in our foreign relations."[20]

Baron Tanaka, on the other hand, in a memorial which he was believed to have sent to the emperor July 25, 1927, said (if the memorial was genuine and if he was its author): "If we merely hope to develop trade, we shall eventually be defeated by England and America, who possess unsurpassable capitalistic power. In the end, we shall get nothing. A more dangerous factor is the fact that the people of China might some day wake up. . . . Our trade with China will be wrecked. Minseito's proposal to uphold the Nine Power Treaty and to adopt the policy of trade towards Manchuria is nothing less than a suicide policy."[21]

Baron Tanaka had reason to fear that the people of China might some day "wake up." Chinese nationalists were already wide awake and well aware of their situation. Tanaka's "positive" policies in all Sino-Japanese relations confirmed them in their conviction that the unification of their nation would be incomplete without the reconquest

[20] Foreign Policy Association, Information Service, Vol. VI, No. 16, p. 281; Vinacke, *op. cit.*, 503-504; Arnold J. Toynbee, *Survey of International Affairs, 1926* (London, 1928), 510.

[21] Minseito was a Japanese political party more liberal than Tanaka's. The Japanese government denied the authenticity of the Tanaka memorial, which purported to be a report of resolutions recently adopted by a conference of civil and military officials concerned with Manchuria and Mongolia; but Japanese policy from 1929 to 1942 followed the lines indicated by it as closely as if based upon it as a blueprint. If the memorial was a forgery subsequently fabricated, its author needed only to describe, as proposals, what Japan had done since 1927. See Carl Crow, *Japan's Dream of World Empire* (New York, 1942), 22-112, and the *Far Eastern Magazine*, I (May, 1938), 345-368.

of Manchuria, the recovery of lost rights there, and the eviction of Japan—which since 1915 had changed its tactics at times but not its ultimate objectives. That meant an eventual test of strength between Chinese nationalism and Japanese imperialism unless one or the other changed its character and purpose.

Japan in Manchuria: The Fourteen Years' War

The Washington conference of 1921-1922 had left Japan in so strong a strategic position that she had little reason to fear attack from any quarter. Her favorable location gave her, too, if not the special interests in China which she had claimed under the Lansing-Ishii agreement, an invaluable geographical advantage in open competition with the West for Chinese raw materials and markets. With the shorter carry, low wages, and low all-inclusive costs of production, transportation, and marketing, her industries and commerce could easily hold their own against all comers in any trading area they chose to enter in eastern or southern Asia, Indonesia, or Africa.

Japanese investments in China, for example, which in 1902 had been only 0.1 percent of total foreign investments there, were 35.6 percent of the total in 1931, second only to the British and only slightly less. Investments by nationals of the United States had increased only from 2.5 percent of the total in 1902 to 6.1 percent in 1931, and United States trade with China had increased only from 8.5 percent of China's total foreign trade in 1912 to 18.8 percent in 1931.[22]

The new aggressive Chinese nationalism was a more serious threat to Japanese trade expansion—and to the economic and political control, backed by military force, which followed trade and industry wherever possible—than the rather remote possibility of armed intervention. Japanese imperialists viewed with apprehension the infiltration of emigrants from other parts of China into Manchuria and the persistent efforts of the Chinese to regain control of the "eastern provinces." Chinese military governors of Manchuria, Chang Tso-lin in 1926 and Chang Hsueh-liang in 1928, had tried to oust the Russians from control of the Chinese Eastern railway. So, foreseeing some similar experience for themselves in south Manchuria, the Japanese did not protest when Russia used force to regain her old position in the north.

[22] F. V. Field (ed.), *Economic Handbook of the Pacific Area* (New York, 1934), 353; C. F. Remer, *Foreign Investments in China* (New York, 1933), 77; Vinacke, *op. cit.*, 478.

By 1931 a thousand kilometers of competing railway lines, connecting with the Chinese rather than the South Manchurian system, had been built into southwestern Manchuria to break the monopoly, reduce the profits, and restrict the expanding economic and political activities of the South Manchurian railway company; and China had defaulted on Japanese railway loans for lines designed to draw the trade of northern Manchuria away from Vladivostok to Dairen.

It was about the ownership of land, however—especially of farm land—that promoters of Japanese colonization in Manchuria were most concerned. Strenuous efforts had been made, with limited success, to encourage the settlement of Japanese farmers there. In 1915 the right to purchase land had been demanded, but only lease-hold rights had been granted, and Chinese obstructionism had made it difficult to secure leases. The Japanese had circumvented the restrictions wherever possible by using naturalized (Chinese) Koreans to purchase land for rice cultivation, with the intention of soon dispossessing them for the benefit of Japanese farmers unable or unwilling to pioneer it for themselves. The Koreans might then, in the words of the Tanaka memorial, "go on opening new fields, to deliver to the convenient use of our own people"—the Japanese.[23]

In 1931 the 29,000,000 population of Manchuria included only 250,000 Japanese, 800,000 Koreans, and 100,000 Russians. Most of the rest, by general definition including Manchus, were Chinese; and Chinese immigrants were still, in the words of the Tanaka memorial, "flowing in as a flood" and jeopardizing Japanese "acquired rights" both in Manchuria and in Mongolia. Like Alice in Wonderland, Japan had to run very hard to stay in the same place. Economic penetration and government-fostered Japanese immigration were not enough.

The Tanaka memorial denied that Manchuria or Inner Mongolia had ever been, historically, Chinese territory; and the militarists were determined, at whatever risk or cost, to make them Japanese.

The principal obstacles in the way, aside from the natural ambition of the Chinese nationalists to occupy and control Chinese territory,

---

[23] The memorial differentiated between Koreans and Japan's "own people"—though Korea had long since been annexed—but made light of the Chinese naturalization of Koreans. Such people had, it said, become Chinese "only in name, . . . for temporary convenience," and would eventually return to the fold, or could be "instigated to military activities" when their numbers reached two and a half millions or more. Then, under pretense of helping to suppress them, Japan could aid them. The world would find it difficult to tell whether trouble was being made by Chinese Koreans or Japanese Koreans; and Japan could always "sell dog's meat with a sheep's head as a sign board."

were the Nine-Power Treaty and the United States. As the Tanaka memorial put it:

The restrictions of the Nine Power Treaty signed at the Washington Conference have reduced our special rights and privileges in Manchuria and Mongolia to such an extent that there is no freedom left for us. The very existence of our country is endangered. . . . The Nine Power Treaty was initiated by the United States. The other Powers that signed it were willing to see our influence increase . . . in order that we may protect the interests of international trade and investments. . . .

For the sake of self-protection as well as the protection of others, Japan cannot remove the difficulties in Eastern Asia unless she adopts a policy of "Blood and Iron." But in carrying out this policy we have to face the United States which has been turned against us by China's policy of fighting poison with poison. In the future if we want to control China, we must first crush the United States just as in the past we had to fight in the Russo-Japanese War. But in order to conquer China we must first conquer Manchuria and Mongolia. In order to conquer the world, we must first conquer China. If we succeed in conquering China the rest of the Asiatic countries and the South Sea countries will fear us and surrender to us. Then the world will realize that Eastern Asia is ours and will not dare to violate our rights. This is the plan left to us by our Emperor Meiji [Mutsuhito], the success of which is essential to our national existence. . . .

After studying the present conditions and possibilities of our country, our best policy lies in the direction of taking positive steps to secure rights and privileges in Manchuria and Mongolia. These will enable us to develop our trade. This will not only forestall China's own industrial development, but also prevent the penetration of European Powers. This is the best policy possible!

The way to gain actual rights in Manchuria and Mongolia is to use this region as a base and under the pretense of trade and commerce penetrate the rest of China. Armed by the rights already secured, we shall seize the resources all over the country. Having China's entire resources at our disposal, we shall proceed to conquer India, the Archipelago, Asia Minor, Central Asia, and even Europe. But to get control of Manchuria and Mongolia is the first step if the Yamato race wishes to distinguish themselves on Continental Asia.

The decisive step was taken in Manchuria the night of September 18-19, 1931. By Japanese account, a military patrol practicing defense exercises along the South Manchurian railway a little north of Mukden was fired upon from a field while investigating an explosion. The explosion had broken the end-to-end connection between two rails of the line, without derailing or delaying the southbound

(10:30 P.M.) Changchun-to-Mukden train, which the patrol had tried but failed to stop for fear it would be wrecked. A Japanese force, said by the Japanese to have consisted of only five hundred men, then attacked and captured the Mukden army barracks, occupied by ten thousand Chinese troops. The only real resistance was offered by the Mukden police, of whom seventy-five were killed.

By Chinese account, the attack was made without provocation. Chinese troops were under orders to avoid conflict with the Japanese conducting night maneuvers around their barracks; sentries were armed with dummy rifles and the garrison offered virtually no resistance but moved around Mukden and withdrew by train toward Peiping.

Clearly the Chinese were surprised and the Japanese were not. Or —if they were in any way surprised by the timing of the incident— they were well prepared and previously instructed to take advantage of any such occasion. The inhabitants of Mukden simply awoke on the morning of September 19 to find their city in the hands of Japanese troops.

Invoking Article 11 of the Covenant of the League of Nations, China appealed immediately to the League Council, then in session, "to take immediate steps to prevent the further development of a situation endangering the peace of nations." On September 30, with Japan's representative concurring, the Council resolved unanimously that both parties should withdraw their troops from the area of conflict. Chinese troops had already been withdrawn. Japan's representative agreed that Japanese troops should also evacuate, as rapidly as circumstances permitted, the area they had occupied outside the authorized railway zone. Finding at its October 13 meeting that Japan, far from withdrawing, was steadily extending the area she occupied, the Council on October 24, acting under Article 11 of the Covenant of the League and Article 2 of the Kellogg-Briand Pact, with only Japan's representative dissenting, demanded the retirement of Japanese troops to the authorized railway zone by November 16. On November 16 it met again and found the Japanese campaign of occupation steadily proceeding. No positive action was taken till December 10, when, at Japan's suggestion, the Council decided to send a commission of inquiry to determine the facts of the situation. This commission, appointed January 14, 1932, and commonly known as the Lytton commission, was composed of the British Earl of Lytton (chosen chairman by his colleagues), Count Luigi Aldrovani of Italy, Henri Claudel of France, Heinrich Schnee, former governor general of German East Africa, and Major General Frank R. McCoy of the United States.

Although recognized by Japan as the principal non-Asiatic objector to her expansionist ideas, the United States did not at first assume the leadership of the movement to restrain her. Diplomatically, in October, 1931, it encouraged the Council of the League of Nations to do everything within the competence of the League to control the situation, assuring the Council of its support for any such steps as the League might take. With only Japan's representative dissenting, the Council then invited the United States to send a representative to participate in its deliberations. For the remainder of the October meeting Prentiss Gilbert, United States consul general at Geneva, represented his government on the Council; but he was there only as an unofficial observer, instructed to vote only on questions involving the Kellogg-Briand Pact, so was not a party to the peremptory resolution of October 24 demanding that Japan evacuate the recently occupied area by November 16.

To most people in the United States, however, Manchuria seemed very far away. Pacifism was general, genuine, and strong. Public opinion, already disturbed by the depression of those years, was almost universally opposed to the assumption of new international commitments involving any threat of warlike action either by or against the United States. Isolationism in the Congress at once reflected and encouraged isolationist opinion in the country. The United States was not represented at the November or December meeting of the League Council, which was therefore then less confident of its support than in October.

The appointment of a fact-finding commission was apparently a rather timid way of temporizing with a situation which should have been immediately terminated; but it enabled the League of Nations to act without the appearance of haste or prejudice and gave the disputants time to end their own quarrel without too much loss of "face" by either if they had been equally and mutually disposed to do so. Meanwhile, the League could not build up its own prestige by asserting authority which it did not possess or threatening positive action which it could not depend upon its member states to take.

The commission found, moreover, as its members had long realized, that the situation in Manchuria was one which could be permanently maintained only if it were mutually profitable—as it was not—and if both parties were content with it—as neither was. Both had grievances. The incident of September 18-19 was the culmination of a long series of unpleasant incidents during which each party had frequently accused the other of unilateral interpretation or disregard of its agreements. The substance of the situation was that Japan was determined to maintain and multiply her "special rights" in Manchuria and elsewhere in China, and China to diminish them. At the end of 1931, in control of most of Manchuria, Japan was openly unwilling to withdraw her troops until agreement had been reached with China concerning the terms of settlement; and China was unwilling to negotiate until the Japanese troops were withdrawn. Impasse.

The ill-organized and ill-equipped Chinese military forces offered little real resistance to the invasion. China's most effective weapon was a boycott of Japanese goods, which reduced Japanese exports to China in December, 1931, to little more than one-third of what they had been in September. In an attempt to break the boycott, the Japanese fleet and army besieged Shanghai, where they met strong resistance, from January to May 5, 1932.

Meanwhile, on January 7, 1932, while the Lytton commission was gathering material for its report and Shanghai was under siege, the "Stimson" doctrine of nonrecognition was announced. The United States government had been kept well informed, by its own diplomatic and consular representatives, of the course and implications of events. By taking a firm stand on the solid ground of the treaties covering the situation, without seeming to put too much foreign pressure on Japanese Foreign Minister Shidehara, it hoped to enable the more enlightened and moderate-minded civilian leaders to regain control of the militarists who, it correctly surmised, were running away with Japanese policy.[24]

The government of the United States, said Mr. Henry L. Stimson, then secretary of state under President Herbert Hoover, in identical notes to the governments of China and Japan, would not consent to any change in the open-door policy or in the Nine-Power Treaty of 1922 which embodied the open-door policy. Nor would it recognize as permanent any other change achieved by use of methods proscribed by the Kellogg-Briand Pact—in other words, by resort to war or the use of armed force as an instrument of national policy, or settlement of a dispute by other than pacific means.

The Stimson doctrine of nonrecognition of territorial or treaty changes effected in a manner inconsistent with the pledges taken by all signers of the Kellogg-Briand Pact was a praiseworthy effort. It sought not only to maintain American treaty rights and privileges in

[24] League of Nations leaders were still nourishing a similar hope.

China, threatened by Japan, and to shield China from further abuse at the hands of her aggressive Asiatic neighbor, but to buttress the foundation of world peace—general confidence in the good faith of nations in the observance of their treaty obligations, which Japan's cynical and lawless action, if unchallenged, would surely undermine. But it was not enough to stop Japan from announcing, on February 18, 1932, the establishment of the "independent" state of Manchukuo.

This puppet state, with which Japan subsequently went through the transparent formalities of recognition and a treaty of alliance but which she kept always under her protection and control, was to include the three Manchurian provinces of China and the border province of Jehol—which was not occupied or controlled until 1933. It was never recognized by the United States or, up to 1936, by any member of the League of Nations but El Salvador (May, 1934). The Soviet Russian government granted it *de facto* recognition in 1934, however, by dealing with it as well as with Japan for the liquidation of Russian treaty rights in the Chinese Eastern railway. Manchukuo had taken over China's interest in that railway. Russia sold hers to Manchukuo for 140,000,000 yen, plus 35,000,000 yen compensation for Russian officials to be dismissed. Japan guaranteed the payments. The transfer of title took place March 23, 1935. China also had an interest, but was disregarded.[25]

Although the Stimson doctrine of nonrecognition did not immediately stop Japan, neither did Japan's temporary victories in Manchuria and elsewhere in northeastern China stop the Stimson doctrine from gaining the recognition which Manchukuo did not gain. At Geneva on March 11, 1932, a special Assembly of the League of Nations adopted the doctrine as its own in a resolution that members of the League should not recognize any new situation, treaty, or arrangement that might be brought about by means contrary to the Covenant of the League or the Kellogg-Briand Pact. Nonrecognition of any territorial arrangement which was not obtained by pacific means, or of the validity of any occupation or acquisition of territory that might be brought about by force of arms, was subsequently written into the Pan-American treaty of 1933 and advertised the illegality as well as the immorality of Japan's undeclared war on China.[26] The idea that the waging of aggressive war, in violation of treaty obligations such as those assumed by signers of the Kellogg-Briand Pact, was a legally punishable crime was a part of the accusation brought for-

[25] Vinacke, *op. cit.*, 525.
[26] See pp. 157-158.

ward against Axis leaders during the great war which followed, and in the war criminal trials of 1946 and 1947.

The report of the Lytton commission was signed in Peiping September 4 and published October 2, 1932. Although its recommendations, if accepted, would have left Japan in a better position than in 1930, it stated plainly that the operations of the Japanese troops during the night of September 18 could not be regarded as measures of legitimate self-defense. The commission reported that Japan had been guilty of aggression and of violation of treaties and of the Covenant of the League. No one had any reason to be surprised by the answers given to the questions asked.

While the Lytton report was on its way to Geneva, and by way of challenge to the League members to make any real use of it, Japan on September 15 formally recognized her puppet state of Manchukuo and announced her alliance with the so-called state she had created. At Geneva Japan won another tactical success securing a postponement until November of the Council's action on the report, then suffered a tactical reverse when the Council referred the matter to a special meeting of the League Assembly in December; for the smaller nations, which enjoyed a greater preponderance in the Assembly than in the Council and were seeking in collective security the safety they knew they could not assure themselves by national self-defense, were more outspoken in their insistence upon disciplinary action than the great powers were.

Meanwhile Japanese troops pushed southwestward into Jehol and northeastern Hopei provinces. While refusing either at Washington or at Geneva to discuss the future of Manchukuo, a question which it called closed, the Japanese government authorized its ambassador to the United States to say to Mr. Stimson that it had no territorial ambitions in China south of the Great Wall. Mr. Stimson reminded the ambassador that Japan had said the same thing the year before about Manchuria, and stated plainly that the United States would support the world's "peace machinery" to put an end to war. The secretary of state was clearly thinking of Japan's invasion of China as a war, although the Japanese diplomats were still blandly calling it only an "incident," as "no war had been declared." It is no wonder that Japan rejected the suggestion of an emergency League committee that the United States and Russia be invited to send representatives to the Assembly when it took up the Lytton report.

With only the Japanese vote cast against it, Siam abstaining, the Assembly adopted the Lytton report on February 24, 1933, whereupon the defeated Japanese delegation walked out of the assembly hall. Although in terms of sanctions the Assembly's action was only an expression of the considered "opinion of mankind," it was a rebuke such as had never been administered to any member of the League, and clearly opened the way to the application of economic pressure or other sanctions provided for by the League Covenant. On March 27, still blandly insisting that she was seeking only the freedom, peace, and prosperity of eastern Asia, Japan notified the Secretariat of her intention to withdraw from the League. Her withdrawal was legally completed in 1935.

Yet economic sanctions were not applied. There were too many uncertainties; and, although there could no longer be any question about the character of Japan's expansionist policy, there was not generally a clear enough realization of its far-reaching implications. The burden of imposing and enforcing economic sanctions, for which neither legislation nor administrative organization was ready, would have fallen upon the great powers—conceivably only on such of the great powers as were members of the League and willing to carry out its policy at their own risk.

On the day following the adoption of the Lytton report by the Assembly, Secretary Stimson notified the League of Nations Secretariat that the government of the United States approved its action. But President Hoover had been defeated in the election of November, 1932. Franklin D. Roosevelt, who became president March, 4, 1933, was known then for his emphasis on a New Deal program to pull his people out of an economic depression, not yet as an internationalist. The other powers did not dare depend upon the United States to join them in applying economic sanctions; and the application of such sanctions, if not universal, would have meant merely that the people who applied them would have lost their trade with the area affected to those who did not participate in their application.

Soviet Russia was neither unaffected by events in Manchukuo nor uninterested in them. She was not, however, a member of the League, and to League members was at the time, diplomatically, an unknown quantity. (She soon sold her rights in the Chinese Eastern railway, compromised with Japan on the navigation of border rivers, and interested herself in Outer Mongolia while Japan pushed on into Inner Mongolia.)

Italy was a member of the League; but it was Mussolini's Italy, already psychologically aligned as a "have not" power with the armed revisionists, soon to appear as Japan's friend at court and later as her ally. Germany was also a member; but it was a politically weakened and internationally undependable Germany in 1931 and 1932 and became Hitler's Germany in 1933, the only great European power to withdraw from the League on its own initiative without having been rebuked by the other members. France was a member; but it was a France racked by economic dislocation and party strife, just entering (with the resignation of the Edouard Herriot ministry in December, 1932) upon a succession of six leftist ministries in fifteen months. France would run no conscious risks and assume no new national responsibilities for the sake of collective security or to save Hopei province from the Japanese. Britain was a member; but she, too, was struggling through a depression and had other troubles nearer home than in Manchuria. Japan had timed her stroke well.

Economic sanctions were already recognized, furthermore, as in fact a form of warfare, involving the risk of a shooting war if the nation upon which they were imposed should resort to the use of armed force to counteract them. That risk the United States was not prepared at that time to take. The risk would therefore have been principally Britain's; and she was not prepared to take it, in the face of a skeptical and possibly unfriendly world opinion, no matter how fervently the spokesmen of the smaller European nations, including Eire, whose share of both risk and responsibility would have been proportionately small, might urge from the comparatively safe vantage point of a speaker's podium in Geneva that someone should do something to stop Japan.

For the first time, on a major issue, a great power had defied the League, and the League had failed to find effective means to coerce a member state which was at once a great power and a malefactor defiant of world opinion and unwilling to abide by its own treaties. The United States had contributed to the general cause of eventual world peace a policy of tremendous long-term potentialities—nonrecognition of changes effected by armed aggression—and the abandonment of the old concept of neutrality which had pretended not to discriminate between an aggressor and a victim of aggression. But it was a pacifist policy, based upon the assumption of the ultimate efficacy of legal and moral principles. Against tanks and guns it was not immediately any more efficacious than the reproachful resolutions adopted in Geneva. Self-assertive and lawless Japanese imperialism defied the world community which tried to bring it under community control. The way of the wicked seemed at first to have prospered. The peace wall of the world community was breached.

REMILITARIZATION OF GERMANY AND REOCCUPATION OF THE RHINELAND, 1935, 1936

Much of the malaise with which the world was affected in the 1930's was a reaction to bad news coming out of Germany. Friends of democracy regretted the downfall of the Weimar republic. They knew that, for a while at least, there would be less tolerance and freedom than under the Weimar regime but hoped that there would be better order and cohesion, increased employment, and a revival of prosperity.

Moderate-minded people outside Germany were more willing to believe and hope for the best about Hitler and his cohorts than the worst. They could not in fact have believed the simple monstrous truth about them if anyone had been able then to tell it. Revolutions, even the most constructive, had usually begun with some destruction and been marred by some excesses, which had been branded as atrocities by émigrés and other friends and relatives of their victims. In that respect, as the apologists for the new Nazi regime never neglected an opportunity to point out, the German revolution had been orderly and comparatively bloodless. (The counterrevolutionaries had not rushed to the barricades.)

The difficulty was in knowing which of many voices to believe. Many of the émigrés, although the revolution of nihilism had proved itself dangerous and too strong for them, soon convinced themselves and assured others that it could not last; it was alien to the thinking, antithetical to the ideals, and repulsive to the emotional reactions of too many of the German people. Hitler said it would last a thousand years, but that National Socialism was not an article for export. He added that the self-respecting nationalism of the new Germany asked only for freedom and equality of status and would never deny to the nationalism of another nation the respectful recognition it demanded for itself.

Freedom for Germany meant to most Germans only freedom from such restrictions—called shackles by the Nazi—as the Treaty of Versailles had imposed upon her. National equality meant equality of opportunity to rearm at will and national *Ebenbürtigkeit*—recognition of a major-power status inferior to none. Denunciation of the "dictated" Treaty of Versailles had always been the theme song of all Nazi propaganda. But would Germany seek revision of that treaty immediately or only eventually and gradually; by negotiation through the League of Nations, by piecemeal unilateral infraction and denunciation, or by war? Nazi spokesmen contradicted themselves and one another every day. Germany wanted only universal peace—and justice for herself—said Hitler to the world in one breath. In the next breath, when speaking to his own people, he relapsed into the more congenial psychology and vocabulary of war.

Was this a new Germany? Or only a recrudescence of an old one which Europe had learned by experience to fear? Looking back upon it later, and back beyond it, some observers saw new meaning and significance in the political ideas of Wagner, of whose music Hitler was so fond—ideas about which Nietzsche had written:

"Some day the German spirit will find itself awake in all the morning freshness following a deep sleep; then it will slay the dragons, destroy the malignant dwarfs, waken Brunhilde—and Wotan's spear itself will be unable to obstruct its course."[27]

The Nazi said that all Germans everywhere should think of Germany as "home." They set up an elaborate organization headed by Professors Karl and Albrecht Haushofer, father and son, to make and maintain contacts with Germans living abroad and with citizens of other countries—naturalized or native-born—of German ancestry or with German family connections. The Haushofers were also proponents of what they called geopolitics—something which meant at best a scientific study of the natural connection between geography, resources, and national policy; at worst, and in fact as adopted and applied by the Nazi, the use of Germans everywhere to provide information which might one day be useful to Germany in war. The periodical *Geopolitik* was edited for some time by the Haushofers, who thus supplied information and theoretical justification for expansionist ideas which the party or army hierarchy had in mind.

The bonds by which Professor Karl Haushofer's "People's League for Germanism Abroad" was expected to bind Germans everywhere to the "fatherland" were more than merely cultural or sentimental. Germans in ceded territories such as the Saar, Alsace-Lorraine, Danzig, West Prussia, Posen, and Upper Silesia were encouraged to think of their separation from the Reich as only temporary. German minorities in Czechoslovakia and elsewhere were constantly reminded that their kinsmen in Germany were sympathetically interested in them. Intensely nationalistic and self-conscious groups were formed among the Germans in South and Central America. They were taught to think of themselves as Germans no matter where they lived and whether or

[27] Quoted from *The Birth of Tragedy*, chap. 24, by Crane Brinton, in *Nietzsche* (Cambridge, Mass., 1941), 40.

not they had found it expedient to pledge allegiance to another national government.

Nor were German-Americans or Germans in the United States to be neglected. Only six months after Hitler had become chancellor, the *Deutscher Beobachter* of New York published a "Summons to the Germans in America":

The folk arises, the assault is launched. Who will still sit like a coward with his hands in his lap? We are done with the disgrace of the alien over-lordship, years-long endured, gone are the days of national indignity and self-surrender.

The German people has again found itself, is taking its fate again into its own hands, has recognized that only in its own strength can it find again the way upward. Out of this consciousness awakes in it the spirit of sacrifice and the enthusiasm with which it takes up the struggle against need and misery. With German thoroughness, with German industry, and with German endurance it will accomplish the tasks that history has imposed upon it, and the world will again be astounded at this German achievement.

And you, German woman, German man abroad? Will you stand back from this struggle? Have not you an obligation also to make your contribution to the recovery of your fatherland?

The response was disappointing, or would have been if the propaganda ministry had been so ill informed as to expect the German-Americans to forget their duty to the United States. A German-American Bund was eventually formed, with imitation-Nazi paraphernalia and ceremonials. German Nazi agents were busy in it and in various "patriotic front" organizations of neofascist type, parading their patriotism and proclaiming their love of peace, their devotion to home, church, and all virtues but tolerance, and their hatred only of anarchy, godlessness, and communism. But most of the German-Americans, thinking of themselves as Americans first and Germans only in ancestry or by association, and prouder of the culture of the older Germany than of the Kultur of the new, refused to be rounded up and *gleichgeschaltet* (lined up) by the Nazi. Some of them proved, during the doubtful period of uneasy neutrality after the outbreak of the war, to be rather anti-British than pro-German. Few of them were Nazi or pro-Nazi. The propaganda ministry had probably expected of them only that they would support all "peace and patriotism" movements and keep the United States from declaring war on Germany if Germany should be at war in Europe. They helped, when the time came, to divide opinion on the question of active participation in the war, but behaved as Americans, not Germans, when the United States became a belligerent.

The months of December, 1932, and January, 1933, in which the crisis provoked by Japan's seizure of Manchuria reached its climax, found the League of Nations already embarrassed by the question of Germany's rearmament and the imminent failure of the Geneva conference on disarmament. As war minister in von Papen's cabinet, General von Schleicher had demanded on August 8, 1932, that Germany be conceded the right to equality with the other great powers with respect to armament. Otherwise, he declared, she would not be represented at any subsequent meeting of the conference. On December 11, 1932, by a five-power declaration, the other powers participating in the conference granted Germany in principle the right to equality of armament, without conceding the validity of the German argument that they themselves were under obligation, by the Treaty of Versailles, generally to disarm. So von Schleicher, who meanwhile had become chancellor, had what was generally considered a diplomatic triumph to his credit.

The disarmament conference reconvened in February, 1933. There the French adhered to their objection to any increase of armament by any nation—including Germany—for a period of four years. There also British Prime Minister MacDonald offered a proposal for a five-year numerical limitation of armies, these forces to be raised by conscription for short terms of service. The MacDonald proposal would have authorized a Russian army of 500,000, and have allowed Germany, Italy, Poland, and France 200,000 each, Rumania 150,000, Spain 120,000, Czechoslovakia and Yugoslavia 100,000 each, others 25,000 to 60,000 each, with colonial powers permitted to maintain supplementary forces in their colonies. The German delegation, however (perhaps deliberately), tied up the conference in endless discussion of technicalities by declaring that Germany would accept equality in what the conference should define as defensive armament only if what it designated as offensive weapons were legally outlawed and abolished.[28]

The feeling of futility with which the League of Nations disarmament conference adjourned in Geneva in June, 1933, was suddenly

---

[28] Hitler later carried this technique a step further by joining Litvinov in publicly advocating immediate general and total disarmament, and by repeatedly proclaiming that Germany was ready at any time to sign a general pact outlawing war. Such a pact would no doubt have served him very well if others had put their trust in it. He would always sign anything and decide afterward whether to honor his signature. He ignored the fact that Germany was then a party to the Kellogg-Briand Pact, which to him was without significance.

turned to consternation when on October 14, 1933, two days before the date set for the conference to reconvene, Germany announced her withdrawal from it as a result of what Hitler called a denial of the promised national equality, and her intention also to withdraw from the League of Nations.

Baron Konstantin von Neurath, who had been head of the German Foreign Office under Chancellors von Papen and von Schleicher and who continued to hold that office under Hitler until 1938, was a seasoned diplomat of respectable ability and long experience. He would have been at home among conventional diplomats anywhere. But nothing could have been more incongruous than the appearance in Geneva of Goebbels and his bodyguards. It was no intuitive realization of that incongruity, however, that caused the German withdrawal; it was the fundamental incompatibility of Nazi principles and policies with those of the law-minded members of the League.

Gustav Stresemann's government had taken pains, when it joined the League, to advertise to its own people and the world that it was not reratifying the hated Treaty of Versailles; but League and treaty were associated in many Germans' minds, and the treaty was anathema. Withdrawal from the League was quite consistent with the general tone of the revisionist propaganda which had brought the Nazi party into power, and was overwhelmingly endorsed by the German voters in a rigged plebiscite November 12; but it caused well-informed, peace-minded, and forward-looking Germans to view the future with dismay.[29]

Nazi Germany was soon busy with rearmament. The government of the Weimar republic had evaded and violated the disarmament clauses of the Treaty of Versailles in many ways.[30] The Nazi regime concentrated at first on economic mobilization and plans for war production. Less than a year after the announcement of withdrawal from the disarmament conference and League of Nations, Dr. Hjalmar Schacht, who as president of the Reichsbank and minister for economics was responsible for economic preparation for war, reported to Hitler that practical war preparation included the stock-piling of materials, new construction of facilities to produce scarce goods, redeployment of industry to safe areas, and influence over fiscal and trade policies. Strict control of all economic activity was required, he

[29] The question put to the voters was: "Does the German people approve the policy of its government as here set forth, and is it willing to declare this policy to be the expression of its own views and of its own will and solemnly to pledge itself thereto?" The *Ja!* vote was announced as 95 percent.

[30] See pp. 96-98, 240-241, 256-267, 261-263, and 283.

said, with special attention paid to the use of scarce materials—
which involved rationing and priority systems.[31]

Two startling revelations of the ruthless and unscrupulous character
of the Nazi leaders were the party purge of June 30, 1934, and the
murder of Austrian Chancellor Engelbert Dollfuss, July 25 of the same
year. The truth about these incidents was more discreditable to the
men responsible for them than the half-truths that were then known.
It was enough to startle the civilized world, however, to realize that
Hitler, in a break with the left wing of his party, had countenanced the
mass murder, by personal proscription and without pretense of trial,
of hundreds of his most intimate associates of earlier years. Among the
victims were Captain Ernst Roehm, chief of staff of the SA or party
storm troopers, Gregor Strasser, who until 1933 had been Nazi
floor leader in the Reichstag, and former Chancellor Kurt von
Schleicher, whose wife was shot with him in their home. Roehm was
a hard-bitten soldier of fortune who neither knew nor aspired to any
other trade. He had known Hitler well when the future scourge of
Europe had been eking out a precarious and unpromising existence
in poverty and obscurity. To Roehm the party leader was neither
superman nor knight in shining armor but a man of less than ordinary
general ability or respectability who by clever use of certain extraordinary personal gifts and the services of his friends had suddenly come
up from nowhere, and who could lose his new position in a day if the
men who had put him into it should decide to put him out of it.
Roehm did not take the trouble to pretend as others, including Göring,
did that the new Hitler who had been elevated to the chancellorship
had suddenly become sacrosanct as a result of his elevation, someone
quite different from the gangster that the old gang had known.

Roehm was also said to be ambitious, to be planning to perpetuate
the importance of the *Sturmabteilungen* (SA) which he had reorganized and trained, to make them part of the army. The army, however—
then known as the Reichswehr, later as the Wehrmacht—despised the
SA and refused to open its service-proud ranks to them. Wanting the
support of the regular officers' corps, and as confident that he could
control and use the generals and admirals as they were that they
could use and control him, Hitler supported them in their refusal.
So Roehm's name was at or near the top of the proscription list, and
Hitler took personal charge of his liquidation. He made a show then of

[31] Ministry of Economics report on economic preparation for war—*die Krieg-
führung wirtschaftlich vorzubereiten.* Nuremberg trial document EC 128. USA 623.
International Military Tribunal, *Trial of the Major War Criminals* (Nuremberg,
1947-1949), XXXVI 158-214.

being outraged by Roehm's gross personal immorality—which he had long known about and ignored without taking the trouble even to condone it.

Gregor Strasser had shown all along some of the same personal independence as Roehm, and had been associated with Roehm in a movement to get on with some of the socialist measures the party promised while it was making its bid for popular support, before gaining control of the government. It had then stressed the socialist as well as the nationalist features of its program. But von Papen, Schacht, Thyssen, and others had brought Hitler the support of the industrialists by offering to insure them against socialism. So socialist Strasser was liquidated.

The object lesson was not lost on the other party leaders, none of whom for ten years thereafter dared seriously to challenge the personal authority of Hitler. The non-German world was somewhat disturbed, but was slower than the Germans were to realize how successfully the chancellor had already entrenched himself in power or how dangerous it was for anyone in Germany to oppose him.

It soon thereafter became apparent that opposition to National Socialism was dangerous also in Austria. There Christian Socialist Chancellor Dollfuss had made himself something of a dictator and in 1933, as leader of an all-party organization called the Fatherland Front and head of a corporate state of fascist type, had outlawed the German-supported Austrian Nazi party. He had also fought as best he could the influence of the German radio, which beamed Nazi propaganda in Austria's direction day and night. But the Nazi opposition persevered underground.

On July 25, 1934, armed parties seized the government radio station and chancellery. In the course of the attack Dollfuss, a devout Catholic, was shot and permitted to bleed to death, slowly, without the religious consolation of the final ministrations of a priest. Within three days the Austrian government had the situation again in hand, and the new Christian Socialist Chancellor, Kurt Schuschnigg, was able for a while to hold his own against constant secret Nazi pressure. His government publicly charged the German government with responsibility for the unsuccessful *Putsch*.

Having failed to complete their larger mission, the seizure of the Austrian government, the murderers of Chancellor Dollfuss were officially disowned by Hitler in the *Völkischer Beobachter* of July 27; but one of them, former Sergeant Major Otto Planetta, at his trial in an Austrian court, proudly proclaimed his party affiliation and his devotion to Germany and to Adolf Hitler. He and several others were executed.[32]

On March 11, 1935, the camouflage cover stenciled "Air Sport League" (*Luftsporthansa*) was pulled off the German army air force. It had been years in process of creation, part of it trained in glider clubs in Germany and part behind the iron curtain of military censorship in Russia, and had been formally reconstituted on March 1. On March 16, by unilateral denunciation without notice or negotiation, Hitler announced by proclamation that Germany would no longer consider herself bound by the disarmament clauses of the Treaty of Versailles but would reconstitute at once a "defense force"—*Wehrmacht*—of 324,000 men, exclusive of the air force and the navy. A peacetime army of that strength was needed, he said, to provide for the security of the Reich in the face of a Russian army of 960,000 men, and of threatening armament increases elsewhere.[33]

As he usually did on such occasions, Hitler called attention in his proclamation of March 16, 1935, to the existence of a ten-year nonaggression pact with Poland, signed January 26, 1934, to his unaccepted offers to conclude nonaggression pacts or general disarmament agreements with other powers, and to his renewed assurances that since the return of the Saar he had no further territorial claim to present to France.[34]

"At this hour," said Hitler's proclamation, "the German Government renews before the German people and before the entire world the affirmation of its resolve never to go beyond that which the protection of German honor and the freedom of the Reich demand, and especially affirms that it wishes in the national German armament to create no instrument of military aggression, but on the contrary to create exclusively an instrument of defense and therefore an instrument for the maintenance of peace. . . ."[35]

[32] After the German occupation of Austria in 1938 a marble tablet on the entrance to the chancellery on the Ballhausplatz, which had become the Nazi *Reichsstaathalterei*, honored the "154 German men of No. 89 SS Standardte" who had "stood up . . . for Germany" there on July 25, 1934, and especially the seven who had "found death at the hands of the hangman." Reported by George Gedye, *Betrayal in Central Europe* (New York, 1939), 132-133.

[33] In 1935 France lowered her recruiting age and lengthened the term of compulsory military service to compensate for the decline of the birth rate during the war years 1915-1918.

[34] In a plebiscite supervised by the League of Nations in the Saar district January 13, 1935, 90 percent of the votes cast were for reincorporation into Germany. In 1947, with French troops occupying and controlling the area and with France demanding annexation, publicly expressed opinion was more favorable to France.

[35] New York *Times*, March 17, 1935, p. 1; R. P. Stearns, *Pageant of Europe* (New York, 1947), 916.

As it had done at the withdrawal from the disarmament conference and League of Nations, Nazi Germany rejoiced; and much of non-Nazi Germany rejoiced with it. The non-German world was apprehensive but not altogether unsympathetic.

"Since the day when Germany collapsed through treason," exulted the Nazi party Statement on Military Policy, March 16, 1935, "since the days in which the Diktat of Versailles was imposed upon her, this is the German people's greatest moment. . . . With the present day the honor of the German nation has been restored. We stand erect as a free people among nations. . . ."[36]

The "conquest of political equality" was to most Germans a substantial triumph. The right to rearm was to them one of the essential attributes of national sovereignty. It had taken on for them a doubled psychological importance while it had been denied them, because it had been denied them by a form of international control. Others welcomed the return of conscription because they had deplored what they called the undisciplined behavior of the younger generation, had remembered that universal military training had once been an integral part of the youth-training system of the nation, and hoped that it might be so again.

Millions of good Germans who would have been horrified to hear themselves called militarists or warmongers were relieved and pleased with the restoration of the army because they had more confidence in it than in the National Socialists, and because they thought they saw in it some insurance against civil war. There had been in the old imperial army a long tradition of aloofness from party politics (disguised as political disinterestedness), a narrowly defined correctness of behavior, financial honesty, and military efficiency. The Reichswehr was generally—and rather generously—credited with having maintained those traditions, and it was supposed that the new Wehrmacht would be equally dependable though perhaps more democratic. The Nazi purge of the "night of the long knives" had left the citizenry shuddering with horror at the thought of a cutthroat civil war for supremacy among rival Nazi subleaders which no one could be sure would not be an immediate consequence of the sudden death of Hitler.

Nazi and non-Nazi alike generally preferred Hitler to his associates. They hoped that he would use the army if necessary to suppress a mutiny among his satraps or his Janizaries, if such an insurrection should occur, and reassured themselves with the unspoken thought that, if he should die or fail, the army which generations of Germans

[36] New York *Times*, March 17, 1935, p. 31; Stearns, *op. cit.*, 916.

had learned to trust, and which for generations had shown itself generally trustworthy, would step into the breach, restore order without exposing them to the horrors of civil war, and give them a new national government of dependable "German" character. That might mean military dictatorship; but people were more afraid of disorder than of dictatorship. They would have been willing to forgo an opportunity to recover their civil liberties and immunities, rather than risk a civil war and the disorder which they so abhorred.

Abroad, the reaction to the remilitarization of Germany was less favorable. Great Britain, France, and Italy immediately filed protests in Berlin. At a conference at Stresa in Italy in April the same three powers conferred on the preservation of the independence of Austria and on a common policy with reference to Germany. Some hopes were entertained, outside Germany, that the so-called "Stresa front" there formed would hold Germany in check. In April the League of Nations Council formally condemned the unilateral repudiation of the disarmament clauses of the Treaty of Versailles.

On May 3 Schacht complained to Hitler that although everything else had been subordinated to armament it was being found difficult to finance the program or to win popular support for it without such a propaganda campaign as might imperil Germany's international position. Soviet Russian Litvinov called Germany's action "a violation of the [League of Nations] covenant and consequently a violation of obligations undertaken toward the other members of the League, constituting a threat to peace." The League of Nations could not, said Litvinov, "close its eyes to facts."[37] Litvinov and his government faced the facts by making a five-year mutual assistance pact with France, May 2, 1935, and one with Czechoslovakia May 16.

Hitler tried to allay the suspicion he had aroused. In an address to the Reichstag May 21 he said that Germany's good will and love of peace were proved by her permanent renunciation of Alsace-Lorraine and her continued readiness to "observe and fulfill all obligations" of the Locarno Pact as long as others did, although he called the continued demilitarization of the Rhineland a harsh condition for her to meet. Germany would also agree, he said, if others would, to limitation of armaments and prohibition of specific weapons or of those useful only for attack.

The Franco-Russian treaty, which was not ratified until March 27,

[37] Alice R. Craemer, "Cooperative Russia," in *Current History*, September, 1946, p. 223. Technically, Germany's withdrawal from the League was not complete until October 14, 1935, two years after her notification of intention to withdraw.

1936, twenty days after the Nazi march into the Rhineland, was so meshed into the obligations of members of the League of Nations and into "existing treaties" such as Locarno as to have made it legally impossible for France to attack Germany without the consent of the Council of the League, unless the Council failed in a crisis to designate an aggressor and so left her free to act on her own initiative. But the German Foreign Office called it a violation of the Treaty of Locarno and used that charge as a pretext when Germany herself repudiated Locarno March 7, 1936, twenty days before ratification of the pact to which she was attributing her own action.

The pact of May 16, 1935, between Russia and Czechoslovakia bound each to aid the other if France did—not otherwise.[38]

In his apparently though deceptively placatory Reichstag address of May 21 Hitler let drop the revelation that Germany would have a fleet 35 percent as strong as the British and only 15 percent weaker than the French. She had been limited by the Treaty of Versailles to a navy of 15,000 men, with no ships heavier than 10,000 tons; but "in anticipation of" a new naval treaty with Great Britain she had already in 1935 a navy of 34,000 men, with battleships, cruisers, and submarines built and building.[39]

Hoping, apparently, in an unrealistic attempt at realism, to forestall further unauthorized revisions of the ratio between her fleet and the German by recognizing those already made without her knowledge or consent, Great Britain announced on June 18, 1935, a new naval

[38] See pp. 179, 515-517.

[39] Testimony of Admiral Erich Raeder, on trial at Nuremberg, May, 1946. See *Current History*, July, 1946, p. 68. A United Press dispatch from Nuremberg May 20, 1946, said 35,000. In 1920 Germany had sold to Japan, in violation of the terms of the Treaty of Versailles, the plans and specifications of two "undersea cruisers," one of them a mine layer. These submarines, built in the Kawasaki shipyards in Japan under the supervision of Dr. Techel, former chief submarine engineer of the *Germania Werft*, and given their test runs by a "retired" German submarine officer, Kaptlt. a. D. Robert Braütigam, were prototypes of those used by Japan in the Pacific war of 1941-1945. A skeleton German organization, posing as a legitimate firm of shipbuilding engineers, was kept intact in Holland from 1922 to 1935, then moved back to Kiel and Hamburg. Torpedo research and experimentation were carried on in Spain and Germany. For Spain, Turkey, and Finland, false-fronted German firms, known, supported, and—when necessary—subsidized by the German admiralty Division of Naval Operations, built submarines of 100, 250, 500, and 750 tons. Trial runs were purposely prolonged to give German officers and crews more training. The first twenty-four 250-ton U-boats assembled for the new German navy in 1935, from parts previously manufactured secretly and stored, were duplicates or adaptations of a model planned by German engineers in 1930, built for Finland, and tried out (with several others) by German seamen and technicians in Finnish waters in 1933 and 1934. And the purchasers usually paid enough for a U-boat to cover the cost of the experimentation necessary to develop and improve the model!

limitation treaty conceding Germany the right to a navy 35 percent as large as Britain's, with cruisers, battleships, and submarines—all denied her by the Treaty of Versailles. Germany seemed temporarily to have succeeded, as Japan seemed to have done, in disposing of the restrictive clauses of an international agreement by the direct and simple process of tearing up the treaty which recorded that agreement. The "Stresa front," already undermined by Mussolini's insincerity and absorption in his own plans for aggression elsewhere and by Laval's subservience to Mussolini (indicated by his agreement of January 7, 1935, to cede 44,500 square miles of French Tunisia to Italian Libya and part of French Somaliland to Italian Eritrea), was further weakened by this British appeasement of Germany with respect to naval power.

From the acknowledged and official beginning of the remilitarization of Germany in 1935 it was but a short and logical—but fateful —step to the reoccupation of the Rhineland by German troops, March 7, 1936. Although the Allied armies of occupation had been withdrawn from the Rhine bridgeheads and the German area west of the Rhine at the end of ten years instead of the fifteen stipulated by the Treaty of Versailles, the reëntry of German troops into those areas or the refortification of the frontier was still contrary to the terms of that treaty, the Treaty of Locarno, and the Kellogg-Briand Pact. The first of these treaties had been imposed upon Germany as a consequence of defeat and accepted by her people only in preference to alternatives which at the time they could not face. The second and third had been freely negotiated on a basis of equality with the other parties, constitutionally ratified, and repeatedly confirmed by constituted German national authorities, including Hitler, as late as May 21, 1935. Neutral observers not unfriendly to the German people could easily understand the Germans' insistence upon recovering full freedom of action within the boundaries of their fatherland and demanding international recognition of that freedom. They were much less seriously concerned about the reappearance of German troops in the German Rhineland than about the brusqueness of the unilateral action by which Nazi Germany tossed aside its treaty obligations by a brazen show of force.

There was more show than force. The Wehrmacht was not yet ready in 1936 to fight a war against a major power. It had been ordered to retreat if the French army mobilized and reëntered the Rhineland to oppose it. It was not opposed. Hitler had estimated the international political situation more accurately than his generals. By a vote announced as 99 percent of the eligible voters the German people expressed by plebiscite their acceptance of the accomplished fact, without expressing publicly the apprehension any of them may have felt over the manner of its accomplishment.[40]

The most outspoken public protest against the German remilitarization of the Rhineland was voiced by the Soviet Russian delegate to the League of Nations, Maxim Litvinov: "One cannot fight for the collective organization of security without taking measures against the violation of international obligations. We, however, do not count among such measures collective capitulation to the aggressor, capitulation in the face of violation of treaties, or the collective encouragement of such violations. . . . I declare on behalf of my government that it is ready to take part in all measures that may be proposed to the council of the League by the Locarno powers and will be acceptable to the other members of the council."[41]

American opinion, which had generally come to consider the Versailles Treaty harsh and in some ways unjust to Germany, welcomed the recovery of German economy and was not generally unsympathetic toward Germany's natural ambition to regain her freedom to exercise all of the generally accepted rights and prerogatives of a sovereign nation within her national boundaries. Much more concern was felt over the ultimate implications of the manner in which those rights were being reclaimed. But opinion at that time would have been divided as to the justifiability of armed intervention to prevent either the rearming of Germany or her military reoccupation of the Rhineland.

Certainly the United States, which had not ratified the Treaty of Versailles, could not have been depended upon to participate in a move to enforce the disarmament clauses of that treaty by force of arms or by a "preventive" war. American opinion, still strongly

[40] The general German reaction was equally favorable and the passive objectors were equally reticent about their objections—if any—when in October, 1936, by unilateral denunciation announced by Hitler in an address, it was made known to the world that Germany had resumed control of traffic through the Kiel Canal and on the Rhine, Elbe, Oder, and Danube rivers, which the Treaty of Versailles had internationalized. Here again, as in the military reoccupation of the Rhineland, no German nationalist could quarrel on principle with the resumption by Germany of sovereign rights within her national boundaries, although no internationalist—German or other—could be quite indifferent to the ultimate implications of the practice of unilateral infraction by show or threat of force. It was not then generally known in Germany that the Foreign Office had negotiated a new agreement restoring the waterways to Germany's control, or that Hitler had refused to sign it, preferring unilateral denunciation.

[41] March 17, 1936. *Current History*, September, 1946, p. 223. On April 1, 1936, Austria denounced the restrictive military clauses of the Treaty of St. Germain and adopted a policy of universal military (or labor) service.

pacifist, had been aroused against Japan but had not gone far beyond the Stimson doctrine of nonrecognition of changes of territorial sovereignty effected by use of armed force. It had not been so aroused against Germany. The enormous iniquity of the National Socialist regime was not generally recognized; and a long and honorable United States tradition of nonintervention in the domestic political affairs of European nations, and an overwhelming American opinion against commitments involving the use of armed force overseas, would have restrained the government of the United States if it had been disposed—as it was not—to participate in a "stop-Hitler" movement backed by a threat of force.

Contemporary noninterventionist American opinion was clearly expressed by Norman H. Davis, who had been chairman of the United States delegation to the League of Nations disarmament conference at Geneva. On May 29, 1934, he said that the United States would not participate in European political negotiations or settlements, and would not "make any commitment whatever to use its armed forces for the settlement of a dispute anywhere."[42]

The subsequent course of events made easy, in retrospect, the observation that, as the principal great powers most immediately threatened, France and Britain should have realized their danger then, and have taken steps to scotch aggression while there was yet time— when Russian help was offered, while Czechoslovakia was available as a bastion and a well-equipped ally, and before the Rome-Berlin Axis had been formed. They had not learned, however, to put their faith in Russia. Her leaders (until after Hitler became chancellor of Germany) had been wont to describe the League of Nations as an anti-Russian combination of capitalist-imperialist states; she had joined the League only after Germany left it; and she seemed to have been converted to a new faith in collective security only by a belated realization of a need of some such salvation. A certain element of opinion in Britain welcomed the recovery of Germany—and was willing to countenance German rearmament—as a counterweight and buffer against "bolshevism." Britain's naval position was then being further menaced by Japan, which on January 8, 1936, had walked out of the London naval conference when her demand for parity with Great Britain and the United States had been refused, and which had previously given notice that she would not be bound by the terms of the Washington naval limitation treaty after the end of 1936.

Despite all that was then known about new armament and the

42 See Barck and Blake, *Since 1900* (New York), 602.

threatening behavior of militarist governments in other countries, pacifism was still strong in Britain. Prime Minister Stanley Baldwin may have appraised opinion accurately when he stated in Parliament in 1936 that if he had said publicly in 1933-1935 that Germany was rearming and Britain must therefore rearm, and had gone before the voters in a general election on that issue, he would have lost the election.[43]

British public opinion was further distracted from world affairs in December, 1936, by the domestic and intra-imperial crisis occasioned by the abdication of the king and emperor Edward VIII. In May, 1937, shortly after the coronation of the new king, George VI, Mr. Stanley Baldwin retired from public life and was succeeded as prime minister by his chancellor of the exchequer, Neville Chamberlain.

Neither France nor Britain could count on the effective aid of the other. Pierre Laval, convinced twenty years before that France could never again stand up against Germany unless strongly bolstered up by others, was busily appeasing Mussolini in the vain hope that he might somehow induce Mussolini to restrain Hitler. So Germany's easy reoccupation of the Rhineland was made easier by Japan's apparently successful defiance of the League and by Europe's preoccupation with the Italian conquest of Ethiopia.

FASCIST ITALY AND WAR IN AFRICA, 1935-1936

The war began in Africa on October 3, 1935, with the bombing of the Ethiopian towns of Aduwa and Adigrat by Italian planes and the invasion of Ethiopia by Italian troops. That invasion was a characteristic act of self-assertion and aggression on the part of Italian fascism; and fascism itself, like National Socialism in Germany, was in a sense the unruly offspring of national frustration.

Italy was nominally one of the victorious powers of 1918, but the victory was won by her allies and not by her. A successful final offensive with American and Allied support in 1918 did not wipe out the bitter memory of defeat at Caporetto in 1917. Angry over the failure of the Paris peace conference to award Fiume to Italy, Premier Orlando and the rest of the Italian delegation walked out of the conference—and were absent when mandates over former German and Turkish territories in Africa were awarded to France and

[43] *British Parliamentary Debates*, 5th series, Vol. 317, p. 1144. See also Winston Churchill, *Second World War*, I, 215-216.

Great Britain, none to Italy. The return to power of Premier Giolitti, who had done what he could to keep Italy neutral in 1914 and had subsequently been called a traitor for having done so, implied a revulsion of public feeling away from the war policy of 1915-1918 and toward the opinion that participation in the war on the side of the Allies had been unnecessary, unwise, and unprofitable. Discharged war veterans were scoffed at as stupid dupes of other powers. A wave of radicalism, soon to call itself communism, swept the industrial towns. Strikes and riots were numerous in 1919 and 1920. Factories (many of them in Milan) were taken over by their employees, who quickly found themselves unable to do business with those which had not been so expropriated. Industrial stagnation, commercial chaos, and some disorder, destruction of property, and loss of life naturally resulted. The national debt increased, and national credit suffered. Premier Giolitti's government postponed its own downfall for a while, but made it eventually certain by enlisting against the "alien, international" radicalism of the left the new, highly nationalistic, ostentatiously Italian radicalism of the right—the black-shirted *Fascisti*, of the party founded by Benito Mussolini in Milan in 1919.

Many of the early *Fascisti* were war veterans, posing as defenders of law and order against the domestic enemies of their country and against the imported virus of "bolshevism" in time of peace as they had once defended their homeland against invasion in time of war. There was propaganda value in their black shirts, reminiscent of the red shirts of Garibaldi's famous "Thousand," especially after Gabriele d'Annunzio had imitated Garibaldi still further on September 1, 1919, by leading a small band of volunteers to seize Fiume as the old liberator had once seized Sicily. The Italian government lost face with its own people by repudiating d'Annunzio to the extent of signing with Yugoslavia the Treaty of Rapallo, November, 1920, by which Fiume was made a free city. In 1924 Mussolini reannexed the city, permitting Yugoslavia to annex its southern suburb Sušak.[44]

In October, 1922, still talking about defending the country against "bolshevism," which by that time had become a much less serious menace than it had seemed to be in 1920, the Fascists staged a demonstration rather grandiloquently called a "march on Rome" and demanded that their leader (*Duce*) be made premier. On a plea of necessity, to avoid civil war, King Victor Emmanuel III refused to

[44] The Treaty of Rapallo was negotiated for Italy by the then minister of foreign affairs, Count Carlo Sforza, who lived in exile during most of Mussolini's regime and returned to his old position in the postwar governments of 1945 and following.

sign the decree which would have declared a state of siege, and acquiesced instead in the establishment of a personal dictatorship by Mussolini. He never again emerged from the eclipse which kept him constantly in Mussolini's shadow until July 25, 1943, when at long last he dismissed the Duce, whose resignation had been demanded by the Fascist Grand Council July 24, and played an inconspicuously ignominious part in Italy's surrender to the Allies. Generals such as Badoglio, who might have led the army in the suppression of Mussolini, and who eventually watched him go as they had watched him come, accepted him as head of the state and their supreme commander, and obeyed him until defeat by forces from outside Italy had overwhelmed him.[45]

Within a few years, step by step, dictatorship of one man in a one-party police state was "legally" established by unconvincing constitutional procedure. Only the government list of candidates for a Chamber of Deputies already bereft of all real legislative power was permitted in an election. That list, of four hundred candidates, was made by the Fascist Grand Council, with power not only to select but to substitute, from a first list of a thousand submitted by the corporations and other associations. In two such elections or plebiscites in 1929 and 1934 the government won overwhelming majorities of the votes cast. In 1939 the place of the Chamber of Deputies was taken by a Chamber of Fasces and Corporations, nominally representative of the Fascist party and the "corporations." Mussolini had power to legislate by decree, and could depend upon the Chamber for confirmation.

Italian fascism was a showy business. There were music, banners, parades, and demonstrations to impress a spectacle-loving people. Everywhere, discipline and militarization were emphasized to restore the national self-confidence, which had been badly shaken in 1917, and revive the flagging spirit of aggressiveness, which Mussolini sometimes called "virility." Mussolini, a vigorous and forceful individual, made a constant spectacle of himself, living strenuously and leading the nation to live dangerously.

A great show was made of utilizing all the productive forces of the nation by combining economics with politics in the "corporative state."

[45] Apologists who seem to have considered other peoples than the Germans primarily responsible for Hitler, and others than the Italians for Mussolini, have apparently underestimated the significance of the facts that in each case it was the dictator's own people who first accepted him and would presumably have fought for their right to do so if others had intervened, and that in each case it was armed force applied by others that eventually broke him.

Producers were organized into nine syndicates, four for employers and four for employees in agriculture, industry, credit and insurance, and commerce, one for professional men and artists. These syndicates were responsible for wages, working conditions, and industrial relations. The president, council, and minor officials of each syndicate were appointed and controlled by the government, which was controlled by the Fascist party.

Economic life was further organized and controlled from 1934 by the formation of twenty-two corporations or guilds, each to be concerned with all phases of production in one field—such as cereals, mining, internal communications, the tourist industry, and so on. Mussolini was the head of each of the twenty-two corporations and of the National Council of Corporations, and appointed the minister of corporations who was nominal director of the system.

Some improvement in the relations of church and state, strained since political unification, was achieved by the Lateran agreement of 1929. The national government recognized Vatican City as a sovereign state and the pope as its sovereign ruler. The pope accepted payment in cash and bonds as indemnity for the loss of revenue and territorial sovereignty over the Papal States absorbed into the kingdom of Italy in the process of unification, and ceased to consider himself (as his predecessors had done) "the prisoner of the Vatican." There were still sharp differences, however, over the control and character of education.

Some significant economic improvements were effected, especially in the draining of swamplands for wheat growing near the silted river mouths and the fight against erosion on the hillsides, and in the utilization of water power for the electrification of transportation and industry. But there was never enough done to keep pace with the food demands of the rapidly increasing population or to make Italy independent of foreign sources of coal and many of the metals needed in her industries. So Mussolini called Italy overcrowded—although he continued to increase the crowding by encouraging his people to keep up their birth rate—and talked boldly of the necessity of territorial expansion.

In a world already fully occupied or claimed—as Hitler was to observe to his generals a few years later—sooner or later the conqueror comes up against the proprietor. So territorial expansion was possible only by conquest or by intimidation tantamount to conquest. Mussolini preferred an easy conquest, in a war which he was sure his untried bully boys could win.

Ethiopia (Abyssinia) was the only area in Africa not in some way protected by direct or indirect connection with a European power, and had been the object of an unsuccessful Italian attempt at conquest forty years earlier (claimed in fact as an Italian protectorate from 1889 to 1896). It was thus a logical first objective in a career of conquest grandiloquently represented to the Italian people—some of whom were less confident of success than Mussolini pretended to be— as destined to revive the glories of the Roman Empire and make the Mediterranean again *mare nostrum*, an Italian lake.

Having decided upon a campaign of conquest, unless deterred by an attitude of determined collective resistance by the other powers— which it did not anticipate, with the League already weakened by the defections of Japan and Germany—the Italian government took advantage of an otherwise insignificant clash of border patrols at Ualual December 5, 1934, to magnify that incident and make of it a cause of war. Ualual was an oasis somewhere near the border between Ethiopia and Italian Somaliland. The exact location of the boundary in that region had never been determined. Except as it included the oasis in Ethiopia or in Italian territory, it was of no great significance to either. Each party involved in the incident may well have believed itself to be fighting on its own soil. Many more critical incidents have been overlooked, and more serious quarrels between nations settled without recourse to war. Conciliation would have been easy if both parties had been conciliatory.

Both parties were members of the League of Nations, and all the procedures provided by the League for the pacific settlement of international disputes were available. Ethiopia was ready to use them. Italy would use them only as a gesture, determined that they should fail. Meanwhile she poured troops and laborers into Eritrea and Somaliland as an ostentatious threat or in obvious preparation for a pincers movement into Ethiopia. Success there would turn the tables on the French and British, whose large and apparently profitable colonial empires Italy had long envied them and coveted, and would pin French and British Somaliland against the Strait of Bab el Mandeb and the Gulf of Aden as Italian Eritrea and Somaliland had been pinned against the Red Sea and Indian Ocean by Ethiopia and the dependencies of France and Britain.

On January 3, 1935, in an exercise of its "friendly right" to bring to the attention of the League a circumstance affecting international relations and threatening to disturb peace between nations, Ethiopia appealed to the League of Nations under Article 11 of the League

Covenant. In March she appealed again, citing Article 15 of the Covenant. But the League, preoccupied with Hitler's proclamation, March 16, of "A Law for the Recreation of the National Defense Forces," was slow to act, hoping meanwhile that the two parties would settle the dispute by arbitration under terms of a general arbitration treaty already nominally in force between them. On September 3, 1935, the arbitration commission reached a decision which would have saved the faces of both sides if both had been willing to accept it, and which clearly left Italy no excuse for continuing to use the Ualual incident as a pretext for a punitive invasion. Ethiopia would have accepted the result of the arbitration; Italy would not.

While Italian preparations for war continued and Ethiopia vainly sought the protection of the world community as organized in the League of Nations, a careful poll of nearly twelve million people was taken in Great Britain, which indicated that 90 percent of those participating thought Britain should continue to work for the maintenance of peace as a member of the League of Nations, acting with and through the League in foreign policy and participating if necessary as a member of the League in the application of economic sanctions against an aggressor. No more than 70 percent favored the use of armed force, by or for the League, to stop an aggressor. Less than 10 percent would have had Britain use armed force independently.

During the same troubled period, giving public and official expression to the general desire of the people of the United States to avoid European trouble at whatever cost, the United States Congress on August 24, 1935, passed a "neutrality" resolution providing that, whenever the president proclaimed as a fact the existence of a state of war between two or more foreign nations, an embargo on the shipment of arms, munitions, and implements of war to any belligerent should be immediately imposed. The president was empowered to designate "implements of war." War materials—i.e., raw materials, oil, steel, and iron—were not embargoed. President Roosevelt expressed some dissatisfaction with the act, but signed it. Citizens of the United States were to be permitted to travel only at their own risk on any vessel owned by nationals of a belligerent.

The strong contemporary trend of noninterventionist opinion was strengthened by the publicity given the findings of Senator Nye's committee of investigation that the United States had been unnecessarily involved in war in 1917, against its interest, by the machinations of the munitions makers and the insistence of some foolhardy individuals upon traveling in what Germany had designated as danger zones.

Isolationists and noninterventionists warned the nation not to repeat what were then rather generally regarded as the mistakes that had once already led to war. So the traditional rights of neutrals to trade and travel outside actual war zones, which had been so stoutly defended by President Wilson from 1914 to 1917, were surrendered unchallenged in 1935 by a people not unmindful of the past but—if the interventionists were right—misguided by it.

The neutrality legislation of 1935 was tantamount to an admission that the United States had no interests outside its own boundaries or territorial waters which it thought worth defending. That its most vital national interest was in the maintenance of international peace was not then, generally, clearly realized. Or an admission of the reality of that interest was countered by the oversimplified but apparently logical argument that the way to keep the peace was simply not to break or threaten it; the way to stay out of trouble was to stay away from areas where trouble was; and the way to discountenance trouble-making was to refuse to contribute in any way to the achievement of its purposes. Unfortunately, in effect, the policy simply licensed lawlessness by proclaiming the determination of the United States not to risk the disturbance of its own peace in defense of the peace or to help the victims of aggression to defend themselves, even by permitting them to overcome their initial handicaps—when attacked—by purchase of arms, munitions, or implements of war for self-defense.

The far-reaching effect of the "neutrality" policy of the United States was shown by subsequent events to have been the indirect encouragement of aggression. The frequency with which Americans were asked in prewar Nazi Germany why the United States had intervened and robbed Germany of her victory in 1917-1918, and whether in similar circumstances it would intervene again, was a convincing indication of a wish to be reassured on that point, to be more confident, as the Nazi leaders eventually convinced themselves, that the United States would not again intervene in time. News of the "peace and neutrality" movements in the United States was good news to the dictators, both in Asia and in Europe.[46]

Meanwhile, upon the suggestion of the Council of the League, France and Great Britain attempted to negotiate a settlement by proposing that the economic policy and financial administration of Ethiopia be directed by Italy under League supervision. Italy rejected

[46] See Sir Norman Angell, Nobel peace prize winner of 1933, *The Steep Places* (New York, 1948), 108: "The aggressor might have been deterred if he had realized earlier that he would be certain to meet the resistance he finally did meet."

the proposal, and Britain announced in September, 1935, that she would support collective action at Geneva if Italy persisted in her Ethiopian adventure along the lines indicated. Italy's answer was the invasion of Ethiopia, as already noted, on October 3.

On October 7 the Council of the League called Italy the aggressor in a war to which it found she had resorted in a fashion contrary to her covenants as a member of the League. The League Assembly then called upon the nations members of the League to impose economic sanctions by prohibiting the shipment of arms or munitions to Italy, not to Ethiopia, by stopping the importation of Italian goods, and by preventing the sale to Italy of certain war materials.

Economic sanctions, however, were in that case not effective. In fact, they could hardly be said to have been tried. No nation had its embargo legislation ready with the administrative organization to enforce it; and some of the most essential war materials, such as coal, iron, and steel, were not embargoed. British and Dutch oil companies were not forbidden to continue to supply the Italian fleet. It was argued that if these companies stopped deliveries they would simply lose the business to their American competitors, without inconveniencing the Italian fleet to any considerable extent, and might invite attack. President Roosevelt proclaimed only two days after the invasion that a state of war "unhappily" existed between Ethiopia and Italy, and announced an embargo on shipment of arms and implements of war to either belligerent. But American sales of materials useful in war although not finished implements of war increased during the first half of 1936, and the general totals did not decrease. Whether Ethiopia, to which the quick delivery of weapons and munitions would have been virtually impossible under war conditions, was from a practical standpoint less seriously affected than Italy by the arms embargo was vigorously debated but never proved.

An effective general embargo on oil shipments would have crippled the Italian enterprise. So would the closing of the Suez Canal. But who would close the canal? Mussolini repeatedly announced that either step would be regarded by Italy as an act of war. The brunt of the fighting would have fallen at first on the British navy, part of which had moved into the eastern Mediterranean and had a base at Alexandria; but Britain definitely did not want to fight at that time or on that issue. Italy, moreover, was known to have some new ships and a new air force and no one knew yet how effective they might be. By January, 1936, Britain was promised armed support in the event of war by Turkey, Greece, Yugoslavia, and—very reluctantly—France. Pierre Laval of France, never daring quite to throw away the friendship and possible protection of Great Britain, yet reluctant to offend Mussolini, who he hoped would some day defend France, either against Germany or against the "Reds" in France, lagged at every step.

So the British foreign minister, Sir Samuel Hoare, who began by eloquently advocating "steady collective resistance to all acts of unprovoked aggression," ended by rather shamefacedly but perhaps prudently joining Laval in first making propitiatory proposals to Italy, then watering down economic sanctions and delaying their general imposition so long that Italy could easily complete her Ethiopian campaign before being seriously inconvenienced by them.

The Hoare-Laval agreements and the failure to implement sanctions promptly and effectively were unpopular in both France and Britain. In Britain in December, 1935, the results of a general election indicated popular approval of the general League policy of the national coalition government led by Stanley Baldwin. But Baldwin had to disavow the Hoare-Laval proposals, accept Hoare's resignation, and appoint in his place as minister for foreign affairs Anthony Eden, already well known and popular as minister for League of Nations affairs and for his consistent support of the principle of collective security and his opposition to appeasement of aggressors. Laval wangled one more vote of confidence in the Chamber of Deputies, then gave way to Socialist Léon Blum.

The war went rather slowly, as the Italians found it necessary to build roads over rugged terrain in a region difficult of access, over which to move their motorized transport, tanks, and heavy guns; but it could have but one conclusion if Italy adhered to her purpose, which was conquest, and if other powers did not intervene. In late April, 1936, organized Ethiopian resistance collapsed. On May 5 Italian forces occupied the conquered capital, Addis Ababa. Emperor Haile Selassie, the Conquering Lion of Judah, had found sanctuary on a British warship; and Mussolini, speaking before a wildly cheering crowd in Rome, conferred upon little King Victor Emmanuel the title of Emperor of Ethiopia. Guerrilla resistance would plague the Italians as long as they remained in precarious possession of the country; but, for a while, they held what they had taken.

The first national government to recognize the conquest was Poland's. Germany also recognized it when making the general Rome-Berlin "Axis" agreement, October 25, 1936. Seven nations, members of the League—Belgium, the Netherlands, Denmark, Norway, Sweden, Finland, and Poland—on July 1, 1936, at a conference at Copenhagen jointly declared that they would thereafter consider the imposition of sanctions noncompulsory. In other words, they would weigh first their own national security and interests, if asked by the League to impose sanctions, and each would define its own obligations and determine its own course. Germany had been as quick to take advantage of the consternation caused by Italy's defiance of the League as Italy had been to trade on the apprehensions aroused by Germany's rearmament and reoccupation of the Rhineland; and fear of Germany had driven the smaller nation states to scatter, abandoning the principle of collective security which they later accused the great powers of having first betrayed.

The League of Nations delayed action until July 4, 1936; then, while formally denouncing the settlement of territorial questions by force, it acknowledged the accomplished fact by suspending sanctions as of July 15. Again aggression seemed to have gone unpunished, and to promise eventually to be profitable; and Mussolini's son Bruno, who claimed credit for some combat flying, compared the blossoming of a bomb-burst with the unfolding of a rose!

BEGINNING OF THE WAR IN EUROPE: FASCISM IN SPAIN, 1936-1938

The war began in Europe in July, 1936, as a civil war in Spain in which partisans of international communism, democratic socialism, German National Socialism, and Italian fascism eventually participated. The republic which was overthrown in that civil war had been the national government of Spain since the abdication of King Alfonso XIII in 1931. The king's abdication had been a consequence of the failure of the military dictatorship which had maintained the form of the monarchy from September, 1923, to January, 1930.

Spain was one of the few continental European nations to remain neutral from 1914 to 1918. The extraordinary demand and high prices for her products, both agricultural and industrial, induced a wartime money prosperity which caused widespread discontent because it was not widely distributed, and a postwar recession when demand diminished. Failure of a corrupt and inefficient government to meet or apparently to grasp the situation led early in 1923 to a strong separatist movement in Catalonia, the eastern province bordering on France and the Mediterranean, its principal city being Barcelona, the leading industrial center of Spain.

A colonial military crisis also faced the government in 1923. The Spanish army, top-heavy with officers and permeated with peculation, had long been one of Europe's worst examples of the baneful influence of an army in politics and of politics in an army. It found itself unable to suppress a handful of rebels in Spanish Morocco, led by the Riffian chieftain Abd-el Krim. A series of indefensible disasters led to an investigation by a committee of inquiry set up by the elected house of the national parliament, the Cortes.

The report of the committee, to have been published on September 20, 1923, was anticipated by one week by General Primo de Rivera, who was able by a coup d'état to establish himself as a military dictator. Parliamentary government was discontinued, civil liberties were suspended, and freedom of speech and press was suppressed. Municipal councils and political appointees (nicknamed *caciques*) in local and provincial government were replaced by military governors. With some help from the French in Morocco, the Spanish army finally suppressed Abd-el Krim's rebellion. The efficiency of the army was somewhat improved. Some effort was made to encourage manufacturing by the adoption of a protective tariff policy, and some new industries were subsidized. Through a special loan fund a few tenants were enabled to purchase the land they worked.

Yet the government was popular only with the more conservative elements among the army officers, some of the landowning grandees, and the Roman Catholic Church. A small but enthusiastic Falangist (Spanish Fascist) party, borrowing features of both its Italian Fascist and German National Socialist models, had but little actual influence. People were increasingly discontented over de Rivera's failure for six years to keep his promise to summon the Cortes and restore constitutional government and civil liberties. The general depression caused a further deterioration of economic conditions and led to the resignation of the dictator in January, 1930. Without de Rivera's strong support the king could not maintain the monarchy; so on April 14, 1931, still trying to maintain the fiction that his exercise of the royal authority was being only temporarily suspended pending a final expression of the people's will, Alfonso XIII fled to France without formal abdication.

The people's will was predominantly republican. Spain was ripe for revolution. Half of her land was owned by one-fifth of one percent of her total population, two-thirds of it by 2 percent. Owing to insufficient rainfall in many areas, erosion, and overcropping without maintaining the fertility of the soil, grain and grass yields were low.

Agricultural wages were also pitifully low; yet rents were extortionately high—as high in certain areas as two-thirds of the crop. Industrial wages were proportionately low, and the irreducible costs of living in the workingmen's quarters of the industrial towns were high.

Much of the land and some urban property were owned by the Roman Catholic Church, an enormously wealthy church dominating the educational system of a largely illiterate and impoverished people. Only half of the adult population of 1931 could read and write, and in some areas the illiteracy rate was as high as 85 percent. The church was not only powerful and wealthy; the secular clergy was paid something by the state, and only the Roman Catholic Church was so recognized. Monasteries and convents, homes of monastic orders, were numerous and heavily endowed with real estate. Some of them were active competitors in production and in the markets in which they sold their products. The Jesuits were especially active in education.

The revolution, then, if it accomplished its objectives, would be certain to diminish the wealth, influence, and special privileges of the capitalists courted by General de Rivera, the great landowners, the officers' caste and the army, and the church. A popularly elected constitutional *cortes* or constituent assembly met in July, 1931, and quickly adopted a republican constitution, which was proclaimed December 10. The constitution guaranteed such traditional civil liberties as freedom of speech, assembly, and the press. A unicameral Cortes or national legislature was to be elected by universal suffrage of citizens twenty-three years old or older. The president of the republic was to be elected for a term of six years by a special national assembly consisting of the Cortes and an equal number of delegates popularly elected.[47] The president was to appoint the prime minister, who, however, was to be politically responsible to the Cortes, so would in effect be chosen by the Cortes. The first president was Alcalá Zamora, the old republican leader, who had also been president of the provisional government. Manuel Azaña was the first prime minister.

The new constitution declared the separation of church and state, foreshadowed the discontinuance of state grants to the Roman Catholic Church and the dissolution of monastic orders which required of their members an oath of obedience to an authority other than the state (notably the Jesuits), and prescribed the nationalization for

[47] The president of the Third French Republic was chosen by a national assembly consisting of the French Senate and Chamber of Deputies, sitting in joint session for that purpose.

secular purposes of the property of such orders. The Socialists and Republicans composing the new government quickly adopted legislation of the character indicated. In 1932 the Jesuit order was dissolved and its property was nationalized. A civil marriage ceremony was required by law, and divorce was legalized. In the same year legislation similar to the French Associations Act of 1901 and separation law of 1905 brought the church entirely under secular control, confiscated its property, and barred its clergy from giving any other than religious instruction.

From the point of view of the previously privileged church, the anticlerical legislation of 1932 and 1933 was bad enough; but the plundering and destruction of the rich monasteries and churches which had been going on since 1931 had been worse. The outraged ecclesiastical hierarchy and papacy refused to countenance a government so actively unfriendly to the church. Some otherwise favorable public opinion, both among Spaniards friendly to the republic but loyal to their church and among Roman Catholics elsewhere in western Europe and in the United States, was alienated. The church was strongly predisposed in favor of anyone in Spain who called himself its faithful son and posed as its defender, and who promised to restore its property and privileges. It fought back vigorously by forbidding the faithful to send their children to the secular schools.

Equally revolutionary programs were undertaken in the fields of army organization and regulations, social security legislation, and landownership and tenancy. A land reform bill of 1932 empowered the government to expropriate large estates, with compensation in most cases based upon the valuations already established for taxation. The land so nationalized was to be owned thereafter by the national government but distributed to landless agricultural laborers or peasant small holders, who would be aided by state loans for the purchase of seed, fertilizer, and tools and the construction of the necessary farm buildings. Urban labor was assured the right of collective bargaining, and a code was drawn up to provide social security benefits. The officer personnel of the army was drastically reduced in proportion to total personnel, and the efficiency of the officers' corps increased by a system of earned promotion. Nine thousand new schools were set up, and far-reaching plans were made for better training and more pay for teachers, and for fifteen hundred new public libraries. Catalonia was granted autonomy, its own flag, and the use of its own language on an equal footing with Castilian Spanish.

Storms of protest were aroused by the government's reform program—from the radicals of the left for whom it did not go far or fast enough, from the reactionaries who were or thought they would be hurt in purse or privilege, and from moderates afraid of the cost and of the alienation of friendly world opinion. The Republican-Socialist coalition was defeated in the general elections of November-December, 1933, and gave way to a conservative coalition, which began in 1934 to put the clock back to 1931 by gradually nullifying the reform legislation enacted since the birth of the republic.

A general strike, called in protest by the parties of the left October 5, 1934, was marked by outbreaks of violence in Madrid and elsewhere and was suppressed only by the use of troops loyal to the rightist coalition government. In 1935 the agrarian reform act was amended so as to make it much less liberal, and the government proposed to amend the constitution so as to legalize the reopening of church schools, the return of the Jesuit order, and the reëstablishment of the Roman Catholic state church. To hold ground against this reactionary trend, a Popular Front coalition composed of left-wing Republicans, Socialists, Communists, anarchists, and radical labor unionists called syndicalists (the first two of these groups generally anticlerical, the others generally atheist) was formed in 1936.

The Popular Front was an artificial and in many ways uncongenial association of elements ranging from the politically democratic and socially progressive Republicans and Socialists, through the Communists (who, in keeping with contemporary Communist policy, were for the first time instructed to coöperate with the more moderate Socialists at the polls and to support the government)[48] to the bitterest enemies of established church and capitalist state, the anarcho-syndicalists. In the new Cortes elected in February and March, 1936, the Popular Front held a substantial majority of the seats. But Manuel Azaña's new cabinet was composed of moderate Republicans, with the Communists and Radical Socialists (as the former were then doing in France) supporting the government but not actively participating in it. In May, 1936, President Zamora, who had tried to reconcile conflicting elements by satisfying none of them, was expelled from office by the Cortes, and Azaña was elected president of the republic in his place.

The new government tried cautiously to resume the reform program instituted in the first two years of the republic and advocated by the

[48] With Hitler in power in Germany the USSR had recently been recognized by the United States and joined the League of Nations. In 1936 French Communists supported the Popular Front (Socialist and Radical Socialist) government of Léon Blum.

Popular Front in its bid for a return to power. But it could not restrain the extremists who resorted almost everywhere to direct and violent action. Churches and convents were destroyed, estates were seized by peasants, and clerical and fascist newspaper offices and party head-quarters were attacked. The reaction ultimately profited more than the revolution from the general disorder. The army led a revolt against the government, which it called communist and atheist. The government was in office by virtue of leftist radical support, but was vulnerable at home principally because of its failure to keep order and protect life, church, and property, and in Catholic and other moderate opinion abroad because of the anticlerical and immoderate character of many of its supporters, both foreign and domestic.

The civil war began July 17, 1936, as an insurrection among the troops of the Foreign Legion in Spanish Morocco, supported by Regular Army and Moroccan colonial contingents. It was led by a former commander of the Foreign Legion, a general staff officer, General Francisco Franco, who had been transferred in March, 1936, to a command in the Canary Islands when the army threatened to revolt unless the government immediately restored order. The insurrection soon spread to the Spanish mainland, where most of the Regular Army officers and perhaps two-thirds of the enlisted personnel of the army soon joined it, although more of the naval and air force officers were loyal to the republic.

In the autumn of 1936, while Franco moved toward Madrid from the south and supplies reached the insurgents from Italy and Germany by way of Mediterranean and Atlantic ports and Portugal, the insurgent General Mola formed what he called a junta or Committee of National Defense at Burgos, and moved on Madrid from the north. Through the winter of 1936-1937 the city was under attack from both sides, but the government armed the populace, formed a new national militia, and made good use of the men and war material that reached it from Soviet Russia.

Within Spain the war was a military insurrection supported generally by people of wealth and privilege—the socially and economically conservative, politically reactionary, and clerical opponents of the republican revolution. These insurgents, who soon took the name of Nationalists, were the declared enemies of the Basque and Catalonian separatist movements and opposed the granting of autonomy or any special privilege to those provinces. The nucleus of the government forces, called Loyalists, was composed of moderate Socialists and Republicans, who as a result of a common fear of fascism were supported by the radicals of the left, such as Communists and Syndicalists, and by the Basques and Catalonians, who preferred Republicans to Nationalists if either had to be accepted as the national authority.

Both sides received foreign aid. Nazi Germany used the area of conflict as a proving ground for the new planes, tanks, and guns with which the rapidly expanding Wehrmacht was to be equipped, and for the novel tactics and techniques of intercommunication by which the exploitation of those weapons was to be coördinated. The men who went with the weapons to demonstrate them and remained to try them out or to instruct the insurgent Spaniards in their use were called "volunteers" when it was impossible any longer to conceal or to deny their presence. They were forbidden at first to reveal their whereabouts or activities to anyone at home, and the families of those killed were denied the patriotic consolation of announcing that they had died in the service of the fatherland; but the survivors of the Condor Legion, upon their return to Germany after Franco's victory was assured, were publicly acknowledged and commended by Adolf Hitler.[49]

Mussolini also sent reluctant "volunteers" by scores of thousands, by regiments and divisions, six or more whole army corps, as fast as they could be diverted from his campaign in Ethiopia. They had so little interest in the errand that they rarely fought effectively and occasionally failed to fight; but their numbers, weapons, motorized equipment, and air power weighted the scales in Franco's favor. They kept the war going, occupied an ever larger area, thus denying it to the Loyalists as a source of supplies, and in 1938 played an important part in the taking of Barcelona and the conquest of Catalonia.

From Soviet Russia came "volunteers," tanks, planes, machine guns, and munitions for the Loyalists, who were joined also by individual volunteers from many lands. Russian aid was most effective in

[49] In a general directive, June 24, 1937, the German defense minister, Field Marshal Werner von Blomberg, wrote that the navy should have plans ready for "Case Richard," a possible war against "Red Spain." For the army and air force, he wrote, it would "remain a matter of assistance to white Spain with material and personnel, as has been the procedure heretofore." Captured document quoted by Mendelssohn, *op. cit.*, 204. General Wilhelm Ritter von Thoma, the German tank leader who commanded the Nazi ground forces in Spain, said after his capture at El Alamein in 1942 that he had "started for Spain the night that General Franco's revolt was to begin." Although he said that he had never had more than six hundred Germans with him at any one time, exclusive of air and administrative personnel, he boasted of having participated in 192 tank actions there. To the Loyalists he was known as "the Butcher of Guernica." Marshal Koniev, Thoma said, was his Russian "opposite number." B. H. Liddell-Hart, *The German Generals Talk* (New York, 1949), 92.

the first year of the war, diminishing in the later years as the Italian navy was able to patrol the Mediterranean more effectively, and as a result of the establishment of a French-British neutrality patrol in the name of nonintervention.

Segments of both French and British opinion were turned against the Spanish republic by the anticlericalism and the social and economic radicalism of some of its policies. General opinion was otherwise friendly to the republic. Neither the Conservative British government of Prime Minister Stanley Baldwin or Neville Chamberlain nor the Socialist or Radical Socialist government of Premier Léon Blum or Camille Chautemps would have chosen to interfere in Spain's affairs. Both feared the international consequences of intervention by any power. So they induced the others to agree to a policy of nonintervention. Germany and Italy at first denied that they had intervened, and agreed not to do so; but Mussolini boasted openly in 1937 of the success of his intervention. Russia used Germany's and Italy's violation of the nonintervention agreement as an excuse for sending aid to the Loyalists. The Loyalists complained that the closing of the Mediterranean to military shipments worked solely to the advantage of the insurgents, whom Germany and Italy continued to supply by way of Portugal, by air, or through the Bay of Biscay ports controlled by Franco.

Some of the volunteers who fought with the Loyalists in Spain were Americans; and funds, clothing, and medical supplies were sent from all over the United States. Although its own Neutrality Act of 1935 did not apply to civil wars, the United States government adhered officially to what on August 6, 1936, the Department of State called its well-established policy of noninterference with the internal affairs of another country. In January, 1937, a new law prohibited the exportation of implements of war to either side. The United States thus denied to the Spanish government a right which it had conceded to belligerents on both sides in 1914-1916 and which had, historically, generally been conceded. The prohibition, moreover, hurt the Loyalists rather than the Nationalists, as the latter were supplied by Italy and Germany while the former found it increasingly difficult to get help from Russia.

The United States neutrality law of May 1, 1937, made all its prohibitions applicable to belligerents in civil wars as well as in wars between nations. Whenever the president proclaimed that a state of war existed, it became illegal to export arms, munitions, or implements of war to any of the belligerents, or to purchase, sell, or exchange any of its securities. By the same law citizens of the United States were forbidden to travel on a ship of a belligerent nation, and it was declared illegal for United States merchantmen to be armed or to carry arms or implements of war to a belligerent. The day President Roosevelt signed the bill, May 1, 1937, he proclaimed that it applied to Spain.[50]

In 1938 the war in Spain went steadily against the Loyalists. By the end of March, 1939, their organized resistance to the overpowering international forces of fascism was at an end. The republic which had been established on democratic principles by the initiative and with the consent of a large but ill-unified majority of the Spanish people had been overthrown by a determined minority supported by authoritarian foreign influences.

The leader of the reaction, General Franco, made himself *Caudillo* or Leader, as Hitler had become *Führer* of Germany and Mussolini *Duce* of Italy. His party, the Spanish Traditionalist Phalanx or *Falange,* dominated the government in a typically totalitarian one-party system. He proceeded at once to restore the property, privileges, and annuities of the Roman Catholic Church, reëstablishing religious schools and religious instruction in all others, readmitting the Jesuits, prohibiting civil marriage and divorce and requiring only ecclesiastical marriage, and giving the rebuilding of churches and cathedrals priority over other reconstruction of which also the country was desperately in need. He proceeded at once to the liquidation of the Loyalists, sending more than a million (perhaps millions) of them to prison or "correction camps" like those of Germany and Russia, to let them make there their prison-labor contribution to his ambitious program of public works. Whether he would eventually pay the mercenaries

---

[50] A new feature of the bill, which had little pertinence to Spain and may have been intended as a warning to Germany and Italy but had a more discouraging effect on France and Britain, was its "cash and carry" provision that the president might enumerate articles which then must not be exported unless first bought and paid for in cash; and even then they could not be exported in United States ships. Here another "neutral" policy encouraged the aggressors, Germany and Italy. They must have known that in another general European war France and Britain would deny them access to North American markets if they could; so their limited cash purchasing power would be of little practical significance, whereas France and Britain, which would have hoped to draw again upon the industrial and financial resources of the United States as in 1914-1918, would be seriously handicapped by the new law.

Nations contemplating the possibility of a war of defense against Germany and Italy were further discouraged by the Johnson Debt Default Act of April 13, 1934, still in effect in 1939. This act made it illegal for any nation in default or in arrears on debt payments to the United States to sell any of its securities in the United States, or for a new loan to be made to it there. Germany and Italy were also in default but in 1937 had no further credit to lose by the Johnson Act, so were not hurt by it.

who had made him, by being useful to them as an ally, remained then to be seen.[51]

The democracies had little ground for satisfaction over the outcome of the Spanish civil war. They could hope for little better than that, if another general war should occur, Franco would cheat his German and Italian benefactors by remaining neutral. The more democratic Western powers had not intervened or wished to intervene; but many of their thinking people were conscious of a feeling of foreboding that, when the bell tolled the death knell of the Spanish republic, it tolled also for them.

JAPAN IN CHINA, 1937, 1938

War broke out anew at the Marco Polo Bridge near Lukouchiao, a village in the Peiping area of China, July 7, 1937. It soon spread southeastward to Shanghai and thence down the coast and up the navigable rivers. Japan's preparation for the resumption of hostilities not only had gone on apace since her withdrawal from the League of Nations (effective 1933, official 1935) but had begun as early as 1920 with the purchase of the plans of the submarine cruiser U-142 and mine-laying submarine U-117 from German shipyards. The sale of these plans was a violation of the disarmament provisions of the Treaty of Versailles; but the German high command approved it and permitted German engineers, technicians, and "retired" naval officers to supervise the construction of these submarines and others like them in the Kawasaki naval yard, and to conduct their trial runs. During the same period (principally between 1925 and 1936 with certain further improvements in its 7.7 mm. Model 99 light machine gun in 1939 and its 47 mm. antitank gun in 1941) the Japanese army had redesigned virtually all its weapons and much of its equipment. The lightness of the newer models, as compared with the old, conserved valuable materials and adjusted their weight better to the small size of the average soldier; but the emphasis upon lightness and maneuverability, and upon howitzers, mortars, and grenade dischargers for indirect plunging fire at short ranges were clear indications (to those

[51] The Nazi had kept a systematic account of the aid they had given Franco, and presented it in due course. He made payments regularly until the Germans were driven out of France in 1944, partially in valuable war materials such as oil obtained from the United States, and broke off diplomatic relations with Germany only on May 7, 1945, the day of her final and unconditional surrender. See Herbert Feis, *Spanish Story* (New York, 1948), and New York *Times*, May 2, 1948.

who knew about them) of preparations for jungle fighting in areas such as Burma, Malaya, and Indonesia.

On September 18, 1934, Japan notified the United States that she would not be bound after the end of 1936 by the naval building restrictions of the Washington conference treaty of 1921.[52] In January, 1936, she withdrew from the London naval conference. In June, 1936, although still asking and being granted permission to send ships "for studies for protection of fur-bearing seals" to Aleutian and Alaskan ports not then open to other nations, she refused to permit the U.S.S. *Alden*, a destroyer on its way to an Asiatic station, to pay courtesy calls at any of the unopened ports in her mandated Pacific islands.

Meanwhile the Japanese population of Manchuria more than doubled, exceeding half a million, and Japanese trade and industrial enterprise had been pushed aggressively in that area. Japan had sent Manchuria 42 percent of its imports in 1929. In 1934 she sent it 64 percent. By 1933 her opium monopoly in Manchuria and Jehol province, China, was the largest single venture of that sort in the history of the illicit traffic in narcotics. In February, 1935, she sanctioned the establishment of a Manchurian oil monopoly, then refused to interfere with it on the ground that Manchuria was an independent sovereign state, called Manchukuo. By 1936, 60 percent of the upper-bracket civil service positions and half of those in the lower brackets in the puppet state were filled by Japanese. It became apparent that United States Ambassador Joseph Grew had been guilty neither of sensationalism nor of serious exaggeration in December, 1934, when he observed that Japan was out to rule the world, beginning with trade control of eastern Asia.[53]

Both Russia and Japan had found it possible either to avoid hostilities or to engage in them at will along the Russian-Manchurian frontier. Russia had sold her stock in the Chinese Eastern railway and was busy double-tracking the Trans-Siberian, strengthening her border fortifications, and building up her Far Eastern air force and army. In 1935 Japan seized a portion of Chahar province of Inner Mongolia

[52] See Chapter 6, pp. 141-144, and 146-148, and Chapter 12, pp. 448-449 and footnote 18.

[53] Diary entry, December 27, 1934: "Their aim is to obtain trade control and eventually predominant political influence in China, the Philippines, the Straits Settlements, Siam and the Dutch East Indies, the Maritime Provinces and Vladivostok, one step at a time as in Korea and Manchuria, pausing intermittently to consolidate and then continuing as soon as intervening obstacles can be overcome by diplomacy or force. . . .

"We should be reprehensibly somnolent if we were to trust to the security of treaty restraints or international comity to safeguard our own interests or, indeed, our own property." *Ten Years in Japan* (New York, 1944), 147.

and incorporated it into Manchukuo. In February, 1936, a small Japanese and Korean force, with trucks, tanks, and planes, made a foray into Outer Mongolia and were quickly driven out. Thereafter the forces confronted each other along the boundary without much large-scale fighting. In March Russia signed a pact of mutual assistance with Outer Mongolia, and it was announced from Moscow that an attack upon Outer Mongolia by Manchukuo would be considered an act of war against Russia herself.[54]

In China aggression would probably be safer, easier, and more profitable, although even in that sadly divided and disorganized country there seemed for a while in 1936-1937 to be some possibility that a united anti-Japanese front would be formed. Conforming to the current Soviet Russian policy of international coöperation, and to the "popular front" tactics of communist parties in other nations in the middle thirties, Chou En-lai, Mao Tse-Tung and other Communist leaders in China offered to join Generalissimo Chiang Kai-shek's Kuomintang in a national front to resist the Japanese invader. The proposed basis of such a fusion would have been the political democratization of the Kuomintang government (which already resembled an oligarchy or a military dictatorship rather than a parliamentary democracy), economic reforms (especially of an agrarian character) for the relief of the poverty-ridden masses, and immediate and vigorous armed resistance to the continued encroachments of Japan. In December, 1936, Chiang Kai-shek was kidnapped by some of his own subordinates led by Generals Chang Hsueh-liang and Yang Hu-ch'eng, to compel him to agree in principle to an arrangement to combine the Communist and nationalist forces. Through the mediation of Madame Chiang Kai-shek and her brother T. V. Soong such an arrangement seemed well on the way toward consummation when Japan, without a declaration of war, reopened hostilities at Lukouchiao on July 7, 1937. Japan timed her action then, as always, so as to prevent the unification of China under any national government which Japan could not control.

The Japanese government's idea of a satisfactory basis of relations with China had not changed much since the presentation of her infamous Twenty-One Demands in 1915. In 1936 the Japanese Foreign Office, prompted apparently by the army, demanded that the Chinese government put an end to all anti-Japanese agitation in China and prevent any recurrence of it, permit the use of Japanese troops with its own against the Communists and along the Inner-Outer Mongolian

[54] Vinacke, *op. cit.*, 545.

frontier, employ Japanese advisers in all branches of its administrative and military establishment, reduce its tariff, and promote economic collaboration with Japan. At every stage of every negotiation with China or with other national governments Japan insisted that what she had already done in Manchuria and other northern provinces of China must be recognized and could not in any event be undone.

The Chinese national government countered with the proposal that Japan should undo what she had done in northeast China, withdraw her troops from Hopei and Chahar provinces, and coöperate with Chinese authorities in the suppression of the smuggling by which the Chinese national authority was being constantly circumvented. Japan, however, was not at all coöperative. A new series of political assassinations by army officers eliminated several of the more conciliatory leaders, such as Admiral Viscount Makato Saito, lord keeper of the privy seal, Finance Minister Viscount Takahashi, and General Yotaro Watanabe. In Berlin November 5, 1936, the Japanese ambassador signed the anti-Comintern pact with Germany which, although ostensibly directed only against the subversive activities of the Communist International outside Russia, served Germany as the basis of a multiple alliance against Russia, and Japan as insurance against Russian interference with further Japanese aggression in China.[55]

It was interference by the United States which would have been principally to be feared if the United States had then been willing to use force. American sympathies were with China but not sufficiently aroused to support any warlike action in defense of China, even against Japan. More than three years earlier, April 18, 1934, Japan had given public notice that she would resent "any attempt on the part of China to avail herself of the influence of any other country in order to resist Japan or . . . to play one country against another, . . . as tending to disturb . . . peace and order in East Asia." So the United States government was cautious. Although no war had been declared and the terms of its own neutrality legislation did not apply unless the president chose to declare them applicable, President Roosevelt by proclamation on September 14, 1937, prohibited the carrying of arms, munitions, or implements of war either to China or to Japan on vessels owned by the government of the United States, and warned the owners of merchant vessels privately owned that they might carry such cargoes only at their own risk. Since the neutrality law if invoked

[55] In Moscow August 23-24, 1939, to negotiate a German-Russian nonaggression treaty, Herr Ribbentrop told Stalin that the anti-Comintern pact had not been directed against Russia but against the western democracies. U. S. Department of State, *Nazi-Soviet Relations, 1939-41* (Washington,1948), 75.

would have prohibited aid to China as well as to Japan and thus have hurt China much worse than it hurt Japan, it was not invoked. The United States granted credit to China, and individual enterprisers and commercial concerns sold to both sides for cash.

Speaking publicly in Chicago October 5, 1937, the president boldly proposed the establishment by peace-loving nations of a quarantine against the spreading epidemic of world lawlessness. War, he said, whether declared or undeclared, was a contagion which if unchecked could involve states and peoples far from its place of origin, a disease against which quarantine measures should be taken for the health of the community. What he said was pertinent to current German and Italian depredations as well as to Japan's attempt to conquer China. It was pertinent, too, to the whole problem of collective security. The nations which wanted peace, said he, could have peace and could live in amity without fear only if they would make a concerted effort to uphold laws and principles upon which alone peace could rest secure.

It was not war which the president was advocating but international action against war, to make aggression obviously unprofitable and its consequences painful and unpleasant to the aggressor. American public opinion did not as a whole react favorably, however, to what he said. The establishment of a quarantine, it was thought, like that of an economic boycott or other economic sanction, would itself be a war-like act having unpredictable consequences, and so would entail not only an immediate danger of war but long-term commitments to other nations which might eventually lead to an involuntary involvement in war. Either alternative was, to most Americans, clearly to be avoided.

The president was subsequently criticized from all sides: (1) for having spoken in an allegedly irresponsible fashion about commitments which he well knew his people did not then want to make, and which he had no constitutional power to make for them without their knowledge and their constitutionally given consent; (2) for having thereafter made only a pretense of being guided by the expressed anti-war opinion of the majority (part of which might later have been more accurately described as anti-interventionist), and having meanwhile conducted foreign policy in an unofficially interventionist fashion which as the world crisis developed into a world war made the eventual involvement of the United States in it ever more probable rather than less probable; and (3), by those who considered collective action against the spread of the prevalent lawlessness and aggression an imperative necessity, for having publicly abandoned his position instead of boldly trying to inform his people more fully about their actual situation until they also saw the need of the quarantine he proposed. On October 15 and half a dozen times within half a year thereafter, German Ambassador Hans Dieckhoff warned his government that, although the United States would not then actually intervene to stop the Japanese in China, it would certainly intervene quickly and effectively if the existence of Great Britain should ever be seriously threatened as a result of involvement in a general war.

The Assembly of the League of Nations was in session at Geneva when President Roosevelt's "quarantine" speech was made. Next day, October 6, 1937, it adopted the report of its Far Eastern advisory committee, which at the request of China had taken up anew the troubled question of Japan's undeclared war on that country. The findings of the advisory committee were unfavorable to Japan, as those of the Lytton commission had been. Upon recommendation of the committee the League called a conference of the parties to the Washington conference Nine-Power Treaty affirming the national independence and territorial integrity of China. The conference met at Brussels November 3-24. Soviet Russia was represented by invitation as an interested party. She advocated immediate and vigorous action against Japan as she had advocated action against Italy in defense of Ethiopia and of the principle of collective security. Germany was invited, but preferred an attempt at independent mediation. Japan refused to attend; but her case was sympathetically presented by the Italian delegation. The United States was represented; but the unfavorable immediate reaction to the president's "quarantine" address made it patently impossible to commit the United States at that time to any policy more definitive than an attempt at mediation. The conference issued on adjournment an innocuous declaration of principles, and submitted to the Secretariat of the League a record of its discussions. The war went on.

Meanwhile pacifist, noninterventionist, and some isolationist sentiment had been increasingly aroused against President Roosevelt by discussion of his "quarantine" proposal. As if to test whether the people of the United States meant any part of what their president had said, or would be psychologically prepared to go to war to make it good, Japanese planes on December 12, 1937, the day of the fall of Nanking to the Japanese, bombed and strafed a plainly marked and easily identifiable United States naval gunboat, the *Panay*, which had just evacuated the last of the United States embassy personnel from the beleaguered city and was escorting some American-owned oil barges away from the combat area, some twenty-seven miles up the

Yangtze River from Nanking. The *Panay* and three other American vessels were shelled from the shore December 11 and bombed, machine-gunned, and sunk at anchor by Japanese planes the next day, with the loss of two men killed and forty-three other casualties.[56]

Fully aware of the possibility that such a step might lead immediately to war, President Roosevelt and his naval advisers discussed the possibility and advisability of naval retaliation against Japan on account of the *Fanay* incident but, knowing that American opinion, although outraged and angry, was not aroused to the point of approving a "preventive" war, made only a sharply worded protest. Japan immediately apologized, promised to prevent the recurrence of such incidents, and late in April, 1938, paid an indemnity of $2,214,007.36 (a little less than two million dollars for property damage and more than a quarter of a million for injuries to persons).

If the destruction of the *Panay* had been planned as a test case to discover how far the people of the United States were then willing to permit their government to go in defense of its prestige and the economic interests of its citizens in China, it served its purpose. Public opinion would continue to disapprove Japanese expansion there, and would resent direct injury, against which the government would vigorously protest; but the United States would not then go to war unless attacked. With the attention of Britain, France, and Soviet Russia more and more engrossed by the threat of renewed Axis aggression in Europe, there was little danger of armed intervention against Japan in China.

If Japan had needed any further reassurance against armed intervention by the United States, she might have found it in a resolution brought into Congress by Representative Ludlow of Indiana December 14, 1937, two days after the sinking of the *Panay*. That resolution proposed, by amendment of the constitution, to deprive Congress of its power to declare war except to repel invasion or in obedience to a mandate to be given it in a national referendum. Strongly opposed by President Roosevelt, the resolution failed in January, 1938, by the rather narrow margin of twenty-one votes, 188 to 209, two-thirds

[56] Reports of George Atcheson, Jr., and the commander in chief, U. S. Asiatic fleet. U.S. Department of State *Papers Relating to the Foreign Relations of the United States: Japan*, I, 532-546. Other reports indicated three killed and as many as seventy-four wounded. United States Ambassador Joseph Grew had left Nanking in the U.S.S. *Luzon* November 22, and had notified the Japanese government December 1 that the completion of the evacuation, effected by the *Panay* December 11, would soon be undertaken. The officer who ordered the attack, Colonel Hashimoto, seemed clearly to have intended to provoke the United States to war so as to rid the Japanese government of civilian influence.

being needed for passage. The strength of the current popular aversion to the idea of a Far Eastern war, and of popular distrust of the president's supposed predilection for a "stronger" foreign policy, was further highlighted by the outcome of a popular poll which indicated that virtually 54 percent of the people of the United States thought that their government and its nationals should get out of China immediately and entirely; only 30 percent were willing to sanction the use of force in defense of rights and interests there, previously acquired.

Those interests were considerable. The United States was at that time taking more than one-fourth of China's exports and sending approximately one-fifth of its imports. But it was concerned also with the abandonment or maintenance of what Secretary of State Cordell Hull called "orderly processes" in international affairs. The interest and concern of the United States in situations throughout the world, wrote the secretary to Vice-President Garner on January 8, 1938, were not measured by the number of American citizens residing in a particular country at a particular moment, or by the amount of investment of American citizens there, or by the volume of trade. There was a broader and much more fundamental interest: that orderly processes in international relationships should be maintained. The United States was deeply interested, the secretary said, in supporting by peaceful means influences contributory to preservation and encouragement of orderly processes.[57] Very few of its people, however, looked with any favor at that time upon the use of any but peaceful means; and Japan was taking advantage of their reluctance to use force or a show of force.

Japan's determination to chart her own course in eastern Asia and the western Pacific without deference to other powers was exemplified in February, 1938, by her rejection of joint United States, British, and French proposals for a mutual exchange of naval building information. These proposals had been prompted by the suspicion, subsequently proved to have been well founded, that Japan was building warships obviously designed for offensive, not defensive, purposes. The Japanese government refused to give either information or assurances concerning the construction of capital ships or cruisers. It declined also a British suggestion of further consultation with other naval powers, although both Britain and the United States had made it clear that they would then feel free, in consultation with other

[57] Quoted by Stanley K. Hornbeck in *Annals of the American Academy of Political and Social Science*, Vol. 255 (January, 1948), p. 134.

parties to the London naval treaty, to use the right of escalation given them by that treaty.[58]

The war party was further encouraged and emboldened by the Czechoslovak crisis of 1938. If Hitler could bring Chamberlain and Daladier to Munich, Japan could safely defy their governments by pushing her conquest of China to Hankow and Canton. On the occasion of the establishment at Nanking on September 22 of a new Japanese-controlled United Council of China, the Japanese government spoke with a truculence quite different from the tone of its apologies for the sinking of the *Panay*. Brusquely rejecting American, British, and French protests against the closing of the Yangtze to commerce, it refused to admit any longer the inviolability of third powers' property in China or to be responsible for any damage done such property during actual fighting.

After Munich on October 15, 1938, an official Japanese spokesman declared in Shanghai: "Japan is fixed in her determination to crush Chiang Kai-shek's regime. We do not intend to take Hong Kong or Singapore or advance southward in the Pacific, but we must and will carry out our program in China. Without the support of Britain and France the Chiang regime would have collapsed long ago."[59]

On Armistice Day, November 11, 1938, Yosuke Matsuoka, who had led the Japanese delegation when it walked out of the Assembly of the League of Nations under censure in 1933, said flatly in a published statement that the best thing the United States, Great Britain, and other countries could do to hasten the coming of peace in the Far East would be frankly to recognize Japan's paramount position in east Asia.[60]

The second phase of Japan's war in China ended with the occupation of Canton October 21 and Hankow October 25, 1938. Most of the Peking (Peiping)-Hankow-Canton railway line and most of the ports, railways, and riverways east of that line had by that time been brought under Japanese control. Control meant exploitation. It became increasingly evident every day that Japan intended nothing less than eventually to dominate and despoil all China and to degrade its people to the level of virtual slavery. Wherever the heavy Japanese hand lay on the land, exchange controls, trade regulations, and the

[58] *Foreign Relations of the United States: 1931-1941*, I (1943), 303-306; *British Parliamentary Debates*, 5th series, Vol. 331, p. 1515. While the others were thinking of 16-inch guns, Japan was putting 18.1-inch guns on *Musashi* and *Yamato*.

[59] U. S. Department of State, *Press Releases*, Vol. XIX, No. 465 (August 27, 1938), p. 426; *Foreign Relations of the United States: Japan*, I, 621-622, 625.

[60] G. Nye Steiger, "China Balks Japanese Conquest," *Events*, V (January, 1939), pp. 56-59.

customs tariff were revised in favor of the Japanese, so as soon to exclude all other foreign enterprise. The opium trade was pushed among the Chinese population by Japanese (often Korean) agents, both for the money to be made in it and for its demoralizing effect upon its victims.

While European international affairs went steadily from very bad to worse, and while noninterventionist opinion prevailed in the United States, the Japanese government felt quite secure in possession of all that it had seized, and safe in rejecting all protests from whatever source. On November 18, 1938, it notified the United States, in effect, that the Washington conference system of the Nine-Power Treaty had been permanently set aside and was not to be restored or used as the basis of further international discussion. Japan, it said, was establishing a new order based upon genuine international justice throughout east Asia. No attempt to "apply to the condition of today and to-morrow inapplicable ideas and principles of the past" would in any way contribute to the establishment of a real peace in east Asia or to the solution of any of the immediate issues there.

The United States reaffirmed in its reply, December 30, 1938, its adherence to the Washington conference system and its own previous policy, despite changes effected by unilateral action of Japan.

> This government is well aware [it wrote] that the situation has changed. This government is also well aware that many of the changes have been brought about by the action of Japan. This government does not admit, however, that there is need or warrant for any one power to take upon itself to prescribe what shall be the terms and conditions of a "new order" in areas not under its sovereignty and to constitute itself the repository of authority and the agent of destiny in regard thereto. . . .
>
> Meanwhile this government reserves all rights of the United States as they exist and does not give assent to any impairment of those rights.[61]

China had not been quite abandoned by her friends; but her enemy was inside the gates. Nearly a third of her territory, including her most populous and productive areas, was in his hands. Her national survival depended upon the ability of her government to organize and control from the new refugee capital Chungking the vast but almost inaccessible and industrially undeveloped area of western China, and to obtain credit and military supplies for it from abroad. In these tasks it was only partially successful. The promised fusion of Communist and Kuomintang forces into a solid front of national defense did not materialize. Chiang Kai-shek was often accused of being readier to use

[61] *Foreign Affairs of the United States: Japan, 1931-1941*, I (1943), 800-820.

his resources to try to control the Chinese Communists than to expel the Japanese. Guerrilla warfare was the most effective form of defense all over China; and in that kind of fighting the Communists were reported to have embarrassed the Japanese more seriously in some areas than the nationalist forces did. But there was no effective coöperation of Communist and nationalist forces. Some supplies were carried with tremendous effort and at heavy cost by truck and caravan by way of Mongolia from Russia, by the newly opened Burma Road to Chungking, through French Indo-China by the Yunnan railway and a truck line to Chungking, and by blockade-running through a few coastal ports and gaps in the Japanese lines; but all these supply routes except the one from Russia seemed likely to be closed at any time. All three were closed, in fact, in the summer of 1940, as an indirect consequence of Axis victories in the European theater of war.

AUSTRIA, 1938

The march of aggression was resumed in Europe in March, 1938, when Hitler Germany occupied and annexed Austria. After the failure of the *Putsch* of 1934 in which Austrian Chancellor Dollfuss was killed Hitler had publicly disowned the Austrian Nazi who had failed.[62] Again, in an address to the German Reichstag May 21, 1935, he had asserted that Germany had no intention or desire to interfere in the internal affairs of Austria or to annex or incorporate Austria into Germany. There was no point, he said, in an "eastern Locarno," as Germany's permanent renunciation of Alsace-Lorraine under the existing Locarno agreement was sufficient proof of her good will and love of peace. But he added that he would gladly enter into general agreements for the limitation of armaments, the prohibition of specific weapons, or the prevention of hostile propaganda or interference in the internal affairs of any nation.

On July 11, 1936, by treaty with Austria, the German government again recognized Austria's sovereign and independent status and agreed not to interfere directly or indirectly in her internal affairs. Austria agreed, however, to "bring her political policies into conformity with the principle" that she was a German state. Austria had already, on April 1, 1936, denounced the disarmament clauses of the Treaty of St.-Germain and had adopted a national service law providing for both military and labor service.

A general "directive for unified preparation of the [German]

[62] See pp. 468-469.

armed forces for war," signed by General von Blomberg June 24, 1937, accurately summarized the existing international situation in Europe by proceeding from the general assumption that Germany need not then fear an attack from any side. The nations west of Germany did not want war; those east of her were not ready for it.[63] But although admittedly in no danger of attack Germany must be ready to "counterattack" at any time, so as to exploit any military or political opportunities which might occur, and must be constantly "in a position to begin war suddenly and by surprise as regards both strength and time." Nazi planning contemplated at that time a "strategic pounce" upon Czechoslovakia rather than upon Austria. In either case the attack would be systematically planned in advance and designed to overwhelm its victim quickly. As it happened the signs were right, from the German point of view, for Austria first.[64]

At a "Führer conference" November 5, 1937, Hitler made clear to his senior subordinates his conviction that "the German question" was a mere matter of *Lebensraum* and could be solved only by the use of force. The land that Germany needed must be seized. Britain, he thought, could no longer be expected to sanction the return of German colonies in Africa; she had lost too much prestige already in the Italian conquest of Ethiopia. Colonies were no solution anyway, nor was world trade; Germany could be cut off from them too easily. Autarchy was in practice unattainable. So it was land near home that must be seized. Granted that there was none unclaimed or unoccupied; Germans must be prepared, then, to fight for *Lebensraum*.

It was necessary to consider, said Hitler, only where the greatest conquest could be made at the lowest cost. By the conquest of Austria and Czechoslovakia, if she compelled a million people to emigrate from the former and two millions from the latter, Germany could gain food for five or six million Germans; and later she could raise

---

[63] The Germans may have been misled as to the military strength of Soviet Russia by their interpretation of reports of "purges" then in progress in Russia.

[64] The above quotations from the Blomberg directive of June 24, 1937, and the references to "Führer conferences" and directives and other official Nazi communications which follow, are based largely upon confidential German documents captured by the Allied armies in 1945. Some of these were introduced in evidence in the war criminal trials at Nuremberg in 1945 and 1946. Some have been printed by the United States Department of State, others by other departments of the United States government. Many have been cited or quoted, as by: Herbert Feis, *The Spanish Story* (New York, 1948); William L. Langer, *Our Vichy Gamble* (New York, 1947); Peter de Mendelssohn, *Design for Aggression* (New York, 1946); Samuel E. Morison, *History of United States Naval Operations in World War II* (Boston, 1947—); Milton Shulman, *Defeat in the West* (New York, 1948); and H. R. Trevor-Roper, *The Last Days of Hitler* (New York, 1947). Many thousands of them are unpublished.

twelve divisions there. France, he thought, was likely to be so tied up with her own social and political tensions as to be unlikely to intervene unless assured of British help. And of this she could not be certain, as the British were preoccupied with Italy and had probably already accustomed themselves to the thought of seeing Germany settle her own problems in her own way. Poland might attack if Germany were at war with France, unless Czechoslovakia were conquered first and a solid German-Hungarian frontier were formed against her. But she would not do so unless she could catch Germany at a disadvantage.

Hitler's advisers were less sanguine than he was. Foreign Minister von Neurath doubted that the Mediterranean war (France and Britain *vs.* Italy) of which the Führer hoped to take advantage was going to materialize. Minister of Defense von Blomberg was not sure that France would be unable or unwilling to defend Czechoslovakia. Army Commander in Chief General Werner von Fritsch was afraid that the Rhineland did not yet have troops or fortresses enough to defend itself successfully if France invaded it. The high command was unready, rather than unwilling, to lead an attack upon either Austria or Czechoslovakia.

Czechoslovakia was well armed and ready. Austria was smaller and weaker. There the risk seemed less. But first the doubters must be eliminated from the attacking force. Von Neurath, a well-informed and experienced diplomat, was replaced as foreign minister by Joachim Ribbentrop, a former wine salesman who had recently been ambassador to Britain. He was less likely to tell Hitler anything that he knew Hitler would not want to hear. Blomberg was dismissed (ostensibly because of a scandal over his marriage to an improper person), then von Fritsch, who had helped get rid of von Blomberg. New names appeared at the top of the table of organization, names of politically-minded soldiers willing to play politics with the Nazi, hoping some day to control them: von Brauchitsch, who followed von Fritsch as commander in chief of the army, Keitel, List, von Reichenau. Of these Keitel was the least able, the least reputable, the least likely to oppose Hitler, and the only one still in place when Germany crumbled under him in 1945.

As Nazi Germany grew bolder, other peoples took alarm and grew less bold. In the United States Secretary Hull found it politic to explain in writing to the vice-president that it was by peaceful means that the Roosevelt administration was seeking the survival of "orderly processes" in international affairs. In Britain Anthony Eden, displeased with the policy of appeasement, resigned as minister for foreign affairs and was succeeded by Lord Halifax, whose views were more like Chamberlain's. Eden's resignation was generally conceded to be a triumph for Mussolini, and Hitler also gloated over it, while opponents of appeasement viewed it with alarm.

France, plagued with strikes, especially in her aircraft industry, had a budget deficit of eight billion francs in 1937 but could not bring her voters to accept either the reduction of government spending or the new taxes needed to bring the budget into balance. From the fall of the Chautemps ministry January 14, 1938, until April 10, when Edouard Daladier managed at last to form a new one, France passed through a period of uncertainty and instability which gave Hitler an opportunity he needed only to exploit. Even in the Daladier ministry formed after the German annexation of Austria had become an accomplished fact, the minister for foreign affairs, Georges Bonnet, hated and distrusted Russia, the one power that had spoken out with any boldness against the annexation.

In the midst of the French ministerial crisis, February 7, Hitler summoned to Berchtesgaden Chancellor Schuschnigg of Austria and his secretary for foreign affairs, Guido Schmidt. Four days later his ambassador to Austria, Franz von Papen, brought them there. At Hitler's chalet Generals Keitel, Sperrle of the Luftwaffe, and von Reichenau were present to help the Führer intimidate his visitors, who under threat of aerial bombardment and armed invasion of their country signed a protocol of virtual surrender. After his return to Austria, however, Schuschnigg, successor to Dollfuss and like Dollfuss a Catholic Christian Socialist, took steps to put the question to his people: "Are you for a free and German, independent and social, Christian and united Austria, for peace and work, for the equality of all those who declare themselves for the people and the fatherland?"

The plebiscite question was so worded that any Austrian nationalist, whether monarchist or republican, could have voted yes; a National Socialist, favoring *Anschluss* with Germany on Nazi terms and a policy of anti-Semitism, must have voted no. The plebiscite was announced March 9 for March 13, but was never held. By a German ultimatum and renewed threats of invasion, March 11, 1938, Schuschnigg was compelled to cancel it. Immediately thereafter he was driven by continued pressure to resign the chancellorship in favor of the Austrian Nazi puppet leader Arthur Seyss-Inquart, who brought in with him an entirely Nazi cabinet. In the morning of March 12 German troops, for which the Nazi pretended that Seyss-Inquart had asked them urgently, were rolling into Austria, under the immediate command of General von Reichenau with orders to treat as "friendly" any Italian troops they might encounter and as unfriendly any Czechoslovaks. Hitler made a point of "returning" in triumph by way of Linz, where he had been unhappy as a boy, to Vienna, where as a young man he had been a miserable failure. The annexation and incorporation of Austria into the German Reich were announced on March 13.

Meanwhile, on March 11 the French ambassador to Italy asked Mussolini whether he was ready to uphold the Stresa pact and oppose a German invasion of Austria by force of arms. He was not. The situation had changed since 1934, when he sent troops to the Brenner Pass as a warning gesture at the time of the murder of Dollfuss. By the Axis agreement and by collaboration in Spain he had become Hitler's partner. Hitler had already notified him by a letter of March 10, borne by Prince Philip of Hesse, of his intention to invade; and he had given Hitler his assent, for which the Führer seemed hysterically grateful. (Hitler was more confident thereafter, and more inclined to dictate to Mussolini than to consult him.) Only Litvinov, in a statement to the foreign press in Moscow, asserted boldly March 17, 1938, that there was "yet time, although tomorrow might be too late" for the other nations to "take a firm and unambiguous stand on the problem of the collective salvation of peace." Litvinov suggested then a conference on collective resistance to further aggression, warning the world that Czechoslovakia was in danger; but others called his proposal premature. The British prime minister had already decided not to guarantee Czechoslovakia, or France in connection with her obligations to that country.

On the heels of the invading army 25,000 German Nazi commissars crowded into Austria to participate in the plundering (called "organization") of the Jews for the enrichment (called "compensation") of old National Socialist party members.

CZECHOSLOVAKIA, 1938-1939

Czechoslovakia was indeed in danger when Germany annexed Austria. It was only an earlier opening which had taken Hitler into Austria first. He was in position there to threaten to attack the comparatively open southern frontier of Czechoslovakia, less mountainous, less strongly fortified, and less easily defensible than the mountain ramparts that had stood between Bohemia-Moravia and Germany for several centuries. By May 30, 1938, a new general directive was ready for the German Wehrmacht, designed to smash Czechoslovakia by invasion within the first four days, whenever the political leadership should find or create a favorable occasion. Swift action, Keitel thought with malevolent satisfaction, would give Poland and Hungary an incentive to take immediate advantage of Czechoslovakia's distress for their own territorial aggrandizement and would convince everyone else that it would be useless to try to prevent the proposed partition. Hitler was determined to attack in 1938, although he admitted to his generals that his hand was not being forced by anyone. The generals thought 1938 too soon, as they assumed that the western powers would intervene, and feared that the German armed forces would then be found unequal to the combined forces of their enemies. They had, of course, to plan against any such eventuality, but Hitler's intuition told him that no military intervention need be feared, and that the engineers and labor corps could be safely used to man the fortifications of the "west wall" then being built.

Other Nazi leaders, although they pretended to share the Führer's view that a general war over the German-Czechoslovak question was improbable, were already contemplating such a war as a possibility without confessing to one another any doubt that, if it came, Germany would win. Their confidence, which may have been to a certain degree synthetic and self-induced, was strengthened by their self-assurance that the United States would not in any event intervene. United States neutrality legislation and numerous expressions of noninterventionist opinion had convinced them that they had nothing to fear from that quarter, no matter what President Roosevelt had said about a quarantine or Secretary Hull about peace and orderly processes. Clearly and repeatedly but in vain German Ambassador Hans Dieckhoff and Counselor of Embassy Hans Thomsen warned their government from Washington that the United States would intervene decisively, as in 1917, if Great Britain were seriously threatened. Similar warnings from Ambassador Herbert von Dirksen in London were similarly disregarded.

Fear that reckless Nazi leadership would involve Germany prematurely in a war which the unready Wehrmacht could not win led several disaffected generals to participate in September, 1938, in a plot to overthrow Hitler. The conspiracy reached into the higher echelons of the general staff, including the chief of staff, Colonel General Ludwig Beck, General (later Field Marshal) von Witzleben, General Franz Halder, chief of staff, Major General Thomas, chief of war economy, responsible for the supply of war material, and Admiral Canaris, chief of military counterintelligence. Like most other conspiracies of similar character, however, this one had in it more of melodrama than of menace to the Führer's safety or position, and was dropped when the prime minister of Great Britain went three times to Canossa (at Berchtesgaden, Godesberg, and Munich) to meet Hitler, thus enabling him to achieve a "solution" of the Sudeten-Czechoslovak "question" and enormously enhancing his popularity and prestige.[65]

Meanwhile the Sudeten German question was made to furnish the desired occasion for intervention.[66] The German element in the Czechoslovak population, although not denied a voice in government or otherwise seriously abused, had been a discontented minority for twenty years, especially vociferous and troublesome under the leadership of Nazi Konrad Henlein since Hitler's rise to power in Germany. Soon after the fall of Austria the dismemberment of Czechoslovakia was heralded by Henlein's demand that the Germans in that country be free to proclaim their German character and their acceptance of National Socialist (pan-German, anti-Semitic, totalitarian) principles, and that areas inhabited principally by Germans be given the unrestricted right of self-determination. These demands were reiterated in uncompromising fashion by the Nazi press and radio.

A Czechoslovak election was held in May without surrender to intimidation, and the western powers at that time offered the Beneš government some encouragement. But between May and September, while a million Germans were called to arms and Henlein renewed the Nazi German and Sudeten German demand that Czechoslovakia cancel her purely defensive alliances with France and Russia on the ground that they threatened Germany with attack, the idea of appeasement gained ground in western Europe.

A crisis was deliberately precipitated by Hitler in an address to the annual Nazi party congress at Nuremberg September 12, 1938. The Czechoslovak government, with the British Lord Runciman act-

---

[65] Witzleben and Canaris were excuted by the Nazi in 1944 and 1945, respectively, for complicity in the attempt to assassinate Hitler July 20, 1944. Halder, who had been cashiered in 1942 for failure on the Russian front, spent some time in concentration camp but was not found to have participated in the July plot of 1944. He was tried by a German denazification court and acquitted September 22, 1948. In his postwar book, *Hitler als Feldherr,* he attributed many of the Wehrmacht's worst disasters to Hitler's amateurish interference with the work of the professional military staff.

[66] See pp. 171-174.

ing as mediator between it and the Sudeten Germans, had granted on September 7 virtually all of the demands of that recalcitrant group, short of the actual right of secession. It had gone as far as it could go without losing all resemblance to a sovereign state and without giving away its German-border regions. These contained many of its richest industrial resources and were bounded by its only historical, most easily defensible, and best-fortified frontier. Hitler, however, demanded for German citizens of Czechoslovakia what he called the right of self-determination, and promised them military protection. They responded at once by demanding the right to secede from Czechoslovakia and join Germany. If they continued their agitation for the right of secession, if Czechoslovakia refused to grant it, and if Germany intervened to "protect" them, war between Czechoslovakia and Germany might be an immediate result and might ultimately involve France as Czechoslovakia's ally and Great Britain as an ally of France. Russia also had defensive alliances with Czechoslovakia and France, the former of these to become effective, however, only if Czechoslovakia resisted an attack and France took the field in her defense. Italy too had her Axis agreement with Germany. So any war might soon become a general one as that of 1914 had done.

The prospect was generally appalling. In the Assembly of the League of Nations delegates from the Netherlands, Sweden, Norway, Poland, Denmark, Belgium, and Finland followed one another in a disheartened and disheartening parade across the podium, each notifying the League that his nation no longer considered itself obligated under Article 10, 16, or 17 of the League Covenant to participate in joint action or to grant foreign troops right of passage across its territory, even in the name or at the request of the League. As their governments had done in the Copenhagen declaration of July 1, 1936, most of them accused the great powers and the League of having abandoned the principle of collective security, and claimed, therefore, the right to return to traditional policies of independence and neutrality. This series of surrenders started the day after Hitler's challenging Nuremberg address of September 12, as if those concerned realized only too clearly that it was the League and the whole system of collective security, as well as Czechoslovakia and her allies, that the Nazi orator was challenging. They must have known that he was declaring a twentieth-century *Kulturkampf* against the fundamental assumptions of Christianity and democracy upon which the pillars of western European civilization were based; but none dared defy him alone, and none trusted another to stand loyally by it in a common defiance.

Many millions, probably a large majority, of the Germans were also deeply disturbed by the threat of a war which they did not want. They had been told incessantly for years that Germany's peace and safety—in fact, her national existence—were threatened by Soviet Russia and by Czechoslovakia, which, they were told, was to be the forward base from which Russia would attack. They had heard countless tales of the abuse heaped upon their German kinsmen in Czechoslovakia. But only a handful of them wanted war at that time. The others assumed that France, Britain, and possibly Russia would intervene if Germany invaded Czechoslovakia. They had not forgotten the blockade and the defeat of 1918; they remembered the alien occupation of the Rhineland and the Ruhr, the inflation of their currency, and the national bankruptcy which had followed. They could contemplate only with the deepest consternation the prospect of another exhausting war against an overwhelming coalition of enemy powers, another blockade and eventual defeat, and a repetition of their experience of the consequences of defeat. They had accepted all of Hitler's triumphs and had gloried in them, but principally because those successes had been achieved by defiance of a divided world and won without a war.

The German Wehrmacht, with bolder leadership than it had had a year earlier, had its plans completed by September 9, down to the last detail of timing of a pincer movement, for the immediate and complete destruction of the Czechoslovak army. Colonel General von Brauchitsch was to command, and Hitler had shown surprising talent as an armchair strategist, especially at showing his generals how he thought it possible either to achieve strategic surprise or to avoid making precisely the attack the enemy anticipated. But the generals were worried and hoped not to have to test their plan in action. Only Hitler was confident; and whether by the intuition of a peculiar political genius or by virtue of an ignorant man's freedom from intellectual prejudice, he had appraised the international situation more accurately than the generals had. Whether Hitler himself, despite his public show of boldness, was bluffing as he had bluffed when ordering the military reoccupation of the Rhineland was something which his potential enemies did not dare at the time to try too hard to discover.

Neville Chamberlain in particular, peace-loving prime minister of a great power militarily and psychologically unprepared for war, convinced himself that the peace of Europe could be purchased only by appeasement of the power that seemed readiest to disturb it. He seemed to think it possible to do business with Hitler, and perhaps desirable that Germany be strengthened as a bulwark against revolutionary Russia. Russia he profoundly distrusted. Indeed, some of his friends thought her more dangerous to their way of life and to the world than National Socialist totalitarianism, of which they knew comparatively little except that it was authoritarian in character, proclaimed itself the mortal enemy of communism, and seemed generally capable of getting practical results.

So Chamberlain, commendably though perhaps imprudently forgetful of his dignity and of national prestige, acquitted himself and his government in advance of any charge which might otherwise have been brought against them of having wanted war or purposely precipitated it, by asking upstart Hitler for a personal interview and going not halfway but all the way to meet him in his chalet at Berchtesgaden September 15 as Schuschnigg had gone on the Führer's imperative invitation in February. Contemporary letters to the London *Times* warmly praised what one of them called the utilization of the vital moment by "the sleepless sentinel of liberty and peace." The government of France knew about his mission and sanctioned it. The government of Czechoslovakia heard of it and trembled.

At Berchtesgaden Chamberlain was confirmed in the belief in which he had gone there: Hitler was a man of his word and would make war rather than withdraw his claim to the Sudetenland, which he would have called abandoning his countrymen to continued persecution by the Czechoslovaks. The German Luftwaffe would not at that time have been capable of bombing either Paris or London off the map, or of seriously damaging either city; but neither Chamberlain nor Daladier was sure of that or dared risk the trial by battle. So it was decided, in accordance with though not on the basis of Lord Runciman's conclusions and recommendations, that Hitler and his Sudeten satellites should be given what they said they wanted. Czechoslovakia must yield without plebiscite the border areas with populations more than 50 percent German. Then, Chamberlain hoped or tried to hope, an international guarantee could be given the smaller, more homogeneous, and therefore healthier state that would remain; and Hitler Germany would be satisfied. To save the peace, they sold the pass.

Chamberlain was a well-meaning but opinionated and self-righteous individual, rather stubborn-minded than really stout-hearted, difficult for his fellow ministers to advise effectively. On his own responsibility, without consulting Foreign Minister Anthony Eden, he had brushed aside in January, 1938, a proposal by President Roosevelt that an international conference be held in Washington to try to solve by peaceful means some of the problems then threatening the peace of Europe and of the world. One of the problems was the recognition or nonrecognition *de jure* of Italy's conquest of Ethiopia, which he had then said he was ready to recognize as part of a general settlement with Italy.

The position of Great Britain was by no means the sole determining factor; but it was important. Immediately after the Hitler-Chamberlain interview at Berchtesgaden, General Keitel sent word orally, September 16, to General Maurice Gamelin, commander of the French army, that Hitler had decided to attack Czechoslovakia. The leaders of the Reichswehr (*sic*: Wehrmacht?), said Keitel, had tried to restrain Hitler but could not do so. Only a resolute stand by Britain, with France, in defense of Czechoslovakia would dissuade him. Gamelin was not ready to take such a stand, or sure that Britain would.

As early as March 20, 1938, the British prime minister had privately "abandoned any idea of giving any guarantee to Czechoslovakia" or to France in connection with her obligations to that country.[67] On his own responsibility at Berchtesgaden he promised Hitler that he would advise Czechoslovakia to cede the border areas in which the German population predominated. After his return his government and the French, with both cabinets divided in opinion, advised Czechoslovakia to yield to Germany's publicized demands before producing a situation for which France and Britain would take no responsibility; and reluctantly President Beneš and his government yielded, with the stipulation that the ceded territory should not be occupied by German troops until its boundaries had been drawn in conference.

The British prime minister, personally taking upon himself the burden of travel and negotiation as if he were his own minister for foreign affairs, had served less as a mediator than as Hitler's messenger. He had, however, secured Czechoslovakia's compliance to Hitler's Berchtesgaden demands, so had reason to be horrified when he reported that fact at Godesberg in the Rhineland September 22, and found that in the midst of the one-sided negotiation Hitler had egregiously and unilaterally stiffened his terms. Although he stated categorically that it would be his last territorial demand in Europe—a

[67] Keith Feiling, *Life of Neville Chamberlain* (London, 1946), 347-348. Repeatedly throughout the crisis, through unofficial personal channels, French Foreign Minister Georges Bonnet reassured Hitler that France would not fight for Czechoslovakia.

statement publicly repeated in a speech in Berlin September 25—the Nazi leader produced at Godesberg a map on which the most vitally important border areas were marked off for immediate German military occupation, with all Czechoslovak troops and border guards to be withdrawn, with all fortifications, munitions and supply depots, and transport and communication systems intact. Only in a few other areas, not vital to the national defense, might plebiscites be held. The boundaries of plebiscite areas and of areas to be occupied immediately without plebiscite were to be dictated by the Germans, not drawn by negotiation.

Here was a *Diktat* indeed. The Beneš government at once declared its terms, in the form in which they had been laid down by Hitler, to be unconditionally unacceptable. Neither France nor Britain would at the moment put further pressure on President Beneš to compel him to accept them. Premier Daladier declared that France would aid Czechoslovakia if she had to defend herself against an unprovoked attack, and on September 26 Great Britain gave France a much stronger assurance of her support in such a war than she had given her before Germany invaded Belgium in 1914; but it was worth less. How much less was indicated by the diffident and apologetic fashion in which Chamberlain broke the news to his people by radio September 27, seeming to find it as "horrible, fantastic, incredible" as he supposed they did that they should be digging trenches and trying on gas masks because of a quarrel in a faraway country between people of whom they knew nothing. He had apparently begun at last to realize the impossibility of doing business with Hitler with any confidence in Hitler's word, but may have hoped that if one more bargain were made with him time might be gained for the necessary war preparations to hold him to it. If he were convinced, he said, that any nation had made up its mind to dominate the world by fear of its force, he would feel that it should be resisted; but war was a fearful thing, and he and his people must be very sure, before embarking on it, that really great issues were at stake. He did not say by what method but "fear of its force" Germany had set out to dominate central Europe or why it should not be resisted, or what greater issue could have been at stake.[68]

Before Chamberlain's first flight to Berchtesgaden, Foreign Com-

[68] *Ibid.*, 372. The Irish-American-born British fascist William Joyce, soon to be known as the traitorous "Lord Haw-Haw" of the Berlin radio, applied in London September 24 for a renewal of his British passport. By the time he got it he had decided that he would not have to use it then; but on August 24, 1939, having heard his master's voice, he secured a new five-year renewal of his passport and slipped away to Germany. Rebecca West, *The Meaning of Treason* (New York, 1947), 24.

missar Litvinov had sent word from Moscow both to France and to Great Britain that Russia would be ready to join them in defense of Czechoslovakia, despite the objection of Poland and Rumania to granting right of passage to Russian troops, hoping that that objection might be overcome by the League of Nations, at least where Rumania was concerned. Again, in the League of Nations Assembly September 21, Litvinov said in part:

Czechoslovakia is suffering interference in its internal affairs at the hands of a neighboring state, and is publicly and loudly menaced with attack. . . . We intend to fulfill our obligations under the pact, and together with France to afford assistance to Czechoslovakia by the means open to us. Our war department is ready immediately to participate in a conference with representatives of the French and Czechoslovak war departments, in order to discuss the measures appropriate to the moment.

The League of Nations was still strong enough, Litvinov continued, to avert or arrest aggression. All that was necessary, he said, was to reaffirm (*réaffirmer*) the obligatory character of such action and for once to bring the machinery of the League into action in conformity with the Covenant. Otherwise the aggressors would soon be so strong that the League—or what was left of it—could not stop them if it tried. The whole value of Article 16, he said, lay in its compulsory character; no league was needed to make one state help another by choice and in its own interest. If collective security and joint resistance to violations of the territorial integrity and political independence of League members were cut out of the League, what "principles," he asked, were left to which members might adhere (as previous speakers at that assembly had spoken eloquently but unconvincingly of doing)? Russia was prepared, he said again, to render Czechoslovakia immediate and effective aid if France, loyal to her obligations, would give her similar assistance but would otherwise accept no responsibility whatever for the events then taking place or for the fatal consequences which might ensue.[69]

[69] League of Nations Assembly *Journal*, No. 10 (September 22, 1938), 132-133. If Litvinov knew that France would really do nothing, and that Russia would not therefore be treaty-bound to do anything, he knew then that he could talk for the record as boldly as he liked without serious risk of having to make good what he said. He had told his Leningrad constituency on June 27 that, although Germany had "openly pursued a mad anti-Soviet policy" of unlimited aggression and had "indulged in dreaming of the Ukraine and even of the Urals," the Soviet Union's indications of the way to check and eliminate aggression had so often fallen upon deaf ears that he considered Russia relieved of responsibility for further developments and free to act as it saw fit. The German ambassador, reporting Litvinov's Leningrad address, interpreted it as an indication that the Soviets were ready then to break with the western powers and to decide in each case thereafter whether their

The course of events in the last week of September, 1938, indicated that Hitler was generally considered more convincing than Litvinov. The Führer permitted Germany's general mobilization order (fully worked out long before) to be made public so as to intimidate Czechoslovakia and its would-be defenders, and announced that his troops would march into the Sudetenland October 1 unless the "question" was "settled" before then. Stating boldly his persuasion that there was no problem so difficult or pressing that it could not be solved by the resort to reason rather than by resort to force, President Roosevelt twice appealed to Hitler to consent to another conference rather than plunge Europe into war by making the invasion as scheduled. Chamberlain, Daladier, and Roosevelt asked Mussolini to use his influence with Hitler for the preservation of the peace. Knowing that Italy was not ready to participate in a general war and could not make sure of a share of the spoils by earning a commensurate share of the expected victory or being strong enough to demand spoils that she had not earned, Mussolini was glad to see the outbreak of hostilities postponed a little longer; so on that rare occasion the Italian Duce played the unusual role of peacemaker (with some appearance of distinction, being a better linguist than the other principals). Whether because of Mussolini's intercession or for other reasons, Hitler announced a deferment of the invasion and arrived in Munich by plane September 29 for the conference.[70] Neither Czechoslovakia nor Russia, which had as valid reasons as anyone for defending Czechoslovakia and for seeing Nazi Germany held in check, was invited to send a delegate; and neither was likely soon or ever to forget such a rebuff.

---

interests required coöperation with Britain and France. U.S. Department of State, *Documents on German Foreign Policy, 1918-1945*. Series D, Vol. I (Washington, 1949), pp. 921-924, 928-929.

Inspector General Jan Syrový, chief of the Czechoslovak general staff, was reported to have said to a British visitor in September, 1938, that his army was ready to fight the Germans alone or in an alliance with the British and the French; not with the Russians. Once in, he said, the Russians could never be got out.

The Russian foreign commissar's eloquent "collective security" address, above quoted, was delivered to the Assembly of the League of Nations. Using Litvinov's already famous phrase, "Peace is indivisible," the Chinese delegate Wellington Koo had urged the same Assembly of the League, September 16, to embargo under Article 17 of the Covenant any further shipments to Japan of arms, munitions, oil, or other essential raw war materials.

[70] The Führer's remark to his generals August 23, 1939, that he was afraid only that some dirty pig would interfere with his plan for an invasion of Poland by proposing mediation may have referred to Mussolini, who in fact sent Ciano to London, Paris, and Berlin from August 31 to September 3, 1939, to inquire about the possibility of mediation. Hitler had chosen the way of force by natural preference, and adhered to it by instinct and conviction.

At Munich the concessions already made in principle were signed, sealed, and delivered, September 29-30. Czechoslovakia was told by her friends to surrender without plebiscite a greater area than had been demanded by Hitler at Godesberg, with fortifications, weapons, factories, supplies, means of transport and communications intact. She was left defenseless. The worthlessness of an international guarantee of her independence and of the integrity of her truncated territory was demonstrated by Poland's immediate seizure of Teschen and the surrounding area with 120,000 Czechs and only 80,000 Poles, and by the alacrity with which Slovakia, led by Joseph Tiso, protégé of Germany, demanded immediate autonomy.[71]

Hungary was only momentarily restrained by Czechoslovakia's Little Entente alliance with Yugoslavia and Rumania. On November 2, with the consent of German and Italian arbitrators Ribbentrop and Ciano, she seized part of southern Slovakia with a population of about one million, some of whom were Hungarians. Immediately after Munich, rather than plunge his country into war against such hopeless odds without allies, President Beneš resigned and went for the second time into exile.[72]

With bated breath and troubled heart the world listened to its radio for the report from Munich. In Berlin the news touched off a hysterically thankful celebration among a people who had been oppressed by dread of another war and who rejoiced not because some new territory had been acquired or even because a diplomatic triumph had been achieved but because no war had been declared. Soon, however, the SA and SS, given new license and operating under orders, indulged in the most violent campaign of plunder and persecution of the Jews unhappy Germany had yet seen. President Roosevelt recalled Ambassador Hugh Wilson from Berlin. For Germans, rejoicing because

---

[71] Hitler told the Polish ambassador September 20 that Germany would be on Poland's side in a war against Czechoslovakia over Teschen, but advised that Poland should not begin military action until after Germany had occupied the Sudeten mountains "because then the operation would be much shorter." Ambassador Josef Lipski to Premier and Foreign Minister Beck. USSR, *Documents . . . Relating to the Eve of the Second World War* (Moscow, 1949), I, 182.

The Russian commissar for foreign affairs, Litvinov, also on September 20, reassured Czechoslovakia that the Soviet Union would render her immediate and effective aid if France remained loyal to her treaty obligation and also rendered aid, or if Czechoslovakia asked the League of Nations to apply Articles 16 and 17 of the Covenant in the event of an attack by Germany. *Ibid.,* 204.

[72] In June, 1948, rather than plunge the country into civil war and possibly into a war against Soviet Russia, again against overwhelming odds and with no real assurance of help, and rather than sign a communist constitution, he resigned once more in great discouragement and went into retirement at his villa outside Prague. There on September 3, 1948, he died.

Germany had won a victory was safer than giving thanks because the victory had been bloodless.

In Paris and London throngs assembled at the airports to greet the men of Munich. Daladier was reported to have feared at first that his people had come to lynch him for his betrayal of them and of their ally; but they were there to acclaim him for having helped to prolong the peace.

Standing beside his plane at a London airport, Chamberlain, looking anything but triumphant, held aloft a paper which he said bore his signature and Herr Hitler's and read it to those who had come out to meet him. It was a supplementary two-party statement signed while the final drafts of the Munich agreement were being prepared:

> We, the German Fuehrer and Chancellor and the British Prime Minister, have had a further meeting today and are agreed in recognizing that the question of Anglo-German relations is of the first importance for the two countries and for Europe.
>
> We regard the agreement signed last night and the Anglo-German Naval Agreement as symbolic of the desire of our two peoples never to go to war with one another again.
>
> We are resolved that the method of consultation shall be the method adopted to deal with any other questions that may concern our two countries, and we are determined to continue our efforts to remove possible sources of difference, and thus to contribute to assure the peace of Europe.[73]

Back at 10 Downing Street, wishing that what he said were true and perhaps half-thinking that it was, the British prime minister told an anxious assemblage outside his residence that for the second time there had come back from Germany to Downing Street "peace with honor," adding: "I believe it is peace for our time."[74]

[73] See Winston Churchill, *Second World War*, I; Feiling, *op. cit.*, 381; *Documents on German Foreign Policy 1918-1945*, Series D., Vol. II, p. 1017.

[74] Winston Churchill was reported to have been sharply critical of Chamberlain's policy at the time. After the war he wrote: "No case of this kind can be judged apart from its circumstances. . . . Those who are prone by temperament and character to seek sharp and clear-cut solutions of difficult and obscure problems, who are ready to fight whenever some challenge comes from a foreign Power, have not always been right. On the other hand, those whose inclination is to bow their heads, to seek patiently and faithfully for peaceful compromise, are not always wrong. On the contrary, in the majority of instances they may be right, not only morally but from a practical standpoint. How many wars have been averted by patience and persisting good will! . . .

"The Sermon on the Mount is the last word in Christian ethics. . . . Still, it is not on these terms that ministers assume their responsibilities of guiding states.

"There is, however, one helpful guide, namely, for a nation to keep its word and to act in accordance with its treaty obligations to allies. This guide is called *honour*. It is baffling to reflect that what men call honour does not correspond

"Peace for our time" may be interpreted as implying a presumably permanent peace established in our time, such as Woodrow Wilson had hoped to see, or peace for a generation, or—on the lips of a man already nearly seventy years old—peace for only a little while longer, not nearly long enough. It is hardly conceivable that to Chamberlain on his return from Munich it could have meant much more than peace purchased by the day at fearful cost, to be used to prepare Britain and to find allies against the time when, as he said later, "Hitler would not have it." He had gone a long way down a steep and treacherous path to avoid a war which he realized too late was inevitable unless Hitler had a change of heart or was overthrown by a German revolution; and Hitler was the last man in the world to repent and change his ways while winning, and the Germans the last people in Europe to revolt against a winning government.

Opinion in the United States was divided: There was hope that the promise of "peace for our time" might yet provide opportunity for a more durable and equitable settlement of the troubled affairs of Europe without war. There was consternation over the disaster to Czechoslovakia, which as the most democratic and progressive of the succession states seemed to most Americans to have deserved a better fate. There was concern for the future of a shrinking world in which war gave way only to the threat of war as the chosen instrument of national policy.

President Roosevelt's estimate of the situation was expressed October 26, 1938, to the New York *Herald-Tribune* Forum: "It is becoming increasingly clear that peace by fear has no higher or more enduring quality than peace by the sword. There can be no peace if the reign of law is to be replaced by a recurrent sanctification of sheer force. There can be no peace if national policy adopts as a deliberate instrument the threat of war."

The practical wisdom or unwisdom of the decision to buy time depended upon the price paid and the use made of what was purchased. The price was high, but the time was not all wasted. Hitler gained control of the indispensable mountain bastions of Czechoslovakia, of the Skoda armament and munitions works at Pilsen, then

---

always to Christian ethics. . . . Here . . . Honour pointed the path of Duty, and . . . the right judgment of the facts at that time would have reinforced its dictates.

"For the French government to leave her faithful ally, Czechoslovakia, to her fate was a melancholy lapse from which flowed terrible consequences. . . . and it must be recorded with regret that the British government not only acquiesced but encouraged the French Government in a fatal course." *Op. cit.,* 319-321.

Europe's best, and of Czechoslovakia's by no means inconsiderable other man-power and industrial resources. What Germany gained the anti-Nazi forces lost; also the well-trained and well-equipped Czechoslovak army and the possibility of immediate and direct help from Russia. In the two years after Munich, the British aircraft industry was expanded and converted to war production. During that period most of the Hurricanes and Spitfires that clawed the Luftwaffe out of the sky over Britain in August and September, 1940, were built and the pilots who manned them so gallantly and efficiently were trained. Germany, however, also made use of the interval to complete and equip her Wehrmacht and to work out Hitler's war plans; so while something was gained, much was lost.

Munich, September, 1938, was the crucial test and turning point of the period. Hitler and his more radical minions such as Foreign Minister Ribbentrop were greatly encouraged. Their prestige among their own people was enhanced. Hitler was confirmed in his opinion that the political leaders of France and Britain were weaklings, men of little courage, and that the peoples of the political democracies had no convictions for which they would fight. "I saw them at Munich," he repeated whenever he found it necessary to reassure his generals that no effective interference by France and Britain need be feared when Germany invaded Poland.

One of those whom the Germans had least cause to fear was the French minister for foreign affairs, Georges Bonnet, whom he had not seen at Munich. Clinging fatuously to the hope that Germany might defend France's Mediterranean islands and Tunis against Italy, as he feared Britain would not do, Bonnet was determined that Hitler should get what he wanted without war, if France had to be kept anesthetized throughout the operation. During the Munich crisis he conferred with the German government more often than with his own, making no secret of his readiness to purchase Hitler's favor by abandoning Czechoslovakia.

In Paris December 6, 1938, Bonnet and Ribbentrop signed a peace and friendship declaration for France and Germany not altogether unlike the Hitler-Chamberlain declaration signed at Munich September 30. The parties pledged themselves to pacific and neighborly relations. Both solemnly recognized as definitive, as it was then drawn, the Versailles boundary between Germany and France, and agreed that no question of a territorial nature remained unsettled between them. The two governments were resolved, they said, to maintain contact on all matters of mutual interest, and to consult each other on difficult international questions.[75]

The French and British leaders whom Hitler so despised and discounted were slow to realize that he was insatiable. They did not then see the interim directive of October 21 in which he notified the Wehrmacht that the future tasks of the armed forces and preparation for the conduct of the war resulting from those tasks would include the liquidation of the remainder of Czechoslovakia and the occupation of Memelland; but they soon saw the remainder of Czechoslovakia liquidated and Memelland occupied by Nazi forces.

One of the first concessions which Beneš's successor Emil Hacha had to make was the granting of autonomy to Slovakia and Ruthenia. But on March 10 he dismissed the Slovakian premier, Joseph Tiso, and declared martial law in Bratislava, the capital of Slovakia. On March 13 the pro-Nazi Father Tiso, who had appealed to Hitler for help, was brought before the Führer in Berlin and was offered Slovakia's "independence" if he would sever her connection with Czechia; and Ribbentrop made the offer more persuasive by showing him a telegram which he said had just been received from Regent Horthy of Hungary to the effect that troop dispositions were already made and that on Thursday, March 16, a frontier incident would take place which would be followed by "the big blow" on Saturday. Horthy hoped to take Ruthenia and part of Slovakia. He added that he would never forget the new proof of Hitler's friendship, and that Hitler could rely on his gratitude at all times.

So Tiso declared Slovakia independent of Czechia. President Hacha of Czecho-Slovakia countered by declaring martial law.

With some difficulty, on March 14 Father Tiso induced the Bratislava parliament to declare Slovakia independent of Czechia and again to make him premier. Next day President Hacha of Czecho-Slovakia was summoned with his foreign minister to Berlin, where they were browbeaten and bullied by Hitler to the point of physical collapse and were induced at last under threat of immediate invasion and the bombing of their capital to accept a German protectorate over the ruined remnant of their state. The protectorate over "Bohemia-Moravia," as the Germans then renamed it, was announced March 16, with the former German minister for foreign affairs, Baron Konstantin von Neurath, as protector. One week later the military forces and foreign

[75] John W. Wheeler-Bennett, *Munich: Prologue to Tragedy* (London, 1948), 164-165, 178, Appendix L; *Documents . . . Relating to the Eve of the Second World War*, I, 284-285; *Documents Diplomatiques Françaises*, 1938-1939, MDCCCCXXXIX, Document 28, p. 33.

policy of Slovakia were also *gleichgeschaltet* (lined up or coördinated) with Germany's by the establishment of another protectorate, which had to cede some further territory to Hungary. Hungary seized Ruthenia two days ahead of schedule, March 14-16. The dismemberment of Czechoslovakia was complete.

PART IV

The Six Years' War

CHAPTER 13

Axis Attack, 1939-1941

POLAND

The Nazi-Soviet Pact of August 23, 1939

The same fateful third week of March, 1939, which witnessed the completion of the dismemberment of Czechoslovakia saw Hitler secure from Lithuania the city and hinterland of Memel, called Memelland, where the existence of a considerable German element in the population gave him the only pretext he needed. He demanded and was granted the city with its hinterland March 21, and entered it in triumph from the pocket battleship *Deutschland* two days later. As President von Hindenburg had done before him, he had gone around Danzig by sea rather than cross the Danzig corridor.

Clearly Poland would be next and German Danzig would be the logical first point of attack. But what could be done in Poland—or for Poland by those who would have protected her—depended upon Russia; and, especially to the western powers, Soviet policy was an enigma. Litvinov, the Soviet commissar for foreign affairs, was known to have told a Leningrad constituency on June 23, 1938 (three months before his last eloquent League of Nations advocacy of the principle of collective security), that his suggestions for the restraint of Nazi Germany had too frequently fallen upon deaf ears among representatives of the western powers, and that he had decided to reserve thereafter full freedom of action and to consider the USSR released from further responsibility for what might transpire in Europe. The German ambassador, Count Friedrich Werner von der Schulenburg, interpreted Litvinov's address as an indication that the USSR was ready then to break with the policy of the western powers and to decide anew in each case which might arise thereafter whether its own interests required coöperation with those powers.

Whether Soviet Russia could or would have done, in defense of Czechoslovakia at the time of the Munich crisis, what Litvinov said again at Geneva in the midst of that crisis that she was ready to do was the subject of conjecture and debate. Chamberlain and some of his advisers mistrusted her and doubted her ability to carry on a sustained campaign against a major military power. They underestimated her productive industrial capacity and supposed that she had been more seriously weakened by the widely publicized series of military and political purges than she proved subsequently to have been. Clearly, however, by not inviting her to the Munich conference, the western powers forfeited their last opportunity to form with her, before being attacked by Nazi Germany, a firm and fast anti-Nazi antifascist alliance. That Russia would accept no responsibility for the consequences of a settlement about which she had not been consulted, but would seek her own security thereafter by dealing separately with friend or former foe, soon became obvious enough.

Soviet publications nearly ten years later repeated an accusation made by Stalin March 10, 1939, that the western powers had tried both at and after Munich to incite Germany to attack the Soviet Union, and had strengthened her then for that purpose. Whether Stalin and his advisers were of that opinion in September, 1938, or formulated the accusation at some later date, their deep distrust might have been intensified by their suspicions about what had been done in their absence, affecting their interests, at that conference. The ultimate consequences of the realienation of Russia by the western powers, if indeed she had been anything but an alien or an outsider during her four-year officially coöperative period, were incalculable.

Although Poland had nonaggression pacts with both Germany and Russia she feared both and, for her own safety, would have given either the impression that the other would defend her. At Berchtesgaden January 5, 1939, the Polish minister for foreign affairs, Colonel Joseph Beck, reminded by Hitler that Danzig was a German city and must some day "return to the Reich," replied cautiously that the problem of Danzig was a difficult one about which Russia was very sensitive. Hitler, probing for an opening but finding none at the moment, assured his visitor that there was no reason for him to fear a *fait accompli* in Danzig.[1]

[1] One characteristic anti-Comintern way to deal with the Russian danger might have been to dispose of Stalin. The Japanese ambassador to Germany, General

Whether she was disposed to defend Poland or not, Russia loomed on Hitler's horizon as the ultimate European continental enemy; but in the spring and summer of 1939 his Russian problem promised temporarily to solve itself. Stalin was determined not to permit the Soviet Union to be used by anyone but himself. In an address to party leaders on March 10 he ridiculed attempts he said France and Britain were then making and had made to incite Germany to attack Russia, and warned his people to beware of letting their country be drawn into conflicts by warmongers accustomed to having others pull chestnuts out of the fire for them.[2]

Russia began in mid-April to negotiate separately but simultaneously with both sides. To Britain in response to an overture made on March 20 she proposed on April 16 a British-French-Russian alliance. On April 17 and May 5 respectively her Ambassador Alexei Merekalov and Counselor of Embassy Georgei Astakhov called at the Berlin Foreign Office to ask whether Germany would permit the Skoda works at Pilsen in Czechoslovakia to go on making arms and munitions for Russia and whether the Soviets would be permitted to continue to maintain a trade commission in Prague. While there the Soviet spokesmen opened also, as if incidentally, the larger question whether there was any reason why ideological differences should prevent Germany and Russia from getting along well together on a normal, in fact a better than normal, footing. There existed for Russia, said Merekalov, no such reason.

Oshima, reported to chief Heinrich Himmler of the Gestapo (secret state police) January 31, 1939, that he had already sent ten Russians across the Caucasus frontier armed with bombs with which to kill Stalin. Several others attempting to enter Soviet territory had been shot at the frontier. International Military Tribunal, *Trial of the Major War Criminals* (Nuremberg, 1947-49), II, 135; Document 2195-PS, *ibid.,* XXIX, 327-328; IMT, *Nazi Conspiracy and Aggression* (Washington, 1946), IV, 852; Milton Shulman, *Defeat in the West* (New York, 1948), 74.

[2] Undersecretary Hencke of the German Foreign Office in his memorandum of the conversations in Moscow on the night of August 23-24, 1939, in which the Nazi-Russian nonaggression pact was finally negotiated, reported that "Herr Molotov" raised his glass to Stalin, remarking that it had been Stalin who—through his speech of March, 1939, which had been well understood in Germany—had brought about the reversal in political relations. U.S. State Department, *Nazi-Soviet Relations, 1939-41,* 76.

It was quite customary for Stalin or Molotov to make policy pronouncements in officially reported speeches to other party leaders or in statements to be published by the Tass agency or in the party paper *Pravda.* The foreign offices of other powers were expected to inform themselves about Soviet policy by reading those reports. Sometimes official international communications were answered only in that fashion. Molotov sometimes seemed surprised and affected some resentment when foreign governments officially ignored or failed to answer or act upon such indirect and unofficial indications of his wishes. Hitler used a similar technique for unilateral denunciation of treaty obligations, usually in addresses to the Nazi Reichstag.

Also hypersuspicious and feeling his way cautiously, State Secretary Weizsäcker made at the time only a guarded response. But within two days of Counselor Astakhov's visit of May 5 to the German Foreign Office a German informer had told M. Coulondre, the French ambassador to Germany, that in order to regain Danzig and rejoin East Prussia to Germany Hitler would soon come to an understanding with Soviet Russia, perhaps for a fourth partition of Poland. The recall to Moscow just then of the Russian ambassador and military attaché was generally interpreted in Berlin as indicating that something important was afoot in the east (*"dass etwas im Osten im Gange ist"*). Astakhov was soon gratified to observe that the German press had changed its tone. The usual attacks on the Soviet Union, he said, had ceased, and he was pleased to note that reports concerning Russia had begun to be quite "objective." He might have noted also that the usual denunciation of the Soviets and their leaders had suddenly disappeared from the standard pattern of Hitler's speeches.

Meanwhile, May 3, Maxim Litvinov, the Soviet's Jewish commissar for foreign affairs, long known as an outspoken advocate of international action to restrain aggression, was suddenly dismissed and was succeeded by Viacheslav M. Molotov. Litvinov had been negotiating with France and Britain for an alliance and a guarantee of Poland but had not found the western powers ready to join Russia in guaranteeing the "protection" of the Baltic states Estonia, Latvia, and Lithuania (which those states for fear of Germany and Russia were unwilling to accept), or to sanction the annexation by Russia of what was then eastern Poland or of Bessarabia, or to give Russia herself a military guarantee against attack by Japan. Litvinov had stood beside Stalin at the usual May Day parade and had received the British ambassador May 2. But on May 4 he was reported to have asked to be relieved of the heavy responsibilities of his office because of failing health. His dismissal was interpreted by Hitler as a propitiatory gesture, and by the German Foreign Office and the French ambassador to Russia as an indication that Russia might be as ready to partition Poland as to protect it. Hitler later told his generals that the dismissal of Litvinov had been "decisive."

The German ambassador to Russia, however, Count Friedrich Werner von der Schulenburg, though a worldly-wise and well-seasoned diplomat, found "Herr Molotov" rather difficult. Molotov would not resume negotiations on economic questions until the "necessary political bases" for such negotiations had been constructed, but neither would he say what those necessary bases were. Both governments, he said, would have to think about that.[3]

Uncertain whether Molotov was trying to tie political discussions to negotiations on commercial matters because he wanted both or because he really wanted neither (although the Russians had themselves initiated the discussion), and knowing that British-French-Russian political and military negotiations were still being carried on in some desultory fashion, the German Foreign Office decided to sit tight until it could be more confident that any proposals it might make would not be used by the suspicious (*recht verdächtig*) Kremlin to exert new pressure on the western powers. Yet on May 23 Hitler wondered aloud in a conference with his chiefs of staff whether Russia would coöperate in "isolating" Poland. If not, he said, Japan must be induced to "attack her at the right time."

On May 30, 1939, the German Foreign Office informed its ambassador to Russia that, "contrary to the policy previously planned," it had at last decided to undertake definite negotiations with the Soviet Union. Further Russian overtures, made partly through intermediaries, were still thought necessary, however, to convince the skeptical German ambassador and Foreign Office that it was a non-aggression pact with Germany for which the Soviets were seriously angling, and that the British-French-Russian negotiations which they were deliberately spinning out were merely for purposes of bargaining.

Hitler had never thought seriously of Poland as a barrier against Russia. It could not resist Russia if it would, he said, and would not fight for Germany against Russia, although it might attack Germany if the latter suffered serious reverses in the west. He had always looked upon it simply as the receiver of stolen territories taken from Germany in 1918 which must some day be taken back, and of other areas which Germans would find useful as *Lebensraum* or living space, so should take when they found it convenient to take them. Britain and France, however, looked upon Poland after the dismemberment of Czechoslovakia as the nation most likely to be next attacked and to resist attack. Upon the initiative of Great Britain, taken March 20, 1939, they announced on March 31 that they would give

[3] The ambassador's report continued: "Herr Molotov had apparently determined to say just so much and not a word more. He is known for this somewhat stubborn manner. I therefore concluded the conversation and stated that I would inform my government. Herr Molotov then bade me farewell in a very friendly fashion." The conversation had been prolonged because Molotov, who spoke only Russian, had requested that the German ambassador bring no translator with him, and Molotov's interpreter "translated very correctly but slowly from the French." *Nazi-Soviet Relations*, 6, 7.

Poland all support possible if she should be compelled to defend herself against any action threatening her independence. On April 5 Poland, which already had a mutual treaty of guarantee with France, concluded a similar one with Great Britain. Calling the British-Polish treaty of defensive guarantee an incitement of Poland to attack the Germans domiciled in Posen and West Prussia, Hitler used that treaty as a pretext to abrogate, April 28, the German-Polish nonaggression pact he himself had made with Marshal Pilsudski in 1934 and the British-German naval treaty of 1935.

The failure of the French and British to bring Russia into their agreement guaranteeing Poland against attack was signalized by the dismissal of Litvinov May 3, 1939. To that failure Prime Minister Neville Chamberlain's profound distrust of Russia and want of confidence not only in her good faith or good will but in her ability to conduct a sustained offensive campaign might have contributed. So did the unreadiness of the western powers to guarantee Russia unconditionally against Japan, and Molotov's insistence that without specific military commitments no general political alliance would be worth making or should be considered made, whether drawn, signed, and ratified or not. The wary foreign commissar was careful not to put France and Britain into a position to exploit a tripartite alliance politically for its moral effect without fulfilling its military obligations in case of war—which the Nazi were assuring him was what he should expect. He knew that they were unready for actual war. He said also that he wanted the alliance to constitute a guarantee against indirect aggression as well as against attack—"indirect aggression" to mean a coup d'état or internal political change favorable to the aggressor in any European state which one of the contracting parties thought it should protect. The French government objected that such a provision might be taken by Russia as license to intervene almost anywhere.

The failure was due more substantially, however, to the fears of Poland, Rumania, Finland, and the Baltic states. Marshal Voroshilov eventually demanded, August 14, that, if Russia were to defend Poland as her ally, Russian troops must have right of access to Vilna, Lemberg, Galicia, and Rumania. Soviet negotiators insisted all along upon a guarantee not only of Poland but of all states bordering upon Russia in the west; but those states were unwilling to accept Soviet "protection"—which to them meant annexation and control—or the guarantee of any group of which Russia was a member. Fearing both but Germany less than Russia, although they already had nonaggression pacts with the latter, Estonia and Latvia signed nonaggression pacts with Germany May 31. Lithuania had already ceded to her Memel and Memelland.

Great Britain had to negotiate separately with Poland and with Russia. If Russia was militarily weak, argued Polish Foreign Minister Beck, an alliance with her would be worthless. If she should prove to be militarily strong she would never evacuate any territory her troops might occupy, even though ostensibly in its defense. Afraid of losing land which they had taken in 1918-1921, neither Poland nor Rumania was willing to have Russian troops on its soil on any terms or to grant them right of passage, although Rumania did not have to answer that searching question in the final crisis. The Nazi soon proved to be more amenable to reason than the western powers about such arbitrary transfers of territory and sovereignty.

The first actual armed aggression after the dismemberment of Czechoslovakia was committed by Italy. On April 8 she sent troops into Albania and, having completed an easy conquest within a week, on April 15 gave the king-emperor, Victor Emmanuel, the new title of king of Albania. The conquest of this long-coveted beachhead in the Balkans put Italy into a much better position to control the Adriatic and the Strait of Otranto, and gave her a base from which to threaten Greece or Yugoslavia. What most startled the world about the seizure was its brazen cynicism. But Germany did not disown her Axis partner. Far from it. A German-Italian military alliance commonly called by Axis publicists a "pact of steel," negotiated in Milan May 6-7, was signed May 22 in Berlin.

Further aroused by the conquest of Albania, Britain and France announced on April 13 that they had offered to help Greece and Rumania defend their independence if they would defend themselves. Similar arrangements were completed with Turkey by Great Britain in May and by France in June, 1939. In what Winston Churchill subsequently called "a spirit of detachment from the facts," and jealous of a "neutrality" at least partially inspired by fear of Germany, Belgium refused even to enter into military staff conversations with France or Britain for her defense against invasion.[4]

Seeking assurance that other neighbors of the fascist states would not be attacked, President Roosevelt asked Hitler and Mussolini on

---

[4] The treaties with Poland, Greece, and Turkey held through the war, although aid to Poland and Greece seemed at first to have come "too little and too late." Rumania, which had not been guaranteed against attack by Russia, renounced the proffered aid against Germany before the war began. Turkey was not invaded. See pp. 590, 819, and 820-821.

April 14 for a statement of their intentions, offering to transmit to other states whatever reassurance they would give him. By way of answer, in the Reichstag, Hitler mockingly called the roll of nations which he had declared he did not intend to attack or seize, and asked rhetorically who then was afraid. The disciplined Reichstag dutifully guffawed when he mentioned Liechtenstein; but none of the frightened neighbors of the Reich dared say that it was afraid.

The resignation of Litvinov and the signature of the Italian alliance prompted opportunist Hitler to bolder action and more talk about creating his own opportunities. The principle by which one evades solving problems by adapting oneself to circumstances, he had said at a staff conference May 23, was inadmissible. Circumstances must rather be adapted to aims. This was impossible without the invasion of foreign states or attacks on foreign property. Living space in proportion to the magnitude of the state was the basis of all power. . . . The choice was between advancement and decline. . . . Further successes could not be attained without the shedding of blood.[5]

At the same conference Hitler told his staff that no repetition of the Czech affair was to be expected; the idea that they could get off so easily again was dangerous. There would be war, and they must burn their boats. It was no longer a question of right or wrong, of justice or injustice, he said, or of treaties, but of life or death for eighty million human beings. The war should be confined to Poland if possible; but if Britain came into it Belgium and the Netherlands must be occupied. Declarations of neutrality must be ignored. The possession of the vulnerable Ruhr basin would determine the duration of Germany's existence. Britain would be unable, he thought, to make war on the continent, and air attack and the German navy would soon cut her life lines. Time would not be on her side, as Germany would not again bleed to death on the continent.[6]

Renewed Russian overtures encouraged Hitler's Foreign Office by the end of May to try again to negotiate seriously for an agreement covering both economic and political relations. Molotov blew first hot, then cold—usually colder when the Germans seemed to be making the advances, as on August 14-15—and continued the pantomime of negotiating at the same time with the western powers, play-

[5] *Nazi Conspiracy and Aggression*, VII, 848.

[6] *Ibid.*, 849-852; Shulman, *op. cit.*, 34. The navy and air force were not then adequately prepared for a war against Great Britain, but plans for the conquest of Poland were complete. On April 11 "top secret" special orders were issued covering food requisitioning in Poland. The Germans living there were to be spared, and any supplies taken from them were to be paid for in German currency.

ing one negotiation against the other. A British-French military mission was then in Moscow at his suggestion, but deadlocked with the Russians over the question of Russian occupation of Polish territory. At last, with startling suddenness, the Nazi got results.

On August 19 Molotov brusquely broke off an interview with the German ambassador with a routine repetition of his own statement that agreement on economic questions must be reached before agreement on political relations could be considered (a literal inversion of an equally uncompromising statement he had made to the same man in the same place on May 20). Then within half an hour, having talked meanwhile with Stalin, or having heard of the completion of a commercial treaty which could not well have taken him by surprise, he summoned Schulenburg again and handed him a draft of a nonaggression pact such as he said his government would then be willing to consider making. The trade treaty which he demanded as a prerequisite had already been negotiated and was signed that day. It provided for the exchange of German machine tools, industrial installations, optical supplies, and armament (including armor plate) for Russian raw materials such as lumber, cotton, grain, oil cake, phosphate, platinum, manganese, chrome, furs, petroleum, etc. The Russian draft of the proposed political agreement was accepted by the Germans as a basis for discussion and was made the basis of a treaty negotiated in the Kremlin by Stalin, Molotov, and German Foreign Minister Ribbentrop. Signed by Molotov and Ribbentrop during the night of August 23-24, 1939, it was variously called thereafter the Hitler-Stalin, Nazi-Soviet, or Moscow nonaggression pact.[7]

The Nazi-Soviet nonaggression pact was what its name implied only in the sense that the parties agreed for their mutual convenience not to attack each other. Both remained free, jointly or separately, to attack whom else they chose. It startled all the world as if it had been a military alliance. It provided that neither power would engage or participate in or support any attack, aggressive action, or grouping of other powers against the other. The two were to maintain continual contact with one another for the purpose of consultation, to exchange information on problems affecting their common interests, and to settle all disputes or conflicts by friendly exchange of opinion or by arbitration. The treaty was concluded for a period of ten years, with provision for its automatic extension for another five-year period un-

---

[7] Ribbentrop told the Russians that the anti-Comintern pact had always been "basically directed not against the USSR but against the western democracies." *Nazi-Soviet Relations*, 75-78.

less one of the parties denounced it a year or more before the expiration of its original term. It was to enter into force as soon as it was signed.[8]

By a secret protocol signed with and part of their pact of August 23, the Moscow treaty makers bisected Europe and apportioned it between them as Napoleon and the Russian tsar had done at Tilsit. Germany agreed that Finland, Estonia, and Latvia were to constitute a Russian sphere of interest. (Overlapping interests in Lithuania were not clearly defined. The Russian interest eventually prevailed.) Germany was to take that part of Poland which lay west of the Narew-Vistula-San River line, Russia what lay east of it, approximately the territory taken from her by Poland in 1920. Each was to suppress all beginnings of Polish agitation against the other.

With regard to southeastern Europe, whereas Russia specifically asserted its interest in Bessarabia, Germany declared itself totally disinterested politically in those areas (*an diesen Gebieten*). So while Russia was licensed by Germany to take Bessarabia from Rumania, the bargain did not stipulate how much farther either of the bargainers might go into southeastern Europe. Germany did not renounce or disclaim any but political interests there, and Russia did not renounce any of her age-old interests either in the Straits or in the Balkans.

While the nonaggression pact, the protocol, and the commercial treaty made possible a mutually profitable short-term arrangement, it was an uneasy and mutually suspicious partnership at best, based on cupidity and bad faith, with innumerable unanswered questions of conflicting interests and unlimited eventual opportunity and occasion for mutual recrimination, more likely to arise from incompatibility of purposes than from misunderstanding. Two expanding imperialisms unlimited could not go on indefinitely as congenial companions in aggression. For both parties, however, it served an immediate practical purpose. To Germany it meant insurance for her rear if her proposed attack upon Poland should lead to war with France and Britain. Russia had got from Germany what the western powers had not been free to promise her: time in which to continue her military preparation against the day when she might be at war with Germany, and a great expanse of territory in which to maneuver in an elastic defense against invasion. To both it meant participation in a fifth partition of Poland.

The day before the Nazi-Soviet pact was signed, Hitler told his generals that it was being signed and that they would soon be making war on Poland. He would give a propagandist cause for the war, he

[8] Neither party ever denounced it.

said; never mind whether the stated cause seemed plausible or implausible. The victor would not be asked afterward whether he had been truthful about the causes of the war. It was not right that mattered, only victory. Right was on the side of the stronger, and eighty million people should get what was their right. They should have no pity but adopt a brutal attitude and act with the greatest severity.[9]

Hitler had told Ciano (Mussolini's Fascist son-in-law and Italian foreign minister) at Berchtesgaden August 11 that he expected to take advantage of "the next Polish provocation" and to make of it a cause of war for the reconquest of Danzig and the corridor and the conquest of Poland. Once he had signed his pact of August 23 with Stalin, he had Poland where he wanted her, and feared only some untimely intervention which might prevent the war he wanted. While Ribbentrop interpreted every new British move as another sign of weakness, Hitler called the Polish-British defensive treaty a provocation, an incitement of the Poles to commit atrocities against the German minority in Poland. He had in fact been warned by his own ambassador that Britain would intervene if he invaded Poland, and that he would find himself at war with Britain no matter how quickly Poland might be defeated.

"It has been alleged," the British prime minister wired Hitler August 23, "that if His Majesty's Government had made their position more clear in 1914 the great catastrophe would have been avoided. Whether or not there is any force in that allegation, His Majesty's Government are resolved that on this occasion there shall be no such tragic misunderstanding. If the need should arise, they are resolved and prepared to employ without delay all the forces at their command. . . . I trust that Your Excellency will weigh with the utmost deliberation the considerations which I have put before you."[10]

A British-Polish alliance was proclaimed August 25; but the German chancellor weighed very light the considerations Chamberlain put before him. "It is not machines that fight each other," he had told his generals only two days before. "We have the better quality of men. Mental factors are decisive. The opposite camp has weaker people. In 1919 the nation collapsed because the mental pre-requisites proved inadequate." In 1939 he, the master, the man of action, the leader the western powers lacked, would see to it that the will to vic-

---

[9] *Nazi Conspiracy and Aggression*, III, 585, 655.

[10] Winston Churchill, *The Second World War*, I, 396; Dirksen memorandum to the German Foreign Office, August 18, 1939; USSR, *Documents . . . Relating to the Eve of the Second World War*, II, 138-143.

tory did not fail. Let no one intervene! He delayed the invasion of Poland nearly a week, however, to "eliminate British intervention" if he could by giving Chamberlain an opportunity to back down. The erstwhile appeaser exasperated him by not backing down. Ciano told Nazi Finance Minister Schwerin von Krosigk that Britain and France would fight. Although as a former Rhodes scholar at Oxford University he should have known Britain better, Schwerin von Krosigk replied that Hitler thought not. (Ribbentrop had told Hitler that the British had no principles for which they would fight.) Ciano told his German visitor he knew Hitler's views but Hitler was mistaken. He had suggested to Hitler a conference in which he said that the Axis party could not fail to win without war because it would be better prepared to face the eventuality of war if the conference failed.[11]

Italy was not ready for war, and would not be ready for three years unless Germany supplied her immediately with munitions and war materials. She feared she might have to defend herself against the French and British. Mussolini reminded Hitler that in their previous meetings they had not envisaged war until after 1942, by which time he said he would have been ready. He had counted on a longer period of peace during which to work out with their mutual friend Franco the partitioning of French colonial North Africa—Morocco to Spain, Tunisia and Algeria to Italy—and he did not like to be disturbed at dinner. Each Axis dictator told the other, however, that he considered an eventual conflict with the western democracies inevitable. It was merely a matter of timing; and the time seemed to Hitler, if not to Mussolini, to be opportune. He made no serious attempt at accommodation with Britain, no honest response to Chamberlain's and Neville Henderson's attempt to find a *modus vivendi*. A beginning had been made, he told his generals August 23, for the destruction of British hegemony in the world. Britain's anti-aircraft defenses then,

---

[11] *Nazi-Soviet Relations,* 79. General Keitel, chief of the Wehrmacht high command, thought Britain would not fight, and that if she did it would not matter much, as Germany could always get oil from Rumania. Admiral Canaris, director of military intelligence, warned Keitel that Britain would fight and that Germany would be hurt by a British blockade. *Nazi Conspiracy and Aggression,* III, 580-582, 665.

The widely experienced Dr. Herbert von Dirksen, ambassador to Britain from May 3, 1938, warned the Foreign Office that the British would fight if Poland were invaded, and would eventually prove to be very formidable. Dirksen was recalled to Berlin for consultation August 13, 1939, and at his own request his name was soon afterward put on the retired list. The Dirksen papers are Volume II of the Soviet publication *Documents and Materials Relating to the Eve of the Second World War.* Volume I is *From the Archives of the German Foreign Ministry, November, 1937-1938.*

he said, were negligible. Two years later she might be found to have strengthened them. He had made the political preparations. The way was open for the soldier.[12]

Blitzkrieg

GERMAN INVASION

Germany was well prepared for a swiftly moving land and air war in Poland, to be won by use of striking power and soon ended without necessity of falling back upon the staying power which only sea power could have given her. She was inadequately prepared for a naval war against Great Britain. Her reckless leaders seemed to have been misled by Chamberlain's propitiatory policies of the Ethiopia-to-Munich period, by Ribbentrop's mistaken judgment, and by their own intuitively induced opinion that, although the British government might make some warlike gestures as a matter of form and face-saving, the British people would not fight and a German-Russian partition of Poland would be sensibly accepted as an accomplished fact when completed. In the face of all the German Führer's talk about bringing Britain to her knees, the record of his policy in action would indicate that he thought she would need only to be beaten but not beaten to her knees to induce her to abandon the alliances which she would realize she could not maintain, and to make peace with him on terms

---

[12] *Hitler-Mussolini Letters and Documents,* 7, 10, quoted by Churchill, *op. cit.,* 398-399; Herbert Feis, *The Spanish Story,* 71; *Nazi Conspiracy and Aggression,* III, 581-586.

Hitler had indicated to Ciano at Berchtesgaden August 12 that the pseudo neutrals should be liquidated one after another, and that Italy might well "cover" Germany by putting pressure on Yugoslavia while Germany eliminated Poland. Ciano, *Diaries, 1939-1943* (New York, 1946), 119; *Nazi Conspiracy and Aggression,* IV, 508-517; VIII, 516-526.

Publicly, Mussolini talked boldly, "Tell Chamberlain," he said to the British ambassador July 7, "that if England is ready to fight in defense of Poland, Italy will take up arms with her ally, Germany." Churchill, *op. cit.,* 387.

During the first three days of actual hostilities Ciano canvassed with the British, French, and German foreign offices the possibility of a belated conference. Lord Halifax, the British foreign minister, said Britain would agree to a conference only if German troops were immediately withdrawn from Poland. Hitler, on the other hand, would not surrender military advantages already won, or enter a conference without prior guarantee of complete success. The conference could not otherwise succeed, said Hitler, since Britain was "determined to wage war in any event." *Nazi Conspiracy and Aggression,* IV, 465.

Stalin was subsequently quoted as having said in a speech in August, 1939, not published then: "If war begins we cannot simply sit back. We shall have to get into the fighting, but we must be the last to join in. And we shall join so as to cast the decisive weight onto the scales, the weight that will tip the balance." Alexander Dallin, "The Fateful Pact: Prelude to World War II," *New York Times Magazine,* August 21, 1949, p. 40.

which he would dictate. That would mean the surrender of her supremacy at sea, and he could liquidate her empire at his leisure by "peaceful" means.

With Colonel General von Brauchitsch in overall command (under Hitler as supreme commander or *Feldherr*), with Colonel Generals von Bock and von Rundstedt commanding the northern and southern army groups respectively and Marshal Hermann Göring the air force (*Luftwaffe*), the Wehrmacht went into Poland on September 1, 1939, with fifty-six divisions, nine of which were armored, and fifteen hundred aircraft. The German ground forces were less generally motorized then than later, but much more generally than the Polish; and the continued dry weather favored the motorized forces, depriving the Poles of the meager protection which they had hoped the fall rains, deep mud, and swollen streams might give them. The Poles fought tenaciously everywhere, especially around Danzig and Gydnia and at Warsaw, but were overwhelmed in a few weeks. Their airfields, bridges, and transportation and communications centers were destroyed by heavy artillery fire and bombing from the air, their army groups were separately encircled or isolated and immobilized. In two weeks' fighting, the Germans took 700,000 prisoners of war and captured or destroyed 40,000 horses, 1600 guns, 8000 machine guns, 800 airplanes, and other valuable equipment in proportion, and reduced a nation to a state of temporary helplessness and despair. Their acknowledged casualties were only 10,572 dead, 30,322 wounded, and 3400 missing.

The "lightning war," so loudly and so long predicted to admonish people to be good, passed from the rehearsal stage to a full-dress performance. Aware of its implications, the Germans photographed the spectacle and used the film, entitled *Blitzkrieg in Polen*, to intimidate the neutrals. Their photography was technically excellent and the picture quite convincing, although the audience reaction was not always what the exhibitors anticipated. Nations at war with Germany later found it useful for the indoctrination of new members of their armed forces.

BRITISH AND FRENCH DECLARATIONS OF WAR

On the day of the invasion Great Britain and France demanded the withdrawal of German troops from Poland. Foreign Minister Ciano of unready Italy talked of an international conference, but the western powers would not entertain any such proposal unless hostilities ceased immediately and German troops withdrew from Poland. Hitler would give up none of the advantages already won, and had no thought of stopping the invasion. Italy at once proclaimed her nonbelligerent status by announcing that she would not take the initiative in military operations. Upon the expiration of their ultimata at 11:00 A.M. and 5:00 P.M. respectively, September 3, Great Britain and France declared themselves at war with Germany. On the same day Australia and New Zealand also declared war. Canada declared war September 10. South Africa and India waited. Eire remained neutral.

REVISION OF UNITED STATES NEUTRALITY LEGISLATION

In the United States people were not urged, as President Wilson had advised them in 1914, to be neutral in thought as well as in deed. Following the failure of his attempts to prevent or even to postpone the war, President Roosevelt proclaimed on September 5 that a state of war existed between Germany and Poland and between Germany and the western powers as allies of Poland. Existing United States neutrality legislation prohibited the exportation of arms or munitions to a belligerent. On September 21 the president called Congress into special session and asked it to amend the neutrality laws, which he said he regretted having signed.

Weeks of lively, often acrimonious, discussion ensued, in Congress and throughout the land. Some, called by their opponents "interventionists," not ready yet to call themselves boldly that but convinced from the beginning that the peace and interests of the United States would be endangered by a Nazi victory, were ready to do something to redress the balance of military preparedness by making arms, munitions, and other war supplies available to the political democracies at war. Others, called by their opponents "isolationists" but most of them more accurately described at that time as noninterventionists, persisted in the attitudes and opinions which had prompted the passage of the neutrality acts—that the United States could and should remain neutral and that the neutrality act was an essential safeguard not only of neutrality but of the peace and most vital interests of the nation.

By votes of 55 to 24 in the Senate October 27 and 243 to 172 in the House of Representatives November 2, the revised Neutrality Act of 1939 was passed. It was signed and made public by presidential proclamation on November 4. The embargo on implements of war was lifted; but United States vessels were forbidden to enter areas designated by the president as war zones; and all ports of the belligerents, the waters around Great Britain, the Baltic and North seas were so designated. So belligerents could have implements of war or other war materials, as other goods, only on a cash-and-carry basis. As in 1914, the trade policy of the United States worked out more advantageously for the maritime powers than for Germany; but Nazi Germany, which had little credit in the United States and very soon had virtually no commercial carriers at sea, chose not to make a major issue of that matter at that time. Hitler told his generals that, because of neutrality legislation, the United States was not dangerous to Germany, and that its aid to Germany's enemies would prove unimportant.

DECLARATION OF PANAMA, OCTOBER 2, 1939

Meanwhile, at Panama October 2, the foreign ministers of the American republics unanimously adopted a policy of hemispheric neutrality. All belligerent non-American nations were warned against hostilities within an American safety or neutrality zone, roughly three hundred miles wide, around the American continents, observance to be enforced jointly or singly by the nations which proclaimed it. Canada was then the only American belligerent.

The Fifth Partition of Poland

NAZI-SOVIET PACT OF SEPTEMBER 28, 1939

Two days after her own invasion of Poland, Germany invited the Soviet Union to occupy the area assigned it, east of the Narew-Vistula-San River line; but Russia was not ready. Hitler had been too quick for her. Although Molotov congratulated him upon the entry of German troops into Warsaw, the Soviet foreign commissar admitted a week later that he and his associates had been surprised by the swiftness of the German conquest. Ever since the signature of the Nazi-Soviet pact the Russian press had been "as though it had been transformed," and anti-German literature had disappeared as if by magic. But more time was required even in Russia to prepare men's minds for such a reversal of direction. Although it was otherwise ready to send troops into Poland in coöperation with the Nazi, who until August had been posted and pilloried all over Russia as the principal national enemy, government must make some excuse to "make the intervention of the Soviet Union plausible to the masses and at the same time avoid giving the Soviet Union the appearance of an aggressor." The Soviet government notified the Nazi September 10 that it intended to declare that Poland was falling apart and that it was therefore necessary for the Soviet Union to come to the aid of the

Ukrainians and White Russians threatened by Germany.[13] The partition pact of September 28 was then made.

LIQUIDATION OF POLAND

On September 17, their government having given Germany four hours' notice and Poland none, Soviet troops crossed the boundary line which had been established between Poland and the Soviet Union by the Treaty of Riga in 1921, pointedly requesting that the Germans fly no planes east of the Brest Litovsk-Lemberg line. The Polish government that day sought sanctuary in Rumania for its members and for such of its armed forces as could escape. It did not ask Rumania to enter the war as its ally, and on September 21 the Rumanian government declared its neutrality.

Stalin rejected the German draft of the announcement of the Nazi-Soviet partition of Poland on the ground that it told the truth too plainly.[14] He was ready enough, however, for the partition, and prepared to proceed immediately to "the solution of the problem of the Baltic states," which meant that Germany might have Lublin and the Warsaw province (as far as the Bug River) but should waive her claim to any part of Lithuania and support the Soviets without stint or limit in Estonia, Latvia, and Lithuania. There would be no residual Poland.

There was no residual Poland after September 28. Germany conceded to Russia her claim upon part of Lithuania, for which the Soviet subsequently agreed to pay Germany 31,500,000 reichsmarks. Russia secured the Drohobycz and Boryslav oil fields and agreed to deliver to Germany, in addition to whatever quantities had already been or might thereafter be agreed upon, crude oil in an amount commensurate with the annual production of those fields, estimated at 300,000 tons. Lublin province and part of the province of Warsaw fell within the German sphere and were incorporated into what the Nazi called their "Government of Poland." Russia promised to facilitate transit traffic, across territories under her control, between Germany and Rumania, Iran, Afghanistan, and the Far East. The mutual promise of August 23 to suppress all beginnings of Polish

[13] Report of Ambassador von der Schulenburg to the German Foreign Office, quoting Molotov. *Nazi-Soviet Relations,* 91. Such a statement would be more plausible when published if German troops had already crossed the Narew-Vistula-San line; but the Russians were soon quite apprehensive lest the Germans forget to withdraw from territory they had occupied east of that line.

[14] ". . . *da es den Tatbestand mit allzu grosser Offenheit darlege.*" Memorandum, Counselor of Legation Gustav Hilger to German Foreign Office, Moscow, September 18, 1939. *Ibid.,* 99, 102-103. See map, p. 82.

agitation against either Germany or Russia was renewed; and a joint attempt was made by propaganda either to end the war or to shift responsibility for it or for its continuance. Intervention by any third power was to be rejected.

Calling their new pact for the liquidation of Poland the sure foundation for a lasting peace in eastern Europe, the governments of the German Reich and of the USSR solemnly declared their conviction that it would serve the true interest of all peoples to put an end to the state of war then existing between Germany on the one side and Britain and France on the other. Both said they would work toward that goal, jointly with other friendly powers if occasion arose. Should those peace efforts fail, they said, Britain and France would be demonstrably responsible for the continuance of the war. "Germany," said Molotov in a speech a month later, "is in the position of a state which is striving for the earliest possible termination of the war and for peace, while Britain and France are in favor of continuing the war and are opposed to peace."[15]

USSR AND THE BALTIC STATES

The Soviet Union acted promptly on the license given it by Germany by the pact of September 28, 1939. On September 29 it signed a pact of mutual assistance with Estonia, with which it already had a nonaggression pact. The new treaty, signed reluctantly by the Estonian foreign minister, who had been summoned to Moscow several days previously for that purpose, gave Russia permission to establish naval and air bases in Estonia and to station troops there. (The bases were soon to be used in war against Finland.) The Estonian government was permitted, however, to retain some semblance of sovereignty in other matters until after the fall of France in 1940. On October 5 a similar pact was signed by the Soviet Union with Latvia, and the Red Army occupied Latvia also. Under the terms of the Nazi-Soviet pact of September 28, scores of thousands of "Baltic" Germans were either repatriated or resettled at the expense of dispossessed Poles (Jews or other) in the German-occupied parts of Poland.

Germany did not ask Russia to wage war openly on France or Britain but expected the Nazi-Soviet pact to be otherwise as profitable to Germany as to Russia. Officially Russia encouraged that expectation. Revising only the wording of a draft copy shown him in advance for his approval, Stalin authorized Ribbentrop to make a public state-

[15] James F. Byrnes, *Speaking Frankly* (New York, 1947), 286; *Nazi-Soviet Relations,* 105-109.

ment of a community of German-Russian interest inimical to the alleged war aims of the western powers. "The attitude of Germany in declining military aid," said the Russian-authorized version of the German foreign minister's remarks, "commands respect. However, a strong Germany is the absolute prerequisite for peace in Europe, whence it follows that the Soviet Union is interested in the existence of a strong Germany. Therefore the Soviet Union cannot give its approval to the Western powers creating conditions which would weaken Germany and place her in a difficult position. Therein lies the community of interests between Germany and the Soviet Union."[16]

Ribbentrop and Admiral Dönitz hoped that Russia would join Germany in putting pressure upon Norway to compel her to permit the Germans to use Trondheim and Narvik as bases for their war on British shipping. The Norwegian bases were to be had only by conquest; but as a substitute the Soviets allowed a German prize crew from the pocket battleship *Deutschland* to bring the American-owned vessel *City of Flint* into Murmansk in October and depart at will. German naval and diplomatic documents referred repeatedly to the use by Germany of a base on the Murman coast, and Russian icebreakers enabled a German raider (*Schiff* 45, *Komet*) to enter the North Pacific by way of Bering Strait. A German request for a Far Eastern base was rejected April 5, 1940, but the German navy was ready in September to "abandon the base on the Murman coast" and to thank the Russians for "valuable assistance."[17]

The First Winter, 1939-1940

THE WAR AT SEA

Anticipating immediate air raids on their ports and urban areas, the British people continued grimly to provide themselves with gas masks and air-raid shelters. Some of their children were evacuated from London. But it was the submarines, as in 1915 and 1917, that first brought the war directly home to them. On the day of the British and French declarations of war an unarmed, unescorted westbound passenger vessel, the *Athenia*, was torpedoed and sunk two hundred miles west of Donegal by a submarine which must have left its base

---

[16] Ambassador von der Schulenburg to the German Foreign Office, October 19, 1939. *Nazi-Soviet Relations,* 126-127.

[17] S. E. Morison, *History of U.S. Naval Operations in World War II,* III (Boston, 1948), 50-51; *Nazi-Soviet Relations,* 185; Winston Churchill, *The Second World War, II.* (Boston, 1949), 595. The *City of Flint,* which had been carrying cargo to England, was released to its owners from a Norwegian port.

before the invasion of Poland had begun. One hundred and twelve lives were lost, twenty-eight of them American. Nazi propaganda promptly accused the British of having sunk their own ship in the hope that Germany would be blamed for it and so would be embroiled with the United States; but Admiral Dönitz, when on trial at Nuremberg after the war, admitted that the Germans sank it.

Hitler issued a public warning that the arming of merchant ships would warrant sinking them on sight, to which the British government replied that it would arm its ships and they would shoot submarines at sight. The German admiralty then issued orders that enemy merchant ships not passenger vessels would be sunk without warning on the assumption that they would be armed. Admiralty orders were that neutrals were to be "specially well treated," but only Spanish vessels were treated especially well. The U-boats were, however, at first kept out of the western Atlantic, so as to avoid direct conflict with the United States. The whole German plan of conquest had been based upon the erroneous but not inexplicable belief, of the validity of which the Nazi leaders had at last convinced themselves and one another, that the people of the United States regretted having intervened and "robbed Germany of her victory" in 1917, without necessity and in the interest only of Great Britain. The assumption was that an older and wiser generation would insist, when again confronted with the same or a similar problem, on their government's remaining neutral and aloof until attacked.

With seldom less than two thousand merchant ships at sea, totaling several hundred sailings per week, the British lost some vessels to the U-boats—65,000 tons in the first week of the war, 40,000 in the second, 21,000 in the third, and approximately 10,000 in the fourth— but they kept their sea lanes in operation. In tankers, vital for their oil and gasoline supply and for the fueling of their fleet, they lost 60,000 tons in the first two weeks but captured 50,000 tons from the Germans. German merchant shipping, meanwhile, estimated by the British at two million tons, had to seek shelter in German or neutral ports; but only two German submarines were sunk by the British in the first four weeks of war.

During the autumn of 1939, many ships were sunk just outside the mouths of British harbors by mines laid on the sea bottom in shallow water and detonated by magnetic controls when ships passed over them. Although a fairly adequate defense against such mines was soon developed, mine sweeping and other defensive measures against mines were heavy tasks throughout the war.

On September 17 the British aircraft carrier *Courageous,* engaged in shepherding into port some of the merchantmen not yet organized into protected convoys, was torpedoed off the southwestern coast of Ireland with a loss of five hundred men. Ireland having remained neutral, the antisubmarine patrol base at Queenstown (Cóbh) which had been so useful from 1914 to 1918 was not available. On October 14, before the defenses of the battle fleet base at Scapa Flow (also used 1914-1918) had been properly secured, a German submarine commanded by Lieutenant Gunther Prien threaded the entrance to the anchorage and sank the British battleship *Royal Oak.* The anti-aircraft defenses of the area had also to be perfected before the base could be fully utilized again by the battle fleet.

Surface raiders also took their toll. In an unequal contest on November 23 the British auxiliary cruiser *Rawalpindi* was sunk between Iceland and the Faeroe Islands by the German heavy cruiser *Scharnhorst.* Meanwhile the German pocket battleships *Deutschland* and *Admiral Graf Spee,* faster than anything the Allies had which equaled them in gun power or defensive armament, and with their eleven-inch guns and heavy armor more than a match in battle for anything equal to them in speed, were at large in the Atlantic. They had sailed from German bases a week before the invasion of Poland, with orders "in the event of war" dated August 4. Each was accompanied by an auxiliary to carry fuel, supplies, and prisoners. The *Deutschland* cautiously cruised the North Atlantic, where she sank two ships, one of them Norwegian, and captured the American-owned *City of Flint,* then returned to Germany. But three British battleships and two cruisers had had to be assigned on her account as additional escorts for the protection of the North Atlantic convoys.[18]

When the *Admiral Graf Spee* made its presence known by sinking ships off the eastern coast of South America and the capes of southern Africa, nine escort, patrol, and hunting groups including a total of twenty-three powerful warships were ordered to run it down. In a running battle off the mouth of the Río de la Plata December 13, 1939, the German raider was heavily damaged and dogged into the neutral port of Montevideo by the British eight-inch-gun cruiser *Exeter*—which was almost totally disabled but not sunk—and the light cruisers (with six-inch guns) *Ajax* and *Achilles.* Another British cruiser, *Cumberland,* came up from the Falklands in time to close in

---

[18] See pp. 96-97. *Scharnhorst,* 27,000 tons standard displacement, 35,000 tons full load, with nine eleven-inch guns and a speed of twenty-six knots, might well have been called a battleship. She was an intermediate step in German warship building between the pocket battleship and *Bismarck.*

with *Ajax* and *Achilles* outside Uruguayan territorial waters off Montevideo harbor. (The action of December 13 had occurred well out at sea but inside the newly proclaimed three-hundred-mile Pan-American defense zone. Protests were lodged with both belligerents.) Unable either to escape or to remain in Montevideo harbor without being interned, Captain Langsdorff of the *Admiral Graf Spee* was ordered, by an admiralty conference in which Hitler, Admiral Raeder, and General Jodl participated, to fight his way to Buenos Aires if he could but otherwise to scuttle his fine ship at the harbor mouth, which he did December 17, after having transferred seven hundred of his men to another German ship at Montevideo. Two days later he committed suicide.

Captain Langsdorff had released in Montevideo the merchant seamen the *Admiral Graf Spee* was carrying, survivors of some of the ships he had sunk. His service ship *Altmark* evaded searchers and roamed the sea till February 16, 1940, when she entered Jössing Fiord, Norway. The British destroyer *Cossack* followed her in. Although told by the captain of a Norwegian patrol gunboat that the *Altmark* had been searched and found to be unarmed and to have no prisoners on board, Captain Vian of the *Cossack* boarded her after a brief fight, found her armed, and released 299 British seamen prisoners. They had not been seriously mistreated and were in good physical condition. Both ships had violated the neutrality of Norwegian waters. The Norwegian government protested bitterly to Britain the next day, but later suggested arbitration. The British estimated that the Germans by then had sunk 218,000 tons of Scandinavian shipping and had taken 555 Scandinavian lives.

THE FRENCH FRONT

On the French front the first winter of the war brought little action. The French rushed garrisons into their Maginot line and patrolled the area in front of it, but did not seriously test the strength of the new German "west wall" opposite them, which the Germans industriously strengthened. Although she had honored her obligation to declare war on Germany, France had not wanted war. Her people accepted it stoically, without confidence or enthusiasm. It had come too soon after 1916; 1918 had only temporarily restored their optimism; and the middle thirties had divided them into mutually unfriendly and distrustful groups to which national unity was but a phrase and the *Fraternité* of their great revolution and their national motto an empty word. France was looking for no trouble that she did not already have;

and although Hitler ordered a general attack on her to be made through Belgium November 12 he postponed it repeatedly during what the newspaper correspondents and radio commentators soon began to call the "phony war."

There were British troops in France from September 4, the first corps ashore by September 19, with general headquarters at Le Mans. For fear of air attack on their cross-Channel communications they went the long way around at first, landing at St. Nazaire, which had been one of the ports used by the American Expeditionary Force in 1917-1918. Later, as their service of supply had not been seriously disturbed, they ventured to use first Cherbourg, Brest, and Nantes, then Le Havre and Dieppe as in 1914-1918. Their front south of Lille was not in contact with the enemy. Units got glimpses of the Wehrmacht only when rotated, a few at a time, with French units on the German border.

THE PROPAGANDA WAR

While Hitler waited for Great Britain to recognize his conquest of Poland and, for fear of war, to ask for terms of peace, he refrained from ordering the air raids which would have angered the British people and stiffened their resolution to go on with the war. The British meanwhile, busy with the war at sea and with their problem of supply, welcomed a period of comparative quiet during which to convert their industries to war production, build airplanes, and train an air force and army. Their air force dropped propaganda pamphlets over German cities assuring anyone who might read them that the Allies had no real quarrel with the German people. The latter were being misled by Hitler into an iniquitous, unnecessary, and ultimately suicidal war, from which they ought to save themselves by refusing to follow such a Führer further. Old or middle-aged German people could have remembered having been told something similar to that in 1918 about their kaiser; but many of them had been disappointed in the peace they had got after sending away the kaiser; and Hitler's regime was incomparably stronger at home, as well as much more ruthless, than the kaiser's had been. Any revolt against it would have been more dangerous and less likely to succeed. And Hitler had not yet lost his war; he had merely not yet won it. So those who did not laugh at the clumsy British propaganda pamphlets did not make themselves publicly heard or in any way conspicuous.

While the world wondered where and when he would strike next, Hitler assured his admirals and generals on November 23 that he had not organized their armed forces with any other intention than to use them to attack. Balancing east against west, he had decided to attack in the west while his eastern front was free. He did not know how long that front would remain free. He had a pact with Russia, to be sure, but pacts were kept only as long as they served the purposes for which they were made, and Russia would keep hers with Germany only as long as she thought it to her advantage—especially if Stalin should die and someone less sensible and less dependable should take his place. Mixing prophecy with heroics as he habitually did, he registered a vow to stand or fall in the struggle and never to survive the defeat of his people.[19]

THE RUSSO-FINNISH WAR

Finland, which had achieved its independence from Bolshevist Russia with German help in 1918, had signed one of Russian Foreign Commissar Litvinov's network of nonaggression pacts in 1932. In October, 1939, on the heels of the foreign ministers of Estonia, Latvia, and Lithuania, the Finnish foreign minister was summoned to Moscow, where Finland was offered, as the others had been, a mutual assistance pact with its powerful neighbor. The offer was accompanied by demands for cessions or leases of territory which would have put Russia into a position, with bases at Hangö and Viborg, to dominate the Gulf of Finland and in time of war with Finland to close the gulf and deny any ally of Finland access to it. Russia would also dominate the Karelian peninsula between the Gulf of Finland and Lake Ladoga, and the northern Finnish seaport Petsamo. Finland refused, and sought in vain for German intercession and support. On November 28 the Soviet Union denounced the seven-year-old nonaggression pact and invaded Finland at eight points. The Finnish army resisted fiercely, skillfully, and stubbornly; and the winter campaign wrought havoc in a Russian army inadequately prepared and ineptly led, while weather and terrain favored the defense. It was not a lightning war but the grinding down and crushing of a small nation by the relentless pressure of a larger and stronger one. The outcome was predictable. Finland was compelled to make peace at Moscow, March 12, 1940, giving Russia more than she had demanded in October, without the compensation in territory which had then been offered. Cessions included Lake Ladoga and surrounding territory, the Karelian peninsula beyond Viborg, a thirty-year lease on a base at Hangö to control the

[19] Speech at a conference of commanders November 23, 1939. *Nazi Conspiracy and Aggression,* III, 572-580.

Gulf of Finland, and what had been Finland's portion of the Rybachi peninsula overlooking Petsamo. Other territorial transfers protected the Russian Murmansk railway by moving the Russian-Finnish border farther from it. Finland lost some of her most densely populated territory, the homeland of 10 percent of her people, and ports on the Gulf of Finland which would be strategically valuable to her more powerful neighbor but had been vitally important to Finland.

The world resounded with unfavorable criticism of the Russian war on Finland and the peace terms imposed, and reëchoed with defense of Russia. No one took seriously the Soviet excuse that Russia was threatened by Finland. The disparity was too great. The Soviet spokesmen, with their Union still officially at peace with Germany, were not then free to say that they thought it necessary in defense of Russia to control the bases and areas they seized, lest Nazi Germany seize and use them in an attack upon Russia, either as an ally of Finland or by violating Finland's neutrality. The same argument was offered, after June 22, 1941, when Russia was at war with Germany, to justify after the act the seizure of the other Baltic states, eastern Poland, and Bessarabia to give the Russian armies a large area in which to maneuver before being driven back if worse came to worst into territory that was part of Russia when the Hitler-Stalin pacts of 1939 were made.

The apparent comparative ineffectiveness of the Russian army in the Finnish campaign was variously interpreted. Some observers, including some of the German, remembering the purges of a few years before in which Russian army leaders had paid with their lives for being caught planning military coöperation with Germany before Stalin had put upon it the stamp of his official approval, readily concluded that the best brains of the Soviet armies—and certainly some of their better ones had been involved—had been liquidated, removed from responsible positions, or so intimidated as to be no longer useful. Others guessed that the makers of Soviet policy had supposed that Finland would surrender without fighting, as her neighbor states had done, and that policy makers and generals were surprised to find they must fight for what they wanted, and so fought ill prepared.

Communists everywhere dutifully defended Russia's policy, as they had defended her 1939 deals with Hitler and her participation in the partition of Poland and the extension of her "protection" to the other Baltic states. Noncommunist world opinion was generally unfavorable. Britain and France considered sending "volunteers" to fight for Finland as Russian Communists had fought for the republic in Spain, but found no way to send them without violating Norway's neutrality while Norway was unwilling to grant them right of passage. When Finland appealed to the League of Nations as the victim of aggression, December 2, 1939, the traditionally timid and slow-moving League promptly expelled the Soviet Union from membership and authorized its Secretariat to coördinate all offers of assistance to Finland.

Japan had been censured by the League and had withdrawn from it. Italy had withdrawn after adverse action and under adverse criticism. Nazi Germany had withdrawn without having suffered any serious affront. Only Soviet Russia was expelled. Most of the men who directed Russian policy in 1939 and experienced that expulsion in 1940 were still in high position at the policy-making level nine years later. Being men of long memories, they seemed still to find it easier to believe that western world opinion was unfriendly both to them and to the Soviet Union than that it was friendly, and to remember the ancient adage that he who sups with the devil at an international conference or in an international organization should use a very long spoon.

SCANDINAVIA AND THE LOW COUNTRIES

Position of the Northern European Neutrals

The northern European nations tried again in 1939 to remain neutral as in 1914; but their position was more difficult. Interested primarily in high-grade Swedish iron ore, so useful in the production of ball bearings and for other purposes requiring steel of finest quality, the Germans were willing at first to work with the Russians to keep Sweden neutral. With a strangle hold upon the Silesian sources of a good portion of Sweden's coal supply they were able to put economic as well as military pressure on her. The Soviets wanted no Swedish intervention in their Finnish war and kept Swedish aid to the Finns on an unofficial humanitarian basis. The Germans meanwhile carried Swedish iron ore in summertime from Lulea by way of the Gulf of Bothnia and the Baltic, and in winter through Norwegian coastal waters down from Narvik.

Hitler always made it clear to his subordinates of highest rank that he intended to invade the continental Low Countries and Norway in 1939. For the protection of the Ruhr, he said, Germany would need weather reporting and aircraft warning stations and anti-aircraft bases in the Netherlands and Friesian islands. To gain assured access to the North Sea and the Atlantic, and for fear Britain might seize

Norway and cut off the flow of Swedish iron ore and nickel via Narvik, Germany must anticipate Britain and herself seize Norway. The Norwegian traitor Vidkun Quisling was in Germany before the war began, begging for money for his Norwegian Nazi party and trying to tie Norway to Germany by pretending that, when war came between Germany and Britain, Britain would unquestionably occupy Norway unless Germany seized it first. In December Quisling was in Berlin again, and although Hitler pretended (to Quisling) not to be interested in Norway if it stayed neutral as he said all Scandinavia should, he gave him twenty thousand reichsmarks in January, 1940, and promised him ten thousand pounds in British currency per month for three months "to combat British propaganda."[20]

A general German directive for the invasion of the Netherlands and Belgium was issued October 9, 1939, the tentative date being November 7. France was to have been attacked November 12; but von Brauchitsch pleaded bad weather and ammunition shortages as reasons for several postponements while Hitler grumbled at the general for being so faint-hearted. In January an officer of a German airborne division, carrying documents to Cologne, made a forced landing on Belgian territory and was captured. Undestroyed documents captured with him revealed plans for the invasion of the Netherlands, Belgium, and France. The Germans again postponed the invasion while they prepared variants of the plans, and Winston Churchill publicly invited the neutrals in their own defense to make common cause with one another and with the western Allies while there was still time. But the Belgian government, pretending to believe that the tame surrender of the documents had been only a German propaganda trick, adhered to its refusal to admit French or British troops or to plan for them to meet the invasion on Belgian soil. Meanwhile noisy elements of the neutral press accused Churchill (then a member of the war cabinet but not prime minister) of trying to involve as many neutral nations as he could to fight Britain's battles for her.

The British-French Supreme War Council seriously considered, in London March 28, the necessity of sending military aid to the Netherlands, with or without invitation, if the Netherlands should be invaded and Belgium should refuse to help. At the same meeting France and Britain gave each other mutual assurances that neither would negotiate or conclude a separate armistice or treaty of peace without the previ-

[20] Address by General Alfred Jodl to Nazi party leaders, November 7, 1943; *Nazi Conspiracy and Aggression*, VII, 924; Alfred Rosenberg, "Brief Report on Activities of the Foreign Affairs Bureau of the Party from 1933 to 1943," *ibid.*, 32-35.

ous knowledge and consent of the other. They agreed then also that Norwegian coastal waters should be mined, beginning April 5, to try to stop the Germans from using those waters as they were doing as a covered corridor not only for their ore ships from Narvik but for warships ocean-bound. The operation was begun off Narvik April 8. The Germans, already on their way, invaded Norway at dawn April 9. Yet, as if they thought that that invasion had been planned and executed in less than twenty-four hours, Reynaud and Daladier of France referred to it as "action in consequence of the laying of mines in Norwegian waters."

In an address on April 5, referring to the German failure to invade France and Britain when they had been weakest in 1939, Prime Minister Neville Chamberlain said that Hitler had missed the bus. His remark had a hollow sound a few days later, but although his government had been warned on April 3 that German forces were then assembled at Rostock for the seizure of Scandinavia, most people in Britain would have found it as incredible that the Germans could transport an expeditionary force up the coast of Norway in the face of British sea power as most Americans later found it that a Japanese naval force could bomb Pearl Harbor without inviting immediate extermination.

On the basis of a conference with the Norwegian Quisling in Berlin December 14, 1939, Hitler ordered the supreme command of the German armed forces to prepare for an invasion of Norway. On January 3, 1940, he "emphasized that the operation must be prepared as quickly as possible." The general directive for the double invasion of Denmark and Norway (code name "Weser Exercise") was issued March 1, slightly revised March 7. The date, to be April 9, was tentatively set on March 16, definitely on April 2. All ships engaged were given British names to mask their identity if challenged, and were to answer Norwegian challenges in English. Ships were to be darkened, except that upon approaching the Norwegian coast they should illuminate the British flags which they were to fly until, except presumably at Narvik, all their troops had landed. The troops were to be kept hidden below decks and were not to be told their destinations until actually approaching them.[21]

[21] Martienssen, *Hitler and His Admirals* (New York, 1948), 50-51; Jodl's diary and Raeder memorandum for Admiral Assmann: *Nazi Conspiracy and Aggression,* I, chap. 9; IV, 392; VI, 883, 892; Churchill, *Second World War,* I, 564, 572. Surviving German generals and admirals maintained in interviews after the war that it was the *Altmark* incident of February 16 that pushed Hitler into making "his only unpremeditated invasion"—that of Norway; but their records contradicted them. An order signed by Field Marshal Keitel January 27 showed that the in-

In Oslo April 5, on the day the Allies had planned to begin the mining of Norwegian waters but three days before that mining was begun, the German minister to Norway showed invited guests the war film *Blitzkrieg in Polen,* with the final caption: "For this they could thank their English and French friends." But the Norwegian government still seemed more concerned lest the British give the Germans a pretext for invasion by mining Norwegian coastal waters than lest the Germans make the invasion on a manufactured pretext or without waiting for one. The pretext was portended by the statements of survivors of the German troop transport *Río de Janeiro,* torpedoed by the Polish submarine *Orzel* off the southern coast of Norway April 8, that they had been on their way to Bergen to help the Norwegians defend their country against the French and British. The British battle fleet, without aircraft carriers, none being then available, at once left Scapa Flow when warned on April 7 that a German fleet was steaming through the Skagerrak, but failed to intercept its enemy. Further warning that the German battle fleet was out was given by the British destroyer *Glowworm,* which at 0830 April 8 radioed that it was engaging two German destroyers off the Norwegian coast near Trondheim and then fell silent. (It was subsequently learned that *Glowworm* had rammed the German heavy cruiser *Hipper* and been sunk. The crippled *Hipper* put in at Trondheim.)

Very early April 9 German troops crossed the Danish frontier at several points, made six sea and air landings elsewhere, and occupied Copenhagen without meeting much resistance. King Christian and his government and people had to submit to German control. Up the coast of Norway, where many had lain hidden for several days or weeks on innocent-looking ore ships, the Germans swarmed ashore. Within twenty-four hours, without using more than two thousand men in any one landing force, and using only three divisions in the initial assault phase, the invaders captured all the principal Norwegian ports. They soon had enough land-based aircraft operating from Norwegian fields to make it extremely hazardous for British naval forces except submarines to venture close inshore. British mines and submarines sank several loaded German transports but never enough to keep the stream of reinforcements from flowing virtually at will. More were transported by air. In the direct approach to Oslo the German cruiser

---

vasion of Norway was being planned at that time. General von Falkenhorst was appointed February 21, after the *Altmark* incident, to command the invasion force; but on March 14 "the Führer had not decided what reason to give" for the enterprise, and was still looking for some justification.

Blücher was sunk by gunfire from shore-based batteries, the *Emden* damaged, and the *Lützow* (former *Deutschland*) driven off; but the town was taken by air-borne troops and others who moved overland from landings down the fiord.

At Narvik there was harder fighting, especially in the harbor and the fiords below. The Germans were once driven from the town but were reinforced and well supplied by air, and held the area around it. The Allies hung on to the harbor until June 9, when, with the Germans moving into France and the Norwegian army ready to capitulate, it had to be abandoned. The British aircraft carrier *Glorious* and destroyer *Acasta* were sunk while participating in the evacuation.

At Andalsnes and Namsos, south and north of Trondheim, the British landed a few troops in mid-April to try to reinforce the Norwegians retiring under constant German pressure northward from Oslo. The German expeditionary force was soon built up to seven well-equipped divisions whereas the British, having sent to France the two divisions they had once earmarked for Finland, had only a few battalions left for Norway, with a token force of French chasseurs but without tanks, antitank guns, or aircraft; so the forces they had landed at Andalsnes and Namsos had to be withdrawn.

The Norwegian resistance movement was intelligent, ubiquitous, and persistent. The Germans occupied the country for five years and imposed heavy burdens on it but did not break the spirit of its people. When further organized armed resistance became hopeless, June 9, King Haakon and his government ordered cessation of hostilities and, escaping by way of Sweden, set up a government in exile in England. The large and efficient Norwegian merchant marine was indispensable to the Allied cause and earned an equally indispensable revenue. But the Germans used Norwegian harbors and airfields as bases for their surface raiders, submarines, and air forces, and from them waged a deadly war on Allied shipping. The conquest of Norway gave them an advantage which they had coveted but not enjoyed in 1914-1918.

The Netherlands and Belgium, May, 1940

Before the Germans invaded Poland Hitler told his high command that the Low Countries must be seized and used as German outposts and bases in the war against Great Britain. From the beginning, all plans for an offensive in the west, including those captured by the Belgians in January, 1940, had included the Netherlands, Belgium, and Luxemburg among the areas to be occupied. Better protection could so be afforded the vital Ruhr industrial region against land or air attack, and by outflanking the Maginot line the Germans could pour troops into northern France through Luxemburg and Belgium as they had done in 1914. Even after the unprovoked invasion of Denmark and Norway, however, Belgium and the Netherlands were careful not to provoke invasion or give the Nazi pretext for one by abandoning their neutral position and admitting French or British troops to help them to defend themselves.

In the early morning hours of May 10, 1940, by land and by seaplane, parachute, and glider, German motorized and air-borne troops in overwhelming numbers attacked the vital strong points in the Netherlands. Dutch airfields were seized by parachute troops and held until garrisons for them could be brought in by transport plane, or were neutralized by bombing. Plans for inundation, an ancient defensive last resort of the Low Countries, were not carried out in time. Canal and river bridges were seized before their defenders could destroy them. The heart of Rotterdam was bombed and burned out as an object lesson, with little other military purpose than to paralyze resistance and demoralize the people. Civilians were not yet inured to bombing, or soldiers to the thought of having their homes bombed behind them and their families driven like hunted animals in flight along the roads or into the fields and forests. Both found the new terror more terrifying than the more familiar horrors of the battlefield, which they were better prepared, psychologically, to meet. Even the shrill screaming of the air brakes on the *Stukas* (*Stürzkämpfer* or dive bombers) made their attacks more horrendous.

Driven out to sea in a small naval vessel and unable to land again on Dutch soil without soon being taken prisoner, Queen Wilhelmina of the Netherlands went to England and set up a government in exile there, May 13, which with the Dutch colonial empire contributed substantially thereafter to the Allied cause. Finding his armies soon reduced to impotence, General Winkelman capitulated for the Dutch armed forces in the Netherlands May 15. Arthur Seyss-Inquart, who as a reward for having delivered Austria into Hitler's hands had been Nazi proconsul (*Reichsstatthalter*) in Austria since 1938, was appointed German commissioner (*Reichskommissar*) for the Netherlands. Although no peace was made by the queen or her government, the Germans were completely in control of the continental European territory of the kingdom. Until 1945 they could use it and its harbors, such of its shipping as they had seized, and whatever food, war materials, and services they could compel its people to deliver.

The invasion of Luxemburg and Belgium was simultaneous and co-ordinated with the attack on the Netherlands. The woods and hills of the Eifel-Ardennes region proved to be less serious logistic obstacles to the mechanized forces of 1940 than they had been to the German armies of 1914 or 1918, and less than the French and Belgians had supposed that they would be. Luxemburg was quickly overrun and the Belgian military frontier was breached at many points, all along its length. The great fortress Eben Emael, which was to have guarded the passage of the Meuse River and the King Albert Canal, fell in two days under a coördinated and well-rehearsed attack of dive bombers, parachute troops, and demolition and assault groups. Within four days the Germans reached the Meuse from Liège to Namur. Within a week, with the Netherlands taken and the King Albert Canal (con-necting the Meuse from near Maastricht with the Scheldt at Antwerp) crossed at many points, they were in Brussels. The Belgian army abandoned Antwerp May 18.

On the day of the invasion, both Belgium and the Netherlands asked for the aid of the Allied troops which they had not previously dared admit to their territories. Only a little British aid reached the Nether-lands; and the French Seventh Army under General Giraud had to move so quickly to occupy in time the islands of Walcheren and South Beveland at the mouth of the Scheldt that they outran their ammuni-tion supply. Within three hours of the receipt of the appeal French and British troops were moving forward into Belgium. As the German general staff had hoped (and General von Blumentritt said afterward that it had been informed from Brussels) they would do, the French seriously weakened their position around Sedan by moving troops northward from that area into Belgium, where the German advance outflanked them before they reached their assigned positions. The British Expeditionary Force was similarly unable to consolidate the positions into which it was rushed without adequate reserves.

By-passing the northern end of the Maginot line between Mézières and Namur on May 15, the German General von Rundstedt thrust a spearhead, based on the Eifel-Ardennes region, across the southern tip of Belgium through the inadequately fortified and thinly held French frontier line near Sedan, already partially denuded of de-fenders by the movement of the French Ninth Army northward into Belgium. On May 18, the day Antwerp fell, that spearhead reached Amiens. By May 27, it pushed on to the English Channel at Abbeville, turned northward, and took Boulogne and Calais. General Giraud, who replaced General Corap as commander of the French Ninth

Army, was taken prisoner with many thousands of his troops. General Billotte of the French First Army group was killed in an automobile accident May 21. The British, French, and Belgian troops north of the Sedan-Abbeville line were cut off from reinforcement or supplies from the south and subjected to converging pressure. An attempt to cut off the strangling arm by hacking at it from north and south between Bapaume and Péronne failed. It held its grip and squeezed. (See maps, between pp. 22-23 and on p. 64.)

King Leopold of Belgium capitulated for his army as of midnight May 27-28. His cabinet, already in exile in Paris, repudiated his surrender; but he set his people an example of submission to superior force. Belgium was not to be free again until 1944, and its man-power and—barring sabotage—industrial resources were until then at the disposal of the occupying power, which knew well how to use them.

FRANCE AND BRITAIN, 1940

France

To Dunkirk, June 4

On the day of the invasion of the Netherlands and Belgium, May 10, British Prime Minister Neville Chamberlain resigned. The leader of the new coalition government was doughty Winston Churchill, who as first lord of the admiralty from 1911 to 1915 had been largely responsible for the fleet's readiness for war in August, 1914, and who had returned to the same office a few hours after the declaration of war in September, 1939. He had learned much and forgotten nothing, and soon proved himself to be an inspiring leader, the authentic voice of the hardiest of his people in adversity. "I have nothing to offer you," he told the House of Commons when asking for a vote of confidence on May 13, "but blood, toil, tears and sweat."[22]

[22] Winston Leonard Spencer Churchill, son of Lord Randolph Henry Spencer Churchill and American-born Jennie Jerome, grandson of the seventh Duke of Marlborough, was born at Blenheim Palace, home of the Dukes of Marlborough in Oxfordshire, England, November 30, 1874. He had served by 1940 a long and arduous apprenticeship for the high office of prime minister. Having entered the military service from Sandhurst at the age of twenty-one, he saw some active service in 1897 and 1898. As a newspaper correspondent, he observed and reported on the Boer War. First elected to Parliament as a Conservative in 1900, he joined the Liberal party six years later. By 1940 he was a Conservative again. After the failure of the 1915 Dardanelles campaign he resigned his cabinet offices and went to France for a period of active service as commander of the Sixth Royal Scots Fusiliers but was recalled to the cabinet by Prime Minister David Lloyd George in 1917 and served first as minister of munitions, then as secretary for war and air minister. In 1921-1922 he was secretary of state for the colonies, and from

In France, Daladier had resigned as premier in March, but had remained as a member of the cabinet of his successor, Paul Reynaud. General Charles de Gaulle, an ardent advocate of mechanization and motorization of the armed forces and of the use of tanks, had then— too late and but little regarded—become undersecretary of state for war. Under pressure of military disaster in May, Premier Reynaud reorganized his cabinet with himself as minister of defense and Marshal Pétain, recently returned from the post of ambassador to Spain, as vice-premier. M. Mandel was minister of the interior. Reynaud then replaced the totally defeated General Corap of the Ninth Army with General Giraud (q.v. above), and called in from Syria General Maxime Weygand, once Marshal Foch's chief of staff, to replace General Gamelin as commander in chief of the French armies and army air force.

Pétain, who seemed never to have recovered from the effects of the defeat which had stared him in the face at Verdun in 1916 and which he had been so nearly ready then to recognize, seemed already to be thinking less of making war than of making peace. He appeared to be acting upon the assumption that the French radicals whom he had always hated had ruined the republic, and that the British, whom he had never trusted, were ready to betray it and leave it in the lurch. France, therefore, should withdraw at once from the war—which he had never wanted—and let the British take such care of themselves as they could. With such traitorous elements in her own population and with such undependable allies, he thought, France could never win a war against the numbers, strength, and discipline of the Germans. Rightist Catholic France must save itself by some sort of reconciliation and collaboration with Nazi Germany for the suppression of atheistic communism in France. He seemed not to consider France morally bound by her agreement not to make a separate peace. Each ally, he argued, was obligated to the other only in proportion to the military aid the other had supplied. Britain, he said, had sent to

November, 1924, to June, 1929, chancellor of the exchequer. He was one of the first to warn the world of the danger of Nazi aggression.

If his accomplishments in other fields had not been overshadowed by his prominence in public life, Mr. Churchill would have been known as a vigorous writer. His *Life of Lord Randolph Churchill*, a biography of his father, was published in 1906, *The World Crisis of 1916-18* (four volumes) from 1923 to 1929, and his *Marlborough* (four volumes) from 1933 to 1938. His *Second World War*, of which the first volume, *The Gathering Storm*, was published in 1948, the second, *Their Finest Hour*, in 1949, and the third and fourth, *The Grand Alliance* and *The Hinge of Fate*, in 1950, was eagerly awaited and widely read. He was an extraordinary chronicler of events in which he had taken part.

France only ten divisions, and could not be trusted not to make a separate peace. Already hopelessly defeated, he thought, France must not bleed to death for Britain, which he thought was equally certain also soon to be destroyed unless she conceded defeat and capitulated.

Reynaud and Weygand were more sanguine than Pétain, although the general shared the marshal's rightist Catholic views, and busied themselves bringing fresh French forces to bear along a northward-facing line across France north of Paris. Some troops were brought from the outflanked Maginot line; others were soon trapped there. North and east of the German Sedan-Abbeville-Calais sickle blade, the military situation of the Allies rapidly deteriorated. The forces around Arras tried, May 21-23, to break out to the southward but failed. The British Expeditionary Force was put on half rations May 23 and faced the prospect of extinction unless it could extricate itself by sea. French forces in the same area faced the same prospect, and the alternatives narrowed down to certainty when King Leopold and the Belgian army capitulated, May 27-28.

Dunkirk was the only way out. By what seemed at the time almost a miracle of improvisation, summoning for the purpose hundreds of tugs, fishing boats, and pleasure craft of all sorts manned by volunteers, shepherded by light naval vessels, and protected overhead by the reserves of fighter aircraft painfully husbanded from the disastrous campaign in France, in which they would have vanished like the proverbial drop of water on a hot stone if they had been thrown into it, the Allies managed to pick up off the beaches of Dunkirk between May 28 and June 4 more than 336,000 men. Two-thirds of those so rescued were British, a few Belgian, the others French. Nearly 700 of the 861 boats used were British, manned by British crews. The Germans claimed 40,000 prisoners at Dunkirk; and 50,000 French soldiers under General Molinié, who by stubbornly engaging seven German divisions around Lille had lessened appreciably the pressure on Dunkirk, had to surrender May 31. All of the heavy guns, supplies, and equipment of the British Expeditionary Force and of the others salvaged with it had been destroyed or left behind to fall into German hands. The men were taken off the beaches almost empty-handed; and they found most of the people in Britain also empty-handed, weaponless. A German invasion of Britain seemed imminent. But the Germans turned southward instead, to complete the conquest of France, which promised to be easier and to lead, indirectly perhaps but certainly, to the making of a victor's peace with Britain.

To Compiègne and Vichy

After the fall of Belgium and the evacuation at Dunkirk the Germans intensified their attacks southward into France, behind and through the Maginot line, which had been weakened by the removal of some of its garrison troops for the war of movement further west. General Weygand could not cope with them. His reserves were soon expended. The general disorganization was so great, and the confident German columns moved so swiftly in the wake of the *Stukas*, with fighter-plane protection, that hundreds of thousands of French soldiers suffered the double humiliation of being surrounded and forced to surrender without the meager satisfaction of having fought effectively.

Watching his opportunity like a jackal, without reference to the Italian king or grand council or to his own military or political advisers, and despite President Roosevelt's best efforts to dissuade him, Mussolini decided May 9 to make war on France. On June 10, the moment having come when he thought he could gain most while doing least, he announced that decision, effective at midnight June 10-11.

In great haste and confusion, along roads jammed with hysterical refugees scourged by machine guns from the air, the French government moved first to Tours, then on to Bordeaux. "This very hour another dictatorship has stabbed France in the back," cried Premier Reynaud in a message to President Roosevelt. But, "we shall fight in front of Paris; we shall fight behind Paris; we shall close ourselves in one of our provinces [Brittany?] to fight, and if we shall be driven out of it we shall establish ourselves in North Africa to continue the fight, and if necessary in our American possessions."[23]

Those were brave words, reminiscent of Clemenceau and similar to the roaring defiance with which, six days earlier, Winston Churchill had braved the threat of an invasion of Britain. But Reynaud could not make them good. At an Allied war conference near Orléans June 11 Churchill reminded Marshal Pétain that they had survived trying times together in 1918; but the marshal only reminded his old ally that they had not at their disposal in 1940 the reserves, many of them British, which had saved them in 1918. Although he joined Weygand June 11 in insisting that Britain should send at once to France the

[23] W. L. Langer, *Our Vichy Gamble* (New York, 1947), 22. Reynaud's "stab in the back" expression, already worn threadbare by German propagandists in their denunciations of the armistice of 1918, was rephrased by President Roosevelt in an address at the University of Virginia: "The hand that held the dagger has struck it into the back of its neighbor."

reserve divisions which they (incorrectly) supposed she had available, and all her fighter air force, holding none in reserve at home, Pétain had decided by June 4 or sooner that France must make a separate peace. To reduce Paris to ruins, he said, would not materially affect the outcome; so Paris was declared an open city and abandoned by the French army June 13. The Germans took possession June 14.

Compelled to confess with obvious chagrin that he could promise only a few planes then and perhaps three divisions in October, Churchill told the French government that, although he could not release France from her obligation or consent to her making a separate peace, he would not reproach her if she made one, *provided*, however, that the French fleet was sent to British ports to make sure it would not fall into enemy hands. He would not send to France, to be destroyed there in a hopeless fight already lost, the last reserves of the Royal Air Force. The British home defense command had said that it must have a minimum of twenty-five fighter squadrons to defend Britain against attack by the Luftwaffe. The real turning point, said Churchill, had not yet come. It would come when those reserve squadrons of the R.A.F. met and broke the Luftwaffe in the skies over Britain; so he would not sacrifice them over France. Meanwhile, fearing retaliation, the French denied the British the use of airfields around Marseilles for bombing raids on northern Italian industrial areas.

At the peak of the crisis Britain made the extraordinary proposal of an organic union with France. Premier Reynaud and General de Gaulle were favorably disposed toward the proposal, Weygand and Pétain opposed. It was rejected, June 15, after very brief and skeptical consideration by a harried and divided group of ministers. Weygand was ready to obey an order to cease fire but would not accept responsibility for giving such an order, although Reynaud offered to authorize him to give it.[24]

After desperate appeals to the United States to declare war on behalf of France, Reynaud resigned. Pétain asked Hitler June 17 on what terms France might secure an armistice, and was instructed June 19 to send a delegation to Rethondes, near Compiègne. With the French already suing for an armistice, June 21, Mussolini launched

[24] A comparison with 1918 is suggested. The German military authorities insisted then that the government secure an armistice, sent a civilian to receive the terms, instructed him to sign regardless of their severity, then accused the civilians of betraying them. See pp. 67, n. 17, and 76.

an offensive against southeastern France; but three French divisions plus frontier fortress troops held the invasion at the Alpine border and halted it at Menton.

Meanwhile at Munich, June 17, Hitler and Mussolini quarreled over the ultimate fate of France and her possessions, with Hitler as the stronger doing the dictating. Spain might have Morocco, except some Atlantic ports which Germany would demand. Italy might take Nice, Corsica, Algeria, Tunis, and Djibouti but might not occupy the rest of France east of the Rhone river as Mussolini wished to do. Germany would take back Alsace and Lorraine and would keep also the Longwy-Briey iron fields, part of Belgium, and the principal ports of Norway. In Africa she would regain or take and keep French Guinea, Sierra Leone, Togoland, Nigeria, the Cameroons (French and formerly German), the French and Belgian Congo, and (formerly German) East Africa.

The harassed French war cabinet spent the interval in interminable discussions of the alternatives to acceptance of such terms as they could get. Once, on June 20, the cabinet decided to move to Algiers and continue the war from there although an armistice must be made for metropolitan France. Daladier, Georges Mandel, minister of the interior, President Jeanneney of the Senate, and Edouard Herriot, president of the Chamber of Deputies, were advocates of that course, and made off for North Africa, most of them aboard the *Massilia*. Marshal Pétain urged, however, that it was the duty of the government to remain in France and share with the French people whatever fate fortune [or Hitler] might have in store for them, on pain of being no longer recognized as the government. Pierre Laval called upon President Lebrun and, by threatening as a member of the Chamber of Deputies to bring charges of treason against him if he left France, bullied the president into abandoning his plan to carry the seals of the republic to Algiers. Under orders from Darlan, upon receipt of news of the signing of the armistice the captain of the *Massilia* refused to take the passengers to Britain and delivered them instead, virtually as prisoners, to the Vichy-controlled French colonial authorities at Casablanca. M. Mandel was arrested by order of General Noguès and interned, and the plan to transfer the government to North Africa was dropped.[25]

[25] A judge who freed M. Mandel because he found no sufficient ground for his arrest was dismissed, and General Noguès rearrested the minister of the interior. Still a prisoner, Mandel was murdered by order of the Germans late in 1944. The execution of his murderers was ordered after the war by the government of liberated France. One of the charges on which Otto Abetz, wartime Nazi high commissioner for occupied France, was sentenced in Paris in July, 1949, to imprisonment for twenty years was joint responsibility, with others, for the murder of M. Mandel.

General de Gaulle escaped in a British plane to Britain, where after the armistice was signed he became the leader of the "Free French" forces, supported by the Allies, continuing the war for France although disowned, outlawed, and sentenced to death by the Pétain government. The unhappy French armistice delegation found Hitler awaiting them June 21 in Marshal Foch's old headquarters railway carriage, which had been taken by the Germans from a Paris war museum and replaced where it had stood November 11, 1918. Then Matthias Erzberger had had to sign an armistice agreement which Hitler had never permitted the world to forget and was intent upon avenging. In a characteristic preamble to the armistice terms, which he had General Keitel read to the French delegation, Hitler aired again his propaganda version of what he said had happened in 1918:

Trusting in the assurances given to the German Reich by the American President Wilson and confirmed by the Allied Powers, in November, 1918, the German Wehrmacht laid down its arms. So came to an end a war which the German people and its government had not wanted, and in which, in spite of an enormous preponderance of power, its enemies had not succeeded in defeating in any way decisively the German army, navy, or German airforce. . . . Word-breaking and perjury had conspired against a people which after a heroic resistance of more than four years had made the one fatal error of trusting in the promises of a democratic statesman.[26]

By the terms of the armistice agreement Germany occupied the northern three-fifths of France and all its English Channel and Atlantic coasts. France was deprived of the sources of 90 percent of its prewar iron output, 90 percent of its sugar-beet production, two-thirds of its coal, half of its wheat, and control of two-thirds of its people.

Free to choose its seat in the unoccupied territory, the Pétain government established a provisional capital in Vichy. All fortresses and coast fortifications in the occupied area were to be surrendered intact, with arms, munitions, contents, and plans. The French government had to obligate itself to turn over harbors, factories, railways, and communications systems, undamaged and in good order, and to compensate French owners for whatever the Germans needed and took from them. The German government stated that it intended, after the cessation of hostilities with England, to reduce its garrisons on the west coast to the essential minimum. It undertook also to give the French government all necessary facilities to enable it to administer

[26] E. Murawski, *Durchbruch im Westen* (Berlin, 1941), 291-322; Langer, *op. cit.*, 54-75. The preamble accused France and Britain of having made war on Germany without cause in September, 1939.

both occupied and nonoccupied areas from Paris but, alleging "technical difficulties," failed to keep its bargain.

The greatest concern was felt in Britain and the United States over the fate of the French navy and air force. Mr. Churchill had tried in vain to induce the French government to send both to Britain, or anywhere beyond the reach of the Axis powers. The United States ambassador had given Admiral Darlan, commander of the fleet, the first of what grew eventually into a long series of sharp warnings that to surrender the fleet to the Germans would mean permanent loss of the friendship and good will of the United States.

Neither Pétain nor Darlan was willing then or later to surrender the French fleet or control thereof to anyone. The armistice terms required that the fleet be assembled in ports to be named, and there demobilized. All warships outside France were to be recalled except those which might be designated to represent French interests in the colonial empire. The German government declared that it did not intend to use the French war vessels in the harbors of the occupied area except for coast defense and mine sweeping.

The principal French fleet was tied up at Toulon according to agreement. The British promptly immobilized the ships caught at Alexandria. To prevent the units at Oran from sailing to Toulon, and so being put again within reach of the Axis powers, the commander of a British task force summoned them to rejoin the British or to move beyond German reach and be immobilized. Upon the French admiral's refusal, the British fired upon and disabled several vessels. Only a few escaped and reached Toulon. By that unpleasant incident Pétain, Darlan, and many though not all other Frenchmen were further embittered against their former allies. Two great new battleships, nearing completion, escaped the Axis dragnet, *Jean Bart* finding anchorage in Casablanca harbor and *Richelieu* at Dakar. Several cruisers and destroyers and the aircraft carrier *Béarn*, with 156 American-made warplanes on board, stayed at Fort-de-France, Martinique, in the French West Indies, under the command of Admiral Georges Robert. The United States warned Germany and Italy sharply, June 17, that it would not, under the Monroe Doctrine, countenance the transfer of any territory in the Western Hemisphere from one non-American power to another.

There was less of the French air force left at the time of the armistice than of the fleet, and its surrender was more complete. All installations in the occupied zone were already operating as if German. All airfields and air-force ground installations in unoccupied

France had also to be turned over to the Germans and Italians, who could require them to be rendered unusable. Non-French planes caught in the unoccupied area were to be seized by the French and surrendered to the Germans. France had to order her airmen to surrender their planes without wrecking them, and to agree to treat as enemy (*feindlich*) any who tried to take off in violation of the surrender order.

France had to promise not to aid the enemies of Germany, and to prevent French soldiers or sailors from aiding them, or Frenchmen from joining their armed forces, or French ships, planes, or arms from going to Britain. So Frenchmen choosing, as did General de Gaulle and the "Free French," to disregard the armistice had to go on not only without the blessing of the government they no longer recognized but under the ban of its official disclaimer and condemnation. Vichy France had to agree, on the other hand, to give Germany and Italy the right of transit "between Germany and Italy" as they might demand. She had also to aid them in various ways, not least humiliating of which was to be the release of all those imprisoned for having aided the Germans, and the surrender to the Gestapo of those whom the Germans should name (i.e., the refugees to whom she had given asylum) in nonoccupied France and its protectorates and possessions. There was no place to hide. French prisoners of war were to remain prisoners until peace was concluded. German industry profited from their presence, and France was weakened by their absence.

The Nazi who had so long and so incessantly denounced the armistice terms of 1918 as too severe and the reparation claims of the Treaty of Versailles as exorbitant required France in 1940 to sign a blank check for the costs of the occupation, starting at 400,000,000 francs per day. Much more was eventually squeezed out of France in war matériel, services, and food and factory production—a German intention indicated in the terms of the armistice only by the provisions that the fugitive population of the occupied area should return, and that the French government should prevent the evacuation of goods from that area.

The armistice terms did not mention territorial cessions. Cessions were planned but were left for the peace.

Although the French had to agree to cease firing immediately, and had already generally ceased, hostilities were not to be terminated until six hours after the signing of a similar armistice agreement with

Italy.[27] The armistice was to hold France until the conclusion of peace, but the Axis powers might terminate it at any time if she failed to meet her obligations under it. Those obligations were indeed onerous.

It was a long armistice. All of the principal Vichy leaders—Pétain, Darlan, and Pierre Laval, vice-president of the council—anticipated an easy German victory over Britain, therefore a short armistice and an early peace. It was to them inconceivable that Britain should be so unrealistic as to persevere against such odds. Darlan did not believe that German invasion of Britain would be necessary. Neither government nor people, he thought, would have the courage to stand up under bombing from the air.

Laval, as a "man of sense," could imagine nothing but a Nazi victory. He thought it realistic for France to propitiate and collaborate with Germany, and to wish her to win quickly, so that peace could sooner be restored. "We have no other road to follow," he told the Chamber of Deputies June 24, "than that of loyal collaboration with Germany and Italy. I experience no embarrassment in speaking thus, for even in peacetime I favored such collaboration." Later he said openly that he hoped Germany would win the war, and privately that he would hail the day when Churchill, Eden, and other British leaders were lynched.

Little less bitter than Laval, Darlan told the United States ambassador that he would never send the French fleet to Britain, for fear Britain would not send it back. A British victory would be as bad for France, he said, as a German. He would rather scuttle the fleet than surrender it to either power. Even in German-occupied Paris there was some collaborationist opinion; but the Nazi, although they thought themselves very clever, were too clever to know how to use it.

Direct diplomatic relations between France and Britain had been broken off, indirect contact being maintained only through the Canadian minister, M. Dupuy, or through the British embassy (Ambassador Sir Samuel Hoare) in Madrid. Hoping to prevent the surrender of the French fleet, however, to hold to a minimum the active collaboration of nonoccupied France with Germany, if possible to prevent the Axis from gaining control of the French colonies and overseas possessions, and at worst to keep open a listening post on

---

[27] The last Maginot line forts were surrendered intact June 30, when French armistice officers were sent to order their surrender.

the German-dominated continent, the United States maintained an embassy at Vichy. Admiral Leahy was ambassador.

The movement to adapt national policies to the apparent realities of the moment was general. Italy prepared to attack the British troops in Egypt. Japan soon went into Indo-China and compelled China and the Allies to close the Burma Road. In an address to the general congress of delegates of the Soviet Union on March 29, Molotov announced that it was the intention of his government "peaceably" to reannex Bessarabia. He expected the announcement to command attention, and Rumanian Ambassador Gafencu duly noted and reported it. But instead of offering at once to cede the territory as the Soviet foreign minister had indicated he expected, King Carol of Rumania turned to Germany for a territorial guarantee. Immediately upon receipt of news of the surrender of King Leopold of Belgium, Carol indicated to his council of ministers that, having seen neutrality broken everywhere, he was ready to abandon it and invoke the aid of Germany against the Russian menace.[28]

King Carol did not know that Germany had already, by secret protocol in conjunction with the Nazi-Soviet nonaggression pact, licensed Russia to take Bessarabia. But there was also Bucovina. In June Molotov let the German Foreign Office know that the Soviets would expect German support for their claim on Bucovina, which he said was inhabited by Ukrainians. Germany would have preferred to guarantee Hungarian and Rumanian territory (except Bessarabia) against the USSR. But the Germans showed no surprise and gave no help or solace to the Baltic states when they were absorbed into the USSR on June 15, or to Rumania when Bessarabia and northern Bucovina were seized by the USSR immediately after the fall of France.[29]

Rumania had not been guaranteed by the Allies against attack by Russia. On July 2, 1940, she renounced her British-French guarantee against German aggression and aligned herself with the Nazi "new order."[30]

As soon as France had clearly come to the point of laying down her arms, Franco of Spain occupied the international zone at Tangier and began to indicate that he was ready, granted certain conditions and concessions, to share with his old allies, the Axis powers, the territorial fruits of their victory. He would want Gibraltar for Spain,

[28] Grigore Gafencu, *Prelude to the Russian Campaign* (London, 1945), 282-283.
[29] See pp. 536, 601.
[30] On July 2 the naturalization of William Joyce ("Lord Haw-Haw") as a German was completed.

and French Morocco, Oran, and part of Algiers, and certain other oddments around Río de Oro in West Africa; and he would need weapons, planes, war equipment, and food, all in advance. In June the Axis did not need his services badly enough to show much interest in his offer, although he protested his adherence to Hitler personally, to the German people, and to the cause for which they were fighting, and though he belabored Mussolini for help in bargaining with Hitler.[31]

The changes in the world mosaic during that momentous summer were not, however, all additions to the tail of the Nazi comet. Three weeks after the German occupation of Denmark, Iceland was occupied, on invitation, by the British. At the same time Greenland asked the United States for protection; and in July an unofficial United States protectorate over Greenland was announced. United States Undersecretary of State Sumner Welles condemned the Soviet absorption of the Baltic states. Far more significant, however, was material United States aid to Britain.

United States Aid to Britain

The people of the United States were not indifferent to the war. Few of them supposed that their safety and well-being would not be affected by its outcome. But noninterventionist opinion was strong, even after the fall of France. Few would have gone to war out of love or admiration for the British Empire. Many were distracted by Japan's continued aggression and increasingly evident expansionist ambitions in eastern Asia and the southwest Pacific. Japan had alerted American opinion by warning the United States and the Allies, just before the German invasion of the Netherlands, that she would brook no change in the status of the Netherlands East Indies, by her establishment on March 30, 1940, of a new puppet "Chinese national government" at Nanking, by her penetration of French Indo-China, accelerated after the fall of France, and by her success in compelling Britain to agree to cut off the flow of supplies through Hong Kong and over the Burma Road from Burma.

Although nearly all its people were still pacifist or pacific-minded, the United States was confronted in the summer of 1940 by a dan-

---

[31] Later in the year, when the Germans turned their attention to the Mediterranean, the discussion of a change by Spain from nonbelligerent to belligerent status was resumed. But Franco always wanted more than Hitler could or would give him, and would do nothing hazardous unless well paid in advance.

gerous situation and a number of brutal questions. Would it be vitally hurt or materially helped by the elimination of the British Empire as a major element in world affairs in eastern Asia and the southwest Pacific? Would it choose to face the prospect of dealing single-handed in that area with a victorious, confident, and bellicose Japan? Could it afford to see Britain eliminated as a counterweight to Nazi Germany in Europe or as a base for a potential counterattack for the liberation of occupied non-Nazi Europe if it should come to that? Could the United States view otherwise than with alarm even the remotest possibility of the appearance in the Atlantic of the combined German, French, and British fleets under Nazi control, using a conquered Britain as a base? President Roosevelt as a candidate for reëlection (for an unprecedented third term) and the Republican presidential candidate Wendell Willkie agreed publicly on the essential point that the vital interests of the United States would be badly hurt by such an outcome of the war in either hemisphere. At the same time both candidates supported the Burke-Wadsworth Act, signed by the president on September 16, while the presidential campaign was in progress, providing for compulsory military training on a selective service basis.

Although the trend of public opinion did not keep pace with the racing thoughts of the alert and global-minded president, it ran in the same direction as more and more people asked themselves the same sober questions, and as one startling Japanese or German victory after another indicated that those questions were not purely hypothetical. People mourned the fall of France, feared the fall of Britain, and began—many of them for the first time—to be apprehensive about the safety of the United States. Better to help Britain and the empire to survive than to face alone, in a fast-shrinking world, the conquerors of Britain and destroyers of the empire.

If President Roosevelt had needed to be told such things the plain-speaking British prime minister would have told him. Writing personally as a "former naval person" to the president on May 15, the day of the German breakthrough across the Meuse which led within a fortnight to the evacuation at Dunkirk, Mr. Churchill pointed out in his usual forthright and dramatic fashion that "the voice and force of the United States" might count for nothing if they were withheld too long. Britain needed immediately, he said, forty to fifty destroyers—old ones would do—several hundred airplanes of the latest type (to be replaced by others already on order and being built in the United States), and considerable quantities of anti-aircraft equipment and ammunition, and of steel. "We shall go on paying dollars for as long as we can," he wrote, "but I should like to feel reasonably sure that when we can pay no more you will give us the stuff all the same." He suggested at the same time that a United States naval squadron visit Irish ports, for fear the Germans might otherwise attempt an air-borne or parachute landing in Ireland.[32]

The month of June was critical for Britain. Her troops had returned from Dunkirk without their weapons or equipment, and the country was nearly destitute, militarily, on the ground. Only the absorption of the Germans in the completion of their conquest of France and their failure to solve the problems of air power, logistics, and an amphibious Channel crossing saved Britain from invasion then.

Aid was soon on its way from the United States, which took immediate steps to send arms to Britain and, as long as France was a belligerent, to France. The army and navy air forces turned in as "obsolete," for immediate shipment to the Allies, new or slightly used fighter planes and fighter bombers, and waited for newer ones from the factories. Out of the arsenals and stock piles, also treated as "surplus," came 600,000 infantrymen's rifles, 80,000 machine guns, nearly a thousand guns of the 75-mm. type made famous by their use in the first world war of the century, a million artillery shells, more than 100,000,000 rounds of rifle and machine-gun ammunition. Anxiously those who knew what was being done watched the convoys bearing arms which might enable the courageous people of embattled Britain to defend their island. Special trains waited at the British ports to carry the weapons with all speed to the reconstituted divisions and the new home guard.[33]

At the end of July, 1940, with the first consignments of small arms in hand but still in a time of "clamant need," Mr. Churchill reminded

---

[32] Winston Churchill, *The Second World War,* II, 24, 25.

[33] "Even though large tracts of Europe and many old and famous states have fallen or may fall into the grip of the Gestapo and all the odious apparatus of Nazi rule," said Mr. Churchill in the House of Commons June 4, just after Dunkirk, "we shall not flag or fail. We shall go on to the end. We shall fight in France, we shall fight on the seas and oceans, we shall fight with growing confidence and growing strength in the air; we shall defend our Island, whatever the cost may be, we shall fight on the beaches, we shall fight on the landing-grounds, we shall fight in the fields and in the streets, we shall fight in the hills; we shall never surrender; and even if, which I do not for a moment believe, this Island or a large part of it were subjugated and starving, then our Empire beyond the seas, armed and guarded by the British Fleet, would carry on the struggle until, in God's good time, the New World, with all its power and might, steps forth to the rescue and the liberation of the old." *Ibid.,* 118; Hansard, *British Parliamentary Debates,* Vol. 361, p. 796.

President Roosevelt of his request of May 15 for some destroyers. In reply it was suggested that some reconditioned over-age United States destroyers might be traded to Britain for long-term leases on some British bases in the Western Hemisphere. Both the neutral character and the legality of the transaction were challenged in the United States, but Attorney General Robert H. Jackson found it legal under an old Supreme Court decision authorizing the president to dispose of surplus navy vessels and unneeded naval material. Although it might have been difficult to prove, if challenged, that the vessels were not needed, it was argued that the whole transaction greatly strengthened the national defense, especially of the Panama Canal. The attorney general called the arrangement constitutional as an executive agreement which would not require Senate ratification, as a treaty would have done. The "neutrality" of the transaction was rather unconvincingly defended on the ground that, although the vessels were being turned over to a belligerent by a nation which had not formally renounced neutrality, they had not been built specifically for that purpose. The undeclared position of the United States was thereafter rather nonbelligerent than neutral. No one expected the Nazi to look upon such aid to their enemy as other than unfriendly; but Hitler chose at that time not to permit his resentment to bring him into war with the United States.[34]

In a series of transfers between September 9 and November 26, fifty old destroyers reconditioned at a cost of $20,478,445 (original cost $75,477,348) were turned over by the United States navy to the British. At the same time, although they were not offered as a *quid pro quo*, ninety-nine-year leases were given by the British on naval bases in the Bahamas, Jamaica, St. Lucia, Trinidad, Antigua, British Guiana, Bermuda, and Newfoundland, invaluable for defense of the waters off the eastern coast.

If the British had not held their own it would have been advantageous to them, as well as to the peoples of the Western Hemisphere,

[34] In *Their Finest Hour*, Mr. Churchill wrote in 1949: "The transfer to Great Britain of fifty American warships was a decidedly unneutral act by the United States. It would, according to all the standards of history, have justified the German government in declaring war upon them. The President judged that there was no danger, and I felt there was no hope, of this simple solution of many difficulties. . . . The transfer of destroyers to Britain in August, 1940, was an event which brought the United States definitely nearer to us and to the war, and it was the first of a long succession of increasingly unneutral acts in the Atlantic which were of the utmost service to us. It marked the passage of the United States from being neutral to being nonbelligerent. Although Hitler could not afford to resent it, all the world . . . understood the significance of the gesture." *The Second World War*, II, 404.

to have the bases in the hands of the United States, which would defend them.

Although Mr. Churchill permitted himself to speak somewhat disparagingly of the "intrinsic value of these antiquated and inefficient craft," he made no secret of the fact that Britain needed then whatever she could get, or that she found them useful. Feelings were aroused in Parliament over his trading away any territory, outright or on lease. So the prime minister found it politic to emphasize in Parliament his personal satisfaction over such a recognition of a community of interest, and over the prospect that the British Empire and the United States would thereafter have to be "somewhat mixed up together in some of their affairs for mutual and general advantage." He was glad to see the United States interest itself in the outcome of the war. To President Roosevelt he spoke of the two peoples as "two friends in danger helping each other as far as we can." He assured the president that it was the settled policy of the British government to offer the facilities in question, as a means of making it easier to protect the Atlantic seaboard, without stipulating for anything in return, no matter whether Mr. Roosevelt found himself able or unable to deliver the destroyers and other war materials.[35]

The swelling stream of war goods shipments put a heavy strain upon the dollar reserves of the United Kingdom and its people. In compliance with United States legislation, those shipments were at first paid for in cash. By November, 1940, the $4,500,000,000 balance with which the country went into the war, augmented by $2,000,000,000 earned by exports and including $335,000,000 worth of British-owned assets convertible into dollars in the United States and requisitioned by the British government for sterling, had been reduced to $2,000,000,000. That would not pay for half of what had then been ordered and not yet delivered, and ten times as much was needed.

On December 8 the prime minister again, as on May 15, asked President Roosevelt outright for assistance in amounts greater than could immediately be paid for. As usual, he referred to his request not as an appeal for aid but as "a statement of the minimum action necessary" to achieve the defeat of "Nazi and Fascist tyranny," which he called "a matter of high consequence to the people of the United

[35] House of Commons, August 20, Hansard, *op. cit.*, Vol. 364, p. 1171; letters dated August 22, 25, and 27. Churchill, *Second World War,* II, 408-412. Only two of the bases, in Newfoundland and Bermuda, were accepted as free gifts "generously given and gladly received." Antigua was offered in addition to the seven bases originally indicated by the United States.

States and to the Western Hemisphere." As for Britain, he would have called it "false economy and misdirected prudence" to have worried too much in such desperate circumstances about what would happen when the dollar supply ran out.[36]

In the face of his knowledge that the tripartite pact of September 27, 1940, was clearly directed at least as much against the United States as against Soviet Russia (Germany, Italy, and Japan having agreed to go to war against any nation then neutral which might make war upon any one of them), President Roosevelt moved as fast as he could move public opinion with him in the direction of unlimited aid to Britain short of open and declared war. At a press conference December 17, with a homely reference to lending his neighbor a garden hose to help him put out a fire, then asking for his hose back but not for pay, he put out the provocative suggestion that the best immediate defense of the United States would be the successful self-defense and survival of Great Britain. In his "fireside chat" by radio December 29, he said:

A nation can have peace with the Nazi only at the price of total sur-render. . . .

Such a dictated peace would be no peace at all. It would be only another armistice, leading to the most gigantic armament race and the most devastating trade wars in history. . . .

It is no exaggeration to say that all of us, in all the Americas, would be living at the point of a Nazi gun—a gun loaded with explosive bullets, economic as well as military. . . . To keep war away from our country and our people . . . we must be the great arsenal of democracy. For us this is an emergency as serious as war itself.

In an address to Congress January 6, 1941, asking for billions of dollars' worth of weapons and supplies to be lent or leased to the nations defending themselves against Nazi-fascist aggression, the president defined "the four essential human freedoms" endangered everywhere by that aggression, which he hoped would be realized and secured in the postwar world: freedom of speech and expression, freedom of worship, freedom from want, and freedom from fear.

House of Representatives bill 1776, popularly known as the "Lend-Lease Act," was introduced January 10. After earnest debate, it was passed by the House February 8, 260 to 165, and by the Senate March 8, 60 to 31. The house accepted certain Senate amendments March 11, 317 to 71. The bill gave the president, until June 30,

[36] Churchill, *Second World War*, II, 557-567.

1943, extraordinary discretionary powers to authorize the manufacture and the transfer, by sale, exchange, or lease, of any defense article for the government of any country whose defense he deemed vital to the defense of the United States. He was left free to determine, with such advice as he might seek (and he sought much) what war materials or weapons should be treated as "defense articles" and what nations should be aided for the reason that their defense was considered vital to the defense of the United States.

Until the United States was a belligerent, lend-lease was a one-way operation, all outgo and no income. The initial congressional appropriation to support it was seven billion dollars. It unquestionably encouraged resistance to the Axis powers and to Japan, especially in Britain at a time when aid and encouragement were welcome. The first appropriation toward it was clearly only an installment on an undetermined and possibly unlimited commitment ($49,096,125,000 by the end of 1945). Its cost in cash was not, however, the principal reason for the concern it caused among the people of the United States. It marked the end not merely of appeasement but of anything that could be called neutrality. It committed the United States to a course of action called "short of war" but not far short of it; and the decisions which might bring the country nearer to "a shooting war" were entrusted to the president, not to Congress, to which the constitution had reserved the right to declare war. There was some personal distrust of the president and widespread apprehension over the extension of the presidential powers, although Congress had consented to the extension for a stated period.

In the five years which followed the passage of the Lend-Lease Act, the British Empire received more than thirty billion dollars' worth of invaluable aid and returned more than six billion dollars' worth in the form of supplies and services to United States expeditionary forces. Each gave the other whatever help it could.

Britain and the Blitz

THE INVASION MENACE

After the fall of France, Britain and her empire stood alone but for the aid of the United States, which was barely enough and arrived only just in time. It was not to be expected that the triumphant German army, fresh from its quick and comparatively easy conquest of Norway, the Low Countries, and France, would be frightened off by the defiance hurled at it, in an attempt to hearten both the French and the British peoples, by the prime minister just after Dunkirk.[37] Either an air-borne or a sea-borne invasion or both, across the Channel or by way of Eire, preceded in either case by bombing from the air, seemed imminent. In the House of Commons, June 18, Mr. Churchill spoke again for his people:

What General Weygand called the Battle of France is over. I expect that the Battle of Britain is about to begin. Upon this battle depends the survival of Christian civilization. Upon it depends our own British life, and the long continuity of our institutions and our Empire. The whole fury and might of the enemy must very soon be turned on us. Hitler knows that he will have to break us in this island or lose the war. If we can stand up to him, all Europe may be free and the life of the world may move forward into broad, sunlit uplands. But if we fail, then the whole world, including the United States, including all that we have known and cared for, will sink into the abyss of a new Dark Age, made more sinister, and perhaps more protracted, by the lights of perverted science. Let us therefore brace ourselves to our duties, and so bear ourselves that, if the British Empire and its Commonwealth last for a thousand years, men will say, "This was their finest hour."

The people braced themselves and did their duty. The bombing—called "the blitz"—did them grievous harm; but the danger of invasion was averted. It was never in fact quite as serious as they then supposed. The Wehrmacht had outrun Hitler's plans. He was not ready in June or July, 1940, to invade England, because he had not supposed that a long war or an invasion would be necessary. He had started the war in 1939 with less than fifty submarines ready, half of which were of only 250 tons each. To have won quickly against Britain he would have needed several hundred, perhaps a thousand. To win the air war over Britain in 1940 he needed more first-rate long-range fighter aircraft than he had, and to carry an invasion army across the Channel and over the beaches he needed special landing craft and amphibians with which no army in Europe was then equipped. Although he shared Göring's confidence in the air arm (Luftwaffe), his advisers would have seen to it that he made, beforehand, more nearly adequate preparations for an invasion if he had seriously supposed he would find it necessary to make one.

The course of events, captured German documents, and postwar interrogation of many of the principals subsequently indicated that Hitler always hoped, until it was too late to hope, that Britain would

[37] House of Commons, June 4. See footnote 33, *supra*.

capitulate without being invaded except by bombers and strafing fighter planes—that the object lessons she had seen, the hardships incidental to the blockade he thought the Luftwaffe could impose, the punishment she would take from the air, and the threat of invasion would be enough to break the morale of her people and to bring them soon to terms.

Before Dunkirk the German armor had mysteriously slowed down. The comparative success of the evacuation had been due to many causes, among which the tenacity of the resistance at Calais, the counteroffensive of the British air arm, the hardihood of the rescuers, and splendid discipline among the rescued were not to be unduly discounted. Abundant postwar German testimony, however, and contemporary German records captured in 1945, which would have been found incredible if taken in 1940, indicated that both armor and air force had been almost unaccountably held back from total destruction of the defeated Allied forces. Army group commander General Gerd von Rundstedt wished to give his armored forces time to regroup, refit, and recuperate after their hazardous and exhausting dash across France. Both he and Hitler thought it essential to refurbish their favorite offensive weapon immediately, so as more effectively to strike or threaten France with it and quickly to deprive Britain of further French support.[38]

The postwar German explanation was that Hitler hoped then to arrive at an agreement with Britain without further military operations against her after completing the conquest of France, so did not wish to drive her beyond the point of no reconciliation.[39]

Not knowing all that was in Hitler's mind, but fully aware of the aroused spirit of the British peoples and of the rapid improvement of their military situation since the nadir at Dunkirk, Mr. Churchill wrote to the prime ministers of the commonwealth nations June 16 in a tone of complete confidence: "I do not regard the situation as

[38] After the war, von Rundstedt blamed Hitler for the failure, charging that the Führer had been misled by maps which showed the terrain around Dunkirk as impassable for tanks. Commander in Chief of the Army von Brauchitsch ordered a vigorous attack. Von Rundstedt delayed the order, while von Kluge and Kleist, commanding the armor, waited for permission to strike.

[39] Statement based upon interrogations of Nazi Foreign Minister Ribbentrop, Baron von Neurath and Dr. Paul Schmidt of the German Foreign Office, General Paul Warlimont, deputy chief of the operations staff of the German high command (OKW), and others, and upon interpretation of internal evidence in the directives of July 2 and 16 and others. Hitler ordered that the air war and invasion should be planned, prepared for, and "under certain conditions carried out if necessary." Similarly, however, on March 11, 1938, he had said that he intended to invade Austria only if other means should fail. *Documents on German Foreign Policy, 1918-1945,* Series D, Vol. I, p. 568.

having passed beyond our strength. . . . I do not see why we should not be able to meet it. . . . I do not think it by any means impossible that we may so maul them that they will find daylight attacks too expensive. . . . No one can predict or guarantee the course of a life-and-death struggle of this character, but we shall certainly enter upon it in good heart." If they had known the uncertainties then beclouding the strange mind of Hitler, and the bickering and hesitation in his high command, they might have entered upon it in even better heart.[40]

THE BATTLE OF BRITAIN

The air war over the English Channel and the southern coastal areas of England, designed to draw out and destroy the British fighter air force, began in earnest July 10, 1940. The Germans were in superior numbers, and their best fighter aircraft had at first the added advantages of greater speed and faster rate of climb. The British fighters were more maneuverable and better armed. An advantage of fighting over or near their own territory was that many of the British pilots, though shot down, and some of their disabled planes, could be saved to fight again. To the Germans, every man or plane shot down was lost. They lost twice as many as the British, but were sending over several times as many.

After ten days of the blitz, Hitler made an ostensible "peace offer," in a harangue to the Reichstag and diplomatic representations by way of Sweden, the United States, and the Vatican. It would have been a one-sided and worthless truce, another treaty dictated by the man who had railed so at the Treaty of Versailles as a *Diktat*; but he said he owed it to his conscience to appeal to common sense. His tone alone, like that of the kaiser in 1916, would have been enough to guarantee that his gesture could elicit only a negative response. He was no vanquished foe begging favors, he said, but the victor speaking in the name of reason. He could see no reason why the war should go on and was grieved to think of the sacrifices it must claim. Britain had only to refrain from interfering on the continent of Europe, and her empire would be guaranteed. The same day, he promoted nine generals, including Keitel, to the rank of field marshal, Jodl to be a general, and Halder and Falkenhorst to be colonel generals.[41]

Hitler's speech of July 19 was heard in Britain, and the British Broadcasting Corporation and press gave him his answer without

[40] *The Second World War,* II, 195-196.
[41] It was just then that Hitler was most indifferent to Franco's unsolicited suggestion that Spain become a belligerent as his ally.

waiting for official prompting or permission. The government did not reply. Its reticence and its perseverance were incomprehensible to Ribbentrop and Hitler.

So the German high command continued to make plans, and the navy to collect self-propelled barges and other improvised cross-Channel transport, for an invasion of southern England. But the plans were not as well coördinated as was usually to be expected of the German staffs, or as carefully prepared as for the invasion of Norway. There was bickering between the three armed forces— jealousies, and recriminations which the supreme command (OKW, *Oberkommando Wehrmacht*) failed to eliminate. The chief of staff of the army, Colonel General Halder, called it suicide to funnel an expeditionary force through the narrow cross-Channel corridor which was all that the naval staff, headed by Admiral Raeder, thought could be held and controlled for the purpose. Hitler compromised. He ordered plans made for landing the Sixteenth and Ninth armies at points all along the coast from Folkestone almost to Portsmouth. Nightly British bombing raids along the French-Belgian-Dutch "invasion coast" destroyed some of the transports, tugs, trawlers, and barges collected there; but enough transport survived the bombing, or could have been brought in, to carry a formidable expeditionary force. Troops and transport had to wait, however, for the air umbrella which must cover an opposed crossing in the teeth of British naval power, and without which no beachhead could be held or exploited. The Luftwaffe must first secure control of the air over the Channel and over England; and that it was unable to do.

"If after eight days of intensive air war the Luftwaffe has not achieved considerable destruction of the enemy's air force, harbors, and naval forces," Hitler wrote to Admiral Raeder on July 31, "the operation will have to be put off till May, 1941." Under the Führer's Directive 17, the air war was intensified in August, directed toward destroying the British air forces, fields, airplane factories, and sources of supply, then at the harbors and at London. Warships and shipping, Göring and Hitler thought, could wait.

More than a thousand German bombers participated in the August and September raids, and more than sixteen hundred fighters. On one of the most crucial days, August 15, the Luftwaffe sent a hundred bombers and forty long-range fighter planes over the Tyneside and lost thirty of them—mostly heavy Heinkel bombers—to seven British squadrons that had been recuperating in the north from constant strenuous fighting in the south. Eight hundred German planes were over southern England that day. Then and again on September 15 the last British reserve squadrons were engaged. During the last week of August and the first week of September, while the issue hung in the balance, the British lost a fourth of their thousand trained fighter pilots and nearly half a thousand planes. "Never in the field of human conflict," said Mr. Churchill in the House of Commons August 20, "was so much owed by so many to so few."

Then in September Göring gave the southern airfields and their defending squadrons a respite by turning his attention principally to London. The German navy would have preferred to see him attack the British navy, naval bases, and port facilities other than those to be used for the supply of the invasion forces. It objected strenuously to the "absolute air war" fought without reference to the needs of the navy or the "Operation Sea-Lion," as the invasion plan was called. But Göring thought that the air war, alone, would soon bring a surrender. Ribbentrop told Stalin on October 13 that Germany had already won the war. The only question left was how long it might take the British to recognize and admit the fact of their country's complete collapse.[42] So, hoping that, when sufficiently softened by pounding from the air and worn down by the constant threats of invasion, Britain would prudently capitulate, Hitler hesitated to take the risk or pay the cost of an invasion. His military intelligence reports meanwhile overestimated Britain's defensive strength as seriously as Hitler and his foreign minister underestimated her tenacity.[43]

On September 15, fifty-six German planes were shot down over Britain. On September 17 the invasion, already thrice postponed, was indefinitely deferred; but ostensible and ostentatious preparations for it were continued as a military and political threat, and the bombing meanwhile went on. On October 15 nearly five hundred planes dropped several hundred tons of high explosive and several scores of thousands of incendiary bombs on London. A month later Coventry was subjected at night to an attempt at obliteration bombing. About four hundred people were killed, and the Germans threatened to obliterate other British cities in their turn. London night after night, Birmingham, Sheffield, Liverpool, and other cities suffered heavy

---

[42] *Nazi-Soviet Relations,* 210.

[43] It would be difficult to determine whether the exaggerated accounts of British readiness to repel attack were the product of German ineptitude or of treason. Admiral Canaris, director of military intelligence, was, until his execution for complicity in the assassination plot of July, 1944, involved in most of the conspiracies against Hitler.

damage and many thousands of civilian casualties. The most destructive fire raid of the winter was on London the night of December
29-30. It devastated great areas. The British countered with night
bombing raids on Hamburg, Essen, Danzig, Dresden, Cologne,
Düsseldorf, Berlin, and other German cities, but "took," that winter,
more than they were able to "give back."

TECHNOLOGY OF DEFENSE

Few of the fears with which the British people faced the prospect
of war went unrealized. Although both sides contemplated the use
of gas, neither chose to be the first to resort to it. New forms of aerial
attack were constantly being tried, against which new defenses had
to be improvised.

Radio was used, both offensively and defensively, in communications and as a direction and range finder. Refinements of the latter
were radar, sonar, and the proximity fuse, in the development of which
American and British ingenuity and experience were eventually
pooled to mutual advantage.

Tampering with German radio beams sent out for the guidance
of night-flying bombers succeeded somewhat in diminishing the
accuracy of night attacks. Aerial barrages of anti-aircraft rockets
and gunfire, and long wire streamers, sometimes with aerial mines
attached, trailing from balloons or parachutes, were ingenious and
expensive experiments. The most effective anti-aircraft weapons were
the fighter plane—some night fighters were used—and radar-directed
guns using shells armed with the proximity fuse. The proximity fuse
would explode a missile if it came near enough to a target. For use
against infantry vehicles, but especially for anti-aircraft, this was
better than a time fuse, the setting of which depended for effectiveness
upon the accuracy of a hastily formed estimate of the range, direction,
and speed of a moving target (which might be taking evasive action),
or a contact fuse, which was effective only if detonated by actual contact with a target. A direct hit on a high-flying plane or on a dive
bomber bearing directly down upon the gunner and presenting its
thinnest silhouette was difficult to score. So the new fuse was a
revolutionary scientific development. Of these most useful weapons,
however, only the fighter plane and an early form of the range and
direction finder were available in the first year of the war, and planes
could not be used over an area where anti-aircraft fire was being
used.

People not actively engaged on air-raid defense duty were usually ordered to take shelter while a raid was on; but the numbers of air-raid wardens and of air-raid precautions (ARP) steadily increased. With the beginning of the incendiary raids more civilians had to stay out during raids, in the streets and on the housetops as "fire watchers" or fire fighters or for rescue work, while trained personnel manned the anti-aircraft defenses. Civilian casualties from June, 1940, to June, 1941, were 43,381 killed and 50,856 seriously injured; but provision for the hospitalization of the injured was always more than adequate.

DEFENSE OF THE SEA LANES

Again as from 1914 to 1918, Britain was partially blockaded, and the problem of keeping the sea lanes open was vital. Although the German submarine and cruiser strength was inadequate to maintain tight blockade, the undersea and surface raiders took a heavy toll of shipping; and shortages of food and war materials were always just around the corner.

Even the harbor mouths and coastal waters were made hazardous for a time by the magnetic mine. This menace to the seafarer was dropped, usually by parachute from a low-flying plane at night, into shallow water where it could lie submerged and invisible in the mud until activated by the change induced in the earth's magnetic field by the hull of a passing ship. This was eventually countered by a demagnetization process known as "degaussing," but at the cost of time and some other inconvenience, and not until after heavy losses had been sustained.

During the summer of 1940 several German raiders disguised as peaceful merchantmen were at large in the Atlantic and one (*Schiff* 45, *Komet* which had completed the northeast passage with the help of Russian icebreakers) in the Pacific. By the end of September, 1940, those in the Atlantic had sunk thirty-six ships, totaling 235,000 tons.

In November the recently completed pocket battleship *Scheer* sortied into the North Atlantic. On November 5 *Scheer* was engaged by the armed British merchantman *Jervis Bay*, on convoy escort duty. Like a wolf among sheep guarded by a devoted dog, the pocket battleship sank the *Jervis Bay* with two hundred men on board, and five ships of the convoy: 47,000 tons, 208 merchant seamen. She then went on to the West Indies and South Atlantic. No such fate as that of the *Admiral Graf Spee* awaited her on that voyage.[44] When she returned to Kiel in April, 1941, she had sunk sixteen ships, 90,000

[44] See pp. 547-548.

tons. The heavy cruisers *Hipper, Scharnhorst,* and *Gneisenau* were also at large in the Atlantic in the autumn of 1940, based on Brest.

In full control of the northern and western shores of France, with land-based planes doing ocean reconnaissance for a submarine fleet based in Bay of Biscay ports, the Germans were in a position to make all Atlantic approaches to the British Isles extremely hazardous. In November Admiral Dönitz of the U-boat fleet moved his command post from Paris to Lorient, and from there directed by radio the first "wolf pack" attacks, with what he called "very good results." The only good defense, except the speed and luck upon which some of the fastest ships depended, going it alone, was the convoy system. Convoy was not a perfect solution, however. Admiral Dönitz said later that it merely bunched his targets for him. Ships lost days of what might have been good steaming time waiting for convoy or proceeding at the pace of the slowest. Their usefulness to their owners was correspondingly reduced. Operating costs were at the same time greatly increased, by rising insurance rates and the higher wages and bonuses without which seamen would not man the ships. Actual sinkings represented, therefore, only a fraction of the total losses and inconvenience imposed upon the shippers by the threat of sinking, and only a fraction of the diminution of deliveries.

There were never enough warships available for convoy escort duty; but more bases for the escorts were also needed. The western approaches, north and south of Ireland, were especially dangerous to the shipping funneled through them to west-coast British ports. Bases were available in northeast Ireland, which was part of the United Kingdom, but not in neutral Eire. Iceland was a valuable base. For convoys around Africa, the Spanish or Portuguese Atlantic islands would have afforded useful escort bases; but none was then available. Wavering pro-Axis neutral dictator Franco of Spain had not given the German navy or Luftwaffe the use of Spanish island bases, or Britain an adequate pretext for seizing them. Portugal's situation was not altogether different from Spain's.

At the western tip of Africa, Dakar in friendly hands would have been an invaluable base, in enemy hands a dagger at the throat. There seemed always to be a danger that a garrison obedient to Vichy France might willingly or unwillingly permit it to be used as an operating or supply base by Axis U-boats, surface raiders, or patrol planes. While so held, it would certainly not help the British but would be at least potentially dangerous to them.

In September, 1940, an attempt was made by a Free French and

British task force to take Dakar. The Free French forces were led by General de Gaulle, who had convinced himself that the garrison would welcome him and join him without fighting. The secret had been badly kept, however. Vichy, warned in time, and sensitive about its sovereignty over what remained of the French colonial empire, had sent three cruisers and three destroyers from the Mediterranean, past the British at Gibraltar, to Dakar ahead of them. The garrison, so reinforced and incited to resistance, obeyed its commander, who obeyed the Vichy government and resisted de Gaulle. Tactical surprise was not achieved. The British naval forces approached Dakar and shelled it, September 23-24-25, but found themselves at a disadvantage against the fortress guns on shore and the fifteen-inch guns of the immobile and uncompleted battleship *Richelieu*, which showed its gun turrets and range-finding equipment to be very much alive. De Gaulle failed to effect a landing, and the attempt was abandoned. De Gaulle went on to Duala in French Equatorial Africa and established himself there.

After the French and British failure at Dakar, President Roosevelt offered to purchase *Richelieu*, which had helped to defend that strong point and port, and *Jean Bart*, a similar great battleship then known to be at Casablanca and reported to be uncompleted. Marshal Pétain replied that he could not sell the ships. Their sale was forbidden, he said, by the terms of the French-German armistice agreement and, even if it were not contrary to the agreement, Germany would not permit it. He promised, however, not to let them be used against the British but to keep them where they were or to notify the president in advance if they were to be moved. If he had sold the ships, he would have hoped to recover them after the war.[45]

The potential value of Atlantic island bases for convoy escorts was again indicated on Christmas Day, 1940, when an outward-bound convoy carrying thirty thousand men to the Middle East was attacked by the German heavy cruiser *Hipper*, off the Azores. The transport *Empire Trooper* was damaged but succeeded in putting into Gibraltar for repairs. *Hipper* was engaged by the cruiser *Berwick* of the convoy escort. Both were damaged, but *Hipper* made off in the mist and returned to Brest.

By the end of 1940 the rearmament of Great Britain had proceeded to the point where sizable troop reinforcements could be sent to join the forces of the other members of the commonwealth, and the British

[45] *Jean Bart* fired on the United States landing forces in November, 1942. See p. 670.

and Indian troops withdrawn from India, in North Africa and the Near and Middle East. The Axis powers, however, were turning their attention also to southeastern Europe, northern Africa, and the Mediterranean.

THE MEDITERRANEAN REGION, 1940-1941

Spain and Vichy France

GIBRALTAR AND THE ATLANTIC ISLANDS

Like other European enemies of Britain, the Axis powers would have liked to take Gibraltar and exclude British ships from the eastern Mediterranean. Then Malta also might have fallen, and Axis contact with North Africa would have been made easier and less hazardous. As Hitler's mind began to turn away from Britain in September, 1940, it naturally turned toward Gibraltar. What he could do there depended, however, upon relations between Franco and Pétain, between Falangist Spain and Vichy France. If he permitted Franco to take Oran, would French North Africa immediately align itself with the enemies of the Axis powers? That would have hurt Germany, which drew supplies from Africa through the unoccupied part of France.

Taking for granted that the United States or Britain would seize the Azores or the Canary Islands if Portugal or Spain became an actual belligerent, Hitler thought it would be expedient and feasible for the Luftwaffe to anticipate the seizure if either of the peninsular nations should abandon its position of profitable and rather pro-Axis technical neutrality. Approached on the subject in Berlin in mid-September, Ramon Serrano Suñer, Franco's avowedly pro-Axis brother-in-law who was soon to be made foreign minister of Spain, indignantly rejected the idea of an alien occupation of any of the Spanish islands but suggested Portuguese Madeira.

The idea of the seizure of the Atlantic islands was not soon abandoned. On October 29, 1940, Major von Falkenstein of the German supreme command staff wrote into the record of a "Führer conference": "The Führer is at present occupied with the question of the occupation of the Atlantic islands with a view to the prosecution of the war against America at a later date. Deliberations on this subject are being embarked upon here."[46]

(In view of persistent reports that the Nazi were about to seize

[46] *Nazi Conspiracy and Aggression* III, 376. This statement was confirmed by testimony of Hermann Göring in his trial at Nuremberg. Hitler's War directive 18 of November 12, 1940, directed the commander in chief of the Wehrmacht to

the Azores, President Roosevelt on May 22, 1941, ordered the United States Navy to be ready in thirty days to occupy the islands; but the operation was not necessary then. In October, 1943, by invoking the six-hundred-year-old British-Portuguese alliance and promising protection if Spain should attack Portugal, the British government secured the use of the Azores as a base with Portuguese collaboration. The United States was then also permitted to use the islands. They proved useful as an antisubmarine patrol base and as a landing and refueling point in the air-ferry and transport service.)

THE PROMISE OF FRENCH COLLABORATION

Plans for an attack upon Gibraltar usually presupposed the use of the German air force and German or Spanish artillery firing from Spanish bases, to drive British ships away from Gibraltar and to deny the British the use of their airfield there, and right of passage for German troops through unoccupied France and Spain. Marshal Pétain told United States Ambassador Leahy that Hitler had asked for right of passage. At conferences with Laval at Montoire October 22, Franco at Hendaye October 23, and Pétain at Montoire October 24, Hitler tried to compromise the interests of his collaborators. Laval professed always to have advocated collaboration with Germany against Britain, which he said had rushed France into war and then given her little help. Franco, who had professed "unchangeable and sincere adherence" to the German leader and the German cause, would "gladly fight at Germany's side," but only if promised Morocco and much of Algeria including Oran, and only if Spain were supplied in advance with weapons, munitions, and food. Meanwhile, the plan must be kept secret lest Britain prevent the delivery of corn and wheat already contracted for in Canada; and Franco refueled German submarines and sent on to Germany part of the American oil he was securing as part of the price of his neutrality, and strategic war materials such as wolfram which he had agreed to sell to the United States or Britain.

Hitler told all three (Laval, Franco, and Pétain) that Spain might take only such part of French North Africa as France might be compensated for out of the colonial possessions of the British Empire. With the stipulation that France should be so compensated, Pétain agreed "in principle" to a policy of collaboration, and specifically to a statement that the Axis powers and France had "an identical inter-

---

study how to "support the Spanish garrison" of the Canaries and seize the Cape Verde Islands immediately, and whether to occupy the Azores. Troops were to be ready to move into Portugal from Spain. *Ibid.*, VI, 957-960.

est in seeing the defeat of England accomplished as soon as possible."
It was agreed that the French government would support, within the
limits of its ability, the measures which the Axis powers might take
to that end.[47]

North Africa and Egypt

The conquest of Egypt was left at first to the Italians, as they
wished. Under command of Marshal Graziani an Italian force outnumbering the British forces there approximately five to one invaded
Egypt in September but was stopped between Sidi Barrani and Mersa
Matruh. General Wavell was in command of the defense. So as to tie
down as much British tonnage as possible and keep British troops
engaged as far away as possible from the German *Lebensraum* and
the Rumanian oil fields, Hitler offered to send a stiffening of German
armored forces to reinforce his ally in Egypt. Knowing, however, that
where the Germans went they took command and credit, Mussolini
declined their help there in October. In December the British went
over to the offensive and by February, 1941, had driven the Italians
out of Egypt and Cyrenaica as far west as El Agheila. Then the Axis
forces in North Africa were strengthened by the infusion of the German *Afrika Korps*, ably led by General Erwin Rommel, while Wavell's
force was weakened by the necessity of sending aid to Greece. By early
April the Axis forces were again in northwestern Egypt; but Italy had
lost her status as an autonomous ally of Germany.[48]

Southeastern Europe

GREECE AND BULGARIA

The last major operation undertaken independently by Mussolini,
without the previous knowledge or consent of the German high command, was the invasion of Greece from Albania October 28, 1940.

[47] W. L. Langer, *op. cit.*, 92-95; Churchill, *The Second World War,* II, 524-525;
Paul   Schmidt,   *Statist   auf   diplomatischer   Bühne*   (Bonn,   1949),   499-506.
Apologists for Pétain subsequently maintained that he hoped not to have to make good
on his sorry bargain. Whether Hitler would have made good on his was debatable.
He was then only about three months away from his "last peace offer" to Britain, in
which he had offered to leave the empire intact. Hitler's intentions as to Belgian
Equatorial Africa in that matter were not then made clear.

[48] Mussolini had insisted that Italian planes should participate in the bombing
of Britain. In the night of November 11-12, 1940, Italian bombers flew their only
mission over Britain, and the British claimed thirteen of them shot down. The
same night, in a strike destined thirteen months later to be comparable with Pearl
Harbor, except that the men involved on both sides at Taranto knew that their

(Hitler and Mussolini were in Florence October 28, but the letter in which Mussolini said he had given his partner a few days' notice had not reached him.) Italian troops reached their point of farthest advance—which was not very far—into Greece in November. By March, 1941, they had been pushed back much farther into Albania than they had ever gone into Greece. Clearly "sawdust Caesar" Mussolini would need help there as well as in Africa; and if the British were to be prevented from threatening the Rumanian oil fields by establishing airfields in Greece, German troops must prevent them.

Italian failures in North Africa and Greece led to the abandonment of grandiose plans which had entertained the German high command and Foreign Office during the winter—to move down to the Mediterranean coasts of both the Balkan and the Iberian peninsulas without fighting for either, then a three-pronged offensive via Gilbraltar (von Rundstedt), Tripolitania and Egypt (von Bock), and Bulgaria and the Dardanelles (List), through Turkey and the Near East to Suez, thus encircling the Mediterranean and excluding Britain from it. If the conquest of Egypt had gone fast and far enough, it might have been possible to close in on Turkey from the south, via Palestine and Syria.

By February, 1941, Operation Felix (Spain, Gibraltar, and the Atlantic islands) as well as Sea-Lion (invasion of Britain) was given up. Hitler and Ribbentrop were trying to incite Japan to attack the United States, so as to deprive Britain of the hope of further American aid, and peace and nonaggression pacts were made with Bulgaria, and soon afterward with Yugoslavia and Turkey—all this as preparation for an eventual invasion of Russia and a quick campaign in Greece. The Greek campaign was an inconvenience which the Germans would presumably have preferred to avoid. But they could not be indifferent to the threat, to Italy and to the Rumanian oil fields, of British troops in Greece, or to the possibility that an Axis campaign through Bulgaria into Greece would arouse Yugoslavia to hostile action.

Bulgaria joined the German-Italian-Japanese alliance March 1, 1941, and German troops—680,000 more or less, already accumulated in Rumania, devouring Rumanian food reserves—moved into Bulgaria. Russia was officially notified by Germany, two days before, that the treaty was about to be signed, that German troops were in

---

nations were at war, a carrier-borne British naval air force based on Alexandria seriously crippled an Italian battle fleet at Taranto. In February the Italian fighter squadrons were sent home from the Channel area.

Bulgaria only to expel British troops from Greece, and that they would be withdrawn when that mission was accomplished, without attacking Turkey; but Russia was not reassured. She had made no secret of the fact that she considered Bulgaria part of her Balkan sphere, not Germany's.

YUGOSLAVIA AND GREECE

On March 27, 1941, the Yugoslav government which had signed the German-Italian-Japanese pact two days before was overthrown. Count Teleki, the Hungarian premier who had concluded a pact of eternal friendship with Yugoslavia in December, 1940, committed suicide April 3. On April 5 the new Belgrade government signed a friendship and nonaggression pact with the USSR. Next day, affronted by that action as Soviet Russia had been by the Bulgarian signature of the tripartite pact, the Germans bombed Belgrade and moved into Yugoslavia and Greece. Invaded from all sides, Yugoslavia was overrun within twelve days, and its government disintegrated. Hungarian and Bulgarian troops reoccupied territories lost to Yugoslavia in 1918. The northwest provinces were annexed outright by Italy or taken over as parts of the pro-Axis puppet state set up at Zagreb by the Croatian terrorist quisling Ante Pavelić, which soon became an Italian protectorate. Stubborn partisan resistance, however, continued, led at first by the Chetniks under General Draža Mihailović, named minister of war by the Yugoslav government in exile in London, and later by the partisans under "Marshal Tito," Josip Broz. Mihailović was materially aided by the British and in 1942 and after by the United States. Tito and his Communist partisans were always aided by the Russians and, in the last years of the war, by Britain and the United States.

The British sent about 45,000 men, including Australians and New Zealanders, to aid the Greeks. Tenacious defensive action by these troops, especially on and around Mount Olympus, delayed the German advance into Greece, and the New Zealanders held the historic pass at Thermopylae long enough to make possible the evacuation of about two-thirds of the expeditionary force. But the Greek army of Epirus surrendered and the Germans entered Athens April 22. By May 20 the remainder of Greece was overrun and its government driven into exile. That was the government of King George II, which the British government had guaranteed in 1939 and which it loyally sought in 1945 to restore.

CRETE

In the last eleven days of May, despite losses so heavy as to cause even Hitler to question their usefulness, German parachute and other air-borne troops captured Crete without benefit of control of the sea. Control of the air was sufficient. The British evacuated seventeen thousand men, but lost fifteen thousand. Although, because of the losses sustained on Crete, Hitler vetoed a proposal for an air-borne invasion of Cyprus, the conquest of Greece and Crete made the Aegean a German lake and threatened the position of the British navy in the eastern Mediterranean. The reconquest of Ethiopia, the restoration of Emperor Haile Selassie to his throne in May, the opening of the Red Sea and Gulf of Aden to American supply ships by President Roosevelt, and the imminent British conquest of Italian East Africa were small gains in comparison.

Near and Middle East

SYRIA

The way seemed open for an Axis conquest of the Near and Middle East, in which the strategic location of Syria would almost inevitably cause that French-mandated area to be involved. Admiral Darlan, successor to Laval as vice-president of the council of the French government at Vichy and at the same time minister of foreign affairs, interior, and marine, was leader and spokesman of a group of French officials who then showed themselves ready to aid the Axis actively, although the United States tried hard to dissuade them.[49]

[49] Ambassador Leahy to Pétain, May 13: "Any military assistance to Germany beyond the strict requirements of the armistice will bring about a permanent loss of friendship and good will of the American people toward France." Public statement by President Roosevelt after conference with Secretary Hull and Sumner Welles, May 15, to the effect that it was inconceivable that the French people would willingly collaborate with the enemy of freedom and popular institutions, which would rob them of their African colonies. (But note Marshal Pétain's radio address the same day.) Secretary Hull to French Ambassador Henry-Haye, May 20. Langer, *op. cit.,* 151, 152, 153.

Darlan hated the British, who he said had repeatedly ruined his family, while the Germans had never harmed them. He was extremely sensitive about his personal and professional prestige and had been irked by a sense of indignity as an admiral in the weaker of the two navies in the British-French alliance; and he would never forget Oran. He was convinced, moreover, that Britain could not win the war and that France would find it prudent and perhaps profitable to propitiate the power—Germany—that seemed destined to dominate the continent. A German victory, he said, would really be better for France than a British victory. *Ibid.,* 117.

PARIS PROTOCOLS

Darlan visited Hitler in Berchtesgaden May 11-12. The business that he did there was indicated by promises already made in Paris, May 3, to Nazi proconsul Otto Abetz and confirmed by the Paris Protocols of May 28. Under those agreements France was to permit the shipment of supplies for the Afrika Korps in French ships with French naval vessels convoying them, if necessary, via Marseilles or Toulon and Bizerte, and their transport from Bizerte to Gabès by the French Tunisian railway or in French army trucks then stored in North Africa. Dakar was to be made available to the Germans as a submarine, naval, and air base. In aid of an anti-British uprising in Iraq, begun May 2, French planes and munitions then in Syria were to be delivered to the Iraqi rebels, and German planes en route to Iraq were to be staged through Aleppo and other Syrian airfields and serviced and refueled there. General Dentz, in command in Syria, was instructed to give the Germans all possible help and to oppose any British attempt at retaliation.

In the face of American warnings,[50] Marshal Pétain broadcast by radio on May 15 an admonition to the French people, approving "in principle" the visit to Berchtesgaden from which Darlan has just returned. Public opinion, the old marshal said, could neither decide nor appraise the course of government. It was, for the French people, he declared, simply a question of following him without mental reservation along the path of honor and national interest.[51]

Counterattack and New Hope for Britain

IRAQ AND SYRIA

Much of what Darlan had promised for North Africa was indignantly vetoed in council on June 6 by General Weygand, in command there, and Admiral d'Esteva, commanding the French naval base at Bizerte; but most of what he had promised as to Syria was done. German planes, given facilities in Syria, aided the anti-British forces in Iraq but—perhaps because of the demands just then being

[50] See footnote 49 above. Hitler would have been highly pleased, of course, to see irreconcilable differences arise between France and the United States, as Churchill was pleased with every new commitment of the United States to the cause of Britain.

[51] Langer, *op. cit.*, 151-152. French Indo-Chinese rubber was then reaching Germany through the agency of Japan and Russia.

made on the resources of the Luftwaffe by the air-borne invasion of Crete—not enough. Pushing up from Basra at the head of the Persian Gulf, British and Free French forces succeeded in reëstablishing a friendly government in Bagdad June 1.[52]

A week later a similar combination of British and Free French forces moved into Syria and Lebanon from Palestine, Trans-Jordan, and Iraq. Frenchmen obedient to Vichy resisted invasion of the mandates by the Allies, including their countrymen. The Free French commander, General Catroux, and the British government proclaimed the independence of Syria and Lebanon. Damascus was captured June 21, and the campaign ended on Bastille Day, July 14. Next day British and Free French forces occupied Beirut.

Two threats to the Near and Middle East were checkmated in Syria and Iraq. Their significance was more apparent later, when an Allied supply route was established from Basra across Iraq for the benefit of Russia. Turkey, freed from danger of invasion, remained neutral. The German invasion of Russia began while the Syrian campaign was in progress, and a British-Russian alliance was formed July 12, three days before Beirut was occupied.

BISMARCK

During the last week of May, 1941, the prospects of the British Empire seemed at their worst since June of the year before. British forces were being driven out of Greece and Crete, barely holding on in Egypt, fighting for Iraq, and not yet able to fight back in Syria. French collaboration with the Germans was at its height. Russia was still sending substantial quantities of essential war materials to Germany. At this point there appeared on the otherwise bleak British horizon two gleams of light and a startling question mark. The light was from the sinking of the *Bismarck* and from President Roosevelt's Pan-American Day address. The question was whether the report that Germany would invade Russia in June was to be believed.

Since the beginning of the war, naval intelligence had had knowledge of two German super-battleships, *Bismarck* and *Tirpitz*, reputedly unsinkable, not yet completed at the outbreak of the war. Bombing raids on the German shipyards might have delayed but had not prevented the completion of the first of these giant ships; and meanwhile Britain's newest, biggest, and best *Prince of Wales* and *King George V* had to be kept at home to guard against a formidable new enemy with

[52] See pp. 371-372 and map, p. 111.

which only they were presumed to be able to contend. In May *Bismarck* sortied from Grimstad Fiord near Bergen, Norway, passed around to the north of Iceland, and entered the North Atlantic with the heavy cruiser *Prinz Eugen* to prey upon the convoys there. Off the coast of Greenland May 24 the two were engaged by *Prince of Wales* and one of Britain's heaviest battle cruisers, *Hood*. *Hood* was hit in a magazine by a single salvo, believed to have been fired by *Prinz Eugen*, blew up, and sank. *Bismarck* was slightly damaged, but drew away and made for Brest. Pursued for two days and nights, repeatedly lost and relocated, slowed down by ruptured fuel tanks and betrayed by the oil slick from them, attacked again and again with torpedoes by carrier-borne planes and destroyers, the crippled giant ship was at last brought to bay four hundred miles west of Brest May 27. Pounded by heavy gunfire from the battleships *Rodney* and *King George V*, she was sunk by torpedoes fired from a cruiser. The British navy had assembled for the search and final combat eight battleships and battle cruisers, two aircraft carriers, eleven cruisers, twenty-one destroyers, and land-based patrol planes. The result had vindicated weapons and techniques; but *Prinz Eugen* escaped, leaving *Bismarck* to take care of itself if it could.[53]

UNITED STATES MOVES TOWARD BELLIGERENCY

Meanwhile, during the second quarter of 1941, the United States government committed itself more and more deeply to the defeat of the Axis powers. On March 30 it seized twenty-eight Italian and two German ships, on the technical ground that their crews had made them a menace to navigation by sabotaging them. Nine Latin-American countries also then seized Axis-owned vessels in their ports. In April, by agreement with the Danish minister in Washington, the United States was authorized to set up military and naval establishments in Greenland to prevent the Germans from doing so and to protect Greenland until Denmark herself should again be free. At the

[53] *Prinz Eugen, Admiral Hipper,* and *Seydlitz* were heavy cruisers, officially of 10,000 tons but actually of nearly twice that displacement fully loaded. They were fast—33 knots or more—armed with eight-inch guns, and protected against vertical bombing by exceptionally heavy horizontal armor plates. They survived many bombing attacks at Brest, in Norwegian harbors, and elsewhere; but *Admiral Hipper* and *Seydlitz* were eventually disabled by bombing in German harbors. *Tirpitz,* similar to *Bismarck,* drew the attention of the British navy and air force until September, 1944, when it capsized under bombing at an anchorage near Tromsö, Norway. *Prinz Eugen* was used as target ship in both Bikini atom bomb tests but was kept well away from the center of the target areas and was not seriously damaged.

same time the United States obtained the right to use thirty-five Danish vessels. On June 6 Congress authorized the U.S. Maritime Commission to use the ships which had been seized. Axis consular and diplomatic representatives protested vigorously. By orders of June 14, 20, and subsequently, their consulates and propaganda-distributing agencies such as the German Library of Information in New York were closed, and Axis assets in the United States were frozen. Germany and Italy retaliated with like action against United States consulates and assets.

On May 24, the day the *Hood* was sunk, the president alerted the navy and marine corps to be ready to take the Azores in thirty days, but reports that Germany would invade Russia in June and had been denied the use of Spanish islands by Franco made it seem safe to wait. It appeared improbable that Hitler would choose to add Spain or Portugal or both to the already lengthening roll of his enemies if he was actually committed to the Russian venture, as he proved June 22 to be. Iceland was substituted for the Azores July 7.

In line with the policy of tightening Western Hemisphere defense, on the day of the sinking of the *Bismarck*, May 27, President Roosevelt in his Pan-American Day address broadcast by radio a warning that the frontier of that defense was being pushed eastward into the Atlantic: "The war is approaching the brink of the western hemisphere itself. It is coming very close to home. . . . It would be suicide to wait until they are in our front yard. . . . We have . . . extended our patrol in north and south Atlantic waters. We are steadily adding more ships and planes to that patrol. . . . Our patrols are helping now to insure the delivery of needed supplies to Britain. All additional measures necessary to deliver the goods will be taken."[54]

Three days later, as if to indicate that the war had indeed come "close to home," German submarines sank nine ships carrying lend-lease supplies in a convoy south of Greenland. On June 9 came word that the U.S. merchant ship *Robin Moor*, carrying general cargo from Brooklyn to Cape Town, had been sunk by a German submarine May 21, seven hundred miles east of Brazil. Given no assistance by the U-boat commander, the crew had drifted in lifeboats for nearly three

[54] S. E. Morison, *History of U.S. Naval Operations in World War II*, I, 67; Robert E. Sherwood, *Roosevelt and Hopkins* (New York, 1948), 29. Some eighteen hundred persons and firms accused of working in the interest of the Axis were blacklisted May 27.

In April and May 20 per cent of the United States Pacific fleet was transferred to the Atlantic, leaving the Pacific fleet inferior in strength to that of Japan in every category of combat ship.

weeks before being picked up. To an official protest, the German government replied only that it would continue to sink every ship carrying contraband to Britain. In a special message to Congress June 20, the president referred to the *Robin Moor* sinking as an act of intimidation, a warning to the United States not to resist the Nazi movement of world conquest, a notification that it might use the high seas of the world only with Nazi consent. On that point, he said, the United States was not yielding and did not propose to yield.

When Russia was invaded by the Germans June 22, the president was ready to declare her eligible to receive lend-lease assistance from the United States. Public opinion was divided as to the wisdom of that move and of the obvious trend toward belligerency. Although Chief of Staff General Marshall warned the country of the danger of permitting its newly organized and incompletely trained army to disintegrate at such a time, a bill to extend for six months the term of service of men who had been inducted for one year under the selective service act, whose term would soon expire, was passed by the House of Representatives August 12 by only one vote, 203 to 202, and by the Senate by a majority of fifteen, 45 votes to 30.

THE HESS INCIDENT AND RUSSIA

The German invasion of Russia was, to many, less surprising than the Nazi-Soviet nonaggression pact of 1939 had been. Although shrouded in mystery as to its origin and heavily cloaked in secrecy as to its outcome, the parachute landing in Britain of the deputy leader of the National Socialist party, Rudolf Hess, in the night of May 10-11, was the news sensation of its day. He had flown alone from Augsburg and said he had come on a personal peace mission. His idea was ostensibly that Germany and Britain should make peace. If he then proposed that Great Britain should join the Axis powers in an anti-Communist crusade against Russia, his proposal was quite consistent with the Mediterranean and Near Eastern plans which had occupied the minds of the Nazi leaders during the winter then just past, and which in the second week of May seemed more likely to succeed than to fail. When his mission—whatever its purpose—was known or assumed to have failed, he was disowned by his Führer as insane. In time, in imprisonment, he evinced other manifestations of real or pretended mental disintegration.

Hess's flight was but one of many warning signs of which the Soviet leaders were always well informed. The German and Italian foreign offices—and presumably the Russian government—knew that on April 24 the British ambassador to Russia had predicted in Moscow that Germany would invade Russia June 22.[55] Considering the Hess incident separately at the time, however, it was difficult to judge whether the enigmatic solo aviator had been seriously sent, was being used as a human trial balloon, was in fact insane, or was only another fugitive from Nazi Germany.

RUSSIA, 1941-1942

Treaty of Convenience, 1939-1941

MUTUAL MATERIAL AID

Hitler was reported by Count Ciano to have remarked to Mussolini October 4, 1940: "My mistrust of Stalin is equalled by Stalin's mistrust of me." The Germans were careful to record in writing such specific agreements as they reached. The general economic mutual assistance agreement of August 19, 1939, was amplified and extended February 11, 1940.[56]

Under the expanded 1940 agreement, the Soviet Union was to deliver to Germany within the next twelve months raw materials in the amount of approximately 600,000,000 reichsmarks, including the 100,000,000 reichsmarks called for by the treaty of August, 1939, principally 1,000,000 tons of grain and legumes, 900,000 tons of mineral oil, 100,000 tons of cotton, 500,000 tons of phosphates, 100,-000 tons of chrome ores, 300,000 tons of scrap and pig iron, 2400 kilograms of platinum, manganese, metals, lumber, etc.

During the first half of the second treaty year the Soviet Union was to make further raw material deliveries of similar character in the amount of 230,000,000 reichsmarks.

German deliveries to Russia were to consist, as before, of industrial products, installations, information about processes, and finished war materials. In the manufacture of these materials Germany would have to draw upon her own stocks of metals used as alloys in making the finer grades of steel; but those stocks were to be replenished by imports from Russia, which within the first eighteen months covered by the agreement was to deliver 11,000 tons of copper, 3000 tons of nickel, 950 tons of tin, 500 tons of molybdenum, 500 tons of wolfram, 40 tons of cobalt. A German Foreign Office memorandum of Septem-

[55] *Nazi-Soviet Relations*, 330.
[56] See p. 535. Also *Nazi-Soviet Relations*, 83, 108, 131, 199-201, 318.

ber 28, 1940, indicated that since February 11 Russian deliveries, one-third of which was grain, had amounted to 300,000,000 reichsmarks, whereas Germany's to Russia had been valued at half that much. In August, Russia had sent materials worth 65,000,000 reichsmarks, Germany materials worth 20,000,000 reichsmarks.

There were to be further important benefits for Germany. The Soviet Union declared itself willing to serve as a purchaser of metals and raw materials from third countries. Germany was given right of transit to and from Rumania, Iran, and Afghanistan, and freight rates on Manchurian soybeans shipped across Russia to Germany were reduced 50 percent. It was part of the agreement that compensating German deliveries might lag from three to six months behind Russian deliveries. They lagged more than that in 1941. New agreements from time to time, as late as January 10 and April 10, 1941, increased the amounts to be delivered.[57]

For about a year beginning March 30, 1940, by Hitler's personal order, delivery of the stipulated war materials to Russia was given priority over delivery of comparable materials to the German armed forces. So confident was Hitler that German war industry could keep the Wehrmacht adequately supplied, as it did; and so essential did his war-industry and economic-warfare advisers consider the materials which Russia was supplying.

Each got what it thought it needed most, paying what it had to pay to get what it wanted. Each preferred to continue the exchange rather than break it off, although each knew that what it was delivering might be used against it. Each knew that it was hurting itself but hoped ultimately to profit by helping itself more than it was hurt.

On May 15, 1941, the German trade expert Dr. Kurt Schnurre reported in a Foreign Office memorandum that although great difficulties were being created by countless rumors of an impending German-Russian conflict, although the German air ministry was refusing to release aircraft promised and already sold to the Russians, and although Germany was in default on various other commitments, especially armament, he was under the impression that he might have got more by demanding more. He considered it indeed a notable performance that, despite the heavy burden imposed upon the Russian people, particularly with regard to grain, the materials contracted for were being punctually delivered:

[57] A questioner in the British Parliament showed some concern lest North American materials reach Germany by way of Russia as some South American shipments were doing. Express train loads of east Asian rubber for Germany were given the highest priority on the Russian railways up to June, 1941.

	In April, 1941		In 1941	
Cotton	8,300	tons	23,500	tons
Grain	208,000	"	632,000	"
Manganese ore			50,000	"
Nonferrous metals				
(copper, tin, nickel)	6,340	"		
Petroleum	90,000	"	232,000	"
Phosphates			67,000	"
Platinum			900	kilograms
Raw rubber from east Asia				
By special trains	2,000	"		
By regular Siberian trains	2,000	"		

Russia was still obligated to "make deliveries in advance" of German deliveries until August, 1941. Meanwhile approximately seventy German engineers and fitters under the direction of Admiral Feige were proceeding according to plan with the construction of the "cruiser L" in Leningrad, with German supplies coming in as scheduled.[58]

MUTUAL MISTRUST

Diplomatically, relations between the rival imperialisms were outwardly polite but often strained. The Russians were unpleasantly surprised by the speed of the German conquest of Poland and had to hurry to occupy their share. The Germans were "correct" but very cool when Russia made nonaggression pacts with the Baltic states, although informed that Russia would expect in that matter "the unstinting support of the German government."[59] Friction arose over the rights of German nationals in the Baltic countries. Officially, Russia was equally "correct." Stalin authorized Ribbentrop to say publicly that the Soviet Union was interested in the existence of a strong Germany and recognized a community of interests between Germany and itself.[60]

There were also divergences of interest. Hitler warned his entourage from the beginning that pacts were kept only so long as they served

[58] *Nazi-Soviet Relations*, 339-341. Göring had told General Thomas in August, 1940, that priority for deliveries to Russia over deliveries to the Wehrmacht would obtain only until the spring of 1941. Göring had been, before the war, the general director of economic mobilization. General Thomas was chief of the war economy department of the German high command and was accumulating "basic facts for a history of German war and armament economy."

[59] German Ambassador von der Schulenburg from Moscow to the German Foreign Office, September 25, 1939, quoting Stalin. *Nazi-Soviet Relations*, 102-103. See also p. 544.

[60] *Ibid.*, 126-127. October 19, 1939. See page 544.

their purpose, and that Russia would hold herself to that one only while she considered it to be to her advantage. He was constantly afraid that someone less sensible than Stalin, less moderate, less amenable to reason, or less reliable might take Stalin's place.

For "political and technical reasons" the German navy gave up a plan to repair warships and outfit auxiliary cruisers in Russian yards. At Molotov's pointed request, it had to agree to keep its ships west of twenty degrees east longitude in the Baltic. Germany agreed to support the extension of Soviet interests toward the Persian Gulf but declined Russian offers to purchase warships *Prinz Eugen*, *Seydlitz*, and *Lützow* and plans for *Bismarck* and *Tirpitz*, although later some guns and gun turrets were delivered and some ship construction done on a partially completed cruiser *Lützow*, renamed *Petropavlovsk*.[61] Hitler vetoed a proposal that his navy try to purchase submarines from Russia.

When the Germans invaded Norway Molotov cryptically wished Germany "complete success in her defensive measures" and quickly showed himself more compliant than Mikoyan had recently been in the matter of deliveries of war matériel. When notified May 10 of the invasion of the Low Countries and France, Molotov remarked that he understood that Germany must protect herself against Anglo-French attack, and did not doubt that she would succeed. The speed of the Nazi conquest of the Low Countries and France, however, and Mussolini's stab-in-the-back declaration of war upon France startled the Russian leaders, who seemed to have expected a longer and more costly campaign. So Russia also moved quickly, into the Baltic states. Her timetable in Lithuania was: June 14, ultimatum; June 15, occupation; July 14, plebiscite, 90 percent pro-Soviet; July 21, unanimous assembly resolution asking admission as a new state to the Union of Socialist Soviet Republics; August 8, acceptance. Similar synchronized steps were taken in Latvia and Estonia. Protests of those states through their ministers to Germany were not received by the Nazi Foreign Office, and they were offered no encouragement to resist, although their ministers and legation staffs were temporarily given sanctuary. The foreign trade specialists in the Foreign Office were concerned over the loss of the Baltic states as sources of food and raw materials essential for war, and continued to cultivate trade relations with Finland; but the policy division decided not to make an issue of it. So Molotov was able blandly to congratulate the German ambassador

---

[61] See p. 545. Simultaneously, the Germans renamed their pocket battleship *Deutschland*, naming it *Lützow*.

most warmly upon the splendid recent successes of the German armed forces, and to explain that the unresisted reinforcement of Russian troops in Lithuania, Latvia, and Estonia had been necessary to put an end to the intrigues by which the western powers had attempted to sow there seeds of distrust between the USSR and Germany.[62]

The Russian occupation of Bessarabia and Bucovina raised more serious questions. As to the former, Germany could not well object in principle, having declared herself at the outset, in the original Nazi-Soviet pact, totally disinterested in it. She could only pretend to be surprised, although she had but the shortest official notice, because on March 29 Molotov had declared before the Supreme Soviet that it was time to find a "solution of the problem" of Bessarabia, and his declaration had been published. For him, as for Hitler, such a statement was enough. Others were to note it and consider themselves adequately informed.

Just then in process, however, of drawing Rumania into the Axis camp and of monopolizing Rumanian oil and grain, the German Foreign Office argued that Rumania must not become a theater of war. It preferred to pose as the protector of Rumania. So it protested that the Soviet claim on Bucovina was new. Molotov counterclaimed that that province was the last missing part of a unified Ukraine, and the USSR took for Ukraine the northern part of the province. The Germans could only register their usual concern for the *Volksdeutsche* (people of German origin) in both provinces in question.

Rumania had a further complaint—that the Soviets were not drawing the new Bessarabian-Rumanian boundary properly, along the Prut River and the lower Danube as established by the Treaty of Berlin (1878), but in such way as to control the islands there and all practical commercial access to the Black Sea at the mouth of the Danube. The question of control of the Danube, and a German ambition to guarantee against Russia (though not against Hungary with regard to Transylvania) the truncated remainder of Rumania, continued to trouble relations between the Nazi and the Soviets. But on June 27, 1940, Germany could only advise Rumania, in order to avoid war with the Soviet Union, to yield to the Soviet government's demand. It yielded; but, in the words of the Rumanian ambassador then in Moscow, "The ultimatum, brooking no delay, came to inevitable maturity a year later."[63]

The German ambassador was not at all apprehensive over the

[62] *Nazi-Soviet Relations*, 142, 152-154.
[63] Grigore Gafencu, *op. cit.*, 73, 289, 293.

arrival in Moscow in May, 1940, of Sir Stafford Cripps as British ambassador. Schulenburg said he saw then "no reason to doubt the loyal attitude of the Soviet Union" toward Germany. In July he was reassured by a report on the Cripps-Stalin interview, given him by Molotov by order of Stalin:

1. Stalin said that he had said to Cripps he saw no danger that Germany would establish a hegemony over the continent [as Mr. Churchill had said in a letter to Stalin that Germany was trying to do].

2. Britain, Stalin said, would welcome a revival of trade with Russia, provided that no British exports were resold to Germany. Russia would continue to export to Germany part of the nonferrous metals she bought abroad, because Germany needed the metals for the manufacture of matériel she delivered to the Soviet Union. She would trade with Britain only on that condition.

3. According to the report, the British government had expressed the opinion that the unification and leadership of the Balkan countries for the purpose of maintaining the *status quo* were rightly the task of the Soviet Union and in the existing circumstances could be carried out only by the Soviet Union. Stalin said he had replied that no power had the right to an exclusive role in the consolidation and leadership of the Balkan countries and that the Soviet Union, although interested in the Balkans, claimed no such mission.

4. Cripps had agreed, Stalin said, that the interests of the Soviet Union in the Straits must be safeguarded. Stalin said he had replied that the Soviet Union was in fact opposed to the exclusive jurisdiction of Turkey over the Straits and to Turkey's dictation of conditions in the Black Sea. The Turkish government, he said, was aware of that.[64]

By the Vienna award of August 30, while the battle of Britain was at its height and when a dozen German divisions were already on their way from France to Poland, Ribbentrop and Ciano permitted Hungary to take Transylvania from Rumania, despite the bitter and violent objection of a Rumanian delegation. The loss of the province cost King Carol his throne and sent him again unmourned into well-cushioned exile. Claiming an interest in Rumania, and objecting that the German foreign minister had participated in making the award without consulting or informing her, Russia also protested; but her protest was rejected. Ribbentrop reminded her that Germany had had very short notice before Bucovina and Bessarabia were seized. It

[64] Schulenburg to German Foreign Office, July 13. *Nazi-Soviet Relations,* 166-168; Churchill, *Second World War,* II, 133-136. Churchill corroborated Stalin on point 1, and did not contradict him on points 2 to 4. In his letter asking Stalin to see Cripps he had offered to "discuss all the great problems" raised by Hitler's bid for power.

must be demonstrated to the Soviet Union once and for all, wrote the Nazi foreign minister to the German ambassador in Moscow, that Germany's standing (*Bedeutung*) and predominant interests in Rumania had led her to guarantee Rumanian territory and existing boundaries. The mere geographical contiguity of the Soviet Union to Rumania could not be invested with a significance comparable with German interests in Rumania. Plans for an invasion of Russia from Rumanian territory were being made in Germany in September, 1940.[65]

When the German high command notified Russia of its intention to send troops to northern Norway by way of Finland, Molotov asked to see the text of the agreement and of all or any secret protocols. When he made the same demand beforehand concerning the tripartite (German-Italian-Japanese) pact signed September 27, 1941, he was told that that alliance was "directed exclusively against American warmongers, . . . to bring the elements pressing for America's entry into the war to their senses by conclusively demonstrating to them that if they enter the present struggle they will automatically have to deal with the three great powers as adversaries." Molotov was assured that the alliance was in no way directed against Russia, that Russia's relations with any or all of the allies were specifically mentioned as not changed, and that there were no secret protocols or other secret agreements.[66]

An article in *Pravda* September 30 indicated that the Soviet government had decided to make the best of a situation with which it was not pleased. Russia, it said, would remain constant and at peace, as far as her doing so depended solely upon her. The article treated the United States as if it were already at war—which was contrary to Hitler's intentions, as he had hoped to dishearten Britain by frightening the United States into an attitude of isolationism, so that Britain would feel isolated.

No matter what Ribbentrop or *Pravda* said, the position of the Soviet Union had changed for the worse. Whereas the Nazi-Soviet pact of 1939 had licensed Russia to play a big role in world affairs, the

[65] Milton Shulman, *Defeat in the West*, 336; *Nazi-Soviet Relations*, 178-187.

[66] *Nazi-Soviet Relations*, 195-204. The tripartite treaty obligated the signers for a period of ten years to assist one another with all political, economic, and military means if any of them should be attacked by a power not then involved in the European war or the Chinese-Japanese conflict. Japan did not declare war when Germany invaded Russia. Germany was not being attacked, and Japan had by then a neutrality agreement with the Soviet Union. Hitler and Mussolini declared war on the United States promptly after Pearl Harbor, and satellite signers of the Tripartite pact dutifully followed their lead.

tripartite pact had imposed limits upon her against her will and without her previous knowledge. She had then to decide whether to stiffen her resistance or to become an active partner in the anti-British alliance. Her decision would depend somewhat upon the inducements offered her by Germany as the price of her alliance and partly upon her leaders' judgment as to which side would win the war, survive, and be better able to reward her for participation or for nonparticipation. The Germans offered inducements either way, but must win the war before their offers could be made good unless Russia simply took for herself what she wanted.

Telling Stalin in a letter of October 13 that the total defeat of Great Britain was already recognized by everyone but the British, Ribbentrop invited Molotov to come to Berlin to discuss the "historic mission" of the four powers, Germany, Italy, Japan, and the Soviet Union, and to adopt a long-range policy by the delimitation of their interests on a world-wide scale.[67]

MOLOTOV IN BERLIN, NOVEMBER 12-13, 1940

Accepting Ribbentrop's invitation, Molotov visited Berlin November 12 and 13 for one of the war period's most momentous conferences. It was his first journey outside Russia, his only meeting with Hitler. Whether by design or by coincidence, the British Royal Air Force greeted him on the first day of his visit with the news of the smashing of an Italian war fleet at Taranto and heavy Italian losses in a bombing raid on Britain.[68] Hitler excused himself from an evening interview, the first day, because of the danger of an air raid, and used the same excuse to break off another on the second day in which he had clearly exhausted himself without wearing Molotov down perceptibly. A long final interview with Ribbentrop the second night was held deep in an air-raid bunker while the British bombed Berlin. If Britain was already helpless, whose planes and bombs were those?

---

[67] *Ibid.,* 207-213. At a Danubian conference of Germany, Italy, Rumania, and the USSR at Bucharest October 28, the day Italy attacked Greece, Russia claimed for herself and Rumania exclusive control of the only useful mouth of the Danube, and the exclusive right to use it for warships. A British objection to the abolition of the old European commission for control of the Danube was rejected by Vyshinsky in language very similar to that used again by him at the Danubian conference of 1948. Russia owed nothing to Great Britain, said Vyshinsky, since she had been excluded by the Treaty of Versailles from all Danubian commissions (although the Soviet Union had not during that period been a Danubian state). Britain, stormed Vyshinsky in 1940 as in 1948, had no business there (although she had done business there since the Congress of Vienna internationalized the Danube in 1815). Gafencu, *op. cit.,* 76.

[68] See p. 588, n. 48.

If Germany had already won the war, what was the "life and death struggle" in which Hitler asked him to remember she was engaged? Neither coward nor fool, Molotov weighed the question whether the Nazi had yet won their war or were destined to do so; if not, Russia need not join the tripartite alliance unless adequately rewarded. He kept his own counsel as to whether he knew that plans for a German invasion of Russia had already been in preparation for three months.

Hitler and Ribbentrop talked as expansively as Ribbentrop had written about the certainty of a German victory and the liquidation of the bankrupt British Empire. Britain was done, they said, and the United States could send her little help. The German navy would stop most of what was sent. Whether the United States entered the war was a matter of no consequence to Germany. No Anglo-Saxon would be permitted to land in Europe. The United States was not interested in saving Britain, but only in securing the British Empire and bases and in "making money" in Europe, whereas it "had no business" in Europe, Africa, or Asia.[69]

More patiently than ever before to anyone, Hitler explained his policies and acts. Troops for Kirkeness had had to be sent through Finland. When their task was finished he would send no more; but Germany needed lumber and nickel from Finland and must protect her iron ore shipments from Sweden. Finland, he said, might even permit the establishment of British or American air bases on her territory. Would Russia then declare war on the United States? Clearly there must not be another Russo-Finnish war.

Molotov would not promise. There must be no more anti-Russian demonstrations in Finland, or German troops in Finland, or dispatching of Finnish delegations to Germany, or receptions of prominent Finns in Germany. Finland was in Russia's zone, and he wanted it outright.

The conversations ranged widely over the earth, with Hitler and Ribbentrop trying to direct them to immense profits to be made as Germany's partner in the liquidation of the British Empire, with Molotov tenaciously bringing them back nearer home to ask for answers to specific questions. He would study the draft of the four-power treaty the Germans had ready for him. Participation in the tripartite pact alliance was entirely acceptable to him in principle, provided that Russia was an equal partner in it; but Russia must have

[69] *Nazi-Soviet Relations*, 207-259. At this point the German record said that "Molotov expressed his agreement." At another, it quoted him as saying that he agreed with what he understood of what Hitler had said. At another, it reported that "the Führer showed great indignation."

concrete guarantees, bases in the Dardanelles and in Bulgaria within easy reach of the Straits, a mutual assistance pact with Bulgaria, and an outlet for Bulgaria to the Aegean. Mere assurances were not enough. "Deeds did not always correspond with words." Germany must leave Finland, Poland, and Bulgaria to Russia and revoke her guarantee of Rumania, which he bluntly said was obviously aimed against the interests of Soviet Russia.[70]

The stated purposes of the proposed new pact were to prevent the war from spreading further, to terminate it quickly, to detach Turkey from her existing international commitments and win her over to collaboration, or to draw a new Straits convention in the interest of the Soviet Union, giving only Black Sea powers the right to send war vessels through the Straits, and if necessary to impose the new convention upon Turkey by the combined pressure of the four powers. Each of the four was to aid the others in economic matters and to supplement and extend existing agreements with them. None was to join or support any combination of powers against any of the others. They would apportion Europe, Africa, and Asia among themselves and those who joined them as allies. Germany was to take central Africa. France would share northwestern Africa with Spain. Italy would dominate northern and northeastern Africa. Japan should do as she pleased with southeastern Asia and the southwest Pacific. Russia was to be free to move southward toward outlets on the Persian Gulf and Indian Ocean. Manchuria was not mentioned.

Molotov was most immediately interested in outlets to the eastern Mediterranean and from the Baltic to the North Sea. The formidable four-power alliance might then have been consummated had not each of the protagonists, particularly Molotov, overreached himself. Hitler would not undo what he had done in Rumania or Finland, or guarantee exits from the Baltic. He would not give Russia control of the Balkans and the Dardanelles, or of the mouths of the Danube. Franz von Papen said in 1945 that in his two Berlin interviews with Molotov Hitler lost the war. If the Soviet Union had lost the war it might have been said of Molotov that in those interviews he gambled away his country's last best chance for forestalling a German invasion;

[70] Hitler asked Molotov whether Bulgaria had asked for a Russian guarantee as he said Rumania had asked for a German one. Molotov did not answer the question. German navy documents used at Nuremberg indicated that Molotov asked Germany to support a Russian claim on Kars and Ardahan, which the Soviets claimed again in 1946. Soviet delegate Vyshinsky supported the claim before the Political and Security Committee of the General Assembly of the United Nations, October 24, 1947.

for it seemed to have been then and there that Hitler's tentative thoughts of an invasion hardened into a decision.

Assuming that Britain would not have had the fortitude to persevere as she was doing or to send troops into Greece, or Molotov the hardihood to bargain so boldly, unless the two had already reached a secret agreement against Germany, and startled by Molotov's talk of the Dardanelles, Hitler ordered November 12 that all preparations for war in the east should continue. The day Molotov left Berlin the German naval diarist noted that the Führer was still "inclined to instigate the conflict with Russia."

DANUBE, BALKANS, AND STRAITS

The king of Bulgaria followed on Molotov's heels in Berlin. Then came Ciano, then Suñer, again obdurate against urging that Spain become a belligerent. Then in swift succession hapless or hopeful representatives of the other southeast European states were summoned to the Nazi capital to sign the tripartite pact, while Russia advertised at the same time her discontent and her helplessness by permitting Tass articles to be published denying that she had approved their action in advance, as the *Hamburger Fremdenblat* had said that she had done in the case of Hungary.

While Bulgaria delayed signing for a little, Russia proposed on November 25, 1940, both to Germany and to Bulgaria, the Russian-Bulgarian mutual assistance pact which Molotov had mentioned to Hitler in Berlin. In what he called and considered a definitive statement of the terms on which the Soviet government would be willing to sign the German-Italian-Japanese pact and withdraw her objection to Bulgaria's signing it, Molotov stipulated that the region south of Batum and Baku, to the Persian Gulf, must be specifically recognized as a center of Russian interest. Japan must give up oil and coal concessions in northern Sakhalin. Molotov specified further that German troops must be withdrawn at once from Finland and that Germany must recognize that Bulgaria was geographically located inside the security zone of the Black Sea boundaries of the Soviet Union. Germany must also recognize Russia's right to conclude a mutual assistance pact with Bulgaria and to establish army and naval bases on the Bosporus and the Dardanelles on long-term lease from Turkey. Bulgaria must acknowledge that the Straits were a vital part of Russia's Black Sea frontier, and obligate herself to aid Russia if Russia's interests were threatened in the Black Sea or the Straits. Russia would on those terms help Bulgaria to take western Thrace from Greece and, if attacked by Turkey, to take also "the European parts of Turkey." Whether for fear of Germany or Turkey or for other reasons, Bulgaria did not accept the Russian offer.[71]

On December 3 the German decision to conduct a siege of Britain rather than attempt an invasion was imparted to heads of departments, and defense of Germany against bombing was for the first time given top priority.[72]

The Führer's Directive 21, December 18, 1940, ordered the armed forces to be prepared by May 15, 1941, to crush European Russia in a quick campaign (Operation Barbarossa) before the conclusion of the war against Great Britain. The stated objective of the invasion was "to establish a defense line against Asiatic Russia from a line running approximately from the Volga river to Archangel." The high command was told that it could count on the active participation of Rumanian and Finnish troops under its command. It was expected that Swedish highways and railways would be available for the use of German troops. One army group was to be assigned primarily to the defense of Norway but also to offensive operations with the Finns to secure the ore mines around Petsamo and cut Russia off from Murmansk and the Arctic Ocean supply route. All orders were to indicate that they were precautionary only, against the possibility that Russia might change her attitude toward Germany.[73]

[71] Harry N. Howard, U. S. Department of State *Bulletin*, XIX, No. 472 (July 18, 1948), pp. 63-78, and *The Problem of the Turkish Straits* (Department of State Publication 2752, Near Eastern Series 5), 14-29 and 47-68; *Nazi-Soviet Relations*, 258-260; Churchill, *Second World War*, II, 587-589. Substantially the same proposals concerning the Straits were put forward by the Soviet government August 7 and September 24, 1946.

[72] The bombing of Britain went on in full fury, but the fear of invasion diminished with the danger. "I cannot feel that the invasion danger is past," wrote the prime minister to President Roosevelt. "The gent has taken off his clothes and put on his bathing suit, but there is an autumn nip in the air. We are maintaining the utmost vigilance." Churchill, *Second World War*, II, 498.

Hitler was then vainly urging Franco to attack Gibraltar January 10. Pétain was on the point of dropping Laval from his government. Laval's portfolios were taken over by Darlan. Collaboration continued to be the order of the day in Vichy, but Hitler scolded Darlan, who was less obsequious than Laval had been.

[73] *Nazi-Soviet Relations*, 260-264. Document from Wehrmacht *Archiv*. Nine copies were made, signed by Hitler and initialed by Jodl and Keitel.

"Stalin must be regarded as a cold-blooded blackmailer," said Hitler to his generals at the Berghof January 9, 1941; "he would, if expedient, repudiate any written treaty at any time. Britain's aim for some time to come will be to set Russian strength in motion against us. If the USA and Russia should enter the war, the situation will become very complicated. Hence the possibility of such a threat developing must be eliminated. If the Russian threat were nonexistent, we could wage war on Britain indefinitely. If Russia collapsed, Japan would be greatly relieved; this in turn would mean increased danger for the United States." Anthony Martienssen, *Hitler and His Admirals*, 93.

There was no change in Russia's attitude of coöperation in the exchange of war materials, but a noticeable stiffening of opposition to the expansion of German military activity in southeastern Europe. While sedulously avoiding provocation that might lead immediately to war, Russia was taking such precautions as she could, and on certain points would yield no further ground. Her Foreign Office gave clear and repeated warning that it considered the territory of Bulgaria and of the Straits as within the security zone of the USSR, and would regard the appearance of any foreign armed forces there as a threat to Russian security. In Moscow, Vyshinsky told the Bulgarian minister that Russia could not support Bulgaria in her adherence to the three-power pact.

Russia, in turn, gave Germany only one day's notice when she signed a friendship and nonaggression pact with Yugoslavia a few hours before the Germans invaded that country without warning and without previous notice to Russia. Germany then professed to be abused; but Molotov explained only that the Soviet government had tried to preserve the peace, and reminded the Germans that they also had said they were opposed to an extension of the war. He called the German invasion of Yugoslavia "very deplorable." Each of two great powers had virtually given the other final warning.[74]

Germany offered no formal objection to the five-year Russian-Japanese neutrality and nonaggression treaty signed in Moscow April 13, 1941, when Japanese Foreign Minister Matsuoka stopped there and in Leningrad for a few days on his return journey after some weeks in Berlin. "South to Singapore" had been in effect the German slogan in Matsuoka's conversations with Hitler and Ribbentrop. The Nazi leaders were confident that the Wehrmacht could handle the Russian armies, and preferred to use their Japanese alliance against the British Empire and the United States. By the new treaty with Japan, the Soviet government recognized the inviolability and territorial integrity of the Japanese puppet state of Manchukuo, and Japan that of the People's Republic of Mongolia. Each agreed to remain neutral if the other

[74] *Nazi-Soviet Relations*, 316-320. Russian deliveries of grains, petroleum, manganese ore, nonferrous and precious metals, and east Asian rubber declined in January and February but "rose by leaps and bounds" in March.

Churchill sent Stalin, April 3, a cryptic but clear enough warning of the significance of German troop movements in the Balkans and southern Poland; but British Ambassador Sir Stafford Cripps failed to deliver it until April 19, then delivered it indirectly, through Vyshinsky, instead of directly to Stalin. Churchill, *Second World War*, III, 358, 360.

Rudolph Hess, deputy Führer of the Nazi party, flew to Scotland May 10, ostensibly to induce the British to overthrow the Churchill government and make peace. *Ibid.*, 48-55.

became the object of hostilities by a third power or combination of powers. The treaty meant that Russia would make no effort to stop Japan in China, so it was somewhat disconcerting to the United States. But by giving the Soviet Union some shadow of security in eastern Asia it improved its position in eastern Europe by partially freeing it from the danger of having to defend itself against simultaneous attacks on two fronts. The Soviet government showed no disposition at that time to attack on either front.

German Invasion of Russia

MOTIVES AND OBJECTIVES

The decision to invade Russia was Hitler's. What devil had possessed the Russians to conclude their friendship pact with Yugoslavia? he asked Ambassador von der Schulenburg. They were only serving notice of their interest in the Balkans, Schulenburg told him; and after all, he had been bound by his pact with them to consult them, but had not done so. Why had they sent so many troops into the Baltic states? That was only the well-known Russian urge for 300 percent security, the ambassador replied, and added that he could not believe that Russia would ever attack Germany.[75]

It was one of Hitler's fixed ideas that Britain was being sustained by the hope of help from Russia and the United States. If, then, he could eliminate Russia and if Japan, freed from fear of Russia by the neutrality pact recently signed, could eliminate the United States, Britain would be left to try to stand alone, and would fall before the Wehrmacht if it did not capitulate.

Hitler knew that Russia was not ready to attack him, and hoped

[75] *Nazi-Soviet Relations*, 330-332. Defense affidavits presented at the war criminal trials at Nuremberg in 1948 offered testimony to the effect that Red Army officers and soldiers had talked freely in the Baltic states of an impending invasion of Germany, and had said that they were there for that purpose.

Ambassador Schulenburg did not underestimate the Russians as Hitler's more congenial and sycophantic advisers did. *The Goebbels Diaries* (New York, 1948) p. 566, said that he was not told until June 21 that Hitler intended to attack Russia. He had done his best in Moscow to combat rumors running out of Germany that war was imminent. Like Kurusu and Nomura in Washington before Pearl Harbor, he could play the part of an innocent abroad more convincingly if kept ignorant. A career diplomat of long experience, wide knowledge, and ability, never a National Socialist by conviction, he was one of those executed for the anti-Hitler plot of July 20, 1944.

The German general staff, on the other hand, though well informed about Hitler's plans, knew little about Russia. It had in its possession the captured archives of Holland, Belgium, Greece, Yugoslavia, and France, but had learned no Russian secrets from them. (Postwar interrogation of Colonel General Franz Halder.) Milton Shulman, *op. cit.*, 62.

that she was not ready to withstand attack. He did not know that she would not attack eventually, although his ambassador assured him steadfastly that she would not fight unless attacked; so he decided to forestall her.

Greed and megalomania, as always, played their part in his decision. He had made himself master of Europe and had looted it. Europe and Asia were feeding Germany; but to remain master of what he had conquered, in the longer war with which he saw himself faced, he must find more food for it. For that he must go to Russia. A suggestion had already come from there that he could have more grain in 1941 than ever, by paying for it under a new economic agreement. But why pay for it? He wanted grain, magnesium ores and other nonferrous metals, and oil in greater and assured quantities, and he was getting them right up to the moment of the attack. But he did not want to go on paying for them with good German steel and war equipment as he had been doing. His insatiable appetite for conquest had grown with easy conquest, and his economic experts were ready with their plans for the exploitation of the new *Lebensraum*. Russia should feed the German armed forces that year, although millions of the Russian people would starve. The economic war planners knew that they would get no more India rubber, tungsten, copper, platinum, tin, asbestos, or manila hemp by the old channels until contact with the East was again established; but they expected to take possession of three-fourths of the armament industry and nearly all of the precision tool and optical instrument industries of Russia, as well as oil, ore, and grain fields, and to make the war pay for itself.

Count Ernst von Weizsäcker, state secretary in the German Foreign Office, recorded in a memorandum of April 28, 1941, his opinion that while Germany might defeat Russia in a military sense it would lose in an economic sense. Passive resistance would prevent the utilization of what was conquered, and the window to the Pacific would remain shut. Britain, he said, was not being sustained by hope of help from Russia but would be encouraged by seeing Germany embroil herself with another formidable enemy. The war would therefore not be shortened by an attack on Russia but might be prolonged; and it could not be made to pay for itself.[76]

Although Hitler had boasted confidentially to his generals that the decision to attack had always been in him, and although National

[76] *Nazi-Soviet Relations*, 333-334. Baron von Weizsäcker was sentenced at Nuremberg April 11, 1949, to seven years' imprisonment on charges of having plotted aggressive war against Czechoslovakia, and of joint responsibility for crimes against humanity.

Socialism was inherently and incurably warlike in character, Nazi propaganda always represented the war on Russia as a crusade against Bolshevism upon which the fate of western European civilization depended.[77]

By radio and loud-speaker announcement, June 14, handed to the German ambassador June 13 and published by Tass June 15, the Russian government denied rumors of trouble with Germany. Molotov afterward reproached Schulenburg for not getting a favorable answer with comparable publicity. Hitler's answer was given privately to his generals in a briefing conference in Berlin June 14: the war was preventive in character, not actually defensive just then, but inevitable.

Mutual recriminations over border violations, mostly by aircraft, led when all was ready, June 22, to an address by the Führer to the German people, telling them that his loyal efforts to maintain peace had been in vain, his patience was exhausted, and their fate had been put into the hands of the army which had invaded Russia that morning. Their ambassador was instructed to say to Molotov that Soviet troop concentrations on the border had become intolerable and that his government had decided to take countermeasures. Molotov was said to have retorted that for an hour German planes had been bombing Russian towns, and that such an attack on a country with which Germany had a friendship and nonaggression treaty was such a breach of faith as the world had never seen.[78]

To his cynical ally Mussolini Hitler wrote, June 21, that while doomed Britain clutched like a drowning man at every straw, hoping desperately for help from the continent to win her war for her as it had so often done in the past, and while the "North American Union" stood behind both Britain and Russia, goading them on and watchfully waiting, he and Mussolini must save Europe from grave danger. The partnership with the Soviet Union had always been uncongenial

[77] In a book published in 1945 Grigore Gafencu, Rumanian former minister of foreign affairs and in 1941 ambassador to Russia, wrote: ". . . It might also avert in time the miserable fate that threatened to fall on the world if the USSR should still be erect and strong at the end of the war." Gafencu, *Prelude to the Russian Campaign*, 167, 173.

Gafencu reported elsewhere that Hitler prophesied to him in April, 1939, that if war ever came victors and vanquished alike would lie, when it ended, under their ruins, and only "that fellow in Moscow" would profit in any way from it. Gafencu, *Last Days of Europe* (New Haven, 1948), 78.

[78] James F. Byrnes, *Speaking Frankly*, 292. See Secretary Hull's response to the Japanese emissaries Nomura and Kurusu in Washington on Pearl Harbor Day, p. 656.

Gafencu's account of the final Molotov-Schulenburg interview, based on the latter's oral report to him, was slightly different in wording but similar in general tenor and content. Gafencu, *Prelude to the Russian Campaign*, 212.

and irksome to him, he said, a break with his background and concepts and with his older obligations. Having struggled through to the last great decision, he felt again spiritually free.[79]

"Now comes this Russian diversion," wrote President Roosevelt to Ambassador Leahy June 26. "If it is more than just that, it will mean the liberation of Europe from Nazi domination . . . and at the same time I do not think we need worry about any possibility of Russian domination."[80]

1941

As Napoleon had hoped to do in 1812, the Germans planned in 1941 to destroy the Russian armies by defeating them, to live off the country, and to find shelter in the towns if winter overtook them. They repeated also Napoleon's fatal error: failure to equip their troops adequately for fighting through a Russian winter. The Russians, on the other hand, made full use, as against Napoleon, of their timeless defensive resources: space which they could trade for time, the devotion and tenacity of their troops, the patient fortitude of their people under privation, their perseverance and ferocity as partisans—and the Russian winter and the mud in spring. As Napoleon had done, the Germans took into Russia with them troops furnished by their allies and satellite states, and found them to be of questionable value.[81]

From Finland, East Prussia, German-occupied Poland, Hungary, and Rumania highly mechanized and mobile forces poured into Russia and the Russian-occupied Baltic states and Poland, and into Bessarabia. Sweden permitted one division to cross Swedish territory to Finland. Much of the Luftwaffe was shifted from the attack on Britain to cover the invasion. The tactical objective was to thrust into, then surround and capture or cut to pieces, the Red armies facing them. It was partially achieved. Hundreds of thousands of Red soldiers were killed, wounded, or captured. At Minsk, in the first week of war, the Germans claimed 290,000 prisoners of war, 2585 tanks, and 1499 guns. Civilians included, Russian casualties soon mounted into millions.

[79] *Nazi-Soviet Relations*, 349-353.

[80] Langer, *op. cit.*, 161. Pétain thought that the Germans would only occupy the Russian provinces near the German border and set up buffer states there, and that that would cause the downfall of Stalin and end the menace of communism.

[81] The Finns fought well. Hungary and Rumania sent, all together, a million men; but their troops usually needed a stiffening of Germans. Later Italy sent whole divisions; but their hearts were not in the enterprise. Franco later sent a worthless Blue Legion of "volunteers." Goebbels complained in his diary in January, 1942, that the French on the Russian front were no longer worth anything, had lost their military punch, and were giving a poor account of themselves.

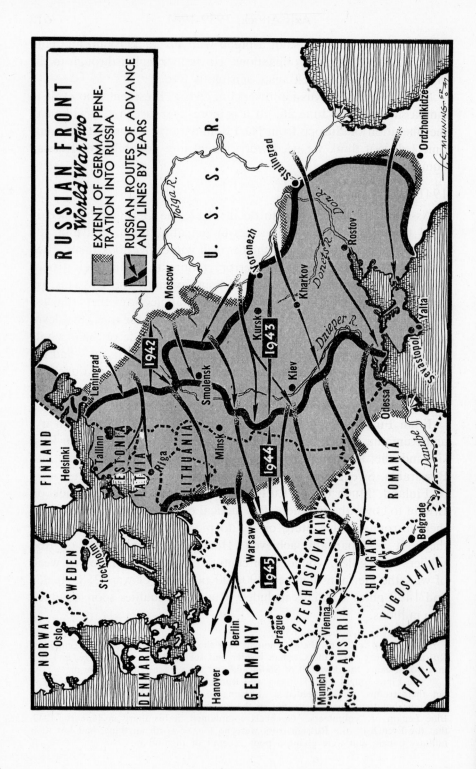

RUSSIAN FRONT
World War Two

EXTENT OF GERMAN PENE-
TRATION INTO RUSSIA

RUSSIAN ROUTES OF ADVANCE
AND LINES BY YEARS

More interested than his generals in the naval, political, and economic aspects of the war, Hitler pressed the northernmost and southernmost prongs of the offensive, seeking to join forces with the Finns by the early conquest of Leningrad, barring Russia from the Baltic, and to gain access to the industrial war materials of southern Russia and the Caucasus. His generals would have given priority to the destruction of Red Army units in the center of the Russian line, and the seizure of the vital transportation center, Moscow. The Führer overruled his generals in August, detaching mobile armored forces from the central armies to expedite the encirclement and capture of Kiev in mid-September, and to reinforce the drive on Leningrad. The army group assigned to the drive on Moscow thus lost some of its speed and striking power, though its infantry attempted the impossible. "We underestimated the Russians," ruefully admitted General Halder after the capture of Narva, August 17. He had reckoned on 200 divisions, and had already counted 360.[82]

Russia was grievously hurt in the first summer campaign. Her troops could hold on for only a few weeks to the areas occupied since 1939. Then they began to lose older Russian territory: Ukraine, which had produced a fifth of Russia's wheat and nearly all of her beet sugar; the Donets Basin, which had produced nearly two-thirds of her coal; iron mines of the Krivoi Rog region, whence had come more than half of her iron; the huge electric power dam and plant near Dniepropetrovsk; the nonferrous metals of southern Ukraine and the Donets and Don basins; the metallurgical industries of such cities as Nikolaev, Kiev, Kharkov, Dniepropetrovsk, Zaporozhe, Voroshilovgrad, and Taganrog; and the northern shores of the Black Sea and Sea of Azov.

The Russians saved some of their industries by moving them out of reach into or beyond the Urals; most of the rest in the areas overrun were destroyed. Some of their people went east with their transplanted industries; others hung on to harry the invaders as partisans; others were reduced by the Germans to virtual slavery where they were or deported as slave labor to Germany. Some of the armed forces saved themselves by withdrawal in a well-planned "defense in depth"; others stubbornly delayed the enemy advance which had cut off and

[82] It was charged at Nuremberg after the war that the northern German army groups had killed 135,567 civilians in three and one-half months, and that 33,771 Jews had been killed in Kiev in two days. Army orders modeled on those issued by Generals von Reichenau and von Mannstein licensed and encouraged the abuse of the people of the occupied area. Peter Calvocoressi, *Nuremberg: The Facts, the Law and the Consequences* (New York, 1948), 74-75, 89.

surrounded them. No other nation in Europe could have lost so much and so many and still have lived.

No other government had survived such disasters and been strengthened by them. Having assumed the titles of prime minister and generalissimo, Marshal Stalin showed himself to be a resolute national leader of great courage, with ability to command loyalty and obedience. The defense of Russia by the Russians transcended communist ideology until the soil of Mother Russia was again free from the invader. The Orthodox Church was again given national sanction, and Christianity was recognized as the religion of many of the people. Military discipline was tightened, army officers were given more authority, and party discipline within the army was temporarily relaxed. The work day and work week were lengthened. People labored to the limit of their endurance in their salvaged war industries and on what land was left to them. Tens of thousands of new tanks, guns, and planes replaced the thousands that were lost or destroyed, and fresh millions of reserves replaced the millions of soldiers killed, wounded, or lost as prisoners of war. The most valuable of Russia's inexhaustible resources was the Russian people, who refused to recognize exhaustion.

Help came from Britain and the United States. On July 12 the Soviet government accepted a British offer of a military alliance, Britain being willing for the time being to overlook ideological incompatibilities and differences of political and economic systems, and Russia being ready to accept help from whatever source.

Late in July, 1941, Harry Hopkins flew from Scotland to Moscow by way of Archangel, as the personal emissary of President Roosevelt, to ascertain what lend-lease supplies the Red Army most urgently needed. Tanks, and steel for making more tanks, was the answer, although Stalin told his friendly visitor that he already had four thousand heavy, eight thousand medium, and twelve thousand light tanks and was then making a thousand per month. Stalin then listed also as urgent Red Army needs light anti-aircraft weapons, aluminum for planes, machine guns, and rifles. The winter line, he said on July 31, would be west of Leningrad, Moscow, and Kiev, probably not more than a hundred kilometers from where it then was.[83]

[83] Robert E. Sherwood, *op. cit.*, 336-339. Stalin told Hopkins then that he would welcome United States troops on any part of the Russian front at any time, under United States command. Later he was less cordial toward that idea.

Stalin asked outright for British troops for the Russian front. "It seems to me," he cabled Churchill September 15, "that Great Britain could without risk land in Archangel twenty-five to thirty divisions, or transport them across Iran to the southern regions of the USSR." Britain did not have so many divisions available

Two months later, in Moscow, Mr. Averell Harriman and Lord Beaverbrook arranged more definitely with Stalin for delivery of lend-lease supplies. Stalin listed again as his most urgent needs tanks, anti-aircraft, and armor plate, and added antitank guns, medium bombers, fighter and reconnaissance planes, and barbed wire. The agreement signed October 1 covered more than seventy main items, from planes and destroyers to army boots (of which the Russians asked for 400,000 per month) and more than eighty kinds of medical and surgical supplies. With an expression of sincere gratitude, November 4, Stalin accepted for the Soviet government a billion-dollar United States loan, without interest, to pay for armaments and raw materials. Repayment of the loan was to begin five years after the end of the war, and to be completed during the following ten-year period. Lend-lease for Russia was announced by President Roosevelt November 7.[84] Supplies were sent through Archangel, Vladivostok, and Iran—Russia's coveted outlet to the Persian Gulf and Indian Ocean serving as an inlet instead, thanks to a friendly Britain and the United States and their hard-won influence with the government of Iran. Hard pressed in October, 1942, Stalin asked that the United States send him *per month* five hundred pursuit planes of the fastest and most improved type, from eight thousand to ten thousand trucks, five thousand tons of aluminum, and from four thousand to five thousand tons of explosives. He called it essential also to secure the delivery within a year of two million tons of grain and the largest possible amount of fats, concentrated food, and canned meat—and twenty to thirty ships to be ceded to the merchant marine of the USSR to carry food to Vladivostok. He had explained his request to Wendell Willkie, who had visited him with credentials from the president.

In mid-October, 1941, German spearheads around Mozhaisk, west of Moscow, were met by fresh Russian reserves—which surprised them—and by the first snow and frost of what proved to be an early and unusually severe winter—which dismayed them. Field Marshal

---

for either enterprise. Any troops sent to Murmansk then, replied Churchill to Ambassador Sir Stafford Cripps, would have been "frozen in darkness for the winter." It would have taken at least three months, he said, to put two divisions into the Caucasus or north of the Caspian, and they would then have been only "a drop in the bucket." Churchill, *Second World War,* III, 462, 465.

[84] Churchill, *Second World War,* III, 394, 397, 400, 639. The announcement caused great apprehension in the United States among those who on religious, ideological, or historical grounds most distrusted communist Russia. Suspicion was slightly allayed by the arrival of Maxim Litvinov, Soviet vice-commissar for foreign affairs, as ambassador to the United States. Total lend-lease to the USSR, through December 31, 1945, was $11,141,470,000.

von Brauchitsch, professionally trained, experienced, and until then successful commander in chief of the army, wished to break off the offensive and prepare a defensive line. Rundstedt and Leeb would have preferred to draw their troops back to the 1940 line across Poland, where they might have found some shelter for the winter. Hitler overruled them all and the offensive was continued until Moscow was nearly half encircled, albeit at some distance, with Germans around Dmitrov north of the capital and Tula south of it. Some of the Soviet government offices were moved as a precaution to an emergency capital at Kuibyshev on the Volga river, five hundred miles farther east. By Hitler's personal order, on December 2, a new offensive was undertaken; but the Russians under Marshal Zhukov counterattacked successfully December 6 and the offensive failed.

For failure and for little faith, Field Marshal von Brauchitsch was relieved of his command, and Hitler became in his own person commander in chief of the army as well as of the whole defense force or Wehrmacht. Colonel General Halder, chief of staff of the army since 1938, was retained in that position until September, 1942.

In the north, before the end of September, the Finns had regained with the help of the Germans the area around Lake Ladoga which they had lost to the Russians in 1940. Russian warships were kept bottled up in the Gulf of Finland, at Leningrad and Kronstadt. The Germans meanwhile had overrun Lithuania, Latvia, and Estonia, and Leningrad was almost though not quite encircled. During part of the winter, with the Moscow railway line cut, Leningrad had to be supplied across the ice of hard-frozen Lake Ladoga. The sufferings of its population were intense, but war work went on. The organizer of the city's heroic defense was a member of the Communist party's highest echelon, the Politburo—General Andrei Zhdanov.

The German right-wing offensive directed by Field Marshal von Rundstedt went at first, through Bessarabia, more slowly than had been expected, but in the late summer and autumn swept across southern Russia where gains of greatest economic importance as well as area were made. In the Crimea only the fortress of Sevastopol withstood attack. German submarines and patrol boats, transported by way of the Elbe, the *Autobahn*, and the Danube, were active in the Black Sea. The line of farthest advance for the year ran in November generally southward from a point south of Moscow, to include Orel, Kursk, and Kharkov, then southeastward to include Rostov, near the mouth of the Don River.

Thinking that the position at Rostov could not be held through the winter, and knowing the probable cost in casualties of trying too late to retreat from it, von Rundstedt asked for permission to abandon it and draw back while there was still time to the line of the Donets River. The high command authorized the withdrawal but was overruled by Hitler, who ordered von Rundstedt to hold Rostov and thought he should go on and take the Maikop oil fields. Protesting that soldiers could not do what the Führer ordered, the old field marshal asked Hitler either to rescind his order or to find someone else to command Army Group South. Hitler removed the recalcitrant von Rundstedt and found someone else, one of von Rundstedt's subordinates, von Reichenau, who lost Rostov, could not try then to take Maikop, and in January, 1942, died of heart failure. Rundstedt was later sent to command the forces in France.

Three of the generals most successful in Poland and France had been broken, two of them permanently, for failure or for trying to argue with Hitler in the Russian campaign. Hitler was inclined thereafter, as the rift between him and the generals with the best professional training widened, to distrust and call "defeatist" all those who doubted that men could do what he demanded of them, and to prefer to listen to and promote those who could pretend a confidence and resolution equal to his own. Men were more than machines, he told them. Wars were won by genius and the exercise of the will, not by numbers or by mathematical calculations of comparative strength. Until then his intuitions had more than once been more accurate, as estimates of general situations involving the imponderables, than his generals' professional calculations had been; so he easily convinced himself during the winter of 1941-1942 that only his "no retreat" orders had saved his armies from disaster. With obvious reference to generals whom he did not name, to a Reichstag which did not question him, he spoke of individuals who failed in critical moments and lost their nerve, and asked for plenary power to act in such cases without regard for "so-called well-earned rights." On motion of Reich Air Marshal Göring the Reichstag gave him "with stormy salvos of applause" the law he wanted. He was already supreme commander of the Wehrmacht and the army; but his arbitrary power over individuals was increased. The winter was none the less disastrous.

Hitler could not control or cashier the weather, although the Reichstag would have authorized it if he had asked. Goebbels conceded, in his diary, 50,000 casualties from frostbite by January 20, and one month later 62,627 more. Total casualties from all causes to February 20 were 1,064,768, including more than 200,000 killed. Shortages of

Diesel and fuel oil were keenly felt in the navy and there was a general fuel shortage at home, while whole armies were immobilized by want of motor fuel. Appeals for warmer clothing for soldiers at the front gave the lie to Hitler's premature public statement, October 3, 1941, that Russia was already so beaten and broken as never to be able to rise again.

How far Stalin was from thinking Russia hopelessly defeated was made clear in conversation with British Foreign Minister Anthony Eden December 16. The prewar position of the Soviet Union, i.e., her position prior to the German attack, with respect to Finland, the Baltic states, and Bessarabia, should be restored. The Curzon line should be the basis of the Soviet-Polish boundary line. Rumania should give the Soviet Union bases, but might be compensated out of former Rumanian territory then held by Hungary. Bucovina would not be returned. Churchill's position then was that Russia's claims in those areas had been recognized only *de facto* and were contrary to the Atlantic Charter, to which Stalin had subscribed. Britain could not recognize them without prior agreement with the United States (which would not then have agreed). Such questions should wait for a peace conference, to be held after the war.[85]

1942, TO STALINGRAD

Until that disillusioning winter, total industrial mobilization for war had not been found necessary in Germany, such a surplus war production potential had been built up, and so much labor and material had been drawn from satellite and conquered countries. War plants had not had to work up to capacity, munition factories had found one shift per day sufficient, much peacetime production of consumers' goods had continued, and Germans had generally found their personal needs for "life as usual" fairly well supplied. Hitler had indeed gone so far as to order the demobilization of forty divisions and the reconversion of some factories to consumer-goods production. A belated recognition of the seriousness of the new situation brought about by failure to win the Russian war by a swift knockout led in February, 1942, to the establishment of the Speer ministry for total economic mobilization. Step by step during the next three years the Speer ministry took over the allocation of war materials, armament production, naval building, and all aircraft production; but by the time the total economic dictatorship of the *Führerstaat* had been established there was little left of Führer or of state.

[85] *Ibid.*, 629, 630.

Meanwhile economic exploiters and political and cultural organizers and archivists followed the armed forces into Russia and the intervening territory to establish the new order there. Although decent individuals among them tried to preserve cultural values, the population generally, and Poles and Jews especially, rued their coming.

A Czech-Slovak-Polish confederation under German leadership was proposed by the Germans in January. The meaning of coöperation between the master race and weaker ones was made clear. "Formal statutes are not considered necessary in developing European coöperation. The country assuming the leadership is declared to have the duty of determining the special needs and capabilities of the weaker countries and of taking their interests into consideration."[86]

Although the Red Army was soon in a position to retaliate and did so, Russian prisoners of war were generally worse abused than others except as the Germans differentiated between "deserters and real prisoners."

When the Nazi were ready in April, 1942, to draft civilians from the eastern occupied area for labor, Goebbels wrote in his diary: "That means of course that they must be fed better than the Russian prisoners thus far. Also, of course, they must be given certain privileges, as their performance will otherwise not be satisfactory."[87]

In April, 1942, came a test of strength between Nazi influence and the influence of the United States in French Vichy. Nazi influence prevailed. In the face of the most vigorous objection from the United States, Pierre Laval, the Frenchman most brazenly subservient to Germany, the one who could best be expected to force a policy of collaboration down the throats of his countrymen, returned to Vichy as premier and (under Pétain) effective head of the state. Darlan held on as commander in chief of the armed forces, responsible directly to Pétain. Laval told the United States ambassador, Admiral Leahy, that he expected and preferred to see Germany win. His policy, which he called one of reconciliation, was, he said, the only one in the interest of a definitive peace. The United States had committed a serious error in entering the war. Only Bolshevism would win by it.[88]

---

[86] U. S., *Foreign Commerce Weekly*, vol. 5-6 (February 7, 1942), p. 9, n. 3.

Göring broadcast a promise to the German people in October, 1942, that if there was to be hunger in Europe they, the Germans, would be the last to starve. That promise he kept.

[87] *Goebbels Diaries*, 157, 182.

[88] Langer, *op. cit.*, 200, 248, 250. Laval did not say how he thought the United States should have reacted to the attack on Pearl Harbor. The United States was ready to break off relations with Vichy, but the illness and death of Admiral Leahy's wife delayed his departure and kept the embassy open as a sort of listening post in an alien land.

Meanwhile in Paris the Nazi cracked the whip. As reprisal for a train wreck in April in which "several" Germans had been killed, thirty hostages were shot. It was announced by the occupation authorities that, unless those responsible for the wreck were captured within eight days, eighty additional hostages would be shot and more than a thousand "communists and Jews" would be put into freight cars and "shipped east." No proof was offered that the hostages were in any way directly connected with the sabotage or other acts for which reprisals were being taken, or personally with the supposed saboteurs. They were merely persons already in custody as known or supposed members of the patriotic resistance, natural enemies of the occupation forces. Many of them were members of the families of those active in the resistance. But the Nazi did not consider it necessary to establish an actual connection except as a means of disheartening one or another. Persons thought to be in sympathy with the resistance were labeled, with little discrimination, communists, de Gaullists, or Jews. Five hundred such persons were deported to an eastern labor camp and ten hostages were shot as an exemplary reprisal when on or about April 21, 1942, a German soldier was killed in Paris.[89]

In May, 1942, German Propaganda Minister Dr. Goebbels was wondering, as Hitler and Ribbentrop had wondered about Britain more than a year earlier, why the Russians had not given up the ghost. "If we had to do with a civilized people in our eastern campaign," he wrote in his diary, "it would long ago have collapsed; but the Russians are quite unpredictable in this as in other matters. They show a capacity for suffering that is simply impossible with other peoples. The men at present in control of the Soviet Union of course know that very definitely and base their plans for the coming summer on this mentality."[90]

Russia had other resources than the amazing endurance of her people; and while waiting for the June sun and wind to dry the deep mud of spring and make roads and fields passable she mobilized them. General Halder told interviewers after the war that when he told Hitler what he knew about Russian tank production the Führer frothed at the mouth, screamed with rage, threatened his chief of staff with his fists, and refused to listen further.[91]

[89] *Goebbels Diaries*, 177-179. For the killing of Reinhard Heydrich, deputy protector of Bohemia-Moravia, in May, 1942, the village of Lidice was destroyed in June and its population exterminated or deported, although Heydrich was generally believed to have been murdered by some of his own German police associates, of whom two were later executed and one committed suicide.

[90] *Ibid.*, 207.

[91] British War Office interrogation, September, 1945. Shulman, *op. cit.*, 69, 70.

Russia and Great Britain signed in London on May 26 a twenty-year treaty of alliance against Germany, providing for postwar collaboration and mutual assistance. Mutually the high contracting parties undertook not to make a separate armistice or peace with Germany or with any ally of Germany, and to act in accordance with the two principles of not seeking territorial aggrandizement for themselves and of nonintervention in the internal affairs of other states. Each undertook not to conclude an alliance or take part in a coalition directed against the other.[92]

From London Molotov went on to Washington to urge the establishment of a second front in western Europe in 1942. General George C. Marshall, chief of the combined committee of chiefs of staff, told him that the problem was primarily one of transport and was just then being seriously complicated by the diversion of shipping to the Murmansk route to carry supplies to Russia—a statement repeated next day by the president. During three months, April to June, 143 ships, 826,000 tons, left the United States for Russia. Of the eighty-four ships that went by way of the North Cape, forty-four reached Murmansk. Twenty-three were lost by enemy action or casualty. Seventeen were unloaded in Scotland.[93]

In a new lend-lease agreement with the United States, June 11, 1942, Russia recognized the principles of the Atlantic Charter.

At a conference in Moscow in mid-August, Stalin bluntly insisted that Britain open a second front in France in 1942.[94] He grudgingly accepted a North African campaign as a substitute, and said he would

[92] In the Security Council of the United Nations, Russian delegate Gromyko objected to the North Atlantic Pact of 1949 on the ground that it was forming a coalition directed against Russia. Its signers took the position that the pact was defensive in character and was not directed against Russia unless she intended to attack one of them, as she said she had no thought of doing.

[93] Sherwood, op. cit., 556, 575; Morison, op. cit., I, 159, 164-165, 198, 200, 367. During that month of May, submarines sank 73 ships, 350,000 tons, in the Gulf of Mexico and the Caribbean, more than world losses in any month prior to February, 1942. In the first six months of 1942 the United States lost more tonnage than in the whole war of 1914-1918.

On the Murmansk route from August, 1941, through 1942, out of 301 ships in 21 northbound convoys 53 were lost; 248 arrived. Out of 232 ships in 16 southbound convoys, 16 were lost; 216 arrived. Up to the end of September, 1943, the Murmansk route had carried 23 percent of United States shipments and a very large proportion of those from Britain to the USSR. About 21 percent of cargoes sent by that route had been lost, 8 percent of those sent by way of Iran, none—by enemy action—of those sent through Vladivostok, although Japan could have stopped them.

[94] The disastrous and terribly costly British reconnaissance raid on Dieppe was made August 19. Stalin had conveniently forgotten the help that Russia had given Germany two years before, when Britain would so have welcomed the opening of a second front in Europe.

"accept gratefully" an Allied force at the south end of his defense line.[95]

By that time the southern end of the Russian defense line was in the Caucasus. By a winter (1941-1942) counteroffensive the Russians had managed to recapture Mozhaisk and perhaps 10 percent of the territory they had lost northwest and southwest of Moscow; but the Germans held on through the winter in "hedgehog" positions around Velikie Luki, Vyazma, Rzhev, Orel, Kursk, Kharkov, and Taganrog, and maintained their sieges of Leningrad and Sevastopol.

Under General Fritz Erich von Mannstein, who had been chief of staff to von Rundstedt in Poland and France and had risen through combat commands in Russia, the Eleventh German Army began the 1942 offensive in the Crimea May 8. Only two weeks were needed to clear again the Kerch peninsula, lost late in 1941. On July 3 Sevastopol had to surrender. Twenty days later Rostov was retaken, and on August 23 Maikop was occupied. The German armored forces and truck-borne infantry were in the Russian oil fields which Hitler had thought they could reach in 1941, but found the wells plugged and the machinery wrecked. They were stopped for three weeks in the heart of the oil fields by shortages of motor fuel, some of which had to be carried to them by a long airlift.

The real goals were farther on: the greater oil fields around Grozny and Baku, the oil pipe line from Baku on the Caspian to Batum on the Black Sea, beyond the Caucasus Mountains, and Stalingrad on the Volga. The loss of Stalingrad would cut off central Russia from its own Caspian-Volga oil barge line from Baku, and from the Allied supply line across Iran to the Caspian Sea.

So as rapidly as possible, against unrelenting resistance, the southernmost spearheads swung southeastward from Maikop toward Grozny; but the base of their salient had had to be broadened. A second summer offensive from Kursk toward Voronezh and along the whole line from Kursk down to Taganrog had closed up by mid-August to the right bank of the Don, from Voronezh to the easternmost "Don bend" nearest Stalingrad. The pursuit of the first objective, the conquest of the Caucasus to supply Germany with oil, was weakened and slowed down thereafter by the diversion of supplies and reinforcements to the second—to cripple Russia by the conquest of Stalin's city, Stalingrad.

Both failed. Inadequately sustained, the southern offensive did not

---

[95] Sherwood, *op. cit.*, 617. No such force was sent. When once the German advance had been stopped, Stalin did not want one. The North African campaign did not satisfy Stalin. He refused, when it was made, to think of it, or of the Sicilian or the Italian campaign which followed it, as a second front or as a substitute for one.

take Grozny or reach the Caspian Sea. The northern drive reached Stalingrad at the end of August but could not take it.

In September, as in 1941, the German general staff would have drawn back from Stalingrad to a shorter line while there was still time, but Hitler would have none of that. He dropped his practiced but pessimistic chief of staff, Colonel General Halder, and replaced him with General Kurt von Zeitzler, who was more optimistic at first but not for long. From October 14 to November 5 a ceaseless grinding attack was pushed, exhausting the men who made it and the munitions carried to them, partly by air, at great cost. Led by General Vassily Chuikov, the Russians turned their city into a redoubt and fought for it stone by stone with whatever weapons and munitions they could bring across the Volga by barge under incessant German fire. It was one of the titanic battles of the century, and a turning point of the war.

The failure at Stalingrad marked the end of the great Axis offensive. Japanese conquest in the southwest Pacific had reached its full stretch and been stopped in the Coral Sea, at Midway, and on Guadalcanal. The British North African counteroffensive had begun at El Alamein in Egypt, October 23-24. A United States expeditionary force had landed in Morocco November 7-8. By November 23 another winter and a Russian counteroffensive, which had begun four days earlier with easy breakthroughs against Hungarian, Italian, and Rumanian troops along the Don River side of the salient below Voronezh, west of Stalingrad, had immobilized and surrounded twenty-two German divisions in the Stalingrad area. The airlift that continued to supply them in starvation fashion, although it lost five hundred planes in the attempt, might have evacuated some of them; but Hitler, who had forbidden their commander, Field Marshal Friedrich von Paulus, to abandon the attack and extricate his forces when he could have done so, ordered him to stay where he was and defend himself. With the 200,000 that were left of his 330,000 men, and with fifteen other generals, von Paulus surrendered February 2, 1943, to Marshal Zhukov.[96]

[96] Hitler called the surrender "cowardly." One of the other generals surrendered was von Seydlitz, a member of a family distinguished in military service for many generations. While prisoners of war, both Seydlitz and Paulus joined a Russian-sponsored union of German officers to advocate, by radio, the overthrow of the Nazi and the making of an immediate peace with Russia. Paulus was a prosecution witness at the trial of the principal war criminals at Nuremberg. Seydlitz did not return home immediately, and the possibility of his continued collaboration with the Russians after the war was the subject of speculation in the west.

General Halder spent the last years of the war in concentration camp in Germany, so did not share the fate of those involved in the July 20, 1944, assassination plot against Hitler.

CHAPTER 14

The United States: From Neutral to Belligerent

NEUTRALITY

Isolationism, Aloofness, Nonintervention

RETREAT FROM 1918

If neutrality meant indifference or impartiality, intellectual aloofness or detachment, then the people of the United States were never neutral in the second world war of the twentieth century, no matter how far they had pushed their government toward neutrality in the period between the wars, hoping to avoid involvement. Almost all Americans felt a quick instinctive sympathy with the victims of tyranny and aggression and hoped to see them soon regain their freedom and their rights. The characteristic American predilection for peaceful, legally established procedure was strong enough to serve as an effective guarantee that the United States would not break the peace by threat or use of armed force, but not strong enough between 1930 and 1940 to induce the nation to commit itself to the use of force to preserve the peace. In that reluctance to resort to the legal or authorized use of armed force in defense of the principle of collective security to prevent or stop aggression, the people of the United States were by no means alone. Only the dictators were ready, and they traded upon the unreadiness of the unready.

Many circumstances had contributed since 1918 to the prevalence of the extremist attitude of isolationism and of more moderate but more widespread noninterventionism. Constant review and revision of the history of the war years 1914-1918 had combined with general disappointment over the impermanence of the peace to produce a rather general attitude of disillusionment and futilitarianism. The United States had not been able from 1914 to 1917 to defend the previously conceded rights of neutrals or to remain neutral itself. As a belligerent, the United States had saved France and Britain from defeat and the threat of imminent destruction and had helped to destroy the Hohenzollern empire. But it had subsequently become fashionable to say that the peace of Versailles had been unduly harsh, and that the French had been vindictive and the British interested only in imperial advantages and profits. To have contributed so materially to so sorry and impermanent a peace must have been a blunder, into which the United States must have been tricked by alien propaganda or its own big-money or munitions men, or misled by its own leaders for nefarious personal reasons. Nothing permanent or constructive had been accomplished, it was said, by intervention in a European war. Nothing useful could be accomplished by intervening in another. War was a malady of which Europe had not been cured by the bloodletting of 1914-1918, a vice to which it was addicted and would always eventually return. To repeat and compound the error of intervention, then, would be egregious error indeed.

Few of those who so inoculated themselves against what they called British or war propaganda realized what useful uncompensated service they were doing the revisionists, or to what an extent they were being prompted by German nationalist propaganda disguised for that purpose as propaganda for a free American policy, for disarmament and peace.[1]

MANCHURIA, 1931

North American public opinion was more nearly unanimous in 1931 with reference to Japan, Manchuria, and China than with reference to Germany or Italy and Europe. Probably three-fourths of the press supported Secretary Stimson's move, first to challenge Japan's seizure of Manchuria as a violation of the Nine-Power China Treaty and the Kellogg Pact, and second for parallel action by the United States to support the League of Nations in any measures short of war which it might take in restraint of unprovoked aggression. There was some expressed objection at home, but not much, to having the United States consul general, Prentiss Gilbert be present at the League of Nations Council meetings in Geneva to discuss enforcement of the Paris Pact, or ambassador Charles G. Dawes at those in Paris for the same purpose. The Stimson doctrine of nonrecognition of changes of

---

[1] See pp. 131-137.

territorial sovereignty made by methods inconsistent with the obligations assumed under the Kellogg Pact (of Paris) was very generally approved. No government, however, could then have led the people of the United States into war against Japan in defense of China's sovereignty in Manchuria. Manchuria seemed far away.[2]

NATIONAL SOCIALISM

Opinion in the United States was startled by the rise of National Socialism in Germany and especially offended by the news reports of anti-Semitism, the revolt against intellectual and cultural freedom highlighted by the burning of books by students in the universities, and the unconvincing Reichstag fire trial—convincing only as evidence that a ruthless and lawless police state had been established. There was no popular demand, however, for intervention by the government of the United States to deny the German people what was generally regarded as their right to accept and obey, or of their own volition to revolt against, a government made in Germany, which had not been imposed upon them by any alien authority. The Germans had convinced themselves and many others that they needed a stronger government than the Weimar republic, and that the Treaty of Versailles had been unjust to them and ought to be revised. It was not difficult to understand the natural aspiration of the Germans to regain for their fatherland as soon as possible full sovereignty within its national boundaries and a position of recognized equality of rights and privileges (*Ebenbürtigkeit*) among the nations. Only the thoughtful and the prescient were aware of a deep sense of apprehension and foreboding lest Nazi intransigence eventually lead Germany into a second general war to reverse the results of the one she had lost in 1918, or over the possibility—which then seemed so remote—that the United States would again inevitably be involved if such a war should come to pass.[3]

THE JOHNSON ACT

Public opinion in the United States was further alienated against the quondam Allies of the Four Years' War against Germany by the hardships of the economic depression of the early 1930's, and by the failure of the debtor nations to resume payment on their debts to the United States after the Hoover moratorium. A debt default act of April, 1934, sponsored by Senator Hiram Johnson of California,

[2] See pp. 456-461.
[3] See pp. 462-476.

made illegal a new loan to any nation in default or in arrears on debt payments to the United States, and prohibited the sale in the United States, by such a nation, of any of its securities.

The curtailment of the credit of the debtor nations did not move them to resume payment on the debts. Not even token payments were made thereafter. Only Finland, which had not defaulted, kept up her payments.

The combined effect of the Johnson Act and of the continued default upon relations between the United States and the nations affected was generally bad. Americans saw money being spent for armament in Europe, as if in preparation for another war, by nations which had not yet paid debts incurred in their last one, although one of them (Great Britain) boasted a budget surplus while the United States government budget showed a deficit. Europeans, on the other hand, saw themselves threatened with aggression by the totalitarian states, while the Johnson Act denied them credit that they needed to overcome their heavy handicap in military preparedness. The unintended but inevitable effect of the act was, therefore, to encourage potential aggressors and discourage potential victims of aggression. Refusal to supply credit for the purchase of means of defense, on the theory that nations which could not find the money would not go to war, did not prevent the imposition of war upon a people by aggression, by a nation which pretended to be destitute but expected to make war a profitable enterprise. The act dashed also whatever hope there was that new loans might revive international trade and restore prosperity.[4]

Neutrality Legislation

ETHIOPIA. ACT OF 1935

In the summer of 1935, while Italy accumulated a quarter of a million troops and laborers in Eritrea and Italian Somaliland and rejected all suggestions of peaceful settlement of her synthetic quarrel with Ethiopia, the United States Congress debated a joint resolution to insure technical neutrality. Although divided on account of the backwardness of Ethiopia, a nation ruled through half-savage native chieftains by an imperial autocrat, the only free nation in Africa in which human slavery still found legal sanction, American opinion generally favored Ethiopia as the object of aggression and was correspondingly unfavorable toward Italy, which was rightly regarded as the aggressor. Although apologists for conquest reviewed the world

[4] See pp. 422-425.

history of aggression, they could find only precedents, no justification.

American opinion was not indifferent to the illegality and wanton wickedness of the war, or impartial in its attitude toward the belligerents. It would have preferred to see the League of Nations take immediate and effective steps to prevent or stop the invasion and settle the dispute by pacific means. The government of the United States had assured the League that it would do nothing to reduce the effectiveness of measures the League might take for that purpose.

Yet the threat of a new war revived memories of involvement in a past one, precipitated by an incident in a faraway place called Sarajevo, which in 1914 had seemed almost, though not quite, as remote as Ualual in eastern Africa seemed twenty years later. That involvement was incorrectly interpreted in 1935 by a large body of opinion, probably majority opinion, as an unfortunate consequence of insistence upon the right of neutrals to trade and travel outside actual war zones, in defiance of proclaimed blockades and war zones. Years of study of the origins of the war of 1914 and revelations of the war aims of the belligerents had led to a realization that Germany's share of responsibility for that war had been less, and the war aims of Germany's European enemies less altruistic, than had been generally known in 1917 or 1918. The consequent reinterpretation of twentieth-century history and dissatisfaction with the largely negative results of United States intervention in the Four Years' War led many people to the conclusion that the attempt of 1917-1919 to influence the course of events in Europe had been a waste of time and effort, and of men's lives.

Logically then, if participation in one European war had failed to prevent another, the United States should not participate in another; and, to avoid involuntary involvement, it should avoid the mistakes and be on guard against the sinister influences which had once drawn it from its neutral position. Testimony taken by the Nye committee was publicized to show, with other expressions of opinion, that the munitions makers and other big-money men, the traders, the travelers, and British or pro-British propagandists had been responsible for the error of 1917. By America First and by many persons not members of that organization, public opinion was thoroughly alerted against being again so misled. Only a minority asked often at that time whether the majority was misleading itself by giving such free rein to its preference for freedom to remain at peace.

Accurately reflecting prevalent majority opinion, the Neutrality Act of August 24, 1935, empowered the president when war broke out between two or more European nations, or during the progress of such a war, to proclaim that a state of war existed in the area affected. With the issuance of the president's proclamation, the Neutrality Act imposed an immediate embargo on arms, munitions, and implements of war. The president was to declare what implements and materials were war materials or implements of war.[5] United States citizens were warned not to travel on vessels of any belligerent nation, or were to travel at their own risk.

SPAIN. APPLICATION TO CIVIL WAR

The Neutrality Act of 1935 expired February 29, 1936, but was then extended to May 1, 1937. While the Axis powers and Russia intervened in the civil war in Spain, and France and Great Britain tried in vain to localize hostilities and maintain the principle of non-intervention although it was soon only a polite fiction, the new United States Neutrality Act of February 29, 1936, tightened restrictions by denying loans or credit to any belligerent. There was little demand that the United States officially intervene. Although opinion was divided, largely because of the extreme radicalism and anticlericalism of some of the Loyalists, there was a preponderance of sympathy for the legally established Loyalist government. There were more American volunteers and more material aid for the republic than for Franco.

Late in 1936, with the war against the republic being more and more taken over by the Axis powers, which were also better able then than formerly to prevent the sending of Russian aid to the republicans, a request was made in the United States for licenses to export planes and other war matériel to the Loyalists in Spain. The government, which had only unofficially discouraged the sale of war equipment or matériel to either party, was compelled then for the first time to say officially whether its neutrality legislation applied to civil wars. That question was answered almost unanimously in Congress by joint resolution signed by the president January 8, 1937. The conflict in Spain was called a war, and the neutrality legislation already passed then made it illegal to sell weapons, other implements of war, or war matériel to either side. As Franco was getting help elsewhere, and the United States was the best source of aid still available to the Loyalists, the neutrality policy of the United States hurt the republic without hurting the insurgents.[6]

---

[5] In the Italian-Ethiopian conflict, unfinished raw materials such as petroleum were not so defined, and were not included among the enumerated articles banned by the League of Nations sanctions. See pp. 481-482.

[6] See pp. 492-493.

The neutrality laws of 1935 and January, 1937, were short-term legislation. The latter would have lapsed May 1, 1937, had not Congress reënacted on that date most of its provisions in what was presumed to be more nearly permanent form. The new law left the president some discretion to determine when or in what circumstances he should proclaim that a state of war existed and declare its embargo provisions to be applicable and in effect. Other provisions of the older legislation were kept and strengthened. It was made illegal for United States ships to carry arms, munitions, or implements of war to a belligerent, or to go armed, or for a citizen of the United States to travel on a vessel of a belligerent. The president was given authority to deny armed merchantmen or submarines of a belligerent the use of ports or harbors in the United States but was not left free to differentiate between civil and international war, between one belligerent and another, or between attacker and attacked. A new feature of the law of May 1, 1937, was the "cash and carry" provision that title to certain purchased commodities, to be enumerated by the president, must be taken in the United States and the commodities paid for in cash before delivery. Enumerated commodities so purchased might not be carried in United States ships.

The enforcement of the "cash and carry" act in the event of a general war between the Axis and the western European powers would be to the advantage of the maritime powers as long as their ready money or quickly realizable cash assets lasted, unless Axis submarines, surface raiders, and air power could cut them off from their sources of supply. Being already without credit in the United States, on the other hand, with few readily realizable assets, and likely as they were to be at once cut off from access to North American supplies, the Axis powers would lose little as a result of the "cash and carry" provision that they would not in war immediately have lost for lack of credit and sea power, and little on which they had depended or based supply plans. So they would ultimately, though not at first, have been less seriously affected than the maritime powers by the application of the act.

On the day of its passage the act of May 1, 1937, was proclaimed in effect for the war in Spain. It was not invoked in the Chino-Japanese conflict in July—which Japan called only an incident, in which there had been no declaration of war, and in which the United States government preferred to be free to aid China although that meant forgoing use of its authority to stop the shipment of war materials by private entrepreneurs to Japan.

Popular reaction to President Roosevelt's "quarantine" speech of October 5, 1937, the *Panay* incident, and the Ludlow resolution clearly indicated that, while not generally uninformed or indifferent to the ominous trend of world affairs, the people of the United States were not ready to assume the risk of war or a new burden of commitments in an attempt to control the course of events overseas. Preferring peace at almost any price, they clung emotionally to their time-honored policy of neutrality.[7]

LEND-LEASE

Britain

Until 1940, and to a diminishing extent until the Japanese attack on Pearl Harbor, the neutrality policy of the United States was based upon the rather general hope or assumption that the United States was free to choose between participation and nonparticipation, between peace and war. People naturally chose peace. People preferred to believe, if they could, that, having had very little directly to do with the immediate causes of the war, they could avoid being vitally affected by its consequences. Such an outcome would be possible only if there were a peace without victory, leaving the balance of power in Europe materially unchanged, or if the characters of the belligerent governments and leaders were so much alike that it mattered little which side won.

From the outset in 1939, but more clearly in 1940, it became apparent that there was to be no peace without victory, and that not only western Europe but the world would be profoundly affected by the kind of peace a victorious Germany would make. The cynical Nazi-Soviet treaty for another partition of Poland was a warning signal. The swiftness and startling efficiency of the German attack were in effect another. The invasions of Denmark, Norway, the Netherlands, Belgium, and France warned the world that Hitler would not stop anywhere until someone stopped him. The fall of France seemed likely to be followed by the fall of Britain.

Could the United States, then, afford to remain neutral? The acknowledged and uninhibited British nationalist and imperialist Winston Churchill used every argument with which his extraordinary resourcefulness and long experience in public life equipped him to convince President Roosevelt that the interests of the United States

[7] See pp. 497-504.

would be adversely affected by a German victory, and that enlightened self-interest would dictate that the United States insure the defeat of Nazi Germany by insuring the survival and ultimate victory of Britain. If the United States permitted Hitler to conquer Britain as he had already conquered other nations, said Churchill pointedly, it would soon find itself in peril.

There was no danger of immediate invasion. The Atlantic was still a broader barrier than the English Channel, which, with the British Royal Air Force in action above and beyond it, was proving itself an obstacle to invasion. A slightly stunned public opinion, how-ever, was slowly realizing that with the British Isles, the Danish, Spanish, and Portuguese Atlantic islands, and French West Africa in its possession a victorious Germany would be in a position to drive American commerce off the Atlantic and exclude it from the Medi-terranean, from Europe, and from Africa. Daily revelations of the character of the Nazi regime indicated that it would be impossible, as the recently returned commercial attaché Douglas Miller said it would be, to "do business with Hitler."[8] There was no reason to sup-pose that American interests would fare any better in Asia or the southwest Pacific if Japan gained control of those areas or a position of paramount interest there.

From the outbreak of the war, American opinion swung under pressure of daily events and an awakening awareness of their sig-nificance, to which awareness President Roosevelt constantly con-tributed, in the direction of material aid to those who would defend themselves against attack by the Axis powers. By a new neutrality act signed by the president November 4, 1939, the "cash and carry" principle was extended to all commodities, but the ban on sale of weapons, munitions, and other war matériel was dropped. Empowered to define combat areas into which United States citizens, ships, and planes were forbidden to go, the president so designated all ports of belligerents, the Baltic and North seas, the waters around the British Isles, and most of the Bay of Biscay. The sinkings by which Germany had attempted to enforce her paper blockade orders in the waters around the British Isles and off the coasts of the Allied countries from 1914 to 1919 had not been forgotten, and the "neutral right" to traverse those waters unless stopped by an effective blockade was abandoned.[9]

[8] Douglas Miller, *You Can't Do Business with Hitler* (Boston, 1941). See also Chapter 13, pp. 462-476, 520.
[9] See pp. 34-42.

The Dunkirk evacuation and the fall of France made obvious the urgent need of Britain for immediate and direct aid. Weapons and planes were sent in such quantity as soon nearly to have exhausted British purchasing power in the United States. Fifty old United States destroyers were turned over to Great Britain, and the United States was given ninety-nine-year leases on certain naval and air bases on British American territory. When British assets readily convertible into dollars for cash purchases of food, military equipment, and supplies approached the vanishing point, a new and unlimited source of supply was opened up by the passage of the Lend-Lease Act, H.R. 1776, March 11, 1941. The first appropriation to put the act into effect was $7,000,000,000; the eventual total was $49,096,125,000.

"This decision," said President Roosevelt March 15, was "the end of any attempt at appeasement in our land; the end of urging us to get along with the dictators; the end of compromise with tyranny and aggression." Its effects were many and far-reaching. By the terms of the act the federal government and its agencies were authorized to purchase or manufacture "defense articles," which might be weapons, munitions, ships, vehicles, building materials, food, clothing —anything useful to a people at war. These commodities might then be sold, lent, leased, or otherwise transferred to any nation whose defense the president deemed vital to the defense of the United States. By thus putting its industrial resources at the disposal of the chosen nations to the detriment of others, the United States was "taking sides"—another momentous step away from neutrality, through non-belligerency, toward the status of a belligerent. Opinion as to the wisdom of the step was sharply divided at the time, but the measure was supported as an act of national self-defense by those who thought it not only prudent but imperative to help the nations which seemed most friendly to the United States to defend themselves against attack by those menacingly less friendly. The aggressors against which lend-lease materials would be used had already broken the world's peace and were threatening the safety and prosperity of the United States.

Under lend-lease, government-purchased supplies were sent to China for use against Japan; sales of scrap iron and gasoline to Japan by individuals and privately owned corporations were soon prohibited. With lend-lease funds the financial structures and military establishments of the Central and South American republics most likely to contribute to hemispheric defense or to furnish bases useful to the United States in war were strengthened. Nations such as Turkey, not yet involved in the war, were militarily strengthened as a safeguard against the danger of attack. Meanwhile many of the principal industries of the United States were converted and geared up to war production before the United States became a belligerent, and the allocation of the output of the oil wells, arsenals, and airplane and tank factories could be at least partially controlled by the agencies responsible for procurement for the armed forces. Lend-lease production was thus made a useful form of industrial and military preparation for belligerency. After the United States became a belligerent, the working principle of lend-lease was that each ally should give each other whatever material or other aid it could, for credit on lend-lease account, but without immediate or cash payment. Lend-leased articles were to be returned or paid for only upon request of the president. In 1917 and 1918 the United States had sold on credit while paying cash for supplies and services; and its relations with the Allies had subsequently been embittered by the "war debts" which resulted.

Lend-lease exports were sent, before the end of 1945, to more than sixty countries or dependencies. Of these exports Great Britain and the British Empire were the first and principal beneficiaries, to a total amount of $30,753,304,000. Britain and the empire were also in a position, however, to make the largest return (sometimes called reverse or return lend-lease) in the form of facilities, supplies, and services to the armed forces of the United States overseas, to a total of approximately one-fifth, or six and one-third billions of dollars, of which approximately two-thirds were supplied by the United Kingdom of Great Britain and Northern Ireland. Only France and her possessions made a larger return in proportion (something less than one-third, but less than one billion.)[10]

USSR

Second on the list of beneficiaries of lend-lease aid was the Soviet Union. President Roosevelt's confidential personal emissary Harry Hopkins flew to Moscow by way of Britain and Archangel in July, 1941, to be told what Russia needed, and U. S. Ambassador Averell Harriman and Lord Beaverbrook of Britain were given a supplementary statement of needs when negotiating in Moscow the confidential protocol of October 1, 1941, under which the lend-lease program was set up.

[10] *Twenty-second Report of Congress on Lend-Lease Operations* (Washington, June, 1946.)

Premier Stalin cabled President Roosevelt November 4:

Your decision, Mr. President, to grant to the Soviet Union a loan in the amount of one billion dollars subject to no interest charges and for the purpose of paying for armaments and raw materials for the Soviet Union is accepted with sincere gratitude by the Soviet Government as unusually substantial aid in its difficult and great struggle against our common enemy, bloodthirsty Hitlerism.

I agree completely, on behalf of the Government of the Soviet Union, with the conditions which you outlined for this loan to the Soviet Union, namely that payments on the loan shall begin five years after the end of the war and shall be completed during the following ten-year period.

The Government of the USSR stands ready to expedite in every possible way the supplying of available raw materials and goods required by the United States. . . .[11]

President Roosevelt announced the new policy November 7. Supplies of food and clothing, essential war materials, tanks, and motor transport vehicles were poured into Russia in generous quantity through roundabout routes by way of Vladivostok, Iran, and Murmansk. On the especially hazardous Murmansk "run," in four years, the convoys lost seventy-seven ships with crews and cargoes.[12]

Stalin remarked to President Roosevelt at the Teheran conference in November, 1943, that without United States production Russia and her allies would have lost the war. Total lend-lease aid to the Soviet Union, to the end of the year 1945, was valued at $11,141,-470,000. Materially, aid to the Red Army was largely a one-way transaction. It used against the Germans the matériel given to it, to the detriment of the Wehrmacht and the manifest advantage of all those at war with Germany; but there was little occasion for the Soviets to give other aid to their allies. Principally in the form of supplies and services to the United States Army Air Force on Ukrainian airfields used for shuttle-bombing of German targets, quite near the end of the war, and to prisoners of war in process of repatriation after liberation in areas overrun by the Red Army, return lend-lease from Russia amounted to about $2,213,000—one against five thousand.[13]

[11] Robert E. Sherwood, *Roosevelt and Hopkins* (New York, 1948). Maxim Litvinov was made Soviet ambassador to the United States November 6, 1941. He held that position until August 22, 1943.

Payments on the loan did not begin in 1950, and the Soviet Union declined then to return lend-leased ships.

[12] John R. Deane, *The Strange Alliance* (New York, 1947), 298.

[13] See pp. 616-617.

China

The supply of lend-lease weapons, vehicles, and materials to China was restricted by the length, vulnerability, and difficulty of the only available supply routes, and by the inadequacy of the terminal and distribution facilities needed in China for the utilization of materials delivered. Although Hong Kong was held by the British until December 25, 1941, Indo-China and most of the east China coast and its other principal ports were in Japanese hands that year, and the Burma Road was China's life line.[14]

The conquest of Burma by Japan early in 1942 closed the Burma Road. For nearly three years thereafter, the air route "over the hump" from India was the sole supply line for China. After the reopening of the Burma Road by the construction of the Ledo Road connection from Assam, some automotive equipment and spare parts could be sent into China by land, but the hazardous air route over the mountain barrier continued until the end of the war to carry lend-lease planes, bombs, and gasoline to the armies of Chiang Kai-shek and to the United States aviators flying from and for China. Lend-lease aid to China totaled $1,335,632,000, much of it after V-J Day, reverse lend-lease $3,672,000. The reverse lend-lease came partly in facilities, largely in the labor of the men who built roads and airfields.[15]

BETWEEN VICTORS AND VICTIMS IN THE FAR EAST

Indo-China and Malaya

The United States was attacked at Pearl Harbor, Hawaii, by Japanese naval air forces on December 7, 1941, because for forty years it had stood in the way of Japan's ambition to despoil China and to dominate the trading area of southeastern Asia and the southwest

[14] See pp. 504, 570.

[15] Military aspects of the China-Burma-India campaign are discussed elsewhere. See also pp. 772-774.

After V-J Day, under command of General Wedemeyer, as a lend-lease operation, the United States air forces in China carried two whole Chinese armies from south and west China, one to the Shanghai area and the other to Tientsin, another from Hankow to Peiping. Vehicles valued at $68,000,000 sorely needed by the Chinese, surplus ammunition valued at $50,000,000, and enormous quantities of clothing and other supplies were lend-leased to China after the surrender of Japan, to help the nationalist government take over Manchuria and other areas Japan had occupied. Much of this material eventually found its way into the hands of the Chinese Communists.

Pacific.[16] Particularly since the beginning of the war in Asia with the Mukden incident of September 18, 1931, followed on January 7, 1932, by Secretary Stimson's declaration of the doctrine of nonrecognition and by the proclamation by Japan on February 18, 1932, of the establishment of the puppet state of Manchukuo, which the United States never recognized, tension between the two governments became more and more serious as Japan continued on her career of conquest and exploitation in China.

In February, 1939, the United States and the western European powers tried in vain to induce Japan to open the Yangtze River to world trade. Japan endeavored to make the opening of that river the price of world recognition of her "new order" in eastern Asia. On February 10, while the United States cruiser *Astoria* was at sea on a friendly mission of courtesy, bearing back to Japan the ashes of Japanese Ambassador Admiral Saito, who had died in Washington, the Japanese occupied Hainan, thus cutting the Hong Kong-Singapore line and diminishing the value of Hong Kong as a British naval base.

Soviet Russia, the object of the German-Japanese anti-Comintern pact, gave China more direct aid in 1938 and 1939 than any other power, besides immobilizing a Japanese army of from a quarter-million to a half-million men on the northern borders of Mongolia and Manchuria, where some tentative hostilities occurred in the summers of both of those years.

Upon termination, January 26, 1940, of the period of notice duly given six months earlier, the United States ended its commercial treaty of 1911 with Japan. No legal obstacle thereafter prevented the proclamation of an embargo on trade with Japan; but to avoid provocation or giving Japan a pretext for aggression the United States refrained at that time from declaring an embargo. The first partial embargo, on various minerals, chemicals, and aircraft engines and parts, was imposed six months later, July 5, 1940. This was followed July 26 by an embargo on aviation gasoline and lubricating oil—a calculated risk based on the knowledge that if cut off from other sources Japan might simply seize the rich oil fields of Sumatra and Borneo.

Meanwhile, on April 15, 1940, six days after the German invasion of Norway and more than three weeks before the invasion of the Netherlands, Foreign Minister Arita of Japan advertised an interest

[16] See pp. 429-434, 440-450, 494-504.

in the Netherlands East Indies by announcing that Japan's prosperity was so closely and mutually bound up with that of the Netherlands Indies that anything—such, for example, as hostilities in Europe—disturbing the *status quo* in the Indies would be deeply disturbing to Japan. Secretary of State Cordell Hull replied that it was the policy of the United States to preserve, not to disturb, the status of the islands.

In June, 1940, the German ambassador to Japan, Dr. Eugen Ott, was asked how Germany would react to an extension of Japanese military activity into French Indo-China and part of the Netherlands Indies. Ott replied that Germany would not object to such a move if Japan would promise to attack the United States if the latter were ever at war with Germany. He suggested Hawaii and the Philippine Islands as points to be attacked.[17]

New notice of impending danger, unless the United States should commit itself to a policy of outright appeasement, was given by the signature on September 27, 1940, of the tripartite coalition of Germany, Italy, and Japan. By the terms of that pact, Japan agreed to accept German-Italian leadership in the establishment of a new order in Europe, and the Germans and Italians hers in eastern Asia. The three contracting powers further undertook to assist one another with all political, economic, and military means if any of them should be attacked by any power not then involved in the European war or in the Chino-Japanese conflict. Soviet Russian leaders were understandably perturbed, but the Germans explained to them that the tripartite pact was directed exclusively at the "American warmongers" to prevent them from prolonging the war by bringing the United States into it at the final stage of the defeat of Britain. That the new coalition was directed against the United States, whether exclusively or not, was clear enough. If the United States should use its fleet to prevent Japan from seizing Malaya or the Netherlands Indies, Germany and Japan were obligated by the treaty to make war on the United States. Japan was similarly bound if United States aid to Britain seemed about to become decisive or should merge into outright war. The United States answer to the tripartite pact was, in effect, the Lend-Lease Act of January, 1941. More immediate answers were new embargoes, September 30, on shipments of iron and steel scrap to Japan, and of other metals, ores, and manufactured articles December 10, 1940, to January 10, 1941. These and

[17] Telegram submitted as evidence in Tokyo war crimes trial, reported by United Press in *Wisconsin State Journal* September 24, 1946.

earlier embargo measures were taken with the knowledge that Japan might pretend to have been forced by them to occupy the Indies to make certain of that alternative source of oil and rubber. Ambassador Joseph Grew reported from Tokyo January 27 that they had started people talking in Japan about a surprise mass attack on Pearl Harbor.[18]

In March and April, 1941, Hitler and his minister for foreign affairs, Ribbentrop, tried hard to induce Japan to take active measures in the Far East so as to divert the interest of the United States from Europe and the Atlantic to the Pacific. They assured Japanese Ambassador Oshima and Foreign Minister Matsuoka that the Soviet Union need not be feared. Germany had not made an alliance with the Soviets, Ribbentrop said, because the Soviets wanted too much —bases in the Dardanelles, a position of preponderant influence in the Balkans, especially in Bulgaria, and the sacrifice of German interests in Finland; but Germany was watching Russia closely and would crush her quickly if she made a wrong move.

Japan was urged by the Germans to attack Singapore. The conquest, she was assured, would be easy with the backing of Germany, whose strength was doubled by unity and redoubled by the genius of Hitler, "who certainly must be considered the greatest expert of modern times on military matters." Britain had already lost the war, they said, although she had not yet had the intelligence to admit it.[19] The United States would not dare send its fleet west of Pearl Harbor, and Roosevelt would be frightened into remaining neutral and discontinuing aid to Britain. Matsuoka replied that Japan did not fear the British and could easily destroy the United States battle fleet, but feared a long war of five to ten years against the United States, with the fleets not committed. Then snatch the Philippines and ruin Roosevelt's prestige, he was told. He need not fear the United States submarines. Ribbentrop had asked Grand Admiral Raeder, and Raeder had told him that Germany would give Japan the benefit of

[18] Joseph C. Grew, *Ten Years in Japan* (New York, 1944), 368; *Foreign Relations of the United States: Japan, 1931-1941,* II, 133; Morison, *History of U.S. Naval Operations in World War II,* III, 60-61. Admiral Kimmel said later that he had been told that United States naval intelligence did not believe such rumors, but it became known afterward that in January, 1941, Japanese Admiral Isoroku Yamamoto ordered plans for an attack on Pearl Harbor to be prepared.

[19] Matsuoka told Hitler that Ambassador Grew had warned him against making the three-power alliance. Although every Japanese Grew had spoken to seemed to think Germany would win the war, Grew had told Matsuoka that they were wrong. Britain would win, and Japan was taking a great risk in allying herself with Germany. *Nazi-Soviet Relations, 1939-41,* 295.

her latest technical improvements in submarines, including periscopes.[20]

As for Russia, Matsuoka said that Japan would permit her to secure an ice-free outlet by way of India or Iran but would not tolerate her on the China coast. War between Germany and Russia was not inconceivable, the Japanese minister was told, and was certain if Russia should attack Japan; so Japan could seize Singapore with impunity, and should do so without first declaring war. She must not attack Russia, however. The destruction of the British Empire and the distraction of the United States were more important.

In the new order to be established, the United States was to be economically excluded from Europe, Africa, and Asia and isolated on the American continent. Hitler told his Japanese colleague that Germany did not want war with the United States but would strike first if Japan and the United States should ever be at war. Nothing was stipulated about who might have attacked whom, or about a defensive war. German soldiers were "naturally" far better than American. Besides, the German submarines and Luftwaffe would see to it that no American soldier set foot on European soil.

Between interviews in Berlin, Matsuoka visited Mussolini in Rome, where the Duce told him that "America" was enemy number one, and must be watched closely but not provoked. Russia was enemy number two. Matsuoka reported further to Hitler that while in Rome he had tried to convince the pope that the United States and especially President Roosevelt were needlessly and maliciously prolonging the war in Europe, while in Asia Japan was fighting neither China nor the Chinese but only Bolshevism.

In a conference in Berlin April 4, 1941, Matsuoka told Hitler that his informants had told him the United States would not fight Japan for the sake of China or of the southwest Pacific if Japan did not cut off the supply of tin and rubber from there. But he thought that it would fight, although it had not threatened to, if Japan entered the war with the intention of participating in the destruction of the British Empire. Japan was free to decide. "If Japan continued in the same fashion as at present, a war with the United States sooner or later would be inevitable. In his view this conflict might better

[20] In less than four years of war United States submarines sank 5,320,094 tons of Japanese shipping in the Pacific. Theodore Roscoe, *United States Submarine Operations in World War II* (Annapolis, 1949), 527-565; Navexos, *Japanese Naval and Merchant Shipping Losses during World War II by All Causes* (Washington, 1947), 468. The Germans were not favorably impressed with the technical efficiency of the Japanese in the use of the new equipment.

occur sooner than later. . . . If Japan proceeded further along the present course she would some day have to fight and this might happen under more unfavorable circumstances." So he repeated his request for "the latest inventions and improvements, . . . for the Japanese navy must make preparations at once for a conflict with the United States."[21]

Soviet-Japanese Neutrality Pact

In Moscow on his way home from Berlin, April 13, 1941, the Japanese foreign minister signed a five-year neutrality pact with the USSR. Each party agreed to respect the territorial integrity of the other, and to remain neutral if the other should "become the object of hostilities on the part of one or several third powers." If the treaty held, Japan was thus insured against the danger of having to fight the United States and Russia simultaneously.[22] As the application of the pact was not limited to the Far East, she did not consider herself obligated under her prior three-power alliance with Germany and Italy to attack Russia if the latter should become involved in the war in Europe. The Germans registered no official objection to the new neutrality pact, either in Tokyo or in Moscow. At the Moscow railway station as Matsuoka resumed his homeward journey, Stalin was exceptionally and demonstratively friendly to German Ambassador von der Schulenburg. The German embassy interpreted his unusual effusiveness as an indication of a wish to remain on cordial terms with Germany.[23]

While the Japanese foreign minister was in conference in Berlin and Moscow, with Hitler for help and with Stalin for neutrality and nonintervention in the event of war with the United States, a series of American-British-Canadian staff conferences in Washington considered the coördination of defense plans to be put into effect if the United States should be involved in the war. Those conferences concluded that Nazi Germany was still the major threat not only to Britain and to Canada but to the peace and safety of the United States. German scientists were known to be constantly at work on new and secret weapons, and it was rightly feared that if the war in

---

[21] Dr. Paul Otto Schmidt's notes. Present: Hitler Ribbentrop, Meissner, Matsuoka, and Schmidt. *Nazi-Soviet Relations*, 314; 281-316.

[22] The USSR denounced the treaty April 5, 1945.

[23] *Nazi-Soviet Relations*, 322-325, 326. The German ambassador reported that he had heard by way of Matsuoka and the Italian ambassador that Stalin had called himself (to Matsuoka) a convinced adherent of the Axis and an opponent (*Gegner*) of England and America.

Europe should be prolonged they might (as Nazi propaganda was promising) produce a weapon which would prove decisive. The ABC staff agreement of March 27, 1941, provided therefore, first, for measures short of war: lend-lease, and to dissuade Japan from further aggression in the Pacific; second, for coöperation when and if Axis aggression forced the United States into war. It was agreed that in the second event the Atlantic and European area would be considered the decisive theater. The principal United States military effort would be exerted there, the operations of United States forces in other theaters being conducted in such a manner as to facilitate that effort. If Japan entered the war, military strategy in the Pacific area would be defensive, the United States battle fleet being used offensively (only) in the manner best calculated to weaken Japanese economic power, and to support the defense of the Malay barrier by diverting Japanese strength away from Malaysia.[24]

At a planning conference on the defense of Singapore and the Far East, April 21-27, 1941, the United States was represented by naval Captain William R. Purnell, chief of staff to Admiral Hart, commander of the western Pacific fleet. No actual war plans were made, but the conference recommended war against Japan by all the powers represented there (Britain and the empire, India, Australia, New Zealand, the Netherlands East Indies, and the United States) if Japan should commit a direct act of war against any of them, or moved troops into Thailand west of Bangkok, or south of the Kra isthmus, or into Portuguese Timor or the Loyalty Islands.[25]

[24] Morison, *op. cit.*, I, 45-47; III, 51. The realism of the ABC appreciation of the Nazi danger was vindicated by the postwar revelation that Hitler had told his senior naval officer Admiral Raeder on July 25, 1941, that although he wished to avoid a declaration of war against the United States while the east front campaign was in progress, he "reserved the right to take severe action against the USA" after he had finished Russia. Meanwhile he would never call a submarine commander to account if he torpedoed an American ship by mistake. Martienssen, *Hitler and His Admirals* (New York, 1948), 117.

[25] Morison, *op. cit.*, III, 55. Neither the acknowledged contemplation of the possibility of involvement in war nor a staff agreement for coöperation if involved was an agreement to go to war, whatever was implied. Both then and later, American opinion was very much alive to the question to what extent the president and his staffs had committed the United States to a warlike course of action before Japan committed the decisive act of war. The biographer of President Roosevelt's intimate adviser Harry Hopkins concluded that urgent and repeated questions by the British as to American intentions in the event of further Japanese aggression in the Far East remained unanswered until the day of Pearl Harbor. Sherwood, *op. cit.*, 259.

Just before Pearl Harbor, Captain Creighton, U.S.N., reported from Singapore to Admiral Hart, commanding United States naval forces in Manila, a conversation with Air Marshal Brooke-Popham in which the British commander had intimated or implied that a pledge of armed support for Britain in any one of several eventualities had been made. Admiral Hart said he had had no corresponding instructions from Washington. U.S. Congress, Joint Committee on the Investigation of the Pearl Harbor Attack, *Pearl Harbor Attack* (Washington, 1946), Part 14, p. 1412.

Meanwhile, in compliance with the major policy decision to treat Germany and her war on the Atlantic convoys as the more immediate and greater danger, the United States transferred approximately 20 percent of its Pacific fleet to the Atlantic. The transfer, effected during April and May, 1941, left the United States Navy in the Pacific inferior to the Japanese in every combat category.[26]

THE ATLANTIC CHARTER

The United States was moving nearer to belligerency in the Atlantic. On April 10 the destroyer *Niblack*, reconnoitering Iceland, made sound contact with a submarine and attacked it with depth charges without result except that the U-boat withdrew from the immediate area. As a part of Hemisphere Defense Plan No. 2, April 24, United States vessels were ordered to report the location of all German vessels found west of Iceland, but not to fire upon them unless fired upon. Beginning July 19 the United States Navy took over the convoy of vessels bound for Iceland.

In mid-August, 1941, at a secret and carefully guarded conference aboard warships of their respective navies at sea off the Newfoundland coast, President Roosevelt and Prime Minister Churchill reached agreement on a general statement of purpose subsequently known as the Atlantic Charter (August 14). In a manner reminiscent of President Wilson's Fourteen Points, the general principles and character of the peace which the two leaders declared their peoples wanted to see made were very broadly outlined: no territorial or other aggrandizement; no territorial or other changes not in accord with the freely expressed wishes of the people concerned; recognition of the right of all peoples to choose their own form of government, and restoration of sovereignty and self-government to those who had been forcibly deprived of them; freedom of access to trade and raw materials; international economic collaboration; destruction of Nazi tyranny, freedom from fear and want; freedom to traverse the high seas; the establishment of a wider and permanent system of general security, and eventual disarmament.[27]

[26] The battleships *Idaho, Mississippi,* and *New Mexico,* the carrier *Yorktown,* light cruisers *Brooklyn, Philadelphia, Savannah,* and *Nashville,* two destroyer squadrons, oilers *Cimarron, Sangamon,* and *Santee,* three transports, and other vessels were transferred. Morison, *op. cit.,* I, 57; III, 57.

[27] See Appendix B. Other nations were invited to endorse the charter, and the Soviet Union was presently one of those which did so. Secretary Hull warned Great Britain December 5, 1941, to make no specific agreements with Russia as to the postwar settlement, and no secret accords contrary to the charter. The Soviet Union was one of the original twenty-six nations which endorsed the principles of the

While the Atlantic conference was in session, Congress debated the extension of the term of selective military service from twelve to eighteen months. Opposition to the bill, as to all measures tending toward preparedness for war or toward participation in the war, was vociferous both in and outside Congress—outside, from organizations such as the America First Committee and influential individuals such as the radio orator Father Charles Coughlin and the enormously popular aviator Charles Lindbergh; inside, from Senators Nye and Wheeler and Representatives Hamilton Fish of New York, Clare Hoffman of Michigan, and many others. Some members of the Congress expressed concern over the imputation of a breach of faith with men who had been called into the service for twelve months only, if they were to be held for a longer term. Some small amends were made by providing for a pay increase of ten dollars per month at the beginning of the second year of service. Others professed to fear the loss of liberty if the military establishment should be so increased when the country was "not at war." Others—pacifists, isolationists, noninterventionists, and a few of the more captious of the Republican members—seemed to the president's friends to be merely "fighting Roosevelt"—and Great Britain. All of the patience, personal prestige, and persuasiveness of the army chief of staff, General George Marshall, was needed in committee hearings to carry the measure by a vote of 203 to 202 in the House of Representatives, 45 to 30 in the Senate.

From September 1 the United States Navy escorted convoys from a point off Argentia, Newfoundland, to the meridian of Iceland. Actual though undeclared war began September 4 when a German submarine fired two torpedoes at the U. S. destroyer *Greer*, which had been alerted by a British plane four hours before and had had sound contact with the submarine for more than three hours but had refrained from initiating hostile action. *Greer* dropped depth charges after the torpedo attack, without result.

The official United States military and naval estimate of the general situation as of September 11 was that the safety of the United States would require military victories outside the Western Hemisphere, by United States forces or others. Germany could not be defeated by the nations then at war with her. Britain and the Netherlands could not defend the southwest Pacific. Japan was be-

Atlantic Charter in the United Nations Declaration of January 1, 1942. The principles of the charter were again reaffirmed by both parties to the British-Soviet twenty-year alliance of May 26, 1942.

lieved to be planning to use the mandated islands as a screen from behind which to attempt to take Malaya, Thailand, the Netherlands East Indies, and the Philippine Islands, probably Burma, and possibly eastern Siberia. With the means then available, she could be stopped in the Pacific only at a great distance from her home islands. Submarine and air raids on British and American naval installations and communications were to be anticipated; but "the principal strategic method employed by the United States in the immediate future should be the material support of present military operations against Germany, and their reinforcement by active participation in the war by the United States while holding Japan in check pending future developments."[28]

Events in the Atlantic continued to indicate the imminence of a serious clash with Germany. On September 27 an American-owned tanker, *L. C. White*, registered as from Panama, was torpedoed off the eastern bulge of Brazil. On October 9 the president asked Congress to permit the arming of merchant ships engaged on missions connected with the defense of the United States. On October 17 the destroyer *Kearney* was torpedoed off Iceland with the loss of eleven men missing, ten injured. The crippled vessel made an Icelandic port, but within a few hours of receipt of news of its having been torpedoed the bill asked for by the president eight days before was passed by the House of Representatives by a vote of 259-138. The first U. S. Navy vessel lost in the war was *Reuben James*, a destroyer sunk while convoying supplies to Iceland, October 31. Only 45 of her complement of 160 men were rescued. The loss of *Reuben James* prompted the Senate to pass, November 7, the bill to permit the arming of merchantmen, which with certain amendments adopted a week later so revised the neutrality laws as to permit American ships to enter combat zones and belligerent ports, and the navy to convoy goods to and from ports in the British Empire.[29]

As a friend and ally of Germany, Japan interested herself in what her foreign minister called the provocative conduct of the United States toward Germany. Matsuoka warned Ambassador Grew in May that if war should break out between the United States and Germany as a result of a German attack on a convoy Japan would consider the United States the aggressor, and war between Japan and the United States would follow.[30]

---

[28] Sherwood, *op. cit.*, 410-418. Neither Pearl Harbor nor Hawaii was mentioned as the objective of a possible attack.

[29] See also pp. 570-576, 594-596.

[30] Grew, *Ten Years in Japan* (New York, 1944), 388-389.

END OF APPEASEMENT

Japanese Stock-Piling

Although, before Germany invaded Russia, Hitler and the German Foreign Office had encouraged Japan to push southward to Singapore rather than northeastward into Siberia, Ribbentrop reversed direction after the invasion and early in July was urging Japan to attack the Soviet Union. President Roosevelt asked Japanese Premier Konoye to deny a rumor then current that Japan was about to make such an attack. Konoye immediately disavowed any such intention and, sardonically playing back to the president his own reference to earnest efforts toward achievement of the high purpose of the maintenance of peace, countered with the suggestion that Roosevelt deny that the United States was about to attack Germany.[31]

Japan, however, went her own way and completed her conquest of Indo-China. July 26, Britain and the United States froze such Japanese assets as they could control. At the same time, without much hope of success, President Roosevelt proposed to Japan that Indo-China be neutralized by agreement of Great Britain, the kingdom of the Netherlands, China, the United States, and Japan. Japan could have been promised access to supplies of rice and fertilizer and to some oil, but would have had to evacuate. She refused.

The oil embargo and the freezing of assets abroad were keenly felt by Japan. She had to import 88 percent of what she used, 80 percent of her total from the United States. Within the year ending March 31, 1941, she had been able to stockpile oil enough for about one year of war. Unable after July 26 to discharge cargoes in the United States, and thus to earn dollars for the purchase of oil elsewhere—in the Netherlands East Indies, for example—she found herself seriously restricted in her stock-piling policy.[32]

The Myth of Encirclement

"Japan must immediately take steps to break asunder this ever-strengthening chain of encirclement," cabled Foreign Minister Toyoda

[31] *Ibid.*, 396-400. Having misjudged Germany's Russian policy, and having lost face when the United States took a firmer stand than formerly, the notoriously anti-American and prowar Matsuoka was dismissed from the ministry of foreign affairs July 16 and was succeeded by Admiral Toyoda.

[32] Morison, *op. cit.*, III, 63. Just then the United States nationalized the armed forces of the Philippines and made Field Marshal Douglas MacArthur of the army of the Philippines commanding general of the United States Army Forces in the Far East.

to Ambassador Nomura in Washington August 4, adding that he was determined to "bring about the purposes of the tripartite pact" (i.e., to make war on the United States if Germany did).[33]

Orally on August 6, Ambassador Nomura gave Secretary Hull a virtual ultimatum: The United States must restore free trade with Japan, discontinue aid to China and British Far Eastern possessions, recognize Japan's new status and regime in Indo-China, and put pressure upon Chiang Kai-shek to negotiate for peace. Japan would then go no farther, would declare it her intention to withdraw her troops from Indo-China after the war, and "at an opportune time" would guarantee the independence of the Philippines, provided that Japanese had rights and privileges equal to those enjoyed there by citizens of the United States.[34]

In mid-August Premier Konoye proposed to meet President Roosevelt in Honolulu or somewhere halfway between the two countries. Rightly suspecting that Konoye expected to use the almost inevitable failure of the conference to convince the Japanese people of the inevitability of war, Secretary of State Cordell Hull preferred to see first whether Japan would so alter her policies that such a meeting might have some prospect of success.[35]

Although he considered such a conference useless while Japan maintained her conquest and military occupation of Indo-China and continued to incite her own press to attack the United States and talk about encirclement by the United States, President Roosevelt agreed to the proposal *only provided* that both sides first state their terms in writing. Secretary Hull offered as basic principles of peace: (1) respect for the sovereignty and territorial integrity of all nations; (2) noninterference in the internal affairs of one nation by another; (3) the open door and equality of commercial opportunity; and (4) no alteration of the *status quo* in the Pacific by other than peaceful means. Premier Konoye said officially that he accepted Secretary Hull's conditions. But Ambassador Nomura explained in Washington that acceptance was not retroactive: Manchukuo and other

[33] Message intercepted and decoded in Washington. *Ibid.*, 6. The United States had just occupied Iceland.

[34] *Ibid.*, 66.

[35] *Foreign Relations of the United States: Japan, 1931-1941*, II, 344, 553 *et passim*; *Memoirs of Cordell Hull* (New York, 1948), 1025-1026. Secretary Hull warned Ambassador Nomura August 16 that the United States government could not for a moment remain silent in the face of such a threat as a Japanese invasion of the South Seas area, which would seriously menace British success in Europe and with it the safety of the Western Hemisphere and of the United States. Ambassador Grew advised the president at the time to agree to a conference comparable with the one he had just held with the British prime minister.

changes already made in China must be recognized as permanent, and Japan would not evacuate Indo-China until after the end of the war. Konoye meanwhile assured his minister of war Hideki Tojo and the navy minister that he would "of course" insist upon the firm establishment of the Greater East Asia co-prosperity sphere and upon revision in Japan's favor of the Nine-Power Treaty guaranteeing the sovereignty and territorial integrity of China.[36]

The conference was deferred. Instead, the president gave Ambassador Nomura on August 17 a warning virtually tantamount in diplomatic language to a threat of war:

This government now finds it necessary to say to the government of Japan that if the Japanese government takes any further steps in pursuance of a policy or program of military domination by force or threat of force of neighboring countries, the government of the United States will be compelled to take immediately any and all steps which it may deem necessary toward safeguarding the legitimate rights and interests of the United States and American nationals and toward insuring the safety and security of the United States.[37]

PEARL HARBOR

Plan to Attack

With the United States government known to be adhering to the basic principles of peace defined by Secretary Hull August 17, the Supreme Japanese War Council decided September 6, 1941, to take the East Indian oil wells if the United States would not open up the Pacific oil line. If that meant war with the Netherlands, British Empire, and United States, so be it. Crude oil inventories were already down from twenty million to fifteen million barrels. Preparations for war must be completed by October 31. As camouflage, Konoye told Ambassador Grew that he accepted President Roosevelt and Secretary Hull's conditions for a Pacific conference.

The Supreme War Council's program of minimum demands and maximum concessions was then, as three months later: (1) settlement of the China incident by Japan without interference; the Burma Road to be closed; no more American or British aid to Chiang Kai-shek; (2) no increase of British or American armed forces in

[36] Konoye's memoirs, quoted in *Pearl Harbor Attack*, Part 20, p. 3999; Morison, *op. cit.*, III, 68; Grew, *op. cit.*, 426.

[37] U. S. Department of State, *Peace and War; United States Foreign Policy, 1931-1941* (Washington, 1943), 714; Charles A. Beard, *President Roosevelt and the Coming of the War, 1941* (New Haven, 1948), 488; Sherwood, *op. cit.*, 356.

the Far East, even in British or American possessions; (3) no interference in Franco-Japanese relations concerning Indo-China; (4) the
restoration of free trade with Japan; coöperation in meeting Japan's
economic needs; (5) assistance in the establishment of close Japanese economic relations with Thailand and the Netherlands East
Indies. Upon those terms Japan would agree: (1) not to use Indo-
China as a base for military operations except against China; (2) to
withdraw her troops from Indo-China after the restoration of peace
in the Far East; and (3) to guarantee the neutrality of the Philippines.[38]

War planning went on apace. On carrier *Akagi* October 5, a
hundred selected pilots representing six carriers, who since September had been practicing shallow-water torpedo drops, were told by
Admiral Isoroku Yamamoto that on December 8 (Tokyo time;
December 7, Hawaii time) they were to destroy the United States
battle fleet at Pearl Harbor.[39]

Called too conciliatory toward the United States, Konoye resigned the premiership October 18, and General Hideki Tojo, an old
Kwantung army man already minister of war, became premier and
head of the Home Office without giving up the ministry of war. Tojo
was less conciliatory. Secretary Hull asked Ambassador Nomura in
vain for clear-cut evidence that the new Japanese government would
abandon aggression and revert to a peaceful program and peaceful
methods.

Instead, Yamamoto's Operation Order No. 1 to drive the United
States and Great Britain from Greater East Asia, the East Indies,
and the Philippines—a plan authorized September 6—was ready
punctually, November 1. Two days later Ambassador Grew advised
his government not to underestimate Japan's obvious preparation
for war or think of it only as saber rattling. Action by Japan which
might render unavoidable an armed conflict might come with dangerous and dramatic suddenness.[40]

[38] Morison, *op. cit.*, III, 68-70; Hull, *op. cit.*, 1102; *Pearl Harbor Attack*, Part 12,
pp. 96-97. The Japanese proposal of a Pacific conference was renewed September 22.
[39] Morison, *op. cit.*, III, 83-86; *Pearl Harbor Attack*, Part 1, p. 645. Naval staff
study of the plan for a carrier strike on Pearl Harbor which Yamamoto had ordered
Admiral Onishi in January to work out was completed by September 13. Pilots and
carrier groups had been training for the attack since August, midget submarine crews
for a year.
[40] *Foreign Relations of the United States: Japan, 1931-1941*, II, 704; Grew, *op. cit.*,
470. The commander in chief of the combined Japanese fleet, Admiral Isoroku
Yamamoto, was notified November 5 by the chief of the naval general staff, Admiral
Osami Nagano, that it was feared that war was inevitable, and that preparations for
war were to be completed by the first part of December. See p. 745.

The ambassador did not exaggerate either the danger or its imminence. Two days after his warning message was sent, a former Japanese ambassador to Germany and signer of the German-Japanese alliance, Admiral Saburo Kurusu, was delegated on special mission to join Ambassador Nomura in Washington. Plans for an attack on Pearl Harbor were already completed and general naval orders issued by Yamamoto. Ambassador Nomura was told by Foreign Minister Togo November 5 that it was absolutely necessary to come to an agreement with the United States by November 25; but the only terms on which Japan was willing to agree included, as on September 6, the abandonment of China and all eastern Asia to the mercy of Japan.[41]

Would the United States fight Japan if Japan attacked Malaya or the Netherlands East Indies? President Roosevelt asked his cabinet November 7. The cabinet was unanimously of the opinion that it would. That day the Japanese Pearl Harbor task force was ordered to rendezvous in the Kuriles, and Sunday, December 8 Tokyo time (December 7 Hawaii time), was designated as Y-day, the estimated day of attack. (The eventual day of the attack was to be X-day. A radio message December 2, X=Y, meant that the attack was to be made on the day originally estimated.) Admiral Nagumo, newly designated task force commander, issued his first operation order November 10; and the ships sailed in echelons from Kure naval base in the Inland Sea November 10-18. Submarines, five of which carried on their decks abaft their conning towers the two-man midget submersibles used and lost at Pearl Harbor, left the Kure base November 11-20, with directions to take positions of readiness for war with the United States.[42]

In Washington November 17 and 20 Nomura and Kurusu reiterated Japan's demands as the price of peace: no more help to China, a free hand for Japan there, recognition of Manchukuo and the Japanese "new order" in China, economic aid and a required quantity of oil for Japan. The deadline previously set was extended from November 25 to November 29, but the demands of November 20 were designated by the Japanese foreign minister to the Japanese

[41] Morison, *op. cit.*, III, 72-73; Grew, *op. cit.*, 471-472. Kurusu and Nomura were later said not to have known that the decision to attack Pearl Harbor had been made, but they must have known that the delay occasioned by Kurusu's mission would be advantageous to Japan in a war which was already on its way.

[42] Ensign Sakamaki, *I Attacked Pearl Harbor*, reviewed by Chicago *Daily News*, December 7, 1949; Morison *op. cit.*, III, 72-73, 86-89; Naval Analysis Division, U.S. Strategic Bombing Survey, *Campaigns of the Pacific War* (Washington, 1946), 19.

ambassador as an ultimatum. "This time we mean it," the note ran; "the deadline absolutely cannot be changed. After that, things are automatically going to happen."[43]

A three-months' *modus vivendi* proposal drawn up by the United States Department of State after consultation with the president, Admiral Stark, and General Marshall, and shown to representatives of the British, Australian, Netherlands, and Chinese governments, was rejected by them November 25 and held in abeyance. The proposal was based on the presumption that Japan would advance no farther by force or by threat of force. It would have provided for a partial withdrawal of Japanese troops from Indo-China, the resumption of trade with Japan with the oil supply rationed monthly for civilian use only, and negotiation for peace in China on principles of law, order, and justice. That Japan would have rejected it was indicated by the renewal that day of the anti-Comintern pact. The Pearl Harbor attack force sailed that day from the Kuriles.

Next day, November 26, Secretary Hull answered the Japanese ultimatum of November 20. The United States maintained the position it had taken at the writing of the Nine-Power Pacific Pact of 1922, when Japan attacked China in Manchuria in 1931, and on August 17 and September 3, 1941. As a basis for a new treaty, Japan must withdraw from China and Indo-China, and from the Axis pact.

Secretary Hull's reply November 26 to the Japanese ultimatum of November 20 was itself subsequently called by critics of the Roosevelt administration an ultimatum—as if it had driven the Japanese to the decision to make war, although the Pearl Harbor attack force had already left its last landfall. Yamamoto's orders to Nagumo to attack Pearl Harbor on X-day could have been revoked by radio and the assault force recalled; but only at the price of a second and greater Munich.[44]

The Japanese uncovered no evidence, then or later, of intention to recall the attack force if Nomura and Kurusu had succeeded in keeping the peace by inducing the United States entirely to abandon

[43] Togo to Nomura, November 22. Intercepted, decoded and handed to Secretary Hull November 23. Hull was seeing "intercepts" of most of the messages exchanged between the ambassador and the Japanese foreign office. Sherwood, *op. cit.*, 421; Morison, *op. cit.*, III, 76, n. 69. Things happened, but not automatically. On November 21 the forces designated for simultaneous invasions of Luzon, Thailand, and Malaya and for attacks elsewhere were ordered to take position at their various points of rendezvous.

[44] The task force sailed from Etoforu Island on the morning of November 26 Tokyo time, 25 Washington time. There is a time lag of ten hours from Washington to Tokyo, five and one-half from Washington to Honolulu. Tokyo is west of the international date line. Morison, *op. cit.*, III, 76, 88-92, 385.

its traditional position and thereafter to sanction and contribute to Japan's career of conquest.

War would probably not have begun between the United States and Japan in December, 1941, if Japan had been willing even then to stop where she was, retain what she had already taken, and desist from further aggression; or if the United States had been ready to abandon China, Indo-China, Malaya, Hong Kong, Thailand, Burma, and the Indies to Japanese control and exploitation at a time when China, France, and Britain were unable to defend them, and soon herself to be denied commercial access to them.

Japan could not well have been expected, and indeed was not expected, voluntarily to give up what she had gained. The United States would not recognize or approve those gains but would not then have attacked or attempted to blockade her to wrest them from her. But neither could the United States well recede from the position it had held throughout the century, in defense, principally against Japan, of the sovereignty and territorial integrity of China, or abandon its Stimson doctrine of opposition to changes of territorial sovereignty effected by other than peaceful means. The United States was in Japan's way.

In his *Memoirs* Secretary Hull subsequently defended as follows the decision to make no further concessions to Japan: "[Accedence to Japan's demands] would have given us peace—that is, until Japan, after strengthening herself through the concessions we should have made, was ready to move again. But it would have denied all the principles of right living among nations which we had supported; it would have betrayed the countries that later were our allies; and it would have given us an infamous place in history."[45]

The decision to stand its ground was made by the United States. The unrevoked and practically irrevocable decision to complete an act of aggression already planned and long in preparation was made by an elder statesmen's conference in Tokyo November 29. Ex-Premier Konoye thought the war unnecessary and unwise. Tojo called it a political necessity, to maintain militarist control of the government, and argued that the severance of economic relations with the United States, with or without war, would mean the impoverishment of Japan; so Japan must seize the resources of Malaya and Indonesia.

A Berlin-to-Tokyo message intercepted and decoded in the United States assured Japan that Germany would of course join in the war immediately if Japan became engaged in hostilities with the United

---

[45] Hull, *op. cit.*, II, 1105.

States. Tokyo replied next day: "There is extreme danger that war may suddenly break out between the Anglo-Saxon nations and Japan through some clash of arms. . . . The time of the breaking out of this war may come quicker than anyone dreams."[46]

On the day of final decision, November 29, the deadline date he had set in Washington, Premier Tojo made an incendiary public address to the effect that eastern Asia must be purged of Anglo-American influence to secure the welfare of the co-prosperity sphere. The decision to make war on the United States, Great Britain and the empire, and the Netherlands was ratified by cabinet council December 1, and operation plans already made for attacks on all three were then activated. The Japanese embassy in Washington was ordered December 2 to burn its codes; the Japanese consul in Honolulu was ordered to report daily on warships in Pearl Harbor and on whether they were protected by nets; and Admiral Nagumo was told that X-day would be Y-day. Berlin was notified December 3 that Japan was about to attack.[47]

In a last-minute attempt to avert war, President Roosevelt appealed directly to Emperor Hirohito of Japan, December 6. Calling attention to the natural apprehension aroused in the Philippines, Malaya, and the Indies by the constant increase of Japanese forces in southern Indo-China, he called upon Hirohito to dispel the darkening clouds. The United States would not invade Indo-China if Japan withdrew; but none of the peoples he had mentioned, said the president, could sit indefinitely or permanently on a keg of dynamite. With his throne resting rather precariously on something closely resembling a keg of high explosive, Hirohito dared risk neither his crown nor his head by openly opposing his militarists. His reply, delivered after Pearl

---

[46] Sherwood, *op. cit.*, 441; Morison, *op. cit.*, III, 77, 78; Beard, *op. cit.*, 530; *Nazi Conspiracy and Aggression*, V, 567; *Pearl Harbor Attack*, Part 35, pp. 657, 658; Hull, *op. cit.*, 1092. Mr. Churchill repeatedly declared that if the United States should be involved in war with Japan a British declaration of war would follow "within the hour."

[47] Morison, *op. cit.*, III, 78, 92. Nazi leaders Dönitz and Göring testified at their postwar trials as war criminals that the attack on Pearl Harbor had come as a complete surprise—"albeit a pleasant one," quipped Göring—to German political and military leaders. Goebbels confided to his diary February 14, 1942, that Nomura and Kurusu had known nothing of the real intentions of their government, and that he (Goebbels) and Hitler envied the Japanese government its ability to keep its servants so completely in the dark. Dönitz, *The War at Sea*, 25, 26; *Goebbels Diaries* (New York, 1948), 86.

The war diary entry of December 6 of the German naval attaché in Tokyo read, in part: "The armed forces have already decided three weeks ago that war is inevitable, even if the United States at the last moment should make substantial concessions. Appropriate measures are under way." International Military Tribunal, *Trial of the Major War Criminals: Proceedings*, XIV. 335-338; XXXV, 622.

Harbor by Foreign Minister Togo to Ambassador Grew, was that he wanted only the establishment of peace in the Pacific and consequently in the world; and the Nomura-Kurusu note of December 7 to Secretary Hull must be his answer to the president.[48]

The final Japanese reply was a war message delivered while the attack on Pearl Harbor was in progress. It was full of accusations against the United States. "In all my fifty years of public service," retorted Secretary Hull to the two envoys, "I have never seen a document that was more crowded with infamous falsehoods and distortions on a scale so huge that I never imagined until today that any government on this planet was capable of uttering them."[49]

Unreadiness at Pearl Harbor—Early Warnings

United States government leaders in Washington could not have been surprised by the outbreak of hostilities by act of Japan without prior declaration of war. The armed forces on Hawaii should not have been but were taken by surprise when attacked without warning early Sunday morning, December 7 (Hawaii and United States time). All army officers and men in the Hawaiian area were well aware that they were on outpost duty, and navy men that the navy should be always ready. Both should have been constantly alert. It would have been impossible with the means then at their disposal to maintain a constant round-the-clock and round-the-compass long-range patrol, and radar search was in its infancy; but, perhaps from overconfidence, they did not make full use of what they had; and liaison between army, navy, and air force, even between their commanders, was imperfect. The senior officers present, Admiral Husband E. Kimmel and General Walter C. Short, could say truthfully in self-defense in retrospect that Washington had failed to realert them in the last few hours prior to the attack, when intercepted Japanese messages, tardily decoded, only half-appreciated, and ineptly handled after their decoding, had warned Washington before Hawaii that Pearl Harbor, not Thailand, the Kra peninsula, or Borneo, was to be the object of the first attack. Both in Washington and in Hawaii, men had often told one another that Japan might attack Pearl Harbor at almost any time. That they permitted the men on duty there to be made the victims of a surprise attack was due not to any trustful

[48] Grew, *op. cit.*, 487-489; Hull, *op. cit.*, 1093-1094, 1099. The president's message to the ambassador informing him about the one to the emperor was delayed several hours by the Japanese cable office before delivery.

[49] *Op. cit.*, 1096.

confidence in Japan's integrity or good intentions but to their under-estimate of her temerity. Having tried to diagnose her intentions on the basis of an inaccurate estimate of her capabilities, no matter how often they warned one another that she might attack somewhere, few had really believed that she would dare attack Pearl Harbor.

The idea was not new. Participating in the fleet problem of 1938, the carrier *Saratoga* had launched a "successful surprise" attack on Pearl Harbor from the same area, using the same tactics as the Japa-nese. The "dead space," between steamship lanes, used by the Japa-nese attack force was known to be a logical route for it to use. The British had demonstrated at Taranto in November, 1940, the deadli-ness of a carrier-borne air strike against a battle fleet in harbor.

Army and navy commanders in Hawaii were alerted by their seniors in Washington November 27 to the danger of impending war but not specifically to a threat to Hawaii, and were directed to take only de-fensive measures. "This dispatch is to be considered a war warning," cabled Admiral Stark to Admirals Hart and Kimmel. "Negotiations with Japan looking toward stabilization of conditions in the Pacific have ceased. An aggressive move by Japan is expected within the next few days. The number and equipment of Japanese troops and the organization of naval task forces indicate an amphibious expedition against either the Philippines, Thai, or Kra peninsula, or possibly Borneo. Execute appropriate defensive deployment preparatory to carrying out the tasks assigned in War Plan L. 46."

Also on November 27, Chief of Staff General George C. Marshall cabled General Short: "Japanese future action unpredictable but hostile action possible at any moment. If hostilities cannot, repeat cannot, be avoided the United States desires that Japan commit the first overt act. This policy should not, repeat not, be construed as restricting you to a course of action that might jeopardize your defense. Prior to Japanese hostile action you are directed to under-take such reconnaissance and other measures as you deem necessary but these measures should be carried out so as not, repeat not, to alarm civil population or disclose intent."

Measures taken and reported by General Short and by the Army Air Forces for which he was responsible were clearly inadequate ex-cept as precautions against local sabotage, and showed that he did not comprehend the situation; yet he was not realerted by General Marshall or ordered to take more appropriate precautions. Secretary of War Stimson and Generals Marshall and Gerow subsequently ad-mitted to a congressional committee of investigation that they should have kept their outpost commanders better informed and have warned them again; but nothing altered the ugly facts that, knowing well the outpost's duty to be ready to meet the enemy and fight him at any time with the weapons made available, the forces occupying the Hawaiian outpost on December 7, 1941, were found unready to defend themselves.

Especially in Washington, strategic decisions vital to national defense were inextricable from political strategy and tactics. Aware of its political responsibility to the electorate and moral responsibility to its people, the administration found it necessary constantly to consider not only how to stop aggression by the tripartite treaty powers but how to rally a deeply divided peace-loving people, many of whom were distrustful of it, in support of a war policy if war resulted from its attempts to stop the aggressors by measures short of war. A preventive war or anticipatory counterattack would have been contrary to American tradition and politically unfeasible. If for no other than political reasons, for fear of those of its own people who doubted the integrity of its administration, the United States had to wait for Japan to strike the first military blow. More afraid of the opposition of its own nationals than of the hostile disposition of the national enemy, in the final days of crisis the administration showed less concern about realerting its outpost commanders than about alarming public opinion prematurely or giving Japan a pretext for accusing it of provocation. The U. S. Navy in the Pacific was directed not to offend Japan.

Thinking that it would be politically expedient for Japan to divide United States opinion still further by attacking British or Dutch possessions in the southwest Pacific but not those of the United States, some members of the president's cabinet expected her to do that. Japan solved the cabinet dilemma and united the people of the United States, as well as the British and Dutch nations, against her by attacking the possessions of all three.[50]

Attack

Launched from a position two hundred miles north of Oahu in the early morning of December 7 (Hawaii time; December 8 Tokyo time) more than 360 Japanese carrier-borne aircraft subjected the

[50] Henry L. Stimson, *On Active Service* (New York, 1948), 389-394; Sherwood, *op. cit.*, 428, 434; Beard, *op. cit.*, 525, 566, 582-584; Sherman Miles, *Atlantic Monthly*, July, 1948; Morison, *op. cit.*, III, 77.

Pearl Harbor naval base and nearby Hickam airfield and installations to a destructive torpedo, bombing, and strafing attack. In a terrible two hours, the United States Navy lost about three times as many men as by enemy action in the Spanish-American War and the Four Years' War of 1914-1918 combined. Its losses, including those of the marine corps, were 2117 killed, missing, and died of wounds, 779 wounded. Army casualties were 218 killed, missing, or died of wounds, 364 wounded; civilians 68 and 35. Three-fourths of the naval planes there were destroyed or disabled, one-third of the army planes. The battle fleet was severely crippled. Five battleships—*Arizona, California, Nevada, Oklahoma, West Virginia*—and three destroyers were sunk or severely damaged, three other battleships, three cruisers, a seaplane tender, and a repair ship damaged. Japan had not yet declared war.[51]

The immediate consolidation of American opinion for war against Japan, effected by the Pearl Harbor attack, and Britain's immediate declaration of war upon Japan created a new dilemma for the Roosevelt cabinet and chiefs of staff. Would the United States simply turn upon Japan, and would the Pacific so engross the war effort as to draw off support and supplies essential to the Atlantic war against Nazi Germany, which had been recognized by the government planners but perhaps not by the public as the greater menace? Great Britain was at war in both areas and needed help against the Axis. Hitler solved that problem by ordering the German navy, December 8, to attack United States ships wherever found, and on December 11 declared war on the United States. As a member of a new German-Italian-Japanese military alliance formed December 11, which pledged each ally to victory over both Britain and the United States and to make

[51] Morison, *op. cit.*, III, 126. Immediately and permanently removed from their commands, Admiral Kimmel and General Short asked for trial by courts-martial to fix responsibility for the disaster for which they were naturally blamed. Their request could not then be granted, although there were immediate and subsequent official investigations. The United States could not afford to publicize the extent of the damage done although President Roosevelt, in his address to Congress asking for a declaration of war, said that very many lives had been lost. The United States could ill afford, moreover, to risk the leakage to Japan of the supremely valuable war secret that it had "cracked" the secret Japanese cryptographic codes. Much valuable information was secured during the war from intercepted enemy messages. The Japanese would have changed their codes and ciphers if they had known that United States cryptographers could read them. Admiral Yamamoto, who before hostilities began had warned his countrymen that a war against the United States could not be won by overrunning its Pacific islands or even its western coast, but only by marching into Washington and dictating peace terms in the White House, was shot down with members of his staff over southern Bougainville, April 18, 1943, by United States airmen from Henderson Field, Guadalcanal, brought to the rendezvous by an intercepted Japanese message. *Ibid.*, VI, 128-129.

no separate peace with either without full mutual understanding, Italy also declared war that day on the United States. Bulgaria, Hungary, and Rumania, under Axis control, followed suit December 12, and Albania December 17.[52]

Accepting the total involvement of the United States in the war as a longed-for guarantee of victory, and "being saturated and satiated with emotion and sensation," Prime Minister Churchill "went to bed and slept the sleep of the saved and thankful."[53]

[52] *Pearl Harbor Attack*, Part 35, pp. 691-692; Martienssen, *op. cit.*, 133-134, Churchill, *op. cit.*, III, 615. In announcing the German declaration of war in the Reichstag December 11, Hitler spent half an hour denouncing the "cripple" Roosevelt and his wife. A foreign observer reported that some Foreign Office and propaganda ministry men applauded. Army and navy men, he said, did not applaud until the end of the Führer's harangue. Arvid Fredborg, *Behind the Steel Wall* (New York, 1944), 58.

[53] Churchill, *op. cit.*, III, 608.

CHAPTER 15

Allied Counterattack, 1942-1945

UNITED NATIONS DECLARATION, JANUARY 1, 1942

The overall turning point of the war was the entry of the United States into it as a belligerent, with the unity of opinion and purpose arising from resentment of the unheralded attack on Pearl Harbor and the prompt Axis war declarations which followed. The military tide did not turn immediately in favor of the Allies. It ran against them, in fact, for six months in the Pacific[1] and a year in Russia; but the decisive element, the industrial and naval strength, eventually the military power, and the influence of the United States, gradually made itself felt in 1942.

Nothing but the aggressions and oppression which had caused it did more than the entry of the United States to unite the world against the Axis powers and Japan. On January 1, 1942, the nucleus of the United Nations was formed, a loose association of twenty-six states at war with the Axis powers. These included the United States; the United Kingdom of Great Britain and Northern Ireland, the other members of the British Commonwealth of Nations, and India; the Union of Soviet Socialist Republics; China; governments in exile of European countries already overrun: Poland, Norway, the Netherlands, Belgium, Luxemburg, Czechoslovakia, Yugoslavia, and Greece; and several of the smaller states of the Caribbean region. The declaration, by which each signatory power subscribed to the principles of the Atlantic Charter and agreed to use all its resources against the common enemy and to make no separate armistice or peace, was left

[1] See pp. 744-753. The British battle cruiser *Repulse* and heavy battleship *Prince of Wales* were sunk by Japanese air attack off the coast of Malaya December 10, 1941.

open for further signatures. Mexico and the exiled governments of the Commonwealth of the Philippine Islands and Ethiopia signed on June 5, June 10, and July 28, 1942, respectively. Iraq, Brazil, Bolivia, Iran, and Colombia joined the United Nations by declaring war on Germany during 1943, Liberia in February, 1944, and liberated France December 26, 1944.[2]

ATLANTIC

Caribbean

Quite aside from the constant threat to the Panama Canal, the Allies needed the active coöperation of the Central American and West Indian republics against the submarine menace. Germany had by that time nearly five times as many submarines as in September, 1939, and soon sixty to eighty of them were operating off the Florida coast, in the Caribbean and Gulf of Mexico, and off the northeast coast of South America. Well supplied by roving tenders and tanker submarines, these German submersibles were soon sinking oil tankers from Aruba and Venezuela and bauxite carriers from South America in such numbers as to become a serious threat to vital shipping space and to supply of essential war materials. With the demand constantly increasing, ships were being destroyed faster than they could be replaced.

On April 1, 122 of Germany's 288 submarines were operational: 19 in the Arctic, 14 of them at sea; 81 in the Atlantic, 47 at sea and 34 refueling and rearming at bases on the west coast of France. U-boat crews were jubilant. They boasted at home that the United States possessed no real defense against them, that they could expend all their torpedoes on their hunting grounds and sink transports with gun-fire on their way home. February, March, May, June, and August were bad months, October and November worse.

Within one week in February the German battle cruisers *Scharnhorst, Gneisenau,* and *Prinz Eugen*, which thanks to clever camouflage and effective anti-aircraft defense had survived repeated bombing attacks in port at Brest, made a successful foul-weather dash up the English Channel to German havens; the great French liner *Normandie*, being readied at a New York harbor pier for troop-

[2] Eight others declared for the Allies and signed the United Nations declaration in February and Saudi Arabia on March 1, 1945, in time to qualify for invitations to the San Francisco United Nations organization meeting. Argentina, Eire, Sweden, Portugal, and Franco Spain remained neutral. Denmark was occupied for five years by the Germans and had no government in exile to sign the declaration for her.

transport service, burned out and rolled over in the mud; and Singapore surrendered to the Japanese.

In May United States tonnage losses of seventy-three ships, 350,000 tons, were greater than world losses had been in any month prior to February, 1942. In the first half of 1942 it lost more shipping than in the war of 1914-1918.[3]

Countermeasures

Gradually countermeasures met the undersea offensive. Improved submarine detection and location gear was developed and installed. The convoy system was more generally enforced, and tightened by the use of escort airplane carriers and destroyer escorts. Off Trinidad from August to November, 42 of 108 unescorted ships were lost by enemy action, 11 of 1354 in convoy. On wind-swept and rocky Ascension Island in the South Atlantic, twelve hundred miles east of Recife, Brazil, a United States airfield was put into operation in July as an antisubmarine patrol base. Roughly equidistant southward from West African Dakar and Freetown and westward from Brazzaville in the Belgian Congo, it was useful also as a staging point for planes being flown to northeastern Africa and the Near East.

Allied shipping losses were still high, but German submarine losses also mounted. Dönitz reported to his Führer August 24 that, of 304 U-boats in operation to that time, 105 had been lost. Average loss was then 2.9 U-boats per month, 4.9 percent per month; man-power losses were 38 percent per year, total to date 3803. Building about twenty submarines per month, with an average daily number at sea ranging upward from 47.7 in March to 105.4 in October, Admiral Dönitz found his U-boat fleet only 10 percent as effective, per boat, by the end of the year as at the beginning. Submarines were being killed faster: twenty-one during the first half of the year, six by United States forces; sixty-four in the latter half, eleven by United States forces. Despite a total loss of nearly two million tons of Allied ship-

[3] Morison, *History of U.S. Naval Operations in World War II,* I, 198, 200, 410; Martienssen, *Hitler and His Admirals* (New York, 1948), 261; Dönitz, *War at Sea,* 31; *Goebbels Diaries,* (Garden City, 1948), 148. The German admiralty claimed its largest number of sinkings, 145 ships, in June, its largest total tonnage, more than 700,000 tons, in November, 1942. The Allies conceded after the war 115 ships in June, 636,907 tons in November. The Germans claimed on July 6, 1942, to have sunk, with the aid of land-based air strength, twenty-three of thirty-four ships in Russia-bound convoy PQ-17. Martienssen, *op. cit.,* 139. One convoy, CS-107, lost fifteen ships November 1-4, 1942. Morison, *op. cit.,* I, 324.

ping in 1942, new construction showed a net gain of 738,000 tons over losses in the last quarter of the year.[4]

The war of the Atlantic was won by the Allies in 1942 in the sense that supplies never ceased to flow by air and sea to the beleaguered enemies of the Axis powers. While its own armed forces were being increased from 2,000,000 to 7,000,000 men and supplied and equipped, and 1,500,000 of those men were sent overseas in 1942, the United States continued to serve as the great arsenal and supply center of the United Nations, using the others' American and European territories as bases for its own operations while supporting theirs. As its president had said of the Atlantic Charter in his "four freedoms" address on the anniversary of the birthday of George Washington, the United States was making its war policy apply "not only to parts of the world that border the Atlantic but to the whole world."[5]

USSR

Lend-Lease

In Moscow as in Washington, Pearl Harbor raised the question whether war materials would continue to be sent by the United States to the other nations then at war with Germany. Stalin did not miss an opportunity to stress the point that the United States could not afford not to go on supplying Russia. "I have received your message informing me of consignments of armaments from the United States for January and February," he cabled the president in mid-January, 1942. "I would like to emphasize the fact that at the present moment when the peoples of the Soviet Union and its army are exerting all their power to thrust back, by their determined offensive, Hitler's troops, the fulfillment of American deliveries, including tanks and aeroplanes, is of the utmost importance for our common cause, for our further successes."[6]

---

[4] Martienssen, *op. cit.*, 139-140, 151-154; Morison, *op. cit.*, I, 259, 311, 324, 380, 403, 407; Dönitz, *op. cit.*, 26. After an unsuccessful convoy action off the northern coast of Norway December 31, 1942, in which the German surface warships failed to distinguish themselves and heavy cruiser *Hipper* was severely damaged without loss to the convoy although a German and a British destroyer were sunk, Grand Admiral Erich Raeder was removed from command of the German battle fleet, as of January 31, 1943. Raeder was succeeded by Grand Admiral Karl Dönitz, until then commander of the submarine fleet. Hitler declared himself ready at that time to scrap his remaining battleships but did not do so. He valued the U-boats, however.

[5] The four freedoms were: freedom of speech, freedom of religion, freedom from want, and freedom from fear.

[6] Sherwood, *Roosevelt and Hopkins* (New York, 1948), 496-497. The tide soon again turned against the Soviets, and ran against them until Stalingrad, but lend-lease deliveries amounted by the end of October, 1943, to 7000 planes, 3500 tanks, and 195,000 motorized vehicles. See pp. 616-617, 637.

Alliance

In London May 26, 1942, Foreign Commissar Molotov and Foreign Secretary Eden signed a twenty-year treaty of alliance between the Soviet Union and Great Britain, restating and confirming military agreements made July 12, 1941. An agreement also made in London June 11 provided for direct diplomatic relations between the Soviet Union and Canada.

Meanwhile Molotov went on to Washington to urge the opening of a second front in western Europe. General Marshall and the president told him that the United States hoped to open a second front in 1942, but that the transport problem was being seriously complicated by ship losses on the Murmansk-Archangel supply route to Russia.

The second front would be stronger, argued Molotov, if the eastern front stood fast; but suppose the Soviets reduced their demands for materials so as to free shipping for a second front, and the promised second front then failed to materialize?[7]

In a conference in Moscow with Winston Churchill and United States Ambassador W. Averell Harriman, August 12-15, 1942, Stalin was more insistent than Molotov had been on the immediate establishment of a second front, and repeatedly referred to what he chose to call Britain's refusal to open one. Wars were not won with plans, he said; if the British infantry would only fight the Germans as the Russians and the Royal Air Force had done, it would thereafter be less afraid of them. He eventually agreed, however, to accept an Allied invasion of French North Africa as a substitute.[8]

Counteroffensive

No non-Soviet expeditionary force materialized on the Russian battle line. Stalin soon dropped from his conversations with the Allies his statement that he would welcome one; but lend-lease supplies poured in across Iran by way of the Caspian Sea and the river Volga. That life line and the Baku oil supply which followed the same routes

---

[7] Sherwood, *op. cit.*, 556, 563, 575; Morison, *op. cit.*, I, 164-165.

[8] Sherwood, *op. cit.*, 617. With ill-concealed embarrassment and difficulty, Mr. Churchill swallowed his resentment of Stalin's uncomplimentary remarks, and refrained from asking him where the second front had been or what the Soviet Union had been doing for the war effort in 1940 while Britain fought the war alone.

In October Stalin wanted monthly: 500 pursuit planes, 8000 to 10,000 trucks, 5000 tons of aluminum, 4000 to 5000 tons of explosives; and within a year 2,000,000 tons of wheat and all the fats, concentrated food, and canned meat the United States could send, with twenty to thirty ships as gifts to carry them to Vladivostok. *Ibid.*, 617, 639.

northward were seriously threatened; but Maikop, Mozdek, and Stalingrad were the points of farthest German advance, points of no return for many thousands of the Wehrmacht. The Baku oil field was successfully defended, the Caspian supply route was kept open, and Astrakhan at the mouth of the Volga was held. Stalingrad was, for Russia, the great holding point and turning point of the war.

While United States troops invaded French northwest Africa and a sustained British counteroffensive drove Axis troops out of Egypt and across Libya, the Red Army began its magnificent counterattack around Stalingrad. The Germans trapped at Stalingrad surrendered ten days after the British captured Tripoli, nearly three months after the Allied landings in Morocco.[9]

Although the geopolitical significance of the North African campaign was not properly to be denied, the numbers of men engaged and the wastage of the Wehrmacht on the Russian front were infinitely greater. Showing great tactical and logistic flexibility, and making good use of the advantages of fighting in their own country in a winter climate to which most of them were inured and for which they were better outfitted than the Germans were, the Red armies attacked ferociously, first at one point and then at another, all along the line. Before the winter offensive was halted by the melting snows of spring, the invaders were driven back four hundred miles from Stalingrad to Novorossiisk, out of the Caucasus except the Kerch peninsula northwest of Novorossiisk. Rostov, Kharkov, Kursk, and Voronezh were retaken with the valley of the Don below Voronezh, and only Kharkov lost again when the Axis forces, hanging on to Stalino and Taganrog, pushed back to the right bank of the Donets.

West of Moscow, German hedgehog positions at Vyazma, Rzhev, and Velikie Luki were cut off and overrun. Leningrad was still partially surrounded from the south, but frozen Lake Ladoga gave access to the city and the siege was raised by reconquest of the eastern approaches in January, 1943.

In mid-July, a few days after the U. S. Seventh and the British Eighth armies invaded Sicily, the Red Army launched a new offensive around Orel. That drive to clear Russian territory, subsequently sustained through the winter of 1943-1944, pushed westward to Lake Peipus in the north without taking Narva, but in a general sense let the Baltic states wait upon the Dnieper and the Balkans. Peoples and industries of the Soviet Union had survived the temporary loss of the grain fields of Ukraine and the best of their coal fields, nickel and

[9] See pp. 668-669.

manganese mines, steel plants, and water-power sites, but government and people were determined to retrieve them.

Kharkov, called the Pittsburgh of Ukraine, was again liberated in August; Smolensk, traditional western gateway, in September; Kiev, the ancient capital, November 6. The Germans hung on as for dear life to the rail center Zaporozhe and the ore centers Krivoi Rog and Nikolaev; but in January, 1944, south of the Pripet marshes, the Red armies crossed the 1939 boundary of Poland and in March the Dniester into Bessarabia (lost in 1918, retaken 1940). By the end of March, they stood along the Carpathian boundary of Ruthenia, which had been part of the territory of prewar Czechoslovakia. In April they liberated the Black Sea port Odessa, and in May the Crimean peninsula and Sevastopol.

Prewar Soviet territory was nearly free, and the Red Army was in better position to invade the Balkans by land from the northeast than the Allies by sea from the Adriatic. Long-term political policy, moreover, and war aims other than the purely military, did more to determine Soviet than Allied military strategy.

Confronted with the necessity of forced evacuation in the east, the Germans stepped up the savagery with which they treated the peoples of the occupied areas. In May, 1943, SS *Brigadeführer* Stroop reported that there was no longer any Jewish quarter in Warsaw. In compliance with Hitler's order of April 23, the ghetto had been destroyed. A week later, because half of the fifty thousand Poles he had been ordered to evacuate had escaped and joined the partisans, the Nazi governor of Lublin was ordered by the SS to evacuate 190,000. In September the Wehrmacht had to give up Katyn, and Goebbels predicted that the Russians would accuse the Germans of having massacred the "12,000 Polish officers" whose bones the Germans had unearthed from a mass grave there, and whom they had accused the Russians of having murdered. In November, to stop the "everlasting grumbling," the Nazi were pronouncing and publishing death sentences for "defeatists"; and Goebbels said the measure had a sobering effect. At the extermination camp at Auschwitz (Oswiecim) by December 1, 1943, 2,500,000 persons had been gassed and burned to death, and 500,000 had died of starvation or disease. These included 20,000 Russian prisoners of war and 100,000 German Jews. The 3,000,000 dead were 70 to 80 percent of all persons sent there. The others, the strongest, had been screened out for slave labor.[10]

[10] Affidavit of the camp commandant Rudolf Hoess, *Waffen SS*, IMT, *Trial of Major War Criminals* (Nuremberg, 1947-1949), XXXIII, 276; XII, 19; XXVI, 628-

NORTH AFRICA

Northeast and Northwest Africa, 1942

ANOTHER FRONT

While the holding engagements of the spring and summer of 1942, which eventually contained the Japanese in the central and southwest Pacific, were being fought; while the Red armies were being pushed back in the Caucasus and to Stalingrad; and while the British were being driven out of Libya into Egypt, thoughts of a so-called "second front" in Europe would have been much in men's minds without Soviet insistence.

The first U. S. Army Air Forces flying fortress (B-17) air raid, over Rouen in August, proved little but that the big bombers could fly home badly crippled. It was only a portent and an inconclusive promise of what the Allied strategic bombing program was eventually to do.

A large-scale British-Canadian reconnaissance raid on Dieppe August 19 demonstrated at great cost in lives the difficulty of direct invasion. Incidentally, it taught the Germans something about the strength and weaknesses of their *Festung Europa* defenses, which they estimated were in general fairly strong.

Meanwhile French North Africa was chosen as a second front or, in Stalin's mind, as a substitute for one (northeast Africa not being counted by him as a major front). That area had never fallen fully under Axis control. Since March, 1941, the United States had sent supplies there, stipulating that no surplus should accumulate or be sent on to Germany or Italy. Observers went with the material wherever possible, to report what they could learn; and shipments were suspended on occasion as a form of economic pressure. Meanwhile, by threat of military occupation the Germans drew supplies of foodstuffs from the area by way of Vichy France, or for direct delivery to Rommel's forces in North Africa. Some trucks, munitions, and gasoline were also delivered when the Germans threatened to occupy Bizerte; but that occupation threat had not yet been carried out when Allied forces landed at Casablanca and Oran.

DESERT VICTORY: WESTWARD FROM EL ALAMEIN

The elimination of the Axis forces from northern Africa was a converging operation. The first decisive military coup was British

---

642; *Goebbels Diaries*, 396, 487, 510. Hoess said that 400,000 Hungarian Jews were exterminated at Auschwitz in the summer of 1944. Hoess was tried and hanged by the Poles in 1947.

General Montgomery's desert victory at El Alamein in northwestern Egypt October 23, 1942. That night General Mark Clark of the United States Army went ashore in Algiers from a British submarine which had carried him from Gibraltar, to arrange if possible through the mediation of United States Consul Robert Murphy with French General Mast and others for an unopposed landing by an Allied expeditionary force. November 2-3, after having held on too long under Hitler's orders to hang on, Rommel's *Afrika Korps* began, under pressure, its long retreat from El Alamein, leaving its hapless Italian auxiliaries without transport, to hold off the advancing British Eighth Army or be rounded up and herded into its prisoner-of-war enclosures. At the other end of the long southern Mediterranean coastline, Allied landings were made at Casablanca in French Morocco and at Algiers and Oran, Algeria, November 8. The new expeditionary force was composed principally of United States troops which had been carried, some by way of Britain, some directly from the United States, by a combined U.S.-British naval convoy operation. It was led by General Dwight D. Eisenhower.

EASTWARD THROUGH MOROCCO AND ALGERIA

The landings were not unopposed. It had been hoped that the armed French forces in Morocco and Algiers might welcome the arrival of United States troops, bringing them an opportunity to rejoin the Allies and free their areas from Axis domination and threat of Axis occupation. With the invader-liberators came the legendary general Henri Honoré Giraud, who in two wars had twice been captured by the Germans and twice escaped. Hoping that French soldiers would rally round Giraud wherever given an opportunity to do so, the Allies had picked him up by submarine off a beach in southern France and carried him to Gibraltar and Oran. They had hoped that he might successfully assume command of French forces in northwest Africa; he had hoped to take command of the entire operation, which he would have preferred to divert to southern France. He knew nothing of Allied plans; and the French officers in northwest Africa refused at first to accept him as their leader. They seemed to prefer Admiral Darlan.

Darlan was in northwest Africa when the invasion began. He was known, as a leading member of the Vichy government, to have collaborated with the Axis in ways and to an extent actively unfriendly and injurious to the Allied cause; but he was believed to be the only man who could bring over to the Allies the French army forces in North Africa and the battle fleet anchored at Toulon, both thought to be loyal to him and likely to obey his orders. He radioed Pétain for authorization to coöperate with the United States. Pétain did not officially acknowledge receipt of the message but ordered all French troops everywhere to resist the invasion, and replied reproachfully by radio to President Roosevelt's radioed request that there be no resistance.[11]

Darlan hesitated till November 10. The landings near Oran and Casablanca were effected in the face of some resistance, which cost the expeditionary forces about two thousand casualties and three days of precious time. The object of the operation was to secure as speedily as possible a position from which to occupy Bizerte and Tunis before the Germans could seize them—as they very quickly did. On the day of the invasion, without Marshal Pétain's knowledge, Pierre Laval gave the Germans permission to cross the territory of unoccupied France and to use air bases in Tunisia. Darlan's "cease-fire" order of November 10, first publicly disavowed by Pétain, then privately approved by secret code, was seized upon by the Germans as a pretext for the military occupation of all France.[12]

The completion of the German occupation of France emphasized the "prisoner" status of Pétain, so made it easier for officers in the French armed forces to consider themselves released from their personal oaths of obedience to him and go over to the side of the stronger. Darlan was recognized November 11 as French high commissioner in North Africa, Giraud as military commander of French forces. Darlan ordered the French fleet to leave Toulon and join the Allies; but Admiral de Laborde adhered to general orders of 1940, failed even to get up steam, and upon approach of German troops November 27 scuttled the ships where they were. It was said that the ships had no fuel and could not be moved. The Germans took Toulon, then handed it over to the Italians. Laval, on the other hand, from Vichy, ordered Admiral Esteva at Bizerte to coöperate with the

---

[11] Langer, *Our Vichy Gamble* (New York, 1947), 349-350; Mark W. Clark, *Calculated Risk* (New York, 1950), 67-132. No "Free French" were wanted by French army leaders in northwest Africa. The unsuccessful attack on Dakar in 1940 had not been forgotten. For that reason, and for fear that through some indiscretion the news of the invasion plan might leak out, the Free French leader, General de Gaulle, was not officially told of the operation until it was already under way. He was partially reconciled with Giraud after Darlan's death. No reconciliation between de Gaulle and Darlan was thought possible. Each called the other a traitor and renegade.

[12] At Casablanca one hit each was suffered by two United States destroyers, two cruisers, and the battleship *Massachusetts*, and about forty landing craft were wrecked. The French lost four destroyers and eight submarines, sunk or missing, *Jean Bart* and three other warships disabled, 490 men killed, 969 wounded. Morison, *op. cit.*, II, 110.

Germans, which he did. Axis forces were given an easy opportunity to establish themselves in Bizerte and Tunisia.

Speed was vital to the success of the North African undertaking, essential if a long and costly campaign was to be avoided. By dealing with Admiral Darlan and using him, Generals Clark and Eisenhower hoped to save time and lives, and in fact saved both; but not enough. The Germans and Italians were in Bizerte and Tunis before them.

Describing himself as only a trustee of authority, but assuming the title of "chief of state" in North Africa, the politically ambitious high commissioner, Darlan, soon set up an imperial council more pleasing to Generals Giraud, Noguès, Bergeret, and Chatel than to anyone else in northern Africa. The council was undemocratic in its views and authoritarian in its methods, and aroused bitter criticism on that account in both Britain and the United States. It was nothing of which a doctrinaire democrat could be proud. Yet Darlan professed to be deeply hurt when President Roosevelt saw fit to defend the policy of using him as a matter of expediency, without commitment as to the character of the postwar government of France or the status of the Colonial empire which it was presumed would be restored to her.[13]

Admiral Darlan's change-over to the side of the Allies was disregarded by Admiral Godefroi at Alexandria; so the British would not let him move his ships for fear they would fall into German hands. Admiral Robert at Martinique also sat tight, under some surveillance. Dakar was occupied by the Allies without a fight, November 23.

TURNING POINT

"It would seem that the turning point in this war has at last been reached," said President Roosevelt in an address November 17. His spirits were buoyed by the successful landings and cessation of French resistance, and by word that the Red Army was holding firm at Stalingrad, that the British Eighth Army was advancing on Bengasi, and that two Japanese battleships and three destroyers had been sunk (at great cost) in furious naval battles around Savo Island, which put an end to Japanese attempts to dislodge United States marines and soldiers from Guadalcanal in the Solomon Islands. A Japanese analyst unwittingly agreed with the president, calling Guadalcanal the "fork in the road which leads to victory for them or for us." "The tide has turned," echoed Field Marshal Smuts from Johannesburg December

---

[13] Darlan was assassinated December 24. Bonnier de la Chapelle, a student described as a de Gaullist, was apprehended and accused, tried by the French December 25, and executed December 26.

20. Churchill was more cautious. "Now this is not the end," said he November 9. "It is not even the beginning of the end. But it is, perhaps, the end of the beginning." With characteristic tenacity and confidence, however, he went on, perhaps in angry indirect retort to the suggestion of an independent federated India: "Let me, however, make this clear, in case there should be any mistake about it in any quarter. We mean to hold our own. I have not become the king's first minister in order to preside over the liquidation of the British Empire."[14]

Conference at Casablanca

CAMPAIGN PLANNING

At a conference at Casablanca in mid-January, 1943, to which Premier Stalin was invited but did not come, plans were outlined by President Roosevelt and Winston Churchill and their chiefs of staff for the invasion of Sicily, to follow the completion of the conquest of Tunisia. Although Mr. Churchill showed a preference for the Balkans as the area in which to launch the first major invasion of what the Germans were calling their fortress of Europe, the joint chiefs of staff agreed at Casablanca that plans should be made for a cross-Channel invasion of northern France in 1944. For lack of landing craft and other essentials, and of shipping space, the necessary build-up for such an operation would be impossible in 1943 if Italy should be invaded and the supply of lend-lease materials to Russia continued and stepped up, as was proposed.[15]

As steps toward a provisional political settlement for French North Africa, Generals Giraud and de Gaulle were induced to meet, shake hands perfunctorily for the news-film cameras, and effect a gruff semblance of reconciliation. At Giraud's request, a prewar French North African official, Marcel Peyrouton, who had helped Darlan overthrow Laval in December, 1940, and resigned as ambassador to

[14] Sherwood, *op. cit.,* 656; Morison, *op. cit.,* V, 287, 292. See also pp. 248-249. Until November, 1942, shipping losses were greater than replacement. By June, 1943, available tonnage equaled that available in 1939. After that, shipping was built faster than it was lost.

[15] "The Russians were hard task masters, difficult to please," reported General Arnold of the U.S. Army Air Forces, with reference to the delivery of 800 planes to the Red Army at Basra by January 31. *Global Mission* (New York, 1949), 405.

British naval losses on convoy duty on the Murmansk run included, by the end of 1942, two light cruisers, four destroyers, four mine sweepers, and a submarine. Total German and Italian submarine strength was then slightly more than four hundred boats, about one-fourth of which were operating in the Atlantic. They were particularly active, naturally, just inside and outside the Strait of Gibraltar; but their sinkings were decreasing elsewhere and their losses mounting, owing to air-borne defense. Morison, *op. cit.,* I, 164, 407; Dönitz, *op. cit.,* 27.

Argentina when Laval scrambled back into power in France, was made governor general of French North Africa. As Peyrouton was said to be a Darlan man, his appointment was unpopular with those— and there were many—to whom the inveterately anti-British Axis collaborationist Darlan had been anathema.

"UNCONDITIONAL SURRENDER"

At a press conference at Casablanca, January 24, with the British prime minister present and concurring, President Roosevelt announced that "unconditional surrender" would be the first prerequisite of peace with Germany, Japan, or Italy. Speaking for both commonwealths, the president informed the newsmen and the world, including enemy peoples, that the United States and Great Britain would not negotiate on any other terms.

The "unconditional surrender" policy provoked serious debate and criticism; but it was not announced on impulse or decided upon without careful consideration. Immediately, it was an answer to both British and American expressions of concern over the Peyrouton appointment just made, and over the president's own recent admission that it was expediency, not democratic ideology, that had prompted him and his advisers to try to use Darlan. Second, it might have done more than it seemed to do to allay the outspoken suspicions of the Soviet Russian leaders that the western Allies were not seriously interested in destroying Nazi Germany, and would make a separate peace at the first favorable opportunity, keeping Germany as a bulwark against communism and letting an isolated Russia bear the brunt of war alone.[16]

The memory of the general acceptance in Germany of the falsified nationalist and Nazi version of the history of the armistice of 1918, upon which the new-war spirit had fed in the period between wars, would alone have gone far toward explaining the surrender demand. Let there be no question, a second time, about who lost the war, no renewal of the charge that an unbeaten German army had been tricked by false promises of a generous peace into a premature capitulation. Let the admirals and generals sign the instruments of their own surrender in the field. Let them not again send a civilian on that errand, then betray him as they had betrayed "politician" Erzberger.

[16] A fantastic rumor was at that time afloat in Germany, of a proposed separate peace and new agreement for coöperation with the Soviet Union, to be followed by the bolshevization of Germany with Goebbels assuming the leadership of the German Communists, and by a stiffening of all fronts against the "capitalist-imperialist" powers, Britain and the United States. Arvid Fredborg, *Behind the Steel Wall* (New York, 1944), 157-158.

Let any part of the Nazi civilian regime that survived the surrender acknowledge its own failure and its responsibility for the ruin it had brought upon Germany.[17] The articles of surrender of the armed forces were not to be permanent treaties of peace. The demand for surrender neither promised nor precluded a reasonably generous peace.

What effect would the "unconditional surrender" have on the morale of the German people and armed forces? Would it bring sooner or postpone the day of their surrender? Stalin said he feared it would stiffen their resistance. While breathing hatred of Hitlerism and the Hitlerites, Soviet propaganda left room always for the implication that Russia would not seek the destruction of Germany or of the German people. While secretly in Washington Soviet Ambassador Litvinov made clear his government's opinion that Germany should be dismembered and East Prussia ceded to Poland, a German-language Russian proclamation disclaimed any intention of the Soviet Union to take any territory not previously Russian, and Stalin was widely quoted in March as having said in an address that the Red Army would stop its westward movement when it reached the German border.[18]

Nazi Propaganda Minister Paul Joseph Goebbels gave all possible publicity to the demand for unconditional surrender, making such use of it as he could to convince the German people that they must fight on to victory, as a merciless dictated peace was in prospect for them if they failed. Privately he welcomed the Allied demand as an aid in keeping war-weary and politically disaffected elements of the population under Nazi control. "If they were to put up a peace program somewhat along the lines of Wilson's Fourteen Points," he wrote, "they would undoubtedly create great difficulties for us." Total mobilization

[17] See pp. 563, n. 24, and 565; Churchill, *Second World War,* IV, 685-691.

[18] British Foreign Minister Anthony Eden, in Washington, discounted Stalin's statement as one made only for its possible propaganda effect inside Germany. Finland, the Baltic states, Bessarabia, and the eastern part of prewar Poland could have been designated as "previously Russian." The Goebbels diary entry of March 6, 1943, indicated German knowledge or belief that those territories had been promised to the Soviet Union, and that East Prussia, Silesia, and the Mark of Brandenburg would go to Poland if Germany should be defeated. *Goebbels, Diaries,* 274; Sherwood, *op. cit.,* 709-711. See also pp. 713-714, 719-721.

In Moscow in May, 1945, Stalin suggested to President Truman's special envoy Harry Hopkins that, if it should become apparent that Japanese resistance was being made more desperate by the demand for unconditional surrender, an offer of acceptable surrender terms might weaken that resistance. The Allies could then impose their will upon Japan afterward, through their occupying forces, and so more easily accomplish their objectives. Sherwood, *op. cit.,* 903; William D. Leahy, *I Was There* (New York, 1950), 383.

was decreed at last in Germany January 28, and thousands of restaurants and many amusement centers for the first time had to close for want of man power. Production of consumers' goods and luxury items, which until then had suffered only limited restriction, was seriously curtailed. Although Göring had broadcast to the world in October, 1942, that if there was to be hunger anywhere in Europe it would be least felt in Germany and the Germans would be the last to starve, the meat ration had to be reduced March 9 "to avoid having to slaughter the last cattle in the Ukraine, [which] . . . would have a very bad psychological effect." Bomb damage was becoming serious. Bombed areas were roped off to bar an inquisitive public from them.[19]

There was a German underground which tried throughout the war to infuse life into the idea that the Hitler regime was not Germany and did not properly represent the German people. Agents of that underground sought diligently to make a deal with the Allies for generous peace terms to be granted Germany if Hitler should be eliminated and his regime overthrown. Survivors of the underground and other anti-Nazi elements of the German population said then and afterward that their hopes to overthrow the Nazi and make peace were killed, and their efforts doomed to failure, by the heartlessness of the demand for unconditional surrender. That demand, they said, played into the hands of the Hitlerites, stiffened resistance, and prolonged the war by implying that the peace would be worse than war.

If the validity of the underground's complaint was judged by the effectiveness of its measures for the assassination of Hitler and the overthrow of his government, to be followed by an immediate request for an armistice and peace, the Allied governments could not have found in that underground a very dependable ally. The war would end when the German army found it hopeless and turned on Hitler to destroy him, or when it was driven back inside Germany and destroyed there. The army was the only German force strong enough to break Hitler's grip on the instruments of control in Germany. While winning, it would not try to break him; when losing, it could not. The Nazi leaders had not the sense of responsibility that prompted Hindenburg, Prince Max von Baden, Ebert, and Erzberger to sue for peace when they knew a war was lost. Hitler grew steadily more fanatical and maniacal, determined to destroy what he could not hold. His obstinacy, which was the determining factor, was in no way affected by the

[19] *Goebbels Diaries*, 258, 278, 285, 305, 325. Hitler and Goebbels scolded at the drunkenness, conspicuously self-indulgent living, profiteering, and peculation of their Gauleiters, SS, and other officials; but they only denounced the malefactors, did not discipline them.

demand for unconditional surrender; and he ruled both army and people until he and they were destroyed. It would therefore have been difficult to demonstrate that the unconditional surrender demand, so logical in the circumstances, had any appreciable effect on the duration of the war.

Tunisia

LAND WARFARE

The strategic objective of the Allied north African campaign was nothing less than the whole northern coast of Africa; so only meager progress could be claimed or counted until Allied armies advancing from the west and the southeast met in Tunisia and liquidated any Axis forces caught between them. Acting promptly in November and December, 1942, the Axis powers used their advantage of position to seize the French naval base at Bizerte and fill Tunisia with troops, soon to be reinforced by the battle-hardened remainder of the *Afrika Korps*, driven across Tripolitania by General Montgomery's British Eighth Army.[20]

In mid-February, 1943, a hard-hitting German counterattack recaptured Faïd Pass, Gafsa, and Sbeitla from the hastily and rather haphazardly assembled French colonial and United States troops that had just taken them. In March the newly reconstituted U.S. Second Corps, commanded by General George S. Patton, drove eastward to retake Gafsa and establish depots for the British Eighth Army, which was soon to outflank the Mareth line and move into Tunisia. General Patton was then removed from command, and General Omar Bradley moved the U.S. Second Corps northward for a drive along the coast to Mateur and Bizerte.[21]

Meanwhile the British broke the Mareth line and captured Gabès March 30, Sfax April 10, Sousse April 12, and Enfidaville April 20.

The Tunisian campaign soon ended after Bizerte was taken by the U.S. Second Corps, Tunis by the British, and Pont du Fahs by French forces, May 7. German air transport managed to fly off a few staff officers and technicians; but many loaded planes were shot down. May 9, General Krause surrendered 25,000 German troops southeast of Bizerte. May 11, the Cap Bon peninsula was cut off at the

[20] The Germans bore the brunt of the fighting during the retreat through Italian North Africa. The Italians, often left in the lurch by their allies, lost more prisoners. Goebbels scoffed at the unverified and unconvincing but official Italian casualty list for November: 300 killed, 23,000 missing. *Diaries*, 324.

[21] General Dwight D. Eisehower was in supreme command, British General Sir Harold Alexander in command of all Allied ground troops, under Eisenhower.

base. May 13, resistance ceased and 150,000 prisoners of war were surrendered by General von Arnim. The total number of prisoners taken was about 267,000. Other Axis losses were 30,000 killed and 27,000 wounded. The principal Allied military effort had been made by the British first and Eighth armies. Total United States casualties for the whole North African campaign were 18,558: 2184 killed, 9437 wounded, 6937 missing and prisoners of war.[22]

Convoy Escorts vs. Submarines

While the Tunisian campaign was at its height, the ceaseless antisubmarine warfare of the convoy escorts reached its peak. During the first twenty days of March a daily average of 116 German U-boats were active in the Atlantic. During that period eighty-five ships totaling 500,000 tons were sunk, 68 percent of them in convoy; and only one U-boat was killed—by a British plane flying from an Iceland base. The enemy never came nearer to disrupting the Allied supply line.[23]

In April and May, however, defensive submarine detection gear and killer tactics and equipment improved more rapidly than submarine attack techniques. U-boat losses in May, 1943, exceeded those of the first three months of the year, having risen from 13 percent to 30-50 percent of all boats at sea. From May onward, the wolf packs were no longer safe from detection and attack, anywhere at sea. Compelled by increased fire power and air power of the escorts to submerge before attacking, they could no longer attack convoys successfully, and were often themselves attacked without sighting a convoy, which was of course at once diverted. Thanks to such vigorous convoy defense, before the end of the Tunisian campaign the United States had transported to Europe and Africa two million men, with material and supplies, without losing a loaded troopship.[24]

[22] Goebbels, in his diary entry of May 9, called Tunisia a second Stalingrad, and ruefully admitted to himself that telling the German people what had happened to Rommel would be no simple matter. Still popular, with a fabulous reputation, Rommel had been brought home long before the end of the campaign. *Diaries*, 360.

Goebbels professed amazement at the "ignorance and irresponsibility" of United States prisoners of war, who had been instructed, if taken, to divulge only personal information such as name, rank, and serial number. He was agreeably surprised at the decent treatment the German prisoners of war received, and surmised that Hitler would immediately but secretly order the unshackling of British prisoners, some of whom had been fettered after Dieppe. Some German POWs had been fettered by the British in retaliation. "We can no longer indulge in a prestige fight with the English in the matter of fettering," confessed the subtle *Doktor*, "since the English hold many more German prisoners in custody than we do English." *Ibid.*, 382.

[23] Morison, *op. cit.*, I, 344, 410; Dönitz, *op. cit.*, 29.

[24] Three transports were lost on their way to Greenland or Iceland, and some were sunk off northern and northwestern Africa after having debarked their troops. Morison, *op. cit.*, I, 409.

Meanwhile an accelerated Allied shipbuilding program outpaced an accelerated German submarine-building program and development of new and improved U-boat types.[25]

STRATEGIC BOMBING

While the Axis submarines failed in their greatest trial of strength to cut the convoy line, and German Admiral Dönitz tried in disgust to relegate the Italian navy to supply-transport duty since it would not fight effectively, and the retreating Wehrmacht, abandoning food and munitions undestroyed, encumbered itself in its forced withdrawal from Russia with plunder from looted homes, the Luftwaffe could not prevent heavy bombing raids on German cities. War production was temporarily stopped or more or less seriously crippled in one industrial center after another.

Recriminations flew thick and fast, particularly around the heads of Field Marshal Göring, chief of the air force, and Field Marshal Erhard Milch, second in command. Göring and Milch attributed their own failure to their former associate Ernst Udet, who had committed suicide in 1941 after an unsuccessful attempt to induce them to put the new jet- and rocket-propelled Messerschmitt fighter planes into mass production. The war in Russia had also played its part, not only by attrition but by creating a continuing demand for planes of the older types, still useful there. So the fast-climbing and faster-flying turbo-jet planes needed for over-the-target protection of German cities were not put into mass production until late in 1943, or available in effective numbers until 1945.[26]

Although continuous "round-the-clock" bombing was rather a threat than a reality in the spring of 1943, it was an ominous threat. The war was beginning at long last to come home to the German people. On April 5 United States heavy bombers escorted by British and Canadian pursuit planes reached industrial centers of Antwerp.

[25] The *Schnorkel*, an underwater breathing device enabling a submarine to run submerged longer and at greater speed, was not ready until 1944. With improved anti-aircraft guns, the wolf packs tried for a while to surface and fight it out with the escorts, but lost too many and soon had to abandon the practice.
Dönitz told Hitler July 8, 1943, that three of the last four German submarines that had tried to pass Gibraltar had been lost. Martienssen, *op. cit.*, 178.

[26] Hundreds of the best new German planes were on the production lines when the war ended.
Goebbels reported (in his diary) that on a tour of inspection of bomb damage in Essen and the Ruhr—on which it was determined that the Krupp works needed better anti-aircraft protection—Milch blamed both Göring and Udet for the Luftwaffe's fighter failure. Goebbels attributed also to Milch at that time an "insubordinate" remark that the Stalingrad army could have been saved, and that Paulus ought to have disobeyed Hitler's orders and saved it. *Diaries,* 320.

The Germans proclaimed that two thousand Belgians had been killed. On April 10 Goebbels admitted privately that the British espionage service was functioning alarmingly well, and that the Royal Air Force was well informed about results achieved. It proved him right in the night of May 17-18 by breaking the Eder, Sorpe, and Möhne dams, causing flood-water damage and loss of power. Only as a result of German treason, Goebbels thought, could the enemy know so well where to strike and what he had destroyed; it must be the work of German Jewish émigrés. As if to prove his point, a heavy raid fell on Altona and Hamburg July 25-26, only two days after their heavy anti-aircraft batteries had been sent away to Italy. The execution of captured fliers, in retaliation and as a deterrent, was considered.[27]

Day and night air raids were increasingly destructive. On May 18 serious damage was done to naval installations at Kiel. In a series of seven British night raids during May, on the industrial centers of the Ruhr—Dortmund (twice), Duisburg, Bochum, Düsseldorf, Essen, and Wuppertal—in addition to industrial damage done, the homes of many thousands of people were destroyed. Unwilling to see compulsory housing of refugees imposed within the Reich—with the concomitant dissemination of information about bomb damage and the consequent deterioration of popular morale—until the housing capacity of German-occupied non-German areas had been exhausted, Hitler ordered at Göring's suggestion that the bombed-out refugees be sent to France, preferably to Burgundy. Many of those deported soon filtered back to the rubble of their homes. By mid-September a million people were evacuated from Berlin.

SICILY AND ITALY

Sicily

STRATEGICAL CONCEPT

The distance from Britain to India by way of Gibraltar and Suez is three thousand miles less than around Africa. While the northern shore

---

[27] Hitler ordered the press to play up the news of the execution in Japan of some United States prisoners taken in the Doolittle air raid on Tokyo. "The English and the Americans would probably not have the nerve to reply with adequate reprisals," wrote Goebbels, "whereas of course we would." Hitler and Goebbels agreed that it was unprofitable to bomb only British harbors and industrial centers, and talked of concentrating on centers of culture and the homes of the plutocracy. Göring could not understand why the Allies ever gave the Ruhr a respite. *Ibid.*, 189-193, 308, 313, 321-322, 340, 341, 382-384, 405, 510.

of the Mediterranean was held by the Axis powers or by powers friendly to them, United States shipments of supplies—to Russia by way of Basra, to India, and to China by way of India—had to make what General Marshall called "a twelve thousand mile detour" around the Cape of Good Hope. Control of the Mediterranean was therefore the next logical objective of the Allied powers after the occupation of North Africa.

It was hoped that Italy would withdraw from the war when she found her long coastline exposed to attack by superior sea and air power operating from the nearest North African bases. Then, from bases in Italy, air power could reach into the Balkans to carry supplies to the Yugoslav partisans still carrying on active resistance, to destroy installations in the Rumanian oil fields from which the Axis powers were drawing three million tons of oil per year, and to bomb Austrian, Czech, and south German war industries, not yet seriously damaged. Whether, after the elimination of Italy, to invade the European mainland through southern France, from the head of the Adriatic, or through Salonika was a question not yet answered. Whether to try to join hands with the Red Army as quickly as possible in Bulgaria or on the lower Danube, to try to anticipate it on the upper Danube in Hungary, Austria, or Czechoslovakia, or to leave the eastern German front to it as its exclusive field of operation while launching the principal United States-British attack on the plains of northern France was a decision involving international political as well as military strategy.

CAMPAIGN

First steps first. Although British-held Malta had withstood years of Axis bombing, the three smaller Italian-held islands near by— Pantelleria, Lampedusa, and Limosa—surrendered under Allied bombing June 11, 12, and 13, respectively. On July 10, 1943, an amphibious assault was made on Sicily.

General Eisenhower was in supreme command, with British General Sir Harold Alexander as deputy commander of Allied ground forces. General Patton's Seventh Army, of which the Second Corps was commanded by General Bradley, landed on the southern coast and fanned out, pushing an armored spearhead northwestward across the island to Palermo, then working eastward along the northern coast. The British Eighth Army, under General Montgomery, landed in the southeast and advanced northward along the east coast. The two armies closed the pincers at Messina after thirty-nine days of fighting, August 17.

By concentrating heavy anti-aircraft protection, the Germans, who had done more than their proportionate share of the more formidable fighting, managed to extricate a considerable portion of their armored forces and air-borne troops across the Strait of Messina to the Italian mainland. They had suffered 37,000 casualties, the Italians 137,000, most of whom were prisoners of war. Allied casualties were 31,158 killed, wounded, and missing.

AIR WARFARE, SICILY AND ELSEWHERE

Most of the preliminary bombardment of Axis strong points in Sicily in preparation for the invasion of Sicily was done from the air. Air-borne troops participated in the invasion, at heavy cost, some of them being fired on by Allied troops as they flew in. Such tragic blunders were due in part to the difficulty of identification, in part to Axis air attacks being made at the same time, and in part to the nervousness of imperfectly trained, trigger-happy troops, who had much yet to learn about the arduous trade of the invader.

While the Sicily campaign was in progress, on July 19, 272 heavy and 249 medium United States planes bombed the San Lorenzo and Littorio railway marshaling yards in Rome and an airfield near by. Crews had been carefully briefed. Churches and historical monuments had been clearly marked on their maps. None was damaged.[28]

In Germany on successive nights, July 27-28 and 28-29, a raid on Essen caused a complete though only temporary stoppage of work in the Krupp munitions works there, and what Goebbels called "the heaviest raid yet" fell on Hamburg. On August 17, the day the Allied pincers closed at Messina, an attempt was made by a 600-plane raid to destroy the highly secret experimental laboratories at Peenemunde on the Baltic coast, where the flying bomb later to be known to the Germans as V-1 (*Vergeltungswaffe* or retaliation weapon) was being developed. The laboratories were damaged but not destroyed. Subsequent bombings—including three by the Eighth United States Air Force in 1944—failed to prevent the completion of the deadly weapon, which the British were to know only too well in 1944 as the "buzz

---

[28] General Lewis Hyde Brereton, *The Brereton Diaries: the War in the Air in the Pacific, Middle East, and Europe, 3 October 1941-8 May, 1945* (New York, 1946), 194-195. Crew members who were members of the Roman Catholic Church were offered an opportunity to withdraw from the raid, but none did so.

Mussolini was required to resign as premier of Italy and leader of the Fascist party five days after the bombing of the Rome railway yards.

bomb.''[29] On August 23, six days after the cessation of hostilities in Sicily, a United States air raid on Berlin deranged the city's transportation for more than two weeks and caused more than a 50 percent stoppage of production in some factories for a longer period.[30]

Meanwhile, on August 1, 164 United States Liberator bombers (B-24's) of 177 that had flown off their bases in North Africa reached their target—the Ploești oil fields in Rumania. Their pilots and bombardiers knew that they had done awesome damage to a principal source of the Axis oil supply. Just how much, they could not then know. Forty-six of their planes were lost over Axis-controlled territory—forty-one as a result of enemy action, five for other causes. Two had fallen into the sea on the way to the target. Seven landed in neutral Turkey and were interned there, one in the sea off the Turkish coast, two on friendly bases. Four hundred and forty men were killed in action or missing; seventy-nine were interned in Turkey.[31]

INTERNATIONAL POLITICS

Although, under the gifted leadership of General Eisenhower, there was good coördination of United States and British naval, air, and ground forces in the campaign in Sicily, unanimity was more difficult to achieve and less perfectly achieved at the highest policy levels.

Disillusioned by defeat in Greece and by the loss of Italian North Africa, and demoralized by successive defeats and the impending loss of Sicily, some disaffected army officers and high officials of the Fascist party, including Dino Grandi and the Duce's son-in-law Galeazzo Ciano, staged a palace revolution at a meeting of the Fascist Grand Council in Rome on July 24. They demanded that Mussolini resign as leader of the party and premier of Italy. The falling Duce refused, but was notified next day by the king, who until then had meekly countenanced him, that his government position had been taken from him. He was taken into custody by the new government headed by Marshal Badoglio, but was rescued by Nazi paratroopers from Gran Sasso in the Abruzzi mountains September 12 and carried off to German-controlled territory. Here he was set up again, September 23, under German tutelage and with principally German support as head of a "Fascist Italian Republic," still—naturally—an active ally of Nazi Germany.[32]

With the deposed Italian Duce and the memory of a fugitive ex-

---

[29] General of the Air Forces H. H. Arnold, *op. cit.,* 498.
[30] *Goebbels Diaries,* 423, 424.
[31] Brereton, *op. cit.,* 200-202.
[32] The fallen Caesar used his restored semblance of authority to order the imprisonment and execution of his faithless son-in-law Ciano. Goebbels noted on

kaiser of imperial Germany apparently in mind, President Roosevelt warned all neutral nations July 30 to give no asylum to "war criminals." Sweden, reading the weather signs aright, withdrew permission, previously granted under heavy pressure, for German troops to pass through Sweden to Finland or to Norway.

The new Italian government of Marshal Badoglio announced at first, officially, that the war would go on; but two days before the end of the campaign in Sicily (i.e., on August 15) an Italian army emissary was in Lisbon to negotiate for peace. Generals Walter Bedell Smith and (British) K. W. D. Strong of General Eisenhower's staff met Castellano and informed him that the only military terms were unconditional surrender. Peace terms were not stated. Stalin was informed August 17 by Roosevelt and Churchill, then in conference in Quebec, and was notified at that time that southern Italy would be invaded somewhere before September 1, and at another point about a week later.

Stalin was not appeased. Annoyed because a second front satisfactory to him had not yet been opened up in western Europe, he had sent an angry message to Churchill late in June, accusing the Allies of deliberate failure and bad faith. Churchill replied as angrily, without consulting Roosevelt. The Soviet commissariat for foreign affairs recalled its Ambassador Maisky from London July 28, announcing that he was being made deputy commissar. A meeting of Stalin and Roosevelt scheduled for July 15, about which Churchill had shown little enthusiasm, did not take place. Stalin, in turn, was unenthusiastic and suspicious about the Roosevelt-Churchill meeting at Quebec, August 17-24. Soviet Ambassador Litvinov was recalled from Washington, succeeded by Andrei Gromyko, August 22. Nothing was said or done by a Russian spokesman to dispel the general impression that the recall of Ambassadors Maisky and Litvinov was an expression of disapproval of the policies or conduct of the governments to which they were accredited. Tantalizing thoughts of a separate peace with the Soviet Union or with Britain, if the two should quarrel seriously, arose again in Nazi minds.[33]

July 27 that Roberto Farinacci, former secretary general of the Fascist party and leader before the war of its most strongly anti-Semitic and pro-Nazi faction, had been "turned over to Himmler to take care of for a while." *Diaries,* 415.

[33] The months of July and August, 1943, were a period of military crisis in Russia. The Germans launched there on July 5, in the Orel-Kursk-Belgorod sector, their last great offensive on that front, analogous in a way to that of July, 1918, in Champagne. Orel and Belgorod were recaptured by the Red Army August 5, Kharkov August 23, Taganrog August 30, Stalino in the Donets Basin September 8. Stalin's temper seemed sometimes, not unnaturally, to be affected by the way the war was going.

Goebbels quickly guessed that as soon as the Allies had gained a foothold in southern Italy they would invade the Balkans. The Germans must, he said, at once dispose several divisions so as to be ready to meet such an invasion. Stalin did not indicate whether any of his irritability was attributable to sensitiveness or uncertainty on that point.

General Eisenhower was instructed to secure the unconditional capitulation of the Italian armed forces and to extract from it the greatest possible military advantage by seizing ports and airfields—Naples, Taranto, Brindisi, Bari, Foggia, Rome, and if possible others farther north—so as to put unrelenting pressure on the Germans in northern Italy, where it was assumed they would hold fast at first. The Badoglio government signed an armistice just before the military invasion of mainland Italy began, so offered no resistance, and surrendered September 8, the day before the first United States troops landed on the mainland. The principal elements of the Italian fleet surrendered at Malta September 9-13. On its way from Spezia to Malta to surrender, the *Roma* was sunk by German bombers, north of Sardinia.

Hoping to insure itself against the severity of the peace terms which it knew the fascist regime had earned for Italy, the Badoglio government maneuvered for an opportunity to declare war on Germany and join the Allies. Unwilling though they were to discourage anyone from fighting Nazi Germany who was so disposed, and aware that there had been friction and ill will between Germans and Italians as allies, the British and United States army leaders were skeptical about how well the beaten and demoralized Italian soldiery, just given a reprieve by the signing of the articles of surrender, would relish a new war against their former allies, the Germans.[34]

The statesmen were equally at a loss. A lifelong subject and servant of a constitutional monarchy, Winston Churchill said he believed that the new Italy should have a government of that type. Germany, he said, would have been stronger as a parliamentary constitutional monarchy after 1918, and the Weimar republic had been weakened by the fact that it was looked upon by many nationalist-minded Germans as an alien instrument of government imposed upon them by a victorious enemy. For analogous reasons, President Roosevelt and

[34] The Germans soon solved that dilemma by disarming the Italians and seizing their equipment and supplies. Long columns of prisoners and laborers were soon on their way to Germany, where they were welcomed by war industries as a new supply of slave labor. The succession government of Italy declared war on Germany October 13, 1943.

most of his advisers were predisposed in favor of a republic. For obviously practical reasons it was necessary that there be a government in Italy capable of delivering what it had surrendered. Those ideological critics in both countries who had been most disturbed by the Vichy gamble and by the policy of "expediency," which they had hoped had been buried with Darlan, were sure to be offended by the thought of any kind of collaboration with ex-Fascists, easily suspected of posing as nonfascist, until so recently the enemy. Another bone of some contention was Italian Count Carlo Sforza, a former minister for foreign affairs, who as an exile from Mussolini's Italy had lived in France until 1940 and thereafter in the United States. Sforza, who said that the king must go, would have been acceptable to most of the president's advisers as foreign minister or even as premier. Churchill did not want him, called him an intriguer and a mischief-maker, but eventually (in December) under some pressure of public opinion gave way on that point.

At their August conference at Quebec President Roosevelt and Mr. Churchill made several momentous policy decisions. They agreed on the draft of a four-power declaration, in which China and the Soviet Union were to be asked to join them, for the establishment after the war of an effective international organization. They set then the target date, May 1, 1944, for the major invasion of northern France, soon to be supplemented—against Churchill's wish and opinion—by an invasion of southern France. They agreed that Great Britain should invoke her ancient close relations with Portugal to secure for herself and the United States the use of air bases and naval installations on the Azores. And they gladly accepted a suggestion from Stalin that there be a meeting of the foreign secretaries of the three powers, soon, in Moscow.

Italy

1943. TO THE GARIGLIANO

Canadian and British divisions of General Montgomery's Eighth British Army crossed the Strait of Messina and landed across the beaches near San Giovanni and Reggio Calabria September 2, 1943. Six days later the U. S. Fifth Army, consisting of the British Tenth and U. S. Sixth Corps, under the command of Lieutenant General Mark W. Clark, landed near Salerno. As in Sicily, General Eisenhower was in overall command of the invasion, with General Alexander as deputy ground force commander.

Meeting comparatively little resistance, the British Eighth Army moved rapidly from toe to heel of the Italian "boot," capturing Bari on the east coast September 13. When its patrols met those of the U. S. Fifth Army forty miles southeast of Salerno, September 16, a united front was formed across the peninsula, from the Bay of Naples to the Adriatic.

The U. S. Fifth Army met stiff resistance around Salerno, where an invasion had been anticipated by the Germans and defensive preparation made. Incredulous at first, then happily surprised that the landings had not been made farther north, the German high command (OKW, *Oberkommando Wehrmacht*) in Italy reacted quickly to the new situation. Its leaders at first anticipated, and feared above all else, an invasion in the vicinity of Genoa, which, if successfully driven home and sustained, could have deprived them of the use of the north Italian plain and industrial areas, and have cut them off from that part of the peninsula south of the Po River valley. Such an attack would have been costly to the invaders; but if successful it would have crippled the defenders. Hitler immediately assumed that he would have to use a parachute division to capture Rome; actually it was occupied without difficulty, September 10, and the Nazi took over the protection of the Vatican City there. Even the first landings in Calabria Hitler professed to regard only as a feint, to be followed soon by the real invasion, around Genoa or in the Toulon area of southern France. So the eight first-class divisions available in northern Italy were not immediately sent to reinforce the eight which, as Allied military intelligence had correctly estimated, were ready to meet the invasion in the south.[35]

When the German defending forces were assembled they outnumbered the Allies. They had also the advantages of the tactical and strategical defensive, including the choice of positions to be defended, in mountainous terrain guarding a few easily blocked northward passages and a number of swift-flowing, often flooded, streams. The whole Allied enterprise in Italy suffered under the further handicap of never being, from a general point of view, more than a secondary operation. While it was being undertaken several of the most experienced and militarily efficient of the United States divisions, such as the 1st, 9th, and 2nd Armored, which had been "blooded" and begun to become battle-wise in the campaigns in North Africa and

[35] Statements attributed to Hitler, and to Rommel, Kesselring, and von Vietinghoff, successive supreme commanders of the Wehrmacht in Italy. Shulman, *Defeat in the West* (New York, 1948), 85; Dönitz, *op. cit.*, 37; *Goebbels Diaries*, 408-409, 425.

Sicily, were being staged out for transport to Great Britain, to train for and spearhead the Normandy invasion of 1944. Supplies, transport, and man power were doled out like iron rations to the armies in Italy, to make possible the build-up in all categories essential to the success of the major operation, based on Britain.

Despite handicaps, and in face of a defense skillfully conducted by Field Marshal Kesselring, which took expert advantage of position and terrain, the Allied line inched slowly forward. Naples was occupied by the Fifth Army on October 1, Foggia by the British Eighth. The Germans then withdrew to delaying positions along the Volturno River. Sardinia was evacuated by the Germans in the face of Italian pressure September 20. French commandos landed on Ajaccio in Corsica September 14, and the island—birthplace of Napoleon Bonaparte—was evacuated by the Germans October 4, when the French entered Bastia.

During the most critical early months of the Italian campaign approximately 300,000 tons of shipping were required to carry the necessary pumping plants and pipe lines—largely recovered from North Africa—machine shops, warehouses, and ground personnel for ten airfields around Foggia, on which the Fifteenth Strategic Air Force was activated November 1 under command of General James H. Doolittle, leader of the first bombing flight over Tokyo. From Foggia the Fifteenth could reach into Austria and the Balkans, and could bomb ahead of the ground forces in Italy; but while its installations and supply depots were being built up, the build-up of the ground forces was considerably delayed.[36]

Reinforced early in November by the U. S. Second Corps from Sicily, the Fifth Army forced a crossing of the Volturno River, and the Germans withdrew to a winter line, already partially prepared, behind the Garigliano and Sangro rivers.

1944. CASSINO TO THE APENNINES

To disrupt communications behind the German lines in the Cassino area, on January 22, 1944, the U. S. Sixth Corps established a beachhead at Anzio, twenty-five miles south of Rome, while the Fifth Army, in which the Sixth Corps had been replaced by a French one under General Juin, attacked across the Garigliano and Rapido rivers near Cassino. The offensive failed in the face of fierce German re-

[36] General Marshall's report: *The Winning of the War in Europe and the Pacific* (New York, 1945), 19. In December General Doolittle went to England to take command of the U. S. Eighth Air Force, and General Nathan F. Twining assumed command of the U. S. Fifteenth.

sistance. The famous abbey on Monte Cassino was demolished, without the conclusive proof needed to justify its demolition—that it had been made into a military observation post and strong point and used for military purposes. Around Anzio also the defense reacted quickly, and the beachhead was surrounded and furiously attacked before it could be expanded. Only on May 23 was a breakout from Anzio effected, to meet other Fifth Army units advancing northwestward along the coast as a result of a coördinated offensive launched May 11 by the Fifth and Eighth armies. Also on May 23, Canadians with the Eighth Army broke through the Hitler line in the Liri Valley.

When the Allies reached the Alban hills the German commander, Kesselring, offered to withdraw his troops from Rome and declare it an open city. The Fifth Army occupied the Italian capital, the first to be so liberated, June 4, two days before D-day for Normandy. German vehicles were strafed on the congested roads north of Rome.

Beyond Rome lay more of Italy—more mountains, more rivers to cross; but in June and July the Fifth Army was called upon to furnish seven experienced divisions, the 45th, 3rd, and 36th United States, one Algerian, three Moroccan, for the invasion of southern France, scheduled for August. Still maintaining the pressure, however, to prevent the diversion of German divisions to other fronts, and to get beyond the mountains and into the Po Valley if possible, the Fifth and Eighth armies pushed on when they could. Tenacious German resistance was met everywhere, especially along the line of the Arno River. But Florence was taken in August after two weeks of heavy fighting by British troops of the U. S. Fifth Army, Pisa by the U. S. Fifth on September 2, and Rimini on the edge of the valley of the Po by the British Eighth September 21. There the Germans hung on to their transpeninsular Gothic line in the Apennines south of Bologna, protecting the Po Valley. Allied attempts to penetrate that line could do little more than prevent the transfer of German strength to other fronts.

In December Field Marshal Alexander moved up to the position of supreme Allied commander in the Mediterranean area, General Mark Clark to command of Allied armies in Italy, the Fifteenth Army Group, and Lieutenant General Lucian K. Truscott to command of the U. S. Fifth Army.

1945. BOLOGNA TO THE BRENNER

In January, 1945, three combat divisions of the Eighth Army followed that famous army's fabulous old commander, Marshal Montgomery, who had gone more than a year earlier, to Europe. One other was withdrawn for service in the eastern Mediterranean, and one to reserve. Three combat groups of Italians assigned to the Eighth during the winter were no replacement for the combat troops withdrawn. Only the strategic air forces were much stronger than the German; but they facilitated the supply of the Allied forces and interfered with the supply of the German.

There was heavy fighting again in Italy in April, 1945. The issue was determined when Bologna was entered from three directions by Fifth Army troops and the British Eighth Army's Second Polish Corps. On April 23-25 the Eighth crossed the Po in force, and the Fifth captured the Ligurian naval base La Spezia. The German armies were virtually destroyed south of the Po, losing most of their equipment in their retreat. Once out into open country, the Eighth Army swept on to Padua, Venice, and Treviso, the Fifth to Verona, Milan, Genoa, and Turin, and into the approaches to the Brenner Pass. Contact was made with the French beyond Savona, and with the Yugoslavs at Montfalcone, northwestward from Trieste. More than 160,000 prisoners were taken by the Allied armies. With what was left of the German forces in northern Italy, General von Vietinghoff capitulated May 2, 1945.[37]

The Fifteenth Army Group in Italy was always a composite, characteristic of the cosmopolitan membership of the United Nations. It included at one time or other, as elements of its Eighth Army, men from Canada, New Zealand, South Africa, and India, a Polish corps, and a brigade of Jewish soldiers principally from Palestine. There were French colonials—Algerians, Moroccans, Goums, and Senegalese— Frenchmen, Arabs, and a Brazilian division. American components of the Fifth Army included a Negro division, the 92nd, and a regiment (the 442nd) of American-born Japanese. The 10th U. S. "mountain" division, long in training in Colorado, did not see the Apennines until January, 1945, but at once gave a good account of itself.

"The entire campaign," reported General Marshall to the secretary of war, "was slow and bitter. . . . Nonetheless, the Italian campaign made a heavy contribution to the successes on the western front, pinning down German forces which Hitler needed badly to reinforce his weakened armies, both in the east and west."[38]

---

[37] The story of an ostensible German proposal to surrender in March, and of an acrimonious argument arising therefrom between Roosevelt and Stalin just before the president's death in April, will be told in another connection. See pp. 723-726.

[38] Marshall, *op. cit.*, 24, 26.

FRANCE AND GERMANY

Strategy: The Point of Attack

POLITICAL OBJECTIVES

A democratic national government can justify a war only as an act of absolute necessity, and even then only if it is designed to achieve a justifiable objective of supreme national importance impossible in the circumstances to achieve by other means: to repel invasion, or to prevent a major disaster or development regarded as a disaster not otherwise to be prevented. For the Allies in the Six Years' War against Nazi Germany the immediate objectives had to be to arrest, dike back, and finally drive back the flood of Nazi invasion, to liberate the territories overrun, and to destroy at its source the cause of the eruption. That could be done only by the defeat and destruction of the armed forces of Germany, of which in 1943 the Nazi-dominated government of Germany was still so fully in control that only dialectical distinctions could be drawn between party and people, army and government. These entities might split apart in total defeat; but the power of the Nazi over Wehrmacht and people was not likely to be broken otherwise than by the sledge-hammer blows of the armies and air forces of the Allies, delivered by virtue of sea power.

The immediate objective, then, had to be the winning of the war by the destruction of the malevolent power that had made the war by first invading the territories of its neighbors. The ultimate objective was the establishment and maintenance of a decent peace. The world-wide peace that should end a global war might have to be made piecemeal, over a period of years, and might have to depend for its maintenance upon a universal or nearly all-inclusive international organization or world government empowered either to enforce or to revise the provisional first terms of the settlement. In comparison with such long-term forward-looking purposes, the mere military winning of the war shrank to the proportions of a short-term objective only. Essential though it was as the necessary first step toward the making of the peace, and however preferable to the clear consequences of defeat, military victory alone would never be enough.

Should, then, the war strategy of the Allies be planned with peace strategy constantly in mind, to serve both military and political long-term purposes? Or should military strategy be based on only military considerations, leaving peace planning to be done when peacemaking had been made possible by the destruction of the immediate enemy?

More specifically, should the principal United States-British invasion of Europe beyond Italy be made through Greece, or through Istria, Trieste, and Styria, or through France? Mr. Churchill favored the Balkans, so that southeastern Europe would be "liberated"—and occupied at war's end—not by the Red Army but by United States and British troops. Such strategy would have made the invasion of Europe into a campaign not only for military victory over Germany but for postwar geographical position with reference to Britain's ally Russia. It would have meant putting political purposes first in the planning of a military enterprise. But how could any military enterprise be justified except as it served a national, i.e., political, purpose? Why not plan the war with a view to the making of peace, and to the character of the peace to be made?

On the issue of the choice of the invasion route and area President Roosevelt accepted and supported the views of his advisers, among whom Secretary Stimson and Generals Marshall and Eisenhower stood firmly together, that a military campaign for geographical and political postwar position vis-à-vis the ally (USSR) of an ally (Britain) would not justify itself if the preponderance of immediate military considerations weighed more heavily against than for it—as they thought it did.[39]

MILITARY CONSIDERATIONS

As the supreme executive political authorities under the constitutions of their respective governments, the president of the United States and the British prime minister were responsible, with their advisers, for the ultimate national policy decisions. It was the duty of their military staffs to accept decisions so made by their supreme commanders and to carry them out with maximum efficiency and minimum loss of life. It was the duty of the military staffs also to counsel the president and prime minister, laying before them, each in the field of his own competence and responsibility, the considerations upon which decisions should be based. In that capacity the president's

---

[39] Such discussions were naturally not published at the time. No one said publicly whether the decision had been based on any consideration or prevision of the probable reaction of the leaders of the Soviet Union to an Allied invasion of the Balkans. Stalin wanted the United States and Britain to make a "second front" in France. He clearly did not want to see them in southeastern Europe. He was always suspicious of their motives, was or seemed to be apprehensive about their ultimate objectives, and violently resented anything which he thought might threaten what he had in mind for Russia. Despite the continuing menace of a dangerous common enemy, the disruption of the alliance was—or seemed to be—always an ominous possibility. That danger seemed especially serious from January to August, inclusive, 1943, when the decision where to invade Europe was being made.

advisers submitted substantial considerations favoring France over the Balkans as the field of the principal invasion of Europe in 1944.

Mr. Churchill favored the Balkans for military as well as for political reasons. That was not his first experience as a member of the cabinet in a war against Germany and Bulgaria, and he remembered: how Germany's allies had failed her at the culmination of the far-flung Mesopotamian and Syrian invasions in which Britain had been accused of having unwisely dissipated her military strength; how Bulgaria had sued for peace in 1918 when invaded from Salonika; how Germany had been weakened by blockade, and her armies had been crippled in the autumn of 1918 by their inability to bring up enough oil products from Rumania; how quickly she capitulated when the collapse of the Austro-Hungarian monarchy opened her territory to invasion from the south. He remembered the carnage of that war in Flanders and could not contemplate taking such man-power losses again. He and his advisers still hoped in 1943 that by a series of attritions, from the air and from the eastern Mediterranean to which their thoughts turned more naturally and traditionally than those of their American associates, Germany could be brought to surrender without being invaded from the west; and many thousands of lives could so be saved. From more recent experience Mr. Churchill remembered Dunkirk, Dieppe, and Britain's plans for defense of her own Channel coast, and spoke eloquently and with emotion of blood-drenched sands and corpses on the beaches. He was convinced only with great difficulty, and had to be repeatedly reconvinced, that the direct way was the best way. When finally committed to the enterprise, he loyally supported it.

The Americans favored France. With the war against Japan in mind as well as Germany, United States war planners had hardily adhered to the decision made before Pearl Harbor to give the war against Germany priority over war against Japan; but to them the direct way to Germany was better because it promised to be quicker. With air cover such as the Luftwaffe could not have provided for a German Channel crossing attempt in 1940, they believed that they could transport an expeditionary force from England and land it in Normandy without prohibitive losses. The English Channel was easier to cross than the Mediterranean. Britain was a better base from which to operate than southern Italy or anything else the Mediterranean area could offer, and France a better theater of war in which to bring to bear the superior weight of man power and machines.

The overland distance to the Ruhr, the industrial production center without which German resistance would soon be paralyzed, was shorter from the west or northwest. Losses would be sustained either way, perhaps faster in a major undertaking in France than in a minor one in southeastern Europe; but one year of heavy fighting in one area might take fewer lives, all told, than a longer war in more areas than one.

Most important of all, perhaps, a full-scale invasion of France would compel the German Wehrmacht to fight on two major fronts simultaneously, as well as in Italy. The nightmare which had haunted Bismarck and the German general staff since the Iron Chancellor's day, the two-front war in which Goebbels would soon be confessing to his diary that Germany had "never had any luck," but which Hitler had so far managed to avoid, would come home to the German people as a reality for the first time since 1917. The Red Army had men enough to cover the eastern front. Let the Allied expeditionary force deploy, then, in the west; and let the Wehrmacht try to withstand them both at once.

So, as the shortest way to military victory in Europe for military reasons, the generals chose France. Intent upon their first task, the winning of the war, they let peace problems wait for other men to wrestle with another day.

The decision to attack through France was confirmed first by Churchill and Roosevelt, then by Stalin at a conference at Teheran, November 28-December 1, 1943. Stalin showed a marked preference at that conference for the proposal of a secondary invasion through southern France, rather than one from the Adriatic through western Yugoslavia, which the British would still have preferred.[40]

[40] Stalin repeated at Teheran the promise already made to Secretary Hull at a conference in Moscow, that the Soviet Union would join the Allies in the war against Japan when Germany was defeated. He did not then say how soon or with what forces.

At the same conference Stalin advised the president to give his people the propaganda treatment if they continued to object to the Soviet Union's retaining after the war the Baltic states and the territory taken from Poland in 1939.

At a conference at Cairo, November 22-25, attended by Chiang Kai-shek but not by Stalin, President Roosevelt and Mr. Churchill had announced that everything which had been taken from China by the Japanese, such as Manchuria, Formosa, and the Pescadores, would be restored to her. At Teheran, as if conscious of no contradiction, the president indicated to Stalin that the Soviet Union might be given access by lease to a free port at Dairen, under international guarantee.

At Teheran a declaration concerning Iran was agreed upon: "The governments of the United States, the Union of Socialist Soviet Republics, and the United Kingdom of Great Britain and Northern Ireland are at one with the government of Iran in their desire for the maintenance of the independence, sovereignty, and territorial integrity of Iran." Great Britain and the Soviet Union had agreed in January, 1942, that both should withdraw their armed forces from Iran within six months after the end of the war.

Preparation

Against the advice of Harry Hopkins and Secretary Stimson, and the known preference of Churchill and Stalin for General Marshall, President Roosevelt on his way home from the conferences at Teheran and Cairo chose General Eisenhower to command the invasion. Admiral King and others in the offices of the combined chiefs of staff in Washington, of which Marshall was chairman as well as United States chief of staff, had convinced the commander in chief that General Marshall could not be spared from the supremely important position he then held. There was no one to replace him. No one else had so clear a comprehension of the whole global pattern of the war, or so firm a grasp of its many problems. No one was more generally respected for ability or integrity of character. General Eisenhower, moreover, was eligible on his record as something of a genius at securing coöperation in composite forces. Field Marshal Sir Alan Brooke had been Churchill's choice until it was decided that an American should command, since Americans would predominate in the invasion forces.[41]

Normandy

D-Day, June 6, 1944

For months before D-day Britain was bursting at the seams with the build-up for it. Provision had to be made for assembling, provisioning, and final training there of 1,533,000 United States troops. The hospital plan called for 124,000 beds. Parks for 50,000 military vehicles had to be found, 270 miles of railroad to be built, and 20,000 railway cars and 1000 locomotives added. The United States air forces required 163 airfields and accommodations for 450,000 men. Thousands of landing craft of various types had to be constructed and assembled to carry the invasion, with hundreds of cargo vessels, and war vessels to protect the others. Materials for the reconstruction of

---

Goebbels guessed or was told that at Teheran: the United States and Britain had asked for Russian airfields for shuttle bombing; it had been agreed that eastern Germany would be ceded to Poland in exchange for "eastern Poland," which would be retained by the Soviet Union. He expressed amazement that leading English statesmen could be so taken in by Stalin, who, he said, would never think of fulfilling his obligations to them. *Diaries*, 542:

[41] General Dwight D. Eisenhower, *Crusade in Europe* (New York, 1948), 168, 196-197, 207-209; Sherwood, *op. cit.*, 802.

the port of Cherbourg, and floating piers ("Mulberries") and old vessels to be sunk as breakwaters to form an artificial harbor, were also got in readiness.[42]

In conjunction with the Royal Air Force, the Eighth and Fifteenth United States Air Forces, still located in Britain and Italy respectively but combined in organization January 1, 1944, as the U. S. Strategic Air Forces in Europe, under command of Lieutenant General Carl Spaatz, did what they could to prepare the way for the invasion. The U. S. Air Forces in the United Kingdom had by that time 3000 heavy bombers and 6500 first-line planes of other types. Heavy losses were sustained, especially in February over Regensburg, Merseburg, and Schweinfurt, where the Luftwaffe made a determined effort to sweep the bombers from the skies; but heavier losses had been anticipated, and prepared for by replacements, than were sustained.

Principal objectives of the heavy winter bombing were the war industries of the Reich, particularly airplane, synthetic oil and gasoline, and ball-bearing plants. As invasion time approached, attention of lighter craft was turned to bridges, railways (especially locomotives), and other means of communication and transport in France, so as to isolate the German forces in the invasion area.

Before dawn of the day of the invasion, air-borne Allied troops were dropped by parachute and glider, inland from the beaches to be crossed, to continue the disruption of enemy communications and interfere with the reinforcement of the area to be invaded. Through the night, across the Channel, and at dawn across the beaches, under adequate air cover, flowed the invasion. The assault area was the lowland of Normandy, on a fifty-mile front between the base of the Cotentin peninsula and Le Havre. While naval gunfire drummed on the coastal fortifications and reached over into the enemy rear areas, General Bradley's U. S. First Army attacked between Carentan and Bayeux, the British and Canadian Second Army under General Sir Miles C. Dempsey farther eastward, toward Caen. Field Marshal Montgomery was in general command of the ground forces of both armies.

Some tactical surprise was achieved by attacking in rough weather, shortly after low tide, when the moon was full, well away from any large harbor and at some points below sheer cliffs, through treacherous

---

[42] Marshall, *op. cit.*, 10, 30. It was not surprising that the Italian campaign and the war in the southwest Pacific sometimes seemed slighted as to supplies. The wonder was that Operation Overlord, as the invasion of France was called, did not absorb everything available.

shallow waters.[43] Lodgments were effected on three beachheads the first day. By June 11 the beachheads had been expanded and connected, and the German attempt to stop the invaders at "the wall" had failed. Prefabricated piers towed across the Channel, with old ships sunk as breakwaters, afforded artificial harbors for the landing of supplies across the beaches. Allied plans then called for the occupation of the area west of the Seine and north of the Loire, and for the liberation of Paris, within ninety days.

The defense was handicapped by uncertainty as to where the principal invasion would occur and differences of opinion between leaders as to whether to attempt to meet it at the "fortress" wall or absorb it by defense in depth. Hitler had anticipated that Normandy, rather than the Pas de Calais region, would be first invaded, although the latter was nearer England, was on the more direct and shorter line to the Ruhr, and was the area from which from June 12 onward V-1 flying bombs were being launched against London. Neither Hitler nor his high command, however, could be sure that the Normandy invasion was not a feint, to be followed soon by a move into the Pas de Calais. The German Fifteenth Army was therefore held until July 25 in the Pas de Calais area while the Seventh Army bore the brunt of the attack alone.

The defense of the coastal region was under the immediate command of the energetic Field Marshal Erwin Rommel, of North African and Italian fame. In the immediate vicinity of the Normandy assault he had at his disposal ten divisions, nine infantry and one *panzer* (armored). Field Marshal Gerd von Rundstedt, hero of the 1939 and 1940 conquests, hero and scapegoat of the 1941 campaign in Russia, commanded all German forces in France, consisting of some sixty divisions of uneven quality. All field commanders were subject to constant surveillance and some interference by OKW—Hitler and his high command headquarters. They were slowed down and restricted in their movements by the necessity of securing OKW approval, and hamstrung by the incessant Allied air warfare on roads, bridges, and troop movements behind their coastal lines. Rommel's armor, in reserve, was too close to be mobile. Rundstedt's was too far away. Harassed by Allied strafing and by fuel and ammunition shortages due to transportation failures, reserves did not arrive in time to prevent the establishment of the beachhead, or in sufficient strength to destroy it as

[43] The Germans made similar use of difficult terrain and bad weather—unfavorable except as it afforded them protection against Allied aircraft—when they counterattacked in the Ardennes in December, 1944.

Hitler ordered. Yet Hitler, at Soissons June 16, with nearly half a million men and 300,000 vehicles ashore in the beachhead, denied the generals' request for permission to retire behind the Seine. A wedge must be driven between United States and British troops, he said, and Normandy must be held at all costs.

Hitler ordered that all harbors also be defended to the death of the last surviving soldier; but Cherbourg was surrendered June 27. Damage to its installations delayed its use by the Allies but was soon repaired. Le Havre was held by the Germans until September 11 but was so heavily bombed by the Allies that its naval base installations were destroyed. Denied the use of its French bases, and forced thereafter to operate from German or Norwegian ports, the German submarine fleet—even with benefit of *Schnorkel* on some of its best boats —lost two-thirds of its effectiveness.

With the capture of Cherbourg and the Cotentin peninsula it was clear that the Allies could maintain their beachhead and would soon be ready to break out of it. Rundstedt advised his government to try to end the war—and was removed from his command, July 2, to be succeeded by General von Kluge. Ten days later Rommel asked again for permission to retreat across the Seine, and was again refused.[44]

July 20 Bomb Plot

Hitler's distrust of his generals and their hatred of him and resentment of what they called his interference with the military command were probably exaggerated by contemporary Nazi commentators such as Goebbels and by the generals in postwar interviews with Allied interrogators. But the mutual antagonism was real. On both fronts Hitler hysterically commanded that every position be held to the last drop of blood of the last defender. To the generals, trying to save what they could of their forces by giving ground, such frenzied orders were the ravings of an amateur gone mad. To him their failures and proposals to retreat were treason or, at best, craven cowardice. Wars were won by strength of will, he said, and only his will was indomitable.

At last, July 20, 1944, the most serious of a long succession of

---

[44] Rommel was injured in the wreck of his automobile, under strafing, July 17. Because of his "defeatist" views, put into writing June 12 and July 15, and of his knowledge and alleged approval of the July 20 plot against Hitler's life, he was compelled by two German generals, one of them Hitler's adjutant Buresdorf, to commit suicide October 14, 1944. See Hans Speidel, *Invasion 1944. Ein Beitrag zu Rommels und des Reiches Schicksal* (Tübingen, 1949); Desmond Young, *Rommel, the Desert Fox* (New York, 1950), 181-189, 204-211.

plots against Hitler's life, made ostensibly with a view to an immediate request for peace terms, culminated in the explosion of a bomb in his headquarters *Wolfsschanze* at Rastenburg on the eastern front. Hitler was slightly injured and four of his companions were killed. The loosely planned revolution was immediately suppressed.[45]

Swift and terrible was Nazi vengeance for the attempt on the Führer's life, which was made the pretext for a six-months' general purge of the disaffected. Renegade Nazi, civil servants, Social Democrats, churchmen, intellectuals, and army and navy officers—both active and retired, including fifty from the general staff—were involved or implicated, and executed when it was thought that torture could wring no more incriminating information from them. Among those executed were: former Colonel General Ludwig Beck, once chief of staff, who had been involved in a pre-Munich plot and had resigned in protest against the invasion of Czechoslovakia; Graf Friedrich Werner von der Schulenburg, former ambassador to the Soviet Union, who had told Hitler that the attack on Russia was unnecessary; Admiral Canaris, former chief of military intelligence, who had misinformed his government about Britain's readiness to repel invasion; Graf Helmuth von Moltke; General Heinrich von Stülpnagel, military governor of France, who disregarded orders to defend or destroy Paris; Karl Goerdeler, former lord mayor of Leipzig, who was to have been a leader in the new government; Field Marshal Edwin von Witzleben, who was to have taken command of the army and who, as a special disgrace, was hanged in civilian clothing; Graf Ulrich von Hassell, former ambassador to the pope; and Graf Klaus Schenk von Stauffenberg, who put the bomb, in a brief case, under Hitler's chair. Nearly five thousand persons were purged. Many scholars and churchmen who had knowledge of the plot but were not active in it survived.

The result of the 1944 purge was the final subjection of the army to Hitler. General orders issued by the new chief of staff, Guderian, prescribed that general staff officers must be judged thereafter on the basis of character, spirit, attitude toward political questions, and readiness to coöperate in the political indoctrination of the junior commanders in accordance with the tenets of the Führer. Political and

[45] On the same day, July 20, 1944, Premier Hideki Tojo of Japan resigned, and Franklin D. Roosevelt was nominated for a fourth term as president of the United States. On June 19 and 20, attempting to disrupt the United States campaign on Saipan, the Japanese lost three carriers, two tankers, and more than 400 planes over Guam and in the Philippine Sea.

personal subjection did not, however, cure the confusion. The Luft-waffe was responsible only to Göring, the navy to Dönitz. The Waffen SS and the Wehrmacht were independent commands. Only Hitler could command them all, none of them another. They competed with one another for equipment and supplies, in the allocation of which it was commonly believed among the others that the parachute di-visions and Waffen SS were generally favored. General Eisenhower noted no change in the morale of the German troops in France as a traceable result of the murder attempt or of its failure.[46]

Breakout and Entrapment: Falaise Pocket

Without the use of a major port in France, and despite bad-weather interruptions of the flow of shipments through their artificial ports on the Normandy coast, the Allies had four armies ready by July 25 to break out of their beachhead there. The Canadian First Army under General Crerar and the British Second under General Dempsey formed what was soon to be known as the Northern Army Group under Field Marshal Montgomery. The U. S. First under General Hodges and (after August 1) the U. S. Third under General Patton, forming what was later known as the Central Army Group, were commanded by General Omar Bradley.

While the British and Canadian armies contained the heavier enemy forces on their front by attacking and then withstanding fierce counterattacks along the Orne River above Caen, General Hodges' U. S. First Army launched an offensive July 25 which broke through at St. Lô and Coutances. Taking quick advantage of the opening so made, General Patton's U. S. Third Army drove swiftly southward along the western side of the Cotentin peninsula through Avranches (July 31), then across the base of the Brittany peninsula through Rennes (August 4) to Le Mans (August 9) and Nantes, thence east-ward up the right bank of the Loire to Angers, August 10.

The Eighth Corps of Patton's U. S. Third Army was assigned the task of overrunning Brittany and taking the coast towns St. Malo, Brest, Lorient, and St. Nazaire, in which some 75,000 German troops shut themselves up and stood siege so as to deny the United States forces the use of their port facilities.

From the hills around Mortain Rundstedt's successor von Kluge could see an inviting opportunity to drive a counterattack through to Avranches and thus to cut off the U. S. Third Army, which had to be supplied through a narrow opening there or by air. A heavy armored counterattack was launched there August 7, supplemented by others

[46] Shulman, *op. cit.,* 135, 143.

against the British and Canadians farther east, and stubbornly continued until August 12; but General Hodges' U. S. First Army held
the Avranches gap open.

The tenacity of the Germans around Mortain made possible an
Allied pincer movement to entrap the German Fifth *panzer* and
Seventh armies. Against determined resistance, which exacted more
Allied casualties for the ground yielded than any other part of that
campaign, the British and Canadian armies fought their way
southeastward by August 17 to Falaise. Elements of the U. S. Third
meanwhile turned northward from Le Mans through Alençon, and in
the evening of August 12 reached the outskirts of Argentan. There
ensued a terrific battle between German armored forces seeking
desperately to keep open the Falaise-Argentan gap to permit the escape of their Seventh and Fifth (*panzer*) armies, recalled too late from
Mortain, and the Allies striving from north and south to close it. Some
of the hardiest and most fortunate of the elements of the entrapped
armies escaped through the gap before it was closed near Chambois
August 20, and made their way eastward across the Seine. August 22
the "pocket" was eliminated. A hundred thousand prisoners of war
were taken, and many thousands more had been killed or wounded
or had lost their equipment. German resistance west of the Seine and
north of the Loire was broken, and the way to Paris was wide open—
for which the original Allied timetable had allowed ninety days, from
D-day, the day of the invasion.[47]

Sweep Across France and Belgium

INVASION PORTS

It was obviously good German strategy if possible to deny the Allies
the use of French and Belgian ports, although Hitler was subsequently
criticized by his generals for having immured 120,000 soldiers in
them. It had been the intention of the Allies, once the invasion got
under way, to supply the United States forces in northwestern France
directly from the United States. Ports such as Brest, Lorient, St.
Nazaire, and Bordeaux had been used by the United States expeditionary force of 1917-1918 and might have been used again; but they were
strongly defended.

---

[47] General von Kluge was removed from his command August 17, replaced by
General Model, and recalled to Berlin. Perhaps because he did not dare face
questioning concerning his knowledge of the July 20 plot against Hitler's life, he
committed suicide August 18. In a memorandum defending his conduct of the
campaign in France he urged Hitler, unless the new weapons won the war soon, to
make up his mind to end it while something of Germany was left. *Ibid.,* 154.

The French undertook the reduction of Bordeaux but did not complete it in time to affect materially the outcome of the war. Brest was taken September 19 by the U. S. Eighth Corps, which had recently been made part of a new Ninth U. S. Army under command of Lieutenant General William H. Simpson; but harbor facilities were found too badly damaged, and Brest was thought by then to be too distant from future fields of operations, to warrant immediate reconstruction. So the Channel ports had to be used, and the importance of England as a base for the whole operation was enhanced. Dieppe was liberated August 31, and tonnage began moving through it September 7. Le Havre fell into Allied hands September 11 and was put into use as a port October 9.

As the Allied armies moved eastward across France their earlier destruction of bridges and railways cost them something in logistics problems. Approximately a million gallons of gasoline per day, with munitions and other supplies and replacement weapons and vehicles were needed to keep the offensive rolling. The supply problem was never perfectly solved. It was especially critical in September and October when as supreme commander General Eisenhower had to decide whether to give supply priority to General Patton's Third Army, racing eastward toward Metz and the Rhine, or to Field Marshal Montgomery's forces, which liberated Brussels September 3 and Antwerp September 4 but had to fight for two months to clear the lower Scheldt so as to give the Allies access to Antwerp from the sea. That port was not put into operation until November 27, and then under heavy fire of enemy flying bombs. Meanwhile thousands of trucks of the Red Ball Express rolled night and day along one-way roads closed to local military or civilian traffic, from the ports to the forward depots. Gasoline was pumped through cross-Channel pipe lines from England to beachhead storage tanks, and some of it thence through pipe lines laid in the wake of the advancing armies. Often the spearheads had to be supplied by airlift.

The ports of southern France, Toulon and Marseilles, were used to good advantage. A secondary invasion was started between Nice and Toulon August 15 by a Sixth Army Group consisting of the U. S. Seventh Army under command of General Patch and the First French Army commanded by General de Lattre de Tassigny. While the U. S. Seventh fanned out eastward to take Nice, northward to Grenoble, and up the valley of the Rhone River, the French First moved westward to free the Mediterranean seaports; then some of it advanced toward

Toulouse and Bordeaux while other French units joined the U. S. Seventh in its drive up the valley of the Rhone.

Harassed also by local French resistance groups, the Germans soon lost their grip on southern France. Southwest of Orléans, September 16, approximately twenty thousand occupation troops, cut off in an attempt to move back to Germany in time, tamely surrendered to the commander of the U. S. 83rd Division. The 1st French Armored Division of the U. S. Seventh Army had already made contact with the 2nd French Armored Division of the U. S. Third Army northwest of Dijon on September 11.

The Sixth Army Group continued to be supplied from Italy, by way of Marseilles and Toulon, for some time after it had passed under the operational control of SHAEF (Supreme Headquarters, Allied Expeditionary Forces), September 15. Fourteen more divisions were subsequently moved in through those ports, which, with the main railway line through Lyons and Dijon, were adequate to maintain the southern army group and at the same time to contribute materially to the supply of the central group until the seaway approaches to Antwerp were cleared.

PARIS

While the Falaise pocket was being eliminated, spearheads of the U. S. Third Army turned eastward to deny the enemy the use of communications lines between the Seine and Loire rivers. Orléans was reached by the Twelfth Corps August 17, Fontainebleau by the Twentieth August 20. By the end of August these advanced units, passing south of Paris, had swept on to a point 140 miles eastward, within sixty miles of the German border. A remarkable feature of this advance was close ground-air coöperation with fighter-bomber groups of the U. S. Ninth Air Force, a group of which was attached to each ground-force column to do reconnaissance for it and bomb and strafe ahead of it. The air force assumed also the task of watching the long open southern flank along the line of the Loire.

With Allied forces at Versailles and threatening encirclement of Paris from the south, the Paris police went on strike, barricades appeared in the streets, and French resistance came into the open. There was some skirmishing in the city; but, content to try to defend itself against the populace, the German garrison of ten thousand men did not try to defend the city or even to destroy its bridges across the Seine, as Hitler had ordered it to do. On August 25 the commandant, General von Choltitz, surrendered city and garrison to General Jacques

LeClerc of the French 2nd Armored Division, which had earned the honor of being the first to reënter the liberated capital of France.[48]

To the West Wall

ALLIED FORCES

September began with thirty-seven Allied divisions on the continent: twenty United States, twelve British, three Canadian, one French, one Polish. There were then in Britain six more United States divisions, three of them air-borne. The combined air forces had at their disposal 4035 operational heavy bombers, 1720 light, medium, and torpedo bombers, and 5000 fighters. The Air Transport Command had more than 2000 transport planes.[49]

No more British divisions were available. They were using all they had; and the national service was calling upon men between the ages of sixteen and sixty-five, women between eighteen and fifty. In contrast, so successful had the Germans been in procuring or requiring services of others that they were only then instituting a sixty-hour work week, closing theaters, music halls, cabarets, schools of music, and art colleges, and combing men out of nonessential occupations.

[48] General LeClerc and his division had made their way northward across the Sahara from Lake Chad to participate in the campaign in Tunis. After some service in England, the division had formed part of the Third Army spearhead at Argentan, whence it was moved to Paris. It made the first contact with the 1st French Armored Division of the U. S. Seventh Army from the Mediterranean, and eventually saw Berchtesgaden. It was uniformed, equipped, and supplied by the United States on lend-lease.

As soon as he could safely do so, General Charles de Gaulle entered the city and with some nationalistic exaggeration congratulated it upon having liberated itself.

General von Choltitz and his immediate predecessor as commandant of Paris, Lieutenant General Wilhelm von Boineburg-Lengsfeld, were court-martialed by the Nazi in April, 1945, for their failure to defend the city or to destroy its bridges but were saved by the general collapse. Boineburg-Lengsfeld, having failed to appear as a principal witness against von Choltitz, escaped from Nazi custody and surrendered to the Americans. Shulman, *op. cit.,* 166-168.

A partial inventory of French *objets d'art* carried off by the Germans from March, 1941, to July, 1944—4174 cases filling 137 railway cars—included 21,903 items such as:

    5281 paintings by the greatest masters.
    684 miniatures and manuscripts.
    683 sculptures, medallions, etc.
    2477 articles of furniture said to be of value to art history.
    5825 hand-made works of art (bronzes, porcelains, majolica, etc.).
    1286 Asiatic works of art (bronzes, porcelains, screens, etc.).

Report of Bereichsleiter Robert Scholz, chief of the special staff for pictorial art. Nuremberg trial document 1015 (b)-PS, IMT, *Trial . . . ,* IV, 89; XXVI, 524-530; *Nazi Conspiracy and Aggression,* III, 666-670.

[49] Eisenhower, *op. cit.,* 289.

German women had not yet been called upon for an effort comparable with what had been required of women in Britain since the beginning of the war.

German Forces

Such elements of the German Fifth *Panzer* and Seventh armies as had escaped the Mortain-Falaise-Argentan encirclement were decimated and disorganized. The commanding general of the Seventh, Hans Eberbach, was captured at breakfast with his staff at Amiens, August 31. Since D-Day approximately one million men of the German army had been in action. Nearly half of those used had been lost, of whom nearly half were prisoners of war—135,000 between the breakout of St. Lô and the liberation of Paris. Of fifty divisions available in June only ten remained as effective units.

By September 4 the number of prisoners of war increased to more than 350,000: 40,000 surrendering to the British in the Pas de Calais and Somme Valley towns, 25,000 to the U. S. First around historic Mons and Compiègne, 11,000 at Namur and Mézières along the Meuse, and 50,000 to the U. S. Seventh in the south of France.[50]

On September 4, the day Antwerp was taken by the British, old Field Marshal von Rundstedt was again placed in command of the German troops in France, replacing Model, who had replaced Kluge, who had replaced Rundstedt. Realist that he was in professional military matters, and more concerned about rescuing the remnants of his armies than about holding French or Belgian territory, he tried to fight only rear-guard actions designed to get his units out intact, "to hold the enemy outside the Reich for a while," and to hope for a favorable turn of political fortune. Except along the waterways to Antwerp, which it took two months of dogged fighting to clear, no solid resistance was encountered by the Allies until they reached Metz and Aachen.

Production of the German V-2 heavy rocket was increased from three hundred in August to seven hundred per month from September, 1944, to March, 1945. This new long-range missile, for which Nazi propaganda had predicted miracles, was first launched from the Netherlands and western Germany in September, 1944. It did extensive damage and caused many casualties in Antwerp, and proved itself a very potent weapon. But it was a less serious threat to the Allies than the jet-propelled fighter airplane then in production despite Allied bombing.

[50] *Ibid.*, 302; Shulman, *op. cit.*, 174-175.

The Luftwaffe could have contributed more to the defense if it had got its turbo-jet fighters into production sooner. Thousands of them were on the assembly lines when the war ended. The air force was seriously handicapped, from September, 1944, onward, also by motor fuel shortages due to the loss of Rumania, with what oil production had been possible there under Allied air attack, and to the persistent bombing of the synthetic oil plants in Germany itself.

The fuel supply of the submarine service was always adequate; but the practice of prefabrication in widely scattered areas failed to prevent Allied bombing from hampering U-boat construction. Of 290 new boats promised between July and December, 1944, only 65 were delivered. The number of submarines in commission declined from 181 in June to 140 in December. The effectiveness of the U-boats in service also decreased. For fifteen merchant ships sunk in January, 1945, fourteen submarines were lost at sea and eight destroyed in harbor by air attack. In March, for twelve Allied ships sunk, eighteen submarines were lost. In April thirteen Allied merchant ships and thirty-three German submarines were sunk, while twenty-four submarines were destroyed in harbor by air attack.[51]

To the Reich Boundary

Less than three months were required by the Allies to break into France and drive the Germans out of the area north of the Loire and west of the Seine. Problems of supply and transport, rather than resistance, were responsible for the fact that three months more were used in closing up to the western German border, behind which the shattered Wehrmacht sought refuge but upon which it could be expected to stand again and fight. If it had been possible to be equally strong everywhere at once the rapid advance of the Allied forces across France and Belgium might then have been continued into Germany.

Without Antwerp or its equivalent a winter campaign would be impossible. There were those who thought, on the other hand, that an immediate invasion of Germany was possible while the Wehrmacht was, so to speak, on the run, and that with the middle Rhine in Allied hands a winter campaign might not be necessary. The decision was to allocate to the Northern Army Group such supplies and transport as were necessary to establish a bridgehead across the lower Rhine at Arnhem, then to clear the Scheldt below Antwerp and close up to the lower Rhine. The result was the eventual opening of the vital supply port for the winter campaign which handled, although

[51] Martienssen, *op. cit.*, 222-226.

harassed by V-bombs and V-2 missiles, an average of 25,000 tons per day; but the advance on the middle front was slowed down for want of sustenance.

Aachen (Aix-la-Chapelle) was taken by the U. S. First Army October 21, Metz by the U. S. Third November 22, Strasbourg the next day by the U. S. Seventh. Then the advance came up against the Siegfried line. Little work had been done upon that defense line since the fall of France, but it was nonetheless a formidable barrier consisting of tank obstacles and concrete forts with interlocking zones of fire. It was strongest in the Saar, where it was three miles in depth, weakest above Karlsruhe and east of Aachen.

North of Aachen and the Ruhr there were only the natural barriers —broad streams and low-lying, often flooded, land. There on September 17—in an attempt to turn the open northern end of the Siegfried line and gain a beachhead beyond the lower Rhine—the First Allied Airborne Army, based in England, dropped the 82nd U. S. Airborne Division around Eindhoven west of the Meuse, the 101st U. S. Airborne around Nijmegen between the Meuse and the Waal, and the 1st British Airborne at Arnhem beyond the Rhine. These units seized roads and bridges and tried to blaze a path, then hold it open, for the ground forces to approach the relatively thin-skinned northwest frontier of Germany. Bad weather, however, interfered with air-borne supply and reinforcement, and strong German defense forces, speedily assembled, decimated the British division dropped at Arnhem. Allied lines in the eastern Netherlands were materially advanced; but the bridgehead beyond the Rhine at Arnhem had to be abandoned. Only about 2400 men of the division dropped there could be brought back across the river. The Allied high command correctly interpreted the experience there as an indication that formidable resistance was yet to be encountered before the Reich could be invaded. The need for Antwerp as a supply port was again demonstrated, and Marshal Montgomery's Northern Army Group turned to clear the approaches to it.

The Germans' estimate of their total loss in prisoners of war from D-day to the end of November was 750,000.

Other Fronts

While the western Allies were occupied in France and Belgium the Red Army was busy in eastern and southeastern Europe. The starting line of its offensive, begun June 23, 1944, was, from north to south, from a point just east of Narva, along the eastern shore of Lake Peipus, east of Vitebsk and Mogilëv, then westward and again southward to include the southeastern portion of Ukrainian Poland and northern Bessarabia. By August 1 the line had been pushed forward to include southeastern Latvia and eastern Lithuania, and in Poland to the east bank of the Vistula opposite Warsaw. There it stood until January 12 while in Warsaw on the left bank an uprising led by Tadeusz Bor-Komorowski ("General Bor"), ordered by the Polish government in exile in London in anticipation of the Russian advance, was sustained for sixty-three days. Two days before the Warsaw rising was scheduled to begin, the powerful Hermann Göring Armored Division passed through the city, eastward, and drove back the Red Army spearheads opposite, which had advanced ahead of the general Russian line. In mid-September some supplies and Red Army liaison officers were dropped by parachute to the insurgents in the city; but the siege was not then raised. The Soviet Union did not recognize the noncommunist London government in exile as the true government of Poland, preferring to set up a communist administration in the area occupied by the Red Army, which the Russians could control and which they therefore called democratic and friendly. The noncommunist Poles and General Bor-Komorowski, on the other hand, were trying to get possession of Warsaw and establish an anti-Soviet administration in it by anticipating by as narrow a margin as possible the liberation of the city from the Germans by the Red Army. Their margin was too narrow. The surrender of "General Bor" to the Germans was announced October 5.[52]

Meanwhile, beginning August 21, the Red Army went into the Balkans. Prompted by Allied bombing of Bucharest and the Ploeşti oil fields in July, and with the Red Army at the gates, young King Michael of Rumania dismissed and imprisoned his pro-Nazi minister Ion Antonescu, August 23, and ordered his army to cease fire against the forces of the United Nations. Thereupon the Germans took their turn at bombing Bucharest. King Michael announced his willingness to surrender unconditionally in the name of the nation and called upon his people to join the Red Army at once in driving the Germans from Rumanian soil. The official armistice was signed in Moscow September 12, 1944. Rumania agreed to furnish at least twelve infantry divisions for the war against Hungary and Germany, to insure

---

[52] Some hazardous but ineffectual attempts were made by the United States and British air forces to drop supplies to the Warsaw insurgents. The Russians did not encourage them.

freedom of movement for Soviet troops in and through Rumania, and over a period of years to pay reparation to the Soviet Union, in oil products, materials, and mechanical equipment to an amount of $300,000,000.[53]

At the northern end of the Soviet battle line Finland announced September 2 that it would break off relations with Germany and request the withdrawal of German troops from its territory. Five days later a Finnish peace delegation arrived in Moscow, where on September 10 an armistice was signed. The Soviet Union regained what it had taken in 1939, plus the promise of reparation.

Bulgaria declared war on Yugoslavia and Greece in April, 1941, and on Great Britain and the United States in December, 1941, but resisted German pressure to declare war on the Soviet Union. In a speech before parliament August 22, 1944, with the Red Army starting its drive into Rumania, the Bulgarian foreign minister stressed his country's traditionally friendly relations with Russia and described the declaration of war against the United States and Britain as a mistake. On August 30 a Bulgarian delegation arrived in neutral Cairo to seek an armistice. Anticipating the signing of the armistice, the Soviet Union declared war on Bulgaria September 5. Although Bulgaria immediately asked Russia also for an armistice and declared war on Germany September 8, the armistice with Russia was not granted until September 9, and Bulgaria was occupied by the Red Army. Allied armistice terms accepted October 11 called for the evacuation within fifteen days of all Bulgarian troops and officials from Greek and Yugoslav territories occupied by Bulgaria in 1941. The official armistice was signed in Moscow October 28.[54]

From Rumania and Yugoslavia it was possible for columns of the Red Army to by-pass northeastern Hungary and threaten Austria from

[53] The coup was planned with Lucretiu Patrascanu (Communist), Juliu Maniu (National Peasants' party), Constantin Bratianu (National Liberal), and Titel Petrescu (Socialist). General Nicolai Radescu, a stanch enemy of the Nazi, became premier in December. In March, 1945, by direct command of Soviet Vice-Commissar for Foreign Affairs Andrei Vyshinsky, Radescu was overthrown and procommunist Peter Groza was named premier. The influence of Anna Pauker, an old-time Communist, increased. Soon Maniu was in prison, Britianu under house arrest, and Petrescu under attack by the communist press. On November 11, 1947, Maniu was sentenced to solitary imprisonment for life, charged with having conspired against the state with representatives of Britain and the United States. On December 30, 1947, the government announced the abdication of King Michael and the establishment of a people's republic.

[54] Edward Riley Stettinius, *Roosevelt and the Russians; the Yalta Conference* (Garden City, 1949), 14. Also in October, 1944, the Allies announced the results of a conference which had worked at Dumbarton Oaks, Washington, D. C., for several weeks on plans to implement the Moscow and Teheran declarations of 1943 of their intention to establish a permanent United Nations organization.

the southeast, but stubborn resistance was met at Budapest until February 13, 1945. Vienna was occupied by the Russians a month later.

At a conference at Quebec September 11-16 President Roosevelt and Prime Minister Churchill initialed on September 15 a proposal, soon to be popularly known as the Morgenthau plan, for the dismantling after the war of the German war-making potential in the Ruhr and Saar industrial areas. The plan indicated an intention to convert Germany into a country primarily agricultural and pastoral in character. Other advisers of both statesmen sharply challenged the wisdom of the Morgenthau plan; and within a fortnight Mr. Roosevelt was ready at least partially to repudiate it.[55]

In the western Pacific in October, 1944, the Japanese tried desperately to break up the United States reoccupation of Leyte in the Philippines. Already restricted in its movements by shortage of fuel oil, with its air force training and replacement program similarly crippled, the imperial Japanese navy lost in a series of furious naval and air engagements known together as the battle of Leyte Gulf, October 23-26, three battleships, one large airplane carrier, three light carriers, ten cruisers, and nine destroyers. It never recovered from those losses and could challenge the United States fleets again only by use of land-based planes.

The first B-29 superfortress air raid on Tokyo was made from Saipan by the U. S. 21st Bomber Command November 24. The war was closing in upon Japan and reaching into her home islands.

Ardennes Counteroffensive

In order to strengthen his Central Army Group to maintain the offensive in the Saar, and his Northern Group to cross the Rhine below Köln (Cologne) and invest the Ruhr, in December General

---

[55] James F. Byrnes, *Speaking Frankly* (New York, 1949), 185, 186; Edward R. Stettinius, *op. cit.*, 40.

During the autumn of 1944 the postwar division of Germany into three occupation zones, with Berlin an international zone within the Russian, was agreed upon by a European advisory commission meeting in London. The French zone was created later, against Soviet opposition, out of territory originally allocated to Britain and the United States—principally the latter. The zoning agreement was confirmed, not made, at the Yalta conference of February, 1945. The postwar status of the western powers in Berlin by international agreement as well as by right of conquest was thus defined before their armies reached the Rhine. The Soviet Union's title to an occupation zone reaching westward beyond the upper Elbe was conceded before the Red Army crossed the Vistula at Warsaw. The western powers' right of access to their occupation zones in Berlin was clearly implied, and subsequently recognized by the USSR, but was less well defined.

Eisenhower maintained only a thin line opposite the rough country of the Ardennes Forest and Eifel mountain region. Four divisions, some of them lately arrived and still unseasoned, were assigned to hold a front of seventy-five miles between Monschau and Trier. The decision to strengthen parts of the line for offensive action at the expense of other parts so weakened and exposed to counterattack was called a calculated risk. Allied intelligence officers knew that a new German *panzer* army, the Sixth, had been formed, last located by them at Köln, but were not well informed as to the extent of the enemy preparation or the point or hour of the attack. The troops in the front lines were surprised by the assault.

The counteroffensive was planned in the greatest secrecy and ordered in detail by Hitler, who was at Adlershorst, near Bad Nauheim, from December 11, 1944, to January 15, 1945, for the purpose. His objective was to drive a wedge between the Central and Northern Allied Army groups to the Meuse within two days, to take Namur and Liège, then to thrust forward to Brussels and Antwerp within fourteen days. He would thus again deny the Allies the use of their most valuable supply port, and trap Marshal Montgomery's Northern Army Group in the Netherlands. Marshal von Rundstedt, who had commanded the successful breakthrough from the same regional base in 1940 which had burst right across France to the sea, logically commanded the operation, but subject always to strict OKW supervision and control. Hitler needed his proficiency but did not trust him. Three armies participated: the *panzer* Sixth under the redoubtable SS-man Sepp Dietrich; the Fifth (Wehrmacht) Army on the left; the reconstituted Seventh to hold the southern shoulder of the salient against the anticipated counteraction of General Patton and the U. S. Third Army from the western border of the Saar.

The attack was planned for December 12 but postponed four days to wait for a period of bad weather. Then, under cover of fog and snow, which blinded and grounded the Allied fighter air force, it was launched with great ferocity by eight *panzer* divisions on a forty-mile front in the early morning of December 16. Many of the front-line United States units were overwhelmed. Rapid progress was made the first day, and some Allied depots were captured. The penetration was soon deep enough to disrupt communication between forces north and south of it; so Marshal Montgomery was put in command of those north of the penetration, including the U. S. Ninth and First armies. General Bradley retained command of forces south of it. The British Thirtieth Corps was assigned the task of holding the line of the Meuse

River and the Liège area; but the counteroffensive was stopped four miles east of the Meuse.[56]

General Bradley drew on the map a line of maximum penetration beyond which he doubted that the offensive could be carried—with only one good east-west road between Stavelot and Bastogne—if the shoulders of the salient held firm and unless the Germans could capture large quantities of gasoline in Allied depots. Confident that Liège and Verdun could be held, he did not order the removal of the depots located there.

The shoulders held firm. Their holding was the work, among others, of the 7th Armored Division of the U. S. Ninth Army at St.-Vith in the north and in the south of the U. S. 101st Airborne Division, rushed from Reims to Bastogne and surrounded there until relieved by U. S. Third Army forces moving up swiftly from the south. A decisive factor in the issue was a change to clear, cold weather December 24, which for two days enabled five thousand Allied planes to strafe the congested roads of the penetration area. The tide turned on Christmas Day at Celles and around Bastogne.

With Allied armies attacking from south, north, and west, Rundstedt was ready by January 2 to withdraw but could not obtain OKW permission to do so until January 9. By January 16, with Allied pincers from north and south meeting at Houffalize, the "bulge" was eliminated.

The counteroffensive, which brought the Germans out of their defenses to fight again a war of movement in the open, was costly to them. Hitler had promised them plenty of gasoline and three thousand planes to keep the skies clear above them. They lost 220,000 men, half of whom were prisoners of war, more than 1400 tanks and assault guns, and 6000 other vehicles. The Luftwaffe lost more than 1600 planes. The Allies, on the other hand, succeeded in turning to their own advantage an encounter which had startled them and threatened them with a serious reverse. The resumption of the principal offensive toward the Rhine was delayed about six weeks, but would then be resumed against a Wehrmacht weakened by its last major counteroffensive effort on that front. Total German losses in the eight months since June 6 were estimated at three million men, half on the western and half on the eastern front. Allied losses in the Ardennes battle

[56] Near Malmédy December 16, some United States prisoners of war from battery B, 285th field artillery observation battalion, were shot by men of the 1st SS *Panzer* Division. English-speaking Germans in United States uniforms and vehicles sought to drive into rear areas and create confusion.

were 77,000 men—about 8000 killed, 48,000 wounded, 21,000 captured or missing—and 733 tanks or tank destroyers.[57]

Immediately after the elimination of the "bulge" the Second British Army resumed the offensive at Sittard and drove ten miles into German territory to the Roer River valley northeast of Aachen. Meanwhile diversionary German attacks southward from the Saar toward northern Alsace and Lorraine were repulsed, and the "Colmar pocket" in Alsace in which the Wehrmacht had been holding on was eliminated. From Strasbourg to the Swiss border the Allies had reached the Rhine. Territorially speaking, the France of 1939 was free. Politically it, or something to replace it, had yet to be resurrected or created.

Yalta to Potsdam

MILITARY SITUATION, FEBRUARY, 1945

A new Russian offensive launched in Poland January 12 put Stalin into an advantageous military and diplomatic position for the international conference convened at Yalta, on the southern coast of the Crimea, east of Sevastopol February 4. The Germans had mustered 150 divisions on their eastern front without moving any from the west, but could not hold. Tannenberg, scene of the greatest Russian disaster of 1914 and site of the tomb of von Hindenburg, German hero of that campaign, fell on January 21. By the end of January the Red Army had broken into East Prussia and stood on the east bank of the Oder from near Breslau to near Frankfurt an der Oder, little more than thirty miles from Berlin; and the Russian conquest of Gleiwitz and Kattowitz (Katowice) denied the Germans access to the coal, steel, lead-zinc, and oil of Upper Silesia. On January 20, the day Franklin D. Roosevelt was inaugurated for the fourth time as president of the United States, a new provisional national government of Hungary signed an armistice with Russia, Britain, and the United States, acting for the United Nations at war with Hungary.

Having freed its own territory from invasion and overrun Poland and southeastern Europe, except Greece, where it had conceded a paramount interest to Britain, the Soviet Union was in position either to continue or to withdraw from the war. No open threat to withdraw and make a separate peace needed to be made; the possibility was always there, and Soviet propaganda proclamations had from time

[57] Eisenhower, *op. cit.,* 364-365.

to time suggested it. Some of Roosevelt's and Churchill's advisers were uneasy in the face of their realization that the United States and Britain needed, or thought they needed, the help of the Soviet Union against Germany and Japan more than the Soviets needed theirs just then against Germany. More certain of his ground than Roosevelt and Churchill, Stalin could use that advantage to outtrade them.

British and United States strategists were of two or more minds as to military strategy for 1945. Churchill, Montgomery, and the British military staff revived an earlier proposal that the principal Allied attack on the western front, to be delivered as early as the condition of the terrain would permit, should be a drive across the Rhine north of the Ruhr and a dash across northern Germany to Berlin. Their theory was that the fall of the national capital would mean the quick collapse of German resistance, and that military possession of Berlin would be a valuable pawn in immediate postwar negotiations with the Russians as to the occupation and treatment of defeated Germany.

Neither assumption was tested or could be proved at the moment. Such a drive from west of the lower Rhine to Berlin would have had approximately ten times as far to go as the Red Army from the Oder; so the Russians might well have reached Berlin first if both had made a race for it.

To have supported and supplied such a drive on Berlin as the British proposed would have required the use of the equipment and resources of the airlift then at the disposal of the Allied high command to such an extent as to have left the remainder of the west German front at a standstill for want of logistical support. At such a price, General Eisenhower did not think the Berlin drive worth the cost. Thinking rather of the conquest of the Ruhr and the war industries of southwestern Germany, and of the destruction of German armies, as his primary objectives, he preferred first to meet and to destroy west of the Rhine as many of the enemy armed forces as he could catch there, then to push several spearheads forward simultaneously, across the Rhine and right across Germany. The transport facilities available, including the airlift, were adequate to supply several such offensives simultaneously from forward bases if the whole line were so moved forward, not otherwise. Although his plan for the broader offensive was criticized as a dispersion of his strength, it offered him an opportunity to use the advantage of superior strength and would not permit the enemy to concentrate as he would have done against an attack in one area only.

At a meeting of the combined chiefs of staff at Malta General

Marshall, en route to Yalta, supported General Eisenhower's plan, which already had the support of SHAEF: (1) close up to the Rhine, destroying in the process as many as possible of the enemy armed forces; (2) cross the Rhine at several points; (3) send a four-pronged offensive across Germany (a and b) north and south of the Ruhr, meeting east of it, then turning northeastward and eastward toward Berlin, (c) by the valley of the Main toward Leipzig to meet the Red Army somewhere on or near the upper Elbe, and (d) to the upper Danube, then southward to the Brenner and eastward to a meeting with the Red Army in Austria and Czechoslovakia.

The most valuable industrial regions would so be the first to be overrun. The northernmost offensive would seal off the Netherlands and the Danish peninsula, Bremen, Hamburg, and Lübeck. With British and Russian forces about to meet on the Baltic coast, presumably somewhere east of Lübeck, German forces in the Netherlands, Denmark, and Norway could wither on the vine. In Germany, meanwhile, the well-bruited Nazi intention to withdraw the most dependable of their military forces to an Alpine redoubt, there to defend themselves indefinitely against the conquerors of their country, would be frustrated. Against the background of such a general offensive, designed to break the enemy's power and will to resist, the military conquest of his capital was not judged by General Eisenhower to be a military objective of primary importance. Political issues which might otherwise have been determined by the outcome of the military campaign, such as the boundaries between occupation zones and the international status of the Berlin occupation zone, had been predetermined in London in September by political decisions soon to be confirmed at Yalta. If agreements already made as to the status of the Berlin occupation zone were to be honorably kept—and it was no part of the province of a military commander to predict that they would be violated—it did not matter much whose army first occupied the city.

It was a matter of the greatest consequence, however, to President Roosevelt's advisers at Yalta that assurance should be given of the Soviet Union's actively joining the Allies in war against Japan as soon as possible after the cessation of hostilities in Germany. Assurances had been given, to Secretary Hull at Moscow in October, 1943, and at Teheran; but the United States military staff, still mindful of the ferocity of the Ardennes counteroffensive and of the naval and air battle of Leyte Gulf, wished them to be made more specific. Neither Iwo Jima nor Okinawa had yet been taken. Long-range bomber bases in the Marianas were being bombed by medium-range enemy bombers from Iwo, and the cumulative effect of the war on Japanese shipping was not yet convincingly apparent. The atomic bomb was not ready, and no one knew what it would do. Long and bitter campaigns in the Philippines and Ryukyus seemed to be in prospect, to be followed by a terribly costly invasion of the Japanese home islands, then conceivably by a final campaign on the continent of Asia against the large self-sustained Kwantung army which Japan was believed to have there, still uncommitted. It was to neutralize that Kwantung army and to furnish southeast Siberian air bases that Russian participation in the war was most urgently desired. Military considerations based upon his advisers' inaccurate estimate of Japan's remaining strength, and upon their overestimate of the need of Russian help against Japan, weighed heavily upon the president at Yalta and influenced the decisions and concessions he found it necessary to make there.

"WE THREE" AT YALTA

At the Yalta conference, February 4-11, 1945, Stalin promised the United States air bases in Hungary and the maritime provinces of eastern Siberia, and again agreed to bring the Soviet Union into the war against Japan within three months after the cessation of hostilities in Germany. It would take three months, he said, to relocate the divisions necessary for such an enterprise, some of which were already moving eastward. It was assumed that the Red Army would go into Manchuria and contain the Japanese forces there. General MacArthur's plans were thereafter based on that assumption.

In return Stalin asked then only that China grant autonomy to Outer Mongolia, with which he soon made a treaty, and that rights and concessions wrested from Russia by Japan in 1904-1905 be restored. It was agreed that Dairen should be internationalized and Russia given a free port there, with her old railway rights in Manchuria and a thirty-year lease on the Port Arthur naval base. The southern half of Sakhalin should be restored, and the disputed Kurile Islands should go to Russia. The United States would use its influence to induce nationalist China to accept the Mongolian and Manchurian settlements here outlined and the Soviet Union would sign a treaty of alliance with that government, disown the Chinese Communists, and help China free itself from the Japanese. Stalin insisted upon a written record of the agreement of the heads of the three great powers that the Far Eastern claims of the Soviet Union should unquestionably be fulfilled after Japan had been defeated; but as the Soviet Union was not then at war with Japan the agreement had to be kept secret. "For fear of leaks," the Chinese government was not then told of it. The president's naval aide, Admiral Leahy, carried the document home and locked it in his secret White House file.[58]

At Yalta President Roosevelt changed his position with reference to giving France a place on the Control Council, representing the principal Allied powers, which was to govern Germany until peace was made. Churchill had suggested it, Roosevelt and Stalin opposed. When Roosevelt moved over to the affirmative, Stalin accepted the decision. Acceptance did not cost him much. The French occupation zone would be carved from the United States and British zones, not from Russia's. A veto would always be as effective in a four-power council as in one of three. And the probability of solidarity among the powers other than Russia was diminished.

No agreement was reached at Yalta as to reparation payment to be required of Germany. Ivan Maisky, former Soviet ambassador to Great Britain, demanded for Russia half of a total of twenty billion dollars in kind, in machinery and factories to be delivered within two years and production within ten. The Russians argued that German heavy industry could well be reduced by 80 percent; the remaining 20 percent could maintain a standard of living comparable with that of the remainder of central Europe. Shares of reparation should be apportioned, Maisky said, according to the participants' contribution to the winning of the war, and in proportion to material losses sustained. That apportionment, he estimated, would give the Soviet Union half or $10,000,000,000 worth, $8,000,000,000 to Great Britain and the United States, $2,000,000,000 to all others. The Russian estimates were not accepted but were taken under advisement as a basis for further discussion by a reparation commission to meet in Moscow.[59]

Although Stalin had broadcast several times that he was at war

[58] Leahy, *op. cit.*, 318; Stettinius, *op. cit.*, 74, 92-96, 351; Sherwood, *op. cit.*, 866-867; Byrnes, *op. cit.*, 42. The promised air bases in Hungary and eastern Siberia were not made available.

[59] The Soviet claims were discussed again but not accepted at Potsdam in July, where the Russians said Roosevelt (who was no longer living) had accepted them. At a foreign ministers' conference in London in July, 1946, Molotov repeated the allegation that Roosevelt had accepted the Soviet reparation figures at Yalta. Sherwood, *op. cit.*, 862; Byrnes, *op. cit.*, 28-29; Stettinius, *op. cit.*, 131, 165, 266-267, 345-346; Leahy, *op. cit.*, 292-293, 302, 313, 316, 320, 322, 355, 420-425.

only with Hitler and the Hitlerites, and had no desire to destroy or dismember Germany, it was he who suggested writing the word "dismemberment" into the Yalta Protocol. In a section of that protocol defining the "unconditional surrender" formula, the three powers claimed supreme authority with reference to Germany and asserted that in the exercise of that authority they would take such steps, including the complete disarmament, demilitarization, and dismemberment of Germany, as they deemed requisite for future peace and security. Stalin was supported by Roosevelt on dismemberment. For fear it would stiffen German resistance, Churchill was doubtful of the wisdom of the policy.[60]

The organization of the United Nations was discussed at Yalta. There was little discussion of the right of any of the three principal powers to veto in the proposed Security Council a motion to take or recommend action. The Russians wanted also, for any of the five powers holding permanent seats in the Security Council, the right to forbid discussion of a question. Revealing his suspicion that discussion in the Council or Assembly of the United Nations might be used to mobilize opinion against the Soviet Union, Stalin reminded the others that Great Britain and France had led the move to expel Russia from the League of Nations in 1939. The United States representatives insisted that all members, large and small, must have the right to be heard. Stalin accepted the principle; but Vyshinsky made it clear that Russia would never agree in practice to the right of small nations to judge the acts of the great powers.[61]

At Yalta President Roosevelt reluctantly agreed to support in the United Nations organization conference, soon to be held, Russia's claim for additional votes in the Assembly for Byelorussia and Ukraine, as for independent nations. Although the British situation was not parallel, with India not yet quite independent but to be a member of the Assembly along with the member nations of the commonwealth, Britain could not consistently veto the Russian claim, however preposterous it might be. One of the president's first comments was that he himself might as well ask for forty-eight memberships for the United States. The Russians, on the other hand, pretended to consider all Latin-American states satellites of the United

---

[60] See protocol, Appendix D.

[61] Sherwood, *op. cit.*, 852; Stettinius, *op. cit.*, 112, 142, 149; Byrnes, *op. cit.*, 37-38. "We three have to decide how to keep the peace of the world," said Stalin at Yalta, when arguing against giving France an occupation zone or a seat on the Control Council, "and it will not be kept unless we three decide to do it."

States, and to be making a material concession when they dropped their claim for a seat for Lithuania.[62]

Ever alert to an opportunity to increase Russian influence at the Dardanelles, Stalin brought up at Yalta a proposal to revise to Russia's advantage the Montreux convention governing the use of the Straits, which he said was out of date. Clearly apprehensive, Churchill suggested that any conference on that subject should be held in London. Stalin said he would be satisfied if the foreign ministers would study the matter and report on it to their governments. The question was left open for a future meeting which was not held.

Iran, concerning which a statement had been issued at Teheran, was not officially discussed at Yalta, and not mentioned in the protocol.

The Red Army ruled in Poland while the conference discussed the boundaries and government of the new Poland to be established. It was agreed at Yalta that the provisional Polish (Lublin) government then functioning should be reorganized on a broader democratic basis with the inclusion of democratic leaders from Poland itself and from Poles abroad. The new government was to be pledged to the holding of free and unfettered elections as soon as possible on the basis of universal suffrage and secret ballot, in which all democratic and anti-Nazi parties were to have the right to take part and to put forward candidates.

As to the area of the new Poland, the three heads of government agreed that its eastern boundary should follow the Curzon line, with some slight digressions. President Roosevelt tried in vain to get Lwów and some oil for Poland. To counterbalance the loss of territory east of the Curzon line, held from 1919 to 1939, Poland was to receive "substantial accessions of territory in the north and west"; but the final delimitation of her western frontier was to await the peace conference.

Polish accessions of territory on the north and west could be made only at the expense of Germany, in East Prussia, West Prussia, Pomerania, Silesia, or regions farther west. Most of those areas had long been peopled by Germans. Unless the German population was to be unceremoniously driven out, new minority problems would be

[62] Stettinius, *op. cit.*, 196-197, 281; Byrnes, *op. cit.*, 39-41; Sherwood, *op. cit.*, 856; Leahy, *op. cit.*, 318-321, 341-342. The agreement to support the Soviet Union's claim for separate seats for some of its member states was not announced at the time or included in the protocol. When news of it leaked out later, great suspicion was aroused in the United States as to possible other secret commitments. Stalin said he would support a United States claim for an equal number of seats in the Assembly, but no such claim was advanced.

created by such cessions; but Stalin blandly observed that there was no serious minority problem where the Red Army had advanced. People usually ran away before the troops arrived. The United States delegation was uneasy about the German-Polish boundary question but could reassure itself with the thought that the final delineation of that boundary was to await the peace conference.[63]

In a general declaration as to liberated Europe, the Yalta Protocol announced that the participating powers intended to assist the peoples liberated from Nazism and fascism to create democratic institutions of their own choice. To foster the conditions in which such institutions could be established, the three governments offered jointly to assist the liberated peoples wherever, in their judgment, conditions required: (1) to establish conditions of internal peace; (2) to carry out emergency measures for the relief of distressed peoples; (3) to form interim governmental authorities broadly representative of all democratic elements in the population and pledged to the earliest possible establishment through free elections of governments responsive to the will of the people; and (4) to facilitate where necessary the holding of such elections.

In their declaration the spokesmen for the three powers reaffirmed their faith in the principles of the Atlantic Charter, their pledge in the Declaration by the United Nations, and their determination to build in coöperation with other peace-loving nations world order, under law, dedicated to peace, security, freedom, and general well-being of all mankind.

The disillusionments of the next five years seemed to be due less to agreements made at Yalta than to willful misinterpretation, misapplication, or flagrant violation of them, with the Soviet Union the principal offender. Critics of President Roosevelt subsequently accused him at worst of having betrayed his cause to Russia or of having been already in his dotage and incompetent, or at best of having fatuously "trusted the Russians" and paid them too high a price for a few days' aid against Japan. He could not, however, disregard the opinion of his military advisers that virtually no price would be too high to pay for Soviet assistance to speed the day of victory over Japan as well as Germany. He was furthermore bidding also, beyond victory, for Soviet membership in the United Nations and for Russian friendship and coöperation in the postwar world—

[63] Stettinius, op. cit., 9, 41; Byrnes, op. cit., 29-33. For all practical purposes for the next five years, the boundary was the Oder-Neisse line. In an agreement with Poland in 1950 a communist-controlled East German government accepted that line as the permanent boundary.

war and peace aims of inestimable potential value. His conviction that he could not afford to quarrel then with Stalin was probably in accord with majority opinion in the United States, which was at that time resolutely favorable to the Soviet peoples, eager to believe the best about them, and hopeful of mutually tolerant and friendly relations with them in the far future. Russian prestige, a product of industry, fortitude, and military prowess, was formidable. An imposing fund of good will for the Soviet peoples had been built up among Allied peoples. Strong elements of public opinion in the United States, neither communist nor procommunist, would probably have taken the president seriously to task if he had quarreled with Stalin at Yalta or failed to safeguard the possibility of United States-Soviet coöperation in war and peace.

The president died before the consequences of the conference were fully to be discerned. His most responsible advisers, however, testified that, although weary with the burden of his office and with the extraordinary exertions of the conference, he was in full possession of his faculties and got more concessions than he made. It would have been difficult, moreover, to point out a significant advantage of the Soviet Union recognized at Yalta which it did not in fact already actually enjoy, or any promised it at Yalta which it could not have gained for itself, by use of its own strength, without the sanction of a conference.[64]

CONQUEST OF THE RHINE

The Allied campaign for the Rhineland and for the Rhine itself was resumed southeast of Nijmegen February 8, 1945, with an offensive by the Canadian First and British Second armies, which with the U. S. Ninth Army constituted Field Marshal Montgomery's army group on the northern wing of the Allied line. Progress was slow because of the waterlogged condition of the terrain. The Germans

[64] As a concession to the views of the United States, Stalin agreed at Yalta that nations not already at war with Germany might qualify for charter membership in the United Nations by signing the United Nations Declaration and declaring war by March 1, 1945. Peru took that step February 11, Chile and Paraguay February 12, Venezuela February 16, Uruguay February 23, Turkey February 24, Saudi Arabia April 12, effective March 1. Argentina declared war on Germany and Japan on March 27. Stalin offered to have Byelorussia and Ukraine sign the declaration also, but withdrew the suggestion when President Roosevelt did not support it. Stettinius, 200-203, 298.

Angered because he had not been at Yalta and because he thought that the official communiqués of the conference had not adequately recognized him and France, General de Gaulle said that it would not be convenient for him to accept an invitation to meet President Roosevelt in Algiers as the president made his way home from Yalta. Sherwood, *op. cit.*, 861; Leahy, *op. cit.*, 327.

had blown up the flood gates of the Schwammanuel dam, the day before the attack was launched, and flooded the Roer River. Stiff resistance was offered by the First German Parachute Army fighting as infantry under General Schlemm. Although inexperienced in their new infantry role, these selected and specially trained young Luftwaffe soldiers had not yet suffered, as so many of the Wehrmacht had, the dishearteningly repeated experience of defeat and retreat; and their morale and combat effectiveness were high. Cleve was taken, however, February 12.[65]

The flooding of the Roer River valley delayed the start of the U. S. Ninth Army, under General William H. Simpson, the southernmost of the three armies in Montgomery's army group, until February 23, when it crossed the Roer River. A week later it reached the Rhine opposite Düsseldorf. At the same time the U. S. First Army under General Hodges also pushed forward. Its Seventh Corps reached Köln March 5.

Two days later, at Remagen above Köln, a small advance unit of the 9th U. S. Armored Division, Third Corps, U. S. First Army, found the Ludendorff bridge across the Rhine only slightly damaged by the demolition charge which its defenders waited too long before setting off. The bridge was immediately seized and troops rushed across.[66]

The Remagen bridgehead was vigorously expanded and exploited. Anticipating an immediate move northward from it against the Ruhr, the Germans thinned out their defense formations on the east bank of the Rhine from Mainz to Mannheim, concentrating them north of Remagen, thus offering General Patton's U. S. Third Army an opportunity also to effect an easy crossing of the river.

The U. S. Third Army captured Trier March 2. In a week it reached

[65] As the German navy found it unprofitable to go on with new construction or repairs which could not be completed quickly, naval personnel was also being weeded out from the bases and put into naval operations or turned over to the army. With veteran army officers and noncommissioned officers, the naval infantry was credited with showing commendable spirit, but its losses were relatively high. The navy was busy evacuating troops from Norway, Finland, Courland, and eastern Pomerania, and two million refugees from the other Baltic states. Its submarine training stations in the eastern Baltic had been abandoned. Dönitz, *op. cit.,* 42-46.

Finland declared war on Germany March 4, as from September 15, 1944.

[66] The death penalty had been ordered by the Nazi for failure to blow a bridge in time, but the bridges were useful up to the last moment to retreating German troops. German artillery and the Luftwaffe tried for ten days after the loss of the Ludendorff bridge before they succeeded in knocking out its central span. By that time the U. S. First Army had its Treadway bridges in use and no longer needed the Ludendorff.

The last German troops to withdraw across the Rhine in formation crossed at Wesel and blew the bridge there March 10.

the Rhine at Andernach northwest of Coblenz and swung southward toward the U. S. Seventh, which on March 15 attacked the Saar salient from the south. Between Mannheim and Mainz, in the night of March 22-23, the 5th Division of the U. S. Third Army crossed the Rhine without formal preparation, against negligible resistance, and established the second Allied bridgehead on the east bank of that river. By March 25 the conquest of the left bank was completed. The month-long campaign had cost the Germans about ten thousand men per day. Their total losses in the west since D-Day had mounted to about two million.

The third assault across the Rhine was made, after intensive artillery preparation, at four places between Rees and a point south of Wesel, in the night of March 23-24. The army group commanded by Field Marshal Montgomery, including the Canadian First, British Second, and U. S. Ninth armies, was aided by forty thousand airborne troops who dropped ahead of them in the morning. The first objective was the Ruhr, which was soon encircled on the north by the U. S. Ninth Army and on the south by the U. S. First, breaking out from its Remagen bridgehead March 25 and meeting elements of the U. S. Ninth near Lippstadt April 1. The Canadian army turned northward to seal off the Netherlands, and the British northeastward toward Bremen and Hamburg.

The fourth and fifth major crossings were made by the U. S. Seventh Army below Mannheim and the French First farther south. When all had joined hands on the east bank of the river they were ready for the final phase of the war, the rush to cut Germany to ribbons by driving motorized forces across it from west to east to meet the Russians.

In four days, March 21-24, from Britain and Italy and from behind the lines in western Europe, the Allied air forces flew more than 42,000 sorties. As the motorized columns thrust swiftly eastward across Germany, reconnaissance, supply, and tactical bombing assumed a new importance, while strategical bombing of enemy airplane factories and synthetic oil plants was continued.

QUARREL OVER GERMAN SURRENDER OVERTURE IN ITALY

On March 9, 1945, SS General Karl Wolff indicated to the Allied commander in Italy that Marshal Kesselring and the German high command in Italy were ready to surrender. General Alexander asked the combined chiefs of staff to authorize him to send one United States and one British officer to Berne to escort the German or tell him he must come to Allied headquarters at Caserta, Italy, to receive surrender terms and instructions. United States Ambassador Harriman notified Foreign Commissar Molotov in Moscow, who raised at first no other objection than to stipulate that three Russian officers must accompany the two Allied officer emissaries. Unless Russian officers participated he would insist that negotiations be immediately terminated. The Allied reply was that no negotiations were in progress in Berne and that none would be undertaken until German emissaries came to Caserta, where Russian observers would be present.[67]

"Utterly unexpected and incomprehensible," Molotov called "the refusal of the United States to admit the participation of the Soviet representatives in the negotiations in Berne." Oblivious of Harriman's denial, he insisted that "the negotiations already begun in Berne be broken off." Both Harriman and General Deane reported adversely on Molotov's domineering tone, and advised against appeasement. Secretary of War Stimson took the position that an enemy proposal to surrender was a military matter, to be accepted as such at any time at the discretion of the competent commander in the field.

There was no negotiation in progress in Berne on March 16 when Molotov insisted that the alleged negotiation be terminated; but a British and a United States officer, without benefit of Russian escort, met Wolff at Locarno March 21 and instructed him to go to Caserta to arrange the proposed surrender. Wolff went instead to Germany to confer again with Marshal Kesselring, who was being transferred from the Italian to the western German front. Harriman informed Molotov of the meeting and told him again that no negotiations had taken place. The foreign commissar again refused to accept the ambassador's statement of fact, and denounced as "absolutely inadmissible" such negotiations "behind the back of the Soviet government," which he said had been "carrying the main burden of the war against Germany."

President Roosevelt then tried, March 24, to carry the discussion past Molotov to Stalin himself. Stalin, he said, must have been misinformed. Officers in the field must be authorized to secure the surrender of enemy troops. No political implications or violation of the principle of unconditional surrender was involved.[68]

[67] No Russian troops were then fighting Italian troops, and none had been in Italy.

[68] The same day, the president urged that Molotov attend the forthcoming organization conference of the United Nations at San Francisco, pointing out that his absence would be construed as indicative of a lack of interest in the objectives of the conference, and that public opinion was more important in the United States than Stalin or Molotov seemed to realize. Stalin later sneered at the "use of public opinion as a screen."

Stalin replied that his military colleagues and informants—who had often been right when Roosevelt's had been wrong—did not doubt that three German divisions had already been moved from the Italian to the Russian front, or that negotiations had taken place between the United States, Britain, and Germany, in which Marshal Kesselring had agreed to open the front and permit the Anglo-American troops to advance to the east, and the Anglo-Americans had promised in return to ease the peace terms for Germany. Consequently, he continued, the Germans on the western front had in fact ceased the war against the English and the United States. At the same time the Germans continued the war with Russia, the ally of England and the United States.[69]

Both the president and Prime Minister Churchill had grave misgivings over the increasingly disagreeable attitude and uncoöperative conduct of the Russians. Both sent strongly worded protests against the accusation that Eisenhower's advance had been made possible not by victory but by a disloyal deal with the common enemy. If Wolff had never intended to surrender but had been trying only to promote dissension among the Allies, wrote the president to Stalin April 4, his maneuver had achieved some success with Stalin. Further, the president frankly expressed his "bitter resentment" against Stalin's informers, whoever they were, for such "vile misrepresentations" of his actions or those of his trusted subordinates. Stalin replied that he had never doubted the president's integrity or reliability.

In cables to Harriman and Churchill on the day of his death, April 12, the president showed his continuing concern but indicated an intention to play down the ugly quarrel with Stalin, rather than play it up. To the ambassador he said: "It is my desire to consider the Berne misunderstanding a minor incident." To Mr. Churchill: "I would minimize the general Soviet problem as much as possible because these problems, in one form or another, seem to arise every day and most of them straighten out as in the case of the Berne meeting.

"We must be firm, however, and our course this far is correct."[70]

The formation of the new Polish provisional government of national unity on a broader democratic basis with inclusion of democratic leaders from Poland and from Poles abroad, which had been agreed upon at Yalta, was deadlocked from April to June. Stalin refused to accept in the new government as colleagues of the procommunist

[69] The Allies were just then mopping up the west bank of the Rhine, and had crossed that river at Remagen, above and below the Ruhr and between Mainz and Mannheim.

[70] Leahy, *op. cit.*, 330-336; Byrnes, *op. cit.*, 53-60.

Lublin Poles, whom he favored, anyone who had been associated with the London Polish government in exile, or who would not accept the Curzon line, with minor rectifications, as the permanent Polish-Russian boundary, or whom he regarded as "unfriendly" to the Soviet Union.[71]

SAN FRANCISCO CONFERENCE: UNITED NATIONS

Beginning with the United Nations Declaration of January 1, 1942, plans were made by the Allies for postwar as well as wartime international coöperation. A move to broaden and make permanent the war association of the United Nations by the establishment of a new international organization of world-wide scope to plan and preserve the peace was initiated in the United States Congress in March, 1943, by Senators Ball of Minnesota, Burton of Ohio, Hatch of New Mexico, and Hill of Alabama. Congress was committed to the principle of collective security (1) by the resolution introduced in the House of Representatives by James Fulbright of Arkansas in June and adopted by the House in September, 1943, by a vote of 360 to 29, favoring "the creation of appropriate machinery with power adequate to establish and maintain a just and lasting peace among the nations of the world, and participation by the United Nations therein," and (2) by the Senate's adoption, 85 to 5, of Article 4 of the Moscow pact of October 30, 1943.[72]

The Moscow pact was drawn in October by Secretaries Hull, Eden, and Molotov, and accepted by the Chinese ambassador to the Soviet Union. The four powers jointly declared that they would continue after the war to act together for the organization and maintenance of peace and security. In Article 4 they formally recognized the necessity of establishing at the earliest practicable date a general international organization, based on the principle of the sovereign equality of all peace-loving states and open to membership of all such states, large and small, for the maintenance of international peace and security.[73]

[71] Stettinius, op. cit., 314.

[72] Article 4 of the Moscow pact was substituted for a resolution introduced by Senator Tom Connally of Texas, chairman of the Senate Committee on Foreign Relations, favoring participation by the United States—by constitutional processes—in a postwar organization to stop aggression.

[73] By Article 6 of the Moscow pact the powers agreed not to employ their armed forces within the territories of other states except for the purposes envisaged in the declaration and after joint consultation.

The powers further declared their intention to destroy fascism and establish democratic government in Italy, to liberate Austria from German control, and to bring to book the Germans responsible for crimes against humanity by sending them back to the countries in which their atrocities had been committed, for punishment under the laws of the liberated countries.

Meanwhile, in July, 1944, upon invitation of the United States, forty-three nations sent delegates to a conference at Bretton Woods to lay the economic foundation for a permanent organization. This conference instituted an International Bank for Reconstruction, capitalized at approximately $9,000,000,000 (of which the United States quota was to be about $3,175,000,000), and an International Monetary Fund of $8,800,000,000 (of which the United States was to contribute $2,750,000,000). The bank was to make reconstruction loans to member nations and to underwrite bankers' loans for industrial reconstruction or the rehabilitation of agriculture. The monetary fund was to stabilize national currencies with reference to one another, and to facilitate international money transfers.

The founders of the League of Nations had waited until the war of 1914-1918 was over, and incorporated its charter into the Treaty of Versailles. With the removal of the common danger, the nations failed, when challenged, to maintain a united front for the preservation of the peace. The establishment of the United Nations was a wartime measure, taken in the hope of capitalizing what was left of the spirit of coöperation engendered by the crisis, and of preserving or approaching some unity of purpose for the peace. Thus at Dumbarton Oaks, Washington, D.C., in August and September, 1944, a conference of delegations headed by United States Undersecretary of State Edward Stettinius, Sir Alexander Cadogan of Great Britain, and Soviet Ambassador Andrei Gromyko drafted the outline of a plan for a permanent United Nations organization. That outline, with the concurrence of Chinese Ambassador V. Wellington Koo, was the basis of discussion at Yalta in February and at the San Francisco conference April 25 to June 26, 1945.[74]

"We the peoples" were named in the opening statement of the Charter of the United Nations as the founders of the organization, acting through their respective governments. But, although a conscious effort was made to create a new organization stronger than the League of Nations, it was another league of national states, not a world federation of peoples, that was established at the San Francisco conference. Its members were national governments rather than peoples, on the principle of the sovereign equality of all members; and it was not authorized to intervene in matters essentially within the domestic jurisdiction of any member state.

Fifty nations signed the charter June 26, 1945, as original members: the forty-six then at war with one or another of the tripartite

[74] See p. 718. For the text of the Charter of the United Nations see Appendix E or Department of State Publication 2353, Conference Series 74.

powers; Byelorussia (White Russia) and Ukraine at the request of the USSR; and Argentina and Denmark, whose representatives were invited during the life of the conference. Membership was open to all other peace-loving states willing to accept the obligations contained in the charter and able and willing, in the judgment of the organization, to carry them out.[75]

The structure of the United Nations resembled that of the League of Nations: a General Assembly (Assembly), Security Council (Council), Economic and Social Council, Trusteeship Council (Mandates Commission), International Court of Justice (Permanent Court of International Justice, commonly called the "World Court"), and a Secretariat similar to that of the League.

The General Assembly, meeting annually, in which each member was entitled to not more than five representatives but only one vote, was empowered to discuss and make a recommendation upon any question brought before it relating to the maintenance of international peace and security. Any such question on which action was necessary was to be referred to the Security Council. The Assembly might also call the attention of the Council to a situation likely to endanger international peace and security.

The Security Council of eleven was made primarily responsible for the maintenance of peace and security. It was to be so organized as to be able to function continuously, each member being represented at all times for that purpose at the seat of the organization. The Republic of China, France, the USSR, Great Britain, and the United States of America were to be permanent members. Six nonpermanent members were to be elected on a rotating basis for terms of two years each, with due regard for equitable geographical distribution, none to be eligible for immediate reëlection. Each member was to have one representative and one vote. Decisions on procedural matters were to be made by an affirmative vote of seven members. On other matters the affirmative vote of seven necessary for a decision had to include the concurring votes of all of the permanent members; hence the right of veto by a permanent member.

The parties to any dispute, the continuance of which was likely to endanger the maintenance of international peace and security, were admonished first of all to seek a solution by peaceful means. The

---

[75] Admission to membership would be effected by decision of the General Assembly upon recommendation of the Security Council, and upon signature of the charter. Poland became a member in 1945; Afghanistan, Iceland, and Sweden in 1946; Burma, Siam, Pakistan, and Yemen in 1947; Israel in 1949; and the Republic of Indonesia in 1950. Eire, Portugal, and Trans-Jordan were rejected by Soviet veto.

Security Council was charged, however, with the duty to determine the existence of any threat to the peace, breach of the peace, or act of aggression, and to make recommendations or decide what measures should be taken to maintain or restore the peace. For that purpose it was empowered to call upon member states to take measures short of war, such as the severance of communication and of economic and diplomatic relations; or, if such measures seemed likely or had proved to be inadequate, for such action by land, sea, and air forces as might be necessary to maintain or restore international peace and security. Member nations obligated themselves, upon call of the Security Council and by agreement, to furnish such forces and to give right of passage to forces so employed.

The charter contemplated the establishment of a military staff committee to advise and assist the Security Council on questions relating to its military requirements and to assume responsibility, under the Security Council, for the strategic direction of armed forces placed at its disposal. National or collective self-defense was recognized by the charter as the exercise of an inherent right.

The Economic and Social Council of eighteen elected members was authorized to make or initiate studies and to make reports with respect to international economic, social, cultural, educational, health, and related matters, for the purpose of promoting respect for, and observance of, human rights and fundamental freedoms.

Members responsible for the administration of non-self-governing territories subscribed in the charter to a declaration of principle that the interests of the inhabitants of those territories were paramount, and that the obligation to promote to the utmost the well-being of the inhabitants of such territories must be accepted as a sacred trust. The trusteeship system was to apply to territories then held under mandate, or to be detached from enemy states as a result of the war, or voluntarily placed under the system by states responsible for their administration. It was to be supervised by a Trusteeship Council, under authority of the General Assembly.

The principal judicial organ of the United Nations was to be the International Court of Justice. The statute of the court was based upon that of the Permanent Court of International Justice created by the League of Nations. Its powers and functions were analogous to those of its predecessor.[76]

[76] An obvious comparison of the United Nations organization with that of the League of Nations was in the attempt to make the new organization stronger than the older one had been, particularly by provision for the use of stronger sanctions, including the use of armed force, to prevent or check aggression. Although it

GERMAN COLLAPSE AND SURRENDER

The first major Allied offensive after the envelopment of the Ruhr was a thrust across central Germany to the Elbe River, with secondary spearheads following it closely on the right and left. For this purpose the Ninth U. S. Army was transferred from Marshal Montgomery's command and Northern Army Group to General Bradley's in the center. Meanwhile the Canadian First and British Second armies under Marshal Montgomery turned northward and northeastward, respectively, to seal off the Low Countries and the Danish peninsula. The U. S. Seventh and French First armies, which crossed the Rhine below and above Mannheim March 26 and April 1, respectively, moved eastward and southeastward across the upper Danube and southern Bavaria, toward Austria and the Brenner Pass. To a new army, the U. S. Fifteenth, under the command of General Gerow, were assigned the miscellaneous duties of containing the German garrisons still holding St. Nazaire and Lorient, of guarding the left bank of the Rhine opposite the Ruhr against German sorties from that beleaguered area, and of setting up military government in occupied enemy territory.

Within a week after the Rhine crossings north and south of Wesel the Ruhr was surrounded, April 1, by the U. S. Ninth Army, which had passed around it to the north, and the U. S. First, which had broken out of the Remagen bridgehead and come down to it from the south. Within two more weeks the pocket had been considerably compressed and cut in two; and on April 16 and 18 the dissevered remnants of its garrison surrendered. The prisoner-of-war count was 325,000, including thirty general officers.[77]

By April 14 the U. S. Third Army had reached Chemnitz, not far southwest of Dresden, near the northwestern boundary of Czecho-

---

failed during its first five years to establish an international police force to enforce its decisions, it called upon member states in 1950 to repel an invasion of South Korea. Its usefulness was restricted during those five years by excessive use and abuse of the veto power in the Security Council, especially by the Soviet Union. The forty-fourth Soviet veto was used September 5, 1950, against a resolution calling upon members to refrain from aiding the invasion of South Korea and to use their influence to end it. Nine members voted for the resolution. Yugoslavia abstained from voting. The forty-fifth Soviet veto on September 12, 1950, caused the rejection of a United States resolution to set up a UN commission to investigate Chinese Communist charges, which the Soviet delegates supported, that United States planes operating with UN forces in Korea had attacked a Chinese airfield in Manchuria.

[77] Eisenhower, *op. cit.,* 406; Shulman, *op. cit.,* 286. Field Marshal Model, who had been responsible for the defense of the Ruhr, committed suicide. He had been known as one of "Hitler's generals," but had failed to stop the Red Army on the Vistula or the Allies on the western front in 1944.

slovakia. A little farther north, elements of the U. S. First Army, already released from the envelopment of the Ruhr pocket, entered Dessau, not far west of the Elbe River. A small bridgehead was established on the east bank of the Elbe at Magdeburg by the 2nd Armored Division of the U. S. Ninth Army April 12, but had to be abandoned April 14. The 83rd Division crossed the Elbe farther south and maintained its position until recalled by previous agreement.

The advance to the Elbe had been rapid. Hoards of government treasure, archives, looted goods, and objects of art had been overrun and taken into custody, sometimes by accident.[78] Concentration camps had also been overrun and their surviving victims liberated. War-hardened soldiers had been stunned and sickened by the grisly evidence of atrocities committed in the camps.

East of the Elbe the Germans counterattacked fiercely in defense of the western approaches to Berlin. The armored United States forces which made or attempted the crossings near Magdeburg were at the end of their tether as to supplies, fifty miles from Berlin, and could have been supplied for a "dash to Berlin" only at the expense of other units still engaged on vital missions. The dividing line between occupation zones, moreover, had already been drawn along the Elbe and Mulde rivers in that region; it was understood by the governments concerned that the armed forces of each should, after the cessation of hostilities, be withdrawn to its own zone of occupation.

The line beyond which United States troops should not advance was drawn by General Eisenhower in direct negotiation with the highest Red Army echelon. Such a line needed to be drawn to avoid accidental hostile contact between forces not well known to one another, advancing toward each other in enemy territory, in circumstances in which accurate and immediate identification might have been difficult and failure to identify would have been dangerous. The line of farthest advance by British and United States forces was in many areas some distance east of the eventual dividing line between occupation zones, but west of points which might otherwise have been reached before the Red Army reached them. The U. S. Third Army, for example, liberated Linz and Pilsen but did not go on to Prague.

---

[78] The archives of the German Foreign Office and records of Hitler's conferences with his generals, admirals, and political lieutenants were among the captured archival materials. Many of them were subsequently published by the Allied governments and have been cited frequently above: e. g., United States Department of State, *Nazi-Soviet Relations, 1939-41,* and *Documents on German Foreign Policy 1918-1945,* Series D, Vols. I and II; and the International Military Tribunal, *Nazi Conspiracy and Aggression,* and *Trial of the Major War Criminals.* They were used by Anthony Martienssen for his *Hitler and His Admirals,* and by many others.

On April 25, the first USA and USSR patrols met and greeted each other at Torgau, between Dresden and Magdeburg on the Elbe River. The German armies of the north and south were separated from one another, and the possibility of their establishing an Alpine redoubt was reduced by the continued advance of the U. S. Third and Seventh and the French First armies into Czechoslovakia and Austria from the west, and of the Red Army from the east.

Meanwhile the Red Army closed up to Vienna, Dresden, Berlin, and Stettin. There was hard fighting for Berlin, and many casualties on both sides. The Red Army artillery added devastation to the extensive damage already done by bombing. The flooding of underground railway stations and tunnels used as shelters added to the horror of the siege. Yet Hitler would not consent to the surrender of the city to save it from destruction or its remaining inhabitants from the holocaust. He himself took refuge in the deep air-raid bunker beneath the chancellery and spent his last nightmarish days ordering armies which existed only in his imagination to rally for a rescue which was no longer possible. He might have escaped by airplane, but refused.[79]

Other leaders realized that the war was lost and urged surrender before complete collapse. Production Minister Albert Speer wrote to Hitler March 18 that, if the nation was not to perish, "some material basis must be preserved on which the life of the people, however, primitively," might be continued. Quite mad by then, Hitler replied, in part: "If the war is lost the nation will inevitably perish. There is no need to consider the basis even of a primitive existence any more. On the contrary, it is better to destroy it ourselves. Besides, those who remain after the battle are of little value; for the good have fallen."[80]

Through Count Folke Bernadotte of Sweden, Heinrich Himmler tried, April 24-25, to arrange for a separate surrender to the United States and Great Britain, not to the Russians. Hitler, he said, had shut himself up in Berlin to perish, had had a cerebral hemorrhage, and could not live more than a day or two longer. Someone else must save Germany.

[79] H. R. Trevor-Roper's *The Last Days of Hitler* (New York, 1947; 2nd ed., 1950) was a careful study, based on the evidence available at the time. Rumors persisted that Hitler had escaped to Argentina, Spain, or Shangrila. Stalin continued for some weeks to say that he believed Hitler was still alive.

[80] Trevor-Roper, New York *Times*, February 29, 1948, p. 50; *Last Days of Hitler* (1947 ed.), 81, 114. Speer lost his position, but was reinstated March 30. He said after the war that on or about April 21 he had recorded in Hamburg and left there with Gauleiter Kaufmann for broadcast a radio appeal to the German people to disobey Hitler's order to destroy everything of value rather than let it fall into enemy hands; but the recorded address was not broadcast until three days after Hitler's death. Speer was sentenced at Nuremberg to twenty years' imprisonment.

Although Himmler was minister of the interior, national leader of the SS, and titular commander of the home front, he was not constitutionally competent to speak for the little government that was left. President Truman replied, however, through Count Bernadotte, that no partial surrender would be accepted. The German armies on the eastern front must surrender also to the Red Army. The Soviet government was immediately informed, and the negotiation was dropped.[81]

April 30 was generally accepted as the date of Hitler's death by suicide in the air-raid bunker beneath the Reich chancellery in the Wilhelmstrasse in Berlin. In his last will and political testament he repeated his well-worn charge that the war had been forced upon him by international politicians who either came of Jewish stock or worked for Jewish interests. As Führer, he formally disavowed and expelled from the party both Himmler, who had offered to surrender, and Göring, who had made an equally ill-advised offer as successor-designate to take over the duties of his office as chief of state. As his successor as Reich president, supreme commander of the Wehrmacht and navy, and minister of war he named Admiral Karl Dönitz. Goebbels was to be chancellor of the new Reich, Bormann chancellor of the Nazi party. Dropping Ribbentrop, he named Arthur Seyss-Inquart foreign minister in the new government. Speer was also dropped, for the second time. Count Lutz Schwerin von Krosigk was reappointed minister of finance. Repeating for the last time his discredited dictum that the military surrender of territory or a town was dishonorable and impermissible, he announced his personal decision not to forsake his capital city but to share the fate of the millions of its inhabitants who remained there. In a final exhortation he stressed, as always, the subordination of the individual to the common good, the duty of obedience, the maintenance of the racial laws, and merciless opposition to "the world-poisoner of all peoples," international Jewry.[82]

Late at night, May 1, Radio Hamburg carried a proclamation from Admiral Dönitz to the Wehrmacht announcing that the Führer had fallen, dying a hero's death at the head of his troops in Berlin, faith-

---

[81] Trevor-Roper, *Last Days of Hitler*, 133-134; Leahy, *op. cit.*, 354-355. Himmler was arrested May 26. Upon being identified, although he was carrying false identification papers, he committed suicide. The day of his surrender attempt, April 25, was the day of the meeting of United States and Red Army patrols at Torgau, and of the assembling of the San Francisco conference.

[82] Trevor-Roper, *Last Days of Hitler*, 177-180, 213. The will included a statement of reasons for Hitler's belated marriage to Eva Braun, who died with him. Goebbels and his wife were among those in the bunker to the end, then on May 1 poisoned their six children and had themselves shot.

ful unto the end to the idea to which he had consecrated his life, the preservation of the peoples of Europe from Bolshevism. As successor to Hitler as head of the state and supreme commander of the Wehrmacht, Dönitz declared his intention to continue hostilities against the United States and Great Britain only as their armed forces hindered him in the defense of eastern Germany against Bolshevism. To that end he demanded discipline and obedience. Next day Stalin announced the completion of the conquest of Berlin.

The disintegration of the German armed forces was accelerated by the death of Hitler, as many of their officers professed that they considered themselves honor bound, as long as he lived, by their oath of personal allegiance to him. For fear of reprisals against members of their families some of them had been afraid to surrender until they knew at last that the Nazi were powerless at home as well as in the field.

The final military collapse came quickly. In Italy on April 29, SS leader Karl Wolff, who had made the first surrender overtures earlier in April, and Colonel General Heinrich von Vietinghoff, successor to Marshal Kesselring as Wehrmacht commander in Italy, signed articles of surrender effective May 2 for the remaining German forces in Italy, numbering about a million men. The senior Allied commander, General Sir Harold Alexander, accepted the surrender in the presence of United States and Russian officers. The German troops then in northwestern Italy were taken into custody by General Mark Clark's U. S. Fifth Army.[83]

On May 1 German General Blumentritt was authorized to try to spare the city of Hamburg by declaring it an open city. Next day he arranged to evacuate it, and the Second British Army immediately occupied it.

On May 3 Lübeck was occupied by British forces, and Admiral Hans von Friedeburg, the new head of the German navy, acting for Dönitz, appeared at Marshal Montgomery's headquarters to ask whether he could surrender to the western Allies three German armies then facing the Red Army on the eastern front, to avoid having to surrender them to the Russians. The request was refused.[84]

Under authority given in advance by General Eisenhower as supreme commander, Marshal Montgomery accepted on May 4 the military surrender in the field of all German troops in northwest Ger-

[83] See p. 690. Clark, *op. cit.,* 426-451.

[84] The preference was real. As in 1918, however, the Germans gambled desperately to the last on the possibility of a quarrel among the powers aligned against them, a quarrel which they strove constantly to promote.

many, the Netherlands, and Denmark. Next day the German First and Nineteenth armies, comprising Army Group B in western Austria, surrendered to Lieutenant General Jacob L. Devers, commanding an Allied army group composed of the U. S. Seventh and the French First armies.

At General Eisenhower's headquarters in Reims, France, in the very early morning of May 7, an instrument of general unconditional surrender was signed by Admiral Friedeburg and Field Marshal Alfred Gustav Jodl of the OKW, General Walter Bedell Smith as Eisenhower's chief of staff, and representatives of the French and Soviet Russian armies. All hostilities were to cease as of midnight, May 8-9. By General Eisenhower's express order, the German emissaries were required to appear at Red Army headquarters in Berlin May 9 and sign a formal ratification of the surrender instrument of May 7. In Berlin, Admiral Friedeburg signed the ratification for the German navy, Field Marshal Keitel for the Wehrmacht, and General Hans Jürgen Stumpff for the Luftwaffe. Air Chief Marshal Sir Arthur Tedder signed for General Eisenhower, and Marshal Grigori K. Zhukov for the Soviet high command. Lieutenant General Carl A. Spaatz of the U. S. Air Forces and General de Lattre de Tassigny, representing the French government, were witnesses. To the Russians, that final act was the only real surrender; and Stalin was not ready until then to announce that the war against Nazi Germany had ended.[85]

War costs could not be counted, weighed, or measured. Whether or what anyone had won was questionable, but no one could deny or doubt that Germany had lost. It was estimated that the German armed forces lost in battle about eight million men, killed, captured, or permanently disabled. Half a million German civilians were killed by bombing from the air, and 700,000 were injured. Thirty thousand of the 38,000 men who served in the German submarines were killed. Two-thirds of nearly twelve hundred submarines put into service were destroyed, including about a hundred scuttled by their crews at the end of the war. One hundred fifty-six were surrendered to the Allies. The last to be accounted for was U-977, which surrendered in Argentina August 17, 1945. British antisubmarine forces were credited with the destruction of 525 German and 69 Italian submarines, United States forces with 174 German and five Italian.

[85] Leahy, *op. cit.*, 357-366. Admiral Friedeburg committed suicide when taken into custody with other members of the former German high command and general staff and of the Dönitz government, May 23, 1945. Field Marshal Jodl was tried as a war criminal at Nuremberg and hanged, October 16, 1946.

The Allies lost to the U-boats 2775 ships, 14,500,000 tons (all causes, 4786 ships, 21,000,000 tons), 54 percent British, 16 percent from the United States; 64 percent of the losses were in the Atlantic. Shipping losses exceeded replacement until November, 1942. The total of 25,000,000 tons available at the outset of the war was not equaled until June, 1943.

As Germany's ally, Italy reported 760,000 military casualties: 60,-000 dead, 500,000 prisoners of war, 200,000 missing; as one of the Allies against Germany from September 8, 1943, to April 30, 1945, 48,078: 17,494 soldiers killed, 9353 wounded, 17,647 missing, and 3584 men killed in the navy.

British civilian casualties at home approximated 150,000; merchant seamen, 30,189 dead, 5264 missing, 4402 wounded, 5556 interned. Military casualties, compounded with those in other theaters of war and with those of other members of the commonwealth and the empire, were more than a million.

Of a population of 3,000,000, Norway lost more than 10,000 lives, including 900 members of naval and air forces and 3200 merchant seamen. Poland had a quarter of a million military casualties and a total loss of 5,000,000 persons, including 3,000,000 Jews. Probably 3,000,000 other Jews were systematically exterminated, and millions of others uprooted. Yugoslavia suffered a loss of 1,685,000 soldiers and civilians, 75 percent in battle with the Germans.

Russian casualties were heaviest of all. The Soviet Union mobilized for the war, all together, 22,000,000 men and women against Germany's 17,000,000, mostly men.[86] Probably from 5,000,000 to 7,000,000 Russian soldiers were killed, wounded, or lost as prisoners of war, and an equal number of civilians killed. Six million homes, of 25,000,000 people, were destroyed. A tenth of the area of the USSR, including half the principal areas of coal, steel, machinery, and electric power production and three-fifths of the iron mines, was at one time overrun by the Germans and at least partially destroyed. German losses were heavier in Russia than anywhere else until 1944-1945.

The United States carried to the European theater of war more than three million men, and used in combat sixty (all but the 13th Airborne) of the sixty-one combat divisions that it sent there. When the

[86] United States mobilization reached a peak of 14,000,000; British, including Commonwealth and Empire, 12,000,000; Chinese 6,000,000. General Marshall, *op. cit.*, 103.

In a conference with Harry Hopkins, Ambassador Harriman, and Charles Bohlen in Moscow, May 27, 1945, Stalin mentioned 5,000,000 casualties. Records were incomplete. Subsequent estimates were higher.

last of those troops sailed away, there were no ready combat divisions left in the United States. Total United States battle deaths in Europe were 160,045, total battle casualties 772,626. The infantry, comprising 20.5 percent of total strength, suffered 70 percent of the casualties, the casualty rate slightly higher among officers than among enlisted men. Improvement of battle surgery and medical care, however, reduced the rate of death from wounds to less than half the 1918 rate, returning 58.8 percent of wounded men to duty in theaters of operations.[87]

POTSDAM CONFERENCE

From May 26 to June 6, 1945, Harry Hopkins was in Moscow as President Truman's personal emissary to join Ambassador Harriman and the State Department's Russian-language expert and specialist on Russia, Charles E. Bohlen, in a series of conferences with Molotov and Stalin. The work of the San Francisco conference was facilitated by the securing, June 6, of Stalin's belated consent to the proposal that the great-power right of veto should not be exercised to prevent a question from being put on the Security Council agenda.

As to Poland, Stalin conceded at the Moscow conference that, as a great power without the aid of which the war could not have been won, the United States was entitled to a voice in the determination of the character of the new government to be formed, as had been agreed at Yalta. He disavowed any intention to sovietize Poland or to collectivize its farms, denied that any Soviet interference had taken or was taking place, and again agreed to broaden the political base of the Polish government by admitting four noncommunist ministers to the provisional Polish government which he insisted must be the base upon which to build. One of those added, he conceded, might well be Stanislaw Mikolajczyk, wartime leader of the London group of Poles in exile. All must be friendly (i.e., acceptable) to the Soviet Union. Hopkins tried without success to secure the release or speedy trial of fourteen "London Poles" held in prison on charges—admittedly not the cause of their imprisonment—of illegal possession and use of radio sets.

Stalin assured Hopkins on May 28 that the Red Army would be ready in Manchuria by August 8, and would attack Japan in August if nationalist China would consent to the changes agreed upon at

[87] *Ibid.*, 107-108. It was announced that the use of plasma, sulfa, penicillin, and similar discoveries helped to reduce the death rate from wounds to less than 4 percent.

Yalta. On this occasion he stated categorically that he would do what he could to promote unification of China under the leadership of Chiang Kai-shek, since no Communist leader was strong enough to unify that country. He said he wanted China to control all of Manchuria as part of a unified national state, and would welcome representatives of Chiang Kai-shek to accompany the Red Army and establish a Chinese administration there as soon as the area was occupied. He agreed that a four-power trusteeship should be set up for Korea under China, Great Britain, the United States, and the USSR.

Stalin's suggestion that it might be easier and equally efficacious to modify the unconditional surrender formula to secure the capitulation of Japan, then to impose the will of the victors upon the vanquished by use of occupying forces, was an indication that he expected the Soviet Union to share in the military occupation of Japan.[88]

By mid-June, 1945, agreement was reached in London that all Allied troops in Germany should be withdrawn to their own occupation zones: the Russian east of a line drawn slightly southwest of south from Lübeck, including Mecklenburg, western Pomerania, western Brandenburg (the area around Berlin), Anhalt, and Saxony; the United States zone comprising Hesse, Bavaria, and the northeastern portions of Württemberg and Baden; the French, southwestern Württemberg and Baden and the Rhenish Palatinate; the British, the lower Rhineland, Westphalia, Brunswick, and Hanover. The German reconquest of Alsace-Lorraine was not recognized, and France reoccupied the Saar.

At the same time United States, British, and French garrisons entered Berlin, where each occupied a sector. Occupation policy was to be administered for the time being by an international Control Council on which each of the occupying powers was represented, with the right of veto. No one challenged publicly at the time the right of each or any of the Allies, as of all, to be in Berlin or to have a share in the government of Germany from Berlin by equal right of conquest.[89]

Provision for free access, by the occupiers of the western zones,

---

[88] Sherwood, *op. cit.,* 884-912. Mikolajczyk was made minister for agriculture and deputy premier in a new Polish provisional government June 23, 1945. After protesting frequently that elections were not free and that terrorist methods were used by the government to intimidate his followers, he fled from Poland October 20, 1947, to London and thence to the United States.

[89] The Russians had previously challenged, then conceded, the right of France to an occupation zone and a place on the Control Council. See p. 830.

to the international occupation zone in which they had an unchallenged right to maintain occupying forces was not only implied but made. Immediate insistence upon a more specific and contractual arrangement for access to the former German capital was not then generally thought necessary. It was, indeed, avoided for fear of its probable adverse effect upon the little that was left of mutual confidence and cordiality in the relations of the western Allies with the Soviet Union, and lest it jeopardize the prospect of success of the forthcoming Potsdam conference. Again as at Yalta, for the sake of the possibility of winning the good will of the Soviet Union and securing its aid in the war against Japan, the spokesmen for the western powers were careful not to quarrel with Stalin; and he was aware of his advantage.

At a three-power conference at Potsdam, a suburb of Berlin, July 17 to August 2, 1945, the United States was represented by its new president, Harry Truman, and a new secretary of state, James F. Byrnes. Some of the president's other advisers, such as his chief of staff Admiral Leahy, General Marshall, and Secretary of War Stimson, had served his predecessor through several earlier conferences, and Byrnes had been at Yalta. Stalin and Molotov, with a large staff, represented the Soviet Union. The British delegation was headed until July 25 by Winston Churchill and Anthony Eden; after July 28, as a result of the outcome of a general election at home, by the new prime minister and minister for foreign affairs, Clement Attlee and Ernest Bevin. No major alteration of war aims or of policy resulted at the conference from the change of leaders of the British delegation.

In a statement of general principles to govern the treatment of Germany in the initial period of occupation, the powers declared that their purpose was to disarm Germany and to extirpate Nazism and militarism in Germany, not to destroy or enslave the German people. Supreme authority was vested in military government, the commanders in chief of the occupying forces to be fully in control each in his own zone and responsible to his own government, all jointly in the Control Council for Germany as a whole.

No other central government was, for the time being, to be established. Decentralization was to be the rule of political life; but local self-government and participation in government on a democratic basis were to be encouraged. Subject to the necessity of maintaining military security, freedom of speech, press, and religion was to be permitted, and religious institutions were to be respected.

Economically, during the period of military occupation, Germany was to be treated as a unit. To that end, common occupation policies were to be established for the regulation of all major phases of economic life. War potential was to be reduced by the demolition or removal of the means of production in excess of what was considered necessary for the maintenance, without assistance, of the standard of living to be permitted.

Reparation claims of the USSR were to be met by removals from the Soviet occupation zone and from appropriate German external assets, such as German foreign assets in Bulgaria, Finland, Hungary, Rumania, and eastern Austria, with respect to which Britain and the United States renounced reparation claims. Reciprocally, the Soviet government renounced all claim to shares of German enterprises located in the western zones of occupation, and to German foreign assets other than those specified. It made no claim to gold captured by Allied troops.

In addition to the reparation to be taken by the USSR by removal from its own zone of occupation, and in exchange for an equivalent value in food, coal, potash, petroleum, and other products, it was agreed that the USSR should receive 15 percent of such usable and complete capital equipment as should be found unnecessary for the German peace economy and should be removed from the western zones; and a further 10 percent of such industrial capital equipment without payment or exchange of any kind in return.

Little was left of the German navy but submarines.[90] Of what surface ships remained, Britain, the United States, and the Soviet Union were to take one-third each. Of the 156 submarines surrendered, each was to take ten. The others were to be destroyed.[91] Merchant ships, except coastwise and inland waterways vessels, were to be pooled for use in the war against Japan, and divided thereafter as a committee should judge equitable. Ships lent to the Soviet Union by Britain and the United States were then to be returned to their lenders.

The conference approved in principle the proposal of the Soviet government that the city of Königsberg and surrounding territory be

[90] *Graf Spee* was scuttled off Montevideo December 17, 1939. *Lützow,* a partially completed cruiser, was traded to the Soviet Union in 1940. *Bismarck* was sunk west of Brest May 27, 1941. *Gneisenau* was irreparably damaged from the air at Kiel, and *Scharnhorst* was sunk by British surface ships off northern Norway in November, 1943. *Tirpitz* capsized under air attack at anchor near Tromsö, Norway, in September, 1944. *Prinz Eugen* figured in the Bikini bomb tests in July, 1946.

[91] Leahy, *op. cit.,* 425. Some of the principal submarine shipbuilding yards, with engineers, technicians, and specifications, and some *Schnorkel*-equipped U-boats of the latest types, were in the Russian occupation zone.

transferred to the USSR. It did not approve the Soviet proposal that the USSR and Turkey should control the Dardanelles. President Truman's counterproposal that free passage for all, through the Dardanelles and on the Rhine and Danube rivers, should be guaranteed by the United Nations was blocked by Soviet opposition. The deadlocked question was referred to a Council of Foreign Ministers, for which provision was made.[92]

The first task of the Council of Foreign Ministers was to be the preparation of a peace treaty with Italy, which had been the first of the Axis powers to break with Germany, had made some military contribution to Germany's defeat, and had joined the Allies in the war against Japan. The council was further charged with the preparation of peace treaties for Finland, Rumania, Bulgaria, and Hungary. President Truman was unwilling, however, to recognize the existing Soviet-sponsored government in Rumania, Bulgaria, or Hungary, or to support an application of any of those nations for membership in the United Nations, until convinced—as he said he was not then convinced—that it was democratic in fact as well as in name, and based on the free will of its people. In a politely euphemistic statement which did not conceal but could have made it easier to bridge over the chasm already opening up between the Soviet Union and the western powers, the three heads of governments said they did not doubt that, in view of the changed conditions resulting from the termination of the war in Europe, representatives of the Allied press would enjoy full freedom (which they did not then enjoy and did not obtain) to report to the world upon developments in the countries in question.

The three governments made it clear that in their opinion the Falangist Franco government of Spain, having been founded with the support of the Axis powers, did not, in view of its origins, its nature, its record, and its close association with the aggressor states, possess the qualifications necessary for membership in the United Nations.

As to Poland, unless the western powers were ready—and they were not ready—to quarrel with the Russians, they had to accept at Potsdam some unpleasant accomplished facts. The Red Army had liberated Poland, and the Polish provisional government created by the USSR was in control. Polite verbiage could only put a fair face on the matter, while optimists might hope that a statement once made public might one day be made true. So the three powers noted that in accordance with the decisions of the Crimea conference the Polish provisional government had agreed to the holding of free and un-

[92] *Ibid.*, 416.

fettered elections in Poland as soon as possible on the basis of universal suffrage and secret ballot, in which all democratic and anti-Nazi parties should have the right to take part and to put forward candidates; and that representatives of the Allied press should enjoy full freedom to report to the world upon developments in Poland before and during the elections.

The three heads of government agreed that, pending the final determination of Poland's western boundary, the former German territories east of the Oder-Neisse line, including Danzig and such part of East Prussia as was not placed under Soviet Russian administration along with Königsberg, should be under Polish administration and for such purposes should not be considered part of the Soviet zone of occupation in Germany. The three heads of government specifically reaffirmed, however, that the final delimitation of the western frontier of Poland should await the peace settlement.[93]

The Potsdam conference recognized that the transfer to Germany of German populations or elements thereof remaining in Poland, Czechoslovakia, and Hungary would have to be undertaken. Millions of German refugees had already been driven in headlong flight before the advancing Red armies, or unceremoniously and often brutally expelled from the reoccupied areas and from eastern Germany. The conference report said that such transfers should be effected in an orderly and humane manner. The Control Council should see to it that the displaced Germans were equitably distributed among the occupation zones; and the governments of Poland, Czechoslovakia, and Hungary should be requested to suspend deportations while the Allied

[93] Poland's dependence upon the Soviet Union was inevitably increased and prolonged by possession of former German territory which she could hope to hold against a revived and reunified Germany only as long as the Red Army would help her hold it or would hold it for her.

Poland's eastern boundary was fixed by a Polish-Soviet treaty February 28, 1945, approximately along the Curzon line, the actual boundary to be drawn on the ground by a mixed commission. Former German territory east of the Oder-Neisse line was turned over by the Russians, April 21, 1945, to an administration representing the provisional Polish government. Stalin was unwilling at Potsdam to change the arrangement already made, but was reported to have told President Truman that the question of the German-Polish boundary was still open and that he was "not committed" on it. In a new treaty with Poland August 16, 1945, he recognized the Oder-Neisse line as the permanent boundary. It was again so recognized by "treaty" agreement between Poland and the east German "government" June 7, 1950. Byrnes, *op. cit.*, 80-81, 191-192; Leahy, *op. cit.*, 406, 423; New York *Times*, August 19, 1945, June 11, 1950; James T. Shotwell and Max Laserson, *Poland and Russia, 1919-1945* (New York, 1945), 85, n. 3.

In a discussion at Potsdam of the rights of Roman Catholics and their church in Poland, Stalin quizzically or scornfully asked Truman and Churchill how many divisions the pope had.

governments examined the report of the Control Council on the care of those deported.[94]

At the beginning of the Potsdam conference, and again a week later, Japan asked Stalin to mediate in her behalf for peace with Britain and the United States. Stalin did not report the first request to his conferees, and told them only after he had rejected both that he had replied to the Japanese that their proposals were too vague to be considered. As the Japanese might have guessed, he was then preparing to make war on Japan and showed no interest in seeing that war ended before the Red Army had taken possession of Manchuria. His chief of staff assured the others present at a special conference at Potsdam that the Red Army would be withdrawn from Manchuria as soon as the Japanese troops there should have surrendered. The second Soviet operation in the Far Eastern area would be the conquest of southern Sakhalin, which Russia had lost to Japan in 1905.[95]

From Potsdam July 26, 1945, the United States and Great Britain summoned Japan to surrender. An atomic bomb had by then been detonated in a desert test in New Mexico, and a list of Japanese target cities for it had been made up by the U. S. Army Air Forces; but no one knew how the new weapon would perform in an air burst over a city such as Hiroshima or Nagasaki. Plans were then being made for an invasion of the principal Japanese islands—Kyushu November 1, 1945, Honshu early in 1946. It was estimated that the conquest of those islands would cost the United States a million casualties. It was to make it unnecessary either to invade the Japanese home islands or to use the atomic bomb that Japan was then summoned to end the war by surrender.

Japan was threatened by the Potsdam Declaration with the destruction of her armed forces and the restriction of her power to her home islands by the lopping off of conquered territories such as Manchuria, Korea, and Formosa. She was warned that war criminals would be tried and punished. She was not threatened with the enslavement or destruction of her people. But on July 28 Premier Suzuki rejected the ultimatum by announcing that it was unworthy of public notice.[96]

---

[94] The westward flow of refugees continued. Western Germany was seriously overcrowded; and the displaced persons problem was critical.

[95] Leahy, *op. cit.*, 415-420.

[96] Stimson, *op. cit.*, 618-620, 625; Leahy, *op. cit.*, 413, 419-420; Byrnes, *op. cit.*, 211-212; 263; Stettinius, *op. cit.*, 96-97; Arnold, *op. cit.*, 492.

CHAPTER 16

The War in the Pacific, 1941-1945

EXPANSION OF JAPANESE-DOMINATED AREA

The Philippines and Malaya

JAPANESE PLANS FOR ATTACK

At six o'clock in the morning of December 8, Tokyo time, when the task force at Pearl Harbor had had time to make its surprise attack, the Japanese high command announced that since dawn of that day Japan had been at war with Great Britain and the United States. The primary objective of the war was to make Japan economically and strategically self-sufficient by seizing possession of what the Japanese leaders called their southern resources area—the Malay Peninsula and the East India islands. But before the island empire of the Netherlands could be attacked, the anticipated interference of the United States—from Guam or the Philippines (also potentially a part of that resources area), and the striking power of the United States Pacific fleet at Pearl Harbor—had to be neutralized. The British base at Hong Kong was also in the way. So on Pearl Harbor Day air attacks were made on Clark Field near Manila and on Shanghai and Hong Kong, and landings that night in Thailand and northern Malaya.

The attacks had been long and carefully planned, and were well prepared, coördinated, and synchronized. A hundred thousand troops were ready in Formosa (Taiwan) and Hainan. Okinawa and French Indo-China were also used as staging areas. Naval bases for the operation were available in the Pescadores islands, at Camranh Bay in Indo-China, and on Palau, Saipan, and other mandated (former German) islands. Oil and gasoline depots were ready at convenient points.

Imperial Japanese headquarters notified the commander of its combined fleet November 5, 1941, that war was probably inevitable. On November 21 all forces were ordered to proceed to their designated rendezvous points. The decision to go to war was made by the government December 1. Army and navy commanders were informed that day of the decision, and on December 2 were notified, as was Admiral Nagumo, commanding the Pearl Harbor attack force, that general hostilities would begin December 8.[1]

LUZON

As at Pearl Harbor, but for less apparent reasons, United States forces in the Philippines permitted the Japanese to strike the first blow. Fog over Formosa delayed the start of the first air strike from there against Clark Field, near Manila. The Japanese forces massed on Formosa for the Philippine campaign expected to be bombed there as soon as word of the Pearl Harbor strike should reach General Douglas MacArthur, commanding in the Philippines. The word reached MacArthur eight or nine hours before the first enemy plane reached him. Yet, to the amazement of the attackers, most of the United States planes were caught in a "defensive" attitude, lined up on the ground. The only radar and radio sender were knocked out in the first assault; so the defense was crippled from the outset by the wrecking of its communication system. Half of the heavy bomber strength of the United States Army Far Eastern air force and a third of its fighter force were destroyed the first afternoon. The remaining heavy bombers were withdrawn to the southward; and navy search planes, also soon reduced to half their initial strength, followed the few surface ships and bombers southward. The rapidly dwindling remainder of the army fighter force had to be used thereafter chiefly for reconnaissance, surrendering control of the air.[2]

The initiative gained with control of the air was soon used by invasion forces already assembled on Formosa and Palau, respectively, to move into Lingayén Gulf, December 22, southeastern Luzon at Legaspi, and southern Mindanao at Davao. All of these had left Japan weeks earlier, and had been poised in readiness at their forward bases astride the Philippines. The well-equipped amphibious forces

[1] Tokyo time, December 7, Honolulu time. See pp. 651, n. 40; 658-660.
[2] United States Strategic Bombing Survey (USSBS), *The Campaigns of the Pacific War* (Washington, 1946), 26-28; General Lewis Hyde Brereton, *The Brereton Diaries* (New York, 1946), 37-67. Thailand signed a ten-year treaty of alliance with Japan December 10, and declared war on the United States and Britain January 25. The United States declared war on Thailand February 5.

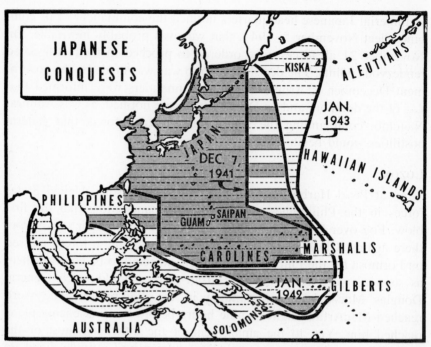

JAPANESE CONQUESTS

KISKA — ALEUTIANS

JAN. 1943

JAPAN DEC. 7, 1941

HAWAIIAN ISLANDS

PHILIPPINES

GUAM · SAIPAN

CAROLINES — MARSHALLS

JAN. 1942 — GILBERTS

AUSTRALIA — SOLOMONS

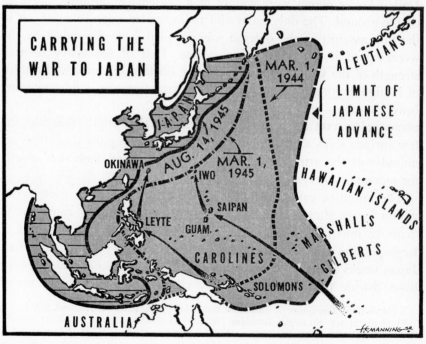

CARRYING THE WAR TO JAPAN

MAR. 1, 1944 — ALEUTIANS

LIMIT OF JAPANESE ADVANCE

JAPAN

AUG. 14, 1945

OKINAWA

MAR. 1, 1945

IWO

HAWAIIAN ISLANDS

SAIPAN

LEYTE

GUAM

MARSHALLS

CAROLINES — GILBERTS

SOLOMONS

AUSTRALIA

F.E.MANNING JR

making the invasion operated at first under cover of carrier-based air-craft. Then the Fifth air army moved in from Formosa and supported ground operations. Manila was declared an open city but was heavily bombed December 27 and 28. Manila and the nearby Cavite naval base were occupied by the Japanese January 2, 1942. The Japanese Third Fleet was free December 31 to return to Formosa to refuel, and then go off to the Palau-Davao area to participate in operations against Borneo and Celebes.

United States and Philippine defense forces retreated to the Bataán peninsula, across the bay from Manila, whence General MacArthur was ordered by President Roosevelt to escape by patrol boat and plane while he could to Australia, which he reached March 15, to plan the eventual return and reconquest. With such support as could be given him by a few submarines and PT (patrol torpedo) boats, General Jonathan Wainwright held Bataán until April 9 and the Manila Bay island fortress Corregidor until May 6, when he was compelled to surrender with the remnant of his forces.[3]

MALAYA

Under protection of overwhelmingly superior strength in land-based air power, the Japanese made good use of their equipment and capacity for amphibious warfare to leapfrog their way rapidly down the Malay Peninsula, making untenable all advanced British airfields and landing at will behind any new line the defense attempted to establish. In a bold attempt to intercept and destroy a Japanese landing force, Admiral Sir Tom Phillips left Singapore late in the afternoon of December 8 with the heavy battle cruiser *Repulse,* sister ship of *Renown* and the ill-fated *Hood,* and the magnificent new battleship *Prince of Wales,* which had reached Singapore from European waters only six days earlier. He had with him four destroyers, no cruisers, no aircraft carrier. He requested but could not be given land-based fighter plane protection over designated areas at times when he estimated that he might be in those areas.

[3] The Japanese treated their prisoners badly; but General Wainwright survived his imprisonment and, with British General Percival, the similarly unsuccessful defender of Singapore, was signally honored by MacArthur at the surrender ceremony on the *Missouri* in Tokyo Bay, September 2, 1945.
The Japanese troops on Luzon were commanded by General Masaharu Homma until March 9, 1942, when for failure to take Bataán Homma was replaced by General Tomoyuki Yamashita. Yamashita faced MacArthur again in the Philippines in 1944 and 1945. Both Japanese generals were subsequently tried and hanged as war criminals, the United States Supreme Court ruling that the powers of the president as commander in chief of the armed forces covered the trial and punishment of prisoners of war charged with war crimes or responsibility therefor.

Informed by submarines that two fine, fat British battleships were out without an air umbrella, Japanese planes, loading at southern Indo-Chinese bases with bombs for Singapore, changed part of their loads to torpedoes and took off. They flew right to Singapore without locating their quarry, which had reversed course and then had turned again as Admiral Phillips changed his plans; but on their way home, December 10, they swarmed on their targets. Both of the great ships went down. Of nearly three thousand officers and men on board, accompanying destroyers rescued two thousand. Admiral Phillips and Captain John Leach of *Prince of Wales* were drowned.[4]

Other Outposts

December was a sad month for the Allies. The United States defense of Guam sent off its last message the day *Prince of Wales* and *Repulse* were lost. Midway was held; but the stouthearted though hopeless defense of Wake Island was overwhelmed the day before Christmas. After seventeen days' siege Hong Kong surrendered on Christmas Day. Meanwhile, December 24, Free French forces under Admiral Muselier seized the French islands St. Pierre and Miquelon, off Newfoundland, and embroiled the United States with both French factions, as Vichy disowned de Gaulle and the Free French while the United States maintained precarious diplomatic relations with Vichy.

Coördination of War Effort

At the suggestion of President Roosevelt, General Sir Archibald P. Wavell was named supreme Allied commander of the southwest Pacific area. The appointment was announced January 2, 1942, but the situation deteriorated so rapidly that the rather reluctant Caesar was never able to organize an effective high command, and the defensive efforts of the Allies were never coördinated. Each nation retained control of its own forces and thought first of its own interests.

[4] Churchill, *The Second World War,* III, 619-623. *Prince of Wales* participated in the pursuit and sinking of *Bismarck,* in which *Hood* was sunk by an explosion following a hit. It carried Winston Churchill to the Atlantic conference, escorted convoys to Malta, and helped to keep watch on *Tirpitz* and *Prinz Eugen.* The armored aircraft carrier *Indomitable,* which was to have accompanied it to Singapore, was temporarily disabled by an accident; so Phillips was sent on without air escort.

Britain felt the loss of these great ships and others and of Hong Kong, and the impending loss of Singapore, as the United States felt Pearl Harbor and Bataán. A supplementary war credit of a thousand million pounds was voted December 16. After a three-day debate in the House of Commons, January 27 to 29, 1942, the government won a vote of confidence by a vote of 464 to 1. The adverse vote was cast by J. Maxton. Mr. Maxton did not speak for or against the motion, and asked the ministers no question during the long discussion.

General Wavell's responsibility included the defense of Burma; but the Japanese crossed the Salween River February 9, and Wavell had to fly off Java to safety at Colombo in Ceylon February 25.

Measures for general high-level coöperation were ultimately more effective: (1) a Joint Chiefs of Staff Committee in Washington, presided over by the United States chief of staff, General Marshall; (2) a Pacific War Council, on which Australia, New Zealand, and the Netherlands East Indies were represented and to which India was soon invited; (3) a Combined Raw Materials Board in Washington for the allocation of materials; and (4) a Combined Shipping Adjustment Board in Washington and London. An Allied Supply Council was set up in Australia May 5.

Under the First War Powers Act passed by the United States Congress December 18, 1941, the president established a War Production Board to stimulate and coördinate war production, and appointed Donald Nelson of Sears, Roebuck to administer it. One of the new agency's first problems was promotion of synthetic rubber production to compensate for the Japanese conquest of most of the sources of the world's natural rubber supply, and to atone for failure to stock-pile in time.

After passing through various organizational phases, the Foreign Economic Administration headed by Leo Crowley became one of the key agencies for waging total war, denying essential war materials to the enemy by preëmptive buying, supplying weapons and materials to allies and potential allies under lend-lease. War production in the United States in 1942 equaled that of Germany, Italy, and Japan. In 1943 it increased 50 percent over 1942. In 1944 it was twice what it had been in 1942. To transport men and materials overseas the War Shipping Administration was given control of ocean-going shipping and, to the great fleet so acquired, added more than four thousand newly constructed ships. To protect shipping, combat enemy war vessels, and replace losses, the navy was enormously increased during hostilities; and repair, supply, and refueling facilities and techniques were constantly improved.

Singapore and the Indies

THE MALAY BARRIER

Without waiting for the fall of Bataán or Singapore, the Japanese moved from Davao in January, 1942, on Celebes and oil-rich Borneo. Methodically they used air power to reach from one forward base to the point chosen for the next, followed it with an amphibious landing well protected by cruisers and destroyers, and built up defensive and offensive strength there for the next step. The seizure, January 10-12, of Tarakan island, close off the northeast coast of Borneo, gave them high-grade oil and, with Balikpapan on the southeastern coast of Borneo, January 23, and Macassar on the southwestern tip of Celebes, taken February 10, control of the Macassar strait.[5] This was the work of their western invasion force. Meanwhile, using paratroops, their eastern invasion force took Menado on the northeasternmost tip of Celebes; then Kendari on southeastern Celebes and Ambon (Amboina), on which was located the second largest naval base in the islands. This gave them freedom of movement through the Moluccan strait. Their next steps, similarly executed, were the seizure of Kupang on the southwestern tip of Dutch Timor, using paratroops again, and of Bali, the island nearest Java on the east. These moves were completed by the end of February and, with the fall of Singapore, opened the way for pincers attack on Java from east and west.[6]

A similar series of landings were made at Rabaul on New Britain and Kavieng on New Ireland January 22; at Lae on New Guinea January 25; and at Gasmata on the southern coast of New Britain February 9.

Throughout this advance, the superiority of Japanese air power was decisive. But the invaders had also the advantages of greater numbers and strength in everything, of the initiative, of superior reconnaissance, of unity of command, and of conducting a planned campaign. Mobile Japanese air forces, both land-based and carrier-borne, were at that time superior in numbers and performance to any opposition they encountered.[7]

Dutch, British, and United States naval and air forces offered such resistance as they could, but never seriously inconvenienced the invaders. They were heavily outnumbered and outgunned everywhere, widely dispersed, and never able to function as a combat team. The United States naval and air forces which had been drawn off southward from the Philippines were based for a time on Java with naval

---

[5] After the conquest of Tarakan, Japan acknowledged herself at war with the Netherlands East Indies. A landing was made in British North Borneo December 17.

[6] Kupang was favorably located as a base from which to intercept reinforcements approaching Java from the east, through the Arafura and Timor seas, or fighter planes being ferried from Australia.

The Japanese landed on Portuguese Timor February 20. Portugal protested the intrusion upon her territory, as she had done when Dutch and British imperial forces occupied it as a safety measure "for duration of the war," December 18, 1941. The Allies could not hold it. Some of the last of the Australians to leave were taken off by United States submarine.

[7] USSBS, *op. cit.,* 29.

operational headquarters at Surabaya. In the night of January 23-24, in the Macassar strait, four United States destroyers sank four large troop transports engaged in the Balikpapan operation but could not halt the movement. A combined United States and Dutch striking force of three cruisers and six destroyers attempted unsuccessfully in the night of February 19-20 to interfere with the invasion of Bali by attacking an enemy force of six destroyers and some transports. One Allied destroyer was sunk, and two cruisers and a destroyer damaged. One Japanese destroyer was damaged, no ships were sunk. The invasion of Bali continued. The Japanese were notably superior in torpedo tactics and training and were equipped with more dependable torpedoes.

Damage to Allied ships and planes was doubly serious, as replacements were not available. Repair facilities, never adequate, rapidly diminished. Base after base was made untenable by enemy air power.

Virtually every ship in harbor at Darwin, north Australia, for example, was destroyed on February 19 in a heavy air attack launched from four carriers by Admiral Nagumo's air fleet force which had begun the war by striking at Pearl Harbor. United States and Australian fighter planes grounded there were destroyed; and reconnaissance seaplanes and their tender had to be withdrawn southward.

Some United States submarines were based at Fremantle and Perth in southwestern Australia, eighteen hundred miles from the nearest navy yard (Melbourne) able fully to accommodate a U-boat of the 1575-ton Pacific fleet type. Others were based on Brisbane on the east coast of Australia, also a long run from the Indies. In September, 1942, they set up an advanced base at Exmouth in northwest Australia, seven hundred miles north of Perth. These submarines levied toll on tankers, transports, supply ships, and escort vessels. But they were frustrated by frequent failure of their torpedoes, and the effect of their depredations was not yet seriously felt.[8]

SINGAPORE

During January the relentless advance of the Malayan invasion force continued. On January 30 the last British troops withdrew from the mainland and breached the causeway leading out to the island on which Singapore was built. Facing seaward and adequately fortified against assault from the sea, the great naval base and fortress

---

[8] Submarine S-36 was grounded on a reef in the Macassar strait January 21. *Perch* was destroyed by depth charges in shallow water in the Java Sea, off Surabaya. *Shark,* which had carried Admiral Hart and his staff from Manila to Surabaya, disappeared in February in the Molucca passage. Theodore Roscoe, *United States Submarine Operations in World War II* (Annapolis, 1949), 69, 74.

proved vulnerable on its land side. In the night of February 8-9 the
Japanese landed on the northwestern coast of the island and maintained their foothold. On February 15, with his men suffering from
shortages of water, food, gasoline, and ammunition, General Percival
surrendered the surviving garrison of more than fifty thousand British
and imperial troops.[9]

SUMATRA, JAVA, AND THE JAVA SEA

The invaders were already established on Sumatra when Singapore
surrendered and opened the western way to an immediate invasion of
Java. There they used parachute troops February 14 to seize the oil
fields before they could be quite destroyed, then followed in with
amphibious landings as usual. The Sumatra wells produced half the
oil of the Indies.

Convinced after the loss of the bastion at Singapore that Java could
not be successfully defended, General Wavell dissolved the hypo-
thetically unified high command on February 25 and flew off to
Colombo in Ceylon. United States General Brereton also took off for
Colombo, using his few remaining B-17 Fortresses and heavy transport planes to fly out air force personnel. The Dutch took over command of the defense of Java.[10]

The Japanese poured into Java at three points: near Batavia in the
northwest, on the north coast east of Batavia, and at Rembang west
of Surabaya, the last big oil center in the islands. In a final attempt to
sink Japanese convoys in the Java Sea a mixed force of five cruisers
and ten destroyers—Dutch, British, Australian, and American—was
cobbled together and attacked, February 27-28. Two Allied cruisers
and three destroyers were sunk. The Japanese lost no ships, and the
occupation of Java proceeded without further organized resistance
after March 1, when five cruisers—Dutch *Java* and *DeRuyter,* United
States *Houston,* British *Exeter* (one of the victors over *Graf Spee*
in 1939), and Australian *Perth*—were sunk while trying to escape
from the Java Sea through enemy-controlled exits.

[9] It was on February 9 that the *Normandie*, renamed *Lafayette*, burned at her
pier in New York harbor. It was on February 12 that the German warships
Scharnhorst, Gneisenau, and *Prinz Eugen* ran the gantlet of the English Channel
with comparative impunity. German U-boats were reaping a rich harvest off the
Florida coast and in the Caribbean. In Burma British withdrawals continued. On
Bataán hope flickered and burned low.

[10] Morison, *History of U. S. Naval Operations in World War II*, III, 336; USSBS,
op. cit., 30. En route from Australia to Chilachap with a cargo of fighter planes,
the seaplane tender *Langley*, the oldest United States aircraft carrier, was sunk
south of Java by land-based planes flying from Kendari, Celebes.

The United States cruiser *Marblehead*, crippled in previous action, escaped from Chilachap on the south coast of Java and was sent to Trincomalee, Ceylon, for repairs. Two modern United States destroyers, *Whipple* and *Parrot*, four old four-stacker destroyers of Division 58, and two United States gunboats survived the campaign for the Malay barrier. The United States lost the cruiser *Houston*, four destroyers, and the seaplane tender *Langley*; Britain *Prince of Wales*, *Repulse*, *Exeter*, and three destroyers; Australia the cruiser *Perth*; the Netherlands cruisers *Java* and *DeRuyter* and six destroyers. The Japanese lost two destroyers to submarine attack; one sank when it struck a mine; none was sunk by an Allied surface ship. Seldom in the history of war had readiness and the initiative paid such premiums. Seldom had so much been won at so little cost.[11]

THE RISING SUN AT ZENITH, 1942

Ceylon

JAPANESE CARRIER STRIKING FORCE

The exploits of Admiral Nagumo's carrier striking force of the First Air Fleet were startling. The core of that combat unit consisted of six aircraft carriers: *Akagi, Kaga, Soryu, Hiryu, Shokaku,* and *Zuikaku*; two battleships: *Hiei* and *Kirishima*; two heavy cruisers: *Tone* and *Chikuma*; light cruiser *Abukuma*; and nine destroyers. After Pearl Harbor, coördinating its movements admirably with those of the other naval and amphibious forces, without losing a ship or having one damaged by enemy action, it struck with devastating effect at ships and shore installations at Darwin, Amboina, Rabaul, and Chilachap, and contributed to other Japanese successes.

COLOMBO AND TRINCOMALEE

From the Java Sea Nagumo's carrier force ranged westward into the Indian Ocean and on April 5 and 9 (the day of surrender on Bataán) severely damaged ships and shore installations at Colombo and Trincomalee on Ceylon. British cruisers *Dorsetshire* and *Cornwall*, aircraft carrier *Hermes,* and corvette *Hollyhock* were sunk in the Indian Ocean by Nagumo's carrier-borne planes. During the week of April 2 to 9 twenty-eight Allied merchant ships, 135,689 tons, were lost in waters around India: twenty-three in the Bay of Bengal,

[11] Morison, *op. cit.,* III, 375; USSBS, *op. cit.,* 30-31, 38-40; Roscoe, *op. cit.,* 76-77.

fifteen of them under air attack; five to submarines off the west coast of India.[12]

Colombo and Trincomalee were the objectives of Nagumo's longest reach to the southwestward. In the four months following Pearl Harbor his far-ranging task force operated unscathed and unchallenged through 120 degrees of longitude. In that period it sank five battleships, a carrier, two cruisers, seven destroyers, and thousands of tons of merchant shipping, and damaged other ships and harbor installations. During its first long run of unbroken success it was rarely sighted by an enemy, or effectively attacked; only its planes appeared. Yet, with its first mission of opening the way completed, it was time for the task force to go home to Kure in the Inland Sea to refit, and to replenish its complement of planes and pilots. The British made it pay a heavy price for its Ceylon and Indian Ocean strikes.[13]

Coral Sea

The conquest of the southern resources area which Japanese spokesmen called essential to the maintenance of Japan as a world power of the first rank was stopped in the air over the Indian Ocean in April, 1942, over Darwin in north Australia and Port Moresby in New Guinea, over the Coral Sea in May, and in the central Pacific near Midway in June. The Hawaiian, Samoan, Fiji, New Hebrides, and Loyalty islands and Midway remained in Allied hands; and advanced United States naval bases were built at Espiritu Santo and at Nouméa on New Caledonia. To set up a defense perimeter and hold what they had seized, the Japanese sent a task force and convoy down from Truk in the mandated Caroline Islands, seized and occupied Tulagi in the Solomons, May 3, then turned westward across the northern arm of the Coral Sea toward Port Moresby on the southeastern coast of New Guinea. Possession of Port Moresby would have given them control of New Guinea and have brought them uncomfortably close to Australia.

A United States naval task force built around the aircraft carriers

[12] In the summer of 1942 German submarines based on Penang, Singapore, and Batavia took over the war in the Indian Ocean, the Japanese concentrating on the Solomons and southwestern Pacific. Morison, *op. cit.,* IV, 197.

[13] Morison, *op. cit.,* III, 383-386; USSBS, *op. cit.,* 31. Only two of Nagumo's carriers were used in the battle of the Coral Sea in May. Many of the planes of the four that were used and lost at Midway were manned by new pilots inferior to those of the first team, expended during the first four months and never adequately replaced.

The carrier striking force reached Kure April 18, the day of the Doolittle token raid on Japan.

Lexington and *Yorktown* entered the Coral Sea from the southeast-ward to intercept the Port Moresby expedition. The outcome of such enterprises in vast ocean spaces, with visibility often restricted by clouds, rain squalls, or darkness, depended often as much upon the success of searching operations as upon efficiency in combat. Each commander naturally tried to find his opponent without being found. Here the uncertainty was increased by the fact that, on the United States side, early reconnaissance had been done by land-based B-17's, and neither ship identification nor intercommunication was perfect.

In the morning of May 7, however, United States carrier planes attacked part of the Japanese transport force and sank its escorting light carrier *Shoho*. Next day the planes of each carrier force attacked the other, each finding its target inadequately protected, with fighter planes away on mission. *Lexington* was sunk and *Yorktowr* damaged. The Japanese carriers *Shokaku* and *Zuikaku,* two that had been with Nagumo from Pearl Harbor to Ceylon, were heavily damaged. The Japanese lost also the destroyer *Kikuzuki,* and suffered damage to other vessels. The United States task force lost also the oiler *Neosho* and destroyer *Sims*.

The Japanese probably inflicted, in the battle of the Coral Sea, more damage than they received; but United States naval officers learned more about carrier protection than the preëminently offensive-minded Japanese, and repair and rebuilding techniques enabled them to take advantage more promptly of what they had learned. *Yorktown* returned from the Coral Sea to Pearl Harbor for repairs and got back to Midway in time. *Shokaku* was not available for Midway, and *Zuikaku* was sent from the Coral Sea to the Aleutians. The principal purpose of the Coral Sea mission, moreover, was accomplished. The southward expansion of the Japanese-dominated area northeast of Australia was stopped; the attempt to take Port Moresby by sea was abandoned; and Milne Bay on the southeastern extremity of New Guinea was occupied by United States forces before the end of August.[14]

Midway, June 4-6

JAPANESE PLANS

The Japanese knew by June, 1942, that their reach eastward and southeastward was not unlimited. But they wanted better outposts, farther out, to guard against the eventual counterattack which they knew was to be expected. For a better defense perimeter and the more

[14] Morison, *op. cit.,* IV, 63, 81; USSBS, *op. cit.,* 52-55, 188.

easily to prevent a repetition of the carrier-borne Doolittle token air raid, they planned, therefore, the seizure of Midway and some of the Aleutian Islands, then the Fijis, New Caledonia, and if possible New Zealand. Having thus cut the United States off from access to the western Pacific, they would then go over to the defensive and see whether the United States, deeply involved in the Atlantic and committed to a major war in Europe, would make the sacrifices necessary to win back what they—the Japanese—had seized so quickly and so easily.

NAVAL-AIR BATTLE

At dawn, June 4, a formidable armada approached Midway. Fleet commander Admiral Isoroku Yamamoto led in person, in the giant super-battleship *Yamato*. He had at his disposal a dozen battleships and six aircraft carriers, including Admiral Nagumo's famous fast-striking force of the First Air Fleet, and a full complement of cruisers, destroyers, and supply ships, escorted by submarines and followed by transports carrying an occupation force. The United States naval staff anticipated the attack but could send to meet it only three carriers, *Enterprise, Hornet,* and *Yorktown,* with a complement of cruisers, destroyers, and twenty-nine submarines, under Admirals R. A. Spruance, T. C. Kinkaid, F. J. Fletcher, and C. A. Lockwood, Jr. The United States strategy was for the carriers to stand off northeast and north of Midway, anticipating that the enemy would attack the island by air, and to launch planes to attack the enemy carriers while their fighters were away.

Unlike Pearl Harbor on Pearl Harbor Day, Midway was well armed and alert. Every plane capable of leaving the ground was in the air when the long-expected air attack was delivered at 6:30 A.M., June 4. When the attack ended, twenty minutes later, seventeen Midway pilots were missing. A third of the attackers were shot down by fighter planes and anti-aircraft fire.

Meanwhile United States carrier planes attacked as planned. By noon three enemy carriers were sinking, and a fourth sank at nine next day; but *Enterprise* had lost fourteen of thirty-seven dive bombers, ten of fourteen torpedo bombers, and a Wildcat. *Hornet* had lost all her torpedo bombers and a dozen Wildcats; *Yorktown* all her torpedo bombers but one, two dive bombers, and three Wildcats. Soon a second strike was launched by the other enemy carriers, which found *Yorktown* with too many of her fighter planes away and damaged her so severely that she had to withdraw from the action. She was sunk by a submarine three days later with her destroyer escort *Hammann*, while retiring toward Pearl Harbor.

Yamamoto turned away to westward. Adverse weather conditions and battle losses limited the effectiveness of immediate pursuit; but two of his cruisers, which had been crippled in a collision during evasive action occasioned by United States submarine *Nautilus* in the night of June 4-5, were overtaken by dive bombers from *Enterprise* and *Hornet* on the second day of his retreat. One of them, *Mikuma*, was sunk. The other, *Mogami*, needed two years to repair. These were the cruisers that had sunk *Houston* and *Perth* off Java on March 1.

The Japanese lost in the battle of Midway four (*Kaga, Akagi, Soryu, Hiryu*) of the carriers that had struck at Pearl Harbor, a heavy cruiser, 253 aircraft, and 3500 men; the United States lost a carrier, a destroyer, 150 aircraft, and 307 men.[15]

The carrier strength of the two forces was now numerically equalized, but Admiral Spruance's own striking power was seriously depleted by the furious action of June 4, and his surface complement was not comparable with Yamamoto's battleship fleet. He had good reason, therefore, to be cautious in pursuit and to avoid being caught in any trap set for him by his redoubtable opponent, who still had at his disposal a powerful surface force. The Japanese Aleutian task force then in the North Pacific with four aircraft carriers including *Zuiho*, detached from the defeated Midway fleet, would have welcomed a carrier battle with Spruance's remaining two. Spruance's prudence was confirmed by Admiral Nimitz, commander in chief in the Pacific area, who recalled him and his carriers from the area.

At the battles of the Coral Sea and Midway naval air warfare reached a new peak. It was carrier-borne plane against shore installations, plane against plane, carrier-borne plane against carrier and other ships. Submarines also operated against surface ships, scouted enemy movements, screened their own, and killed cripples and their escorts, but did not play the finally decisive part in battle action. Battleships (Japanese), cruisers, and destroyers escorted carriers but did not fire upon one another. Yet without them the carriers could not have ventured as they did.

[15] Morison, *op. cit.*, IV, 104, 131, 159, 255; USSBS, *op. cit.*, 58-77. Army air force and marine corps planes flying from Midway played a considerable part in reconnaissance and in engaging enemy planes, but did little damage as bombers of ships. Dive bombing was more effective and less costly at Midway than torpedo bombing; and the need of better fighter protection for torpedo bombers was emphasized. Carrier *Soryu*, disabled by carrier planes and awaiting tow, exploded and sank after U.S.S. *Nautilus* administered the coup de grâce by torpedo attack.

Midway was one of the decisive battles of the war. It was the central Pacific turning point. Japan was stopped and turned back. The United States gained the initiative, and her opponent could never regain it.

Aleutians

While the Midway operation was in progress the Japanese raided Dutch Harbor, Alaska, on June 3 and 4, and seized Kiska, Attu, and Agattu in the Aleutian Islands. By-passing Kiska, United States and Canadian forces regained Attu and Agattu, little less than a year later. Kiska was evacuated by its invaders under cover of fog, July 29, 1943, and occupied by a United States and Canadian assault force August 16, 1943. Fearful of attack by the northern route, the Japanese strengthened their defenses in the Kuriles, Karafuto, and Hokkaido.

The Solomons

Guadalcanal

The point of furthest Japanese advance in the Solomon Islands area was Guadalcanal. There the Nipponese were met by the 1st U. S. Marine Division, which landed east of Lunga Point August 7-9 and took immediate possession of an unfinished airstrip soon renamed Henderson Field. The United States forces also occupied Tulagi, August 7. Henderson Field, near the northern coast of Guadalcanal, surrounded on the west, south, and east by enemy-held territory, was the center around and over which fierce fighting raged for six months, and from which marine corps, army, and naval air forces operated over disputed sea and island areas to the northwestward, toward the principal Japanese base in the area at Rabaul.

There were fierce air battles over Henderson Field. Unable to capture it, the enemy would if possible make it untenable and useless by constant bombing. Land-based fighters and bombers were staged down from Rabaul through fields on the intermediate islands, such as Buin Field on Bougainville. On September 28 the field was raided by sixty-two planes. Twenty-three bombers and a fighter were shot down without United States losses. The score was then more than two hundred Japanese planes lost, thirty-two American. In the period October 16 to 25 ten enemy planes were shot down by anti-aircraft fire, 103 by fighters; United States losses, fourteen planes. On October 24, twenty-four Grumman fighters, operating on gasoline flown in to them by the day, shot down twenty fighters and a bomber. Next day seventeen enemy fighters and five bombers were shot down; but by October 26 the field had left, available, only twenty-three fighters, sixteen dive bombers, and one torpedo plane.

At night the field was frequently the target of gunfire from offshore, from destroyers carrying enemy reinforcements or from battleships and cruisers sent down from Rabaul on bombardment missions.

The story of Guadalcanal was an epic of heroism on the part of the men, who fought mud, mosquitoes, malaria, shortages of food and supplies—and a stubborn enemy—to survive, to check the enemy's progress at that point, and to begin there the long process of rolling back the invasion of the southwest Pacific area. It was an especially notable chapter in the history of the United States Marine Corps (USMC) which long bore the brunt, though by no means all, of the hardships of the campaign. Its outcome depended not only upon the valor, tenacity, and skill of the ground troops and airmen committed there but upon the success of the frequently disheartening but always indomitable efforts of the navy to reinforce and supply them, and to protect them against systematic shelling from the sea, while interfering in all ways possible with the supply and reinforcement of their adversaries.

NAVAL-AIR ENGAGEMENTS

The principal Japanese operational base for the Solomons area was Rabaul on New Britain, with support available from Kavieng on New Ireland and Truk in the Carolines, and with forward rendezvous points at Buin on Bougainville and in the Shortland islands. The Japanese had thus an enormous logistic advantage over their United States naval adversaries operating on a shoestring from far-off and half-adequate Espiritu Santo and Nouméa. Both were served by coast and air watchers on islands throughout the area, equipped with radio sending apparatus. These were useful to the Allies as air-raid warning lookouts but could not always detect night movements of enemy barges or other small water craft. Some information gathered by long-range planes flying from Australia was forwarded to United States naval intelligence; but identification was not always accurate, and communication channels were roundabout and too often slow.

Fumbling for information, and futile searches for an approaching enemy, ended all too often in surprise encounters in which previously rehearsed maneuvers, executed in perfect unison by seasoned task forces already long accustomed to operating as tactical units, paid the Japanese rich dividends. For almost every engagement in the Solomons campaign, on the other hand, Allied naval headquarters had to enter a scratch team hastily extemporized for the occasion. Inevitably their teamwork was inferior to that of the experienced and well-drilled enemy team. The substantial United States advantage of the equipment of some of its ships with search-radar apparatus of the latest type was often nullified by failure to make full use of it or to interpret quickly and accurately enough what the radar screens revealed, whereas on virtually every occasion the enemy made instant and expert use of torpedoes.

Savo Island, August 8-9. Immediately after the USMC landing on Guadalcanal the enemy moved to break off the unloading of supplies for the marines and to destroy the transports that had brought them. A mixed force of two British and four United States cruisers and four destroyers patrolled the narrow waters south and east of Savu island, in separate divisions of three cruisers and two destroyers each. They were inadequately warned of the imminent approach of the expected enemy; their officers and men were weary from long watches on the alert, some of them asleep; and their senior officer in command (Admiral Crutchley, R.N.) was in conference aboard the *McCawley*, off the landing beach, with Admiral Turner and General Vandegrift, in command respectively of the landing force and the marines ashore. Their officers and crews were surprised and confused. In an encounter with seven enemy cruisers, three United States heavy cruisers (*Quincy, Vincennes,* and *Astoria*) and one Australian (*Canberra*) were sunk, and major damage was suffered by United States heavy cruiser *Chicago.* Allied losses included 1270 men killed and 709 wounded. The only Japanese loss was a cruiser torpedoed by a United States submarine, S-44, on its return to Kavieng. The transports unloaded their men on Tulagi and Guadalcanal and departed; and the troops they had landed, with part of their supplies, remained.[16]

Eastern Solomons, August 23-25. Having failed to dislodge the Americans from Guadalcanal, the Japanese turned to reinforcement of their own forces there. A United States carrier force moved to intercept the reinforcement in waters northeast of the island. In an encounter of carrier plane against carrier, far out at sea, the Japanese carrier *Ryujo,* destroyer *Mutsuki,* and a transport were sunk; ninety Japanese planes were shot down. The convoy went on to its destination, but its commander reported that piecemeal reinforcement was too costly to be continued. The United States task force lost twenty aircraft, and the carrier *Enterprise* suffered bomb damage. The veteran

[16] Morison, *op. cit.,* V, 17-64; USSBS, *op. cit.,* 105-108; Roscoe, *op. cit.,* 152.

Japanese carriers *Shokaku* and *Zuikaku* and the United States *Saratoga* had part in the action, and United States *Wasp* was ordered up in reserve. A serious weakness in radio communication was revealed by crowding of the air waves, through failure to reserve different wave lengths for incoming combat intelligence and fighter reports and outgoing fighter direction.[17]

While serving with *Hornet* as distant escort for the 7th regiment, USMC, reinforcement for Guadalcanal, United States carrier *Wasp* was sunk northwest of Espiritu Santo September 15, and the battleship *North Carolina* and destroyer *O'Brien* were damaged by submarine torpedo attack. All but one of *Wasp's* air-borne planes were recovered by *Hornet*. *North Carolina* was repaired at Pearl Harbor. *O'Brien* sank on the way home, October 19. The convoy reached Guadalcanal September 18, and unloaded 4000 men, with equipment and supplies, in twelve hours.

On October 15, four thousand troops of the United States Americal division reached the island. Japanese strength there had by then been built up to about thirty thousand.

Cape Esperance, October 11-12. Undeterred by the battle of the eastern Solomons, the Japanese used a steady stream of fast destroyers, usually at night to avoid observation and air attack, to build up and supply their forces on Guadalcanal. Their usual route between New Georgia and Choiseul and Santa Isabel was soon known to Americans as "the slot," and their destroyer supply train as the "Tokyo express." Occasionally some cruisers made the run, to keep the way clear for the destroyers and to shell Henderson Field and other United States installations on Guadalcanal. They were watched and harried but never stopped by United States patrol torpedo boats from Tulagi.

One such bombardment task force—four heavy cruisers and a destroyer—bearing down toward Cape Esperance on the western extremity of Guadalcanal, was surprised and attacked in a night engagement off Savu island by a United States force of four cruisers and five destroyers under Rear Admiral Norman D. Scott. One United States destroyer, *Duncan*, caught in a cross fire between the opposing forces, was sunk. There was confusion on both sides. The commanding Japanese admiral, Goto, was killed by a shell which destroyed all his charts and wrecked his ship's communications apparatus. The Japanese heavy cruiser *Furutaka* and a destroyer were sunk by gunfire in the engagement, and two more destroyers by planes from Guadalcanal next day; but Japanese destroyers landed troops and

[17] Morison, *op. cit.,* V, 79-107; USSBS, *op. cit.,* 111-113.

heavy artillery at Tassafaronga, and Americans on Guadalcanal were shelled again from the sea October 14.[18]

Santa Cruz, October 25-27. To protect and support their supreme effort to take Henderson Field, which very nearly succeeded on October 25, the Japanese sent down from Truk and Rabaul in the last week of October the largest naval and air armada they had collected for one operation since Midway. It was led by the ubiquitous Vice-Admiral Nagumo and included four battleships (*Hiei, Kirishima, Kongo,* and *Haruna*), four carriers, and cruisers, destroyers, and submarine scouts in proportion.

To intercept the imposing enemy fleet by use of carrier-borne planes, two United States carrier task forces formed around *Hornet* and *Enterprise* moved into the area west of Santa Cruz island, east of San Cristobal, southeast of Guadalcanal. In a carrier-plane engagement on October 26, with her own striking planes away, *Hornet* was caught by dive bombers and torpedo bombers from *Shokaku* and *Zuikaku,* and crashed by two suicide-diving pilots of bomb-loaded planes. The carrier soon had to be abandoned and sunk by United States destroyers. The United States also lost destroyer *Porter,* torpedoed by submarine, and seventy-four planes. *Enterprise,* battleship *South Dakota,* and cruiser *San Juan* were damaged. *Saratoga* was the only United States carrier left in the area fit for action. The Japanese lost a hundred planes, no ships. *Shokaku* was knocked out of the war for nine months; carrier *Zuiho* had her flight deck damaged; and heavy cruiser *Chikuma* was seriously crippled. The Japanese battleship fleet was untouched.[19]

Naval Battle of Guadalcanal, or Savu III and IV, November 12-15. The tide turned in the Solomons in mid-November, 1942. Finding destroyers unsatisfactory as carriers of heavy tanks, artillery, and other equipment, and of troops in such numbers as seemed necessary for the reduction of American resistance on Guadalcanal, the Japanese collected in and around the Shortlands a fleet of heavy transports with 10,000 replacements and 3500 special attack troops. Two battleships (*Hiei* and *Kirishima*) with strong cruiser and destroyer support were sent down from Truk and Rabaul to protect it.

In the night of November 12-13, in the familiar waters around Savo island, northwest of Guadalcanal—which had by then earned the nickname of "Ironbottom Sound"—Admirals D. J. Callaghan in *San*

---

[18] Morison, *op. cit.,* V, 147-171; USSBS, *op. cit.,* 115-118.
[19] William D. Leahy, *I Was There* (New York, 1950), 118; Morison, *op. cit.,* V, 199; USSBS, *op. cit.,* 119-124.

Francisco and Norman Scott in *Atlanta* ran their cruiser and destroyer columns into headlong collision with *Hiei* and *Kirishima* and fifteen destroyers which were running in to shell Henderson Field. Fortunately the high-explosive bombardment ammunition with which the Japanese had ready-loaded their guns was not of the armor-piercing variety; but their torpedoes, as usual, were deadly. In the inevitable confusion of a slam-bang night-collision battle, the damage was serious enough.

The United States cruisers managed to concentrate their fire at close range on *Hiei* long enough to disable it. It was bombed and torpedoed next day by Henderson Field planes and was then scuttled by its crew. The raiders lost also two destroyers. Admiral Callaghan was killed on *San Francisco,* which suffered major damage. Admiral Scott went down with the search-radar-equipped light anti-aircraft cruiser *Atlanta.* The new light anti-aircraft cruiser *Juneau* was badly damaged, and was torpedoed by a submarine next day as she limped back toward Nouméa with *Helena* and *San Francisco.* Four United States destroyers were also sunk. Next night enemy cruisers returned to shell the airfield on Guadalcanal.

On the fourteenth the Japanese transports approached the island. Eight of them were sunk and four beached at Tassafaronga under attack of USMC planes from Henderson Field and a strike flown from *Enterprise,* which had effected emergency repairs and returned within reach of the area.

In the night of November 14-15, again in Savu strait and west of Savu island, battleship met battleship and slugged it out with radar-directed sixteen-inch guns. The battleship U.S.S. *South Dakota* drew most of the Japanese fire, which left Admiral Willis A. Lee in the new battleship U.S.S. *Washington* free to concentrate on the enemy *Kirishima,* which was sunk, as was one more Japanese destroyer. In that engagement the United States lost three destroyers: *Benham, Preston,* and *Walke.*

United States warship personnel and cruiser losses in the third and fourth battles around Savu island were heavier than Japan's—the United States lost seven destroyers, Japan three; but the loss of two battleships, and of thousands of men on the twelve transports sunk or beached, discouraged the Japanese leaders. As one of them said, it was for them "the fork in the road" which led to "victory for them or for us."[20]

[20] Morison, *op. cit.,* V, 225-235, 258, 281-292; USSBS, *op. cit.,* 125-129. "The tide has turned," said President Roosevelt, November 17. The landing in North

Tassafaronga, November 30. Finding large convoys, however protected, too easily vulnerable, the Japanese returned after the naval-air battles of mid-November to the use of destroyer-transports at night to supply their troops on Guadalcanal. Apprised of the approach of an unusually large supply-destroyer force, a United States task force of five cruisers and six destroyers moved westward into Savu strait in the night of November 30-December 1. Eight destroyers were intercepted. One, which was caught closest to the United States cruisers, disobeyed instructions and returned their fire, so made itself their one good target and was sunk by gunfire. The others made a quick, previously rehearsed turn in the darkness, fired torpedoes, and escaped. United States cruiser *Northampton* was sunk by torpedo, and major damage was done by torpedo to three others: *Minneapolis, New Orleans,* and *Pensacola.* One enemy attempt to replenish the supplies of his ground troops was thus frustrated—at a very high price.[21]

Summary. In January, 1943, the Japanese expended several hundred more aircraft (six hundred from November 18 to February 8) in continued attacks on Henderson Field, but tried only to keep their ground forces on Guadalcanal supplied. In February they reversed the direction of the Tokyo destroyer-express to evacuate the island. The evacuation of from twelve to thirteen thousand men, mostly at night, was effected in the first week of February, with considerable damage done to their destroyer-transports by planes based on the island. Having completed a sweep of the island February 9, General Patch radioed to Admiral Halsey that the Tokyo express no longer had a terminus there.

Sixty thousand men of the United States Army and Marine Corps were committed on Guadalcanal; 1592 were killed in action, many more incapacitated by wounds and disease; and the cost in planes and pilots was heavy. The Japanese committed 36,000 men and evacuated only about a third of them. Of the others, a thousand became prisoners of war, nine thousand died of disease. More men than were evacuated were listed as killed or missing.

Africa had been made secure. The demands upon naval strength and shipping occasioned by the war in Europe made doubly creditable the achievements of the southwest and central Pacific commands, with the few ships and limited facilities that could be found for them.

[21] Morison, V, 293-315; USSBS, 139-140. While escorting transports for Guadalcanal January 29, 1943, United States heavy cruiser *Chicago* was torpedoed off Rennell island by a carrier plane, revealing an improved Japanese night-air-attack technique. *Chicago* sank January 30; 1049 of her men were rescued. The four transports, and five more February 4, arrived and unloaded unmolested. Morison, V, 351-363.

At sea the struggle for the Solomons cost the United States and Japan twenty-four ships each. The United States lost 126,240 tons: two carriers, eight cruisers, and fourteen destroyers, with such of their men as could not be rescued, and many others on warships not sunk. Japan lost 134,839 tons: two battleships, one light carrier, four cruisers, eleven destroyers, and six submarines.[22]

Japan was not much inconvenienced by the loss of some thousands of infantrymen or artillerymen. She was more sensibly affected by the loss of warships and their crews, which could not readily be replaced, and by the temporary loss of the services of damaged vessels necessarily withdrawn for repair. She was mortally hurt, however, only by the depletion of her land and naval air strength. All her subsequent defensive efforts were weakened as a result of losses sustained in the Solomons campaign. She spent prodigally there between two and three thousand aircraft with trained combat crews. She had not thereafter enough aviation gasoline, training facilities, planes, or time to train replacement pilots equal in efficiency to those lost in 1942 in the Indian Ocean, at Midway, and over or around the Solomon Islands.

SEVERANCE OF JAPANESE COMMUNICATIONS, 1943-1944

Submarines—The Silent Service

Before the setting of the sun which rose war red over Hawaii on Pearl Harbor Day, the order went out from the chief of the United States naval staff to execute unrestricted air and submarine warfare against Japan.[23]

As battleships and air force installations had been the targets of the heaviest attack, the submarine base and repair facilities had suffered little damage. The Pacific submarine fleet could therefore proceed at once on the many missions assigned to it.

---

[22] Morison, *op. cit.,* V, 333, 364, 372.

[23] Agreements to restrict the use of the submarine as a blockade weapon against merchant shipping were made by the five principal naval powers at the Washington and London naval conferences of 1921-1922 and 1930. But Japan notified the other parties in 1934 that she would not be bound by the naval limitation treaties after December 31, 1936. Without undertaking to pass upon the question of the extent to which a state of war between the United States and any foreign country affected the operation of treaty provisions between them, the United States Department of State listed the treaty signed at Washington February 6, 1922, limiting the use of submarines and noxious gases in warfare, "not yet in force" on December 31, 1941. It was to have become effective only on the deposit at Washington of the ratifications of all its signers, and France had not ratified it. Japan was not a party to the naval treaty of March 25, 1936. Department of State publication 2103, *Treaties in Force . . . on December 31, 1941* (Washington, 1944), 43. See also, above, p. 144.

Of a total of 111 submarines, plus seventy-three then being built, the navy had at its disposal in the Pacific area fifty-five large and eighteen medium submersibles. Japan, which at the London conference of 1930 had been conceded the treaty right to parity with Britain and the United States in total submarine tonnage, had about sixty. The number of the United States submersibles increased as the war went on; the number of Japanese fleet-type submarines was approximately maintained and an average of from forty to forty-five were kept continuously in operation, while the imperial navy's surface ships were nearly all destroyed. A large number of midget submersibles were built for coast defense, but little used.

The typical fleet-type United States submarine displaced about 1575 tons. With a cruising range of ten thousand miles it could carry seven officers and seventy men on a cruise of thirty to sixty days. Three—*Argonaut*, *Narwhal*, and *Nautilus*—displaced 2700 tons each and could serve as supply and troop transports. Cruises averaged from six to seven weeks, half of the time being spent in transit between base, be it Brisbane, Fremantle, Perth, or Pearl Harbor, and operating areas. Pearl Harbor-based boats often "topped off" their Diesel-fuel loads at Midway.

The submarines of both navies were driven by Diesel motors when on the surface, electrically when submerged. The storage batteries which furnished the power for propulsion when submerged had to be charged and recharged by running on the surface. A Japanese admiral claimed credit for having invented a breather tube which would permit the use of Diesels when submerged—if not beyond its depth—before the Germans developed the *Schnorkel*; but neither Japanese nor United States submarines were equipped with anything of the *Schnorkel* type during hostilities. The exhaustion of the batteries, choking gases given off by them when anything went wrong, and the danger of explosion and fire from broken electrical circuits were ever-present hazards of the service. The Japanese had the benefit of German designs, models, and technical advice in submarine construction and operation, but the Germans were not proud of their Oriental pupils in that school.

The Japanese fleet-type submarines were slightly larger than the American: from 1600 to 2200 tons. They were generally faster on the surface (twenty-four knots as against twenty), slower submerged (eight knots as against nine). They were said to be less easily maneuverable under water, and unable to dive as deep. They lagged behind their United States counterparts in radar equipment, radio communications, and the electronic search and sound gear which served as eyes and ears to both, under water or when for any other reason their skippers could not see. The Japanese had, on the other hand, two very great advantages: numerous bases near their operating areas, eliminating the long runs to and from base which the United States boats, even those based in Australia, were regularly compelled to make; and more reliable torpedoes.

The torpedoes with which the United States submarines and smaller surface ships were equipped in 1942 had been designed primarily for use against enemy warships, more or less heavily armored. Some of them were equipped with electric detonators, which often failed in service to be activated, as they were designed to be, by proximity to a ship's hull. Others, with contact fuses in their war heads, often failed to make contact, even when correctly aimed and fired, because their depth-regulating mechanism was faulty and they ran too deep, passing beneath their targets; or they might make contact but fail to explode because their fragile firing pins broke without detonating them. Others "porpoised," i.e., surfaced and dived again. One circled and sank the submarine—*Tang*—that fired it. Fewer defectives were found among the torpedoes used in the later years of the war.[24]

Submarining was a lonely service, usually silent while on mission. Boats commonly operated independently in the first years of the war, often in groups of three in the last years. Orders and information could always be received by radio, but danger of enemy interception and decoding limited the use of that means of communication. Reports could be made by radio but, like launching a torpedo, only at the risk of betraying one's position. Communication between submarines operating together was possible but subject to the same limitations. The submarine's function was generally to penetrate the

---

[24] *Tang* was lost, however, in the night of October 24-25, 1944. Twelve men managed to surface from the stricken ship, of whom nine swam until morning and were picked up by the Japanese. One of the nine survivors, Commander O'Kane, was awarded the Congressional Medal of Honor in April, 1946. From February 17 to October 24, 1944, *Tang* rescued twenty-two men and sank twenty-two enemy cargo vessels, a tanker, and a transport, 93,824 tons. Only *Tautog*, with twenty-six from April 26, 1942, to January 20, 1945, sank a larger number. Only three— *Flasher, Rasher,* and *Barb*—destroyed more tonnage. *Flasher's* twenty-one vessels, 100,231 tons, all in 1944, included two tankers of more than ten thousand tons each, a transport and two cargo ships of six to seven thousand tons each, and a 5700-ton light cruiser. *Rasher's* eighteen vessels, 99,901 tons, from October 9, 1943, to August 19, 1944, included on August 18, 1944, a tanker of nearly ten thousand tons and an escort aircraft carrier of twenty thousand, and next day a 17,537-ton transport. *Barb's* seventeen vessels, 96,628 tons, all in 1944, included the double killing on September 16 of an 11,177-ton tanker and a 20,000-ton escort aircraft carrier.

enemy's defenses, to injure him wherever possible, and usually not to give battle but to elude pursuit—to operate by stealth and strike without warning. The silent service could not afford to talk; too much useful information might be given gratuitously to the enemy.

Submarine missions were of many various kinds. Submarines carried Philippine government gold and important persons off the islands, food and ammunition to Corregidor. They maintained contact with whatever resistance movements there were throughout the war area and carried supplies to them. They scouted enemy-held islands by landing parties on them, by mapping their shorelines and charting surrounding waters, and by photographing them. The periscope was used as a telescope and range finder when running at periscope depth, camera-rigged for photographing the results of torpedo shots or enemy installations along shore, or hoisted to widen the skipper's range of vision on the surface. The submarines operated a seagoing rescue service, especially along the heavy bomber routes and along the fighter-bomber air lane between Iwo Jima and Japan. Their operations with the carriers and battle fleets were much more than incidental; but their most important service was cutting the life lines of Japan by sinking her cargo ships, tankers, and transports.

Japanese submarines were used with the fleets against carriers and cruisers, and occasionally on nuisance missions such as carrying an airplane for a reconnaissance flight over the northwest United States coast or lobbing shells into California or an island beyond the imperial surface navy's reach. They were not used very effectively against United States convoys, transports, or naval tankers. In 1943 and later more and more of them were sent to carry supplies to island garrisons marooned in areas of which their air and surface forces had lost control.

Submarine rarely fought submarine, although Allied submersibles sank twenty-five Japanese and five German U-boats in the Pacific during the entire war, and it happened that the last Japanese submersible destroyed, I-373, August 12, 1945, was sunk by United States submarine *Spikefish*—*Spikefish*'s only victory. The last major ship lost by the United States Navy in the war, heavy cruiser *Indianapolis*, was torpedoed east of Leyte July 29, 1945, by Japanese submarine I-58. Eight hundred and eighty men lost their lives. The last Japanese ships sunk by submarine were two coast defense frigates torpedoed in the Sea of Japan, off the southwest coast of Honshu during the forenoon of August 14, 1945, by U.S.S. *Torsk*.[25]

[25] Roscoe, *op. cit.*, 488-490; Morison, *op. cit.*, VI, 69.

War of Attrition and Blockade

Japan's capacity to sustain her population, maintain war production, and defend the area she had seized depended upon her ability to exploit the resources of that area—to carry home raw materials, to supply her armed forces scattered over a vast expanse of ocean, and to replace the materials expended. For all these purposes she needed ships. In peacetime her economy had depended heavily upon sea-borne trade, and upon her merchant ships' earnings as carriers. In wartime to be able to continue to carry for herself became the indispensable condition of survival.

The island empire entered the war with approximately six million tons of merchant shipping. The civilian economy needed half of that to maintain itself; but more than two-thirds of all that was available was allocated at once to the armed forces, leaving always something less than enough, a little less at first than two million tons, for civilian purposes.

Wherever Japanese ships were to be attacked, United States submarines followed them. Off the entrances to passages between islands in the Philippines, in East Indian waters, in the South China Sea, all along the China coast—particularly at the northern entrance to Taiwan (Formosa) Strait—off the northwest coast of Luzon and the east coast of Japan, and finally into the Yellow Sea and the Sea of Japan itself and along the west coasts of Kyushu and Honshu, the submarines pursued their quarry.

The highest total number of submarine-days spent on offensive patrol in operating areas in one month in 1942 was 512 each in November and December; 55 ships attacked in December, 159 torpedoes expended; in 1943 in August, 858 days, 105 ships attacked, 387 torpedoes expended; in September, 697 days, 112 ships attacked, 461 torpedoes; in 1944 in October, 1306 days, 230 ships, 799 torpedoes; in 1945 in June, 1067 days, 147 ships, 522 torpedoes. In July, 1945, the number of targets—military or other—diminished sharply. In August only fifty-nine ships were attacked. There were fewer Japanese vessels afloat then.

New Japanese ship construction could not keep pace. Starting at 27 percent of losses from all causes in 1942, it reached its peak at 877,372 tons, 49 percent of losses from all causes, in the first half of 1944. In the second quarter of 1945 it was 15 percent.

Imports of essential raw materials declined proportionately. Iron ore, iron, and steel reached their peak in 1941, bauxite in 1942;

scrap iron reached 2,104,000 metric tons in 1940, 360,000 tons in the next four years, 12,000 tons in 1945. Imports of rice and other grains and flours increased until 1942, then declined. Raw rubber reached its peak in 1941, declined in 1942, and rose again in 1943 to equal the import of 1941. Total imports of bulk commodities were highest in 1940; but 1941 was nearly equal to 1940 *minus* scrap iron.

Of 611 Japanese naval vessels destroyed by United States forces during the entire war, 1,822,210 tons, submarines sank 201 vessels or 540,192 tons. Of 2117 merchant vessels sunk, 7,913,856 tons, submarines sank 1113, or 4,779,902 tons. Of a total of 2728 vessels, 9,736,068 tons of Japanese shipping and naval vessels sunk by the armed forces of the United States, U. S. submarines sank 1314 vessels, 5,320,094 tons. The total Japanese merchant shipping sunk considerably exceeded the amount available at the beginning of the war. More than three and a quarter million tons were constructed during the war, and little was left. More than half of the staggering total was accounted for by United States submarines.[26]

Maps showing where enemy vessels were sunk and where the hunters, who were always also the hunted, lost their lives in the pursuit—grounded, blown up by mines, or shattered by enemy gunfire or depth charges—looked very much alike. The symbols clustered thick around the headlands and the entrances to or exits from the straits, drawing ever closer to Japan. Of the 288 United States submarines that saw active duty, fifty-two, just less than one of five, were lost—a number nearly equal to the number of the larger fleet type available in the Pacific when the war began. They carried with them 3505 men, 13 percent of the enlisted men and 16 percent of the officers who went down into the sea in ships.[27]

REDUCTION OF JAPANESE-DOMINATED AREA, 1943-1944

Southwest Pacific

NEW GEORGIA

Although the Japanese were eliminated from Guadalcanal, they continued in 1943 to consolidate their airfields and bases in the islands to the northwest. The first major counteroffensive action taken

[26] U.S. Army and Navy Assessment Committee, *Japanese Naval and Merchant Shipping Losses During World War II from All Causes* (Washington, 1947), vi, vii; Roscoe, *op. cit.,* 523.

[27] The Japanese lost 130 submarines and had only fifty-eight left when the war ended, many of which were not at sea or fit for service. Including those scuttled at the time of the collapse, the Germans lost 801, with 30,000 men; Italy 85.

by the United States South Pacific forces was the conquest of New Georgia. Losses in July included the light cruiser *Honolulu* and destroyer *Gwinn*, and damage to light cruiser *St. Louis*. Munda was taken August 5 and used as a base for further operations. The conquest of the island was completed October 9. New Zealand troops occupied two of the Treasury Islands October 26.

NEW GUINEA

A Japanese attempt to land invasion forces at Milne Bay at the southeastern extremity of New Guinea was frustrated by United States naval forces in the battle of the Coral Sea in May, 1942. In July the Japanese landed strong forces at Buna-Gona and Sanananda on the northeast coast of the island and began to push southward overland toward Port Moresby. During the last week of August they landed troops at Milne Bay but were driven off with heavy casualties by Australian troops. It was their first forced evacuation of territory they had occupied. Australian and United States troops of MacArthur's southwest Pacific command based in Australia blocked also the difficult jungle and mountain route to Port Moresby and pushed the Japanese back toward Buna.

Lack of overland routes on New Guinea compelled both combatants to depend almost entirely upon air and sea transport. A large Japanese convoy was destroyed in the Bismarck Sea March 1-4, 1943, by land-based American and Australian planes. More than three thousand men went down with the twelve vessels sunk, which included eight loaded cargo-transports and four destroyers; 2734 survivors were rescued by Allied destroyers and submarines. The incident demonstrated again that a fleet or convoy within reach of land-based air strength must carry its own air cover.

At the end of June, 1943, MacArthur's combined forces began the long process of island-hopping and leap-frogging along the northern coast of New Guinea that was eventually to carry them back to the Philippines. Landings were made on Woodlark and Kiriwina islands and at Nassau Bay, June 30. Buna was taken July 23, Salamaua and Lae September 4, Finschhafen September 22. From each point taken, men and supplies were staged forward to the next, while frequent bombing neutralized the strong enemy air base at Wewak. In December Rabaul, already partially neutralized by carrier-borne air strikes and by the seizure of neighboring islands, was isolated by the seizure of Arawe and Cape Gloucester, in southwestern and northwestern New Britain; and some Japanese naval air strength was withdrawn from Rabaul. Then the Admiralty Islands were seized in February and March, 1944.

In late April, after weeks of Allied air preparation, a jump of four hundred miles was made to airfields at Hollandia and Aitape. By May 27 the advance reached Biak island. Noemfor island was occupied July 2, and Sansapor at the northwestern extremity of New Britain July 30. In July General MacArthur had at his disposal ten divisions: four United States and six Australian. An amphibious landing on Morotai in the Moluccas September 15, 1944, was the final westward thrust prior to the invasion of the Philippines.

Borneo was not to be liberated until May-July, 1945; but the Malay barrier was broken from the south. Some hundreds of thousands of Japanese troops were by-passed and cut off in New Guinea, New Britain, New Ireland, and other islands to be disposed of by the various processes of attrition except as they could be meagerly supplied by submarine or subsist off jungle country. They were thereafter a negligible factor in the war, with no capacity for organized offensive action. The way was open for large forces to move up to the Philippines. Davao, in southern Mindanao, was less than four hundred miles away.[28]

India, Burma, China, 1943-1945

PLANNING CONFERENCES, 1943

China was represented at the Trident conference in Washington in May, 1943, by T. V. Soong, and figured prominently in its deliberations. Generals Stilwell, Chennault, and Wedemeyer were also present. Stilwell, the highest-ranking United States Army officer who could speak Chinese and who knew China from many years of service there, was then army chief of staff to Chiang Kai-shek and was pushing hard for the building up of ground forces there, under his own command. Chennault, commander of the U. S. Fourteenth Air Force in China and former leader of a volunteer organization there called the "Flying Tigers," wanted priority for gasoline, planes, and bases for a much larger air force. Soong wanted vigorous prosecution of a campaign in Burma to reopen the Burma Road; but landing craft

[28] USSBS, op. cit., 173-190; Morison, op. cit., VI, 54-65. Wesley Frank Craven and James Lea Cate (eds.), The Army Air Forces in World War II, IV, The Pacific— Guadalcanal to Saipan (August, 1942 to July, 1944) (Chicago, 1950), 148-150. General MacArthur moved his headquarters from Brisbane to Hollandia September 7, and reorganized his ground forces as the Sixth and Eighth armies, under Generals Walter Krueger and Robert L. Eichelberger.

for amphibious operations there were not then available. Chiang Kai-shek accepted Allied aid as an earned right, but not tutelage, either as to the character of his government or as to use of the aid given him. The problem was further complicated by other questions: whether the nationalist Kuomintang government or the Chinese Communists could better be depended upon to offer effective resistance to the Japanese, and whether nationalists and Communists could be induced to present to the invader a united front, as they were not then doing. Stilwell had little confidence in Chiang Kai-shek and Chiang cordially disliked the tactless and disrespectful Stilwell. Chennault found the generalissimo more congenial. One of the decisions of the Trident conference was to step up the quantity of aviation gasoline being flown over "the hump" from India.[29]

In August a conference—called Quadrant—at Quebec established a new southeast Asia command, naming Lord Louis Mountbatten supreme allied commander in that area and Stilwell deputy commander. Because of continued personal incompatibility and mutual distrust between Chiang Kai-shek and General Stilwell, the latter was replaced in the autumn of 1944 by General Albert C. Wedemeyer. The combined Royal and United States combat air forces, including the U. S. Tenth, were commanded by United States General George E. Stratemeyer.

INDIA-BURMA THEATER, 1944

During 1943 and 1944, at the end of one of the most precarious supply lines in history, the United States continued to support the reorganization, reëquipment, and retraining of the Chinese nationalist army and, simultaneously, a campaign for the reconquest of Burma and the building of a road across northern Burma to connect with the old Burma-China road. At the expense of prodigious United States-British-Indian-Chinese exertion, mountains of supplies were unloaded at Calcutta, pushed up the Brahmaputra Valley, and many of them flown across northern Burma and the hump of the Himalayas to China. By January, 1945, the Himalayan air route alone was carrying 46,000 tons a month.

In October, 1943, two Chinese divisions reëquipped and trained

[29] The conference set May, 1944, as the target date for the invasion of northern France, and authorized an operation for the seizure of the Azores unless Portugal could be persuaded by negotiation to grant the use of bases in the islands. Upon the strength of promises to protect Portugal against reprisals or against attack by Spain, permission to use the bases was granted in October. Sherwood, *op. cit.*, 729-740.

by General Stilwell in northeastern India moved into the Hukawng Valley in northern Burma. They were joined in February, 1944, by a United States infantry combat team familiarly known as Merrill's Marauders. In May these forces captured an airfield at Myitkyina, while General Wingate's British and Indian jungle troops blocked the Irrawaddy Valley. All of these movements were supplied by air, often by parachute air-drop. Early in 1944 an attempted Japanese invasion of northeastern India, which if successful would have cut off all Allied forces in Burma from support except by air, was checked around Imphal by British and Indian troops. From then on, through 1944, the Japanese slowly but surely lost ground in Burma.

The Ledo—renamed the Stilwell—Road was completed, and the first convoy of trucks carrying war material across Burma from northeast India reached China January 28, 1945. By then Japan's China Sea supply lines to her troops in Burma had been cut. The British and Indians further undermined the Japanese position in central Burma in February by taking Meiktila. Mandalay fell to the British March 21, and Rangoon May 3. Lord Mountbatten estimated that the campaign in Burma had cost the Japanese 300,000 casualties, including 97,000 dead.

CHINA, 1945

In China in May, 1944, and in April, 1945, hoping to make it impossible for the United States air forces in China to reach out across the China Sea to join hands with those operating over the Philippines and Ryukyus, the Japanese launched their last major offensives of those years, against the areas in which United States airfields were located. The 1944 offensive overran seven of those fields. Until the Marianas base was made available in June, 1945, United States B-29 Superfortresses flew from Chinese bases to Japan. In 1945 General Stratemeyer commanded the Tenth and Fourteenth U. S. air forces at Linchow and Kunming, and the rehabilitation of the nationalist armies continued, while the Allies vainly continued their efforts to induce nationalists and Communists to join forces politically and together take the offensive against their common enemy. Living largely off the land, however, Japanese armies occupied much of China's most fruitful area until ordered by their government to surrender in September, 1945.[30]

[30] Marshall, *The Winning of the War in Europe and the Pacific* (New York, 1945), 56-62.

Central Pacific, 1943-1944. The Mandated Islands

The Gilberts

It was estimated at the Quebec conference of August, 1943, that General MacArthur's combined Allied forces should be ready for a Philippines campaign in the autumn of 1944, and that a combined United States army-navy-marine corps offensive, predominantly a naval movement westward from Hawaii under the general responsibility of Admiral Nimitz, by way of such islands as would need to be used or neutralized, should reach the Ryukyus in the spring of 1945. Both movements were made within the periods estimated.

As a preliminary step, some of the Ellice Islands were occupied in August and Baker Island was reoccupied in September, 1943. Air bases speedily set up there were busy for the remainder of the war.

The British-mandated Gilbert Islands were seized by the Japanese in December, 1941, and fortified. The defenses of one of them, Tarawa, were made particularly strong. Logs, iron, reinforced concrete, and a heavy covering of earth were used to protect gun emplacements in dugouts virtually impervious to bombs or plunging shellfire, vulnerable only to close-range attack with hand-directed fire or explosive missiles. The 2nd U. S. Marine Division, landing on Tarawa November 21, 1943, found the island stubbornly defended by interlocking lines of fire from weapons in cunningly concealed and sheltered emplacements, and sustained 20 percent casualties among its fifteen thousand combat troops before it could secure the island. Of nearly five thousand Japanese garrison and labor troops, 146 prisoners were taken. At the same time part of the 27th U. S. Army Division took Makin, in the same island group, less stubbornly defended, with fewer casualties. Undefended Apamama island was occupied by men landed from a submarine November 20. The whole operation was supported by nine hundred carrier-based aircraft. The escort carrier *Liscome Bay* was torpedoed and sunk by a submarine. Light cruiser *Independence* survived a torpedo hit.

The Marshalls

From the Gilberts the offensive moved westward to the Japanese-mandated, formerly German, Marshall Islands. There the U. S. 7th Division, which on June 2, 1943, had taken Attu in the Aleutians, and the 4th Marine Division landed January 31, 1944. By February 4 they had completed the reduction of the defenses of Kwajalein and Majuro, atolls with excellent anchorages.

While carrier planes raided Truk, Ponape, and the Marianas, Eniwetok was taken February 19-23 by the U. S. 27th Division and a USMC combat team operating out of Kwajalein.[31]

With the Admiralty Islands soon also in United States hands, the great central Pacific Japanese naval base at Truk could be attacked by air from north and south, as well as by carrier-borne aircraft. So neutralized, it could be by-passed, well to northward, without necessity of a direct naval attack upon it, which could have been costly. In a carrier air strike at Truk February 16 and 17, 200,000 tons of merchant and naval shipping were destroyed, with a large number of aircraft. Finding Truk useless as a base, all major Japanese naval vessels abandoned it and retired to the Palaus or to their home islands. The entire air strength of that portion of the Japanese First Air Fleet found in the Marianas on February 22, 120 planes, was destroyed. Except at Brunei Bay and Singapore, the imperial fleet was back where it had started—with less strength left.

The Western Pacific, June-December, 1944

THE MARIANAS

Saipan and Tinian in the Marianas were mandated to Japan in 1919. Guam, a United States possession acquired from Spain in 1898, was seized by Japan in December, 1941. The Fifth U. S. Marine Amphibious Corps, consisting of the 2nd and 4th Marine divisions, landed on Saipan June 15, 1944, followed by the 27th U. S. Infantry Division. Nearly a month of extremely bitter fighting ensued before the conquest of the island was completed. From July 21 to August 10 the 77th Infantry Division, the 3rd Marine Division, and another USMC brigade fought for the reconquest of Guam. Tinian took nine days. Before the fighting stopped, bulldozers, great earth-movers, and coral-rock crushers were busy making runways for the B-29 superfortresses that were to use them as bases for the long-range strategic bombing of Japan. The first major B-29 air strike went off November 4.

NAVAL-AIR BATTLE OF THE PHILIPPINE SEA

When the first landing was made in the Marianas, while heavy fighting for Saipan was in progress and while Guam, Tinian, and

---

[31] Eniwetok handled approximately seventeen hundred arrivals and departures during August, and one day had 144 ships in its lagoon. USSBS, *op. cit.,* 219. See maps, between pp. 8-9, and 754-755.

Rota were still in Japanese hands, a Japanese fleet sortied from San Bernardino and Surigao straits, south of Samar and Leyte in the Philippines, to attack the invading forces and destroy the ships that had brought them. Vice-Admiral Mitscher's fast Task Force 58 of the U. S. Third Fleet was on guard to prevent interference with the invasion.

Both combatants had learned to increase the efficiency of carrier-borne planes by giving them, wherever possible, alternative landing fields ashore, as *Enterprise* had done in the battle for possession of Guadalcanal. Admiral Ozawa hoped to use that tactic to advantage. Approaching the Marianas from the westward through the Philippine Sea June 19, he launched at his longest reach the most powerful attack yet made against United States surface forces, instructing his pilots, whose fuel tanks would be nearly empty when they made their attack, not to try to return to their carriers but to land on Guam or Rota. Refueled and rearmed overnight ashore, his comparatively in-experienced and imperfectly trained replacement pilots could return to their carriers next day, shuttle-bombing the United States fleet both going and coming.

Informed of the approach of the enemy fleet by a series of reports from submarines *Harder, Redfin, Flyingfish, Seahorse,* and *Cavalla,* Admiral Mitscher elected to stay near Saipan to protect the men on the island. He cleared his decks for the use of fighter planes by send-ing off his bombers and torpedo planes to rendezvous to eastward; so his fighters were in position to fly cover for the carriers and for Saipan, and to shoot down enemy aircraft homing on Guam and Rota. For a loss of twenty-six planes and twenty-four pilots and air crewmen, they destroyed 383 enemy planes. Anti-aircraft shot down nineteen.

Ozawa retired in the night to westward. Mitscher followed, and overtook him only by launching 216 planes in midafternoon, June 20, at a distance of 250 miles at the risk of their being overtaken by darkness or of seeing them exhaust their fuel supply before they could return to the carriers. Mitscher had to light up his carriers with beacons to guide them home, and recovered only 116 of the 216 planes he had launched. Eighty aircraft were ditched, twenty shot down, thirty-eight men lost.

Although the enemy surface fleet was not destroyed, three Japanese aircraft carriers and two tankers were sunk, two of the carriers by submarines. One of these was the veteran busy bee *Shokaku,* sunk by *Cavalla* on the submarine's first patrol. The other, *Taiho,* tor-pedoed by *Albacore,* was Japan's newest, the largest in the world,

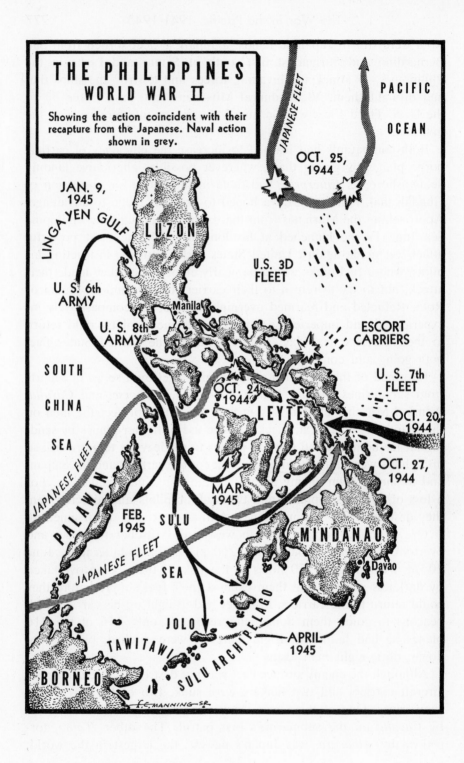

THE PHILIPPINES
WORLD WAR II

Showing the action coincident with their recapture from the Japanese. Naval action shown in grey.

31,000 tons. Major damage was done to four other carriers, battleship *Haruna*, and cruiser *Maya*. The trained air groups of the three carrier divisions engaged were so decimated that Japanese naval aviation was nearly finished as a factor in the war. The battleships *Indiana* and *South Dakota* took some slight bomb damage in the attack of June 19.[32]

THE WESTERN CAROLINES

The Palau island group in the western Carolines were the western-most of the Japanese-mandated former German islands, near enough to serve the Japanese as a base for their original invasions of the Philippines and the Netherlands Indies. They and Yap, on which the United States had a lease on a cable station between the wars, were well worked over in September by carrier planes from Admiral Halsey's fast-moving U. S. Third Fleet, in a sweeping operation which destroyed that month, there and elsewhere, an estimated total of two thousand enemy aircraft.

The 1st USMC Division landed on Peleliu in the Palau group September 15, and the 81st Infantry Division on Angaur, south of Peleliu, two days later. The conquest of both islands, except snipers hidden out in caves, was completed by September 30. Ulithi was occupied September 21, and an advanced naval base was established there which proved useful in subsequent naval operations around the Philippines. Husbanding its waning strength, the Japanese fleet did not interfere with the conquest of the Carolines.

The conquest of Peleliu coincided chronologically with that of Morotai, south of Mindanao, by the 31st and 32nd divisions, of the Southwest Pacific Command. The two great offensive movements were ready to meet and concentrate for a time on the Philippines.

LEYTE ISLAND

While running interference for the Peleliu and Morotai landings by bombing enemy installations in the Philippines, Admiral Halsey gained encouraging information about the state of Japanese defenses in the islands which prompted him to suggest that the invasion of Leyte island, planned for December 20, be made October 20. The admiral's suggestion was forwarded with favorable recommendations

[32] *Ibid.*, 209-272; Roscoe, *op. cit.*, 379-383. Within one month Admiral Nagumo was killed on Saipan; Premier Tojo resigned; Admiral Shimada was replaced as Japanese Navy Minister by Admiral Nomura; Franklin D. Roosevelt was renominated for a fourth term as president of the United States; and an attempt was made to assassinate Hitler.

by General MacArthur and Admiral Nimitz to the joint chiefs of staff, then in conference at Chateau Frontenac, Quebec, and was immediately approved by them. Troops already battle-loaded for Yap and other intermediate landing points were diverted to join the others in an immediate move on the major objective.

In a series of preliminary air strikes on Okinawa, Luzon, and Formosa Task Force 38 provoked the most violent enemy air resistance so far encountered, and made itself the enemy target, east of Formosa, in the fiercest battle of the war to date between ship and land-based aircraft. In these engagements the Japanese lost, in the air and on the ground, 650 planes. Comparable damage was inflicted upon their shops, factories, and bases. Task Force 38 lost seventy-six planes in combat and in operational accidents.

The disparity in losses was only partially due to the fanatical zeal of the Japanese pilots to injure their enemy. They were third- and fourth-string substitutes, unseasoned and inadequately trained. Their factories could turn out planes faster than the schools could turn out skilled pilots. Their training schedule had been foreshortened by the urgency of their need, and by lack of motor fuel for training planes. The United States carriers, on the other hand, were getting better fighter protection than two years earlier, and had greatly improved their communications and combat-control techniques. Japanese losses of air strength in October, 1944, on Okinawa, Formosa, and Luzon—with the breakdown of communications in battle, and the failure of land-based forces to contribute effectively to the supreme naval effort—helped materially to determine the outcome of the battles for Leyte island and Leyte Gulf.

An armada of 53 assault transports, 54 assault cargo ships, 151 tank landing craft, 72 infantry landing craft, 16 rocket-launching ships, and 400 assorted amphibious craft carried the U. S. Sixth Army to Leyte October 20, under an air umbrella of planes from eighteen escort carriers. Six battleships, with cruisers and destroyers, served as naval escort, with carrier task forces also on guard at sea. Leyte Gulf swarmed with ships as the troops went ashore south of Tacloban.

The military problem for the reoccupying force was to seize and hold the island as a base for further operations. For the Japanese the problem was to reinforce the island garrison, which was done principally through the west-coast port Ormoc. They put in the best they had. General Tomoyuki Yamashita, victor at Singapore and on Bataán, returned from Manchuria to take charge of defense of the Philippines, bringing after him from Shanghai one of the finest Japanese divisions, the 1st, of the touted Kwantung army. The defense sustained frequent heavy losses in persistent attempts to send reinforcements by water to Ormoc. The offensive was always handicapped by high winds, violent rainstorms, deep mud, and lack of decent roads.

United States troops closed in at the end of November on Limon in the northern part of the island. Ormoc was captured December 11 after a new landing on the west coast near the town by the 77th Division. Japanese resistance on the island was crushed by the end of 1944.

Leyte Gulf

The Japanese high command realized that holding the Philippines was vital to the continuation of the war. If the Allies regained the Philippines they could close the China Sea to Japanese ships, with or without Hainan, Hong Kong, Shanghai, or Formosa. With the sea lane to the southward closed, Japan would be cut off from the oil of Sumatra and Borneo and could be strangled. If the fleet continued to be based—as much of it then was—close to its oil at Singapore and Brunei Bay on Borneo, it could not be armed from home. If it was brought home it could not be fueled from the Indies. As Admiral Kurita put it, there would be no sense in saving the fleet at the expense of the loss of the Philippines.

So the decision was made at the highest levels to commit the last line of naval defense, the battle fleet, in a decisive engagement to break up the Leyte invasion. The target of the counterattack was the transports and supply ships crowded into Leyte Gulf. To reach its objective the attack must break the cordon of defense maintained around the Leyte area by the U. S. Seventh and Third battle fleets.[33]

Admiral Toyoda knew when the first rangers landed, in the evening of October 17, on the islets in the mouth of Leyte Gulf, to secure the entry. Immediately he set his fleets in motion toward the area indicated. Down from their bases in the Inland Sea and the Pescadores and up from the Singapore area the surviving warships were summoned to what their commanders knew might well be—and

---

[33] The Seventh, under Admiral Kinkaid, came up from the southwest Pacific with MacArthur, the Third under Admiral Halsey across the central Pacific under the general direction of Admiral Nimitz. The Japanese combined fleet was serving under its third commander in chief, Admiral Toyoda. Admiral Yamamoto was shot down over Bougainville in April, 1943. Admiral Koga went down with a seaplane in a storm, March 31, 1944, in an attempted flight from Palau to Davao.

what proved to be—their last rendezvous as a fleet. On October 20, Leyte landing day, the principal Japanese battleship and cruiser force was replenishing its fuel tanks at Brunei Bay in northwest Borneo; Admiral Ozawa with a combined carrier-battleship-cruiser force designed to appear as the principal attack group, but so poor in planes that it could serve only as bait for a diversion, sailed southward from the home islands; and all available submarines were ordered south from Formosa to watch the entrances to water passages through the Philippines.

United States submarines were also watching the passages, and radioed timely warnings of enemy fleet movements off Borneo, Palawan, and Manila. The reports were correctly interpreted as indicating that the largest battleship and cruiser group coming up through the South China Sea from Brunei Bay would approach Leyte Gulf either by the southern route, by way of the Sulu and Mindanao seas and Surigao Strait—i.e., south of Negros—or by the northern through the Sibuyan Sea and San Bernardino Strait, north of Samar. The latter was thought more probable. The Japanese were planning to approach by both routes; but the U. S. Third and Seventh fleets had time to prepare to defend both. Two Japanese support groups tried the southern approach, one coming down from the Ryukyus and Pescadores, the other up from Brunei Bay by way of the Sulu Sea.

Vice-Admiral T. Kurita, with a central attack force of four battleships including the two giants *Musashi* and *Yamato*, eight cruisers, and eleven destroyers, was to push through the Sibuyan Sea and San Bernardino Strait, then turn southward to Leyte Gulf, where he would be met by a supporting attack force approaching through Surigao Strait. It was hoped that the battleships and carriers coming down from the north, though more imposing than formidable, might create a diversion.

Kurita had trouble getting through. Off Palawan, before turning eastward into the Sibuyan Sea, he lost two heavy cruisers, *Maya* and *Atago*, to submarines *Dace* and *Darter*. A third, *Takao*, was disabled for duration and sent back to Brunei Bay with an escort of two destroyers. Some confusion of command ensued while Kurita transferred with his staff to *Yamato*.[34]

In the Sibuyan Sea, October 23, Kurita's fleet was attacked by planes of the United States carrier fleets east of the islands. He lost

---

[34] *Darter* ran aground. *Dace* rescued her crew and *Nautilus* destroyed her by gunfire. Roscoe, *op. cit.*, 392-395.

there one of his giant battleships, *Musashi*—63,000 tons standard displacement, nine 18.1-inch guns, speed 26 knots, but not immune to bombs or torpedoes. Once he turned back; but he turned again, threaded the familiar San Bernardino Strait at high speed in the darkness, the night of October 23-24, and appeared off Samar in the morning.

Meanwhile two uncoördinated support attack forces came to grief south of Leyte. As the Japanese warships filed through the narrow Surigao Strait, the old battleships of Rear Admiral J. B. Oldendorf's task force of the U. S. Seventh Fleet, guarding the convoys in the gulf, crossed their course in a manner like the crossing of a T. Of the first group, Nishimura's, two battleships, a cruiser, and three destroyers were sunk, largely by gunfire. Some of the later damage was done by collisions and torpedoes. Japanese casualties were estimated at more than five thousand. No one got through. A crippled destroyer limped away but was found and sunk next day.

The eastern exit from San Bernardino Strait was well guarded October 24. Next morning it was unguarded. Kurita's luck had changed. He had expected to have to fight his way out. Unaware that the diversionary force including battleships, cruisers, and carriers which was approaching from the north was only a toothless decoy, and having been given greatly exaggerated estimates of its strength, and of the damage done to Kurita in the Sibuyan Sea, Admiral Halsey rushed off in the night with his fastest and strongest, including Mitscher's Task Force 38, to meet the new threat. Off Cape Engaño he met it with ninety ships against nineteen and destroyed it, sinking all four of its carriers. Then he rushed back, already too late.

The sacrifice of Japan's last aircraft carrier task force as a diversionary target was the end of the voyage for that part of her navy; but it diverted United States Task Force 38 from the defense of Leyte Gulf at a critical moment. While Halsey was gone Kurita attacked a weak Seventh Fleet outpost of light escort carriers, destroyers, and destroyer escorts—all that then stood between him and his quarry in Leyte Gulf.

The destroyers attacked boldly with guns and torpedoes, and laid smoke screens while the escort carriers launched attack planes and fled to windward to be hidden by the smoke. One United States carrier, *Princeton*, two escort carriers, *Gambier Bay* and *Saint Lô*, and a destroyer escort were sunk. Three Japanese heavy cruisers were disabled by aircraft and one by a destroyer's torpedo. *Yamato's* superstructure, radar, and radio communications gear were so wrecked as to blind, deafen, and partially isolate her. Reconnaissance planes failed to return. The fleet had no air cover. Little information or help was received from ashore; and the U. S. Third Fleet might return at any time. The leader feared a trap. So Admiral Kurita, who until then had pushed on with such hardihood under great adversity with the central attack force for which all else had been sacrificed, reversed course within reach of his objective and retraced his way through San Bernardino Strait.[35]

Carrier-based and land-based planes harried the retiring Japanese fleets October 26, killing crippled ships and running total enemy losses up to three battleships including *Musashi*, four aircraft carriers including *Zuikaku*, ten cruisers, nine destroyers, and a submarine: 305,710 tons, 45 percent of the tonnage committed. The Japanese battle fleet never fought again as a fleet.[36] The United States fleets lost 36,600 tons, 2.8 percent of tonnage committed.

LUZON

While the conquest of Leyte island was completed in December, 1944, the U. S. Seventh Fleet escort carriers moved into the Sulu Sea in support of a task force of two regiments which landed on the southern coast of Mindoro. Sensitive to any new threat to their South China Sea life line, the Japanese had expected Palawan to be the object of the next attack; so Mindoro was lightly held and quickly taken. Airfields were at once established for the protection of an amphibious expedition to Luzon, and feints were made to indicate that the landing would be made on the south coast of that island.

In early January, 1945, a U.S. Sixth Army assault force gathered on its transports east of Leyte and threaded the recently Japanese-controlled Surigao Strait and the Mindanao and Sulu seas. As the landing fleet turned northward off the west coast of Luzon, its mine-sweeping,

[35] *Princeton*, the first fast United States aircraft carrier lost since *Hornet*, two years earlier, was sunk by land-based planes.

The last surviving carrier of the Pearl Harbor task force, *Zuikaku*, was one of the four of Ozawa's diversionary force, all sunk October 25.

The first organized *Kamikaze* suicide attacks were made by fifty-two Japanese planes in the battle off Samar. Making mere guided missiles of their bomb-loaded planes, one-way pilots crash-dived them on their targets. One helped sink escort carrier *Saint Lô*.

Survivors of *Gambier Bay* and screening vessels sunk were not picked up for two days. Many of them died awaiting rescue. Forty-five survivors of destroyer *Johnson* were seen alive in the water but not found. Comer Vann Woodward, *The Battle for Leyte Gulf* (New York, 1947), 216.

[36] USSBS, *op. cit.*, 280-321. See also C. V. Woodward, *op. cit.*, and James A. Field, *The Japanese at Leyte Gulf: The Sho Operation* (Princeton, 1947), 1947.

bombardment, and escort carrier groups were attacked by land-based Japanese suicide-diving planes, despite the efforts of planes from the United States fast carrier force to keep the Luzon airfields blanketed. On January 6, sixteen ships were hit. Ten of them suffered serious damage. The landing was made successfully, however, at Lingayén Gulf January 9. Sixty-eight thousand troops were landed along fifteen miles of beach that day, and a comfortably deep beachhead was established. Surprised and confused by General MacArthur's succession of swift moves, the Japanese failed to concentrate their opposition at the landing point rather obviously indicated by topography, where they themselves landed in 1941.

Deploying a portion of his combat troops in position to defend the beachhead against strong enemy forces in the hills to the north and east, the United States commander pushed an armored spearhead, as the Japanese had done three years before, southward to Clark Field and Manila. A second landing was made at Subic Bay on January 29, which quickly sealed off the Bataán peninsula at its base. Two days later the U.S. 11th Airborne Division made an amphibious west-coast landing at Nasugbu, south of Manila. Within another week the 1st Cavalry and 11th Airborne divisions were closing in on Manila from north and south; but resistance continued there until February 23, and parts of the city were destroyed. Parachute and amphibious landings were made on Corregidor on February 16, and enemy resistance on the tunneled island ceased about two weeks later. Manila Bay was soon thereafter open.[37]

COMPLETION OF REOCCUPATION OF THE PHILIPPINES

The reconquest of Palawan island in late February provided airfields for the policing of the South China Sea. Landings made against feeble resistance at the landing points on Panay, Cebu, and Negros during March were followed by stubborn and prolonged fighting in the hills. The reconquest of Mindanao took from March to May. Tarakan and Borneo were retaken by Australian and Netherlands East Indies troops in May, Brunei Bay and adjacent airfields by Australians on June 10, Balikpapan in July. Resistance on Luzon continued through the summer; but the area under United States control was steadily expanded by forces converging from Legaspi and Manila and pushing northward and northeastward from the central Luzon plain. The

[37] Marshall, *op. cit.*, 76-79. An unknown number of Japanese, in excess of 4,215, were killed on Corregidor. United States casualties were 136 killed, 8 missing, 531 wounded.

Cagayan Valley was swept clear by July 1. Japanese losses in the Philippines were by that time 317,000 killed and 7236 captured, against United States casualties of approximately 60,628 killed, wounded, and missing.[38]

To both belligerents Luzon meant more than Luzon, and to Mac-Arthur more than a victorious return. It meant position and the virtual closing of the South China Sea. In mid-January a fast United States carrier force ran the strait between Formosa and Luzon and swept southward along the China coast to Hong Kong and Camranh Bay, sinking forty-seven ships including seven large tankers, a total of 150,000 tons. Access to the southern resources area and its oil was progressively denied to Japan.

In four months, in defense of the Philippines for the sake of access to the resources of the area she had seized three years earlier, Japan's military and naval leaders sacrificed most of her surface fleet and seven thousand aircraft. As a desperate last resort they then turned to bleeding tactics, suicide attacks; but even *Kamikaze* pilots had to take off on their one-way missions inadequately trained, for lack of motor fuel. Her surviving battleships and cruisers, similarly hamstrung, huddled at scattered anchorages in the Inland Sea to await their turn at suicide or carrier-borne air attack.

CARRYING THE WAR TO JAPAN, 1945

Long-Range Bombing

THE UNITED STATES B-29

The long-range bomber called the B-29 "superfortress," brought out by the United States Army Air Forces in 1944, was a new threat to Japan. It could fly farther and carry a heavier load of explosives, with a larger crew and more armament for its own defense, than either of its predecessors, the Liberator or the B-17 or flying fortress. From Chengtu in China or from the Marianas, it could reach the home islands of Japan in a flight of less than eight hours. Radar equipment enabled it to bomb with some accuracy—though often with less than enough to satisfy those responsible for its use—in darkness, through clouds or overcast, or from altitudes beyond the reach of ordinary anti-aircraft fire. Carrying incendiaries as well as explosives over the highly inflammable bamboo-built cities of Japan, it brought fire and terror to whole urban areas, and destruction to war industries

---

[38] *Ibid.,* 83. See map, p. 778.

and shipyards. Only Kyoto, of Japanese cities of over 100,000 population, escaped its lethal attention.

THE MARIANAS

The first big B-29 strike went off to Tokyo from Saipan in the Marianas November 24, 1944. Thereafter, the raids steadily increased in frequency, in numbers of men and planes involved, and in destructiveness. The distances, however, although not beyond the capacity of such a plane operating at maximum efficiency under favorable conditions, were enormous for one partially disabled by enemy action or mechanical failure, or with wounded men aboard. Some losses were taken by enemy action over Japan, more by fuel failure or forced ditching of planes on the long return flight to Saipan. Bomber flights from Saipan to Tokyo were often intercepted by enemy fighters from Iwo Jima. The range was too great for United States fighter escort planes. United States installations on Saipan were occasionally bombed by Japanese planes from Iwo Jima. The full realization of the potentialities of the Marianas as a bomber base clearly called for the conquest of Iwo.

Iwo Jima

Iwo Jima was the first Japanese possession to be invaded in the war. It was a small, evil-smelling, sulfurous volcanic island, ugly, and valuable only for its strategic location with reference to the air or sea approach to Honshu from the south or the southeast, less than eight hundred miles from Tokyo. It had two airfields and as an ocean outpost useful to Japan was bombed occasionally, as if for practice, through 1944 by planes of the United States carrier fleets engaged in the Marshalls, Marianas, and Carolines operations. It was defended by a garrison of something more than twenty thousand men, under command of General Todamishi Kuribayashi. Late in 1944 it was marked for conquest.

The Iwo operation was primarily naval. The 3rd, 4th, and 5th divisions of the United States Marine Corps trained for it in the Hawaiian Islands, as did the communications personnel of the Army Air Forces who were to set up, maintain, and operate the radio-teletype contacts with the heavy bomber force headquarters on Saipan and the Iwo airfields when they should be taken. A fleet of 495 ships carried an assault force of 75,144 men and 36,164 garrison troops. It was covered by seven old battleships, four heavy cruisers, and fifteen destroyers. Just before the invasion, February 16-17, and again on February 25, 1945, a fast carrier force of 118 ships including eight battleships and seventeen aircraft carriers with 1170 embarked aircraft made the first carrier-based raids on the Japanese home islands in the vicinity of Tokyo.

After a long period of saturation bombing and bombardment, a landing was made on the southeast shore of Iwo February 19, 1945. It soon became apparent that although the intensive preparation had pulverized the surface of the ill-favored island, its elaborate and well-protected underground defenses had not been seriously disturbed. From concealed and comparatively undamaged emplacements in the face of an extinct volcano, Mount Suribachi, which dominated one end of the beach, and from similar emplacements in the face of a hill at the other end, a murderous cross fire was poured into the landing zone, where the marines were for a while pinned down. Wreckage of equipment in a jumble of supplies made the area a beachcomber's paradise after the guns firing into it were silenced; but it was purgatory while the heat was on. Thousands were wounded there, and hundreds died.

Nearly four weeks of vicious fighting followed. The last Japanese sortie was made March 16, ten days after the island had been called secure; and for weeks thereafter, rather than surrender, die-hard defenders were being burned or blasted out of hiding places under ground, from which they had ventured forth at night or sniped by day.

The defense of Iwo Jima cost the Japanese the lives of an estimated total of 21,304 men, of whom 13,234 were counted and buried by the United States forces. Two hundred and twelve were taken prisoner. United States casualties, naval losses not included, were 4590 killed, 301 missing, 15,954 wounded. Total enemy and United States casualties were nearly equal in number. The disparity was in the numbers of the dead.

The use made of Iwo Jima went far toward balancing its fearful cost. The first airfield taken was at once put into operation under occasional mortar fire from the enemy holding higher ground. The number of lives saved in emergency bomber landings alone exceeded the number lost in the conquest of the island. Installations on Saipan were no longer bombed by planes from Iwo. No longer intercepted by fighter planes from Iwo, from April 7 the B-29's picked up fighter escort there for their protection to and over their targets. Crippled planes, or planes with wounded men aboard, could land on Iwo on their return. Heavier bomb loads could sometimes be carried, with the possibility of topping off at Iwo. Soon Iwo Mustang fighter planes were flying strafing missions of their own. A submarine and seaplane lifesaving service was maintained from the island to Japan. A meteorological service station was set up there, and aerial reconnaissance constantly carried on. As long as the war lasted, and for several months thereafter, Iwo was the hub and center of the heavy air-borne traffic of the western Pacific.

Okinawa

CONQUEST

From the conquest of Iwo Jima, while the reoccupation of the Philippines by the southwest Pacific area forces proceeded, the strategic assault forces of the United States central Pacific area turned their attention to Okinawa. Okinawa was the largest island in the Ryukyus, large enough to accommodate several great airfields when taken and to serve as a staging area for large numbers of troops for further operations. It offered excellent anchorages and sites for naval installations, lay athwart Japan's sea and air routes to Asia and the South China Sea, and was less than 350 miles from her home islands. The island was expected to be stubbornly defended and it was. It was more strongly garrisoned and gunned than United States military intelligence had estimated, and its defense was well planned and tenacious.

To provide an anchorage and seaplane base, nearby Kerama Retto was seized first, March 26, by the U.S. 77th Division. To prevent naval interference Japanese warships and naval installations in the Inland Sea were bombed by carrier aircraft March 19 and 24.

The Okinawa operation was one of the most difficult and costly of the Pacific war. The expeditionary force consisted of 1213 ships and 451,866 ground troops, covered and supported by a United States fast carrier force of eighty-two ships and a British carrier force of twenty-two. The British bombed Formosa and other Japanese bases.

A comparatively easy landing was made on the southwestern coast of Okinawa April 1. Driving right across the narrow island, the marines turned northward and the army infantry divisions southward, where the latter encountered the principal enemy resistance in well-prepared defensive positions, burrowed into caves in the limestone and coral cliffs and ready to pour fire down the ravines. Within a week four divisions were ashore and Wontan Airfield was available for marine corps fighter planes. Within three weeks the northern part of the island was secure and the marines could join the army infantry in the south. Strong artillery support came constantly from the heavy guns of battleships offshore and from carrier planes. Yet organized resistance was not fully quenched until June 21. Probably more than 110,000 Japanese had by that time been killed on the island and about 7500 taken prisoner. United States casualties ashore were 7213 killed and 31,081 wounded. Three days before the end, with his battle virtually won, the United States commanding general, Simon Buckner, was killed.[39]

THE FLEET THAT CAME TO STAY

Both by sea and by air the Japanese resorted to suicide attacks to interfere with the Okinawa operation and to sell their island as their lives at the highest possible price. On April 6 their one remaining giant battleship, *Yamato*, with light cruiser *Yahagi* and eight destroyers, sortied through Bungo Channel east of Kyushu and proceeded down through the East China Sea under orders to approach Okinawa from the northwest and attack United States shipping there. Neither *Yamato* nor her escort was expected to return, but it was considered more consistent with the traditions of the imperial navy to send them out than to conserve them or have them await destruction in the Inland Sea. Other warships in operational condition would have gone out—and down—with them if there had been fuel oil for all. The 2500 tons necessary for the limited operation undertaken were procured only with great difficulty.

Yamato and escort were sighted by United States submarines *Threadfin* and *Hackleback* as they made their exit from Bungo Channel in the late afternoon of April 6. Next day they were discovered and attacked by United States carrier planes in the East China Sea between Kyushu and Okinawa. Holed in her starboard side by a torpedo, *Yamato* took five bomb hits and nine torpedoes in her port side, capsized, and sank. *Yahagi* and five destroyers were also sunk. Three destroyers limped back to Sasebo sorely damaged. Japanese gunfire knocked down ten United States planes. Eight United States pilots and eight aircrewmen were lost. Cruiser *Hancock* was hit but not sunk by a *Kamikaze*.

The heaviest United States losses afloat off Okinawa were occasioned by *Kamikaze* diving-plane attacks. The tiniest radar picket boats, far out on the perimeter of the operations area, were not too small to

---

[39] *Ibid.*; USSBS, *op. cit.*, 326. General Marshall's estimate was 109,629 Japanese killed and 7871 prisoners; the USSBS, 131,000 killed and 7400 prisoners.

be smothered by them; the anti-aircraft fire of the largest battleships and best-armed anti-aircraft cruisers was not fierce enough to deter them. Day after day they came, ten times in great organized attacks. Never had the United States Navy lost so many ships in so short a time: thirty-six were sunk, twenty-eight of them by air attack, of which twenty-six were victims of the *Kamikaze*. None lost, however, was larger than a destroyer. No transport was lost.

Over the Ryukus and Kyushu during the Okinawa campaign the Japanese lost more than 7800 planes, of which more than 3000 were shot down by United States naval and marine corps planes, 400 by naval anti-aircraft, 558 by B-29's. Operational losses were reported as 2655, an indication of insufficient pilot training and inefficiency of their last-string ground crews. *Yamato* took down 2498 men.

In addition to ships sunk, United States losses afloat, attributable to the Okinawa operation, from April 1 to July 1 were 368 ships damaged, 763 planes lost, 4907 men killed or missing, and 4824 wounded.[40]

The price was high. The prize was a new base near Japan from which to mount the final offensives which seemed likely to be necessary.

Climax and Surrender

BLOCKADE AND BOMBING

Through July and August, 1945, the naval and air blockade of Japan continued, intensified by the mining of some of her harbor mouths and coastal waters. On March 19, June 22, and July 24 and 28, two thousand carrier-borne and Okinawa-based United States planes completed the destruction of the warships in her Inland Sea. During July and August nineteen Japanese warships and eight railroad ferries were sunk and two ferries beached, nineteen warships and two ferries damaged. It was during this final period that United States submarines first entered the Sea of Japan to attack the last remaining shipping lines to the Asiatic mainland. Six times in July and thrice in August, planes of the United States fast carrier force of fourteen carriers, eight battleships, fifteen cruisers, and fifty-seven destroyers struck at the Japanese home islands. Five strikes were at Tokyo. A British force of four carriers, a battleship, six cruisers, and seventeen destroyers operated with the United States fleets. From new airfields

[40] USSBS, *op. cit.*, 324-327, 340; Hanson Baldwin, New York *Times*, March 26, 1950, pp. 62-64, 67-69. Cruiser *Pittsburg*, carrier *Hornet* (VIII), and eight other ships were damaged by typhoon June 4.

on Okinawa hundreds of heavy bombers and strafing fighter planes joined hundreds from the Marianas and Iwo Jima in incessant hammering, with hundreds of thousands of tons of bombs, at her industries and transportation system. Seven times in July and once in August coastal targets were shelled from the sea. Against a total Allied loss of 258 planes to enemy anti-aircraft and 104 in operational mishaps, 1386 Japanese planes were destroyed in the air and on the ground and 1980 operationally.[41]

It was obvious that the capacity of the armed forces of Japan to resist invasion was being sensibly diminished. But her army, in the home islands and in eastern China, Manchuria, and Korea, was known to have five million trained men left; and it became apparent that the remaining resources of her air force were being husbanded for *Kamikaze* attacks and landings on the Okinawa airfields, and to resist invasion.

It was assumed that invasion of the home islands to compel surrender would be necessary. Two major invasion operations were planned, one on Kyushu in November, 1945, and one on Honshu about four months later. It was estimated that the invasions might cost the Allies a million casualties. Whether another war must then be fought against the Kwantung and other Japanese armies on the Asiatic mainland would depend upon the will and the capacity of those armies to continue hostilities—which were little doubted—and upon whether Russia made a timely entry into the war as her leaders had repeatedly but secretly declared that she would do.

HIROSHIMA AND NAGASAKI

For years, in a race of death rather with the Germans than with the Japanese, British and American scientists labored to produce a new type of bomb using the heat and explosive energy of atomic fission. On July 16, 1945, a bomb of the new type was detonated at a desert proving ground in New Mexico and found to be terribly effective. How destructive it would be if detonated in midair over a city or an industrial center, or whether it could be so detonated, remained to be proved in practice. The decision to use it was made on military grounds, in which an estimate of its effect on enemy morale outweighed ethical and moral considerations.

The decision to use the atomic bomb was based, as such wartime decisions must usually be based, upon incomplete information about the enemy. It was known that the blockade was steadily

[41] USSBS, *op. cit.*, 351.

strangling Japan and that the bombing was crippling her industries and transportation system, but not how near she was to the end of her resources or how soon she might collapse. It was known that the entry of the Soviet Union into the war, if and when it came, would deal a lethal blow to any Japanese hope of a negotiated peace without victory or defeat; but with or without Russian intervention there was urgent reason to bring the war to an end at the earliest possible moment. It was known that there were a peace movement and a peace party in Japan, but the die-hards were still in control and were believed likely to retain control until the emperor himself moved to surrender. It was thought that the use of the atomic bomb would shock the mikado into making that vital move, that he could then be used by the Allies to procure the immediate surrender of his armies and the acceptance of the surrender terms by his people, and that the war could so be soonest ended.

Honorably accepting his share of responsibility for the decision, United States Secretary of War Henry L. Stimson wrote afterward:

We had developed a weapon of such a revolutionary character that its use against the enemy might well be expected to produce exactly the kind of shock on the Japanese ruling oligarchy which we desired, strengthening the position of those who wished peace, and weakening that of the military party. . . .

Hiroshima was bombed on August 6, and Nagasaki on August 9. These two cities were active working parts of the Japanese war effort. One was an army center; the other was naval and industrial. Hiroshima was the headquarters of the Japanese army defending southern Japan and was a major military storage and assembly point. Nagasaki was a major seaport and it contained several large industrial plants of great wartime importance. . . .

In order to end the war in the shortest possible time and to avoid the enormous losses of human life which otherwise confronted us, I felt that we must use the Emperor as our instrument to command and compel his people to cease fighting and subject themselves to our authority through him, and that to accomplish this we must give him and his controlling advisers a compelling reason to accede to our demands. This reason furthermore must be of such a nature that his people could understand his decision. The bomb seemed to me to furnish a unique instrument for that purpose.

My chief purpose was to end the war in victory with the least possible cost in the lives of the men in the armies which I had helped to raise. In the light of the alternatives which, on a fair estimate, were open to us I believe that no man, in our position and subject to our responsibilities, holding in his hands a weapon of such possibilities for accomplishing this purpose and saving those lives, could have failed to use it and afterward looked his countrymen in the face.

More than a hundred thousand people died in Hiroshima and Nagasaki as a result of two bomb bursts. A comparable number died in Tokyo in fire raids of the type which in the year of grace 1945 had come to be known as "conventional," involving several hundred B-29's and several thousand tons of bombs, including napalm incendiaries. If two of the former meant less of the latter, then the all-inclusive overall atrocity, war itself, would be sooner ended.[42]

USSR's ENTRY INTO THE WAR

The use of the atomic bomb at Hiroshima did not bring the immediate surrender which those responsible for the momentous decision to use it hoped it would. While the mikado and his advisers hesitated, two more heavy blows were struck. The Soviet Union declared war on August 8, and on August 9 an atomic bomb was dropped on Nagasaki with results more devastating than at Hiroshima. The action of the USSR had been presaged by statements made by Stalin at Teheran, Yalta, Potsdam, and elsewhere, and was taken precisely when Stalin had promised that it would be taken—three months after the termination of hostilities in Germany. The Red Army used the interval to move to the Far East the additional divisions, equipment, and supplies it needed for a quick and easy conquest of Manchuria, southern Sakhalin, and Shimusu and Paramushiro in the Kurile Islands, all of which it overran within two weeks. Red Army troops entered Korea August 12.

V-J DAY AND TOKYO BAY, AUGUST 15 AND SEPTEMBER 2, 1945

Under the triple impact of two atomic bombs and the Soviet Union's entry into the war, the Japanese government let it be known on August 10 that it was ready to surrender militarily, with the understanding that the prerogatives of the emperor as sovereign in Japan should be preserved. The Allies replied August 11 through the United States secretary of state that the emperor should remain and retain his title, but that from the moment of surrender his authority and that of his government to rule the state should be subject to the supreme commander of the Allied powers.

Beyond unconditional military surrender, cessation of hostilities, and disarmament, the general Allied terms as published in the Pots-

[42] *Harper's Magazine,* February, 1947; *On Active Service* (New York, 1948), 612-633.

dam Declaration of July 26 were already known: limitation of Japan's sovereignty to her home islands; occupation of her territory by the Allies; liquidation of war industries; trial and punishment of war criminals; freedom of speech, thought, and religion; and removal of obstacles to the revival and strengthening of democratic tendencies among the people. They had been ostentatiously ignored by Premier Suzuki when announced.[43]

At midnight August 14-15 President Truman and Prime Minister Attlee were able to announce that the surrender terms had been accepted. Next day the emperor gave the cease-fire order to his troops. The instrument of surrender was handed to representatives of the Japanese armed forces by General MacArthur at his headquarters August 19. The Kwantung army in Manchuria surrendered to the Red Army August 21. United States troops took over the Atsugi Airfield near Tokyo August 29 and began the occupation of Japan. The Yokosuka naval base at the mouth of Tokyo Bay was occupied August 30 by the United States Marine Corps regiment which had been overwhelmed in the invasion of the Philippines. The British landed at Hong Kong August 30, but formal Japanese surrender there was not effected until September 16.

Aboard the United States battleship *Missouri*, at anchor in Tokyo Bay, the instrument of surrender of the Japanese imperial government, general headquarters, and all of its armed forces was signed September 2, 1945, by Mamoru Shigemitsu of the Foreign Office and General Yoshijiro Umezu for the armed forces. General MacArthur signed as supreme Allied commander, and Admiral Nimitz for the armed forces of the United States. Generals Wainwright and Percival, who had surrendered Bataán and Singapore in 1942, were present.

Separate surrenders of scattered units were subsequently signed: for the southwest Pacific area off Rabaul September 6, to General Chiang Kai-shek at Nanking September 9, on Borneo September 10, at Rangoon and on New Guinea and Malaya September 13. United States troops landed in south Korea September 8 to receive the surrender of Japanese troops there south of the thirty-eighth parallel of latitude, while by arrangement between the governments of the USA and the USSR Soviet troops accepted the surrender of those north of that parallel.[44]

The war cost Japan more than five and a half million casualties, of

---

[43] See p. 743.

[44] So arose, somewhat fortuitously, an unnatural geographical division of Korea which, by failure of the occupying powers to achieve a mutually acceptable occupation policy or agreement as to the character of the government of a unified Korea after evacuation by their occupation forces, led to a world crisis in 1950.

whom more than half a million were civilians. Army and navy deaths, including *Kamikaze* and other suicides, were about half a million, civilian deaths more than 200,000. Of her twelve battleships she had one left; of twenty-two carriers and escort carriers, none operational; of forty-three cruisers, none operational; of 165 destroyers, twenty-six heavily damaged; of 104 submarines, twenty-two, six of them German. Her merchant shipping losses exceeded by a third the tonnage with which she started the war, and replacements by new construction were less than two-fifths of losses. Personnel losses on her ocean-going merchant marine were 116,000, of whom 27,000 were dead and missing.[45]

The United States sent 1,250,000 men to the Pacific. The victory there cost in men's lives 41,322 dead, 170,596 total casualties.[46]

[45] Roscoe, *op. cit.*, 492; report by surrender envoys, Chicago *Daily News*, August 22, 1945.
[46] Marshall, *op. cit.*, 107; Hanson Baldwin, New York *Times*, January 11, 1948, p. 31.

CHAPTER 17

The Problem of Freedom from Fear

THE FRUITS OF VICTORY

The fruits of victory were Dead Sea fruit, bitter to the taste. Moral and physical weariness lay heavy on the victors, weakness on the liberated. Despair and social disintegration prevailed in the devastated homelands of the vanquished. Occupation of former enemy territory was a thankless task and aid to former foes as to wartime friends a continuing burden for which compensation could scarcely be expected.

It seemed all too likely that, as Stalin had said at Yalta, the peace would be made and kept only as "the three" of Yalta made and kept it; but such unity of purpose as had been temporarily achieved between the principal powers lately allied or associated in the war was soon lost. President Roosevelt died in April, 1945, worn out, disillusioned, and disturbed over his apparent failure to win and hold the confidence of Stalin. The people of Great Britain, with peacemaking and long-deferred reforms at home in mind, chose in July, 1945, another leader than the lion-hearted one who had led them through the war. The new president and the new premier found Stalin and his associates more difficult to understand or deal with in peacetime than their predecessors had found them while at war and faced by a common danger. National objectives of the Soviet Union and of the western powers diverged; mutual suspicion, always present, came stark and ugly into the open; and the tone of international intercourse, especially between the Soviet Union and the western powers, deteriorated. The behavior of the Russians indicated that so far as the Soviet Union was concerned, far from having ended as the western world would have chosen to assume that it had done, the war had only passed into another phase. Occasional expressions of the same opinion in the United States were publicized in Russia.

The Face of Death

THE THREAT OF WAR

Communist propaganda revived, after the danger of attack by Germany and Japan was past, the Marxist theory that capitalism and communism were naturally, inevitably, irreconcilably at war. That did not mean necessarily that warfare must be waged incessantly by military means, but that the incompatibility and the threat of war were constant. The "capitalist" democracies were pictured as the putative aggressors, the communist "peoples' democracies" as the only true friends of peace. To the peoples of the western world, who for the second time in the twentieth century had hoped that the end of a war might mean the end of war, the thought of a third such experience was abhorrent. They shrank before the threat of it, as they shuddered at the memory of the last.

THE FEAR OF ATOMIC WARFARE

In the conclusion of a statement of his reasons for recommending the use of the atomic bomb against Japan, former Secretary of War Henry L. Stimson wrote for publication in *Harper's Magazine* in February, 1947:

As I read over what I have written, I am aware that much of it, in this year of peace, may have a harsh and unfeeling sound. It would perhaps be possible to say the same things and to say them more gently. But I do not think it would be wise. As I look back over my five years of service as Secretary of War, I see too many stern and heartrending decisions to be willing to pretend that war is anything else than what it is. The face of war is the face of death; death is an inevitable part of every order that a wartime leader gives. The decision to use the atomic bomb was a decision that brought death to over a hundred thousand Japanese. No explanation can change that fact and I do not wish to gloss it over. But this deliberate, premeditated destruction was our least abhorrent choice. The destruction of Hiroshima and Nagasaki put an end to the Japanese war. It stopped the fire raids, and the strangling blockade; it ended the ghastly specter of a clash of great land armies.

In this last great action of the Second World War we were given final proof that war is death. War in the twentieth century has grown steadily more barbarous, more destructive, more debased in all its aspects. Now, with the release of atomic energy, man's ability to destroy himself is very nearly complete. The bombs dropped on Hiroshima and Nagasaki ended a war. They also made it very clear that we must never have another war. This is the lesson men and leaders everywhere must learn, and I believe that when they learn it they will find a way to lasting peace. There is no other choice.[1]

The reception given such books as David Bradley's *No Place to Hide* and John Hersey's *Hiroshima* by the reading public of the United States was an indication of the earnestness with which thoughtful people were questioning both mind and heart as to whether deliberate, premeditated destruction by use of such a weapon as the atomic bomb was necessary, whether it was justifiable even as the least abhorrent choice, whether the United States had forfeited the moral leadership of the Christian democratic world by resorting to it. Of two things thoughtful people were more clearly aware than ever: that the face of war was the face of death, and that they abhorred it. It was part of the tragedy of the twentieth century that others took advantage of their known abhorrence, traded upon their often demonstrated and very real reluctance to go to war, and deprived them of the enjoyment of the peace they had thought they had earned by victory in war. Peace-loving people hoped that eventual conflict between communist and noncommunist half-worlds would be found to be as unnecessary as it seemed to them to be unreasonable and unwise. Only radical communist theory said otherwise; but radical communist theory and a professed fear and hatred of the "capitalist" nations prevailed in the public policy statements of the Soviet Union.

Eventually it was announced that Soviet scientists had produced an atomic bomb. It was revealed that vital secrets of the production of the bomb and the materials from which it was made, in Canada and the United States, had been betrayed in wartime to Soviet agents. So the fear of eventual reprisal quickened the reasoning of the moralizers. The threat of war was widely considered in the western world a threat to the survival of civilization itself.

Trials of War Criminals

QUESTIONS OF LAW AND COMPETENCE OF THE COURTS

The searching questions asked, because questions of conscience as well as of policy were raised, throughout the victorious western world

[1] Also in *On Active Service* (New York, 1948), 633.

in the postwar years as to whether that world had done civilization and the law on which it rested a service or a disservice by use of the atomic bomb were matched by similar challenges of the legality, the moral justification, and the wisdom of the trial of the most prominent of those accused, and the punishment of those found guilty, of crimes against peace, war crimes, and crimes against humanity.

Experience was one determinant of policy but offered little precedent for the punitive action contemplated. In similar circumstances in January, 1920, an international council of premiers called upon the queen of the Netherlands to surrender ex-Kaiser Wilhelm II of Germany for trial by an international court as a war criminal. Among the offenses for which the victors of 1918 proposed to hold the former kaiser morally responsible were the cynical violation of the neutrality of Belgium and Luxemburg, the hostage system, mass deportations, systematic devastation of territories, unrestricted submarine warfare, and acts committed by the German authorities against noncombatants in German-occupied non-German territories.

In addressing their unusual request to the government of the Netherlands, which refused it, the powers conceded that the case under discussion did not fall within the lines of a public accusation of a fundamentally legal nature, but called what they proposed to do an act of high international policy, imposed by the conscience of the universe, for which the procedure was provided in order to give the accused such guarantees as had never been known before in international law.[2]

The decision to bring the war criminals of 1945 to trial was made during the war by the Allies, and each of them had its list of those to be indicted. Government leaders making the decision were not indifferent to the likelihood that the right of the victors to try the vanquished would be challenged on legal, procedural, moral, and practical grounds. Their troops had fought a long war, much of it ruthlessly, against a ruthless enemy, and had been charged by the enemy with the commission of atrocities. Should the punishment of atrocious criminals, then, wait for the appearance upon earth of the perfect ones, without sin and virtuous above reproach, who by their immaculate goodness should be qualified to judge the wicked?[3]

[2] U.S. Department of State, *Papers Relating to the Foreign Relations of the United States. Paris Peace Conference, 1919*, IX (Washington, 1946, publication 2599), 888.

[3] While advancing into Russia the Germans accused the Russians of the murder of more than ten thousand Polish officers and other prisoners found in a mass grave at Katyn, near Smolensk. German ammunition alleged to have been found with the corpses could have been, but was not proved to have been, some sold to the

Experience with Weimar Germany had shown that it was useless to ask the defeated enemy to try his own.[4] Should neutrals then be asked to conduct the trials? What neutrals? Would a nation which had precariously maintained neutrality and avoided active involvement in the war be willing to involve itself so controversially at war's end but before the peace was made? Learned judges could be found in Switzerland; but would they be learned in the laws of the nations in which the crimes in question were alleged to have been committed, or interested in establishing new precedents and definitions in international law? Judges from neutral nations would have to depend in last resort upon Allied prosecutors or lawyers from the liberated nations.

Must action always wait upon precedent? An *ad hoc* international military tribunal was created as an act of policy, to administer and give force to existing international treaties and international law, and deliberately to set a precedent by bringing individuals to trial for acts and policies of their national governments for which they were accused of having shared responsibility. Nazi organizations with thousands of members—the leadership corps, *Schutzstaffel* (SS), *Gestapo*, and security police (*Sicherheitsdienst*, SD)—were put on trial and found guilty, as well as individuals. As used by those who had stood in high places under the Nazi and Japanese regimes the military underling's stereotyped defense that he had acted illegally or inhumanely only under orders which he could not disobey, or that he was not personally responsible for acts of his subordinates, was challenged.

The competence of the court and the legality of its acts were questioned by scrupulous nationals of Allied countries, as well as by the accused and by their friends. Some recalled the ancient maxim that no act was legally punishable which before it was committed or was alleged to have been committed had not been defined as a crime, with a legally established penalty. It was generally conceded that much of the law under which the accused were tried had existed and been generally recognized before the war—the Kellogg-Briand Pact, for

---

Russians by the Germans between 1939 and 1941. The Germans tried in vain to persuade the International Red Cross or some other neutral agency to investigate the atrocity. The Russians denied the accusation and accused the Germans, but broke off relations with the Polish government in exile in London when it raised the question. The USSR never invited an investigation. The "argument from silence" subsequently arose when Russia did not make its Katyn charge a part of the public indictment of the Nazi leaders before the international tribunal at Nuremberg. See *Goebbels Diaries* (Garden City, 1948), 318; Churchill, *op. cit.*, IV, 757-761.

[4] See pp. 94-96.

example, with its general renunciation of war and its obligation to settle all disputes by peaceful means. No one doubted that that treaty had been violated; but it was a new thing to punish persons for acts of nations; it was a new court, created after the offense, which was to judge them; and agents of other governments than their own would administer the sentences of those convicted.

"Crimes against humanity" was a phrase too vague for definition; but the crimes which had been committed against great segments of mankind were almost too outrageous for human comprehension. There was no international law against genocide, the killing of a people. The prewar world had not been conscious of the need of one, as attempted genocide had scarcely been imagined.

Prevalent opinion was that neither legalistic objection nor self-abnegation should obstruct the course of justice, and that less than justice would be done if, the peoples having made the sacrifices and endured the hardships of the war, and the soldiers and millions of other victims having died, the men criminally responsible for war atrocities and for the war itself were permitted to go unpunished for lack of ready-made machinery or precedent for their trial and punishment.

THE NUREMBERG TRIALS

Twenty-four of the principal Nazi offenders were indicted as major war criminals before an international military tribunal at Nuremberg, Germany, in October, 1945, on four counts: (1) participation in a common plan or conspiracy to commit crimes against peace, war crimes, and crimes against humanity; (2) commission of crimes against peace, in planning, initiation, or waging of a war of aggression; (3) commission of war crimes through violation of the laws or customs of war; (4) commission of crimes against humanity through the murder or enslavement of civilian populations before or during the war, or persecution on political, racial, or religious grounds.

The trial began November 21, 1945. The fallen Nazi leaders were given what they had consistently denied their unfortunate opponents —a long and patient trial, without physical torture or mistreatment, with benefit of German counsel of their own choosing, and with abundant opportunity to testify in their own defense. Their own records—correspondence, published proclamations, official documents, stenographic reports of leaders' conferences, affidavits, statistics, and documentary films, captured by the Allies in quite unprecedented quantities and acknowledged by the accused—testified eloquently against them. Most of them tried to put the blame for everything on Hitler, who was dead. Some pleaded ignorance of atrocities of which the judges were convinced they could not have been unaware, others only inability to prevent what they said they had not approved. The generals pleaded obedience to orders in the transmission of orders for which they said they had not been responsible.

Three were acquitted: former Chancellor Franz von Papen, former Reichsbank president and Economics Minister Hjalmar Schacht, and radio propagandist Hans Fritsche. The acquittal of Schacht and von Papen was generally unpopular. Both drew comparatively light sentences, subsequently, in German denazification courts; and Schacht, who had managed to be found in a concentration camp at the time of the collapse, was eventually successful in a long series of appeals. Both carried a heavy burden of responsibility for Hitler's rise to power and for his abuse of power; but direct participation in the crimes listed in the indictment was not, in the opinion of the court, proved against either of them.

Three of those accused escaped trial: Martin Bormann, secretary of the party, whereabouts unknown, condemned *in absentia*; Gustav Krupp, head of the steel and munitions complex of that name, because of advanced age and illness; and Robert Ley, former head of the Labor Front, who committed suicide in his cell soon after his indictment.

Three were given life-term prison sentences: Rudolf Hess, former deputy leader of the party, who feigned insanity; Walther Funk, Schacht's successor as Reichsbank president and economics minister; and former Grand Admiral Erich Raeder, commander of the navy until January, 1943.

Four were given shorter prison terms: Baldur von Schirach, former youth leader, twenty years; Albert Speer, former minister of armaments and war production, twenty years; Konstantin von Neurath, former foreign minister and Protector of Czechoslovakia, fifteen years; former Grand Admiral Karl Dönitz, leader of the U-boats, Raeder's successor as commander of the fleet, and designated to succeed Hitler as chancellor, ten years.

Twelve, including Bormann *in absentia*, were sentenced to be hanged. Former Reichsmarshal Hermann Göring cheated his executioners by swallowing poison just before the hour set for his execution. Ten were hanged: Joachim Ribbentrop, former minister for foreign affairs; former Field Marshal Wilhelm Keitel, chief of the high command; former Colonel General Alfred Jodl of Hitler's military staff;

Ernst Kaltenbrunner, former head of the Nazi security police; Alfred Rosenberg, former official Nazi ideologist; Hans Frank, wartime governor general of Poland; Wilhelm Frick, former minister of the interior; Arthur Seyss-Inquart, first Nazi chancellor of Austria and wartime commissioner for the Netherlands; Julius Streicher, former editor of the anti-Semitic newspaper *Der Stürmer*; and Fritz Sauckel, director of the wartime slave labor program. The day of their execution was October 16, 1946—two days less than a year after their indictment.

In the ten-months' trial of the major war criminals five million words of testimony were taken—partly for the record. The trial wrote into the record a history of wickedness and crime which until then had been, and would otherwise soon again have been, beyond belief. A socially responsible attempt was made to establish, by unparalleled precedent if necessary, the fundamental though not yet universally acknowledged principles that the waging of aggressive war in violation of existing treaty agreements and of international law was a crime for which individuals could be brought to trial before an international court and punished if found guilty, and that obedience to alleged superior orders was not an acceptable defense against charges of atrocious crimes against persons. The western world was long beset, however, by doubt about the wisdom of what had been done, and cynics said to one another that the anticipated aftermath of every future war would be that the leaders of the losers would be liquidated.

JAPANESE AND OTHER TRIALS

Doubt about the wisdom of trial by conquerors did not stop the trials. In United States military courts or in international military tribunals set up on the Nuremberg model for the purpose, about a thousand further cases involving approximately three thousand defendants were tried. Most of them were convicted and 724 were given death sentences: 462 in Germany, 124 in Japan, 131 in China, the Philippine Islands, and Guam, seven in Italy. Many of the prison sentences were subsequently reduced.

The Japanese former leaders executed included former General Kenji Doihara, who commanded in the attack on Mukden in the Manchurian incident of 1931; former General Hideki Tojo, who was premier when Pearl Harbor was attacked; a former war minister, General Seishiro Itagaki; and former commanders in Burma, the Philippines, and Nanking, Generals Kimura, Homma, Muto, Yamashita, and Matsui. Admiral Shigetaro Shimada, navy minister at the time of Pearl Harbor, former army Chief of Staff Yoshijiro Umezu, who signed the instrument of surrender for the armed forces, and former Colonel Kingoro Hashimoto, who ordered the shelling of the *Panay* and the British gunboat *Ladybird* on the Yangtze in 1935, were sentenced to life imprisonment. Admiral Isoroku Yamamoto, who as commander of the fleet ordered the attack on Pearl Harbor, was killed during the war. The former chief of the naval general staff, Admiral Osami Nagano, and former Minister for Foreign Affairs Yosuke Matsuoka died before the trials ended. Mamoru Shigemitsu of the Foreign Office, who signed the instrument of surrender for the government, was sentenced to seven years' imprisonment. The United States Supreme Court refused appeals of the former Japanese war lords on the ground that their sentences had been imposed by international military tribunals beyond the jurisdiction of the court. Eleven nations participated in the trials.[5]

THE ELUSIVENESS OF SECURITY

Revenge was not sweet. All were relieved, but few were otherwise gratified. An attempt was made to establish in international law the principle that the commander of an army was responsible for the conduct of his subordinates and punishable for crimes committed by them against inhabitants of a combat area or an occupied country, or against prisoners of war. Exemplary penalties were imposed upon former commanders whose men had offended the decency developed in struggling humanity in the long course of its striving toward civilization. Whether these admonitory punitive examples would do more to prevent war or promote peace than the heads of the leaders of a slaughtered garrison, set on pikes on the walls of a medieval town, one did not know. One knew that the feeling of security that one sought was not in him. One wondered how far civilization had been set back and security undermined by war, and whether punishment of war lords who failed would deter future aspirants from trying. One wondered how peace could be made in a world in which men who walked always in fear tried to use fear itself as their instrument. One wondered how long shining armor would protect those who wished peace, and what use would be made of the period of grace it vouchsafed them.

[5] United Press dispatch, Tokyo, November 12, 1948; *Wisconsin State Journal,* December 20, 1948. The Japanese trials ended in October, 1949. Shigemitsu was paroled in November, 1950.

PARTIAL PEACE SETTLEMENT

The Long Armistice

UNITED NATIONS

As planned at the organization meeting of 1945 in San Francisco, representatives of the fifty-one original members of the United Nations convened in London January 10, 1946. The United States was represented by Secretary of State James Byrnes, former Secretary Edward Stettinius, Senators Connally and Vandenberg of the Committee on Foreign Affairs, and Mrs. Eleanor Roosevelt, world-minded widow of the late president. Norwegian Trygve Lie was elected the first president of the organization—known then as UNO (United Nations Organization) later as the UN (United Nations)—for a five-year term. Paul-Henri Spaak of Belgium was the first president of the Assembly. The first nonpermanent members of the Security Council, elected by the Assembly, were Egypt, Mexico, and the Netherlands for one-year terms, and Australia, Brazil, and Poland for terms of two years. Organization was completed by the election of members of the Economic and Social Council, the judges of the International Court of Justice, and the nucleus of a permanent Secretariat. New York was chosen as the site of the permanent headquarters of the organization.

Meeting for its twenty-first and last session at Geneva from April 8 to 18, 1946, the League of Nations made way for its successor by transferring to the United Nations its buildings and other assets and such of its functions as the UN had already undertaken to assume, and voted itself out of existence. The International Labor Office (ILO) and United Nations Educational, Scientific, and Cultural Organization (UNESCO) continued to function under new auspices in fields developed under the aegis of the League.

International Court of Justice. Judge Green Haywood Hackworth of Kentucky, a former member of the Permanent Court of Arbitration at The Hague, was one of the justices chosen for the new World Court.[6] The court met at The Hague from April 3 to May 6, 1946, to organize itself and formulate rules of procedure. Its first case, referred to it by a Security Council resolution of April 9, 1947, was a dispute arising out of mine damage to two British destroyers, with some loss of life, in Corfu Channel, October 22, 1946. The

[6] The judges' normal term of office was fifteen years. To start the rotation, lots were drawn. Justice Hackworth drew a six-year term. In the face of bitter Soviet opposition on November 1, 1950, the Assembly extended Lie's term as president for a period of three years.

decision was announced April 9, 1949, two years after the case was referred to the court by the Council. Albania was ordered to pay an indemnity of £843,947, but had the slender satisfaction of a court ruling, without indemnity, that the British had violated her sovereignty by sweeping the waters of the area afterward to determine the nature of the explosions.

Upon request of the Security Council or the Assembly the court rendered advisory opinions as the former "World Court," the Permanent Court of International Justice, had done for the League of Nations. At the end of 1949 it had pending three international cases and three requests for advisory opinions. One of its advisory opinions was that a member state could not properly vote against the admission of a candidate for membership for reasons other than those indicated by the charter.

When the first UN assembly reconvened at Flushing Meadow, Long Island, October 23 to December 15, 1946, four new member states were elected: Afghanistan, Iceland, Siam, and Sweden. Five others—the Albanian People's Republic, the Mongolian People's Republic, Trans-Jordan, Eire, and Portugal—applied but were not elected. Soviet Russia led the opposition to the election of Eire. The admission of the Republic of Indonesia September 28, 1950, raised the total membership to sixty.

Trusteeship. A Trusteeship Council to take the place of the League of Nations Mandates Commission in the supervision of the handling of non-self-governing areas and peoples was set up. Trusteeship agreements covering formerly mandated areas were submitted and approved: Australia for New Britain, New Zealand for western Samoa, Belgium for Ruanda-Urundi, Britain for Tanganyika and those parts of former German Kamerun and Togoland which were previously mandated to Britain, France for the parts of the erstwhile German Kamerun and Togoland which were formerly mandated to France. The Assembly declined to authorize the Union of South Africa to incorporate into its own territory its formerly mandated territory, once German Southwest Africa. The Union of South Africa declined to transfer the mandated territory to the status of a trusteeship, but continued intermittently to submit information concerning its administration of it. In 1947 the United States was made trustee for the former Japanese-mandated islands.

Atomic Energy Commission. An international Atomic Energy Commission was established by a General Assembly resolution of January 24, 1946, to inquire into all phases of the production, control, and use of the energy released by atomic fission, with a view to the promotion of the peaceful use of such energy and the prevention of its use in war. The commission had before it (1) a United States proposal presented by elder statesman Bernard Baruch for the establishment of a rigorous system of inspection and enforcement, but not for the destruction of existing stocks of atomic weapons or the immediate international outlawry of their use in war, and (2) a Soviet Russian proposal presented by Andrei A. Gromyko for an international convention prohibiting the use of atomic weapons in warfare but providing for only domestic enforcement of the prohibition. The Soviet Union wished to see the destruction of the existing (United States) stocks of atomic weapons, but hardly refused to agree to international inspection of any sort generally deemed likely to be effective.

With representatives of Poland and the Soviet Union abstaining, on December 30, 1946, the commission adopted for submission to the Security Council a report incorporating the United States proposals. Action in the Council was blocked by Russian opposition. The United States position was that the great-power veto should not be applicable to a resolution for inspection or enforcement; the representative of the Soviet Union argued that the veto power provided by the charter must be retained.

Iran. The veto power was not applicable to proposals to hear or discuss complaints of nation against nation; and free use was made of the Assembly and Security Council as world forums for the presentation of such complaints. The government of Iran addressed to the Security Council on January 19, 1946, an allegation that Red Army troops were being kept in Iranian territory after the date agreed upon with Iran, Britain, and the United States for their withdrawal, and that the USSR was intervening in the internal affairs of Iran. The Council received and considered the complaint in the face of Soviet Union opposition. In protest against the consideration of the complaint, the Russian representative on the Council absented himself while the complaint was under discussion; but the offending Red Army troops were removed from Azerbaijan.

Greece. Two days after the receipt by the Security Council of Iran's complaint against the USSR, the Soviet representative brought in a complaint against the presence of British troops in Greece and the Ukrainian representative complained against the presence of British troops in Indonesia, as threats against peace and security. A motion to appoint a commission to investigate the latter complaint was defeated, and the Council declared the matter closed. The Ukrainian representative, however, reopened the Greek question August 24 by accusing Greece of violation of the Albanian frontier and persecution of minorities. The Greek government then on December 6 accused Albania, Bulgaria, and Yugoslavia of supporting Communist guerrillas in northern Greece.

A UN investigation commission reported June 25, 1947, that the three nations accused had supported guerrilla warfare in Greece and had kept their frontiers open to partisans engaged in it. The *ad hoc* commission recommended the establishment of a permanent commission. Within the commission, France accepted the report but not the recommendations. Eight nations accepted both. Poland and the USSR rejected both. In the Security Council July 29 a United States resolution to accept the findings and implement the recommendation of the commission failed with nine votes for and two against, because one of the negative votes was cast by the USSR. Poland voted with the Soviet Union. The United States then carried its resolution to the UN Assembly, which adopted it October 21 by a vote of forty to six, with ten abstentions.

The 1949 Assembly adopted a resolution asking members to impose an arms embargo on Albania and Bulgaria as long as the two countries continued to give aid to guerrillas in Greece, and asked the two countries to desist from interference in the internal affairs of Greece.

Indonesia.   The Japanese troops which surrendered in the Netherlands East Indies in 1945 were told to maintain order there until Allied troops could take over. Much of their military equipment fell into Indonesian hands. Dutch troops in sufficient numbers being unavailable, British troops moved into Batavia September 29, 1945, under instructions to confine the occupation to a few of the larger cities and not to interfere with local administration, which was already largely in the hands of the nationalist movement led by Achmed Soekarno and later by Sutan Sjahrir. The Dutch authorities refused at first to deal with the nationalist leaders, and there was fighting between natives and the British and Dutch occupying forces. Some United States lend-lease equipment was used by both of the latter.

On February 10, 1946, the government of the Netherlands proposed that a self-governing Indonesian commonwealth be established, to be voluntarily associated as a member of a federation with the Netherlands. By a truce agreement signed at Linggadjati after months of negotiation alternating with hostilities, the Dutch and Indonesians agreed that an autonomous United States of Indonesia should be formed under the Dutch crown, to become a sovereign state by January 1, 1949. Member states were to be a Republic of Indonesia, East Indonesia, and Dutch Borneo. Soekarno was the first president and Sjahrir premier of the Republic of Indonesia.

The Linggadjati agreement was ratified by both parties and was implemented in 1947 except in Sumatra and Java, where the Sjahrir cabinet had to resign as a result of differences between the general administration and the new Republic of Indonesia. A United States offer of mediation was rejected by the republic. Dutch forces went over to the offensive and occupied eastern and western Java and southern and eastern Sumatra. Seeing in the conflict a danger to world peace, the UN Security Council called on both parties on August 1 to end hostilities, offered to mediate the dispute, and set up a Good Offices Commission of three members, from Belgium, Australia, and the United States. Through the good offices of the commission a new truce agreement was signed aboard the United States transport *Renville* January 17, 1948. The sovereignty of the Netherlands was to be recognized until the United States of Indonesia was organized.

On May 26, 1948, the Indonesian republic, acting as if it were already a sovereign state, made a consular agreement with the USSR. On June 12 the republic was recognized by other Soviet-dominated nations. The Netherlands protested that the treaty with the USSR violated the interim *Renville* agreement. The other Indonesian states were ready to form an all-Indonesian government, with or without the republic, to take over authority from the Dutch lieutenant governor general and his cabinet. In September a communist revolt broke out in central Java. Negotiations with the Netherlands foreign minister, D. U. Stikker, and other members of the cabinet of the Netherlands in the republican capital Jogjakarta broke down.

In December, 1948, the Netherlands government moved troops into the republican areas of Sumatra and Java and captured and interned the president and cabinet of the republic and the commander in chief of its armed forces. Upon motion of the representative of the United States, the UN Security Council on January 28, 1949, condemned the military action of the Netherlands as a violation of the *Renville* truce agreement. It called upon the Netherlands to withdraw its troops from the former republican areas, release the captured republican leaders, and restore the government of the republic at Jogjakarta.

The government of the Netherlands refused at first to yield to the injunction of the Security Council but eventually accepted a compromise suggested by the Council March 23 on motion of the representative of Canada that hostilities should cease forthwith and that representatives of the Netherlands, the republic, and the Indonesian federalists agree to meet at a round-table conference at The Hague, ready to accept the findings of that conference. The Netherlands accepted the recommendation, evacuated Jogjakarta June 24, and agreed to the restoration of the republican government there July 6. Hostilities were terminated August 10 in Java and August 14 in Sumatra.

By agreements signed at a round-table conference at The Hague November 2, 1949, the kingdom of the Netherlands transferred sovereignty over its former territorial possessions in the East Indies, except Dutch New Guinea, to the Republic of the United States of Indonesia. The new federated republic accepted a statute of union with the kingdom of the Netherlands to assure coöperation in the field of common interests by semiannual ministerial conferences. The formal transfer of sovereignty, marking the end of Dutch rule in the Netherlands Indies, was effected at Amsterdam and Batavia (renamed Jakarta) December 27, 1949. Achmed Soekarno was elected president of the new federal republic at Jogjakarta December 16, 1949. Mohammed Hatta was its first premier. It was admitted to membership in the United Nations September 28, 1950.

Palestine-Israel. Palestine was often on the agenda of the United Nations as the date of the termination of the British mandate, May 15, 1948, approached and passed.[7] It was the whole agendum of a special session of the Assembly beginning April 28, 1947, which set up a special committee of representatives of eleven countries to report at the regular session beginning September 1. Having tried in vain to reconcile conflicting interests and keep the peace in Palestine, Britain supported in the September session the special committee's recommendation that the mandate should be terminated and the independence of Palestine achieved. The Assembly adopted, November 29, 1947, a plan for the partition of Palestine into Jewish and Arab states and an international city of Jerusalem, the three to be linked by an economic union effective upon termination of the British mandate. A UN Palestine Commission appointed under the Assembly resolution of November 29 reported March 19, 1948, that it was unable to accomplish its mission because of the uncoöperative attitude of the mandatory power, which was unwilling to admit it to Palestine until May 1.

The new state of Israel was proclaimed by its prime minister,

[7] See p. 369.

David Ben-Gurion, immediately upon the termination of the British mandate, May 15, 1948, and was recognized that day by the United States and two days later by the USSR. Chaim Weizmann was provisional president until elected president February 17, 1949. The seat of government was established at Tel-Aviv.

The UN Assembly authorized the appointment of a mediator between Arab and Jew in Palestine, and a truce was effected on the basis of Security Council resolutions of May 29 and July 15, 1948.

As United Nations mediator, Count Folke Bernadotte of Sweden, first proposed, June 28, a Palestinian union with local autonomy for each part. Both parties rejected the proposal. UN Secretary General Trygve Lie asked for an armed force of a thousand guards to preserve the peace, and the mediator urged both sides to prolong the truce.

On September 17, 1948, Count Bernadotte and one of his observers were assassinated in Jerusalem by Jewish dissidents, who escaped. The government of Israel at once outlawed all terrorist organizations. Ralph J. Bunche of the United States succeeded Count Bernadotte as mediator. Count Bernadotte's report, posthumously presented to the UN Assembly at its annual session, recommended recognition of Israel, but with certain boundary revisions which neither Israel nor the Arab states would willingly accept.

Largely through the patient, tactful, but forceful efforts of Dr. Bunche, armistice agreements between Israel and her neighbors were signed, the first with Egypt on January 6, the last with Syria July 20, 1949. The principal problem then left unsolved was the status of Jerusalem. The UN Assembly preferred that the Holy City be internationalized under UN trusteeship, to which Israel and the Arab states did not then agree. Israel was admitted to membership in the United Nations May 11, 1949.[8]

Kashmir. A conflict between Pakistan and the Dominion of India over the border state of Kashmir (84,500 square miles), controlling the passes to central Asia, was brought before the Security Council by India in January, 1948.

The maharajah, Sir Hari Singh, finding himself and the ruling Hindu minority in Kashmir faced with a rebellion of the Moslem majority and an incursion in considerable numbers of the Moslem tribesmen of the northwest frontier, had acceded to India and appealed for help. India had sent help, and accused the Pakistani of aiding the rebellious Kashmiris.

The Security Council sent a commission to Kashmir, which was un-

[8] For his work as mediator, Dr. Bunche was awarded the 1950 Nobel peace prize.

able to bring about the withdrawal of either the Indian troops or the invading tribesmen, or to conduct a plebiscite. However, it reported to the Security Council in January, 1949, that a cease-fire order had been issued by both sides January 1. In March Admiral Chester W. Nimitz was appointed UN administrator to conduct a plebiscite; but the UN commission reported at the end of 1949 that Indian and Pakistani troops were still in Kashmir and the plebiscite could not yet be held.

Berlin and Korea. See below.

Negotiations, Conferences, and Treaties

COUNCIL OF FOREIGN MINISTERS, MOSCOW, DECEMBER 16-26, 1945

Whereas the United Nations was expected to interest itself in matters of general concern, the business of drafting terms of the immediate peace settlement was reserved for the principal victorious powers. It was decided at the Potsdam conference of July-August, 1945, that treaties of peace with Italy and the other late European allies of the Axis powers should be drafted by the foreign ministers of the principal Allied and associated powers, meeting from time to time at their respective capitals. Many other questions were referred to the same group.

At the first foreign ministers' conference at London in September, 1945, the United States, Great Britain, the Soviet Union, France, and China were represented. The conference ended without having reached agreement as to whether the representatives of France and China should participate in discussion of terms of peace with nations with which they had not been engaged in actual hostilities.

At Moscow, December 16 to 26, 1945, the British and Soviet foreign ministers and Secretary Byrnes, meeting without their French and Chinese colleagues, continued the discussion of the making of peace treaties. They decided that the treaties made with any of the former European satellites of Germany should be drafted by the representatives of only those former belligerents whose representatives had already signed the armistice agreement with it. That decision excluded China. France might participate fully in the making of the treaty with Italy but only in discussion of the others. The United States, which had not been at war with Finland, might discuss but could not vote on the terms of the treaty to be made with Finland. The treaty drafts so prepared would be submitted to a general conference of the five principal powers and sixteen others—Australia, Belgium, Brazil,

Canada, Czechoslovakia, Ethiopia, Greece, India, the Netherlands, New Zealand, Norway, Poland, Ukraine, South Africa, Byelorussia (White Russia), and Yugoslavia—which had actively waged war with substantial forces against the Axis powers and their European allies. The recommendations of the general conference would then be taken into consideration in making the final peace treaties by the states which had originally signed the armistice agreements. Renewed but unconvincing assurances were given the British and United States representatives at the Moscow conferences that the postwar governments of Rumania and Bulgaria were genuinely democratic and representative in character, and that legal guarantees of freedom of utterance, religion, association, and elections were adequate and were being faithfully observed.

Three long ministers' conferences were held, one in London and two in Paris, before the meeting of the Paris peace conference of 1946 to draft the treaties to be presented to that conference.

PARIS PEACE CONFERENCE, JULY-OCTOBER, 1946

Unlike its prototype of 1919, the general peace conference of the twenty-one nations which had recently been at war with Germany and her allies, meeting at Paris July 29, 1946, was only advisory in character. It could express a preference when offered alternatives, and could criticize and recommend to the' powers which had signed the armistice agreements; but the latter would write the final treaty terms.

There was full and free discussion, much of it in public and fully reported to a world audience, some of it—perhaps for benefit of the audience—rather acrimonious. Preliminary draft treaties with Italy, Rumania, Bulgaria, Hungary, and Finland, to be considered by the conference, were published in advance. Small powers as well as great were permitted to vote on all five treaties, article by article, and to put their views on record from the world podium in plenary sessions. Spokesmen for the defeated powers were permitted to address the conference before its commissions settled down to the business of studying the proposed treaty terms, and to appear before the commissions as advocates but not as negotiators.

Public demonstrations of the apparatus of open diplomacy and democratic procedure in the conduct of international business did not dispel the atmosphere of mutual fear and suspicion in which the conference met. Listeners were regaled with the most violent accusations of sinister ulterior motives and hostile intentions they had yet heard voiced in public, in the new language of diplomacy. Speakers for a

Slav bloc echoed the polemics of Molotov and Vyshinsky against the alleged warlike intentions and containment or "encirclement" policy of the more democratic capitalist western powers. Spokesmen for the west denied the accusations brought against their governments and peoples and spoke bluntly about the behavior of the USSR, but understated their resentment of Russian resumption of active promotion of Communist revolutionary activities outside the recognized territorial boundaries of the Soviet Union. In an almost interminable succession of votes, clause by clause on treaty after treaty, the six members of the Slav bloc—Byelorussia, Czechoslovakia, Poland, Ukraine, the USSR, and Yugoslavia—cast their votes solidly against fifteen, Molotov against Bevin of Britain, Bidault of France, and Byrnes of the United States.

COUNCIL OF FOREIGN MINISTERS, NEW YORK, NOVEMBER-DECEMBER, 1946

The Paris peace conference of 1946 adjourned October 15. Its recommendations were generally incorporated by the Council of Foreign Ministers into the treaties finally drafted by them at their fourth long conference of the year, New York, November 4 to December 12, 1946. The treaties were signed for the United States in Washington by Secretary Byrnes on his last day in office, January 20, and for the other powers in Paris on February 10, 1947.

TREATIES, FEBRUARY 10, 1947

Italy. Although Italy was the first of Germany's allies to withdraw from that alliance in defeat and join her enemies, it was remembered that she was the first to join Germany in 1940 in attacking France, and that Mussolini and the hardier Fascist faction gave further aid to Hitler after the Duce's deposition by his own people in 1944. The new republic of Italy which was formed July 14, 1946, under the leadership of a Christian Democrat premier, Alcide de Gasperi, and Socialist Pietro Nenni, deputy premier and minister for foreign affairs, had to accept stern terms of peace.[9]

[9] The treaty was ratified by the constituent assembly July 31, 1947, but did not go into effect until September 15, as the USSR did not ratify it until August 29. The republican constitution was approved and the last United States and British troops were withdrawn December 22. The constitution was promulgated on Christmas Eve, 1947. The first president under the new constitution, Luigi Einaudi, was elected by the two houses of the national parliament May 11, 1948. Prefascist and antifascist Foreign Minister Count Carlo Sforza, who had been president of the first postfascist provisional parliament, returned as a member of the Badoglio cabinet and Foreign Office in a sixth de Gasperi government.

No attempt was made to collect in cash full compensation for damage done to the nationals of the Allies who were eventually the victors; but reparation in kind was to be made to Yugoslavia in the amount of $125,000,000, $100,000,000 to the USSR, $105,000,000 to Greece, $25,000,000 to Ethiopia, $5,000,000 to Albania. Italian armed forces were limited to: an army of 250,000 including 65,000 *carabinieri*; a navy of two battleships, four cruisers, four destroyers, and thirty-six auxiliary vessels with a maximum personnel of 22,500; and an air force of 150 transport planes and 200 fighter planes of all types—no bombers.

Italy had further to cede the Dodecanese Islands to Greece; Fiume, the Istrian peninsula, and much of Venezia Giulia to Yugoslavia; the Adriatic island of Saseno to Albania; and certain small northwestern border areas to France. Trieste, between Italy and Yugoslavia, and a natural Adriatic outlet for the trade of the hinterland as far north as Austria, was provisionally set up as a free territory under United Nations guarantee. The restored independence of Ethiopia was recognized.

Italy had also to renounce in favor of Great Britain, the USSR, and the USA all claim to her former colonial possessions in northern and east Africa, although she hoped that some of them might eventually be restored to her under a United Nations trusteeship. Temporarily the colonies in question were left, as they then were, under British military occupation and political control.

An Assembly resolution of the United Nations provided in November, 1949, that a UN commissioner and an international council should draw up a constitution for a united Libya (Cyrenaica, Tripolitania, and Fezzan) and should supervise its establishment as an independent state by January 1, 1952. A UN *ad hoc* committee resolution of October 19, 1950, recommended by a vote of fifty-three to one, with France opposed and the Soviet bloc not voting, that a Libyan national assembly should convene before January 1, 1951, and establish as soon as possible a provisional government to which authority should be progressively transferred under the guidance of the UN commissioner and commission. The committee resolution reaffirmed an earlier UN Assembly resolution that Libya should be admitted to membership in the United Nations as soon as it was established as an independent state. The Assembly adopted the resolution November 17, 1950.

Italian Somaliland was returned to Italy under UN trusteeship for a period of ten years, after which it also was to be given independence. Decision as to Eritrea was deferred.

Hungary. Hungary had to agree to pay in goods the equivalent of $200,000,000 to the Soviet Union and $50,000,000 each to Czechoslovakia and Yugoslavia. Northern Transylvania, taken from Rumania with Axis sanction in 1940, was returned to Rumania. A bridgehead of territory on the right bank of the Danube, opposite Bratislava, was ceded to Czechoslovakia with southern Slovakia, annexed in 1938. Eastern Ruthenia (Carpatho-Ukraine), annexed at Czechoslovakia's expense in 1938 and 1939, was occupied by the Red Army and became part of the territory of the Soviet Socialist Republic of Ukraine. The repatriation of populations of Czechoslovakia and Hungary was left to direct negotiation.

Rumania. Rumania declared war on Germany when invaded by the Red Army in August, 1944, but could not escape the consequences of having made war on Soviet Russia as Germany's ally. By the treaty of 1947 she had to agree to pay material reparation to the USSR in the amount of $300,000,000, and to confirm her Soviet Union boundaries of 1940, i.e., to confirm the involuntary cession of Bessarabia and northern Bucovina to Ukraine of the Soviet Union, and of southern Dobruja to Bulgaria. She was compensated only by the return of northern Transylvania by Hungary.

Bulgaria. Bulgaria did not join Germany against Russia; Russia declared war on Bulgaria only when ready to invade. So Bulgaria was required to agree to pay in reparation only $25,000,000 to Czechoslovakia and $45,000,000 to Greece. She lost no territory, but was again frustrated in her desire to gain direct access through western Thrace to the Aegean. Greek claims in Macedonia were rejected. Friction with Turkey, which had not led to open war, continued.

Finland. Finland paid the penalty for her unsuccessful attempt as Germany's ally to avenge her 1939-1940 defeat at the hands of Soviet Russia. She was compelled to cede to the Soviet Union her only Arctic port, Petsamo, her part of the Rybachi peninsula west of Murmansk, and the vital Karelian peninsula, with land around Lake Ladoga and the port of Viborg (Viipuri). The USSR gave up its lease on Hangö (Hanko) but took a fifty-year lease on a naval base at Parkkala on the Gulf of Finland between Hangö and Helsinki. Finland agreed to pay Russia the equivalent of $300,000,000 in reparation.

ONE WORLD OR TWO?

European recovery after the war was retarded by economic exhaustion and dislocation, and by political uncertainty. Uncertainty grew principally out of the inability of the principal western powers to maintain with the Union of Soviet Socialist Republics even the appearance of friendly relations that had been temporarily achieved during the war. It had in fact undergone a change before the cessation of hostilities, as the certainty of success became increasingly apparent and the day of final victory approached.

Lenin had told Communist party members: "We are living not merely in one state but in a system of states, and the existence of the Soviet Republic side by side with imperialist states for a long time is inconceivable. One or the other must ultimately triumph."[10]

In a political campaign speech in Moscow February 9, 1946, Stalin closely followed the Lenin line of the incompatibility of capitalism and communism and the inevitability of capitalist-communist conflict:

It would be incorrect to think that the second world war arose by chance or as the result of the mistakes of such and such statesmen, although there certainly were such mistakes. In actual fact the war arose as the inevitable result of the development of world economic and political forces on the basis of contemporary monopoly capitalism. Marxists have declared many times that the capitalist system of world economy conceals within itself elements of a general crisis and military ramifications, that in view of this the development of world capitalism in our time is being carried out not in the form of a steady and even forward movement, but through crises and military catastrophes.[11]

Communist terminology called Britain and the United States "capitalist" and "imperialist" countries; and Soviet foreign policy appeared to British and American observers to be based upon the assumption that Russian interests were inimical to theirs. The Soviet leaders behaved and usually spoke as if they assumed that, the postwar period being one of crises and catastrophes for the capitalist powers, the time was opportune for a return to the policy of expanding communism—if indeed that policy had ever been abandoned. Catastrophe for capitalism, which would give world communism a favorable opportunity, would meanwhile come the sooner if the crisis occasioned by the war were but prolonged. Communism could perhaps wait longer and more confidently than capitalism could for the peace. "We are a patient people," said Stalin; and his government did not hurry. Insisting upon unanimity, apparently, only to prevent unanimous agreement, they seemed to many of those whose duty it was to deal

---

[10] See Walter Bedell Smith, *My Three Years in Moscow* (New York, 1950), 325.
[11] *Pravda*, February 10, 1946.

with them to be deliberately delaying the peace settlement, which was generally regarded as prerequisite to general recovery.

Truman Plan

Russian foreign policy returned in the first postwar years both to the active support of revolutionary communism in other countries and to the territorial expansionism of the tsars. The latter return took the form of pressure on Greece and Turkey.

GREECE

Greece had in 1939 an alliance with Great Britain, which had promised before the war to protect Greece from Axis aggression if she would defend herself—as she did, successfully against Italy, unsuccessfully against the Axis combination of Italy, Germany, and Bulgaria. In 1941 Britain tried loyally but in vain to keep that promise. Greece so fell naturally into the small sphere of influence which Stalin was willing during the war to concede to Britain while claiming for Russia a prior and paramount interest in Rumania, Bulgaria, and Yugoslavia.

It was the prewar Greek monarchy with which Britain made an alliance in 1939, which she kept alive as a government in exile during the Axis occupation of the country, and which returned with British sponsorship and support when the Axis troops withdrew in 1944. That government, however, was anathema to a strong Communist guerrilla force in Greece, called the National Liberation Front or—from its Greek initials—the EAM, which had fought the alien enemy persistently. Looking upon the none too liberal or efficient returning émigré government as both enemy and alien, the EAM was disposed to make life as uncomfortable and uncertain for it as it had done for the Axis occupation.

Gradually, with some help at first from British troops, the royal government in Greece extended the area under its control. In December, 1946, it brought to the attention of the Security Council of the United Nations its complaint that its Soviet-dominated Communist neighbors, Albania, Yugoslavia, and Bulgaria, were keeping their frontiers open to fugitive rebels and were supplying and supporting the Communist guerrillas in Greece. The Security Council was prevented by a Soviet Russian veto from taking action. The UN Assembly sent a fact-finding commission.[12]

[12] See pp. 227-231.

TURKEY

Turkey lived dangerously through the war, preserving until March, 1945, sometimes quite precariously, the technical neutrality of a nation alternately cajoled and threatened by the Axis, courted by the Allies. She was a beneficiary of lend-lease aid from the United States, and an uneasy neighbor of the Soviet Union. One of her periods of greatest danger was in 1940-1941, before Hitler's decision to invade Russia, when the high-echelon Nazi planners were talking of an envelopment of the Mediterranean and a push through Asia Minor toward Iran and India. Another threat, less obvious but serious if real, lay in Molotov's proposal to Hitler in Berlin in November, 1940, that the Soviet Union join Germany in the war. One of the Soviet stipulations was that Germany and the other members of the tripartite alliance support the USSR's demand for bases in and near the Bosporus and Dardanelles.[13]

Danger to Turkey at the Straits reappeared when her twenty-year nonaggression pact with the Soviet Union expired in 1945 and was denounced by the Soviet Union. The Soviets opened a propaganda campaign for the return of Kars, Ardahan, and other territory, and broached the question of a revision in their favor of the Montreux convention authorizing Turkey to police the Straits, although Britain and Russia had confirmed that convention August 10, 1941. On the alleged ground that the Straits might be attacked by an enemy of the USSR against which Turkey might not be strong enough to defend them, the USSR wanted bases there.

The Soviet demand, if granted, would have made Russia mistress of the Straits. The imperial Russian government had set itself essentially the same objective in 1914 and 1915. It was the same demand which, approximately five years before, Molotov asked Hitler to support and Hitler rejected. The Allies were unwilling to discuss it at Yalta, and rejected and dropped it at the Potsdam conference, where the Russians refused to accept as a substitute the international "free passage for all" guarantee advocated by the United States for the Straits, the Danube, and the Rhine.

TRUMAN DOCTRINE

With Turkey under Russian pressure on her northern frontier and at the Straits, and from Bulgaria in Thrace, and with Greece harassed by Communists within and without, President Truman made on

[13] See pp. 110-113 and 741-742, U.S. Department of State, *Bulletin,* XIX, No. 472 (July 18, 1948), p. 63.

March 12, 1947, the portentous policy pronouncement that it was a national interest of the United States to prevent the extension of Soviet influence into Greece or Turkey. The president asked Congress for, and was given, authority to grant assistance to those two countries in the amount of $400,000,000. Military equipment and supplies were sent to both. A military mission went to Greece. Both governments were enabled to maintain themselves and hold their ground.

The Truman policy was patently one of containment. Prevented by the Russian veto from acting effectively through the United Nations to check the spread of Soviet power and influence, which the USSR was actively extending unilaterally outside the United Nations, the United States took the considered but incalculable risk of unilateral action, also outside the United Nations. By so doing, it acted in reluctant recognition of the fact that, the political objective of an effective one-world organization having not yet been attained, it was incumbent upon the noncommunist nations wanting peace in a world at least partially free from communist control to restrict as they could the area to be brought under Soviet domination. If "one world," partly communist and partly noncommunist, was not then to be had, then one of two worlds—the noncommunist and the communist—was preferable to none. Meanwhile the possibility of eventual arrival at a tolerable *modus vivendi* between the two uncongenial parts of the world would be enhanced if the eastern bloc did not go on gaining ground in Europe at the expense of the west. As the west saw it, it had to restrain Russia if possible.

Marshall Plan

Realizing the risk involved in unilateral action by the United States to implement the Truman doctrine of containment of Soviet Russia, and the disadvantage of adherence to any policy essentially negative in character, Secretary of State George C. Marshall proposed on June 5, 1947, a positive, forward-looking policy to complement it by making a consistent effort to immunize western Europe to communism by promoting its economic recovery. The Marshall plan was in a sense, but in only a limited sense, successor to the wartime relief organization UNRRA.

UNRRA

The United Nations Relief and Rehabilitation Administration was formed in Washington on November 9, 1943, by representatives of forty-four allied and associated nations then at war, to provide food, clothing and shelter, and aid in the prevention of pestilence and the recovery of health to the populations of areas liberated by the armed forces of the United Nations. Former Governor Herbert H. Lehman of New York was its first director general. During and after the war, UNRRA was actively engaged throughout the liberated areas, supplying seed, livestock, and machinery for the restoration of agriculture and industrial production, as well as immediate relief and medical and surgical supplies.

In 1945 and 1946 UNRRA sent to Europe and the Far East more than one and one-third million dollars' worth of supplies. The United States furnished 90 percent of the food and paid 72 percent of the operating expenses. At the end of 1946 it discontinued its support. Its withdrawal was occasioned less by loss of interest in the relief of obvious distress than by a growing realization of its cost, the spread of skepticism as to whether those being helped were doing all they could to help themselves, and the uncomfortable knowledge that UNRRA supplies were being used in eastern Europe to support communist regimes unfriendly to the United States.

ECA AND OEEC

The Marshall plan recognized that aid was still needed, but proposed to help principally those nations that most actively aided themselves. Although no political controls were stipulated, it was generally assumed that the United States was offering aid to its friends, as a counterpoise to political domination by the USSR. Secretary Marshall suggested a coördinated continental European reconstruction program in which Britain, France, and the USSR were all invited to participate, with the full coöperation of the United States. Soviet Foreign Commissar Molotov attended, with Bevin and Bidault, the first conference of three foreign ministers at Paris to consider the invitation. There he objected to the proposal, however, on the ground that it would infringe upon the sovereignty of participants, and accused Bevin and Bidault of splitting Europe when he withdrew from the conference. The USSR not only did not further participate but prevented Czechoslovakia from participating in the conference of sixteen nations which met in Paris in July, 1947, to draw up a plan for general economic recovery with Marshall plan support. The USSR encouraged Communists everywhere to denounce and sabotage the program as a manifestation of United States imperialist aggression. Although the central and eastern European states with communist-dominated governments had accepted UNRRA aid and found it useful, they also held aloof. Austria, Belgium, Denmark, France,

Greece, Iceland, Ireland (Eire), Italy, Luxemburg, the Netherlands, Norway, Portugal, Sweden, Switzerland, Turkey, and the United Kingdom of Great Britain and Northern Ireland participated. Sir Oliver Franks, later British ambassador to the United States, was a leader in the work of the conference.

Of the $22,440,000,000 which the conference estimated that the European Recovery Program (ERP) would need in food, fuel, raw materials, and capital equipment within four years, the United States Congress appropriated on April 3, 1948, an installment of $6,800,000 for the first fifteen months, to be supplemented by subsequent appropriations, and authorized the establishment in the United States of an Economic Cooperation Administration (ECA) to administer it. Paul G. Hoffman was the first ECA administrator. The European organization to screen the requests of participating governments for aid, and to elaborate a long-term economic plan for coöperation and recovery was the Organization for European Economic Cooperation (OEEC).

A direct agreement was made with the United States as to the use of the funds or materials given by each nation receiving aid. Each participating nation was authorized to sell ERP materials to its own people, and to use the funds so raised to buttress its credit and bolster its economy. Aside from its general interest in the economic recovery of Europe, the United States hoped to secure in return and to stockpile some essential raw materials.

ECA and OEEC reports soon indicated that some recovery was evident and more in prospect, and that Marshall plan aid was contributing materially both to recovery and to a reviving spirit of confidence. Whether recovery would continue, however, if Marshall plan aid were discontinued, how long the aid would therefore need to be continued, and what the ultimate total cost might be, were perplexing questions. Russian and other communist opposition to the program soon assumed the proportions of a new menace to the peace, called in popular parlance "the cold war."

Cominform

SOVIET SPHERE OF INFLUENCE

While the western powers planned and worked to keep western Europe free from communist control, the Communists took control and strengthened Russian influence in east central and southeastern Europe.

Disillusioned since 1938 as to the reality of western aid, former

Premier and President Eduard Beneš and Jan Masaryk, son of the first president of Czechoslovakia, acting for the Czechoslovakian government in exile, made a treaty of friendship and mutual assistance with the Soviet Union December 12, 1943. They hoped to make their centrally located and economically westward-oriented country serve as a bridge between east and west in Europe.

Finland, Poland, Rumania, and Bulgaria fell under the control of the Red Army when it invaded them in 1944. Deeply committed militarily as it was at the time in France, and politically interested in Italy and Greece, the British government had little choice but to agree to a temporary division of southeastern Europe into provisional spheres of influence roughly coterminous with the areas occupied. Similarly committed militarily in France, and not in a favorable position to veto the arrangement, the United States, with serious misgivings, concurred. At the armistice the western Allies preserved approximately their preferred position in Italy and Greece; and Russia kept hers in eastern Europe and the Balkans, north of Greece and Thrace.

Confronted then with the fact that Russian influence and communism were for the time being paramount in the countries overrun and held by the Red Army, the men responsible for United States and British policy had to recognize that situation. They regarded it, however, and their recognition of it, as only temporary, subject to change when peace followed armistice, and when the free and fully democratic elections which had been promised should be held. Then they supposed that strong noncommunist, nonfascist, democratic elements which they knew existed would take their places in reconstituted governments.

The few elections held did not produce the changes anticipated and hoped for by the west; and western protests against undemocratic election procedures and the unrepresentative character of the new governments were rejected.

Communist Control

The second step in the extension of Russian influence in her European sphere of influence was the consolidation of communist control in the hands of a closely knit and disciplined Soviet-sponsored minority. Noncommunists were not at first excluded from parliaments, cabinets, or other government positions; but Communists usually first got control of the police and key positions such as ministries of the interior, foreign affairs, and defense in what were called united-front governments combining all democratic nonfascist elements. From those positions they infiltrated others.

The strongest noncommunist parties numerically were generally the Agrarian and the Socialist. The Agrarians were usually interested in land reform to break up the remaining great estates, and would have modernized and mechanized agricultural production by encouraging the development of coöperatives among small holders. Collectivization had, therefore, usually to be held for a while in abeyance. Urban proletariats were ordinarily ready for socialization of the principal industrial resources and means of production, but not for complete communization. It was prudent, then, for the first postwar governments in the Soviet sphere of influence to occupy the high ground and strong points, so to speak, by communizing at first only the basic industries and utilities, banks, and insurance companies, while private ownership and trading continued elsewhere; but the general trend was toward more complete communization, and the opposition was subjected to a constant grinding process of attrition.

The degree of industrialization already attained and the proportion of bourgeois elements affected were highest in Czechoslovakia; but for reasons of other than economic policy President Beneš readily took some Communists into the Czechoslovak cabinet. Klement Gottwald was premier in 1946, Antonin Zápotocký speaker of the parliament, Jan Masaryk nominally minister for foreign affairs but with a Communist undersecretary, Beneš president with limited powers.

The third step in the consolidation of communist domination within each national government was the transition from participation as one of several minority groups in government coalitions, called united fronts, to assumption of complete control by the elimination of the other parties. In Yugoslavia, where Marshal Tito had an army of his own, and Poland, where President Boleslaw Bierut was carried into power by the Red Army, the opposition was never very dangerous to the new regimes. But in Yugoslavia General Mihailović, who as leader of the Chetniks and minister of war of the royal government in exile did not coöperate with Tito's Communist partisans, was brought to trial and executed on charge of treason in 1946; and Roman Catholic Archbishop Aloysius Stepinac of Zagreb was sentenced to eleven to sixteen years' imprisonment and confiscation of property on charge of wartime collaboration with the Axis puppet government in Croatia.

The Yugoslav monarchy was abolished November 29, 1945; the Bulgarian by plebiscite of September 8, 1946; the Rumanian December 30, 1947. Power passed in Bulgaria into the hands of the veteran Communist leader Georgi Dimitrov, in Rumania into those of Premier Petru Groza and Anna Pauker, minister of foreign affairs, in Hungary into those of Matyas Rakosi.[14]

Members of the various Agrarian or peasant small holders' parties generally outnumbered Communists in southeastern Europe in the middle forties and resisted collectivization, which they feared would reduce them to the status of a rural proletariat. When the Communists secured control of the machinery of government and the police, they attacked the Agrarians relentlessly. Noncommunist members of the cabinet coalitions were forced out of office as enemies of the people and traitors to the new peoples' democracies. Agrarian leader G. M. (not Georgi) Dimitrov escaped from Bulgaria, but Nikola Petkov was executed. Premier Ferenc Nagy of Hungary and former Premier Stanislaw Mikolajczyk of Poland, both peasants' party leaders, fled in fear for their lives in 1947 and sought asylum outside their homelands. Socialist leaders, less strong and so less dangerous, generally fared better personally but not politically.

On November 3, 1950, the General Assembly of the United Nations adopted a resolution introduced by the member from Australia censuring Bulgaria, Hungary, and Rumania for their refusal to fulfill their treaty obligations in the field of human rights, which had been confirmed by the International Court of Justice, and noted with anxiety the continuance of serious accusations against the three governments. Only the USSR and Ukraine voted in the Security Council in September, 1949, to nominate them for membership in the United Nations.

COMMUNIST INFORMATION BUREAU

The Soviet Union's answer to the anticommunist aspect of the Marshall plan was the further consolidation of Russian influence in eastern and southeastern Europe through the Communist Information Bureau (Cominform), a Council for Economic Mutual Assistance, and an inclusive network of alliances. The Cominform, formed at Belgrade in September, 1947, took the place of the Communist International which had been officially abolished in May, 1943. The use of the Cominform as an agency to insure uniformity of policy toward the west and of both policy and method in internal affairs was demonstrated by general denunciation of Marshal Tito for disobedience of its instructions when in 1948 Yugoslavia got out of line.

[14] Georgi Dimitrov was one of the defendants in the Berlin Reichstag fire trials of 1933. He died in Russia in July, 1949.

The Marshall plan did not prohibit or actually stop trade with non-participating countries; but Russian trade with the other nonparticipants increased in the first years from less than 5 percent of her foreign trade to more than half of her exports and more than a third of her imports. The Cominform countries sent to the Soviet Union in those years approximately twice as much in goods as it sent to them. The difference was partially balanced in the cases of Hungary and Rumania, as in that of Finland, by reparation payments due.

A series of dual mutual assistance pacts made from 1947 to 1949 bound all members of the Cominform and the Council for Economic Mutual Assistance together, each to each of the others and all to the USSR, in a network of alliances.

Communist and Russian influence continued to be strengthened. In Hungary in 1949 Joseph Cardinal Mindszenty, well known as an obstinate and outspoken enemy of communist control of education and of the collectivization of the land, much of which was owned by the church, was accused of treason, conspiracy with foreign enemies of the republic, and violation of the currency laws, and was sentenced to life imprisonment. A new parliament adopted a constitution closely modeled, as were those of the other so-called "peoples' democracies," on that of the Soviet Union. Three former Communist leaders, including former Minister of the Interior Laszlo Rajk, a veteran of the communist intervention in the civil war in Spain, were hanged for treason in October and five others were given prison sentences. For having deviated from the Cominform policy and the party line, Rajk was called, at his trial, a nationalist deviationist and an agent of western imperialists. The abjectness of the confessions of both Rajk and Cardinal Mindszenty, quite at variance with their defiant attitude and courageous conduct prior to arrest, was strongly reminiscent of the behavior of those accused in the Moscow purge trials of 1936-1937.

In Poland in 1949 power was well concentrated by grace of Soviet Russia in the hands of President Boleslaw Bierut, Premier Josef Cyrankiewicz, and the new minister of defense, Marshal Konstanty Rokosowski (formerly Konstantin Rokossowsky), put at Poland's disposal by the Red Army and the USSR. Rokosowski was made a Polish citizen by decree, and commander in chief of the Polish army. Most of the other officers of the Polish army, although many of them were of Polish origin or family background, had made their military careers in the Red Army.

Bulgaria was politically sovietized in 1948. Under a new church law adopted in February, 1949, a number of Bulgarian Protestant churchmen were brought to trial on charges of having worked against the democratic institutions of the state and engaged in espionage in the interest of the western imperialists whose churches supported them financially as a missionary enterprise. Embalmed as Lenin's had been, the body of Georgi Dimitrov was brought back from southern Russia where he died, and his successor Vulko Chervenkov read over it a funeral oration copied from Stalin's of 1924 over the body of Lenin. For enforcing against Soviet citizens some of the regulations imposed upon other aliens, and so betraying his shameful assumption that Bulgaria might have interests of her own apart from or at variance with the interests of the Soviet Union, Traicho Kostov, second secretary of the Communist party under Dimitrov, and principal organizer of the new Bulgarian economic plan, was accused of deviation, insincerity toward the Soviet Union, and insincerity in self-criticism. Kostov was brought to trial December 7 on charges of espionage, conspiracy, and high treason. He was found guilty, sentenced December 14, and hanged in Sofia on December 16, 1949.

Czechoslovakia went far during the years 1945 to 1947, inclusive, toward completion of radical social reforms and revolutionary nationalization of resources and industry without quite destroying democratic political liberties; but it was abruptly transformed in February, 1948, into a "people's democracy" of the Soviet-approved type. The change was made without direct intervention of the Red Army and with little disorder or violence—except to the liberties and susceptibilities of those who opposed the change.

President Beneš recognized the change in legal form February 27, resigned June 7, and died in retirement on September 3. On March 10 Foreign Minister Jan Masaryk, who in 1947 accepted an invitation to a conference in Paris to set up the Marshall plan, then after a flying visit to Moscow withdrew his acceptance of the invitation, was found dead beneath a window from which he had jumped or been thrown. The new communist government announced his death as a suicide.

Masaryk and Beneš were the last prominent official representatives of the old democratic Czechoslovakia of the period between the wars. The pre-Munich minister of defense, General Jan Syrový, who said in 1938 that the Czechoslovak army would not welcome the Red Army as an ally, was sentenced in 1947 to twenty years' hard labor. In 1948 Klement Gottwald succeeded Beneš as president, and Antonin Zápotocký followed Gottwald as premier. Vladimir Clementis took Masaryk's place as foreign minister. As in other Cominform countries, there were Catholic Church and party purges in Czechoslovakia in 1948 and 1949. A Czech newspaper was the first to publish announcement that Yugoslavia had been expelled from the Comintern. In 1951 it was announced that Clementis had been arrested for treasonable activity in the interest of the western powers.

Only Yugoslavia rebelled. Tito had an army before the Red Army arrived on its liberating mission in 1944, and he and his party needed less help from Russia to get control of their country. They showed early signs of nationalist deviation from Cominform policy both in the matter of collectivization of peasant landholdings and as to the filial acceptance of Russian methods within Yugoslavia and the preëminence of Russian interests in world affairs as well as in commercial relations with other members of the Comintern.

On June 28, 1948, anniversary of Sarajevo and traditionally a day of great national significance to the Serbs, the Prague *Rude Pravo* published a Cominform communiqué to the effect that Yugoslavia had been expelled from that organization. Within two years, commercial treaties and alliances with the culprit state were canceled by the others of the Cominform. But Tito made few concessions to them, and only a few propitiatory gestures toward the noncommunist western powers. More often than not, as if its difficulties with the Cominform were only family squabbles that should not affect relations with the outside world, Yugoslavia voted with the others in support of Soviet Russian policy in international conferences and forums such as the Security Council and Assembly of the United Nations and the 1948 conference on control of the Danube. In October, 1949, the Soviet Union supported Czechoslovakia rather than Yugoslavia for a seat on the Security Council of the United Nations. Yugoslavia won the election by a vote of thirty-nine to nineteen.

CONFERENCE ON CONTROL OF THE DANUBE, 1948

At the Paris conference of 1946 the western powers insisted that a subsequent conference be held to take up the question of new guarantees of freedom of transit on the Danube, to replace the prewar international convention and preserve the international character of that river, which the United States would have preferred to see completely internationalized. Articles providing for the conference were included in the treaties of peace with Hungary, Bulgaria, and Rumania.

The nations met at Belgrade from July 30 to August 18, 1948. All of the riparian states but Austria, with which no peace treaty had been made, were represented: Czechoslovakia, Hungary, Yugoslavia,

Bulgaria, Rumania, Ukraine; also Britain, France, Russia, and the United States. As leader of the Soviet delegation Commissar Andrei Vyshinsky controlled a solid bloc of seven delegations and dominated the conference. Although Yugoslavia was already out of favor in the Comintern, and Vyshinsky and the leaders of other Comintern delegations made some openly anti-Tito statements, publicly, outside the conference, the Yugoslav delegation did not break ranks or get out of step within the conference.

As chairman of the conference, Vyshinsky set the tone of the meeting at the outset by excluding the use of English as an official language. If the British and Americans were displeased, he said, the door by which they had entered was still open, and they were free to leave. It was clear that he intended to maintain his contention that the regulation of traffic on the Danube was the affair of riparian states only— and the USSR.

The new convention drafted at Belgrade conceded the principle of freedom of navigation, but kept the machinery of regulation entirely in the hands of the riparian states, with Rumania and Yugoslavia in control of the Iron Gate and Rumania and the USSR (Ukraine) of the river's mouth. Britain, France, Belgium, Germany, Greece, and Italy lost the rights they had enjoyed as members of the prewar regulating commission. Protesting against the voiding of their treaty rights, France and Britain refused to participate in the final vote. The United States voted alone against the convention, the disciplined Slav bloc of seven for it.

Berlin Blockade and Airlift

ACCESS TO BERLIN

As a result of military developments Berlin became an international occupation zone in May, 1945, located like an island well within the previously agreed-on Russian zone of occupation. It was agreed by the Allies that the Berlin international zone should be jointly governed by a four-power Control Council of commanders in chief of the occupying forces, whose decisions were to be unanimous as a guarantee of appropriate uniformity of action in the separate zones. A four-power statement of June 5, 1945, indicated that the Control Council should also "reach agreed decisions on the chief questions affecting Germany as a whole."[15]

"Agreed decisions" among the British, United States, and French

[15] New York *Times,* September 7, 1947; *supra,* pp. 714-715, 738-739.

commanders were not difficult to reach; but, especially after Marshal Zhukov was recalled, the Russian member of the *Kommandatura* often disagreed with the other three. Unanimous decisions affecting Germany or the Berlin zone itself were therefore difficult and rare. The right of the western Allies to be in Berlin on a completely equal footing with the Russians was not then questioned, however. The right to be there meant the right of access, which was granted: access by canal, railway, road, air, telegraph, and telephone.

Blockade

No progress having been made toward completion of a German peace treaty or toward the establishment of a uniform occupation policy, the western Allies proposed at a conference in London in March, 1948, that a federal government of western Germany be established, to include their three occupation zones. Marshal Vasili Sokolovsky, successor to Zhukov as Russian commander in Berlin, walked out of the Control Council there, proclaimed that the western Allies had no right to be in Berlin, and imposed restrictions on train traffic between the western zones and Berlin. Those restrictions were tightened into a complete ground blockade in June, when the Allies introduced a new currency to reduce inflation and check illegal trading.

The Allies countered with an airlift, which kept west Berlin supplied while the Russians cut off the supply of electric current and of food. Later the Allies retaliated further by closing the eastern frontier of the western zone to interzonal trade.

Negotiations

In direct negotiations in Moscow beginning July 30, 1948, Great Britain, France, and the United States proposed to withdraw the western-zone currency from circulation in Berlin, provided that four-power control of the east Berlin bank of issue could guarantee a sufficient supply of currency and credit for occupation costs and business needs in west Berlin, provided that trade between Berlin and the western zone and with other countries, then controlled by the Russians, could be supervised by a four-power commission, and provided that the blockade was lifted. Stalin agreed orally to all of those proposals and referred the agreement to Molotov for drafting. Molotov made difficulties.

The Soviet foreign commissar said that, by violating the agreement to administer all Germany as a unit, the Allies had forfeited their right to be in Berlin and could have access to the city only as the Russians chose to give it to them. He tried also to tie the continuance of negotiations on the Berlin blockade question to an indefinite postponement of the federalization of western Germany. A second interview with Stalin secured a draft of a directive, details of which were to be worked out by the Control Council in Berlin, to lift the blockade and resume trade, with four-power control of currency in Berlin and of trade with western Germany and with other countries. Marshal Sokolovsky returned to the Control Council for a few meetings only to sabotage that agreement as Molotov had done.

It appeared that the Russians were deliberately prolonging the negotiations until winter weather and the long hours of darkness soon to be expected in the Berlin area would so retard the operation of the airlift that cold and hunger, affecting some two and a half million people in the Allied sectors in Berlin, would force the hands of the Allies. United States Ambassador Walter Bedell Smith came to the conclusion that Stalin must be capable of contradicting himself and even, on occasion, of deliberately deceiving his auditor.[16]

On September 22, 1948, the western powers terminated the negotiations until the blockade should be lifted. A week later they laid the issue before the Security Council of the United Nations as a threat to peace. With Vyshinsky representing the USSR in the Security Council, ready with his veto, the Council failed at first to effect a settlement of the problem. Then the Assembly tried; but the Assembly committee's report was not taken up in the Council. The USSR was too powerful, and its attitude uncompromising.

AIRLIFT AND END OF BLOCKADE

The airlift carried Berlin through the winter. By May 12, when the blockade was lifted, 1,583,686 tons of supplies had been flown in, 1,214,339 by United States aircraft and 369,347 by British, at a cost of $170,000,000. Additional supplies flown in during a tapering-off period raised the total to 2,323,738 tons by the end of September, 1949.[17]

The thaw came in the spring, after the western powers had shown convincingly their determination not to be bullied or badgered out of Berlin, after the airlift had demonstrated that west Berlin could and would be supplied by air, and after the signing of the North Atlantic

[16] Walter Bedell Smith, *op. cit.*, 62.

[17] The captured documents of the German Foreign Office, in process of screening by an Allied team of scholars for partial publication, were flown to England for safer keeping.

Pact (q.v., *infra*). The facilities of the United Nations for amicable adjustment of disputes were always available but were only incidentally used. The first break in the ice jam of the Berlin blockade sector of the "cold war" came in informal conversations between Jacob A. Malik (USSR) and Philip C. Jessup (USA) in New York, where both men had spoken for their governments in the UN Assembly and Security Council throughout the crisis. It was not the facilities that failed.

Agreement in principle was reached May 4 that the blockade should be lifted on May 12, and that the Council of Foreign Ministers should meet again to discuss basic terms of policy with reference to Germany and Austria. The blockade was lifted as agreed, and the council met in Paris from May 23 to June 20, 1949; but little progress was made toward drafting terms of peace for Germany or Austria. Both countries continued under occupation, while the world tried to stabilize a state of instability.

FEDERALIZATION OF WESTERN GERMANY

The republican federalization of Germany west of the Russian zone was completed by the adoption of a federal constitution by a parliamentary council at Bonn on May 8, 1949. The basic law provided for a federal diet or Bundestag, members of which would be directly elected for a four-year term, and a federal council or Bundesrat, composed as the Weimar council had been of members of the state governments. Parties like the Nazi, which by their aims or by the behavior of their supporters were calculated to damage or destroy the fundamental free democratic order, were declared unconstitutional. To avoid the too frequent or irresponsible overthrow of the government, another weakness of the Weimar republic, the constitution provided that the Bundestag must choose a new chancellor by majority vote before it could, by a vote of no confidence, ask the president to dismiss the old one.

Elections to the federal diet were held August 14. In September Theodor Heuss was elected president of the federal republic, and a former mayor of Köln, Konrad Adenauer, leader of the Christian Democratic (largely Catholic) party, became chancellor. Adenauer's government was a coalition of his party with the Free Democratic (Liberal) and the German parties.

The adoption of the Bonn constitution was evidence of failure of the Russian attempt to prevent the federalization of west Germany by blockading Berlin. Immediately after the lifting of the blockade, an election was held throughout the Russian-occupied zone of Germany and east Berlin, with a single zonal list of candidates, to choose a people's congress. In October a German Democratic Republic was proclaimed in the Soviet zone. Wilhelm Pieck was elected president by the two houses of the congress, and Otto Grotewohl of the Socialist-Unity party (*Socialistische Einheitspartei Deutschlands*, SED) formed a government, the key ministries of which were held by Communists.

The situation of the German people was uncomfortable, the future uncertain and unpromising. The former German territory east of the Oder-Neisse line seemed likely to be lost to Poland for as long as Russia chose to help Poland hold it. Polish settlers soon replaced on the land the millions of Germans dispossessed and driven out. No German could contemplate but with dismay the thought of a permanently divided Germany. The question in west Germany was whether one would prefer a reunited Germany, communist-controlled, or freedom from communist control in a truncated part of a divided Germany. An interim choice seemed to be continuance of the occupation.

Life went on, but under difficulty. The understandable insistence of the occupation authorities upon considering eligible for office or other positions of responsibility only those free from the taint of National Socialism meant, all too often, government and administration by greybeards or incompetents whom the Nazi had not thought worth recruiting for their use. The occupation authorities announced that they intended to dismantle only the surplus factories which had built up Germany's war potential beyond her peacetime needs. But Germans soon objected that the dismantling program was being carried beyond all reason in disregard of the hard facts that, cut off as it was from food supplies from the agricultural areas of eastern Germany, west Germany needed to manufacture more than before for export, and that despite war losses the population of west Germany had increased with the migration of millions of displaced or repatriated Germans.

As the threat of war between east and west increased, the question of rearming western Germany, or of permitting it to rearm itself, arose. West Germans, living in the first danger zone, debated whether they wished to be rearmed. In east Germany a very strong communist-controlled police force alarmingly like a reincarnated Nazi SS was formed, trained, and equipped in military fashion.

The North Atlantic Defense Pact

Fear of communist aggression led apprehensive thinkers in western Europe to review the failure of the "peace-loving states" to combine in time to prevent aggression in Manchuria, Ethiopia, Spain, or Poland in 1931-1939. The lesson some such thinkers thought they had learned was that the aggressors who first attacked their neighbors might not have taken the risk of making those attacks if they had known they would meet precisely the resistance which eventually they met. If so, then let others who might contemplate aggression know in good time that it would be met with adequate force.

Failure of the United Nations to achieve in its first years the power, prestige, and effectiveness as a world peace agency which its sponsors hoped it would achieve was marked by the failure of its members to provide the international armed force, under its control, which its charter contemplated. It seemed at first to be, in that respect, only another League of Nations. The continuing international tensions of the postwar years, however, contributed to the growth of a rather general opinion that, in the world as it then was, peace was to be secured only by a preponderance of power, if necessary of military power, in the hands of those who wanted peace.

Soviet Russian and Cominform spokesmen and Communists everywhere spoke constantly of fighting for peace and at the same time threatened war; spoke of democracy and screamed imprecations at politically more democratic nations; circulated peace petitions and talked of disarmament and inevitable revolution, and war to the death between communism and capitalism. The result was to reawaken in the western world a sense of danger, and a realization of the continuing necessity of collective action for security—a necessity half-forgotten in the period of relaxation after the war.

BENELUX UNION: BELGIUM, THE NETHERLANDS, AND LUXEMBURG, 1948

The economic problems of recovery came first for the Low Countries. Such problems were less serious in Belgium than in the kingdom of the Netherlands, but in Belgium there were political considerations also. Luxemburg was incorporated into Germany during the war, but its government in exile returned at once after liberation and resumed its close currency and trade ties with Belgium. Queen Wilhelmina of the Netherlands returned to a grateful and loyal people and ended gracefully a reign of fifty years by abdicating in favor of her daughter Juliana. The Netherlands were hard hit economically by losses in the Indies and by diversion of Rhineland trade to Hamburg and Bremen. King Leopold of Belgium could not at first return. Too many of his people remembered without pride the fascist trappings and in effect pro-German policy of his prewar Rexist party, and his capitulation in 1940 with his army. To preserve domestic peace, when he returned in 1950, he was required to name his son Prince Baudouin regent, and to promise to abdicate in Baudouin's favor when the prince came of age.

The Benelux union of Belgium, the Netherlands, and Luxemburg was a tariff union. The agreement was drafted in 1946 in accord with a convention signed in London in 1944, and went into effect January 1, 1948. It provided at first for a common tariff on foreign trade, not for free trade between the members of the union or for uniformity of excise taxes, or for a common currency. Although the treaty made provision for an economic union only, the recognition of common interests of which it was itself an indication was carried over into the international political sphere, and the three nations went together into the Western Union of 1948 and the North Atlantic Pact of 1949.

Western European Union, 1948

The declared intention of the Soviet Union and the Cominform to wreck the European recovery program called the Marshall plan, in which they refused to participate, was alarming to the peoples of western Europe and drove them to seek in regional agreements and alliances, within the framework of the United Nations but without dependence on it, much as if it were not there, the protection which they feared it could not give them. Such a general and military alliance was formed by Britain, France, and the Benelux group, for a period of fifty years, at Brussels March 17, 1948. No international armed force or integrated military command organization was at first available. Although a military committee was authorized to make plans for the common defense, it was clear that the armed force at its disposal was not at all imposing, and would be inadequate to meet an attack of the Red Army through Germany.

Council of Europe

The old Briand idea of a United States of Europe was revived after the war by one of his pet creations, the European Parliamentary Union, and received support from such distinguished individuals as Mr. Winston Churchill and Edouard Herriot of France. Under further sponsorship of the Western European Union the statute for a sort of parliament of Europe, to be called the Council of Europe, was signed in London May 5, 1949, by men from Britain, France, Belgium, the Netherlands, Luxemburg, Ireland, Italy, Denmark, Norway, and Sweden.

The first meeting of the council was at its headquarters at Strasbourg August 10, 1949. Greece, Turkey, and Iceland were invited to join the organization, and the Saar and western Germany were later offered associate membership. The organization thus approached universality as to membership, but was only a forum. It could discuss and recommend but not legislate, or stop aggression. It was only too clear that, no matter how western Europe planned or what its statesmen said to one another or to the press, it could not stop the Red Army without help from the United States.

THE NORTH ATLANTIC TREATY

The Truman and Marshall plans were proof that the United States was not indifferent to the course of events in Europe, and the airlift showed that it was in Berlin and Germany to stay while it considered its presence there necessary in its own interest and for the peace and safety of Europe and the world. The North Atlantic Defense Pact was the product of its decision that the Soviet threat of force must be met by a show of force.

While the Western European Union was being formed and the Cominform consolidated, and while the airlift was being extemporized to beat the Berlin blockade, the United States Senate adopted in June, 1948, a resolution brought in by Senator Vandenberg: that the United States encourage and participate in mutual collective security arrangements affecting its own security. It was informally proposed through diplomatic channels that the United States and Canada join the members of the Brussels-pact Western European Union in a defense pact for the security of the North Atlantic area. Negotiations were continued through the winter of 1948-1949, and a treaty was signed in Washington April 4, 1949.

The parties—Belgium, Canada, Denmark, France, Iceland, Italy, Luxemburg, the Netherlands, Norway, Portugal, the United Kingdom, and the United States—reaffirmed their faith in the principles and purposes of the United Nations and their desire to live in peace, then declared their resolution to unite their efforts for collective defense and for the preservation of peace and security. They agreed to maintain by self-help and mutual aid their individual and collective capacity

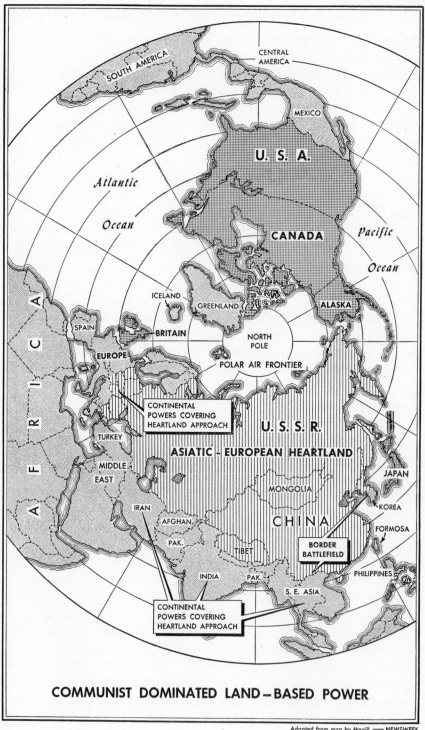

COMMUNIST DOMINATED LAND – BASED POWER

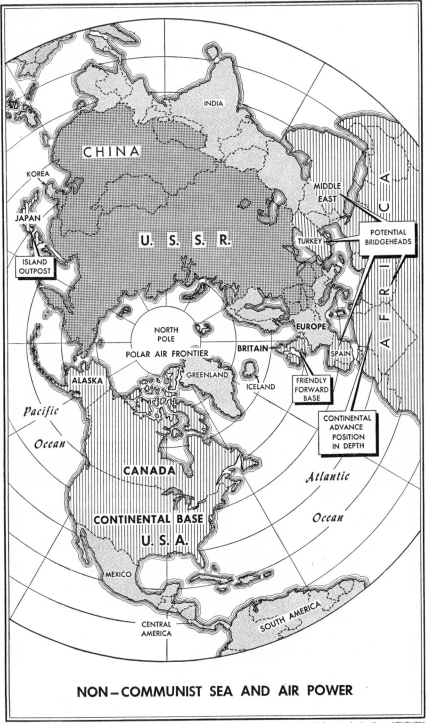

NON – COMMUNIST SEA AND AIR POWER

Adapted from map by Magill —— NEWSWEEK

to resist armed attack, and to consult together when threatened. An armed attack against the territory or armed forces of any of them, including occupation forces, in Europe or North America or north of the tropic of Cancer in the Atlantic, should be considered an attack against them all. Other European states might, by unanimous agreement of the parties, be invited to accede to the treaty.[18]

Litvinov said for the USSR in the Assembly of the League of Nations in 1938 that the way to stop armed aggression was to meet it with armed force. His successors called the North Atlantic Pact an indication of intention to commit aggression. The makers of the alliance called it a defense measure, hoping that a show of force and readiness to use it would prevent aggression and keep peace.

Before any member of the defensive North Atlantic alliance was attacked or called upon to aid another, all were summoned by the Security Council of the United Nations, as members of that organization, to help the Republic of South Korea resist attack from North Korea.

KOREA, 1950

Civil War in China

CHINA'S EIGHTEEN YEARS' WAR

War occupied China eighteen years, beginning at Mukden in 1931 and returning to Manchuria in 1945, unfortunately not ending there but spreading as a civil war and revolution. For a promising short period in 1937 and 1938 nationalist and communist China made common cause against the Japanese; most of the time they fought one another, or harried the Japanese separately. United States war leaders were disturbed by what they learned of the quantities of military supplies furnished with great effort by the United States for use against the Japanese that were wastefully and ineffectually used by Chiang Kai-shek against the Chinese Communists. Their sympathies were further alienated by what they learned about financial corruption as well as inefficiency and reactionary ideas on political, economic, and social questions, prevalent among favorites and officials in high places. Reports that the Communists could arm and equip themselves with American weapons and vehicles sold or too easily surrendered to them by nationalist generals on the run threatened at times to dry up the sources of supply.[19]

[18] See Appendix F.
[19] See pp. 452-461, 494-504, and 772-774.

The Yalta agreements concerning China were incorporated in a Russia-China treaty in August, 1945. The Soviet Union recognized the nationalist government of Chiang Kai-shek as the government of China, which implied no further aid to Mao Tse-tung and the Chinese Communists. China agreed to the Soviet Union's regaining, after the expulsion of the Japanese, the treaty rights taken from imperial Russia by the Japanese in 1905: the use of a naval base at Port Arthur and a free port at Dairen, and railway rights in Manchuria. Manchuria was to be returned to China.

When Japan surrendered, the Chinese Communist forces were concentrated principally in northern China, nationalists in the south. The Communists got possession of considerable quantities of Japanese military equipment, and of the Peiping-Mukden railway. The Russians treated Japanese capital investment in Manchuria as war booty, dismantled much of it and moved it out, then let the Communists take over, as the latter were in better position to do than the nationalists. The Russians would not permit nationalist troops to land at Port Arthur or Dairen. The United States Air Transport Command flew in a small United States-equipped nationalist army; but that army could occupy only the southern part of the province and could not hold that indefinitely. It lost Mukden in October, 1948.

The United States was interested primarily in seeing an effective national government established in China, able to maintain itself, establish order, and accept responsibility for the obligations which a national government could be expected to assume. If compelled to choose between a communist and a noncommunist government, it would presumably and not unnaturally have chosen the latter, as the one with which it would probably be more likely to be able to deal with some confidence. That meant supporting Chiang Kai-shek, whether it had full confidence in him or not.

For analogous reasons but without public explanation or, at first, acknowledgment of its policy, the USSR chose Mao Tse-tung and the Communists, although it had officially disavowed them by making its 1945 treaty with nationalist China.

MARSHALL MEDIATION

Hoping to end the long civil war without further devastation, in December, 1945, President Truman asked the recently retired army chief of staff, General George C. Marshall, to undertake a mission of reconciliation in China. The old soldier tried for a year. His only success was a truce during which an all-party congress at Chunking rewrote the constitution of 1936, which had never been accepted. The new constitution was promulgated by Chiang Kai-shek December 31, 1946, after acceptance by a national assembly at Nanking which Communists were not invited to attend. The constitution was to go into effect one year later, but the communist-controlled parts of China did not participate in the November, 1947, elections; and the national assembly, although elected from nationalist areas, found that it had no real legislative power or control of government.

COMMUNIST ASCENDANCY

Neither side was willing to compromise. The nationalist government tried to fight communism with force rather than reform, and failed. Many of its military and civil leaders were inefficient and corrupt. Aid from the United States, continued through 1948, sifted through their fingers or lined their pockets, while the economy of the country continued to deteriorate and the military situation went from bad to worse. The United States appeared to have bought into a bankrupt business which it could neither revive nor liquidate. As the nationalist government progressively lost the respect and earned the hatred of millions of its people, the United States was hated also for supporting it. The bombing of a communist-held Chinese city by nationalists using United States equipment and ordnance was likely to be resented as an "American bombing." By the end of 1949 communist ascendancy, except in the last nationalist stronghold on Formosa, was virtually complete. The USSR withdrew its recognition of the nationalist government in October, 1949.

THE RECOGNITION QUESTION

Many national governments, one of them the British, recognized the communist regime as the *de facto* government of China. The United States did not so recognize it. The USSR made a treaty of friendship and alliance with it, signed February 14, 1950. With Soviet support, it had already taken up the cudgels for recognition by the United Nations.

In the Security Council of the United Nations on December 29, 1949, the USSR challenged nationalist China's right to hold China's seat on the Council. The Canadian chairman ruled out the protest as an item not on the agenda. On January 10, 1950, the Soviet delegate, Jacob Malik, walked out of the Council meeting when it refused to give immediate consideration to his resolution to exclude the nationalist Chinese delegate, T. F. Tsiang. Two days later, the Council voted his resolution down, six votes to three: the USSR, India, and Yugoslavia for; the United States, China, France, Cuba, Ecuador, and Egypt against; Britain and Norway abstaining. Malik walked out of the Council, and a few days later out of the group discussing control of atomic energy, and did not return until August 1. After similar attempts to exclude the representatives of nationalist China, all of which were similarly rebuffed, the representatives of the Soviet Union followed Malik's example and walked out of various UN committees. The USSR was in default from January until August on its obligation as a member of the Security Council to be represented there at all times.

Division of Korea

In June, 1950, the United Nations faced a severe test of its strength and determination when South Korea was invaded from North Korea. In that crisis it did what the League of Nations had not dared to do, and probably could not have done if it had dared to try: called upon its members to oppose the aggression with their armed forces under its auspices.

MILITARY OCCUPATION

The Red Army entered north Korea August 8, 1945; United States troops landed in south Korea a month later. The Russians were authorized to accept the surrender of the Japanese troops north of the thirty-eighth parallel, while those south of that line surrendered to the Americans.

So far as the United States forces were concerned, the location of the line was a matter of circumstance and convenience, but it was soon treated much like a national boundary as the two occupying powers found very little area of agreement in which coöperation proved possible. Neither wanted to see Korea divided, but neither would see it entirely controlled by the other.

The occupying forces had other problems than their relations with each other, although those relations were indeed a problem. The Japanese had governed Korea with a heavy hand, in their own interest, and through Japanese officials. They had stamped out every movement for independence or self-government and had systematically guarded against the appearance of a native leader group or class. The few tame Koreans whom they had used as underling officials were for that reason suspect in the eyes of the United States occupation. Potentially capable native leaders and administrators were hard to find. Of trained, able, experienced ones there were nearly none.

The Russians were better prepared to establish a new order quickly in Korea than the Americans. Tsarist Russia had been interested in Korea half a century before, and the USSR was interested. For them Korea did not seem so far away. A swarm of political commissars and civil affairs experts went in with the troops and initiated or promised changes of the sort calculated to win the support of a considerable element of the population, such as land reform. They set up local government of the Soviet-approved type, communist-controlled, and trained and equipped an army quite disproportionate in size to the size or wealth of the population, much larger than was needed for defense against anything South Korea could send against it.

In South Korea government moved less swiftly. The republic was noncommunist and based on popular election, but made slow headway against political and economic problems. The army was equipped only for defense against infantry attack with infantry weapons, less adequately trained than the North Korean, and less thoroughly politically indoctrinated. North Korea, close to great water-power sources along the Yalu River, was more highly industrialized. When alien occupying armies were withdrawn, the North Korean government was better able from the outset to maintain itself or to wage war without help than the South Korean.

The United Nations interested itself in the possibility of ending the geopolitically unnatural division of Korea on the democratic basis of a general election under safeguards to insure its freedom. North Korea would not coöperate or admit to its territory the commissioners sent out; but a UN commission was available in Seoul in June, 1950, to observe and report what happened there.

INVASION OF SOUTH KOREA

Trained North Korean troops equipped for offensive action with tanks, guns, and vehicles of Russian make, and ably led, invaded South Korea June 25, 1950. They captured the South Korean capital in three days. With the sanction and in the name of the Security Council of the United Nations, *minus* Russia, United States troops were sent in by air and sea to help the South Koreans defend themselves, while United States and Australian planes flew from Okinawa and Japan to clear the air of Russian-made planes which supported the North Koreans.

Britain at once placed at the disposal of the United States such naval vessels as she had in Japanese waters, and soon sent up some troops from Hong Kong. Air and sea power were on the side of the defenders, strength and readiness of ground forces on the side of the invaders.

If the United States had planned an invasion of Korea as Malik and the Chinese Communist premier and foreign minister, Chou En-lai, accused it of having done, its forces would have gone in in greater strength and better prepared.

To commit combat units to action piecemeal, to fight a retarding action against superior numbers and equipment, and to build up strength while retiring are difficult military operations. All of those things the defending forces in Korea had to do and did well; but they were compressed into a small perimeter around their entry and supply port Pusan before they accumulated the necessary strength to take advantage of superior sea and air power to make an amphibious landing near Seoul and pinch off the principal supply lines of the North Korean forces. A quick breakout from the Pusan perimeter then followed.

Once the invasion had been rolled back and North Korea largely overrun by troops carrying the United Nations flag, the outcome depended primarily upon the seriousness and extent of Chinese communist or other intervention. The Russian representative in the Security Council of the United Nations called the UN forces the interventionists. The United States tried to keep the China question separate from the Korean, and Korea from Formosa, while the Soviet Union maneuvered in the United Nations organization to connect them.

Collective Action to Restrain Aggression

SECURITY COUNCIL

The Security Council of the United Nations met immediately when notified of the invasion of South Korea. It found North Korea guilty of a breach of the peace, told it sharply to recall its troops, and ordered an immediate cease-fire throughout Korea. Nine nations voted for the resolution: Britain, China, Cuba, Ecuador, Egypt, France, India, Norway, and the United States; none against it. Yugoslavia abstained from voting. Russia, maintaining her walkout since January, was absent. The United States' attempt to limit its commitments by neutralizing Formosa while the Korean issue was being settled was used by Chinese communist and Soviet propaganda to tie the three issues together: Korea, Formosa, and recognition.

On June 27 the Security Council requested the United States and other members of the United Nations to send armed forces to repel the invasion of South Korea. Troops, planes, and ships were already on their way. Seven votes were cast for the resolution, one (by Yugo-slavia) against. Russia was absent, India and Egypt did not vote. The North Korean government angrily protested that the action was illegal, as no representative of that government was present when Korea was discussed, and as the representative of the USSR was not present when the vote was taken.[20]

By a vote of seven to none, with Egypt, India, and Yugoslavia abstaining and Russia absent, the Security Council on July 7 authorized the United States to establish a unified command for the United Nations forces defending southern Korea. General MacArthur was named supreme commander, and flew thereafter the United Nations flag, with that of the United States. Reports were submitted from him regularly to the Security Council. Scores of offers of ships, base hospitals, planes, and troops—the latter generally in token numbers—were received, and many were accepted. In May, 1951, fifteen nations were participating under the United Nations banner in Korea, forty-one contributing.[21]

In August it was the Soviet Union's turn to hold the chairmanship of the Security Council, and its delegate Jacob Malik, who had not been far away, returned to serve as chairman. His first move, on which he was defeated by eight votes to three, was an attempt to unseat the nationalist Chinese delegate, who he said represented no one, in favor of one from communist China. He tried also in vain to have a North Korean delegation heard and spokesmen for South Korea ex-cluded by the Council. Chou En-lai cabled the secretary general that the communist Chinese government insisted upon being seated in the United Nations as the government of China, and would send a delega-tion to the Assembly in September. He also announced that China would not stand idly by and see North Korea overrun.

Spokesmen for South Korea let it be known that they expected the forces which had freed them from invasion to turn over to their government at the earliest possible moment full civil authority over all Korea. In October the United Nations Assembly accepted responsibility

[20] After returning to the Council later, Malik introduced a resolution to strike out of the Council report as illegal all actions taken during his six months' absence. The motion, which would have been tantamount to a reversion to the eighteenth-century Polish practice of "exploding" a diet, failed.

[21] To the UN forces Britain had sent, in addition to naval and naval air forces, some 6000 troops; Turkey 5200; Australia, Canada, France, Greece, New Zealand, the Philippine Islands, and Siam approximately 1000 each; the Netherlands 650 and a destroyer. More than half of the total, and a larger proportion of the weapons and matériel, had been supplied by the United States. The Republic of Korea was reported at that time to have about 100,000 men in the field.

for the settlement then apparently in prospect. The Assembly resolution proposed that all appropriate steps be taken to insure conditions of stability throughout Korea by (1) a unified, independent, and democratic government, and economic rehabilitation; (2) a UN commission for unification and rehabilitation; and (3) plans to be developed by the UN Economic and Social Council for relief and rehabilitation in Korea.

Impressed by the August demonstration of obstructive tactics in the Security Council, and remembering that the prompt action taken there on June 25 could not have been so promptly taken, if at all, if the Soviet delegate had been there with his veto, the Assembly adopted on November 3 a resolution to make it possible to by-pass the Security Council if necessary to get quick collective action. The resolution authorized the convening of the Assembly on a few hours' notice, to use armed force to be put at its disposal by the member nations to stop aggression if the Security Council failed to stop it.

As Chou En-lai had said it would, Red China intervened. A winter of bitter warfare swept the Korean peninsula. By a vote of forty-seven to seven (the Soviet bloc, India, and Burma), with eight members (Afghanistan, Egypt, Indonesia, Pakistan, Sweden, Syria, Yemen, and Yugoslavia) abstaining, the United Nations Assembly adopted on February 1, 1951, a resolution naming communist China an aggressor in Korea for aiding North Korean aggression there.

TOWARD COLLECTIVE SECURITY

Born of war, as the League of Nations was, the United Nations sought as the League had sought to prevent war by promotion of the general welfare and by peaceful settlement of international disputes. Its founders planned that it should be provided with stronger sanctions than the League had had at its disposal, the ultimate sanction being armed force with which to command obedience to its decisions and to prevent or punish acts of unprovoked aggression. Its commission on the ground called the invasion of South Korea an act of unprovoked aggression. South Korea was its creature, legally established as an independent state under its sponsorship and protection. The United Nations could have claimed no authority thereafter, its protection would have been but a feeble thing, grave injustice would have been done if not condoned, and the fear of aggression would have stalked the world unchallenged, if it had not taken steps to defend in South Korea the principle of collective security to which it owed its own existence and by which it was to be justified.

By taking the lead in the Korean enterprise and assuming the heaviest share of the burden and risk, the United States did for the United Nations in 1950 what no member did for the League of Nations when it was challenged by the Japanese, the Italians, and the Germans. Other nations which also wanted peace aligned themselves with it, as it identified its interests with theirs. The issue depended as much upon their strength, unity, and courage as upon the justice of their cause.

Appendixes

APPENDIX A

The Fourteen Points and the League Covenant

THE FOURTEEN POINTS

President Wilson's Address to Congress January 8, 1918

I. Open covenants of peace, openly arrived at, after which there shall be no private international understandings of any kind but diplomacy shall proceed always frankly and in the public view.

II. Absolute freedom of navigation upon the seas, outside territorial waters, alike in peace and in war, except as the seas may be closed in whole or in part by international action for the enforcement of international covenants.

III. The removal, so far as possible, of all economic barriers and the establishment of an equality of trade conditions among all the nations consenting to the peace and associating themselves for its maintenance.

IV. Adequate guarantees given and taken that national armaments will be reduced to the lowest point consistent with domestic safety.

V. A free, open-minded, and absolutely impartial adjustment of all colonial claims, based upon a strict observance of the principle that in determining all such questions of sovereignty the interests of the populations concerned must have equal weight with the equitable claims of the government whose title is to be determined.

VI. The evacuation of all Russian territory and such a settlement of all questions affecting Russia as will secure the best and freest cooperation of the other nations of the world in obtaining for her an unhampered and unembarrassed opportunity for the independent determination of her own political development and national policy and assure her of a sincere welcome into the society of free nations under institutions of her own choosing; and, more than a welcome, assistance also of every kind that she may need and may herself desire. The treatment accorded Russia by her sister nations in the months to come will be the acid test of their good will, of their comprehension of her needs as distinguished from their own interests, and of their intelligent and unselfish sympathy.

851

VII. Belgium, the whole world will agree, must be evacuated and restored, without any attempt to limit the sovereignty which she enjoys in common with all other free nations. No other single act will serve as this will serve to restore confidence among the nations in the laws which they have themselves set and determined for the government of their relations with one another. Without this healing act the whole structure and validity of international law is forever impaired.

VIII. All French territory should be freed and the invaded portions restored, and the wrong done to France by Prussia in 1871 in the matter of Alsace-Lorraine, which has unsettled the peace of the world for nearly fifty years, should be righted, in order that peace may once more be made secure in the interest of all.

IX. A readjustment of the frontiers of Italy should be effected along clearly recognizable lines of nationality.

X. The peoples of Austria-Hungary, whose place among the nations we wish to see safe-guarded and assured, should be accorded the freest opportunity of autonomous development.

XI. Rumania, Serbia, and Montenegro should be evacuated; occupied territories restored; Serbia accorded free and secure access to the sea; and the relations of the several Balkan states to one another determined by friendly counsel along historically established lines of allegiance and nationality; and international guarantees of the political and economic independence and territorial integrity of the several Balkan states should be entered into.

XII. The Turkish portions of the present Ottoman Empire should be assured a secure sovereignty, but the other nationalities which are now under Turkish rule should be assured an undoubted security of life and an absolutely unmolested opportunity of autonomous development, and the Dardanelles should be permanently opened as a free passage to the ships and commerce of all nations under international guarantees.

XIII. An independent Polish state should be erected which should include the territories inhabited by indisputably Polish populations, which should be assured a free and secure access to the sea, and whose political and economic independence and territorial integrity should be guaranteed by international covenant.

XIV. A general association of nations must be formed under specific covenants for the purpose of affording mutual guarantees of political independence and territorial integrity to great and small states alike. . . .

TEXT OF THE COVENANT

(These articles include (in *italics*) amendments to Article 6 (in force from August 13, 1924), Articles 12, 13, and 15 (instated September 26, 1924), and Article 4 (instated July 29, 1926). Paragraphs are numbered according to the resolution adopted by the Assembly on September 21, 1926.)

The Covenant of the League of Nations

The High Contracting Parties,

In order to promote international co-operation and to achieve international peace and security

> by the acceptance of obligations not to resort to war,
>
> by the prescription of open, just and honourable relations between nations,
>
> by the firm establishment of the understandings of international law as the actual rule of conduct among Governments,
>
> and by the maintenance of justice and a scrupulous respect for all treaty obligations in the dealings of organised peoples with one another,

Agree to this Covenant of the League of Nations.

ARTICLE 1

1. The original Members of the League of Nations shall be those of the Signatories which are named in the Annex to this Covenant and also such of those other States named in the Annex as shall accede without reservation to this Covenant. Such accession shall be effected by a Declaration deposited with the Secretariat within two months of the coming into force of the Covenant. Notice thereof shall be sent to all other Members of the League.

2. Any fully self-governing State, Dominion or Colony not named in the Annex may become a Member of the League if its admission is agreed to by two-thirds of the Assembly, provided that it shall give effective guarantees of its sincere intention to observe its international obligations and shall accept such regulations as may be prescribed by the League in regard to its military, naval and air forces and armaments.

3. Any Member of the League may, after two years' notice of its intention so to do, withdraw from the League, provided that all its international obligations and all its obligations under this Covenant shall have been fulfilled at the time of its withdrawal.

ARTICLE 2

The action of the League under this Covenant shall be effected through the instrumentality of an Assembly and of a Council, with a permanent Secretariat.

ARTICLE 3

1. The Assembly shall consist of Representatives of the Members of the League.

2. The Assembly shall meet at stated intervals and from time to time as occasion may require at the Seat of the League or at such other place as may be decided upon.

3. The Assembly may deal at its meetings with any matter within the sphere of action of the League or affecting the peace of the world.

4. At meetings of the Assembly, each Member of the League shall have one vote, and may have not more than three Representatives.

ARTICLE 4

1. The Council shall consist of Representatives of the Principal Allied and Associated Powers, together with Representatives of four other Members of the League. These four Members of the League shall be selected by the Assembly from time to time in its discretion. Until the appointment of the Representatives of the four Members of the League first selected by the Assembly, Representatives of Belgium, Brazil, Spain and Greece, shall be Members of the Council.

2. With the approval of the majority of the Assembly, the Council may name additional Members of the League whose Representatives shall always be Members of the Council; the Council with like approval may increase the number of Members of the League to be selected by the Assembly for representation on the Council.

2 *bis. The Assembly shall fix by a two-thirds majority the rules dealing with the election of the non-permanent Members of the Council, and particularly such regulations as relate to their term of office and the conditions of re-eligibility.*

3. The Council shall meet from time to time as occasion may require, and at least once a year, at the Seat of the League, or at such other place as may be decided upon.

4. The Council may deal at its meetings with any matter within the sphere of action of the League or affecting the peace of the world.

5. Any Member of the League not represented on the Council shall be invited to send a Representative to sit as a member at any meeting of the Council during the consideration of matters specially affecting the interests of that Member of the League.

6. At meetings of the Council, each Member of the League represented on the Council shall have one vote, and may have not more than one Representative.

ARTICLE 5

1. Except where otherwise expressly provided in this Covenant or by the terms of the present Treaty, decisions at any meeting of the Assembly

or of the Council shall require the agreement of all the Members of the League represented at the meeting.

2. All matters of procedure at meetings of the Assembly or of the Council, including the appointment of Committees to investigate particular matters, shall be regulated by the Assembly or by the Council and may be decided by a majority of the Members of the League represented at the meeting.

3. The first meeting of the Assembly and the first meeting of the Council shall be summoned by the President of the United States of America.

ARTICLE 6

1. The permanent Secretariat shall be established at the Seat of the League. The Secretariat shall comprise a Secretary-General and such secretaries and staff as may be required.

2. The first Secretary-General shall be the person named in the Annex; thereafter the Secretary-General shall be appointed by the Council with the approval of the majority of the Assembly.

3. The secretaries and staff of the Secretariat shall be appointed by the Secretary-General with the approval of the Council.

4. The Secretary-General shall act in that capacity at all meetings of the Assembly and of the Council.

5. *The expenses of the League shall be borne by the Members of the League in the proportion decided by the Assembly.*

ARTICLE 7

1. The Seat of the League is established at Geneva.

2. The Council may at any time decide that the Seat of the League shall be established elsewhere.

3. All positions under or in connection with the League, including the Secretariat, shall be open equally to men and women.

4. Representatives of the Members of the League and officials of the League when engaged on the business of the League shall enjoy diplomatic privileges and immunities.

5. The buildings and other property occupied by the League or its officials or by Representatives attending its meetings shall be inviolable.

ARTICLE 8

1. The Members of the League recognise that the maintenance of peace requires the reduction of national armaments to the lowest point consistent with national safety and the enforcement by common action of international obligations.

2. The Council, taking account of the geographical situation and circumstances of each State, shall formulate plans for such reduction for the consideration and action of the several Governments.

3. Such plans shall be subject to reconsideration and revision at least every ten years.

4. After these plans shall have been adopted by the several Governments, the limits of armaments therein fixed shall not be exceeded without the concurrence of the Council.

5. The Members of the League agree that the manufacture by private enterprise of munitions and implements of war is open to grave objections. The Council shall advise how the evil effects attendant upon such manufacture can be prevented, due regard being had to the necessities of those Members of the League which are not able to manufacture the munitions and implements of war necessary for their safety.

6. The Members of the League undertake to interchange full and frank information as to the scale of their armaments, their military, naval and air programmes and the condition of such of their industries as are adaptable to warlike purposes.

ARTICLE 9

A permanent Commission shall be constituted to advise the Council on the execution of the provisions of Articles 1 and 8 and on military, naval and air questions generally.

ARTICLE 10

The Members of the League undertake to respect and preserve as against external aggression the territorial integrity and existing political independence of all Members of the League. In case of any such aggression or in case of any threat or danger of such aggression the Council shall advise upon the means by which this obligation shall be fulfilled.

ARTICLE 11

1. Any war or threat of war, whether immediately affecting any of the Members of the League or not, is hereby declared a matter of concern to the whole League, and the League shall take any action that may be deemed wise and effectual to safeguard the peace of nations. In case any such emergency should arise the Secretary-General shall on the request of any Member of the League forthwith summon a meeting of the Council.

2. It is also declared to be the friendly right of each Member of the League to bring to the attention of the Assembly or of the Council any circumstance whatever affecting international relations which threatens to disturb international peace or the good understanding between nations upon which peace depends.

ARTICLE 12

1. The Members of the League agree that if there should arise between them any dispute likely to lead to a rupture they will submit the matter either to arbitration *or judicial settlement* or to enquiry by the Council, and

they agree in no case to resort to war until three months after the award by the arbitrators *or the judicial decision* or the report by the Council.

2. In any case under this Article the award of the arbitrators *or the judicial decision* shall be made within a reasonable time, and the report of the Council shall be made within six months after the submission of the dispute.

ARTICLE 13

1. The Members of the League agree that whenever any dispute shall arise between them which they recognize to be suitable for submission to arbitration or *judicial settlement*, and which cannot be satisfactorily settled by diplomacy, they will submit the whole subject-matter to arbitration or *judicial settlement*.

2. Disputes as to the interpretation of a treaty, as to any question of international law, as to the existence of any fact which, if established would constitute a breach of any international obligation, or as to the extent and nature of the reparation to be made for any such breach, are declared to be among those which are generally suitable for submission to arbitration *or judicial settlement*.

3. *For the consideration of any such dispute, the court to which the case is referred shall be the Permanent Court of International Justice, established in accordance with Article 14, or any tribunal agreed on by the parties to the dispute or stipulated in any convention existing between them.*

4. The Members of the League agree that they will carry out in full good faith any award *or decision* that may be rendered, and that they will not resort to war against a Member of the League which complies therewith. In the event of any failure to carry out such an award *or decision*, the Council shall propose what steps should be taken to give effect thereto.

ARTICLE 14

The Council shall formulate and submit to the Members of the League for adoption plans for the establishment of a Permanent Court of International Justice. The Court shall be competent to hear and determine any dispute of an international character which the parties thereto submit to it. The Court may also give an advisory opinion upon any dispute or question referred to it by the Council or by the Assembly.

ARTICLE 15

1. If there should arise between Members of the League any dispute likely to lead to a rupture, which is not submitted to arbitration *or judicial settlement* in accordance with Article 13, the Members of the League agree that they will submit the matter to the Council. Any party to the dispute may effect such submission by giving notice of the existence of the

dispute to the Secretary-General, who will make all necessary arrangements for a full investigation and consideration thereof.

2. For this purpose the parties to the dispute will communicate to the Secretary-General, as promptly as possible, statements of their case with all the relevant facts and papers, and the Council may forthwith direct the publication thereof.

3. The Council shall endeavour to effect a settlement of the dispute, and if such efforts are successful, a statement shall be made public giving such facts and explanations regarding the dispute and the terms of settlement thereof as the Council may deem appropriate.

4. If the dispute is not thus settled, the Council either unanimously or by a majority vote shall make and publish a report containing a statement of the facts of the dispute and the recommendations which are deemed just and proper in regard thereto.

5. Any Member of the League represented on the Council may make public a statement of the facts of the dispute and of its conclusions regarding the same.

6. If a report by the Council is unanimously agreed to by the members thereof other than the Representatives of one or more of the parties to the dispute, the Members of the League agree that they will not go to war with any party to the dispute which complies with the recommendations of the report.

7. If the Council fails to reach a report which is unanimously agreed to by the members thereof, other than the Representatives of one or more of the parties to the dispute, the Members of the League reserve to themselves the right to take such action as they shall consider necessary for the maintenance of right and justice.

8. If the dispute between the parties is claimed by one of them, and is found by the Council, to arise out of a matter which by international law is solely within the domestic jurisdiction of that party, the Council shall so report, and shall make no recommendation as to its settlement.

9. The Council may in any case under this Article refer the dispute to the Assembly. The dispute shall be so referred at the request of either party to the dispute provided that such request be made within fourteen days after the submission of the dispute to the Council.

10. In any case referred to the Assembly, all the provisions of this Article and of Article 12 relating to the action and powers of the Council shall apply to the action and powers of the Assembly, provided that a report made by the Assembly, if concurred in by the Representatives of those Members of the League represented on the Council and of a majority of the other Members of the League, exclusive in each case of the Representatives of the parties to the dispute, shall have the same force as a report by the Council concurred in by all the members thereof other than the Representatives of one or more of the parties to the dispute.

ARTICLE 16

1. Should any Member of the League resort to war in disregard of its covenants under Articles 12, 13 or 15, it shall *ipso facto* be deemed to have committed an act of war against all other Members of the League, which hereby undertake immediately to subject it to the severance of all trade or financial relations, the prohibition of all intercourse between their nationals and the nationals of the covenant-breaking State, and the prevention of all financial, commercial or personal intercourse between the nationals of the covenant-breaking State and the nationals of any other State, whether a Member of the League or not.

2. It shall be the duty of the Council in such case to recommend to the several Governments concerned what effective military, naval or air force the Members of the League shall severally contribute to the armed forces to be used to protect the covenants of the League.

3. The Members of the League agree, further, that they will mutually support one another in the financial and economic measures which are taken under this Article, in order to minimise the loss and inconvenience resulting from the above measures, and that they will mutually support one another in resisting any special measures aimed at one of their number by the covenant-breaking State, and that they will take the necessary steps to afford passage through their territory to the forces of any of the Members of the League which are co-operating to protect the covenants of the League.

4. Any Member of the League which has violated any covenant of the League may be declared to be no longer a Member of the League by a vote of the Council concurred in by the Representatives of all the other Members of the League represented thereon.

ARTICLE 17

1. In the event of a dispute between a Member of the League and a State which is not a Member of the League, or between States not Members of the League, the State or States not Members of the League shall be invited to accept the obligations of membership in the League for the purposes of such dispute, upon such conditions as the Council may deem just. If such invitation is accepted, the provisions of Articles 12 to 16 inclusive shall be applied with such modifications as may be deemed necessary by the Council.

2. Upon such invitation being given the Council shall immediately institute an inquiry into the circumstances of the dispute and recommend such action as may seem best and most effectual in the circumstances.

3. If a State so invited shall refuse to accept the obligations of membership in the League for the purposes of such dispute, and shall resort to war against a Member of the League, the provisions of Article 16 shall be applicable as against the State taking such action.

4. If both parties to the dispute when so invited refuse to accept the obligations of membership in the League for the purposes of such dispute, the Council may take such measures and make such recommendations as will prevent hostilities and will result in the settlement of the dispute.

ARTICLE 18

Every treaty or international engagement entered into hereafter by any Member of the League shall be forthwith registered with the Secretariat and shall as soon as possible be published by it. No such treaty or international engagement shall be binding until so registered.

ARTICLE 19

The Assembly may from time to time advise the reconsideration by Members of the League of treaties which have become inapplicable and the consideration of international conditions whose continuance might endanger the peace of the world.

ARTICLE 20

1. The Members of the League severally agree that this Covenant is accepted as abrogating all obligations or understandings *inter se* which are inconsistent with the terms thereof, and solemnly undertake that they will not hereafter enter into any engagements inconsistent with the terms thereof.

2. In case any Member of the League shall, before becoming a Member of the League, have undertaken any obligations inconsistent with the terms of this Covenant, it shall be the duty of such Member to take immediate steps to procure its release from such obligations.

ARTICLE 21

Nothing in this Covenant shall be deemed to affect the validity of international engagements, such as treaties of arbitration or regional understandings like the Monroe doctrine, for securing the maintenance of peace.

ARTICLE 22

1. To those colonies and territories which as a consequence of the late war have ceased to be under the sovereignty of the States which formerly governed them and which are inhabited by peoples not yet able to stand by themselves under the strenuous conditions of the modern world, there should be applied the principle that the well-being and development of such peoples form a sacred trust of civilization and that securities for the performance of this trust should be embodied in this Covenant.

2. The best method of giving practical effect to this principle is that the tutelage of such peoples should be entrusted to advanced nations who by reason of their resources, their experience or their geographical position can best undertake this responsibility, and who are willing to accept it, and

that this tutelage should be exercised by them as Mandatories on behalf of the League.

3. The character of the mandate must differ according to the stage of the development of the people, the geographical situation of the territory, its economic conditions and other similar circumstances.

4. Certain communities formerly belonging to the Turkish Empire have reached a stage of development where their existence as independent nations can be provisionally recognised subject to the rendering of administrative advice and assistance by a Mandatory until such time as they are able to stand alone. The wishes of these communities must be a principal consideration in the selection of the Mandatory.

5. Other peoples, especially those of Central Africa, are at such a stage that the Mandatory must be responsible for the administration of the territory under conditions which will guarantee freedom of conscience and religion, subject only to the maintenance of public order and morals, the prohibition of abuses such as the slave trade, the arms traffic and the liquor traffic, and the prevention of the establishment of fortifications or military and naval bases and of military training of the natives for other than police purposes and the defence of territory, and will also secure equal opportunities for the trade and commerce of other Members of the League.

6. There are territories, such as South-West Africa and certain of the South Pacific Islands, which, owing to the sparseness of their population, or their small size, or their remoteness from the centres of civilization, or their geographical contiguity to the territory of the Mandatory, and other circumstances, can be best administered under the laws of the Mandatory as integral portions of its territory, subject to the safeguards above mentioned in the interests of the indigenous population.

7. In every case of mandate, the Mandatory shall render to the Council an annual report in reference to the territory committed to its charge.

8. The degree of authority, control, or administration to be exercised by the Mandatory shall, if not previously agreed upon by the Members of the League, be explicitly defined in each case by the Council.

9. A permanent Commission shall be constituted to receive and examine the annual reports of the Mandatories and to advise the Council on all matters relating to the observance of the mandates.

ARTICLE 23

Subject to and in accordance with the provisions of international conventions existing or hereafter to be agreed upon, the Members of the League:

(a) will endeavour to secure and maintain fair and humane conditions of labour for men, women and children, both in their own countries and in all countries to which their commercial industrial relations extend, and for that purpose will establish and maintain the necessary international organizations;

  (b) undertake to secure just treatment of the native inhabitants of territories under their control;

  (c) will entrust the League with the general supervision over the execution of agreements with regard to the traffic in women and children, and the traffic in opium and other dangerous drugs;

  (d) will entrust the League with the general supervision of the trade in arms and ammunition with the countries in which the control of this traffic is necessary in the common interest;

  (e) will make provision to secure and maintain freedom of communications and of transit and equitable treatment for the commerce of all Members of the League. In this connection, the special necessities of the regions devastated during the war of 1914-1918 shall be borne in mind;

  (f) will endeavour to take steps in matters of international concern for the prevention and control of disease.

ARTICLE 24

1. There shall be placed under the direction of the League all international bureaux already established by general treaties if the parties to such treaties consent. All such international bureaux and all commissions for the regulation of matters of international interest hereafter constituted shall be placed under the direction of the League.

2. In all matters of international interest which are regulated by general conventions but which are not placed under the control of international bureaux or commissions, the Secretariat of the League shall, subject to the consent of the Council and if desired by the parties, collect and distribute all relevant information and shall render any other assistance which may be necessary or desirable.

3. The Council may include as part of the expenses of the Secretariat the expenses of any bureau or commission which is placed under the direction of the League.

ARTICLE 25

The Members of the League agree to encourage and promote the establishment and co-operation of duly authorized voluntary national Red Cross organizations having as purposes the improvement of health, the prevention of disease and the mitigation of suffering throughout the world.

ARTICLE 26

1. Amendments to the Covenant will take effect when ratified by the Members of the League whose Representatives compose the Council and by a majority of the Members of the League whose Representatives compose the Assembly.

2. No such amendments shall bind any Member of the League which signifies its dissent therefrom, but in that case it shall cease to be a Member of the League.

APPENDIX B

The Atlantic Charter

DECLARATION OF PRINCIPLES, KNOWN AS THE ATLANTIC CHARTER, BY THE PRESIDENT OF THE UNITED STATES AND THE PRIME MINISTER OF THE UNITED KINGDOM.

August 14, 1941

Joint declaration of the President of the United States of America and the Prime Minister, Mr. Churchill, representing His Majesty's Government in the United Kingdom, [who] being met together, deem it right to make known certain common principles in the national policies of their respective countries on which they base their hopes for a better future for the world.

First, their countries seek no aggrandizement, territorial or other;

Second, they desire to see no territorial changes that do not accord with the freely expressed wishes of the peoples concerned;

Third, they respect the right of all peoples to choose the form of government under which they will live; and they wish to see sovereign rights and self-government restored to those who have been forcibly deprived of them;

Fourth, they will endeavor, with due respect for their existing obligations, to further the enjoyment by all States, great or small, victor or vanquished, of access, on equal terms, to the trade and to the raw materials of the world which are needed for their economic prosperity;

Fifth, they desire to bring about the fullest collaboration between all nations in the economic field with the object of securing, for all, improved labor standards, economic advancement, and social security;

Sixth, after the final destruction of the Nazi tyranny, they hope to see established a peace which will afford to all nations the means of dwelling in safety within their own boundaries, and which will afford assurance that all the men in all the lands may live out their lives in freedom from fear and want;

Seventh, such a peace should enable all men to traverse the high seas and oceans without hindrance;

Eighth, they believe that all of the nations of the world, for realistic as well as spiritual reasons, must come to the abandonment of the use of force. Since no future peace can be maintained if land, sea, or air armaments continue to be employed by nations which threaten, or may threaten, aggression outside of their frontiers, they believe, pending the establishment of a wider and permanent system of general security, that the disarmament of such nations is essential. They will likewise aid and encourage all other practicable measures which will lighten for peace-loving peoples the crushing burden of armaments.

APPENDIX C

Declaration by United Nations

January 1, 1942

A JOINT DECLARATION BY THE UNITED STATES OF AMERICA, THE UNITED KINGDOM OF GREAT BRITAIN AND NORTHERN IRELAND, THE UNION OF SOVIET SOCIALIST REPUBLICS, CHINA, AUSTRALIA, BELGIUM, CANADA, COSTA RICA, CUBA, CZECHOSLOVAKIA, DOMINICAN REPUBLIC, EL SALVADOR, GREECE, GUATEMALA, HAITI, HONDURAS, INDIA, LUXEMBOURG, NETHERLANDS, NEW ZEALAND, NICARAGUA, NORWAY, PANAMA, POLAND, SOUTH AFRICA, YUGOSLAVIA.

The Governments signatory hereto,

Having subscribed to a common program of purposes and principles embodied in the Joint Declaration of the President of the United States of America and the Prime Minister of the United Kingdom of Great Britain and Northern Ireland dated August 14, 1941, known as the Atlantic Charter,

Being convinced that complete victory over their enemies is essential to defend life, liberty, independence and religious freedom, and to preserve human rights and justice in their own lands as well as in other lands, and that they are now engaged in a common struggle against savage and brutal forces seeking to subjugate the world,

DECLARE:

(1) Each Government pledges itself to employ its full resources, military or economic, against those members of the Tripartite Pact and its adherents with which such government is at war.

(2) Each Government pledges itself to cooperate with the Governments signatory hereto and not to make a separate armistice or peace with the enemies.

The foregoing declaration may be adhered to by other nations which are, or which may be, rendering material assistance and contributions in the struggle for victory over Hitlerism.

DONE AT WASHINGTON January First, 1942

The signatories to the Declaration by United Nations are as listed above.

The adherents to the Declaration by United Nations, together with the date of communication of adherence, are as follows:

Mexico	June 5, 1942	Ecuador	Feb. 7, 1945
Philippines	June 10, 1942	Peru	Feb. 11, 1945
Ethiopia	July 28, 1942	Chile	Feb. 12, 1945
Iraq	Jan. 16, 1943	Paraguay	Feb. 12, 1945
Brazil	Feb. 8, 1943	Venezuela	Feb. 16, 1945
Bolivia	Apr. 27, 1943	Uruguay	Feb. 23, 1945
Iran	Sept. 10, 1943	Turkey	Feb. 24, 1945
Colombia	Dec. 22, 1943	Egypt	Feb. 27, 1945
Liberia	Feb. 26, 1944	Saudi Arabia	Mar. 1, 1945
France	Dec. 26, 1944		

APPENDIX D

Yalta Protocol

Report of the Conference

For the past eight days, Winston S. Churchill, Prime Minister of Great Britain, Franklin D. Roosevelt, President of the United States of America, and Marshal J. V. Stalin, Chairman of the Council of People's Commissars of the Union of Soviet Socialist Republics, have met with the Foreign Secretaries, Chiefs of Staff, and other advisors in the Crimea.

The following statement is made by the Prime Minister of Great Britain, the President of the United States of America, and the Chairman of the Council of People's Commissars of the Union of Soviet Socialist Republics on the results of the Crimean Conference:

The Defeat of Germany

We have considered and determined the military plans of the three allied powers for the final defeat of the common enemy. The military staffs of the three allied nations have met in daily meetings throughout the Conference. These meetings have been most satisfactory from every point of view and have resulted in closer coordination of the military effort of the three allies than ever before. The fullest information has been interchanged. The timing, scope and coordination of new and even more powerful blows to be launched by our armies and air forces into the heart of Germany from the East, West, North and South have been fully agreed and planned in detail.

Our combined military plans will be made known only as we execute them, but we believe that the very close working partnership among the three staffs attained at this Conference will result in shortening the War. Meetings of the three staffs will be continued in the future whenever the need arises.

Nazi Germany is doomed. The German people will only make the cost of their defeat heavier to themselves by attempting to continue a hopeless resistance.

The Occupation and Control of Germany

We have agreed on common policies and plans for enforcing the unconditional surrender terms which we shall impose together on Nazi Germany after German armed resistance has been finally crushed. These terms will not be made known until the final defeat of Germany has been accomplished. Under the agreed plan, the forces of the three powers will each occupy a separate zone of Germany. Coordinated administration and control has been provided for under the plan through a central control commission consisting of the Supreme Commanders of the three powers with headquarters in Berlin. It has been agreed that France should be invited by the three powers, if she should so desire, to take over a zone of occupation, and to participate as a fourth member of the control commission. The limits of the French zone will be agreed by the four governments concerned through their representatives on the European Advisory Commission.

It is our inflexible purpose to destroy German militarism and Nazism and to ensure that Germany will never again be able to disturb the peace of the world. We are determined to disarm and disband all German armed forces; break up for all time the German General Staff that has repeatedly contrived the resurgence of German militarism; remove or destroy all German military equipment; eliminate or control all German industry that could be used for military production; bring all war criminals to just and swift punishment and exact reparation in kind for the destruction wrought by the Germans; wipe out the Nazi Party, Nazi laws, organizations and institutions, remove all Nazi and militarist influences from public office and from the cultural and economic life of the German people; and take in harmony such other measures in Germany as may be necessary to the future peace and safety of the world. It is not our purpose to destroy the people of Germany, but only when Nazism and militarism have been extirpated will there be hope for a decent life for Germans, and a place for them in the comity of nations.

Reparation by Germany

We have considered the question of the damage caused by Germany to the allied nations in this war and recognized it as just that Germany be obliged to make compensation for this damage in kind to the greatest extent possible. A commission for the compensation of damage will be established. The commission will be instructed to consider the question of the extent and methods for compensating damage caused by Germany to the allied countries. The commission will work in Moscow.

United Nations Conference

We are resolved upon the earliest possible establishment with our allies of a general international organization to maintain peace and security. We believe that this is essential, both to prevent aggression and to remove the political, economic, and social causes of war through the close and continuing collaboration of all peace-loving peoples.

The foundations were laid at Dumbarton Oaks. On the important question of voting procedure, however, agreement was not there reached. The present Conference has been able to resolve this difficulty.

We have agreed that a conference of United Nations should be called to meet at San Francisco in the United States on April 25, 1945, to prepare the charter of such an organization, along the lines proposed in the informal conversations at Dumbarton Oaks.

The Government of China and the Provisional Government of France will be immediately consulted and invited to sponsor invitations to the conference jointly with the Governments of the United States, Great Britain and the Union of Soviet Socialist Republics. As soon as the consultation with China and France has been completed, the text of the proposals on voting procedure will be made public.

Declaration on Liberated Europe

The Premier of the Union of Soviet Socialist Republics, the Prime Minister of the United Kingdom, and the President of the United States of America have consulted with each other in the common interests of the peoples of their countries and those of liberated Europe. They jointly declare their mutual agreement to concert during the temporary period of instability in liberated Europe the policies of their three governments in assisting the peoples liberated from the domination of Nazi Germany and the peoples of the former Axis satellite states of Europe to solve by democratic means their pressing political and economic problems.

The establishment of order in Europe and the rebuilding of national economic life must be achieved by processes which will enable the liberated peoples to destroy the last vestiges of Nazism and Fascism and to create democratic institutions of their own choice. This is a principle of the Atlantic Charter—the right of all peoples to choose the form of government under which they will live—the restoration of sovereign rights and self-government to those peoples who have been forcibly deprived of them by the aggressor nations.

To foster the conditions in which the liberated peoples may exercise these rights, the three governments will jointly assist the people in any European liberated state or former Axis satellite state in Europe where in their judgment conditions require (A) to establish conditions of internal peace; (B) to carry out emergency measures for the relief of distressed peoples; (C) to form interim governmental authorities broadly representative of all democratic elements in the population and pledged to the earliest possible establishment through free elections of governments responsive to the will of the people; and (D) to facilitate where necessary the holding of such elections.

The three governments will consult the other United Nations and provisional authorities or other governments in Europe when matters of direct interest to them are under consideration.

When, in the opinion of the three governments, conditions in any European liberated state or any former Axis satellite state in Europe make such action necessary, they will immediately consult together on the measures necessary to discharge the joint responsibilities set forth in this declaration.

By this declaration we reaffirm our faith in the principles of the Atlantic Charter, our pledge in the declaration by the United Nations, and our determination to build in cooperation with other peace-loving nations world order under law, dedicated to peace, security, freedom and general well-being of all mankind.

In issuing this declaration, the three powers express the hope that the Provisional Government of the French Republic may be associated with them in the procedure suggested.

Poland

A new situation has been created in Poland as a result of her complete liberation by the Red Army. This calls for the establishment of a Polish provisional government which can be more broadly based than was possible before the recent liberation of Western Poland. The provisional government which is now functioning in Poland should therefore be reorganized on a broader democratic basis with the inclusion of democratic leaders from Poland itself and from Poles abroad. This new government should then be called the Polish Provisional Government of National Unity.

M. Molotov, Mr. Harriman and Sir A. Clark Kerr are authorized as a commission to consult in the first instance in Moscow with members of the present provisional government and with other Polish democratic leaders from within Poland and from abroad, with a view to the reorganization of the present government along the above lines. This Polish Provisional Government of National Unity shall be pledged to the holding of free and unfettered elections as soon as possible on the basis of universal suffrage and secret ballot. In these elections all democratic and anti-Nazi parties shall have the right to take part and to put forward candidates.

When a Polish Provisional Government of National Unity has been properly formed in conformity with the above, the government of the USSR, which now maintains diplomatic relations with the present provisional government of Poland, and the government of the United Kingdom and the government of the USA will establish diplomatic relations with the new Polish Provisional Government of National Unity, and will exchange ambassadors by whose reports the respective governments will be kept informed about the situation in Poland.

The three heads of government consider that the Eastern frontier of

Poland should follow the Curzon line with digressions from it in some regions of five to eight kilometres in favour of Poland. They recognize that Poland must receive substantial accessions of territory in the North and West. They feel that the opinion of the new Polish Provisional Government of National Unity should be sought in due course on the extent of these accessions and that the final delimitation of the western frontier of Poland should thereafter await the peace conference.

Yugoslavia

We have agreed to recommend to Marshal Tito and Dr. Subasic that the agreement between them should be put into effect immediately, and that a new government should be formed on the basis of that agreement.

We also recommend that as soon as the new government has been formed it should declare that:

(1) The anti-Fascist Assembly of National Liberation (Avnoj) should be extended to include members of the last Yugoslav Parliament (Skupschina) who have not compromised themselves by collaboration with the enemy, thus forming a body to be known as a temporary Parliament; and,

(2) Legislative acts passed by the anti-Fascist Assembly of National Liberation will be subject to subsequent ratification by a constituent assembly.

[There was also a general review of other Balkan questions.]

Meetings of Foreign Secretaries

Throughout the Conference, besides the daily meetings of the heads of governments and the Foreign Secretaries, separate meetings of the three Foreign Secretaries, and their advisors have also been held daily.

These meetings have proved of the utmost value and the Conference agreed that permanent machinery should be set up for regular consultation between the three Foreign Secretaries. They will, therefore, meet as often as may be necessary, probably about every three or four months. These meetings will be held in rotation in the three capitals, the first meeting being held in London, after the United Nations Conference on World Organization.

Unity for Peace as for War

Our meeting here in the Crimea has reaffirmed our common determination to maintain and strengthen in the peace to come that unity of purpose and of action which has made victory possible and certain for the United Nations in this war. We believe that this is a sacred obligation which our Governments owe to our peoples and to all the peoples of the world.

Only with the continuing and growing cooperation and understanding among our three countries and among all the peace-loving nations can the highest aspiration of humanity be realized—a secure and lasting peace which will, in the words of the Atlantic Charter, "afford assurance that all the men in all the lands may live out their lives in freedom from fear and want."

Victory in this war and establishment of the proposed international organization will provide the greatest opportunity in all history to create in the years to come the essential conditions of such a peace.

Signed: WINSTON S. CHURCHILL

FRANKLIN D. ROOSEVELT

J. STALIN

February 11, 1945

APPENDIX E

Charter of the United Nations

[The preamble and first two of nineteen chapters of the Charter of the United Nations, adopted at San Francisco, California, June 26, 1945, follow.]

We the peoples of the United Nations determined

    to save succeeding generations from the scourge of war, which twice in our lifetime has brought untold sorrow to mankind, and

    to reaffirm faith in fundamental human rights, in the dignity and worth of the human person, in the equal rights of men and women and of nations large and small, and

    to establish conditions under which justice and respect for the obligations arising from treaties and other sources of international law can be maintained, and

    to promote social progress and better standards of life in larger freedom,

and for these ends

    to practice tolerance and live together in peace with one another as good neighbors, and

    to unite our strength to maintain international peace and security, and

    to ensure, by the acceptance of principles and the institution of methods, that armed force shall not be used, save in the common interest, and

    to employ international machinery for the promotion of the economic and social advancement of all peoples,

have resolved to combine our efforts to accomplish these aims.

    Accordingly, our respective Governments, through representatives assembled in the city of San Francisco, who have exhibited their full powers found to be in good and due form, have agreed to the present Charter of the United Nations and do hereby establish an international organization to be known as the United Nations.

CHAPTER I

Purposes and Principles

ARTICLE 1

The Purposes of the United Nations are:

1. To maintain international peace and security, and to that end: to take effective collective measures for the prevention and removal of threats to the peace, and for the suppression of acts of aggression or other breaches of the peace, and to bring about by peaceful means, and in conformity with the principles of justice and international law, adjustment or settlement of international disputes or situations which might lead to a breach of the peace;

2. To develop friendly relations among nations based on respect for the principle of equal rights and self-determination of peoples, and to take other appropriate measures to strengthen universal peace;

3. To achieve international cooperation in solving international problems of an economic, social, cultural, or humanitarian character, and in promoting and encouraging respect for human rights and for fundamental freedoms for all without distinction as to race, sex, language, or religion; and

4. To be a center for harmonizing the actions of nations in the attainment of these common ends.

ARTICLE 2

The Organization and its Members, in pursuit of the Purposes stated in Article 1, shall act in accordance with the following Principles.

1. The Organization is based on the principle of the sovereign equality of all its Members.

2. All Members, in order to ensure to all of them the rights and benefits resulting from membership, shall fulfil in good faith the obligations assumed by them in accordance with the present Charter.

3. All Members shall settle their international disputes by peaceful means in such a manner that international peace and security, and justice, are not endangered.

4. All Members shall refrain in their international relations from the threat or use of force against the territorial integrity or political independence of any state, or in any other manner inconsistent with the Purposes of the United Nations.

5. All Members shall give the United Nations every assistance in any action it takes in accordance with the present Charter, and shall refrain from giving assistance to any state against which the United Nations is taking preventive or enforcement action.

6. The Organization shall ensure that states which are not Members of

the United Nations act in accordance with these Principles so far as may be necessary for the maintenance of international peace and security.

7. Nothing contained in the present Charter shall authorize the United Nations to intervene in matters which are essentially within the domestic jurisdiction of any state or shall require the Members to submit such matters to settlement under the present Charter; but this principle shall not prejudice the application of enforcement measures under Chapter VII.

CHAPTER II

Membership

ARTICLE 3

The original Members of the United Nations shall be the states which, having participated in the United Nations Conference on International Organizations at San Francisco, or having previously signed the Declaration by United Nations of January 1, 1942, sign the present Charter and ratify it in accordance with Article 110.

ARTICLE 4

1. Membership in the United Nations is open to all other peace-loving states which accept the obligations contained in the present Charter and, in the judgment of the Organization, are able and willing to carry out these obligations.

2. The admission of any such state to membership in the United Nations will be effected by a decision of the General Assembly upon the recommendation of the Security Council.

ARTICLE 5

A member of the United Nations against which preventive or enforcement action has been taken by the Security Council may be suspended from the exercise of the rights and privileges of membership by the General Assembly upon the recommendation of the Security Council. The exercise of these rights and privileges may be restored by the Security Council.

ARTICLE 6

A Member of the United Nations which has persistently violated the Principles contained in the present Charter may be expelled from the Organization by the General Assembly upon the recommendation of the Security Council.

NOTE: Seventeen following chapters of the charter outlined the organization and procedures of the United Nations, and means of amendment and ratification.

APPENDIX F

North Atlantic Treaty

Signed in Washington, D.C., April 4, 1949

Preamble

The Parties to this Treaty reaffirm their faith in the purposes and principles of the Charter of the United Nations and their desire to live in peace with all peoples and all governments.

They are determined to safeguard the freedom, common heritage and civilization of their peoples, founded on the principles of democracy, individual liberty and the rule of law.

They seek to promote stability and well-being in the North Atlantic area.

They are resolved to unite their efforts for collective defense and for the preservation of peace and security.

They therefore agree to this North Atlantic Treaty:

ARTICLE 1

The Parties undertake, as set forth in the Charter of the United Nations, to settle any international disputes in which they may be involved by peaceful means in such a manner that international peace and security, and justice, are not endangered, and to refrain in their international relations from the threat or use of force in any manner inconsistent with the purposes of the United Nations.

ARTICLE 2

The Parties will contribute toward the further development of peaceful and friendly international relations by strengthening their free institutions, by bringing about a better understanding of the principles upon which these institutions are founded, and by promoting conditions of stability and well-being. They will seek to eliminate conflict in their international economic policies and will encourage economic collaboration between any or all of them.

ARTICLE 3

In order more effectively to achieve the objectives of this Treaty, the Parties, separately and jointly, by means of continuous and effective self-help and mutual aid, will maintain and develop their individual and collective capacity to resist armed attack.

ARTICLE 4

The Parties will consult together whenever, in the opinion of any of them, the territorial integrity, political independence or security of any of the Parties is threatened.

ARTICLE 5

The Parties agree that an armed attack against one or more of them in Europe or North America shall be considered an attack against them all; and consequently they agree that, if such an armed attack occurs, each of them, in exercise of the right of individual or collective self-defense recognized by Article 51 of the Charter of the United Nations, will assist the Party or Parties so attacked by taking forthwith, individually and in concert with the other Parties, such action as it deems necessary, including the use of armed force, to restore and maintain the security of the North Atlantic area.

Any such armed attack and all measures taken as a result thereof shall immediately be reported to the Security Council. Such measures shall be terminated when the Security Council has taken the measures necessary to restore and maintain international peace and security.

ARTICLE 6

For the purpose of Article 5 an armed attack on one or more of the Parties is deemed to include an armed attack on the territory of any of the Parties in Europe or North America, on the Algerian departments of France, on the occupation forces of any Party in Europe, on the islands under the jurisdiction of any Party in the North Atlantic area north of the Tropic of Cancer or on the vessels or aircraft in this area of any of the Parties.

ARTICLE 7

This Treaty does not affect, and shall not be interpreted as affecting, in any way the rights and obligations under the Charter of the Parties which are members of the United Nations, or the primary responsibility of the Security Council for the maintenance of international peace and security.

ARTICLE 8

Each Party declares that none of the international engagements now in force between it and any other of the Parties or any third state is in conflict with the provisions of this Treaty, and undertakes not to enter into any international agreement in conflict with this Treaty.

ARTICLE 9

The Parties hereby establish a council, on which each of them shall be represented, to consider matters concerning the implementation of this Treaty. The council shall be so organized as to be able to meet promptly at any time. The council shall set up such subsidiary bodies as may be necessary; in particular it shall establish immediately a defense committee which shall recommend measures for the implementation of Articles 3 and 5.

ARTICLE 10

The Parties may, by unanimous agreement, invite any other European state in a position to further the principles of this Treaty and to contribute to the security of the North Atlantic area to accede to this Treaty. Any state so invited may become a party to the Treaty by depositing its instrument of accession with the Government of the United States of America. The Government of the United States of America will inform each of the Parties of the deposit of each such instrument of accession.

ARTICLE 11

This Treaty shall be ratified and its provisions carried out by the Parties in accordance with their respective constitutional processes. The instruments of ratification shall be deposited as soon as possible with the Government of the United States of America, which will notify all the other signatories of each deposit. The Treaty shall enter into force between the states which have ratified it as soon as the ratifications of the majority of the signatories, including the ratifications of Belgium, Canada, France, Luxembourg, the Netherlands, the United Kingdom and the United States, have been deposited and shall come into effect with respect to other states on the date of the deposit of their ratifications.

ARTICLE 12

After the Treaty has been in force for ten years, or at any time thereafter, the Parties shall, if any of them so requests, consult together for the purpose of reviewing the Treaty, having regard for the factors then affecting peace and security in the North Atlantic area, including the development of universal as well as regional arrangements under the Charter of the United Nations for the maintenance of international peace and security.

ARTICLE 13

After the Treaty has been in force for twenty years, any Party may cease to be a party one year after its notice of denunciation has been given to the Government of the United States of America, which will inform the Governments of the other Parties of the deposit of each notice of denunciation.

ARTICLE 14

This Treaty, of which the English and French texts are equally authentic, shall be deposited in the archives of the Government of the United States of America. Duly certified copies thereof will be transmitted by that Government to the Governments of the other signatories.

In witness whereof, the undersigned plenipotentiaries have signed this Treaty.

Done at Washington, the fourth day of April, 1949.

BIBLIOGRAPHY

Allen, Robert S. *Lucky Forward. The History of Patton's Third US Army.* New York, 1947.

Allied Commission for Austria. *The Rehabilitation of Austria.* 2 vols. Washington, 1949.

Allied Forces. Report by the supreme allied commander, Mediterranean, to the combined chiefs of staff on the operations in southern France, August, 1944. Washington, 1946.

Allied Forces. Report by the supreme allied commander, Mediterranean, to the combined chiefs of staff on the Italian campaign, 8 January, 1944, to 10 May, 1944. Washington, 1946.

Allied Forces. Supreme Headquarters. Report by the supreme commander to the combined chiefs of staff on the operations in Europe of the Allied Expeditionary Force, 6 June, 1944, to 8 May, 1945. Washington, 1946.

Almond, Gabriel A. (ed.), *The Struggle for Democracy in Germany.* Chapel Hill, 1949.

American Russian Institute. *The Soviet Union Today.* New York, 1923.

American Russian Institute. *The USSR at War.* New York, 1943.

Amery, Julian. *Sons of the Eagle.* New York, 1949.

Anders, Lt. Gen. W. *An Army in Exile: The Story of the Second Polish Corps.* New York, 1949.

Anderson, Evelyn. *Hammer or Anvil: The Story of the German Working Class Movement.* London, 1945.

Angell, Norman. *The Steep Places.* London, New York, 1947.

Anonymous. *U.S.A.* Munich, 1940.

Arnold, General of the Armies H. H. *Global Mission.* New York, 1949.

Bailey, Thomas A. *Woodrow Wilson and the Lost Peace.* New York, 1945.

Baldwin, Hanson W. *Great Mistakes of the War.* New York, 1950.

Baldwin, Hanson W. *The Price of Power.* New York, 1948.

Ball, M. Margaret. *Post-War German-Austrian Relations: The Anschluss Movement, 1918-36.* London, 1937.

Baltzly, Alexander, and Salomone, William. *Readings in Twentieth Century European History.* New York, 1950.

Balzak, S. S., Vasyutin, V. F., and Feigin, Y. G. (eds.). *Economic Geography of the USSR*. New York, 1949.

Barck, Oscar T., Jr., and Blake, Nelson M. *Since 1900: A History of the United States in Our Times*. New York, 1947.

Barmine, Alexandre. *One Who Survived; the Life Story of a Russian Under the Soviets*. New York, 1945.

Baykov, Alexander. *The Development of the Soviet Economic System*. Cambridge, England, 1946; New York, 1947.

Beard, Charles A. *American Foreign Policy in the Making, 1932-1940*. New Haven, 1946.

Beard, Charles A. *President Roosevelt and the Coming of the War, 1941*. New Haven, 1948.

Beloff, Max. *The Foreign Policy of Soviet Russia, 1929-1941*. 2 vols. New York, London, 1947, 1949.

Beneš, Eduard. *My War Memoirs*. London, Boston, 1928.

Bernstein, Victor H. *Final Judgment, the Story of Nuremberg*. New York, 1947.

Bernstorff, J. H. v. *My Three Years in America*. London, 1920.

Bisson, Thomas A. *America's Far Eastern Policy*. New York, 1945.

Bisson, Thomas A. *Japan's War Economy*. New York, 1945.

Bisson, Thomas A. *Prospects for Democracy in Japan*. New York, 1949.

Black, C. E., and Helmreich, E. C. *Twentieth Century Europe*. New York, 1950.

Bloch, Marc. *Strange Defeat*. Oxford, 1949.

Blum, Léon. *For All Mankind*. New York, 1946.

Boldt, Gerhard. *Die letzten Tage der Reichskanzlei*. New York, 1948.

Bonsal, Stephen. *Suitors and Suppliants. The Little Nations at Versailles*. New York, 1946.

Bor-Komorowski, T. *The Secret Army*. London, 1950.

Bourke-White, Margaret. *Half-way to Freedom*. New York, 1949.

Bradley, David. *No Place to Hide*. Boston, 1948.

Brandenburg, Erich. *From Bismarck to the World War*. London, 1927.

Brandt, Karl. *Germany, Key to Peace in Europe*. Claremont, Calif., 1949.

Brecht, Arnold. *Federalism and Regionalism in Germany; the Division of Prussia*. New York, 1945.

Brecht, Arnold. *Prelude to Silence: The End of the German Republic*. New York, 1944.

Brereton, General Lewis Hyde. *The Brereton Diaries*. New York, 1946.

Brinton, Clarence Crane. *From Many One*. Cambridge, Mass., 1948.

Brinton, Clarence Crane. *Nietzsche*. Cambridge, Mass., 1941.

Brogan, Denis William. *The Era of Franklin D. Roosevelt*. New Haven, 1950.

Brogan, Denis William. *France Under the Republic. The Development of Modern France* (1870-1939). New York, 1940.

Burchett, Wilfred G. *Wingate's Phantom Army*. Bombay, London, 1947.

Buss, Claude A. *War and Diplomacy in Eastern Asia*. New York, 1941.

Byrnes, James F. *Speaking Frankly*. New York, 1947.

Calvocoressi, Peter. *Nuremberg: The Facts, the Law and the Consequences*. New York, 1948.

Campbell, John C. (ed.). *The United States in World Affairs, 1945-1947*. New York, 1947.

Campbell, John C. (ed.). *The United States in World Affairs, 1948-1949*. New York, 1949.

Carr, Edward Hallett. *International Relations Between Two World Wars, 1919-39*. London, New York, 1948.

Carr, Edward Hallett. *The Soviet Impact on the Western World*. New York, 1947.

Carroll, Malcolm. See Germany, *Auswärtiges Amt*.

Carroll, Wallace. *Persuade or Perish*. Boston, 1948.

Cave, Floyd A., and associates. *The Origins and Consequences of World War II*. New York, 1948.

Cecil, (Lord) Robert. *A Great Experiment*. London, 1941.

Chamberlain, Neville. Biography. See Feiling, Keith.

Churchill, Winston. *The Second World War*. I, *The Gathering Storm*. II, *Their Finest Hour*. III, *The Grand Alliance*. IV, *The Hinge of Fate*. Boston, 1948-1950.

Churchill, Winston. *Secret Session Speeches*. New York, 1946.

Churchill, Winston. *Victory; War Speeches by the Right Honorable Winston S. Churchill*. Boston, 1946.

Ciano di Cortelazzo, Count Galeazzo. See Gibson, Hugh.

Ciechanowski, Jan. *Defeat in Victory*. Garden City, 1947.

Clark, Grover. *Economic Rivalries in China*. New York, 1938.

Clark, General Mark. *Calculated Risk*. New York, 1950.

Clay, Lucius D. *Decision in Germany*. New York, 1950.

Coulondre, Robert. *De Staline à Hitler*. Paris, 1950.

Crankshaw, Edward. *Russia and the Russians*. London, 1947; New York, 1948.

Craven, Wesley F. (ed.). *The Army Air Forces in World War II*. I, *Plans and Early Operations January 1939-August 1942*. II, *From Torch to Pointblank, August, 1942, to December, 1943*. IV, *The Pacific: From Guadalcanal to Saipan*. Chicago, 1948-1950.

Crow, Carl (ed.). *Japan's Dream of World Empire: The Tanaka Memorial*. New York, 1942.

Dallin, David J. *The Real Soviet Russia*. New Haven, 1947.

Dallin, David J. *The Rise of Russia in Asia*. New Haven, 1949.

Dallin, David J. *Soviet Russia and the Far East*. New Haven, 1948.

Dallin, David J. *Soviet Russia's Foreign Policy, 1939-42*. New Haven, 1942.

Dallin, David J., and Nicolaevsky, Boris I. *Forced Labor in Soviet Russia*. New Haven, 1947.

Dean, Vera M. *Europe in Retreat*. New York, 1939.

Dean, Vera M. *The United States and Russia*. Cambridge, Mass , 1947.

Deane, John R. *The Strange Alliance*. New York, 1947.

Dennett, Tyler. *Americans in Eastern Asia*. New York, 1941.

Deuel, Wallace R. *People Under Hitler*. New York, 1942.

Deutsch, Harold G. "Strange Interlude: The Soviet-Nazi Liaison of 1939-1941," *The Historian,* Spring, 1947, pp. 107-137.

Deutscher, Isaac. *Stalin: A Political Biography*. New York, 1949.

Dickens, Admiral Sir Gerald. *Bombing and Strategy*. New York, 1949.

Dirksen, Herbert V. *Moskau, Tokio, London. Erinnerungen zu 20 Jahren deutscher aussenpolitik, 1919-1939*. Stuttgart, 1949.

Dönitz, Karl. *Die U-bootswaffe*. Berlin, 1940.

Duff, S. Grant. *German and Czech*. London, 1937.

Dulles, Allen W. *Germany's Underground*. New York, 1947.

Dulles, John Foster. *War or Peace*. New York, 1950.

Duranty, Walter. *USSR. The Story of Soviet Russia*. New York, 1944.

Eade, Charles (compiler). *Speeches of Winston Churchill*. New York, 1945.

Ebon, Martin. *World Communism Today*. New York, 1948.

Eichelberger, Lt. Gen. Robert L. *Our Jungle Road to Tokyo*. New York, 1950.

Eisenhower, Dwight D. *Crusade in Europe*. New York, 1948.

Eisenhower, Dwight D. Report by the supreme commander to the combined chiefs of staff on the operations in Europe of the Allied Expeditionary Force, 6 June, 1944, to 8 May, 1945. New York, 1946.

Evatt, Herbert V. *The United Nations*. Cambridge, Mass., 1948.

Eyck, Erich. *Das Personliche Regiment Wilhelms II*. Zurich, 1948.

Fabian, Bela. *Cardinal Mindszenty. The Story of a Modern Martyr*. New York, 1949.

Fairbank, John K. *The United States and China*. Cambridge, Mass., 1948.

Farr, Philip. *Soviet Russia and the Baltic Republics*. London, 1944.

Faulkner, Harold U. *From Versailles to the New Deal*. New Haven, 1950.

Fay, Sidney B. "The German Balance Sheet," *Current History,* August, 1948.

Fay, Sidney B. *The Origins of the World War*. 2 vols. New York, 1928, 1931.

Feiling, Keith. *The Life of Neville Chamberlain*. London, 1946.

Feis, Herbert. *The Road to Pearl Harbor*. Princeton, 1950.

Feis, Herbert. *The Spanish Story*. New York, 1948.

Field, F. V. (ed.). *Economic Handbook of the Pacific Area*. Garden City, 1934.

Field, James A. *The Japanese at Leyte Gulf*. Princeton, 1947.

Fischer, Louis. *The Life of Mahatma Gandhi*. New York, 1950.

Fischer, Ruth. *Stalin and German Communism*. Cambridge, Mass., 1948.

Fisher, Harold H. *America and Russia in the World Community*. Claremont, Calif., 1946.

Fitzgerald, Walter. *The New Europe; an Introduction to Its Political Geography*. London, 1946.

Flechtheim, Ossip K. *Die Kommunistische Partei Deutschlands in der Weimaren Republik*. Waterville, Me., 1948.

Fleming, Denna F. *The United States and the World Court*. Garden City, 1945.

Foerster, Friedrich W. *Europe and the German Question*. New York, 1940.

Foltz, Charles. *The Masquerade in Spain*. Boston, 1948.

France. Ministry of Foreign Affairs. *The French Yellow Book*. New York, 1940.

France. Ministry of Foreign Affairs. *La Politique Allemande v. Turquie 1941-1943*. Paris, 1946.

François-Ponçet, André. *Souvenirs d'une Ambassade à Berlin*. Paris, 1946.

Friedrich, Carl J. *Inevitable Peace*. Cambridge, Mass., 1948.

Fuller, John F. C. *The Second World War*. New York, 1949.

Gafencu, Grigore. *Préliminaires de la Guerre à l'Est, de l'accord du Moscou (21 août 1939) aux hostilités en Russie (22 juin 1941)*. Freibourg, 1944.

Gafencu, Grigore. *Prelude to the Russian Campaign*. London, 1945.

Gafencu, Grigore. *Last Days of Europe*. New Haven, 1948.

Gandhi. See Nehru.

Gantenbein, James W. (ed.) *Documentary Background of World War II*. New York, 1948.

Gedye, George E. R. *Betrayal in Central Europe*. New York, London, 1939.

Germany. Auswärtiges Amt. *Amtliche Urkunden Zur Vorgeschichte des Waffenstillstandes 1918*. Berlin, 1924.

Germany. Auswärtiges Amt. *Documents and Materials Relating to the Eve of the Second World War*. New York, 1948.

Germany. *Das nationalsozialistische Deutschland und die Sowjetunion, 1939-1941. Akten aus dem archiv des deutschen auswärtigen amts*. Washington, 1948.

Germany. Foreign Office. Library of Information. *Documents on the Events Preceding the Outbreak of the War*. Berlin, 1939; New York, 1940.

Gibson, Hugh (ed.). *The Ciano Diaries*. Garden City, 1946.

Gierson, Philip. *Books on Soviet Russia, 1917-1942*. 1945.

Gilbert, Felix (ed.). *Hitler Directs His War*. New York, 1950.

Gilbert, Gustave M. *Nuremberg Diary*. New York, 1947.

Gisevius, Hans Bernd. *To the Bitter End*. Boston, 1947.

Goebbels, Joseph. *The Goebbels Diaries, 1942-1943*. Garden City, 1948.

Gooch, G. P. *Studies in German History*. New York, 1949.

Gordon, David L., and Dangerfield, Royden. *The Hidden Weapon*. New York, 1947.

Gouzenko, Igor. *The Iron Curtain*. New York, 1948.

Grant Duff, Sheila. *German and Czech; a Threat to European Peace*. London, 1937.

Great Britain. Foreign Office. *The British War Blue Book*. New York, 1939.

Great Britain. Foreign Office. *Documents on British Foreign Policy*. London, series.

Great Britain. Foreign Office. Imperial (British) Defense Committee. *History of the Great War*. London, New York, 1920-1945.

Greenfield, Kent R., Palmer, Robert R., and Wiley, Bell I. *The U.S. Army in World War II*. Washington, 1947.

Greenwood, Harry Powys. *The German Revolution*. London, 1934.

Grenfell, Captain Russell. *The Bismarck Episode*. New York, 1948.

Grew, Joseph C. *Ten Years in Japan*. New York, 1944.

Griswold, A. W. *The Far Eastern Policy of the United States*. New York, 1938.

de Guignand, Frederick F. *Operation Victory*. New York, 1947.

Guilland de Benouville, Pierre. *The Unknown Warriors*. New York, 1949.

Gulick, Charles A. *Austria from Hapsburg to Hitler*. Berkeley, 1948.

Gunther, John. *Roosevelt in Retrospect*. New York, 1950.

Halder, Franz. *Hitler als Feldherr*. Munich, 1948.

Halder, Franz. *Hitler as War Lord*. New York, London, 1950.

Halperin, Samuel William. *Germany Tried Democracy*. New York, 1946.

Hamilton, Thomas J. *Appeasement's Child. The Franco Regime in Spain*. New York, 1943.

Harper, Samuel N., and Thompson, Ronald. *Government of the Soviet Union*. New York, 2nd ed., 1949.

Harris, Seymour E. *The European Recovery Program*. Cambridge, Mass., 1948.

von Hassall, Ulrich. *The von Hassall Diaries*. New York, 1947.

Hayden, Joseph R. *The Philippines, a Study in National Development*. New York, 1942.

Hayes, Carlton J. H. *Wartime Mission in Spain, 1942-5*. New York, 1945.

Hinton, Harold B. *Air Victory: The Men and the Machines*. New York, 1948.

Hitler, Adolf. *My Battle*. New York, 1943.

Hitler, Adolf, and Mussolini, Benito. *Les Lettres secrètes échangées par Hitler et Mussolini*. Paris, 1946.

Hoare, Sir Samuel, (Viscount Templewood). *Complacent Dictator*. New York, 1947.

Holmes, General Julius C. "Eisenhower's African Gamble," *Collier's,* January 19, 1946, p. 27.

Hornbeck, Stanley K. *The United States and the Far East.* Boston, 1942.

Hoskins, Halford L. *The Atlantic Pact.* Washington, 1949.

Hough, Frank O. *The Island War.* Philadelphia, New York, 1947.

Howe, Quincy. *A World History of Our Own Times.* I (of three). New York, 1949.

Hughes, Emmet J. *Report from Spain.* New York, 1947.

Hull, Cordell. *The Memoirs of Cordell Hull.* New York, 1948.

International Military Tribunal. *Nazi Conspiracy and Aggression.* 8 vols. Washington, 1946.

International Military Tribunal. *Trial of Major War Criminals: Proceedings.* 40 vols. Nuremberg, 1947-1949.

Isely, Jeter A., and Crowl, Philip A. *The U. S. Marines and Amphibious War: Its Theory and its Practice in the Pacific.* Princeton, 1951.

Jackson, Robert H. *The Nuremberg Case.* New York, 1947.

James, Sir William M. *British Navies in Second World War.* London, 1946; New York, 1947.

Janowsky, Oscar I. *Nationalities and National Minorities.* New York, 1945.

Jasny, Naum. *The Socialized Agriculture of the USSR.* Stanford, 1949.

Jaspers, Karl. *The Question of German Guilt.* New York, 1947.

Johnson, Amanda. *Norway, Her Invasion and Occupation.* Decatur, Ia., 1948.

Jones, F. C. *Manchuria Since 1931.* New York, 1949.

Jones, George E. *Tumult in India.* New York, 1948.

Kammerer, Albert. *La vérité sur l'armistice.* Paris, 1945.

Karig, Walter, Harris, R. L., and Manson, F. A. *Battle Report.* New York, 1948.

Kase, Toshikazu. *Journey to the Missouri.* New Haven, 1950.

Kato, Masuo. *The Lost War.* New York, 1946.

Kelsen, Hans. *The Political Theory of Bolshevism.* Berkeley, 1949.

Kenney, George C. *General Kenney Reports.* New York, 1949.

Kerner, Robert Joseph (ed.). *Czechoslovakia.* Berkeley, Los Angeles, 1945.

Kerner, Robert Joseph (ed.). *Yugoslavia.* Berkeley, 1949.

King, Ernest J. *The U.S. Navy at War, 1941-5.* Washington, 1946.

Knaplund, Paul. *The British Empire, 1815-1939.* New York, 1941.

Koestler, Arthur. *Promise and Fulfilment: Palestine, 1917-1940.* New York, 1949.

Kohn-Bramstedt, Ernst. *Dictatorship and Political Police: The Technique of Control by Fear.* London, 1945.

Komorowski. See Bor-Komorowski.

Konovalov, Serge (ed.). *Russo-Polish Relations.* Princeton, 1945.

Kordt, Erich. *Nicht aus den Akten.* Stuttgart, 1950.

Kordt, Erich. *Wahn und Wirklichkeit*. Stuttgart, 1948.

Kühlmann, Richard V. *Erinnerungen*. Heidelberg, 1949.

Kulischer, Eugene M. *Europe on the Move*. New York, 1948.

La Fargue, T. E. *China and the World War*. Stanford, 1937.

Lacina, Vaclav. *In Czechoslovakia Now*. Prague, 1946.

Lane, Arthur Bliss. *I Saw Poland Betrayed*. Indianapolis, 1948.

Lange, Friedrich. *Ostland Kehrt Heim*. Berlin-Leipzig, 1940.

Langer, William L. *Our Vichy Gamble*. New York, 1947.

Langer, William L. *Seizure of Territory*. Princeton, 1947.

Langsam, W. C. *The World Since 1914*. New York, 6th ed., 1948.

Laserson, Max M. *Russia and the Western World*. New York, 1945.

Latourette, Kenneth S. *History of Japan*. New York, 1947.

Latourette, Kenneth S. *Short History of the Far East*. New York, 1946.

Lattimore, Owen. *Pivot of Asia: Sinkiang and the Inner Asian Frontiers of China and Russia*. Boston, 1950.

Lattimore, Owen. *Solution in Asia*. Boston, 1945.

Lattimore, Owen. *The Situation in Asia*. Boston, 1949.

Lattimore, Owen and Eleanor. *The Making of Modern China*. New York, 1944.

Lauterbach, Richard E. *Danger from the East*. New York, 1947.

Lauterbach, Richard E. *These Are the Russians*. New York, 1945.

Leahy, Fleet Admiral William D. *I Was There*. New York, 1950.

Lee, Dwight E. *Ten Years: The World on the Way to War, 1930-1940*. Boston, 1942.

Lehrman, Harold Arthur. *Russia's Europe*. New York, 1947.

Lenin, Vladimir I. (Nicolai). *Imperialism*. New York, 1939.

Lichten, H. E. (collaboration). *Phantom und Wicklichkeit*. Frankfort, 1948.

Lilge, Frederic. *The Abuse of Learning*. New York, 1948.

Lochner, Louis P. *What About Germany?* New York, 1942.

Lochner, Louis P. (ed.). *The Goebbels Diaries, 1942-1943*. Garden City, 1948.

Lowdermilk, Walter C. *Palestine, Land of Promise*. New York, London, 1944.

Lutz, R. H. *The Fall of the German Empire*. Stanford, 1932.

Macartney, C. A. *Hungary and Her Successors*. New York, 1937.

Macartney, C. A. *National States and National Minorities*. London, 1934.

MacDonald, Mary. *The Republic of Austria, 1918-1934: A Study in the Failure of Democratic Government*. New York, London, 1946.

McCune, G. M. *Korea Today*. New York, 1950.

McNair, Harley F. (ed.). *China*. Berkeley, 1946.

McNeill, William H. *The Greek Dilemma: War and Aftermath*. Philadelphia, 1947.

Magidoff, Robert. *In Anger and Pity*. New York, 1948.

Mandel, William. *The Soviet Far East and Central Asia*. New York, 1944.

Margolin, Arnold D. *From a Political Diary: Russia, the Ukraine, and America 1905-1945*. New York, 1946.

Margolin, Leo J. *Paper Bullets, a Brief Story of Psychological Warfare in World War II*. New York, 1946.

Markham, Edwin M. *The Allied Occupation of Japan*. Palo Alto, 1948.

Markham, R. H. *Tito's Imperial Communism*. Chapel Hill, 1947.

Marshall, George C. *Biennial Reports of General George C. Marshall, Chief of Staff of the United States Army, to the Secretary of War, July 1, 1939 to June 30, 1943*. Washington. The Infantry Journal, 1943.

Marshall, George C. *Biennial Report of the Chief of Staff of the United States Army to the Secretary of War. July 1, 1943 to June 30, 1945*. Washington. The Infantry Journal, 1945.

Marshall, George C., Arnold, H. H., and King, E. J. *The War Reports of General George C. Marshall, General H. H. Arnold, and Admiral Ernest J. King*. Philadelphia, New York, 1947.

Martienssen, Anthony. *Hitler and His Admirals*. New York, 1948.

Mason, John Brown. *The Danzig Dilemma*. Stanford, 1946.

Massing, Paul W. *Rehearsal for Destruction: A Study of Political Anti-semitism in Imperial Germany*. New York, 1949.

Maximilian, Prince of Baden. *Erinnerungen und Dokumente*. Stuttgart, 1928.

Maximilian, Prince of Baden. *The Memoirs of Prince Max von Baden*. New York, 1928.

May, Arthur James. *Europe and Two World Wars*. New York, 1947.

Meinecke, Friedrich. *The German Catastrophe*. Cambridge, Mass., 1950.

de Mendelssohn, Peter. *Design for Aggression*. New York, 1946.

Merriam, Robert E. *Dark December*. Chicago, 1947.

Meyer, Cord. *Peace or Anarchy*. Boston, 1947.

Middleton, Drew. *The Struggle for Germany*. Indianapolis, 1949.

Mikhailov, Nicolai N. *The Russian Story*. New York, 1945.

Mikolajczyk, Stanislaw. *The Pattern of Soviet Domination*. London, 1948.

Mikolajczyk, Stanislaw. *The Rape of Poland*. New York, 1948.

Miller, Douglas P. *Via Diplomatic Pouch*. New York, 1944.

Miller, Douglas P. *You Can't Do Business with Hitler*. Boston, 1941.

Miller, John, Jr. *Guadalcanal: The First Offensive*. Washington, 1949.

Millington, Herbert. *American Diplomacy and the War of the Pacific*. New York, 1948.

Millis, Walter. *Road to War. America, 1914-1917*. Boston, 1935.

Millis, Walter. *This Is Pearl*. New York, 1947.

Molotov, Viacheslav Mikhailovich. *Problems of Foreign Policy; Speeches and Statements, April 1945-November 1948*. Moscow, 1949.

Montgomery, Field Marshal Sir Bernard L. *El Alamein to the Sangro River*. New York, 1949.

Montgomery, Field Marshal Sir Bernard L. *Normandy to the Baltic*. Boston, 1948.

Montgomery, John F. *Hungary: The Unwilling Satellite*. New York, 1948.

Moore, Barrington, Jr. *Soviet Politics. The Dilemma of Power*. Cambridge, Mass., 1950.

Moore, Harriet L. *Soviet Far Eastern Policy, 1931-1945*. Princeton, 1945.

Moore, Wilbert E. *Industrialization and Foreign Trade*. New York, 1946.

Moorehead, Alan. *Montgomery, A Biography*. New York, 1946.

Morgan, Lt. Gen. Sir Frederick. *Prelude to Overlord*. New York, 1950.

Morison, Samuel E. *History of United States Naval Operations in World War II*. I, *The Battle of the Atlantic*. II, *Operations in North African Waters*. III, *The Rising Sun in the Pacific*. IV, *The Coral Sea, Midway, and Submarine Actions (May, 1942-August, 1942)*. V. *The Struggle for Guadalcanal, August, 1942-February, 1943*. VI, *Breaking the Bismarcks Barrier, 22 July 1942-1 May 1944*. Boston, 1947-1950. (More volumes to follow.)

von Muralt, Leonard. *From Versailles to Potsdam*. Hinsdale, Ill., 1948.

Murawski, Erich. *Durchbruch im Westen*. Berlin, 1941.

Mussolini, Benito. See Adolf Hitler.

Mussolini, Benito. *Memoirs*. London, 1949.

Namier, Lewis B. *Diplomatic Prelude, 1938-9*. New York, London, 1948.

Nansen, Odd. *From Day to Day*. New York, 1949.

Nehru, Jawaharlal. *Nehru on Gandhi*. New York, 1948.

Neumann, William Louis. *Making the Peace, 1941-1945: The Diplomacy of the War-Time Conferences*. Washington, 1950.

Nevins, Allan. *The New Deal in World Affairs*. New Haven, 1950.

Nevins, Allan. *The United States in a Chaotic World*. New Haven, 1950.

Newman, Bernard. *Balkan Background*. New York, 1935.

Newman, Bernard. *The Captured Archives: The Nazi-Soviet Documents*. London, 1948.

Newman, Bernard. *Russia's Neighbor—the New Poland*. London, 1946.

Nuremberg Trials. See Victor H. Bernstein, Peter Calvocoressi, International Military Tribunal, Robert H. Jackson, Royal (Br.) Institute of International Affairs, Henry L. Stimson.

Olden, Rudolph. *The History of Liberty in Germany*. London, 1946.

Oliver, R. T. *Why War Came in Korea*. New York, 1950.

Parker, James. *The History of Palestine*. New York, 1949.

Peffer, Nathaniel. *Basis for Peace in the Far East*. New York, 1942.

Peterson, Maurice. *Both Sides of the Curtain*. London, 1950.

Plivier, Theodor. *Stalingrad*. New York, 1948.

Poole, DeWitt C. "Light on Nazi Foreign Policy," *Foreign Affairs*, October, 1946, pp. 130-155.

Pratt, Fletcher. *The Marines' War*. New York, 1948.

Pratt, Fletcher. *War for the World*. New Haven, 1950.

Pudleston, W. D. *The Influence of Sea Power in World War II*. New Haven, 1947.

Radin, George. *Economic Reconstruction in Yugoslavia*. New York, 1946.

Rauschning, Hermann. *The Revolution of Nihilism*. New York, 1939.

Rei, August. *Nazi-Soviet Conspiracy and the Baltic States: Diplomatic Documents and Other Evidence*. London, 1948.

Reinsch, Paul S. *An American Diplomat in China*. Garden City, Toronto, 1922.

Remer, Charles F. *Foreign Investments in China*. New York, 1933.

Roberts, Stephen H. *The House That Hitler Built*. New York, 1938.

Roosevelt, Franklin D. *The Public Papers and Addresses of Franklin D. Roosevelt*. 4 vols. New York, 1950.

Root, Waverly L. *Secret History of the War*. III, *Casablanca to Katyn*. New York, 1946.

Röpke, Wilhelm. *Internationale Ordnung*. Zurich, 1945.

Röpke, Wilhelm. *The Solution of the German Problem*. New York, 1947.

Roscoe, Theodore. *United States Submarine Operations in World War II*. Annapolis, 1949.

Rosinsky, Herbert. *The German Army*. Washington, 1944.

Rossi, A. *The Russo-German Alliance: August, 1939-June, 1941*. Boston, 1951.

Roucek, Joseph S. *Central-Eastern Europe, Crucible of World Wars*. New York, 1946.

Roucek, Joseph S. (ed.). *Contemporary Europe*. New York, 1948.

Rougier, Louis. *Les accords Pétain-Churchill; histoire d'une mission secrète*. Montreal, 1945.

Rudin, Harry R. *Armistice, 1918*. New Haven, 1944.

Sasuly, Richard. *IG Farben*. New York, 1947.

Schapiro, J. Salwyn. *The World in Crisis*. New York, 1950.

Schechtman, Joseph B. *European Population Transfers, 1939-45*. New York, 1946.

Schechtman, Joseph B. *Population Transfers in Asia*. New York, 1949.

von Schlabrendorff, Fabian. *They Almost Killed Hitler*. New York, 1947.

Schmidt, Paul. *Statist auf diplomatischer Bühne*. Bonn, 1949.

Schneefuss, Walter. *Deutschtum in süd-ost-Europa*. Leipzig, 1939, 1941.

Schuman, Frederick L. *Soviet Politics at Home and Abroad*. New York, 1946.

Schuschnigg, Kurt. *Austrian Requiem*. New York, 1946.

Schwartz, Harry. *Russia's Post-War Economy*. Syracuse, 1947.

Seraphim, Hans-Günther. *Die deutsch-russischen Beziehungen 1939-1941*. Hamburg, 1949.

Seton-Watson, Hugh. *The East European Revolution*. London, 1950.

Seton-Watson, Hugh. *Eastern Europe Between the Wars, 1918-1941*. Cambridge, England, 1945.

Settel, Arthur (ed.). *This Is Germany*. New York, 1950.

Seymour, Charles. *American Diplomacy During the World War*. Baltimore, 1934.

Sheele, Godfrey. *The Weimar Republic*. London, 1946.

Sheppard, W. E. *Britain at War*. London, 1947.

Sherman, Admiral Frederic C. *Combat Command. The American Aircraft Carriers in the Pacific War*. New York, 1950.

Sherwood, Robert E. *Roosevelt and Hopkins*. New York, 1948.

Shotwell, James T. *The Great Decision*. New York, 1944.

Shotwell, James T. *What Germany Forgot*. New York, 1940.

Shotwell, James T., and Laserson, Max. *Poland and Russia, 1919-1945*. New York, 1945.

Shub, David. *A Biography: Lenin*. Garden City, 1948.

Shulman, Milton. *Defeat in the West*. London, 1947; New York, 1948.

Smith, Howard K. *Last Train from Berlin*. New York, 1942.

Smith, Robert A. *Divided India*. New York, 1947.

Smith, Sara R. *The Manchurian Crisis, 1931-1932*. New York, 1948.

Smith, Walter Bedell. *My Three Years in Moscow*. New York, 1950.

Somerville, John. *Soviet Philosophy*. New York, 1946.

Sontag, Raymond J., and Beddie, James Stuart (eds.). *Nazi-Soviet Relations, 1939-41*. Washington, 1948.

Speidel, Hans. *Invasion 1944. Ein Beitrag zu Rommels und des Reiches Schicksal*. Tübingen, 1949.

Spender, Stephen. *European Witness*. London, 1947.

Spengler, Oswald. *The Decline of the West*. New York, 1926, 1928.

Spengler, Oswald. *The Hour of Decision*. New York, 1934.

Spengler, Oswald. *Today and Destiny*. New York, 1940.

Stalin, Iosef Vissarionovich. *Problems of Leninism*. Moscow, 1940.

Starr, Chester G., Jr. *From Salerno to the Alps*. Washington, 1948.

Stebbins, Richard P. *The United States in World Affairs* (IV of series). New York, 1950.

Steiger, George Nye. *The Far East and the Second World War*. New York, 1944.

Stern, James. *The Hidden Damage*. New York, 1947.

Stettinius, Edward R. *Roosevelt and the Russians; the Yalta Conference*. Garden City, 1949.

Stilwell, Joseph W. *The Stilwell Papers*. New York, 1948.

Stimson, Henry L. "The Challenge to Americans," *Foreign Affairs,* October, 1947.

Stimson, Henry L. "The Decision to Use the Atomic Bomb," *Harper's Magazine*, February, 1947.

Stimson, Henry L. *The Far Eastern Crisis*. New York, 1936.

Stimson, Henry L. "The Nuremberg Trial; Landmark in Law," *Foreign Affairs*, January, 1947.

Stimson, Henry L., and Bundy, McGeorge. *On Active Service: In Peace and War.* New York, 1948.

Stolper, Gustav. *German Economy, 1870-1940.* New York, 1940.

Stolper, Gustav. *German Realities.* New York, 1948.

Strakhovsky, Leonid I. (ed.). *A Handbook of Slavic Studies.* Cambridge, Mass., 1949.

Straubel, James H. *Air Force Diary.* New York, 1947.

Streit, Clarence K. *Union Now.* New York, 1949.

Swisher, Earl (ed.). *Pacific Islands.* Boulder, Col., 1946.

Tardieu, André. *L'année de Munich.* Paris, 1939.

Templewood, Viscount. See Sir Samuel Hoare.

Timasheff, Nicholas S. *The Great Retreat.* New York, 1946.

Tolischus, Otto L. *They Wanted War.* New York, 1940.

Tolischus, Otto L. *Tokyo Record.* New York, 1943.

Tompkins, Pauline. *American-Russian Relations in the Far East.* New York, 1949.

Torrès, Henry. *Pierre Laval.* New York, Toronto, 1941.

Towster, Julian. *Political Power in the USSR, 1917-1947.* New York, 1948.

Toynbee, Arnold J. *Civilization on Trial.* New York, 1948.

Toynbee, Arnold J. *The Prospects of Western Civilization.* New York, 1949.

Toynbee, Arnold J. *Survey of International Affairs, 1928.* London, 1928.

Trevor-Roper, H. R. *The Last Days of Hitler.* New York, 1947.

Trewartha, Glenn T. *Japan: Physical, Cultural, and Regional Geography.* Madison, Wis., 1945.

Turnbull, Archibald S., and Lord, Clifford L. *History of United States Naval Aviation.* New Haven, 1949.

USSR. Information Bulletin. *The Sixteen Soviet Republics.* Washington, 1945.

USSR. Ministry of Foreign Affairs. *Documents and Materials Relating to the Eve of the Second World War.* Moscow, 1949.

United Nations Secretariat, Department of Public Information. *Everyman's United Nations.* New York, 1948.

U.S. Chief of Counsel for the Prosecution of Axis Criminality. *Nazi Conspiracy and Aggression.* Washington, 1946. See International Military Tribunal.

U.S. Congress. Joint Committee on the Investigation of the Pearl Harbor Attack. *Pearl Harbor Attack.* 40 parts. Washington, 1946.

U.S. Department of the Army, Historical Division. *Anzio Beachhead, 22 January-28 May 1944.* Washington, 1948.

U.S. Deparment of the Army, Historical Division. *Okinawa, the Last Battle.* Washington, 1949.

U.S. Department of the Army, Historical Division. *The United States Army in World War II*. Washington, 1947.

U.S. Department of the Army, Historical Division. *Utah Beach to Cherbourg, 6 June-27 June 1944*. Washington, 1948.

U.S. Department of State. *Documents on German Foreign Policy, 1918-1945*. Series D, Vols. I, II, III. Washington, 1949.

U.S. Department of State. "Germany, the Soviet Union, and Turkey During World War II." Harry N. Howard, *Bulletin*, XIX, No. 472, July 18, 1948.

U.S. Department of State. *Nazi-Soviet Relations, 1939-41*. Washington, 1948.

U.S. Department of State. *Papers Relating to the Foreign Relations of the United States. Paris Peace Conference, 1919*. 13 vols. Washington, 1942-1947.

U.S. Department of State. *Peace and War; United States Foreign Policy, 1931-1941*. Washington, 1943.

U.S. Department of State. *Prelude to Infamy: Official Report on the Final Phase of U.S. Japanese Relations October 17 to December 7, 1941*. Washington, 1943.

U.S. Department of State. *The Spanish Government and the Axis*. Washington, 1946.

U.S. Department of State. *The Treaty of Versailles and After*. Washington, 1947.

U.S. Department of State *United States Economic Policy Toward Germany*. Washington, 1946.

U.S. Department of State. *United States and Italy, 1936-1946*. Washington, 1946.

U.S. Department of State. *United States Relations with China, with Special Reference to the Period 1944-1949*. Washington, 1949.

U.S. Joint Army-Navy Assessment Committee. *Japanese Naval and Merchant Shipping Losses During World War II by All Causes*. Washington, 1947.

U.S. Office of Naval Intelligence. *Führer Conferences, 1939-1940*. Washington, 1947.

U.S. Strategic Bombing Survey. *The Effects of Air Attack on Japanese Urban Economy*. Washington, 1947.

U.S. Strategic Bombing Survey. *The Fifth Air Force in the War Against Japan*. Washington, 1947.

U.S. Strategic Bombing Survey, Naval Analysis Division. *The Campaigns of the Pacific War*. Washington, 1946.

U.S. War Department. *Nazi Party Membership Records*. Washington, 1946.

Untersuchungsausschuss der d. *Verfassungsgebende Nationalversammlung und des d. Reichstages, 1919-1929*. Berlin, 1925-1930.

Valentin, Veit. "Vorgeschichte des Waffenstillstandes," *Historische Zeitschrift*, 1926.

Vansittart, Robert G. *Bones of Contention*. London, 1945.

Vernadsky, George, and Karpovich, Michael. *A History of Russia*. 2 vols. New Haven, 1943, 1948.

Vinacke, Harold M. *A History of the Far East in Modern Times*. New York, 5th ed., 1950.

Voznesensky, Nikolai A. *The Economy of the USSR During World War II*. Washington, 1948.

Vyshinsky, Andrei Y. *The Law of the Soviet State*. New York, 1948.

Vyshinsky, Andrei Y. *Lenin and Stalin, the Great Organizers of the Soviet State*. Moscow, 1949.

Wallbank, T. W. *India*. New York, 1948.

Walsh, Edmund A. *Total Power. A Footnote to History*. Garden City, 1948.

Weber, Alfred. *Farewell to European History*. London, 1947; New Haven, 1948.

Weinrich, Max. *Hitler's Professors*. New York, 1946.

Welles, Sumner. *We Need Not Fail*. Boston, 1948.

Werth, Alexander. *The Year of Stalingrad*. London, 1946.

West, Rebecca. *The Meaning of Treason*. New York, 1947.

Wheeler-Bennett, John W. *Munich: Prologue to Tragedy*. London, New York, 1948.

Williams, Francis. *Socialist Britain*. New York, 1949.

Wilson, Field Marshal Lord (Henry). *Eight Years Overseas, 1939-1947*. London, 1950.

Winn, Godfrey H. *Convoy to North Russia*. London, 1937.

Wiskemann, Elizabeth. *Czechs and Germans*. New York, 1938.

Wiskemann, Elizabeth. *Prologue to War*. New York, 1940.

Wiskemann, Elizabeth. *The Rome-Berlin Axis*. New York, 1949.

Wiskemann, Elizabeth. *Undeclared War*. London, 1939.

Wolfe, Bertram D. *Three Who Made a Revolution*. New York, 1948.

Wolfe, Henry C. *The Imperial Soviets*. New York, 1940.

Wolfers, Arnold. *Britain and France Between Two Wars*. New York, 1940.

Woodward, Comer Vann. *The Battle for Leyte Gulf*. New York, 1947.

Woodward, Ernest L., and Butler, Rohan (eds.). *Documents on British Foreign Policy, 1919-1939*. London, 1946—

Woodward, Ernest L., and others. *Foundations for World Order*. Denver, 1949.

Wright, Gordon. *The Reshaping of French Democracy*. New York, 1948.

Wright, Quincy (ed.). *A Foreign Policy for the United States*. Chicago, 1947.

Wuorinen, John H. *Finland and World War II, 1939-1944*. New York, 1949.

Yanaga, Chitosi. *Japan Since Perry*. New York, 1949.

Young, Desmond. *Rommel, the Desert Fox*. New York, 1950.

Zacharias, Ellis M. *Behind Closed Doors: The Story of the Cold War*. New York, 1950.

Ziff, William Bernard. *Two Worlds*. New York, London, 1946.

Zweig, Ferdynand. *Poland Between Two Wars*. London, 1944.

Index